Huxley

Huxley:
From Devil's Disciple
to Evolution's
High Priest

ADRIAN DESMOND

§

HELIX BOOKS

PERSEUS BOOKS

Reading, Massachusetts

ISBN 0-7382-0140-5

Library of Congress Catalog Card Number: 99-60005

Published in Great Britain by Michael Joseph Ltd. Paperback edition published by Penguin Books, London.

Perseus Books is a member of the Perseus Books Group

Cover design by Bruce W. Bond

1 2 3 4 5 6 7 8 9 10—03 02 01 00 99
First paperback printing, March 1999

Find Helix Books on the World Wide Web at
http://www.aw.com/gb/

Contents

Illustrations   *page* vii
Acknowledgments   xi
The Apostle Paul of the New Teaching   xiii

PART ONE: THE DEVIL'S DISCIPLE

1825–1846
Dreaming my own Dreams

1   Philosophy Can Bake No Bread   3
2   Son of the Scalpel   18
3   The Surgeon's Mate   36

1846–1850
The Devil and the Deep Blue Sea

4   Men-of-War   53
5   An Ark of Promise   66
6   The Eighth Circle of Hell   86
7   Sepulchral Painted Savages   111
8   Homesick Heroes   129

1850–1858
Lost in the Wilderness

9   The Scientific Sadducee   149
10   The Season of Despair   172
11   The *Jihad* Begins   195
12   The Nature of the Beast   216

v

Contents

13   Empires of the Deep Past   231

1858–1865
The New Luther

14   The Eve of a New Reformation   251
15   Buttered Angels & Bellowing Apes   266
16   Reslaying the Slain   292
17   Man's Place   312

1865–1870
The Scientific Swell

18   Birds, Dinosaurs & Booming Guns   339
19   Eyeing the Prize   361

PART TWO: EVOLUTION'S HIGH PRIEST

1870–1884
Marketing the 'New Nature'

20   The Gun in the Liberal Armoury   385
21   From the City of the Dead to the City of Science   411
22   Automatons   433
23   The American Dream   463
24   A Touch of the Whip   483
25   A Person of Respectability   495
26   The Scientific Woolsack   507

1885–1895
The Old Lion

27   Polishing off the G.O.M.   537
28   Christ Was No Christian   562
29   Combating the Cosmos   583
30   Fighting unto Death   600

Afterword: Huxley in Perspective   615

Abbreviations   645
Notes   648
Bibliography   751
Index   783

Illustrations

1. The earliest known daguerreotype of Tom Huxley. (*By courtesy of Sir Andrew Huxley*)
2. Huxley's self-portrait as a student. (*T. H. Huxley to H. Heathorn, n.d., HH 79, Archives, Imperial College, London*)
3. *Punch*'s satire on 'sons of the scalpel'. (*Punch*, 2 [1842], 149)
4. Charing Cross Hospital about 1840. (*Charing Cross Hospital, Medical Illustration Group*)
5. The studious Huxley, aged twenty. (*Sketch by T. H. Huxley: Family Correspondence, Archives, Imperial College, London*)
6. The newly commissioned sailor, billeted in the 'Hulks'. (*Sketch by T. H. Huxley: Family Correspondence, Archives, Imperial College, London*)
7. Assistant Surgeon Huxley, RN (*By courtesy of Sir Andrew Huxley*)
8. HMS *Rattlesnake* off Sydney Heads. (*Painting by Oswald Brierly, National Library of Australia, Canberra*)
9. Henrietta Heathorn, painted by Thomas Griffiths Wainewright the Poisoner. (*By Courtesy of Sir Andrew Huxley*)
10. Hacking through the scrub with Kennedy's light party. (*Sketch by T. H. Huxley: Archives, Imperial College, London*)
11. The gallery of Huxley's Museum. (*Reproduced by permission of the Director, British Geological Survey, GSM 1/105*)
12. Huxley raging against the world. (*Archives, Imperial College, London*)
13. The Irish physicist John Tyndall. (A. S. Eve and C. H. Creasey, *Life and World of John Tyndall* [Macmillan, 1945])
14. The hawk-eyed Huxley in 1857. (L. Huxley, ed., *Life and Letters of Thomas Henry Huxley* [Macmillan, 1900])
15. Tom and Nettie on honeymoon. (*Sketch by T. H. Huxley: Archives, Imperial College, London*)

16. The young lecturer drawing a gorilla skull. (*The Library, Wellcome Institute for the History of Medicine, London*)

17. The clever frontispiece to Huxley's *Man's Place in Nature*. (T. H. Huxley, *Man's Place in Nature* [Macmillan, 1894])

18. The first known skull of Neanderthal Man. (*Archives, Imperial College, London*)

19. Huxley's jokey sketch of Neanderthal as an ape man. (*Archives, Imperial College, London*)

20. The tiny bird-like dinosaur *Compsognathus*. (T. H. Huxley, 'On the Animals which are Most Nearly Intermediate Between Birds and Reptiles', *Popular Science Review*, 7 [1868], 244)

21. Huxley's caricature of a giant dinosaur *Cetiosaurus*. (*T. H. Huxley to J. Phillips, n.d./146, Oxford University Museum*)

22. On London's School Board. (*Archives, Imperial College, London*)

23. The 'Science Schools' Building in South Kensington. (*Archives, Imperial College, London*)

24. The Laboratory in 1893. (*Archives, Imperial College, London*)

25. A Haeckelian lineage for mammals. (*Archives, Imperial College, London*)

26. The ancestral mollusc curling its shell. (*Archives, Imperial College, London*)

27. Huxley Eikonoklastes in New York. (*Archives, Imperial College, London*)

28. O. C. Marsh's table of fossil horses. (T. H. Huxley, *Collected Essays*, 4:130)

29. A projected five-toed ancestral horse, 'Eohippus'. (*Archives, Imperial College, London*)

30. Huxley in Birmingham. (*By courtesy of Hilary Buzzard*)

31. The sectarian turmoil. (*Archives, Imperial College, London*)

32. The Inspector of Fisheries. (*By courtesy of Angela Darwin*)

33. Marian Huxley's painting of John Collier painting her. (*By courtesy of William Collier*)

34. H. G. Wells apeing Huxley. (*By courtesy of M. J. Wells*)

35. The Right Honourable T. H. Huxley in his Privy Councillor's suit. (*By Courtesy of Clare Huxley*)

36. Huxley presenting his droll side. (*By courtesy of Michael Huxley/Richard Milner*)

Acknowledgments

MY HOME CRITIC Nellie Flexner deserves special credit for reading reams of manuscript and improving the flow of the text. Jim Moore was always on call. He also read a large portion of the book and happily answered my telephone queries about blasphemy trials or Bishop Wilberforce's grandmother. While Bernie Lightman kindly commented on the 'Afterword' and sections dealing with Huxley's agnosticism.

I owe a great debt to Huxley's great granddaughter Angela Darwin, who is currently transcribing Henrietta Huxley's letters to T.H.'s sister in Tennessee. These frank family letters are an invaluable resource. Angela fed me transcriptions and braced herself for questions of the kind: 'Did Henrietta allude to the socialist mob attacking Huxley's bus in 1886?' 'Why did she change vicars?' 'Did she mention Oscar Wilde turning up one night?' (Imagine the stir caused by this velveteen embodiment of the new Hedonism, whose salvation by sin was a snub to Huxley's rational Puritanism.) The queries went on, I am afraid, but Angela was very understanding.

My main research centred on the 5,000 Huxley letters in the Archives of Imperial College, London. Anne Barrett's help here went beyond the call of duty as she supplied information and esoteric articles. I actually used a splendid microfilm of these letters, supplied by Research Publications Ltd, PO Box 45, Reading RG1 8HF, UK. These fifty-four reels allowed me to trawl through Huxley's daily correspondence in the wee hours and gain an intimacy which could not otherwise have been attained. I am grateful to Cristina Ashby at Research Publications for her generosity.

Not that it is exactly *easy* to decipher Huxley's scrawl. His handwriting is notorious among scholars. When he was in a rush (which was always), it resembled one of his drunken crayfish which had fallen into the ink pot and staggered across the page to its doom. Compositors constantly complained, as did Huxley when they took enterprising stabs at his words. 'Your printers are abominable', he told the editor of *Nature*. 'They make me say that "Tyndall did not see the *drift* of my statement", when I wrote "*draft*" as plainly as possible'. After twenty years, my sympathy is still with the printers.

Many other scholars and Huxley family historians discussed their specialities with me: David Allen talked on Huxley's medical in-laws; Ralph Colp on illnesses; Eric Holloway on microscopes; Sophie Forgan on that 'fungoid' spread of buildings (as H. G. Wells had it) at South Kensington; John Laurent on New South Wales; Robert Ralph on drunken John MacGillivray; Giacomo Scarpelli on points Italian; Jim Strick on spontaneous generation; William Collier on John Collier; Martin Cooke on Henrietta Huxley; and Mario di Gregorio on Huxley's marginalia. Others who rallied or supplied material include Ruth Barton, Peter Bowler, Derek Freeman, C.G.Gross, Boyd Hilton, David Knight, Richard Milner, Ron Rainger, Evelleen Richards, Marsha Richmond, Nicolaas Rupke, Simon Schaffer, Jim Secord, Sonia Uyterhoeven, Antonello la Vergata, Mary P. Winsor and Alison Winter. Jim Secord and Evelleen Richards at the Huxley Centenary Conference at Imperial College in 1995 inspired me to wrap up my major conclusions in a separate section. A reflexive 'Afterword' connects the narrative text to the latest Huxley historiography.

To the following archivists and scholars I extend my thanks, for access to archives, help and hospitality, and to the libraries themselves for permission to quote from manuscript material: the American Philosophical Society for supplying a microfilm of their Huxley letters; Howard Hague, Charing Cross and Westminster Medical School; John Thackray at the British Museum (Natural History); Ian Lyle, Royal College of Surgeons of England; Perry O'Donovan of the Darwin Letters Project, and the Syndics of Cambridge University Library; Frank James and the Royal Institution archives; Gill Furlong and Victoria Lane at University College London Manuscripts Library; King's College, London, archives; Graham McKenna, British Geological Survey; C. A. Piggot, Royal Botanic Gardens, Kew; Gina Douglas, the Linnean Society of London; Reg Fish and his successor Ann Sylph, Zoological Society of London; Mary Sampson, The Royal Society; David Webb, the Bishopsgate Institute, London; Virginia Murray at John Murray (publishers); Christine Weideman and Judith Ann Schiff for permission to cite from the Othneil Charles Marsh Papers at Yale University Library; Joan Grattan, The Milton S. Eisenhower Library, Johns Hopkins University; Stella Newton, Oxford University Museum; Gillian F. Lonergan, Co-

Acknowledgments

Operative Union, Manchester; Jennifer Jeynes, South Place Ethical Society, London; Solene Morris, Darwin Museum, Down House (permission to publish is courtesy of English Heritage, who now own Down House); AnneMarie Robinson and the University of London Library, Senate House; the British Library; the Wellcome Institute for the History of Medicine, London, and the National Library of Australia, Canberra.

Angela Darwin made available pen-and-ink sketches from the family letters. A number of the portraits, paintings and sketches have not been published before. They are still in private possession and for permission to include them I am grateful to Sir Andrew Huxley, Clare Huxley, Richard Milner\Michael Huxley, William Collier, and Hilary Buzzard. Likewise my thanks go to the Archives at Imperial College, London, for the liberty to use many photographs from their collection.

G.P. Darwin kindly allowed me to quote from Charles Darwin's correspondence. And Sir Andrew Huxley graciously consented to my publishing extracts from his grandfather's letters.

The Apostle Paul of the New Teaching

'MY GOOD & KIND agent for the propagation of the Gospel', Darwin called him, 'ie the Devil's gospel'. Thomas Henry Huxley became Darwin's Rottweiler, instantly recognizable by his deep-set dark eyes and lashing tongue. Where Darwin held back, Huxley lunged at his limping prey. It was he, not Darwin, who enraptured and outraged audiences in the 1860s with talk of our ape ancestors and cave men. Listeners were agog in a prim, evangelical age. These were terrifying, tantalizing images. 'It is not the bishops and archbishops I am afraid of', Samuel Butler once said. 'Men like Huxley . . . are my natural enemies'.[1] No-one stirred passions like Thomas Henry Huxley.

Huxley was one of the founders of the sceptical, scientific twentieth century. We owe to him that enduring military metaphor, the 'war' of science against theology. He coined the word 'agnostic' and contributed to the West's existential crisis. All of this makes him look so modern that we want to snatch him from his age. Today his agnostic stand seems obvious. But yesterday it was an immensely daring, motivated, ideological position. That plodding zoological autocrat, Richard Owen, called him a pervert with 'some, perhaps congenital, defect of mind' for denying Divine will in Nature.[2] Who can realize the prissy, patronage-based, undemocratic, sermon-dominated, Anglican-controlled, *different* society Huxley faced, and faced squarely?

He remains a saint to some, a sinner to others. He had a huge, multitalented intellect and seemed to run ten lives simultaneously. 'Brilliant' was George Eliot's word for him, but even she wondered where this *agent provocateur* would strike next. He had a stiletto of a pen. 'Cutting up monkeys was his forte, and cutting up men was his foible', the *Pall Mall Gazette* noted. The alternative, for Huxley, was 'to lie still & let the devil have his own way. And I will be torn to pieces before I am forty

xiii

sooner than see that'.[3] He was built 'on the high pressure tubular boiler principle', and adoring students came from every continent to see this social engineer thundering onto society's mainline like an unscheduled express. George Eliot thought he was out of control half the time. The corpulent cosmic theist John Fiske travelled from America and understood him perfectly:

> I am quite wild over Huxley. He is as handsome as an Apollo . . . I never saw such magnificent eyes in my life. His eyes are black, and his face expresses an eager burning intensity . . . He seems earnest, – immensely in earnest, – and thoroughly frank and cordial and modest. And, by Jove, what a pleasure it is to meet such a clean-cut mind! It is like Saladin's sword which cut through the cushion.[4]

Huxley is a contextual biography, for want of a better word: as often as not it looks up from street level to provide a fresh perspective on the people's scientist. At the outset my goal was to write it in a way that would humanize science and its history in order to make it accessible and interesting. As such the historiography remains hidden, however much it shapes our picture of T.H. Huxley, and the theoretical issues only become overt in a separate Afterword. Even so, the book is intended as a contribution to the new contextual history of science. It looks at evolution's use in order to understand the class, religious or political interests involved. It raises questions about new practices and new workplaces. How did England's vicarage view of a designed, happy world in 1830 become the cold, causal, and Calvinistic evolutionary vista of 1870—that passionless cosmos reflected in an impersonal laboratory?[5] Put simply, *Huxley* shows the external world changing with the social world. It shows Huxley marketing the 'new Nature' to give his low-status professionals more esteem in an Oxbridge-dominated culture. This is a story of Class, Power and Propaganda.

Such an approach allows me to paint an unashamedly *social* portrait – to pan across London's splashy streets to catch Huxley in action, to locate him firmly in a reforming, industrializing, urbanizing, -Dickensian Britain, with its slums, its trade unions and its great debates on evolution, emancipation and moral authority.

Thomas Henry Huxley came from nowhere, proud, pushy, a new Luther looking for a pulpit. He seemed half mad at times, messianic at others. An outsider with a cutting tongue and a chip on his shoulder, he would claw his way from London's dockside slums to the presidency of the 'Parliament of Science', the British Association for the Advancement of Science, and then be hailed as the great prophet of the new technocracy in America. He rose with the muddy-booted engineers, the industrial Dissenters hacking at the obstructive Anglican edifice. His life is a chronicle of the rising middle classes. It is also the tale of a society in crisis, out of which came today's scientific world.

He was born into an age of bishops in cauliflower wigs deliberating on God's goodness in Nature. At the end he was riding a penny-farthing through a new world, lit by electricity and criss-crossed by telephone wires. He left a secular society probing human ancestry, a society led by intellectuals proudly wearing his 'agnostic' badge.

The wrenches as England industrialized told in his gritty, tub-thumping, scientific life, with its hunger and pain, and its campaign for a new intellectual aristocracy. Beatrice Webb saw 'a strain of madness in him'.[6] Indeed the whole family had its ups and down – scandals, traumas and asylums were as much a part of his private world as the medals, presidencies and praise.

There was a flawed perfection to Huxley as no other eminent Victorian. Contradiction wrapped themselves up in his tall, wiry frame: he was the great educational reformer who had next to no formal education; the sceptic who made Biblical phraseology his stock-in-trade ('Pope Huxley', the *Spectator* dubbed him); the materialist with a messianic streak. He tailored evolution to middle-class needs. He harangued, he applied it to man and mind, even worse he took it to the masses. And yet he had excruciating trouble assimilating Darwin's doctrine of Natural Selection himself.

'Extinguished theologians', ran one of his wonderfully bloodcurdling slogans, 'lie about the cradle of every science as the strangled snakes beside that of Hercules'.[7] For a century historians have debated, championed and denounced Huxley's 'war' on theology. But why did he rise like Saul to 'smite the Amalekites' – these enemies of his scientific Israel? And how are we to interpret the 'warfare' anyway? As rational science triumphing over holy obscurantism? At the dawn of the twenty-first century 'reason' seems a precarious, value-laden yardstick, and one which has an infuriating habit of changing allegiance. In Huxley's young day, it lay with the natural theologians. Not only is the 'warfare' image hackneyed; so is the reaction to it – the harmonious history born in the 1970s, which smooths over the Victorian conflict. The point is not to deny the struggle, any more than to refight the good fight. It is to understand why an angry outsider used science as a weapon to claw power, and to appreciate the social currents that swept this rapier-wielding doubting Thomas to the summit.

Those swirling currents were industrial Dissent. If biography can have a thesis (a subject tackled in the Afterword), this is *Huxley*'s – he was at the extreme cutting edge of an alienated and excluded radical Dissent. To dub him 'The Devil's Disciple' in Part I is to use a provocative title with multiple meanings. The Devil was Darwin. But, as in George Bernard Shaw's play, Huxley turns out to be doing the Lord's work,[8] riding the crest of a radical Dissenting secularism, which wanted fair play for non-Anglicans: the moralizing 'agnostic' began by ridding society of its idolatry and ended up establishing a rival evolutionary priesthood.

Ultimately this is a story of how scientists, with their agnostic evolutionary beliefs, came to hold such a position of authority in the twentieth century. But it is the nuances that make history interesting. We have to capture the rich texture of Huxley's emotional, religious and scientific life, trace his Unitarian friendships, his industrial backers, his oscillating relationship with the workers, his broad alliances with an avant garde raging against the privileged Anglican Church. If we see him developing a rival profession of science, with its ideological roots in industrial Dissent, the antagonisms begin to clear up.

And we can only do that by prising open the closed areas of his life. The teenage Huxley is unknown: no papers have been published on his shadowy medical origins, no books entitled *Young Huxley*, no Ph.D theses on his opium-hazed teachers or his skew-hatted student days.[9] Darwin's gentrified opulence was never his. Huxley's birth above a butcher's shop spoke for itself. His was a world of sots and scandals, of debts and ne'er-do-wells. He was a man on the make, a 'plebeian', he said. We have to track him through the slums that made Dickens shudder, through a turbulent student world – of Gin Palace lowlife and fiery medical democrats. Understand the Church-baiting, reforming 1830s and 1840s and Huxley's public emergence in 1851, 'soul sickened and sceptical', makes sense.

The newer approaches to science, emphasizing its class and social underpinnings, push us further in this direction. Only a backcloth of steam factories, professionalization, imperial expansion, liberal Dissent and *laissez-faire* will allow us to appreciate why Huxley's New Model Army of outsiders pledged its allegiance, not to the old aristocracy and clergy, but to the new captains of industry and the professions.

The young hothead scrambled to the top of his profession; indeed he *made* a profession of science. With him the 'scientist' was born. The word only came into vogue from the late 1870s to describe a struggling professional, systematically probing Nature, paid to research, engaged on an unprecedented open-ended quest. Huxley boosted the 'Scientist's' profile by trenching on the clergy's domain, raising the territorial tension by equating authority with technical expertise. He was the self-perceived poor boy, one of Thackeray's thrusting blades, trying to turn so much 'symbolic capital' – the medals and kudos – into real cash.[10] His conversion of knowledge into a paying commodity was a major step in the making of a salaried scientist. In Darwin we see an older ideal, the wealthy, self-financed gent whose home was his laboratory – and in Huxley twentieth-century corporate science in the making.

Science had a new breed of star performer. Huxley transported audiences to strange dinosaurian worlds and conjured up alien pithecoid people. Bushy-bearded labourers with blistered hands flocked to his talks on our ancestry. He drew the sort of crowds that are reserved for evangelists or rock stars today. Two thousand were turned away from St Martin's Hall in London one Sunday when he delivered a 'lay sermon' on material salvation (the outraged Lord's Day Observance Society promptly stopped the lecture series). He was the most scintillating scientific missionary to stand on a soap-box.

Bishops' wives were astounded that he wasn't a sort of scientific Jack the Ripper; 'and yet', one exclaimed, 'I hear that he is a devoted husband & an affectionate father'. Behind the headlines lay this quieter Huxley, the family man, the teacher, the fossil expert who showed that dinosaurs were the ancestors of today's birds. Here too we see the *realpolitik*. Everyone knows of his clash with a purple-vested Bishop Wilberforce in 1860, when Huxley declared that he would rather have an ape for a grandparent than a bishop who prostituted his gifts. But who knew that the two were quietly working together in the Zoological Society, sacking drunken keepers and arranging exhibits?

If he caricatured eminent bishops we cannot simply cheer or hiss, we have to ask why. His singular sort of science – based on a non-miraculous, cause-and-effect Nature – was for battering down seminary doors. Evolution cradled within an agnostic framework seems obvious today, precisely because we have inherited the victor's mantle. But it was far from obvious in 1870. Then the English public schools and universities shunned science as useless and dehumanizing. Their world was of character-forming Classics and Theology. Oxford and Cambridge were finishing schools for prosperous Anglicans. Against 145 Classics Fellowships at Oxford in 1870, there were four in science.[11] The stacked odds explain Huxley's single-minded assault on the ivy seminaries using his newly-professionalized forces.

Huxley's satires of Anglican supernaturalism and Oxbridge privilege have helped to distort our view of the Victorians. Just as Oscar Wilde parodied Huxley's Puritan generation, so Huxley caricatured Bishop Wilberforce's day. He saw strangled priests around evolution's cradle and lampooned Gladstone's first-century beliefs; and he finally made Christ himself rebuke Victorian Christianity. This was black propa-

ganda for his rival scientific priesthood. And successful too: he persuaded sceptical, Classically-trained politicians that science was
essential to an industrial nation. It became an arm of the state, controlled by Huxley. But his scientists incorporated all their mid-Victorian
prejudices into the new civil service biology.[12] The slamming lab doors
shut out the women and workers and priests. Inside the lab, the new
man, having trouble with the 'new woman', could bolster Darwin's gendered and class image of evolutionary 'reality'.

Biography gets us around the sepia image of a static, strait-laced Victorian age. We can plot one man's trajectory through a seething century
– indeed, understand why the laces slowly straightened as the old radicals became the new reactionaries. So in Part 2, 'Evolution's High
Priest', which takes the story from 1870 to Huxley's death in 1895, the
sets change. The Darwinians were in place and underpinning the new social order. We find Huxley deflecting the spotlight from his own ideological assumptions.[13] He made 'neutral' science a moral Saladin's
sword. And a political one: he recast Darwinism in the middle of the
Great Depression (1874–96) to contain his workers' Leftward drift –
turning open-competition radicalism into a darker Social Darwinism.
And as the bottom dropped out of history and the Victorians peered,
horrified, into the unfathomable abyss of geological time,[14] it was the
silver-haired Huxley who cast a stabilizing anchor from the evolutionary
ship.

The social order was increasingly professional as the second industrial
revolution got underway after 1870. Northern capital was flowing into
London, but the steel barons were investing in more than the stockmar-
ket.[15] Quakers and Congregationalists, munitions manufacturers and
factory free-traders were funding Huxley. These social alignments become more explicit as we get beneath the scientist's neutral veneer.

The Victorian era was 'hinged' about 1870 with the industrial retooling. So was Huxley's life. He moved to the forerunner of London's Imperial College, honed a new laboratory biology, and started training
schoolmasters for the industrial regions. It was the beginning of that
base-up reconstruction which ensured science's take-off. Money was
switching from charity to education, the street arabs were being swept
into schools, the Divinely ordered society was becoming Darwinianly
ordered, and the middle classes were beginning to look to Nature for
their ultimate explanations. There was Huxley at every turn. The *Pall
Mall Gazette* saw his hand 'in all the moving subjects of the day'. By the
time the knighted legions stood over his grave in 1895 there had been a
total re-evaluation of knowledge. Science and the middle-class professionals were in. Evolution had become 'natural'.

This is the human story behind these sea-changes. Huxley was long crushed under an inverted financial pyramid, chocked with boozy relations. The sober Darwinian was trying to hold the lid down, trying to usher in a new scientific morality as the gin-sodden floozies threatened scandal. Here was the reverse side to Huxley's public face. And it remains partly hidden. Huxley's extended family is unknown to historians, and my account throws up more questions than answers. Given the tragedy of his daughter Mady's illness and death, one wonders what lay behind his sister-in-law's shriek 'No wonder you drove Mady mad'. Was this just the deranged raving of a widow high on chloral and gin? More needs to be done on the relationship of these talented Victorian daughters with their pressured, patriarchal fathers.[16] If nothing else, tragedy and trauma provide a continuity after 1870 as the rational tornado worked like ten men to support dozens of dependants.

The sexagenarian scourge continued to fascinate, just as the *enfant terrible* had. There was more to Huxley than a brilliant early-peaking scientist. He continued to change hats, becoming the supreme cultural critic – part political fixer in private, part matinée idol in public; charismatic from his holier-than-thou agnosticism, authoritative from his command of the 'new Nature'. He had his finger on the pulse; or rather he speeded up the pulse, making the Victorian heart thump with his goading talk of the 'sin of faith'. It explains why Beatrice Webb, arriving late on the scene, should consider him 'greater as a man than a scientific thinker'.[17]

But we cannot snap judge so chimerical a character. He had the confidence to remake himself with the times. The idiosyncratic *enragé* becomes the stern moralizer. The self-perceived 'plebeian' transforms into the powerful Privy Councillor. The scientific radical rebukes Liberal Prime Ministers and takes tea with Tory ones. And every now and then the scowling mask shatters, to reveal a smile (so rarely captured in photographs). It was the beam of a brilliant boy, having arrived in Olympus. The last two photographs typify the contrast: the public face of the Privy Councillor, and the endearing – and disarming – 'phiz' that was, perhaps, ultimately the man.

That Victorian shrine, the *Life and Letters of Thomas Henry Huxley*, is a splendidly cracked monument, like an old imperial statue, good in its day for inspiring the troops, but now covered in historiographic vines. In 1900 it did not matter that the letters were bowdlerized and contracted.[18] As we approach 2000 it does, and retranscribing his 5,000 letters, diaries and manuscripts housed at Imperial College in London has enabled me to discover how many of Huxley's famous *bons mots* were Victorian misquotes.

The *Times* claimed that no one could 'estimate the forces which have been at work to mould the intellectual, moral, and social life of the century' without appreciating T.H. Huxley. It is crucial today, as the aftershocks of the great Victorian crisis of faith rumble on in the West, to understand this 'apostle Paul of the new teaching'.[19] To understand, in short, the making of our modern Darwinian world.

Part One
The Devil's Disciple

1825–1846

Dreaming my own Dreams

1

Philosophy Can Bake No Bread

THE LANKY 15 year-old sidled down fetid alleys, past gin palaces and dance halls. Sailors hung out of windows, the gaiety of their boozy whores belying the squalor around them. The boy's predatory looks and patched clothes seemed in keeping. But his black eyes betrayed a horror at the sights: ten crammed into a room, babies diseased from erupting cesspits, the uncoffined dead gnawed by rats. The scenes would scar him for life.

In 1841 young Tom Huxley was in a twilight world. For a highly strung, sensitive lad the degradation was numbing. Daily the drug-grinder's apprentice threaded his way through East London's hovels. He carried a little muslin bag, but his drugs proved useless when the people 'were suffering from nothing but slow starvation'.

The century's worst recession had left mass unemployment. It showed in the haggard faces of his patients. Each wretched garret brought sorry sights, of bedridden seamstresses with no better food than 'bread and bad tea'. How could he suggest a healthy diet? One deformed girl, nursing her sister, 'turned upon me with a kind of choking passion. Pulling out of her pocket a few pence and halfpence, and holding them out, "That is all I get for six-and-thirty hours' work, and you talk about giving her proper food"'. Tom trudged ahead of the Grim Reaper, unable to stay his scythe. He watched the paupers succumb, mortality statistics scratched on the 'ledgers of death'.

Night-time found him in his tiny dockside surgery, venting his anger. The wide-eyed boy who loved metaphysics and religion and dreamed his way into the immensity of geological time asked himself: how could a 'solitary Philosopher' be 'happy in the midst of poverty'?[1] The pleading faces were to haunt him for life. They put the moral fire into his drive for a New Reformation. Christianity had failed the starving. Politics had failed them. The young evangelical would look for a new sort of salvation.

Thomas Henry Huxley's was an ignominious beginning. Not for him Darwin's silver spoon; he had no fortune to inherit, no family tradition to uphold. He was born on 4 May 1825 above a butcher's shop in Ealing, a small village 12 miles west of London. His father was an 'active intelligent man', but intelligence hadn't gained him success. Tall and dark, George Huxley bequeathed to his youngest son a quick temper and a 'glorious firmness which one's enemies called obstinacy'. He passed on little else, except a talent for drawing, which would give Tom his eye for capturing a rainforest or a reptilian fossil. George had been teaching mathematics at Ealing School for 18 years when Tom was born. It was a minor public school, relying on Classics and discipline to stiffen the backbone of the Anglican nation, and already in precipitous decline. At the time of Waterloo it had boasted 300 pupils, and George had taught John Henry Newman (the future Catholic cardinal) before that. From the school the Newman brothers had acquired their intense evangelical bias. But the fall in its fortunes had left George Huxley penniless.

His father's neglect bred a bitterness in Tom and he compensated by doting on his mother. Rachel was 'a "Cockney" born within the sound of Bow Bells' (although of Devonshire descent) and already 40 when she gave birth to Thomas Henry, her sixth and youngest surviving child. The boy's love for her was 'a passion'. He 'laid awake for hours crying because I had a morbid fear of her death – her approbation was my greatest reward and her displeasure my greatest punishment'. From his mother came 'the tone of his inner spiritual life', a pious, moral, questing, questioning spiritual life, never content, never at rest. The boy's emotional submergence was total. He had his mother's slender build and black eyes, and even the twiddling movements of her fingers. Her lightning intuition was his: 'things flash across me', she would say. That trait would serve Tom well as he rose to become a star performer in the Victorian firmament. Maternal wit and paternal temper formed an explosive combination. They left Tom quick and sharp, with a short fuse and a low flashpoint.

This mental ferocity had its matching exterior. Tom's piercing eyes and penetrating stare were set off by a raptorial mouth. His boyhood years did nothing to diminish this predatory look. He grew lean and gangling, with straight black hair and a permanent sarcastic expression, signalling a lethal bite. It went with the mocking surplice, as the boy turned his collar back to front and preached 'to my mother's maids in the kitchen'.[2]

The Huxleys were a strange, impassioned family, permanently at odds, with no vice or virtue that was not exaggerated in the youngest member. Being 'much younger than the rest', Tom rarely saw his brothers and grew up 'while they were little more than strangers to me'. He was heroically alone, or so an inner voice told him – paternal neglect and poverty leaving him 'without [much formal] education and without friends of my own age, left to quench my own running thirst for knowledge as I but might'. A battling mentality gave him inner strengths, but the insularity bred a bitter streak. Cocooned in his mental world, he became introspective and 'one of the most secretive thin-skinned mortals in the world'.

Of his three brothers, James was four years older and 'the only one for whom I felt any inkling of affection'. Jim and Tom were lookalikes, the identical hot-tempered, hyperactive pair who 'can't take things easily'. Both were feisty, but Tom had the laconic edge. The oldest brother, George Knight Huxley, was the staid one, already on his way to becoming a barrister and businessman when Tom was a toddler. He would subsidize the others in their hours of need: 'my sage and prudent brother', Tom called him. 'The truth is . . . we are all three too much alike to get on well. Our intense though hidden selfishness lies at the root of each of our characters, and is the source of its good & its evil'. It gave them a 'determination & force of character'.[3] It also put the poison into their clashes. The third brother, William, was eventually estranged by one of these boiling feuds and Tom never saw him again.

The sympathy and security came from his raven-haired sister Lizzie. Indeed, 'of the surprising six people who sprang from our father & mother', Tom always told her, 'you and I are the only two who seemed to be capable of fraternal love'. Nine years older, she was a mother figure and adored accordingly. Like so many daughters in large households, she was the unsung heroine. She helped with Tom's religious training and, speaking French and German, fired the boy's interest in Goethe. Theirs was an intense bond, never to be broken. Tom was more detached from the elder sister, Ellen, and when her life took a disastrous turn he could only 'marvel' that she and Lizzie 'sprang from the same stock'.[4]

At the age of eight, in 1833, Tom started in his father's school, and a 'Pandemonium of a school' at that. Twenty-four months there was the only schooling he had in his life. By now Ealing School had dwindled to 40 pupils. The fall in standards was even more evident and the masters 'cared about as much for our intellectual and moral welfare as if they were baby-farmers'. Burly louts terrorized the younger lads, although 'bullying was the least of the ill practices'. He must have studied Ovid and Virgil, music and mathematics, but all he could remember was laying out the class tough, William Poideoin. The wiry Tom had always been victimized, 'but there was a wild-cat element in me which, when roused, made up for lack of weight' and, notwithstanding a black eye, 'I licked my adversary effectively'.[5] This David and Goliath image would become an emblem of a life's struggle in a hostile society.

The school's decline crippled Tom's father. His '28 years faithful service' counted for nought; his fees collapsed and in 1835 he abandoned teaching.[6] George, at 55, took the family north to his native Coventry, armed with a letter of recommendation from old boy Newman.

So Tom spent his early teens footloose in the silk-weaving city of Coventry. Here his grandfather had owned 'a large old inn' while raising his family on a farm a few miles from the city, but he had died in debt and both had been sold 30 years before Tom's birth. The city was small enough to amble around in an hour. Hemmed in by commons and landed estates, it had become ingrown and choked. Rows of half-timbered houses hid hives of congested courts containing most of the 30,000 inhabitants. Every house had its loom, turning out fancy ribbons for the lower classes. Down endless terraces Tom saw them, little bent men pressed against clattering looms, with women and children winding the silk.

George Huxley took over Coventry's new Savings Bank. This should have been a wise move, as retrenchment in Parliament was mirrored by penny-pinching in private life, and the 'old stocking gave way to the savings-bank'. Everywhere the ethic was evident: the Huxley family arrived to find the ribbon masters sweeping the Anglican gentry out of the Town Hall after the first civic elections, and selling the corporation silver to pay for reforms. The bank was no less a symbol of thrift and self-sufficiency.

But the weavers never trusted it. A leaked word from the bank about their savings and the boss might cut their wages. And anyway they had their own friendly societies, legalized in 1836. Dozens sprang up in local pubs; here the weavers kept their own company, as they downed a pint and paid in their pennies.[7] Not that they could make any deposits, with the onset of a recession in 1837. The Ealing boy became used to 'their dialect and ways', and to their sallow faces (the silk's delicacy allowed them no windows or winter fires), but he saw few in his father's bank.

With his father struggling, Tom was thrown on to his own devices. He had no more schooling, 'nor sympathy in any intellectual direction'. It left him with a biting resentment. His sisters eked out a living with a dame school. Six year-olds would attend for a year before becoming winders on their fathers' looms. But as the corner shops collapsed and families starved on one hand-out loaf a week – plus a little 'mother's mercy' (opium) to 'deaden the gnawing wolf within' – the pennies for education vanished.

Tom recoiled into a fantasy world, escaping into a secret realm of science, 'dreaming my own dreams'. At 12, rummaging through his father's library, he encountered James Hutton's *Theory of the Earth*, that aimless eternal earth, wheeling on, with no signs of a beginning and 'no prospect of an end'. Voyaging through the vastness, Tom became withdrawn, his emotions confused. From his nightly cosmic wanderings came 'Joys and anticipation', where daily reality brought only disappointment in 'all those whom I had reason to love and value most'. Cynical and sad, he saw 'absolutely nothing to bring me into contact with the world – and I hated and avoided it'.[8]

He could ramble over the surrounding commons, past villages 'black with coal dust . . . and broken by Dissent'. But each cottage showed the same sickly occupants. Peering through their windows revealed scenes of appalling filth, with pregnant 16 year-old daughters destined for a life of drudgery. Tom did not need to be told by the sour-stomached critic Thomas Carlyle that society had to be cleansed. But reading the essayist did give him a sense of religious mission which owed nothing to a decrepit theology. Young Tom learned that new heroes were needed – Great Men with a sense of destiny.

Carlyle also taught him the heroic quality of work. Play was not for Tom, nor any of the 'pursuits of boys of my own age'. Carlyle breathed the Alpine air of German romanticism and Tom took up the language. It was another fortification; scholarly airs could shield a sensitive soul. Friends found him 'pretending to make hay with one hand, while in the other he held a German Book!'[9] The turgid tomes were mischievously hidden at picnics, but the ribbing only increased the boy's aloofness.

Intellectually stifled, he sought out older men, ribbon masters. But still this upstart David showed his slingshot mentality. Even among these manufacturers he 'was too proud to be treated as one whit of less importance than they'. But his mentors were indulgent and well versed, Unitarians and Independents, marginal men developing new forms of knowledge. Their Chapel science was based on natural causes rather than the Anglicans' miracles. Such materialism went with the wheeze-and-snort of steam. No supernatural lore to underpin the status quo for them: the ribbon masters' earthy science was to move society on. It was to usher in the cotton millennium. Power-looms went with dissent. Often they went with doubt: it was 'an age of darkness, and yet of brightness . . . *Steam, iron, smoke, egoism, doubt*, and *distrust*, are all alike in colour'. In Coventry the future George Eliot lost her Puritan faith. And here Thomas Huxley's religious pilgrimage began.

In one businessman, George May, Tom found a sympathetic ear and an appealingly irreverent approach. The Lord's Day was not so much for observance as to argue the ground of all existence:

> Sunday. Hinckley. Had a long argument with M[r].
> May on the nature of the soul & difference between
> it & matter[.] I maintained that it cannot be proved
> that matter is *essentially* – as to its base – different
> from soul. M[r]. M. wittily said, soul was the
> perspiration of matter – We cannot find the
> absolute basis of matter we only know it by its
> properties neither know we the soul in any other
> way . . .[10]

This ethereal talk was set against a background clatter. Three new steam factories went up in Coventry in 1836–8. Steam power promised a new destiny. It might even have been Tom's. Stephenson's locos were speeding faster every year, too fast for Coventry, bypassed as the first London-Birmingham railway in 1838 took away its road trade. But it was electricity that fascinated Tom. He jotted memos in a hand-stitched notebook – 'make a galv. battery' or 'try the exp[t]. of a simple galvanic current', wondering if he could crystallize carbon. He was always seeking components, causes, mechanisms. His imagination stretched to the heavens, looking for ultimate particles or 'speculating on the cause of colours at sunset'.[11]

But industry was not to be Tom's destiny. Every Coventry lad became an apprentice. It was a peculiar city, where only those who had served a seven-year indenture (in any trade) could become voters. For a boy fascinated by philosophy, his apprenticeship could only be in medicine. Even then he faced an ethical dilemma, studying while the poor starved. He justified himself with an epigraph in his notebook: 'Philosophy can bake no bread; but it can procure for us God freedom & immortality. Which now is more practical Philosophy or Economy'?[12] It was a question for life.

Both sisters married medical men in 1839. The urban build-up created an urgent need for doctors. The silk-paternalists had opened a second dispensary, where the weavers picked up their drugs for a penny-a-week subscription. An old part-timbered house was even being converted into Coventry's first hospital. Tom tunnelled the cheapest way into the cheapest profession, burrowing behind brother Jim. Lizzie's husband, 39 year-old surgeon's son John Salt, had already apprenticed Jim. Even before Ellen's marriage, her own beau John Charles Cooke was teaching Tom the trade.

Cooke was a beer-swilling, opium-chewing man of massive medical lore, a rambunctious entrepreneur who could teach anything for a fee: anatomy, obstetrics, pharmacy or forensic medicine. While training Tom he was editing a huge compendium of medical lectures. Not just *any* lectures, but those of the flamboyant John Elliotson: a fierce materialist who saw the brain pour out thoughts as the liver does bile – a *provocateur* whose outrageous Spinozaism took away the soul and the 'consoling' Christian hopes 'of the despised and the miserable'.[13] Elliotson was a brilliant innovator, whose mesmeric experiments were positively theatrical. (Too much so even for London's 'godless' University College, which sacked him after his hypnotized patients caused havoc.) Cooke never shied away from heresy or hard work.

Tom began at 13 under Cooke, not gently, in deference to his tender years, but traumatically. The lad entered a dissecting room to find a naked cadaver – a cold body and a dead brain which had once glowed with hopes and desires. His morbid curiosity 'overpowered all other feelings'. He stood for hours, transfixed by the gruesome probing as the corpse was dismembered. The human gore was emotionally shattering. He fell into a strange lethargy.

For weeks he deteriorated, 'poisoned' somehow, until he looked 'thin and ill'.[14] His distraught parents sent him to a friend's farm, where the catharsis of haymaking carried him back to an innocent past and worked its healing power. Farmyard smells would always remind him of his rebirth on those sweet autumn mornings, even if the scars never quite healed.

He began questioning the meaning of evil and death. How did it square with God's beneficence? It did not, according to Southwood Smith's *Divine Government*, that Unitarian bible which Tom read at George May's. This was a provocative book – a plea that poverty and distress were signs that society had taken a wrong turn and that reform was a divine duty. 'Agree with him partly', Tom jotted on 25 October 1840. But wouldn't the Unitarian's denial of Christ's divinity and miracles have an 'injurious effect on morals'?

Coventry exposed Tom to a biting sectarianism. He heard the shrieking denunciations of Anglican privilege – to tithes and church rates, to the Church monopoly on Oxbridge education and professional posts. These were the corrupt fruits of State endowment. Radicals saw the Church continuing to 'commit fornication, until the Dissenters tear her ... from her ILLICIT EMBRACE' with the State. Tom was among defiant, proud men whose resistance to the Church had been unprecedented. Some 50,000 summonses a year had been issued by the clergy to prise tithe money out of the Dissenters. After reading Southwood Smith, Tom had 'a long talk with my mother & father about the right to make Dissenters pay church rates – & whether there ought to be any Establishment – I maintained that there ought not in both cases'.[15] He was learning the morality of civil disobedience.

In the anatomy schools the sectarian factions were buzzing with discontent. 'I hate all people who want to found sects', Tom jotted. 'It is not error but sectarian error – nay & even sectarian truth w^h. causes the unhappiness of mankind'. Yet he could not keep his fingers out of the fire. In an age when students dabbled in immensities, he argued passionately about Creation. So intense were the discussions on 'medical metaphysics' during classes that one teacher was 'afraid that ... *common physic*, by which so many of us "live, and move, and have our being," will fall to the ground!'[16]

Now Tom had to think seriously about common physic himself.

*

At 15 he took his first real look at the Great Babylon. Both brothers-in-law had gone to London, Salt to practise, Cooke to teach. On 7 January 1841 he followed them down.

In Buckingham Palace the popular young Queen Victoria, three years on the throne and only 21, had just married Prince Albert. In Parliament peers still ruled and patronage guaranteed all things. Lord Melbourne was Prime Minister, and the great Whig salons held power – but only just. The reform drive of the 1830s – with its acts to widen the middle-class vote and democratize the town halls, and its bills to benefit Dissenters (who had even been forced to marry in Anglican churches) – had petered out. In 1841 Sir Robert Peel was set to put the Conservatives back on the government benches. Not that the 'benches' were much for Tom to look at, being in the patched-up portion of the Houses of Parliament, which had been gutted by fire in 1834.

London – haloed in a 'sublime canopy' of smoke, with its gas-lit streets and islands of gentrified opulence. Fashionable carriages paraded through Hyde Park flaunting their wealth. The world's largest city, a sea of 2 million faces, bred a numbing awe. One could drown in the 'ocean stream of life' flowing down Regent Street. Nothing matched the elegance of Mayfair, or Nash's stucco terraces around Regent's Park. Opulence, anonymity and round-the-clock activity gave the city an excitement unknown in the provinces.

But Tom saw little of this salubrious side. Cooke had apprenticed him to Thomas Chandler, a lowlife doctor in the East End. There the gloomy waves were of the hovelled poor, wallowing in filth and disease. He had entered a dark world, penetrated only by missionaries shocked by the 'moral degradation'. London had its vile excesses too.

That January Tom found himself alone in a tiny Rotherhithe surgery. The horrors he saw there were to mark him for life. The East London poor were as little known as 'the savages of Australia'. Yet no aborigine, he later remarked, was 'half so savage, so unclean' as these troglodyte tenement dwellers. Rooms were putrid from overflowing cesspools. Even sanitation pioneers such as Southwood Smith (who took Dickens to see the fever nests) needed a 'dose of fanaticism, as a sort of moral coca', to stomach the sights.[17] Starvation left the children emaciated and typhus killed them. Even death brought its own shame. Wasteland burials were so common in Rotherhithe that rotting bodies were thrown up with each new interment. It was a macabre winter.

Thomas Chandler was a reforming practitioner,[18] a former House Surgeon at University College Hospital and full of Elliotson's hypnotic techniques. Tom watched him mesmerize his delirious patients, passing his hands rhythmically over their faces, putting them into a calming sleep. The trance was a 'marvellous remedy' for gnashing fits and incurable tics, his speciality, and he had plenty of twitching maniacs to practise on.[19]

Tom must have sensed the shambles around him. Mesmerism, though it gave the underprivileged General Practitioners more power, was a two-edged sword. People were getting hold of it. Young girls sleepwalking on stage were turning the practice into a sexually charged side-show attraction. Street 'patterers' carried lurid placards announcing a new pamphlet 'The Diabolical Practices of Dr --- on his Patient when in a state of Mesmerism'.[20] While reformers were trying to police medicine, circumscribing it in their own professional hands, lay performers were running amok.

In the nine years since the 1832 Reform Bill the medical ranks had been in revolt. They too wanted a widening of their power, a say in the running of the elite licensing bodies, the Royal Colleges of Physicians and Surgeons. General Practitioners were unionizing and attacking the knightly hospital consultants who ran the colleges like rotten boroughs. Chandler's mesmerists were milling with the rest outside the porticoes of the Oxbridge-Anglican Establishment. Tom was swept along, listening to the shouts for talent before rank, watching as his medical class tried to gain a say.

The turbulence tossed the boy about. A boy he still was. 'I have had my trowsers seated', he told his mother, 'but I have grown lately & they are outrageously short – the best wear I am sorry to say very badly – wear white & shabby – But Nelly inspected me the last time I was in London ... & I dare say you have received an "*official*" account'.[21]

There were breaks in the gloom for Tom: Jim might arrive, or he would visit a theatre with 'Aunt Lizzy' (his mother's cousin Eliza Knight). But by day the youngster steeled himself for his slum rounds. His surgery was on Paradise Street, itself a sick joke. He was a hundred paces from the water's edge, traced down dark alleys between the warehouses and pubs. Here, on a sewage-slimy Thames, as belching smoke and river fog blended into choking pea-soupers, one drew 'gloom with every breath'.

The deformed garret-dwellers showed the need for a new kind of regeneration. The Church was a rich man's luxury, irrelevant here. 'I dare say there ain't ten out of a hundred gals what's living with men', a costermonger said, 'what's been married Church of England fashion'. The Bible held no hope and word-of-mouth ignorance acquired mythic proportions. But there was a dumb perspicacity on the streets, and a casual incredulity about rich folks' notions. One ragged girl had heard:

> that the world was made in six days: the beasts, the birds, the fish, and all . . . There was only one house at that time as was made, and that was the Ark for Adam and Eve and their family. It seems very wonderful indeed how all this world was done so quickly. I should have thought that England alone would have took double the time.[22]

A new foundation for living was needed, a new way of controlling mores and freeing people. Factory workers were marching, demanding the vote and annual ballots, uniting in support of the democratic People's Charter. Tom read Carlyle's *Chartism* on this 'bitter discontent grown fierce and mad'. Riot police were no solution; society had an obligation to the destitute. Duty to the working classes was *Chartism*'s message. Something had to step in where Christianity had failed. The seething slums, Tom said, gave 'a terrible foundation of real knowledge to my speculations'. Science had to pay social dividends.

He sat grinding drugs in his apothecary's shop, reading: 'in that little narrow surgery I used to work morng after morng & eveng after eveng', ploughing through 'that insufferably dry & profitless book Humes *History* [of Great Britain]. how I worked against hope through the series of thefts robberies & throat cutting in those three first vols'. The despair mirrored his surroundings. Rotherhithe was notorious for the knife-wielding gangs in its criminal slums, and its underbelly of 'whores, pandars, crimps, bullies'.[23] But the real obscenity was the middle-class indifference to this ocean of poor.

'*Cursed is the ground*' indeed. Engulfed by drunks and whores the boy became guilt-ridden. He anguished over the 'deep draught of abomination I took'. Remorse led to mental flagellation, that evangelical comfort: 'I confess to my shame', he said, 'that few men have drunk deeper of all kinds of sin than I'. He had to regenerate himself before he 'earned absolute destruction'.

Guilt came from being middle-class among the destitute. The starving were mostly decent people, whose only crime was poverty. 'I see no fault committed that I have not committed myself', he jotted (it was Goethe's aphorism). He remained a Puritan in this moral rectitude and resignation, but he could never accept the notion of innate depravity. There had to be hope. He moved closer to Southwood Smith's view of earthly salvation. Acquiescence in the face of such poverty was a sin; 'redeeming the people from a degraded condition is a duty', Smith had insisted. Welfare and educational programmes must bring society back in line with God's benevolent intent.[24] Tom had begun his own regeneration. Monastic study would put him on the road to redemption.

He spent nights tackling chemistry and history, then came Latin and Greek. He would work his way out of the quagmire. He set his sights on University College, that emblem of Dissenting aspiration, with its radical French sciences and Benthamite economics, all a snub to Oxford and Cambridge exclusivity. By April 1841 spare hours were devoted to algebra, geometry and physics. Letters went off to his mother: 'I got the books all right', but is 'there not a Latin Grammar at home, & an Euclid? I am glad my father sent Hutton for I like it much the best but the college requires Euclid'.

Lists tumbled out of him, read this, read that, followed by admonishing progress reports. By the summer he was deep in physiology, having dumped Hume's *History* 'in utter disgust & despair'. Like all self-improvers he had faith in book learning; education became a passion, as it did with so many radicals seeking 'bread, knowledge and freedom', convinced that self-improvement was a path to power. The new steam presses had caused prices to plummet, and with the newspaper tax down to a penny (the hated tax was a failed government initiative to crush the pauper press) the streets were awash with radical prints. Swamping them was the *Penny Magazine*, 200,000 subsidized copies a week to divert the masses with more innocuous knowledge. Tom flew high and low, ploughing through Müller's *Elements of Physiology* while picking up insect trivia in the *Penny Cyclopaedia*.

There was no wilier product of the 'Steam Intellect' society than Tom Huxley. His workbench discipline was extraordinary. Week in, week out he kept up a punishing schedule: on Tuesdays and Thursdays physiology, on other weekdays a 'chronological abstract of reigns', evenings of arithmetic, Saturdays devoted to chemistry and physics, with an hour's German each day. In between he grappled with Guizot's *Civilization in Europe* and built electromagnets. Always he pushed harder: 'I must get on faster than this', he chivvied himself as he fell behind in Ancient History, 'and let me remember this – that it is better to read a little & thoroughly than cram a crude undigested mass into my head'.[25]

With an intellectual head of steam Tom packed his books and escaped the ghetto late in 1841. He moved in with sister Lizzie and John Salt. At 14 Euston Place, next to the new Euston Station, they were close to University College Hospital. Tom and Jim, that identical pair, were living in tandem. As Jim left Salt's apprenticeship and went to Gloucester Lunatic Asylum as dispensing chemist, Tom moved in. Lizzie was protective towards her little brother. She pushed him on, sure of his bright future.[26] Here family life was more congenial, and Tom adored her year-old daughter Jessie, who was just starting to walk.

Euston Place was a medical enclave. It saw the comings-and-goings of professors and swaggering students with their '"loudly" dressed' look. Tom's other brother-in-law John Cooke was a neighbour at No 18.[27] He had come down to teach across the road at a cut-price anatomy school, Sydenham College. This was among the last of the private schools, set up behind University College Hospital. 'Dingy purlieus' these places were, often converted houses, offering cheap courses to lure students away from the hospitals. They were breeding grounds for dissidents, their angry teachers engaged in a dirty war with the elite surgeons. The drop in student numbers during the depression only exacerbated this rivalry. Survivors like Sydenham College were clinging on at the bottom end of the market.

Tom took the affordable option. He enrolled at Sydenham College in October 1841. More floats from his brothers-in-law saw him through – £4 for the medicine course, £5 for chemistry, £2 for Cooke's forensic medicine class.[28] A 'mildewy appearance' marked his fellows: plaid trousers, long hair topped by stove-pipe hats, the reek 'of full-flavoured Cubas'. Add to this dissolute air a proud and opinionated voice, and that was Tom. At night deep-dish discussions grew slurred in the grogshops as the hot topics were aired: mesmerism, medical reform, Chartism, the poor laws, and not least the reflex arc – that new concept pioneered at Sydenham College (and slated by the medical barons as soulless and 'mechanistic', because the reflex jerk was not under conscious control: the body was acting as an automaton). Not to mention the eternal verities: *Punch* lampooned the students' tipsy forays into metaphysics, with skew-hatted reprobates prodding one another: 'What you say about Corporeity is all very well, but it presupposes the idea of

– (hic) – absolute spirituality and transcendental – (hic) – perfection . . .'[29] The topic was Tom's to a tee.

In these back-street schools flaming politics were fuelled by emancipatory science. The Dissenting teachers spat at rank and wealth; some worked in gin palaces or brought petitions for their pupils to sign. They made morals cultural products, they made thought a function of brain matter, and they claimed the entire mental realm for the new medical expert. They were tearing the spiritual halo from mind and nature and usurping the role of the priest. These angry Dissenters demanded professional parity with the State-supported clergy. No wonder Dr Arnold at Rugby School saw a generation of 'materialist atheists of the greatest personal profligacy' being raised in this Sodom and Gomorrah.[30] But most of all the firebrands screamed defiance at the 'medical aristocracy'.

That was even true of the urbane coffee-drinking Marshall Hall, founder of Sydenham College and discoverer of the reflex arc. As head of a radical ginger group, the British Medical Association, he damned the College of Physicians for its Anglican exclusivity:

> Can anything be imagined more preposterous, more
> iniquitous, more *immoral*, than this mingling of sacred
> things with profane, of religious with medical distinctions
> and privileges? Of religion it is a mockery; it is hypocrisy
> . . . it is intolerance; it is, in a word, the same fire which
> consumed the bodies of our fellow-men in Smithfield![31]

Tom heard the call for merit before Church privilege. Hall was trying to open up the top jobs to talent. He could be seen in college, dissecting turtles to prove his reflex arc, although outside his science and politics were derided by conservatives.

While the top hospitals trained the gentry's consultants – those 'plundering monopolists' who took the plum jobs at the Royal Colleges – Tom's school taught the humble GPs. These were destined for the inner cities. They were the new men who soul-searched about slums and sanitation, who used the new secular sciences as a tool for education and liberation. And for their pains, they were despised as a 'low born cell-bred selfish' mob. Tom was clearly gazing up from below.

The medical world wasn't all demos and debauchery. Of course the press and pulpit focused on those 'anencephalous abortions of the human race' found drunk in class, but usually billiards and smoking were the worst excesses. Even these were eschewed by Tom. He stood apart 'isolated among my fellows, in habits, in thought and still more by poverty'. Not 'by any means shy, in fact, quite t'other', but he was 'as sensitive as a woman, as proud as Satan and as poor as a church mouse'.[32]

Still, like *Punch*'s drunks he began 1842 grappling with imponderables. Studying muscles and bones only sent him soaring into the clouds. Trying to pigeon-hole all knowledge as either 'physical' or 'metaphysical', he stopped short at 'morality'.[33] The boy had been buffeted by so many winds that he no longer knew whether morality was a cultural product or God's gift; the former, he began to suspect. He had become a radical; long-haired still, but with a straight stovepipe and sober breath.

2

Son of the Scalpel

TOM NOW LOOKED THE part, a serious study in shabbiness, his cast-off clothes tailored to his cut-price school: 'a very pale, thin, lanky, ugly body with dreadfully long hair which no persuasion would induce me to cut, and a generally neglected style of attire'.[1]

But still Lizzie saw in her Bohemian brother the family's deliverance. 'My highest hopes are centred in that boy', she always said.[2] In April 1842 she was vindicated: Tom took his first certificates of merit at the Sydenham College awards.

Fortified, he pushed on after Easter, registering for the spring botany course. Or perhaps he was egged on by Cooke, an expert on medicinal plants. His new teacher, like so many in these parlous private schools, was an idiosyncratic outsider – or rather an insider turned out, an Oxford-trained clergyman who had lost his vocation and was looking to a new salvation. This was Richard Hoblyn. A kindly soul with a friendly face, Hoblyn was now eking out a living by writing chemistry manuals and books on steam engines, and teaching botany to top up.[3] (When all else failed he went into business with Cooke, cramming London University applicants for their entrance exams.)

Unable to afford the 3d bus fare, Tom strode the four miles from Euston to Chelsea to hear the nurseryman's son and University College lecturer John Lindley at the Physic Garden.[4] He hiked over two or three times a week, always finding Lindley ruddy-faced and hearty, in stark contrast to his students. Occasionally Tom was defeated in his trek. On 2 May 1842, two days before his 17th birthday, demonstrators taking the 30-foot Chartist petition to Parliament brought the capital to a standstill. Flyers went up everywhere, crowds waved tricolours. The depression was hitting London hard, with mass unemployment, and the 100,000 Chartists in a one-and-a-half-mile column blocked all routes. It was orderly, but ominous.

A different sort of flyer forced Tom's pace later in May. The Worshipful Company of Apothecaries announced its yearly competition for medals. (Apothecaries were the lowest of the disintegrating medical estates: drug compounders and General Practitioners, the shopkeeping class of medical men.) Tom looked 'longingly at the notice'. Salt urged him on, and Tom entered his name, telling no one else but Lizzie, fearfully ambitious but terrified of appearing vain. ('Virtue . . . aware of itself is sickly', he copied out of Carlyle.) He put in long hours for a young hand, from 8 am. until midnight.[5] He mined out Cooke's library and set into the nation's. Ten minutes away lay the British Museum. He marched past the Grenadiers guarding its entrance, past the rubble (the new wings were under a forest of scaffold), past masons sculpting stone colonnades, past horses turning giant cement mixers. He signed the visitors' book, glanced at the giraffes on the stairway, and headed for the library to lose more hours in the *Annales des Sciences Naturelles*.

For three summer months he kept up this regime. In the process he swept off Hoblyn's prize at Sydenham College, winning a book, *La Botanique*. As a diversion he pored over his homemade batteries, puzzling at the currents breaking up chemical solutions.[6] But the pace of each 'long hot summer's walk over to Chelsea' showed where his ambition lay – in the Apothecaries' medal.

On exam day, 1 August, he was a disembodied wreck. How he got to Apothecaries Hall in Blackfriars – 'Rhubarb Hall' to the students – he never knew. All he recalled was Lizzie throwing her slipper after him for luck. He sat, the youngest of six, at a long table, the candidates glaring 'at one another like strange cats in a garret'. Paper and plants were placed in front of each at 11 am. The invigilator opened his *Times* to read of the Chartist unrest. And there Tom sat, only the spine-tingling 'Scratch, scratch, scratch' disturbing the still air. At 4 pm. the others finished, but he and a rival asked to carry on, furiously competing, his fellow looking like 'an attorney's clerk writing for his dinner'. Tom, cramp in his hands, collapsed exhausted at 8 pm., his rival at 9 pm. It was his first public exam, an unprecedented eight hours of writing, and he would never forget it. Lizzie and Salt waited up, worried, and 'Great were the greetings . . . when I got home'.[7]

*

Brother Jim was muddling along at Gloucester Lunatic Asylum and the boys cogitated on their careers. Doubtless it was Cooke again who saw the opening. London's newest teaching hospital, Charing Cross, offered six free places a year.[8] Their father could scarcely afford the servant's-wage sum of £42 a year fees. So Jim and Tom, the identical hyperactive pair, continued their careers together: they both applied for free tuition.

Free scholarships were for the sons of destitute gents. Embarrassed vicars and surgeons applied for their boys, whose 'station in society gave them a just pretension'. Respectability was the watchword: two clergymen had to vouch that Tom's father was a distressed teacher 'unable to defray the expense'. Unlike the grubby back-street schools, Charing Cross was not prepared to open the floodgates to tinkers and chimney sweeps. Consultants feared the 'irruption of the Gothic hordes'. Even corner druggists were edging out the few labourers who had a foot on the slippery professional slope. Hospital managers looked into Huxley senior's 'station in society' and his sons' 'classical education' and 'moral character'.[9]

That August the 'Gothic hordes' were a sensitive subject. Tens of thousands were massing on London's commons; a General Strike paralysed the cotton towns as a protest against wage cuts. Demonstrators were shot in Preston, after a hail of stones stopped the Mayor reading the Riot Act. The clashes came closer, much closer: crowds jeered the columns of Grenadier Guards on their way to Euston Station to crush the northern strikers. Screams of 'Bloody Butchers' curdled the air. Outside Salt's house in Euston Square the troops had bayonets fixed. Yards from Tom's window baton-wielding police bludgeoned a path into the station. For a week in mid-August the family was besieged; daily the battalions ploughed their way in. Daily the crowds shouted 'Don't go and slaughter your starving fellow countrymen'. It was a confirmation that reform had failed the labouring classes. Subjected to workhouses and wage cuts, denied the vote or a decent living, they were clenching their fists. 'Nature, God, and reason, have condemned this inequality', announced the Chartist proclamation on 17 August.[10] It was a thought. What *did* Nature say of social inequality?

Through the uproar the boys continued to canvass the clergy's vote. Jim was safe in Gloucester, although even here a commotion arose as a demagogue was summonsed for a show trial. George Holyoake, young, fluent and provocative (or, in the *Times*' view, a 'miserable-looking lad' indulging in an 'absurd harangue') inflamed

Gloucester Crown Court by denying God. He added injury to the insult by suggesting that rich parsons go on half pay during the depression. In a nine-hour speech he toed the line of his gutter rag, the *Oracle of Reason* (penny trash which demanded a priest-free democratic society and used evolution to oust a patrician God). On 16 August the judge recognized the 'enormity' of Holyoake's blasphemy and jailed him for six months, leaving no doubt that cloth-cap atheism was taken as an attack on the Anglican State. There were no such scruples about the Church for Jim. He topped the clerical requirements by lining up five reverends as referees, which at least showed willing. But, like Tom, he was running up debts and had begun tapping Salt again. Charing Cross promised a career, he reassured Salt, and a chance to liquidate 'both principle and interest'.[11] Tom's thought exactly, with the country crumbling and the strike biting.

Salt and Cooke added their references, and stranger voices were heard. Father scrounged from his Ealing old-boys. The down-at-heel ex-master again doffed his cap to well-to-do pupils. By now there was no mightier High Church voice than that of John Henry Newman. He was enormously influential, fighting Church reform and reinstating Church ritual (even if he stood on a precipice, ready to jump over to Rome). The boys were a generation younger than Newman, born long after he had left Ealing. But their father still begged an endorsement for them, as he had once for himself.

Tom was happier pulling himself up by his own bootstraps. Everyone thought he had lost the Apothecaries' prize. Salt appeared one day with a dejected expression, having heard that the winners were University College men. 'Lizzie came to comfort me and I believe felt it more than I did'.

> What then was my surprise on returning home one
> afternoon to find myself suddenly seized and the whole
> female household vehemently insisting on kissing me. It
> appeared an official-looking letter had arrived for me, and
> Lizzie . . . could not restrain herself from opening it. I was
> second [and] to receive a medal accordingly.

The prospect of a silver medal on top of his Sydenham College prizes ensured his place at Charing Cross. On 6 September 1842 the managers took the unprecedented step of admitting both brothers.[12] So on 1 October 17 year-old Tom Huxley and superannuated Jim joined the sons of the surgeons and clergy as free scholars.

*

Charing Cross Hospital was solid and classical, shouting its philanthropic importance in the salubrious Strand. Building work had
only finished in 1834, as the New Poor Law was put into place and
the workhouses planned. At no time in the nineteenth century did
sick paupers need more help. (The rich had their five-guinea
consultants.) Fitting out the wards had taken the rest of the
decade. These had been lean years for a charity serving London's
swelling army of poor. When the Huxleys arrived the hospital was
only just out of the red.

Decimus Burton's building stood on a small triangular strip, its
main entrance on Agar Street (a short new road running off the
Strand). Tom Huxley took rooms at No. 9, facing the porticoed
entrance.[13] From here he could see the wan faces of the destitute
crowding round the waiting room.

The plan had been grand: the first modern hospital, dispensary
and medical school built as one. It sounded fine in the prospectus;
in reality Huxley found only three upper floors finished and then
some of the wards empty. The so-called 'medical school' was a
few rooms in the basement between the morgue and the chapel.
Frugality was the key. Cost-conscious managers ran it on a tight
budget, as befitted a retrenching workhouse age. Huxley suffered
with his patients: coal fires were extinguished at dusk as the
gaslights went on. Budgeting even hit his canteen lunch. To 'avoid
trouble and waste' it was always beef and it was always boiled.[14]
No fish or pork was served, and no vegetables but potatoes and
rice, each unappetizing platter saved by a little beer.

At least underground the din was muffled. The widened Strand
with its new shopfronts was drawing Oxford Street's crowds, but
nothing penetrated the sombre air of the morgue. Above was a
crush of carriages, the clatter of iron rims on cobbles, so deafening
that the Strand had just been experimentally resurfaced with
wood. All around were entertainments, from gentlemen's clubs to
the notorious Coal Hole, where carousers shouted their obscene
'evidence' during mock stage divorces. By day *Morning Chronicle*
hacks rushed to their offices. At night revivalists preached at the
'profligate wretches' about them. They could be heard praising the
Lord for reclaiming sots, or applauding missionaries from the
heathen colonies. Well-meaning prigs, Huxley thought them; so
many 'Stigginses', like the po-faced reverend in *Pickwick Papers*,
wheedling money out of passers-by to provide 'the infant negroes
of the West Indies with flannel waistcoats'. All life was here, from
the hymn-singers of Exeter Hall to the 'gay' girls whistling a

different tune outside. Huxley must have agreed with Dr Johnson: 'the full tide of existence is at Charing Cross'.[15]

Opposite on the Strand stood the rebuilt Hungerford Market. Its cavernous interior stretched down to the Thames, a jostling confusion of stalls and barrows, with women in bonnets and shawls shouting their wares. Huxley could rummage for old clothes, or fresh vegetables, or descend to the vaults for his whelks and fish – and coming out, he could pick up tea in the corner grocery.

The Strand improvements were not the only sign of civic pride. It was never as fashionable as Regent Street, but more interesting, with its kaleidoscopic facades. The real transformation was occurring in front of St Martin-in-the-Fields church. Nests of ramshackle houses had been cleared to make a huge open space. Huxley could stand on the site and look down Whitehall, or over to Pall Mall, or up to the new National Gallery. This was Trafalgar Square in the making. The people were being pushed out: imperial architecture and municipal pride had no place for the mangy poor.

The other end of the Strand was different. There the stench of social deprivation remained. Squalid, sewage-filled alleys made up the vile no-go rookeries around Drury Lane, whose sick and wounded swelled the hospital's casualty list – so much so that some gentlefolk saw the charity attracting this 'Lazarhouse of disease' back to the affluent end of town.[16]

For the hard-up pupils lured by the bright lights, there were non-medicinal leeches. Money-lenders clustered round the college, turning long-term students into long-term debtors.[17] Not that Tom needed them: Cooke could be tapped, and brother George was good for £30 floats.

At the hospital the surgeon daily walked the wards, dragging 'a miserable tail of a dozen joints'. By year's end the trailing students had seen a thousand patients from the rookeries and road crashes. Eight thousand were treated in Huxley's first year, gashes and building accidents, pouring in from every scaffolded site down to the Houses of Parliament (gutted by fire in 1834), not to mention the crushed limbs from the sewers being laid in the West End. Dickens, who had worked near by, was horrified by the 'ghastly appearance of the hapless creatures' in casualty. 'In one bed, lay a child enveloped in bandages, with its body half-consumed by fire', in another a woman 'in a heavy stupor', her face 'stained with blood'. One girl from the ghetto, thrashed so brutally by her man, died before his eyes. From these gin-sodden rookeries came endless stabbings and beatings. It was a sad fact that cases of 'personal violence' made up the third largest category of casualties.[18]

The 'Dame of the Wards' (matron) ensured a rigid regime, policing her untrained nurses and under-fed poor. Huxley withstood the spartan conditions and mercifully missed reveille: no patient was to be in bed after 7 am., all were to be scrubbed and ready for breakfast at 8 am., no swearing, no 'gross or filthy conduct' by staff or patients, no drunken visitors, no smoking. The squad of domestics doubling as nurses was drilled as tightly. They wore uniforms but they were poorly paid; the sots smuggled in gin for a tip, and fallen angels were regularly cast out. Huxley missed morning prayers in the wards, but not the vicar of St Martin-in-the-Fields on his rounds, performing his own spiritual surgery on the ungodly hovel-dwellers.

Just before 9am. Huxley fought his way through the out-patients (the waiting room was inside the Agar Street entrance), past the gaunt faces and emaciated bodies. Saddest were the hunchbacks and tykes with club-feet, come because the hospital specialized in deformities.[19] Others were dejected, turned away for simply being starving. Some did get in later, by the back entrance. They lay ready, boiled and flayed, for his 11 am. dissections. Unclaimed pauper corpses and workhouse dead were marked down for the medical school. This amid the outcry that, for the crime of being poor, the sentence was dismemberment:

> A worse than felon's doom! for when his life
> Returns to God! then, then the bloody knife
> Must to its work – the body that was starved,
> By puppy doctors must be cut and carved.[20]

And in the depths of the depression there was no shortage, particularly when the first snows fell.

Dissecting Drury Lane's dead was not for the squeamish. Huxley's teachers warned of this disagreeable duty, but he was becoming inured. Not so others, who fled in terror, faced by decapitated heads, hovered over by bloody scalpelled hands – the first fledgling reaction of ashen youths wanting to 'breathe again the salubrious atmosphere of the streets'.[21]

Huxley learned one lesson during these subterranean days. The *Lancet* rammed it home: nothing was to be seen except by dissection. While bad surgeons walked the wards reading 'from other people's bad books', life and death stared them in the face: 'medicine is a *trade*, and not a *science*', the *Lancet* insisted (jabbing at the elite consultants); the apprentice must learn by application.[22] Look for yourself – it was a motto he learnt for life.

On 9 November Huxley attended the Apothecaries' prize-giving 'and bore my share in both pudding and praise'. He collected his silver medal, querying the vanity of prizes. But he told himself that the real 'charm of success lay in Lizzie's warm congratulation'.[23] She in turn prophesied great things 'touching the future fortunes of "the boy"'. Her joy turned sour eight days later. At the height of the depression, with disease and starvation endemic, Lizzie's daughter Jessie died of scarlet fever. She was not two-and-a-half; it was Tom's first sight of death in the family and he was devastated. He could never look back on this period without 'Mental pain' erupting from the 'seething depths'.[24]

It was the beginning of his Charing Cross career and Huxley ground on in a gloom. He threw himself into work and derived inspiration from the strangest source: a godfearing teacher whose lectures were steely cold and whose former life had been too hot. This was the diminutive, lonely Thomas Wharton Jones. Every afternoon Huxley watched this drab, clerk-like man enter, wearing rusty broad-cloth. He stood at a table's edge, 'with downcast eyes, and fingering his watchchain', and talked a cold, clinical and enthralling physiology.[25] The Scots accent betrayed a haunted past. At Huxley's age he had been Robert Knox's assistant when the one-eyed, gold-waistcoated, civic-skewering Knox had the largest anatomy class in Edinburgh. Here, tragedy had turned to public notoriety. As the mob poets shrieked:

> Burke's the murderer, Hare's the thief
> And Knox the butcher who bought all the beef . . .

It had been Wharton Jones and two other assistants who opened the back door to Burke and Hare, unwittingly paying for their sacked-up murder victims. Knox barely escaped the mob after the chilling trial, nor were his assistants spared. A traumatized Wharton Jones fled, wandering from city to city for ten years. He specialized in eye surgery; but like Knox he always looked wider, studying the giant eyes of squids too. And he became an adept embryologist, making his name in 1835 by describing the nucleus in the human ovum (barely seven years after the unfertilized egg itself was discovered).

This had secured him the Charing Cross post. He had only been at the hospital a year when Huxley arrived. It was perhaps fitting that Thomas Wharton – named after the Chairman of the Board of Excise – should twiddle his chain and talk with a clerk's precision. 'Singularly dry and cold in form', Huxley called the lectures, 'but admirable in logical construction, and full of knowledge derived from personal observation'. Their breadth was remarkable. He had Huxley studying the teeth of foetal sharks, feather growth and the sutured jigsaw of the perch's skull. Wharton Jones 'never had any notes' but his talks could have been printed straight off.[26] He was a sad, solitary figure, but Huxley never felt 'so much respect for anybody as a teacher before'.

From such a man Huxley could learn the fastidious side of microscopy. He followed his teacher's interests, examining the formation of blood corpuscles. He kept abreast of the new German cell theory – that all living tissue was composed of discrete cells – and the debates on their central nuclei. He felt the excitement as anatomists finally described the egg's fertilization and the development of a 'rudimental embryo'.[27] So engrossed did he become that while others relaxed in the courtyard his head could be seen silhouetted in an upstairs window peering through an eyepiece. He was in an unused ward fitted up as a museum. The constant frame suggested to one beery wag a pub board, 'The Sign of the Head and Microscope'.

Even up here it was hard to concentrate. Financial crises had forced the hospital to sell some of its street frontage. Pubs and newsagents flaunting pornographic prints lined its sides. Next door conjurors performed in the 'Polygraphic Hall', and the audience's roar carried up to Huxley's museum. Then, after dark, the sleazy nightclubs on Chandos Street at the back opened up, their clientele of 'seedy Dick Swivellers' attracting the patrolling prostitutes. Old tutors knew the pitfalls. They fretted about students, doubled over dismembered corpses. They feared that this charnel-house work would blight the young bud and drive the tyro into these 'saloons to seek the company of harlots and drunkards'.[28]

Huxley's days dragged on. He struggled in for 9 am. chemistry classes, then dissections, with afternoons of physiology, medicine and surgery, followed by physics at 6.30 pm. The *Lancet*'s advice was never to burn the midnight oil. But 'I am like the owls', Huxley said, 'nocturnal natured, and as they can't mouse so I can't work at an other time'.[29] He lurched between backbreaking work and bone-idleness. Slaving at night left him doodling by day. 'I worked extremely hard when it pleased me, and when it did not ... I was extremely idle (unless making caricatures of one's pastors and masters is to be called a branch of industry)'. Quick-witted, he darted from subject to subject, endlessly questing, pursuing his fancy. 'I read everything I could lay my hands upon, including novels, and took up all sorts of pursuits to drop them again quite as speedily'. His intellect, 'rather acute & quick than grasping or deep', made the craft side of medicine a chore.[30] But in an age looking for certainty it was suited to the exactitudes of physiology and the cold logic of chemistry.

That logic was deftly chopped by Huxley's other favourite, George Fownes. He was fresh from Germany's best chemical laboratory at Giessen. He returned with a Ph.D. (a degree unheard of at home). He also returned with the latest German techniques to reduce proteins to their constituents and synthesize bodily byproducts. Chemistry was encroaching on the organic realm for the first time. Fownes was doing what once was thought impossible, making the materials of life. He committed Charing Cross to this laboratory-based 'organic chemistry'. The school's President talked of the science's 'grandeur', and Tom felt it. Fownes had him boiling egg albumen, adding alcohol, passing electric currents, simulating the body's chemistry. He dissolved flesh with alkalis and digested it with acids, like the Germans looking for the molecular basis of muscle activity.[31]

While his teachers used German methods, their overview remained quintessentially English. For them, every atom of the universe functioned perfectly because it was Divinely designed. Fownes was deep in his *Chemistry as exemplifying the Wisdom and Beneficence of God* while Tom was boiling flesh. The book argued that the proximity of Britain's iron and coalfields was providential. For Wharton Jones the body's perfect plan pointed to the same Celestial Draughtsman. 'Profound philosophy!' barked Knox at these 'design arguments' in 1843. Huxley heard the guffaws from the radicals who 'breathed a doubting theism'. Divine design was passé. A 'vile' joke 'peculiar to British physiology', cackled Knox, and 'downright nonsense' as a serious explanation. Wharton Jones, seeking absolution long after Burke was hanged, loathed Knox's stiletto wit. He praised the eye's camera design, and God as a sort of Supreme Fox Talbot. The Establishment applauded; Huxley's two mentors each received the 100-guinea Acton Prize of the Royal Institution, given for books on the Divine in nature.

But Huxley had moved with the cotton Dissenters and Unitarians. He could never accept chemical formulae as God's handwriting

– nor spiritual design as a satisfying explanation of life. He delved into the original German sources and emerged much harder-headed. Atop his student notepad sat a quote from the Zurich anatomist Jacob Henle:

> To explain a Physiological fact means in a word to deduce its necessity from the physical and chemical laws of Nature.[32]

But then hadn't a disapproving Carlyle noted this stark tendency in the age?' Freewill, he said, has 'withdrawn into the dark', and the 'spectral nightmare of . . . necessity usurps its throne'.[33]

But Huxley's fascination with the functional architecture of nature showed. Jim watched his young brother walk off with the awards. At prize-giving on 1 May 1843 Revd J. W. Worthington presented him with Fownes' chemistry and Wharton Jones' physiology medals, praising his 'extraordinary diligence'. As always the vanity of prizes left him cold, and he scratched on the back of Wharton Jones' diploma, 'Well, 'tis no matter. Honour pricks me on'.[34] This nervous indifference was no consolation for Jim, who had to be content with a good conduct note.

Spare hours were now spent a mile away, in the refurbished Royal College of Surgeons. The building was only five years old, yet Huxley marched past doric pillars already 'blackened with coal-smoke'. He sat in the magnificent 90-foot museum, sun streaming in through high alcove windows, lighting three-storey book-lined walls. Twelve thousand exhibits – endless deformities, surgical curios, pickled platypuses and chimpanzee parts – made it the richest vein of morbid and comparative anatomy in town: 'every-thing the imagination of man can conceive'.[35] In pride of place were fossil giants, ground sloths and huge armadillos. And facing them a skeletal notoriety, the human giant, O'Brien, snatched and skeletonized against his dying wish.

Restocking costs were still £3,000 a year, and it showed. In the library was every German source. Here Huxley delved into the latest French tome on the latest subject, 'electrophysiology', his interest piqued by Wharton Jones. Fools knew that electric shocks made hanged felons move, but their betters hardly knew why. Wharton Jones pictured muscles composed of stacked discs sur-rounded by nerve fibres. The current turned them into electro-magnets, whose attraction caused the muscle to tighten. Given this breathtaking analogy, and the bravado with which steam-cranked society saw its designs in nature, one suddenly understands Huxley's delight in the 'mechanical engineering of living machines'.[36]

It was not only the 'engineering part of the business' he loved. The 'architectural' side appealed too – what he called 'the wonderful unity of plan' in the myriad 'diverse living constructions'. Medical London was a powerhouse of this 'philosophical anatomy'. All molluscs were reducible to a common blueprint, all vertebrates to another, insects and crustaceans to a third, starfish to a fourth: it was the law of the age, unity in diversity. Detecting the plan behind the varied fins, fingers and wings gave Gradgrind anatomists their *raison d'être*. This was *the* science in the great Babylon. The 'all-pervading unity' of life was 'one of the most sublime truths in nature'. Animals were not built by Creative whim, but constrained by morphological laws. Legislative Whigs combined with laconic radicals to hail this new zoology based on '*Law* and *Order*'.

Huxley joined them. The spiritual had lost its power. Leafing through his old Coventry notebook one day, he fell on his remark about the Unitarians' anti-miraculous nature injuring morals. 'God help you goose', he scribbled, laughing at his naivety.[37]

Like all great truths the Archetypes of Life could mean anything to anyone. Here, in the conservative College of Surgeons, the grave Richard Owen was beginning to put a new gloss on these groundplans. Owen was diffident, shy – his radical enemies said sly (by which they meant the pet of society patrons). Seven years the Hunterian Professor, he was a brilliant zoologist 'with brains enough to fill two hats'. Chimpanzee anatomy, platypus reproduction, giant moas – he was master of them all, and now turning to fossils. He had caught the public imagination by christening the 'dinosaurs'. He then provoked a gasp by proving that tiny marsupials lived alongside them. Huxley watched Owen escorting the greats around his museum, at once charming and obsequious. In a Chartist age he was the Tory favourite: a scourge of red Lamarckians (and the recipient of a £200 pension from Prime Minister Sir Robert Peel for his pains). It made him the darling of Carlyle's set. They delighted 'in Owen, with all his enthusiasm for fossil reptiles'. A 'tall man with great glittering eyes' was Carlyle's generous comment on Owen's goggle-eyed looks. More generous still, he claimed that he had learned more from Owen 'than from almost any other man'.[38] Owen was to please even more. He was planning to put a definitive shine on these abstract groundplans of life –

turning them into Creative Ideals, pure images existing only in the Divine mind. As the unknown Huxley sat in the library, watching, Owen was in his room upstairs planning his magnum opus on the vertebrate Archetype.

The College of Surgeons overlooked the leafy square of Lincoln's Inn Fields. Huxley would walk to it through the new Tuscan colonnades of Covent Garden market, slipping on the stew of cabbage leaves, weaving among the pie men and flower girls. In an evening he might wander through theatreland, watching the swells stream in to see Edmund Kean in his latest production.[39] Perhaps he stopped at the Bohemian Wych Street pub, The Shakespeare Head. The haunt of artists, hacks and students, it was owned by the editor of *Punch*. The publican was perfectly placed to lampoon medical low-life:

> Son of the scalpel! from whatever class
> You grind instruction just enough to pass

from Charing Cross you come, and every college, 'Thirsting alike for half-and-half and knowledge'.

> Though to cheap hats and boots thy funds incline,
> And light rough Chesterfields at one pound nine;
> Though on the virtues of all plants thou'rt dumb,
> Save the *Nicotina Tabacum*,
> (*Pentandria Digynia*! – Lindley – mum!)[40]

Not really Huxley. He bought his 'half-and-half' at the bar, even if he had not learned to puff cheap Chesterfields. *Punch* twitted the tyro surgeons, who drank themselves into a stupor while talking tipsy metaphysics. But Huxley's quest for the two valued commodities of the age – bread and knowledge – was earnest. And he knew more of Lindley's Physic Garden than its tobacco plant.

Only one route to the College of Surgeons made an indelible impression on him, and that was the shortest one, through the cesspit of courts and alleys around Drury Lane.

> Alleys nine or ten feet wide, I suppose, with tall houses
> full of squalid drunken men and women, and the pavement
> strewed with still more squalid children. The place of air
> was taken by a steam of filthy exhalations; and the only
> relief to the general dull apathy was a roar of words –
> filthy and brutal beyond imagination – between the close-
> packed neighbours, occasionally ending in a general row.

Thousands crammed these tenements, sometimes 20 to a room, six to a bed, with buckets as toilets and the stench overpowering. Among them 'the rotting, uncoffined bodies of the dead remain where they died'. A few days in a 'festering London August' and corpses were 'quivering with maggots', which at least kept them out of the puppy doctors' paws. One in four children died. The surviving urchins scraped horse manure off the Strand crossings for a living, to allow silk-chokered gents to pass unsullied. Huxley stole past twopenny doss houses, where the sexes slept together on filthy floors. Here the gangs made life difficult, and rats made it lethal. 'All this,' he puzzled, 'almost within hearing of the traffic of the Strand, within easy reach of the wealth and plenty of the city'. Here he was, a penniless scruff. 'Nobody would have found robbing me a profitable employment'. He passed the down-and-outs unmolested. But he did wonder why, in the depression with the Chartists inflaming passions, the hovel did not explode and the beggars go on a looting spree.[41]

While society forgot the poor, reformers were busy cleaning the middle-class Augean stable. Even the conservative College of Surgeons capitulated. For 20 years its 'self-perpetuating, tyrannical' council had withstood the wrath of Thomas Wakley's battling *Lancet*. But in 1843 the crochety councillors were finally subjected to elections. 'Old Corruption' was dying around Huxley. The new men, Huxley's men – GPs and Dissenting teachers representing the urban industrial areas – moved in with their gutsier science.[42] Talent and training were to replace rank and wealth. Huxley saw a new world in the making.

But still the poor were denied a voice and damned to their hovels. Gentlefolk assuaged their guilt by giving coppers to voluntary hospitals like Huxley's, which were left to pick up the pieces. Minds as well as bodies were healed at Charing Cross, which specialized in mental problems, of special interest to Jim Huxley. Students went free to hear the humane mad-doctor John Conolly at Hanwell Lunatic Asylum, and to see his unmanacled inmates (a libertarian approach Jim was to copy later).[43]

Tom was watching more corporeal surgery. The operating theatre was tiny; the patient strapped, screaming, the 'dreadful shrieks . . . resembling the bellowing of a wild animal' as the knife cut. A poor devil lay on the slab, gas lights above. The students clustered sweatily around, packed in tiers overlooking the table. The cutting was swift; it had to be with trauma the greatest killer. Buckets caught the dripping blood, the sawdusted floor mopping up the spurts. The event was almost as shaking for the students as for the patient. Elsewhere, Huxley's old teachers were pioneering painless approaches. Chandler was still exploiting mesmerism's *'tranquillizing* effect', greater than 'the largest "safe" dose of opium'. His flamboyant friend Elliotson had moved on to mesmeric surgery, giving 'painless amputations' his theatrical cachet.[44]

Jim was hearing different screams. He was doing well in midwifery, picking up a certificate of merit in 1844.[45] He had plenty of practice, in the maternity ward and at home, where Lizzie gave birth to another baby, Flory. Tom too was often around, the perfect babysitter who practically adopted the girl. He was strangely comforted by her cries, seeming to work best under domestic pressure.

Back in the Strand he found a new friend among the 1844 intake, Joseph Fayrer. And a new exotic horizon: Fayrer had sailed in from Bermuda. He was five months Huxley's senior but had seen the world. His father had commanded the largest steam ships sailing to New York. Joseph was a hardy hand: Trinidad, Havana, Jamaica, he had visited them all as a midshipman in his father's paddle steamers. As the freezing pea-soupers set in and the 'soft black drizzle' of soot cast its 'funereal pall' over Charing Cross, he fired Huxley with stories of sparkling Caribbean seas, 'where the water was clear as crystal' and 'the fish, corals, and seaweed were visible in its depths'.[46] He had been paralysed by poisonous sea-urchin spines and had swum among sharks. It was after seeing surgeons working on yellow fever victims in Bermuda that he had decided to come home and study medicine.

Like Huxley, Fayrer stood in awe of the great engineers. The students could always indulge their passions at the Adelaide Gallery. Here were chugging steam engines, and an 'oxyhydrogen microscope' that was said to magnify three million times.[47] Replica paddle boats sloshed up and down a 6,000 gallon tank. But the *pièce de résistance* was the ultimate deterrent: a Perkin's steam-operated machine gun firing 20 rounds a second down the 100-foot gallery.

Fayrer became a firm friend. The two often worked through the night, not that darkness brought quiet. Even at 2 am. the Strand reverberated to the drays dragging vegetable wagons from Waterloo Bridge to Covent Garden. Theatres were their only relaxation. They shunned the raucous student life: 'hardly anything would induce me to dance', Huxley said, or 'to go to such a thing as a party'.[48] While Fayrer fired him up with steam ships in hot seas, he tempted Fayrer with physiology. They sat side by side, watching the chain-twiddling Wharton Jones. In May 1845 Fayrer followed Huxley by taking the physiology prize. In fact he scooped the awards, winning a £15 scholarship for two years.

In 1845 all three of Tom's brothers married, leading to a certain matrimonial confusion. None quite agreed with the others' choices. William so disparaged George's Mary that Tom cut him dead (and they remained estranged for life). Tom's defence of Mary reached a point of passion. Every time he saw her 'she looked prettier than ever with just the same bright eyes and merry laugh'. He called the 'loveable little creature' his 'sister'. Confusion was caused by Jim's wife being another Mary, so George's wife became 'Polly'. Confusion turned to chaos for the girls. Tom was the spitting image of Jim, but Polly's problem was voices: she 'often fails to distinguish between my voice and George's for which I laugh at her immensely'.[49]

Tom's reservation was about Jim's wife. Jim was sharp, full of the world and its ways. But as to an intellectual match, 'I doubt whether he has married wisely'. She was 'a very good creature, and manages his house capitally, but she is nothing more'. No luminous wit to 'brighten a husbands path'. No bon viveur: 'Brought up in a remote country town, under the eye of her father an old clergyman, she has no notion of making her friends amusing'. After a while he sensed that even Jim felt 'frightfully uneasy at times'. Not that Tom – the last unmarried offspring – would make a better catch. He gazed wistfully into the future, only to see himself 'doomed to be a dreadful spoon of a husband'.[50]

Evidently in late 1845, a most extraordinary and unaccountable scandal broke around Lizzie and Salt. Whatever happened, it was hushed up; and so successfully that no historian has managed to penetrate it (few, indeed, have even known about it). There was clearly a fear of social disgrace and ostracism, with Tom more paranoid than most. His mother never forgave Salt for dragging 'your poor unfortunate sister' into the gutter, as she told Tom: 'believe me I can almost hate the man for his unprincipled conduct towards all who have befriended him'.[51] Jim broke off from Salt, and George considered himself compromised. Tom was the only one left to help Lizzie. Did Dr Salt administer some heroic drug overdose that killed a patient? Surely, in light of their eventual clandestine flight from the country, it was nothing so mundane as a financial scandal? (Medical men were well known in the bank-ruptcy courts, and it was hardly a crushing social stigma.) The event, whatever it was, was traumatic and terrible and would split the family for life.

Tom blotted out the horror, drowning himself in the gigantic surgical tomes now dropping from the steam-presses. By day he trundled on like an automaton, anatomizing his way through the animal kingdom. Insects and centipedes were teased apart. He became absorbed in snails and even more the extraordinary multi-generation lifecycles of flukes and jellyfish.[52] By now he was being invited to Wharton Jones' tiny town house. At home his teacher's outer crust cracked to reveal a volcanic interior. He veered from the sublime to the ridiculous, from germinal vesicles to jams and galoshes. He talked of his own huge unfinished text on eye surgery (to be praised and damned as gloriously definitive and 'absurdly pedantic'). The air was charged as he launched thunderbolts against rival embryologists. In an age of clashing intellects he was already embittered, a little man with a huge rage. Backbiting and infighting were occupational hazards before the rise of professional adjudicators. Huxley sat, sipping tea, listening to him rant 'with more energy than worldly wisdom'.[53]

Huxley continued his journey around the human body. He was still silhouetted in the museum window, measuring the layers in the hair follicle. All year he had been doing it, unable to believe his eyes, convinced he had found a new membrane. He had. The Germans had missed it: right up against the hair shaft, a single layer of cells, 'very delicate and pale'. He could even see their nuclei '1-2000th of an inch' long.[54] Wharton Jones wanted him to publish, suggesting the *Medical Gazette*, sober and sedate like himself (and a regular reporter of his lectures). So a short note was prepared; Wharton Jones polished the prose and Huxley perfected the drawing. Students regularly fired off missives to the medical press, grumbling about cantankerous surgeons or school costs. But rarely one 'On a Hitherto Undescribed Structure', in the human hair or elsewhere. The 20 year-old held his breath and posted his paper.

Huxley's years as a long-haired student were ending. Most boys went into practice at this point, but he still longed for the academic world. In August 1845 he walked down the Strand to London University's offices in Somerset House. Here, in a stark hall, he put himself through Part 1 of the Bachelor of Medicine exam. The affable University College physiologist William Sharpey was impressed, awarding him the gold medal for anatomy and physiology.[55] But Huxley never managed to sit Part 2. After three years he had finished his hospital training. His free scholarship had expired and he needed to pay his way.

At 20 he was too young to obtain a College of Surgeons' licence to practice.[56] He was deep in debt, having borrowed £2 a week for three years to cover food and rent. He owed sums to Cooke, and to dependable George. He had glittering golds but no gainful employment. He needed pay, and fast.

On 28 November 1845 he picked up an 8*d Medical Gazette* and there was his note on the new hair membrane. Wharton Jones was delighted. He incorporated 'Huxley's Layer' into his lectures and blew his protégé's trumpet. 'There's something for you at your time going down to posterity', chortled Jim.[57]

3

The Surgeon's Mate

H OW COULD HUXLEY MEET his mounting pile of debts? The solution came from his nautical friend Joseph Fayrer. He suggested the sea. The sick bay afloat had its appeal; Her Majesty would pay, while his other liege lady, Nature, could be followed lasciviously around the globe. The Navy fostered scientific assistant surgeons. Look at the son of Kew Garden's Director, Joseph Hooker, who had stepped off HMS *Erebus* in 1843 after his Antarctic herborizations. Or the young crustacean expert Harry Goodsir, not long gone with Sir John Franklin to the Canadian ice packs, searching for the North-West Passage. So good did it sound that Fayrer took his own advice; he enlisted himself.[1]

Huxley saw the benefits. An assistant surgeon's lot had improved by 1846. He was now saluted as a subaltern, with pretty good pay at 7s 6d a day. These were minor points, but medical reformers had fought for them furiously, and they were still fighting on other fronts. He would have to endure abominable conditions, and it was a high-risk career; the death rate among surgeons' mates in the West Indies and Africa was notorious.[2] But who else would pay him to anatomize voraciously around the world?

Fayrer goaded him into writing personally to the Physician General of the Navy, Sir William Burnett. It seemed 'rather a strong thing to do', but a poor boy without patrons had little option. A long confab on 31 January 1846 'ended in our concocting a letter'. Huxley duly excused himself:

> Having a great desire to enter the Medical Department of
> Her Majesty's Naval Service and being at the same time
> totally unprovided with any friendly influence by which

the attainment of my object might be accelerated – I take
the liberty of addressing myself directly to you as the
Head of the Department . . .[3]

The entry requirements were stiff. He had the necessary certificates, everything from surgery to botany, proof of a year spent in human dissection, six months apprenticed in pharmacy and so on. He cut his hair and collected references: Wharton Jones told of his medals and Sharpey gave a 'very high opinion of his abilities'.[4] Huxley added that a 'Silver Botanical Medal was awarded to me by the Apothecaries Company' and that the university had given him a gold. 'I have paid especial attention to Microscopical Anatomy' and he pointed Sir William to his discovery published in the *Gazette*. His credentials looked good.

And to the top brass. At the bottom of the acknowledgment from the Naval Medical Office was a note from Sir William to see him at Somerset House. 'I thought that looked like business', and so it was. Sir William, 67, had started as a surgeon's mate himself and had survived the battles of the Nile and Trafalgar to receive a CB and four war medals. He was a kindly reformer who had recently bettered the pay and position of the assistant. A spruced Huxley sent his card ahead. Sir William emerged, 'a tall shrewd-looking old gentleman, with a broad Scotch accent'. He clutched Huxley's card. 'The first thing he did was to return it, with the frugal reminder that I should probably find it useful on some other occasion. The second was to ask whether I was an Irishman. I suppose the air of modesty about my appeal must have struck him'.[5] The Physician General was satisfied, and made arrangements to give the brash aspirant his final *viva*.

The College of Surgeons tested the Admiralty's medical men first, issuing 'fitness' certificates. He also needed a vicar's note vouching for his 'good moral character' and another testifying to his competence in the Classics.[6] He had diplomas everywhere, his life summed up in pieces of paper.

But at least he was progressing. Salt himself had fled the country, leaving Lizzie, heavily pregnant, to have her baby and follow on. The shadow falling over the family was darkening. Tom was losing his favourite sister, who had pushed him on and thrown her shoe after him for luck. The backbiting intensified as Jim turned on Salt, leaving more bad blood. In secret one February day Tom took Lizzie and the children across the Channel to Antwerp. She went, babe in arms, with the maid holding Flory. The flight was precipitous: Lizzie had not even registered baby Edith, no one had booked accommodation and Tom had to tour the lodging houses.

He took the night ferry back. It docked at 7.45 am. on Thursday 19 February. He rushed to Charing Cross and by 11 am. had gathered up his certificates and received 'the order to go for examination before the College of Surgeons'.

It was hard to concentrate. He reassured Lizzie the next day that he was home 'safe and sound and without sea-sickness'. But the return had made him more paranoid. The pilot had asked him 'if I knew who it was that came over in the vessel who wanted private lodgings'. He had been at one of the residences Huxley had tried. 'Is it not odd?' Tom asked. 'I should advise you to keep to yourself and the children as much as possible out of the way of the people belonging to the Victoria [the English ship] – which lies not very far from you – and Elizabeth [the maid] should be particularly careful not to pick up any English acquaintance – she would not be a difficult person for anyone to pump'.[7]

Everything conspired to stop Huxley joining up. No Board examined at the College of Surgeons on the following Friday, 27 February, so he had to bide his time. He was now itching for his shillings.[8] His *viva voce* at the College on 6 March was a perfunctory affair and accordingly cheap at two guineas. He passed routinely.

A few days later he went before Sir William and, finally, on 13 March 1846, the pallid landlubber became a 'Jack Tar', a sailor. Officially he was put on the books of Nelson's old flagship, HMS *Victory*, that functional shrine in Portsmouth Harbour. Actually he was to take up residence in the largest hospital in the world, Haslar Naval Hospital in Gosport, across the harbour. He had what he wanted, 7s a day. 'So you see all the prophets' noses are rubbed the wrong way', he laughed to Lizzie.[9] At last he could chip away at his debts.

But nothing was so simple. He now added an 'agent' (a sort of finance company) to his creditors, borrowing to buy his kit. What with dress uniform, cashmere waistcoats, cocked hat, 'rich gilt town-made Sword, £4', and so on down to twelve boxes of boot blacking, he found himself forking out £46 2s 6d. That was four months' pay and money he could ill afford.[10]

Queen Victoria's Navy was 'the right arm of England', flexing its muscles before the world. The 'Senior Service' still gloried in

Nelson and Trafalgar as it policed the seas and upheld the *Pax Britannica*. It was opening up new colonies, helping to turn 'White Men's Graves' into hospitable little Englands. Reform was in the air; press ganging was dying and so were the disciplinarians. And the future held new challenges as iron-cladding, steam furnaces and screw-propellers custed timber and sail. But behind the poster romance lay the usual 'drudgery, boredom, danger, and misery' below deck.[11] The assistant surgeon would find out for himself.

Haslar was a huge, century-old, red-brick hospital facing the sea. With three storeys and wings 500 feet long, it could accommodate 2,000 patients in 80 wards. Fever cases had their own isolation units and a mad-house treated the Navy's insane with a new sensitivity. It was built on a promontory, with a jetty into the harbour, so that the casualties could be landed direct. From here Huxley could gaze across the grey waters to the wharves at Portsmouth, or watch the square-riggers being fitted out.

Huxley was swamped amid a torrent of surgeons fresh from their ships or awaiting commissions, and miffed that his new chief, Sir John Richardson, '"Old John," as we irreverent youngsters called him, took not the slightest notice of my worshipful self'.[12] Sixty year-old Sir John was a taciturn figure. In his day he had dressed gunshot wounds during the Peninsular War against Napoleon and sailed on Franklin's first polar expedition. Haslar's museum was his creation, and chocked with the spoils of countless voyages. Of course he had noticed his new assistant. Even as Huxley decried 'the churlishness of the chief', Sir John was trying to get him a good survey ship, or a better shore posting.

One day Sir John 'heaped coals of fire on my head by telling me that he had tried to get me one of the resident appointments, much coveted by the assistant-surgeons'. He wanted the brilliant microscopist in his own museum. 'I was within an ace of being appointed' too, Tom told Lizzie. But an Admiralty man 'put his spoke in the wheel on behalf of a friend of his & so I am out of it'. No favoured shore posting. 'However', said Sir John, 'I mean to keep you here till I can get you something you will like'. And that explained why Tom was not 'packed off to the West Coast of Africa like some of my juniors'. He had been spared the worst fever-ravaged posting in the Service. But packed off he would be: 'mother is not very well', he informed Lizzie, 'and the probability that I shall be off some time or other, instead of stopping here for a twelvemonth, does not brighten her'.[13]

*

Succumbing to the paranoia as the Salts fled, Tom addressed Lizzie's letters to 'Miss Knight'; 'let me know whether I may write to you directly', he said. Salt had taken the alias 'Dr Scott'. Every subterfuge was practised to keep the family skeleton from springing out of the closet. Tom even feared some tampering with the mail. Better not 'send any more letters to me', he advised his sister, 'in case of accidents'.

'Mrs and Dr Scott' moved to Cologne incognito. As Huxley looked to his own commission, Lizzie was worried sick, but still defiant. 'We did what the time compelled us to and believed it no concern of anyone's', she told him, sending greetings on his 21st birthday. 'They cannot judge fairly if they would'. Salt was having trouble scraping a living 'but we do not despair'. Where it would end she did not know. Emigration schemes were canvassed, but even finding travel information frightened her, for fear she would tip her hand and then 'everyone w^d know'.[14]

Huxley was facing his own uncertain journey. His destination too was some distant land, at the farthest reach of the Navy's long arm.

At Haslar he heard the stories of capricious sea captains. There were spit-and-polish men, sacrificing comfort to 'smartness and show'. The press depicted their 'perfect despotism', so out of keeping with the age. They were autocrats, for better or worse – and the worst forced their surgeons to suffer 'much vituperation, and abuse, without the power of retaliation' or, at least, not without being cashiered. At sea there was no come-back, as one irate surgeon wrote: 'I have seen a captain's fist . . . shaking near a subordinate's face, when, had it been on shore, and in plain clothes, the latter might have eaten him, boots and all'. For a headstrong Huxley holding his tongue would be a tall order. Even full surgeons lived in 'hot, narrow, and confined' cabins aboard frigates, 'like large coffins', close to the gun-room. And why? another asked: 'in order to give the captain's steward a large berth' aft. As he said, 'the captains will soon have half the ship to themselves'.[15]

Huxley began to wonder what his own captain would be like. But not for long. The Arctic and Indo-China surveyor, Captain Owen Stanley, contacted Richardson, hoping to pick up one of his best charges with a flair for science. It was Huxley's break, especially as Sir John 'has shown himself for some reason or another a special good friend to me'. It was 'an *exploring expedition* to New Guinea (not coast of Africa, mind)', Huxley reported to Lizzie in May; 'would I like that? Of course I jumped at the offer'. He had fallen on his feet – a captain with a penchant for science, who was not prepared to underrate his junior surgeon. And New Guinea, 'a place almost unknown'.[16] Tales were already rife about the mist-shrouded tropical island. Captain Francis Blackwood had just returned from the region in HMS *Fly*, with stories of suspected inland ranges, exotic birds and warlike natives.

With the Season in full swing the aristocratic Stanley was recruiting his officers in town. He trained back and forth, dividing his time between Portsmouth dockyard and the London soirées. Huxley was given leave to come up for an interview.

He was ushered into Stanley's presence. The captain was short and stocky and impenetrably reserved, like many a sea captain – a lonely, unmarried, grey-haired old man for his 35 years. Only occasionally did the brusque outer crust crack to reveal a kind, insecure soul. The saturnine Stanley had seen the empire forged at the sharp end. He had climbed the ranks as the Navy roamed the globe, his life a microcosm of imperial endeavour. At 15 he went to Patagonia, where he learned to survey. (His ships brought back the Fuegian 'savages' who were to return on the *Beagle* with Darwin and FitzRoy.) He had searched for the North-West Passage, and sailed the brig *Britomart* to north Australia (1837–43), planting the flag to pre-empt the Dutch. He had helped to secure New Zealand, seizing it from under the eyes of the French and out of the hands of the Maoris. He was seasoned to hot and cold. He had been crushed in the Arctic ice for ten months, and trapped in tropical Burma for longer.

It showed. He looked burned out. He was broody and suffered bouts of 'suicidal despair'. He flew high and low, sometimes reserved, at other times wild-tempered. He was a good surveyor, if unadventurous, and 'a thorough scientific enthusiast', Huxley noted. What Huxley did not know was that ambition had got the better of Stanley, whose 'bruised self-esteem' showed that he had never quite succeeded. He was ignominiously surveying British rivers when the *Rattlesnake* command came through.

In his two interviews Huxley began to get the man's measure. Stanley, like his father, was an 'aristocrat to his very finger-tips', from a line of heirs and heiresses. Or, as the mate put it, he was 'an exceedingly gentlemanly gentleman'.[17] The Stanleys were leading Whigs and liberal Anglicans, steering the ship of state, and ruling the waves as naturally. His father had loved the sea, but ended up on the 'Dead See', the bishopric of Norwich, given him by the Whigs and nicknamed for its dilapidated state. The family were noble Whigs all, tolerant of Dissent, full of *noblesse oblige*. With his brother Arthur leading the Anglican reformers at Oxford, and a cousin in Melbourne's ministry, the helm seemed Stanley's by right. But Huxley was constitutionally suspicious, however civil the skipper to his scientific young surgeon.

The *Rattlesnake* was to continue HMS *Fly*'s work along the cloud-covered shores of New Guinea. Huxley was promised full leave to collect New Guinea's exotic animals. 'Depend upon it unless some sudden attack of laziness supervenes, such an opportunity shall not slip unused out of my hands'. He had high hopes, as the skipper 'shows himself altogether very much disposed to forward my views in every possible way'.

Stanley was recruiting the veterans of Blackwood's three-year voyage. 'I am progressing with my list of officers', he reported, portraying them with Dickensian candour. 'Mr Suckling, First Lieutenant, an old and steady, good officer, though somewhat deaf. Mr Ince, a fat, laughing, good-humoured sailor, who was out with Captain Blackwood in the *Fly*, is Second Lieutenant. Mr Dayman, a very clever and intelligent person who went out with James Ross in the *Erebus*, is the Third Lieutenant, and assistant Surveyor. Doctor Thomson, a young man, fond of botanical pursuits, is the surgeon, and a Mr Huxley, a very good naturalist, is the assistant surgeon . . . ' He had, he said, 'every reason to be satisfied'.[18]

So had Huxley. He was reassured by Stanley's technical bent and saw promotion if he stuck to his scientific last. 'So that altogether I am in a very fair way, and would snap my fingers at the Grand Turk'. Stanley introduced him to the scientific lions: first, to the pride's imperious leader Richard Owen, whose new *Lectures on the Comparative Anatomy and Physiology of Vertebrates* started and stopped with fishes. Bring home fish brains was Owen's advice. Then to John Edward Gray, the British Museum peon, a closet taxonomist who twinkled at the sight of pickled invertebrates. He and Richardson were currently dividing up the spoils of Captain Ross' Antarctic Expedition; if any obscure barnacle was a desideratum, Gray would know it. Best of all was an opening to the irrepressible Edward Forbes at the Geological Survey.[19] Jokey and gangly, laughing as he threw his long hair back, Forbes was instantly approachable. His own survey had been to the Aegean; he was an expert on the starfish and sea slugs in the deep-sea dredge. There was no one better to show Huxley the ropes.

Huxley was dying to leave, to see the tropics, taste their fruits; not least to start dissecting and making a name for himself. He knew that he would suffer 'privations and petty vexations'. He had read the *Lancet* editorials deploring the assistant surgeon's lot. The marine officer straight from school messed in the ward-room with the lieutenants, walked their weather-side of the deck, and had a cabin and servant. Not so the junior surgeon. He could be the most educated man aboard, four years in medical school, and yet be barred from the ward-room and denied a berth, given only a hammock. Worst of all, he had to sling it in the gun-room with the midshipmen, boys all, 14 or 15 year-olds. The *Lancet*, wanting education rewarded, in the Service and out, was furious. The junior surgeon was dripping with 'professional diplomas'. And for what? To be 'thrust into a filthy, dark den, called the midshipmen's berth, among a set of noisy, half-educated school-boys'. Huxley would have to sleep, work and eat with the 'middies'. And the word was that these pranksters had 'a great antipathy to studious habits'. He looked at his armful of certificates and wondered if his good intentions were for nought.

An aristocratic high command pooh-poohed this 'namby-pamby, brooding discontent'. Gun-room discipline and class divisions were what counted. Why should the assistant surgeon mess with his 'better-paid superiors'? For the old guard it was not education but breeding that counted. As one peppery old gent said, before long the 'cook's-assistant' will be making demands![20]

Huxley sat in his room at Haslar, no pitching, no yawing, no hissing wind or shrieking middies. Before him a new £13 microscope (his first £37 quarterly cheque on 1 July was used for anything but settling debts). Here was the way to study a bee's muscles, quietly. He teased out the nerves of a slug. It was filigree work, requiring intense concentration.[21] How would he manage on a rolling ship, crowded and cramped?

The shillings continued to slip through his fingers. Charting unknown regions, he had expected a library on board. But the Admiralty supplied no books. He had 'carte blanche from the Captain to take as many as I please', but they were 'ruinously expensive' for an assistant in hock, 'though a mere dewdrop in the general cost of the fitting-out of a ship ... A hundred pounds would have well supplied the *Rattlesnake*'.[22] And so went the rest of his cheque. The Service was proving somewhat expensive.

*

Her Majesty's Ship *Rattlesnake* was stripped to her timbers in Portsmouth dock when Huxley first saw her. She lacked the striking power of her reptilian namesake. Twenty-eight-gun frigates of her class were already obsolete. 'Donkey' or 'jackass' frigates they were laughingly called by the old salts who had seen active service. Nor did the surveyors have much clout. They might have the most hazardous jobs during peace time, but 'the officers of "*regular*" men-of-war, as they delight to be called, pretend to think surveying a kind of shirking – in sea-phrase, "sloping"'.

The ship was small, 113 feet and 503 tons, with a complement of 180 officers and men. She was 44 years old and her timbers showed it. Launched in 1822, she had seen hard service 'chasing pirates and privateers' and as a troopship in the Chinese Opium Wars.[23] Most recently she had been off New Guinea, only to return in a rotting state. The fastidious Stanley was supervising a massive refit.

His orders, in a word, were to secure northern Australia for British settlement and make the surrounding seas safe for British merchantmen. In practice this meant surveying the Torres Strait – the passage between northern Australia and New Guinea – which was used by ships returning home via India from Sydney and the South Seas. He was to mark channels through the reefs (notorious as a ships' graveyard), to enable square-riggers to beat through the Strait at night. He was also to assess sites for new British colonies. The Admiralty feared that foreign traders could pass unseen through the Strait; it wanted local garrisons and coaling stations, and regular patrols to keep watch for French ships. Imperial vigilance was a prime part of the mission.

With emigration peaking, propeller-driven steamships were expected to be a major part of future traffic, reaching Sydney via Singapore through the Inner Passage, inside the Barrier Reef. Here the steamers would be protected from the Pacific swell. Most ships still steered outside the reef because of the risk of wrecking. Certainly no merchantman out of the colony would chance the Inner Passage, with the sun's glare on the water ahead masking the white foam. The inner channel had to be 'well swept and its dangers marked out'. This was Stanley's second priority.

Also on the South Seas route – and awaiting exploitation by gold miners and whalers – lay the haunting island of New Guinea. Stanley was to chart its southern shores and the archipelago off its eastern tip. These were not such friendly waters, and the Sea Lords warned him to 'guard against the treacherous disposition of their inhabitants'. Huxley knew he would meet savages. The *Fly*'s men talked of charcoal-painted Papuans and scare stories of head-hunters abounded. What terrors awaited them behind the luxuri-ant camouflage at the water's edge no one knew. But the Admiralty realized the potential for exploitation. The *Rattlesnake*'s naturalists – like so many before them – were to send New Guinea's riches to the British Museum. Here 'zoological *patriots*' would christen and claim its rainforest inhabitants, on the gilded principle that 'once an animal is named and described, it becomes . . . a possession for ever'.[24]

By now all the 'unpeopled regions of the earth' were seen as British territory. The 'surplus' poor from the industrial slums were being shipped in huge numbers to the colonies, 400,000 a year during the depression. The figure was expected to rise with the Irish potato famine worsening; and with prospective steam lines putting Australia 'little more than a month's voyage' away that continent was looking attractive.[25] Surveying vessels were a bridge-head, opening up territories as well as maintaining links and policing the little Englands. The *Rattlesnake* was to act as banker as well, carrying £50,000 in gold coin for the Cape Colony and £15,000 for Mauritius.

The ship was commissioned on 24 September 1846, but the Sea Lords were tying up Stanley's refit with red tape. While waiting Huxley escaped to that peripatetic 'Parliament of Science', the British Association for the Advancement of Science, which was holding its jamboree at nearby Southampton. All his new contacts were there. Owen dominated the proceedings with his numbingly technical talk on the vertebrate groundplan or 'Archetype'. Here too was Forbes, the voice of the British Asses' 'Dredging Commit-tee' (he had even dredged his way along the coast to the Southamp-ton venue). There was an irreverence about Forbes that Huxley found appealing. Rollicking was the word; unlike Owen, Forbes was positively playful, sparing nobody with his *John Bull* squibs.[26] Forbes talked jellyfish and starfish. He even gave Huxley a prize, an *Amphioxus* dredged from the sand: a strange transitional creature, not a fish for it had no heart, nor a head proper, yet with a lamprey-like notochord and nerve chord running its length. Where it stood was a mystery, which increased when Huxley saw its invertebrate's blood.

Huxley's commission came through on 2 October. Still the *Rattlesnake* was unready, so he and his 'fellow prisoners' found themselves remanded in the Hulks, the penitentiary ships in the harbour. Now he understood Dr Johnson's quip, that 'being in a ship is being in a jail, with the chance of being drowned'. For generations these rotting warships had housed the Gin Lane reprobates on their way to Botany Bay. They were the staging posts for leg-iron men convicted of pilfering food or swearing trade union oaths. Their decks squelched blood and tears; in the air the crack of the cat-o'-nine-tails and stink of torn flesh. With transportation suspended, the sailors were left with the stench. Tom posted his brother George a maudlin cartoon of his cell under the motto 'Am I not a man & a brother?'

Aboard the *Rattlesnake* Stanley's rearrangements were drastic. He jettisoned some cannons and two actually ended up in his cabin. He was making the most of the available space; 'having only eight guns on the main deck, I have arranged all the officers' cabins and the Mess place there, the midshipmen occupying the gun-room below. A poop extending as far as the wheel gives us an excellent chart room, with plenty of light and air'.[27]

Coming aboard at last, Huxley was delighted to find that Stanley had planned the crew's quarters meticulously. Against all the prognostications, he had his own cabin (or rather an alcove off the gun-room), and a cot, while he could stow his books and set up his microscope in the chart-room. Even so it was not the lap of luxury. Given a berth six feet by seven, crammed with cot, clothes, desk, chest, cocked-hat box and rifle, there was scarcely room to turn. Nor to stand: 'I really doubt whether Jonah was much worse accommodated'. Huxley's 5 feet 11 inches left him disadvantaged, with 'the height of the lower deck . . . 4 feet 10 inches. What I am to do with the superfluous foot I cannot divine. Happily, however, there is a sort of skylight into the berth, so that I shall be able to sit with the body in it and my head out'.[28]

Thrust among 22 high-spirited youngsters, he appreciated the complaints. Surgeons' mates were 'the *dry nurses* of the navy', there to keep the boys in check. Stepping into the gun-room he saw why: two were troublemakers, another pair were the worse for wear after a fight. There was a mischievous glint in the eye of Philip Sharpe, the son of an old clergyman. But at least Tom could escape to the poop. 'In an ordinary frigate if a fellow has the talents of all the scientific men from Archimedes downwards . . . they are all lost. Even if it were possible to study in a midshipmen's berth, you have not room in your "chat" for more than a dozen books'. But Stanley had transformed the poop 'into a large chart-room with bookshelves and tables and plenty of light. There I may read, draw, or microscopise at pleasure'.[29]

The *Rattlesnake* was towed out of dock later in the month and moored in harbour. Here the work continued. She sported new cannons from Woolwich arsenal, and Stanley boasted that she had 'the best supply of instruments that a surveying ship ever sailed with'. Pride of place went to the 17 gleaming chronometers, for use in fixing longitude and the location of wrecking reefs. She carried a decked boat, the *Asp*, which could be hoisted on and off, as well as 'two gallies, thirty-two feet long; a very fine pinnace and two first-rate cutters, so that in the boat department we are well off'.[30]

On 21 October Stanley mustered the ship's company. Huxley now met his messmates for the first time. The officers seemed 'very gentlemanly', and he hoped that their shared interest in science would foster camaraderie. 'The requisite discipline is kept up', he told Lizzie, 'but not in the martinet style'. Common pursuits meant they had 'more respect for one another' than in men-of-war.

There seemed no lack of *ex officio* naturalists. The Navy's paid collector was the rugged, bushy-bearded ornithologist John MacGillivray. Only three years older than Huxley, 'Jock' MacGillivray was already a veteran. He had been with the *Fly* and was itching to go out again after only six months. Huxley had heard the tittle-tattle. Gray at the British Museum slated MacGillivray as an 'ignoramus', telling Cooke as much.[31] But his credentials were good: his father was professor of natural history at Aberdeen, and John was well-versed by the Zoological Society's bird artist and erstwhile Australian traveller, John Gould.

Among the supernumeraries was Stanley's personal collector, James Wilcox, on board to stock the museums in the bishop's Norwich diocese. But the man Huxley warmed to was the surgeon. 'My immediate superior, Johnny Thompson [sic], is a long-headed good fellow without a morsel of humbug about him'. Thomson was a rucksack and rifle man. He was another avid collector, keen to augment his cabinet and to record events, bringing his daguerreo-type camera for the purpose. He was a candid Scotsman, with an 'even and amiable disposition' to offset Huxley's hot temper. They would get on well. 'One friend on board a ship is as much as anybody has a right to expect'.[32]

Two weeks before sailing Huxley bade farewell. He stayed with George on Regent's Park and picked up last-minute tips from

Forbes. His brother threw a farewell party, with Fayrer making a speech and Tom *debuting* in his uniform. The real leave-taking was more poignant. He clasped his mother goodbye on 19 November; always embarrassed by emotional displays, he was choked by her 'gut tearing sentimentality'. His father was 66 and fragile, and Tom knew that five years could be forever.

The family he left was badly fractured. He had outgrown his parents and outdistanced his brothers. Lizzie's exile had taken her on to Bonn. Cut dead by James and the rest, she castigated their 'mental aberration on the subject of my husband'. Cooke's teaching had flopped and he was drowning his sorrows in beer and opium, and 'Ellen is not getting on better' (she too had hit the bottle). 'The ladies are not in the ascendent in our family', said Lizzie; nor, it seemed, were their husbands.[33] Tom's departure would only speed the break-up.

Back in Portsmouth the ship was a buzz. Ratings rushed around; everywhere smelled of polished wood and tarred rope. Chests of tea and casks of rum were coming aboard. The tub became a creaking Noah's Ark: crates of ducks and chickens, corralled sheep and yapping gun dogs, winched on to the sounds of the fiddler and accordionist practising their shanties. It was bursting with provisions and bristling with marines (sentries for the shore parties on hostile shores). Loved ones were coming and going in tears. But it was the last supernumeraries who added the incongruous note.

As Huxley had been warned, Stanley began commandeering half the ship. He settled his steward in a large berth and his butterfly collector in another. He made room for the Revd Robert King, son of his old superior in the *Adventure* and the *Beagle* in South America, Phillip Parker King, who was now living in Australia. Unknown to the Admiralty, Stanley had even planned to take his mercurial brother Charlie to Hobart, where he was to be the Governor's Private Secretary. Charlie, a Royal Engineer and social catastrophe, had just blighted the family name by marrying a banker's daughter, Eliza Clayton, who would have been *nouveau riche* had she had money ('No money *at all*' and worse, 'a voice like a vulgar person who wishes to speak *genteelly*'). Hobart seemed a suitable place for them. The plan only fell through because of the *Rattlesnake*'s delays, forcing the newlyweds to take a merchant ship. But Huxley found other Stanleys settling in.

A nice cruise to Madeira, the bishop believed, would do his recuperating daughter Catherine good. And of course she would need her sister Mary as a chaperon. Notwithstanding the crush,

Stanley gave over two more of his cabins. Huxley, squeezed in the ship's bowels like Jonah, watched in horror. One cabin was set up with cots as their sleeping quarters, another made into a pleasant dressing room, which the young ladies were decorating with pictures. The idiosyncratic Stanley again forgot to tell the Admiralty. Rough-cut swabs, wondering what sort of survey they were signed up for, saw the girls bring a little of the Bishop's Palace aboard: a sofa, and a piano which played Bohemian Quadrilles, and all the finery, right down to silver wine labels engraved with the Stanley crest, 'two for port, two for sherry, and two for Madeira – we mean to be very grand'.[34]

There was a criminal profligacy to it in 1846, as the Irish potato famine intensified. They were sailing as starvation ravaged the rural communities. Death now stalked the hovelled poor, who subsisted on bread and potatoes, forcing untold thousands more to America and the colonies. The ship seemed safely removed, a floating autocracy. Each man was at his station, protected by the *noblesse oblige* of the bishop's son on the bridge. On 27 November the bishop himself came aboard to bless their endeavour.

1846–1850

The Devil and the Deep Blue Sea

4

Men-of-War

HUXLEY SAILED ON 1 December 1846, leaving the *Lancet* campaigning for better conditions. Education demands rank: it was a cry dear to his heart. He was even being cited himself:

> Some of the best educated young men in the profession are at present acting as naval assistant-surgeons, and 'denizens of the midshipmen's berth' . . . On looking over the navy list, we find, that such men as the younger HOOKER, the botanist, and HARRY D. GOODSIR, are assistant-surgeons; and also several graduates and undergraduates of the University of London. Among these, we may mention, T. H. HUXLEY, a medallist of 1845 . . .[1]

But in an odd way Huxley preferred the middies' mess. Like MacGillivray, he was deep in debt and scrounging. Living was cheaper in the gun-room. He would only have to fork out 30s a month, barring drink. That would save a pound on the extravagances of the ward-room.[2]

The bishop's entourage accompanied the ship along the south coast, past Dorset's blue lias cliffs and Devon's smugglers' bays. The *Rattlesnake* put in at Plymouth, where the £65,000 treasure trove was brought aboard. Knowing the captain's commission, cocky Midshipman Sharpe calculated his 'nice little share' and reckoned it 'paid for his outfit'. The middies' impecunious minder, who had begged, borrowed and begrudged £46 for his, could only wonder at the corruption.

The bishop's farewell sermon was preached against the backdrop of Devonport docks. Workers poured out of the gigantic store-houses to hear it. Huxley was lost amid a thousand listeners: port families and 'rough sailors whose eyes were dimmed with tears'. Then he scribbled a farewell note to his mother. His cabin was homely with 'my gay curtain and the spicy oilcloth'. And he had his modicum of privacy. But then, Cooke's example notwithstanding, 'If I had no cabin I should take to drinking in a month'.[3]

With the world facing him, he sat in his berth making resolutions. On 10 December, after the treasure chests had been stowed and the instruments calibrated, he started a diary: 'Thank God! fitting out is at last over. We have no more caprices to fear but those of the wind – a small matter after having been exposed to those of the Admiralty'. Plans tumbled out of him. He was leaving England as a student, with one eye on pay and one on his 'future prospects', for careful 'observation may enable me to *become* a teacher'. He had to annexe some remote corner of the animal kingdom, as Victoria's Navy was annexing the world. Specialize, that was the trick. Study what nobody else could, the 'perishable or rare marine productions', the sort that rarely reach England – take them over and make them his own. He had in mind the delicate gelatinous animals, jellyfish and their relatives. These he could dissect, draw and discard as they sailed along. Simply naming and claiming new animals could be left to the closet taxonomists at home: 'what I *can* do and they *cannot*' is anatomize fresh filamentous corpses on the high seas.

He would make the most of the voyage: scoop out fish brains, as Owen advised, and, donning his hat as a philosophical anatomist, dissect every mollusc from cuttlefish to clam to see if they shared the same plan. He would dissect the trepang too, that huge commercially harvested sea slug of the Barrier Reef, and barnacles and worms and corals and fish parasites . . . He slapped his diary shut with a defiant flourish: 'All these are things which I can attend to myself and in which I neither interfere with nor need the assistance of any one else'.[4] He had a dogged determination to go it alone. The young idealist, with an outsider's faith that talent could triumph, faced a new dawn.

The next morning, 11 December, the crew bade their farewells. Huxley cut his moorings. Great white shrouds of sail were unfurled and HMS *Rattlesnake* left English shores. The noise as the canvas caught the wind erased all thought of land: creaking joists, lashing waves, officers screaming and men shouting, the ensemble drowned by the wind in the rigging. Out in the Channel the tempests forced him to eat his words about the Admiralty and its blusterings. Nothing had prepared him for the Atlantic storms. As the weather worsened the *Rattlesnake*'s shoddy workmanship became evident. The scuppers, carrying run-off water from the decks, were inefficient. The gales sent thunderous waves crashing over her bows, and nearly every hatch leaked, leaving the main and lower decks flooded. For days the old tub was pitched and tossed. The provisions were ruined. Not that the middies cared for food, lying about groaning. Water sloshed from side to side carrying 'everything that was movable'. Huxley dodged the crashing debris. Desks 'were completely resolved into their elements', gun-cases smashed and even 'the unfortunate ducks were picked up dead in bucketfuls'. The *Rattlesnake* had been turned out in 'a disgraceful state'. He had expected the sturdiest ship for a dangerous survey. But the Sea Lords had provided 'the slowest, clumsiest' and leakiest ship ever to 'wear the pennant'.[5] The passage to Madeira was mercifully quick but remarkably uncomfortable.

The Portuguese island of Madeira, off the African coast, had been the traditional first stop on circumnavigations since Cook's time. The vineyards and whitewashed villas came as a welcome sight to the sailors standing on waterlogged decks, and a stopover allowed the crew to fix the leaks. Eight days out from a snowy December England, and Huxley was in a world of balmy breezes and banana plantations.

While Stanley took his sisters partying, Huxley sat in the pews of the cathedral. On Christmas Eve he watched the Catholic festivities, less with a sense of anthropological mission than with evangelical anger. To puritanical Englishmen Catholicism conjured up the miseries of the 'shiftless' millions in Ireland. It put the moral spite into their anti-Popery. The rationalist scorned this prostitution of human reason. To the young sailor priests and prostitutes were all of a piece, only standing on opposite sides of the sacred divide. At Mass the 'chanting' was 'of a most vile description'. It was 'difficult to say who evinced more indifference to what was going on – the choristers or the people and Santa Maria! ... I was glad to get away, even at the risk of being whisked off by some of the Portuguese pimps who hail you at every step'.[6]

Christmas Day was spent on the island, dominated by its volcanic cloud-covered summit and plummeting mist-filled ravines. Huxley and the ship's purser clambered up the Curral Mountain on horseback, along hair-raising ledges, 'with a perpendicular rock on our right and an equally perpendicular precipice on our left, our hold on terra firma being entirely confined to some five feet of rough stones'. He was concentrating too hard to be terrified. At the top he stood in awe, his 'enjoyment of the sublime and beautiful' marred only by a more primal hunger.[7]

'Mountain scenery is new to me', he mused, but it would become a lifelong obsession, and the signs of violence forced strange reflections. On 26 December, as the ship sailed on a warm breeze, Huxley dwelt on the dark, mocking disguises of Romantic Nature:

> Nature is a true tragedian – her most painful throes, her
> wildest struggles have all within them some element of
> beauty – even in death she covers her face, like Caesar,
> with a graceful mantle. So in this island, a huge monument
> of some awful volcanic phenomenon – made up of wild
> peaks and intervening deep gullies and ravines.

It was as if she was disguising the awful plunges with cotton-wool clouds. The picturesque town of Funchal overlooking the bay was the same. It seemed a fair 'whited sepulchre' city from afar, 'but all stinks within'. On mountain tops and in sherry-sipping society, the cynic saw superficial friendliness disguise a primal savagery.

Huxley's reverie was interrupted by the Master at Arms calling, 'Three bells, sir'. He was on his way. The lush tropics of Rio de Janeiro awaited.[8]

On the last day of the year, Huxley recorded a latitude of 21° 12' – they had crossed the Tropic. They ploughed on, through shimmering phosphorescent seas, caused by myriad luminous jelly-fish which he netted for dissection. The *Rattlesnake*'s sails caught the Trade Winds on 2 January 1847. Flying fish skimmed the water's surface. They littered the decks in the morning, but nothing else did: he searched in vain for the fine reddish dust that Darwin had reported on the *Beagle*'s deck 15 years earlier.[9] The long weeks of the Atlantic crossing were spent examining the haul from his tow net. One day it would be bristle-jawed arrow-worms, confusing creatures whose relationships were unknown. Another it was sea squirts (which shot water jets on being handled), and even droplets of water proved to be positively alive with pulsing water-flea-like crustaceans.

Huxley's microscope was set up in the chart-room. Here he was in familiar surroundings. His money had gone on books, which lined the walls: Buffon's natural history, innumerable novels, old student notebooks, tomes on zoology, German philosophy, Dante and Horace in Italian to teach himself the language, 'and there I sit' and work 'much as though I were in my rooms in Agar Street'. With the exception, of course, that he now had a growing audience. He watched the voracious arrow-worms swim around 'with their heads buried in some unfortunate' sea squirt. His microscope was an escape hatch; it transported him into an exotic world of beautiful diaphanous beings, pulsing and phosphorescing. The trouble was the queue of swabby faces wanting to peer down into it. It was true about the 'noise and frivolity' of the mess. Delicate dissections were hard enough on land. On a rolling ship, surrounded by prying eyes and practical jokers, they needed the patience of Job, or at least 'the toil and labour of a moral Sisyphus'.[10] His gawping middies wanted to see 'something pretty', and he bored them with incomprehensible microscopic sights so as to be left alone.

After passing the Cape Verde islands, 300 miles from tropical Africa, the frigate was rocked by a momentary earthquake, but little else shattered the peace. 'Our friends the flying fish have quite left us, and sharks, dolphins and pilot fish have taken their place'. The mugginess made it impossible 'to rake together any thoughts in this hot noisy berth'. In the calms the canvases flapped uselessly, and Stanley took the opportunity to take deep sea soundings, or try to. Spun yarn weighted with 384 lbs of lead shot, fed out for 38 minutes to a depth of 2,600 fathoms, still failed to hit bottom. At one point the obvious happened, and Huxley reported that, 'alack and alas . . . the splicing came undone and away went the lead minus line, to investigate for himself. He has however not yet returned to report, and strong fears are expressed that he has absconded'.[11]

Then they were buffeted by squalls, sheets of rain accompanied by thunder and lightning, with waterspouts visible in the distance. Again the water in his cabin was 'wish-washing about'. The sick list grew, the old salts with rheumatism and boys with puffy feet. They stood outside his sick bay, most of them illiterate, a gruff bunch scorned from the upper deck as 'degenerate, despicable, immoral, and barely distinguishable from the common criminal'. Huxley saw them no differently at first. 'What a precious pack I have to deal with', he mused as he lanced feet. 'Save the necessary courtesies of life, I shall make it my business to have very little to do with them'.

Worse was yet to greet him in the surgery. They crossed the

Equator on 13 January – 'usual tomfooleries observed', he jotted of the heathen Saturnalia. He and the doctor suffered first, being ducked and drenched, and Huxley dished out the same to 'the unhappy beggars who had to follow'. His infectious spirit struck the midshipmen and Philip Sharpe audaciously doused the captain. (Huxley was beginning to like their style.) But the ducking had tragic consequences. The sick list grew 'in consequence of the Neptunizing'.[12] Two novices contracted pleurisy, writhing with chest pains and fever for days. Huxley watched helplessly as one succumbed, the first death on a long voyage, and a terrible irony under the circumstances.

Into the southern Atlantic and he caught his first Portuguese man-of-war, the poisonous *Physalia*. These were the invertebrate yachts of the high seas, with their beautiful sails and long deadly tentacles. He picked up his specimen by its five-inch vivid blue float, careful of its poisonous tentacles (hence their name 'sea nettles'). He had a day to examine it, for in the equatorial heat it was 'semifluid & stinking' by the next morning.[13] But that was time enough to correct the 'horridly superficial' observations of the French zoologists. He was becoming his own man, and on the way to his first *Rattlesnake* paper.

A week later they approached Rio, sailing past golden sands and fringing palms. The harbour was crowded with everything from hollow-log canoes to 'felucca-rigged boats', with merchantmen standing off. Aromatic scents carried on the sultry air as Huxley came up to catch his first sight of the New World. It beats Madeira 'into fits', he burst out as he saw the city on 23 January; it must rival 'the Bay of Naples for the title of the most beautiful place in the world'. For a week they remained at Rio, the crew visiting its shops and squares, and the markets with their exotic fruit and fish. 'They must eat queer things', he said as he saw the cuttlefish and hammerhead sharks on the stalls. In 90° temperatures they examined the unhewn-granite buildings. The richer streets rivalled those in Europe, and 'feather-flower' bouquets of humming-bird plumes could cost a fortune.[14] Outside town the whine of the cicadas grew deafening, and Huxley marvelled at the colossal saxhorn snails clustering on pawpaw hedges and the enormous gaudy butterflies fluttering through the banana groves.

But the drawbacks were shocking. The stench on the beach was offensive, but even more overpowering was the moral stench of slavery. Along unsewered streets the blacks trudged, their backs glistening, pulling carts or humping crates. Gangs marched to the beat of a tin rattle. Some had iron collars, others masks of tin, padlocked from behind. MacGillivray was stunned at the 'extreme brutality' of the masters. Huxley was chastened by the blacks' resilience. 'I have a much greater respect for them than for their beastly Portuguese masters'. He compared the slaves to 'the corresponding class in England, the manufacturing and agricultural poor', the workers demanding their own 'emancipation'. It was a pity, he thought, recalling the horrors of the potato famine, that a 'few of the hungry Saxon millions now famishing in England' could not seize this 'vile, ignorant' nation and transform Brazil into a 'second Indian Empire'.[15]

Huxley and MacGillivray hardly escaped the stench of slavery at sea. The boat they hired to dredge the beautiful Botafogo Bay was crewed by slaves, who were made to work by 'dint of bribery and ridicule'. The genial Forbes had taught Huxley the trick of dredging, and what he lacked in equipment he made up for in ingenuity. Gauze meat covers doubled as sieves, and the results were spectacular. This was no choppy Southampton; the azure waters of the palm-fringed bay were 80° and the pair pulled up 45 species of molluscs, starfish, anemones and the primitive little sand-burrowing *Amphioxus*. They sat examining their catch against the spectacular backdrop of Sugar Loaf Mountain, the warm waters lapping at their feet.

Huxley made fast friendships, the first with MacGillivray. They explored everywhere together. Being 'Naturalists', *officio* and *ex-officio*, they 'had or pretended to have a more or less naturalistic' goals. But 'our investigations always took in the end a chemical turn, to wit, the examination of the nature and properties of a complex liquid called Sherry Cobbler. Oh Rio, thou Sodom-and-Gomorrha in one, town of stinks and beastliness, thou shalt be saved not because of one just man, but because of the excellence of the iced drink'. The sultry days saw them climbing the mountains. They gloried in the fierce tropical storms, watching the solid lightning bolts strike the peaks. Or they spent them dredging, decamping afterwards to a tavern to consume sherry and pigeon.

'Cobblers or no cobblers, however, our liege lady Nature was not neglected'. He examined the reproductive organs of the burrowing *Amphioxus*, and kicked himself for failing to make out the blood circulation. The pair dredged bivalve lamp-shells from the bay on sailing away from Rio on the morning of 2 February, and further out started hauling in nets full of jellyfish.

'By the way', he wrote to his mother (who had just moved down from Coventry to live with the Cookes), 'tell Dr. Cooke with my kindest regards that old Gray is a lying old thief. Many of the things he told me about MacGillivray e.g. his being an ignoramus in natural history etc. etc. having proved to be lies'.[16]

On the long haul to the Cape of Good Hope they took soundings daily and recorded the water temperature at depth. Albatrosses, gliding on long narrow wings, brought the men to the gun rails. 'We don't at all keep in mind the fate of the Ancient Mariner, inasmuch as whole broadsides of small shot and rifle bullets are fired at them daily, but they don't keep to their part of the affair, never coming "for food or play" to the mariner's holla'. Little else distinguished the days in mid-ocean. Huxley could only tell them apart by his harvest. Some days saw a passing armada of Portuguese men-of-war, or the purple-and-white-striped crests of penny-sized *Velellae* ('little sails'), with their tiny tentacled rims.[17] These 'siphonophores', or sea nettles, were jellyfish relatives and the oddest animals, seemingly simple but infuriatingly complex. Nobody could agree about them. Was each a single organism? Or was it a complex colony of many individuals united, one the gas bag, others modified as stinging tentacles, still more the food-ingesting or siphon polyps (hence the group's name), all specialized for single tasks and subordinated to the whole?

The sailing gas-bags had Huxley taking to a boat and trailing his net. Early on, he dropped his drawing book from the starboard quarter boat, and had to watch his unique record of this pelagic life sail away itself. There was nothing for it but to start his dissections afresh. Mercifully many thumb-sized seasquirts or 'Salpae were taken today in the towing net', he logged on 23 February. 'They were of the same kind as those of w[h]. I had previously made (& lost!) drawings'. These sketches were of inordinate complexity. It could take a month to dissect every part of a man-of-war; even then the filigree work could be infuriating. And it all supposed a constant supply. In this perishable climate 'You get a day's work out of your specimen and on the morrow he is rotten'. He needed a regular supply of corpses. 'If Dame Nature will send me one every day I shall do'. Unfortunately she could be profligate one day and parsimonious the next. But at least light breezes in notoriously rough waters bought Huxley the time, and he planned a paper on the man-of-war, to be posted home from the Cape along with his first £40 savings.[18]

The light winds bore the *Rattlesnake* on 8 May into Simon's Bay, on the tip of southern Africa. With the ship moored the storms started to lash the Cape. The gales kept the crew in Simon's Town for a month, although Huxley put the detention down to the 'ball given by the Admiral [of the British Naval Headquarters] on the 7th [April]'. Not that the junior surgeon was to be left out. He too donned his £6 10s dress suit and attended the soirée. 'This was a very creditable affair', about the only one of their stay. 'The "fair Afrikanders" did honour in point of good looks to their native land and danced bravely'.

But it was his only light relief. Simon's Town was a 'dull, dreary' place dominated by the naval dockyards. 'Nothing but officials, stall-keepers and Malays to be seen'. The military installation itself was buzzing; the Boers had made their Great Trek into the interior, and the British were engaged in the 'Caffre War' against the natives, and planning their policy of segregation. But the war meant little to Huxley beyond extortionate prices in the shops. While the officers took coaches the 23 miles to Cape Town, Huxley's South African experience was reduced to foraging along the sea shore.

Still, his haul of molluscs dredged up in the dreary harbour paid dividends. He dissected their nerves and found Owen's descriptions to be wrong. Moreover the nerve patterns of diverse molluscs, from squids to mussels, suggested a common plan – and another paper was in the offing, one putting him up with the elite philosophical anatomists. A 'grand' unifying paper this time – a huge 'monograph of the Mollusca' 'based on examination of at least one species of every genus'.[19] It was hopelessly ambitious – even Huxley realized that 'my eyes are bigger than my belly' – but the Simon's Town stopover allowed him to anatomize his way through another branch of the animal kingdom.

His eyes were getting bigger all the time. The tyro was intent on restructuring the whole of invertebrate creation. He projected papers on jellyfish, sea anemones, siphonophores and the homologies of the heads of crustaceans, insects, spiders and millipedes ('Modest notion this and about enough for the five years in itself'!). It dawned just how much there was to do, with every microscopic dissection of a minute corpse taking days amid pitches and rolls. But it was good to have an obsession. 'I should assuredly go clean daft' aboard ship 'had I nothing to do'.

The man-of-war paper *was* finished. In it Huxley routinely made the sea nettle a single individual composed of 'organs', which he described minutely.[20] Stanley – who had a habit of wandering in to watch Huxley at work – suggested he send it to the bishop. The Whig Lords, before career 'scientists' controlled their own house, ran science as they did the State. Noblemen included trusteeship in their public calling. They ruled the faunal empire at the Zoological Society; they held the British Museum's natural treasures in trust for the nation. Even so, the societies were racked by dissension as the new radical democrats and capitalists swept in, demanding accountable specialists at board level. But the vestiges of rotten borough corruption persisted, with appointments the gift of Lords temporal – and abstruse papers recommended by Lords spiritual.

Bishop Stanley had for a decade been the figurehead President of the Linnean Society. Huxley let the captain send the paper, but he was quietly cynical. Probably 'the Bishop will get it printed in the *Linn. Trans.*, by no means on account of any inherent merit, but because it is the first fruits of his son's cruise'. Not that he really doubted the value of his work, but he hated nepotism. When Stanley sent it from Simon's Town, he told himself that the satisfaction was in the work – which was as well, because he would be ignorant of its fate for a long time. The bishop's people had it, and 'They may do as they like with it'.[21]

Finally, with the £50,000 in chests carried ashore to replenish Cape Town's war-torn coffers, and with the 'all engrossing "Caffre war" dinned into our ears from morning to night', the crew were happy to weigh anchor.

For 24 days they tacked across the Indian Ocean. Typically they experienced 20-foot waves, so that even on 'calm' days Huxley's microscope had to be lashed to the table. But occasionally the calm was shattered by north-easterly gales and mountainous seas, making work impossible for the hydrographers as much as Huxley. On 2 May 1847 the tropic birds heralded a nearby reef and before dusk the look-outs spotted Bamboo Mountain, their first sight of Mauritius. Darwin had rhapsodized in his *Journal* about the island's 'air of perfect elegance', and Huxley had great expectations. At night they could see bright moonshine on glittering sands. The *Rattlesnake* came round to the northern end of the island and Huxley awoke on his 22nd birthday to a brilliant blue sky, transparent turquoise water and the 'handsomest of tugs' to tow them into Port Louis harbour.

And yet, restricted to ship on his first day in this palm-fringed paradise, he fell into a black mood. He was still adrift and dispossessed in his nihilistic thoughts – thoughts of chance and circumstance:

> Twenty-two years ago I entered this world a pulpy mass
> of capabilities, as yet unknown and save for motherly
> affection uncared for. And had it not been better altogether
> had I been crushed and trodden out at once? Nourishing
> me up, was as though one should pick up a stray egg,
> unconscious whether dove's or serpent's, and carefully
> incubate it. And here I am what a score of years in the
> world have made me – such a bundle of glorious and
> inglorious contradictions as men call a man.

In Port Louis harbour he stewed in his berth, suffering the stench of putrefying jellies. He was an outsider aboard ship as much as in scientific society. Yet he was looking for the way in, a way to make his mark, a way to escape the religious and social chains of the past: 'Morals and religion are one wild whirl to me – of them the less said the better. In the region of the intellect alone can I find free and innocent play for such faculties as I possess'. Only uncovering the truth in nature 'allows me to get rid of the "malady of thought"'. He had found a way in; he would share in the democracy of intellect.[22]

The dislocated sailor perked up on finding his shore legs. The island's sorcery worked a spell; the primitive charm he expected from Saint-Pierre's Rousseauesque tale of love in paradise, *Paul and Virginia*. Port Louis was a tropical splash of colour, an exotic, ethnic mêlée. One passed 'silks and satins of the French lady' here, 'the richly embroidered drapery of the Hindus' there, and everywhere 'turbaned Musselmen, Cingalese, Chinese with their tails carefully stowed away in their caps'. Urbane equestrian shows were held against the spectacular mountain backdrop. Even the Indian convict labourers had fiercely noble expressions. Bearded Moors traded with Parsee merchants and young Creoles smoked cheroots on street corners. Market stalls were crammed with a hundred-odd species of brilliantly hued fish. 'In truth it is a complete paradise', he regaled his mother, 'and if I had nothing better to do, I should pick up some pretty French Eve (and there are plenty) and turn Adam'. She knew her Tom, but he reassured her, '*N. B.* There are *no* serpents in the island'.

The isle was a Gallic temptress, which the stiff-lipped English after 40 years of colonization had failed to subdue. And British sensibilities were still shocked. MacGillivray was horrified to see coolies and cane cutters working on the sabbath – although it probably reinforced young Huxley's less parochial outlook. Here too was a place to die, or at least to catch insects: the cemetery 'is one of the most beautiful places I have seen', with its rock tombs garlanded with fresh flowers, and graves overhung with acacia blossoms, buzzing with life.[23] The mêlée extended unto death. There was no sense of Christian universality, but Muslims and Confucians and Hindus each following their own rites.

Not that sentimentality got the better of Huxley. He made a determined show of keeping it at bay. If this curable romantic made a pilgrimage to the tombs of Paul and Virginia, it was only for the glorious hike. Down Saint-Pierre's lilting cabbage-palm avenues, that 'holy temple' where the young lovers admired 'an Intelligence that is infinite, all-powerful and the friend of mankind'. But still Huxley plucked two roses to scent his cabin.

The wiry Huxley was indomitable. Even in the heat he strode 35 miles to Chamarelle Falls and back, sustained by pork brawn and sardines. He took in tow the purser and Revd Robert King, the one having to be carried across streams because of his sore feet, the other adding to his burden by filling his bag with exotic snails. Not for Huxley renting a horse, or borrowing the Surveyor General's stately elephant, as Darwin had done. The subaltern's group 'trudged, full of life and spirits'. And every new vista, from mango plantations to the 350-foot jungle-chasm falls, indeed, 'the firm earth' itself after 'weeks reeling at sea, intoxicated me'. (His 'pocket pistols filled with strong waters' and wayside stops for 'vin ordinaire at sixpence a bottle' helped.) It was, he admitted red-cheeked, 'one of the most pleasant trips I ever had'.[24]

The ship sailed on 17 May with the captain, capricious as ever, carrying £4,000 in bullion for Hobart. This was at the Governor of Mauritius' request, but it meant Stanley disobeying Admiralty orders and delaying the survey. Of course, there was another reason, besides his commission; he could surprise his brother Charlie and Eliza in their colonial home. He plotted a course for Tasmania, 5,000 miles across the Indian Ocean. The *Rattlesnake* tacked south in the 'loveliest weather'. They passed great whales, one 50-foot finback rising majestically out of the water 30 yards away and showing 'his real size to us'. Again Dayman tried to take deep sea soundings, and Stanley even employed an ingenious scoop to bring up some hitherto unseen sea-bed. But to no avail; after feeding the line out for two hours, to a depth of almost four miles, it snapped. By the time they caught the westerlies they were so far south in mid-winter that Huxley was feeling the cold. The galley fuel ran short and the fires were quenched at four each afternoon.

The consequences were unthinkable to an Englishman: 'No hot grog, tea at half-past three, and other abominations'.

'I had one of my melancholy fits this evening', he recorded on 22 June. The blue devils had now turned into black depressions, and they were striking with ferocious regularity. It took him an hour and a half stalking the poop deck, adopting his usual remedy, 'a good "think" to get rid of it'. He looked to his inner strengths, his scientific work, and took comfort from his gelatinous conquests. An hour of planning cured him. Across the Indian Ocean he had been studying the most transparent, troublesome, 'strange and whimsical forms'. Or trying to: *Diphyes* was a ghostly creature, like the man-of-war but with the float replaced by two swimming bells. It was farthing-sized and all but invisible, 'so transparent, that in the water, one sees nothing of it . . . Taken out of water, it looks as if it were composed of two elegantly-cut pieces of very clear glass'.[25] Detach the two parts and they float off by themselves, raising again the question of individuality. Another paper was the tonic he needed, and he planned to post it home from Sydney.

On 24 June, after 28 days at sea, came a welcome sight, the 'jolly face and English tongue of the old pilot' who saw them into Storm Bay in Tasmania. Past the huge basalt pillars at the mouth of the estuary he guided them. Sailors at the gun-rails could spot warehouses in the coves, a tiny fort, and everywhere a patchwork of green and fallow fields. It seemed so quintessentially English. Six and a half months out of Plymouth, on the other side of the world, and the talk was of the furnished cottages, rosy children and real pianos. 'And this in a place where fifty years ago you would have seen nothing but naked savages or kangaroos'.

The next morning they could see the church spires of Hobart 'peeping out from among the trees'.[26] Of all the little Englands scattered across the globe, none recalled so much the mother country. It was all a sea-weary sailor needed.

5

An Ark of Promise

AS A PORT OF CALL Hobart was unscheduled. The captain surprised his brother Charlie on 25 June 1847. But he found Eliza as uncomfortable at Government House as she had been among the Stanleys at home, and rudely snubbed by the Governor's wife. Huxley had a grand view of these social manoeuvrings at the soirées. And there were plenty of these. In fact, Hobart was 'a round of lesser and greater debaucheries'.

Huxley walked Hobart's chilly winter streets, gazing up at Mount Wellington, with its thick eucalyptus cover. After so long at sea English tea and fireside chat were a godsend. Fresh from London he was lionized – which meant being invited into local homes, served by 'ticket-of-leave' men (convicts free to work as they please) and pumped for gossip. The poor boy, socially deprived as he saw himself, loved it: Tasmania 'was without question one of the best places we have sojourned in. The people are very hospitable – really hospitable'.

For a colony barely 40 years old and 12,000 miles from home, it was surprisingly *au fait* with medical developments. The local surgeons initiated him into the latest painless surgery. Mesmeric operations he knew all about, like Chandler's, using hypnosis as an anaesthetic. But as he left England word was arriving from Boston of a rival anaesthetic, ether. The anti-mesmeric surgeons were lauding it. It was a wonderful 'Yankee dodge' to dislodge Elliotson's populists and put the power back into the hands of the professionals. An equally theatrical 'etherial epidemic' was sweeping Britain, with druggists' placards blaring 'Painless Extraction of Teeth'. But it was here in Hobart, only eight months after the Boston announcement, that Huxley 'saw an ether operation for the first time'.[1] Populist he might be, but he was looking to professional rewards, and this procedure gave the surgeon greater command over his patient.

The reception in Hobart raised Huxley's expectations of New South Wales. Eight days later they made their way into Sydney's Port Jackson Harbour, past beautiful coves, their sloping shores surrounded by 'wattles and myrtles with glistening sheen of dark green leaves', the sapphire sea 'so clear, that at thirty feet below, the bed of white sand was visible'. Sailors pressed the gun-rail. To port was Woolloomooloo Bay with its bustling wharves, backed by terraces of stone houses with windmills on the hills. They stood off a neatly clipped park, no surer sign of English civilization. Here they anchored, in Farm Cove, alongside the merchantmen.

Huxley was excited at the 'prospect of obtaining news from home after seven long months of absence'. A boat came out 'with a cartload of letters and newspapers, but no line for me'. It heightened his sense of isolation, of friendlessness in a lonely port. 'I damned everything and everybody' and 'sat down to dinner in a temper that Satan need not have envied'.[2]

To make matters worse, he was kept aboard at first. He was put to work with the ratings, scrubbing and painting. Not for him Darwin's evening stroll through the salubrious part of town. (But then Darwin had travelled as the captain's gentleman companion, rather than a seven-shilling subaltern.) Huxley knew the treats in store. Darwin's *Journal* pictured the whirligig of Sydney life, with the broad streets a crush of smart carriages and starched livery servants. Nothing had prepared Darwin for this 'paradise to the Worshippers of Mammon'. What worried him was the indiscriminate wealth. Ex-cons once broken on the wheel could be worth tens of thousands, and this raised the awful impossibility of telling a man's respectability.

Huxley hardly shared Darwin's fears. When he did get ashore he found the fashionable quarter even more opulent after ten years. Civic pride now competed with colonial snobbery. There was a new architectural grandeur. Town houses of polished stone and red cedar looked important. They stood on gaslit streets. An elegant Government House had been built, along with new 'iron and brass foundries, shipyards, breweries and shops "emulating those of Bond Street"'. Even a university was talked of. But the seamy underbelly of the city was the same, and much better known to the Jacks. Cheap grog in the sleazy pubs on the Rocks drew all sorts. Stocking-capped sailors mixed with prostitutes and ex-cons, and everywhere cabbage-hatted squatters sat about, fresh from their sheep runs. Drunks lay around in fustian-jackets and 'rooskin caps, while their stockingless women smoked Irish pipes, or danced on beer-stained tables.

Drink remained the national pastime, occupying the gents no less than the Jacks, and the 'Gins' (aborigines) inhaled the same alcoholic haze. Ale houses and breweries were everywhere, explaining why half the government revenues came from alcohol sales. The stocks about town were well tenanted by the tramps unable to afford the fine 'for indulging too freely at the shrine of Bacchus'. But for all the 'likker', it remained a fascinating, irritating city, a 'maelstrom of crime and drunkenness, brutality, bigotry and snobbery', but no less of opulence, gaiety and colonial endeavour.[3]

Huxley made up for his own forced labour aboard ship by 'calling, and being called upon – Govt. Balls and the like'. The young officers were courted by the colonial ladies, eager for the gossip. Donning his dress uniform, he threw himself into Sydney's dissipations, soiréeing at the new Government House with his midshipmen. Lizzie heard of his gaiety: 'What think you of your grave, scientific brother turning out a ball-goer and doing the "light fantastic"?' Periodically it palled, as the high life caught up with him. 'I managed three balls and two dinners in the course of a week. I can't say I liked all this'. Outwardly he remained cheerful, explaining the 'method in my madness'. Lonely in a foreign port, where there was 'not a soul who cared whether I was alive or dead', he forced himself to 'pick up a friend or two among the multitudes of the empty and frivolous'. In private he was considerably more cynical. It was social ship-scrubbing, so much extra 'humbug', necessary perhaps, 'but on the whole it was a dog's life, altogether making a toil of pleasure'.[4]

With a 15-foot draft the *Rattlesnake* was too deep for close reef mapping. For this Stanley had inherited a shallow-draft tender left in Sydney after the *Fly*'s expedition, the *Bramble*. But it was so decayed that a lengthy refit was necessary, while a second tender was sold off as useless. Even more useless were the officers manning the boats. Stanley 'packed them all off home' and re-manned the *Bramble* with his *Rattlesnake* men.

For three months the ships were buzzing with fitters and joiners in Farm Cove. Nearby merchantmen unloaded British factory goods and took on wool for the return journey. Not all plied a colonial trade. Sydney controlled an empire within an empire.

Hundreds of tons of sandalwood were shipped to China for incense. And stranger cargoes could be seen: dried trepangs, the Barrier Reef sea slugs, destined for Chinese drug emporia.

Midshipman Sharpe reckoned that these months 'were about the best I ever had'. Bush picnics, Saturday fishing trips and soirées: sometimes with Captain Stanley, whose Sydney friends stretched back to his *Britomart* days, sometimes with Huxley, who enjoyed the junketings, despite himself.

Stanley stepped off the ship straight into a religious dispute. Like the Whig bishop, he saw no threat in Dissent, nor in its demands for equal rights with Anglicans; and fresh in port he agreed to chair a Dissenters' meeting to found a Seamen's Chapel. The High Church *Australian* damned him for joining their 'sacrilegious' ranks. What! Does he believe that any 'possessor of a black coat' can 'marry and baptize'?[5] And he, not merely an 'epauletted Son of Neptune', but an epauletted son of a *bishop*! Huxley, born into a sectarian age, watched the papers trade insults. Twelve thousand miles and nothing new: the same catcalls of 'bigotry'. Stanley backed out, leaving the *Sydney Morning Herald* to add injury to insult by concluding that he was spineless to boot.

Huxley spent his time more productively. He had caught more *Diphyes* coming up the coast and he began his new paper, 'far more considerable in extent' than the last. Its title, he informed Lizzie, would be the self-important 'Observations upon the Anatomy of the Diphydae, and upon the Unity of Organisation of the Diphydae and Phosphoridae'. ('There!' he added. 'Think yourself lucky you have only got that to read' that and not the paper itself!) Again he was using common structures to relate all these 'sea nettles' through one grand blueprint.[6] Three months gave him time to finish and it sailed off, like the last, to His Lordship at the Linnean.

It was followed by a letter to Forbes, announcing that he was corralling all the supposedly 'widely separated families' of polyp and medusa-bearing animals. He was uniting them all: the stinging hydras, sea anemones, sea nettles and jellyfish.[7] He was bringing them together in a new class; but such are the ironies of life that a Göttingen zoologist Rudolph Leuckart, barely two years his senior, anticipated him in an epochal book at precisely this moment, calling them all the 'Coelenterata'.

Away from the microscope the desolate partying continued. The lonely sailor was scouring the ballrooms for 'a few pleasant acquaintances'. He cruised the dance halls and crashed private parties. But rather than pick up a few shallow friends, he fell prey to a consuming passion.

She had hair of 'Australian silk'. Perhaps she was pretty, he could not decide. She did not know a fish from a frog but she had a ferocious talent, spoke German, loved poetry and philosophy, and the Polka. He first met Miss Henrietta Anne Heathorn at a party. She was leaving but he still waylaid her for a dance; 'my brother in law', she recalled, declared 'it impossible as his wife my sister had already gone to put on her wraps & the horses c^d not be kept waiting. Never mind said Mr Huxley – we shall meet again & then remember you are engaged for the 1st dance'. His deep-set dark eyes mesmerized her. They 'had an extraordinary way of flashing', she noted, 'when they seemed to be burning – His manner was most fascinating'.[8] While gadding about he had already met her brother-in-law, the businessman William Fanning. Fanning was married to Henrietta's half-sister Oriana and Henrietta herself kept house for them in New Town, 'a pretty house at Cook's River'.

The girl with silky hair was constantly surprised by her subaltern with flashing eyes. At the next Government ball, 'suddenly I saw him opposite me in a quadrille dancing with my sister. In the refreshment room we met & chatted so long that the man who brought me there had gone away'. Dances ruled the calendar in Sydney. They were social fortifications for a beleaguered elite, where matches were made and new arrivals could be mined. Two more passed; each time she scanned the blue-jackets for 'that delightful doctor', and each time she found him. The last was at the parsonage. 'What an eve of glamour it was'. He pinched a wishbone from his companion's plate and 'we pulled then wished & danced. He uttered magic words – before he left he begged of me the red camellia I wore'.[9] Huxley stole away, looking for all the world like a raven-haired romantic – indeed returning to his berth to preserve the bloom.

In his own diary he cloaked his emotions. The charade of interminable dances, he jotted, 'thank God, was checked by a serious . . . illness which lasted some three weeks'. His recuperation was inimitable, a 100-mile ride under shadeless gums up the coast past Newcastle. He was presumably invited by his outward-bound companion, Revd Robert, the fourth son of Captain King. The captain was a towering figure in the colony, the son of a former governor, and running an enormous farming and mining operation, the Australian Agricultural Company. Huxley rode to the company's estate at Port Stephens, where the Kings had a beautiful house called 'Tahlee'. The ubiquitous captain ran one of the colony's scientific salons. Frequently in London, he was as likely to be found bent over the barnacles in the Zoological Society's museum as discussing maritime affairs. (It was in the zoo that King had taught Darwin how to use preservatives.) King and Huxley had molluscs in common and the sea at heart, and they struck it off. The captain saw the surgeon away with packages, letters and another introduction to Richard Owen at home.

Huxley rode on with another son, Philip Gidley King, to his house at Stroud, 20 miles away. Philip had been one of the *Beagle*'s middies. At 30, he was running the company's stud farms and their approach to Stroud was heralded by fields of prize cows. Of course Huxley overdid the journey and paid for it. He was laid-up with chronic rheumatism in his foot, which kept him bedridden for days. The march was typical of the way he attacked everything, knocking himself out. And so there he lay, disgusted but grateful for King's 'kind-hearted attention'.[10]

His absence baffled Henrietta. Only later at a *Rattlesnake* picnic did she learn that he was ill up-country. Friends playing Cupid would constantly ask the middies 'whether Dr Huxley had returned'. She waited. 'Exquisite' picnics and parties passed. 'I began to think all that had gone before was my imagination & that his was just a sailors way'.

Arriving back, Huxley was 'glad to find that I had been inquired after by the New Town folks' – all 'instinct I suppose, for I could not have told myself why at the time'. Henrietta was way ahead of him.

In late September he found an excuse to call at Fanning's house, 'Holmwood'. Henrietta was caught unawares: she was upstairs when she heard hooves galloping up the drive and a servant 'looked out of the Bulls eye window & exclaimed Its Doctor Huxley'. Huxley joined her two half-sisters for lunch, but Henrietta 'was paralysed & c^d only get down' after they had adjourned to the drawing room. Even more paralysing, 'of all subjects the one under discussion', said Huxley, 'was my reception into the family'. It was coy, talk of '3 sisters . . . going about without a protector' and him offering his services to Henrietta. 'My heart leaped', Huxley said. 'But I thought to myself, Tom, you are a fool . . . and you have only seen one another four times'. He walked with them, twining flowers round her bonnet. She slipped on a branch and he pulled it away 'saying . . . so would I remove all hindrances from your path in life'.[11]

Impulsive in all things, he was as good as engaged at their fifth meeting. He had chanced his arm, and his life's course was plotted. The outsider, true to form, had found love in the colonies. The sober cynic, scratching the surface of a hollow pleasure-seeking society, had uncovered a heart as emotionally and intellectually full as his own. It surprised her; it certainly staggered him.

Nettie he called her, or 'Menen'. She was poetical, artistic, religious and well read. Two years' schooling in Neuwied on the Rhine meant they talked the same language. 'I had not the least idea of the true meaning of Science,' she admitted. 'Something of art, something of literature I knew but of science not an iota'. But 'the happiness of being together swallowed up everything else'. He drew her into an unimagined world, stranger than Australia. He unveiled the cosmos, explaining the elegant laws of chemical affinity and the unifying archetypes of animal life. He opened a door 'to undreamt of possibilities', revealing scientific dramas 'that were like fairy tales'.[12]

She would smooth the rough edges and soothe that 'scornful contempt for his fellow creatures'. Nettie was two months younger than 'Hal', having turned 22 on 1 July, 'but she is *in fact* as much younger than her years as I am older than mine'. He loved her 'Saxon yellow hair', although 'appearance has nothing whatever to do with the hold she has upon my mind for I have seen hundreds of prettier women. But I never met with so sweet a temper, so self-sacrificing and affectionate a disposition'. Her only folly was to leave 'her happiness in the hands of a man like myself, struggling upwards and certain of nothing'.[13]

But struggle and uncertainty marked the middle classes moving across the empire. Henrietta's family had been there: her mother's father had been a physician in Barbados, her grandmother (born on Antigua) had married three times and Nettie had been born in the West Indies (illegitimately, so she later discovered). She was an imperial outsider, a hardened match for Tom's marginality. She had been brought up in the hop-growing district of Kent by an aunt, her paternal grandfather having been a brewer in Maidstone. With 200 grog shops in Sydney, Australia looked like a Dionysian dream. Her father had taken over a 100-foot, three-storey flour and timber complex, Woodstock Mill, close to the village of Jamberoo, 90 miles south of Sydney.[14] He added a brewery, drawing water from the Minnamurra river, and converted the cooperage to produce beer barrels.

Nettie had followed her father out, arriving with her mother and half-sister before Christmas 1843. They travelled on a bullock dray from Wollongong to Woodstock, sitting on sacks stuffed with maize husks, stopping only to quench their thirst from sponge-like ferns in the tree forks. She had never seen such sights: 'gum-trees two hundred feet' high draped with 'snake-like' lianas, and 'lofty cabbage palms' whose canopy blocked out the sun.

For Nettie Woodstock was a steam-engine 'fairyland'. Like Hal she loved the 'whirr of machinery' and she crept into the mill to watch the ox-drawn cedar logs in the teeth of the saw, spraying perfumed sawdust.[15] But her mother wept bitter tears at the hardship, and Nettie was reduced to unpicking her own dresses. Not that she remained long. Her youngest half-sister Oriana came out two months later and was married to Fanning in the Woodstock parlour. The couple set up home in New Town, where Nettie joined them.

This is where Hal found her. Fanning's became a second home, evenings around the fire there reminding him 'of the happy old days at S[alt]'s'. Here he encountered Nettie's father, 'a curious man of strong natural talent evidently, but rather ingenious than sound'. With a French frigate in port, one final Government ball gave them the occasion to talk openly. Or rather not, as they paced about outside, pretending to take the air: 'No word of love was spoken but we understood one another'. Huxley, stiffly attired in his dress uniform, beat around the bush furiously, 'half mad with excitement'. And so ended his first Sydney spring, precipitously, with an engagement after six dances.

Huxley had his emotional mooring at last. In his unsettled way he was settling down, and away from the dance floor Nettie found quite a different soul, 'earnest and silent'. 'You have', he said, 'tied your fate to that of a young poor, I had almost said, friendless, man, rich in nothing but his love for you'. It focused his mind, and fitful nights worrying over his prospects 'brought on my old nervous palpitation'. They would marry when he made full surgeon. This he expected sometime after his return, accelerated by 'his scientific work, for this was the inducement held out by the Admiralty to energetic subalterns'. Science could still be his salvation. With renewed energy he dissected a simple relation of the cockles and mussels, *Trigonia*, and posted his findings to Forbes.[16]

Nettie's presence rekindled almost religious emotions in Huxley.

Absolved, he would rise, 'nobler and purer', 'banishing evil from my thoughts'. The long-haired student from the medical garret would start again, the font within cleansed. She had 'sweetened the very springs of my being which were before but waters of Marah, dark and bitter'. So began 'a new era', one 'of much more importance than all H. M. navy put together'. The three months up, he had to agree with young Sharpe: 'the most pleasant I have ever spent, and fraught with events'.[17]

The *Bramble* had already left port. Stanley wanted to test the tender and her 36 crew. He had kept on her commander, Lieutenant C. B. Yule, a 'very good fellow', whose knowledge of New Guinea 'will be invaluable'. At the Governor's request they sailed her 240 miles south to the whaling station at Twofold Bay, to survey the site for a new customs house. (The Sea Lords in London were monthly more infuriated by his idiosyncratic behaviour.) He found the landscape artist Oswald Brierly languishing there, managing the whaling works. Brierly was well salted, having sailed the world on an adventurer's yacht, and Stanley brought him aboard to record the *Rattlesnake*'s progress in New Guinea.

Dayman was taking soundings in Port Jackson to see if the channel could accommodate a battleship. The first major dry dock east of Bombay, big enough to berth a steamer or warship, was being built on Cockatoo Island, north of Sydney. With Britannia's need to secure the region for immigration and trade, everyone expected men-of-war to become common sights soon. As the *Bramble* and *Rattlesnake* joined up, the time of parting came. Hal left Nettie a miniature of himself, which she placed under her pillow, and he was gone.

At daybreak on 11 October 1847 they sailed out of Sydney Harbour to map the passage up to the Barrier Reef. He 'felt downhearted'. The 'pain of parting from her was the feeling uppermost in my mind. But I am not one of those who "put finger i' the eye" and whine over the unavoidable'. He would look on the positive side and keep her 'ever present with me in my wanderings . . . an ark of promise in the wilderness of life'.

He might have been 'more outwardly content' now, but it did not stop him letting out 'a great general growl' about the shipboard separation 'as I walked up & down [with Dayman] during his watch'.[18] As they tacked north to the Inshore Passage, between the mainland and Barrier Reef, Huxley tried to get back to his thimble-sized comb jellies. But it proved difficult. They hit a

squall, with terrifying lightning bolts, but the real maelstrom was
in his mind. He wrote back to Nettie on the '5th day of the
Hegira'. Sydney might have been his Mecca, his place of rebirth,
but the prophet feared the impression he had left. He had been
talking religion with her, the previous Sunday after church, leaving
her under a dark cloud.[19] Now he forlornly tried to make amends,
as the 'matter . . . so deeply interests us both'. But he still sounded
like a Calvinistic product of London's low-brow anatomy schools.
The student had emerged from the radical chaos of the 1830s and
1840s like so many, full of rational Dissenting ideas about nature,
as non-miraculous and subject, as one Dissenter said, to '*Law* and
Order'. He had pushed on, delighting in Sir William Hamilton's
logic in proving that reason could not reveal God, because it could
not tear aside the veil of phenomena (Hamilton used intuition for
his evidence of the Divine). Huxley realized that the human mind
was trapped by the limitations of thought and language, and
hemmed in by physical evidence. Going beyond Hamilton, he
refused to treat the Divine outside the reach of the senses as
anything but an ungraspable dream.

How to explain it to Nettie? It is not *what* we believe, but *why*
we believe it. Moral responsibility lies in diligently weighing the
evidence. We must actively doubt; we have to scrutinize our views,
not take them on trust. No virtue attached to blindly accepting
orthodoxy, however 'venerable' – and certainly not for its social
status (Anglicanism, as the State religion, still carried enormous
privileges). Who could respect a person who would 'gratify a
selfish ambition by adopting and defending the first fashionable
error suited to his purpose'? Better to be 'one of those who would
spend years of silent investigation in the faint hope of at length
finding truth'. Huxley was on his way to defining a new relationship between Man and 'the great deep sacred infinitude' of Nature
(as Carlyle had it), helped by the expanding vision of Victorian
science.

He trod gingerly with Nettie. His was an honest doubt, he
claimed. It was an admission that one could only go so far,
stopping short of Genesis myths and miraculous interventions,
Afterlife and Atonement. It *was* legitimate to 'doubt, in all sadness
of heart, and from solemn fear to tread where the fools of the
day boldly rush in'. But he repudiated the flaming atheists, the
slum demagogues who were fired by socialist dreams. Those
wretches used their politicized atheism to destroy the Anglican
social fabric – 'those miserable men, whose scepticism is the result of

covetousness & who pitifully exhibit their vain ingenuity for the mere purpose of . . . disturbing the faith of others'.

He ended with a powerful image of the Reformation, when protesters indicted the corrupt Papacy and sought a morally cleansed basis of belief. 'I can only say in Martin Luther's ever famous words, "Hier Steh Ich – Gott helfe mir – Ich kann nicht anders" ["Here I stand – God help me – I cannot do otherwise"]'.[20] At Holmwood, Nettie was not comforted.

The ship arrived at Moreton Bay on 17 October 1847. A local steamer had sunk in the south passage to this 20-mile-wide bay, drowning most on board, and Stanley's surveyors spent time marking a safer north entrance. Huxley went off shooting, tagged by two 'gentlemen in black', friendly Morton Islanders, bagging 'ten fine cockatoos, whose edible excellencies I mean to try at breakfast'. The sight of the flat munching faces of dugongs or sea cows caused excitement, no less than the aborigines harpooning them in Brisbane River. A new porpoise was also spotted, although killing it was a native taboo, and MacGillivray refused rather than 'outraging their strongly expressed superstitious feelings'. (Only later did he learn why. The aborigines worked with the porpoises to catch shoals of mullet – the porpoises driving them inshore, allowing huge numbers to be speared, themselves weaving safely in and out of the natives' legs.)

On board, the crew entertained the aborigines, the men and women all naked, save only a 'small fringe in front' on the young girls. The married women were evident by the loss of the last joint of the right-hand little finger.[21] The industrious MacGillivray started to build a lexicon of aboriginal sounds. Huxley set off with Stanley up the Brisbane River in the *Asp*. The blue-and-white flowering vines at the jungle's edge gave way to 'picturesque' country near Brisbane itself. This was a 'veritable Garden of Eden'. It was perfect pastoral land, and the squatters' wool was cried out for by the English mills. But the shifting sand banks made the Brisbane River a treacherous artery, and Stanley's brief was to find a safer way of transporting the wool to the waiting ships.

Stanley and Huxley parted in Brisbane, which had only recently been freed from its vicious military rule. Huxley hired a horse and a squatter guide and decked himself out. What with corduroys, 'a cabbage tree hat' and moustache, 'no one could have distinguished me from a genuine squatter'. (Darwin would have flinched. He dismissed the squatter as 'the horror of all his honest neighbours', the contemptible ex-con who 'steals a few animals, sells Spirits without a licence, buys stolen goods & so at last ... turns farmer'.) No such scruples for Huxley, setting off in squatter's guise for the Darling Downs. 'I shall not soon forget the exhilaration of my spirits as we rode through the bush', free from all worries about 'such things as ships'. Up the Brisbane River they galloped to see the wool depots. By the next day they had reached the Dividing Range, and on the third had 'the stiffest ride of all – forty-five miles', their brains baked and gullets dry. Through dense bush they rode, lassoed by vines, laughed at by kookaburras. The last pass proved 'one of the toughest climbs . . . I ever had'. The scene on the way to the Darling Downs was worth it: majestic eucalyptuses, strangler figs built on flying buttresses, 'whimsical festooned creepers' hanging 'like a fantastic drapery', and 'a deep stillness reigned over all, broken only now and then by the sweet musical chime of the bell-bird'.[22]

Coming back was even sweeter. Nettie's first letter caught him at Brisbane. He sat reading it behind a sack in the *Asp*, stuck on a mudflat. She talked of her love, 'deepened and confirmed', and whatever her religious worries 'I have no misgivings'. 'Thank you, thank you a thousand times', he intoned, 'it is all, all I could wish'. He had not been romancing in a dream, 'the story of our love is a true story'.

Many a lonely sailor found love in town or among the rocks. Huxley was not alone in his affair. The *Bramble*'s surgeon Archie McClatchie had paid court to Nettie's best friend Alice Radford. At sea the shipmates had 'dreadfully long "yarns"' about the girls, with Archie tweaking Huxley about tying the knot on his 'struggling fortunes'.[23]

The *Rattlesnake* hauled off on 4 November. They sailed past coral islands colonized by breeding seabirds, stopping only to survey Port Curtis on Harvey Bay, near the Tropic of Capricorn. In London Gladstone had planned to turn this superb ten-mile-wide bay into the major port for 'North Australia'. (And to start a new convict colony to take the pressure off Tasmania.) A year earlier settlers had founded the town of 'Gladstone'. But before the first nail had been hammered, its fate had been sealed a world away. The Conservatives had been swept from office in 1846 and the incoming Whigs scotched the idea. Huxley entered a ghost town of eerie relics: piled bricks, posts marking the '"Government-house," wheel ruts in the hardened clay ... with a goodly store of empty bottles strewed about everywhere'.[24] As the grog-swilling settlers had pulled out, so an older life had returned, the emus and kangaroos leaving tell-tale tracks across the mudflats.

Aboard, the chart-room was quiet, the middies away, and Huxley pored over the mud from the dredge. It was full of fern-like *Plumularia*, branching colonies of tentacle-waving polyps, the 'sea firs' so abundant in these waters. And dragged from its burrow was a superficially clam-like *Lingula*, a sort of 'living fossil', its shell indistinguishable from those in ancient rocks.[25]

Then he and MacGillivray took off for Facing Island, out in the Bay. In 90° temperatures they waded the swamps and sedge grass, sending oystercatchers flying. Flocks of noisy blue mountain parrots flew between gum trees as the men cooked black duck 'bush fashion' for supper. The land was good only for game in the sailors' eyes, and MacGillivray returned to shoot a 22-pound Australian bustard for his messmates' supper. As always the ship was a sanctuary in these hostile waters; poisonous sea snakes infested the harbour, and enormous sharks would break surface to shred fish hooked from the *Rattlesnake*'s stern. But the towing net yielded treasures: endless jellyfish, including the two-foot *Cephea*, like an enormous all-seeing umbrella with its eight red eye dots.[26]

Three hundred miles further on a storm forced them into the Percy Islands. The sailors arrived on the main island to find the gum scrub graced by flocks of black and white cockatoos, and scattered turtle carapaces signalling aboriginal feasts. They left it smouldering. Someone set fire to the long grass, trapping the naturalists who barely escaped to the boats. On deck all they could do was watch the blaze for days until nothing remained. They pushed on to Captain Cook's Whitsunday Passage (near modern Proserpine). Ashore the lagoons were dry and cracked. Metallic flashes caught the eye as the crew searched for water in the brush. The captain's servant shot a yellow-breasted sunbird, with its steel-blue throat. MacGillivray too was out with his gun, hunting for the most extraordinary of birds, megapodes. In clearings these 'brush turkeys' could be seen scraping great mounds of vegetation, in which the females would lay their eggs and, unique among birds, let the fermenting greenery do the incubating.

The bizarre beauty of the place only emphasized their distance from home. On Saturday 11 December Huxley had been away for a year – 12 months that had seen black despair and a bright light. He had mastered the sea nettles, but not his feeling of alienation, and his loneliness only increased at the thought of Nettie. That day found the *Rattlesnake* off Cape Upstart (near today's Bowen) and the perfect present was yet to come. No water could be found. The pools located by the *Fly* were dry. In fact almost no fresh water had been detected anywhere inside the tropics and the crew were rationed to six pints a day in the heat. The captain had no choice but to stop surveying the reefs and turn the ship back. It was a 'red mark' day, Huxley scribbled. He would see his sweetheart again. 'Sydney in five weeks! Bravo'.[27]

But everything bedevilled them. A powerful trade wind battered the square-rigger; then they were becalmed. The *Asp*, charting inshore, found inaccuracies on the Admiralty map. Sheltering during a squall on Keppel Island led them to more unknown reefs, which had to be mapped. On Christmas Eve, Huxley came on deck for his 10 pm. constitutional, to be greeted by a cacophony of shouts as a poop officer spotted foam a cable's length ahead: ' "Breakers on the lee bow", screamed a lookout. "Hands about ship. Down with the helm", and round went the old ship like a whisk', past the prettiest coral reef. A few moments more and Christmas Day would have been spent as a castaway on Curtis Island. The mix of heart-stopping drama and slack canvas infuriated him:

> Christmas Eve! a time that one has been used to consider
> as . . . an occasion of pleasant meeting among friends.
> And here I am in this atrocious berth without a soul to
> whom I can speak an open friendly word. But it is all
> good discipline doubtless . . . for I find myself getting
> more and more satisfied and content with my own sweet
> society and that of my books.

The frustration was relieved by Carlyle and the teeming crustaceans. Carlyle was a bit of a crustaceous philosopher, whose books were devoured by Huxley as quickly as 'by the mighty hordes of cockroaches in my cabin'. Carlyle warned him against 'a dead brute Steam-engine' view of nature, built of mechanical checks and balances, pain and pleasure drives, utility and fatalism, with 'all soul fled out of it'. That way lay 'the black malady', scepticism. Contentment could only come from Nature's poetic praise of the Godhead.[28] But perhaps the greatest lesson he learned from reading Carlyle was that real religion, that emotive feeling for Truth and Beauty, could flourish in the absence of an idolatrous theology.

Christmas Day was shadowless under the Capricorn sun. Huxley was nostalgic for snowy mornings, church music and childish excitement.

> There shall be no more Christmas days or festive days of
> any kind for me in a ship. It is a cruel mockery to call a
> drinking bout among a parcel of people thrown together
> by the Admiralty 'spending a merry Christmas'. It is a
> more than Egyptian feast, for *all* the guests are skeletons.

Two years earlier he had been sitting by the fire with the family. That, 'alas! was but the last ray of a happy sun, followed by a dark night of misfortunes'. Lizzie's banishment preyed on his mind. It was now complete in its peculiar way. Word reached him that the 'Scotts' had crossed the Atlantic to New Orleans. Even here their hopes were fading, their plan to buy a farm and start afresh in some semi-civilized territory. Dreams require cash: Lizzie had done her best 'with G^{eo} to induce him to spare a trifle', but they had sailed empty handed. George still received 'pitiable' letters 'from America . . . in which *she* is made to appeal to my feelings to avert actual starvation', all because of 'her vagabond husband'. Tom's mother was crushed. 'God help them for . . . what can be the end of all his strange doings'? His doings became stranger: from New Orleans they had trekked to the backwoods – social ostracism sending them to the farthest reaches. And still there was secrecy; only Tom knew their final destination, Tennessee.[29] 'Oh Lizzie! . . . what endless misery hast thou seen'. The ship rolled along, his gloom accompanied by bumping waves; 'you and I were the only two I believe who really loved and therefore understood one another'. Her image seemed to fade, the sound of her voice drowned by the wind in the canvas: 'we may never meet again'.

As the year ended they blew into Moreton Bay and filled the kegs. All hands watched the *Bramble* return from Brisbane with the mailbags. That afternoon, 6 January 1848, the weather brightened. 'I got half a dozen letters, one from Sydney which was almost more than I had ventured to hope – and that I read first – so true is it that a man shall leave his father and his mother and cleave unto his – ah! would I could call thee – wife'. But Nettie was in black. The Governor's death had put the colony in mourning, and it turned her thoughts to their eternal destiny:

> I hope dearest that I may die before you . . . I was thinking
> I could not bear you to be taken and me left alone . . .

God forbid this and may the day be very far distant before
this dread separation shall come. May we love and grow
old together and dying may we meet again in Heaven.[30]

Heaven could wait; it was their earthly separation that frustrated
Hal. The next morning, the skipper brought equally welcome
news: 'that the [man-of-war] Paper had arrived, had been perused
by Prof. Forbes who was "delighted" . . . with it, and was to be
read before the Linnean Society'. Perhaps he was sailing into
glory.[31]

All eyes were now on Sydney. For five hours on 13 January 1848
this was literally true. The *Rattlesnake* lay becalmed, 'sails flapping
against the mast – in sight of the Heads'. 'Would that the good
ship *Rattlesnake* were the veriest old smokejack of a steamer', he
grumbled as a 'Hunter River steamer' chugged past, only an hour
from disgorging its passengers. It was a sign that the days of
canvas were numbered. The sailing ship *Rattlesnake*, by 'sweeping'
the Inner Passage, was ironically making the sea safe for the
steamers. He found the issue a talking point in Sydney the next
day. Plans were already afoot for a railway to siphon the flood of
steamer-born immigrants away from Sydney. How far away
nobody could tell, although an exploring party at that moment
was blazing a trail across the continent to the Swan River Settlement (Perth).

Given shore leave, he was 'off to New Town' to make up for
three months' separation. The two weeks were awash with colour
and excitement. Hal and Nettie, along with most of the colony's
50,000 inhabitants, joined the festivities as Sydney celebrated its
60th anniversary, culminating in a regatta on 26 January. Every
ship was dressed, lights sparkling; 'we gave a grand turnout', he
admitted, proud of his adopted city.

The euphoria ended on 2 February, when 'I found myself out at
sea again'. Stanley had set out for the Bass Strait at the new
Governor's request, to inspect the lighthouses between Tasmania
and the mainland. The smooth water of the Strait was cathartic
and endless *Oceanea* jellies left Huxley 'content with the world'.
He even dropped his mother a teasing note, suggesting he might
turn 'colonial' and leaving her to guess why.[32]

But as usual the warm glow turned into a hot stew. In the thick
mist at Port Phillip the thermometer topped 90°. But there were
compensations. Inside, the Port was alive with sails, acres of white
canvas and blue medusae. The magnificent harbour, wide and

deep enough for 'half a dozen navies', saw a fleet of merchant vessels ready to take on wool. And, on the ripple line, 'Vast numbers of a large "sea-jelly" (*Rhizostoma Mosaica*), gave the water quite a milky appearance'. Huxley was now blinkered by more than love. Dismissing the country, and writing off the seaside village of William's Town as 'a few weatherboard houses', he cocooned himself aboard, pulling up and drawing the football-sized, tentacle-less jellies.[33]

Only when the temperature fell by 30°F did he stir. He put ashore with McClatchie at a 'rickety pier' attached to a William's Town tavern. They lubricated themselves and took a mail cart the two miles to Melbourne. 'I must say I was very much surprised, knowing that the place had been not more than ten years in existence, to observe its size and the many tall chimneys which rose near the river – evidently indicating manufactories of considerable size'. These tallow works had attracted colonists and the city already boasted 12,000 people. 'There are several very good hotels. We went to the Royal, procured horses, [and] rode about the Town'. Everywhere were 'bullock-teams and drays recently arrived with wool'; everyone hurrying, with 'few loungers like ourselves in the streets'. It oozed prosperity. The talk was of independence from New South Wales (which was soaking up the revenues) and the creation of a self-governing state, Victoria. They arrived with a grand ball imminent, but Huxley declined this time; 'faith'! he exclaimed, 'I'm getting staid'.

The wind in their teeth, they sailed on 21 February to Tasmania's northern coast, dominated by Mount Valentine, 'bold and grand in its outline'. Huxley set off to explore the 'cheerful' region around Port Dalrymple. The effect of crossing the Bass Strait had been to bring them closer to home. 'Everything from the rosy-faced girls and children to the fruit trees bent down under their weight of apples or pears put us in mind of England'. He took the steamer up the 'picturesque' River Tamar the 40 miles to Launceston. It was 'exceedingly pretty country . . . very like some of the middle counties of England'. Yellow stubble fields greeted him everywhere, the harvest just in, and galloping down shady lanes left him with an exhilarating homesickness.

In Port Dalrymple everyone was busy. Dayman with his chronometers, MacGillivray shipping sunbird skins to John Gould at London's Zoological Society,[34] and below decks Huxley was finishing his most ambitious paper, based on his hundreds of jellyfish nettings.

The jellies had a simple stomach suspended under an umbrella-like bell. Microscopically the stomach wall appeared as two 'foundation membranes', an inner, ciliated one and an outer, denser one. Huxley made these layers and the gelatin-like mass sandwiched in between the defining features of medusae. Every jelly's muscles, sex organs and tentacles stemmed from a precise part of a membrane. Then he went on to relate the jellies themselves to the stinging *Hydra*-like polyps and men-of-war and plumularian sea firs. *All* shared this two-layer plan, their membranes only folding differently. To prove that the tentacles or sex organs of *Physalia* and the jellies were homologous he caught every growth stage, and then watched these parts emerge from the same layers in the embryo.

What did this say about jellies? They had been lumped by default with single-cell amoebas on one hand and starfish on the other in Cuvier's rag-bag group, the 'Radiata'. From 12,000 miles away the assistant surgeon was breaking into this 'lumber room' of ill-assorted creatures; he was regrouping the two-layer stinging animals into a great discrete class of their own. From down under he was turning nature upside down.[35]

Nettie, a sensible girl who liked Schiller and penned love poems, must have asked 'Why jellyfish?' And he must have led her self-importantly from these pulsing 'nastinesses' to the great problem of existence, contrasting his tiny truths of creation with the sand-castle sophistries for which men were willing to die. The tiny truths were real bricks which would build a palatial foundation to Truth. They were the stanzas of Nature's great poem; and only by reciting the ultimate sonnet could we gain a rational set of mores and a real meaning to life.

Huxley planned to post the opus to Sir William Burnett, to present to the Royal Society, not out of 'sycophancy', but because 'I owe the old man much, and would do this as a simple matter of respect'. He made it sound like a favour to the old gent. But in truth he was rationalizing his use of silver-haired patrons. The stakes were high. The Royal Society was the upper tier of English science, nigh-on 300 years old and able to confer enormous prestige. Curiously, at this moment it was suffering a corporate version of Huxley's own angst. His reluctant relations with the Burnetts and bishops reflected the wider antagonisms of British science. The Society's courtly days were ending. Its old loyalties to Crown and Church (typified by Burnett and bishop) were fading with the influx of capitalists, doctors and academics.[36] Its new backers were merchants and empire builders; its new gods utility and service to the state; its new priests, the technocrats and specialists. Men like Huxley were taking over, disdaining salon politics and society patrons, contemptuous of the spider-stuffing clergy and blue-blooded dilettantes. Half-way round the world he caught the metropolitan mood exactly, even if he had to swallow his pride and play the game for the moment.

This was to be his make-or-break paper, and on it his scientific fate would ride. If it succeeds 'I shall go on accordingly'. If it flops 'I will give these things up and try some other channel towards happiness for dear Menen and myself'.

At sea on 3 March an unprecedented 10½-knot speed shook the scuttlebucket, 'jury-rigged as she was' for slow surveying. Huxley's tremors were inside. He thought on pride and vanity. A driven man, wanting scientific recognition, he was twisted by guilt, the fear of ambition. His volcanic moods were fuelled by thoughts of Nettie and the need to be noticed, and brought to flash point as he tweezered medusae. 'I am content with nothing, restless and ambitious . . . and I despise myself for the vanity, which formed half the stimulus to my exertions'. 'Oh would that I were one of those plodding wise fools who having once set their hand to the plough go on nothing doubting'.

Stumbling on the granite outcrops and 'mutton bird' burrows of Goose Island left him feeling a plodding fool. He was greeted at dusk by 'clouds' of these returning shearwaters, flitting past his head 'like spectres in the gloaming'. As darkness fell, and the crew set about clubbing the birds in a bloodthirsty scrum, he peered through Stanley's telescope, seeing a nebula for the first time and becoming lost in the blackness of space.

'I must say this for the skipper – oddity as he is, he has never failed to offer me and give me the utmost assistance in his power'. Stanley brimmed with *noblesse oblige*, but his kindness left Huxley uneasy. On the run up to Sydney Stanley came into the chart-room, watched him drawing medusae and offered again to post the paper to the bishop. It prompted Huxley into musing on his own attitude. 'I often fancy that if I took the trouble to court him a little we should be great friends – as it is I always get out of his way and shall do so to the end'. Huxley was his own man, his fierce independence bordering on social contempt, taking pride in his class and his talent. His dark eyes flashed defiance. Rank for him was earned by grit and ability, not appointed from on-high. He met social hauteur with intellectual snobbery. 'That same stiffneckedness (for which I heartily thank God) stands in my way with others, my "superior" officers'. Were he to kow-tow they 'would I am sure think me what is ordinarily called a "capital fellow" i.e. a great fool'.

It was nobody's fool who beat up the south coast. The fates of course mocked him. Just as the frigate tacked north for Sydney, the wind chopped to the east, lashing them with rain and forcing them in to Cape Howe. 'If I were a Catholic I would invest a little capital in wax candles to my pet saints'.[37] But Nature was no capricious dame, to be appeased by the gods. His life was now planned: to understand the eternal truths behind her superficial veil. Knowledge of a secular nature, there lay the new source of power. It was not to be delegated by episcopal patrons, but seized by plebeian hands.

6

The Eighth Circle of Hell

IT WAS A TIME of trysts. These were 'fairy days' for Nettie, when midshipman Sharpe 'was Mercury to me and Hal', carrying notes and arranging rendezvous. The ship's arrival in Sydney on 9 March 1848 had given them another seven weeks' grace.

Hal caught up with the gossip. He heard about the three clergymen who had deserted to Rome, leaving Nettie's church unattended. Distant Sydney was shadowing Oxford, as the Tractarians moved to more ritualistic Catholic practice. 'How very dreadful', she exclaimed, sharing his dislike of anything 'Romish'. 'I cannot imagine any sensible person turning Catholic, it is repugnant to common sense'.

Huxley could never escape the whirl of religion. 'What wonderful and beautiful sights have already met your view', his mother exclaimed, 'there is something so fresh and refreshing in your letters, so unlike the worldliness and care of everyday life'. She hoped that his chance 'to contemplate the wonders of Nature' away from the Church-haters and Chartists would fortify him, hoped:

> that whilst your mind is young & free to judge of the God
> of Nature by his Works and Providences, you may also
> find an inward witness to strengthen those same
> convictions e're you return to the Land of your Birth, and
> mix again, as you 'must do,' with the Scoffer and the
> Unbeliever. I say 'must do,' because they seem to me to
> stalk about more arrogantly than ever. May God bless
> you my dear Tom, for he alone can keep you from such
> Adversaries.[1]

*

The lovers were soon visiting the 'fine shops in George Street and Pitt Street, where French silks' were cheaper than in London. They strolled in the Domain (the public gardens), taking in the military band or watching Sydney's elite disport themselves in their expensive carriages. Then tea on the verandah, yellow loquats and peaches, so plentiful that they were fed to the pigs. The land seemed to Nettie an 'earthly Paradise'. And now she had her Adam, even if he offered more bitter fruit. But even that – Hal's scepticism – might abate with 'God's blessing'.[2]

But paradise was littered with ruined archangels. Huxley met his share of these sad souls, petty criminals spared the gallows, boys sent out for burglary. Transportation to New South Wales had been suspended, but this was still a prison colony. Iron gangs worked on the roads, their grey and yellow uniforms standing out. Convicts took on every wretched duty: on the sheep stations, in shops and as servants. Even as portrait painters: for all of Nettie's disdain she was painted in pastels by Thomas Griffiths Wainewright the Poisoner. (Actually he was transported for forgery. The sickly aesthete, now broken on the road gangs, had exhibited at the Royal Academy before trying to obtain his inheritance ahead of time.)

The servants were Nettie's bugbear. Decanters had to be locked up, and desk drawers. Once a drunken butler pointed a gun at Will and had to be led away struggling. Uppity maids and tipsy recidivists were all the gossip:

> Domestic troubles – a new housemaid arrived the night
> before, sent word before breakfast – she didn't think she'd
> like the place and forthwith left – all the other servants
> believing her crazed. Really I never knew such a
> discontented race.

'Of all the minor miseries of life there is in truth one transcending all, that of being dependent on your cook'. But having to brook the cook's wild turkey without bread sauce was nothing to Huxley's shock in the stable. He met the groom. The face was familiar, a bit older and hardened; it was William Poideoin, the bully who had given him a black eye at school. Poideoin was a rarity among the pilferers and prostitutes, but not the first public schoolboy Sydney had seen. He 'occupies the post of half clerk – half ostler to a stable man here. He recognised me and I commiserated [with] him greatly (from his own account) until I heard . . . that he had been "sent out" (colonial for transported which is impolite) and had one or two colonial convictions since'. Ticket-of-leave men were all on the make, and Poideoin, grubbing for references from 'Respectable parties', tried to tap Huxley 'for old school fellows sake', without much success.[3]

Tom told everyone at home. But his letters carried more startling news. He dropped his mother a line about the engagement. Lizzie learned of the romantic side, how they 'managed to fall in love . . . in the most absurd manner after seeing one another – I will not tell you how many times, lest you should laugh'. George's was a more jaded account: 'Jim is my great comfort', Tom joked of his medical brother, mad-doctoring again and a model of family virtue, complete with a baby daughter, Katy. Look at him, 'he committed a similar folly about the same time of life – with a coarse lookout and now le voilá', transformed into 'a respectable, corporative, bunch-of-seals sort of man' (a crack at Britain's growing civic pride and mayoral regalia). The vision was horrifying and appealing. 'You are right in imagining the astonishment of us people at your essay in the tender business', Jim replied, 'especially our mother, who . . . scarcely thought the world as yet contained the properly adapted article for you'.

Immediate marriage was out. He was not going to copy MacGillivray, who was crushed by debt yet crazily rushing into marriage (love-sick sailors quickly succumbed in the colony). A Malthusian poor-house society showed no mercy on the improvident. Huxley was not prepared to sink in penury like his brothers-in-law (a sticky topic, with George now bailing out Cooke): 'were she Venus & the Graces rolled in to one I am not sufficiently fond of love in a cottage, to hurry into marriage upon a hundred & twenty seven pounds ten shillings and no pence per annum. Vice to be hated needs to be seen, they say. If poverty were substituted for "vice" the proverb would be more veritable – so we have made up our minds to wait like prudent folk'.

His hope remained science and the Service. He intended to 'write myself into my promotion' and 'I have the strongest persuasion that four years hence I shall be married and settled in England. We shall see'.[4]

It gave his make-or-break paper a new urgency. This was not just jellyfish esoterica; it was his deliverance. If he could hold the Sea Lords to their word about rewarding scientific assistants, he could jump the queue to full surgeon – or, if not, obtain an academic post in London. Either way it was his future and he invested enormous energy in it. He talked incessantly of these hopes, but Nettie never fully understood. Living in the real world, of planters and brewers, she found the idea bizarre, that 'a description of a marine creature should win him fame', let alone the funds 'that would enable us to marry'.[5]

In mid-March the paper was ready. It went first to a beautiful new mansion, Elizabeth Bay House, the best scientific salon in Sydney. This was the home of the austere bachelor William Sharp Macleay, out in the colony eight years to help his father (a former Colonial Secretary). Huxley rated Macleay 'one of the first anatomists of the present day'. He was also 'the most extraordinary old fellow I ever met with . . . talk of what you will from Church history to Colonial politics – on the number of joints in a beetle's hind leg – he is equally ready. And his black eyes twinkle in the midst of his yellow wrinkled physiognomy'.[6]

At Macleay's salon you could find Captain King and an enthusiasm for insects. Here was also heard more arcane talk. Long before, as an Embassy attaché in Paris, liquidating British claims at the end of the Napoleonic Wars, Macleay had devised a peculiar geometric arrangement for his beetles. He classified all organisms in sets of five, which he pictured on the circumference of a circle. He saw five classes of animals, joined in a ring, each class with five orders, ultimately ending up in myriad circles of five linked species. This elegant pattern was considered a piece of Divine neatness – or more commonly as Macleay's '*Quinarian* nonsense'. But it was no nonsense to Huxley, searching for the sublime patterns in nature. Macleay's 'circular system' would influence him enormously over the next decade.

Macleay had devised it in the aftermath of the French Revolution. As an Embassy attaché he had seen the social shambles caused by the ragged revolutionaries, and it was in this context of post-war Paris that his new science packed its ideological punch. The English upper classes blamed the Revolution on the poisonous philosophies of the Enlightenment. And the naturalist singled out for most venom, the man who 'vomited' his 'abominable trash' over a profligate Paris, was Jean-Baptiste Lamarck. Lamarck's evolutionary theory was damned as scientific excrement, fouling the wellsprings of society and subverting Church authority. Lamarck, professor of insects and worms at the Paris Museum of Natural History, had seen animal life rise unaided on the earth, one species transforming into another, rather than being Created miraculously. He envisaged twin evolutionary streams rising from the same base – one passing through the worms towards the insects, the other from polyps to molluscs. In the reactionary Regency, Macleay emasculated the system at a stroke. He bent Lamarck's two streams into a circle, destroying the force of his upward-moving nature (which ultimately made mankind an evolved ape), while leaving the idea of continuity intact.[7] He bastardized the system, sending nature round in circles. Mankind was spared a soul-destroying ape ancestry.

Huxley was set thinking by Macleay, pondering nature's geometry as he prepared his 'Medusae' paper. The circles appealed to his aesthetic sense. He had a 'strong appreciation of the Beautiful in whatever shape', and in Nature's circular symmetry the beauty seemed transcendent. Lizzie learnt that 'the celebrated' Macleay 'werry much approves what I have done'. It was a good signal and ended an autumn of optimism. 'I tell Netty to look to being a "Frau Professorin" one of these odd days, and she has faith'.[8]

Huxley was more modern than Macleay. He took a developmental approach to the classification of life. He would show the organs of jellyfish and men-of-war developing from the embryo in the same way, to prove that they were related. All had a common two-membrane structure – indeed, Huxley casually noted towards the end of his 'Medusae' paper, these jellyfish membranes bore the same physiological relation to one another as did the two cell layers in the early vertebrate embryo. And that was a breathtaking connection – sweeping across creation from the man-of-war to Man himself.[9]

As always there was the hoary problem of placing the paper. Oddly enough, George on business in Versailles had run into the Bishop of Norwich. There could have been no more inspired coincidence; nor a more agreeable tip-off. Tom's mother reported that they 'travelled in the same carriage . . . The Bishop identified His Name with yours immediately', leading to a bumpy conversation about sea jellies 'in which you figured most agreeably amongst the Bishops observations'. It was, said his mother, 'Honey to my Heart'.[10] And to Tom's. Now he knew that he was being noticed.

His qualms vanished. On Stanley's say so, he again targeted 'the Nautical Bishop – I want him to get [the new paper] read at the Royal Society . . . If a thing is worth any thing it's worth making the best of'. And on that principle he wrote to Sir John Richardson, asking him to back the bishop. George he dragooned even more shamelessly. 'As you have met the Bishop and know him would you mind calling upon him some time or other to ascertain the fate of my unfortunate . . . progeny?' He needed feedback. 'The Bishop will tell you what competent men say . . . and let me know "nothing extenuating["] I am not likely to "die of an article" a la Keats'.[11]

In the event Stanley sent it with his dispatch to Admiral Beaufort (the chief hydrographer), to be passed on to the bishop. Perhaps this was to make amends, to take the wind out of their Lordships' sails after his own peregrinations. Anyway the message went with it, that his young surgeon 'is very anxious to have [it] read out at one of the learned societies – the Royal in preference'.[12]

Would it share the fate of Noah's raven, never more to be seen – or was it his dove? With the paper gone, he girded his loins. Before him lay the long haul. Every man-jack would be a hirsute Noah before they finished on the reef, 'making straight the path of the steamers'.

> For the next ten months Her Majesty's Ship will be a kind of lay monastery – a floating hermitage – free from all the deceits of the world the flesh (save of a black & woolly nature) & and devil . . . For ten mortal months we shall do nothing but cultivate our beard – fry our liver – and make acquaintance with great numbers of marine unpleasantnesses.

But at least in the watery wastes he could show a profit: 'where there is nothing to be bought you can't spend . . . I shall have some seventy or eighty pounds in my pocket on our return & be able to pay off old scores'.[13]

The 'fairy days' were at an end. Nettie steeled herself for the uncertainties ahead. She was 'fearful lest you meet with attacks from the natives'.[14] No one underrated the dangers, or the fevers that swept the sick bay. She reconciled herself to long silences as the ship made its laborious way to Cape York, on the north-eastern tip of Australia.

Stanley now added a barque to his mini fleet of mother ship, deck boats and tender. The *Tam O'Shanter* carried an exploring party, destined to blaze the trail overland, through the hot, trackless bush all the way from Rockingham Bay (near the modern town of Ingham, in northern coastal Queensland) to Cape York, 600 miles north as the cockatoo flies. While the donkey-frigate earned its name, continuing to mark a channel for the steamships inside the northern stretch of the Barrier Reef, the overland party would cut its way through the unexplored bush, mapping, collecting plants and animals, recording aboriginal tribes and so on, to join up at the Cape.

Stanley had helped plan the overland expedition, qualified only by his sea captain's omniscience. The barque was packed with provisions, 28 horses, 100 sheep, wagons and every breed of hardy explorer. Led by the indomitable Edmund Kennedy, who had searched the central Australian deserts for rivers and knew the North Australian interior, the party included the botanist William Carron (Macleay's gardener), Thomas Wall the naturalist, a store-keeper, shepherd, three carters, four labourers and a Hunter River aboriginal guide, Jackey Jackey. There was enormous optimism about this trip. Kennedy was a good leader, religious, supportive and full of enthusiasm. It was to be a 'pilgrimage of discovery'.[15]

The *Rattlesnake* sailed out of Sydney on 29 April 1848. Immediately Huxley's tumultuous emotions overcame him. As the ship cast off he opened his diary with the refrain 'I have no heart to write'. It set the tone for the long voyage. It should have been a challenge as he entered the richest coral sea in the world. By his own admission the opportunities were 'such as none but a blind man would fail to make use of'. And he had plenty of time, for they were to map reefs by means of a monotonous series of triangulations and explore tropical islands for the 600 miles of the Inner Passage, between the Barrier Reef and the mainland.

Five days out, on 4 May, Huxley took stock. The flotilla had struggled 150 miles against adverse currents. The wind had died, the sea was a 'blue mirror'. He peered in, reflecting on life, or rather on the pulsing jellies, still hoping to claim this corner of creation. Medusae gave way to marriage. 'My birthday again. What an immense change has this twenty-third year made in me! Perhaps ... it will turn out to be the most important in my life. My first year of sea-life – my first year of scientific investigation ... my first year, last but not least, of love'. He reread Nettie's letters, and scooped out a 'beautiful' *Stephanomia*, a sea nettle with a whole column of swimming bells, and spent his birthday studying it.[16]

The 1,500-mile trip to Rockingham Bay gave him time to learn Italian, which he found easy. It took him away from the wretch-making smell. The meat packers had failed to seal the containers, leaving them with half-a-ton of putrefying flesh, which would have crawled over the side by itself had it not been fed to the sharks off Port Bowen. On 21 May they reached Rockingham Bay, an inlet

18° south of the Equator. The land was lush during the rains and the water holes full. For a few it was heaven. As the ship circled the bay – Goold Island – the Family Islands – Dunk Island – Doctor Thomson continually took off ashore. 'The time passes on very comfortably,' he nodded; every island had its collectables and shells. 'With a perpendicular sun the perspiration pours down off me and my clothes are as wet as if I had walked through a pond'. His dark-eyed assistant had a more pained expression. Huxley began niggling. 'Rain, Rain!' he growled:

> The ship is intensely miserable. Hot, wet, and stinking.
> One can do nothing but sleep. This wet weather takes
> away all my energies. I do not mind dry heat to any extent
> but to be steamed in this manner is too much for me. I try
> to pass the time away in thinking, sleeping and novel-
> reading, which last is a kind of dreaming.

He lay in his Turkish bath, lost in the anonymous *Ranthorpe*. (It was actually written by George Henry Lewes, later George Eliot's lover, both of whom Huxley would come to know well.) He identified with the wounded aspirations of its rough diamond hero. Through salty eyes he stared into a cracked mirror. It was a clichéd story, but for a moment he was back on the Strand. He was standing in Percy Ranthorpe's shoes – that sold-out dramatist and poet, hating himself for believing that 'merit unheralded wins no victory, unpatronised, gains no attention'. But deep down Ranthorpe, like Huxley, another 'poor, dreamy boy, self-taught, self-aided', knew that there was only real 'dignity in intellectual rank'. It left Huxley with a niggling self-doubt. 'Have I the capabilities for a scientific life'? If he had, there was 'something holy' in using them. But to strive with no gift, pushed on by patrons, 'no Bedlam fool can be more worthy of contempt'.[17] As he stewed in his sweat, the doubts boiled up in his brain.

Even the jellies lost their attraction. Only the natives now piqued his interest. Ashore he painted the aborigines, and they painted him, thumbing bars of red paint across his forehead. He felt their flat elongated beards. They stared back at his own facial adornment, only marginally less remarkable. He had grown 'a peak in Charles I. style', which gave a *'triste* expression to my sunburnt phiz'. Like most sailors, he was faintly bemused by the 'savages'; it was a jittery, nervous reaction. The young man from Ealing gave a condescending laugh at the sight of them struggling with pipe and baccy. He shared that sense of civilized hauteur, perhaps because they were unaccountably threatening, less physically than culturally. What did he make of these naked 'gins', who looked upon white men as '*marki*' or ghosts of their ancestors?[18] He stared into their eyes during painting sessions. Fads and taboos gripped every culture. But here the alterations were painfully physical; the right upper incisor was knocked out during childhood and the septum of the nose perforated for a bone; bodies were covered with extraordinary whirling cicatrices or ornamental scars, and there was no clothing but an occasional armlet or girdle of twisted human hair, perhaps with an opossum tassel.

Fierce currents forced the barque to stand off 500 yards. Kennedy's supplies were ferried over. The fiddler played a 'stamp-and-go' shanty as the horses were hauled over the gunwale and their heads lashed to a boat, ready to be swum ashore. On the beach the 89 surviving sheep were gathered by the shepherd. A ton of flour and 600 lbs of sugar were off-loaded; three carts, four tents, canvases, gunpowder, shot. The ferrying was endless. All the boats were involved: guns, blankets, books, axes, pack saddles, 40 chains, three kangaroo dogs. Nobody would say they came unprepared for a four-month journey through the bush.[19] The 13 hardened men helped by the crew set up camp close to a fresh water creek. Carron the plant collector wandered off to pick specimens, the storekeeper checked his mountain of provisions.

The team was to trek north between the Dividing Range and the coast to Cape York, where they would rendezvous with the *Rattlesnake* in October. Kennedy invited Huxley to join the reconnoitring party, to scout out the terrain for a few days. Loath to pass up an opportunity to see the natives, he set off with Kennedy's 'light party' on 30 May. He was desperate for a 'modicum of adventure'. At base camp 'we had a capital breakfast à la bush – damper [unleavened bread], tea and chops to wit – and by 9 o'clock were mounted and off, exploring and no mistake'. The four looked the part, billy cans dangling from belts. 'Each man had pistols in his holsters and a double-barrelled carbine slung by his side, cartridge belt and etceteras, so that, though I fear no sergeant would have marched though Coventry with us as "regulars", we should not have been badly equipped for a guerilla raid'.

They beat a path through the tall grass, but along the ridges the going got tough. Too tough; they began to realize how impenetrable the bush was. Irritating rattans – prickly palms – cut them at each turn, while huge buttressed trees and enormous screw pines blocked their way. Epiphytes or air-plants perched in the tree forks, but the hanging briers were ready to snare anyone who gazed up. Fenced in by ridges they beat their way back to base camp to try again the following morning. The next day was no better. Even following a river bank was fruitless, the forest was impenetrable. Aborigines appeared from nowhere at one point, only to scatter; but Huxley could hear the 'coo-eys' on all sides as they watched unnoticed, and he imagined the sensation 'produced by a spear between the shoulders'. They ploughed on, becoming bogged in creeks and tea-tree marshes, continually backtracking, constantly cut off by rivers. Eventually they bivouacked close to the shore. It might not have been successful, but it beat the tedium of dissection. And Huxley saw his aborigines: that night a group 'came very cautiously sauntering with their hands behind them'. He engaged them in a sort of self-mocking gesticulatory conversation. 'I bound my handkerchief round the head of one, and obtained in return some sliced edible root wrapped in a leaf. They invited me to their camp but I declined as Kennedy did not wish to have any close intercourse with them'.

Before the light failed the rains hit again, torrential downpours. They tried to dash back to base camp, but the rivers were rising. They floundered a third of the way over and retreated in face of the swirling waters, convinced that 'soaking was better than drowning'.

Two abortive attempts to penetrate the interior boded ill. The next day they started the last, up the coast, across open savannah, with red kangaroos scattering through the tall grass. But they were soon caught in the brush again. 'The same rope-like climbers, the same prickly rattans, the same dense high forest'. They hacked through for a mile, making impossible progress, only to find their way barred by a river. Kennedy decided to start the real expedition from its far bank and they returned to camp to prepare. He wanted Huxley to travel with them, and if

> the Service would have permitted I certainly should have done so – two or three months in the bush would have set me up in strength for the next three years . . . I rather like Kennedy. He is evidently a man of grand determination.

But a surgeon's mate was not his own man, and the skipper prevailed. After an evening carousing in Kennedy's tent, Huxley saw the party off the next morning. It was 5 June as the crew watched the exodus, some with foreboding, others seeing a moment in the continent's history. The exploring party disappeared in search of a promised land: a confident Kennedy at the head, the convoy of carts, sheep, horses, with 'the rear brought up by the indefatigable Niblet [the ticket-of-leave storekeeper]', the whole bearded procession 'patriarchal-looking and imposing'.[20]

Now Stanley's flotilla began its painstaking survey. The plan was to zig-zag the 600 miles up the Inner Passage to achieve an unbroken series of triangulations. The surveyors took theodolite readings, moving from island to island; the *Asp* charted the coast-line, the other boats took depth readings near the reefs, while the *Rattlesnake* sounded the centre of the channel. It was to be the most exhaustive sweep, in every sense, taking four and a half months. And it gave Huxley an unparalleled opportunity to study one of the most exuberant seascapes on earth.

Before them lay an exotic world. Quiet emerald lagoons contrasted with Pacific breakers outside the Barrier. Along shallow coral banks the Jacks scattered. They paddled through tidal pools and combed the sparkling waters for trophies. In the lagoons they found themselves dwarfed by bizarre sea sculptures, giant sea fans and towering staghorn corals. Below them stony brain corals sat impassively. Everywhere were harlequin colours, dazzling flashes of butterfly fish, shocks of sapphire and yellow. Coral polyps waved orange and pink tentacles, and whole shoals of brilliant reef fish turned as if one, creating a bewildering optical illusion.

They landed on 37 coral islands, stopping hours here, a week there. Shooting parties went to one, scouts searched another for water. MacGillivray bagged birds, Thomson collected shells and the sailors searched for conches. Then they would move on, the look-outs blinded by the sun's glare off the sea, watching for foam ahead.

It should have been a lifetime's experience for a tyro setting out to conquer the invertebrate kingdom. The dappled shallows were shimmering with life. Hidden in the undersea forests enormous clams slotted between sea fans, octopuses lodged in crevices, feather stars walked on a thousand feet and feathery tube worms waved a thousand arms. Jewelled flatworms fluttered like marine butterflies. Here was the new world of echinoderms and molluscs – speckly sea cucumbers looking like deflating cushions and brilliant sea slugs, some a foot long. They would creep along the bottom, flaunting their crimson and yellow-red trimmings, or flounce through the water in blazing butterfly strokes.

But beauty turned into monotony, and the surveying routine

into a grind. Huxley's scientific notebook remained blank. It was too hot to sleep. He lay mouldering in his sweaty cabin. It wore him out just watching the cockroaches; 'a sudden unanimous impulse seems to seize the obscene thousands which usually lurk hidden in the corners of my cabin. Out they rush, helter-skelter, and run over me, my table, and my desk'.[21]

His creaking timbered world began to close in. Tiny nuisances preyed on his mind. Even when he was fired up, niggling problems ground him down again. Not that there was active opposition to his work.

> But it is a curious fact, that if you want a boat for
> dredging, ten chances to one they are always actually or
> potentially disposed of; if you leave your towing-net
> trailing astern . . . it is, in all probability, found to have a
> wonderful effect in stoping the ship's way, and is hauled
> in as soon as your back is turned; or a careful dissection
> waiting to be drawn may find its way overboard as a
> 'mess'.[22]

His diary entries became brief, lazy and late. He ignored the wildlife. And in the stultifying heat he ignored the most stunning coral on earth.

So began Huxley's descent, his dark gloom contrasting with the coral sea's brilliance. Off Dunk Island he lay listless, listening to the rain. He finished a novel as MacGillivray chased huge purple butterflies and gigantic black and gold spiders. Jock returned with five kinds of starfish and 12 crustaceans, some new, and flycatchers, ready to be shipped to Gould.[23] But Huxley could not be roused. It was the same at each stop. They sailed on to the Barnard Islands (near modern Innisfail), where MacGillivray found a gorgeous rifle bird, with metallic green throat and velvety black surround.

On the mainland Huxley and MacGillivray did run into aborigines, with 'necklaces, and cylinders through their noses', who 'seemed very desirous of making our acquaintance'. It shook Huxley from his apathy for a time. A new group appeared, with black paint across the eyes, bartering armlets for ship's biscuits. And nearer to Double Point the ship's team obtained a green-painted boomerang, never before seen in this region.

But Huxley's interest in the reefs was petering. Great lethargic gaps began to appear in his diary; in mid-June he passed the Frankland and Fitzroy Islands (off modern Cairns) without comment

No word about the huge headed flying fox with ringed eyes, even though MacGillivray found a rookery so full that branches were bending under the weight of bats. He shot dozens, their cries of pain like the 'squalling of a child'. Huxley stopped all notetaking. Many of his resolutions had come to nought: to collect fish brains, fish parasites and breeding barnacles. And the sad fact that, sitting on the world's finest reef, he was unable to shake his lethargy and look at the coral polyps could only have deepened his gloom. Sweltering on the sun-drenched beaches he sank further into despair.

The azure seas were teeming with reef fish. Small patrolling sharks would pass the paddling sailors. Ashore egrets dashed through the scrub snapping up skinks, past wild nutmeg, round screw-pines. The mound-incubating megapode birds could be seen scraping their huge fermenting nests. The brush turkeys were killed for the pot; pomegranates were picked, yams dug and coconuts were shot from the palm tops for drink. Naturalizing came easy; so much awaited discovery. MacGillivray collected unknown snails; indeed half the ship's company combed the beaches for cowries and spider shells, adding more ballast to the hold.[24] But the junior surgeon was never as committed a naturalist as MacGillivray. He had no interest in new birds or snail variations. His passion was the micro-structure of medusae, looking inside, not out, and the clammy heat had killed that.

The cloistered world within a man-o'-war's timbers was a prison – 'perfect isolation between the blue of the sea and the blue of the sky', a sailor lamented. 'The life without you is monotonous and empty', the life within becomes obsessional and dementing. 'Everywhere, the ship is the old Europe we are vainly trying to escape from'.[25] But no escape was possible. It was the familiar prison each returned to from the desiccating reefs.

Huxley craved human company. The months and steam-heat were taking their toll. He was lonely for Nettie. Nature was a soulless comforter. He had no interest in pickling new fruit bats and rifle birds to please the closet taxonomists at home. That wasn't serious science. Nor did he change when Nature came to him – in the shape of the unknown species of kangaroo that obligingly swam over to escape a dingo and lived on deck for a few days.

Craving human contact, he devoted pages of his diary to some sails sighted one day – more space than to all the siphonophores combined. Sails in this uncivilized region acquired a mystique, unrivalled by anything in nature. They meant humans and intrigue. A lifeboat with a shipwrecked crew? A cruiser with dispatches? A boarding party returned with tales 'of natives and attacks and wounds and distressed crews'. A 25-ton cutter, out from Sydney to search for sandalwood, had been ambushed off the Palm Islands. Huxley was ferried over 'laden with lint and bandages', and he listened to the story as he plastered the master's fractured skull: of a dawn attack by 30 aborigines armed with waddies and boomerangs, the fight with cutlass and pistol to regain the deck, and the turning point as the crew retook the swivel gun amidships. Such dramas were the making of legend. Huxley thought on the dying throes of the 'gentlemen in black', shot through the throat, with morbid fascination.

Life and death was everything and nothing out here. Shipboard life was a sort of sleepwalking for Huxley. Its surreal aspect was heightened by his immersion in Dante's *Paradiso* at night and 'three-water grog' by day (his quarter-pint rum ration).[26] Dante was his escape, his voyeuristic adventure. He mulled over sudden death, and survival, the stimulus of the minute. He still regretted not travelling with Kennedy, even though the overland party had failed to show at the rendezvous points. But he was too lethargic to think of it now.

It was a somnambulant period, as the flotilla moved its monotonous way up the coast. Up past the mangrove-lined Trinity Bay (site of modern Cairns), past swampy islands with huge salt-water crocodiles, along untold reefs, a haven for blue mantis shrimps with snapping jaws and sea urchins with spines like knitting needles. They made Low Island, with its signs of native turtle feasts. Nothing had induced him to open his diary for six weeks. Except now, on 7 July, when he scribbled the four strained words 'Anchored under Low Ids', only to snap it shut again.

He recoiled within, rereading Nettie's letters, thanking her a 'thousand times'. He told of his 'crisis' and 'fits of mental and bodily irritability'. Highly strung, like all the family, with a boiling intellect that teetered sometimes towards madness, he lay a prey to heat and worry. His mind became a maelstrom. There was no escape; even his clammy studies of the Low Island jellies and sea slugs disintegrated. The humidity left him prostrate. Thoughts of Nettie tormented him through the night. He wrote one long love letter for three months. 'Oh God this horrible absence! I cannot reconcile myself to it with all my philosophy'.[27] They passed Cape Tribulation, its name catching the mood, while the Hope Islands seemed a mariners' joke – except to Jock, who delighted in their *Halcyon* kingfishers.

At length the ship reached Cape Flattery in late July. Here Huxley escaped to scale the peak of Lizard Island 78 years to the day after Captain Cook himself had climbed it. Down below, MacGillivray found still more unique snails and came to the conclusion that every islet had its peculiar species. He returned armed with the 'showy golden blossoms' of a low-spreading tree *Cochlospermum*, bags of poisonous snakes and the porcelain shell of a Pacific cowrie, the first to be seen in Australia. Nor, he boasted, had he returned from any of the 37 islands 'without some acquisitions to the collection'.

His haul only emphasized Huxley's despondency. The heat addled his brain. Even teasing out the cowrie's nerves proved a strain, as sweat trickled into his eyes. For weeks one island blurred into another. Imagine 'months shifting from patch to patch of white sand . . . living on salt pork and beef, and seeing no mortal face but our own sweet countenances' obscured by long beards. The six weeks left 'a perfect blank in my memory'. At least Dayman's team had a job to do. They were 'living hard and getting fatigued every day', but the rest 'were yawning away their existence in an . . . orchis-house'.[28]

Boredom in paradise became the norm; or was it hell? Lizard Island had been his Mountain of Purgatory. On leaving it he swapped Dante's *Paradiso* for the more congenial *Inferno*. Expelled from the undersea Garden of Eden, with its eerie staghorns and stony brains, his soul descended through its own circles of despair. Dante provided a grim counterpoint to the ordeal on the reef. Sailing from Lizard Island, he heard the 'cries and shrieks of lamentation'; he heard the damned in limbo, stripped like himself of the beatific vision, separated from those he loved.

The medieval journey matched his torment. Off the mangrove-fringed Howick Islands, he was oblivious to the skies blackened by flying foxes and the shoreline traces of turtle feasts. But he had the smell of roasting flesh in his nostrils. Under the blazing sun the Pilgrim descended into the Eighth Circle of Hell, the awful *Male-bolge* – the ditches stuffed with pimps and popes, the 'steaming stench . . . disgusting to behold'. The 'soles of every sinner's feet were flaming'. Even Huxley drew breath, the furnace air burning his lungs. 'I think I never read anything so horribly distinct' before. Dante 'describes Hell like a practical *Times* reporter'. 'I don't wonder at the Italian women thinking that he had actually been down to Hell'. The Pilgrim roasting on the reefs was trapped in his *Bolgia*, unable to escape, only to meditate on his sins.

All around great ungainly pelicans were plunging into the emerald waters. But he was in the infernal kingdom, watching black fiends fish sinners from the boiling pitch. He missed the real sport. Parties combed the Claremont Islands with a setter. Quail provided targets for the 'First of September' shooters, imagining themselves on the moors as the season opened. While the plump Torres Strait pigeons 'appeared on the table at every meal, subjected to every possible variety of cooking'. And signs of exhausted turtles dragging themselves up the beaches led to caches of leathery reptilian eggs for breakfast.

September wore on, with no sign of Kennedy at the rendezvous points. He too was being tested by fire.

Dante poked fun at the Pilgrim. 'May your guts burn with thirst that cracks your tongue'. And they did. No terrors in the *Malebolge* could match this damnable voyage. Caught between the devil and the deep blue sea, Huxley locked himself below. 'We are laying at present under Sunday Island . . . I have not been ashore and don't care to go, what's more'.

The circle was complete, for it was on Sunday Island on 30 September that he finished the *Inferno*. Like the Pilgrim, he finally emerged from this 'trench of misery'. He made his 'way back up to the bright world' and came ashore for the shoot at Cavin Cross Island, although the splattered entrails matched the worst excesses in Dante. 'The poor birds were very tame and the shooting was simple butchery . . . I had nothing to do but load and fire as fast as possible'.[29] The blood lust became so intense that one midshipman shot at the captain, thinking him fair game.

Four days later the *Rattlesnake* reached Cape York. The crew were weary, some had scurvy. Stanley was mentally drained. The isolation of command was beginning to tell. But he pressed on: keeping them at work, clearing out old wells on the beach and pumping aboard 75 tons of fresh water. Then came more soundings. The boats went off to map the coast. Others were ordered to Albany Island, off the Cape, which was being considered as a coaling station for the steamers.

Huxley met MacGillivray's 'old acquaintances', the Cape aborigines. Huge numbers arrived from the islands, 150 men, women and children, including Papuans who were friendly with the Cape people. MacGillivray, compiling his aboriginal dictionary, sat with them round a fire, eating their shellfish and mealy plums. Like

Huxley he was a smoker, but their smoke-filled bamboo pipe, three feet long and as thick as a man's arm, made him nauseous. More came in, bringing him a new phalanger, 'quite tame, and very gentle', with short, silky, grey hair and, the oddity, a bald tip to its tail.[30]

The steamy days ticked away with no sign of Kennedy. MacGillivray spent his time packing a crate for John Gould, a cornucopia of unknown birds, a riot of emerald, topaz and jonquil-yellow feathers, so important to a bird artist.[31] He went out shooting in the jungle, scouring the lush Asian palms, or searching the open eucalyptus valleys, moving between 12-foot high termite mounds. Glorious honey-suckers, sunbirds, purple-throated orioles and king-fishers splashed with 'sealing-wax red': all went off to the Zoological Society, packed with flying fox pelts and the pet phalanger skin.

The arrival of a provision ship from Sydney meant supplies – sheep, bread, limes to counteract the scurvy and, best of all, mail. Hal opened Nettie's first, but every letter was dominated by 'the news that a Revolution has again convulsed France'. She even feared that 'we shall be enveloped in War' and that he might be recalled. His mother reported that 'Louis Phillipe has abdicated ... and the "on dit" is that the whole French family are in England'.[32] Jim, a political animal like Tom, sent a blow-by-blow account: of Court corruption and the clampdown on liberty, resulting in a mob bursting 'into the Tuilleries'. 'There were 100,000 troops in Paris at the time – yet was it a bloodless revolution'. The democrats turfed the 'old rogue' 'out of throne & country', but the revolution devoured itself as provisional governments rose and fell, none finding 'favour in the eyes of the mob' until the 'representation [was] doubled & any blackguard of 25 is eligible to sit'. At this even Jim lost sympathy. 'They are in a terrible financial mess and the provisional Gov'. has got the Herculean task of satisfying the many headed – wherein every class interest wants everything for itself'.

Huxley wondered if the London rookeries he had once walked had exploded. At 'present old England rides the storm in safety', said his mother, although there were 'fears for the immediate future owing to the frequent outbreaks of the horrid Chartists and other disaffected ones'.[33]

But Cape York was a world away. The late mail only prompted Huxley to wish that the revolutionaries 'who are going to make a democratic New Jerusalem of Europe would turn their attention towards the Anglo Australian line of packets, and reform them' first. From the bush the tumultuous events in Europe seemed remote. The civilized world might be tearing itself apart, but with news five months old no one really knew. And his mother still hoped that his exotic experiences were having a devout effect: 'enriching your mind and forming your Character for a high destiny both in this Life and that which is to come'.[34]

On 2 November they could wait no longer for Kennedy and weighed anchor. Huxley was beginning to be glad that he had not walked overland: 'Fancy my disgust at finding the ship gone'. The *Rattlesnake* tacked west, sailing across the Gulf of Carpentaria to the mangrove-covered bays of Port Essington (in what is now Arnhem Land). 'We dropped anchor opposite a high cliff . . . on top of which was perched a ruinous-looking block-house with a few pieces of cannon mounted on its top, the firing off of which would I verily believe have blown down the whole concern'. The sinking feeling was reinforced by the Commandant's gig which came out to greet them, bearing apologies that all the marine officers were ill.

The ten year-old settlement was as sick as its garrison. Stanley had been present at its founding in 1838, when the prefabricated shacks and Government House were erected. It was to have been the seed of a 'second Singapore'. 'Victoria' the colony had been christened, the first in honour of the new Queen. It was a government attempt to colonize the north coast – to control the Torres Strait traffic and provide for merchantmen poaching Dutch trade in the East Indies. Now it was a rotting shanty town. The buildings were termite-ridden. The Government House had been wrecked in a hurricane. Even the dogs had disappeared inside the giant crocodiles. It was the most 'miserable ill-managed hole in Her Majesty's dominions'. The settlement was too far up the inner harbour, away from the sea breezes. As such it was 'fit for neither man nor beast', the 'fearful damp depressing heat' leaving everyone 'a prey to ennui and cold brandy-and-water'.

In this decaying hothouse intrigues proliferated. The result was as much 'caballing and mutual hatred' among the troops 'as if it were the court of the Great Khan'. Orders came laced with vitriol. The 'commandant is a litigious old fool always at war with his officers, and endeavouring to make the place as much a hell morally as it is physically'.

Fevers were rampant, caused by bad food and unbroken toil, the men like mad dogs being worked in the midday sun. There was nothing in the *Inferno* to match: the poor squad was prodded by fiends and tortured by fire. Two years earlier 60 troops had arrived. At parade Huxley counted 'just ten men present. The rest were invalided, dead, or sick'. The hospital holding the fevered was a living hell. It was close by a putrid lagoon, positively steaming at 90° like a '*hot* salt bath'.[35] The roof leaked in the monsoons, forcing the surgeons to operate under tents. Abandonment of the settlement was imminent and the colonists prayed daily for deliverance.

It had no saving graces except its pineapples, growing like weeds. But the steaming shallows were 'a hotbed for medusae'. The harbour was alive with marble-like spherical jellyfish, *Bougainvillia* (named after the French explorer), and Huxley bobbed in his tropical bath plucking out specimens.

If he was suffering for his science, religion still plagued him and the symptoms again showed. A shipwrecked missionary, Father Angelo, had lived here a few months and tried to drive the spirits out of an aboriginal nature. MacGillivray knew the difficulties. He never doubted the natives' intelligence, although like all whites he judged them on their mimicry of Western ways. They had little to thank the settlers for, least of all the drink 'to which they have become passionately addicted'. But God was harder to imbibe than grog. That dogged explorer Edward John Eyre, the first white man to cross the empty immensity of the Great Australian Bight, developed a sympathy for these 'shadowy-characters of the never-never', but he had gone to New Zealand knowing that not a 'single real and permanent convert to Christianity has yet been made'.[36] Given the fact, the pragmatic MacGillivray placed Christianizing second to civilizing. The missionaries were at least rendering the shores safe for shipwrecked sailors.

The souls of the natives held no interest for Huxley. What intrigued him was the fate of the man sent to save them. As always he had his eye on the sects of his own culture. For months Father Angelo had learned the aborigine's tongue and taught his bemused charges Latin prayers. Huxley learned that the man was 'wholly without religious feeling, well acquainted with theology and a strong stickler for the doctrine of his church'. Nothing reinforced his prejudices about papism and its militia more. The priest was 'a *soldier of his church*, i.e. like most soldiers he did his duty religiously but cared not two straws for the quarrel in which he fought'. The military metaphor, honed by Huxley's anti-Catholicism and suspicion of the warring sects, was becoming pointed.

Like the buildings, the priest had crumbled in this hell-hole. Just before the *Rattlesnake* arrived he had died, as MacGillivray put it, blasphemously denying God.

All their minds were turning. In mid-November they beat a retreat and 'it was like escaping from an oven'. The *Rattlesnake* put to sea before the monsoon. The skies were already heavy, with lightning on the horizon at night. Bearing west again, they could make out the cloud-covered summits of the 'magnificent island' of Timor. They took the westward route round the Australian continent, 'listlessly and lazily'. It was a slow return, gruelling to even the hardened hands. Provisions ran low and each hungry man became an angry man. Even the good-natured Doctor could 'vomit forth a whole bellyful of bile against some unfortunate messmate, and what a pleasing relief followed upon this medical treatment'. His assistant sympathized, too often indulging in the treatment himself.

Both noticed Stanley's deterioration. His demeanour was changing with the strain. For 22 years, man and boy, he had been surveying hazardous shores. Like surveying captains before him, brittle perfectionists all – Pringle Stokes of the *Beagle*, who shot himself in Tierra del Fuego, and FitzRoy on Darwin's expedition, who broke down in Valparaiso – Stanley teetered on the brink. Emotionally drained, he was overworked and obsessive, refusing to delegate the simplest task. He had grown distant from his officers, 'constantly snarling at them from an ungovernable temper'.

It took them over two months to sail back to Sydney. Christmas Eve passed with Hal reminiscing again about 'dear Old England'. He was 'tossed and tumbled like a pea in a pill-box', and the loneliness left him with 'a great mind to take a dose of Laudanum tonight and sleep all through tomorrow'.[37]

By the time they reached 30° south they hit a revitalizing cool wind, 'and my energies, well nigh extinguished for some time . . . are beginning to be restored'. Suddenly released, he started taking an interest in the *Velellae* and *Physaliae* again, filling reams of paper. The captain sailed past the Swan River settlement (site of modern Perth), disappointing everybody by not stopping. But in the breeze Huxley was tweezering and probing and jotting. Out of the tropics he could think.

And in the cool he perked up. The penitent was being led by a beatific vision. Nettie's divine light would lead him out of limbo, up through the heavenly spheres to paradise. The Pilgrim's isolation, like Dante's, was ending. He was on his way 'home', to his Beatrice. A year earlier they had just met and his desires 'seemed a dream'. Now 'I have a "sober certainty of waking bliss"'.[38]

The ships reached Sydney on 24 January 1849 in a deplorable state. Nine months in the tropics had left them rotting. A crawling mass of cockroaches blackened the rigging and crunched underfoot. They swarmed, shivered Midshipman Sharpe, 'over tables at meals, flying into candles, dropping and crawling all over you when asleep'. As a drastic remedy the *Bramble* was sunk in Mosman Bay for a week, then hoisted out, free, at least for a while. Huxley was not much healthier, arriving 'little better than a walking Lots' wife', and February found him 'chiefly engaged in putting a large supply of wholesome food into me'.[39]

As the refit began, Huxley started three months' leave. The city was scorching. On the north shore 'a hot wind blew – a brick-fielder, so called because the wind passed over certain old brick-fields'. The girls wore cool white and the houses had closed shutters, with wet blankets behind. The cabbies had their own way of cooling off. Huxley limped back aboard one night. '*We* did *not* get drunk', he explained to his mother, 'but our cabman did – and consequently your son was busily engaged about two o'clock this morning in extricating himself from a bouleverse'd cab by the windows'.[40]

He was hit by a tidal wave of home news. 'Your picture of the present state of the family is like a Daguerreotype', he replied to George, 'but it is decidedly not flattering. Very few warm tints and a great breadth of shadow'. As always the impecunious Cooke looked portly in focus. He is 'growing quite fat', Ellen admitted, but 'I can't say he is growing rich'. Fat and floundering. His partnership with Richard Hoblyn, cramming students for their exams, was a flop, so that George was now bankrolling him too. 'The worst', grumbled George, 'is that he is not a whit the better while I am so much poorer'.[41] Tom had heard it all before: the family seemed doomed to fall backwards off the financial fence; sinking fortunes were their fate. It mustn't be his.

His father was frail and Tom feared 'there is but small chance of my ever seeing him again'. His mother was as lively as ever, and fishing for information about his fiancée. He was now distant, and his prim responses made no bones about Nettie's place beside him. He sat down on 1 February to give her a full account of Henrietta – her hair, her uncertain looks, her 'womanly' mind:

With my present income of course, marriage is rather a
bad look out, but I do not think it would be at all fair
towards Nettie herself, to leave this country finally without
giving her a wife's claim upon me. I could not, in common
delicacy, ask her to follow me to England without such
were the case. But there are difficulties on all sides.[42]

The task was to convince George, who was financing successive
married Huxleys and loath to keep the last. Tom agreed that
marriage was a 'hazardous act' (MacGillivray had stepped ashore
to find himself a father). But he could not ask Nettie to England
unmarried, only to find himself posted 'to the West Indies or
China'. 'Ulysses endeavours to reach his Penelope would be nothing
to mine – and I have the additional disadvantage of not being a
hero'. So his idea was 'To marry just before we leave Sydney',
then to leave Nettie with her parents while he established himself
in London. They always had his '138£ a year'; it might not set
them up salubriously, but 'it will keep us both from the gutter'.[43]

Sydney was home from home; 'my friend Fanning's house is
as completely my home as it well can be', he told his mother.
'And then Nettie had not heard anything of me for six months,
so that I have been petted and spoiled ever since we came in'.
He had thought of jumping ship. But to do what? Become a
colonial doctor? London was the centre of the world and the
pivot of imperial science. That was where he had to be. 'It is
very unlikely I shall ever remain in the colony', he reassured
her.

While he was thinking of the future, Nettie was contemplating
marriage: 'Isy [her half-sister Isabel] is persuading me to get
married – and Willie [Fanning] won't say one way or the other –
and I – there are so many reasons for and against I know not what
to say'. Neither knew how long they would be apart after Hal left
for home. 'Much must depend upon how things go in England. If
my various papers meet with any success, I may perhaps be able to
leave the service'.[44]

But would they meet with success? At home Cooke had been
chasing around for news. He 'called both at the Royal and the
Zoological Societies', Tom's mother reported, 'but could not hear
tidings of your Papers'. George too was trying to track down the
'wandering scientific babes'. His shipboard brother feared that
'somebody has turned out the cruel uncle to them'. His need to
know had nothing to do with 'vanity': 'all my worries at present

are intensely practical' – and he spelt them out as brutal propositions.

> 1^{stly} that I am an Ass^t. Surgeon in the Navy, and by
> way of Lemma to that, that I might nearly as well break
> stones on the road; 2^{ndly} that I want to get my
> promotion when I get home or else get out of the
> service altogether & 3^{rdly} that I have no interest or
> visible means of making other people help me either to
> the one end or the other: 'arfal' as the clown says, I
> must help myself.

With no patronage strings to pull, his papers had to shout his name. He had no other way of jumping the Navy List to promotion, or of picking up a scientific job, or of bringing Nettie over. The logic was stark.[45]

All the while Hal was watching Nettie with Alice, Ory's three year-old daughter. She adored Ory's children, sighing 'If dear Alice were only my own'. Hal, now one of the family, stood godfather to Ory's new baby boy. It tied the cords tighter and the baby claimed a special place in Nettie's heart. 'The love that one has for a child is such a tender holy love', she believed. Hal teased her for it, while secretly knowing 'that I should love the mother of my children even better than my dear mistress'.[46]

If children had to wait, at least they were together for the moment. Not that the euphoria was to last. It was overshadowed by news from the north.

A schooner docked on 5 March with three skeletal survivors from Kennedy's overland party. Sydney was agog. At a court hearing they presented a pathetic sight, 'pale and emaciated, with haggard looks'. In a trembling voice, one of the survivors, Carron, told a horrifying tale of despair.

It had taken them six weeks just to clear the swamps of the base camp region. Straightaway it proved too much for the shepherd, who ran off and had to be hauled out of an aboriginal camp. As they hacked through the strangling undergrowth the horses collapsed, the sheep died from the wet of continual river crossings and the men came down with malaria. The three-horse carts crashed around on the tree-strewn jungle floor and had to be abandoned. Of the 800 lbs of goods packed into each, the axes, saws and specimen boxes were jettisoned and everything else crammed into saddle bags. By August the storekeeper Niblet was very ill; a month later midday temperatures were topping 100° and even one of the kangaroo dogs died of heat exhaustion.

Huxley listened as the story reached its horrifying dénouement. It took them five months to trek 400 miles. Only nine horses remained and the labourers humped enormous crates through the jungle on their backs. Behind them, where once was a flock, trotted a solitary sheep. On 11 November they killed it and shared the flesh in a last supper. Realizing the hopelessness of the situation, Kennedy left eight men under Carron at Weymouth Bay. He and Jackey struck out with the remaining three, taking seven horses, pushing on the last 150 miles to the Cape to fetch help.

Tragedy dogged their every step. Near Shelburne Bay one carter accidently shot himself in the shoulder; another was too ill to go on and both were left, cared for by the third. Kennedy and Jackey ploughed on alone. Near Escape River, not 20 miles from their destination, they were tracked for days by aborigines. Kennedy fell with a spear in his back. Jackey buried him amid the leaves of the scrub floor and walked on, taking the long route round the hostile tribe. Eight days later, on 23 December, Jackey, lame and exhausted, struggled into the Cape.

A rescue party found nothing of the three Shelburne Bay men but their clothes. At Weymouth Bay, Carron's group camped by a brackish creek, and waited. Where aborigines could live off the land, white explorers, carrying all the trappings of Western civilization, could only starve. One labourer, weak and emaciated, died on 16 November, a carter four days later. Gloom gave way to a sort of 'sluggish indifference'. In 110° temperatures the flesh of the last horse rotted within two days. They were surrounded by armed aborigines, sometimes taunting, at others bearing rancid fish, once attacking with barbed spears. Another week on, and the shepherd 'withered away . . . without pain or struggle'. Fate mocked them: they actually spotted the *Bramble* passing the bay one day, but frantic rocket-firing failed to attract it. The last vestige of hope dashed, they sank into a terminal lethargy. One labourer struggled to the creek and sat down to die on its bank. They found him the next morning but had no strength to dig a grave. On 28 December Niblet and the naturalist died and were covered with leaves.

The macabre scene had the air of a malarial hallucination, bodies bobbing in the creek, in the bushes. Nothing seemed real. They had lost their will and 'withered into perfect skeletons'. Jackey and the rescue team found armed natives everywhere, rotting corpses, and Carron and one labourer barely alive. Carron's elbow and hip bones were poking through his skin. Fearing an attack, they carried the botanist swiftly out of camp, clutching his seeds. He left his precious plants and his diary behind.

These poor souls had suffered and died for their science and their survey. Huxley thought of Kennedy, a 'fine noble fellow', and what might have been. To 'have perished by starvation or the spears of the natives . . . You may be sure I am not sorry to return home'.

The jolt served to strengthen his resolve. Like everyone he was haunted by the tragedy. A brig, searching Weymouth Bay, found Wall's and Niblet's skulls, which were taken to Albany Island for burial.[47] Kennedy's body was never recovered, only the half-chewed remains of his papers, buried by Jackey. These were brought to Stanley, but they only undermined his mental state more. Huxley steeled himself for the last leg of the survey, thankful to be alive.

7

Sepulchral Painted Savages

'AM I AT SEA or dreaming?'

The *Rattlesnake* left Sydney harbour on 8 May 1849 and sailed north, this time destined for New Guinea. Hal left Nettie a knot of grief and frustration. She had heard of the 'fierceness' of the Papuan natives and worked herself into a state, imagining Hal 'exposed to their attacks'.

The dreaming carried him up the coast. He settled into his somnambulistic routine, lost in Nettie's letters in the momentary calm, 'then comes a roll . . . the timbers creak, the pigs squeal, the fowls cackle, two or three plates fly with a crack out of the stewards pantry' and the cook's curses brought him back to reality.

He had a ruder awakening after Moreton Bay (Brisbane). Steering through the Coral Sea, the heavily laden ship was hit by a cyclone. The *Bramble* lost her stern-boat and separated from the *Rattlesnake*, which was itself 'plunging and rolling in the heavy seas like a log'. The shoddy caulking left the gun room and Huxley's cabin flooded. He sided with the men, blaming it on the officers, who should have been ''tending to the ship, 'stead o' givin pic-nics in Sydney harbour'.[1] Then the tiller rope gave way and the ship broached to and was hit by three huge waves broadside.

Far from the cyclone, Nettie sat at home with his old letters:

> They are never-failing sources of comfort . . . Ah how I
> love him – with my whole soul – with all the truth and
> devotion that ever urged a woman's heart. My desire is to
> become good and excellent as the being he imagines me –
> my happiest dreams are of a peaceful home with him to

love and care for – my hopes, his advancement in temporal and eternal blessings.

His own dreams returned with the glassy seas, and by June his diary entries were taking a lyrical turn. He gazed at her picture at night and then walked the deck: the 'little waves plish-plash with a pleasant murmur against the side', but he was absorbed as 'a thousand thousand thoughts chase one another through my brain', and always Nettie became 'at last directly or indirectly the object of my meditation'.

He huddled over his microscope. He had plankton enough to keep him absorbed: sea urchin larvae, sea nettles and comb jellies, a pulsating, flashing, jerking mass of life, a world within a world seen through his eyepiece. And endless tiny stalked polyps, *Tubularia*, which turned up in every ocean at every latitude. He was still listing them, only to discover one day when the tide dragged his net under the hull that they were actually 'attached in large masses to the ship's bottom!'[2]

Then the steaming downpours began. It was back to being 'sweated and stewed & bedeviled under the sun ... living like romany d--- [dogs] domiciled in a wooden hutch'. He sat 'melting though half-stripped' in his 'orchis-house'. But no orchid-fancier had to endure this botanical sauna day after day. 'Hot, wet, rainy, muggy', he logged on 9 June, as he shut himself away with his increasingly exotic trawl, 'singular' sea butterflies (gaudy swimming slugs) and bizarre crustaceans with long frontal spines.

The stewing heat drew out Stanley's insecurities. He suffered morbid fears about the terrors of the interior. Cannibalism obsessed him. Nor was it surprising with the lurid tales of New Guinea's head-hunters. The dismemberment of Kennedy's men had left them all with a nightmare.

Sight of the Louisiade Archipelago off eastern New Guinea on 10 June restored Huxley's faith that they were moving on: jungle-covered mountainous islands obscured by clouds. The island chain stretched away eastwards from New Guinea, and the *Rattlesnake* followed it to the furthest tip, Rossel Island, which loomed up a 'rich, leafy mass, of all shades from indigo to grass green'. Even its rugged peaks remained jungle-strewn, and shrouded all day 'by a fleecy cloudy canopy'. Huxley knew 'nothing more beautiful than a cloud resting upon a mountain peak, like the head of a delicate girl resting on the broad shoulder of an old warrior'.[3]

On 13 June Stanley was 38 and logged: 'a better day could not be chosen for the commencement of our survey!' Proper charts would finally allow British merchantmen to sail these waters safely. On maps the Archipelago, like New Guinea itself, was a mass of blanks, vague shores, uncharted reefs and missing islands. Yet this was the trade route to the East Indies and the Pacific – the route taken long before by Captain Blyth with his precious bread-fruit plants.

Rossel Island stood at one end of a huge 30-mile lagoon. They could see coconut palms and huts, and offshore the sails of native canoes. They needed sheltered anchorage inside the lagoon, away from the Pacific breakers. But the only entrance was a narrow channel, 200 yards wide, with razor-like coral banks on either side. The *Rattlesnake* squeezed through, 'passing within a stone's throw of roaring breakers on either hand', the leadsman singing 'out his "Deep nine" or "By the mark fourteen"', with everyone holding his breath. They were safe.

Well, not all. 'The skipper's black dog "Native"', Huxley wrote, 'committed suicide last night, by walking into the sea out of the main chains. The skipper and his dog had this in common, that they liked one another, and were disliked by every one else'. Stanley's jagged nerves and bellowing rages were wearing – as were his jitters about the natives. Here they were friendly enough, turning up in their ten-man canoes with carved bows and outrigger. They bartered yams and coconuts for axes, pilfering the odd one like the most 'dexterous London thieves'.

The month was spent exploring the islands in what they called 'Coral Haven'. Huxley went with MacGillivray, Simpson and Brierly to see the islanders, waving green branches as the recognized sign of peace. His account of the first parleys was laced with parochial wit, giving it a mocking tone. His mixture of plebeian patter and derring-do disguised a deeper unease among these 'savages'. Having lured the fishermen to the beach by antics, he was greeted by 'one bright copper-coloured gentleman who appeared like Paul to be "the chief speaker" bearing a green branch in his hand'. Huxley laid down his gun 'and had a very interesting and polite interview with friend coppery and two other gentlemen who were quite black and had large fuzzy heads of hair with combs a foot long, narrow and very long-pronged, stuck into the front of their very remarkable coiffure. Brady had given me a red cap which was much coveted by all, but I made one of the fuzzy-headed gentry give me an ornamented chunam-gourd for it'.

Huxley was in an alien world and showed few of MacGillivray's anthropological insights. His reaction swung between astonishment, embarrassment and condescension, as it did for most European travellers. He identified two 'races', some natives being black and 'fuzzy-headed; others again were of various shades of copper colour' with close-cropped hair. 'Their only clothing was a long leaf curled up behind into a most absurd appendage like a bustle'. 'And the septum of the nose was ornamented – save the mark! – with a long white bone or some such thing stuck through it'.

But he excelled in his chatty accounts of an individual's quirks. He was the Ealing boy facing spirits from another world, wrestling for understanding. There was the 'old gentleman' who 'had lost his nose, which imparted an expression of soft and pleasing melancholy to his countenance'. Another's foot was swollen to gigantic proportions with elephantiasis (giving Huxley first-hand experience of diseases never seen by normal surgeons). He lampooned their 'ugly mugs', although 'some of the young nymphs were comely enough'.[4]

The mess buzzed at the sight of a 'blackie' with a human-jaw bracelet. This 'singular piece of *bijouterie*' had everyone offering hatchets, mirrors and handkerchiefs in exchange, but he would not 'part from it for love or money'. Like all sailors, wanting their trophies (on Darwin's *Beagle* in New Zealand it was shrunken heads), the *Rattlesnake*'s ratings were busy trading for human jaws. Otherwise it was jade hatchets and totem figureheads, swapped for axes and hats. On another island the natives wore necklaces of human vertebrae. Whether they were 'the memorials of friends or trophies of vanquished foes', the bleached bones were enough to make Stanley shudder.[5] It increased his morbid fear and made him reticent about any sort of contact. Huxley and Thomson saw it as a crisis of nerve.

Huxley and his messmates spent these sunlit days 'tucking up our duds' and wading the shallows. They picked their way through the mangroves, watching hermit crabs and 'queer little leaping fish' (mudskippers). His workload was light, although his duties were more exotic than any Charing Cross demonstrator's. No Strand surgeon had to treat a sailor writhing in pain after standing on a poison-spined frogfish.

On shore they watched sacred kingfishers and sulphur-crested cockatoos among the palms. The mound-incubating megapodes were common, 'running about the thickets, and calling to each other like pheasants'.[6] Shooters bagged them, a staple for the pot. Regular searches were made up mangrove creeks for water. On these Huxley was able to see the jungle's edge, with its pitcher plants full of sweet water and 15-foot tree ferns, although the scene had to be appreciated through swarms of biting flies.

By now he was having difficulty restraining his sarcasm about the skipper. Stanley went with Brierly and Huxley to sketch the tree-fern luxuriance of a creek. Huxley was a lightning artist with a good eye. But seeing Stanley's child-like sketch 'I nearly burst out laughing'. 'That he had neither smell nor hearing nor taste sufficiently refined to enable him to distinguish one sensation from another, sulphuretted hydrogen from Millefleurs, "God save the Queen" from "Old Dan Tucker" . . . I knew long ago, but now I find that his eye is equally defective'.

Huxley's bravado ashore disguised a deeper unease. At the centre of Coral Haven was 'Pig Island', named from an incident on 20 June. The larking sailors landed, 'looking well to our "ammunition of war"', and were surrounded by 40 or so armed 'hullaballooing' villagers. The crew knew nothing of native customs. The agitated villagers threw an appeasing pig at their feet, at the same time surreptitiously lifting Huxley's gun. 'I looked big and blustered a little, they drew together and scowled, handling their spears', wrote a tense Huxley, 'so I pretended at last to be satisfied, and forming in battle-array, Simpson as advance guard, Brierly and I carrying the pig, and MacGillivray as rear-guard, off we marched'. They broke into a nervous laughter 'at the absurdity of the scene'. And thus 'piggy and his carriers, squealing and laughing', hastily made for the boat.

But Stanley shied away from contact. Whatever his phobias, inland penetration was not his brief; indeed his orders were to 'guard against the treacherous disposition' of the natives. His quailing appalled Huxley and Thomson. When the captain did land he looked 'as stupid as a stockfish'. It was not only the skipper's sketching that Huxley impugned, but his savvy during the exchanges and, ultimately, his nerve. A reckless Huxley sneaked away from one beach bartering session and followed a jungle path, stumbling on to a native village. He returned to fetch a jittery Stanley. But the captain insisted on an armed escort, and even then was 'anxious to get away, wandering about in a regular fidget'. What incensed Huxley was the captain's boast about his 'communication with the natives' and that, having met them ashore, '*I don't think it necessary to go [again] myself*'. Huxley lambasted the 'little man' as a regular 'Sir Joshua Windbag'.

Sunday 1 July was Nettie's 24th birthday. That day her emotions got the better of her: Fanning passed on Hal's present, Schiller's works, 'with a note from dearest Hal. So surprised and overcome was I that I wept for many minutes . . . I longed that he were by to thank and tell how much how very much I loved him'. A thousand miles away Hal lay in his bunk, brooding, doubting. What was he? A man of massive knowledge to most people, a mixture of horse sense, street patter and profound philosophy set off by the sharpest critical faculty.

> I might have made a good critic, and an accomplished
> man. As it is what am I? A hotch potch of knowledge and
> ignorance, fact and fiction picked up from all the highways
> & byways of knowledge cheek by jowl with the most
> absurd ignorance at which a schoolboy might blush . . .
> There are few men who do not know a great deal more,
> and that in a better manner than I do, & there are very
> few books and still fewer men in whose learning I do not
> find some fallacy.[7]

The next day the *Rattlesnake* hauled off, zig-zagging west from reef to reef inside Coral Haven. Parties landed on each island, searching for water and bartering axes and cotton nightcaps for yams. The hold was filling fast. On Brierly Island (named after the ship's artist) 368 lbs of yams were swapped for 17 axes. Huxley, the unfulfilled engineer, watched the outriggers as much as the natives, sketching them and insetting details. He joined the barter parties and inveigled his way into villages, sketching scenes, sharing coconuts, amazed at the native's kiln technology and ability to turn out earthenware pots '18 inches across'.

On other islands more than deals were struck. Joannet's skirmishing natives sought to impose their own trading terms. Dayman's men opened fire and the 'crack and whistle of the shot' sent natives crashing over the galley's side. Huxley patched spear wounds and axe cuts. It was this 'treacherous attack' by friendlies known to have been out to the *Rattlesnake*, Stanley told the bishop, that firmed his resolve: no parties would be sent to the interior. No bird-of-paradise or exotic bloom was worth the 'sacrifice of one human life'.[8]

When the canoes deserted the frigate, there were other visitors. All hands came to the side one night to see the ship surrounded by swarming, fluorescing, 100-segmented worms giving off a 'brilliant greenish light'.[9] Huxley threw himself back into this pelagic life with gusto in the absence of native contact. He was now dissecting daily, minute worms and jellies and sea nettles; and if he got bored there were always parasitic crustaceans to pick off his catch. A few 'nastinesses' could keep him from 'utter stagnation'.

Nastiness was ever present. Tragedy lurked below decks. The ship's carpenter, whom he had been treating since Sydney, was buried on Middle Island on 2 August. Life seemed cheaper in the torrid zone, so far from home. The crew made a fire over the grave, to conceal it, lest his jaws end up as native ornaments.

> The traces of Death's hand at sea are soon obliterated;
> you die in the morning, and in half an hour your cabin is
> nailed up, and folks are speculating as to who will have
> your vacancy. You are buried or thrown overboard in the
> afternoon; the next day your traps are sold before the
> Captain, and the day after you are forgotten. There is
> hardly room for the living on board a ship, so that no
> wonder that the dead find no resting place in it.[10]

In mid-August, after sailing 300 miles from Coral Haven, they sighted a hazy 'blue mountain mass' on the horizon ahead – this was the awesome '*Dowdee*', the New Guinea mainland. For the first time they faced the real unknown. Few had seen it, none had explored it. It was, 'perhaps, the very last remaining habitable portion of the globe into which European cruisers and European manufacturers had not penetrated'.[11] Its north coast was unmapped, and its south coast had to be charted before it could be opened up. On this huge, lush, jungle island were peoples uncontacted by the outside world.

The mountainous land was enveloped in dense white cloud, impenetrable and mysterious. Huxley, straining for a view, played the jaded Jack Tar. 'Time was when I should have made this a red day ... when I was young and a little enthusiastic'. 'There lies before us a grand continent – shut out from intercourse with the civilized world, more completely than China, and as rich if not richer in things rare and strange. The wide and noble rivers open wide their mouths inviting us to enter. All that is required is coolness, judgment, perseverance, to reap a rich harvest of knowledge and perhaps of more material profit'.

And 'a little risk'. The alluring rivers could seduce, invite them into dark creeper-strewn traps that would close in behind, a throttling jungle where alien eyes watched every turn. The cynic cut in: the poor boy, wondering why he should suffer, unrecognized and unrewarded. Too much was demanded of frontier science.

Where did it get Carron, plucked from his own private hell? Why take risks? Facing the shrouded mysteries of New Guinea forced strange reflections. Huxley started a deranged dialogue with himself in the sultry heat: what was 'the advancement of knowledge and the opening of wide fields for future commerce to my comfort'? The seven-bob subaltern was paid for bandaging boils, not breaking new ground; 'it's all very well for young fools' to talk of the nobility of knowledge, but 'You get no thanks for that' and the 'pay [is] just the same'.

He snapped out of his strange mood instantly. 'Admirable reasoning! but Cortes did not reason thus when he won Mexico for Spain nor the noble [Rajah] Brooke when he conquered a province [Borneo] in a yacht'. It was the leitmotiv of Huxley's young life: the need for danger money at the forefront of science. Trained explorers need to be recruited, as all specialists struggling with nature. Pay for the 'wounds and contusions' in the fight to advance knowledge. Push people to the limit, yes; but reward them.

'Mysterious currents' forced them to stand off for days, unable to anchor, the shrouds around the mountains tantalizingly visible on the horizon. Occasionally the clouds would clear to reveal stupendous green jungled summits; 'I never saw the like before', Stanley admitted, 'far more magical, far more sudden'. But he was not tempted to go in. For the last two weeks in August the *Rattlesnake* lay at anchor off Brumer Island.

The island looked glorious through the spy glass. From under dipping coconut fronds came a stream of natives in huge catamarans. The contact promised much; these boats were of a new type, three logs, anything up to 30 feet long, lashed together by rattan cords. The central log was exquisitely carved and painted red and white at the bow and stern. These Papuans seemed well disposed and were the first actually allowed on board the *Rattlesnake*. They shinned up a rope, their enormous hair combs appearing before their blackened faces, peering over the gun rail. They were impressive in their strangeness, with high white-striped cheeks, high-crowned skulls, flat circular earrings and a stick through the nose. In their canoes they seemed taller. On deck they shrank to five foot four, dwarfed by their ten-foot polished spears, and purple amaranth flowers in their hair hardly made them fearsome. On board they clustered, chewing betel nuts and spitting black saliva through black teeth, protesting their friendship by touching their noses while pinching their navels.

Eventually 100 a day were turning up, some carrying hornbill heads or cassowary feathers for trade. On board an 'amusing vagabond' would stick his cowrie shell necklace in his mouth, to heighten the effect of his charcoal face and white-painted brows, put on 'a grotesque attitude' and start beating a tin pot. To the laughter of the crew the drummer, fiddler and fife-player struck up a shanty and joined in. For Huxley the novelty superseded serious study. There were none of Darwin's probing questions, about their origins, about the enigmas of God's handiwork, or the meaning of savages for civilized, sherry-sipping man. For the moment Huxley was just another sailor laughing at their 'grimaces and antics'.[12] Not that he lacked the opportunity. He mischievously led one inquisitive Papuan down the hatch to the ward-room, where the officers were sipping wine. They might refuse a surgeon's mate his rightful place, but hardly his eerie sepulchral-painted guest, with nose sticks and hair comb, who was by now fearfully clutching Huxley's hand. So they seated him in an armchair and offered him a glass. And there he sat, nervously enjoying himself.

MacGillivray went on with his lexicon. There was plenty of time to question them on the names of common objects. Most days the canoes would arrive, with the natives bringing cooked yams as calling cards. They seemed kind and soon understood the Victorian proprieties. But kindness invited its own reward, and they were scurrilously cheated by 'Honest Jack' – and greeted by 'torrents of choice Billingsgate' (fishmongers' foulmouthing) if they reciprocated. Men brought boys to look at the strange ship. Out of a huge 27-man canoe stepped one venerable chief. Huxley thought him not 'unlike the Bishop of Norwich' (old chiefs apparently being the same everywhere). The skipper did his best to impress. He lit blue lights at night, giving the ship a ghostly glow, or fired rockets, and mystified them with scenes of civilized life on his £25 magic lantern.

Sometimes tattooed women came too, dressed in red-and-green-dyed grass skirts. The crew draped them in gaudy regatta shirts and they would 'dance for our amusement' on the quarterdeck. Huxley never considered the common denominator of his own stovepipe-hatted sex and the coppery-combed 'gentlemen', but he saw 'how perfectly women are women all the world over', with 'the same incessant flow of small talk'. 'And to complete the resemblance they all persisted in kissing and hugging an impudent young varlet of a ship's boy', then taking a 'roguish delight' in inspecting the black smudges on his white face. One aspect was not shared with civilized women and must have seemed barbarous to Huxley: MacGillivray noted that 'they appeared to be treated by the men as equals and to exercise considerable influence over them'.

On 19 August the cutters were dispatched to the island, with Huxley, MacGillivray and Thomson along. The captain's orders were to find water, but all were keen to see a village. With natives holding their hands, they marched up a snaking craggy path towards the island's central ridge. Led like blind men, they stopped at the top and for the first time saw a breathtaking view: high jungly hills on each side and spread out before them lush coconut groves and the 'curious gables of the native huts', set off by the 'wide ocean with a tremendous line of rollers' in the distance.[13]

The whole village turned out for the procession. Men in hair combs and cassowary feathers were beating out rhythms on drums or 'roaring' into huge bamboo pipes, so that it turned into the 'most hideous uproar imaginable'. Huxley moved freely among the huts, sketching the charcoal-blackened women. Here was a strange Arcadian beauty. Untouched people; not necessarily noble savages, but apparently happy ones. They lived in a land of plenty, ready to share their bananas and guavas and coconuts. They were to be envied their 'primitive simplicity and kind-heartedness'. Where was that 'malady of thought' afflicting industrial England? He realized that 'civilization as we call it would be rather a curse than a blessing to them'. Huxley knew the fate in store for them, slamming the 'mistaken goodness of the "Stigginses" of Exeter Hall, who would send missionaries to these men to tell them that they will all infallibly be damned'.

Stanley's timidity was now the talking point. He never ventured ashore. In two weeks parties were allowed to visit the island only twice, for a couple of hours each. There was no reconnaissance, no collecting. We 'have not been permitted to take the slightest advantage of the opportunities afforded' us, moaned Huxley. Proper exploration of the island could have provided a dry run, readying them for New Guinea. But no; 'we knew as much of its botany, similarly zoology, when we anchored, as we do now'. The New Guinea 'mainland was not half a dozen miles off and there appeared to be some promise of a large river. Not a boat was sent to explore the coast . . . if this is the process of English Discovery, God defend me from any such elaborate waste of time and opportunity'.[14]

With no exploration, Huxley had to content himself with sketching the canoes of inquisitive visitors. Or scissoring sea slugs. Nights would find him 'sitting in my hatch – which opens into the common den where the rest of the menagerie divert themselves', candle burning, sweat pouring, writing up his notes or reading the 'wonderful' *Wilhelm Meister*, Goethe's 'cold & glassy' reflection of life. He liked novels of disillusionment.[15]

Morale was collapsing again in the heat. September found them moving along the New Guinea coast. Days they spent 'coquetting with the shore', unable to find an anchorage. One moment they were in 100 fathoms, too deep for an anchor, the next in six and stirring up the mud dangerously. Nerves jangled as it became clear that Stanley was afraid to land. Some took to grog and vice: a seaman was lashed for drunkenness and a midshipman for 'unclean and indecent behaviour'. All hands were summoned to watch. The men were tied to the grating, with the surgeons behind. They were needed, with the 'cat' able to knock a man down and lacerate his back. Huxley's insubordination was more private. He kept his complaints about the failure of the 'little man's heart' to himself. He escaped Stanley's lashing tongue when others were verbally whipped. 'I am sick of the brute! He has been like a little fiend all day, snubbing poor old Suckling in the most disgusting manner, and behaving like a perfect cub to all about him'.[16]

With the crew on a knife edge, fights with the Papuans were flaring up. Huxley heard that the equally 'gallant and humane commander' Yule in the *Bramble* had fired at angry natives, who through a mix-up had given a pig and received nothing. Still, the continual barter was revealing some interesting items: on 5 September two live *Cuscus* were traded 'for an axe a-piece'. These rare phalangers – grey-coated, naked-tailed, opossum-like marsupials – now joined the ship's company. Gentle, slow and nocturnal, they lived curled up asleep in the corner of the hen coop by day, forepaws over nose. At night they came alive, eating coconut and lapping pea soup, their huge reddish-yellow eyes giving them good night vision. As Huxley strolled on deck for his 10 pm. constitutional, and Stanley smoked his cigar, the night-watch allowed the *Cuscus* to climb the rigging.

Between deals they scudded westward, slaking their thirst with hot rainwater streaming off the sails. ('It's what a wine merchant would call a "full-bodied" drink by the time we get it'.) The mugginess reminded them of a 'vapour bath'. 'It rains continually', Huxley complained, 'heavy clouds hang over the land in bands almost down to the shore, their white fleece shewing beautifully against the blue side of the mountains'. They pushed on past Cape Rodney in mid-September, never landing, remaining between seven and 30 miles offshore. Finally on Thursday 20 September they put in under some red cliffs. It was 'so like a place near Preston, to which I went the day Charlie was married', noted Stanley, 'that I called it Redscar'. On Sunday morning Huxley rose to the sight of sunrise over the majestic New Guinea summits. The range had been growing steadily as they sailed west; now it assumed spectacular proportions. It 'can hardly be less than 10,000 feet high', he guessed, and some 'thirty or forty miles inland'.

What did Huxley think of the 'little man' appropriating the entire New Guinea mountain chain? (It was christened 'Owen Stanley's Range'.) Naming might be 'possessing', but this was imperial arrogance run amok. Huxley was sick of Stanley's conceit. Too timid to step ashore, he sailed past claiming the distant mountains! Peaks and islands were called after the officers – parcelled out by the skipper. The assistant surgeon even found one of the 40-odd islands in the Calvados Group named 'Huxley Island'.[17]

The Papuans now were smaller, with hair 'frizzled up into a mop projecting backwards'. But their canoes stood off and no waving of red rags would lure them in. Nor were shore parties allowed. Everyone moaned as the chances slipped away. Even more galling, on 25 September, when the *Rattlesnake* moved a few miles along the coast, Papuans with pigtails tied with dog-toothed rosettes came out from a river's mouth to invite them ashore. They 'were civil enough', though heavily armed, and the fact that they were ignorant of iron showed that Stanley had an opportunity for virgin contact.

But no. The ships sailed on another 30 miles, to anchor off Yule Island, named in honour of the *Bramble*'s 'gallant' commander. Even this stopover lasted only a few hours. Buffeted by heavy seas, they were uncomfortable at anchor and finally, on 27 September, after six weeks cruising along New Guinea's coast, never once setting a foot on the mainland, Stanley plotted a course due west, across the Great Bight of New Guinea, back to Cape York in northern Australia.

It 'makes me sick', Thomson fumed. He considered the four months a fiasco. The French had passed these shores but not penetrated the interior. Here was the crew's opportunity to be 'considered discoverers; but this was denied us'. 'And now we have left this great *terra incognita*'. 'I cannot now conceal my chagrin'. Huxley was never able to collect the bird-of-paradise he had promised Lizzie's daughter Flory.

For four days they sailed across the Coral Sea, past islands on the northern extremity of the Great Barrier Reef – past Bramble Key, with its huge booby and noddy colonies. A resigned crew arrived at the benighted Cape York on 1 October, and Huxley scribbled his last dyspeptic note for two weeks: 'No provision ship, no letters. I won't swear'.

The provision ship arrived the next day with five months' mail. Nettie told him that the Fannings were moving to England. *Punch* kept him laughing and the *Times* was long out of date. Yesterday's news made him feel remote. Not *so* remote that his bank manager could not find him, even at the ends of the earth. Salting away his shillings had left him no richer. Still £140 in the red, he concluded that 'the sooner I desert and go to California the better'.[18]

Then came even more astonishment. After all the worrying, he had positive sightings of his intellectual offspring. He was over-joyed by his first direct message from Forbes on 'the fate of my scientific efforts'. 'They are it appears to be printed and he promises, in his own words, "to see that they are done justice to". At the same time he speaks of . . . my establishing for myself "a high name as a naturalist"'. Huxley trumpeted the news to Nettie, knowing that a paper in the Royal Society's *Transactions* would increase his prospects.

A letter from Jim added more. He had spotted two notices of his brother in the *Athenaeum*: his two year-old paper 'On the Anatomy of Diphyes' had been read at the Linnean Society on 16 January 1849, and in the 10 March issue: 'Meetings for the ensuing week:- Zoological. "M^r. Huxley R. N. On the animal of Trigonia"'. Tom had waited to hear this for so long. Not even the Linnean paper being attributed to 'W. Huxley Esq' could dampen his euphoria. So, said his practical brother, your 'mind is bent on Scientific pursuits', how would it 'be converted into daily bread'?[19] Jim suggested he become a mad-doctor, bread before science, but Tom had fixed his sights.

Buoyed up, he sent Forbes another screed, arguing again that the lowly stinging animals were all of a kind, which he proposed to call 'Nematophora' (from the 'nematocysts' or stinging cells). He was the first to see that all the hydras and jellies and sea nettles and anemones were two-layered. His little truths were becoming bigger, as he began to corner whole chunks of creation. He suspected, too, that his stinging animals could be arranged in some sort of geometric pattern, to show their relationships. There must be 'a great law hidden in the "Circular System" if one could but get at it . . . but I, a mere chorister in the temple, had better cease discussing matters obscure to the high priests of science themselves'.[20]

Huxley's joy contrasted to Stanley's blank countenance. Ten days after recalling his brother's wedding at Redscar Point, he heard that Charlie was dead from a stomach infection, leaving Eliza widowed and alone in Tasmania. But Stanley's mind was turning; he made no mention of it, showed no grief. He was withdrawing, his reason becoming impaired.

The monotony of Cape life was suddenly broken two weeks later. Huxley was now to learn far more of the intimate details of aboriginal customs, and from an unexpected insider source.

The sailors were dumbfounded to see among the aborigines a 'white woman disfigured by dirt and the effect of the sun on her almost uncovered body'. They stood in disbelief, staring, as she came forward, slightly lame, with inflamed eyes, 'and in hesitatingly broken language cried "I am a Christian – I am ashamed"'. A cutter brought her out to the ship, accompanied by her 'brothers'. Slowly, over the days, she told her story 'in half Scotch, half native dialect'.

She was *Teoma*, which turned out to be Thompson, Barbara. She was only 20, a tinsmith's daughter from Aberdeen, who had come out with her father when she was eight. At 15 she had run away with a sailor to Moreton Bay. After marrying they had sailed to the Torres Strait to make a living scavenging off the wrecks. But a squall capsized their cutter, drowning everyone except Mrs Thompson, who was rescued by natives out turtling. As a white *marki* (ghost) she was adopted as an elder's reincarnated daughter. For five years, as one of the 'jumped-up-alive', she was treated well and lived on Prince of Wales Island in the Strait. She spoke the language of her 'brothers' fluently and adopted their manners so as to present 'a most ludicrous graft of the gin upon the white woman'. She had sung ballads to herself at night to try to retain her old language, but even now found it difficult 'to translate her native thoughts into plain English'.

Like all the aborigines, she had known of the *Rattlesnake*'s presence, and she told Huxley of Kennedy's death. Now MacGillivray had a 'native' translator to add the more awkward concepts to his lexicon. She poured out astonishing stories, of tribal attacks, the cutting-and-carrying of heads, the *marki* deities and animistic beliefs of her people. She gave Huxley and MacGillivray their first deep insights into aboriginal culture. *Teoma* joined the ship, settling into the captain's workshop, surrounded by calico presents. 'Poor creature!' said Huxley, 'we have all great compassion for her and I am sure there is no one who would not do anything to make her comfortable'.[21]

The naturalists set off ashore. Seaforthia palms towered 80 feet above them. Along the rivers they collected seeds of tiny banana and ginger plants for Sydney's Botanical Garden. MacGillivray found the 'play houses' of the bower birds, large stick-canopied tunnels, their entrances littered with attractive objects, where the male indulged in 'strange antics' to lure the female. He collected one precarious bower and actually shipped it lock-stock-and-barrel to the British Museum. He and Wilcox, the captain's collector, sent more imperial treasures to Gould: a trove of beautifully prepared kingfishers, *Cuscuses*, lovely wrens, flycatchers, honey-eaters, iridescent starlings and spectacular crimson-cheeked black parrots.[22]

But this wasn't for Huxley. He stole off for a month's adventure in the *Asp* to chart the islands around Bligh's Channel at the western entrance to the Strait. His party went heavily armed, hearing from *Teoma* that a renegade white man, thought to be an escaped convict from Norfolk Island, was leading a tribe on Mulgrave Island, raiding vessels and terrorizing the islands. This proved the need for a garrison settlement here, to make the Cape a port of refuge, a coaling station, a trading post and a missionary centre. Stanley brooded on the outrages. Before leaving the Cape he visited Albany Island and the graves of Wall and Niblet, or what remained of Kennedy's men. He was now obviously unstable.

Time hung heavily and Huxley spent the last steamy month at the Cape poring over fleshy sea squirts (or salps). He had hauled in hundreds of these flask-shaped creatures at Redscar Point, and here at the Cape 'the sea was absolutely crowded' with them. Alive they defensively spurted a stomachful of sea water at him; dead no kin readily claimed them. They were anomalies, apparently with no close relations. Tradition made them strange molluscs, and all the stranger for his observation that the free-swimming embryo of one, an *Appendicularia* from New Guinea, had tail muscles like a tadpole's.[23] (It was a hint of the most astounding relationship ever to be uncovered in the animal kingdom; the sea squirt larva would eventually be linked to the fish. Within 20 years it would be made the evolutionary bridge between the invertebrates and the backboned fish, reptiles and mammals.)

But the strange salps said something else to Huxley at the Cape. He always found two types together, so distinct that they looked like separate species. But they were not; one was actually producing the other, long chains of them could be seen emerging from it. The chains detached and inside each member a foetus developed – which itself grew into the original solitary form! This lifecycle was seen as an 'Alternation of Generations', just as hydras produce medusae, which breed hydras. But not by Huxley: at the Cape he argued that the first salp simply budded off the second. The chains floating away were not *individuals*, but detached reproductive organs, bits of the parent no less (zoöids he called them). These were the sex organs of the mother salp living independent lives!

Nothing was stranger, that an individual could exist in 50 free-swimming parts! So were the millions of aphids springing from one female by parthenogenesis nothing more than bits of her? A more provocative Royal Society paper was on the way.[24]

Nine weeks at the Cape were enough. Not that sailing would be better, with the *Rattlesnake* doubling back to New Guinea. But with *Teoma* aboard at least Huxley had a guide to aboriginal culture. They set sail on 3 December and that afternoon reached Mount Ernest Island in the Strait. Huxley got ashore and shouts of *Poud! Poud!* and offers of biscuits to an old man bought him his ticket to the local village. He passed a strange enclosure, with houses fenced in low bamboo, and was warned that it was 'a place to be feared'. (It was a sacred site, according to *Teoma*, for initiation into manhood, and any woman looking at it would be executed.)

The old man led them further into a magical clearing, 'arched over by magnificent trees and so shaded and cool, with a "dim religious light" pervading it'. The great canopy deflected 'the hot sun' and in the 'silence and the gloom' he imagined himself in a great cathedral. Huxley, always set pondering by religious expression, stood before 'a strange fantastic sort of monument in this savage sanctuary'. Through his mind flashed fantastic images of 'horrible savage rites' and alien gods, yet the clearing seemed so still and 'utterly peaceful'. A great screen of mat was adorned by reddened spider shells and at its base 'flat stones of all shapes carved and painted with hideous human faces'. In the shade he sat down to sketch this ancestral funerary monument, pleasing the old man by his attention. It was haunting. 'I never shall forget the beauty of the place; while in it I felt as if listening to beautiful music'.

He came even closer to the dead on Darnley Island. Stanley refused to come ashore, but Huxley penetrated the coconut fringe on the 'bright white beach', passed clumps of 'shimmering bamboos' standing sentry, and entered the beautiful village of Mogoor. He wandered among the 'whimsical-looking beehive-shaped' huts and picked up trophies. His native minder 'had no objection to pilfer his ancestors' skulls and basely sell them'. Nor Huxley to buy them, of course. He came away with three.

The people were 'gentle and polite'. The women were treated kindly, and so were strangers. Huxley was offered a *coskeer*, a wife; not that Nettie needed to be jealous, with polygamy the norm throughout the Straits. Still it was ironic, for this was about the closest he would come to nuptial bliss in the southern hemisphere. While he refused a wife, MacGillivray accepted a new species of *cuscus*, brought in tame in a 'nice bamboo spindle-shaped cage'.[25] The old man who parted with it pleaded that it be cared for properly, but MacGillivray skinned it nevertheless. Wives and *cuscuses*: the white *marki* ghosts were showered with gifts. They were higher beings, and such they must have appeared, striking lucifer matches and shooting birds from the skies.

Bramble Key was the last island before New Guinea. They remained there for three days, stocking up. Some raided the tern colony for eggs. Others collected spinach; and 17 turtles were taken during the night as they plodded, exhausted, back to the sea after egg-laying. The massive reptiles, 280 lbs apiece, were manhandled aboard ship to be kept alive for food. The terns' eggs were a treat. But Huxley called the spinach 'filth' and the island something worse. 'Its hot, damp, muggy, rheumatic, disgusting, and abominable'.

Christmas dinner was better, a turtle feast during the thundery monsoon off Redscar Point in New Guinea. Then a post-prandial stroll on deck to admire the mountains. Rolling in an awful swell they had to drop a second anchor. Table-topped Mount D'Urville at 13,000 feet seemed to be adversely affecting the weather, as the disintegrating Stanley was affecting the crew. None was unhappy to leave. The *Bramble* stayed on to finish the survey, while the *Rattlesnake* cast off on 29 December, sailing back along the coast. As the new year 1850 rolled in they scudded east, all eyes astern, as clearing skies revealed majestic jungle-covered mountains up to 120 miles away.

Duchateau Island natives came alongside at dawn on 8 January, 'confound them', said Huxley, 'for they disturbed my slumbers'.[26] He had lost interest. Stanley had too. He finally cut southwards, to Sydney. 'Today finishes eight months' away, Huxley jotted. 'A month hence we must be in Sydney. I dare not think about it'.

8

Homesick Heroes

THE BRITTLE PERFECTIONIST was cracking. Captain Stanley looked ravaged and no one questioned his cut-and-run policy. He had been racked for months. The flood of anxieties, about the reefs, the savages, the safety of his crew and the worth of his work, had pushed the 'little man' to the brink. The crash came with horrifying violence.

Sailing away from the Louisiade he had a seizure, leaving him partly paralysed. As he dragged his leg, his mind began to wander. Then came the vitriolic outbursts. His 'waspish' temper 'became unbearable' and Thomson showed alarm as Stanley snapped heads off. The doctor pleaded with him to relinquish command or he 'could not feel . . . responsible for his life'.

Stanley's fastidiousness deserted him. He seemed not to care anymore, his mind gone, his body paralysed, his brother dead. He ignored badly charted wrecking-reefs in the Coral Sea. This, as MacGillivray said, was practically criminal for a surveyor with 17 chronometers on board.

The run to Sydney was painfully slow. Light winds dogged them. 'We have made about 600 miles in the last fortnight', Huxley logged on 24 January 1850; 'we are about 800 miles from Sydney, and might be there in a week. But so we might a week ago. Uncertainty and suspense seem my lot. Patience! Patience!' On 4 February they were still lying becalmed, 30 miles off Sydney Heads. Only six hours away but no breeze to blow them in. He had not heard from Nettie for five months and the frustration was showing. 'The Fates can surely not tantalize any longer'.[1]

These were the moments that Nettie dreamed of yet dreaded, as the *Rattlesnake* hove into sight. In her 'bitter fancies' she feared that he would not step off, that 'a letter black-edged and sealed' would arrive in his stead. It was her recurrent nightmare. 'The gnawing of despair . . . Oh God, whatever I deserve, avert this evil from me'.

But the *Rattlesnake* arrived and once more Hal stepped lively ashore. He had survived New Guinea. So had *Teoma*, now transformed into Mrs Thompson once more. She was reunited with her parents and Hal expected to find her a '"Lioness" in the good town of Sydney and a source of great glorification & turkey-cock gobbling for us'. Others were less fortunate. Stanley looked haggard. Staggering on deck to take the mail from a sombre Robert King he received another body blow, word from the Bishop's Palace that his father had died the previous September. He showed no sign of shock, but his anguished inner cry was almost his final one.

The captain had done his work. He had proved the absence of any stray reefs off New Guinea. He had taken the first step in opening these regions to the whalers and gold prospectors. But it was never enough for a man consumed. One desire 'rules all his actions', noted Thomson, and Huxley understood it well, 'the wish to rank amongst the . . . *savans* of England'. Scientific pre-eminence was the intellectual badge of a gentleman. It 'fills his mind by day and is the subject of his dreams by night'. But the captain was to be disappointed, the doctor recognized, for he is 'a superficialist in all his knowledge'.[2]

Hal stepped into the Sydney sun to find everything changed. Holmwood was abandoned and the Fannings already on the seas to England. Nettie was in the next cove, lodging with Mrs Griffiths at Woolloomooloo. He would troop the few hundred yards across the beautiful public gardens to meet her. Then 'we descended to the little summer house on the rocks and talked even to my heart's content of our home and all that we would make it'.[3]

They watched the ships as Hal caught up with nine months' news. He heard of the balls, the races, and the day Nettie came home to find the boozy cook setting the house on fire, the butler drunk in the road, the children covered in soap-suds and the baby smashing eggs on the bed. But what could a brewer's daughter expect in a tipsy ticket-of-leave society? By the water's edge she briefed him on the events half-a-world away: 'War, nothing but war', with Louis Napoleon's march into Rome to restore Pope Pius IX. Hatred of the Catholic French put her in mind of the new clergyman, who looked like 'a romish priest'. But her father's financial troubles at the brewery seemed more immediate – as did marriage.

Huxley was glad to be off the ship. After being parboiled in the gun-room for months he could let off steam. He enjoyed a wild dash with shipmates to Parramatta. Darwin had cantered here ten years earlier, taking the Great Western Road on the south side of Port Jackson. But his was a civilized jaunt with the stream of 'Carts Gigs, Phaetons & Horses'. Nothing so sedate for Huxley; he rowed over to the north shore and then cracked the whip, scattering swarms of green budgerigars.

> You can't fancy what a mad ride we had out here. We
> came up the North Shore way (about eight and twenty
> miles) in about 3 hours & a half galloping, jumping,
> singing and shouting like four 'wilde jäger' Luckily its a
> very solitary road and I don't think there were any
> spectators of our follies. If there had been they would
> certainly have imagined us just escaped from Tarban Creek
> [the local lunatic asylum].[4]

He was not always a quiet hot-head. Parramatta was a small town, with 17 pubs (he stayed in the 'commodious' Woolpark Inn), a racecourse, barracks and the notorious Female Factory, which had successfully turned generations of pilferers into 'alcoholic sluts'. Ships' surveyors routinely brought their chronometers for checking to the observatory at Parramatta, but Huxley's was no staid party cradling precision instruments.

The home news was of the usual pecuniary disasters. 'Poor Cooke', wailed George, 'he is in a desperate state. He has clung to teaching till it has entirely failed him ... they have the utmost difficulty to exist from day to day'. Rock-steady George was wailing about himself too. The crash of 1847 had wiped him out. Railway shares had collapsed, banks had folded, even the Bank of England was threatened: 'my fortune is gone', he told Tom. 'The panic ... knocked down my property to half its value. The French revolution in 1848 gave me another blow, and the very large sum I have advanced to the different members of the family to start them in the world not being forthcoming I am completely crippled'.

Huxley's sources of income were disappearing. And the moral pressure was building; his parents were leaning on George and James, but Jim too had run into difficulty and was cutting his 'allowance to the old folk one-5th'. Mother thought Tom ought to start contributing. Her 'claim is a moral one equally on all of us', George warned, even as he fought Tom's corner and pleaded that 'it was not fair till you had time to get clear'. But Tom felt the pressure. He could *not* get married, he *had* to earn. He had heard the word: McClatchie, back in England and visiting George, reported to 'D^r. Tom that your Brother looks on your matrimonial Alliance (*at present*) as an imprudent speculation'.

George continued to root for Tom and his strange science. 'You will have heard of the Bishop's death. I must try & get at his execs & learn if they had any papers of yours'.[5]

While Hal watched his pennies, Nettie's worries were other-worldly. On the surface all seemed smooth. The Sydney Heads 'with a thousand sun-sparkles' looked 'tenfold more beautiful' with Hal beside her. But there were emotional undercurrents, and sometimes the swell broke surface. At moments their eternal life arm-in-arm no longer seemed so secure:

> Oh if I only . . . felt assured that Death would be to us but a dark gate which led us to eternal happiness, what peace would possess me . . . And my friends – my Father, my Mother, the one believes not and the other believing is not so mindful of heavenly things as I would she were – and he, dear Hal – God guide him to the perfect light for I am often very unhappy about his sentiments – I have so much need of leading unto holy things . . . that I fondly hoped he would have been the guide and instructor unto more perfect ways – but here my hopes have borne bitter fruit. Something has come over me of late; I cannot pray as fervently as I did.

Her sombre thoughts would fly away as he arrived at the door. On 7 March they attended a ball at Government House, Huxley in his dress uniform and cocked hat, Nettie breathless: 'to dance . . . with him it is bewitching – he holds me so that I scarcely touch the ground – I danced incessantly but never once felt tired'. Other nights were spent at home. On 12 March 'We all had a round game of cards in which Hal most provokingly won all from me and asserted that his influence over me was so constant that it was exemplified even in the smallest things – then he impertinently whispered in my ear, "Give me a kiss". How his eyes flash sometimes!'[6] Then he ran across the Botanical Gardens to the ship.

*

Stanley was aboard. At 38 he was a pathetic sight, wizened, 'prematurely old'. He had written telling his widowed sister-in-law Eliza 'to lose no time in joining the ship'. He had fitted up her cabin and was comforted by their shared grief. Now he looked to London and a shore posting. High things were expected – an Admiralty desk was talked of, perhaps even Beaufort's at the Hydrography office. Of the last 26 years Stanley had spent 22 at sea, which was enough for one lifetime.

At daybreak the next morning, 13 March, he was found unconscious on his cabin floor. He had suffered an 'epileptic paralytic fit' and fallen on his head. Huxley cradled him, but there was nothing he could do. Stanley died in his arms at 7.40 am.

Waves of remorse struck the men as they realized what Stanley had been suffering. He had finished his survey in torment. 'But he died', Huxley wrote, with 'the end attained', and his epitaph was the thanks of endless mariners who were to thread their way through the maze of coral reefs. 'Which of us may dare to ask for more?'[7]

Sydney society shuttered its windows on 15 March. Flags were flown at half mast. HMS *Rattlesnake* had 'her yards a'cockbill [disorderly] and topped in opposite directions, instead of being quite square and trim'. The coffin was lowered into the pinnace, which proceeded across the harbour to the north shore, followed by boats bearing the cream of Sydney society. A visiting ship in port, HMS *Meander*, fired a 38 gun salute, one for each year of his life. Ashore Huxley proceeded behind the coffin, the *Meander*'s band playing a dirge, and Revd Robert King read the service.

The next day, Huxley was in church again. On 16 March Nettie's half-sister Isabel was married. Nettie was somewhat disapproving, with Isy an old maid of 38 and her husband 20. But Hal acted 'Papa' and gave the bride away, even if he sat in the pew (as always foul tempered during church services) uttering 'the greatest absurdities in the gravest possible manner'. Here he met Nettie's mother for the first time, and 'so "snaked"' her 'that she was deep in her praises of him'.

It highlighted his own problems. Hal told his mother that he had made up his mind: 'I determined that we should be terribly prudent and get married about 1870, or the Greek Kalends, or, what is about the same thing, whenever I am afflicted with the *malheur de richesses*'. If sudden wealth, or at least a steady job, was the desideratum, then another piece of tittle-tattle raised his hope:

I heard from an old messmate of mine at Haslar the other day that Dr. MacWilliam, F.R.S., one of our deputy-inspectors, had been talking about one of my papers, and gave him to understand that it was to be printed. Furthermore, he is a great advocate for the claims of assistant surgeons to ward-room rank, and all that sort of stuff, and, I am told, quoted me as an example! Henceforward I look upon the learned doctor as a man of sound sense and discrimination! . . . I find myself getting horribly selfish, looking at everything with regard to the influence it may have on my grand objects.[8]

The time for leaving was drawing close. After Stanley's death the last survey was abandoned. Huxley had his wish, to get home early, but not in the way he expected. Yule had taken command, with orders to proceed directly to England by the fastest route. His appointment by the *Meander*'s captain infuriated Sydney's naval commander, who considered this his prerogative. It left Yule jittery and unsure of his position, and eager to be off.

The dam of pent-up emotion was continually breached in these fraught days. A teasing Hal made Nettie cry by taking back his miniature. ''Twas so mean of him'. 'I could cry that I shall not clasp it tonight as usual'. He 'was tyrannizing – he knew I could refuse him nothing'. Two days later a box arrived for her and there it was, 'set in a pretty little locket which I could wear. I kissed it again and again . . . I was so very very happy and yet I could not stop my tears'.[9]

He was an emotional despot. But she was angelically susceptible to 'those strange piercing glances which, odious snake, he has never yet found to fail'. Glances like Medusa's own: 'I wish to talk but your eyes wont let me', she once complained. 'Hal, dear Hal . . . You draw out my thoughts and feelings – and appropriate them most tyrannically – and yet 'tis perhaps one of the things that has bound me with stronger love to you. You *are* a tyrant still conquering by strength where influence fails'.

In their last weeks together the idyll was tainted by flashes of the future. The frustration showed in his capricious moods, fitful one minute, fond the next. There were stolen kisses as Mr Griffiths went out to smoke his cigar, and more on a drive under the pretext of taking the children out.[10] It was a time for parting presents, a turtleshell comb from the islands, and a daguerreotype taken by Thomson, showing Hal in his uniform.

He handed over his diary, his account of the Coral Sea inferno and New Guinea natives. 'It tells of the wanderings of a man among all varieties of human life', he explained, 'from the ballroom among the elegancies and soft nothings of society to the hut of the savage and the grand untrodden forest. It should tell more. It should tell of the wider and stranger wanderings of a human soul, now proud and confident, now sunk in bitter despondency – now so raised above its own coarser nature by the influence of a pure and devoted love'. But it was a history of the outer man, not of his inner soul.

One inner feeling now clouded his thoughts. It 'hangs like an incubus over me'. For two or three years they would not see one another, and the cloud would 'remain until the dreaded separation is over, and Hope has again become the only possible comforter'. She cried at the thought of it. 'Three years – they seem immeasurable – how often will my heart sicken and long to rejoin him and know it must wait and weary'.

At times they were paralysed by emotion. Doubt vied with desire. Hal would go gloomy, his moods swinging, fearing the failure of his scientific plans, fearing they might drift apart in the storms of life and love. He poured out his heart, worrying about 'having overrated his ability'. And should he fail, he asked Nettie 'if I w^d still . . . esteem him as before – for said he to be loved from compassion would be unbearable'. Money, he had to make the future promise it. It was the straw he clung to as the moment of parting came. Science had to pay.

Near the end they were constantly together, riding, dining, cuddling on the rocks. The storm clouds broke on Saturday 27 April, the 'bitter day'. A sailor brought word that the ship was to sail on the Tuesday. Hal led Nettie quietly into the drawing room to prepare her. 'I have not cried today', she jotted on Sunday 28 April, 'but the heaviness at my heart seems to weigh me down – and I am so cold'.[11]

They sneaked a few hours alone on Monday night. 'Every now & then as I sat talking,' Hal wrote, 'the thought that I had to part from you shot through me like a cold pain'. 'I could have fallen on your neck and wept like a child'. The next morning he sent gifts, more turtle combs, copies of Carlyle, 'a letter for you written in the days of desolation on the New Guinea coast', and a note declaring that 'I never knew how much I loved you, dearest, till last night'.

It was clear the sailing would be delayed but 'I . . . dare not come ashore again. If I did I should never leave you. I would have given the world last night to return and lay my head upon your dear shoulder once more, and give you one more long, long embrace'.

Nettie spent a tearful Tuesday watching 'the old ship from the verandah' through a glass. By night she could see the square-rigger out in the bay with 'all the little boats clustering like busy ants around it'. She watched the endless provisioning 'in a kind of stupor'.[12]

He broke his vow and ran over for the last time, on Wednesday night. But the moment of farewell was strained. Both knew the years of painful separation that lay ahead. They tried to smile and disguise the inner hurt, but 'there was something horribly absurd in our doing so'. Nettie handed him her diary – and he was suddenly gone, leaving her savouring his 'dear words and dearer kisses'.

Huxley ran from Woolloomooloo 'in a strange unnatural state of excitement'. Ran mindlessly, breathing fast, confused, fearing that he would miss the ship, wanting to. The 'exertion seemed cooling & calming to me and I was collected enough by the time I got on board'.[13]

Everything was chaos. The ship was crammed, with invalid marines from the abandoned Port Essington, the *Bramble*'s crew, wives and children. Mrs Charles Stanley in black was mourning the old captain, and Mrs Yule was accompanying the new. They were sailing overcrowded, with upwards of 230 people on board.

That night the loading continued. Officers barked, sailors swore, shouts of 'One, two, three – haul!' accompanied the crash of cargo in the hold. The last crates of goats, chickens and ducks were winched on. The frigate seemed more like a farmyard. Screeching cockatoos and parrots were brought aboard, and the usual quota of cats and dogs. 'All was in confusion – visitors, duns & dirt were everywhere'. An inebriated MacGillivray staggered 'on board in the middle of the night & was put under arrest – his wife and child came about 2 A. M. '

Hal went to bed only to toss and turn, and before he knew it 'about ½ past seven we began to get the anchor up'. He too was straining with his spy glass. 'I watched you in the verandah this morning', he jotted in one last note, handed to a departing boat. 'Good bye – God bless you my own darling'.[14]

It was a scorching morning on 2 May 1850 as they waved goodbye to the crowds on Farm Cove. The sea was glassy. Then a 'breath of wind came hot as from a kiln from the northwest, the sails were loosed and we were on *our way home*'.

'I went up on the poop and found several who like myself had come to take a last look'. There was Mrs Stanley, tall and sombre in black. The laden ship pulled out slowly. They passed Woolloomooloo Bay. Hal desperately trained his signalman's glass on the houses and saw Nettie on the balcony:

> with glass directed towards the old ship. Did she see me? I know not. All I know is that the figure stayed there until we were far down the harbour . . . I watched & watched until we were between the heads and then as the house now a white speck was shut in by the south head I turned away and saw no more of Sydney. I said to myself that I had done with looking back. Goodbye Sorrow, come Hope.
>
> And therefore I went down with Simpson to have a glass of champagne – &, silently, I drank to *our* success & happy reunion.[15]

He watched as first Port Jackson and then the coast itself vanished. 'I saw the last of the land of Australia . . . a dark grey line along the horizon backed by as splendid a sky as ever the setting sun lighted up'.

> We part friends, O land of gum trees. I have much, much to thank you for.[16]

Yule stood on the bridge, making haste to retain his bars. He still feared being intercepted and replaced. 'At sunset the lookout man was specially ordered to turn his regards astern – he could see no sail & I think that now Cap Yule begins to think himself safe & breathes easily'.

Huxley had become an old salt, pronouncing on the passengers like a hardened sea dog. With children running everywhere, he relished the squalls. 'All the women save Mrs Stanley below & all the children sick – thank God'. Perhaps not relished; his 25th birthday was a washout, with water slopping in his cabin. 'Such a vile night – half a gale of wind – the ship rolling heavily and no sleep to be had. Oh the vile odour, oh the noises!' The preserved meats were giving off a stench again, not that he could concentrate

on this olfactory offence for the din of creaking bulkheads, screeching parrots and swearing sailors.

The talk was of them heading for Chile to fix the leaking stern-
post. It might not sink the ship but it certainly spoiled the biscuits.
The storms kept the 'ladies all thoroughly done up – or rather
down & invisible'. But when they eased, one 'good lady' Mrs
Crawford threatened more damage with her singing. The cacophony inspired the dogs and then the parrots joined in. The
desperate middies got up a fiddle and fife session to drown her
out, 'but the remedy was as bad as the disease'.[17]

To the old salts' disgust they had turned into a passenger liner.
Some fell to the 'seaman's snare'. MacGillivray staggered the
decks, clutching a bottle rather mournfully. Or he could be found
'moralising as he sat contemplating himself in his looking-glass.
Ah Jock! You're up to your old tricks again tonight'.[18] It disgusted
his old drinking mate.

The reality of sea life was ever present. On 6 May one of the
forecastle men died of blood poisoning in Huxley's sick bay. He
had scratched himself with a splint of bone on serving the beef. It
seemed nothing, but he was dead within days. Huxley felt helpless
as he reflected on the doctor's culpability: 'am I not more or less
guilty of this man's death from want of knowledge? The responsibility of the physician is something fearful'. Who would doubt the
need for a more practical physiology, or a greater reward to spur
on its devotees? But for now there was an awful fatalism to his
job. 'We shall have two or three more deaths before reaching
England. It is distressing to pass men and know that their doom is
already fixed, they, poor fellows, unconscious as sheep before the
shambles'. Mercifully he was distant from the men. It was the
same in the haybarn all those years ago, when he sat alone. Now it
was so in the sick bay.

In his candlelit berth he sat in solitary splendour. He devoured
the Whig historian Thomas Babington Macaulay's epigrammatic
Essays in between drawing up classificatory charts linking all
known invertebrates. Or he indulged in imaginary chit-chat with
Nettie. A sleepless, gale-tossed 48 hours was lost reading her
journal. He followed her innermost feelings, 'of the aching that
gnaws within my heart ... but you know dearest by your own
heart all the agony I feel. Let us rather turn to the bright future
than dwell over the sad present'. So violently was the tub rolling
that the water was up to his knees. He 'did not have to go down
"the rocks" to my bath in the morning but stepped out of bed

1. (*Above*) The earliest known daguerreotype of Tom Huxley, as a medical student in the early 1840s.

2. (*Inset*) Huxley's self-portrait as a student: 'a very pale, thin, lanky, ugly body with dreadfully long hair'.

3. (*Right*) *Punch's* satire on the dissipated 'sons of the scalpel'.

METAPHYSICS.

4. Charing Cross Hospital about 1840. It is the triangular building on the right, seen from the Strand.

5. The studious Huxley, aged twenty, possibly in his Agar Street lodgings.

"am I not a man + a brother?"

6. (*Above*) The newly-commissioned sailor in October 1846, billeted in the 'Hulks' (the old prison ships in Portsmouth harbour), while the *Rattlesnake* was fitted out.

7. (*Right*) Assistant Surgeon Huxley, RN.

8. HMS *Rattlesnake* off Sydney Heads.   9. (*Inset*) Henrietta Heathorn, a brewer's daughter in the convict colony. This portrait was painted by Thomas Griffiths Wainewright the Poisoner.

10. Hacking through the snagging scrub with Kennedy's light party. The nearest figure is Kennedy, the next Huxley.

11. (*Above*) The gallery of Huxley's Museum in Piccadilly.

12. (*Opposite, above*) Huxley raging against the world - or at least the *Pall Mall Gazette*, with Tyndall looking on in trepidation.

13. (*Opposite, below*) The Irish physicist John Tyndall, whose own flamboyant pantheism caused a storm. Tyndall and Huxley 'formed a sort of firm' in the public mind.

14. (*Above*) The hawk-eyed Huxley in 1857.

15. (*Left*) Tom and Nettie on their honeymoon. Never a moment lost, Huxley spent it dredging in Tenby Bay, South Wales.

right into it'.[19] The crew wanted to put 'into New Zealand to have this vile leak in the after gunroom stopped, but Yule is afraid of being intercepted I believe and wont take a hint'.

Huxley was now squelching in his shoes and joined the others in making a formal complaint. They had been due to sail past the mountainous cliffs on New Zealand's northern tip, but at the North Cape Yule relented and turned for the Bay of Islands, by Cape Brett. Albatrosses heralded their passage down the coast and after dark on 16 May they entered the Bay.

The next morning the ship anchored off Russell. It gave Huxley an unexpected look at New Zealand. The village was pleasant, with a luxuriant, fern-covered backdrop. (Its 30-odd houses were new, and this 'calm & peaceful' feel belied the fact that Chief Heki had gutted the original settlement five years earlier during the Maori War.) Ashore Huxley found the tattooed Maoris a fierce and 'athletic' people, although the women's 'gaudy cotton prints' looked incongruous. Eyre, drained of his 'warmth and colour' by the Australian wastelands, was Lieutenant Governor of the colony, but still sympathetic to the people and, indeed, married himself in a double Maori ceremony.

During recaulking Huxley's party took the cutter 11 miles up the high-banked Kidi Kidi river. For the last two miles a Maori boy guided them, or rather took a 'cross cut' through endless bogs, 'dancing on' ahead as they lumbered through the swamps. But the result was worth it: 80-foot waterfalls, with a huge cave sculpted by the pounding water, its floor and walls a dense carpet of luxuriant ferns and mosses.

But Huxley was more engrossed in the missions than the *manuka* bushes. He wanted to find out 'what missionary life was like' for himself. So he trudged on ten miles to the mission centre at Waimate. A forced pace in the 'chill & bracing' air, through 'fine country . . . covered everywhere with high ferns', put him there by moonlight on 18 May. It was a school and church station of 40 whites and many Maoris, including the great Heki himself. He was welcomed with '*tea unlimited* and a blazing fire' and was 'agreeably surprised' by the missionaries. He had expected a certain '*straight-hairedness* . . . & methodistical puritanism but I find it quite otherwise'. They were 'quiet, unpretending, straightforward folks desirous of doing their best for the people among whom they are placed'. Much of their straight-hair had been torn out, as they were outwitted by the wily Maoris. Old chiefs, prompted on the temporal benefits of Christianity, would reply, 'You've forgotten the big rats', the ships' rats running amok, a parry that appealed to Huxley. Still, with a log fire and a rat-catching cat on his lap, he found even a mission homely.

He returned to the ship in torrential rains, muddy and bedraggled, 'my horse & I went head over heels together' down a clay bank, he explained. But it did not dampen his enthusiasm: 'I like the look of New Zealand'.[20]

The *Rattlesnake* raced on south-east, towards Cape Horn on the tip of South America. No Homeric heroes, these, returning the adventurous way. Every man-jack wanted a hasty end to the ordeal. The homesick sailors had one thought in mind, English soil beneath their squelchy shoes. Spirits were buoyant. Huxley and Thomson paced the deck, lost in plans. Thomson was returning to the baby he had never seen, Huxley to uncertainty. After four years as surgeon and mate their heart-to-heart threw up the unspoken truths. Huxley had a great respect for the man, but 'my hot temper had not always permitted me to act with perfect justice towards him and though we never quarrelled, I felt as I told him that was more owing to his even & amiable disposition than to my deserts'.

Johnny Thomson met him more than half-way. He was awed by his assistant's cynical wit and cutting brilliance. Thomson faced down his own pride to admit, as Huxley wrote in his diary, 'that although placed by the service as my superior he had never forgotten that I had far the advantage in intellect and knowledge'. Huxley, flattered, disclaiming 'in sorrow how untrue it was', nonetheless recorded it. He was getting the measure of his worth.

But would the world recognize it? For days he planned his first London moves. It took gall for an assistant surgeon to dictate terms to the Sea Lords. He would go to Sir William Burnett and request a year's shore posting to write a book on his oceanic men-of-war. And still richer, 'I shall tell him that I cannot afford to lose a . . . year's pay'. Therefore 'will he manage the matter so that I may be nominally attached to some naval Hospital'. In short, he wanted half pay for an indefinite leave, with no duties! Huxley for his part would ask this on condition that the great guns – Owen and Forbes – vouched for his work.

Of course, 'living in London may be a *poser*', certainly on three shillings a day. But nothing daunted, he could lodge with George. Who knew? By the end of 1851, when the *Rattlesnake* was originally due to return, he might have a book in press.

It was getting cold now. But the moon in June looked a little lovelier for the luciferous *Pyrosoma* 'shining like white hot cylinders in the water'. Millions of them – the 'fire-body' *Pyrosoma* was another sea squirt, with its hard cylinder wall covered by luminous buds. The ship ploughed through them, phosphorescing like 'lesser moons'. It induced a trance: the sea glowed and dimmed, as if approaching and receding. Waves of 'soft bluish light' spread out 'as far as the eye could reach on every side'. But the moment he dropped a net in 'they dived down' and, millions or no, he ended up with a single specimen.[21] Still that was enough to let him finish his sea squirt paper for the Royal Society.

As they approached Cape Horn the weather worsened. Hail pounded the ship. Snow fell on 23 June – the first seen by the voyagers in four years – light flurries to start, and then blinding sheets. Huxley had bounced from an orchid-house to an ice-store and expected to shatter. The bitterness was 'nipping me up into a sort of animated mummy'. He became bluer and stiffer with each league. The ship began to freeze; the decks disappeared under snow, and ice hung in 'great stalactites about our bows'.

They were to 'double the dread cape' in mid-winter. The sun struggled only 10° above the horizon and gave no heat. Huxley's teeth chattered; wrapped in Nettie's 'beautiful comforter & wristbands', bundled in his great-coat, he determinedly stamped the deck for two or three hours a day. Out there, in the snow, with a lashing spray, the wooden tub seemed a pitiful liferaft in the icy vastness. It was 'desperately cold' now, 22°, with a fierce wind from the Antarctic.

Mrs Stanley was confined to her cabin and he would pop in to check on her. She might have seemed a vulgar parvenu in the Bishop's Palace but, an upstart himself, Huxley found her cultured and well-read, which counted above blood-line. He cared for her budgerigars, and she lent him 'Lamartine's Histoire des Girondins to say nothing of "Mary Barton"', with its evocative 'descriptions of the working classes in manufacturing towns', which he knew so well from his Coventry childhood.[22]

After rounding the Horn against glacial blasts and ferocious waves, the *Rattlesnake* beat up the Patagonian coast to the most desolate of colonial outposts. They anchored in the Falklands on an icy 8 July. The 'Ultima Thule', this, 'and no mistake'. The bleakness of Port Stanley was heightened by a snow-blanket over the treeless wastes. 'How can I describe to you "Stanley" the sole town, metropolis & seat of government'? he asked Nettie. 'It consists of a lot of black low half weatherboard houses, scattered along the hill sides . . . One barn-like place is Government House', another was the squalid barracks of the pensioned Irish soldiers, 'fretting to death' and bitter at having been duped into serving in such a godforsaken hole.

Here was Captain Sulivan, Darwin's old messmate on the *Beagle*. He had surveyed the islands and was now settled here, trying to make a living raising cattle, while shipping Darwin South American fossils. He is a 'fine energetic man', Huxley admitted, but to bring his wife 'to such a desolate place' verged on cruelty. The town was an abomination. The weather was no better. It was one of the most savage winters on record. The thermometer fell to 18° at night and the water froze as the ratings swabbed the decks. 'The only thing to be done is to eat, eat, eat'. To keep body and soul together, 'You consume a pound or so of beefsteak at breakfast and then walk the decks for an appetite at dinner, when you take another pound or two of beef or a goose . . . By four o'clock it is dark night – and as it is too cold to read the only thing to be done is to vanish under blankets as soon as possible and take twelve or fourteen hours sleep'.[23]

To add to his misery he caught mumps as they sailed. He lay in his bunk for ten days, cogitating on existence and calculating his extortion of the Admiralty's coffers. Letter posting became a serendipitous affair. If the lookout spotted a ship Huxley scribbled one on the chance that it could be sent aboard. Off Montevideo on 8 August they passed the *Phoenician*, 44 days out of England and Sydney bound, and Hal rushed a dozen lines.

Late August saw them back in the tropics, 'bowling along at a fine pace'. Through great sheaths of floating gulf weed they ploughed, 'a world in itself', full of shells, pipefish and planktonic crustaceans. Hal was back where he started, pulling in purple Atlantic *Velellae*. England was now only weeks away. He could visualize the great Babylon. 'I long to be home'.[24]

By October 1850, after voyaging 40,000 miles, they were less than three weeks from Plymouth. Neptune blew a 'splendid westerly gale' and the ship buzzed with excitement. There was a spring in every Jack's step, packing and crating, preparing trophies and tall stories – and reflecting. Almost four years they had been away. They had seen the ends of the earth, stood on blistering coral sands, fought through snagging gum scrub, swum in Papuan lagoons, been greeted as *marki* ghosts. They were 'about the last voyagers', Huxley supposed, who would meet 'people who knew nothing of fire-arms'.

He gazed at his 'ugly phiz' in the mirror. It was sunburnt and bearded and told a tale. Every man was returning 'his own Columbus', with stories of 'a southern cloud-land full of strange wonders'.

They thought on friends who had not returned. In the sick room he had stared death in the face so often. He had seen sailors succumb to pleurisy, blood poisoning and disease. He had held dying men in his arms, the skipper among the last. And yet for all of medicine's grave responsibility, he was not committed to the healing art so much as to a helping science, and a more material way to salvation.

He thought of his early censure of the crew, and how unjust he had been: after all, 'they turned out very good fellows'. But it was a different ship now – Yule commanding, MacGillivray splicing the main brace, his middies grown men and looking to commissions of their own. But it remained a microcosm of aristocratic tyranny, like a floating Tsar's court in an age that had dispensed with despots. Still, the 'Service has done me a world of good by case hardening me – knocking me about until I don't mind kicks'. It strengthened his self-discipline, while years of waking up 'on a soft plank, with the sky for canopy and cocao and weevily biscuit the sole prospect for breakfast' gave him a new appreciation of the civilized luxuries.

Landlubbers knew nothing of sailors' privations: they who must 'submit more strictly than Dominican or Franciscan to the three monastic vows – who see for months no civilized faces, but their own tanned and bearded visages – who feast with the thermometer at 90°, upon salt-junk, and (*horribile dictù*) three-water grog'. Like any swab he had sunk to the depths; he had sailed through hell, only to be saved by the girl with hair of 'Australian silk'. He had suffered loneliness verging on desperation. He had gone for months without letters, without knowing whether England's rookeries had blown themselves apart in a Chartist Revolution. Now he was coming home to a settled land: Jim reassured him that the country had steered wide of the European revolutions and, what 'is vastly to the credit of our liberal system of government, has escaped all internal broils herself'.[25] The storms had blown over.

He had gone out 'sick of the world, of its petty intrigues, its lesser and greater selfishnesses & dirt-eating' and found kindness in the colonies. He had voyaged in search of security, and found it.

Nettie's emotional support came with a ray of Australian sunshine. Sydney had turned the introvert about. The long-hair who never danced and shunned parties left the city adept at the light fantastic. 'People tell me, that I am full of fun that they cannot look at me without imagining some joke is going on'. But 'they only see my head'; inside nothing had changed. The heart 'still belongs to the poor proud student and longs, surely longs for the quiet home – the wifes dear smile and all the prattle of the fire side'.[26]

The poor proud student gazed at more than his own grizzled phiz. Staring back were his three savage skulls from Darnley Island. Here was his most enduring memory: of naked Papuans, 'Man-eaters and sorcerers', as the old travellers said, 'among whom divels walke familiarly'. And so it seemed from their fiendish looks, the mop of 'frizzled hair' and 'huge plaited pigtail' strung with teeth. But whatever the sinister human-jawed armlets, Huxley had faced no demons. He had found only villagers, friendly and gentle. The Papuans' 'kind treatment of their women', their pottery and canoe building and the 'grace of design displayed in their carved works' showed a 'capacity for development'. Was this how the 'growing science of Ethnology' should deal with these charcoal-painted people, as 'essentially children' growing towards the civilized ideal?

He had fewer kind thoughts about Australia's 'hopelessly irreclaimable savages'. He recalled *Teoma*'s horror at the infanticide and decapitation, and thought darkly on the men who had killed Kennedy. Had the Papuans and aborigines sprung from the same peoples, who swept down from Asia? What to do with Australia's savages? He pondered this in a barbarous mood. He had no truck with the philanthropic evangelicals and their 'Aborigines Protection Society'. No good could come from these bleeding hearts peddling their paper, the *Aborigines Friend*. Australia's nomads were blind to the Victorian ideals of private property, free-trade and Piccadilly fashion. His squatter's morality was evident; his final solution smugly horrifying. Their 'elimination . . . from the earth's surface can be viewed only with satisfaction, as the removal of a great blot from the escutcheon of our common humanity, by all those who know them as they are, and are not to be misled by the maudlin philanthropy of "aborigines' friends"'.

Genocide and progress were ugly bedfellows. Yet this was the 25 year-old who lamented even more the missionaries' coming. The superficiality of his contact, which bred thoughts of genocide, also led to reflections on the gentle New Guinea people. He looked with 'sadness to the time ... when the peaceful idyllic simplicity of a life without care and without reproach, such as glides along in these Papuan Isles – the very Paradise of Lotus Eaters – ... shall be defaced by the obtrusion of the Polynesian "scourge of God" – the white man. To substitute what? "The blessings of civilization" – which means for the dark race, labour, care, drunkenness, disease, and ultimate subjection and extinction'.

As he peered into the future the arcadia vanished: the islands were 'one vast "witness," that it were better for the Papuans to "walk familiarly with the devils" they have' than face the white man's demons.[27]

Other mementos littered his cabin: the carved turtleshell, remnants of molluscs and sea ferns. The ship had gone out with treasure for the colonists and come back with the empire's riches. Its hold was crammed with sequined sunbirds and glorious honey-eaters, beauty enough to grace Gould's *Birds of Australia*. MacGillivray had his crates of bats and bowers, his pin-boards of butterflies, boxes of snails and a pickle-emporium of crabs and molluscs. All were ready to be described, named and claimed by London's zoological specialists. They were bringing back the biggest haul of tropical 'corrallines' ever to reach Britain – a mix of sea firs, plumed hydroids, stalked organisms with hundreds of connected stinging-celled polyps along their arms, and twig-like moss animals.[28] As the ship sailed on the Gulf Stream, Huxley pondered these composite creatures. The simpler the animals the stranger the question. Was the tiny tentacled polyp or the whole fan-like plume the individual? Were these colonies, or one individual with a thousand waving buds?

He had his knotty questions. He had his notebooks. He had gone out with his 'proud oversensitive, and totally undisciplined mind' and learned to knuckle down to hard work.[29] He had brought back 180 sheets of drawings, and page after page of salty, sweaty description of diaphanous sea nettles and planktonic molluscs, of the blood system of transparent crustaceans, of the anomalous bristle-jawed arrow-worms, of two new orders of sea squirts and 40 genera of jellyfish – enough for a career, but could a career be carved out of such things? Security came not only from love, but from intellectual success. Could he make enough money from science to bring Nettie over? And what *had* been the reception of the papers he had posted home?

He looked ahead with trepidation. The family news boded ill: George doubted he would 'see the Old Man again'. His father was frail after 'an apoplectic fit' and not expected to live. The feeling against the Salts was as strong as the day he left. Tom's mother had lost all sympathy after Salt 'beggared Miss Knight' (borrowing more money). Then Jim sent word that Lizzie and Salt had lost a baby boy 'under very distressing circumstances'.[30] In four years Tom had not had a line from America and he longed for news.

He hardly knew what England held. And he had 'been leading such a semi-savage life for years past' that he wondered if he would ever settle down. He was candid with his mother. 'Time was when I should have looked upon our return with unmixed joy; but so many new and strong ties have arisen to unite me with Sydney . . . You must not be angry, my dear Mother; I have none the less affection for you . . . only a very great deal for a certain little lassie whom I must leave behind me'. 'We have . . . a thousand difficulties in our way, but like Danton I take for my motto, "De l'audace et encore de l'audace et toujours de l'audace"'.

And audacity brought him back to the Sea Lords. He was ready to lay down the law to the gold braid. With the new meritocratic ethos sweeping medicine, he was looking for promotion as a reward for scientific excellence. He had to make money from science to bring Nettie over. Few had done it before. Wealthy gents were philosophers by vocation, disdaining pay with its taint of trade. But times were changing; a new generation was coming out of London's medical schools, out of the godless college in Gower Street, the sons of industrialists, merchants and Dissenters, defiant against Oxbridge and the old paternalist order. They could turn a penny if they could make science a new profession.

As the ship scudded along Huxley's thoughts turned and turned again to Nettie. He clung to her image, the only fixed point in his shifting world. When would he see her 'Saxon yellow hair' again? He reread her letters, red-lining them where her 'little heart speaks out'. He also kept another secret memento, in memory of their first dances: that wine-red camellia.

Zephyrs chased them across the North Atlantic, a calm end to a tempestuous voyage. The gentle breeze 'bids fair to carry us home'.[31]

1850–1858

Lost in the Wilderness

9

The Scientific Sadducee

NOT FOR HUXLEY the mariner's folly, flipping guineas into the deep to thank Neptune for deliverance. But emotionally he was just as extravagant. After the long homeward haul the very rigging quivered with excitement. All hands strained for a sight of industrial Devonport. At last, on 23 October 1850, its smoke-stacks appeared over the horizon. After 40,000 miles on a jury-rigged, rotting scuttle-bucket, through hell-and-high-water, past interminable reefs and endless little Englands, he was back.

That day he 'saw English green fields' for the first time in four years. Not that he noticed, firing off letters, asking 'news of a certain naughty sister of mine', Lizzie in Tennessee. By now Yule had a ship full of impatient souls. Beating up the Channel, they were dogged by contrary winds and chased by the blue devils.[1] But Huxley put the time to use, planning his naval blockade of the Admiralty.

Past the White Cliffs his spine stiffened. He drew up a report for the hydrographer Sir Francis Beaufort. Another went to Sir John Richardson listing his discoveries, asking about 'a nominal appoint-ment' to a Thames ship in order to write them up. Officers routinely went on half pay until they were recalled.[2] But what surgeon's mate had the gall to dictate stronger terms to the Sea Lords? He wanted to remain on leave, and on half pay until he had finished. Nothing less would do.

They put in at Sheerness docks, ten miles down river from Chatham. More dusty grainstores and cranes, bluecoats and bark-ing officers – and the first real feeling he had arrived: 'I was standing in the midst of a group busily talking . . . when I felt my arm touched and lo! there stood my brother James'. It was the same

149

fierce-eyed Jim, mistaken by everyone on board for Tom, 'chuckling at having been the first to see me'. His asylum was close by, in Maidstone, and he had caught the ferry down to intercept the *Rattlesnake*. 'I ran away with him for five minutes' and 'returned to the ship not quite sure whether I had been dreaming or not'.

Finally, on 2 November, after nine days slow hauling, the old frigate moved up to Chatham and to our 'joy, we found ourselves fairly at home'. Here were more friends; first to come aboard was his old friend Archie McClatchie, engaged to Nettie's friend Alice. He looked 'stout and is happy as the day is long', but then he had written for Alice to come, 'Happy Dog!' At McClatchie's another pinch roused Tom from his dream. A servant 'announced "Mr Huxley"' and in strode 'no other than my Brother George & Polly'. Polly was a sight for sore eyes, 'prettier than ever', clutching at him and fussing, lost in emotion and insisting that he come and live with them. The party migrated over to Jim's that night, where the celebrations really began. 'How we talked!' – and the questioning, about the savages, Australia, but most of all Nettie. They were all ears for Tom's tales. Everyone agrees 'that the cruise has done me a world of good'. The sunburnt sea dog was 'voted by acclamation the *handsomest of the family* Ahem!' The mariner had returned, 25 years old, feeling considerably more ancient. The absence had affected his heart too; 'they seem to me to be more likeable than they used to', he said. But then he guessed that the change was 'chiefly in myself'.

His father had survived, although he hardly recognized his son. Nothing had prepared Tom for the sight. He went to London on Monday and found him 'dreadfully altered' and 'mentally an utter wreck'. 'It is painful to me to look at him'. Tom's mother had lost her front teeth and sunken cheeks aged her. Otherwise she was 'just the same amusing, nervous, distressingly active old lady'.[3]

Others recalled times past. The stories about Cooke were true: 'The Doctor is fat & bloated as a prize pig'. At 39 he was burned out. It pulled Tom up to see the plump doctor in lean times, working himself to death, easing his pains with beer and opium. 'I am told that for the past four or five years they have been on the verge of penury'.[4] It reinforced Tom's image of science as adversity; of London as a rich man's arena. With no jobs for men of science, few students enrolled in courses and poor teachers could not survive on the fees. Cooke was a sorry proof that professing science did not pay. Huxley saw the steep climb ahead.

*

Yet everywhere seemed more salubrious. Wide streets, white stone, the West End oozed prosperity. His old haunts were now full of imperial buildings: Nelson stood on his column in Trafalgar Square, Whitehall was becoming the hub of empire. The Gothic Houses of Parliament were positively exuberant. The new Lords was 'magnificent', 'it looks like an Indian Cabinet'. The modern Babylon thrived on its self-importance. A Great Exhibition was about to gloat on it, and the huge glass-curtain Crystal Palace housing the exhibits was already under construction in Hyde Park. Steam enveloped everything: King's Cross and Paddington stations were in the making. Travellers fought through the throng of 'gay' girls at the new Waterloo station to take their first train ride to the seaside at Brighton. Traffic might snarl up on smoggy November streets, but still everything was dizzyingly fast: having waited months for letters he could hardly cope with ten posts a day. After the loneliness of the sea Huxley faced tidal 'waves of people silently surging' down streets. Perhaps this faceless anonymity was worse. Certainly the 'solitude of men seems a greater threat than the wilds I have been used to'.[5]

He rushed with the crowd, calling at the Admiralty, cap in hand. Sir William Burnett was 'ready and willing to do anything' – which meant passing him along to Beaufort. Sir Francis was ready and willing, except to dip into the Admiralty's coffers. Huxley moaned that the Sea Lords 'approved my plans, patted me on the back' and turned him down flat. Where Darwin, the privately-financed companion to Captain FitzRoy, received £1,000 after a nod to the Chancellor from his Cambridge tutor John Stevens Henslow – enough to buy the experts to write his lavish five-volume *Zoology* of the *Beagle* voyage – the surgeon's mate was denied £300. Beaufort hoped he would write a book 'creditable to himself, to his late Captain . . . and to Her Majesty's service'. Huxley choked on the words: 'Publish if you can, and give us credit for granting every facility except the one means of publishing'.[6]

How to move from surgery to pure science, with no means? He was not a member of the gentry, living off his railway shares, like Darwin. He had no Tory patrons, like Richard Owen. Huxley had to make his way on a servant's pay of 6s 6d a day. It would hardly buy him into big-time science. Even less would it subsidize a tome on the man-of-war, winning him a paying position and Nettie's passage over. Such treatises were inordinately expensive. The 150 engravings in Darwin's *Zoology* had soaked up his £1,000; Owen was to cost his work on the extinct giant sloths at £700. Six and sixpence would not even settle old scores – and this was the rub. Having sent endless cheques home, Huxley arrived to find himself *still* £100 in debt.[7]

Back at the ship came better news. It was from the breezy naturalist Edward Forbes, the Geological Survey teacher who had shown him how to dredge. Huxley warmed to the erratically brilliant Forbes, a man free from the 'besetting sins' of pedantry and jealousy. No mortal was a more curious mix: a mollusc expert who cheered Huxley's 'diametrically opposed' notions; an Anglican idealist who could sympathize with 'a wounded spirit tortured by unbelief'. He was a paradox, a bon viveur who straddled the divides. And Huxley welcomed his outstretched hand: 'Up to his eyes in work he never grudges his time if it be to help a friend on'.[8] Perhaps it was because Forbes had walked the mean streets himself. The son of a bankrupt banker, he had scrimped for a living, adding a post at the Geological Survey to his Botany Chair at King's College. Even now, crushed by work, his wife expecting a baby any day, he found time to sift though MacGillivray's spiral-shells from the Coral Sea – casually immortalizing his young admirer in the process. A minute new one, 1/24th of an inch long with translucent whorls, he christened *Chelotropis Huxleyi*. It was the sort of immortality Huxley never mentioned. But it meant a lot.

This was the Forbes who invited Huxley to town. Up he went again, to hear about his papers, his doves, flown from the ark. Forbes overwhelmed him with news: the Medusae paper had been not only read but *published* in the Royal Society's *Philosophical Transactions*, 'the first scientific publication in England', Hal boasted to Nettie. There were cut-outs of his *Trigonia* paper, read by Forbes into the Zoological Society's *Proceedings*, abstracts of the Man-of-War paper communicated by the bishop to the Linnean Society, copies of the *Diphyes* paper. Even his Cape York letter to Forbes had appeared *in toto* in the *Annals and Magazine of Natural History*! Forbes showered him with offprints.[9] It transpired that his name had been appearing everywhere – or rather 'William Huxley's' as the Linnean had it!

Forbes took him to dine with the geological elite, which gathered regularly in one of the Strand's 'dingy but cosy dens', Clunn's Hotel. Here Huxley met the heroic hammerers who had cracked the chaotic old strata. Among them strutted the 'Silurian King', Sir Roderick Murchison, a self-aggrandizing military man turned geological imperialist. Cast in the Napoleonic mould, he had tracked his 'Silurian system' into the heartland of Russia, conquering scientific territory as British goods conquered the world. Of course the old soldier had 'too much Sang froid'. His 'great talent' was topped by his 'great conceit', which Huxley put down to his '3–4,000 a year and a house in Belgravia'. (No modest house at that: 'all grey & gold . . . with arabesques like those of Pompeii', which even Ruskin admitted was 'coming it rather strong'.) Very different was another diner, the bureaucratic Benthamite Sir Henry De la Beche, the man who had put his Geological Survey staff in uniform and paid them a wage. These knights of science lionized the young sawbones, but 'Didn't I feel a minnow among the Tritons!'[10]

Straight off the ship, Huxley found himself welcomed by the geological gentry. These were the men who had unravelled the oldest fossil-entombing strata. They were reaching back to the first Days of Creation. That in itself made their science modish and put it under public scrutiny. Although they had restricted their activities to mapping outcrops and plotting ancient environments, by 1850 dangerous new questions were being asked. How to explain the succession of fossil dynasties, from the Silurian trilobites to Owen's mighty dinosaurs, from the first Jurassic shrewlike mammals to recent humans? No one was more sensitive to this issue than Huxley's main companion that night, Charles Lyell.

Lyell was clubbable and cultured; a friend to peers and Prime Ministers, and recently made Sir Charles by Queen Victoria. He was a lawyer by training and a gentleman by status: he lived on his capital and made geology his vocation. For 20 years eight editions of his *Principles of Geology* had delighted and infuriated. It debunked the notion of cataclysms rocking the primeval earth. Here the past and present landscapes were sculpted by the same slow and steady forces. That was his foundation, but on it stood a wobbly superstructure. Lyell argued that life had not progressed at all. He feared that a grand ascent from acorn worm to ape to Anglo-Saxon would encourage a barbarous evolutionary explanation, the sort touted by artisan atheists. These street-corner socialists would make man only a better sort of brute. They would deny him recompense in a future life and make him fight for it in this. In the 1830s such vicious logic had scared the urban gentry. So Lyell the lawyer called in an expert witness, Nature: he tried to convince the jury that no progression had occurred. It was a brilliant tirade against a criminal transmutation. But it smacked of special pleading. And, as everybody asked, if birds and mammals had always existed, why were their fossils not found in the oldest rocks?

Most geologists thought the remedy worse than the threat. For Murchison the successive strata housed increasingly high lifeforms. Only if they 'found the print of an aldermanic Robinson Crusoe's foot' in ancient Silurian sandstones would he 'knock under'. The geological clergy wanted a Creative progression as a sign that God had continually advanced life. A directional fossil record was proof that man was in His mind from the start. It affirmed the onward march, from the first Day of Creation to the last Day of Judgment. Lyell's fossil fiction seemed perversely unchristian. And that, by a curious twist, was what made it appeal to his young listener at Clunn's Hotel that night. Lyell was 'a most agreeable man', admitted Huxley, and his obstreperous palaeontology even more appealing.

It was 'a delightful evening', Huxley's first among the elite. Forbes topped it off by telling him that the government was now granting the reformed Royal Society £1,000 a year to aid research and publication and 'that as much as I wanted could be provided'. Suddenly the cherry seemed within his grasp. Only days ashore and backing for his book seemed secure.

As always voices whispered, niggling about the taint of patronage. 'God knows I care little enough for distinction', he told Nettie, except 'as it bears upon our prospects'. And he still had to gain the time to write. Being the man of the moment only reinforced his bullish mood. 'An appointment for 3 or 6 months I could get now, but, true to my old habits I must carry my point and have the year I determined upon'.[11]

His last days aboard were all 'bustle and confusion'. Chatham bristled with activity. The supernumeraries escaped in their carriages, with them his black-laced favourite, Mrs Stanley. Crates were carried off, wives wept and a stream of sailors drank away their back pay. But Tom was lost in the letter he had wanted for so long, from sister Lizzie. It spoke of 'sorrow and misfortune'. He could visualize Tennessee, 'from the baking and boiling and pigs squealing' to the backwoods privations. But there was a new baby to 'efface the bitterness' of two losses. 'God knows, my dear sister, I could feel for you. It is as if I could see again a shadow of the great sorrow that fell upon us all years ago'. He offered to stand godfather 'though I fear I am too much of a heretic to promise to bring him up a good son of the church'. 'Tell Florry that I could not get her the bird with the long tail, but that . . . I will send her some pictures of copper-coloured gentlemen with great big wigs and no trousers, and tell her uncle loves her very much and never forgets'.[12]

On 9 November he was paid off and the pendant hauled down. It was a glorious day, with 'the bells ringing lustily'. 'And now', he regaled Nettie, 'I am a free man caring neither for blue coat nor red'. The sea was behind him; ahead lay a more uncertain course among the land sharks. He wrapped his skulls, packed his notebooks, thanked his middies and moved from his creaking alcove to George's house. At 41 North Bank, just off the promenading Regent's Park, he would be close to his parents in St John's Wood, and to the crowds at London Zoo, come to see Europe's first hippopotamus and Tasmanian tigers. But tucked away on a back street the house was oddly quiet. 'I look out upon a garden where in the morning I see thrushes and blackbirds on the grass and no whisper of the roar of the great Babylon reaches my ears'. After years of waves and wind it took some adjusting. Not that he minded the fussing of the scampish Polly, who 'has taken possession of me for a time'.[13]

The reunion with Fanning and Ory in their Paddington villa was ecstatic. Willie rushed up 'and snuggled onto my knee as if he had left it only yesterday'. Huxley became one of the family. He dropped in often, to sit at dinner feeling Nettie's arm 'stealing round my neck'. It brought them closer even as it twisted the knife.

In some ways he was happier with colonials. They were '*real* people free from humbug and affectation'. In an age of 'Steam and Cant', before the squires of science were ousted by the young Turks, he found sycophancy and pomposity on opposite sides of the class divide. But no bootlicking for him – 'I am under no one's *patronage*, nor do I ever mean to be'. It was the leitmotiv of his life, this former East End apprentice, fiercely proud of his self-made image. But his attitude brought massive insecurities. He needed bolt-holes, shields against the world; or rather a real home of his own. He craved security, 'some one in whom I can place implicit confidence, whose judgment I can respect, and yet who will not laugh at my most foolish weaknesses, and in whose love I can forget all cares'.[14]

What he called 'humbug', silver-haired gents knew as salon politics. For generations patronage had guaranteed all things: touching a Lord's arm tipped pounds from the public purse, access to an archbishop opened doors in the British Museum. But this world was dying. Huxley sensed it as he began his scientific rounds. He hardly needed his introductions to the great Richard Owen, having moved straight into Owen's Royal Society circle. Owen had a high cultural reputation as a brilliant comparative anatomist, and a relatively low status as Hunterian Professor in the College of Surgeons, at the council's beck-and-call. Contact between Huxley and Owen was inevitable, not least with Owen specializing in parthenogenesis. Owen symbolized an age in transition – he had come up through the ranks, using hard work and noble patrons, and grace-and-favour would come no higher than Queen Victoria's present of Sheen Lodge in Richmond Park. But he was turning Liberal like the country, and he too was looking for 'pudding' to substantiate the praise.[15]

On 20 November Huxley asked to be posted to the Guard Ship HMS *Fisguard* on the Thames at Greenwich. He needed time, and 'less than a year would be wholly insufficient to my purpose'. Everyone went overboard to help. 'Old John' drummed up Admiralty support. Forbes swore that 'more complete zoological researches had never been conducted during any voyage'. Owen wrote to the First Sea Lord. The Royal Society Grant Committee came out 'strongly in favour of my "valuable researches" (cock-a-doodle-doo!!)'. The society's secretary, Thomas Bell, was a modest naturalist, as easy describing Darwin's *Beagle* reptiles as monographing British crabs, but he shone as an administrator. He was breathing life back into the old lady after the savaging by reformers. He invited Huxley to dine 'and meet a lot of nobs'. Outwardly Huxley took it all in his stride; inwardly he was 'considerably astonished'. Even as he forswore patronage, the top brass were pulling strings. Hands that were feeding him would one day be bitten, but for the moment the bulldog pup was slavering. He was staggered at his reception 'among these grandees'.[16]

Such a salvo went off that the Sea Lords made signals to surrender. On 29 November they appointed him 'Additional Assistant Surgeon' to the Commodore's ship *Fisguard* – and then granted him six months leave on half-pay, renewable. Huxley knew whose broadside had hit the Admiralty's mizen. He told Thomson (back in Edinburgh acquainting himself with the three year-old he had never seen) that Owen's letter had done it.[17] That day too Owen heard from their Lordships that the insistent young subaltern had what he wanted.

His foot was on the first rung of the ladder. 'I wonder how

many steps I shall get up before I am either stopped or get a tumble'. The pay was nothing to get married on. Every mate griped that it would not 'permit him to keep two messes'. So he hoped for a speedy promotion; the average wait was over ten years, but a book would show that he wasn't average. Better still would be a job offer. 'Don't you feel I am on the high road to become a mighty "spider stuffer" as Fanning has it? If stuffing fleas will lead me to my end I am greatly prepared to stuff them'.[18]

So within the month he had it all – a local ship and extended leave if he worked at his science. The chance would be a fine thing; everyone wanted to hear his tales of jawbone-wearing savages. 'I am not naturally a gregarious animal', said the sailor, but the social whirl staved off loneliness. He enjoyed evenings with Fanning, dinners with 'Mercury' (Mr Sharpe) and his 'nice old clergyman' father, even a trip to Nettie's Aunt Kate to hear stories of her childhood. And night-time camaraderie came in the shape of Forbes' boisterous Red Lion Club (named after a pub). Its hell-raisers irreverently shadowed the starchy British Association and Royal Society. It was a tavern vent, a safety valve for the engines of Victorian pomposity. Here the tyros blew off steam. Songs and jokes sent them into a roar as they lampooned an unctuous stuff-shirt science with its plum-in-mouth sermonizing. (The power of sermons in Victorian society explains the pervasive 'cant' which Huxley so hated.) He revelled in its 'Pantagruelistic aspect', set off by Forbes' inimitable squibs, satirizing the official banquets with their '"butter-boat" speeches'.

The endless engagements overwhelmed the landlubber. 'If people would . . . not invite me out to dinners and parties, I should be getting on very well'.[19] One more ball, he swore, then work, back to his fleshy squirts and fiery *Pyrosoma*, readying his paper for the Royal Society.

These should have been honeymoon days as Huxley found his shore legs. But he flew high and low. One moment he was cocky: 'I don't know and I don't care whether I shall ever be what is called a great man. I will leave my mark somewhere'. A moment later he was crushed, wearied by 'this sharp intellect . . . incessantly rolling the Sisyphus-stone of its own queries'. He was too eager: 'one must wait, wait patiently', he groaned. At times he feared he was going nowhere and dragging Nettie with him, and then his anger turned to misanthropic fury. Messmates envied his appointment, but he only hated them 'for congratulating me on my good fortune'.[20]

And underneath he *was* lonely. Nettie's absence was crippling him. He imagined her 'bright smile – a kiss – one of the thousand nothings that make life something'. The passing winter saw him turning paler and more cynical. His meteoric rise among the rich ironically destabilized him more – 'from money to friendship', he now reasoned, 'it is not so much getting as keeping'. An increasing pugnacity masked a deepening insecurity. Success was easy. The drug grinder hovering on the doorstep of the Royal Society had to turn it 'to account'. He stood at the castle drawbridge 'ready to fight . . . or be blown into oblivion'. 'I *have* drawn the sword, but whether I am in truth to beat the giants and deliver my princess from the enchanted castle is yet to be seen'.[21]

Nettie's letters were taking four months to arrive, even longer now, given events. The traumatic news was of her father's financial crisis and his arrest and acquittal in Sydney. Following this the family had trekked 120 miles to Bathurst – a township on the banks of the 'miserable' Macquarie. Here, in treeless sheep country 2,000 feet above sea level, where she found the winter numbingly cold, Heathorn had started brewing again.[22] It increased Huxley's sense of isolation. 'Morning and evening I think of you as I look up at your dear face hanging there in my room', he wrote on 1 February 1851. He was becoming obsessive. He saw her everywhere. She was the heroine of his novels; she had Jane Eyre's 'passionate nature hidden under a mask of self content'; her 'half tearful' look stared at him from Millais' Pre-Raphaelite paintings.[23] He could not escape her.

He was languishing in the shadow of the voyage. He reminisced with newly promoted Captain Suckling and heard that Dayman was taking his own ship to the Cape. Everyone was doing well; even MacGillivray was a driven man, writing a *Narrative of the Voyage of H.M.S. Rattlesnake*. Huxley supplied the drawings, but the camaraderie was gone. The bleaker moments still haunted him. Mrs Stanley sent a few books from the captain's *Rattlesnake* library. She even enticed him over to meet the family, but he called a halt to this hob-nobbing: back at home 'the old lady' was 'inclined to be patronising' and 'I don't put up with that from anybody'.[24] Freed from naval etiquette he no longer had to hold his tongue. Sardonic to the last, he mocked Yule's talk on the voyage at the Geographical Society. MacGillivray followed Yule, 'and I looked on, and laughed'.

He moved through the great Babylon with the air of a moral assassin, stalking his limping, humbugged prey. He had Thack-

eray's *Pendennis* in hand, that 'fling against powdered-head and
... plush breeches', as the *Athenaeum* put it. Huxley revelled in
this exposé of society's 'chaos of folly, vice, and charlatanry'. It
caught the mood, 'the Byronic despair, the Wertherian despondency' of the men fighting their way up. It portrayed an age of
greed and doubt after the fall of the old moral certainties – the
virtue-less mercenary void Huxley found himself floating in. 'You
would not like it', he warned Nettie, 'it reveals too mercilessly the
mean & selfish side of our life. But it is true'.[25] Others cheered the
'mocking Mephistopheles'. The book appealed to alienated spectators like Huxley, 'soul sickened and sceptical'. It evoked his Grub
Street anguish. Dickens was for dilettantes; he is 'not a great artist
and rarely dips much below the surface'. But *Pendennis* – that
captures 'more nearly than any book I know the condition of the
thirsting young men'.

Huxley sided with the thirsting men: men from the ranks, the
trades, the cotton towns, the Dissenting outskirts. Not for him the
medal-festooned Murchison – Major Pendennis incarnate – nor
the forelock-tugging Owen. Not for him the 'roaring young blades
from Oxbridge'. He gravitated to an earthier breed, chaps from
the anatomy theatres who saw science as a mission and self-
aggrandizement as a sin, new men with new values.

The *Dreadnought*'s surgeon George Busk and builder's son
Edwin Lankester were two such. 'They are people quite of my
sort', part of the Red Lion pride whose dens he favoured. (So
much so that Lankester's boy Ray came to worship Huxley as his
'father-in-science'.)[26] They were fellow medical men with a biological interest and social conscience. Lankester was a giant of a man
with a soft Suffolk accent. Like Huxley he was an apothecary's
apprentice who had left school at 12; and he had known garret
starvation. But he had fought his way to a Heidelberg doctorate,
and he was still fighting. Hack work and *Daily News* pieces on
medical reform had kept him afloat. At Greenwich, where the
Dreadnought was berthed, they talked with Huxley of public
health and science for the people. They translated pioneering
German works and enthused over the invisible oceans of life
opened up by the microscope.

They made good sounding boards. Busk was sifting the *Rattlesnake*'s haul of sea ferns (one of which he christened *Plumularia
Huxleyi*). Huxley continued to argue the toss over these creatures.
He still considered the man-of-war a single organism, its parts
only so many 'buds' – even if some of the buds swam away to

start life anew! (Busk shared his interest, having translated a Danish book on 'Alternation of Generations'.)

There was another attraction at Greenwich, Busk's wife Ellen. She stood apart from the run of whale-boned matrons; a naturalist, freethinker, sharp witted, a 'playful' soul who showed 'evidence of suffering'. He took her into his confidence, telling her alone of his 'fair-haired ladee'. She became his 'favourite and ally'. He portrayed her as 'tall very refined', 'with black hair' and 'a most singular pair of penetrating grey eyes'. A 'sort of Egyptian priestess I fancy her', he said, spellbound.[27] She was refined like Mrs Stanley, well-read rather than well-bred. In polite circles words were spoken about her. Whatever Thackeray's stab at the stigma surrounding socially inferior wives, Huxley could hear the odd disparaging remark, the odd closing door.

He liked gutsy rationalists; he was secure among the industrial intelligentsia (Lankester's wife Phebe was the daughter of a Manchester cotton king). For 15 years, since they had swept into the town halls, Dissenters had been prying the professional institutions out of Anglican hands. They resented the Church's privileges, its Oxbridge exclusivity, its divine justification of the status quo and its damnation for all who disagreed.

By 1850 the Dissenters and rationalists had moved in from the fringes to become London's avant garde – and Huxley would meet them all, men such as George Henry Lewes (author of *Ranthorpe*) and Herbert Spencer. 'Secularism' was their watchword, coined by the former firebrand George Holyoake who was now settling into cigar-smoking respectability with the literary radicals on Lewes' weekly, the *Leader*. Dissolvent literature was their rage, books that eroded the clerical cement in the Anglican edifice. They pitted the Dissenting vision of a reforming society against the bishops' rigid hierarchies. Everywhere Huxley felt the meliorist ethic – improvement on earth rather than redemption in heaven. These were the real Pendennises, breaking the old shackles. They wanted scientific standards for judging truth, standards in their hands, legitimating their own claim to intellectual authority. The 'crisis of faith' was a collision of creeds, a product of the rents and changes in an industrializing society. 'The result is everywhere the same', Huxley said. 'Every thinking man I have met with is at heart in a state of doubt, on all the great points of religious belief. And the unthinking men ... are in as complete a state of practical unbelief'.[28] It was agonizingly congenial.

A dissident himself, Huxley was not afraid of the friction as he rubbed shoulders with the 'bigwigs'. He was closer to scientific peerage than he knew. The reformed Royal Society only admitted 15 new Fellows a year; fewer were aristocrats and more were active researchers. The Council was looking for seriousness and scientific commitment. For his part Forbes was looking to get Huxley in. 'I had no idea that it was at all within my reach', Huxley said in surprise, but his papers spoke for him.[29] His doves had found not only a new land but friendly natives.

Still he was hungry. Still he seethed about the lack of paid openings. Science should be a salaried meritocracy, not a dabbling ground for the foppish aristocracy. 'I am sick of writing, weary of longing. The difficulties of obtaining a decent position in England ... seem to me greater than ever they were'. It was a *cri de coeur*, as always aimed at Nettie. 'To attempt to live by any scientific pursuit is a farce ... A man of science may earn great distinction – great reputation – but not bread. He will get invitations to all sorts of dinners & conversaziones, but not enough income to pay his cab hire'.

Radicals had been shouting as much for 20 years. But his cry had a personal ring. Every delay set back the day when he would feel Nettie's 'dear arms round my neck'. He could not consult her; soliloquies were sent off into the blue. Five months later in the Bathurst brewery they were a faint echo. He tried to grasp 'the immense distance in time that lies between us' as he wrapped her birthday present months ahead – itself as ghoulish as a Papuan jaw ornament: his entwined hair with a rattlesnake clasp, 'equal to anything in Thebes or Memphis for symbolic meaning'.[30]

A world away Nettie never understood his goal. Who else saw his salvation in the Salpae? But salvation required working at. His new Royal Society paper was ready in late March. He squirmed in the Society's meeting room in Somerset House as the Secretary read it monotonally. Portly Lord Rosse, famous for the huge six-foot-reflector telescope at his castle in Ireland, looked incongruous in the President's chair, 'more like a gentleman farmer'. All around, his forerunners gazed down sternly from the walls. Members sat uncomfortably on 'cold benches', the tyros wishing themselves 'merry round the [Red Lion] table' instead. The old noblemen probably found Huxley sharp, uncouth, uncompromising and charming. He found the dullness of the occasion appalling. 'I had no idea it was half so painful a process to listen to your own productions'.[31]

Still he had to step up production, 'or this precious year of seed time will bring forth no harvest'. North Bank had its warmth: if he fell into one of his 'hypochondriacal fits' Polly was on hand to talk 'consolation in her simple way'. But it was 'altogether *too* comfortable'. On his own he could 'effect twice as much'. So he decided to 'emigrate to some "two pair back", which shall have the feel and manner of a workshop'. He set out in April's sooty drizzle. He traipsed muddy streets, past horses 'splashed to their very blinkers'. Even grimier were the bedsits themselves. 'I want some place with a decent address, cheap and beyond all things clean. The dirty holes that some of these lodgings are!' And 'such servants with their faces and hands not merely dirty but absolutely macadamised'.[32]

Between landladies he dropped in on Forbes. It was mid April and the man was in a state. He was arranging fossils in De la Beche's splendid new Museum of Economic Geology in Jermyn Street. The museum, with its plum Piccadilly frontage, was being finished in time for the opening of the Great Exhibition. The Geological Survey had moved here, to be linked to a School of Mines, where Forbes would teach. The lot, run with factory discipline, would bring expertise to the mining industry. The Italian Palazzo building was the first 'in Britain which is entirely devoted to the advancement of science'. At last Huxley had found a sign of government initiative – a huge State investment to train the next generation of engineers, metallurgists and geologists. The last licks of paint were going on, the opening day barely a month away.

Huxley had called on the offchance, but the news left him elated. Forbes confided that he was 'all right' for the Royal: the *enfant terrible* had been elected a Fellow, the youngest of the candidates. He had beaten the hardy hands. He had beaten his examiner at Apothecaries' Hall all those years ago; more awkwardly, he had beaten his naval superior, the *Fisguard*'s surgeon. Told the news he 'looked as cool as a cucumber'. The poor boy was to take a seat in the upper house of science and 'sport a tail' to his name, FRS. Recognition came no stronger. But for 'all my cucumbery appearance', he confessed to Nettie, 'I could not sit down ... after the news. I wandered hither and thither restlessly half over London'.

The cost of the Royal Society Fellowship, £14 a year – over a month's pay – seemed prohibitive, but he hoped 'to make it worth the money'. This was to be no plume in his hat. He would 'turn it to advantage'. Having infiltrated the old boys' world he intended to turn it upside down. 'Will you take this step my darling' as proof 'that I have not worked utterly in vain?' He was one stop nearer his goal, and 'by no intrigue'.[33] A child of the 1840s could say no more.

The moment of elation saw him into his own 'den' at the end of April. It was close by, on Regent's Park, a sitting room and bedroom, cheap at '13 & 6d. per week'. His landladies were 'three virgins, long of nose and spinsterful of aspect'. He suspected these daughters of darkness the second he scanned his lounge, an eye-opener on the foibles of spinsterly free-spirits left over from the Regency. 'On the mantlepiece are four statuettes two of Voltaire & Rousseau and two others of a little boy and a little girl in very scanty clingy garments'. Over them hung a great gaudy painting of Waterloo, with soldiers knee-deep in gore 'sticking one another through & through'. He removed this abomination and a non-plussed Nettie now gazed down on the nymphs. He arranged his books, stood his microscope 'in a commanding attitude upon the little table' and carried on dissecting.[34] He had his neutral bolt-hole, a place of refuge after taking on the world.

He was now on his own. His parents were near by, but his father was 'as one dead' and his mother's 'marvellous indiscretions' kept him distant. Lonely, he bought a piping bullfinch, only to suspect that it was painted; the poor bird refused to sing 'but moped and died and is a joke against me to this hour'. He gave a quiet inner scream, 'Oh I am so sick, so weary of this life without love'.[35] The one he did care for was as distant as ever. 'I have left you now a whole year,' he sighed on 2 May 1851. Twelve months to the day since he had sailed from Farm Cove on a hot breeze, watching Nettie's image fade. It was still fading.

His melancholy fits were arriving with monotonous regularity. The sea dog was having trouble settling down. A life of science seemed so much self-indulgence. It wasn't a proper job, it was 'utter vanity', or rather bedsit frippery. Sometimes he craved work that would 'involve sacrifice and danger' to prove that he was alive. The next day, 3 May, he was bucked up. He thanked Owen 'for the honour of the F.R.S.', but the taciturn Owen answered in his Lancastrian accent, ' "No, indeed you have nothing to thank but the goodness of your own work." For about ten minutes I felt rather proud of that speech'. 'The only use of honours . . . is as an antidote to such fits of the blue devils'.

For ten minutes too he warmed to Owen. He cooled as quickly. Owen 'is a queer fish, more odd in appearance than ever'. He has been 'amazingly civil to me', but there was something in his manner, acquired in the town houses of the gentry. 'He is so frightfully polite that I never feel thoroughly at home with him'.[36]

On 4 May Huxley turned 26 and found Dante's devils at the door once more. He retired to his serpent's den, exploding in frustration: 'there is no chance of *living* by science'. Look around, University College's down-at-heel zoology professor Robert Grant takes home £39 a year! His counterpart at King's had long emigrated. Such poverty created a 'shabby-genteel' caste, as Dickens called them, teachers with frayed cuffs, slumming it with whores and thieves in Camden Town. Even the best looked a bit darned and patched. 'Owen who has a European reputation . . . gets from his office as Hunterian Professor £300 a year! which is less than the salary of many a bank clerk'. (Admittedly that ignored his crown pension and grants, which took it over £700, but Owen's perks were exceptional.) Such sums spoke volumes about the value of science, when a society doctor could earn £3,000, a good lawyer £15,000 and the Canon of Christ Church, Oxford £1,000 for no effort at all. What value now 'the beauty of Nature and the pursuit of Truth'? 'A man who chooses a life of science chooses . . . a life of *nothing*'. Huxley took comfort where he could: he *had* penetrated the *sanctum sanctorum*. He might lack a parson's riches, but 'I cannot blame myself. It is the worlds fault and not mine'.[37]

How to change the world? His plight was made more pointed by the economic upturn. The hungry 1840s were over. A new buoyancy was evident as middle-class incomes rose. Boom times lay ahead: the years of *Pax Britannica* and sterling imperialism. Hyde Park's 'great Exhibition of Exhibitions' gloated in this industrial promise. The Exhibition had just opened, a testament to commerce and consumerism. It was crammed with everything from the latest engines to collapsible pianos, a cornucopia of the new and astonishing. Ten thousand exhibits proved that Britain really was the workshop of the world. Viewing them, Prince Albert gave praise to modern science! – and here was Huxley, the scientific aspirant, unable to afford 'three pounds for a season ticket'.

Only when the gate price dropped did he buy a shilling ticket. He entered the colossal Crystal Palace, past the single 24-ton block of coal, standing homage to the source of Britain's wealth. The glass transept was loftier than 'the vaults of even our noblest cathedrals'; its sheer size beggared the imagination. Thousands stood in reverential awe. An age which had lost its faith found a new technological salvation. It was the 'great Temple of England', Nettie heard:

> 50,000 people worship there every day. They come up to it
> as the Jews came to Jerusalem at the time of the Jubilee.
> In the meantime their profound teachers are disputing
> about 'prevenient Grace' and whether they shall be taught
> at all unless they will swallow all 39 articles. If Satan can
> laugh I think he must do so at the perplexities of the
> English bishops at the moment. If they try to mend their
> house they know it will come about their heads – so their
> only recourse is to sit quite still, and get the world in
> general to do the same – rather a difficult tack in these
> days.[38]

It reinforced his view that a new scientific curia was needed, men who could preach rational science and real salvation.

Civvy street seemed brighter to a rising star with an FRS. Some days he woke up 'startled' at 'the wondrousness of life'. Others he woke with a hangover. A week's fling after receiving his Fellowship saw him at Lankester's and Fanning's, dancing 'till half past three'. Bleary mornings were spent reviewing books on starfish and daydreaming about his own Barrier Reef experiences with their kin, sea cucumbers (which defensively shot out their stomachs when handled). He wrote polemics to prove that the 'generations' of medusae from hydroid parents were really buds or 'zoöids'. (He posted one to Darwin, introducing himself. But the Kent recluse doubted whether 'creatures having so plainly the stamp of individuality as have many of your zooids will ever cease to be called individuals'.) Finally he rounded the week out at Lord Rosse's on Saturday, where he made his debut as a Fellow. 'Prince Albert was there and all the scientific nobs', a glittering array of medals and knighthoods. Everyone was kindness itself, even the 'King of Siluria'.[39] Murchison grasped Huxley's hand and said 'he was delighted to be of any service' in the grant matter.

Huxley's phenomenal rise did little to mellow him. At times his cynical mistrust seemed self-fulfilling. No sooner was his Fellowship announced than he lost his Royal Society grant. The Committee argued that, as a serving officer, he should be funded by the government. And so the grisly business began all over again. 'I am not disappointed', he said, for Lord Rosse and Murchison have

offered to back 'any application I may make to the Treasury'.⁴⁰
But it began his second six-months leave on a sour note.

Others were faring no better. MacGillivray was by now struggling with the *Narrative*. Huxley was so badgered about the book
that he made inquiries of the 'mud-volcano himself'. MacGillivray
was in dire straits; 'old Suckling beat up his quarters lately' and
was so struck by Jock's distress 'as to leave £5 for him'.⁴¹ At one
point John Gould found the drunken MacGillivray in jail and had
to bail him out. 'I have done all I can', said Huxley, asked by the
publisher to pry chapters out of him.

Hal's strength came from Nettie. 'Cynic and sceptic as I am, by
nature and by culture, what Thackeray has so justly & strikingly
called a Sadducee – I cling by our love as a certainty, a mysterious
reality'. Love had shown him that there was more to the world
than 'need, greed & vain glory'. But need if not greed was the
name of the game; so off he went to the British Association in July
as a one-man pressure group. Everyone had given him the same
advice. Richardson told him to get the 'British Ass' to 'untie the
Treasury purse'.⁴² Forbes was blunter: he should stand on a
soapbox and shout, or 'make myself notorious somehow'. That
was no problem. He went to the meeting at Ipswich, a beautiful
town of timber-framed Tudor buildings, not 'to advance science,
but to be "advanced" myself'.

A world stood between this meeting and his last. Before the
voyage in Southampton he had gazed at all the 'somebodies'. Now
he was a 'somebody' himself, and treading the boards to tell of his
Rattlesnake arrow-worms: 'I know all about the scenery and
decorations and no longer think the manager a wizard'.

The company was good. He met a lean Orangeman, John
Tyndall, an out-of-work physicist. There was a passion to Tyndall,
as any Irish Protestant who had once thrilled to fanatics calling up
the 'martyred sons of the reformation from their blood-stained
graves'. He was self-consciously 'lower class', and self-made; the
£1-a-week surveyor had saved enough to study under the great
Bunsen at Marburg, the picturesque German town where Luther
had stood his ground. He was five years Huxley's senior and still
in debt after his Ph.D. – another second-class citizen damned by
his career choice. Germany had turned him into a romantic pantheist; for Tyndall, as for his hero Carlyle, 'the universe is the blood
and bones of Jehovah'.⁴³ Tyndall, making his own pilgrimage
away from Protestantism, would take central place in Huxley's
coterie, a friend for life.

Joseph Hooker completed the evangelical triad. He was an imperial botanist and the only one whose future looked secure. 'His father is director of the Kew Gardens', making him the heir apparent, Huxley noted in envy. Hooker's peripatetic existence had been even more exotic. Fired by Cook's epic voyages, he had spent six years bouncing 'like a glass tumbler' from snowdrifts to steamy tropics. He knew the attractions of Sydney, and life in an alcove stuffed with fermenting plants. Three summers in the Antarctic ice-smasher *Erebus* had only whetted his appetite. Not even an engagement to Frances Henslow, daughter of Darwin's mentor, the Cambridge professor of botany, could stop him setting off again to collect Himalayan plants. His capture by an anti-British ruler had a regiment marching in to annexe southern Sikkim for the Crown. 'Do you remember hearing of Hooker's being detained prisoner among the Sikhs?' Hal asked Nettie. His fiancée had waited four years. 'How I envied Hooker', Huxley sighed; 'at this very meeting he sat by her side. He is going to be married in a day or two'.[44] 'I know somebody who would go and be taken into captivity twice over if he thought such a happy termination would follow'.

The sea brought Huxley and Hooker together, naval surgeons who knew the ways of their 'Lords of the Foul Anchor'. But Hooker had the Kew advantage; as the director's son he had picked up an easy £1,000 to publish his *Flora Antarctica*. Even now he was on a £400-a-year Department of Woods grant to finish his New Zealand flora and publish his Himalayan findings.

At Ipswich royalty itself conspired against Huxley. As he walked out to talk on the 'brilliantly coloured' men-of-war and the little *Velella*, with its sails like two 'elegantly shaped piece[s] of cut glass', he counted 20 listeners. The Court retinue had caused an exodus; Prince Albert had arrived and 'turned the heads of the good people of Ipswich'.[45] He pressed on regardless, drawing sweeping circles to illustrate his classification of the stinging 'Nematophora'. (He knew now Leuckart had named them 'Coelenterata' but thought his reasons wrong and stuck to his own name.)

Huxley's 'trumpeting' paid off, with the 'big-wig' President (the Astronomer Royal, George Airy) lining up the Association behind the Royal Society on his grant application. But they all urged him to ease up. The President-elect Colonel Edward Sabine had him to lunch on Wednesday 15 July. Sabine was an unflappable 63 year-old, famous for his magnetic surveys of the globe (indispensable to a naval power; he was behind the *Erebus* voyage to the Antarctic). He 'spoke cheeringly, and advised me by no means to be hasty, but to wait'. Huxley did not have to wait long for more puffs from the irrepressible Forbes. The *Literary Gazette* reported his praise for Huxley's Man-of-War paper. 'Polly is so proud of it that she has been carrying it about in her pocket', Hal told Nettie; 'she means to send you a copy of it so I shall spare my modesty'.[46]

Friday's papers held out even more promise. A job offer on the first page of the *Athenaeum* jumped out at him. He dropped Nettie a note:

> Thomas H. Huxley Esq. F.R.S.
> Professor of Natural History in the
> University of Toronto

> How do you think that would look my pet? . . . As for myself I feel happier than I have since I left you for it seems to me as if the cloud had begun to lift.

Centrifugal forces were flinging the marginal men out to the colonial edges. He would join the thousands spreading across the empire, hard-up professors and hapless paupers – perhaps even friend Tyndall, himself applying for the physics chair at Toronto. By now Canada was only two weeks' steaming time from Liverpool. The university was new and the pay perfect; '350£ Halifax is something over 300£ English'. Forbes and Fanning told him to try for it; even cautious George was converted by Polly. His heart urged him on – it had been six weeks since he had heard from Sydney. In Toronto he could settle his debts and send for Nettie. He began 'to dream dreams' again. Wiser minds knew that nepotism usually decided these matters, but his head was in the clouds. The FRS spoke for him, and what it did not say the references from the best men would. Now, 'if they only have fair play'.[47]

Buoyed up, he threw himself at *Hydra* and sponges with renewed vigour. Then he swanned off to join Busk and Lankester on the Suffolk coast at Felixstowe, where the Lions were summering 'with their lionesses'. Dredging as usual gave way to satanic discussions with his 'Egyptian priestess', Ellen Busk. Huxley's fascination and fear of strong women showed. In an age that pegged ladies as crippled religious dolls, it came as a revelation that she combined 'womanly feelings' with a razor-like rationality. ('In fact', Hal told Nettie, 'I am not sure that your big dog is not a little bit afraid of her scratch'.) There was none of the 'Missionari-ness' of Victorian matrons about her. She knew doubt and 'its darkness'. She too saw the destruction of orthodoxy as 'the only hope for a new state of belief'. Huxley thrived on the sea-mist of rationalism, bewitched by Mrs Busk. He pushed such a view on Nettie, sidelined in Sydney. 'I do not say think as I think, but think in my way', he advised her. 'Fear no shadows, least of all in that great spectre of personal unhappiness which binds half the world to orthodoxy'.[48]

His Toronto references were accumulating into a 'Who's Who' of zoology. 'They are from the 16 first men in Great Britain & France' – from the towering Owen to the reclusive Darwin (who knew Huxley by reputation), from the Secretary of the Royal Society to the President of the BAAS. There was praise for his strident language as much as his mastery of the arcane. No competitor could match them, 'whatever private influences they may have'.[49]

But he knew how the game was played: old school tie, manners before talent. Not to be outflanked he had Eliza Stanley ask the head of the clan, Lord Stanley at the Foreign Office, to add a titled word. Huxley's forelocks were unaccustomed to such tugging. But His Lordship obliged, writing to the Earl of Elgin, Governor-General of Canada, who would choose a professor from the Senate's shortlist.

Thus ended 'another act in the Tragicomedy of my life', he wrote after posting his references on 16 October. He oozed confi-dence, even drifting into messianic musings – 'tracing my own life back I could almost fancy myself set apart ... for some special purpose': alone as a boy, isolated aboard ship, separated from his love and suffering his own 'forty days journey into the wilder-ness'.[50] Was Toronto the Promised Land? 'What does nature want with me'?

Whatever it was, nature had a crushing sense of timing. That night he heard from Fanning that the colonial Governor was planning a natural history chair for the new Sydney University. 'Old Mrs Fanning was quite enthusiastic about it and prognosticates that I am to be Professor at Sydney instead of Toronto'. So, off he went to the Colonial Office the next day, swearing that 'if they will give me £400 a year ... I am their boy'. Fanning continued to inquire about the 'spider chair for Botany Bay'. He boggled at Huxley's references: 'So many lies would almost get a devil into the kingdom of Heaven', never mind a scientific reprobate into the convict colony.[51] Hal could be back anatomizing jellyfish in Port Jackson, by Nettie's side. 'It almost takes my breath away'.

He could join the exodus, the hordes attracted by the gold strikes. Nettie talked of nothing else now. Finds of 16-ounce nuggets had drawn 2,000 to the 'diggins' near Bathurst. The Australian gold rush was turning it into a boom town. The bedlam was unnerving for a girl translating Schiller and practising the piano: everywhere 'busy hands & eager eyes, thirsting with an unquenchable thirst for the glistening treasure'.[52] Hal pictured her trooping off herself, 'pick on shoulder'. But her accounts grew fraught, talk of fights, price hikes (loaves a shilling apiece) and constables quitting with gold fever. Still, with the wealth flowing back to Sydney, a £400 chair looked increasingly feasible.

He no longer knew which way the empire would pull him. Colonial comings and goings were now part of life. In October Nettie's friend Alice sailed in to marry McClatchie. She stayed with George and Polly and this triggered old memories. Time was 'I never saw her without knowing that you were not far off', Hal reported back. Unnerved, he wondered when he would settle into his 'genial philosophical state again'.[53]

As his frustration grew his provocations rose. In his den with the three virgins he was working on the whimsical 'wheel-bearers', microscopic rotifers (so called from the crown of cilia at one end, whirling like wheels). At Busk and Lankester's Microscopical Society he used them as a miniature 'fulcrum whence the whole zoological universe may be moved'.[54] He was still smashing up Cuvier's rag-bag of invertebrates, the 'Radiata'. Since Huxley's rotifers resembled flatworm larvae, and since Johannes Müller had shown that starfish larvae were also worm-like, Huxley now put them together in another discrete assemblage of life. He called it the 'Annuloida'. He was lumping together all the worms, flat-worms, rotifers *and*, outrageously, starfish as a related group. He was practising his provocations in this tiny alcove of creation. But then had Forbes not told him to make himself notorious?

It was grinding night-and-day work, with no recompense. He felt as if truths were cranked out of him at no cost to society. He looked at his brother, leaving for the City at 10 am., and Polly's laughable way of 'cossetting him when he comes home – "poor fellow he is so hard worked". I work as hard again and get no cossetting!' But he was hooked. Science was his opiate, leaving him poor but wanting more. Whether it 'has been a poison which has heated my veins or true nectar from the Gods life giving, I know not, but I can no longer rest where I once could have rested'. Nature's shot gave him a 'sense of power'; and he needed the surge of strength as he kicked at society's door.

It opened an inch and he beheld the Holy Grail. On 7 November he heard that he had been 'within an ace' of getting the Royal Society's 'valuable gold medal'. In a tie-break the 50-guinea Royal Medal had gone to a raddled old worker, George Newport, a deft dissector who had shown that the sperm actually penetrates the egg in fertilization. Newport was a real craftsman, surely the only former wheelwright ever to graduate to the Elysium. Huxley could not begrudge the nugget to such a man, 'old enough to be my father'. Still he was flabbergasted: off the boat a year and glimpsing the gold that 'such men as Owen & Faraday are glad to get'.[55] For another brief second he was flying high.

The year had seen lurches and swings. Daily poverty gave the gold its glint; the daily grind gave him his short-term goals. To George the businessman young Tom seemed to be directionless: the City, industry, a medical practice, that was where one earned money. Yet Tom had fixed his sights. He would scrabble for any university chair that would pay him to practise science. Even the cynic softened occasionally at his sense of achievement. Twelve months to the day since the *Rattlesnake* was paid off, the angry young man looked back. Like some foreigner, awed by the waves of humanity in the great Babylon, the sailor still despaired of the scientific 'scratching to keep your place in the crowd'. Yet the FRS had put him 'at the pit door of this great fools theatre', and now starfish, rotifers and pig-headedness placed him 'not far from the check-taker'.[56]

10

The Season of Despair

CHRISTMAS FOUND HUXLEY climbing the walls of a new den. The news from abroad left him 'as savage as a bear'. The Sydney chair never materialized, and the mail on 29 December 1851 had him growling uncontrollably. A Canadian contact tipped him off that nepotism would win out in Toronto. References from the world's best paled beside the qualification of another candidate, 'a Brother of a Gentleman holding a high position in the Prov^l. Govn''. 'Of course he will have it', snapped Huxley: merit meant nothing.

He began his descent once again, shattered, wrecked on more reefs:

> Into what lies I have deceived myself about devotion to
> Science and the cultivation of the Intellect . . . It is all a
> sham . . . I could stamp and cry aloud for powerless
> vexation.[1]

In a fit he tried to make a killing another way. Despite his debts he borrowed more to flutter on his brother's gold-mining speculations. The fever was infectious. Hadn't Pendennis' father made a mint on copper mines and turned a brass-button gentleman, ignoring his drug-grinding origins? These were boom and bust times. 'Fanning himself is deep in an Australian Gold Mine', George was backing a 'Californian Gold mine – the West Mariposa', but then he was as 'wily as any fox – with a vast amount of experience to boot' (which meant he had already 'made and lost one fortune'). But Huxley's fever quickly broke and he swore he would 'never be such an ass again'.[2]

Others were in the same boat, eyeing the same reefs. An impecunious Tyndall had applied for the physics chairs at Sydney and Toronto. The young Turks were shadowing one another. Huxley offered him introductions to his Sydney friends. And he supported Tyndall's nomination for the FRS, but he was losing his own faith in the fellowship's influence.

Only gents with a fortune seemed to be faring well. Look at Darwin in his manor at Downe, the 'complete Kentish hog'. He was the last of the virtuosi, his home a laboratory: a specialist in everything – worms, flowers, flukes, glaciers and volcanoes. (Huxley knew nothing of his covert work on transmutation.) Darwin kept to himself, with Hooker and Lyell his conduits to London society. Inherited wealth had allowed him to wander the world's unknowns, moving from distant lands to the deep recesses of man's mind, looking for the 'key to unlock those secret chambers where the great laws of his nature are revealed'. More mundanely it had bought him time to write on coral atolls and Andean uplift, and now to churn out tomes on every known barnacle. One 412-page volume had just arrived by post, a present from Darwin who realized that young Huxley was too poor to pay.

Darwin was another old salt who placed Sydney among the '100 wonders of the World'. He had even shot 'platypi' on his ride to Bathurst.[3] But his voyage had been a pampered cruise by comparison with Huxley's. No duties, no middies; he had been a self-financed companion to the aristocratic captain. He had collected at leisure and dined ashore with ambassadors. (Such preferential treatment had galled the *Beagle*'s surgeon-naturalist, who had quit and shipped home.) But for all that, Darwin had known the blue devils, and he had seen a new world in the making, a natural world.

Huxley was thinking about his own voyage again, revelling in MacGillivray's *Narrative*, which had just been published. Given the earlier *brouhaha* it was a 'very creditable' affair. But the illustrations! – 'they have murdered mine in the engraving'. He parcelled up a copy for Nettie, to remind her of more tempestuous days. It took him back to Sydney docks; it even tempted him back:

> I was talking seriously with Fanning the other night about
> the possibility of finding some employment of a profitable
> kind in Australia, storekeeping squatting or the like. As I
> told him any change in my mode of life must be *total* . . . I
> will not attempt my own profession. I should only be led

astray to think and to work as of old, and sigh continually
for my old dear and intoxicating pursuits. I wish I
understood Brewing, and I would make a proposition to
come and help your father.

Why try to soar to intellectual heights? Why not clip Pegasus'
wings and force him to trot like any carthorse? In bleak moments
Huxley even believed that his impoverished origins had 'unfitted
me for ever taking any very high position'. And what of Nettie's
sacrifice on his scientific altar? He saw her 'wasting her youth'
in 'cheerless suspense'. Yet how could he forgo his dream? To
emigrate now would be to fail 'in the whole purpose of my
existence'. It would be 'a sin and a shameful thing'.[4]
He clung to his successes. The glimpse of gold left an afterglow
in his eyes. Sabine told him again 'that a brilliant prospect lay
open for me here if I would only wait', but with the debts piling it
seemed hopeless. The blizzards in 1852 saw him in 'doubt perplex-
ity and utmost despair . . . I am neither Stoic nor Martyr, and even
if I were I can get no clear perception of what is right to be done'.
Personal ambition went with a stabbing need to raise the appreciation of science:

> My brothers understand ambition and profit. Fanning
> understands ambition. None, not even you Menen, seem
> to comprehend the noble love of intellectual labour for its
> own sake – as an end of life. Nay as I dont doubt that like
> the rest I should turn from it at the first temptation for
> the flesh pots, I had better say no more about it.[5]

Through the winter he drove on in a demoniacal haze, writing his
master work on molluscs, planned on the voyage and executed for
an eternity. With his *Rattlesnake* haul of sea butterflies and
pelagic periwinkle relatives he was equipped. He would show that
all molluscs – from squids to snails to whelks – are modifications
of a basic archetype or plan. He was creating order out of Nature,
making it a 'harmonious whole'; and in a Romantic age establishing the coherent pattern of Nature meant the possibility of drawing
moral conclusions, which could give science a new political potency. For the moment, though, he was in his corner, simply
arguing that the squid's arm was a homologue of the snail's foot.
Not, he insisted, that his 'archetypal' mollusc had a real Platonic
existence. It was no effigy in God's mind, even if Owen had seen it
there. It was an abstraction. It summed up 'the most general

propositions' concerning molluscs. The paper was a model of diplomacy, the sort that would establish his credentials as a 'philosophical anatomist'. It has 'taken me a world of time, thought, and reading' and is 'the best thing I have done'.[6]

His exposure at the Royal Society was getting him noticed. He became that 'promising young man', spotted by the old scholar of Chinese Sir George Staunton, who treated him to a tour of the House of Lords. It even got him an invitation to talk at London's fashionable venue, the Royal Institution.

Here the Friday night lectures were glittering affairs. Smart carriages would line Albemarle Street in Piccadilly. The socialites flocked in, more for the soirée to come than its zoological *hors d'oeuvre*. The institution was part of the Whig educational empire, run by technocrats, the few who saw science as essential to an efficient society. Michael Faraday was there, dreaming sublime dreams of electromagnetic force fields. By now the Institution's utilitarianism was tempered by a crowd-pulling dilettantism, and on Fridays 400 was a good crowd. Huxley's talk was scheduled for 30 April. It was 'considered a "crack" thing' and his self-assurance grew in proportion: 'all the bigwigs Faraday Owen Lyell &c give these lectures' and he was 'ready to go in with any of them. "The wind is tempered to the shorn lamb" in my case means "impudence rises with the occasion"'.[7]

Impudence it would be. Here Owen had baffled the fashionable ladies with his talk on flukes and medusae, or rather, his account of their multi-generation life-cycles; and whomsoever Owen could baffle, Huxley could mystify. He took on Owen's knotty problem. The larval fluke inside a snail host can multiply asexually into 200,000 sporocysts, each of which releases a new sort of swimming larva to infect mammals, including humans. Here they reproduce in the blood or liver, laying eggs which pass out and start the cycle over again. So, were these generations of different *individuals*?

No. He would contradict Owen from the same platform. He would argue that these 200,000 are successive free-living parts of the original individual. They were so many independent buds. It was a hard line to toe. And Owen was not known for his grace in the face of contradiction. He was 'feared and hated' for his sledgehammer responses. 'The truth is he is the superior of most & does not conceal that he knows it', and this was his problem, an insecure nature masked by arrogance. Huxley was working on Owen's subject, '"*Parthenogenesis*" which he told me he considered one of the best things he had done!' The sneer showed his delight at playing David; his slingshot aimed at the six-foot Goliath protecting the dons and deans. Owen had given him a lot of help, and 'I am as grateful as it is possible to be towards a man with whom I feel it necessary to be always on my guard'.

So his public début – like his life – was to be on a point of controversy. He told Faraday that his approach would 'considerably modify the theory of Zoology'. 'I suppose', Faraday retorted, that 'if you are . . . to oppose anybody you have thought well over it'. Huxley had, and he had upped the stakes; 'a success may do me a world of good', equally a failure might see him roasted alive.[8] Given the sable-and-feather mix of scientific gents and society ladies he would take his 'profound subject, and play at battledore & shuttlecock with it, so as to suit both'. Owen was being forced on to court.

In fact Owen was forced to play a number of games at once. Huxley finished his paper on molluscs with a cryptic admission that he could trace no progression from one type to another. Indeed he could see no progression in nature *at all*. Privately, his bizarre image was of an immutable archetype at the centre of a Ptolemaic sphere, on which sat all the slugs, squids, whelks and mussels. They were all equidistant from the centre (and the whole cluster sat in galactic isolation from all the other archetypal clusters). This strange amalgam of Macleay's circles and continental archetypes showed a man groping for symmetry and order in nature.[9]

Exhausted, he crawled to the end of his mollusc paper, feeling like one of his sea slugs. To get it in print, however, would require 'a little manoeuvring on my part'. Paranoia now masked the pugnacity, understandably with him destroying Owen's best work on parthenogenesis. The melodrama played out in his mind. He told Nettie on 15 March that if it were refereed by 'my "particular friend" Prof. Owen . . . it will not be published. He won't be able to say much against it but he will pooh-pooh it to a dead certainty'.

Why? Because for 20 years Owen has been 'the great authority on these matters, and has had no one to tread on his heels'. He portrayed Owen nailing up 'No Poachers' notices around his preserve, barring trespassers. In truth Huxley wanted his own blood-soaked banner: 'you will smile at my perversity dearest. I have a certain pleasure in overcoming these obstacles and fighting these folks with their own weapons'. Hostilities would commence, with atrocities committed on both sides, the nastiest 30-year feud in Victoria's reign. But this was merely the reveille, waking the belligerents: Owen, nodding to cloth and gown, his Divine Archetypes a bulwark against rationalist attack, his Natural Law an edict from God. And snarling at him a frustrated Huxley, one of the new Puritans thundering against Anglican thraldom.

The struggle was symptomatic of a wider divide, a reflection of massive urban and industrial developments. But its fury came from Huxley's own rage.

There was the more immediate cause of his paranoia. The previous day, talking to Owen, Huxley's hot head had got the better of him. They were discussing the great Berlin zoologist, Christian Ehrenberg, an expert on unicellular animals, the protozoa. Huxley saw the man as 'a sham'. Ehrenberg denied that many of the protozoans he studied were in fact plants, algae; and he maintained in the same 'oppressive manner' that his single-cell amoebas were miniature higher animals, with granules corresponding to every organ. In Huxley's view the 'man's hobby-horse' had 'run away with him'. Owen rose to the defence. But then Owen was 'a man of (scientific) property himself', a Tory who had defended the realm with the Honourable Artillery Company during the Chartist years, when rioters had been bent on destroying the old order. Of course he 'takes the conservative side', snapped Huxley. When in the

> argument I showed up Ehrenbergs want of judgment and
> candour and above all, his unwarrantable sneers at every
> body else he saw that he could much better pardon
> Ehrenbergs injustice & severity, than that of any *young
> man* who should think fit to say sharp things about him. I
> saw the hint but didn't choose to take it. I laughed – Ah, I
> said, I see you are a great conservative. His reply was
> 'And so will you be after you are forty–' which let me into
> the whole secret of his advocacy of Ehrenberg – it was a
> fellow feeling – a sort of who knows what established
> authority these young men will attack next? We must put
> 'em down. I suppose if I say anything more about
> Ehrenberg I shall have him bearing down upon me – but I
> don't mean to stop or go out of my way for all that.[10]

Owen took this deft punch on the chin. He never did referee the mollusc paper, but neither did he damn it. Rather he read it with 'great pleasure' as a work 'after my own heart'.[11] He was still extremely polite.

*

Toil calmed Huxley down. He turned in a paper on zebra tape-worms to the Zoological Society. Everybody was 'amazed . . . at his complete mastery'. He made a horribly complex subject easy, showing with lightning sketches how the parasite transforms as it migrates around the zebra's body. In the audience a young un-known, Alfred Russel Wallace, marvelled at his 'wonderful power'.

Huxley found that 'the more I work the better my temper seems to be'. The time was his own now. His parents had moved to Jim's asylum, where there was round-the-clock supervision for his father. Before leaving, his mother parcelled out the family keep-sakes and gave Tom an 'old fashioned broach' containing a lock of her hair for Nettie.[12] He teased her about these 'testamentary dispositions'; but she only responded by passing on the toys she had 'put aside for me – "When I had a nursery"'.

He was eking out an existence, translating, cataloguing the sea squirts in the British Museum. It was pin money and not enough. Nineteen plates for his book were ready to be engraved, but the £200 cost of this six-month labour intensive process was beyond him. He needed the grant. He harassed the Astronomer Royal; he harangued the First Sea Lord.[13] But to no avail. Still he met rejections across the board.

He reached another low ebb. He was 'half mad' with worry, and 'equally wild at thinking of the long weary while' since he had kissed Nettie. 'Help me darling', he cried time after time. Then came the crushing blow. On Wednesday 14 April a telegraph sent him to Kent to find his mother dead. She had suffered a heart attack and died at 4.30 that afternoon. Tom arrived near midnight, numbed, clutching his imbecile father. She had been so 'active and youthful' and at 66 'her bright black eyes and lively manners made her seem younger'. In his quivering state he thought of her pro-phetic parting gifts. Her pride, his success, they merged into one desperately reassuring dream. 'She loved me I believe better than any of her sons and fancied she had a right to be proud of me'.

> I am very sad . . . this has opened the floodgates, and the
> whole meaning of existence has sucked out & drowns all
> other feelings. For me there is neither certainty of faith
> nor any consolation – but only a stern summoning of all
> my courage to bear what is inevitable. Belief and
> Happiness seem to be beyond the reach of thinking men in
> these days but Courage and Silence are left.[14]

The sons stood over her grave in Barming Churchyard on Monday

19 April. Tom was still in his 'hideous dream'. Father was there, paralysed and feeble. They 'feared the shock might kill him' but a 'vegetable existence' put him beyond feeling.[15] (He survived three more years in the asylum.) For days Tom tried to function. His Royal Institution début was looming. 'I cannot put it off, and yet I feel unable properly to collect my faculties'. He knew how proud his mother had been about it. It was too late to back out. He worked in a pall of gloom. He considered what it meant to be an 'individual' – as only an invertebrate anatomist could, used to parthogenetic aphids and men-of-war that come apart.

His nerves created waves in the nihilistic void and the lecture somehow shook itself together. He would stand alone, opposing every zoologist on the knottiest problem of the age. A letter from Nettie on the morning of 30 April was a good omen. But every passing hour brought a fresh desire 'to break down, and then go and hang myself'. That night he stood backstage, more anxious than 'I ever have been in my life', thinking of how his mother 'would have entered into my nerves!' The born sermonizer, the boy who had reversed his collar and preached to the kitchen maids, was awaiting his ordination. George and Polly were out there, and the Fannings – and in the front rows the cream of London science: Forbes, Faraday, Wharton Jones and a 'whole lot of "nobs"' besides. The hour struck. In he marched, 'heart beating like a sledge hammer'. Suddenly he knew the felon's fear before the noose tightened.

He took a breath and cast a spell. He conjured up a tropical breeze and slapping sails; they stood off the New Guinea coast, looking up at 'that hot and copper sky – and below into the deep blue'. No disgusting ocean where:

> Yea, slimy things did crawl with legs
> Upon that slimy sea.

That was Coleridge's poetic 'libel upon [its] delicate and peaceful inhabitants'. The modern mariner found beauty and truth in its depths; and a simplicity to its life that posed the profoundest problems. The audience watched men-of-war 'floating idly along', or 'whole fleets of the Velella – with its curious sail . . . twisting about with every breath of air'. He pulled in the towing net and everyone peered at its contents. They saw brilliant-hued floats. They watched a bit bud off and drift away as an offspring, and he teased them – 'Is it an animal? – or is it only *part* of an animal?'[16]

Few accepted that individuals could exist in two or 200 parts;

the applause at the end was more for his ingenuity, even if friends confirmed that he had 'triumphantly demolished' Owen's 'whole system of Alternation of Generations'. Nor was it a polished performance, judging by one letter which complained that, whatever he was good for, it wasn't lecturing. But his ordination was over, and 'Thank Heaven'. 'After the Royal Institution there is no audience I shall ever fear'.

He crashed to the ground afterwards, 'very very tired'. He collapsed and slept and grieved his grief without worrying about work. He did nothing but sleep for days, mooching in a nihilistic gloom. He roused himself with Keats' poem *Endymion*, 'the dreamiest of dreamy legends full of glorious imagery, and inspired by love'.[17] Now he only had Nettie.

Unreal weeks passed, his brain anaesthetized; 'my life rolls on – work – work – work – with very little to vary it'. He had become an expert in the arcana of life. He refereed articles on starfish and sea slugs. He corrected the proofs of William Benjamin Carpenter's *Principles of Comparative Physiology*. Carpenter was a Unitarian and the Professor of Forensic Medicine at University College, and his book – which denied any miraculous tinkering in nature – was to Huxley's taste.[18] Lunching with the 39 year-old Carpenter would have reinforced Huxley's sense of the value of his expertise. Carpenter was fighting to end society's dominance by Oxbridge. He wanted talent and training rewarded. The time had come to put London's science specialists into the top jobs. Huxley was Carpenter's sort of expert, and Carpenter was Huxley's sort of man.

Meanwhile the grant business turned from fiasco to Whitehall farce – a case of missing memorials, wrong doors, officious Under Secretaries. Sir Charles Trevelyan at the Treasury sent him to the Prime Minister; but the PM's personal secretary had lost the memorial from Lord Rosse, and by now the Royal Society had mislaid its minutes as well. He traipsed corridors and sat in antechambers, doggedly determined, however bootless it seemed, his mood summed up by the expression on his new photograph: 'horribly savage & sulky looking'.

Absence was making Hal's memory of Nettie grow fainter even as his heart grew fonder. His correspondence became tardy. He missed Nettie's birthday. Another link snapped when the Fannings shipped back to Australia in August. They twisted his arm to join them, join the 80,000 other emigrants this year, lured by the gold.

But the great, intoxicating, intellectual Babylon had spoiled him; no jogging existence would now do, with 'the great problems of existence set hopelessly in the background'. The last sight of a tearful Ory will, Huxley said, 'throw me into myself more than ever'.[19]

A sniff of 'fresh Professorships' kept him going. With a thousand visitors expected at the pretty new Queen's College during the British Association week at Belfast, he borrowed money from George to go, determined to keep his ear to the ground. And his face to the fore: more confident now, he took to the podium 'for about three quarters of an hour without break', chalky hands waving as he sketched an archetypal sea squirt on the blackboard.[20] Afterwards he steamed to the Giant's Causeway, taking secret pleasure in the swell which sent the mighty philosophers to the side. He strolled the shore with Owen, dwarfed by the huge basalt columns reaching into the Atlantic where giants had once stepped. Owen and Huxley: the giants were of intellect now, world experts divided over the rule of the animal kingdom. Here they stood together, polite and mistrustful, on the final balmy day before the long cold winter.

In September Huxley took a last trip into the past. Two days deputizing for his old teacher Thomas Chandler brought the memories back: the little East End drug shop, his privation and dissipation. Maudlin thoughts choked him: 'you cannot fancy', he told Nettie, 'what a deep draught of abomination I took. From drinking deeper ... my sweet one, you saved me'. He liked to think of himself reclaimed, his new life dedicated to nature and truth. But *real* dissipation was her visiting cousin Alfred, caught creeping out for nights on the tiles, 'addicted to drinking & only fifteen!'[21]

Sots and sad recollections characterized the period. His first job offer came from a struggling private medical school. It was one of the gasping survivors. Founded by an irascible surgeon, George Dermott – a political bruiser who dictated notes in a gin palace – it was a Dissenting relic with no future (it promptly died). But there could be no backstreet lecture-grubbing for Huxley. He wasn't going to be dragged down like Cooke. The 'spectre of a wasted life has passed before me'. He had a 'vocation', and no man of the cloth felt a greater 'duty to follow it'.[22] His rise in this 'boiling scathing world' left him demanding something better.

Nettie told him to follow his heart, and that was set on a university chair. The death of Jock's father, William MacGillivray, professor of natural history in Aberdeen, sent Huxley to Owen and Forbes for references once again. George chuckled at Tom's 'chimerical' desires, but he was determined to take his place in the new intellectual world. 'The past two years' had proved 'that the dreams of my childhood and the aspirations of my manhood were . . . not mere fancies'. They 'were the expression of a hidden force'.[23]

On 7 November he was vindicated. It had been blowing a gale for weeks. 'I had a deuced bad cold . . . it was a beastly November day and I was very grumpy'. But the word came: he had his 'scientific knighthood', the Royal Medal. It filled an enormous longing. It was confirmation of the poor boy's right to walk the public bridleway of science. It would raise his 'status in the eyes of those charming people, "practical men"', who sniggered at his intellectual aspirations.[24] The 50-guinea nugget was proof that science *could* confer prestige in a world looking to rank and wealth. As the downpours continued and Forbes contemplated building an Ark, Huxley had already found his Ararat.

Preparing to be garlanded, Huxley finally felt part of the English nation. The gloss of gold replaced the dross of alien detachment. A new chauvinism punctured his blasé exterior. He caught the mood of national pride, now erasing the class hatreds of the 1840s. Before his investiture he even revelled in the spectacle of Wellington's state funeral. Friends were aghast at 'the national extravagance of spending 400,000 on a dead man', an Iron Duke, hero of Waterloo or no.[25] But Huxley sat in an icy St Paul's Cathedral feeling an inner glow. There he stayed from eight until three, watching the Gothic beams play on the 'best of our people'.

His own ceremony at Somerset House was as much political theatre. At the Anniversary Dinner on 30 November Lord Rosse awarded the medal. Behind him the bewigged past Presidents looked more benign in their frames, and the faces of the 60 Fellows quite exuberant. Huxley told of his lonely years at sea and of his dove: 'it has this day returned not indeed with an olive branch but with a twig of the bay – and a fruit from the Garden of the Hesperides'.[26] He hinted at his portfolios of *Rattlesnake* drawings and vowed to justify the award when the government 'of this *great* country' ceased its great deliberation and afforded him the few pounds to publish.

On that litigious subject he was still fuming. Three weeks earlier he had waylaid Owen, requesting yet another recommendation, this time to shake up the Home Office. Time passed with no sign of it. He was livid. Then he met Owen:

> I was going to walk past, but he stopped me, and in the blandest and most gracious manner said, 'I have received your note, I shall *grant* it.' The phrase and the implied condescension were quite 'touching' – so much that if I stopped a moment longer I must knock him into the gutter. I therefore bowed and walked off. This was last Saturday. Nothing came on Monday or on Tuesday, but on Wednesday morning I received 'with Prof. Owen's best wishes', the *strongest and kindest testimonial any man could possibly wish for*! . . . I gave up any attempt to comprehend him from this time forth.

To be the butt of such hauteur was galling. Owen was a gentleman on the Civil List, now settled royally into Sheen Lodge, and he acted the part. 'How sad it is', someone wrote, 'to see great genius combined with such a want of generous feeling'. Forbes could only agree. Owen 'is certainly one of the oddest beings I ever came across', he told Huxley, '& seems as if he was constantly attended by two spiritual policemen, the one from the upper regions & the other from the lower'.[27] But well might Owen have been getting a little lax; Huxley's requests for references were arriving weeks apart! Owen was backing Huxley to the hilt and to what avail?

The rains continued. Rivers overflowed and lakes covered the patchwork south of England. The Thames was set to flood as Huxley steamed down to Greenwich for Christmas with the Busks. Busk and Huxley were joining forces, turning an honest penny by translating the latest German tome on cells and tissues, Albert Kölliker's *Manual of Human Histology*. As a student text it would pay about £180, enough 'filthy lucre' to make the drudgery bearable.[28] With his writing finally showing a profit, Huxley promised Lizzie something in Tennessee ('Scott' had never been able to practise among the whites; he could only get work treating slaves).[29] 'Don't expect anything vast, but there is corn in Egypt'. He had seen it.

Others had too. A query about sea squirts from the *Economist* piqued his interest. It led him to another schoolmaster's son, a political pamphleteer with cosmic aspirations, Herbert Spencer. Spencer was the sub-editor of the *Economist*, a bumptious man with a breathless vision of an upward-sweeping nature. All he lacked was the proof of this evolutionary progress. Owen disappointed him. Like any self-respecting secularist Spencer hated Owen's Archetypal Holy of Holies and ended his course in 'complete disbelief'. And so he had turned to Huxley. He needed information on the 'production of composite animals by the union of simpler ones'.[30]

Where better than the free-trading *Economist* to find an odd rapport? Huxley indulged Spencer's utopian flights, passing this former railway engineer over to Tyndall with a line from Faust, as 'Ein Kerl der speculirt'.[31] A learned pact bound the tormented trio, who bartered their souls for beauty and truth. Spencer too had known poverty. He had toyed with emigrating. When Huxley was walking the East End hovels, Spencer was donning his Chartist cap and decrying all 'despotisms, aristocracies, priestcrafts'. While Huxley was learning surgery, Spencer was dabbling in more emancipatory sciences, from self-help phrenology to cosmic evolution. With his own phrenological bump of 'self-esteem' he should have been a preacher. But like Huxley in a new age, his tub-thumping was to the glory of the great Unknown. Spencer's, like Huxley's, was a fratricidal relationship with theology. He penned the stodgy sermons as Tyndall led the pantheistic hymns and Huxley preached hell-fire warnings about the unpardonable sin of faith.

Spencer was another child of the 1840s who had learned his politics around the Lord's table. Derby-born into a Chapel culture, he had a searing distrust of the privileged, State-endowed Church. He was still carrying his Nonconformist placard demanding fair play and reform, only now he projected this moral imperative on to the universe. Change was guaranteed: the growth of civilization was 'all of a piece with the development of the embryo or the unfolding of a flower'.[32] Progress through open competition was a 'law underlying the whole organic creation'. It alone could bear 'Humanity onwards towards perfection'.

Huxley found a freethinker whose evolutionary ideals packed a moral punch. Spencer's 'Development Hypothesis' was hot off the press. It ran in the *Leader*, that radical standard born of the hopes of 1848, putting the libertarian in uneasy alliance with the socialists. Spencer was an anarchist who decried all State intervention, whether it was State education for the poor or State privileges for the parson. To Huxley the first was as chilling as the second was cheering.

So began a turbulent friendship. Huxley would end up bursting Spencer's overblown balloons, but a secular iconoclasm bound them at a deeper level. Huxley also had Spencer to thank for his entrée into London's avant garde – that brilliant, anguished group which converged on publisher John Chapman's weekly soirées in the Strand, opposite Spencer's office.

At its hub was the Svengali-like Chapman, mesmerizing with his Byronic looks and the more attractive for flouting convention.[33] Marian Evans (soon to be launched as the novelist George Eliot) was part of his tumultuous household, although her ménage with the philandering Chapman, his compliant wife and jealous mistress was understandably uneasy. Fears that free thought meant free love were hardly allayed by the likes of Chapman. He was a druggist's son and a medical radical in an age which bred them with fearsome dispositions. And he published sensational books. Howls rose with each title: Marian Evans' translation of Strauss' *Life of Jesus*, which made the Gospels a 'misty chaos of contradiction and uncertainty'; Francis Newman's harrowing account of his retreat from Christianity, *Phases of Faith*; the lapsed Anglo-Catholic J. A. Froude's *Nemesis of Faith*; Spencer's finger-wagging to government in *Social Statics*. The climax came with a real proclamation of atheism – for many readers their first encounter with the unimaginable – *Letters on the Laws of Man's Nature and Development* by Harriet Martineau and Henry Atkinson, whom even Darwin's relatives considered 'two criminals'.

The charismatic Chapman was headhunting in 1853. He had revamped radical London's quarterly, the *Westminster Review*. He was casting around for 'advanced thinkers', not to shock, but to 'sap and undermine' a lumbering orthodoxy. He approached Huxley, who offered an account of the lonely cockroach-infested life on the Louisiade. Huxley's review of MacGillivray's *Narrative* added a dash of exotica in a day when businessmen 'run over to India, or to Australia . . . without remark'. It sounded creaking timbers, smelled of grog, sweated in the '*hot* Scotch mist' and fired six-pounders at Sea Lords and soul-savers alike. What Chapman could decipher of the illegible script he liked and he took it on spec, offering Huxley his own scientific column. Here at last was a chance to wield his stiletto pen. Only as an afterthought did he ask about the pay. Chapman was bankrupting himself financing the cause. He offered terms Huxley could not refuse – '12 guineas per sheet (ie. 16 pages)', Huxley whistled to Nettie, and it 'promises to be a guinea a page by and bye'.[34]

Spencer and Chapman drew Huxley into a web of radical friendships. At the soirées he mixed with the literary freethinkers.

He could gaze on Froude's melancholy countenance or savour Newman's 'angelic sweetness'. Here were fellow-travellers William Benjamin Carpenter, the philosopher John Stuart Mill and the convicted atheist George Holyoake. With Huxley 'becoming celebrated in London' his February début created a stir, as Marian Evans noted. He was a glass-case zoological anomaly, a sharp 28 year-old intent on making his way by pure science. For her part Evans was now standing beside G. H. Lewes, a smallpox-scarred veteran with a more political need to popularize science. So this was the dissipated spirit behind *Ranthorpe*. A stare of seeming malevolence made Lewes a 'sort of miniature Mirabeau'. But the good-natured critic, actor, Germanizer and *Leader*-writer struck Huxley with his dramatic tongue:

> I say . . . that if astronomy must destroy theology, it will . . . deepen religion. There is no man in whom the starry heavens has not excited religious emotion; . . . whatever may be the litanies most suitable to his mind, under some form or other, man cannot help worshipping when under the canopy of the 'cathedral of immensity'.

The talk was reasoned and outrageous: disestablishment, democracy, the tyranny of marriage, biblical criticism, evolutionism – every emancipatory 'ism' to destabilize Anglican society. Spencer's anarchic individualists debated with Holyoake's atheist socialists. Then all would join Lewes to demand a liberating theory of 'development', a hammer to break the creationist shackles. On this Chapman even quizzed Owen, intrigued by the ultimate mystery, the way in which 'successive species have been introduced'.[35]

Huxley landed feet first in the throng, but he soon shuffled off to the rim, no doubt with a disapproving glare. Carrying a cross for real science, he scorned the developmental crudities of so many Lotharios. A perceptive Marian Evans reassessed this aloof spectator, with his love of '*paradox* and *antagonism*'. She saw that his personality was reactive: 'its being beckoned in one direction may incline it to turn off in another'. At times he seemed driven by his own bull-headedness. But perhaps that was the price for such 'brilliant talents'.

Afternoons were spent with Spencer and Lewes at the zoo, evenings at the opera. Lewes seemed comfortably familiar, long-haired 'and rather worn-looking', full of *risqué* jokes: a 'loose-tongued merry-hearted being with more sail than ballast', Carlyle called him. It showed as he fell prey to Huxley's wit. At dinner

one day Spencer's guests described the difficulty of writing, and
Lewes announced, 'I get up steam at once. In short, I boil at low
temperatures', only to have Huxley flash back, but 'that implies a
vacuum in the upper regions'.

Huxley found a man swopping women and swopping Owen's
Platonism for Comte's positivism, shearing science of its woolly
theological coat and paring the corpse down to the factual bone.
(Science for the French philosopher Auguste Comte rested on
'positive' facts constituted into a hierarchy of natural laws. Advocating a 'Religion of Humanity' and technocratic priesthood, he
gave science its most sanctified sectarian ethos as the only True
Knowledge.) Lewes' insistence on facts was only marred by his
insistent factual blunders. As for his addiction to evolution, Huxley
had 'no objection whatever' while it was '*an hypothesis merely*' –
meaning he saw not a tittle of evidence. But others felt the way the
wind was blowing. If evolution be true, Lyell reasoned, trying to
gain a crumb of comfort, 'the whole geological history of the globe
is the history of Man'. Radical London was reverberating to this
new hymn. That Unitarian-turned-atheist Harriet Martineau (the
belle laide once inseparable from Darwin's elder brother Erasmus)
raised her eyes while translating Comte in 1853:

> We find ourselves suddenly living and moving in the midst
> of the universe – as a part of it, and not as its aim and
> object. We find ourselves living, not under capricious and
> arbitrary conditions . . . but under great, general,
> invariable laws, which operate on us as part of a whole.

The avant garde was struck by the startling reality. To this end
Lewes, Spencer and Huxley began emasculating Owen's anatomy,
even as the cloying *Quarterly* was lauding it. None doubted that
Owen was 'the greatest living comparative anatomist'; it only
made them more cynical about his Divine Archetype. This was no
blueprint for Creation. Romanticism was *passé*. To a new breed it
was a bad mixture of pomposity and mysticism. In Germany too it
was dismissed by an atheistic underground. Carlyle's romanticism
had been an escape from 'the evils of industrial and materialist
society'.[36] But the men from the engine sheds and medical manufactories saw their salvation in the industrial order. They needed to
strip off the metaphysical gloss and liberate science, leaving it
supposedly value-free and serviceable to its new industrial masters.
The three zoo-going rationalists were deconsecrating Owen's
universe.

This brash crowd was making the world safe for Darwin, who was still sitting in silent agitation on his theory of evolution. Darwin emerged from his Kent retreat on 6 April 1853 to attend a Geological Society meeting, which is probably where Huxley first saw him: broad-set, beetle-browed, with a beaming face and Shropshire accent. Enthusiasm oozed as he declared himself 'a man of one idea', barnacles 'morning & night'. Normally a reticent gent, he offered Huxley his sea squirts from the *Beagle* voyage, and then prompted him: 'it is very indelicate in me to say so, but it would give me *great* pleasure to see my work reviewed by any one so capable'. 'Upon my honour', he exclaimed in his self-effacing way, 'I never did such a thing before'. And then with unaccustomed bravado he dropped Huxley a list of his oddest findings for inclusion.

The mollusc paper came in return. Darwin, from a line of freethinkers and Unitarians, swore by material causes. He too eschewed archetypal ideas as so much verbiage. He too detested the Platonic imagery of 'Owen, Agassiz & Co'. Visualizing an archetype 'in *your* sense', he assured Huxley, as simply the common denominator of all vertebrates or molluscs, 'is one of the very highest ends of Natural History'. But not *the* highest. Huxley supposed a fixed abstraction, but could he not imagine an archetype '*undergoing* further development'?[37] Think of it as a hypothetical *ancestor*, a generalized forerunner from which any number of specialized descendants could evolve. Huxley, the 'architectural' man, interested in anatomy and geometry, not fossils and geology, missed the point.

While Huxley slid in and out of the best social circles and gloried in the kudos, the struggle for a chair had turned into a killing drudge. It was made worse by the separation from Nettie – three years now. Without a job, merit and medal would mean nothing and 'my small light will be ignominiously snuffed out'. Toronto was officially given against him and Tyndall in 1853. Within weeks a chair at King's College in the Strand slipped from his grasp. 'I have got very old . . . in the last two years', he moaned. Continual bouncing from elation to depression meant that 'a good deal of the spring & elasticity has gone out of me'.[38] Mental collapses seemed to regulate his life and 1853 saw the final precipitous trough.

Yet to the world he was thriving. At 28 he was a Royal Medallist, lionized by the 'big wigs' at Royal Society soirées as much as by Lewes' radicals. He seemed brilliantly combative to George Eliot and dashing to Ellen Busk; he was hungry, determined, and they knew he was on the way up. With the young bloods, he was sliding into a position of power. The proof came with his elevation to that star chamber, the Royal Society Council. He also 'propped' Tyndall's 'faltering soul' by announcing his own Fellowship. In fact for a man with no work prospects he showed some brass in directing Tyndall to the top job, telling him he should be 'looking to Faraday's place'. Tyndall, the poetic pantheist, knew that these moves were 'guided by the gods'. He too had been crushed by rejections, but for once justice was done. He gave such fighting talks on magnetism at the Royal Institution that Faraday secured his professorship there. Providence, said Tyndall on hearing a whisper that he would even follow Huxley with the 1853 Royal Medal, evidently 'intends to build us a Toronto at home'.[39]

Huxley too was held by the gravitational pull of the great metropolis. He needed its vibrancy and shared in its self-importance. Here were bookshops on every corner and the treat of first nights. No colonial hideaway would do; science at the centre was 'discussion and debate, politics and action'.[40] The metropolis meant brimming museums and rich institutions; it meant legislating scientific laws rather than collecting local taxes. 'My course of life is taken', he announced. 'I will *not* leave London – I *will* make myself a name and a position'.

Quite how had yet to resolve itself. That perennial grumbler Charles Babbage (who had successfully fleeced the government of thousands to build his calculating machine) complained that science was not a profession. There was no educational standard, no scientific civil service, not even a word for its practitioners. Opportunities were scant. Zoology was still an adjunct of medicine, and its chairs were pitifully undervalued.

But change was coming. The adulation of Mammon during the 1851 Great Exhibition gave science a new set of values. Savants rushed to hitch their demands to Victorian consumerism. Another trooper drilled by De la Beche in the School of Mines, the chemist Lyon Playfair, saw the way ahead. For him 'searchers after truth' were nor dreamy idealists. They were 'the "horses" of the chariots of industry'. Huxley loved the rhetoric, the more because it got results. In 1853 a Government Department of Science and Art was established to oversee the training of the nation's arts and science teachers. Huxley hoped that it would break the Latin stranglehold, so that a schoolboy would in future know 'the difference between ... the contents of his skull and those of his abdomen'. Playfair, appointed the Secretary for Science, became an ally in place. Cultivate him, Huxley told Tyndall; he 'has great influence and will have more'.[41]

While the future looked up, Huxley's money worries were as immediate as ever. Turning a 'prose labourer' was the quick option. No longer the night-owl, he was up at 8 am., at his desk all day and slumped in bed by midnight, too tired for parties. Medical reviews, German translations, long articles for cyclopae-dias and encyclopaedic articles for the *Westminster*: the list went on. He had become a 'penny-a-liner', his speed dictated by dead-lines. He honed his prose, giving his brilliant *bon mots* their vernacular edge. As a 'scientific jackal for the public', he acquired a butcher's knack of displaying the flesh from disembowelled books as tasty morsels. Readers salivated at his political sprint through comparative anatomy. In one of his sharpest anonymous pieces, he talked of the fall of the 'ultra-speculative "red" biol-ogists' Geoffroy and Oken, the old radicals who demanded a common archetype for all animal life (giving men and amoebas equality on good revolutionary principles). But a new generation had taken over 'the Temple of Science' and, true to British Liberal principles, given each animal class its sovereign archetype. The keenest social metaphor enlivened the driest *System der Thierischen Morphologie*.

His production line kept the wolf from the door. What little surplus it generated went to Lizzie, needier herself and now 'in possession of another possible President' (a new baby boy). Off went a draft for $135, amassed, he hastened to add, 'by mine own sword'.[42] He would collect later, say 'twenty years hence', when he would come over 'on the possibility of picking up something or other from one of my nephews at Washington'.

Huxley's translations were tuned to contemporary needs. Chap-man's clique wanted to make man and morality as natural as climate and cosmos. It wanted laws that stretched from stars to society. But to find them it was forced to plunder the microscopic realm, Huxley's realm.

The key turned up in the work of a brilliant Estonian embryolo-gist, who had trained at Würzburg and settled in St Petersburg. Karl Ernst Von Baer had described how the foetuses of chicks, lizards and dogs all diverged and specialized away from a common homogeneous 'germ'. The notion of specialization and division of labour was elastic enough to satisfy everyone. It became the watchword; it explained embryos; it explained evolution; it explained the co-existence of creatures in a habitat, like so many trades in the same tenement; it explained an industrial society based on division of labour – for Spencer it explained everything. Growth from homogeneous to heterogeneous was the 'law of all progress'.

It was even the flirtatious babble of lovers, Marian Evans' come-hither call to Spencer. She would, she swore, presently 'be on equality, in point of sensibility, with the star-fish and sea-egg ... You see I am sinking fast towards "homogeneity" and my brain will soon be a mere pulp unless you come to arrest the downward process'.[43]

The towering edifice rested on Von Baer. He was acquiring heroic status among the cognoscenti. But they were reduced to cannibalizing and recycling secondary sources. Von Baer's work rested in German obscurity. So Huxley set to, translating the relevant texts.

Huxley actually stuck to the letter of Von Baer's law, damning its extrapolation to heaven and earth. Yet even the cautious Owen was extending it to the cavalcade of fossil animals. Life's historical progression mirrored the growth of the embryo; it became increasingly specialized. To prove it Owen plotted the progress of the horse from its ancient five-toed antecedent to today's single-toed thoroughbred.[44] It was no 'evolution', no damnable 'Development', indeed how the Word became Flesh he did not know, except by a 'predetermining Will'. (Lewes did; in the *Leader* he appropriated Owen's fossils for his own evolutionary ends.) Huxley, loathing Owen and his progressive-incarnation mysticism, shied away.

Moreover he believed that Von Baer himself had pulled the rug from under this 'progressive development' nonsense. Von Baer's study of the embryos of the great groups – the vertebrates, molluscs, starfish and insects – had shown each to be based on a unique archetypal plan. They could not be stacked into a chain, none was 'higher' than any other. Nor could Huxley embrace the 'progression of animal forms in time'. Almost all geologists accepted a fossil ascent from fish to man. But not Huxley. His deconsecrated palaeontology was deeply nihilistic and defiantly anti-Creative: no progress, no meaning to fossil life, no Christian comfort. For Huxley, almost uniquely, man was no 'modulus and standard of the creation', no end point, merely an 'aberrant modification'.

He became absurdly provocative. Murchison wanted to see a footprint in ancient rock as proof that man had always existed? Well, Huxley said, with mammals turning up in Triassic beds, he soon expected 'to see a bit of palaeozoic pottery'.[45] He stood the joke on its head. Belief in Palaeozoic man, splashing among the trilobites, put him in a minority of one.

Black clouds heralded the summer's end, pulling a sombre veil over the year. An emotional monsoon was imminent. The first winds had buffeted Huxley in May 1853. He ticked off three years of desperation. He was at his wits' end, diverted into dreary reviewing, rocking himself neurotically to the refrain, 'I can get honour in science, but it doesn't pay, and "honour heals no wounds"'. The wounds were festering. The civility of the Sea Lords had worn thin and in June they refused another leave: six months would see him back in service. He railed at Nettie, thinking she doubted him. Her apparent misgivings gnawed at him until he broke down in July. In an outburst he branded their marriage 'no better than a mockery'. Twelve thousand miles away Nettie recoiled, pleading that 'your words cold & sharp as steel harrowed my very soul'.[46] Isolation and strain, like Stanley's on the bridge, were pushing him to the limit.

The rage gave his reviews a jagged edge. His first *Westminster* column blasted the craze for séances. It hurled the money-changers from the temple of science, that 'Witch *Sabbat* of mesmerists, clairvoyants, electro-biologists, rappers, table-turners, and evil-worshippers in general'. Spiritualism, which was sweeping across the water from pentecostalist New York to emasculate the secular movement, was fit for ridicule.

> If it were true that our poor souls, instead of retiring into
> their rest after the weary fight of this world, were to be at
> the beck and call of every tobacco-squirting 'loafer' who
> chose to constitute himself a medium, would not those of
> us who have any self-respect sooner become dogs, and
> perish with our bodies?

The expert was reclaiming the temple for the priests of reason. Rival vendors in the intellectual market were being condemned to Hades. There was only one true saviour: Science. The trumpet-charge of Huxley's campaign for a policed and professional science had been sounded.

Unfortunately he then blew a new tune, swung round, and

lashed his own camp followers. He brushed off Lewes' own book on Comte with a two-page list of errors. He was serving notice that the temple was off-limits as much to scientific amateurs. The jobless savant was lauding it over the dramatic dilettante, biting his head off with a clean carnassial chomp. He hauled Lewes' headless corpse over the coals, branding him a book-learner. It sent Chapman's group reeling. Marian Evans, the sub-editor (now Lewes' lover and about to elope with him to Germany), implored Chapman not to print 'such a *purely* contemptuous' piece. It was an 'utterly worthless unworthy notice', a jab at one of their own.[47] But it went out uncut, as much a comment on Huxley's mental state as Lewes' slipshod science.

At the height of this crisis came a new edition, the tenth, of the bestselling *Vestiges of the Natural History of Creation*. 'Time was', he exploded in the most savage review he would ever write, 'when the brains were out, the man would die'. *Vestiges* was brilliant journalism, a pot-boiling synthesis of the fringe sciences. It was cleverly crafted to unite the secular factions under the banner of 'Development'. But the science was second-hand and Huxley loathed the book's blundering pretension. It was also visionary, sweeping from the coalescence of planets, the first 'chemico-electric' generation of living globules, through the fossil fish and ancient reptiles, the 'vestiges' of the title, to the perfection of man.

Huxley knew that the anonymous book was pegged on the Edinburgh publisher of low-brow miscellanies, Robert Chambers. The pernickety expert who could not get a job choked on its sales. For nine years the bestseller had been 'greedily swallowed' 'to the great glory and no small profit' of its author. There spoke a bitter specialist living from hand to mouth.

In his foul mood Huxley snubbed the journalistic old-hand; he derided Chambers' talk of 'creation by law' as empty verbiage. These laws looked like spiritual movers behind the scenes, which left the fossil succession an act of God. Transmutation 'is a perfectly legitimate' idea, Huxley reaffirmed, but the will of God was no explanation. In a fit Huxley threw down the book as 'so much waste paper'.

With *Vestiges* citing Owen, Huxley sarcastically stepped in 'to save the learned Professor's reputation'. Owen, trying to balance his rejection of transmutation with acceptance of fossil progression, was crucified again. Ancient armoured fish were the pretext, but the whipping showed how much deeper it went. Huxley parted from *Vestiges* 'in a very bad humour',[48] and he parted from the year in equally bad grace, having upset Nettie, alienated Evans and infuriated Owen.

But the storm was passing and the sun could be seen on the horizon. Nettie's reassuring letters exorcized his fears and the first hints of a real job raised his self-esteem. 'You must pray', he wrote to her on 1 January 1854, 'that I may never have another year' like the last, 'or I shall become altogether as the nether millstone'. 'I have been unjust', he apologized, 'but will never be so again'.[49]

11

The Jihad Begins

There is always a Cape Horn in one's life that either one
weathers or wrecks one's self on. Thank God I think I
may say I have weathered mine – not without a good deal
of damage to spars and rigging though, for it blew deuced
hard on the other side.

Huxley had rounded his Cape after three years of storms. Three
years in a 'set-teeth sort of mood' which had left a permanent
grimace; three years 'when Martin Luther's saying – "If there were
as many devils as there are tiles upon the housetops, I will go"– was
the only fit expression of my habitual temper'.[1] Now in 1854 one
coup after another eased the grimace into a more pleasing grin.

The new year was icy enough for the Cape. In sub-zero temperatures the Thames froze and snow drifts paralysed even 'this
monster of a city'. But 7 January saw a thaw and Huxley reached
a post box to send Nettie a cheery update. The job front looked
good. Wharton Jones was ending his stint as Fullerian Professor at
the Royal Institution and Huxley was tipped to succeed him. That
'is £100 a year', he said. And Forbes was expected to be called
away to Edinburgh. There the old professor, Robert Jameson, 50
years in the post, had withered into a 'baked mummy'. Now, 'too
ill to lecture but too stubborn to retire', he was wished on his
way.[2] Should Forbes go, Huxley anticipated his place in the
Museum of Economic Geology. He knew the slips 'twixt cup and
lip, but he was still a knot of excitement.

The thaw revealed his first *Westminster* number, already on the
news-stands. It cheered Darwin. There was Huxley's review of his
barnacle monographs, and praise for the recluse as brilliant 'an

observer of nature on the small as on the large scale'. Huxley described Darwin's discoveries: how the barnacle larva develops a huge hump like Mr Punch, which oozes cement and glues it to a ship's bottom. And how female stalked barnacles hide a host of degenerate males under their shelly skirts. Darwin was pleased and Nettie perplexed, but Hal told her not to bother with it as 'it is all science and will only bore you'.[3]

Even the calamities were turned to advantage. On the day of the thaw the Sea Lords finally ordered him back to active service. The call-up came as the international crisis deepened, and Huxley assumed 'they will try to get rid of me by ordering me to the Black Sea'. The Crimea was dominating events. The Turks had resisted Russia's demand to protect the Orthodox Christians in the Otto-man Empire. The Russians had swept across the Danube Delta. With the sinking of the Turkish fleet the press at home whipped up anti-Moscow hysteria. Britain had vast naval superiority, '114 effective war steamers' noted Huxley.[4] The public called for the nation to prove itself. In January 1854 the British and French flotillas entered the Black Sea. Assistant Surgeon Huxley RN of course expected a man-o'-war posting.

Not that he had any intention of resuming service. Science was his career now. And so began a cat-and-mouse game with the Sea Lords. He kept recalling their promises to scientific officers, they kept ordering him to Portsmouth. (In fact not to fight but to join the training ship *Illustrious*. 'However', he noted in February as the allies issued an ultimatum to Russia, 'once in their claws there is no telling what might become of me'.) He put his failure to finish his book down to their refusal to fund him. But 'their Lordships saw no reason to alter their decision'.

> *My* Lordship said to himself 'No more so do I' and stuck
> the order on his mantlepiece . . . Luckily for me the
> 'Illustrious' is in the Home station so nobody can accuse
> me of an objection to face the Rooshians.[5]

With hostilities inevitable, strange commissions came his way. Chapman wanted a report on Sultan Schamyl's guerrilla war against the Cossacks in the Caucasus, east of the Black Sea. Huxley knew 'no more about Schamyl than the man in the moon', but for weeks he pored over reports of the Islamic resistance, 'dreamt about it & woke up thinking about it'. He rallied to Schamyl's *jihad*, berating the Cossacks' attempt to replace the 'youthful vigour' of Islam with the 'degraded idolatry of the Greco-Russian Tsar worship,

misnamed Christianity'. It fitted the Russophobia of the moment.
But his slant was revealing. He pointedly sided with the Sufis,
whose asceticism and striving for truth contrasted with Orthodoxy's 'gew-gaw saints' and its 'besotted priests' fawning over the
patriarch as 'God upon earth'.

These were months of hawkish patriotism. The press was pitting
English liberty against Tsarist tyranny, and Huxley put Schamyl
'beside our own Cromwell' as a religious liberator. The metaphor
was unmistakable, writ large by a warrior launching his own holy
war. Indeed Schamyl seemed strangely familiar, with 'his silent
earnest ways, intense determination and love of knowledge'. There
went Huxley in dervish clothes, a man apart, asking what Nature
wanted of him.

Huxley himself was rising through the ranks to become a field
commander in what he saw as science's 'war' against a corrupt
theology. His reports of atrocity and sacrifice show how much of
his image of science came from the real battlefield. War was a holy
duty. Schamyl's cry became Huxley's *idée fixe*: fight or succumb.
The Sultan was binding a Muslim nation through new ideals, and
Huxley's 'scientific Young England' would play up an orthodox
Anglican 'threat' in its own call to arms (rejuvenation through war
was a British national theme after 1854). There was power in
Schamyl's sword.

Huxley was not against Russian imperialism. Indeed the 'aggression of a nation of higher social organization upon those of lower
grade' was one of the 'conditions of human progress'. That was a
bloody ethic of the age, soon to be sanctified in Darwin's work.
The point was to redirect the Russian bear's gaze towards the
Asian 'wastes where his claws may find exercise advantageous to
humanity'.

The work was to Huxley's taste and Chapman praised its 'vigour'.
It is 'the best thing I have written'. And since 'I shall get £30 for it . . . I
don't mind how much more of the same is offered me'.[6]

His gung-ho air belied the ominous developments on his doorstep. Being Huxley there was no silver lining that could not resolve
itself into a cloud. Deep in 'Schamyl', he watched his brother
George collapse as a financial scandal threatened ruin and
imprisonment:

> the sudden and unexpected break out of one of the
> partners in a great London Bank – a man who twelve
> months ago was known to be worth £150,000 – has

involved him in ruin and I fear still worse for it turns out
that some of the people with whom he has been connected
in trying to save themselves have made most improper
uses of moneys with which they were entrusted. And my
brother and others equally ignorant of all this are legally
though of course not morally responsible for their acts.

Huxley's head swirled with memories of the Salt scandal. He had
struggled from the Inferno to see the stars, only to find another
'abyss opening under ones feet'. George knew the stigma a jail
sentence would carry and his mental state 'bordered upon insanity'.
Huxley cared nothing 'for the opinion of the world . . . but I know
its practical effects & I see one more difficulty thrust in a path
which assuredly needed not to be more rugged'. Being a banking
scandal it was hushed up, but it put the bristling indignation into
'Schamyl'. 'When you read it', he told Nettie, 'try to find any trace
of what was boiling in the writer's head'.[7]

The Russians crossed the Danube and Britain declared war on
28 March. Huxley was still fending off the Navy. He used every
delaying tactic, furious at their broken promises. Early in April
their Lordships threatened to scratch his name from the List. He
wished them to the devil and was duly struck off for disobeying
orders. He cocked-a-snook at their Lordships. His final judgment:
'they got the worst of it in logic and words, and I in reality and
"tin"'.[8] But without regular pay the tin was all-important.

As a civilian he could be funded by the Royal Society, which
now offered £300 to finance his book. He worked furiously,
becoming 'more & more anchorite every day'. Science required
factory discipline, 'steady punctual uninterrupted work'.[9] His
scientific-artisan image was being forged, a work-bench mentality
far from the leisured aristocratic ideal. After a day spent teasing
apart the intestines of bivalve shellfish (brachiopods) or probing
their 'hearts' (in fact reproductive organs, as he was first to show)
he would write 'for five or six hours' into the night.

But his spirits were rising. Word that Nettie's father was coming
over – and that Nettie would accompany him – gave Huxley the
final boost. Turning inside out like an emotional sea cucumber, he
found his bottomless pit of pessimism become an endless font of
optimism. He knew 'that we *must* after all these weary trials have
many happy years to go through together'. He marked four heroic
years by posting a coral broach. 'I little thought years ago that I

should only be able to send you symbols of my love on your birthday in '54. – I hoped rather to have waked you with a kiss'. Twelve thousand miles of separation was the ultimate Malthusian restraint: no marriage, no kiss, no spoken word in all that time. But then, as an upright young man in a society without safety nets, the parish-magazine mores were his: no marriage without means. The fear of grinding poverty with a succession of babies made it axiomatic. Even with Nettie coming, the engagement would have to continue 'so long as . . . we can't afford to be married'.[10]

Soon after his 29th birthday he talked at the Royal Institution again, hoping that it would 'earn the Fullerian Professorship for me'. He was desperate for the pay. The wealthy Directors of the Institution could barely credit it: 'what's the use of a hundred a year to him?' asked one. Huxley simply sighed, 'I suppose he paid his butler that'.

He had a gift on stage. He would bend the geometry of a man's arm to produce a bird's wing, or remodel a snail to reveal a squid, showing that all vertebrates, as all molluscs, were variations on a theme, just as the words hemp and *hennep*, or cannabis and *canapa*, were modifications of a mean. But was there a deeper unity to life? Could we connect men and snails the way that linguists connect the words hemp and cannabis, by using known letter changes among the Indo-Germanic races? Yes, by means of the embryo. Von Baer had depicted molluscs, vertebrates and insects starting 'their development from the same point', as similar foetal germs. Words and worms, life was a grand unity. It was awesome stuff for the fashionable audience (which included 'the fair widow M[rs] C. Stanley'). The chair looked within his grasp and 'my 30th year begins well'.[11]

How well he hardly knew. The pace of events caught him out. Jameson died and Forbes was called away a couple of weeks later. He left the Government School of Mines in Jermyn Street precipitously, two lectures into his own natural history course. On 25 May Huxley just as precipitously took over, lecturing 'twice a week on Mondays & Fridays'. 'Called upon so very suddenly to give a course of some six & twenty lectures, I find it very hard work, but I like it & I never was in better health'.[12]

Offers now seemed to cascade down upon him. He tramped the circuit, débuting everywhere. As a government employee in Jermyn Street he had no trouble teaching a parallel course for the Department of Science and Art at Marlborough House in mid-June. In July he started at Albemarle Street's City rival, the London Institution, in its imposing Finsbury building – drilling the merchants and bankers with more esoteric lore. (It was founded by business-men looking to the commercial application of science.) His piece-rate pay began to accumulate. 'Six lectures x five guineas' at Marlborough House; 'ten guineas a piece' in the City.[13] Of course the pressure mounted with the money. The strain regularly drove him to bed, exhausted. 'Lecturing you find hard work'? Tyndall asked. 'So do I, no work harder'.

Occasionally the old pain and alienation told in these talks, putting the teeth into his deconsecrated Calvinism. They were bared before the unsuspecting crowds at St Martin's Hall on 22 July. His seemingly innocuous subject, 'The Educational Value of the Natural History Sciences', was in truth ultra-sensitive. He was vindicating in public what he had been forced to justify to George and Fanning in private – the worth of spider knowledge. Physiology promoted health and happiness. But what value worms? Huxley was justifying his existence. His 'Scientific Calvinism' was a modifi-cation of Southwood Smith's in the *Divine Government*, which he had read as a boy. For Smith the prevalence of evil showed that society had strayed from God's intent and needed to be reformed. For Huxley 'Pain and evil' came with a crushing inevitability. They were impartial and inescapable. The physical 'Government of this universe' meant 'that its pleasures and pains are . . . distributed in accordance with . . . fixed laws'. But people needed a wider purview to appreciate it. To see pain 'woven up in the life of the very worms' would help them face it with 'more courage and submission'. His Schamyl-fatalism rationalized a harsh reality. Science offered a 'Carlylean center of indifference', a way of bearing up to war's carnage or nature's wastage.

There was a brighter side, a Romantic ray to pierce the gloom. The overriding happiness and harmony of life were 'refutations of that modern Manichean doctrine, which exhibits the world as a slave-mill, worked with many tears, for mere utilitarian ends'.[14] The universe was one of order. The *Bauplan* of archetypes and the beauty of azaleas were part of its regularity. They were inexplicable in functional terms. Huxley owed a great debt to the Romantic morphology of the 1840s, when the radicals with their immanent archetypes and laws had challenged Owen's conservative idealists, who made them the Thoughts and Desires of a Divine Craftsman. For Huxley, standing at the deathbed of romanticism, *Bauplans* and beauty were secular aspects of nature. But beauty for its own sake? Darwin would say something about that.

*

Even as Huxley spoke the 'oceans of disgust' were receding, leaving an enriched soil. In late July the Director of the Government School of Mines, Sir Henry de la Beche, made his appointment as natural history lecturer permanent. After the years of drifting he had his institutional anchor, even if it 'would have given me £100 a year only'. But Forbes had two other posts at the school. At first the geology professor at University College agreed to take over Forbes' additional course, on fossils, and also his job as 'Chief Palaeontologist', in charge of the museum fossils.

'Happily for me', Hal told Nettie, the professor pulled out, struck by 'a sort of moral colic' as the university frowned on his split loyalties. Huxley wanted this palaeontology lectureship as well (to double his money), but no arm-twisting would induce him to accept the museum job. It was a prestigious post but beyond his interest. Fossils were crucial to a museum of economic geology: the Geological Survey crew mapping the country used them to identify strata and *that*, said a utilitarian de la Beche, led to coal finds and understanding soil types. In short it was a plum job going at the right moment. But not for Huxley, who saw fossil curation as a diversion. So Sir Henry reluctantly upgraded Forbes' blue-collar assistant John Salter, a brilliant drudge – a Gradgrind who knew each of the 10,000 Palaeozoic fossils in the museum – but a prickly evangelical, and unstable. Everybody thought it 'simply ridiculous'. Huxley got the second lectureship,

> and so in the course of the week I have seen my paid
> income doubled. Listen to my title little girl & be in awe –
> I am '*Lecturer on General Natural History at the
> Government School of Mines*' Jermyn S^t . . . So after a
> short interval I have become a Government officer again,
> but in a rather different position I flatter myself. I am
> chief of my own department & my position is considered
> a very good one.[15]

So Huxley found himself in that grand, three year-old palazzo building with its prestigious Piccadilly frontage. On the ground floor was a huge auditorium, lit by six enormous cathedral-like front windows. Upstairs were the exhibits and galleries. Though it had few pupils at first (schoolboys drilled in Latin were ill-prepared to enrol), Jermyn Street was to train an elite core of industrial chemists, metallurgists and engineers. It was run with workshop discipline. Its laboratories analysed ores and coal, its naturalists looked at marine stocks and resources, its geologists surveyed mineral deposits. Huxley, with his anti-utilitarian bent, found himself in the most utilitarian institution in the country. It was to be his Archimedean point, the position he would hold for life, from which he could move the world.

It was a good place to be as the world began to wobble. The whole social ethos seemed to be on the slide. Professionalization was becoming the key in every sector. The lions-led-by-lambs slaughter in the Crimea was to spark an outcry against an incompetent aristocratic high command. Like everyone else Huxley chafed at this 'imbecility' at the top. Why should birth guarantee leadership (and what value leadership with Lord Cardigan commanding the Light Brigade from his luxury yacht in Balaclava Bay)? The sale of commissions was damned; jobs-for-the-boys were damned. Talented men were needed, men honed by competition. A Commission called for Civil Service places to be made competitive. The Inns of Court began to set exams. The ethos affected science, giving technical education a new cachet. In an attempt to tap the 'reservoir of unfriended talent', the Mechanics Institutes were affiliated to the Society of Arts and exams introduced.[16] These years marked a turning point. Patronage was being replaced by opportunity; allegiance to Church and Crown by service to the State. Huxley's men were coming in from the cold.

He was in place, the new-breed spokesman for science, articulate, self-serving and patriotic, with a lashing tongue and laconic wit. Where once was a closed door, he heard creaking hinges. Out came beckoning fingers. He began accumulating posts like a clergyman collecting livings. But he was no absentee vicar. He galloped ceaselessly round his parishes even if, 'as the jockeys say, the pace is severe'. Each letter to Nettie totted up afresh, as if continual counting would prove them to be no phantasms: £200 from Jermyn Street; Marlborough House, 30 guineas; London Institution, 60 guineas; the *Westminster*, 40 guineas; £50 for 'additional Lectures in Jermyn S.'; student fees, '40 or 50£ probably', an offer to teach at St Thomas' Hospital. Then came books: a *Manual of Comparative Anatomy* promised to Churchill, the British Museum's sea squirt catalogue, his book on the oceanic men-of-war (which his friend Edwin Lankester's Ray Society – set up to publish these sorts of unprofitable monographs – had agreed to print). By the autumn he was reckoning on £500 a year. 'A hundred & fifty pounds or rather more will about clear off my old incubus of a debt', leaving enough to 'make ourselves happy in a small way'. It might not carry him far up the slope of gentility, even with income tax at 7*d* in the pound. In fact, a married man 'cannot live at all in the position which I ought to occupy under less than six hundred a year'. But it was an extraordinary turnaround.

Four years after the *Rattlesnake* voyage he had struggled ashore. He took a last backwards glance. 'It has been a strange history that of these past years, full of dreams & nightmares, but I feel now . . . that I have been right in doing as I have done, in spite of all the pain it has cost us'. 'So my darling pet', he ended his letter to Nettie, 'come home as soon as you will – thank God I can at last say those words'.[17]

It was a more confidant government naturalist who set off in August for a holiday in Tenby, on the South Wales coast. Back to the Atlantic spray, to the rich shores of the Pembroke peninsula, where he could banish 'dyspepsias and hypochondrias and all my other Town afflictions'. Three months in this picturesque fishing village saw the landlubber swopping his sallow skin for a suntan, and taking stock among the tidal pools.

Even Tenby became a paying proposition. He had intended to 'do oceans of work' on sea squirts, but Sir Henry – a dab hand at transforming holidays into reconnaissance trips – put him on a piece-rate to survey the depths. A £50 cheque showed that he could do no wrong. The company was good too. With cholera sweeping through Piccadilly (where samples from the contaminated Broad Street pump proved at last that it was a water-borne disease), the city emptied and the Busks and Carpenters joined him. They took a communal cliff-top house away from the fashionable end of town, with their own 'steps down the cliff face to the sands'. More tranquil now, he would rise before dawn to watch the sun appear over the Carmarthen hills. Out to sea the 20-ton smacks could be seen trawling for herring. By day he joined them, dredging in eight fathoms, eating the whelks and dissecting the sea slugs and sea squirts. Then at dusk a stroll to 'see the slant rays of the sunset tipping the rollers as they break on the beach'. It left 'even *me* at peace with all the world'.[18]

He found an unlikely ally in a local doctor, Frederick Dyster. Unstuffy aldermen with penchants for marine worms were not common, and Huxley relished his find. The two scoured the rock pools and the friendship was sealed when Huxley designated their new feathery-gilled tube-worm *Protula Dysteri*. Christian Socialist aldermen were even rarer. Dyster backed the labouring unions and promoted workers' education, and he did his duty with articles on popular science for the *Christian Socialist*. Like the movement itself, he was well-to-do; he had a French maid, a deaf wife and a wealthy practice where the poor were treated free. But Huxley was never able to take the gold chain seriously. Nothing could stop him proposing that the town-father put his paupers to work collecting worms 'at so much a species'. Nor, as they sat by the fire, could he refrain from playing the Devil's advocate, to wit, 'a horrible Sadducee & sceptic in matters moral & political'. It was the honest basis for a revealing correspondence.

Cold weather brought Huxley back, and London closed in. 'Chimney pots are highly injurious to my morals', he reflected, 'and my temper is usually in proportion to the extent of my horizon'.[19] The grind meant swirling his *Westminster* sword. All the great debates got his cutting treatment. He sliced through the 'hot controversy' over extra-terrestrial life, accusing both the Scots Presbyterians (for) and Anglican dons (against) of basing their views of 'the Heavens' on their understanding of 'Heaven'. The new geological worlds at home were more his arena now. The novice palaeontologist pushed deeper into this *terra incognita*. Here too he found the natives squabbling. Murchison's Silurian empire was annexing the strata below. He was incorporating Revd Adam Sedgwick's fossil-rich Upper Cambrian rocks into 'his Lower Silurians', enraging old Sedgwick. It taught Huxley that stratigraphy was a matter of consensus. With impudent delight the tyro who loved a fight played the consummate diplomat: he suggested that the arbitration of 'Brachiopods will be found better than bombs'.[20]

The quarterly column had its theme: the lack of any progress from 'low' to 'high' animals in the fossil record. And he made his reasoning clear. The old cosmogonists, as he put it, wanting a Divine beginning and Six Days of miraculous Creations, had based their geology on 'the Mosaic account – but churchman and layman now unite in admitting that, if Moses were ever really in possession of the laws of geology, they must have been written on the tablets which he broke and left behind on Sinai'. It was quintessential Huxley, sarcasm with a serious point. A landscape dotted with progressionist castles showed 'that the want which' Genesis 'satisfied still lives'. The Owens and Sedgwicks needed an ascent from Silurian fish to Victorian Anglo-Saxons, to prove that man was in the Divine mind at the outset.

But negative facts were shifting sands, and a poor foundation for these towers. No evidence of Palaeozoic people did not mean evidence of no Palaeozoic people. Only a fraction of the world's Silurian rocks had been sampled. True, they revealed an undersea garden of trilobites and crinoids. But no one could infer camels or condors or cities from Pacific dredge samples today. Nor would anyone see the panoply of ancient life until the Silurian continents had been discovered.[21] Huxley was still looking for his Palaeozoic pottery. For him there was no comforting ascent. The fossil record still had no Christian meaning.

Quarter after quarter he delighted and incited. He picked another hot potato. Were the human races cousins, 'varieties of one species', or different species? And did the latter legitimate slavery? The crisis over American slavery was building. 'Uncle-Tom-mania' was sweeping Britain (with 1½ million sales since 1852, *Uncle Tom's Cabin* was the century's bestseller), and Huxley was musing on racial origins – that tinder-box that was shortly to ignite. In an increasingly racist age, when even the *Times* understood the economics of Southern slavery, Huxley was not joining the 'negro' cause. But he damned the scientific apologists of the murderous slave-owner Simon Legree in *Uncle Tom's Cabin*. Were 'the negro . . . a metamorphosed orang' it would not justify slavery. We are 'bound to put down the slave-holder', not because of his 'cousin-hood with his victim' but because this 'brutality . . . degrades the man who practises it'. He warned 'the Legrees of the south' that science would not sanction 'their atrocities'.[22]

Thomas Henry Huxley had emerged a public man. His pieces were hard sea-biscuits for secular consumption. But it was tough going alone. He was over-extended, dyspeptic and in need of a comrade with a barbed pen. He turned to Tyndall, convincing him to take over the 'critical analytical or anything else-you-please-ical' reviews of the physics books, egging him on with the ungratifying observation: 'What idiots we all are to toil & slave at this pace'.[23] Chapman, now bankrupt, had faced pressure to amalgamate the *Westminster* with the Unitarian *Prospective Review* (in which case Huxley would have resigned). To prevent it the atheist Harriet Martineau had put up a £500 loan, which kept the review afloat. Chapman, up and running again, enlisted Tyndall, and the *Review* took on a more uncompromising tone.

The success of Huxley's coterie showed in the way the Royal Society's medals were falling. After Huxley's in 1852 Tyndall was nominated in 1853, and now it was a draw between Hooker and Forbes. These were the champions of his 'scientific Young England', demanding standards and status. Huxley found himself in a 'queer position', faced with a choice between Hooker and Forbes. So he played 'a sort of Vicar of Bray' and voted each way.[24] The 'bauble' in the event went to Hooker, for his work on the distribution of plants, a sad choice given events.

For months Forbes had written from Edinburgh, telling of his huge class and glorying in 'the most wonderful scenery in Europe'. Then all went quiet. He sent one strained letter on 8 November, talking of pain and weariness. Ten days later Huxley found Forbes' brother in Jermyn Street, preparing to rush north. The next morning, 19 November, came a telegraph. Forbes had died in agony at 5 pm. the previous day.

So departed the jovial soul who had made the public Huxley: the man who had eased him into Jermyn Street and on to the British Association boards, who had taught him to dredge and to shout. 'I owe him so much, I loved him so well', Huxley lamented. The autopsy revealed 'a large *chronic* abscess in one kidney', he told Hooker. 'His life must have been hanging on a thread for years'. Huxley performed his cathartic duties, asking Hooker to pass the news to Darwin, writing an obituary for the *Literary Gazette*, collecting for a bust and a 'Forbes Medal' at the School of Mines. But really he was helpless. 'I think I never felt so crushed by anything before'.[25]

In this stunned state, he found himself targeted. A group of Edinburgh professors pressured him to fill his dead friend's shoes. The calls came with indecent haste, days after the death. Its suddenness had led to a scramble, with every 'eminence on crutches' hoping to compete. Not surprisingly, for it was the best-paid natural history post in Britain, an 'El Dorado', Lyell dubbed it. With classes compulsory for medical students, the professor could add £600 in fees to his £1,000 stipend. Huxley half-heartedly entered the list. Professors no longer had to pledge allegiance to the Church of Scotland, but the chair remained the object of sectarian feeling. Still, he told Hooker, 'there is a mortal difference between 200 & 1000 a year'.

'I dread leaving London & its freedom ... for Edinburgh and "no whistling" on Sundays'. The northern Athens was in decline. Its own tartan army of graduates had marched south to found the London University, now a federal colossus drawing students from the four corners. For them, as for Huxley, London was 'the centre of the world'. As the race hotted up, he cooled even more. He feared turning from a 'genuine worker' into 'a mere pedagogue'.

I feel much like the Irish hod-man who betted his fellow
he could not carry him up to the top of a house in his

hod. The man did it, but Pat turning round as he was set down on the roof, said 'You've done it sure enough but bedad I'd great hopes ye'd let me fall about three rounds from the top' – Bedad I'm nearly at the top of the Scotch ladder but I've hopes.[26]

He did fall. He urged de la Beche to hire a 'competent Naturalist' (himself) for the Geological Survey attached to the School of Mines, someone to dredge the British waters. The Director's forte was reconstructing the ancient environments, and Huxley presented his 'Coast Survey' as an aid to this; after all, the distribution and depth of modern shellfish gave the best clue to the habitats of their archaic forerunners. Another £200, he said, and 'I shall be strongly tempted to stop in London'. De la Beche succumbed and persuaded the Board of Trade to give Huxley his additional post.

Huxley threw over Edinburgh. The extra £200 would leave him in comfort. He might have to 'renounce the "pomps & vanities"' on £700 a year 'but all those other "lusts of the flesh" which may beseem a gentleman may be reasonably gratified'.[27]

His brief – to assess Britain's marine resources – would enable him to become 'something better than a Caledonian pedagogue'. And his pay put him up with the top-earning 'British Cuvier', Richard Owen. Huxley's plans took on their own Cuvierian grandeur. He dreamed of his own faunal empire, of organizing networks of collectors and having 'every species of sea beast properly figured & described in the [Survey's] Reports'.[28]

Nettie had seen out the old year visiting ships, looking over the *Waterloo* and booking cabins. She had packed amid scares of Russian ships sighted off the Heads. She would sail past new harbour fortifications, leaving behind her old colonial life. Hal expected her in May 1855. 'I look forward to our marriage as the beginning of life in its proper sense', he wrote. And the beginning of their properly delineated roles. 'You shall teach me something of your gentleness and patience . . . and I will teach you something of the great problems that are stirring the world'.[29] He rented them a narrow terraced house, 14 Waverley Place, St John's Wood, ten minutes from George and Polly's. Three floors allowed plenty of space for his library and dissecting room. The *Eyre Arms* on the corner was a mixed blessing, but otherwise it was a quiet cul-de-sac and well placed, just off the Finchley Road, with its Atlas omnibus into town.

With Nettie sailing, Huxley launched into his courses. A new classification became their basis. He had dispensed with the classic four branches of animal life – the four endorsed by the old gods of the Elysium, Cuvier and Von Baer, and still taught by Owen. Huxley's *Rattlesnake* shufflings led to five sub-kingdoms. The single-celled animals were separated off as Protozoa (a category common in Germany); he was finally calling his jellyfish and men-of-war Coelenterata – their two membranes, now termed endoderm and ectoderm, being like the earliest embryonic layers of the next group, the Vertebrata; molluscs he left; and the last, the Annulosa, was stuffed with insects, crustaceans, spiders, millipedes, worms and starfish. But not even this questionable lumping stopped him denouncing Owen's 'thoroughly retrograde' alternative.[30] From day one his students were subjected to a provocative view of life, delivered in blistering tones.

His London Institution talks in February and March 1855 were no less radical. The syllabus promised to knock any number of comfortable conventionalities: 'Vital Forces' were placed at the molecular level, plants and animals were made identical at the nucleus level, individuals were made to exist in many parts, 'Progressive Perfection' was called a will-o'-the-wisp. One City stalwart, the librarian Edward Brayley, 'who knows a thing or two more than God almighty', thought it 'the most heretical Syllabus he has seen'.[31]

His City duty done, he declared himself 'sick of the dilettante middle class' and turned to the cloth-caps.[32] De la Beche, an 1830s radical swearing by merit and education, ran yearly lectures for artisans. On winter nights hundreds packed the huge ground-floor auditorium, paying 6*d* to sample each professor in turn. The plebeian thirst for 'bread, knowledge and freedom' had not abated, and the jammed theatre at night contrasted to its half-empty state by day.

  Dyster put Huxley in touch with the Christian Socialist educator Revd F. D. Maurice, and Huxley sent a block of tickets to his Working Men's College in Red Lion Square. Others trying to tame socialism came to him. Charles Kingsley was a Hampshire rector famous for *Alton Locke* (an evocative novel of hovel life). His new book, *Glaucus; or, The Wonders of the Shore*, was a moral tale masquerading as a ramble among the Torquay rocks. It was muscular Christianity to fire the hordes on their first train ride to the seaside. Huxley was reviewing *Glaucus* when its author tapped on his museum door. Kingsley had scorned Lewes and the *Leader*'s overture, fearing the taint of 'bigamy and atheism', but he grasped Huxley's hand. These theologians had impeccable credentials. Maurice had been sacked from King's for demoting Hell to a temporary holding cell, and Kingsley was a votary at 'Nature's shrine'. He could turn science into poetry and a stammer into a 'brilliant flash of words'.[33] His Anglican unorthodoxy was appealing, even if he justified change to save the status quo, and if his 'clods' were taught that 'true socialism, true liberty, brotherhood, and true equality (not the carnal, dead level equality of the communist . . .) is only to be found in loyalty and obedience to Christ'.

Huxley's audience was taught something different. The tub-thumper was preaching old-time hellfire. He damned this 'idolatrous age', this society,

> which listens to the voice of the living God thundering
> from the Sinai of science, and straightaway forgets all that
> it has heard, to grovel in its own superstitions; to worship
> the golden calf of tradition; to pray and fast where it
> should work and obey; and, as of old, to sacrifice its
> children to its theological Baal.

Evangelicalism fired his sermon. He was turning the heathen to righteousness, making Science the Path. Maurice's co-operators swelled his audience – working-class socialists who were becoming interested in spiritualism after failing in the 1840s to create a democratic, co-operative society, in the hope that the spirit forces would put the nation back on its Millennial track. 'The theatre holds 600 & is crammed full', he reported. 'I believe in the fustian & can talk better to it than to any amount of Gauze & Saxony'.[34] But his words were an exorcist's and branded the spirit-rappers.

Infidel socialism was rampant on the factory floor. The extent of working-class atheism told as parsons urged bosses to sack freethinkers, often to find that they were the entire workforce. It told in the census revelation that only half the nation went to church, and next to none from the ghettoes. It told in the three days of rioting this June against a Sabbatarian Bill to stop London's Sunday trading. But most of all it told in the pauper press. Utopian socialist editors attacked 'Priestcraft' and promoted democracy. Demagogues looked through Lamarckian spectacles at fossil life rising by its own exertions, pushing the animal chain 'from below' (a 'power to the people' metaphor). And atop the chain, they saw humans progressing towards a bright co-operative future.

Huxley's workers were familiar with this indigenous street science. On corners, vendor hawked *The London Investigator* in 1855, with its evolutionary propaganda on the 'Origin of Man'.[35] This was gutter science to smash the Anglican state. 'Knowledge is power' was no idle slogan bandied about in illegal prints. Agitators demanded a progressive, technical education to ready them for the day they took control.

Such artisans converged on the school. But its teachers were supplanting this street literature. Huxley genuinely wanted 'the working classes to understand that Science & her ways are great facts for them'. He too believed that science could reveal history's moral. It

> prepares the student to look for a goal even amidst the
> erratic wanderings of mankind, and to believe that history
> offers something more than an entertaining chaos – a
> journal of a toilsome, tragi-comic march no-whither.

Then whither? Not to Millennial Peace, a global Harmony Hall. He had 'no confidence in the doctrine of ultimate happiness'. Nor would nations cease their conquests. News of the slaughter at Sebastopol, flashed home by telegraph, was proof in point. The bitter Dr Knox (reduced to living as an itinerant hack after the Burke and Hare scandal) was doom-mongering about the 'inexorable laws of racial antagonism'. And even Huxley saw the Crimea as part of a centuries-long 'trial of strength' between the Turkish and Russian races 'now being finally decided'.[36]

On the other hand history did not sanction a clerical state, backed by a Bible as a sort of 'special constable's handbook', as Kingsley had it. An 'active scepticism' ensured against such tyranny; doubting was a duty when all knowledge was provisional.[37] Science was only knowledge well organized and well tested. And that made Nature's own education the best guide.

Physiological laws provided the precepts of behaviour. They demanded obedience from the masses, said Huxley pulling a corporation face (writing to Alderman Dyster). He would show 'that physical virtue is the base of all other, and that they are to be clean & temperate & all the rest, not because fellows in black with white-ties tell them so, but because these are plain & patent laws of nature' – in short, drunkenness brings its own destruction.[38] Nature was the new moral sanction. And the new professionals –

trying to transform values as much as the old priests – would ensure that the querulous classes were bound by its judgments. The switch from priests to professionals left the unemancipated almost where they were.

For Huxley, the only way forward was a competitive, technocratic society, with the science professionals at the helm.

Some workers argued back. Most were enthralled. A few complained of the gobbledegook, being used to the fiery clarity of their own orators. But it only aided the tyro in honing his technique. The plebeianizing of Huxley's prose would be a long, dialectical process.

He emerged from his courses exhausted, debt-free for the first time in 15 years, to find Nettie off the English coast. His anxiety gave way to 'desperation at the continuous East Winds'. But on 6 May 'a westerly gale' blew and his heart leaped at the thought of their meeting. It had been five years since that night in Sydney when he dashed for his ship. For five years they had not spoken. For five years they had not seen one another's face. 'I am another man altogether & if my wife be as much altered, we shall need a new introduction'.[39]

The westerlies brought them together, the ecstatic moment coming days later. They touched for the first time since 1850. They wrapped themselves in each other's arms, emotionally choked, together again. But the moment was overshadowed; his idealized image of her, forged from years of longing, was shattered. She *was* altered, terribly; her features were drawn. She had been ill in Sydney and badly served by a quack; and violent gales on the high seas had made her worse. 'Oh this life!' he groaned, the devil 'mingles with all our happiness'.

He installed her parents close by in Regent's Park, and settled her in at George and Polly's, where she could have rest. She needed only care. Dashes between lectures were now punctuated by visits to her. 'God help me. I discover that I am as bad as any young fool who knows no better'; but for the lectures 'I should be hanging about her ladyship's apron strings all day'.[40] As she improved his cynicism gave way to gaiety, leading students to wonder what had become of his 'philosophership'.

It was the best of times, as Nettie recovered and more of the world fell his way. '1000 congratulations' Hooker pealed, referring to Nettie but also welcoming the *enfants terribles* – Huxley, Tyndall and Busk – into the Philosophical Club (that dynamic dining-circle-cum-think-tank inside the Royal Society). Hardly *enfants* any more, terrible or otherwise; they were over 30 and becoming established. Hooker in May became his father's assistant, given a house next to Kew Gardens where he could 'plunge into the Haystacks' of dried Himalayan plants. And they were bending Huxley's 'scientific Young England' into shape. The learned bodies were awash with new blood and Hooker hoped that the infusion would 'resuscitate' even the comatose Linnean. He was fighting the obstructionist 'old fogies' here and complaining of their 'imbecility'. Plans were laid for the tighter vetting of manuscripts, open discussion of papers and dedicated zoological and botanical *Journals*.[41] The gentlemanly ethos was doomed.

To confirm his meteoric rise, Huxley joined Tyndall at the Royal Institution. In July he took the Fullerian Professorship for three years, putting another butler's wage in his back pocket. 'May the gods continue to drop fatness upon you', Tyndall jollied him, and may the 'next great step' be all 'your . . . rebellious heart can desire'.

His rebellious heart was being tamed. With Nettie improving the bachelor was heard chanting, 'Oh that there were no such things as pots & pans'. On £800 they could marry and move into Waverley Place immediately. Phebe Lankester was overjoyed at seeing the tearaway 'tied up'. Carpenter sent his 'intense condolence' along with a '*walnut-wood* book-slide' and inquired 'the time fixed for execution'. 'I terminate my Baccalaureate & take my degree of M. A. trimony (isn't that atrocious?) on Saturday July 21', Huxley laughed. Even he shared the ubiquitous Victorian sense that the brute was being humanized. 'After the unhappy criminals have been turned off there will be refreshment provided for the sheriffs, chaplain & spectators'.[42]

Sir Henry preferred his hammerers single, an unattached corps devoted to the rocks. But should the unfortunate happen, he was not averse to dispatching lieutenants on surveying honeymoons (both Forbes and Salter had put on boots and taken their brides to north Wales). The wheelchair-bound De la Beche had died in April, but the ethic lived on. Huxley told Dyster to expect the newlyweds in a Tenby dredge by late July, 'and I am ready to lay you a wager that your vaticinations touching the amount of work that *won't* be done, don't come true'. 'So much for wives – now for *worms* . . . '[43] With 63 year-old Murchison, the Tory 'King of Siluria', taking over the Survey, Huxley saw uncertainty ahead and advised Dyster, as his 'right reverend father in Worms & Bishop of Annelidae', to publish elsewhere.

Nettie had stepped off the boat straight into a brawl, the first in a line that would last her married life long. 'There is no doubt I have a hot bad temper', Hal had warned her. 'If I hate a man, I despise him', and he detested no one more than Owen. Huxley's slick whipping of Owen in the *Vestiges* review had caused everyone to draw breath. 'By Heavens', Darwin whistled, 'how the blood must have gushed into the capillaries when a certain great man (whom with all his faults I cannot help liking) read it!'[44] It did; Huxley and Owen toppled into a petty world of tit-for-tat. Denunciations flew thick and fast. Arcane anatomical disagreements over the lamp-shell's heart blew up as the wedding preparations proceeded and Owen's *Lectures on the . . . Invertebrate Animals* was published with a snipe at Huxley's 'blindness'.

'Busk and I *roared*' over Owen's 'absurdities', wrote Carpenter five days before the ceremony. He egged Huxley on, having no love of Owen's idealism. As a Unitarian Carpenter accepted immanent natural causes for all mental and physical events; and although his image of fossil specialization was like Owen's, *he* believed that life's progress would one day find its material explanation. Carpenter sent a swift warning of the slur so that, 'if you wish to call him out, you may do so *at once*, rather than after the honeymoon is over'. He offered himself as a second. The 'best proof you can give of your full possession of eyesight, will be to put a bullet into some fleshy part of your antagonist'.[45] No intellectual duel marred the event. But it was a foretaste of things to come.

The banns had been read at the local Anglican church, All Saints, on the Finchley Road. And so, after an eight-year engagement – during which they had seen one another for a matter of months – the day arrived. Saturday 21 July 1855 was a perfect summer morning. The dull and rather large church looked brighter for the flowers. In the pews sat everybody who meant anything to Tom: his brothers, the Heathorns, Fanning's parents. There were the haggard Ellen (and presumably an opium-hazed Cooke) and his scientific confidants Hooker, Carpenter and Tyndall. 'As we knelt at the altar, he holding my hand to his lips', Nettie recalled, 'a great beam of jewelled light fell upon us from the coloured windows'. The sweet moment was savoured. She gazed at her new name in the registry book through 'a mist of amazement'. At last 'we had reached the Promised Land'.[46] Her parents gave a quiet breakfast at North Bank and that afternoon the newlyweds set off.

It was a leisurely trip to Tenby, with lashings of summer rain. Via Oxford and Warwick they went, then down to Stratford to see

Shakespeare's tomb before crossing into Wales. At Dyster's for a fortnight Hal was so doting that the French maid called him *un vrai mari*. The couple took lodgings in August and became a regular 'Darby & Joan'. They looked the part: on warm mornings he would carry Nettie to the beach (she was too weak to walk over the rocks). But Darwin's warning that 'happiness, I fear is not good for work' was unduly pessimistic. Dyster lost his bet – by early August Nettie was a Survey widow as Hal took to the dredge. He left her with the visiting Busks, and she caught up with the lost years talking to Hal's Egyptian priestess.

No Darby and Joan were ever so bizarrely occupied. Each morning Dyster popped in 'and found us in the back verandah my husband, coat off & shirt sleeves tucked up dissecting' a dogfish, pulling a new tapeworm from its gut 'whilst I wrote down its description'.[47] She refused to be excluded, however incongruous a honeymoon it turned out.

To complete his Survey report Huxley taxed the quarrymen working the limestone 'bone caves'. But it was a nearby drowned forest, emerging at low tide, that provided the best opportunity for understanding the process of fossilization. He dug around the trunks, knee-deep in silt, studying plant interment and slicing sections for Hooker.

He sailed on two or three days each week, his tiny boat dwarfed by the trawlers. Reaching mid-Channel his catch piled up: a new flatworm, bristle worm, crustacean, tapeworm and sea squirt. Through heavy seas he pulled as the months turned chilly. At night he would trudge home cold, thinking it 'wonderful how light the house looks', ready to dissect his haul.[48]

A dissection mirrored his life, fast and brilliant. He assimilated in days what took others months, including Darwin. On 11 August a piece of flotsam drifted into harbour covered with goose barnacles, *Lepas*, their blue-tinged shelled bodies connected to the driftwood by a stalk. Barnacles were in the limelight. Not long before they had been ranked as molluscs (they did look like mussels). But the barnacle was, 'in reality, a Crustacean fixed by its head, and kicking the food into its mouth with its legs' – those wafting feathery feet familiar in the acorn barnacles on seaside rocks. The sedentary barnacles were related to the shrimps that scurried around them. Knowing this, Darwin had been reappraising the group since 1846. He had ended up with 1,100 pages of dense monographs and a reputation as the blinkered 'Professor Long' in a Bulwer-Lytton novel. Nine years' work brought a startling conclusion: that a duct leading from the stomach was an ovary and, even odder, that part of the ovary produced cement to glue the adult to its rock! He sent a sceptical Huxley his preparations. But two days with his flotsam *Lepas* and Huxley had detected the 'true ovaria' in the stalk.[49]

The heartaches were over. By 1855 the 30 year-old had achieved those goals that had inspired him for eight years – marriage and a job in science. Or three jobs; he had shot past his peers and was vying with the top earner Richard Owen, about to become the new £800-a-year head of the Natural History Collections in the British Museum. Huxley was brusque, daring, clubbable and energetic, rubbing shoulders with Lyell's knights of science at one level, pulling the bearded working classes behind him on another. His power was growing, on the council of the Royal Society, in the reviews, as the ubiquitous 'Professor' popping up on every platform. He was as sharp as his scalpel, Darwin said, 'a very clever man'. But Darwin did wonder where Huxley's *science* was going – it seemed to be directionless.

Darwin had been sending monographs intermittently, and using Huxley as a conduit to the German zoologists. They were still fairly distant, and only in 1855 did Darwin's address soften from 'My dear Sir' to a warmer 'Dear Huxley'.

Huxley's drift was worrying. The bulldog pup was straying in the wrong direction. Darwin chuckled at the 'exquisite & inimitable' way he handled 'a great Professor', but this back-slapping concealed more than it revealed. Owen's fan-like, ramifying image of fossil life actually suited Darwin's evolutionary purpose. It was Owen – not Huxley – who was unwittingly playing John the Baptist to Darwin's Christ. Darwin tried a gentle remonstrance. He thought Huxley 'rather hard on the poor author' of *Vestiges*. And Huxley's denial of any progress in the fossil record left Darwin positively 'grieved'.[50] Huxley was proving himself a brilliant disappointment.

It was time to invite the tearaway to Downe for a 'pumping' session.

12

The Nature of the Beast

HUXLEY'S EMOTIONAL TYRANNY turned to tenderness inside the family. *Un vrai mari* he was, upholding family virtues, disdaining Chapman's libertinism. Not that it was a conventional household: Waverley Place was unremittingly scientific, what with 'his occupation, his friends, his books'. Nettie 'attended little by little' becoming, like so many scientific wives, an unsung helpmate. She sketched, translated and proof-read. By morning she would blow up diagrams, then 'a hasty lunch, & [with] the cab at the door I would be just in time to get them hung at the Royal Institution'.

Thus the girl whose pleasure had been poetry entered a 'Fairy Land of Science'. She brought intellectual strengths. 'In this utilitarian day, when the old forms of spiritual existence which once ennobled mens lives are become effete', he agreed, one must 'cherish the ideal in the world of Art'. And wasn't Nature herself ultimately

> a poem; not a mere rough engine-house for the due keeping
> of pleasure and pain machines, but a palace whose
> foundations, indeed, are laid on the strictest and safest
> mechanical principles, but whose superstructure is a
> manifestation of the highest and noblest art.

Hal, more and more the mechanical engineer, trotted Nettie around the foundations, giving disquisitions on the unseen forces and eternal verities, and the universal truths embodied in the tiniest diatom. Bit by bit she came to understand 'the great problems that underlay the dissection of even a fish or plant, or the identification of a fossil . . . It was a revelation that ennobled the world I lived in'.

All the while she healed his emotional wounds, switching from invalid to nurse. Hal was crushed by headaches after lecturing. As he charged through the animal kingdom, clawing power by clawing knowledge, the stress built up. He was forced to spread himself wide over physiology, palaeontology and marine zoology, not knowing in 'what branch of science I should eventually have to declare myself'.

Money remained tight as he met his debts and paid his dues. 'Societies & Clubs' cost him 'a mint'. There was one more now, as he joined the Survey men, sitting as a block in the Geological Society. The squeeze threw Nettie onto her own resources:

> My bush life in Australia had taught me to turn my hand
> to anything so that I could cook, paper a room, polish a
> floor, and make a dress & make myself generally useful.
> Owing to this I was able to get on quite comfortably with
> two maid servants and [had] many a pleasant little dinner
> with just [a] few guests in my dining room. From the first
> Dr Tyndall was the most intimate and in a short time we
> were Brother John, brother Hal, and Sister Nettie to one
> another.[1]

Herbert Spencer lured Huxley out for walks; Hooker came with 'Bloaters & ... Pears'. Mercury himself, now Lieutenant Sharpe, dropped by with feather flowers for Nettie in January 1856, recalling old Sydney days.

But word of another messmate was chilling. MacGillivray had 'damned himself', abandoning his wife and children and shipping back to Australia. He had been drummed out of the Service as an alcoholic and was living as a down-and-out. Huxley found his wife sick with consumption, on to 'her last shilling & contemplating the workhouse'. He collected £50 for her passage home. At least with parents in Australia 'there will be more hope for her children than in an English poor-house'. It was the decent thing, putting a little money into her hand and seeing her aboard ship. Later he heard that she had died two weeks away from Sydney.

The sight of social wrecks had him craving support. Home was a sanctuary, its traditional values his security. Hence Hal and Nettie's staid roles: he would lead, be 'your guide as well as your lover'. Hers was the soothing balm, to ease the pain as he battered at authority. He would smite the Amalekites and she 'help me ... in my battle'.[2] 'Battle' said it all. His psychology was adversarial.

He had to confront some embodiment of evil. So past the portcullis of Waverley Place he rode, his lance pointing at Belial himself, Richard Owen.

The lance struck Owen's *Lectures*, to Carpenter's cheers. In a slashing review Huxley slated Owen's zoology as old hat and his self-glorification as unseemly.[3] Partly it was brinkmanship, the angry *parvenu* showing his superiority. Partly it was pique – his own work having been ignored by Owen and his protégés. Whatever, the die was cast. However much was 'good & kind' in Owen, Huxley would now draw out the worst.

Although in part it was personal animosity, in reality the brawling was a bloody repercussion of the ideological divide. Huxley's clique was carving a scientific profession. Old patrons were snubbed as the young Turks fought for self-determination, old theologians abused as they made a show of dissociation. It was to be a self-validating profession. No split loyalties would be tolerated: clerical geologists were like 'asses between bundles of hay', Hooker said. Hence Huxley's hatred of Owen's 'unscientific realism of "Archetypal Ideas"'. It turned Nature's patterns into God's thoughts and surrendered the lot to natural theology. The new men needed an enemy to give cohesion to their ranks. And the imperious Owen was perfectly cast.

Owen was settling into the British Museum in 1856. But onlookers jibbed at his plans. 'Of course Owen would be the Autocrat of Zoology & Palaeontology', Carpenter said. Patrician dictatorship was no model for professional science. He must be made accountable 'to a body of scientific men, who are competent to estimate and criticise his proceedings'.[4] Duty to colleagues as much as to facts was explicit in the call for higher standards. Old-style patronage had to be replaced by peer review and state sponsorship.

Owen was the best palaeontologist in Britain. He had written 100 books and papers on fossils alone, christening the dinosaurs, studying the first mammals, describing fossil reptiles, New Zealand moas and Australian marsupials. Palaeontology was approaching its Victorian apogee – in a few decades 40,000 fossil animals and plants had been named. It was the equivalent of finding a new continent of creatures, underground. The rise and fall of ancient dynasties was generating intense public excitement, making this subterranean world the place to be.

Huxley now swept into palaeontology too. At first he was

pushed by the job. On taking over, Murchison had found no proper fossil catalogues. Salter was ineffectual, prone to depressions and fits of 'self-righteous piety', which everyone blamed on his 'damned religion'. His assistant William Baily kicked 'at everything like order & discipline'. So Murchison asked Huxley to take on the work. Huxley set out to master the fossil collection over the winter so as 'to be *no* longer at the mercy of my subordinates'.[5] And so he ended up doing the palaeontologist's job that he had originally turned down.

In the *Westminster Review* Huxley kept nudging 'higher' life back in time, convinced that there had been no progression. He would hail the world's oldest reptile, found by Lyell in the Nova Scotia coalfields during his American tour.[6] Or he would show that ancient trilobites were just as complex as today's king crabs.

Darwin watched. The last straw came when Huxley mauled even his friend Carpenter's evidence for a progressing fossil life. Carpenter's ancient life was more generalized. And so was Darwin's — but his ancients were *real* ancestors. Transmuting through aeons of time, adult animals had gone on specializing while the embryos remained largely unmodified, retaining their ancestral looks.[7] To Darwin it made evolutionary sense.

He was worried enough to meet Huxley head on — to hear first-hand his doubts about fossil progress. Darwin canvassed a meeting at his Kent home. He organized these periodic 'pumping' sessions, when younger naturalists were taxed (but not told why). At Downe Darwin could control events without putting himself in jeopardy. Here society had to accept him on his own terms.

Others were lined up. The Hookers were to arrive on Tuesday 22 April 1856. Hooker was a long-time confidant, one of the few to be let into Darwin's belief in transmutation ('it is like confessing a murder', Darwin had told him in 1844, and given the gentry's fear that such a bestial science would aid the socialist levellers it must have seemed like a criminal betrayal). At first Hooker had dismissed transmutation. But after being bombarded by Darwin for ten years he was teetering. 'Oh dear, oh dear', he sighed, 'my mind is not fully, faithfully, implicitly given to species as created entities *ab initio*'. With some trepidation, he was coming round to Darwin's '*Elastic* theory'. At any rate, the idea of 'Creation' was 'no more tangible than that of the Trinity & . . . neither more nor less than a superstition'.[8]

For almost two decades Darwin had been sitting on his theory.

He had conceived it in 1837–9, during the tumultuous years of riot, recession and clergy-baiting, when the squires saw themselves holding a lid on a seething, slum-ridden cauldron. It was reforming Malthusian science for a reforming poor-house age. It was also revolting to a besieged Anglican elite. The creation of species was proof that God intervened in Nature, as through the clergy He was supposed to intervene in society, upholding the paternalist order. To deny God's intervention invited catastrophe. 'Once grant that species' mutate, Darwin himself wrote, and the 'whole fabric totters & falls'. His mentor Revd Adam Sedgwick blamed the French Revolution on such 'gross (and I dare say, filthy) views'.' The quiet, affable Darwin risked being branded a class traitor. It was a sickening dilemma. So the recluse had kept his peace for two decades, drafting his wife a note, asking her to publish on his death. Perhaps he would rather have died first.

The years had seen some changes to his theory. Barnacles had taught Darwin that species were '*eminently* variable'. He now knew that variation was the rule, rather than the exception. This meant that competition between the variants operated constantly, not only when the environment fluctuated. He also had a better idea of how a species splits into two. Just as factories employed a specialist workforce, nature favoured a division of labour. Competition pushed variants to seek new openings. They diversified like skilled trades in a market, rubbing shoulders but minding their own business. Darwin, a laissez-faire Whig with a portfolio of industrial shares, saw the same laws shaping the creation of wealth as the production of life. By 1856 his factory metaphor was complete.

The time was right for him to go public. Democratic reforms had put Dissenters into the Town Halls. Unitarians now donned mayoral regalia, advancing their rational, cause-and-effect views of nature, unlike the old supernaturalism. As the Duke of Wellington had feared, power was passing from the Anglican gentry to cotton kings and shopkeepers, 'many of them [Unitarians and] atheists'.[10] Accelerating production left the country feeling prosperous. Society was quiet, people were optimistic. The Chartist scare had evaporated, and with it Darwin's fear of being branded a traitor. The recluse, part-Unitarian himself, was emerging into a safer world. A world where *Westminster* reviewers hailed evolution and Huxley's clique was poised to take power. The moment was opportune. At this gathering he would test the waters.

Another to arrive was the rector's son Thomas Vernon Wollaston. He was a good barometer of conservative feeling: well-to-do, a Cambridge man, currently arranging his beetles in the British Museum. Studies on Madeira had shown him that isolation and climate change could cause beetles to vary. This limited 'power of self-adaptation' was the thrust of his new book *On the Variation of Species*. At Downe Darwin hoped to lead him further. Counterbalancing Wollaston should have been the Tory-hater Hewett Watson. A fierce radical, he was applying fashionable demographic techniques to plant populations. Watson would need no leading; like many atheists he was a transmutationist already, a 'renegade', in Hooker's words.[11] Only his failure to turn up prevented the sparks flying.

Huxley was squeezed for time, with a Royal Institution talk on Tuesday 22 April and a lecture on the Friday. Then there was the inaccessibility of Darwin's hamlet. Although only 16 miles from St Paul's, Downe was the 'extreme verge of [the] world', and chosen by Darwin for that reason. But Darwin promised his carriage at Sydenham station for the nine-mile drive. And with illness the norm at Downe, Emma added that Nettie 'sh^d. have a comfortable arm-chair in her bedroom, so as to live upstairs as much as she liked'.[12]

Hooker was eager to get Huxley along. But *he* wished to talk strategy. He wanted to bring 'about more unity in our efforts to advance Science'. They now had 'sufficient command over the public, as Examiners'. They were even penetrating rival headquarters. (The War Office had Tyndall and Huxley testing candidates for Royal Artillery commissions.) As he spoke their grip was tightening. Carpenter was about to become the new high-profile Registrar of London University. It meant resigning his Examinership in Physiology and Comparative Anatomy, leaving Huxley to step in.

They talked of a corporate shield to protect their gains. Professional status meant ousting the 'pitiful botchers'. It meant controlling knowledge through their own journal, getting science into the classrooms, forming a club – some 'intellectual resort' where they could sojourn.[13] Ultimately, it meant selling themselves as knowledge-brokers. The men on their way to Darwin's were marking out a profession. They were distancing themselves from the vicar-naturalists, sneering at the Cambridge old boys. And, incongruously, awaiting them at Downe was squire Darwin, Cambridge-trained for the Church and about to provide their legitimating philosophy, a naturalistic science of creation with a competitive edge.

The Huxleys travelled on Saturday 26 April, across the chalk Downs, less desolate with the arrival of spring. Their first visit found Downe a sleepy hamlet of thatch and timber, where farm hands doffed their caps. Near by stood a magnificent new mansion, 'High Elms', testifying to Sir John Lubbock's banking fortune. (Darwin would cajole Sir John, London University's first Vice-Chancellor, into backing Huxley as an Examiner.) Down House itself was an ugly brick building fronting on to a small lane, which Darwin had brazenly lowered to protect him from view. It was big enough for his brood of seven, and a perfect rustic retreat. The inside had a frayed, lived-in look. There was little opulence to show for Darwin's fortune; nothing to suggest that he had just sunk £20,000 into the Great Northern Railway, or owned a farm in Lincolnshire.[14]

To Darwin, Huxley was a man of jutting jaw and searing wit; brilliant on a podium, or so he had heard. True, he was no naturalist, no Gilbert White, however fearsome an invertebrate anatomist. Above all he seemed brash and self-assured. Darwin, for his part, was never quite what he seemed. Apparently hearty, he was invalided by incessant vomiting fits. Seemingly outgoing, he was always self-absorbed. And his days ran like 'clockwork' amid a chaotic mess of skeletonized pigeons and dismembered ducks.

Emma Darwin, his wife, was the granddaughter of the pottery patriarch Josiah Wedgwood. She was a little severe, religious, well educated and musically talented (having studied the piano under Chopin). At Downe she fulfilled her parish role, dispensing bread tokens to the poor and gin-and-opium concoctions to the sick. Their home too was a hospice, where she doctored her sick husband. That Saturday they dined at seven, with Emma shepherding relays of servants. The banker's son John Lubbock joined them – very much Darwin's protégé, already dissecting waterfleas and their eggs and following Huxley's work closely.[15]

The next morning came the pumping. Darwin sat in his study near the marble fireplace. Behind him was a book-lined alcove with tiers of pouches, into which he popped notes. At the window a mirror allowed him to spy visitors coming up the drive. Here he was secure, and he had his questions ready: why did Huxley not see fossil animals as more generalized? Trace back today's single-toed horse and we arrive at the small, three-toed Eocene herbivore *Palaeotherium*, with its full set of teeth.[16] Could he not imagine following it further back to some primitive five-toed mammal?

And why did he deny that ancient animals could be intermediate between living groups? Didn't the camel-like *Macrauchenia* that Darwin had pulled from a Patagonian cliff-face point equally towards modern llamas and tapirs?

No. Huxley's answers were inscrutable. He never shared Darwin's field approach, where competition led to progress – or his utilitarianism, which made every structure serve some end. In fact Huxley did not think in terms of *origins* at all. Geometry, not genealogy, fascinated him: the surreal beauty of nature's secret architecture. Species were not to be explained historically, by messy mutations and supposed progression. They had to be appreciated as abstract anatomical patterns. Even then his image of their configuration was bizarre. He pictured species clustered on the surfaces of spheres, each with its central archetype. No animal was nearer the centre; none was more general; fish, reptiles, birds and mammals were all equidistant from the abstract vertebrate type.[17] Molluscs had their distinct sphere, as did coelenterates. And with the spheres unconnected no trilobite could illicitly jump the gap to call itself a fish.

Darwin was nonplussed. He did not tip his hand, simply saying 'that such was not altogether his view'.[18] Huxley had constructed a cosmos of Ptolemaic perfection, of crystalline spheres, brittle and useless to Darwin. He was not thinking in historical terms at all, of bloodlines, family trees, lost ancestors and the kinship of life. His was a defunct world of sublime impenetrability. It might have given no concession to Christian apologists or rabble-rousing Millennialists, but it was no less absurd to Darwin.

After lunch came a walk. Darwin would lead the way in his great coat. It was a beautiful stroll, through acres of gardens. Ten year-old Georgy and young Franky charged about playing Crimean War games. As with Darwin, the gardens were never what they seemed. The greenhouse was packed with saltwater tanks full of seeds, pods and dead birds with stuffed crops, which took some explaining. It was one of his brilliantly humdrum experiments. He was proving what botanists had doubted: that seeds could survive the crossing to oceanic islands, to start the process of colonization.[19] They did not need lost continents to travel over. Summoning up some missing Atlantis (as Forbes had done) to convey British seeds to the Azores struck Darwin as ludicrous. He had pepper seeds surviving five months in brine, long enough for currents to carry them across.

Next door was his real pride, the fancy pigeons. Come, see

them, he said, 'the greatest treat ... which can be offered to [a] human being'. He had 90 birds and every British breed. The aviaries were aflutter with cooing tumblers and pouters with ballooning breasts. Darwin's quirkiness must have struck Huxley. With his hatred of pottering dilettantes, he hardly knew how to take this farmyard science. Pigeons were a labourer's hobby, Darwin admitted it. He supped with pipe-smoking fanciers in gin palaces, picking up tips, 'hand & glove', he said, with 'Spital-field weavers & all sorts of odd specimens of the Human species'. He had an ulterior motive. His Nature was composed of myriad tiny variations. He was showing how skilled artisans could accentuate the slightest variation through selective breeding, pinching and bustling to build new strains, turning an original dove into the equivalent of 'fifteen good species'.

To confirm it he measured beaks and bones. I 'am watching them outside', he explained ghoulishly, '& then shall skeletonise them & watch their insides'. Decaying carcasses were strung up, and a 'fetid odour' rose from rotting corpses in retchmaking potash solutions. Everyone's flesh was creeping, even Darwin's: 'It really is most dreadful work'.[20]

Darwin's reason for starting this grisly business would have struck Huxley as even more horrifying. Darwin wanted to show that hatchlings were 'more normal' than their coiffed parents, that they were more generalized and nearer to the ancestral form. He was working on the premise that individual development held a mirror to ancestral history – that history, like embryology, was a case of increasing specialization. The work was a direct rebuttal to Huxley himself.

The guests ambled on. Hooker and Huxley resumed their planning. Darwin tried to whittle away at Wollaston's faith in immutable species. But for Wollaston beetles only varied *within fixed specific bounds*. To suggest that they broke these bounds and transmuted into new species was 'monstrous'. Darwin's work posed a moral 'danger': it denied God's intervention, that guarantor of the Anglican status quo.[21] Darwin's hopes were dashed and he later recoiled bitterly. Nothing was so 'rich, considering how very far he goes, as his denunciations against those who go further ... Theology is at the bottom of some of this. I told him he was like Calvin burning a heretic'.

After the guests left Darwin unpicked Huxley's objections. Huxley himself came away with no inkling of Darwin's theory of natural selection, but he sensed change in the air. His next *Westmin-*

ster column praised Hooker and Wollaston. These pioneers were tackling the 'chaotic assemblage of facts' about animal and plant distribution. According to Hooker's *Introductory Essay on the Flora of New Zealand*, half of the 100,000 known flowering plants were probably varieties; and Wollaston had shown how malleable insects were. Could these variants continue changing until they became new species? Hairline cracks were ruining Huxley's spheres. For the first time he conceded 'that the whole subject of the influence of climate, habits of life, and other external conditions, as well as of the capacity for variation inherent in each type of form, requires a thorough re-investigation'.[22] It was a small step, the first in a long march to a new world – a world far more hospitable to a rationalist ideologue. Darwin noted it. He logged the 'change in Hookers & Huxley's opinions', and he planned to draw these young Turks further into his heterodox camp.

A garbled account of the meeting had Huxley shifting further. Lyell heard that the Sunday plotters 'grew more & more unorthodox'. Word had it that the entire group laughed at the notion of immutable species. But not so: transmutation for Wollaston remained morally dangerous, and for Huxley geometrically difficult. Others refused to believe that Darwin himself would stretch varieties too far. Lyell's in-law Charles Bunbury, another Cambridge-trained squire, doubted that Darwin would 'assert an *unlimited* range of variation: he would hardly, I conceive, maintain that a Moss may be modified into a Magnolia, or an oyster into an alderman'.[23]

He would. Three weeks later Darwin laid plans to publish his theory after the years of waiting. The world was tumbling. Lyell was desperately rationalizing the birth of humans from ape parents; and at the Philosophical Club he found Huxley, Hooker and Tyndall veering towards transmutation. It showed in Huxley's lectures, running in the *Medical Times*. They had a quizzical air: if each species came from a 'single pair', whence that pair? 'Created' – what does that mean?

> . . . we have not the slightest scientific evidence of such unconditional creative acts; nor, indeed, could we have such evidence; for, if a species were to originate under one's very eyes, I know of no amount of evidence which would justify one in admitting it to be a special creative act independent of the whole vast chain of causes and events in the universe.

And assuming a natural emergence 'there can be no doubt that some form or other of that hypothesis – not less abused by its supporters than by its opponents – called the "Theory of Progressive Development" will present by far the most satisfactory solution'. The words were published on 17 May, three weeks after the Downe meeting. Huxley realized he had been wrong-footed. He was turning, knowing that his secular needs could be well served by transmutation (which could be opposed to supernatural creation), even if it had no jot of 'demonstrative evidence in its favour'.

Could individuals be successively modified? After the Downe weekend he saw no reason why not. After all pigeon breeds differ 'as widely from one another as do many species'.[24] Darwin had taught him that.

Huxley's about-face warmed Darwin. He devoured the lectures. So did Hooker, who found them 'overwhelming', 'like the old Scotch wife who said, "Ae, it was a grand discourse, I couldna understand the ane half of it"'. But it was not their 'revolutionary' nature that struck Darwin. It was Huxley's gall. He mauled Owen in the lectures. Mere mention of his name had 'the old adam in T. H. H.' rising to fight, such 'is the nature of the beast'. Owen's 'Archetypal Ideas' were consigned to oblivion; his parthenogenesis was denounced and his classification derided. Then came a dig at Ehrenberg's 'pertinacity'. Every tyro, of course, had 'to raise his heel against the carcase of the dead lion', but Huxley was baiting the living pride. The lectures were 'too vehement' for Darwin who held to an older etiquette. Huxley had hoped to be put up for the Athenaeum Club, the haven for London's literati. But in Darwin's eyes the butchery made blackballing a real possibility, especially with Owen voting.

> Cannot you fancy him, with a red face, dreadful smile &
> slow & gentle voice, asking, 'Will [you] tell me what M^r.
> Huxley has done, deserving this honour; I only know that
> he differs from, & disputes the authority of Cuvier,
> Ehrenberg & Agassiz as of no weight at all'.

Brilliant science was not enough. The Athenaeum stood for talent and character, not talented character assassination. The lectures stayed Darwin's hand: 'we had better do nothing, to try in earnest to get a great Naturalist into [the] Athenaeum & fail, is worse than doing nothing'.[25]

The problem was 'the way our friend falls foul of every one'.

Darwin was thinking of another with his feathers ruffled. Hugh Falconer was fresh from the plaster-white City of Palaces – Calcutta, that 'belvedere of a ruling race'. The Director of the botanic garden in the imperial capital had made his name resurrecting a Miocene menagerie from the Siwalik foothills of the Himalayas, everything from gigantic giraffe-like *Sivatheriums* to the first-known fossil monkey. Darwin found the repatriated Falconer 'indignant' at Huxley's attack on the prince of palaeontologists, Georges Cuvier.

Cuvier had made function the be-all of animal structure, and British theologians then made perfect structure the proof of a Wise Designer. What of the common plan among vertebrates? Huxley taunted the old fossil hod-men. It had no function. He queried Cuvier's boast that, because all the body parts were functionally integrated, he could build an entire beast from a single bone. What if Cuvier had found a fossil bear's bone? Would he construct a flesh-eating polar bear or fruit-eating brown bear?

Falconer rose to the challenge, relating the teeth of his Siwalik bears to their different habits – then came fossil hogs and dogs. He showed in each case how the body's organs are correlated and co-adapted to a specific lifestyle. Pick any part and you can predict the rest. He finished with Cuvier's prize fossil from Montmartre: part of a crushed skeleton which this 'law of correlation' had shown to be an ancient opossum.

The raptorial Falconer talked 'as if he had eaten Huxley without salt & left no bones at all'. But Huxley's bony frame lodged in Falconer's craw. Huxley rammed his point home, that no one could predict the number of a lion's teeth from its stomach. One had to consult the feline blueprint; this had been built up methodically from a study of all the big cats, and 'no further reason' for this pattern could 'be given than for the law of gravitation' (ruling out a theological gloss). 'By Jove', chortled Darwin, Falconer 'will find this pungent'. And in his new Fullerian course, Huxley promised to take 'Cuviers crack case of the 'Possum of Montmartre as an illustration of *my* views'.[26]

Huxley was honing his skills as a controversialist. All knew it. The tyro was mugging the old men. It was a job he relished, trashing reputations and received wisdom – and perhaps essential work if Darwin's big book was to sweep the world before it.

Darwin himself ground on, terrified at going public, wishing '*most heartily*' that he had never started. He was on to the 'causes of fertility', a huge chapter which would stretch 'to 100 pages MS.' Huxley was taxed on hermaphrodite jellyfish. Did these cross fertilize, rather than impregnate themselves? Surely so, for inbreeding must doom an animal in the 'severe struggle for existence'. How then? Did sperm accidentally wash into the mouth? A ribald Huxley thought the 'indecency of the process' was 'in favour of its probability, nature becoming very *low* in all senses' among the jellies. It fitted Darwin's image of a profligate, wasteful nature, based on overproduction and struggle, with success going to the best variants or breeding accidents. Perfection, design, the old certainties were dead, along with a vicarage view of life's buzzing contentment. Nature's depravity and violence screamed against a sublime Providence. Huxley's reply had Darwin blurting out, 'What a book a Devil's Chaplain might write on the clumsy, wasteful, blundering low & horridly cruel works of nature!'[27] There was no 'might' about it. Darwin had donned his satanic surplice, his Bible for a new nature was under way, and some of Huxley's cynicism was rubbing off.

In August an exhausted Hal escaped with Nettie to the Alps, on the principle that recuperation came from a hard climb. Lectures were also racking Tyndall, who joined them. (A fellow teacher at Jermyn Street, the geologist Andrew Ramsay, should have gone with his young wife Louisa, but Huxley had so 'alarmed Louisa by . . . his want of faith' that 'she worked herself into a fever' and they cried off, fearing what he might say half way up the Matterhorn.)

The crystal-tipped peaks served an aesthetic need, but the drive was initially intellectual: Huxley and Tyndall wanted to understand the veined structure of glaciers. And Huxley was fulfilling a dream. The sub-tropical Curral Mountain on Madeira had whetted his appetite and he was dying to see snowy summits. From Basle's cathedral belfry they espied the Alps, and with elated irreverence each scratched a line on its great bell:

> The biggest bell
> Twixt heaven and hell
> this tongue can tell.

At Interlaken they hired two donkeys, sat Nettie on one like 'Sancta Maria', and with a fussing Hal 'der heilige Joseph' marched to Grindelwald. They trekked on, the scenery breathtaking, through the Wengern Pass, stopping at a primitive wooden inn below the Eiger, where they lay awake listening to the booming avalanches.

By now Nettie, who was five months pregnant, was barely able to move, so they settled her back at Interlaken, while Hal and Tyndall took off for the Rhône Glacier. Alpine climbing was entering its heroic phase; the great peaks were unconquered; ropes and picks were rarely used, only an alpenstock (walking stick). But on the ledges Tyndall's wiry tenacity came into its own. He was one of the most 'daring mountaineers you ever saw,' said Huxley, so 'we have christened him "cat"'. Reaching the 'ice cliffs', they scaled an adjacent rise, crossed on to the glacial crags and ate their 'frugal dinner in a manner which made the pomp of emperors poor'; 'indescribable magnificence', was Tyndall's exclamation. Looming up was 'the mighty mass of the Finsteraarhorn', and behind it the Matterhorn 'rose like a black savage tattooed with streaks of snow'. The Irish pantheist was rhapsodic: 'the shadow of the Finsteraarhorn caused the vapours to curdle up, and to flow with great velocity into the valley of the Rhone. Here however the sun still shone, and the vapours were licked up as fast as they came'. Huxley was euphoric: the massive grandeur sent the psyche dwindling and giddy. The two kept climbing, until Huxley's shoes were 'knocked to pieces'. An excruciating 11-hour ascent to Riffelberg revealed 'the most glorious sight I ever witnessed', a cloudless view of the Matterhorn. The splendour carried him home, where he was 'monomaniacal on the subject'. It was 'one of the most thoroughly successful undertakings of my life'.[28]

The momentum swept him on. No sooner back than he tramped off again, through the fishing villages of north Devon and Cornwall, then over to Wales, studying raised beaches for his 'Report on the Recent Changes in Level in the Bristol Channel'. He thrived on it 'so long as I walk eight or ten miles a day'.[29] It kept him out of smoggy autumnal London, out of the fray. The Caldy cliffs energized him, put a spring in his step, a cocky note in his voice. And he sounded it on his arrival home.

'There is going to be a set-to at the Geological' on 5 November. 'The great O. versus the Jermyn St Pet, on the Method of Paleontology'. But on Bonfire Night Huxley found himself the Guy, caught in his attempt to blow-up Owen and Cuvier's autocratic parliament. Owen produced a precious inch-long jaw with three molars – all that was known of one of the first mammals, the Jurassic *Stereognathus* – and all that was needed to deduce its nature. Owen pictured it as a tiny pig relative, and then his tone changed.

Stereognathus was functionally harmonious and predictable because prehistoric nature was a progressive expression of Divine Intelligence. That was the issue – life's wise design. He glared at Huxley and the temperature rose. Deviants who denied it manifested 'some, perhaps congenital, defect of mind'. These were deviants who perverted 'the Young'; 'Lucretian' misfits whose 'doctrine subversive of a recognition of the Higher Mind' threatened Anglican society and called for 'prompt exposure'.

Word of the flare-up reached Hooker, who told Darwin:

> Owen I hear committed a cutting telling & flaying alive
> assault on Huxleys adaptation views at the Geolog. Soc.
> & read it with the cool deliberation & emphasis & pointed
> tone & look of an implacable foe. – & H. I fear did not
> defend himself well (though with temper) & perhaps had
> not a popular champion in Carpenter who barbed him.[30]

The festering hatred meant that relations could never be normalized, even without the ideological divide. The rolling scrap took Huxley through the birth of his son. In the emotional build-up he did resolve to make amends: 'to give a nobler tone to science; to set an example of abstinence from petty personal controversies'. It was New Year's Eve 1856. He was twiddling his fingers, full of good resolution but directionless. For three years he must continue mastering every branch of biology and geology:

> 1860 will then see me well grounded and ready for any
> special pursuits . . . In 1860 I may fairly look forward to
> fifteen or twenty years 'Meisterjahre,' and . . . I think it
> will be possible in that time to give a new and healthier
> direction to all Biological Science.
> Half-past ten at night.
>   Waiting for my child. I seem to fancy it is the pledge
> that all these things shall be.
>   Born five minutes before twelve. Thank God. New
> Year's Day, 1857.

His mother named the Christmas boy Noel. He had her looks, 'large blue eyes golden curls clear fair skin & regular features'.[31] But would the pledges made in his honour be redeemed? '1860 will show'.

13

Empires of the Deep Past

BABY NOEL WAS 'JOLLY to a degree'. But his father's resolution about avoiding controversy quickly crumbled. It couldn't have been otherwise. Huxley's cadre was moving into power, but everywhere they met Owen's imperious presence. What the scientific parvenus lacked in social strength they made up in moral posturing: hence Huxley's hallelujah, that finally 'the Lord hath given this Amalekite unto mine hands'.

Owen was to deliver guest lectures on extinct animals in Jermyn Street. His talks always attracted the Good and Great. It was galling to see them swan through the school, sundry lords, the Duke of Argyll, Dr Livingstone, fresh from the Zambezi, to be shown the 'intelligence of the Creative Power'. On the strength of this Owen announced himself as 'Professor of Comparative Anatomy & Palaeontology, Government School of Mines' in the *Medical Directory*. That was effectively Huxley's title and he took it as a slap in the face. 'Of course I have now done with him', Huxley seethed in January 1857, 'I would as soon acknowledge a man who had attempted to obtain my money on false pretences'.[1]

While Owen drew the socialites, Huxley retreated among the cloth caps. The flyposters for his working-class lectures were drawing crowds of 500, 'and the fellows are as ... intelligent as the best audience', in fact 'they *are* the best audience ... & they react upon me so that I talk to them with a will'. And he took pains to make them 'participants in my train of thought – not to shove information down their throats as if they were Turkeys to be consumed'.

Word of his lecturing prowess was out, the excitement, the controversy. His Fullerian audience doubled. Hooker sat in. So did

Herbert Spencer. Having published *Principles of Psychology*, which unashamedly embraced 'the genesis of mind in all its forms, sub-human and human', Spencer expected much from Huxley's topic, 'The Physiology of Sensation'. So much so that he did the outrageous for a man who absorbed facts through his skin: he bought a notepad.

'I will make people see what grandeur there is . . . in Biological Science', Huxley said of this course. And what uncertainty. He led his audience through a maze of dissected nerves and severed heads and abandoned them in a philosophical void. He taught that idealism (mind is the only reality), materialism (matter alone exists) and dualism (the two somehow interact through the human conduit) are all unprovable and irrefutable positions. 'I can fancy your turning round . . . as the Israelites did upon Moses and asking "Why hast thou led us out into the wilderness to die?"' But he was kicking away the philosophical crutches on which the gouty gents hobbled, those who castigated materialists as 'knaves'.[2] (They had their reason: artisan atheists, by denying a spirit world and abusing a corrupt clergy, had given materialism a seditious air.) Huxley was legitimating a responsible new breed of experts, the Tyndalls and Playfairs, Carpenters and Darwins, men who studied the material causes of culture and cosmos.

What interested him more and more now were fossils. He started another course for his students, but it took the inevitable toll. Headaches plagued him; 'its no joke', he told Dyster. 'My miserable body is getting shaky again notwithstanding early rising and a six mile walk every day'. 'Oh for a deep breath of a westerly gale on Caldy cliffs'.[3]

By the late 1850s fossils had become central to the debates over creation. Singular new ones were being construed in innovative ways. Owen set the pace. He had come to visualize a continuous creation, rather than so many separate acts. For him Divine Will animated Nature, pushing it forward continuously. 'Natural Law' was short for 'God's Fiat' and His writ runs smoothly now, as it has since the Beginning. Proof of its contingent action lay in life's rambling progression and spread into every niche. No transmutation could explain this, no inexorable Lamarckian ascent.

One fossil Owen hailed as spectacular: the metre-long amphibian *Archegosaurus*. This heavy, salamander-like creature from Bavaria's Carboniferous coalswamps was the most important find since the pterodactyl. Owen announced at Jermyn Street that it connected the fish and land vertebrates, 'linking and blending' them. He talked of the 'march of development' from lungfish via *Archegosaurus* to the first land-living amphibians.[4] This disclosure in Huxley's school on the eve of the *Origin of Species* shows how ready Owen's palaeontology was for an evolutionary gloss.

British expansion in South Africa allowed Owen to announce another surprise. After the Boers had trekked out of the scrubby Karroo plateau, army roadbuilders moved in. They found the region 'richer in fossil remains than it was ever thought'. Huxley was on the Geological Society Council when Owen exhibited one ferret-sized reptile skull with unheard-of features: nipping incisors, stabbing canines and chewing molars. This was a mammal's dentition! The 'weasel-reptile', *Galesaurus*, Owen dubbed it, admitting that the predator made a most 'suggestive approach to the mammalian class'.[5] It was the first hint of an unknown group of extinct mammal-like reptiles.

'Annectant' amphibians and progressive reptiles: these concepts fired the imagination. The age gave them life. As Owen envisaged a creative stream, so Spencer turned it into a torrent. From stellar development to steam power, all was a blur of forward motion. For millennialists biological development held the promise of future perfection. Many a night Huxley and Spencer walked home together, Spencer praising the 'beneficent necessity' of evolutionary and social progress. It was a stop-go walk as the cosmic philosopher was knocked down and 'continually got up again'.

Britain's own mood was buoyant. Industry and the 'economic miracle' left per capita income twice that of Germany. The export of machinery to the rest of the world was staggering, and when the railway engineer Robert Stephenson died his body was borne past throngs of silent mourners to Westminster Abbey. After the Indian Mutiny of 1857 the crown had annexed the East India Company's land. The Queen now ruled India. Great credit booms financed new companies, putting more people into work. Forty thousand commuted daily into London, which was already seized by traffic jams. As incomes rose Samuel Smiles proclaimed in his *Self-Help* that any virtuous Briton could become a gentleman. Social progress seemed inevitable, the end point of a cosmic evolutionary process.

Bold works shouted it. Henry Buckle's *History of Civilization* had society rising like fossil life, shaped by circumstance, subject to statistical laws. Buckle typified the revolt against an aristocratic history driven by Divine whim. 'Buckle the Great' (as Huxley mocked him) was another 1840s radical grown respectable, now speaking the *Westminster*'s language. He articulated its climactic belief in 'one glorious principle of universal and undeviating regularity'. Whether the vital phenomena of life or the vital interests of society, Huxley quipped, every 'disorderly mystery' was becoming an 'orderly mystery'.[6]

Buckle's was the first of the mythopoeic extravaganzas, a gigantic tome with its replacement naturalistic cosmogony. Spencer would perfect the technique, leaving Darwin and Huxley to fill in the fine texture and Tyndall to capture the cosmic warp and weave. Credos were becoming the rage.

Presidents of the Geological Society caught the mood. It affected spry 63 year-old Colonel Portlock (Huxley's backer for the fellowship). Portlock was a veteran of the 1812 War with the United States. He had a 'frame and nerves of iron' but no Iron Duke mentality. Acts of Creation were outmoded, he announced in his Presidential Address. Nature was no Absolute Monarchy, ruled by Divine caprice. God was a sort of Divine Samuel Smiles, helping Nature to help itself. Owen's 'march of development' suggested that new life was continually created by the 'action of physical circumstances'.[7] With Presidents paying court, Owen looked supreme. An early *rapprochement* of his 'speculative Palaeontology' with Darwin's theory seemed likely.

The succession of species had to be explained, and Huxley was now as adamant as Spencer that transmutation was the only option.

At this point Darwin posted fragments of his 'big book', *Natural Selection* as he was set to call it. Odd pages arrived, glimpses that gave no sense of the whole. Darwin was 'like Croesus overwhelmed by my riches'. Each point – the overproduction of life, the random appearance of variants, their struggle for resources and the survival of the best (this sequence was the gist of his theory of 'natural selection') – would be bludgeoned home by bountiful examples. Through 1857 he ploughed, proving that 'large genera' (those with many species) are expanding and the 'manufacturing' sites of varieties. Nature was a superior Spitalfields weaver. He picks feathers, she screens 'every nerve, vessel & muscle; every habit, instinct, shade of constitution'. Nothing got past unless 'it gives some advantage'. Put less anthropomorphically, limited resources force the variants into a civil war. On the battlefront, the less fit are slaughtered and only those with an edge live to found new dynasties.

Such competitive individualism was part of the age. Tennyson's life 'red in tooth and claw' had wiped the smile off nature's face. Only from 'death, famine, rapine, and the concealed war of nature' could 'the highest good' come, 'the creation of the higher animals'. Perfect adaptation was a delusion, part of the defunct argument for a wise design. Individuals were blemished and locked in a struggle. A bloodthirsty leer crept over the face of Nature. Darwin's sickness seemed in keeping. The grind was racking him. The fear of breaking cover stretched him taut and occasionally he snapped. His retreats to a Farnham spa became more frequent, and the sanatorium doctors found him a pitiful sight, 'crushed with agony', sick and shaking.[8]

He would ask Huxley to verify a 'little point'. Did the specialized organs emerge first in the embryo? He would send the relevant pages without 'troubling you ... in what way the case concerns my work'. (Not surprisingly with Darwin tying up embryonic development and evolution.) Darwin was still intimidated; nor did Huxley's mordant wit reassure him: 'The animal body is built up like a House', he replied, first the frame, not 'the cornices, cupboards, & grand piano'.[9] Paragraphs were tricked out to inoculate *Natural Selection* against this sort of sarcasm.

Darwin did confide his 'heterodox notions', saying that classification should 'be simply genealogical'. For him reptiles, birds and mammals were the living tips of the vertebrate tree, whose dead trunk stretched back into the remote past; they inherited their common features from the same, extinct, fish-like ancestor. But Huxley – though looking at fossils these four years – still thought timelessly. He had trouble breaking away from the archetypes, those common-denominator abstractions around which all animals, living and fossil, might be clustered. Classifying was not about 'pedigree & possible modifications', he replied. The 'pedigree business' had 'no more to do with pure Zoology, than human pedigree has with the Census'.[10] Classification was an arrangement for the living, not an appeal to the dead.

Huxley still had to be convinced by Darwin of a branching evolution. True, he held Darwin in high esteem. In class he called the 1,000-page barnacle book 'one of the most beautiful and complete anatomical and zoological monographs which has appeared in our time' ('you will turn my head', Darwin replied). But the monograph was descriptive. *Natural Selection* would be another matter, an evolutionary tome with a utilitarian core.

To sway an anti-utilitarian with a venomous bite was never

going to be easy. Huxley denied the 'doctrine that every part of every organic being is of use to it'. What of the hummingbird's lustre? It had no purpose, save to give nature's poem a beautiful cadence. Sea urchin shapes might tickle our geometrical fancy, but it was 'absurd' to think that they 'are any *good* to the animals'.

> Who has ever dreamed of finding an utilitarian purpose in
> the forms and colours of flowers, in the sculpture of
> pollen-grains, in the varied figures of the fronds of ferns?

Darwin had, and he cringed. So was beauty created for humanity's sake?, he asked in *Natural Selection*. That would 'be fatal to our theory'.[11] Are the fantastic shapes of rotifers for microscopists to admire? No, they are useful to their owners, or had been to their ancestors.

It was imperative to turn Huxley. He was a force in his own right, a charismatic leader. His *corps dramatique* was breaking into the old coteries. Huxley's presence in the societies was felt even when he was not a member, as at the Linnean. This had just moved to the prestigious Burlington House, near his Piccadilly museum. Before meetings he would dine with Hooker, Carpenter and Busk, the new secretary, to plan the old dame's facelift.

He was also helping to reshape London University, that educational 'Holy Roman Empire' with its catholic embrace of colleges. The science departments were fragmented and spread among Medicine and the Arts. But these time-honoured faculties of Arts, Theology, Law and Medicine were 'utterly inadequate' by 1858. No longer could 'Academic bodies' afford 'to ignore Science as a separate Profession'. With material progress the new Messiah, it was an emotive plea. 'What knowledge is of most worth?' echoed Spencer. 'The uniform reply is – science'. What do the ironworks cry out for? asked Carpenter – trained chemists. Tyndall, Lyell and Playfair were equally voluble. The pressure paid off. In 1858 the university created the first Faculty of Science and B.Sc. degree, complete with its progressive cachet.[12]

Huxley's word counted. His star was rising and about to twin Darwin's in the firmament. Together they were elected to one of the most prestigious scientific bodies in Germany, the Imperial Academy of Naturalists in Breslau, 'God forgive them', laughed Hooker. It was Darwin's first European accolade. Hooker told Huxley not to 'get intoxicated on the honour!' But that did not stop him from 'standing upon [his] head'.[13]

The 'cotton millennium' had found its scientific prophets.

Huxley and Tyndall were firing imaginations in a world 'where nothing need remain unknown' and everything could be bettered. They enthralled listeners, whose second sons with their B.Sc.s would keep Might enslaved to Right. Their prospering audience had grown up with steam, gaslight and change. They sped on 60 mile-an-hour expresses, their life a blur of motion, like Turner's *Rain, Steam, and Speed*, thrown out of focus by the hurtling engine.

Dickens inevitably linked 'science and the public good'. And in 'an age of express trains, [and] painless operations' 'such as our grandfathers and grandmothers never dreamt about', the telegraph was 'the most wonderful'. The major towns were connected. Submarine cables ran under the English Channel. Yet the ultimate challenge remained an Atlantic cable. In the summer of 1857 Dayman set off in the frigate *Cyclops* to fix the route. Huxley versed his surgeon on ocean-floor dredging.[14] Within weeks Huxley was examining the mud, a pale-coloured ooze from 12,000 feet (composed of myriad raspberry-shaped shells, all that remained of minute planktonic creatures called *Globigerina*). As he studied this shelly silt, wondering if he was gazing at the source of the world's chalk rocks, *Cyclops* and the 'Wire Squadron' set off in the first (unsuccessful) attempt to feed out an Atlantic cable.

A couple of weeks later Huxley arrived home from his second onslaught on the Alps, bedraggled but with his shakes steadied. Lightning trips were possible now, with a rail link depositing him at Geneva in 39 hours, 'weary but triumphant'. He had gone to confirm his doubts about the supposed fissures permeating glaciers. But it was an emotional sojourn among the ice cliffs. Tyndall was there, fraught himself, suffering a 'rascally brain'. With him was a mathematical friend, Thomas Hirst, dragged away after the burial of his young wife. Climbing had become a drug to ease life's pain, and it was 'a set of dirty sunburnt snowblind wretches' who emerged from their ascent of Mont Blanc. Or in Huxley's case two-thirds of an ascent; only days after arriving he was out of training and stuck at 10,000 feet, where he bivouacked 'on a pinnacle like S⁺. Simon Stylites – & nearly as dirty as that worthy saint must have been'. Here he perched, alone for 17 hours, the desolate glory of the snowface sharpening his anxiety as the others became long overdue. Nettie heard how the madcap Tyndall had managed to conquer the summit in treacherous conditions. 'See what you gain by being a bachelor', she wrote to him. 'No vision of a wife to restrain you from glory – or a snowy burial'.[15]

Huxley charged at aphids the way he charged at the Alps, horns out, treating Owen as a great monolithic impediment.

One major article would wind up his invertebrate work (he was now moving wholly into fossils). Hooker and Busk wanted progressive papers on the Linnean agenda, and Huxley arranged his finale here on 5 November. It was a brilliant explosion on aphid parthenogenesis. 'Polemically', he told Dyster, 'it was . . . the most effectual smasher that has yet come down on the "neb" of my Eminent friend'. The languid-looking Owen was pelted for his 'ignorance writ large'.

It was another case of ideological worlds colliding. To Huxley and a generation of gutsy rationalists Owen's views were archaic. He accepted a residual 'spermatic force' in the female aphid, who continues to deliver (as do her offspring) without mating, until it is exhausted. Some attenuated force!, laughed Huxley, when the progeny of one aphid after ten generations could weigh (were they all to survive) more 'than the whole population of China!' Mystical forces infuriated him. These 'intellectual opiates' no longer soothed the scientific brain. Do gunners explain 'the propulsion of a bullet by saying it was "trigger force"?' Huxley saw the asexual broods on his geraniums as so many buds or zoöids, and their production curtailed by cold weather, not spent spirits.

The paper went off to Darwin, 'profiting by a weeks rest & hydropathy' at his spa. Having long done with 'life-forces', he loved this demolition work. But like all of literary London, he was agog at Huxley's temerity. In fact 'your Father confessor trembles for you'.

Tit-for-tat hatreds were now structuring every move. Huxley, as George Eliot observed, was inordinately reactive, and Owen as stubbornly responsive. Aphids might not amount to much on the cosmic scale, but Man was the measure of all things. Huxley and Owen, the mandarins of science, were moving towards the apotheosis. Lyell might have rationalized the first humans 'stealing quietly into the world', sired by apes, but Owen had not.

Darwin was deep in *Natural Selection* when Owen seized the initiative. Our brain was so distinct, he said in 1857, that he was divorcing mankind from all other mammals. Henceforth we would keep our own select company in a crowning new subclass, the Archencephala ('ruling brain'). Darwin, an unbudging relativist, wondered 'what a Chimpanzee w^d. say to this'.[16] More to the point, what would Huxley?

Owen was a senior statesman of science, fêted by Oxford University with an honorary Doctorate, decorated by the French with the Légion d'Honneur. No one knew more of apes. He had been dissecting London Zoo's corpses since 1830. The orang's foot showed that it could not stand erect and be counted a man, and the chimp's brain that it lacked the intelligence anyway. Every aspect of their prognathous faces and quadrumanous frames emphasized the unbridgeable chasm 'between *Man* and the *Ape*'. Only people were adapted to house 'a rational and responsible soul'.[17]

Owen was sensitive on the issue. Lyell was agonizing over an ape ancestry when the crunch came: news of a human-sized 'oak ape' *Dryopithecus* from French Miocene rocks. 'If Man was develop.^d out of any ape it was from the Dryopithecus', Lyell gulped, '& a million or more of years have been required for it'. The fossil was so human-like that 'tho' extinct perhaps for a million years' it might fool students in their College of Surgeons exams.[18] It didn't fool Owen. He was horrified, dismissing the creature as a gibbon and Lyell's suggestion as silly.

The burly Owen was built to stamp on such nonsense. He shared the fears of his Oxbridge patrons. Lamarck's suggestion that apes had only to move on to the plains, stand to see, free their hands and enlarge their brains to become men and women was execrable. What of morality? Was reason only the better part of brute instinct? The very hint would poison society. Moral responsibility was a gift carrying the promise of future rewards. Remove the fear of damnation and what is to stop the masses from rising up to redress their grievances? Species might turn over, but it was no self-creation. A caring Providence worked by other means.

The strains became visible with the début of a new ape. The gorilla, black and 'indescribably fierce', had not been known long. Owen himself had four tribal-fetish skulls obtained from an old ship's captain. They were daubed in sacred paint, making that 'scowling physiognomy' look even more menacing. But stabbing canines and overhanging brows were marks of the unreasoning brute.[19] These 'forbidding' beasts were not men in the making.

The militants on the streets were already heralding mankind's monkey origin. They learned about the latest finds in the pauper press and the worker-run Halls of Science in the industrial cities. Red Lamarckians saw life pulling itself up unaided – monkeys turning themselves into men, and men transforming their own social troop. There was no God on high delegating power through his clergy. Tory churchmen still saw Creation as the Divine sanction of the status quo. For this reason atheist demagogues – like Robert Cooper and the *Reasoner*'s sub-editor John Watts, who toured the country talking on the 'Origin of Man' – gloated over human ancestry.[20] Apes were paraded in their penny-trash papers and a new ape was grist to the mill. (The first gorilla seen alive had been sold as a chimp at Liverpool docks in 1855. It drew gawping crowds with Wombwell's travelling menagerie, the mistake only being discovered when it was stuffed.)

Hence the gentry's fears. Where would moral authority reside if man did not come from his Maker's hands? The squires looked to Owen. Britain's foremost comparative anatomist was well connected. He had seen his portrait hung alongside Cuvier's in Sir Robert Peel's gallery and he joined Gladstone for breakfast. Owen reassured them that no hideous parody could dull the lustre of the divine species. But a Cambridge don persisted: how does the anatomist explain human superiority? Is the hand or tongue really that different, 'or is the mind working on almost the same anatomy'?[21]

That was the problem. So Owen switched to a cerebral approach. Humans were moral agents and must have unique brains. In 1857 Owen (undoubtedly aware that Darwin was writing his 'big book') pointed to the huge cerebral hemispheres. They overlap the cerebellum, extending so far back, he claimed, that they divide into a unique third lobe. Into this extends a cavity (the 'lateral ventricle') with a peculiar 'posterior horn' and a singular structure projecting from its floor, the 'hippocampus minor'. No one knew what they were for, but apes, Owen claimed, lacked them. He seemed to have found the peculiar pieces to justify mankind's rational uniqueness.

Huxley was flabbergasted. Owen's classificatory edifice stood 'like a Corinthian portico in cow-dung'. Huxley's group believed that Owen had made a colossal error. They assumed that his preserved ape brains must have hardened into distorted shapes (although Owen was aware of the problem).[22] 'Man . . . as distant from a Chimpanzee' as 'an ape from a platypus!' exclaimed Darwin. 'I cannot swallow' that.

In 1858, as London Zoo received its first preserved gorilla in a cask, Huxley added a new lecture to his Royal Institution course. Not so much a lecture, 'The Distinctive Characters of Man' was a broadside which would prove decisive in the Darwinian debate. Behind him were pictures and brains, with humans placed ignominiously beside gorillas and baboons. Looking at them he made his provocative claim, shortly to become famous:

> Now I am quite sure that if we had these three creatures
> fossilized or preserved in spirits for comparison and were
> quite unprejudiced judges we should at once admit that
> there is very little greater interval *as animals* between the
> *Gorilla* & the *Man* than exists between the *Gorilla* & the
> [baboon] *Cynocephalus*.

Skeleton or cerebrum, it made no difference. The devil dared him and he proclaimed in public what Darwin thought in private.

> Nay more I believe that the mental & moral faculties are
> essentially & fundamentally the same in kind in animals
> & ourselves. I can draw no line of demarcation between
> an instinctive and a reasonable action.

True, in cultural terms the gap was 'infinite'. But it is speech, not some spiritual gift, which makes man 'a reason*able* being'. It was the source of our 'unlimited intellectual progress'. But that did not disguise the fact 'that to the very root & foundation of his nature man is one with the rest of the organic world'.[23]

Huxley finished his Royal Institution course croaky and 'bedeviled'. Morality and apes were now explosively mixed and awaited only a fuse. Darwin, ten chapters and a quarter of a million words into *Natural Selection*, was sidestepping human origins 'as so surrounded with prejudices'.[24] But Huxley ensured that mind and man remained in the polemical picture. His gladiatorial stand was not only pushing him into Darwin's camp, but on to its skirmishing defences.

His fearsome talents were still getting him noticed. He had hardly mellowed, but he now roared into the Athenaeum Club. Murchison put him up and wrote:

> I had a success as to you that I never had or heard of
> before. 19 persons voted & of these 18 voted for you &
> no one against you. You of course came in at the head of
> the poll; no other having i.e. *Cobden* more than 11.

It meant more money. 'Hoorar', cheered Hooker, conspiring to get Busk and Tyndall elected next – pay up quickly and come 'on

Monday night & help to swamp the Parsons & get Buckle in'. Buckle's science might have been 'bosh' (invited to dinner Huxley declined 'as I have too much of the Arab about me to eat a man's salt & then pitch into him'). But the whiff of a backlash had him rushing to Buckle's aid.[25]

The group still lacked a house organ, and Huxley kept thrusting his foot into doors. He did get his men a voice in the smartest weekly of the age. A column in the *Saturday Review* would align his scientific upstarts with Trollope and Bagehot. They were liberals; true, not of Mill's stamp, being wary of any democratic diluting of talent, but their assaults on plum-in-mouth pomposity had one preacher fulminating that 'man is born for the love of God and the hatred of the *Saturday Review*'. That was good enough for Huxley. He collected his own 'corps (d'elite!)' and signed them up. It should be 'a salutary influence in this quack-ridden country' gloated Tyndall at the Royal Institution, promising 'to perform my share of the business'.[26]

Only when Hal's own Royal Institution course ended in March 1858 did he find time to register his and Nettie's new baby, already six weeks old. After Noel he had wanted a girl, and Tyndall, more and more the atomic determinist, rejoiced: 'Pon my soul – I dont often swear thus – the gods are very kind to you. Things could not have happened more nicely if you yourself had been the patentee of the molecular architecture'. The devout Emma Darwin stood godmother. Jessie Oriana they named the baby, the latter after Nettie's sister. The Jessie spoke for itself; it had been 13 years since Lizzie's loss and Huxley was finally effacing the past. 'We could not make you a godmother', he wrote to Lizzie, although 'this is a better tie than that meaningless formality'.

But the past was always there, decaying in the shape of Cooke. Lizzie heard about the decline of 'Ellen & her husband'; 'she has not learned wisdom with age', he was drinking himself into an early grave '& now I think they cannot go much further'. Cooke died in September 'a bloated mass of beer & opium', 47, intestate and penniless.

'Chronic enlargement of the liver' the death certificate read, an epitaph for a life poisoned by drink. But Huxley thanked the man for his helping hand. And he knew the 'wear & tear of incessant occupation' that had driven Cooke to his grave. He was grinding down himself. The dissections were interminable, with nothing taken on trust: 'if Hal had but a little rest occasionally . . . ', Nettie lamented. But no. Waverley Place was a bustle. Toddler Noel was turning into a 'stout little Trojan', nothing like his raven-haired father in looks, but like him taking on the world 'as if he were its master'.

Huxley worked through the tears and tantrums. Herrings were examined for the Fisheries Commission, sea-nettles for his book. This he had picked up again, years late. It had a title now, *Oceanic Hydrozoa*. He pored over his 'travel stained cockroachy notebooks & drawings of 1847–8–9–50', that tropical aromatic memento from a world away. But a decade left him feeling 'like the editor of somebody else's posthumous work'. His changes since those barricade days reminded him of France, herself grown into a secure stodginess. Ten years had even sown a little silver in his hair. Otherwise his 'phiz' was the same.[27] Baby Jessie's 'nose is the image of mine', he lamented, and time has 'by no means softened the outlines of that remarkable feature'.

The old world passed away with Cooke, and Huxley threw his door open to the new. His dinner parties saw the rising talent. Guests were non-plussed to find the most formidable talents of the age, Tyndall, Spencer and Mill, facing them across the table. The Hookers would arrive, or the Carpenters. And the Busks, despite the gentle friction between Ellen and Nettie. Friction and jealousy produced a hint of electrostatic *frisson*: 'She was very gentle & kind & even called me "dear"', Nettie told Hal. 'She doesn't know how I'd love her if she were only straightforward about you'.[28] The prickly air was set off by their diametric temperaments. Tall, dark Ellen was 'quick and intelligent' with 'a self-possessed rather blunt but honest manner', a female Tom in truth; but, said Hirst, making his choice at dinner one day, 'she has not Mrs. Huxley's depth and warmth'.

Cooke's failure only highlighted Huxley's success. His 'Croonian Lecture' confirmed it. This was a gala night in the Royal Society's calendar, ill paid but well starred. On a midsummer evening, 17 June, Huxley stood in the Great Hall of Burlington House (the society's spacious new site). He was looking less shabby now in his frock coat, but just as fearsome, with scowling eyes and black hair swept over his ears. Richard Owen was in the Chair and the 'nobs' viewed Huxley – or rather his tongue – with some trepidation. His talk on the skull was clinical and slick. The insiders knew what he was up to: burying a wizened old morphology and giving a forceps delivery to the new. The birth of a new embryological

anatomy was overdue and he dragged it screaming into a secular world to join its German *Bruder*. He focused on one superannuated belief: that the skull was made of distended vertebrae
(an idea championed by Owen and the older anatomists in
London). The Königsberg embryologist Martin Rathke had already
noted the skull's distinct foetal origins, so it could not be a
continuation of the spinal segments, each the embodiment of an
Ideal Vertebra. Such mysticism was 'fundamentally opposed to the
spirit of modern science' anyway. Huxley heroically refrained
from mentioning Owen by name. But that was the least he could
do with his crimson-cheeked protagonist fuming in the Chair.

Everywhere the old romanticism was in retreat: poets were
rejecting Wordsworth's 'spiritualization of Nature'; anatomists
were spurning life's Divine archetypal halo, and Huxley gave a
hearty push to the cultural swing. He ceremoniously knocked off
Owen's vertebral crown.

Spencer joined the regicidal clamour, making his own 'tremendous smash' of Owen's Platonism (like any ex-Unitarian). But
Spencer was dextrously decapitating Owen while standing on his
shoulders. He cut off the archetypal head but kept the progressive
body. He still needed an image of progressing life, and he saw it
evolving by the piling of '*adaptations upon adaptations*'. The
specializations acquired during an individual's life were fixed and
passed on. And this acquisition of skills carried over as cultural
evolution in humans.

The day after the Croonian Hooker received a note. 'I wonder
how Ricardus, "Rex anatomicorum", feels this morning', Huxley
wrote. 'I am deuced seedy but that is just punishment for irreverent
democrats'.[29]

Darwin was feeling worse. For 20 years he had been terrified of
going public. Having finally screwed up the courage to write, he
opened a letter from the Far East that morning. He scanned what
seemed like a précis of his theory; 'all my originality', he cried in
disbelief, has been 'smashed'.

It was from the affable Alfred Russel Wallace out in the Malay
Archipelago. Wallace had occasionally sent jungle fowl skins, but
he was a world removed in every sense: a hard-up collector gone
native, shipping exotic butterflies and birds to a dealer, packing a
1,000 beetles per box to make it pay. He was a former builder's
apprentice and surveyor, whose politics came from the socialist
Hall of Science and evolution from *Vestiges*. He was another 1840s

activist, outraged by wealth and organized religion. And his sojourn in the Indies had only increased his socialist faith in morality as a cultural product and mankind as an evolved animal.

Socialist spectacles gave his nature a pink hue. For him the environment expunged the unfit, not competition; and *his* evolution would realize the ideal of 'perfect man'. But Darwin had no inkling of this utopian vision. All he saw were a few rice-paper pages and an apparently identical theory: 'if Wallace had my M.S. sketch . . . he could not have made a better short abstract!'[30]

An emotional vortex sucked him down. Lyell and Hooker stepped in, acting the consummate diplomats, arranging a joint communiqué of Darwin and Wallace's theory of natural selection at the Linnean (where Busk and friends could control events). It was Darwin's first public pronouncement. But his concern was swept away by grief as his retarded 18 month-old son, Charles Waring, succumbed to scarlet fever. The baby was buried on the day of the reading, 1 July. The Darwins lined the graveside, leaving Hooker and Lyell to quell any rumbles among the Linnean fellows.

Huxley was not a member of the Linnean. But he worked behind the scenes. He vetted the documents establishing Darwin's priority. At last he had an overview of natural selection. He realized why he had been shown all those plumed, ruffed pigeons. Fanciers can spot nuances of colour or shape 'inappreciable to an uneducated eye', and tease them out by select breeding. Nature was only a more ubiquitous selector. Her feedback system was like 'the centrifugal governor of the steam engine', Wallace's letter said, 'which checks and corrects' automatically.

Darwin explained how. Human overpopulation was prevented by disease or famine. So it was with every species. Unchecked a pair of birds could multiply ten million fold in 15 years, or elephants overrun the earth in a thousand years. But predation and starvation take their toll. The grim reaper was vigilant, scything down the weak and ill-fitted. 'Only a few of those annually born can live to propagate their kind', Darwin argued. And in the scramble for resources a 'trifling difference' can 'determine which shall survive & which perish'.[31] The winners were those with some chance adaptation, fitting them to changing conditions (this was 'natural selection'). Only they thrived to breed, passing on their new trait. Since Silurian times 'millions on millions of generations' have transmuted this way. Huxley tried to assimilate the first thumb-nail sketch of Darwin's theory. Its whole naturalistic emphasis was glorious, but some details worried him, such as the relentless emphasis on micro-adaptations and the severity of the struggle. He thought it over.

As Huxley pored over the pages a 'panic-struck' Darwin fled to the Isle of Wight, taking his children away from the fever. Having broken cover he began a full article for the Linnean *Journal*. But the inevitable happened; it swelled uncontrollably. Anyway the 'subject really seems to me too large for discussion at any Society, & I believe Religion would be brought in'. Soon he was back to a 400-page book, an 'abstract' of *Natural Selection*, which he would call the *Origin of Species*. He turned down Hooker's offer of a Linnean grant. He preferred to go over professional heads and reach out to the public. For all his leanings Huxley delighted in empirical British achievement, and English gents came no more dogged than Darwin. His relentless utilitarianism – his demand that every curlicue and hue of the oddest orchid must function in order to be selected – made Huxley wince, but he relished Darwin's snatch at the supernatural:

> Wallace's impetus seems to have set Darwin going in earnest and I am rejoiced to hear we shall learn his views in full, at last. I look forward to a great revolution being effected. Depend upon it in Natural History as in everything else when the English mind fully determines to work a thing out it will do it better than any other.
>
> I firmly believe in the advent of an English epoch in science & art which will lick the Augustan . . . into fits.[32]

Spencer, lodging in the street next to Huxley's to aid their Sunday strolls, was also cranking up. Having broached the origin of mind in *Principles of Psychology* he mooted a ten-volume treatise on everything else. All knowledge was to be tackled in terms of development, or, as he was calling it, 'the evolution point of view'. The pair thrashed it out on their walks to the Finchley countryside. Huxley was notoriously 'chary in his praise', perennially pricking Spencer's theoretical balloons, but he backed his 'modern "novum organon"'.

Others were moving: even Owen in his pontifical address as President of the British Association in September 1858 assuaged conservative fears. The 'continuous operation of Creative power' need cause no fear, he announced. New species might emerge consecutively, but with Natural Law an expression of God's Will, 'our science' is still 'connected with the loftiest of moral speculations'. Owen loathed transmutation, and his notion of 'continuous Creation' would be critical in the years of Christian reconciliation.[33]

As Darwin geared up to publish, Huxley's banner was unfurling on another front. The move to fossil reptiles was inevitable. It was enough that Owen had charge of 'Nature's crowning race', the intimidating dinosaurs. Their Mesozoic empire was firing the Victorian imagination. It had come to light within living memory and assumed an apocalyptic aura, dramatized in John Martin's 'Gothick' paintings. To Tennyson the annihilation of these Brobdingnagian dinosaurs was a sobering reminder of earthly transience. His nature was indifferent, crushing individuals and empires indiscriminately. Dinosaurs were forcing Victorians to break out of their small, circumscribed world. But deep time, like deep space, Tennyson's 'terrible Muses', brought its own insecurity. Those 'dreadful Hammers!', Ruskin wrote of the geologists, 'I hear the clink of them at the end of every cadence of the Bible verses'. It drove some to despair, but left Huxley with his cosy alienation, secure in nature's 'vicious disregard'.[34] The High Churchman Henry Mansel was right in his *Limits of Religious Thought*: God could no longer be found in the rocks, only in revelation.

The Crystal Palace had its 'mausoleum to the memory of ruined worlds', stocked with Owen's life-size dinosaurs, 30-ton concrete models built like reptilian rhinoceroses. But Huxley took satisfaction in the news from America. In Connecticut huge three-toed fossil footprints were being ascribed to dinosaurs walking on their hind legs.[35] This was the most alien of concepts: bipedal creatures with 18-inch footprints and six-foot strides. It was the shape of things to come.

Huxley moved to the dawn of the 'Age of Reptiles'. He focused on the yellow sandstones of Elgin, in the north of Scotland. These were presumed to be Devonian in age – deposited as sediments when lungfish were life's apex and lush club-moss forests were spreading over newly emerged continents. The first discovery (in 1851) of a 4-inch 'lizard' skeleton had Lyell 'inebriate with joy'. Jubilant, too, were the Moray antiquarians led by the Minister of Birnie, Revd George Gordon, in whose parish this oldest of reptilian tombs lay. Such fossil firsts gave their Morayshire, 'the fairest spot on earth', an international importance.

It had locals scouring the quarries, but their next find, a

heavy-scaled creature, *Stagonolepis*, wiped the grin off Lyell's face. Its scutes were suspiciously like a crocodile's from the much later Mesozoic period. By 1858 Gordon was shipping regular consignments to Jermyn Street (thanks to Murchison's payments), keeping the preparators busy with friable limbs and jaw casts.

Huxley diagnosed another 'wonderful reptile', 15 feet long with a 'swinging tail'. And when he cried 'A tooth! A tooth! my kingdom for a tooth!' Gordon triumphantly obliged – allowing Huxley to confirm what his collectors suspected. *Stagonolepis* had socketed teeth, making it an advanced reptile, unlike lizards but like dinosaurs and crocodiles. Its spine and armour were indeed 'eminently crocodilian'. But crocodiles in ancient *Devonian* rocks?

Huxley introduced *Stagonolepis* at the Geological Society and left one overriding impression. Crocodiles must be reptilian Methuselahs, primeval creatures surviving little changed for untold aeons. He remained Lyell's heir. Spencer called the meeting 'a triumph for Huxley, and rather damaging for the progressive theory, *as commonly held*'.[36] Spencer was still trying to think his way round Huxley's obstacles. But what evolutionary view could Huxley accommodate?

His fossil expertise got him the Secretary's post of the Geological. More bureaucratic work, Nettie grumbled; he cannot stop, and he 'looks very tired & worn . . . for he never spares himself'. 'You cannot think what he has got through this past year'.

In 1858 Huxley stood on the threshold. He finally finished *Oceanic Hydrozoa* in September at a manic pace, as Nettie complained, giving it 'five weeks of 6 hours p^r diem during his seaside holiday (?!)'.[37] It ended an era of struggle, of furious highs and forlorn hope, of cynicism and crowning achievement. Had Huxley died on the eve of the *Origin* – of kidney-failure like Cooke, or crushed by a banking scandal like George who was wasting away with phthisis – and had friends collected his *Literary Papers* as they did for Forbes, he would have been remembered as a brilliant invertebrate anatomist who teased out the two layers of jellyfish, an idiosyncratic anti-progressionist, a prophet awaiting Silurian Man, an iconoclast, a scathing critic with a chip on his shoulder. How the world would really remember him the next few years would tell. The subaltern had risen through the ranks, competent in ever-expanding fields. The government officer was ready for whatever his 'scientific Young England' expected.

1858–1865

The New Luther

14

The Eve of a New Reformation

SIX YEARS EARLIER Nettie's sister Ory and her husband William Fanning had left Hal an insecure tyro. Now back from Sydney, they found a confident, hardworking teacher, but just as proud and pugnacious and doing what he had always prophesied, capitalizing on knowledge. The years had seen a transformation. Domestic anchorage gave him a new joy and stability. He doted on his little 'monkey', Noel. This 'bright eyed golden haired mannikin' was 'the apple of his father's eye and chief deity of his mother's pantheon, which at present contains only a god and goddess. Another is expected shortly, however, so that there is no fear of Olympus looking empty'.[1]

They also found him wielding power. Huxley's organizational flair was apparent. He was the whipper-in: 'it is no use putting any faith in the old buffers', he mused, 'hardened as they are in trespasses & sins'. With the *Quarterly Review* talking of moving the British Museum's natural history collection to a separate museum – giving Owen 'a temple of his own' – Huxley formed a 'Committee of Public Safety' and petitioned the Chancellor with alternative plans. His Danton was played to perfection. He expected 'oceans of trouble & abuse, but so long as we gain our end, I care not a whistle whether the sweet voices of the scientific mob are for or against me'.

His ginger group wanted a national museum, but not one under Owen's control. Theirs was to be a Temple of Reason. No republic had a more zealous Minister of Justice. Huxley arranged low-brow support for their people-friendly museum in Robert Chambers' *Journal* and high-brow coverage in the *Quarterly*. He even roused Prince Albert and *The Times*. 'Can you get at the

"Household Words"'? he asked Hooker. 'If only one knew that snob Dickens'.²

A national museum with research facilities would signal the changing ethos. They were no longer 'Gentlemen of Science', parsons and squires with their parish distractions. Quite what the salaried squad was no one could say for sure. Not 'Naturalists', any 'fool who can make bad species and worse genera is a "Naturalist"! save the mark!' Not 'Biologists', too 'foreign' and tainted by 'perversion' (Lamarck had coined the term). Nor 'scientists', an unfamiliar word. They were 'Scientific men'.³ Less gentle, but still with a duty to their own. The Committee showed its benign face as Hooker and Huxley set up a distress fund, a sort of Civil List for the stretched new man.

By January 1859 word was out about Professor Huxley's provocative night-time talks. Artisans flocked to them from all over London. Nobody talked so openly as Huxley; at least no 'nob'. Nobody dared say that humans and animals '*must* have proceeded from one another in the way of progressive modification'. This was now Huxley's firm line. Fired by their own infidel orators and Baptist evangelists, they quizzed him on the 'religious' implications. At a time when teachers were part of a tacit conspiracy not to ship intellectual arms across the class divide, Huxley's forthright response was eagerly reported in their trade journal, *The Builder*.

He fashioned a low-caste Dissenting image of science. The testimony of Nature was for all to hear. No priesthood had privileged 'access to her deepest secrets'. Every man his own pastor: it was a message for the Baptists as much as the democratic masses. Indeed every man must examine the 'mysteries' of existence for himself to keep Britain great; any nation 'hood-winked and fettered' by church dogmas and denying the 'free application of the intellect' would be 'rotten within'.⁴

Thirty years of Dissenting siege against a knowledge-monopolizing, State-supported Church had come to a head. But this was no attack on *religion* per se; a sceptical science merely purified theology by stripping off the concreting myths. Carpenter's Unitarians railed just as hard against Anglican supernaturalism and the State powers of the bishops. For all of them the Bible encoded history's moral truths. Huxley saw 'in these truths the result of a long & loving, if sorrowful, study of man's nature and relations – the stored wisdom of many generations ... Thou shalt love thy neighbour as thyself is the Law of Gravitation of Society'.

For 30 years the Anglican monopoly of the bench, the town halls, the hospitals and Oxford and Cambridge had been eroded, with the final disabilities on Jews being removed in 1858. During that time radicals had tried everything to undermine priestly power. Some had even deployed a self-sufficient Lamarckism to illegitimate the Creationist base of the Church (which was seen as God's pocket-borough, maintained, like Nature, through His personal intervention). Free trade was demanded in divinity as much as in corn. In 1859, with Britain poised to sign Cobden's epochal free-trade agreement with France, Huxley's scimitar was the latest cleansing weapon. He was undercutting the spiritual sanction of a rival profession, reforming God's rotten-borough. *Religion* was not the problem:

> My screed was meant as a protest against Theology &
> Parsondom . . . both of which are in my mind the natural
> & irreconcilable enemies of Science. Few see it but I
> believe we are on the Eve of a new Reformation and if I
> have a wish to live thirty years, it is that I may see the
> foot of Science on the necks of her Enemies. But the new
> religion will not be a worship of the intellect alone.

It would have the Christian ethics of love and duty – the old moral core, left after science had stripped off the mythic excrescences. The day the Whig Dissenters invaded the town halls in 1835 this scientific offensive was on the cards. Huxley, with his adversarial psychology, simply made it the more violent. Any new Unitarian Mayor could have said it, 'there is no safety in trying to put new wine into old bottles'. No 'disinterested Hebrew scholar', Huxley wrote, could render Genesis 'reconcilable with the most elementary . . . facts of Geology'. And if parsons think it 'permissable to turn and twist the Scripture phraseology' to ensure a fit, 'I for my part will undertake to prove that rape, murder & arson are positively enjoined in Exodus'.

The 'origin of man' had proved a cutting weapon in pauper hands. Now Huxley would appropriate it for his professionals. He had deliberately raised the subject, 'claiming my right to follow whithersoever science should lead'. 'After all', he told Dyster, 'it is as respectable to be modified monkey as modified dirt'.[5]

Dust of the earth or chimps in the trees – he had polarized the issue before the *Origin of Species* was out. Darwin had hoped to avoid the human question, but Huxley was making mud-or-monkey the fighting issue. At his spa, Darwin was tormented by a swimming head and 'severe vomiting'. (Worrying about the *Origin* 'is the cause', he admitted, 'the main part of the ills to which my flesh is heir'.) Reading Huxley's *Builder* article hardly perked him up. The parish gentleman feared an unseemly fray. He planned to reassure the *Origin*'s publisher (John Murray) that 'my Book is not more *un*-orthodox, than the subject makes inevitable. That I do not discuss origin of man. – That I do not bring in any discussion about Genesis &c'.

Darwin trudged on, in sickness and gloom. Through the domestic traumas at Downe, through the rages of Mrs Grut the governess, 'more "gruttish" than ever'. In March he sent Hooker a 90-page chapter on the spread of life. Even this was fraught.

> By some screaming accident [Hooker told Huxley], the
> whole bundle . . . got transferred to a drawer where my
> wife keeps paper for the children to draw upon – & they
> have of course had a drawing fit ever since. – I feel
> brutified if not brutalized for poor D. is so bad that he
> could hardly get steam up to finish what he did.

Darwin stoically set back his press date. 'I *have* the old M.S.', he calmed Hooker, 'otherwise the loss would have killed me!' From a distance Huxley turned the tension to farce, ordering Hooker to stand on his 'head in the garden for one hour per diem for the next week'.[6]

But how distant was Huxley really? Darwin spoke as if the *Origin of Species* would require religious conversion, so what of the evangelist on his own hellfire crusade? 'Hooker, who is our best British Botanist & perhaps best in World, is a *full* convert', Darwin wrote to Wallace. 'Huxley is changed & believes in mutation of species: whether a *convert* to us, I do not quite know'. But Huxley was 'a wonderful man'. He kept Darwin on his toes. 'When I feel myself chasing wild geese', Darwin said, softening Huxley up, 'you always rise before me'. Darwin was proving that homologous parts (say the hand, flipper and wing) derived from a common ancestor and were produced by 'real changes in the course of time'. It meant that Huxley's discrete subkingdoms were not so discrete any more – that his mollusc, vertebrate and medusa archetypes had themselves evolved from 'one primordial created form', and that his curious analogy between jellyfish and human embryonic membranes might be a sign of real affinity.

True to form Huxley pointed out a 'flaw' in Darwin's reasoning.

The tumblers and runts interbreed; fanciers had yet to pull their pigeons so far apart as to form real species, with sterile hybrids. But Darwin called his 'a mere rag of an hypothesis' with as many 'holes as sound parts'. The point was that 'I can carry in it my fruit to market'. Not that the naturalist, with his tortured 'prostration of mind & body', could walk much at all. Seeing his 'miserable' prose in proof, he had started rewriting until his health 'quite failed'. And through it all he feared that Huxley would give the rag 'such a devil of a shake that it will fall all to atoms'.[7]

'So do not be too ferocious', he quailed on 2 June 1859. His letter was opened by Huxley as he prepared for the Royal Institution. He was set to lecture on 'Persistent Types', 'living fossils', survivors from Silurian times like the club-mosses and burrow-living bivalve *Lingula*. It seemed that he was about to give Darwin's rag a shake. But no, he held it aloft to signal his change. For the first time he dovetailed their world views. He built an idiosyncratic half-way house, which he hoped would rise into a great temple. Like Solomon he saw nothing new under the sun, no new groups of animals since Silurian times. Therefore an evolutionary explosion must have occurred in the 'pre-geological' period, before the oldest Silurian rocks had settled as sediments.

The new Secretary of the Geological Society was taking on the empire's fossils in 1859, unpacking the crates from missionaries and explorers, governors and garrison commanders. The steamers were unloading increasing numbers, marked for the London museums. Huxley's work reflected the galloping colonization of the globe. Archaic amphibians from Australia, extinct tusked reptiles from the Cape, fossil penguins from New Zealand, he conquered them all. He was publishing as fast as his preparators could etch out the bones.

More Elgin reptiles came from George Gordon in Scotland. An excited Huxley himself sat down 'knife & chisel in hand' to reveal a six-foot, stout-limbed, plant-eater with a crushing 'pavement of teeth'. *Hyperodapedon Gordoni* he christened it, tickling the vanities to ensure more specimens. But the gesture disguised a blow to the Moray men, who had prided themselves on having the first created reptiles. Its kin were 'unquestionably *Triassic* forms'. Elgin's rocks were not ancient Devonian at all, but much later Triassic sediments, laid down during the 'Age of Reptiles'.

Huxley's suspicions sent Lyell to Elgin, and the region, he reported, 'more than justifies your scepticism'.[8] It was the final irony: Huxley, the palaeontological Peter, the rock of Lyell's non-progressionist Church, put the Elgin saurians back into a progressive sequence, back into the 'Age of Reptiles'. Huxley had hammered the last nail into Lyell's geological coffin. After 30 years defending the anti-progressionist faith Sir Charles accepted an ascending fossil series and looked to Darwin for its explanation.

A tortured Lyell began to tease at the issues with Huxley. The problem was to explain the great classes of animals. With no fossil intermediates connecting today's vertebrates and molluscs and insects, where was the proof that they had come from a common stock 'in the course of 1000^{ds}. of generations'? Was some 'creative' cause responsible for these huge jumps? Did transmutation only produce the variety once the great blueprints were established?

No, said Huxley – think of it another way. There were no intermediate forms, so perhaps '*transmutation* may take place without *transition*' – by leaps, leaving no string of middle stages (an idea that squared with his discrete crystalline spheres). Look at the sudden appearance of Ancon sheep, a long-bodied strain with 'short bandy legs', once bred in Massachusetts for the canny reason that they could not jump fences. Or hexadactyl humans (like Robert Chambers who, with his extra finger and toe, amputated at birth, joked that he was returning 'to the reptilian type'). Here were new forms appearing 'at once in full perfection'.

Natural 'monstrosities' ruled out any supernatural need. 'Creation' for Huxley was as much ideological effrontery as philosophical absurdity. Who, he asked Darwin and Lyell, imagined elephants flashing into being from their component atoms? It was contrary to experience, he told students. His atomic elephant was a clever caricature. Yet many who were branded 'Creationists' never thought in these terms. Owen's God worked to a Divine blueprint, the great groundplans of life, and His Word was made flesh by Natural Law (even if this was interpreted as a Divine Edict). Huxley had made straw men of the 'Creationists'. He had distilled his professional, dissenting strategy against the privileged Anglican Church into a Manichean Evolutionist *vs* Creationist slogan, us-*vs*-them, and he was now one of 'us'. Few saw him changing the rules of engagement.

Huxley's propaganda coup was not lost on Darwin. He ended the *Origin* by slating 'the blindness of preconceived opinion' – for who could believe that 'in the earth's history certain elemental atoms have been commanded suddenly to flash into living tissues?' Huxley had put the sting in the *Origin*'s tail.

Lyell braced himself to 'go the whole orang'. If evolution be true 'we shall in time discover extinct fossil varieties of Men', Miocene monkey-like men. But Huxley still wondered. What if mankind went back a long way? Couldn't Lyell imagine humans dodging Jurassic dinosaurs?⁹ What if people had existed since Silurian times? We would never find our monkey ancestors.

By now Huxley was trying to write his *Oceanic Hydrozoa* while reading other people's manuscripts. Putting the *Origin* proofs down, he would pick up Hooker's *Flora of Tasmania*, with its botanical support for Darwin. He finally finished his own preface in July 1859, eight years after the voyage. For five years all the plates bar two had been finished. During those years the Ray Society (which was to publish it) had been saved from bankruptcy – and during those years a succession of Germans had gone 'to the shores of the Mediterranean and made sad havoc with my novelties'.¹⁰ Huxley's first book, and the delay had cost him priority.

He posted the preface and the family left to spend August on the 'Paradise of Arran'. They took a Glasgow steamer down the Clyde and out to the Scottish island. Here, on the sheltered Lamlash Bay, with its smooth clear waters, Hal did what he loved, indulged in the lottery of the dredge. Carpenter had found the bay, with its 'treasure' of rare starfish and sea lilies. It was a teeming marine nursery, with larvae 'by *hundreds*': young worms and jellies.¹¹ It was a calming moment, time to draw breath before the coming storm. All sights were now on the publication of the *Origin*.

At home Darwin suffered a 'terrible long fit of vomiting' as he let go of his 'abominable volume'. The anxiety left him 'miserably unwell & shattered' and in no condition to face a hostile world. On 2 October he fled on a three-day journey to Ilkley on the desolate Yorkshire moors, there to hide out at a spa for two months until the furore over the *Origin of Species* had died down. Such absenteeism was to characterize his life from now on. The family joined him, only to sit out an early winter in 'frozen misery'. Darwin's internal exile was marked by hope and despair. Awaiting the first sight of his book he had 'an awful "crisis"', 'one leg swelled like elephantiasis – eyes almost closed up – covered with a rash & fiery Boils'. Now he understood Huxley's fascination with Dante. It was 'like living in Hell'.

He sought reassurance, touching his friends in letters. 'I shall be *intensely* curious to hear what effect the Book produces on you', he cajoled Huxley. 'I am far from expecting to convert you to many of my heresies; but if . . . you & two or three others think I am on the right road, I shall not care what the mob of naturalists think'.

The 'mental rumpus' affected Hooker no less in these weeks. He was moving house; with his wife and children away he 'avoided suicide' in the run up to the *Origin* and *Flora of Tasmania* by 'working extremely hard with my head hands & legs'.[12] His catharsis came from potting seeds.

Lyell was edging forward, desperately worried about a bestial human origin. ('It is this which has made me so long hesitate', he conceded.) He mooted to Huxley 'a race of savages at first with small cranial development & out of this the negro & white races ... being evolved'. But he was straining. His lingering need for the 'intervention of creative power' to supercharge the process made Darwin cringe: 'I cannot see this necessity', he replied. It would make his mechanism superfluous. 'Grant a simple archetypal creature, like the ... [lungfish] Lepidosiren, with the five senses & some vestige of mind & I believe Natural Selection will account for production of every Vertebrate animal'.[13]

In November Darwin faced his nemesis – the moment he had dreaded for 20 years. The world was about to peer into his soul. Here he was, a renowned naturalist, pillar of the parish, Justice of the Peace, fearing execration as an atheist. He was so over-wrought he didn't know what to expect. He knew that old Oxbridge friends would 'fulminate awful anathemas'; 'you will long to crucify me alive!', he told Falconer in his self-abasing way. He was now lame in his spa at Ilkley, with a swollen face that left him 'worse than when I came'. He clung to Hooker's enthusiasm and Lyell's support, and 'If I can convert Huxley I shall be content'.[14]

Huxley's copy of the *Origin* arrived in mid-November. For the first time he saw the book in its entirety. The remorseless emphasis on adaptation was still a shock. No student of Carlyle could be happy with crass utilitarian explanations, yet here life's chances were calculated on cost/benefit principles. It was a messy, competitive, individualistic approach, with the winners thrown up in the scuffle, at odds with his own search for innate developmental laws. Yet the book explained why modern life was based on so many set plans: these were inherited from common ancestors. And Huxley could salvage something of his old views. Natural selection did not demand that life continually progress, only that animals anchor themselves into niches. So his persistent types, 'living fossils', survived in niches which never changed.

But the details were never of overriding importance to Huxley. Whether or not the *Origin* pointed to a Golden Calf, it led his Israelites out of the wilderness. Huxley put it best in a parable:

> 'My sons, dig in the vineyard,' were the last words of the
> old man in the fable: and, though the sons found no
> treasure, they made their fortune by the grapes.

Any viable mechanism of life's succession would enable his professionals to reap a rich harvest. The *Origin* extended the natural realm; it increased 'the domination of Science', and the annexed territory required its colonial governors. Before them lay an unknown land. 'If we thought ourselves knowing dogs before you revealed Nat Selection', Hooker told Darwin, 'what d– – –d. ignorant ones we must surely be now'.

There was no more infuriating, enlightening book. It had no references, no illustrations. More an encyclopedia, to Huxley's thinking, needing endless readings for the meaning to seep through: an 'intellectual pemmican – a mass of facts crushed and pounded into shape, rather than held together by the ordinary medium of an obvious logical bond'. Exposition was not Darwin's *forte*, he was defeated by commas and daunted by grammar. But there was 'a marvellous dumb sagacity' to the man, 'and he gets to the truth by ways as dark as those of the Heathen Chinee'. Huxley worked his way through, annotating, and by the nth reading he began to transcend the 'humdrum and prosaic' and enter the 'vast and mysterious', awed by the terrible grandeur of Darwin's vision.[15]

As ill-luck would have it Huxley's *Oceanic Hydrozoa* came out within weeks of the *Origin*. As a short-print run, subscription-only Ray Society monograph, it was lost in the mêlée. All eyes were now fixed on the *Origin*. Darwin was on tenterhooks: 'I long to hear what Huxley thinks', he told Hooker on 20 November. The following day he heard. Huxley 'is vastly pleased with it', Hooker wrote. He was even thinking of turning over his next Royal Institution talk to the book. Darwin's mood brightened. How 'unspeakably grand if Huxley were to lecture on the subject'.

A public stand became imperative after the *Athenaeum* fired a 'contemptible' opening shot at the *Origin*. The book was a snub to the clergy and an insult to humanity. Was nihilism now to rule? What else could be said of a monkey-made-man? – he 'was born yesterday – he will perish tomorrow'. Darwin was furious at the way the reviewer 'sets the Priests at me & leaves me to their mercies'. It was crucial to play up the rival moral of evolution. To show progress through open competition, all that handicapped Dissenters had demanded in society. And Carpenter did: the 'War' in Darwin's Nature, he said, led inevitably 'towards the progressive exaltation of the races engaged in it'.[16]

'Since I read Von Bär nine years ago no work on Natural History I have met with has made so great an impression upon me', Huxley rallied Darwin. The dervish had heard the call and was 'prepared to go to the Stake' for parts of it. Like Carlyle's hero Mohammed he sharpened his 'claws & beak' to tear at 'the curs which will bark & yelp'. The new Reformation seemed closer than he had thought. He reminded Darwin that 'some of your friends . . . are endowed with an amount of combativeness which (though you have often & justly rebuked it) may stand you in good stead'. Now Darwin was glad of it. Never one to enter the public fray, he needed a champion as Huxley needed a cause.

The two, so utterly unlike, seemed made for the occasion. Darwin's jubilation took a more traditional turn. 'Like a good Catholic, who has received extreme unction, I can now sing "nunc dimittis"'.

Having heard that his old Cambridge mentor, the blunt Dalesman Adam Sedgwick, 'laughed till his sides ached at my Book', Darwin clung to the *arriviste* men still more. He egged Huxley on. No more raised eyebrows at his savagery: 'What a joke it will be if I pat you on [the] back when you attack some immoveable creationist!'

He started arming Huxley with skulls and 'splendid *folio* coloured drawings' of fantails and runts for his lecture. Nettie produced her usual stockpile of pedagogical pictures. Those bizarre breeds held the illustrative key – 'those dreadful pidgeons', laughed Falconer, on which Darwin practised his 'leger-de-main'. Then Darwin sent parts of the precious *Natural Selection* manuscript, although he doubted if Huxley could 'make heads or tails of it'.[17]

The *Athenaeum* left a bitter taste. Huxley had a standing invitation to contribute to the new liberal *Macmillan's Magazine*. He plunged in, neutralizing the *Athenaeum* in the middle-brow monthly. It was an exuberant piece, out in two weeks, which praised Darwin's 'singularly original and well-stored mind'. Only the *Origin*, which had life stopping and starting as the environment stagnated or changed, could explain why the 'cockroaches of the carboniferous epoch are exceedingly similar to those which now run about our coal-cellars'. Huxley put 'the best thinkers of the day' on Darwin's side. He meant his group. Busk, Tyndall, Hooker and Carpenter all came over with the School of Mines lecturers. Hooker rallied the horticulturalists in the *Gardeners' Chronicle*, making nature a sort of Sublime Nurseryman, always weeding and improving. Carpenter roused the Unitarians, taking his line that miracles were absurd, God interrupting Himself. The Almighty's great law unleashed at Creation was wonderfully revealed in Darwin's world of 'order, continuity, and progress'. Darwin cooed at having 'got a great physiologist on our side. I say "our" for we are now a good & compact body'.[18] And he bubbled in his spa at Huxley's 'delightful & honourable compliment'.

The radicals were awed. Chapman thought the *Origin* 'one of the most important books of this century'. He too approached Huxley for an article. By now the *Westminster* was listing badly, and Huxley the lifelong debtor found himself in an unaccustomed role as creditor. But Chapman was planning a salvage operation, turning debts into shares in a new Westminster Publishing Company. He pressured Huxley about reviewing the *Origin*, which would cause a 'mental revolution', and about saving the *Westminster*, which had already done so.[19] So Huxley raised his credit limit and tailored a review for the avant garde.

Here the *Origin* emerged 'as a veritable Whitworth gun in the armoury of liberalism'. Britain, the world's mightiest industrial economy, was turning liberal as the Dissenters' ideals of free trade and fair competition became the cultural norm, and a gun-running Huxley was selling the *Origin* as a replacement for Dissent's old weaponry. He was tying the book to the forces of 'progress'. Such talk stirred the patriotic breast: in 1859 the *Origin* was vying for attention with Italy's war of unification and the home-grown Volunteers, the rifle clubs springing up in the panic over Napoleon's intentions. *The Times* resounded to Tennyson's booming voice:

> Ready, be ready to meet the storm!
> Riflemen, riflemen, riflemen form!

Darwin's muzzle-loader would keep Britain Great. And the *Origin* came highly recommended, said Huxley: 'bigots denounce it with ignorant invective; old ladies of both sexes consider it a decidedly dangerous book, and even savants . . . quote antiquated writers to show that its author is no better than an ape himself'. Perfect for the literati, who revelled in the shock of the new. The *Origin* underpinned the *Westminster*'s demand for fair play and the selection of the best. Complacent parsons could no more claim privileged status in society than inspired understanding of the universe.

> The myths of Paganism are as dead as Osiris or Zeus, and
> the man who should revive them . . . would be justly
> laughed to scorn; but the coeval imaginations current
> among the rude inhabitants of Palestine . . . have
> unfortunately not yet shared their fate, but, even at this
> day, are regarded by nine-tenths of the civilised world as
> the authoritative standard of fact . . .

Huxley was preaching to the converted when he called 'the cosmogony of the semi-barbarous Hebrew . . . the incubus of the philosopher'. No *Westminster* reviewer doubted it. The prophet looked to the sky for an omen: 'Not a star comes to the meridian at its calculated time but testifies to the justice' of the scientific cause. With this Heavenly sanction the Sultan of biology slaughtered the orthodox. And after the carnage he gave thanks, as 'Extinguished theologians lie about the cradle of every science as the strangled snakes beside that of Hercules'. The orthodox army of occupation was left 'bleeding and crushed if not annihilated'.[20] This was *Jihad* oratory, designed to raise a cry of 'Mashallah!' in the crowd.

Stump oratory was no place for caveats. Huxley was exuberantly endorsing the naturalism of Darwin's vision, not the fine points of his theory. Nothing was said of Darwin's infinitesimal variations, each selected for its adaptive advantage. Nor did Huxley mention that his own belief in large-scale mutations, his Ancon sheep, actually negated them. Or that the Home Counties rabbits which happily overran the Australian outback belied Darwin's vaunted adaptation. Then again, until spaniels and greyhounds refused to cross he considered Darwin's analogy between domestic breeds and wild species incomplete. And Huxley still had trouble with Darwin's genealogical approach to classification. 'Huxley demurs', Darwin confided to Hooker, '& says he has nailed his colours to the mast, & I would sooner die than give up, so that we are in as fine a frame of mind to discuss the point, as any two religionists'.

Huxley's bravura performance was in support of Darwin's evolutionary naturalism, not the minutiae of his mechanism. Darwin had created a new nature for the new professionals. And the more loudly Huxley applauded, the more heartily Darwin hailed 'my good & admirable agent for the promulgation of damnable heresies'.[21]

Others brought their own web of ideological beliefs to bear. Habituated to his workers' heresies, Charles Kingsley the Christian Socialist had come to see 'that it is just as noble a conception of Deity, to believe that he created primal forms capable of self-development'. But as for Darwin's mechanism – his ruthless competition between accidental variants – Kingsley could never allow 'chance and selfishness to rule the fortunes of the human race'. The *Origin*, he admitted to Huxley, 'startled many preconceived judgements of mine'. As muscular and militant in his own way, he thought that Huxley's *Macmillan*'s piece 'said what ought to be said' and would 'keep the curs from barking'. And for his part, he would continue to follow Darwin's 'villainous shifty fox of an argument, into what soever unexpected bog & brakes he may lead us'.[22] But it firmed up his view that 'Nature must be counteracted, lest she prove a curse and a destroyer', that co-operative human ethics stood outside, reflecting the sublimity of the City of God, not the savagery of the Roman arena.

The big question mark hung over the head of Richard Owen. A towering zoologist, his *basso* presence intruded everywhere. He will 'bitterly oppose us', Darwin guessed, for he seeks the good grace of 'the aristocratic world'. Owen stood apart ideologically. His 'continuous creation' and specializing fossil life might fit the bill. But he found Darwin's imperfect Nature, based on struggle and slaughter and chance and accident, simply repugnant.

Even after receiving a '*most* liberal note' from Owen, Darwin still suspected that he would be 'dead against us'. The shifting allegiances would ensure it, or rather Huxley's public stand. The Princes of Light and Darkness needed their celestial antipodes.

Darwin found out for himself. En route back from Ilkley in December he met Owen. Owen had now digested the book, where he found himself painted a reactionary. He was 'savage & crimson at my having put his name with defenders of immutability'. The elbowing had hurt, and Owen knew the culprit: he would have absolutely no truck 'with your Huxleys', he told Darwin, and he said it with such 'arrogance [as] I never saw approached'.[23]

Darwin's fraught daily life was relieved by the Boxing Day *Times*. The Thunderer, flag-bearer of the nation, carried an enormous review. Brilliant witticisms, bon mots, praise for the man whose barnacle books showed that he had 'not entered the sanctuary with unwashed hands' – it had to be by Huxley. It was, bar the opening. Huxley's tentacles now penetrated every literary crevice. The staff reviewer, daunted by the 'immensity' of Darwin's developing creation, against which

> The windy ways of men
> Are but dust which dries up
> And is lightly laid again

(meaning he was scientifically illiterate), had thrown up his hands and turned the rest over to Huxley.

> I wrote it faster than ever I wrote anything in my life – the last column nearly as fast as my wife could read the sheets. But I was thoroughly in the humour & full of the subject . . . I earnestly hope it may have made some of the educated mob who derive their ideas from the 'Times' reflect and whatever they do, they *shall* respect Darwin & be d– – –d to them.

Huxley's Dickensian knack for turning arcana into vernacular came into its own. Bank Holiday readers were taken to the Baker Street Bazaar to behold 'bloated preposterous pigs, no more like a wild boar or sow than a city alderman is like an ourang-outang'. Then to a Seven Dials feather club to see such *outré* pigeons that, were they 'known only in a fossil state, no naturalist would hesitate in regarding them as distinct species'. It was a streetwise exposition of artificial selection – or what people could do to change domestic breeds. And in nature where there were too many mouths to feed, a similar selection operated. Struggling individuals were 'like the crew of a foundered ship, and none but good swimmers have a chance of reaching the land'. Nature picked the best.

'The old Fogies will think the world will come to an end', crowed Darwin. 'I should have said that there was only one man in England who could have written this Essay & that *you* were the man'.

The *Times* flagged Huxley's continuing shift. The old fogies heard that the rocks housed a 'regular succession of living beings', and as 'a broad fact, the further we go back in time the less the buried species are like existing forms'. Where was the effrontery in Darwin's vision? All life is obviously related, he said, putting a new shine on his old embryological ware. 'Not only men and horses, and cats and dogs, lobsters and beetles, periwinkles and mussels, but even the very sponges' begin life as indistinguishable germs. Then they

> march side by side along the high road of development,
> and separate the later the more like they are; like people
> leaving church, who all go down the aisle, but having
> reached the door some turn into the parsonage, others go
> down the village, and others part only in the next parish.[24]

Outrageous perhaps, with the sponges arrested at the vestry while men and monkeys marched on, parting only later in their embryological journey.

Huxley had a provocative gift. He was marketing Darwin's ideas, becoming the recluse's 'hard-working unpaid agent'. Huxley's alignment kept Owen at a distance, and every insulting smack increased his alienation. 'Upon my life I am sorry for Owen', Darwin wrote, 'he will be so d–––d savage; for credit given to any other man, I strongly suspect is in his eyes so much credit robbed from him. Science is so narrow a field, it is clear there ought to be only one cock of the walk!'[25]

With Huxley's *Westminster* review of the *Origin* posted off in December, the 'Committee of Public Safety' reconvened. Speculation was rife about that old dame, the *Quarterly Review*. How would it serve up the *Origin* to the fox-hunting squires? Lyell advised Murray (coincidentally also the *Quarterly*'s publisher) to give the review to a palaeontologist. Hooker said the same to the *Quarterly*'s editor, the cordial Norfolk rector Whitwell Elwin. (Elwin had actually refereed the *Origin*, quaintly advising Darwin to publish a coffee-table book on his 'delightful' pigeons first! More quietly he complained to Murray that 'between the ascertained facts & Darwin's conclusions there is a vast gulf which is bridged over by *unproved assumptions*'.) With the *Origin* out regardless, and Elwin lost for a reviewer, Huxley looked set to snatch the big prize.

But by the year's end he had 'heard nothing and I have my doubts whether Elwin & Murray will think me *tall* enough for the job'. Size was irrelevant; as Elwin told Murray, he wanted 'a really competent & *impartial* enquirer but I have some reason for thinking that Huxley is not that impartial'.[26] Nor would the shires have tolerated one of Huxley's secular sermons. In 1859 nature still had a moral force, and ruling on science remained the duty of their lordships, spiritual and temporal.

15

Buttered Angels & Bellowing Apes

THE *ORIGIN OF SPECIES* tantalized a prim generation. In the freezing weeks after publication it appeared in the unlikeliest places. Commuters coming to hear Huxley's lecture even snapped up the second edition on Waterloo Station. News-vendors, usually with nothing but trashy shilling novels, were touting this Royal Green 15*s* tome.

It was the 'Book of the Day', Owen conceded. Love it or loathe it, the *Origin* could not be ignored. Wollaston, Huxley's fellow visitor at Downe, felt a 'cold shuddering' and turned hostile. Though Darwin was careful not to say it, the *Origin* ultimately meant that man, 'with all his lofty endowments and future hopes, was ... never "created" at all, but was merely ... a development from an ape'. But without the promise of Heaven or the fear of Hell, why should we live a good life? Huxley knew that this was the crux, even as he trashed Wollaston's 'stupid review'.

For or against, the reactions were intensifying. One embarrassing old botanist told Darwin he would continue to read the *Origin* 'as I do the precepts of Christ & the parable of the prodigal son, till my eyes fail me'. The ecstatic highs were only matched by the abusive lows. Others damned the book, fearing that the loss of Creation's moral purpose would 'brutalize' humanity. They compared Darwin's fantastic mechanism to 'Bishop Wilkin's locomotive that was to sail with us to the Moon'.[1] With the stones 'beginning to fly', an agitated Darwin was relieved to see Huxley's *Times* review reprinted in the *Gardeners' Chronicle*.

The *Origin*'s sales galvanized conservatives. The *Athenaeum* demanded show trials to denounce Darwin in 'the Divinity Hall, the College, the Lecture Room, and the Museum'. It meant in

Oxford and Cambridge; wicked London was far too suspect. Indeed the School of Mines staff swung behind Darwin, giving him his first corporate support. They moved too fast for Murchison. But his 'sympathies were with the Conservatives', groaned Huxley, as his boss toyed with standing as London University's first MP (the seat itself symbolizing the growing power of Huxley's Dissenting technocrats). Murchison protested that he was in favour of any 'improvements which our advanced state of Society demands, provided they do not carry us into Democracy'.[2] But Darwin's book did not seem much of an improvement. No 'Silurian King' could accept a levelling theory that made a monkey of his kin.

The chief was outflanked in his own school. The geology teacher Andrew Ramsay had no stomach for a nature made of 'small miracles'. In the museum, Salter glued rows of Devonian and Carboniferous lamp-shells on to a board, copying the family tree in the *Origin*. Its 'beautiful branching gradation' staggered even Darwin, who viewed it on a visit to Huxley's museum one day.[3]

It raised expectations about Huxley's own Royal Institution talk. This was London's first major lecture on the *Origin*, at a West End venue, and delivered by the devil's disciple himself – 'you best & worst of men', as Darwin hailed him. Everyone expected an incisive flash, that explosive mix of provocation and perspicacity which marked his appearances.

Darwin plied him with pigeon skeletons. He even dispatched Huxley to a Piccadilly pigeon club, where velvet-waistcoated fanciers vied with their gaudy breeds. And despite his 'accursed health' he came to town to talk to him. There was no disguising Darwin's hopes for this lecture. Like a hyperactive Alpine goat Huxley had followed Darwin to the precipice and made the long leap – where even Lyell and Carpenter faltered – to a belief that all life stems from '*one* primordial form'. But few dared follow Huxley on human origins; even Lankester admitted that 'it was not given us to know how God first formed man'. Darwin now claimed Huxley as his 'warmest & most important supporter'.

Others too were lagging. Talking of Hal, Mrs Dyster wrote to Nettie:

> I was quite prepared for his siding with Darwins Views, & I can also believe that you enter also into these *with* your husband's help & spirit. *Mine* inclines greatly to [Darwin's] . . . theory, & I fear he is disappointed that I cannot like or understand it.[4]

A stirring patriotism shaped these weeks, moulding the very lecture itself. A grey-uniformed Huxley, gun slung over his shoulder, Tennyson's Arthurian epic *The Idylls of the King* in his hand, composed to the sound of trumpets. He had joined the home-grown Volunteers, the self-financed rifle corps composed of merchants and professionals. Napoleon's invasion scare and the Crimean fiasco had the *Times* demanding that the captains of industry and commerce be put in uniform, the proven best, thrown up by a cut-throat competition. Patriotism and liberalism locked hands as brigades of barristers and businessmen turned sharpshooters. There were Civil Service Corps and Solicitors' Corps, and had Huxley had his way there would probably have been a Science Corps. It was no professional army, but it was Huxley's army of professionals.

Everywhere there was a warm glow in Britain's greatness. Tennyson was evoking Camelot's past glory. Huxley, wrestling with the *Origin*, wallowing in the *Idylls*, portrayed science as an imperishable Excalibur. No metaphor escaped him, and certainly not one tying science to a booming Britain. When he called the *Origin* a Whitworth gun in the liberal arsenal, he was evoking the national mood. 'I am drilling for [the] Rifles', he told Dyster after praising the *Idylls*, and will '"pot" with my first shot the man who should dare to find fault . . . with any tittle of the book'.[5]

Huxley switched his drill day and on Friday 10 February 1860 faced his audience at the Royal Institution. He had distributed tickets to the Darwins, Spencer and Carpenter. They were all there, in the packed tiers of seats overlooking the little stage. The dignitaries occupied the front few rows. Owen was there, and of course Huxley spotted a bishop. On the walls were Nettie's blown-up pictures and on the table distorted and distended pigeon skulls. Darwin had even paid a fancier to bring in his curious coiffed breeds and there they were, show baskets full of puffing pouters, strutting fantails and 'pretty Toy Pigeons'.[6]

And this should have been the gist of his talk – the analogy between the fanciers' skill in drawing out tufts and top-knots, and Nature's mechanism for selecting the best wild variants. But no. Huxley spent too long defining a species and lost the audience. And when he did point to his pigeons ('in Mr Darwin's view the products of a long series of experiments in producing species') it was for another reason. He compared their origin from a wild dove to the descent of today's horses, rhinos and tapirs from the dog-sized Eocene *Palaeotherium*. Even then he threw in his *caveat*, that fanciers had yet to pull their pigeons so far apart as to produce real species; 'by & bye' they might, he admitted, but until then it seems 'to me impossible to admit that the doctrine of the origin of species by Natural Selection stands upon a totally safe & sound physical basis'.[7]

Darwin was nonplussed. He expected Huxley's Whitworth to be sputtering rounds with deadly precision, not to find the General leading a blundering Light Brigade. A fiasco, Hooker called it, which was a 'pity', as Huxley 'intended to have backed the book but unfortunately managed to damage it'. Not that the radicals noticed. It was Huxley's thrilling climax that moved a reporter from the *Reasoner*. He was used to street demagogues undermining Church and Creation, but to hear a man of science was astonishing. It was 'a most exciting and even solemn occasion'.

Huxley damned the sanctimonious meddlers who would stifle troublesome research. And, yes, Darwin's work meant that 'all living things & man among the rest must have arisen from one stock'. He railed against the moral cowardice that would prevent us from accepting it:

> And there is a wonderful tenacity of life about this sort of
> opposition to physical science. Always crushed it seems
> never to be killed, and after a thousand defeats it is as
> rampant now as in the days of Galileo.

The talk ended with an emotive flourish. The gun and grey dress were not only to bar Napoleon, but his priests – to make Britain safe, rational and great. Never was Huxley's sharpshooting more accurate. 'I had a Bishop & a Dean among my auditors', he explained, 'and, to please *them*, I wound up with the most energetic protest in favour of Science *versus* Parsonism that is likely to have reached their ears'. It had the desired effect. 'The High Church orthodox' sought the salubrious air outside. The bishop's entourage left comparing the 'building in Albemarle Street 1860 with the Paris Pantheon' in revolutionary 1791, a shrine to bloodthirsty atheism.

In his flag-waving finale, Huxley moved from 'the little Canutes of the hour enthroned in state & bidding the great wave to stay' to the scientific steamboats bringing a 'thousand treasures' on the rationalist tide. It was all 'very bold', Darwin muttered, as he listened to the gladiatorial metaphors that were his General's stock-in-trade.

For Huxley, Britain's destiny was to see a new Protestant reformation. The moral edifice would not collapse with these fresh truths. It would be undergirded. Britain

> may prove to the world that for one race at any rate
> Despotism & Demagogy are not the necessary alternatives
> of polity – that freedom & order are not incompatible –
> that Reverence is the handmaid of Knowledge – that truth
> is strength & that free discussion is the very life of truth.

Square up to science, he said embellishing this piece for publication. 'Cherish her, venerate her, follow her methods faithfully . . . and the future of this people will be greater than the past'.

> If you do otherwise I fear the day will come when our
> children will see the glory of England vanishing like Arthur
> in the mist & cry too late the woeful cry of Guinever:
>
>> It was my duty to have loved the highest
>> It surely was my profit had I known
>> It would have been my pleasure had I seen.[8]

Science was the real patriotism; it armed Britain with greater intellectual firepower. There spoke a man who had known a decade of debt, who had struggled to secure a science post, only to find it lacking in prestige. He was turning the patriotic tables, turning a reactionary Latinity into treason. Tying science to national salvation, in defiance of the other-worldly sort, was astute policy. If strength lay in Truth, then the country's well-being hinged on the expert's health. The nation needed him.

It was an intoxicating performance (even if Darwin doubted the value of patriotic poetry in an exegesis of the *Origin*). But there was little of Darwin's book in it, and nothing on selection. Darwin grew jaundiced.

> I succeeded in persuading myself for 24 hours that
> Huxley's lecture was a success. Parts were eloquent &
> good & all *very* bold, & I heard strangers say 'what a
> good lecture'. I told Huxley so . . . [But] after conversation
> with others & more reflection I must confess that as an
> Exposition of the doctrine the Lecture seems to me an
> entire failure . . . He gave no just idea of *natural*
> selection.[9]

Huxley was defending a rational explanation of life, not the nuts and bolts of selection. He was not equipped to talk on Darwin's ecological approach. He was no field naturalist juggling messy variables: he had no time for variation, survival rates and island isolation. He was rooted in embryology, with its belief in innate developmental pathways.

There were other obstacles in his way to accepting natural selection. Many critics saw in Darwin's Nature the 'sordid motives' of utilitarian society. Its core was naked survivalism: overproduction, struggle and death, a free-for-all with every individual clawing down his neighbour. In Darwin's 'horridly cruel' nature every part must serve a purpose or be cut down; only from death on a genocidal scale could the few progress. As Hell fell into disrepute, Nature was becoming more hellish.

Huxley wanted competition, but not this utilitarian shadow of workhouse society. He had never accepted Nature as a sweated 'slave-mill' run 'for mere utilitarian ends'.[10] His was a nobler vision of 'Harmonious order'. Raised within the romantic tradition and a rung lower than Darwin's great folks, Huxley had seen society at the sharp end. He could not afford to share his friend's heartless image. Even as he championed evolution, he softened selection.

Huxley's onslaught on 'Parsonism' simply raised the temperature. He was driving in his wedge, splitting off science for his men. He had turned the *Origin*'s factual arcana into an ideological arena. Not that Tory bishops – whose own science testified to a static, Created order – were unhappy with an ideological killing ground. They took up equally entrenched positions. What a 'sneer by the Bishop at Huxley', Darwin noted cryptically in a letter to Hooker. Within days of the lecture Lyell 'had a good half hour's argument with the B[isho]p of Oxford, Wilberforce', who thought Darwin's book 'the most unphilosophical he had ever read'.

Owen had 'gazed with amazement' at Huxley's diagrams comparing the origin of fancy pigeons with a evolution of horses and tapirs from a *Palaeotherium* parent. For years the languid giant had been shoved and goaded. This red rag finally sent him charging. Darwin was expecting 'many & bitter sneers from him', and Huxley ensured them. At the Royal Institution Huxley had mooted man's ape-like frame. Only he who was 'devoid of soul' and unconcerned 'about his own relations to a Creator' could find solace in a bestial human ancestry, raged Owen. And to claim that 'England owes her greatness' to such poisonous philosophy! More truly it 'parallels the abuse of science' at root of the French Terror.

Owen now came out bitterly against the *Origin*. He had received endless protests about it, from as far away as Livingstone in Africa, from as high as the Duke of Argyll in the Cabinet. As the senior statesman of science, his pronouncement was eagerly awaited. The *Origin* was a flash in the pan, he said, to be 'forgotten in 10 years'. The book might be, but Darwin hoped that with Huxley, Carpenter and Hooker on board 'the subject will not'.

Darwin was disheartened as the attacks began 'falling thick & heavy', despite Huxley's reassurance that 'the platoon-firing must soon cease'. In fact the conservative bullets began spraying ever wider. Even Huxley and Tyndall's Alpine climbs were made a laughing stock in the *Athenaeum*. It was a 'detestable article . . . about Tyndall – sneering at his veracity – & very disagreeable about Huxley', said Darwin. 'I look at the Editor as a spiteful old woman, who has taken, what my Brother calls her D.B. degree (ie damned bitch)'. Unable to fight his corner, Darwin relied on his Volunteers. Thank goodness, he told Hooker, for 'Lyell, yours, Huxley & Carpenter's aid'.[11] 'By myself I sh^d. be powerless'.

But this cadre, like the ill-assorted Volunteers, wrangled at the rifle range. All wanted to break the 'ecclesiastical domination' of Oxbridge to give 'the progressive sciences . . . fair play'. The urbane Lyell, writing a book on human antiquity himself, railed against the '30,000 [clergymen] who are sworn to read & interpret' Genesis 'in a certain way not favourable to geology, all paid by the State'. How to break the hold of the sermon? Get science into the classroom, Huxley answered; give schoolmasters a new vocational training, involving 'physical science & Nat^l Hist^y'.

But how, the old Unitarian persisted, to rationalize society at the very hearth place? Why were women barred from science? Radical Unitarians had already opened a 'Ladies' College in Bedford Square, where Carpenter taught. Lyell wanted to open the Geological Society as well. Let them into all the 'places of education to hear both sides discussed'. Wives might be proof-readers, translators, illustrators – like Nettie the best of help-mates. And for Darwin's Volunteers, who 'have a good deal of fighting to do', they kept the home fires burning. But this was it; Huxley saw science as masculine combat. Nor was the Geological 'a place of education', but a forum 'for adepts'. He began to look a rather ragged champion of fair play. In fact on women's rights Lyell thought he looked embarrassingly like 'the B[isho]p. of O[xford]'.

The coalition's seams were showing. The Unitarians talked emancipation, as Huxley's professionals strengthened their male meritocracy. Huxley – once furious at finding doors slammed in his face – now secured the inner sanctum. It would only be opened when daughters learnt something more than domestic skills at their mothers' knee. The school bench had to replace that maternal limb:

> I am far from wishing to place any obstacle in the way of the intellectual advancement and development of women. On the contrary I dont see how we are to make any permanent advancement while one half of the race is sunk, as nine tenths of women are, in mere ignorant parsonese superstitions. And to show you that my ideas are practical I have fully made up my mind . . . to give my daughters the same training in physical science as their brother . . . They at any rate shall not be got up as man-traps for the matrimonial market. If other people would do the like the next generation would see women fit to be the companions of men in all their pursuits.[12]

Women had to be schooled in science. And society had to lose its crippling prudery, to allow a more open approach to the body. The age's delicacy about even bee reproduction was notorious. (Rather than expurgate his talks Huxley refused to teach Bedford Square's 'virgins, young and old'.) Huxley himself planned a training programme. How hard he thought the task – or how much he underrated women's capacity – was shown by his eventual Ladies' course. It was a modified children's class.

When Huxley's *Westminster* review of the *Origin* appeared in April 1860 Owen found his divine archetype derided as 'verbal hocus-pocus'. Darwin was beginning to revel in Huxley's lethal pen, agreeing with 'Lyell that your extinguished Theologians laying about the cradle of each new science &c &c is *splendid*'. Who cared that the review hardly 'advances [the] subject'?

Of course it rebounded in Darwin's face. Days later the Huxleys arrived at Downe. They found Darwin bleary after losing a night's sleep. Owen's *Edinburgh* response was out. 'I am thrashed in every possible way', moaned Darwin. Twenty-five years' friendship lay shattered. 'I wish for . . . auld lang syne's sake he had been a little less bitter'. Anonymity could not cloak the review: 'Some of my relations say it cannot *possibly* be Owen's article, because the Reviewer speaks so very highly of Prof. Owen. Poor dear simple folk!'

They paced the grounds, talking over the German translation of the *Origin* (Huxley had all the contacts). Past the pigeon loft, now emptying, past the rabbit carcasses rotting comfortably. All the while they mulled over Owen's 'malignant' attitude. Owen had been hurt by the ape jibes, insulted by the 'preposterous' lampoon of animals flashing into existence. Darwin and Huxley had polarized the options: either rhinos were miraculously reassembled atoms or transmuted *Palaeotheriums*. Owen's continuous creation and transitional fossils had been shunted aside. For a Superintendent at the British Museum it rankled. Owen's overweening conceit demanded an overkill response. The newspapers egged Owen on. An *Athenaeum* reviewer scoured his new book, *Palaeontology*, for some pontifical pronouncement but found him 'hidden in the valley of dry bones'. Too cautious, it complained. Huxley has said enough 'to freeze us'. 'Is Prof. Owen, then, to be reserved'?

Owen abominated Huxley's soulless gorilla-ancestry. Was blood to run in the gutters as the 'Goddess of Reason' was installed in St Paul's Cathedral? (Aha! wrote Huxley's protégé George Rolleston, 'I have heard that allusion of his to the enthronement of the Goddess of Reason at Paris I don't know in how many Sermons'.) Gentlemanly onlookers were aghast. It was not '*becoming* in one Naturalist to be bitter against another – any more than for one sect to burn the members of another'.[13] But Huxley's sect, with its excommunications and conversions, its bible and corpus, indeed with Darwin's palpitating corpse, needed its stakes.

Through it all, Huxley continued teaching. He ran classes for schoolmasters at Marlborough House, now moved to South Kensington, as part of his plan to get science into the classrooms. He taught them to make the mundane exciting. And what was more mundane than a fishmonger's lobster? They crowded around as he fingered its segments, drawing back at his breathtaking conclusions on the unity of life. Before they exhaled he had whisked them away to glimpse its ancestors. To a time before men, before mammals or reptiles even; to an exotic land where its six-foot ancestor *Pterygotus* scavenged 'along the muddy shores of the Old Red Sandstone seas'.

Excitement was one way to inveigle science on board. Relevance was another. Such was the medieval mediocrity of Britain's public schools that Classics and mathematics were deemed sufficient for life. A Centurion's son from AD 400 'transplanted' into one of these moss-encrusted institutions 'would not meet with a single unfamiliar line of thought'. (A lovely touch, said Darwin, who hated the 'stereotyped stupid classical education'.) Yet 'modern civilization' was based on a scientific revolution. Deny that, Huxley said, and Britain's lead 'is gone tomorrow'. Science shows

> that the ultimate court of appeal is observation and
> experiment, and not authority . . . she is creating a firm
> and living faith in the existence of immutable moral and
> physical laws, perfect obedience to which is the highest
> possible aim of an intelligent being.

Authority was there, of course, in the Scientific Priest's robes. And morality rested in acknowledging his Laws. (Who is to wonder that Owen recalled the Temple of Reason, where *curés* were dragged to confess their charlatanerie?) Huxley's was an old Enlightenment gambit, and veterans as old as the Enlightenment had seen it fail before. George Grote, fêted for his *History of Greece* ('fetid' Carlyle thought more apt for this unspiritual outpouring) liked Huxley's Calvinism. Children should respect these 'immutable moral & physical laws'. But what chance when the Bible in our 'schools, inculcates a faith not only different, but contrary'?[14]

Mundane work now meant crocodiles, to help Huxley fathom the Elgin fossils. He planned to look at Oxford's during the BAAS meeting there in June 1860. 'Your Bedroom is furnished as you desired!' his Christ Church disciple George Rolleston wrote. 'Your Crocodile's skull clear as driven snow'.

One ally amid the dreaming spires was more than any sadducee could desire, and Rolleston better than he dared hope. They had met in London, after the vicar's son had switched from his Classics course at Pembroke College to St Bartholomew's Hospital. A bit plummy at first, he toughened up in Huxley's *embrouillé* medical world. He scorned the shrouded symbolism of the Oxford Movement and spurned the mystical garb of Owen's archetype. By 1860 Rolleston was back at Christ Church, demanding reform, demanding the admission of Dissenters. Though a brain specialist, he still ran his papers past the master. In turn Huxley was backing him for Oxford's Linacre Chair of anatomy. Owen, of course, was

promoting a rival candidate, Rolleston reported, out of 'antagonism . . . to you'.

As 21,000 Volunteers paraded before Queen Victoria in Hyde
Park on 23 June 1860, Huxley was putting his rifle away. He
anticipated no target practice at Oxford. Nettie was to wait for
him at her sister Isy's in Reading. And so on 27 June Huxley set
off for Rolleston's 'Sash windowed Squareboxlike House' in Christ
Church. Here his reptiles lay ready in their Gothic haunt, scutes
polished and jaws in pieces.

His reputation preceded him. The *Westminster* essay on Darwin
had passed round High Table. Prompted by Rolleston, the progressive Vice-Chancellor Francis Jeune, another Pembroke man, had
read it 'to his own gratification'. He had passed it to that 'great
liberal large-hearted man' Henry Liddell, the Dean of Christ
Church, who was not big-hearted enough to appreciate Schamyl's
satire on the orthodox explanation of life – 'Mashallah! it so
pleases God!' But he considered the subject 'a "tremendous"
one'.[15] Pembroke's liberal phalanx treated Huxley to dinner that
night.

The British Association met for a week in a different town each
year, and each year Huxley found the meetings 'duller'. The public
flocked in, thousands of top-hatted gents and ladies in their new
tent-like, crinoline dresses. They milled around the venue halls, as
always impatient, wanting not only to see the scientific lions, but
to hear them roar. On Thursday morning, 28 June, huge numbers
gathered at the Zoology section. The Bishop of Oxford looked on.
There was an expectant buzz, a feeling that the Darwinian issue
would be aired. 'I determined to buck them', Hal explained to
Nettie. He refused to perform, even though called upon. 'I did not
think that a fit place to discuss the question. However, it was no
good, Owen got up and made a very clear speech attacking
statements of mine indirectly', and so 'I got up, and girding on my
armour, went at it'.

Owen had maintained that a gorilla's brain was closer to a
lemur's than a man's (denying Huxley's claim at the Royal Institution). And such distinct cerebral hemispheres, he implied, militated
against humans having evolved. The Glasgow anatomist Allen
Thomson had just dissected a chimpanzee's cerebrum and written
to Huxley confirming its 'extraordinary resemblance to the human
brain'. No Continental expert doubted it, and so Huxley jumped
up with a flat contradiction. Falconer had never seen 'such a set
down'.

'So you had been battling with the Archetype', Nettie replied, 'you were quite right to try to evade the fight', but under the circumstances 'he must be fought'. It was the bell for the longest knock-down fight over an anatomical point in Victorian times. Darwin heard of this tugging over his 'absent body'. He had stayed away, secure in his Richmond spa, where his body was falling apart unaided. Vomiting and headachy, he lived vicariously through the news. 'Your interests', Falconer reassured him, 'were most tenderly watched over by your devoted Elèves'.

'I am none the worse for being stirred up a little', Hal admitted. Life was no longer dull, but 'you could not expect to have a row every day of the week'.

By Friday Huxley was 'as tired as a dog'. He was 'eternally in a bustle', speaking at more meetings than he intended, 'but you know it is not easy for me to keep quiet when anything is going on'. He had given a convoluted paper on sea squirt eggs. That was the hottest topic he cared for: the source of the first embryonic cells to appear. (He tracked them back to the huge dividing egg-nucleus.) It was 'raining cats & dogs' and he was ready to quit and take the 4 pm. Saturday train to Reading.[16] Isy and Nettie promised better company than the Bishop of Oxford. The buzz was now about Saturday's session on Darwinism and society, where the rhetorical flourishes were expected.

On Friday he got out once in the rain 'to look at some of the chapels which are very beautiful'. He ran into the Edinburgh publisher Robert Chambers of all people, the author of the evolutionary *Vestiges* which Huxley had so savagely trashed six years earlier. When the BAAS had last met at Oxford, in 1847, Chambers had been humiliated by the Bishop of Oxford for the 'foul speculations' in *Vestiges*. He knew the pain a lashing tongue could inflict. Then the bishop had carried his scientific flock. But these were new times. With Church and science fractured into liberal and orthodox camps, the old smug consensus was dead. An avant-garde was prepared to lash back. Hence Chambers' 'vehement remonstrances' about Huxley's 'deserting them'. Chambers, once humiliated by Huxley himself, convinced him to stay on. By the time Huxley dined at the Vice-Chancellor's that night he was girding his loins again.

The Saturday meeting drew a huge public crowd, 700, some said 1,000, showing that expectations were high. So many in fact that it had to be switched to the long west room of Oxford's new Gothic revival museum. Hooker (yet to attend a meeting) 'swore as usual

I would not go in; but getting equally bored of doing nothing I did'. Huxley too sauntered in, beneath the angel guarding the entrance.

Inside a flood of light from the glass-roofed atrium played on the jostling crowd. Raucous students were packed at the back. Everywhere were dons and academics. The white chokers of the clergy dominated the centre: this, after all, was their 'temple', glorying in that holy Nature, through 'which the Author of the universe manifests himself to His creatures'.

The chairman was Hooker's father-in-law, Henslow. On the podium was the purple-vested Bishop Samuel Wilberforce, there as a BAAS Vice-President (a courtesy in his own see). He was a mathematician and ornithologist, and loquacious. But being in his own diocese did not guarantee him applause. To a few he was a 'finished Philistine'. The Church needed strong progressives, the liberal *Telegraph* said, rather than these 'old style Tories' who have not budged 'one iota beyond their ancient notions'.[17] Church liberals hated Wilberforce's hard line, as he condemned their softpedalling on miracles. He castigated the 'seven against Christ', the liberal Anglican contributors to the innocent-sounding *Essays and Reviews*, whose critique of the Genesis myth and biblical literalism inflamed more passions in a year than Darwin managed in a lifetime. The Darwinian boat was now bumping along on the ferocious waves already pounding the orthodox Church. But Huxley's reception was just as uncertain. His quips about 'extinguished theologians' alienated many, and there were murmurings about his 'irreverent freedom'.

Speeches and reports were dispensed with quickly. Student bellows rose. At times the crowd seemed to control the event, turning it into a piece of participatory theatre. Refutations of Darwin came and went; Huxley, called on, sarcastically admitted he held 'a brief for Science, but had not yet heard it assailed', and sat down. The crowd bayed for more; the bishop was called by name and finally obliged. He ranged widely, on the *Origin*'s unphilosophical character, on Egyptian mummies disproving change, on fancy pigeons, on the line between man and the animals. Then in a jovial mood, he tried to brighten two hours in a stuffy room with an ad-lib. Student laughter drove him on. In the heat of the moment no one could remember his precise words. But he twisted round and – referring to Huxley's gorilla put-down of Owen two days before – asked him whether the apes were on his grandfather's or grandmother's side.

It was a high-risk strategy. Sedgwick too had panned the *Vestiges* to protect 'our glorious maidens' from its wickedness. Maidens symbolized the chaste; the lurking evil was draped in the black cape of the bestial transmutationist. Wilberforce was playing on sensibilities, raising the inviolability of Victorian womanhood. Huxley could have made flippancy look like vulgarity. But he steered clear of the quagmire.

He waited, stage-managing the event just as much. And when the shouts for him climaxed, he rose. 'A slight tall figure stern and pale, very quiet and very grave' – 'white with anger', some said. He

> had listened with great attention to the Lord Bishops speech but had been unable to discern either a new fact or a new argument in it – except indeed the question raised as to my personal predilection in the matter of ancestry – That it would not have occurred to me to bring forward such a topic as that for discussion myself, but that I was quite ready to meet the Right Rev. prelate even on that ground. If then, said I the question is put to me would I rather have a miserable ape for a grandfather or a man highly endowed by nature and possessed of great means of influence & yet who employs these faculties & that influence for the mere purpose of introducing ridicule into a grave scientific discussion, I unhesitatingly affirm my preference for the ape.

That was enough for the raucous students. There followed

> inextinguishable laughter among the people, and they listened to the rest of my argument with the greatest attention. Lubbock & Hooker spoke after me with great force & among us we shut up the bishop & his Laity.
>
> I happened to be in very good condition and said my say with perfect good temper & politeness. I assure you of this because all sorts of reports were spread about e.g. that I had said I would rather be an ape than a bishop &c.[18]

'Soapy Sam' stood alongside Owen in Huxley's demonic Pantheon. He was everything the squad detested. Huxley's troops were hammering the wedge deeper between science and theology. They had not taken over the barracks to have a Tory bishop use 'his position & his lawyer faculty' to force them back into a moral harness. Huxley had an 'unmitigated contempt' for Wilberforce's tactics. What value science if it had to be approved by rank and wealth? What of integrity? This was not religious obscurantism blinded by a radiant science. If there was light, it came from the sparks caused by the political friction. Huxley oozed Puritan self-righteousness. He made the scientific man seem more principled, more earnest. Moral rectitude was his; 'truth' was defensively ringed by his New Model Army. And before it stood the embodiment of corruption, a purple-frocked bishop with a 'splendid nature debauched by society'.

Perceptions of the event differed so wildly that talk of a 'victor' is ridiculous. Huxley believed himself 'the most popular man in Oxford for full four & twenty hours afterwards'. But even Hooker thought that he had not managed to 'command the audience' and that in the electric air – when even 'Lady Brewster fainted' – it was *he* (Hooker) who subsequently 'smashed' Wilberforce 'amid rounds of applause'. And that it was *he* who was 'congratulated & thanked by the blackest coats & whitest stocks in Oxford' (the liberal clergy). In the chaos the punchdrunk combatants failed to see the jaunty Wilberforce leaving. He bore 'no malice', convinced that he had floored Huxley. He was punning happily as he saw the droll side:

> . . . now a learn'd Professor, grave and wise,
> Stoutly maintains what I supposed were lies;
> And, while each listening sage in wonder gapes,
> Claims a proud lineage of ancestral Apes.
> Alas! cried I, if such the sage's dreams,
> Save me, ye powers, from these unhallowed themes;
> From self-degrading science keep me free,
> And from the pride that apes humility![19]

The public relished the performance. Such acts it loved to see: intellectual tempests which swept away the 'the courtesies of life like a sou'-wester'. It was as stirring, the press said, 'as the Battle of Farnborough or the Volunteer Review'. At a party that night someone wished it could happen again, only to be pulled up by Huxley, 'Once in a life-time is enough'. But it was not. Darwinians needed victories to counter the bad press. The fight was talked up, each time with bloodier results. And not only by the Darwinians. With the furies raging over *Essays and Reviews*, liberal Churchmen like the Vice-Chancellor thought the bishop 'got no more than he deserved'. Rolleston, the meeting's organizer, shared his contempt. He intended to have his own 'slap at the Base Bishop', he told

Huxley, 'before he recovers the cudgelling you have given him'. Wilberforce was being pushed towards the slag heap of 'extinguished theologians'.

In his rest home, Darwin heard from Falconer 'how the Saponaceous Bishop got basted and larded by Huxley'. Darwin chivvied Huxley for his version. Drained by the howling reviews, he revelled in Huxley's retelling. 'I have read [your letter] twice & sent it to my wife & when I get home shall read it again'. 'But how durst you attack a live Bishop in that fashion? ... Have you no reverence for fine lawn sleeves?' Darwin delighted in the witty repartee, even if it blotted out all talk of runts and tumblers.

Only one thing did Darwin enjoy more: Owen's 'basting'. They all suspected Owen of backing the bishop and making 'him strike whatever note he liked'. Owen, lodging at the bishop's palace, obviously chatted about Darwin's book – and Huxley's review. But knowing his faith in 'continuous creation', and his tree of life with its archetypal roots and fossil forks, he might have been coaxing Sam beyond the Six Days to a more informed opposition. But he suffered by association as the bishop resorted to 'round-mouthed, oily, special pleading'.[20]

Exhausted, Huxley crept to the station the next morning to catch the Reading train. He left an ally in place. Rolleston became the Linacre Professor and pledged 'never to give you cause to regret the share you have had in my promotion'. And as proof he started a home mission:

> I tell my friends here that if they would only believe that
> God is Almighty there would be no difficulty in reconciling
> Darwin with the established Creed. But people will not
> believe in this, the Second Article of the Apostles' Creed;
> and they persist in binding down Omnipotence to such a
> line of operation as they, poor mannikins, think they
> could carry out.

Rolleston still had 'a great deal of Oxford slough to shed'.[21] But Huxley thought it helped him blend in among the vipers.

Back in London's secular air, Huxley began a paper to claim the human domain. 'On the Zoological Relations of Man with the Lower Animals' was a landmark production that summed up the Victorian condition. Or exacerbated it, some said. What *were* man's ties to Nature?

> Theologians and moralists . . . impressed by a sense of the
> infinite responsibilities of mankind, awed by a just
> prevision of the great destinies in store for the only earthy
> being of practically unlimited powers . . . have always
> tended to conceive of their kind as something apart,
> separated by a great and impassable barrier.

But anatomists,

> discovering as complete a system of law and order in the
> microcosm as in the macrocosm . . . have no less steadily
> gravitated towards the opposite opinion, and, as
> knowledge has advanced, have more and more distinctly
> admitted the closeness of the bond which unites man with
> his humbler fellows.

Did it matter? For whatever mankind's parentage, whether archangel ruined or ape risen, 'his duties and his aspirations . . . remain the same'. No claim to Divine parentage will

> change the brutishness of man's lower nature; nor, except
> to those valet souls who cannot see greatness in their
> fellow because his father was a cobbler, will the
> demonstration of a pithecoid pedigree one whit diminish
> man's divine right of kingship over nature; nor lower the
> great and princely dignity of perfect manhood, which is
> an order of nobility, not inherited, but to be won by each
> of us, so far as he consciously seeks good and avoids
> evil . . .

Hooker thought these remarks would be 'balsam to many short witted & honest but timid enquirers'.[22] Actually it looked as though they were aimed at Lyell. At least they were more comforting than Darwin's crumbs. Darwin could offer Lyell no such ' "consolatory view" on the dignity of man'. Darwin, ever the relativist, demoted man and deprivileged the present. His vision was cosmic and shocking. Nineteenth-century gents stood at no special point in geological time in his view. 'I cannot explain why', he tweaked Sir Charles, 'but to me it would be an infinite satisfaction to believe that mankind will progress to such a pitch, that we sh^d. be looked back at as mere Barbarians'.

Huxley the essayist became Huxley the anatomist. From imponderables he switched to resolvables. All he could really clear up, he said, were the claims about anatomical uniqueness. So he delved into the neural arcana. Each of Owen's esoteric points about the 'unique' human cerebrum was refuted; every known expert was subpoenaed to prove that apes possess the cerebral lobes and bumps of their human betters. Rolleston sent dissection notes. So did others, while pleading to be kept out of 'controversy with the great potentate'.[23]

Brains, apes and human destiny wrapped themselves up in one disconsolate package and deepened the crisis already racking Victorian intellectuals. By now every review did what Darwin dreaded – extended evolution to humanity in order to slate it. Lascivious stories sold tabloids. Hacks wanted evidence that man 'came forth, in his complete humanity, from the womb of an ape'. Such carnality was a self-refutation. Even Owen was pestered on the point. One Episcopalian, writing a reprisal article on 'The Creative Week' for Wilberforce's *Replies to 'Essays and Reviews'*, asked him. Was Adam produced 'supernaturally . . . *through* the . . . womb of the Ape'?[24]

The Tory *Quarterly* – the review of the *Origin* that Huxley had angled for – had not fallen to an impartial critic. Hooker was staggered at Murray's eventual choice, Bishop Wilberforce. It might have been what the worried shires wanted, but hadn't the age of arbitrating bishops passed? 'The Article itself is astounding': where should he begin, with its 'appalling ignorance of the rudiments of Science, or incredible blunders'? What was Murray doing 'entrusting a Scientific book to an ignorant intemperate Reviewer'?

Darwin scribbled 'rubbish' in his copy. Against the sentiment that 'all creation is the transcript in matter of ideas eternally existing in the mind of the Most High', he jotted 'mere words', Owen's – the sort that sounded hollow to Darwin's Unitarians and secularists.[25] Not that it mattered. Huxley's scientifics were capturing the liberal press. And the story of 'Huxley, the Bishop & the Ape' was spiralling into legend. One rector, quick off the mark to use natural selection in his study of Saharan larks, was so angered at Darwin's deification by 'his prophet Huxley' that he recanted and rejoined the bishop. Huxley, that dark avenging angel, Darwin's 'good & kind agent for the propagation of the Gospel ie the Devil's gospel', was partitioning the world along his own lines. The burst from his Whitworth was scaring the rectors back to their own trenches.

He made a show of ousting those with a dual calling – clergymen with a scientific bent. If it meant denigrating, so be it. The professional demarcation dispute hit a low note as Huxley's pugnacity rubbed off on others. Why should science play host to the 'ignorant priest'?, asked Hooker. 'I say ignorant advisedly, for I hold' the clerical geologists 'to be as really *ignorant* of the fundamentals of Natural History as I am of Church History'.[26]

At this moment a journal dropped into the group's lap. The Dublin-based *Natural History Review* was crashingly unsuccessful. Worse, it was broadly anti-Darwinian. The proprietors wanted to sell it and Huxley drooled. Given his pool of talent it could be provocative; turn its orientation, make it 'mildly episcopophagus', and it could even pay. He roped in Lubbock and Rolleston, those 'plastically minded young men' (meaning Darwin's men). Then the older hands, Busk and Carpenter, were brought on board. Hooker, knee-deep in his own botanical 'midden-heap', was too busy, but he nominated his 'plastic' young assistants who would join for the glory of it. With this line-up, Huxley told him, 'you & Darwin & Lyell will have a fine opportunity if you wish it of slaying your adversaries'. Sobering up some months after Oxford, he was more circumspect. He wanted 'articles *for* & *against*' the *Origin*, he said, so as to leave no doubt 'that the review is a "Champ libre"'.

Darwin and Lyell, those wealthy virtuosi whose living rooms were laboratories where they could lavish time on innovative tomes, called it madness. Original research was what counted, carrying the imprimatur of a gentleman. Yet all around them the academic world was compartmentalizing. It needed specialist journals. To Huxley, a penny-a-liner on other people's papers, a rushing ideologue, with a talent for organization and a desire for power, the prospect of his own journal was appealing. But even Hooker was 'aghast' at the extra donkey work and told him to get a '*paid* subeditor'.[27] But there was no money in the kitty; indeed there was no kitty. Lyell prophesied that Huxley would end up carrying the load – 'quarterly mischief' he called it.

True, the piles were mounting. Starting was easy, but Huxley was finding it 'more & more difficult . . . to *finish* things'. His fascination with one of the first vertebrates to have appeared on the earth, the bizarre armoured fish *Pteraspis*, was driving him to study all Devonian fish. (Brilliant work this: he traced the coelacanths back to a flourishing Devonian group of lobe-finned fish – 'Crossopterygians' he called them, archaic fish which, he hinted in a flash of insight, probably had lungs.)[28] Nights were spent drilling, although why the 'volunteer-soldiering . . . does not kill you',

Darwin puzzled, 'I cannot understand'. If the rifles didn't, everyone expected that the journal would.

Torrential rains heralded the start of Huxley's holiday in August. He took the six-week break at home to clear the backlog. Here his only plague was a curly head poking round the door, wanting to play. Noel, three, was articulate and inquisitive, Jessie was toddling and precocious, 16 month-old Marian completed the blond conspiracy. Nettie, five months pregnant, looked forward to her next Christmas baby. There was a new togetherness as Hal's first holiday at home turned into a second 'Honeymoon'. Evenings were spent proof-reading Spencer's *First Principles* (the start of his ten-volume 'synthetic philosophy'). Hal passed the pages to Nettie, who liked their calm tone.

She read of the 'Unknowable', that mysterious reality beyond the reach of the senses. The 'web and woof of matter and force' had woven a 'veil which lies between us and the Infinite', in Hal's words. Huxley delighted in tracing the concept of the 'Unknowable' to the High Churchman Henry Mansel's *Limits of Religious Thought* (published in 1858). Since man's finite mind could never contact God directly, Mansel argued, we are in no position to question His inspired Word. Mansel was supporting Revelation, but Huxley saw him sawing through the plank on which he was sitting. So did Spencer, and in *First Principles* the 'Unknowable' replaced God Himself.

Nettie took Spencer's book in her stride. She had plunged into a society in crisis, 'destitute of faith, yet terrified at scepticism', as Carlyle had it. She saw it torn by Dissent and teased by the avant-garde. She lived with a devout man and found (as the same Carlyle said) that his 'deep sense of religion was compatible with the entire absence of Theology'. No husband 'manifested more of the moral presuppositions of a Puritan evangelicalism'. Yet, her Hal admitted, '99 out of 100 of my fellows would call me Atheist'. All around her values were transforming – no longer was worth linked with birth; or virtue with the Anglican communion. Nor did morality rest in using church creeds – about the created hierarchies in Nature and Society – to maintain the status quo.

She took the toddlers to Christ Church in Lisson Grove each Sunday. Here Kingsley's friend the Christian Socialist, Revd Llewelyn Davies – Church reformer, female emancipator and co-founder of the Working Men's College – drew intellectuals from far and wide. Nettie sat with them amid its giant Corinthian columns, listening to Davies' reforming sermons. She was happy with Davies (and Davies thought Christianity could only learn from the evolutionary movement). Nettie knew the mood as she scanned Spencer's sheets on the 'Unknowable'. Huxley surprised Spencer by thinking them quite good. Someone had to publish the big evolutionary picture, and only Spencer had the cosmic gall.

'I have not been away this autumn & don't mean to from being very well & jolly', Huxley told the Tenby folk on a wet 9 September. 'My wife is as well as N° 4 will permit . . . N°s 1, 2 & 3 are flourishing'.[29]

Six days later the bottom fell out of his world. On Thursday 13 September little Noel lured him out of the study for a romp. Then it was off to bed, and Noel kissed his father goodnight. Later he woke up, 'sick & feverish'. They soothed him back to sleep, but by morning Hal found him 'very ill', headachy, with a flushed face and a rash. Jessie too showed scarlet fever symptoms. But Noel had no sore throat, and the doctor thought the violence pointed to 'gastric fever'. Jessie was only mildly affected and the baby escaped. Noel's rash reddened and erupted and peeled. The frightened tears gave way to shivering as his pulse quickened and the 'little fellow gradually became delirious'.

Hal could not understand the virulence. 'It was as if the boy had been inoculated with some septic poison'. Nettie was frantic and Hal beside himself as Noel's 'restless head, with its bright blue eyes and tangled golden hair, tossed all day upon his pillow'. Desperation gave way to trauma as they stared the unimaginable in the face. All Saturday he thrashed in his bed, deranged, burning up. His father began to see 'typhoid symptoms', confusing him the more. They sat by the bedside, watching helplessly, hopelessly, mopping his brow. At 7 pm., just as the sun was setting, there was a sudden violent attack. It lasted two hours. They were an instant and an eternity. And then 'we had a dead child in our arms'.[30]

Nettie was crushed and bewildered. Two days earlier her 'hope & darling' had been horse-playing, his eyes twinkling. Those blue eyes now stared, vacant and fixed. A hysterical collapse gave way to numbness, a mindless incomprehension of this outrage on Divine justice. She subsided in agony, her head 'one hot patch of pain'. Hal saw her going out of her mind. Stoically he walked Nettie 'up & down outside the house to let the rain fall' on her 'burning head'. Then she retreated to her room.

Hal's grim resilience got him through the hours, but then came a deep sadness: 'we have lost our poor little son, our pet and hope'. 'The four corners of my house are smitten and I stand face to face with base patience & resignation'. That night Hal gently carried Noel into his 'study, and laid his cold still body here where I write'. He began to slip back into the inferno. Outside the gales continued, but inside a mental tempest left him groping for a stable rock to cling to.

> I could have fancied a devil scoffing at me ... and
> asking me what profit it was to have stripped myself of
> the hopes and consolations of the mass of mankind? To
> which my only reply was & is Oh devil! truth is better
> than much profit.

The rock became the bedrock of knowledge, and Nature laid her healing hand. Like Job he took solace in his religious stand.

> I have searched over the grounds of my belief and if wife
> and child & name & fame were all to be lost to me one
> after the other as the penalty still I will not lie.

He sat in the study facing the tiny body. His emotions were unleashed as he looked back to that New Year's Eve 1856, when he had sat at the same desk and pledged on his son's birth to give 'a new and healthier direction to all Biological Science'. He had found redemption on his son's death. There was no blame, only submission to Nature, and that brought its own catharsis. Therefore, 'I say ... without bitterness – Amen, so let it be'.

Old friends were away: Hooker was examining the cedars on Mount Lebanon and Spencer composing chapters in Scotland. But Tyndall joined the funeral procession at 11 am. on Tuesday, 'stunned & bewildered'. Just as he worked alongside Hal now as Jermyn Street's Professor of Physics, so they stood together in their 'holy leave-taking'. Hal had bought a plot beneath an oak in St Marylebone Cemetery, Finchley and paid extra to have Noel buried 12 feet deep. As he watched the tiny coffin lowered the huge depth the sublimated anger turned to outrage at an insensitive Church. The minister was not at fault, but he

> read as a part of his duty the words 'If the dead rise not
> again let us eat & drink for tomorrow we die' I cannot
> tell you how inexpressibly they shocked me – [the
> clergyman] had neither wife nor child or he must have
> known that his alternative involved a blasphemy against

all that was best & noblest in human nature. I could have
laughed with scorn. What! because I am face to face with
irreparable loss . . . I am to renounce my manhood, and
howling grovel in bestiality? Why, the very apes know
better, & if you shoot their young, the poor brutes grieve
their grief out & do not immediately seek distraction in a
gorge.[31]

Catharsis also came from writing letters, but only Kingsley's
brought such an emotive reply that Huxley opened his heart.
Kingsley, settling in to the Chair of modern history at Cambridge to
combat the 'Spinozaist tendency of the time', thought Huxley's ordeal
'something horrible, intolerable, like being burnt alive'. But the 'void'
would 'be refilled' hereafter, while in our earthly years we must 'make
ourselves worthy of the re-union'. Noel would be reborn.

Our physical body was irrelevant, Kingsley urged: 'I dare say I
am descended from some animal from whom also the chimpanzee
has sprung. I accept the fact fully, & care nothing about it'. What
mattered was our 'moral nature w^h. can . . . initiate the noble, the
beautiful, the merciful, the just'. This moral self was 'nearer to a
God than to a Chimpanzee', and if Nature's scythes 'can kill the
Chimpanzee, they cannot . . . kill me'.[32] The self survives, Noel
survives in the Lord's sight, awaiting their reunion.

This emotional blackmail provoked Huxley's 'savage, splendid,
and sympathetic' reply. Belief was sacred, he responded, and that
put a moral premium on assessing all the evidence, whether it was
for Immortality or Evolution. For Huxley, science taught the
Christian truth 'of entire surrender to the will of God' – one had
to accept the teachings of Nature and give up all prior prejudice.
'Sit down before fact as a little child', he urged Kingsley. 'I have
only begun to learn content & peace of mind since I have resolved
at all risks to do this'.

Huxley's epistle to the Cantabrigians made belief in immortality
a sin in the absence of evidence. He warned of the delusion that
the 'moral government of the world is imperfect without a system
of future rewards & punishments'. Every bit the religious visionary,
he made heaven and hell a part of Nature itself. Theft or murder
bring their own penalty on the earth, inasmuch as they damage the
moral man. 'The gravitation of sin to sorrow is as certain as that
of the earth to the sun'.[33] He was weaving morality into the very
fabric of the cosmos.

*

Through the daily sorrow he trudged, leaving a stricken Nettie upstairs. He busied himself with distractions. He readied the *Natural History Review* for its launch on 1 January 1861. At least with subscriptions 'coming in very lively' he was 'sanguine of success'. Darwin proofed Huxley's trumpet-blast 'On the Zoological Relations of Man' and trilled 'Your term "pithecoid man" [ape-like man] is a whole paper ... in itself'.[34] That bugle call would signal the *Review*'s new direction.

It was Kingsley who continued to bring Huxley back to life. Huge epistles passed between them, as the muscular moralists hacked to the bedrock of one another's being. Their frankness was almost embarrassing. Kingsley knew that 'Theology, metaphysic & the rest of it are actually dying' as 'the thinking portion of mankind' takes to the scientific high ground. He himself yearned to join the crusaders of science. 'Them I love, them I trust, with them I should like, had I my wish, to live & die'. But the more he strained for the new, the more he sought the moral gem in the old. He too was locked in 'struggle of w^h. I never talk ... I never opened my mind to any one as I have now to you'.

It reanimated Huxley's 'useless carcass'. By October he was sleeping again. Outside the miserable rain battered the windows. After three months of ruined crops every pulpit echoed to prayers for fine weather. But not Kingsley's; he fired a national debate by refusing 'to ask that God should alter the course of the universe'. Instead he prayed for spiritual 'light', tapping the moral realm. Huxley believed that moral intercession was as questionable as a fair-weather 'blessing'. But he turned down Kingsley's request to write on prayer for *Fraser's Magazine*. More controversy and he feared he would 'break down'. The endless work in editing the review and liaising with printers and writers was draining him; although he still had enough spark to send Kingsley a prospectus 'with a prayer for help if you can give us any'.[35]

He knew he would have to 'drift into the stream again'. Indeed, hearing that Hooker had returned, sworn to a new serenity, he remonstrated that 'for men, constructed on the high pressure tubular boiler principle, like ourselves', that meant 'to lie still & let the devil have his own way. And I will be torn to pieces before I am forty sooner than see that'.

He was already being torn by the sight of Nettie. Emotional winds were buffeting them both. On 11 December at 9.45 pm. she gave birth to another son. It helped to ease the pain even as it turned the knife. Leonard, she called him, 'because it held our lost boy's name'. Another son was 'a great blessing', but she remained crushed. For his part, Hal scarcely knew whether 'it was pleasure or pain. The ground has gone from under my feet once & I hardly know how to rest on anything again'. Nettie could see the dagger twisting and conspired with Tyndall to get Hal away. That meant one thing. In unprecedented Boxing Day frosts, when the thermometer plummeted to − 17°, Busk and Tyndall marched him off to the rarefied air of the Welsh mountains, reaching Snowdon on 28 December. The grandeur of it matched 'most things Alpine'.[36]

He arrived back on a sombre 31 December. It would have been Noel's fourth birthday and he found Nettie no better. She 'mends but slowly', he sighed to Hooker.

The next morning the first number of his *Natural History Review* was launched. 'What a complete & awful smasher (& done like a "buttered angel")', Darwin crowed as he imagined the effect on that 'canting humbug' Owen. Huxley sent Wilberforce a copy, marking his paper as 'justification for the diametrical contradiction with which he heard Prof. Huxley meet certain Anatomical Statements' at Oxford. (His Lordship typically received it with 'great pleasure'.) Huxley's polemic carried the review. As Lyell said, the 'public will at present devour any amount of your anthropoid ape questions'. Lyell persuaded the Athenaeum Club to subscribe. Hooker thought it could even sit on coffee tables − but for one dread, 'Anatomical' pictures. No one dared flick a page for fear of what 'will turn up next', mortified by the thought that 'it may be a Uterus'. Who could run the risk of the 'children, guests &c' glimpsing it? So pander to the prudes 'who regard Anatomical Plates as repulsive', Hooker said.[37] Cut them out.

Proprieties ruled society. Huxley acknowledged the point in his reply to Hooker. He mooted christening Leonard, and even more sheepishly asked Hooker to stand godfather.

> You know my opinions on these matters . . . So if you
> consent, the clerk shall tell all the lies for you & you shall
> be asked to do nothing else than to help devour the
> Christening feed, and be as good a friend to the boy as
> you have been to his father.
>   My wife will have the youngster Christened although I am
> always in a bad temper from the time it is talked about until
> the ceremony is over. The only way of turning the farce into
> a reality is by making it an extra bond with ones friends.

At times one had to live a lie to live at all. Hooker and Darwin (a godfather as well), were as willing to be hung for sheep as lambs and swore in person to 'renounce the Devil & all his works'.[38]

Nettie came downstairs for the first time on 5 January 1861. Grief had left no room for elation at Leonard's birth, and with Hal back to his punishing schedule she was back to brooding. She forced herself out of the house on 8 February to hear him at the Royal Institution, but it was by 'the grace of god & her own will'.[39] Her pitiable state shocked the Darwins, who saw in her face the agony they had felt on their own Annie's death ten years earlier.

Darwin offered a fortnight's rest in Kent. His image of Downe life in all its morbid glory was alluring. Convalescent gloom shrouded the family. The house 'is dreadfully sick & melancholy. My wife lies upstairs with my girl & she would see little of M^{rs}. Huxley, except at meal times'. Eighteen year-old Etty, still weakly a year after catching typhoid, was attended by a bevy of nurses, with a teary Emma trying 'not to give way to despondency'. Nor would Nettie see much of Mr Darwin himself, so stomachy 'that I never spend the whole evening even with our nearest relations'. Treat it 'as if it were a country inn', he insisted; or, better still, a sanatorium.

So in March a grieving Nettie, three tiny children, trunks and a nurse set off from the new palatial, glass-roofed Victoria Station. They found Down House an infirmary where no one got well; here illness was the norm and health a strange affliction. Emma Darwin was a ministering matron, soothing with physic and spiritual balm in her rest home. She was pious, a little distant at first; or, as Nettie said, 'a dear kind soul' in a rather 'unobtrusive way'. Emma was as pained by Charles' ethical departure from Christianity as Nettie had been by Hal's professional hostility. So there was comfort in her words – and strength in her faith that 'suffering & illness is meant to help us to exalt our minds & to look forward with hope to a future state'.

Left to herself in this strange sanatorium, where the family turned up like guests for their evening meal, Nettie still brooded on Noel. She wondered if she would ever 'be clear minded again', or love her other 'darlings as I did him'.[40]

16

Reslaying the Slain

> Cook had got up some chops . . . for me in wonderful
> style last night, when I went home after my Lecture. Said
> Lecture let me inform you was very good – Lyell came &
> was rather astounded at the magnitude & attentiveness of
> the audience.

Huxley stayed in town, polishing his 'Rifle & Bayonet' and honing his intellect. These Thursday nights in March 1861 saw the Tory nightmare realized as he taught the great unwashed of their gorilla ancestry.

The fliers for his new course brought the artisan élite in droves. Lyell, preparing his *Antiquity of Man*, squeezed incongruously among the carters and was astonished.

'My working men stick by me wonderfully', Hal cheered Nettie at Downe. 'By next Friday morning they will all be convinced that they are monkeys'. The cloth-caps needed no persuading. For decades their gutter presses had proclaimed man's bestial origin. By now the *Reasoner* was arming infidels with facts on fossils and flints to counter 'Theological Theories of the Origin of Man'. Its running mate, the *National Reformer*, was shattering the 'man and beast' dichotomy. Huxley was riding a crest. The pauper presses were devouring the *Origin* as they had the *Vestiges* and French Revolutionary tracts before it. All were grist to their mill. Red Lamarckians saw the '*divine* origin of man' as a supernatural sanction to keep '*the masses in the mud*'. Of course they rallied to any professor who would connect man to the 'under-world of life'.[1]

These flaming atheists had a biting cynicism; 'life is nothing and nothing life', ran a slogan knocking the pretensions of the port-swilling squirearchy. Privately Huxley distanced himself from these 'cynics who delight in degrading man'. The 'absolute justice' he saw in nature was invisible to the demagogues (as it was to Darwin). But he needed the working-class constituency. So he tailored his talks, luring the cabbies and costermongers. First came a little iconoclasm, then praise for their sceptical spirit. He peered into the chimpanzees' cage and came 'face to face with these blurred' mirror images. The apes forced a sudden 'mistrust of time-honoured theories' about our own vaunted place. 'It is as if nature herself had foreseen the arrogance of man', he said in his best broadsheet style, 'and with Roman severity had provided that his intellect by its very triumphs, should call into prominence the slaves, admonishing the conqueror that he is but dust'.

Six hundred packed his great theatre in Piccadilly each week, with many more turned away. Men fresh from the workshops; at least here their place had not been 'usurped by [the] smug clerks' who had overrun the Mechanics' Institutes. They sat 'rapt & still'. Huxley was not the 'phrase-making *poseur*' they usually saw on the rostrum. This was serious. There was a breathless silence; then at the end came 'thunders of applause', which rumbled on after the professor had gone for his chops.

For his workers evolution was self-betterment. The race was hauling itself up by its hobnailed-boot straps. The image conferred dignity on humble origins. As one firebrand put it, from the 'progress of the past we look forward, with inexorable confidence to the achievements of the future'. Theirs was a co-operative march towards the millennium. But Huxley's Elysian metaphor was a mite different. He likened society's stuttering advance to an insect's ecdyses: periods of repressive restraint, Dark Ages, broken by dramatic moults when the old integument was cast off. For fleeting moments the old constraints vanished and the cultural grub puffed itself up in the rationalist air. The Renaissance and the French Revolution had seen such moults, and the creaking showed that another explosive showering of old shell was imminent. On Huxley's metaphor, history was not rambling, open-ended and Darwinian but guided on its own embryonic track with a set destination, when the chrysalis opened to reveal an adult butterfly. But this goal was less a socialist New Jerusalem than a scientific New Reformation. Maybe the butterfly 'state of Man' was 'terribly distant', he told his men, but every moult moves us closer.

Unlike the scoffers he believed that there was a sanctity to mankind. People might have arisen *from* brutes, but they are 'assuredly not *of* them'. An ape ancestry implied no 'brutalization', he said, his eye on Lyell perched warily among the weavers. We can 'leave the brooding' over degradation 'to the cynics and the "righteous overmuch" who, disagreeing in everything else, unite in blind insensibility to the nobleness of the visible world'. In fact,

> thoughtful men, once escaped from the blinding influences
> of traditional prejudice, will find in the lowly stock whence
> Man has sprung, the best evidence of the splendour of his
> capacities; and will discern in his long progress through
> the Past, a reasonable ground of faith in his attainment of
> a nobler Future.[2]

At Downe Emma Darwin 'was very kind & sympathising', and she eased Nettie's 'great pain'. The Darwins took to precocious Marian, now almost two. Being her father's daughter she 'wins golden opinions, but will not be tempted into any demonstrations of affection'. As Nettie relayed the day's doings to Hal, Marian would sit on her lap 'holding a dry pen' and trying to draw Pater, while complaining that 'I can hardly make a man'.

The misery of the place was wonderfully infectious. Hal advised Nettie not to 'go strolling too far carrying great babies', but she had little opportunity. It was blustery and wet and everyone had colds. Trapped inside, the children became trying. Downe sent Jessie into a 'most capricious & irritable mood'. Darwin took it heroically, at least until the Tennyson poems came out.

> Only fancy, M^r. Darwin does not like poetry & prophesies
> that you will get over your liking for it [Nettie wrote to
> Hal]. I fear he has not so good an opinion of you since I
> mentioned your taste for it. Let us pray for his conversion
> & glorify ourselves, like true believers.

Almost nightly Nettie gave readings, joined by Emma and sickly Etty, who ventured downstairs for an hour. But 'M^r. Darwin doesn't think anything of it! I suppose he has worked his poetry into his life, for I cannot believe he has no poets corner in his heart'. Shortly Darwin took to hiding upstairs.

Do stop 'subjecting poor Darwin to a savage Tennysonian persecution', Hal joked. 'I shall see him looking like a martyr & have to talk double science next Sunday'.[3]

The science was ape brains and more to Darwin's taste. It was also a public talking point. As Hal praised his workers as the sons of monkeys, the presses were rolling on Saturday's *Athenaeum*. The adventurer and gorilla hunter Paul du Chaillu was touring England, exhibiting his grisly haul of decapitated heads. (Faithful to Owen, he sold most of them to the British Museum.) His theatrical depictions of the majestic manlike-ape caused a sensation. He showed the proud beast, charging, pounding its chest, falling in a hail of bullets. Owen capitalized on du Chaillu's talk at the Royal Institution, following him on stage to point out that the gorilla's brain lacked a human-like cerebrum and hippocampus. The *Athenaeum* ran his reassuring words. Huxley responded with rapier speed, publishing a rebuttal to Darwin's cry 'too civil'. 'It is a good joke that since Owen attacked me, I . . . feel more inclined to clap anyone on the back, than to cry hold hard!' That reassured Nettie: 'To think that the mild Darwin should hurrah'![4] The public awaited each week's lunge and parry, wondering what would become of society if apes were found with hippocampuses.

Huxley rushed to get the April *Review* out. He worked harder with the *Gardeners' Chronicle* calling it 'a capital Review badly edited'. (They should 'thank God it is no worse', he piped up, still trying to juggle ten things at once after the tragedy.) Rolleston's refutation of Owen went in. But his proof that apes had a hippocampus was so chivalrous that Hooker thought him frightened 'of giving offence to God, Oxford, Orangs & Owen'.[5]

In the middle of it all Hal brought Nettie home. Seven months since Noel's death and she was still 'ill & weak from fretting'. The Darwins had been a release, but seeing the old house and Noel's bedroom she began 'running back again fast'. Hal was at his wits' end and now 'alarmed about her'.[6] Another spell away was the answer; borrowing the Folkestone home of the Secretary of the Royal Institution, Hal turned Nettie round. On Saturday 6 April 1861, as the *Athenaeum* ran Owen's haughty reply, he took her with the three children and two nurses to the Kent coast.

Londoners' jaws were agape. They watched Hal wind up the slanging match 'in disgust' the following Saturday. 'Life is too short' to go on 'slaying the slain', he finished. And with that the squibs started. One whimsical nonentity found its way into *Punch*:

Says Owen, you can see
The brain of Chimpanzee
Is always exceedingly small,

> With the hindermost 'horn'
> Of extremity shorn,
> And no 'Hippocampus' at all.

Ending up

> Next HUXLEY replies,
> That OWEN he lies,
> And garbles his Latin quotation;
> That his facts are not new,
> His mistakes not a few,
> Detrimental to his reputation.
> 'To twice slay the slain,'
> By dint of the Brain,
> (Thus HUXLEY concludes his review)
> Is but labour in vain,
> Unproductive of gain,
> And so I shall bid you 'Adieu!'[7]

A touchy burlesque had finally raised Huxley into the public consciousness. What began in earnest ended in satire, releasing the valve on a fraught situation. The squib's authorship leaked. 'I would give you fifty guesses & you should not find out', he prodded Hooker. Darwin too was astounded. It was Owen's patron, a Church-and-State stalwart in the House, Sir Philip Egerton, well known at the School of Mines for his fossil fish cabinet – 'and the fact speaks volumes for Owen's perfect success in damning himself'.[8]

Every Saturday Hal went to Folkestone. At first Nettie was 'too weak to move off the sofa', but in a couple of weeks the sea air had raised her spirits. She began to walk, sometimes with Hal along the white cliffs, looking out towards France, or with George and Polly. Everyone hoped that her renewed strength would 'relieve the tension of her mind'.

Hal rushed back each Monday, into the office for more lectures and meetings. By now du Chaillu's gorillas were a tabloid obsession. Macabre tales of ferocity circulated, and salacious stories of women-snatching. Here was a giant black ape walking upright, 'stopping at intervals to beat his huge breast and roar'. The beast exerted a 'terrible fascination'. The gorilla became overloaded with sinister symbolism – *Punch* made every Irish patriot a Mr G. O'Rilla fit to be shot down. Du Chaillu returned to Africa to catch Owen a live gorilla. Huxley met with du Chaillu before he left, but he was unimpressed, finding nothing but 'inexplicable confusion' behind the hunter's mask.[9]

Respectable society had never been so provoked over its beliefs. What was it to be human? Were anatomists and butchers to be the new sages? The old sage was horrified. Huxley called on Thomas Carlyle on 30 April. Having spent the radical years slaying material- ist dragons, the hard-bitten hero was not about to tolerate prepos- terous monkey-men. But with the multi-authored *Essays and Re- views* questioning the existence of miracles (the book, out for a year, was still kicking up a storm), the bickering over brains left everyone wondering who were the true interpreters of humanity. Onlookers forlornly tried to disentangle the issues. Owen's backers saw the 'absurdity' of the hippocampus debate, when next to nothing was known of cerebral functioning. Huxley's Broad Church colleagues agreed. For Rolleston our 'diviner life is not a mere result of the abundance of our convolutions'. Nor did cerebral similarities say anything about ancestry. But the attorneys were playing to the crowd. Owen tried to swing support by blackening Huxley as an 'advocate of man's origin from a transmuted ape'.[10] He made human ancestry hinge on the cerebral point. Therefore Huxley's proof of the hippocampus in apes seemed a vindication of mankind's bestial origin.

'People are talking a good deal about the "Man & the apes" question', he informed Nettie. 'Some think my winding-up too strong'. Darwin called it 'truculent' (even though he himself was now 'demoniacal about Owen'). But how else to expose those who 'prostitute Science'? No wonder that it was thought 'strong – it was very', she replied.

> I think had I been at your elbow when you penned it I
> would have asked you to omit it, not from any fear – or
> least thoughts of injustice – but as a matter of policy –
> however Owen did certainly want a word or two of most
> severe censure from a man of courage, after starting what
> he must know to have been false.[11]

Huxley deliberately reduced the question to one of 'personal veracity'. He was fighting for the moral high ground, but he also knew that moral courage was the issue consuming the Anglican mind in the wake of *Essays*.

The *ancien régime* was being eroded from the inside. Liberal *Essay*ists, condemning miracles as atheistic (for breaking the links in God's causal chain), shared Huxley's belief that morality lay in the search for evidence. One *Essay*ist, the ultra-liberal professor of geometry at Oxford, Baden Powell, argued that an unbroken chain back to Creation was evidence of Divine intent. The *Origin* was a theological crutch; grasp it, he urged, and praise 'the self-evolving powers of nature'.

Wilberforce's mace forced the *Origin*'s and *Essays*' supporters into an uneasy alliance. Huxley, Hooker and Carpenter even had Captain Stanley's younger brother, Revd Arthur Stanley, the Canon of Christ Church, elected to their elite Philosophical Club, where he might be enlightened on the heat of a moon-beam or the existence of fossil humans. Stanley believed that the Bible should be interpreted like any other historical book. It led to a close camaraderie; a brotherhood of the beleaguered that might not have survived fair-weather conditions. Stanley confided to Huxley that the enthusiastic *Edinburgh* review of the *Essays* was his, which sent Huxley rushing to the Athenaeum library. The article struck him as 'a very clear defence', even if 'it would not be difficult to make mince-meat of it'.[12]

Wilberforce and twenty-five bishops wrote to the *Times*, complaining of the *Essays* and threatening to indict the authors for heresy. Lubbock started a counter-petition, which praised the book for trying to put the Church's teachings on a 'firmer' footing. Lyell, Busk, Carpenter and Darwin signed. But at Oxford Rolleston refused, no lover of *Essays*. So did Huxley, Hooker and Ramsay, who actually agreed with the hard-line bishops that 'the position of the Essayists [*was*] untenable for Clergymen'.[13] As astute strategists, they knew that this reconciliation wrecked their professional strategy, which relied on confrontation.

Hal dreaded Nettie coming 'back to the old scenes', fearing another of her 'relapses'. Mrs Hooker suggested a house move, in fact that he 'cut St John's Wood altogether' to break the morbid connection. The Waverley Place rent was paid until March 1862, but Tyndall and Hirst came to the rescue and took over the lease. By mid-May Hal had found a larger house near by in Abbey Place, big enough for a growing family and a retinue of domestics. He was determined 'to put the top on her cure'.[14]

So in June 1861 a reinvigorated Nettie returned to a new home. Because of the move, money problems remained critical. Nettie's mother settled in, while Mr Heathorn sailed to Sydney to sort out the £35,000 debts resulting from his brewery's collapse. But Hal was 'only too happy to feel a little free from sorrow' at last. Apart from 'a lunatic neighbour', life was returning to normal. Becoming

hectic, in other words; more and more of the *Review* was falling
on his shoulders, as Lyell had predicted. Unless he watched over
everything 'it goes wrong'. The 'paper is bad, the cover is bad, the
type is bad, & the general get up loose shabby & dogseary'. He
sacked the printer and upgraded everything. 'We must fly high if
we mean to do well'.[15] He lost hours proofing, only to rush home
to fix the overflowing cistern and catch the water dripping through
the ceiling. But that was life.

By now the Darwinians were on top of every aspect of human
origin. While Huxley dissected apes, Lyell prepared his *Antiquity
of Man*. Sir Charles had toured the archaeological sites in England
and looked at the hand-axes excavated by the customs official
Boucher de Perthes in France. These had convinced him that
early man had indeed used flint weapons to kill extinct hippos
and hyaenas. Lubbock was publishing on Stone Age shell
mounds in Huxley's *Review*. Falconer was excavating flint knives
in a Brixham cave, on England's south coast. Here he had found
his famous bear's arm-bone sharpened as a stave. Like an ageing
professor, Lyell was gathering up all this evidence for his
book.[16]

But where were the humans who had hunted cave bears? A
beetle-browed skull cap had turned up in 1857 in the Neander
caves near Düsseldorf. Before anyone had seen it, wild rumours
abounded – Spencer had heard that 'this skull, mark, *is intermediate between that of the gorilla and that of man! . . .* After this,
anything else would be bathos'. Its swept-back forehead and
massive brow ridges pointed to a brutal 'Neanderthal Man' as the
bear hunter. Or so the anatomist Hermann Schaafhausen specu-
lated when he described the skull. This and the stout limb bones
had illustrators depicting 'horrible' prognathous cave dwellers,
squat chimp-men wielding axes and sipping half-warmed pots of
hyaena blood. Busk translated Schaafhausen's paper for the
Review, and even he set Neanderthal Man's overhanging brows in
outline beside a chimpanzee's skull.

Lyell began omnivorously collecting information on this too. He
tapped Huxley, wanting him to illustrate the skull's peculiar
features. In exchange Sir Charles acted as go-between with its
owner, the school teacher Karl Fuhlrott. He sent Huxley's list of
questions and received back photographs, measurements and a
cast.[17] Huxley inexorably moved on to study fossil man, as if he
had the time.

*

There were not enough hours in the day. By now he was deep in his winter courses and rushing between council chambers. Nettie hardly saw him. In a blue moon he might take her to a Jenny Lind concert. But otherwise his presence was a passing blur and he became known as the 'lodger' at home. Even his Saturday nights were spent in Jermyn Street, initiating students in the 'First Principles of Physiology'. He had become a 'mere lecturing pump eternally pouring out floods of discourse'. It was draining him. 'If one had but two heads', he said, '& neither required sleep!'

The one he had did not know which way to turn. The hares he set running darted in every direction. And around every corner he found them breeding furiously. By now Britain's mining operations had become vast. Coal fired the furnaces of the industrial north, and the black-face and 'black-lung' miners digging into these swamp seams disinterred their inhabitants. The Carboniferous corpses – most from the ironstone under the coal – came to Jermyn Street. Huxley checked consignments for fish and continually found something else: squat crocodile-like creatures, 'labyrinthodonts', the earliest amphibians (named after the labyrinthine folding of their tooth enamel). Industry was shining a light on the first vertebrates to lumber out of the methane-bubbling swamps – archaic armoured salamanders 'which pottered, with much belly and little leg, like Falstaff in his old age, among the coal forests'. In spare hours Huxley polished 'coal vertebrae' and shiny skulls, christening them appropriately. 'Anthracosaurus is a good name', Lyell wrote on hearing the latest arrival from Airdrie's Iron and Steel works. And so fish gave way to amphibians.

Lyell wished 'we could multiply you by five'.[18] Huxley's own production was indeed on an industrial scale. But everything had to be squeezed around the lectures. Fuhlrott's Neanderthal package arrived as Huxley was leaving for Edinburgh. It had to wait until he had given his man-and-apes pep-talk to a tough tartan workforce.

He came alive at these confrontationist moments. He never really expected to 'be stoned and cast out of the city gate'; he knew his working men too well. He packed the Queen Street Hall in January 1862, breaking all records (and the Philosophical Institution's run of safe, arty lectures). Among the querulous classes he found 'sinners enough in "Saintly Edinburgh"'. The evangelical *Witness* never understood this fustian enthusiasm. It was appalled at the applause when 'their kindred to the brute creation was most strongly asserted'. But Huxley talked their language. If great truths began as blasphemies, then he intended to blaspheme. Here was a new sort of intellectual hero, emulating the old agitators, 'flouting the novelty of his views instead of smuggling them in'. Edinburgh's workforce loved it.

It was a gentle blasphemy. 'I told them in so many words that I entertained no doubt of the origin of man from the same stock as the apes'. The *Witness* went into spasms. This was the 'vilest and beastliest paradox ever vented in ancient or modern times amongst Pagans or Christians'. Huxley revelled in the kicks and sent clippings to Lyell, Hooker and Darwin to prove 'that my labour has not been in vain'. There was an exuberance in this mock martyrdom. 'I made 'em listen', he boasted to Dyster, '& only after I was gone did the 'Witness' visit me with large & liberal cursing. Life has its joys, my son, if we earn them!'[19]

With the profanities pealing like bells he returned to the fossils. Even more did cave humans whet the public appetite. What were they? What were *we*? Semi-apes wielding hatchets? The cognoscenti's excitement was seeping through to the public. Here were the Ice Age humans that many said never existed. Huxley was looking at the first shattered skulls.

Lyell obtained another, the Engis skull, from the Meuse valley in Belgium. It was as old as the mammoths and yet modern in shape. What could Huxley say? – 'a fair average human skull, which might have belonged to a philosopher, or might have contained the thoughtless brains of a savage'. He turned back to the massive-boned and scowling-browed Neanderthal. That was different.

He settled in to the College of Surgeons. Here was London's chief stockpile of skulls, gruesomely stacked in a shrine to ethnic exploitation. He contrasted endless aboriginal relics with Neanderthal's 'degraded' cranium, pioneering new ways of bisecting and measuring skulls for easier comparison. 'The *Neander-thal skull*' emerged as an '*exaggerated modification*' of the lowest of the '*Australian skulls*'.

Ape brains and Neanderthal bones had the making of an esoteric bestseller. By the time he stood on the Royal Institution podium on 7 February 1862, his talk 'On the Fossil Remains of Man' was the teaser for a book. There never was a more startling lecture 'bearing on the *great question*', someone in the audience remarked. An august audience it was, as usual. Even the Catholic Cardinal Wiseman sat among the dignitaries, which led the wisecrackers to

expect that, after such illumination, he would grant Huxley an
' "Indulgenza plenaria"!!!'[20] What Wiseman actually granted was
less generous than absolution. And anyway Huxley relished his
sins.

Huxley was a power in the School of Mines. He cruised over the
Director's head and contacted the Chairman of a Commission
looking into its running, setting out his views on curriculums and
examinations. The school was a model state enterprise of hard-
core intellects, all of a mind on the *Origin*, *Essays* and money for
merit. The loose set of dogs had become a tight pack, and Huxley
expected everyone to pull his weight. Salter had degenerated into a
technician in his own department, and Huxley considered him 'the
veriest "filius canis" I ever had to deal with'.[21] Salter's outbursts
grew worse. 'Damn your eyes', he once shouted, taking a swing at
Huxley, who had found his fossils left out overnight! The unhinged
evangelical, despised by everyone from the doorman to the Director, was sacked. He picked up his Bible and fossil books and
descended into madness; deserted by his wife, he eventually jumped
into the Thames.

Huxley took over every menial role. He was prodigiously active
in the school, and a good meeting organizer in the societies. What
was drudgery to others had an urgency for him as he set about
restructuring science from the base up.

His vulturine eye locked on to the Zoological Society, with its
exotic cadavers. His swoop was swift and silent. Made a Fellow in
1860, he joined Wilberforce as a Vice-President in 1861. Huxley
and the bishop sat together to sort out finances, sack drunken
keepers and oversee a stream of imperial acquisitions. Every telegram – such as Wallace's on 19 March 1862 to say that he was
returning from the Malay Archipelago with two living 'Paradise
Birds' – set them into motion. Through the public shrieking this
quiet collaboration continued, unheralded, unknown.

Noble prelates saw the government of science as part of their
civic duty, and they provided links to the Zoo's society patrons.
Wilberforce came to the council meetings, but not the separate
scientific sessions, so he missed Huxley's talk on the Zoo's dead
spider monkeys – their brains sectioned to show the hippocampus.
Then again he missed Owen's on the peculiar Madagascan aye-
aye, with its Fagin-like middle finger, long and scimitar'd for grub-
hooking. This was perhaps as well, for whatever Owen's doubts
about Darwin, he quietly admitted here 'that the attempt to

dissipate the mystery which environed the origin of species' could only bring 'great collateral advantages to zoological science'.[22] This was realpolitik; the workaday reality behind the Manichean headlines, unseen through the smoke of battle.

At the Geological Huxley's rise was as fast. As Secretary he read reports and arranged meetings; his own papers on the earliest fish and amphibians seemed more like spirited '*viva voce* account[s]' to Lyell's in-law Charles Bunbury. Huxley was no hammerer; indeed geology, once the proud Queen of the Sciences, had become a concubine in his view, her purpose simply to help zoologists 'reconstruct the history of past life'.

The President, infirm and in Florence, asked Huxley to deliver the 1862 Annual Address. It was vintage Huxley, aimed at the fogies to 'flutter their nerves'. As always he set off to support Darwin, to demand of his critics: 'Now, Messieurs les Palaeontologues, what the devil *do* you really know?' And as always he skewed off.

The night showed him at his idiosyncratic best. Darwin's ramifying tree-image of evolution still had not sunk in. In fact the talk had nothing to do with Darwinism. Huxley did not try to trace newts and lungfish back to their common Devonian ancestor. Instead of concentrating on origins, he harped on the sharks' and crocodiles' long unchanging history. He could not shake his ten-year-old belief that the fossil record showed no progress. His talk, like so many, was a brilliant flash, and when the audience regained its sight 'there were many private protests'. Old Bunbury got the message, that 'the resemblances [of past and present life] are much greater' than the differences.[23]

So did Darwin. Huxley's claws risked maiming his friends. His fossil papers left not the slightest hint that he was Darwin's bulldog. In Edinburgh's museum he had found more labyrinthodonts mixed with the fish; that they were mistaken for one another should have suggested something to Darwin's right-hand man. But no. He used *Anthracosaurus* to show that amphibians had passed through prodigious periods unchanged. It was the greatest irony that those closest to Darwin could not give him the fossil back-up he needed – while it was Owen who was investigating the similarities between lungfish and amphibians.

'I want you to chuckle with me over the notion I find a great many people entertain', Huxley wrote delicately to Darwin, 'that the address is dead against your views'. But Darwin didn't chuckle at this strange exhibition. Even if natural selection could account for life standing still, Huxley's synopsis seemed so one-sided. 'I cannot help hoping', Darwin remonstrated, 'that you are not quite as right as you seem to be'.[24]

Huxley returned to his book. He peered at humans and apes from every side: he rounded up the best eye-witness accounts of living apes and examined embryonic growth. By the red letter day, 5 May 1862, he had a title, *Evidence as to Man's Place in Nature*. He had polished his stunning working-class talk for inclusion. The edge was deceptively shiny, but still jagged enough to draw blood. And it gushed out with his stab at Owen's cackhanded talk of the 'ordained continuous becoming of organic forms'. To the new rationalists Owen's clumsy words sounded quaintly evasive (Owen meant that a Prescient Intelligence produced new species by natural law – which he accepted as an expression of Divine Will). Huxley extracted his capital from Owen's metaphorical mystification. The 'first duty of a hypothesis [is] to be intelligible', he wrote, 'this may be read backwards, or forwards, or sideways, with exactly the same amount of signification'.

On that auspicious 5 May Hal's daughter, Rachel, was born at 1 am., raven-haired like him, the first to defy the blond conspiracy. Some hours later her proud father posted the first two chapters of *Man's Place* to Williams & Norgate for setting.[25]

Huxley was about to utter the greatest profanity since Copernicus moved the earth from the centre of the universe. He would move man from the centre of creation. But it was hard to be provocative with friends like Kingsley. So what? said Kingsley, hearing that his forebear

> was the ancestor of a gorilla – if so, I compliment my
> ancestors on having had wits enough to produce *me*,
> while my cousins have gone & irremediably disgraced
> themselves, by growing *four* hands instead of 2; & not
> being able to do the 3 Royal R's to this day.

But Cambridge professors of this stamp were rare, and Huxley expected a rougher ride from a prim society in the midst of an evangelical revival. He was writing the third chapter, on fossil men. Here was the heavy-browed Neanderthal. Huxley cut through the chimp-man nonsense and assessed its 'ape' features as entirely superficial. The brain was the normal size for a 'savage'. Its stout limbs suggested a cold-climate adaptation to glacial Europe, like one of Darwin's Patagonians. 'In no sense' was it 'intermediate between Men and Apes'. Provocation for Huxley took another form. If Neanderthal does not take us nearer the ape, 'Where, then, must we look for primaeval Man? Was the oldest *Homo sapiens* pliocene or miocene, or yet more ancient'? How much further back must we go to find the 'fossilized bones of an ape more anthropoid, or a Man more pithecoid'?[26] He was preparing the world for ancient semi-humans.

With work and travel he had no time for more than a three-chapter book. No multi-volume doorstopper for him; no *System of Philosophy*, nor even a 500-page *Origin* – but a pithy set of pamphlets, tracts for the times. He took the manuscript every-where. It wasn't only his wife who saw a blur these days; no one had him in focus. He lived a life based on express timetables. His was the first generation able to move with whistle-stop speed. He could open 1862 with a flying visit to Edinburgh, and after the 'frightful blackguarding from the "Witness"' plan to set the 'Irish Holy Willies' straight in Dublin.[27] In July he thought the Matter-horn would cure his rheumatism. In August he tramped Scotland for the Fisheries Commission. Then he tramped the British Associa-tion at Cambridge on his own business, and he topped off the year with a lightning trip to the Isle of Wight. The criss-crossing railways had not only transformed the land, putting every town within earshot of the chuff-and-chunter, but also accelerated the pace of life. Huxley trained 4,000 miles this year without taking time out of a hectic schedule. No one in history had commuted like this and still held down a regular job.

Or rather two. The vicar of science with his plural livings was incapable of turning down a new parish. Especially a plum parish like the Royal College of Surgeons, with its rich, cadaverous museum. It had been 20 years since the long-haired student had first seen Owen there – walking between the cow-sized armadillo and giant ground sloth, colossal fossils at the entrance which stood testament to Owen's fame. Now Owen's old job fell into Huxley's lap. It was a sweet turn, which capped the anti-Platonic swing at the college.

Huxley had already helped the stolid 30 year-old Crimea-veteran William Henry Flower become Conservator in the museum. A brewery owner's son (and how Huxley sympathized), Flower was a Broad Anglican in the Baden Powell mould. Indeed, Powell was his wife's brother-in-law and William had kept a three-day vigil at Powell's deathbed in 1860. Flower too praised evolution as a cleansing solvent, dissolving the dross which had 'encrusted'

Christianity 'in the days of ignorance and superstition'. Like Powell and the Unitarians he called miracles atheistic for breaking God's causal chain. (Tellingly, Rolleston was always asked the same question when he lectured on Darwinism, 'Was I an Atheist or a Unitarian'?) Darwin had restored the Divine Government's 'greatness and grandeur'. Flower stood with Rolleston, not exactly happy with Huxley's 'combative character', but backing him to the hilt, convinced that Owen offered nothing 'like a theory of creation'.[28]

Huxley supported these liberal Anglicans who disdained the Archetype's 'antique dress'. He had Rolleston elected a Fellow of the Royal Society. 'I go bail', Huxley told Darwin, drumming up support for Flower's FRS, for his 'being a thoroughly good man'. Huxley was consolidating his hold on a broad Darwinian party.

Hence it was Flower, only months in the College of Surgeons himself, who reported the news to Huxley,

> that 'there's not a man in all Athens that can discharge Pyramus' (*i.e.* the Hunterian Professorship) but you . . . I am exceedingly rejoiced myself at the prospect of the new 'Hunterian Professor,' though I don't know what *our* illustrious predecessor will say.

After two decades, Owen had made the college one of the most prestigious in Europe. German princes had it on their itinerary. The world's biggest – dinosaurs and extinct New Zealand moas – were born in his little room upstairs; here the 'Age of Reptiles' took hold, Jurassic mammals came to life and the amphibians found their origin. The college's acquisitions were the most prized anywhere, from platypus eggs to chimpanzee brains. But Owen could only watch as Huxley's supporters moved in. This abrupt transfer of power was a sign of the times, signalling the collapse of his empire of 'Archetypal Ideas'.[29] In five years the Royal College turned from a bastion of Platonism into a bulwark of Darwinism.

Huxley received the news of his Hunterian professorship in Switzerland and took a detour on his way home to look at Dijon's giant armadillo *Glyptodon*. He was already planning his inaugural address on the Surgeons' own showpiece skeleton.[30]

Not that he could sit still when he arrived home. He packed *Man's Place* back into his bag and turned around for Scotland. Playfair had co-opted him for the Royal Commission on Fisheries (his first Royal Commission). So his August holiday was spent steaming up the squally Scottish west coast, talking to the drift-netters at loggerheads with the trawlers' crews. He was looking at ways of increasing yields, and whether stocks could be sustained if fry were taken. The old fishing villages had barely changed for centuries, and it left him acutely aware that he held the livelihoods 'of a great many poor people' in his hands.[31] Of course, his book came home in September, a bit salty but not a word longer.

Man's Place fired the final shot at Owen's misshapen ape brain. Courtly souls were appalled as Huxley accused the intransigent Owen of perjury. But he had to 'get a lie recognised as such'. He needed a spectacle to expose that 'mendacious humbug'. 'I will nail him out like a kite to a barn door', he promised, 'an example to all evil doers'.[32] He was smashing the post-Waterloo consensus which made man sacrosanct and any science touching him a reverent and special case.

At the Cambridge BAAS in October, Huxley – as Chairman of the Zoology Section, 'King in Section D', as Kingsley had it (the section that had seen Wilberforce speak two years earlier) – had an ape brain brought in and Flower dissect out its hippocampus. The nailing was to be a public crucifixion. Of course the newspapers were full of it: everyone wanted more on the 'tremendous issues of life'. Huxley gave Darwinism its exposure and the papers reported him:

> The Times in its leader sailed as near the wind as they
> dared [noted Lyell]. The satire about the Chinese
> ennobling remote ancestors was keen enough . . . Lady
> Bunbury went home from the discussion with Kingsley &
> asked him if he did not think they had been too hard on
> Owen. He said no, I think he deserved the thrashing he
> has got.[33]

A deflated, self-opinionated Owen had his own explanation of Huxley's needling. 'Do you remember the story of the clever young Athenian who had an itch for notoriety?' Owen asked the Oxford professor of medicine. 'He sought the Oracle, and asked "What shall I do to become a great man?" Answer: "Slay one"!'[34]

Hooker thought the proofs of *Man's Place* 'amazingly clever'. Lyell too was dazzled by them. The old Unitarian had been buffeted by the Darwinian gale and hardly knew where he stood. Talk of human evolution titillated and tormented him. The pages were 'a great treat', even though he had been terrified of seeing their like for 30 years. But Huxley's jibe about an opposing army of '*emasculate* monks' was in atrocious 'taste & will do no good'. Lyell urged him not to send 'these *dangerous* sheets to press without Mrs Huxley's imprimatur'. The 'naughty' phrases were struck out. Lyell wanted him to go further, to camouflage his scepticism so as not to ruffle 'peoples feathers'. Do not write as if you were 'running counter to their old ideas'. It was a tall order, effectively a countermand to the militant strategy of the young guard. Nor would Huxley contemplate pandering to the 'peace & make-things-pleasant party'.[35] That was collusion with the peers and parsons, and Huxley promised collaborators a 'hot locus in the lower regions' if he became 'Commander in Chief in their universe'.

He stoked the furnaces too energetically for many. Having set the moral tone he was astonished to find Owen proposed for the Royal Society Council in November. Since 'one of us two is guilty of wilful & deliberate falsehood', he told the Secretary, William Sharpey, 'I did not expect to find the Council . . . throwing even a feather's weight into the scales against me'. But even-handed, genial Sharpey was not blinded by moral outrage; while he saw the 'surpassing beauty' of Owen's archetypes, he thought that Darwin's explanation can only 'exalt our conceptions of creative wisdom'. Owen's appointment was routine. No, stormed Huxley, the question was 'whether any body of gentlemen should admit within itself a person who can be shown to have reiterated statements which are false & which he must know to be false'.

The accusation 'is a *very painful* one', said 74 year-old President Sabine, the chivalrous soul who had helped Huxley in the lean years. The new men had over-stepped the bounds of taste even as they drew in the bounds of science. But Huxley's hounding was deliberate. If 'Truth' legitimated the group's right to self-determination, it had to be seen to be the final arbiter. A gentleman's pact not to pursue the matter was no good. They had to expose the 'grossest piece of scientific knavery ever perpetrated' to undermine Owen's whole toadying counter-ideology.[36]

Owen was appointed to the Council but lost his stature. The world knew it when the papers praised his 'chivalric devotion to error'. And Huxley had proved his point with a tenacity that cost him votes. His tenaciousness raised cheers among the gutsy new breed. But the conservative press saw truth in veneration and decency and experience, not in anatomical facts. Owen's posterior lobes took second place to Huxley's posturing. See how he 'crows and struts', the religious papers sneered. 'Here, then, we have the highest authority in England – the so-called British Cuvier', the *Patriot* railed, 'publicly contradicted by his juniors'. No dirty war has its winners, but the social dislocation and changing values of an industrializing, secularizing society left very real casualties.

Rumours began to fly that Huxley ate babies for breakfast. Some saw only his scything intellect, as if he were a religious vandal and home wrecker. 'And yet', whispered Mrs Tait, wife of the reforming Bishop of London, 'I hear that he is a devoted husband & an affectionate father'. It was an awful incongruity for the orthodox, who equated domestic virtues with Christian principles and equated atheism with immorality. In the old world, science had sung a Divine hymn and supported the Anglican status quo. Huxley represented the new order, whose science offered a new set of upright non-Anglican values. In his own mad pugilistic way, he was proving that evolutionary heterodoxy did not equal moral delinquency.

Still his moral campaign flummoxed the old men. 'Huxley is an exceedingly clever man, and rather an agreeable one; and I believe a good man', old Bunbury recognized, 'but I cannot take very cordially to one entirely without veneration'.[37] Huxley's devotion was of a messier, more modern and ill-defined sort, to the architecture of nature and melioration of ills, but there was no lack of feeling as his eyes filled with tears before the shrine of reason.

His theatrics drew the crowds, happy to see 'their boy' take a poke at the high and mighty. Workers turned up in droves, awed by an intellect able to conjure up exotic pasts, dilate on future glories and maim the hated orthodoxies in between. And Huxley did not disappoint. He drilled through the muddy accumulations of untold aeons to show them the evolution of life. He had his hodmen sink an imaginary shaft beneath the school's foundations, through the gravel beds with their elephant remains and cave tigers ('Rather curious things to fall across in Piccadilly!'). Through the London clay, littered with tropical palms, past turtles, which had paddled in warm lagoons where his workmen now sat on a chilly November night. Through hundreds of feet of sea-floor chalk, with its snapping ichthyosaurs, those reptilian dolphins, down to the deepest beds and first fish. The chain-gang exercise was carried off with plebeian panache.

Huxley was rushed, with no time or inclination to polish and publish these lectures, and such 'a 'umble minded party' that he never imagined that they would sell anyway. But his workers thrived on piracy. An enterprising hack took shorthand notes and rushed the pages to Robert Hardwicke's shop at 192 Piccadilly. Hardwicke was a dab-hand at cost-cutting and 'adventurous' publishing, and he distributed the printed lectures in fourpenny weekly parts.

Piracy was a long and dishonourable tradition. What quicker way to make money while democratizing knowledge? Times were more sedate now and there was a careful gentility to Hardwicke's move (he even asked Huxley's permission). Incomes were rising, steam presses and steam trains were sending cheap books country-wide, and Huxley found his lectures peddled enthusiastically to the elite mechanics and alert clerks addicted to the new *Popular Science Review*. (The sixties saw an explosion of low-brow miscellanies, including Hardwicke's *4d Science Gossip*.) Huge bundles were shifted in the Socialist Hall of Science in the Tottenham Court Road. The radicals loved Huxley's 'spirited, lively, familiar' style; the more so as he was 'confirming our own view of the universe'. But for Huxley it was galling. 'Now, I lament that I did not publish them myself and turn an honest penny', he groaned. Hardwicke 'is advertising them everywhere, confound him'.[38] He ended up having to buy his own pamphlets to post to Darwin.

Week by week they hit the news-stands. No one seemed put off by the top-heavy title, *On Our Knowledge of the Causes of the Phenomena of Organic Nature*. Huxley was making the profoundest science exciting to workers – something that the haughty gents who 'are far above receiving, or earning, weekly wages, have ... failed to attain'. He was plebeianizing the *Origin*.

By 8 December the professor had worked his way right into the crevices of Mr Darwin's thought. After two years of groping and rationalizing, Huxley finally made his back-alley fanciers connect with Darwin's 'struggle for existence'. Their own pigeon selection simulated Nature's weeding and sifting. Huxley tried to use 'struggle' guardedly, 'because some people imagine that the phrase seems to imply a sort of fight'. But in his vivid allegorical way he only heightened the bloody impression. He pictured Napoleon's rag-tag army retreating from Moscow. It arrived at the Beresina river, demoralized, 'everyone heeding only himself, and crushing through and treading down his fellows' to get across, the fittest alone making it – 'every species has its Beresina', he said. Whatever his workers thought of this bleak image, Darwin clapped.

The pamphlets were 'simply perfect', and with Huxley coming round Darwin threw them down

with the reflection, 'What is the good of my writing a
thundering big book, when everything is in this green little
book so despicable for its size?' In the name of all that is
good and bad I may as well shut up shop altogether.

Like all bootlegs they acquired a mystique. With a flourishing low
scientific culture they chalked up impressive sales. Appleton even
had a New York edition out within months, with *On the Origin of
Species* astutely prefixed to the title. Lyell was horrified at Huxley's
loss of royalties and in January 1863 advised him 'to rescue the
copyright of the third thousand'.[39]

But with Christmas past Huxley's mind was on *Man's Place*.
That too was about to hit the stalls.

17

Man's Place

'HURRAH THE MONKEY BOOK has come', Darwin cheered on 18 February 1863. He was driven to distraction by Lyell's *Antiquity of Man* and its strangulated efforts to come to terms with the *Origin*. Huxley promised better things. Lyell 'never rises to the magnificence of Huxley's language', Hooker had to agree. You can read *Man's Place in Nature* '1000 times with fresh delight'.

It was a bad time to publish. The American Civil War had closed Lancashire's cotton mills and the transatlantic book trade was depressed. And Gladstone's economic forecast only put the publishers 'more out of spirits'. With science books aimed at city dwellers and the industrial midlands, everybody prophesied an appalling season.

Not that Williams & Norgate was known for its hard sell. *Man's Place in Nature* sat on a specialist list, appealing to Oxbridge Latinity more than Yankee liturgies. The publisher's titles ranged from Arabic grammars and Sanskrit studies to catalogues of Silurian fossils and (after Huxley's arm-twisting) Spencer's *System of Philosophy*. But Huxley was happy to be wedged between the Old Testament exegetes. And being the *Natural History Review*'s publisher, Williams & Norgate did have the trade contacts.

Huxley's name and the inflammatory subject sold the book. His clever frontispiece itself set teeth chattering. Here was 'skeletonized Man' tripping ahead of his 'grim relatives', the loping train of 'grovelling apes' 'as gleesome as if they were going in procession' to the Palace. This was to become a skeletal icon, caricatured to this day as an ad-man's dream. But that belies its shocking début. It put off the high-brow reviewers. Worse, the book was no technical tome, with its delicacies shrouded in Latin, but written in punchy street prose. That prickliest subject, humanity's origin from ape-like ancestors, was being broached first among the people. And they loved it, even at six shillings. The shops were doing a roaring trade, finding these 'fairy tales of science ... as eagerly demanded' as Wilkie Collins' sensationalist thrillers.

Within a week the publishers were preparing a second thousand, and Huxley called in corrections from 'Miss Henrietta Minos Rhadamanthus Darwin' (sickly Etty, the Darwins' literary stylist). Darwin himself never ceased 'to admire the clearness & condensed vigour' of Huxley's prose. As for the rousing finale of the working-class lecture, 'I declare I never in my life read anything grander'. Like a fine day, a book should end with this sort of 'glorious sunset'.[1]

January's new liberal weekly was the *Reader*, run by Kingsley's Christian Socialist comrade Thomas Hughes, author of *Tom Brown's Schooldays*. It was a new pie which left Huxley looking for an unoccupied finger to poke in. Not finding one he co-opted Dyster's. Tenby's alderman duly wrote his first review, taking his tone from Hal's letters (why should we prefer to be 'modified mud rather than modified monkey') and was gratified to hear Lyell call it 'the best thing that had yet appeared' on *Man's Place*.

Engels tipped off Marx (who knew all about Huxley's workers' lectures), telling him *Man's Place* was 'very good'. Old troopers joyously ran extracts in the *National Reformer*. In full-page editorials they talked of Italy's bloodshed 'to destroy long-standing abuses' and America's war against slavery – and in England the mightiest 'revolution' of all, 'a revolution of mind' signalled by *Man's Place*. The *Reformer*'s was real class warfare with the 'hideous and ugly' Church, a 'war to the death' against 'the tyrants of the mind' and property.[2] Huxley found himself drafted by some coarse drill sergeants.

He dodged the draft and shook this disreputable army. He looked for a gentlemanly engagement with orthodoxy. But for a moment the press seemed stunned into silence by his atrocities. (Wilberforce thought them so extreme as to have saved the Church from self-destruction.) And what response there had been showed an unaccountably 'just appreciation' of the evidence. Polite Oxford was positively diplomatic. The dons were delighted 'to find how very long it must have been ... since we were "Pithecoid"', not that they believed 'we got here by that road'. And Rolleston was 'simply enraptured'.

Huxley was 'astonished to find how little abuse the book has met', only the evangelical *Morning Advertiser* 'having opened fire as yet'. Soon enough the religious tabloids started up. Neanderthal was the '"man" who is without the "living soul", spoken of in Genesis', reckoned the *Advertiser*. The Quakers' *Friend* doubted that he had 'any closer connection with . . . Adam than have the possible inhabitants of the Moon'. Even so they knew that Huxley was defiling 'the sanctity . . . which enshrouds our being'. But these barking 'dogs of St. Ernulphus' were as politically toothless as the radical ranters. What mattered was the urban middle classes, living off the fruits of industry, prosperous, aspiring. Huxley's material explanation of life accompanied the inventions that were changing it so fast. He published as the first underground railway opened at Paddington and London's gigantic new sewage system was set to flush out the medieval diseases. In the world's largest city people were small and life was hectic; change was becoming the norm, and here, in its Piccadilly heart, *Man's Place* dug up the last medieval obstruction. It put modern society at the end of a long whirligig of historical progress.

Huxley's 'lowly-origin, noble-future' image made no sense to the aristocracy. Where was 'our heraldic pomp, our vaunted nobility of descent'? But it summed up bourgeois destiny. Our rise 'reads very much like a Law Lords pedigree in the Peerage', someone saw: 'a remote ancestor' in William the Conqueror's day. 'Seventy fourth in descent a Wig-maker – and then the full-blown Chancellor or Chief Justice'.[3]

Nor did the book do the Huxleys any harm. They were rising past the wig-maker stage themselves. A month later the Court physician was making discreet enquiries about Mrs Huxley's maid Fanny Moore, as a wet nurse for Princess Alice's baby. Hal even found himself paraded alongside the 'other worthless individuals' in Lovell Reeve's *Men of Eminence*. George Grote saw him going to the top – President of the British Association, no less. With the appreciation came the demands: institutes wanted Neanderthal casts. An old shipmate, Revd Robert King, who had jellyfished off the *Rattlesnake* stern with Huxley, wanted ancient flints.[4] And he fished in deeper waters for information on how gorilla-men were to be squared with Genesis.

But the book's rationale still flummoxed many. The 'compensation of future progress will be poor comfort to most of your readers blinded, I suppose, as I am "by traditional prejudices"', was old Lyell's gentle lament. 'I forget the exact words of Popes line about the angels "who view a Newton as we view an ape"'. But angelic future archaeologists looking back on us as savages was cold comfort. We have lost the 'noble pedigree which we dreamt of'.[5]

That was the tone of the reviews, a muted howl; 'candid though heretical', groaned the *Athenaeum*. Some did wonder how he could leave mind and speech out of the story, since it was these which gave Professor Huxley 'that power to instruct, amuse and illustrate, by which he is raised immeasurably above the cleverest ape'.

In the reviews Lyell's *Antiquity* was often roped to *Man's Place*, the one making man 'a hundred thousand years' old, the other giving him 'a hundred thousand apes for his ancestors'.[6] Some lashed these books to the *Essays* as well, with their re-evaluation of Genesis. Society was being swept by tidal waves of dissolvent literature. Old worlds and old documents: the same scientific and historical techniques were being used in their interpretation.

The *Essays* recognized it. Even more extraordinarily, so did the Cornish Bishop of Natal (that new imperial see, created in the lush veld of Africa). The erudite John William Colenso's flock included ostrich-feathered Zulu princes. He stood up for Zulu rights. He allowed converts to live polygamously. He compiled a Zulu-English dictionary – but when he tried to translate Genesis and explain its contradictions he ended up doubting its truth himself. His *Pentateuch* was a sensation; a six shilling tome like Huxley's, but 10,000 were snapped up on publication (showing how much more the Genesis myth meant than the Neanderthal reality). Colenso was derided as a nigger-lover whose charges had paganized him. He was ridiculed for his anti-imperial faith that all men stood equal before God ('what, then, is the good of being a Christian?').[7] In the new Cape Town cathedral he was about to be publicly deposed as bishop. Even now he was in London, appealing against the sentence.

A Zulu bishop who doubted Genesis certainly appealed to Huxley, the more so when he spotted his ruddy face in his own college congregation. (Times *had* changed; Owen had counted Wilberforce's in his.) Colenso listened as Huxley broke up the invertebrates into ever more primary groups, seven now, escaping further from Owen's giant archetypal clusters which seemed such a block to evolution.[8] Or he examined Flower's dissection of a gibbon brain, displayed on a table to show the supposedly absent hippocampus. Intrigued, Huxley visited Colenso's house off Hyde Park (a far cry from his Pietermaritzburg cathedral opening on to the veld). *Man's Place* and the *Pentateuch* seemed odd bedfellows. But they were whipping the 'whole country' into controversies, the *Telegraph* said, over which the Wilberforces 'have lost their hold'. Who doubted a changing world when these books 'are torn from the hands of Mudie's shopmen as if they were novels'? Church heterodoxy was keeping pace with scientific heresy. The realignments told as Rolleston and Stanley petitioned Parliament to end Oxford's Anglican exclusivity and Colenso offered his mitred service to the *Reader*.[9]

The sparks from Huxley's and Lyell's books rekindled the embers of the ape-brain debate, which sputtered like a damp squib. The most sensible commentary on it came in a riotous broadsheet (littered with knowing touches). In this tavern farce, a couple of 'bone and bird-stuffing' costers Tom Huxley and Dick Owen were hauled up before the beak. The scruffs had been caught scrapping, with Huxley yelling you 'lying Orthognathous Brachycephalic Bimanous Pithecus'.

> LORD MAYOR. Are you sure you heard this awful
>   language?
> POLICEMAN X. Yes, your worship . . .
> LORD MAYOR. Did you see any violence used?
> POLICEMAN X. Yes, your worship. Huxley had got a
>   beast of a monkey, and tried to make it tread on
>   Owen's heels – and said 'twas his grandfather . . .
> LORD MAYOR. Did Owen appear much annoyed by this
>   outrage?
> POLICEMAN X. He behaved uncommonly plucky, though
>   his heart seemed broke . . . Never saw a man so mauled
>   before. 'Twas the monkey that worrited him, and
>   Huxley's crying out, 'There they are – bone for bone,
>   tooth for tooth, foot for foot, and their brains one as
>   good as t'other . . .
> As there appeared to be no case against Owen, he was
> allowed to be sworn. Hereupon, Huxley demanded to
> be sworn likewise, but Owen objected, declaring that it
> was impossible to swear a man who did not believe in
> anything . . . Owen, however, was directed to take the
> book in his right hand, whereupon Huxley vociferated,
> 'He does not know a hand from a foot' . . .

'Tom Huxley and his low set', known to include the escaped convict, alias 'John William Natal', played on in the pauper press. On trotted Hooker, 'in the green and vegetable line', 'Charlie Darwin, the pigeon-fancier, and Rollstone', cheering on their barrow boy.[10] Nor did the drunks in the stalls miss the punch-line. Big Dick Owen was one of 'these here standstill Tories', but a nip from 'Uxley's monkey got him going!

The farce, in all its serious forms, toured the globe. At each stop Owen's fortifications were strengthened by the established power brokers. In America the Yale geologist James Dwight Dana thought that our arms were freed for intellectual 'and spiritual service'. Clasped hands were the reverent concomitant of an overarching cerebrum. Wiser Germans hedged their bets. The embryological old-hand Rudolph Wagner supported Owen's ideology and Huxley's facts. But then he believed that brains held no evidence of evolution and science had no impact on faith. And he hoped that getting Huxley into his Göttingen Royal Society sent no message about Darwinism.[11] None wanted to see Huxley suck any Darwinian sustenance out of Owen's brain, but the neural nutriment always seemed to be rising up the straw.

The farce ended in the antipodes, where it played to Melbourne's packed houses. Fresh out from Britain, Owen's protégé George Halford introduced himself as professor of medicine with a talk on the ape's grasping toe. It endeared him to Melbourne's exclusives. With patronage controlled by the Presbyterian Church and an anti-Darwinian Governor he ingratiated himself with the claim that *Man's Place* 'might have been written by the devil'. Huxley's supporters (one straight from Jermyn Street) relayed this 'vulgar claptrap'.[12] As the *Athenaeum* had run pieces on the head, so the Melbourne *Argus* publicized debates on the foot. Halford's pamphlet *Not Like Man* was shipped to London to complete the world cycle. Here the *Lancet* abhorred its coarseness, the one aspect that had not changed during its 25,000 mile trip.

But the serious political appropriation began on the Continent. It was the barking dogs which had German insurgents pricking up their ears. Huxley had always been one of the few British zoologists spared the 'contemptuous comment' of German critics. The barricade socialist Carl Vogt – exiled to Geneva after the 1848 revolution – applauded *Man's Place* as a 'beautiful little book'. He even requested Busk's Stone Age skull illustrations for his own *Lectures on Man*. This would blend Darwinism with his belief in the separate origins of the human races. It would also scrape the depths, with 'simious' skulls from the Dark Ages scurrilously labelled 'Apostle skulls' on the fancy that they belonged to retarded monks. Vogt remained a bruiser. He reported that a 'crowd of young savants had come out' for Darwin in Germany and 'we must support the battle against all the champions of the old school'.[13]

By the time the arch-materialist (and member of Vogt's 1848 corps) Ludwig Büchner asked if he could translate *Man's Place* in July, he found that Victor Carus had done the job.[14] And the *Stellung des Menchen*, out within months, caused a sensation.

Russian militants were even more enthusiastic. Revolutionary politics in the Tsarist autocracy gave Darwin and Huxley an underground cachet. The socialist awakening in the early 1860s saw a stream of banned books smuggled in – easy enough with a bungling censor and so many exiles wandering the West. The student lawyer Vladimir Kovalevskii came to London in 1861–2 to look for books to 'awaken the masses'. He was devoted to the émigré activist Alexander Herzen, and the Russian secret police spotted him at the anarchist Michael Bakunin's London home.[15] He returned to St Petersburg to set up a press specifically to translate Huxley's working-class lecture *On Our Knowledge*, along with books by Darwin, Lyell and Buckle.

But the real interest was in *Man's Place*. Nihilists saw ape origins mock Orthodox spiritualism and relativize moral values, undermining the Tsarist state. They had two separate editions of *Man's Place* in preparation before a Russian *Origin* had appeared. They might have had difficulty with Darwin's competitive, weak-to-the-wall ideology, but Huxley gave them no qualms.

With no despot in Buckingham Palace, the surge of messianic materialism was less splenetic in Britain. But there was a hardening of attitudes as the authorities chased the *Essay*ists and Colenso. Tyndall himself was turning into a glorious cosmological force, gobbling up the ancient heavens in an alarming manner. He swept to the stars, then turned to the Delphic atoms for ultimate answers. Huxley aped his incurable determinism, summing up John's favourite query: 'Given the molecular forces in a mutton chop, deduce Hamlet or Faust therefrom'.

Tyndall's dramatic demands only grew. The one-time pantheist saw us all as souls of fire and children of the sun. He turned atomic evolution and the conservation of force into breathtaking conundrums. The *Origin*, he teased Nettie, merely reflected the ephemera of life.

It is only nibbling at the great question and until Darwin
shews intellect, genius, morality & religion to be latent
among the molecules of a quartersize loaf, and until he is
able to express human affections – the love for example
which you bear to that unhandsome Hal . . . in terms of
the combustion of a tallow candle, I shall take the liberty
of treating his literary productions with sovereign
contempt.[16]

These new explorers were colonizing a vast depersonalized galaxy.
Colenso did not hold a candle to the real dilemma of the age,
Huxley told Kingsley. 'Whether the Gospels are historically true or
not' was a matter of 'small moment in the face of the impassable
gulf between the Anthropomorphism (however refined) of Theology & the passionless impersonality of the unknown &
unknowable'.

As Tyndall flew higher, Hal planted his feet more firmly on the
ground. He matched Tyndall's endless cosmic optimism with
boundless scepticism. 'I know nothing of Necessity, abominate the
word Law', he said in his regular sparring with Kingsley:

I don't know whether Matter is anything distinct from
Force. I don't know that atoms are anything but pure
myths. Cogito, ergo sum is to my mind a ridiculous piece
of bad logic[,] all I can say at any time being 'Cogito'.
The Latin form I hold to be preferable to the English 'I
think' because the latter asserts the existence of an Ego –
about which the bundle of phenomena at present
addressing you knows nothing.

'Is this basis of ignorance broad enough for you?' Whether it was
Kingsley's souls secreting matter, or Mr May's matter perspiring
souls, Huxley had been thrashing at these clingy gossamer cobwebs
masquerading as knowledge since he was a boy. The only sensible
'axiom' was that '*materialism and spiritualism are opposite poles
of the same absurdity*'. Huxley shifted the emphasis from the
ground of existence to the 'great game being played' on it:

the wiser among us have made out some few of the rules
of the game . . . We call them 'Laws of Nature' and
honour them because we find that if we obey them we
win something for our pains. The cards are our theories
. . . But what sane man would endeavour to solve this

problem: given the rules of a game & the winnings to find
whether the cards are made of pasteboard or gold leaf?[17]

By shifting from reality to the rules, Huxley was stacking the deck
in his own social poker game. And Kingsley knew it.

The coarsest attacks on *Man's Place* were closest to home. As the
American Civil War raged the doom-mongering about racial conflict inspired a charismatic reactionary with a Ph.D, James Hunt,
to found the Anthropological Society. Hunt and fellow Confederate
sympathizer Charles Carter Blake damned bleeding-heart liberalism and missionary philanthropy; with equality 'a mere dream',
they abominated talk of black suffrage (and Huxley's fellow-travel-
ler John Stuart Mill *was* talking about it), and the socialist
environmentalism which spawned the 'rights-of-man mania'. The
society was set up in 1863 to measure and maximize racial differences. In their white supremacist view, humanity was so many
warring species. They denounced all talk of common ancestry;
black and white men, Hunt proclaimed, came from different
'species of apes'.

Hunt was hissed at the BAAS for his slaving views. But he hit
back from his racist base and used Nature's 'ironclad laws' to keep
the slaves in chains. In the wake of *Man's Place*, ancestral purity
was an emotive issue. White men had their own bloodline and
Blake accused Huxley of polluting it and using his 'eloquence' in
'lowering "Man's place in nature"'. Naked racism was endemic in
the age: even Lyell had balked at the thought of black ancestors:
wasn't it repugnant to 'nearly all men'? Surely to teach it 'w^d.
ensure the expulsion of a Prof.'? Huxley proved him wrong but
that did not stop the hate mail. Darwin himself was pelted by
'those of us who respect our ancestors & repudiate ... the
contamination of Negro blood'.[18]

The first number of Hunt's *Anthropological Review* carried
Blake's 'coarse attack' on *Man's Place*. Huxley instantly resigned
his Honorary Fellowship and dismissed them as 'quacks'. The
battering continued in the *Edinburgh Review* as Blake compared
Huxley to his rabble, holding aloft d'Holbach's inflammatory
System of Nature (that inspiration to the democrats during the
French Revolution).[19] He saw Huxley sliding into a cesspit of
'absolute materialism' and 'atheism' from whose boggy depths the
cosmos was 'quite unintelligible'.

The war had thrown up a rival faction which threatened the

Darwinian hegemony. Huxley switched to the 20 year-old Ethno-logical Society (a more benevolent, protectionist forum whose adepts had always looked to a single origin for the races and environmental causes of their diversity). In the old abolitionists' stronghold Lubbock took over the Presidency, and Busk backed him on the Council, as did Huxley, not that he had much truck with the old philanthropy.[20] The religious and racist complexities of human origins were leaving Huxley's clique feeling more be-sieged than ever.

Summer days saw him snowed under with manuscripts, with a glacier's weight of labyrinthodonts and fish crushing him. The added burden of the *Natural History Review* finally overcame him. Realizing that it had failed to 'appeal to the masses' he lost interest and had the 'Commissariat' hire two editors. 'In spite of working like a horse', he explained to Darwin, 'or if you prefer it, like an ass' 'I find myself scandalously in arrear'. He had publishers hanging on his every promise, and each was promised a textbook. Williams & Norgate were announcing his students' *Atlas of Com-parative Osteology* (that medical sepulchre of skulls, broken down to illustrate his ideas on their homological parts). Churchill was publishing his College of Surgeons' lectures as a book. *That* 'will be out very shortly', he boasted to Hooker. 'N.B. This is not one of my ordinary book promises in which shortly may mean 7 years'. He was pestered by magazine editors for articles 'which you know you can knock off in a moment'. Giant armadillos, evening lectures on zoology and trips to provincial institutes took up any spare hours, while 'Colensoism and botheration about Moses' filled in the minutes.[21] The back burners were steaming, the front burners boiling over, and uncooked morsels sat in pots all over the stove.

And there they remained as he traipsed around Tyneside on fisheries business (Huxley was diligent in his commission duty, although the pay eased his way). His return only saw matters made worse. He talked to Macmillan about turning his Saturday night physiology lectures into a textbook as well.

Every publisher's advance brought him nearer a break-even point. But still he reckoned without more family tragedy.

'My poor old brother & I never had an angry word in our lives', he sobbed as he oversaw the undertakers. George had been support-ive from the day Tom stepped down the *Rattlesnake* gangplank;

the one who had loved little Noel as his own and made North Bank a home-from-home. To Tom the loss was 'larger than I had imagined'. George had gloried in his brother's rise; eating his words as Tom made his name – and his pay – by science. But he had 'been at deaths door' with tuberculosis for years and, although only 53, had wasted pitifully. The 'horror of the thing was the way of his death', Tom said sadly. Brother Jim was isolated in every sense in his asylum. He was becoming withdrawn himself, leaving Tom to carry the load.

George's business affairs were in a mess, and Tom had to let 41 North Bank, with all its memories. Then he made the final sacrifice for the brother who had given him so much. He sold his most treasured possession, the memento that had ironically proved to George that there was money in science. Tom sold his Royal Medal. Its £50 gold value cleared the debt.

The role of family banker and educator had already devolved on Tom. His sister Ellen, Cooke's widow, was drinking away his annual allowance. Then came her 'pathetic letters' begging for more. The nagging fear that 'some awful scandal' would break around her always kept Tom on edge. He was paying for Ellen's daughter Alice to study at Nettie's old finishing school in Germany. (She was expected to be a governess.) He sent Lizzie cheques in America. Brother Jim's daughter Katy, now 16, was also dependent on the family purse. Jim's first marriage had been a disaster 'and ended in a virtual though not a legal separation'. After Katy's mother died, Jim had remarried another 'woman who was much his inferior in social position & education'. The stepmother disliked Katy and virtually cast her out. So Hal and Nettie opened their door. 'She is really a very good girl', and her situation was very sad, Hal admitted, but his salary was stretching thinner all the time. This retinue of dependants left huge worries. With his massive output he had earned £1124 7s 10d in 1862 and he still ended the year £227 in the red.

The care of George's widow Polly and Heathorn's brewery debts now increased the burden. With the birth of baby Nettie on 21 September 1863 Hal had five children of his own and they were 'a devouring fire, eating up the present and discounting the future'. Given their mother's pernicketiness, there was also a fast turnover of cooks, nannies, maids and nurses (they trooped in regularly from an agency, and just as regularly out again).

It wasn't only with a heavy heart that Tom had George buried alongside Noel. It was with a realization that so many now depended on his science. Professionalism and power were no longer a tyro's ideal. They were the family's bread-and-butter. He trudged back to Tynemouth, borne down by 'sorrow & worry of every description'.[22]

He was counting the pennies again in March 1864 as Churchill published his *Lectures on the Elements of Comparative Anatomy*. The book's turnaround staggered everybody; Huxley had devised, dissected and delivered his Hunterian lectures on the classification of life, and cast them into a 300-page book, all within 12 months.

Before anyone had read it he was deep into his 1864 course. He burned the midnight oil, studying the college's skeletons or bottled embryos in his top-floor room. Flower watched him dissect: nothing flashy or 'finikin', but rapidly going 'to the point he wished to ascertain with a firm and steady hand'.[23] In the still of the night – as the gaslights played eerily on the giant's skeleton – he was the only soul about. In his quiet 'oasis', only the bell of Lincoln's Inn Chapel reminded him of the passing hours.

The next day would see him announcing his findings 'in that famous black gown with the red facings'. Scott 'will recollect [it] very well', he told Lizzie proudly. In Scott's day it was draped about Owen. Huxley was now delivering Owen's lectures as well as his own in Jermyn Street. He was driving himself into the ground. 'How often I have wished that he had some capital that he might do only original work', Nettie sighed, '& that he might rest, when he did not feel well'. The leisured Darwins were cruising along nicely on £10,000 a year interest. Nettie had seen them: the squire pottering, poking at his seeds, strolling around the Sand-walk; Emma reading Huxley's *6d* pamphlets to 12 year-old Horace, and ending with the refrain: 'I wish he would write a book'. Not *Lectures*, a proper book, 'something that people can read; he does write so well'. But a huge tome was the product of freedom and fortune. Everyone sympathized. 'If he had leisure like you and me', Lyell wrote, 'what a position he would occupy!' It was hard for Nettie not to be envious, seeing Hal 'eaten up with work'. 'Had he like Darwin ... private means – what work in his own special line' he might accomplish. 'But is of no use wishing for the impossible'.[24]

Huxley had hoped to generate income in America. But with war tariffs and a new US income tax sales were slow. He tapped Spencer's contact Edward L. Youmans, an energetic evolutionary salesman and go-between for English authors. Huxley's Appleton editions of *On Our Knowledge* and *Man's Place* had met with enthusiasm from 'earnest progressives', Youmans reported, but

> they were shamefully abused by the majority of the papers
> in which they were noticed. Agassiz the scientific autocrat
> of this continent led off in his organ the Atlantic Monthly
> . . . and the signal being given from the Cambridge
> watchtower the clergy echoed and re-echoed it . . . from
> one end of the land to the other.[25]

The war in America was spreading its hardship. With cotton supplies interrupted, famine raged in Lancashire. But for Lyell and Darwin the price was cheap. 'If the result . . . could be the abolition of slavery by the year 1900', Lyell said after Lincoln's Emancipation proclamation, 'it would be worth a heavy debt and many lives'. Tory doom-mongering about a black insurrection made it a hard line to hold. Even Huxley's *Saturday Review* expected a slave revolt of 'unrelenting ferocity'. It pushed much of the British press on to the Confederate side, to the uncomprehending dismay of New Yorkers.

Support for the North ranged from Darwin's warm sentimentality to Huxley's cool politics. Huxley was from the cynical generation which scorned the 'nigger philanthropists'. True, the abolitionists had appeal. They escorted fugitive, chain-rattling slaves to mass rallies to whip up support for the North. But in the 1860s they faced a harder racism. It was reinforced by the Arthurian folk myths of national character. And the evangelical revival fostered a new ethnocentrism, with its image of the 'unregenerate savage'. The onus switched from breaking the slave's chains to saving his soul. Stiggins' ideal of Christianized negro gentlemen seemed to be receding.

Huxley had to fight for his pro-North principles with a cold logic. He was up against a hysterical war propaganda, with the Tory *Standard* tarring his North-loving, nigger-releasing traitors as

> Atheists, Socialists, advocates of 'free love', or universal
> licentiousness, of women's rights, and every other
> abomination or absurdity which found favour in infidel
> France, in philosophical Germany, and in democratic
> America, but which religious and loyal Englishmen abhor
> and loathe.[26]

In another way Huxley trod on eggshells. Lizzie was now in

Montgomery, Alabama. Her husband, Dr Scott, was practising again, having been employed as the post surgeon. His Confederate forces had been routed in Tennessee after Grant's victory at Chattanooga. Their 15 year-old son Tom – the boy Huxley had never seen – was assisting his father in the army hospital. Lizzie's agonizing accounts had Tom's 'warmest sympathy, so far as the fate of the south affects you'. 'My heart goes with the south', he explained, but 'my head with the north'. There was none of Darwin's fury at the slave's plight; the shifting attitudes told in Tom's words:

> I delight in the energy and self-sacrifice of your people;
> but for all that, I cannot doubt that whether you beat the
> Yankees or not, you are struggling to uphold a system
> which must, sooner or later, break down.
>
> I have not the smallest sentimental sympathy with the
> negro; don't believe in him at all, in short. But it is clear
> to me that slavery means, for the white man, bad political
> economy; bad social morality; bad internal political
> organization, and a bad influence upon free labour and
> freedom all over the world . . .
>
> All this must jar upon you sadly, and I grieve that it
> does so.[27]

He had been fighting the point publicly for months, after raising it in his Hunterian Lectures. There was nothing in the anatomy of blacks to justify slavery, and only absurdity in the belief that they were a separate species. The smoke of battle wafted through the College of Surgeons. He spoke as no egalitarian, but he held that slavery was corrupting and the North is

> justified in any expenditure of blood, or of money, which
> shall eradicate a system hopelessly inconsistent with the
> moral elevation, the political freedom, or the economical
> progress of the American people.

He waved Hunt's ugly parody of a paper, 'The Negro's Place in Nature'. Its 'preposterous ignorance' spoke volumes about 'the slaveholding interest'. He ripped into its idiocies: that ape-like blacks had elongated heels and could not stand upright, and hair that originates in three follicles! One African doctor James Horton wondered if Hunt had actually seen a black man. An escaped slave, William Craft, made sure that Carter Blake had; he stood upright at the 1863 BAAS, his 'handsome presence' contrasting with the 'mean-looking' Blake, and chopped up his ape-comparisons to rapturous applause. Huxley's anti-slavery rationalizations weren't too strong for the Ladies' London Emancipation Society, which repackaged them in a penny tract.

Hunt, that 'low bred ill instructed imposter', was loathed by the Darwinians. 'I dare say the brute is paid by Confederates to lie as he does', Rolleston seethed. He actually was. The Anthropologicals had a Confederate agent on their Council, who used a slush fund to channel money from the Richmond government.

Huxley never rested his liberation case on anatomy. But the *Reader* applauded his 'doctrine of freedom' and concluded that he had made 'his physiological definition of the Negro's place among men equivalent to an earnest plea for Negro emancipation'.[28]

Huxley made the most of the surgeons' resources. His workroom was a charnel house strewn with peeling lemur muscles and gorilla tendons. But the topic everyone wanted to hear about was cave men. In class he insisted that Neanderthal was no more a 'missing link' or 'midway' to an ape than someone who walked '1 mile [up] the North Road was midway between London & York'.

So where were the ape-men? Wallace was for sending dyak-led expeditions to Borneo to find them. The region was in imperial hands and being opened up as a coaling station on the India-Sydney run. Its lignite deposits had been shown in Huxley's lab to be perfect steam fuel, and Lyell agreed that Borneo's caves might contain equally precious deposits of 'extinct ourangs, if not the missing link itself'.

What fossils existed were being wrenched this way and that. Carter Blake considered the Neander man a deformed hermit who hid out in the caves. Others made him the first non-sapient human – *Homo neanderthalensis*.[29] Or even a distinct genus, a semi-conscious being languishing in 'brute benightedness', ape-like and without any conception of his Creator.

Such extremes were unlikely. Huxley obtained a cast of Neanderthal's brain, and it was much bigger than expected. So big that it 'might have contained the brains of a philosopher', said the Duke of Argyll, the Lord Privy Seal who took as much interest in Nature's laws as Palmerston's and clung to any proof of a more exalted past. But the public's mind was set. As Busk worked on a second Neanderthal skull in the summer of 1864, from a quarry in the Rock of Gibraltar, the press pictured a brutish ape-man. Despite squashing this gothic fiction, Huxley could not resist dashing off a sketch of the hairy new *Homo Herculei Columnarum*, with grasping toes, brutal stoop and tail stump![30]

He was 700 miles north in August 1864, passing huge granite outcrops screaming with sea birds. Leaving the Orkney Islands off the north Scottish coast he headed to the Shetlands on the clanking Fisheries vessel *Salamis*. He gripped the rails as it churned through the North Sea swell. Always he was a distant Londoner, and the local fisher-folk were reticent about talking to Commissioner Huxley. But he did his best, investigating net-meshes, fry and the damage done by beam-trawling.

The Shetlands wilderness gave a new perspective to life in the bustling metropolis. The horizons closed in as his train chugged past 'miles of house-tops'. Three million people now lived in London's sprawling terraces. Huxley was back to the traffic jams and rush hours, 'hideous, vicious, cruel, and above all overwhelming', as Henry James exclaimed of this 'dreadful, delightful city'.[31]

In November 1864, after years of abortive efforts,[32] Huxley finally created an invisible club. He brought together a robust group, all of a mind on Darwinism and Colensoism. He needed to pull his cadre together. Work was a centrifugal force pinning them to their posts. We 'have not seen your ugly old phiz for ages', he would write to Hooker, 'and should be comforted by an inspection thereof'. Hooker's father at Kew was ailing, and he himself was rushed off his feet by 'concerns domestic, scientific, social & official'. He stopped setting the teachers' botany exams for the 'Science & Tarts Department'. Huxley swore by science exams as the best form of accreditation; he was even trying to get them extended to middle-class schools, spreading science's power base right into the heart of the classroom. With the Oxbridge classicists condemning any concession to the industrial middle classes as 'a dangerous state of things', he needed Hooker's help.[33]

Huxley called a meeting at St George's Hotel, close to the Royal Institution, on 3 November. The greatest constellation of New Reformers came together. Hooker was lured in, and the omnipresent Tyndall (he and Hal had become 'a sort of firm' in the public mind). There was Hirst (about to take the physics chair at University College), Busk and Lubbock, and Spencer too. The group was completed by Edward Frankland (Tyndall and Hirst's fellow student at Marburg, and the new chemistry professor at the Royal Institution). These men had grown up on the perimeter, in London's medical schools, German universities or around the midlands Chapel; Lubbock being the oddity as an Old Etonian. None was Oxbridge educated; but this *was* an elite. They were the new intellectual clerisy, slim and fit after an evolutionary sauna. Not all the members were academics – Spencer lived by the pen, Lubbock by the ledger. And to the eight the mathematician and Queen's Printer William Spottiswoode was later added. In clubbable London this was the most elite club of all, with nine members and a closed entry book.

'Amongst ourselves there is a perfect outspokenness', Hirst said. And they showed it. Militancy was increasing on all sides, and they met as the conservative outrage grew at *Essays and Reviews*' non-miraculous Christianity. Two of the *Essays*' authors had been convicted of heresy. When the judgment was overturned on appeal, 'dismissing hell with costs', there was uproar in the parishes. Wilberforce drew up a petition declaring that 'the whole Canonical Scriptures' was the literal 'Word of God', and almost half the nation's clergy signed. He presented it to the Church Convocation, which formally condemned the book.

A group of evangelical chemists, led by Capel Berger, the Plymouth Brethren paint manufacturer, took their own petition to the BAAS, demanding that the Association 'maintain a harmonious alliance between Physical Science and Revealed Religion'. They were sick of Huxley's 'dangerous clique' baiting parsons with the glee 'a small boy feels when he is tying a tin kettle to a dog's tail'.[34]

Wilberforce's Convocation and Berger's petition put the fire into Huxley's night conclave in November. All present shared a 'devotion to science, pure and free, untrammelled by religious dogma'. And that explains some noticeable absences. The older Unitarians Lyell and Carpenter were out.

No other nine-member Club could have written 'a scientific Encyclopaedia'. No other nine members could have staffed a German Technical University. But that was not the most significant point. This was no longer an outsider cadre trying to break in, but an insider caucus spreading out. For all its scientific exclusivity, the club had direct access to the City, Parliament, medicine, industry and the liberal Church – to the cultural heart of the country. Huxley's irregulars had become a National Force.

Various clever names were canvassed, none cleverer than Huxley's 'Blastodermic Club'. (It sounded like hellfire but referred to the germ of 'future organization'.) Anonymity suggested '*x*' to Mrs Busk (that unsung hero, one of the background wives – or *yv*'s, as the joke went – occluded from view). The image of mock freemasonry appealed and 'X' was adopted. As the masters of cultural politics, they would snatch Science from noble patrons' hands and put it on a par with Medicine and the Church. They would dine at 6 pm. on the first Thursday of each month, and then take a post-prandial stroll to the Royal Society, which met at 8.30, where their plans for altering Council procedures would soon tip the balance of power.[35]

Liaising with them were Flower and Rolleston. The liberal Church was still pacing liberal Science. Stanley was now '*the* Dean' to the group: the new Dean of Westminster. He was godfather to the Flower children and invited them to romp in the warm Deanery after chilly services. The Abbey opened its doors to the X. When Tyndall wrote against miracles in Lewes' new *Fortnightly Review*, Stanley – having to conduct a cattle plague ceremony – asked him to devise a 'prayer in which the heart might express itself without putting the intellect to shame'. And, finding a Roman sarcophagus in the crypt, he brought Huxley in to verify that its occupant was genuine.

It was Stanley who recommended the *Antiquity of Man* to Queen Victoria, although presumably not *Man's Place*. But Huxley's tome was finding its own royal by-way. In Berlin Lyell learned that the Princess Royal of Prussia was 'very much *au fait* at the "Origin" and Huxley's book'.[36] Whether or not the Queen was amused, profane fingers were touching the throne. The Dean even invited Ramsay to investigate the Abbey's Coronation Stone; like the zoologist who would dissect a nightingale to understand its song, the hammerers analysed the sandstone to cut through its myth-shrouded origin.

Ahead lay peaks to be scaled. The Xs were an indomitable bunch, used to Alpine faces – Huxley and Tyndall had introduced Lubbock to the exhilaration of the climb a couple of years earlier, marching him 12,000 feet up the Galenstock in five hours. But the deepest crevasses lay in Piccadilly. Lubbock and Carpenter had tried to obtain the Royal Society's 'ancient olive crown', the Copley Medal, for Darwin in 1862 and 1863. But the old gents had bridled at 'crowning anything so unorthodox as the "Origin"' and pointedly honoured his old Cambridge teacher Adam Sedgwick instead in 1863. Even though the reformers secured it for Darwin in 1864, the President Sabine doctored his speech and removed the *Origin* 'from the grounds of our award'. 'Lord have mercy on S.', was all Hooker could say as a furious Lubbock, Huxley and Busk tore into him. Huxley now mooted cutting the President's election term.

As the ruffled feathers subsided, Darwin – his stomach heaving at a hint of controversy – had Busk pass the medal to his worldly brother Erasmus, who found it 'rather ugly to look at, & too light to turn into candlesticks'. But it came with Huxley's blessing. And that, replied Darwin, was 'the real medal to me & not the round bit of gold'.[37]

The X's second act was to issue a notorious manifesto. The opportunity arose with another paper. Tom Hughes, working with Nettie's Revd Llewelyn Davies and about to become Lambeth's Liberal MP, wanted Huxley to shake up the loss-making *Reader*. Tyndall joined Hal on the board, as did Darwin's statistical cousin Francis Galton, eager for experience of 'seamy' hack work. The editor Norman Lockyer was a born organizer, as befits a clerk in the War Office. He had 'his heart in the business' and his 'science already in the right groove'. The weekly would become a stump for science, bigger than the *Westminster*'s, better than the *Saturday Review*'s; a proper publicist's soap-box, putting science right up with the *belles-lettres* in British culture. The *Reader* might be a 'pig in a poke', but the Xs could pull him out '& make him a comely grunter'. It was revamped and recapitalized, with Spencer touting £100 shares. Hughes and Davies paid up, as did five X-Clubbers. By late November they had 'it in hand'. Huxley was 'a director of the Reader Cº. (limited)'.[38]

Circumstances shaped the conditions for Huxley's manifesto. The buy-out coincided with Disraeli's exotic performance in Oxford's Sheldonian Theatre. What with Darwin, *Essays*, Colenso and Huxley, 'Materialism', Disraeli knew, was 'in the ascendant'. To his cherubic delight it left the bishops' privileges teetering on the truth of the Old Testament. That had the Church's Jewish defender flouncing around in an outrageous wideawake hat, winding up the Tory faithful: 'Is man an ape or an angel?' he asked Wilberforce. 'My Lord, I am on the side of the Angels'. The Xs relished *Punch*'s depiction of this Jewish angel, even if it did dignify a 'disgrace to the country'.

Further afield, the conservative mood was hardening. In Europe, liberalism meant emancipation, anticlericalism, unfettered science and freedom of conscience. There was a romance to it: London's Whig Duchesses adored the Italian liberator Garibaldi, whose victories did so much to unify Italy, on his 1864 visit. Mobbing crowds of 500,000 equated liberalism with liberation. No one could deny the mood. One man tried: a good, inept, undiplomatic soul, Pope Pius IX. Horrified at events (not least the threat to the Papal States from Italian troops) he issued an encyclical and Syllabus of Errors. It damned the 'evil' age, with its 'free progress of science'. He refused to reconcile Rome with such 'progress, with liberalism, and with modern civilization'. Political impotence was sending the Pope towards a proclamation of Papal infallibility.

No one doubted that His Holiness had Darwin in mind. Nor that Huxley was a spectre. Not, anyway, after Cardinal Wiseman issued a Pastoral denouncing those who would put 'a solitary cranium . . . in the scale' against Scripture. And hadn't Huxley given men 'the matured intelligence' and women the 'ripened graces' of baboons? But the Pope had attacked English liberalism, and Britannia whipped her skirts behind the Whitworth gun, to flirt with fusilier Huxley. The 'Pope is a glorious old ass', he smiled, 'and I trust he may live a thousand years to go on doing us good'.[39]

It dictated the *Reader*'s snorting response. The covert policy was one of 'slashing attacks to right and left'. As the proprietors took turns to write anonymous leaders, the grunter's broad backbone creaked. With Huxley's on 31 December 1864 it snapped. His rival 'encyclical' on 'Science and "Church Policy"' sent his Anglican partners into a spin. The Church Policy was of course Disraeli's, and the editorial a thunderous attack on his 'electioneering' buffoonery. Huxley damned 'political intriguers', and none more than Disraeli, whose 'grotesque' pandering to the political bishops left him 'patronizing Science for its froth and scum' – its steam engines and telegraphs – while 'scorning its essence and the foundation of its human worth'. He pilloried Disraeli's belief that 'the scoffing light-horsemen of the eighteenth century have been beaten off, and the old traditions have emerged from the smoke not much hurt', when truly 'the broken squadrons of Voltairean cossacks fly only to disclose the heads of solid columns of warriors, disciplined', armed and ready.

The military metaphor got its edge from these party political tensions. This was no church-baiting in a social vacuum. Nor was religion at issue. Her 'unshakeable throne' was in the 'deeps of man's nature', and from it comes our sense of awe at nature's grandeur. But Genesis, the 'old traditions', the incarnations of gods, Disraeli's angels – 'theology' in a word – that was a debased branch of history, amenable to test, indeed tested and found wanting. As such, science had no 'intention of signing a treaty of peace with her old opponent, nor of being content with anything short of absolute victory and uncontrolled domination over the whole realm of the intellect'.[40] Never had such a demand been heard in a respectable weekly. It stretched the Xs' ecumenical alliance to the limit.

Rolleston withdrew his support. The '"old Traditions" are' *not* 'likely to be absorbed or superseded' by science. And the 'Unknowable' was a provocative misnomer, when God 'has partly revealed Himself' in Jesus Christ.[41] The fainthearts were dropping away, Huxley told Darwin, but 'the revolution . . . is not to be made with rose-water'.

Huxley's scepticism ran deeper than even this piece let on. During the evangelical revival, with atheism execrated as a social evil, he built a camouflaging stockade with philosophically defensible supports. Look again, he urged Rolleston. 'The fact is that you have read into the article what you know or think you know of my opinions . . . there is not a word in that article opposed to any forms of belief in a revelation of the Unknowable . . . All that I affirm is that all these beliefs & traditions will have to find a scientific basis & that those which cannot . . . will have to go'.[42] Huxley was not reaching for common ground, but annexing it.

Darwin twigged that the 'capital' piece was Huxley's doing. On receiving Huxley's New Year photograph the next day he replied, 'it makes you look too black & solemn as if facing a bench of Bishops'.[43]

Huxley's son Leonard was not to be lost in a 'harem of sisters'. Another boy was born two weeks later, on 14 January 1865. 'He is to be our Benjamin the child of our old age'. Hal and Nettie were coming up for 40, with six children, and Henry, as they called him, was to be 'positively the last – and a counterpoise to his brother who would otherwise be ruined by the worship of his mother & sisters'. Or Hal hoped the last. But, he told a clerical friend, the 'trees of the Lord are full of sap'.

Nettie was flourishing, 'bless her old heart'. She had her work cut out, organizing a house full of domestics and children, always entertaining and always pregnant. She had returned to her old 'energetic' state, Hal reported. 'And she had need [to]; for what with Servants & what with the price of butcher's meat the mother of six children has a severe struggle in life'. And she had to minister to Hal. The 'lodger' spent his nights among the workers or 'amidst the "lights" (& livers too)' of his lab, only to stagger home late, moaning 'Lectures, Lectures, lectures till I am well nigh lecture mad'.[44] And she would apply 'hot iron & mustard poultices' to ease his aching shoulders.

Those scapulas were overworked as he waved diagrams in his huge auditorium. In 1865 his interests were shifting again. As he demonstrated his skull-bisecting innovations to the Ethnological Society he moved further from ape origins to the living races. Having made human history open-ended with *Man's Place*, raising new possibilities about the origin and antiquity of today's peoples, he became the target for barrow excavators and midden-mound explorers.[45] Archaeologists sent boxes of skulls, and expats shipped aboriginal relics to compare with Neanderthal man.

As usual he tested his new course, 'The Races of Mankind', on his Monday night workers first. (He brought his own reporter this time.) His working men were adoring. One would crave an autograph 'to show my mates'; cabbies refused his fare ('proud to have driven you, sir'). All felt that he has 'done me and my like a lot of good'. Street atheists were delighted that 'science was still marching in their direction' and that the professor was 'among the first friends of our faith'.[46]

Others lacked his savvy with this sort of audience. At times the grave Owen seemed to lack any political sensitivity. When *he* lectured the radical Quakers in industrial Newcastle and

> kept the whole assembly waiting for a long while, he
> apologized by saying, 'I have been detained at
> Ravensworth Castle'. Lord Ravensworth being a strong
> Conservative this Flunkeyism greatly disgusted the self-
> made men who received Gladstone as a King & have
> covered the Tyne Banks for 20 miles with Alkali works &
> Ship Yards.[47]

But Huxley was more sensitive. His workers even took up a collection once, thinking he was not paid for his talks. He sometimes looked as though he needed it. Rheumatic arms were nothing to the poisoned fingers as he grasped nettles. After our animal ancestry, race and class were the new emotive issues.

Emancipation and citizenship were the great questions, for black slaves *and* oppressed whites. But he faced a hardening climate. Even the *Saturday Review* pictured the Bethnal Green hovel-dwellers as a permanent 'caste apart'. The pauper was stuck in 'the condition in which God has placed him, exactly as the negro is expected to remember the skin which God has given him'. Enslaved blacks and downtrodden whites were coming to be seen as 'perpetual inferiors', fit only 'to toil that another may reap the fruits'.

At times the exotic faces on Bloomsbury and Piccadilly streets belied this denial of any faculty for improvement. Hindus were graduating in medicine from University College. (And, the ultimate irony, its first ever prize in English Law was taken by a Trinidadian ex-slave.) Japanese students were sitting chemistry classes there in 1865.[48] Nor did Britain's own 'under-world' see itself perpetually bonded. Huxley's workers expected nothing short of millennial progress culminating in the vote.

Between the expectations of labour and race and the fears of the elite Huxley's was the mediating voice; the judicial interpreter of Nature's discriminatory laws. The rights of working-class women – the slaves of the slaves – only pushed liberalism harder. The education of women was a pressing problem. He knew it. His own cook was illiterate and he had to read recipes 'to her *slowly*'.[49] Huxley turned 40 on 4 May 1865 as Lee and the last Confederate generals surrendered in America. 'The question is settled', the slaves were freed, leaving the 'laws of social gravitation' to operate unhindered. Stability was ensured, he wrote in his *Reader* piece 'Emancipation – Black and White', for it is

> incredible that, when . . . our prognathous relative has a
> fair field and no favour . . . he will be able to compete
> successfully with his bigger-brained and smaller-jawed
> rival, in a contest which is to be carried on by thoughts
> and not by bites.

That was his line – on workers, on blacks, on women – freedom for the oppressed, with the oppressor reassured that 'Nature's old salique law will not be repealed, and no change of dynasty will be effected'. To each side he pleaded natural laws and Cobdenite fair competition, making his the priestly mouthpiece of power brokerage. Of course women's education had to come. The booms as the persistent young Elizabeth Garrett hammered on London University's door had an awful echo. Let them graduate, injustice should not be added to inequality, he urged, and 'the "golden hair" will not curl less gracefully outside the head by reason of there being brains within'.[50] Let them have careers – Nature will hold them to a new station.

Incitement for one side, soothing balm for the other; Huxley made 'Nature' speak through his new priesthood. Black ancestors, workers' unions, women's education – it was a frightening time for timid souls. With the Church-sanctioned hierarchies shattered in Heaven and on Earth the old certainties were gone. Huxley was inscribing Nature's laws on the Tablets now. Obedience to his science was the Word from the Mount, keeping the command structure intact.

This was not power to the people. It was power to the professionals.

1865–1870

The Scientific Swell

18

Birds, Dinosaurs & Booming Guns

HUXLEY'S LABORATORY WAS a necrophiliac's delight, with its peeling tendons and pickled brains. And the 'General', as his students nicknamed him in the late 1860s, was positively intimate with his bones. He would hang his arm over the shoulder of a skeleton and take its hand as he talked. Then, turning to the blackboard, with a flash of strokes and smudges, he would transform one animal into another before their eyes.

Everybody's pupils became his protégés. His science was modern and tinged by the controversial. His responses were fast and as often as not Biblical. The ornithologist Alfred Newton, shrieking from the surgeons' gallery that he had found extinct great auk's eggs, would hear Huxley's shout that Newton 'was like Saul who went out to seek his father's asses and found a Kingdom'. A pugilistic fame put Huxley in the papers almost weekly. As the General organized flanking attacks on a posturing Disraeli or plodding Owen, or moved against the cotton racists or reactionary church, as he strove, above all, to put science's Whitworth gun at the front of Britain's cultural armoury, he grew in legendary status among the students.

University men migrated over for his lectures in Piccadilly or Lincoln's Inn Fields. They talked of his 'agreeable voice', and his homely style, which made abstruse subjects sound 'natural'. Flashes of 'caustic humour' would put 'an extra gleam in his bright eyes', or a 'gravity of look' would give a point depth. He 'never posed, was never starched, or prim' and it made the difference. Proficiency had come with age. No longer did he get up to speak with 'my tongue cleaving to the roof of my mouth'. Nor did he cling to his manuscript 'as a shipwrecked mariner to a hencoop'. Practice had given his public talks the fluidity of poetry readings – hence Dickens' joke, putting a false book-back on his shelf, marked '*The Collected Poems of T. H. Huxley*'. Of course Huxley's 'lucidity' had all the 'legerdemain of the performer'. Off-the-cuff ease required working at; like his writing, its didactic simplicity was the result of hard labour. But all the students agreed that the General had no equal.

Rarely, however, did he moot evolution in class. Nor, despite those fathers 'who dreaded sending young men to him, fearing lest their [sons'] religious beliefs should be upset', did he broach theology. Only occasionally did he lapse (and the students waited for those moments). He might point to the heart's mitral valve, 'so called', he said, 'from a supposed resemblance to a bishop's mitre. You know the thing I mean – a sort of cross between a fool's cap and a crown'. And since no student could remember which side of the heart the valve was situated, he introduced his mnemonic aid, 'a bishop's never in the right'.

From students they went on to become devoted assistants and his wickedest critics. But only Sharpey's gold medallist at University College, the fast-tongued physiologist of radical Baptist stock, Michael Foster, dared call the proofs of Huxley's *Lessons in Elementary Physiology* too dense, 'no offence I trust marm'.[1] Having pioneered the plebeian prose and cloth-cap homily, Huxley was expected to churn out racy textbooks too.

One student turned out a sadder antagonist. The tormented liberal Catholic St George Mivart was already a lecturer at St Mary's Hospital in Paddington. Mivart was well-to-do, born in his father's Mivart Hotel – later famous as Claridge's – and brought up among its noble clientele. He caught the excitement, studying lemurs with Huxley in the wake of *Man's Place*. Huxley proved 'a good friend indeed – firm, generous, energetic, loyal and affectionate'. Mivart was captivated by those 'dark eyes, bright and full of expression'. They would 'light up' as the two strode home for dinner, deep in philosophy and Darwinism and 'the possibility of the medusa having been an ancestral form of man'. But Huxley's Puritan chat of the violation of evidence and the 'sin of faith' troubled his pupil.

In Jermyn Street the courteous Mivart sat adoringly at the master's feet. For a time Mivart felt himself 'a thorough going disciple of the school of Mill, Bain & H. Spencer'. But the convert to Rome was racked in these encyclical years. Between the reactionary Pope and the militant Darwinians he found little solace. The

General hardly helped by visiting Catholic seminaries, darting admiring glances at the hard-line Jesuit militia – *our* 'great antagonist', he called it, 'which is able to resist, and must, as a matter of life and death, resist, the progress of science and modern civilization'.

Huxley's 'moral mischief' put his Catholic admirer on the spot. Mivart agreed that a dead chimp was comparable to a dead human. But man's 'moral & religious nature', with its hopes and aspirations, its promise of immortality and salvation, sets him further from a gorilla than the 'Ape differs from a lump of granite'. The split was to open up into a devastating divide. Mivart was not to genuflect much longer before bishop Huxley.[2]

Huxley's protégés were sliding into place. He pushed 'tooth & nail' to get them into chairs from Galway to Casale. He had them fighting in Melbourne. He had them in Glasgow's Hunterian Museum, undermining the old Whigs – that dying breed, like Prime Minister Palmerston himself, 'opposed to "new fangled things"'. Enrico Giglioli was back in Italy as professor of natural history at the Tecnic Institute of Casale, looking for a brave Italian publisher for *Man's Place*. Near by in Turin, he reported, the Catholic zoologist Filippo de Filippi was mining out the book and championing 'our descent from "Apes"', at least as far as our material bodies went. But like all of the old boys Giglioli was nostalgic for his youth under Huxley and desperate to get back to London 'in the midst of the scientific movement'.[3]

The Xs were beginning to control that movement. Off duty they took their YV's on moonlit trips down the Thames, stirred by Huxley's renditions of Tennyson. Darwin was a sort of corresponding country member. Old Sir Charles Lyell was sidelined, the more because he had obviously 'plundered' Lubbock's paper on prehistoric shell mounds for his *Antiquity of Man*. (Sending Lubbock, 'like all quiet & mild men', Huxley told Hooker, 'about twice as "wud" as Berserks like you & me'.) But there was another very telling grudge.

Ellen Busk had a rapier-intellect which rather spiked the tradition of religiously demure wives. So while Sir Charles regularly 'pumped [Busk] dry of his knowledge', Lady Lyell cut Ellen dead. She would not call, though they lived down the street, nor invite the Busks to her parties. The Huxleys resented it. Hooker saw Mrs Busk as 'a most thoroughly accomplished clever person', and 'more of a Lady' than all the fluttering socialites who flocked 'to

Lady L's soirees'.⁴ It was a further reminder of the X-Clubbers'
socially inferior origins. Ellen's was a new world, of gutsy George
Eliot novels with their trader and surgeon heroes, a world which
saw Elizabeth Garrett return from Paris the first woman Doctor of
Medicine. Talented women were forcing their own way into the
new aristocracy.

But Sir Charles' generation was moving aside. The Xs were the
new power. With the death of Hooker's father in 1865 the State
bought his herbarium and library, making Kew a public institution
and Joseph Dalton Hooker its Director. Lubbock became Sir John
on his own father's death and looked to a Parliamentary career.
Hooker flinched at this 'awful waste of time, of energy, of brain,
of life'. But Huxley backed him.⁵ Not that it helped. Midway
through Lubbock's first West Kent campaign in 1865 Williams &
Norgate brought out his *Prehistoric Times*. It flummoxed the hop-
growers, who thought familiarity with stone-age rubbish tips not
the best qualification in a candidate. He lost handsomely.

Huxley knew that progressive science would eventually find its
voice in the House. It was finding it everywhere else. Rationalist
books were dropping off the presses. Man's aboriginal savagery,
man's rise, man's rational goal, nothing seemed taboo after *Man's
Place*. As a sofa-bound invalid, Darwin had his long-suffering wife
recite from William Lecky's *History of Rationalism*. Huxley had
to like Lecky's saga of disappearing miracles. It 'just missed being
a first class work – But the man is very young & I have great hope
of him bye & bye'. Hooker added Lubbock's and Edward B.
Tylor's *Early History of Mankind* as the year's 'really excellent
works'. Both turned the empire's savages into stone-age relics, like
Huxley's 'living fossils' trapped out of time in the colonial back-
waters. These people provided snapshots of our primitive past.
This wasn't Darwinism with its adaptive spread into richly unique
niches. Tylor's single ladder was climbed by all cultures; we had
hauled ourselves nearly to the top, while aborigines were on the
lowly rungs, reminding us of our past.⁶ The idea resembled
Huxley's ontogenetic track. It suited the empire's growing image
of its native 'children', to be tended by white 'adults'. The Xs took
to this Quaker's son who declared war on the savage superstitions
surviving in his own culture. And Tylor shared the X-Clubbers'
terrible need to emancipate us from our superstitious past.

The club's own rationalist efforts weren't doing as well. The
Natural History Review had become too technical and inward-
looking; this specialist biological journal with its Darwinian bent

was foundering. It never did appeal to the masses, as Huxley had wanted. He was long 'out of concert with it & wash my hands of it. My share of the loss is £25.0.0 & I can't afford luxuries of that kind'. He was still roping in the best talents for the liberal *Reader*, with its wide arts, literature and science coverage – and the brightest was that physiological Turk Michael Foster, who impishly called Huxley 'Captain'.[7] But with too many Captains and precious few crew, the *Reader* ship was doomed too. It had listed after Huxley's cannonade at the Church, when the Christian Socialist commodores took to the lifeboats. Now it headed for the rocks.

Worse was in store when the new navigator came on board. Huxley's militancy had only encouraged a more aggressive takeover. One of Hunt's henchmen Thomas Bendyshe was angling to buy it out. 'I should be very sorry to see the Reader pass into his hands', Huxley told Lockyer. They halved its cover price to 2*d* and boosted the adverts, but to no avail. By autumn 1865 the ailing paper was 'bound over to Satan'. The wealthy Darwin was worried about getting his money back as the ship went down for good. A poor Huxley was sorrier about the lost opportunities. 'The N. H. R. & the Reader are the first & last journals I . . . ever mean to be connected with'.[8]

There was no ignoring the 'Cannibal Club', as Hunt's rival dining élite dubbed itself. By the end of the Civil War they were a wretched power in literary London. Theirs was a phenomenal rise, with the notorious specialist in Arab erotica Richard Burton aboard. They revelled in their repugnance. A savage's skeleton hanging in the window announced their rooms. Inside, meetings were brought to order with a negro's-head mace, and in an unsavoury reaction to the prudery of the age (and to the Ladies' nights at the Ethnological) their erotic excursions verged on the pornographic. They explored phallic symbols and sexual taboos with a freedom unknown elsewhere. They out-marginalized the Darwinians, and out–numbered them, and in their struggle for hegemony threatened to impose their own rival ideology of 'man's place' on society. They claimed '700 to 800 Fellows and a yearly income of £1,500 to £1600' (only later was it realized that they were cooking the books), three-fold the Ethnological's numbers. Lubbock and Huxley's society was bringing in barely £320 a year. The Darwinians might have seemed a model of family propriety by comparison, but they were alive to the danger posed by the cult's extremists.

With the Confederacy in tatters Hunt's men had lost their *raison d'être* and seemed tempted to submerge their infamy. Huxley too was weary of infusing life into the Ethnological. He called the warring factions a 'scandal'; and, as the *Saturday Review* saw, his authority to talk on human origins would be sapped so long as the experts were seen to 'quarrel among themselves'. A takeover was imperative to foster an image of solidarity. Huxley even put up a pontoon bridge for his regulars to march over. In his lectures he ceased referring to 'races', and used 'stocks' to cut through the preconceptions, and talked of them as 'persistent modifications'. But Hunt – that 'Turkey Buzzard', as Rolleston labelled him – feared that Huxley was out to 'crush' them, a qualm increased by the killing look in Lubbock's eye.[9]

In a topsy-turvy world Wallace the 'emancipating' socialist spelled out the main reason for uniting. The Ethnological – that philanthropic crowd-puller with its bevy of anti-slavery ladies – crimped his style. He saw the men-only Anthropological as 'a good protest against the absurdity of making the *Ethnological* a *ladies'* Society. Consequently many important & interesting subjects cannot possibly be discussed there'.[10]

The pulpit delicacy of Victorian sexual mores gave Huxley his own troubles at the Ethnological. With the straitlaced matrons he had to guard his tongue: no mooting the body to bring a flushed cheek, no sexual customs (a fainting subject) – so many taboos made his own culture an absurd subject for study. They certainly made a mockery of serious 'Ethnology'.

He rose to the challenge. He countered the pulpit's sway with his own 'lay sermons'. They drew the ladies; in fact they drew unprecedented crowds now. The Sunday League's flyer announcing that he was to launch its 'Sunday Evenings for the People' sent London into a flurry. The poor were admitted free and others fought for tickets. And who could object to the 'wonders of science' instilling a new 'reverence' in those who did not attend worship?

Two thousand milled about Covent Garden on the night of 7 January 1866, finding St Martin's Hall full. Inside was 'packed to suffocation'. 'Every part of the great Hall was crowded – every foot of standing room was occupied'. Fifteen months earlier Karl Marx had founded the First International here, when it rang to the cheers of Parisian workers. His daughter Jenny had waltzed in the Hall at communist meetings. Now she squeezed in again. With the 'leading names in science, Huxley (Darwin's disciple) at the head' setting the sabbath alight, 'dull England' did not seem so dull any more.

'Sacred Music' played Huxley in, a booming church organ pumping out Haydn's 'Creation' to heighten the sense of awe. ('You may live to see me a Bishop yet', he told Dyster.) With its echo fading he began his hymn. Science was tearing through the 'fine-spun ecclesiastical cobwebs' to behold a new cosmos, in which our Earth is merely an 'eccentric speck' – a world of evolution 'and unchanging causation'. It invited new ways of thinking. It demanded a new rationale for belief. With science's truths the only accessible ones, 'blind faith' was no longer admirable but 'the one unpardonable sin'. Huxley was sacrificing the old authority on nature's 'altar of the Unknown'.

His vision of science promised intrigue and exotic horizons. It was imperial and expansive. He knew he could move multitudes, and he carefully carried his congregation. He guided them 'through a new country', breathlessly, 'like a skilful charioteer', the *Leader* said, 'pulling up with the utmost ease' to show 'magnificent views of the broad and fertile kingdom of Natural Knowledge'.[11] It was a revivalist meeting with its ecstatic highs; the 'Kingdom of Nature' was at hand, and 'a nobler discourse on a nobler theme was never delivered'. Lost amid the hallelujahs was its serious function, as Darwin's laity imputed the old moral laws to the cosmic fabric itself.

Jenny Marx exulted in this 'genuinely progressive' sermon, at a time 'when the flock are supposed to be grazing in the house of the Lord'. Huxley was reclaiming those whose sabbaths had been spent 'bawling a hymn to "Jesus, Jesus, meek and mild"' or passed 'in a Gin Palace'. The sermon cascaded into a tear-jerking finale, and an outraged clergy watched Huxley depart with the audience brought to tears by the 'Creation'.

The womenfolk loved it. Here was the handsome Huxley, greying at the temples, black eyes flashing, the Puritan tease. Evolution to a prim generation was titillating. Ladies young and old were flirting dangerously. 'My mother (aged 75) is delighted with your sermon', Lewes wrote, running it in the *Fortnightly*, '& foresees a change in Religion coming'. (Huxley had made up with Lewes and often dined at the Priory, Lewes and George Eliot's rose-clad house in familiar North Bank. Still, Hal told Tyndall, you could always tell a Lewes review: 'nobody else could be so clever & so ignorant'.)[12]

Huxley's 'Lay Sermon' brought a catcall 'Atheist' from the *Spectator*. He wearily responded that 'Atheism is as absurd, logically speaking, as polytheism' – incapable of proof or disproof – but he clearly needed some alternative label to license doubt and throw the opprobrium back on to the 'sin of faith'. Owen berated these 'extremist views'. Having hoodwinked costermen into believing they were chimps, Huxley was arousing their wives. His 'contemptuous relegation' of the 'Supreme creative Will' was not for pretty ears.[13] Nor did the Lord's Day Observance Society think so. Incensed by this sabbatarian mockery, it stopped the 'Sunday Evenings for the People'.

The rush of the night seemed a hallucination the next day. In the cold light Huxley huddled over black bituminous amphibians. He had the 'scent of . . . carboniferous corpses'. From Irish collieries he ferreted out amphibians, sinuous eel-like creatures, with tiny legs and flat shield-shape heads for slithering through the shallows. In six years he had etched out more of the earth's first land vertebrates than any man living. With the Devonian land insects turning up – mayflies and grasshoppers – one could hear the buzz and snapping jaws of this ancestral fauna.[14] By night or day, it was the time to be alive.

Technical papers streamed from the press, and honours replaced the obloquy. From Paris' Société d'Anthropologie to St Petersburg's Imperial Academy, via the appreciative German academies, foreign fellowships came Huxley's way. He even felt a prophet in his own land, or at least a Sassenach sage, as he travelled to Edinburgh on 2 April 1866. He met up with Tyndall, escorting the wild, sleepless Carlyle; and there, with Carlyle fortified by a nip launching into a 90-minute extemporization, all three were awarded honorary Doctorates of Law. But the mixed feelings for Huxley told in the 'cheers and slight hisses'.[15]

Edinburgh's boos were drowned by the sound of the universities on the march. The oldest dames were donning new clothes; a bill before Parliament would even permit non-Anglican fellows at Oxford and Cambridge, presaging the fall of the entire Church monopoly. These moss-encrusted institutions, 'half-clerical seminaries', he called them, 'half race-courses', were modernizing. To his goading question, 'What are the Universities doing for Science?', a Cambridge group responded by founding a *Journal of Anatomy and Physiology* and demanding a contribution. Cambridge was rushing to catch up with London. With a chair of zoology founded in 1866, it was barely 40 years behind. But the capital kept its lead as Huxley dissected his way through the animal kingdom. In 1866 he began on the whales. Outside the classroom he added the evolutionary lustre:

> No doubt whales had hind legs once upon a time . . . my friend Flower the Conservator . . . will show you the whalebone whale's thigh bones in the grand skeleton they have recently set up. The legs, to be sure, and the feet are gone, the battle of life having left private Cetacea in the condition of a Chelsea pensioner.[16]

Huxley's annexation of London science capped his academic career. Capped was correct. This year he put another hat on. He took the Fullerian Professorship at the Royal Institution again. It was his third concurrent London professorship, a unique feat and probably never to be equalled.

Audiences flocked to hear him. The journalist Eliza Lynn was 'intoxicated' by Huxley's talks in his 'Court of Paradise', the Royal Institution. Here and in the School of Mines and College of Surgeons Huxley continued to collate the world's peoples with the surety that came from imperial conquest. With the navy patrolling the seas he could order the human parts he wanted, treating Her Majesty's Ships like zoological privateers. Occasionally the grave robbery called for Britannia's tact. Captain Watson would sail in with Patagonian chieftains' skulls plundered 'as privately as possible in order that the Natives might not know that any of the Graves of their ancestors had been disturbed'.[17] Or the *Nassau* would sail out with Huxley's shopping list of Fuegian skulls, and a reminder to pick up fossils of a rhinoceros-sized guinea pig (*Toxodon*) spotted at the Straits of Magellan.

Plunder of skulls was one thing, his old Charing Cross classmate Joseph Fayrer's offer was another. Rather than lecturing on indigenous races, come and see them: Fayrer, in the Indian medical service, invited Huxley to the City of Palaces, Calcutta, to compare a sample of all the Asian peoples rounded up by the Asiatic Society of Bengal. Brazen collation was the goal, as if stamping and ranking the races would result in a more orderly empire. For one mad moment the round-up seemed feasible. With railway barons laying tracks to rush troops to the Indian troublespots, Fayrer could transport his ethnological zoo; and Calcutta was rife with bureaucrats, ready to photograph and process. You 'do things on so grand a scale in India', Huxley replied in surprise, but what with lectures and little ones his own participation was out of the question.

Baby Henry had not been the last. Nettie, coming up for 41, already suffering from swollen veins and the stress of her extended family, had added 'another small humanity to the six who already pervade this house'. Abbey Place was bulging as the cots came out and new nurses arrived to look after newborn Ethel. Jim's daughter Katy was still with them for the holidays (during term time she was at Nettie's old German finishing school, paid for by Hal). Nor was life eased by the builders and dust and sheaths of scaffold as they were forced to build new rooms on top to accommodate the growing horde.[18]

So India was out. Barring a weekend dash to Dublin to finger black coal fossils, it was all the *pater familias* could do to catch up with the 'miles of work in arrear'. His age was telling. He knew it when Edith, the newborn baby that his sister Lizzie had carried on her precipitous flight 20 years earlier, had a babe of her own. 'How do you feel as a Grandmother?' he asked Lizzie. In Montgomery they had struggled through the war, robbed by itinerants after the slaves' emancipation. Lodgers made up their earnings. One who was put up after the siege of Atlanta was Albert Roberts, a young newspaper man come to work on the *Montgomery Mail*. His first sight was of Dr Scott, 'a distinguished gentleman in uniform', and 'a beautiful lady, likewise English'. Mrs Scott (Lizzie) 'was adorable', but the attraction for Edith proved greater. 'Give our love & congratulations to Edith', Tom wrote after hearing of her and Albert's baby. 'I read her husbands articles with great pleasure'.

Intrigue still surrounded Scott. Huxley had answered an executor's notice in the *Times*, inquiring after relatives of a deceased Mrs Salt. Her son John had been unknown to her for two decades; the estate came to only £250, but it was a lifeline in post-war Montgomery. After a rigmarole proving his relationship they had their inheritance. It took Tom back to the dreadful days when the couple fled. And here was his favourite sister an 'adorable' grandmother.

> I can quite understand all your feelings. Jess is but eight
> but I talk savagely . . . about my prevenient hatred of the
> long-legged puppy whom she will some day or other think
> more of than of her father & mother.[19]

Huxley was ending his own racial round-up at the Royal Institution in June 1866 as Germany's war of unification began. The Prussian advance 'swept on like a heavy spring tide', trapping his translator Victor Carus in plague-ridden Leipzig. One of Huxley's fellow examiners was with the Prussian troops as they surged across 'nearly the whole of northern Germany'. Do 'you want any Teutonic skulls' he asked, 'with perhaps a rifle bullet included'? More than the odd bullet. The Prussian needle guns proved decisive. Austria was defeated in July at the Battle of Königgrätz. With the peace, Carus finally got a letter out to ask Darwin and Huxley for their biographies to include in a German encyclopedia, now to cover a greater Germany. Everyone wondered how much greater. As the English went over for the 'Annexation Rejoicings', they found a new world power in the making.[20]

The propagandists of Germany's brand of *Darwinismus* knew it. Darwin's doctrines were spreading with British liberalism,[21] as free trade and secularism were taken up by radical unifiers in Italy and Germany trying to forge strong national identities.

The bombastic Ernst Haeckel at Jena was transmuting the *Origin* into a patriotic form. He had been evangelizing the Germans ever since standing up for Darwin at the Congress of Naturalists at Stettin in 1863. Haeckel had made Jena a 'citadel of Darwinism'. He cut an extraordinary figure. In his early 30s, he had a passion for nature's beauty that was religious and a fiery rhetoric that was inspirational. He would escort flocks of students through the Thuringian hills, dilating on the splendours of nature and *Darwinismus*. This Extraordinary Professor of Zoology at Goethe's old university, Huxley told Darwin, was 'one of the ablest' in Germany.[22]

Haeckel stretched Darwin's struggle for existence to society itself. This was the punch in his *Generelle Morphologie*, a 1,000-page double-decker, written to drown his sorrows after the death of his wife. *Darwinismus* drove the best 'peoples irresistibly onward', he insisted. It presaged a new Teutonic destiny. Neither 'the weapons of the tyrant nor the anathemas of the priest' could stop German progress now. Like all radicals, he saw a supine nobility wiped away in the struggle – dogs and aristocrats, he snorted, were all the same in the womb. His *Darwinismus* sanctioned a strong state, with free speech and free trade invigorating its people.

Jena's comparative anatomists were busy drawing evolutionary trees. But Haeckel's was something of a magical wood, with the missing ancestors modelled on living embryos. Huxley beat through the book's thicket of makeshift trees. Each of Haeckel's

family trees was a racially related group sharing a common ancestor, born of the same warring struggle as the new Germany – or
what he called a 'phylum'. All creatures in a phylum are bound
together, the fit survivors, sharing a common bloodline purified by
battle. It consecrated his Messianic ideal of the German *Volk*.
'While the booming of guns at the Battle of Königgrätz in 1866
announced the demise of the old Federal German Diet and the
beginning of a splendid period in the history of the German
Reich', he said welcoming Bismarck to Jena, 'here in Jena the
history of the phylum was born'.[23]

For the moment Huxley could only browse through the book.
As usual he faced a torrent of lectures, three waves combined into
a 100-foot breaker which hit him as it had the gale-tossed *Rattlesnake*. 'If I could only break my leg', he sighed, 'what a lot of
scientific work I could do'.[24]

In England things were moving fast. The British Association meeting in 1866 was a triumph. With Huxley, Wallace and Galton
pulling strings, Tylor tracing civilization to its savage roots,
Hooker satirizing the primitive tribe which had led the British
Asses by the nose until 1860, the papers saw Darwin's theory
'everywhere in the ascendant'. Even the President, physicist and
barrister William Grove, pleaded that gradual evolution was constitutionally sound; it obviated the threat of revolution and was in
the best interest of the State.[25] Suddenly the reform of Nature
sounded frightfully British.

A Harrow schoolmaster struck another chord. Revd Frederick
Farrar proclaimed that 'the important question for England was
not the duration of her coal', but her stock of science teachers.
That was Huxley's sort of talk. Farrar was part of the liberal fall-
out from Maurice's Christian Socialist explosion. He was a science
sympathizer whose work on the evolution of language tickled
Darwin enough to recommend him for an FRS (and to send him
Huxley's 6*d* pamphlets as a bonus).

Farrar and Huxley got up a Committee to force the issue of
science in public schools. With Farrar's contacts and Huxley's
know-how they intended 'knocking on the head' the excessive
Latin versing.[26] If there were no texts Huxley would write them. If
the most important facts of life concerned one's body, his *Elementary Physiology* would provide a fillip. Huxley, cheated of the best
years of schooling himself, would ensure that his 'scientific Young
England' fared better.

Now even Harrow toffs with Latin-filled heads looked on an alien 'wire-scape', as telegraph wires criss-crossed the skyline. They read of reptilian empires more exotic than the Roman, of human antiquities more ancient than the Bible's, of evolution more stirring than Genesis. Daily the newspapers played up the living dramas, as Brunel's gigantic *Great Eastern* paid out the enormous tonnage of telegraph cable from Ireland to Newfoundland. They lived when the first electrical messages crossed oceans at 288,000 miles a second. The revolution was being forced on the old seminaries, its lusty cries drowning out the morbid echo of dead voices.

At the BAAS Huxley had gained the 'Anthropologists' a limited hearing and it paid off in the merger negotiations. The duplicitous Hunt, presumably seeking legitimacy, even offered Huxley the presidency of the amalgamated society.[27] But events overtook the power brokers. The deal was in the final stages when a black uprising in Jamaica blew back in Huxley's face. A local revolt in the cane-cutting colony had been ruthlessly crushed. Jamaica was a patchwork of ramshackle estates, owned by absentee landlords and eyed by the destitute blacks. Eyre was Governor, the man once admired by Huxley for crossing the Great Australian Bight. But the gold-braid-encrusted Lieutenant Governor of New Zealand had become the stiff-necked Governor of this half-evacuated colony. Grievances about high prices, social injustice and squatters' rights had sent machete-wielding militants into Morant Bay's courthouse to hack the hated magistrates to death. White fears flashed back to the atrocious massacres in Haiti and the crackdown was brutal. Eyre's troops were loosed and 439 blacks were cavalierly shot in passing or hanged after impromptu court hearings.

The reprisals went on for weeks, culminating in the half-caste demagogue of Jamaica's Assembly, William Gordon, hanging from a yard arm. This Native Baptist minister might have been a 'poor type of small political agitator', Huxley admitted to Kingsley, who knew Eyre, '& very likely was a great nuisance to the Governor', but 'English law does not permit good persons, as such, to strangle bad persons, as such'. Huxley had done with Carlyle's Great Men as sacred makers of History. There had to be equality before the law. Eyre's 'preposterous subalterns' had illegally executed a man. The Governor approved and was as

> responsible for Gordons death as if he had shot him
> through the head with his own hand. I daresay he did all

this with the best of motives, & in a heroic vein[.] But if
English law will not declare that heroes have no more
right to kill people in this fashion than other folk, I shall
take an early opportunity of migrating to Texas or some
other quiet place where there is less Hero worship &
more respect for justice.[28]

'The sight of heaps of dead bodies in Demerara' sent shivers down
the liberal spine. Spencer's father died hallucinating about Eyre's
atrocity. Anti-slavers found new hackles rising. Mill's liberals
called it murder, and Huxley was asked to join their Jamaica
Committee, formed to prosecute Eyre and wipe the blood from
Britannia's robes.

But it was a divisive issue. Had Eyre not prevented a white
bloodbath? Or a worse fate for the colony's 'tenderly nurtured
women'? Lurid images blended with a belief that English law did
not apply to a '*naturally* wild . . . inferior race'. Out of this potent
concoction came the Eyre Defence movement. It put a strain on
old friendships. Hal watched Tyndall join, and Nettie heard
'brother John' turn down a dinner invitation because he was
pledged to the repatriated 'Eyre and his wife'. The cracks began to
show. It was the only moment in Huxley's and Tyndall's life when
'each of us would have been capable of sending the other to the
block'. Kingsley too called the prosecution 'detestable' (his grandfather, a Barbados judge, had been ruined by emancipation). And
even Hooker thought that any population dangerous to the empire
must be 'subject to the same nemesis'.[29] The *Pall Mall Gazette*
despicably pinned Huxley's 'nigger' politics on to his 'peculiar
views' of ancestry. No one who saw a hairy chimp 'as "a man and
a brother"' would balk at giving blacks the same 'sympathetic
recognition'.

The taunts pushed Huxley to the front of the Jamaica Commit-
tee. He served with Mill, Francis Newman, Tom Hughes, Spencer
and that veteran Rochdale radical turned Birmingham MP John
Bright. Behind them in this alliance of philanthropy and reform
stood Lyell, Darwin and Wallace. Authority was not absolute in
Jamaica, any more than it was in Oxford. No man was above the
Civil Law, as no Wilberforce could invoke powers above the
Natural Law.

One enterprising ex-slave, Moses Moore, read of Huxley's talks
in the *Antislavery Reporter*. Moses had worked his passage from
Guiana and was living at the West India Docks, speaking on

plantation life to raise the money for an education. He sent his 'thanks Sir as emanating from the heart of a "genuine negro"'. (The racists claimed that clever blacks were not pure 'Africans' but of mixed blood.) He wished Huxley's sense would prevail among the planters, 'who have placed the negro race as only two removes from apes'. A slave's praise highlighted Huxley's distance from the hardliners. He would give subject peoples the same rights under English law. But Hunt's cannibals lambasted the Government for recalling Eyre and Huxley for arraigning him. Jamaica revealed the political chasm again and the merger was aborted. Not that Huxley was 'personally sorry to be free of them'.

Race and class were emotively linked by Hunt's clique. It claimed that equality was as bad for a savage as a street arab. A little education would breed dangerous aspirations. The vote would be lethal. The 'nigger' is in 'Jamaica as the costermonger is in Whitechapel . . . a savage with the mind of a child'. By contrast, Huxley was not only talking on ethnology at the Mechanics' Institute, but ending with a collection to ease the 'appalling distress' of the East End jobless, Hunt's Whitechapel 'savages'. Vivid were Huxley's memories of the dock slums, although a long 25 years had elapsed since he had sidled past the derelicts to his Jamaica Street surgery. He put his pennies into an open-top skull on the table, and the cranial vault was soon brimming with coins. It infuriated the reactionaries. The Anglo-Saxon gentry needed to be vengeful masters. The underworld cauldron had to be contained, by martial law if necessary. There could be no charity or freedom for these irreclaimables. The issue was sensitive, with reform on the agenda in 1866. 'We do not admit of equality even among our own race', Hunt's anti-democrats ranted.[30]

But why? radicals countered. Old Chartists and new trade unionists were uniting in a Reform League to push for suffrage. Even Gladstone, impressed by the Lancashire weavers' stoicism during the Civil War layoffs, thought that workers had earned the right 'to come within the pale of the constitution'. Mill's Committee swung its weight behind reform. Mill himself had taken Westminster for the radicals at the 1865 election, Bright was barnstorming in the north, and the Jamaica Committee bumped along on the reform bandwagon. These nights Huxley would sit around with fellow mountaineer and failed ordinand Leslie Stephen, 'denouncing God, Eyre and the British aristocracy by the hour'. The 'Jamaica Row' is rumbling on, he told Lizzie on 1 December, and 'there is to be a Reform demonstration on Monday of 200,000 people – So times are lively'.[31]

In January 1867 a craggy, long-bearded Darwin descended from Olympus and turned up in Jermyn Street. He was viewed as Zeus by the surprised students, and he looked the part as he toured the building with Huxley. The Royal School of Mines now led Britain in applied science education. Huxley's lectures towered over University College's, where that Restoration relic Robert Grant still taught a defunct 1830s zoology in a frayed swallow-tail coat. The small intake belied the school's importance. It was a 'seeding' establishment. Out of it came a select group of industrialists and academics, and its galleries were a shining example 'of what a museum ought to be'. Darwin had pulled his coddled youngest son Horace out of Clapham School. The boy had a mechanical turn and his father browsed though Huxley's prospectus.[32] Huxley himself would shortly put his own nephew 'young Jim' through the school, acting *in loco parentis* as Jim senior became more mentally muddled, shut away in his asylum in Kent.

Haeckel had toured the galleries three months earlier. Afterwards Huxley had wined and dined this Coryphaeus among German naturalists, and the Abbey Place troop kept a 'lively memory' of their larger-than-life guest. Huxley and Haeckel were like conspiring generals, with Hal 'as deeply interested' in the *Morphologie* as Haeckel was 'in his ape-theory'. The camaraderie came from a shared combative attitude; but Haeckel, used to the barricade socialist Carl Vogt's scurrility, found Huxley's 'Attic wit' of a 'much finer grain'. No doubt, too, the dinner conversation turned on their other mutual interest, jellyfish (it had to, with Haeckel calling his own house 'Villa Medusa'). Hal introduced him to the Xs. And Haeckel seems to have undergone something of a mystical experience on meeting the 'Jove-like' Darwin. The venerable patriarch stood silent and slightly flabbergasted, with a flowing beard like Moses on the mountain, as Haeckel boomed his embarrassing, gushing greeting in German.[33]

New Year 1867 saw Darwin 'swearing at each sentence' of Haeckel's *Generelle Morphologie*, hoping Huxley would arrange a translation. 'The German is too difficult for ordinary mortals', Darwin moaned. Even Huxley with his fluent German found it 'uncommonly hard'. Huxley had bullishly resisted Darwin's genealogical approach to classification. But now Haeckel was sending him 'genealogical tables' as well. Haeckel's evolutionary 'trees' were based more on embryonic relationships than Darwin's messy field approach, and they finally converted Huxley. 'Whether one agrees or disagrees' with Haeckel, he said, it was 'more profitable to go wrong than to stand still'.[34]

Even on holiday Huxley could not escape Haeckel's influence. Like all middle-class families the Huxleys trooped off to the seaside each summer. In 1867 it was the quaint village of Swanage on the south coast, six hours away by train and bumpy omnibus. And not content with seven children from ten years to 18 months, with attendant nurses and maids, they were joined by Haeckel's barnacle-specialist, Anton Dohrn. Haeckel's pupils venerated Darwin and Huxley. Like the master, Dohrn recalled 1859 as the turning point of the century, with the Italian War of Unification and the end of the Papal States counterpointing the intellectual bombshell of the *Origin*. Dohrn was shortly to found a unique marine laboratory at Naples, where European zoologists could study the larvae of the warm Mediterranean waters and solve the ancestral riddles.[35] But for the present Huxley and Dohrn fished in cooler Swanage seas. They all remembered it as a time of laughter. Up early for lobster breakfasts, then out with the dredge, while at night the herd of seven children was taught 'bovine vocalisations' by the affable Dohrn, leaving Harry toddling round the house shouting 'Mroo'.

The laughter continued at Haeckel's lamentable jokes about a 'gaseous' God.[36] But the *Morphologie*'s big message about racial ancestries had its impact. It finally forced Huxley to connect his ancient lung-bearing Crossopterygian fish with the first labyrinthodont amphibians – in other words, to show how fish grew limbs and slithered out of the water.[37] He had caught up with Owen. But Huxley's next innovation would overhaul his enemy dramatically. It was the most unexpected piece of ancestor-hunting yet.

Birds and reptiles had interested Huxley for some time. His working men were always the first to know of his innovations and they heard about the chicken's relationship with the tortoise in November 1866. He taught them that the scaly-legged birds were an 'extremely modified and aberrant Reptilian type'. The stork and the 'snake it swallows' sat together in the professor's new vertebrate 'province', which he called the 'Sauropsida'.[38]

In spring 1867, his 24 lectures to the surgeons were devoted to this great reptile-bird ground plan. But that did not make ostriches and crocodiles any likelier-looking bedfellows. However odd to the cloth-caps, it was odder to Owen, who denied it. But Huxley made it seem more reasonable at a stroke. He suggested that dinosaurs had a bird-like heart and lungs and even 'hot blood'.[39] (He probably got the idea from a young palaeontological Ishmael and former piano-tuner's apprentice Harry Seeley, who had proposed that pterodactyls were 'hot-blooded'.)

But Huxley was only thinking in terms of ground plans. His ideas had no evolutionary twist yet. Nor did they on 7 April 1867, when he completely reclassified the birds on the basis of their palate bones at the Zoological Society.[40] Even now he thought that birds were not *literally* modified reptiles, simply that both were based 'upon one and the same ground-plan'. He was still thinking in static structural ways.

Then came the conversion. He finished the last of his Royal Institution lectures on 8 June 1867 and finally had time to give Haeckel's *Morphologie* its due. He studied the book assiduously and the impact was profound. The racial lines and fossil roots transformed his thinking – his notebooks blossomed with avian classificatory trees, a riot of snaking lines and crossings-out.[41]

Linking the living birds into a 'tree', he informed Cambridge's professor of zoology Alfred Newton – a dedicated ornithologist despite his hip disease and walking sticks – was just a step 'in the progress towards the ultimate goal, which is a *genetic classification*', a real blood line, showing how fossil and 'living beings have been evolved one from the other'. He had once told Darwin that was impossible; now it seemed obvious.

He narrowed his sights to partridge and pigeon heraldry, demonstrating how, on 'the Evolution theory', it could be depicted 'by a genealogical tree, or *phylum* as Haeckel calls it in his remarkable "Generelle Morphologie"'. He traced the birds to 'a single primitive stock', like a nobleman following his birthright to the Norman barons.[42] It had taken Huxley a gruelling seven years to come to terms with the most profoundly historical aspect of Darwin's *Origin*.

Having got rid 'of my incubus' – meaning the bird paper, but he might as well have meant his anti-genealogical millstone – he could march faster across the new land. But it was an accidental find that determined his direction.

Huxley was still immersed in fossil reptiles. From every little England the coffins came. As one of his suppliers George Gordon said, his Elgin reptiles 'in days of old must have had cousins scattered over the face of the earth as widely as Queen Victoria's subjects are at the present day'. Her Majesty's colonists were busily despatching them home. From Bengal had come bizarre two-tusked reptiles (dicynodonts). Even better had come from a postman with rounds along the Cape's Orange River. His box of bric-à-brac, 'as in Pandora's', had its treasure at the bottom. Here Huxley found broken 'thigh bones of a great Dinosaurian reptile as big as Megalosaurus and probably nearly allied to it'.[43] This was the first definite dinosaur from Africa. And with only thighs, what else could Huxley christen it, but *Euskelesaurus*, the 'good-legged dinosaur'?

But hind limbs did not a dinosaur make. What did this giant really look like? Owen's life-size dinosaurs in the Crystal Palace grounds stood like scaly rhinos.[44] But this image, like the concrete models, was cracking.

Huxley was in Oxford's museum on 24 October 1867, looking at the dinosaurs made famous by the late William Buckland (the hyaena-keeping, practical-joking Oxford geologist who had introduced the first 'giant reptile' *Megalosaurus*). He noticed a misplaced bone among the 'precious relics'. Having spent a year surrounded by bird skeletons, he saw that this was part of the pelvic girdle, the ilium, and so bird-like as to be astonishing.[45] The avian-shaped hip had never been noted before. It was the catalyst that set him on to the most spectacular of all pedigrees – a dinosaur ancestry for the birds.

His escort that day was Buckland's successor. Old John Phillips had been rather brushed aside by the Darwinians; the faster they rushed, the more he seemed a fuddy-duddy. His review of the *Origin* had been 'weak, washy, stilted stuff', and Huxley had condemned him 'to that part of Hell which Dante tells us is appointed for those who are neither on God's side nor on that of the Devil's'.[46] But in 1867 he was proving himself a live old buzzard, always able to come up with the right fossil bone, and equal to Huxley's quips.

With Phillips' bones, Huxley started pushing the birds back towards the dinosaurs. He dismantled Owen's rhinocerine bulwarks, rebuilding the monsters to avian specifications. Huxley was doing what the critics had demanded: transmuting one major class into another.

His excitement was muted at first. Just as he began, scarlet fever swept through the Abbey Place household. For three months they were 'like lepers'. Nettie was fraught, her mind numbed by the memory of Noel's death, her body 'pretty nearly worn out with nursing day & night'. On 25 November her 'little black eyed girl Rachel was attacked, just as we thought we were safe', but she was the last. Michael Foster's 'prescription of sal ammoniac' did wonders and, Hal told him, 'my wife blesses your name continuously'.[47]

Free of lectures and the fever, Hal spent Christmas in the British Museum's valley of bones, reassembling a powerful, 30-foot herbivore, *Iguanodon*, as a biped. The novelty of a full-size dinosaur up on its hind legs struck him. 'The restoration looks wonderful', he told Phillips, 'a sort of cross between a Crocodile & a kangaroo with a considerable touch of a bird about the pelvis & legs!'[48]

He also looked at that fabulous feathered fossil *Archaeopteryx*. This primitive reptilian bird had been bought on Owen's orders in 1862, to enhance his museum's European reputation (and to enable him to describe it). A bird with a long bony tail and four unfused fingers caused a sensation; 'startling', the papers called it – and the exorbitant £400 price-tag only increased its notoriety. Huxley's ethnological friend John Evans, manager of a pulp mill and a flint expert (a man who 'knows the wickedness of the world and does not practise it', and what better reference coming from Huxley?), detected a jaw with teeth, and then the brain case. After that, friends expected him to find 'the *fossil song*' as well, 'impressed by harmonic variation on the matrix'![49] Evans declared that the fossil's bearing on the 'Origin of Species must be evident to all'. It was enough to have Lyell pleading with Huxley as early as October 1862 to examine the fossil.

But Huxley had trouble with Owen's Jurassic bird. He never said much about it and only examined it at Christmas 1867 to show that Owen could not tell the right foot from the left.

Ironically, *Archaeopteryx* ruined Huxley's neat line between tall ostrich-like birds and giant strutting dinosaurs. With his lingering belief in the 'persistence' of animals, he looked for evidence of *oldest* birds – and Hitchcock's Triassic footprints suggested that big moa-like birds were already living alongside bipedal dinosaurs. For Huxley, *Archaeopteryx* was in many ways 'more remote from the boundary line between birds and reptiles than some living Ratitae [flightless birds] are'.[50]

But dinosaurs were huge – the three-ton *Iguanodon* was much too big to be a bird ancestor. And even more mountainous creatures were coming to light. Phillips' new *Cetiosaurus* (the aptly named 'whale reptile'), removed from local Jurassic rocks in 1868, had thigh bones as tall as a man, making it the 'largest

animal that ever walked upon the earth'. Huxley might 'hunger &
thirst' after such a 'Frankensteinosaurus', but these monsters could
hardly have evolved into birds.[51] There *were* tiny dinosaurs in
existence. Haeckel's colleague at Jena, Carl Gegenbaur, noted the
delicate bird-like leg and ankle of the first – and tiniest – of them,
the chicken-sized *Compsognathus* (from the fine lithographic slates
of Solnhofen that had preserved the traces of *Archaeopteryx*'s
feathers). Huxley pushed *Compsognathus* into the limelight as the
'missing link' between birds and dinosaurs and wondered if it was
itself feathered.

He pulled all the evidence together on a wintry evening, 7
February 1868. The Royal Institution socialites entered his lush
world of Jurassic palms. 'Those who hold the doctrine of Evolution', he began with a new confidence, 'and I am one of them',
believe that today's discrete classes of animals – including birds
and reptiles – have come from a common stock. But to find it we
have to go back to a balmy Jurassic past, to a lagoon at Solnhofen.
Flapping clumsily overhead was a heavy *Archaeopteryx*. And at
the water's edge, a diminutive dinosaur, hopping like a bird, neck
bobbing, snatching prey with its small arms.[52] The talk was a *tour
de force*. At last one could visualize how tiny dinosaurs with long
hind limbs passed by degrees into ancient flightless birds (of which
kiwis and rheas are their 'scanty modern heirs'), and these via
Archaeopteryx's kin into the song birds heralding today's dawn.

It was the crowning moment of his palaeo-work. His first
constructive use of the past had revealed a sensational pedigree.
(Or one of his most 'sensational tricks', Owen growled.) The mid-
brow papers responded to the propaganda coup. His triumphalist
talk was run in the new *Popular Science Review* and *Geological
Magazine* as well as the faithful old *Annals and Magazine of
Natural History* (Darwin's bedtime reading). Huxley, the anatomist interested in the laws and proportions of form, had taken the
decade to adjust to Darwin's emergent evolution. He had moved
from life's abstract geometry to its dynamic ancestry.

But he had come round and he carried the world with him. In
New Jersey bipedal dinosaurs were also turning up. An ambitious,
26 year-old Quaker, Edward Drinker Cope, had resurrected a
fearsome, 20-foot reptile, with a 31-inch thigh but only 12-inch
upper arm. This was his 'leaping' *Laelaps*, named after Diana's
hunting dog, turned to stone in mid-jump. Cope, who would
initiate America's own dinosaur boom, immediately accepted its
avian affinity. Even 68 year-old Phillips was convinced. 'The more

I reflect on the monsters', he told Huxley, 'the more grows my faith in their struthious [ostrich] affinities'. But he could hear his predecessor turning in his grave. 'What would dear old Buckland have said' to his terrible reptiles being cousins of the robins?[53]

Two weeks after the Royal Institution triumph Huxley wrote to Haeckel:

> I am engaged [in] a revision of the Dinosauria, with an eye to the 'Descendenz Theorie'. The road from Reptiles to Birds is by way of Dinosauria to the Ratitae [flightless birds]. The bird 'phylum' was struthious, and wings grew out of rudimentary forelimbs.
>
> You see that among other things I have been reading Ernst Haeckel's *Morphologie*.[54]

19

Eyeing the Prize

'IF HE HAS A FAULT, it is that, like Caesar, he is ambitious'. The *Spectator* was right, of course. The poor boy was still scrambling out of the ghetto. His ascent had been like a furious alpine climb. But by 1868 Huxley had scaled his way to the summit. He had come a long way since his birthday above a butcher's shop.

He was a new middle-class hero, whose wit tingled with patriotism and whose wisdom served the Dissenting elite. His ferocity was a reflection on the intransigent old order. Unable to call up professional backing, refusing to tug on patronage strings, he had forced his own way into society, pinking the old gents and pushing them aside with 'that slashing rapier of his': 'cutting up monkeys was his forte, and cutting up men was his foible', the *Pall Mall Gazette* observed. But the immovable grindstone of society had honed his blade.

There was another public side, and 1868 was a watershed there too. Thirty years earlier, the long-haired apprentice had been horrified by the dockland degradation. These no-go areas of starving wretches continued to haunt society. But Huxley's outstretched hand had turned the menacing labourers into backers for his Great technocratic Britain. 'I am a plebeian', he reassured them, 'and I stand by my order'.[1]

The 'plebeian' became Principal Huxley in 1868, head of his own Working Men's College. His benefactors were Maurice's ubiquitous Christian Socialists. There could be no more concrete proof of their good intentions, however questionable Huxley thought their co-operative politics. On 4 January he inaugurated this small South London college, which was situated across the Thames, on the Blackfriars Road. Lubbock and Tyndall sat on the council, while John Ruskin and Tom Hughes provided the library. To the classrooms were added a coffee lounge where burly mechanics could pore over their *National Reformers*, or touts could offer tickets for Monday nights in Jermyn Street:

> Sixpence for the course – a penny for a lecture by Huxley!
> You have never heard anything like it, my boys. Only
> remember the theatre holds but six hundred, so be in time.

Evening classes for women were planned, and a kindergarten for the tots who were usually written off as gutter-urchins.

In '*your* College', a wellwisher assured him, 'Scientific training' could only lead to 'the greatest literary excellence'. The workers saw it preparing them for power. And Huxley, inaugurating this 'South London Working Men's College', did nothing to disabuse them. There is not a pin to choose between 'your average artisan and your average country squire', a local paper reported him saying. The country would be no 'worse off under one regime than under the other'.

He was swinging the masses behind his professionals. He spoke to them in parables, rationalizing his pitch for power. His opening speech took the form of a game-playing metaphor. If life was a chess match, school should teach us the rules:

> The chess-board is the world, the pieces are the
> phenomena of the universe, the rules of the game are what
> we call the laws of Nature. The player on the other side is
> hidden from us. We know that his play is always fair, just
> and patient. But we also know, to our cost, that he never
> overlooks a mistake, or makes the smallest allowance for
> ignorance. To the man who plays well, the highest stakes
> are paid . . . And one who plays ill is checkmated –
> without haste, but without remorse.
>
> My metaphor will remind some of you of the famous
> picture in which Retzsch has depicted Satan playing at
> chess with man for his soul. Substitute for the mocking
> fiend in that picture a calm, strong angel who is playing
> for love, as we say, and would rather lose than win – and
> I should accept it as an image of human life.

Huxley's romantic personification of Nature had a dramatic punch. It needed to, for he looked on an extraordinary audience: behind the Christian Socialists sat rows of hard men, straight from Southwark's jam factory and engineering site. Leather traders and felt-hat makers dotted the scene, probably some Baptists and Methodists, but mostly freethinkers. A 'brigandlike' assembly, or so it seemed, with 'fine massive foreheads' draped in wideawake hats. These 'great bearded fellows with the signs of labour on their horny hands' had no time for philosophical niceties, and he gave them none.[2]

He made an angel of Darwin's anthropomorphic Natural Selection. Man's challenger was no longer God, but Darwin's godlike Nature, which scrutinized every gambit, every move. Only the scientist was investigating Nature's rule book; only he could be society's new schoolteacher.

Away from the sea of wideawake hats, Huxley was also wooing the other side. His address was spruced up for *Macmillan's Magazine* (itself synonymous with Christian Socialism at times). He persuaded bosses that it was in their interest to educate workers. Only an awareness of Nature's moral order could tame the political passions, and nothing less would stabilize capitalist society. The founding of the Trades Union Congress in 1868 gave his words their force. Widespread agitation had led to the second Reform Bill only months before, giving the better-off workers the vote. Across the Channel France was racked by strikes on the eve of the Commune. Touchy manufacturers heeded his plea for the democratization of knowledge. Investment in this sector would yield social dividends.

> A workman has to bear hard labour, and perhaps
> privation, while he sees others rolling in wealth and feeding
> their dogs with what would keep his children from
> starvation. Would it not be well to have helped that man
> to calm the natural promptings of discontent by showing
> him, in his youth, the necessary connection of the moral
> law which prohibits stealing with the stability of society –
> by proving to him, once for all, that it is better for his
> own people, better for himself, better for future
> generations, that he should starve than steal? If you have
> no foundation of knowledge, or habit of thought, to work
> upon, what chance have you of persuading a hungry man
> that a capitalist is not a thief 'with a circumbendibus?'

Like a line of parsons stretching back to Paley, Huxley was reconciling man to his place. It was a self-serving plea, hitching the nation's progress to his élite's; and such had the social centre of gravity shifted that his was now the voice of moderation. The 'true voice of Jacob', Tyndall called it, so 'different from either howling radicalism or hidebound, stupid Toryism'.[3] The Dissenting middle classes who put technology at the social hub had put Huxley there too. His Evolution had become the ameliorating ideology of the industrial order.

Lines of parsons awaited Huxley. Having squeezed them from science, he had no scruples about stretching its cosmic moral to their domain. Indeed, he was asked to. At last he had 'the chance of preaching just one sermon to the parsons in exchange for the thousands they have preached to him', joked the *Saturday Review*.

Farrar invited Huxley to lecture the City clergy at their anti-quated conference centre, Sion House. It was a 'very odd meeting' in 'as odd a place'. Not even Londoners had heard of this anonymous building near the medieval city wall. What better than to have Huxley put some fire into its moribund meetings? Rows of vicars undoubtedly fidgeted as he undermined the biblical chronology ('6,000' years was chalked on a slate beside him). They heard him take the story back past Joseph, past the Pyramids, past their Nile mud limestones, past their nummulite fossils to an immense antiquity. And, according to the conciliatory *Saturday Review*, they received the Word with equanimity (apart from 'two eccentric parsons' who denounced geology as the devil's work), and proved it afterwards with 'a pleasant half-hour over muffins and tea'.

The *Review* was a mite eager. One vicar apologized the next day for the City clergy's 'rudeness & roughness which stood in painful contrast with the calm dignity, & gentlemanly quietness of your own manner'.[4] Evidently it was just short of a genteel tea. But even he agreed that Huxley was jeered for stating 'conclusions which no competent judge doubts'.

It showed the changing temper of the times. But so too did the Xs' link-up with Maurice's men. Tyndall 'could hew' the orthodox 'to pieces before the Lord in Gilgal', but the Stanleys and Kingsleys 'are so gentle & noble'. And Christian culture's *rapprochement* with science lay with these churchmen. More than Christian culture was tinged by the new science. The Hebrew scholar, the Berlin-educated Marcus Kalisch, exiled in Britain after 1848, asked Huxley to proof-read his *Commentary on Leviticus*.[5] Everyone now consulted this expert on pre-Adamite creation.

On holiday in 1868 at that 'out of the way place' Littlehampton, on the south coast, Hal could be seen strolling along the sands with Nettie, reading her his paper 'On a Piece of Chalk'. The Sussex resorts were now the holiday haunt of the London bourgeoisie, with mothers, maids and children settled into the new boarding houses during the week, joined by their husbands at weekends. Crinolined ladies in their multi-layered, bustled skirts watched the couple saunter past, Nettie, the perfect layman's advocate, stopping to criticize a point of style, or suggesting a better colloquial expression.

Then Hal left to deliver it at a BAAS fringe meeting. In 1868 the delegates gathered in 'the ancient city of Churches', Norwich. A quaking Hooker was President, his resolve strengthened by Tyndall, who told him it was 'a duty that the gods have laid upon you'. Norwich must 'have been as wicked as Gomorrah', a wag observed, for there was surely 'a Church to every family'. Now it was set to receive the real 'Priesthood of Science', as the *Reasoner* dubbed Huxley's arrivals.

Huxley lured the Continentals over: Carus from Leipzig and Carl Vogt from Switzerland. Indeed, Vogt's scurrility and the *Reasoner*'s anticlericalism seemed to set the tone, and not only on the fringe. Hooker in his presidential pulpit lambasted 'that most dangerous of all two-edged weapons, Natural Theology' (with its attempt to deduce God's attributes from nature). 'Rank infidelity' was becoming synonymous with Darwinism, the *English Churchman* noted in sadness.[6] The jargon of factory infidels and emancipating Dissenters had become the stock-in-trade of an under-valued and under-capitalized Science.

Huxley was a whirlwind. He promoted his bird-like dinosaurs, and paid his dues on that score. Re-examining his mid-Atlantic ooze, brought back by Dayman ten years earlier, he detected specks of jelly with his latest high-power microscope. With Haeckel guessing that an amorphous albumen was the primordial living matter, Huxley saw himself looking at the primal slime life of the abyss. He christened his inchoate jelly-creature *Bathybius Haeckelii*. The exuberant Haeckel fired up Huxley, who went on to depict a pulsating film of protoplasm carpeting the 'whole sea bottom from the Persian Gulf round Cape of Good Hope & away by S^t. Helena to England'.[7] Haeckel assumed that this primal life was chemically generated in the depths. Huxley doubted it, but the striking image of a 'continuous scum of living matter' circling the globe seemed to cap the materialistic world view.

Darwin's 'reign was triumphant' at Norwich, said the *Guardian*. Certainly the 'terrible "Darwinismus"' 'crept out when you least expected it'. Even the Hindu-temple expert and Calcutta factory owner, James Fergusson, 'Stolid as an Assyrian Statue' himself, stirred it into his discussion of Buddhist stupas. 'I am preparing to go into opposition', Huxley joked to Darwin about the dwindling number of adversaries. 'I can't stand it'.

More accurately, it was an evolutionary naturalism that stole the show: a visionary naturalism in Tyndall's case. Tyndall was blasting the 'Tories . . . who regard imagination as a faculty to be feared'. His own was positively rioting. Flabbergasted workers were teased with his techno-vision of conscious robots and laboratory-built babies. There was a futuristic beauty to his cosmos. Like a religious visionary, he *saw* the life-giving atoms 'and felt their pushes and pulls'. In his galaxy all forces were convertible and even consciousness had its 'correlatives in the physics of the brain'. This poetic materialism was enough to drive the mild Mivart to damn Tyndall's 'creed – "I believe in One Force"'. But there was a magnificent determinism to it: an awareness that we are all children of the Sun, and that love and pain were 'once latent in a fiery cloud'.[8] It was the stuff of dreams.

Huxley's talk at Norwich was no science fiction, but just as fantastic. In the Drill Hall he initiated his workers into the sea bed's surprises. By now the style was the man; perfect, pellucid. He took his navvies through 'the masonry of the earth's crust' to find the source of the chalk in the carpenter's breeches. For 90 minutes he never halted. He pictured the rain of dead *Globigerina* building up 1,000 feet of chalky sea-bed over the Cretaceous aeons. Then the huge swimming reptiles vanished, and the ocean floor rose up in the 'whirligig of time' to become the lush land where Norwich's fossil elephants would roam. Huxley's best lectures were odysseys, and he ended with the option, Evolution or Creation, as he always did when reaching out ('Choose your hypothesis; I have chosen mine'). It had an impact in this workers' stronghold. The Professor was like the Methodist fanatics, playing to the bushy beards. They yearned for an emotionally expansive science in their secular world, and he was a fisher of souls.

A man got up and said 'they had never heard anything like that in Norwich before'. Never 'did Science seem so vast and mere creeds so little'.[9]

The sermon itself had an oceanic feel. The *Reasoner* ordained Huxley's men to the 'Priesthood' in recognition of this mythopeic vision and Puritan zeal. They were the new brimstone pastors. Enemies saw them retaining the Old Testament benefit of a 'scientific hell', into which 'those who persist in rejecting the new physical gospel' might be cast. Huxley, that 'Roundhead who had lost his faith', conveyed enormous power and urgency.[10] No bearded listener doubted that this sceptical priesthood carried the blood-stained banner of the Reformation.

By the end of the decade Huxley's essays were breaking all records. They were carrying the *Fortnightly*. His electrifying piece 'On the Physical Basis of Life' in February 1869 sent it into an unheard-of seven editions, and the cheques kept coming in. 'No article that has appeared in any periodical for a generation' caused such 'a sensation', said John Morley, the new editor keen to make evolution the *Fortnightly*'s creed.

It was based on a lecture that itself consummated the decade. 'Physical Basis' had inaugurated a Sunday Evening series in Edinburgh, and eye-witnesses confirmed that it was just as sensational. That night Huxley made 'Protoplasm' a household word.

It was the stuff of plant and animal cells, indeed of the slimy depths themselves, but his gothic image of 'quivering disembodied life' took it beyond the mundane. 'Science is almost sublimated into poetry', someone said of protoplasm's 'rushing and roaring' maelstroms inside the cell. It was the unifying matter of life, common to men and algal mats. Huxley showed bottles of smelling salts and carbonic acid, the constituents of protoplasm. Even though living protein was a strange manifestation of these chemicals, it was no more to be explained by a mystical 'vitality' than hydrogen and oxygen becoming water was to be explained by some occult 'aquosity'. The audience sat rapt, and 'you might have heard a pin drop', such was 'the *intense* interest'.

Accept this, he goaded them, and 'you are placing your feet on the first rung of a ladder which, in most people's estimation, is the reverse of Jacob's'. For if the 'dull vital actions of a fungus' are the properties of its protoplasm, so *all* of life's activity is the result of its molecular forces – even the lecturer's thoughts as he talked. Pious Presbyterians knew he was trenching on the sacred. The timid, he continued,

> watch what they conceive to be the progress of
> materialism, in such fear and powerless anger as a savage
> feels, when, during an eclipse, the great shadow creeps
> over the face of the sun. The advancing tide of matter
> threatens to drown their souls . . .

The audience seemed 'almost to cease to breathe, so perfect was the stillness'. Then he released them. Matter and spirit were only imaginary states, raised into ideological spectres. Materialism involved a 'grave philosophical error' because ultimate reality was undiscoverable. It was no more fathomable than the politics of moon-men. He was having his cake and eating it: using 'materialistic terminology' while abjuring 'materialistic philosophy'. The gasp gave way to a burst of applause, its intensity for the 'impressive earnestness of his tone' as much as anything. A listener familiar with the scientific greats, not only 'of this country, but also of France & Germany', announced 'that Mr Huxley surpassed them all'.[11]

The Xs lapped up 'the "lunar politics"'. Morley lapped up the lucre, as the *Fortnightly* presses kept rolling. New York's tabloid *The World* ran a screaming headline 'New Theory of Life'. Melbourne's printers pirated the *Fortnightly* as 'proteinaceous' fever struck the colony, and enterprising restaurateurs offered luncheons of the 'best cooked' 'Physical Basis of Life'. The religious appreciation was sparse, even if protoplasm 'makes the whole world kin', but refutations from three continents appeared 'more times than there are copies of his article'.

After that triumph Huxley planned to combine his essays into a book. 'The public may thank me', Nettie said, 'for I have long been urging Hal to collect & publish them'. It could only be called *Lay Sermons*, with its exultant vision of the new scientific cosmos. It too would break the bounds as an intellectual bestseller. 'People complain of the unequal distribution of wealth', Darwin declared, but it was a far greater 'injustice that any one man sh^d. have the power to write so many brilliant essays ... There is no one who writes like you'.[12]

Everywhere his writings were having an effect. As a besieged Pope was about to declare himself infallible, *Man's Place* appeared in Italy. Mivart was travelling to Rome at the time. He had begun to 'execrate' Huxley's use of the *Origin* 'as a means of impeding Man's advance towards his "end" whatever may have been his "origin"'. What he witnessed reinforced his view. He was 'amazed and saddened', he told Darwin, 'to see our friend Huxley's "Man's place in nature" for sale at most of the railway stations amongst a crowd of *obscenities*'.[13] Clearly the pauper-press fascination extended all the way to Milan.

With Parliament finally looking at scientific education, Huxley stepped up his agitation. Whither a nation which sent its school-leavers into medicine and industry armed with a knowledge of Jewish history and Syrian geography? He wanted an all-embracing 'earth knowledge' taught, to keep Britain ahead of Germany.

Nothing of its kind was known, so the General interrupted a hectic schedule to develop a course, calling it 'Physiography' (a sort of physical geography). He launched it at the London Institution, before an enthusiastic audience of boys and masters, among them Jess, Leonard and Marian.[14] Hal had a magical touch with children; he took them on an imaginary journey down the Thames, explaining the waters, the breezes, the hills – indeed the planet – as an interconnected whole. No schoolboy could kick a stone again without knowing the prehistoric tale it had to tell.

Hal's own brood was growing. Darwin would drop into Abbey Place occasionally to 'demoralise' his favourite Harry.

> I often think of your little man & can fancy I see him now
> with the spoon sticking perpendicularly out of his mouth
> & his eyes as roguish eyes as those of an angel. As Mrs
> Huxley won't sell him she might loan him to us & I w^d
> return mine with his manner highly polished.

Harry's big brother Len was his mother's 'great darling'. At nine he was still under a private teacher. He needed 'hardening physically by contact with boys', but like his father he was 'a clever, cool, imperturbable lazily persevering fellow', and 'very affectionate'. The older girls showed the passing years. Jessie was 'a fine strong limbed healthy girl', and at 11 already tall, 'only half a head shorter' than her mother.

They softened up the cynic. The children 'ripen wonderfully and make life ten times better', Hal had to admit. The house was a hive; 18 year-old 'young Jim' was seconded to the family for three years. (His father's health was 'shattered'; Jim was pensioned off from his asylum and now struggling even to pay the Jermyn Street fees.) Young Jim paced down Baker Street to his chemistry classes with Uncle Hal every day, cool and confident like all the young Huxleys, 'a very charming fellow & steady punctual & hardworking'.

Uncle Hal was 'definitely getting older', when he had 'time to think about it'. He finished the 1860s as he had begun the 1850s, ploughing through 'more work than is good for him'. He cried out for 'two heads or a body that needed no rest'. But all he got were more marching orders. Even on holidays he had to dart away to one institute or another. Or he was pinned to his desk, breaking only for a 15-mile afternoon hike.[15] He was coming up for 45, his hair silvering, a little fatter-faced. The famous physiognomy was losing its fierceness even as it gained a higher profile.

In 1869 the king-maker ascended the presidential thrones himself. Not one, of course; being Huxley, he had to run a gamut of societies simultaneously.

The old generation was handing over the sceptre. Poignancy marked Huxley's Presidential Address to the Geological Society on 19 February 1869. Murchison was absent, mourning his wife. 'My battle of life is nearly fought out', he sobbed the day before. He had wanted to attend, 'the more so as the 19 Feby is my birthday when I complete my 77th year & when I anticipated to be able to testify to the apostles how exalted a Chief you make'. It was a touching gesture to the new 'Chief'. 'May you live long to advance science'.

The neuralgic Lyell, 72 himself, advised Huxley on protocol, acting as his Parliamentary Private Secretary. To his own inauguration Sir Charles had invited the Archbishop of Canterbury and Sir Robert Peel '& both of them came'. That was a world before, and Huxley seemed unlikely to add an Archbishop or Disraeli to his list. Still someone had to say grace and Lyell suggested one of Huxley's radical clerics.

The times showed in his choice. After Huxley charged his glass to the Queen, John Bright was put down to toast the 'Commons', Dean Stanley the 'Church' and Tyndall the 'Physical Sciences'.[16] There was no more unholy, uncomfortable, pleasant party.

Bright was a spellbinding orator, the only one who 'ever really held me', Huxley admitted. But that night he had come to hear Huxley. Like a good radical speech, his was the cry of the underdog tyrannized. In his address Huxley defended Darwin against the holier physicists of Scotland. Darwin had reckoned on hundreds or even thousands of millions of years for natural selection to work in. Sir William Thomson, one of the dazzling Victorian intellects, propounder of the laws of thermodynamics, the entrepreneur who oversaw the laying of the Atlantic cable, deplored this cavalier call on time. Thomson calculated from the earth's rate of cooling that only 100 million years had elapsed since crustal condensation. And that was 'preposterously inadequate' for Darwin's higgledy-piggledy build-up of chance variations, added Thomson's cable-laying partner Fleeming Jenkin.

Huxley revelled in his role of defence counsel. 'Biology takes her time from geology', he retorted. Whatever the earth's age, and the accumulated rock strata suggested that it was immense, Nature has worked her results in it. His air infuriated another Thomson colleague, Peter Tait. The 'dashing' Huxley was like his 'Trades-Unionists', with a 'handloom-weaver's' hatred of the machines brought in to help him. His 'crab-catching' science should welcome the data-crunching might of the physicist. And so saying, Tait dropped the earth's age to a trifling *'fifteen* millions'.[17] That, at least, made Darwin realize 'how devilish a clever fellow Huxley is', for goading the engineers into refuting themselves.

Only 18 days later Huxley delivered another sweeping address. As the new President of the Ethnological Society he turned his attention to the empire. For years he had been showered with rice-paper letters, telling of hairy Burmese, or bizarre uses of the feet, or enclosing photos of Victoria's far-flung tribes. Huxley's colonial network of correspondents grew yearly, and at Sir Gilbert Scott's new, ornamented Colonial Office, Lord Granville talked of his plan to photograph the natives of every dominion.[18]

He streamlined the Ethnological and restricted women to special events. The journalist Eliza Lynn, 'intoxicated' by Huxley's revivalist science and accepting his view of women's 'natural' limitations, found herself excluded and complained bitterly. But it brought the Ethnological into line with the other male bastions. Huxley's own hardliners were purged and, with Hunt's death in 1869, he was free to move against his rivals. The rats were already deserting the Anthropological ship as the cooked books came to light (and a £1,000 debt). Huxley had a mole in place: a friend, the coral expert (and former Mayor of Colchester) Martin Duncan. The urbane Duncan, a little out of place among this 'rough lot', tipped Huxley off about each closed-door session, down to its 'prehistoric Billingsgate', or foul-mouthing.[19] But the merger and the clean-up were on track.

As he ascended the Presidential thrones, Huxley traded in his other chairs. His heir-apparents had been groomed. That loyal prince Michael Foster took over the Royal Institution domain, while Flower was told to 'make thy shoulders ready for the [Hunterian] gown, and practise the goose-step in order to march properly behind the mace'.[20]

The Xs marched behind him. The club was back in formation, their strange freemasonry having survived a civil war.[21] By 1870 the key positions were in the Xs' grasp. (With Faraday lying in Highgate Cemetery – no hallowed ground in Westminster Abbey for this simple man who had made the modern age with his electro-magnets, although the Xs were trying to place a monument there[22] – Tyndall now stood in his shoes at the Royal Institution.) To these key posts they added a key journal, a successful one, finally, after all the abortive efforts. It had a magazine-format, *Reader* or *Saturday Review*-style, but was dedicated to science. It was sustained by adverts for books, binoculars and toothpaste. Lockyer was the liberal editor, Macmillan the liberal publisher; the price was pegged at 4*d*, and the title fixed. 'What a glorious title, *Nature*', a mathematician rejoiced. 'It is more than Cosmos, more than Universe', it took us to the heart of 'mind and matter'. This was Huxley's long-time dream. Experience kept the weekly popular to start. To that end he opened the first number on 4 November 1869 with Goethe's aphorisms:

> Nature! We are surrounded and embraced by her:
> powerless to separate ourselves from her, and powerless
> to penetrate beyond her.
>   Without asking, or warning, she snatches us up into her
> circling dance, and whirls us on until we are tired, and
> drop from her arms.

The opener was purple and pantheistic and seemed to Darwin 'as if written by the maddest English scholar'. Huxley was still out to confound. It was a Nature that gloried in protoplasm and dinosaurs; a Nature that transcended the specialisms of science. This *Nature* was to be a broad cultural forum. It was a winning format; and it won despite piracy in America and competition from an Oxford-based monthly, the aloof *Academy*, with its call for German-style research (its first number carried Huxley's review of Haeckel). 'Darling Hal is as busy as usual', Nettie grumbled, 'I may say rather more so [because] two new Periodicals are just starting "Nature" & "The Academy" in each of which he has an article'.[23] But it was *Nature* that spoke for the London new wave.

Still this group had no label. Huxley dodged 'Atheist', 'Materialist', even 'Nihilist' for his know-nothing response to reality. But the label that proved hardest to peel off was 'Positivist'.

Positivists recognized the sensory limits of knowledge, and they were a devouring force in 1869. Morley was with them, and Lewes. Mrs Llewelyn Davies' brother was one, as was her brother-in-law, the history professor at University College, Edward Beesly. Theirs was a ritualized secularism. They were turning Comte's philosophy into a Religion of Humanity. It was a surrogate theology which recognized no God, but gratified a religious need: a kind of Roman Church with mankind as its object of adoration. (The positivist pontiffs Richard Congreve and Frederic Harrison had been educated among Oxford's Anglo-Catholics, which made them doubly suspect.) Huxley, dining with Beesly and Harrison at George Eliot's house, was dismayed at their talk of restricting research to social ends. Who could predict the fruits of science? Once 'practical men' had laughed at philosophers for asking 'why a frog's leg twitches . . . and yet therein lay the bud of the electric telegraph'.

He saw his liberated science under the thumb of a new set of social jesuits. Mankind's emotional needs were not to be satisfied by empty ritual, but by the real awe of Nature's deep mystery. He had no time for Comte's 'superstitious infidelity'. 'Catholicism *minus* Christianity', he called it, which promptly became the *bon mot* of the age. A squealing Beesly lamented Huxley's 'hard & damaging blow . . . From almost everyone else this would not matter. But from a man of your eminence and known emancipation it amounts to something like putting Comte on the Index Expurgatorius'. Comtists had seen themselves facing the same orthodoxy, 'blunting the enemy's steel', ready for Huxley's lunge. Beesly had never expected Huxley's long knife in his back.

But with archbishops already associating secular knowledge with positivism, Huxley had to distance himself. The ersatz Church was putting the ritual into unbelief, luring converts from Huxley's ascetic scepticism. The 'very air' seemed 'full of Comtism' to Kingsley.[24] Huxley was trying to make it seem like a bad smell.

Huxley's scientific civil service needed its own brocade banner. 'Atheist' was out, there being no disproof of God; and anyway, it was a red republican flag, a political weapon to smash the spiritual basis of privilege. On Mondays he had his share of agitators demanding the unfrocking of priests. He could not be seen to countenance the destruction of the entire Anglican cultural fabric.

The lack of a label became embarrassing when Huxley exhibited himself at that theological zoo, the Metaphysical Society. James Knowles, architect-about-town, and the Poet Laureate Tennyson, whose hideaway cottage he was designing, were gathering living specimens of every sect, the most distinguished dialecticians of their age. Nowhere but in liberal London could Anglicans and Catholics, positivists and pantheists, Unitarians and unbelievers sit down in a grand gesture to debate God's existence. Lubbock approached Huxley in April 1869.

There is to [be] a preliminary dinner on Wednesday (21ˢᵗ.) next at Willis' Rooms at 7 Oclock

There will be about a dozen there, including [the Catholic] ArchB. Manning, Dean Stanley, Tennyson, [Harriet's Unitarian brother James] Martineau, [the Anglo-Catholic W. G.] Ward of the Dublin Review, [Walter] Bagehot of the Economist & [the religious critic R. H.] Hutton of the Spectator.

I have been asked to invite you, will you drop me a line to say if you can & will come.[25]

Nothing could keep him away. By the time the Metaphysical met in Willis' (a venue for literary lectures), Huxley had rejected everybody else's clothes and felt naked. All about him 'were *-ists* of one sort or another; and . . . I, the man without a rag of a label to cover himself with'.

What could he call himself? He was shifting power to an élite whose authority rested in right reasoning, not mythical realities. He had already dropped the 'Unknowable' as the last remnant of idolatry. (It had begun to acquire its own mystique. And when the *Spectator* apologized for rendering it 'Unknowable God', the term obviously had to go.) Yet in Willis' Rooms a cacophony of voices proclaimed that they 'had attained a certain "gnosis"', like the second-century gnostics who professed sparks of divine knowledge. That night he came up with '*Agnostic*'.

It was another pitch for his professionals. It switched the emphasis to the scientific method and its sensual limitations. Agnosticism was made for the moment. Even in his own camp it was necessary. The Cromwellian head of Darwin's New Model Army found his Ranters and Levellers pulling apart: some voted for Haeckel's monistic materialism; others watched Wallace turn to séances and spiritualism. (Wallace was the latest disillusioned socialist to appeal to the spirits to put society back on its millennial course.) Agnosticism enabled the Protector to stand aloof as he surveyed his forces on a neutral parade ground.

He could also lecture the clergy with clean hands. He portrayed agnosticism not as a rival 'creed', but as a method of inquiry. The sciences, he told the Young Men's Christian Association, 'are neither Christian, nor Unchristian, but are Extra-christian', in a word, 'unsectarian'.

That, too, filled a need. Since his slum days he had blamed a divisive sectarianism for the world's ills. His was a sect to end all sects: an attempt to clamber on to a higher moral plane, to escape the priests and paupers, Comtists and Christians. Agnosticism was a many-coloured philosophical cloak, allowing him to mask his deep doubt and indulge in moral brinkmanship. The word would push alienated intellectuals off the defensive for the first time since the French Revolution.

The sceptic's air of 'moral infallibility' flummoxed the opposition. The irony of an Infallible Head of the Church Agnostic was not lost on the *Spectator*, which dubbed him 'Pope Huxley'.[26]

As the social axis shifted in late Victorian times, agnosticism was to become the new faith of the West.

Huxley now faced archbishops as an equal across the Metaphysical table. But Catholic qualms about debating with the Devil were as nothing to those of the British Association for the Advancement of Science about choosing an agnostic pope as President.

The 'General Council' met in a fraught session on 23 August 1869. The outgoing President, Disraeli's confidant and North Devon's Tory MP, Sir Stafford Northcote, had invited Huxley to stay at his country seat during the 1869 Exeter meet. But even he hoped to thwart Huxley's succession. He tried to engineer a palace coup, offering the chair to another Tory grandee Lord Stanley, whose constituency was near Liverpool's 1870 convention site. When word leaked out the press damned this 'ignoble piece of Philistine hypocrisy'. But His Lordship refused the ignominy of being trounced by Huxley on a vote. Twenty years earlier surgeon Huxley had grudgingly nodded to another Lord Stanley. Now the nobleman grudgingly nodded to him. Rank moved aside for 'the mouthpiece of English science'. Northcote was forced to announce Huxley's presidency, even if, the *Times* noted, he 'seemed to feel some little doubt of the perfect wisdom of the choice'.

Hal was at home when the news came. Stanley 'repudiated their having any P. but a Scientific man', Hooker crowed, and 'Lubbock seconded [your nomination] with spirit'. Like everything else, Hal's presidency was born in controversy.

The *Times* feared that Huxley would act the wild partisan and shatter the BAAS's history of deference and consensus. He would 'be in as difficult a position as Mr. Bright in the Ministry'. However 'discreet' Huxley 'may be in the absence of opposition', it concluded, 'his best friends tremble for him'. 'The Times & Co regard you as a wild bull', Tyndall laughed; 'the Times & Co are I fear somewhat asinine'.[27]

The presidency was the acme of Huxley's young career. It crowned a decade which had seen more intellectual turbulence than any since the Regency. Darwin's statesman was to take the dispatch box in the 'Parliament of Science'. Twenty years earlier Huxley had marvelled at the 'big wigs' running the show, now he was a 'big wig' himself. At last he could write his own 'Queen's Speech', and he promised to 'show how pretty-behaved I can be'.

The papers poked fun at the *Times*. So, 'Mr. Huxley is very "indiscreet"', laughed the *Spectator*. And, 'even worse', is inclined 'to talk English'. What! would Northcote smother 'the one grand controversy now raging among cultivated men' over 'whether the Supernatural exists at all' and 'go on telling decorous little lies'?

'If only we had an "indiscreet" Archbishop! – but that being impossible, let us be thankful that we shall next year have an indiscreet President of the British Association'.[28]

Poor boys rarely became president, but then devil's disciples were not often elected pope. It was a testimony to Huxley's biblical dexterity and agnostic astuteness that he could juggle so many soubriquets and still not be pinned down. The Holy Father revelled in his title as the thinking nation genuflected. The Church's prestige was passing to his evangelical professionals, and the pay and power would sustain the first generation of career 'scientists', trained, standardized and accredited. Henceforth men of letters would assess him with a proviso: he 'is really a most agreeable man', said Leslie Stephen, 'considering that he is a scientific swell'.

Huxley remained an 'angry, humorous, unbalanced' soul. And he still toiled like three men, even without three professorships. It seemed he had to, and that only the centrifugal force of his Geological, Ethnological and workers' rounds kept him from caving in. His financial and mental health was underpinned by perpetual motion. Not so for brother Jim, retired, crumpling, although no one yet called him mad. Adversity was Hal's drug; he thrived on it – he had never hit the bottle like Ellen, or fled like Lizzie. It catapulted him out of the sty, and the passing images of a bloated Cooke and exiled Scott had only shot him faster. Old friends had dropped away. MacGillivray was gone: two years dead, 'alone and destitute' in a Sydney hostel, a drunken hobo, 'father and mother unknown' it read on the death certificate.[29] Fate had strange ways, turning one into a tramp and the other a president.

The real wonder was that Huxley came out secure. Marriage

had been his 'heroic remedy'. It was his addictive defence against the world, and it beat 'opium eating'. Abbey Place gave him the energy for his tub-thumping forays. The enchanted castle had turned into a rather stodgy family fortress, and the maiden Nettie into a rather harassed mother with haemorrhoids. But inside its walls he was a different man. The contentment showed as he sat on the sofa and teased his 'special pet' Ethel. If 'you [could] see him with his seven children . . . playing with them as heartily as if he were a child himself', Nettie told Lizzie.[30]

'You cannot think how stout he is getting', Nettie added. The changes in the mirror matched the self-important shape of his city. He marched across a new London. The festering river of his dockside days now ran through the smart imperial capital, bounded by an elegant Thames Embankment. The shapeless city of that soulless era had a new focus in Whitehall and the growing temple of intellect in the west, South Kensington. While the new palazzo complex off Downing Street, the Colonial and Foreign Office, was a reminder of Britain's growing empire.

It had been an imperial progress to match Hal's own. He had seen it at the sharp end. He had shown his 'jacket blue & the beautiful cockade' in steamy ports. Crates of bones and rocks now marked the path of his graduates as they surveyed their way across continents. This wealth of fossils had enabled Huxley and Owen, those competing Hammurabis codifying the laws of life, to reveal the origin of birds and mammals – even if neither accepted the other's conclusions. But Owen now stood aside like an embarrassing old Prime Minister. Huxley was the focus of attention in 1870. 'In his great genius, of which his . . . good-humour is the most conspicuous feature', even the *Spectator* could feel 'a cordial pride'.[31]

The publication of *Lay Sermons* took him into the world of *belles-lettres*. He was a breathtaking essayist, whose seemingly simple prose silhouetted the immensity of his subject. With his 'common-sense cleverness', he could concoct a world on the back of a *Globigerina*. People saw him not merely as the apologist of the evolutionary vision, but as the visionary. By 1870 science *was* Professor Huxley. He made the pace of evolution as exciting as a Waterloo express. He was naturalizing morals and vitalizing molecules, imputing justice to Nature to enable his X-men to bask in its glory. The riddles of existence that had racked the pauper presses in his student days now tantalized his respectable audiences.

This man from nowhere had made science fashionable and himself indispensable. Even Oxbridge masters consulted him about new posts. On his agnostic, neutral ground he could shake hands with university modernizers and church reformers, literary radicals and dissident artists. These were the emerging intellectuals capti- vated by his discoveries of primitive man, and discovering 'how much of man, not least his religion . . . was still primitive'. They were the vanguard, seeking to fuse the best of Christian ethics with the beauty of modern science.[32]

Britain's new intellectuals would become aloof. But not Huxley. The 'plebeian' never really escaped grub street (not, at least, while Ellen was drinking away '220 p^r an.' of his hard-earned cash, or while seven children and sundry nieces remained a consuming fire). He was never to know the opulence of 'literary leisure'. 'But', Nettie sighed, 'we must submit'.[33] For all of that, his witty uncouth- ness served him well. It let him move from mechanics' meetings to Lewes' lunches, and still enjoy tea with Matthew Arnold at Harrow.

He continued to slide between worlds. His Liverpool Presidency in 1870 had its salubrious side, and a certain lording was necessary as he attended banquets and toured the city in the Mayor's stately coach. But he slipped away with Lubbock to look at the Liverpool no one wanted him to see. Into 'thieves' dens, doss houses, [and] dancing saloons' they dived, to be accosted by a bloody-nosed drunk in one. Thirty year-old ghosts haunted him as he moved among the 'unwashed, unkempt, brutal people' of this Atlantic trade port. He was back in docklands again.

Why did they not riot and loot the shops 'before the police could stop and hang a few of them'? It seemed an obvious question in the month that Paris fell to the revolutionaries. But his detective escort was lackadaisical: 'Lord bless you, sir, drink and disease leave nothing in them'. Epidemics silenced the starving in their insanitary slums. The angry apprentice rose up in Hal. It reanimated his ideal of a reformed Nature in an educated Britain knitting the nation together. The professor returned, shaking, to upbraid the toffs who gathered for a glimpse of him. You talk

> of political questions as if they were questions of Whig
> and Tory, of Conservative and heaven knows what [the
> *Liverpool Mercury* reported him saying]; but beneath there
> was the greater question whether that prodigious misery

which dogs the footsteps of modern civilisation should be allowed to exist . . . He believed that was the great political question of the future.

Huxley on the presidential platform was sedate. No panegyric on Darwin, no pounding of the clergy. On a serious subject he could be serious. The Franco-Prussian War was raging, but its toll paled besides the tens of thousands killed yearly by scarlet fever in the 'bloodiest of all wars'. Perhaps he was thinking of his own curly-headed Noel, who still brought a tear after ten years. He talked humbly of yeast from spores, multiplying in fermentation vats, and of the possibility of spore-like germs explaining these explosive epidemics. Science, he promised, would end this 'massacre of our innocents'.[34]

Philosophy could bake no bread. And it was the sober reflection of 30 years that it could not prove God or immortality either. But the revelations of science were assuming the lineaments of the Divine. And as the philosopher fingered the bread, and looked at its active yeast, he could promise freedom: freedom from disease and misery. 'Pope Huxley' was still offering salvation.

Part Two

Evolution's High Priest

1870–1884

Marketing the 'New Nature'

20

The Gun in the Liberal Armoury

NETTIE WAS DAY-DREAMING. At Liverpool in 1870, she was riding in the Mayor's 'great gilded swinging coach', amid the glitz and pomp. Beside her was Hal, the city's guest of honour, lionized as President of the British Association for the Advancement of Science. Suddenly she went cold, fearing that she would wake up and 'see the whole affair transformed into rats mice & a pumpkin as Cinderella did'.

But the bubble was not to burst, nor would she return to rags. Thomas Henry Huxley's rise from slum doctoring to Prime Minister of Science was real. Potent forces had created a new phenomenon, a star spokesman, a cultural critic who took Nature as his text. Huxley was the celebrity of the moment whose 'noble phiz' graced *Vanity Fair* and the *Illustrated London News*.[1]

Those sweeping forces were religious as much as secular. Huxley's Darwinian naturalism welled up with a rising radical Dissent. The Northern industrialists, muddy-booted chapel-goers, swore by science and technological progress. Theirs was a wheeze-and-snort Dissent to undermine the miraculous props under the Anglican throne. While Dissenters talked of the 'sin of conformity', Huxley stretched it to the 'sin of faith'.[2] He took Dissent to its 'agnostic' limit, discarding the last idolatrous trace.

Dissent was still eating away at the Church's State privileges. Even Oxford and Cambridge, so long the symbols of wealth and rank (a tassled cap had remained a sign of noble birth at Oxford until 1870), were losing their Anglican monopoly. On 16 June 1871 Gladstone finally repealed the hated Tests Acts, letting non-Anglicans take degrees at the ancient universities. Here was all that Dissenters had demanded for 50 years – with the exception of disestablishing the

Church, severing it from the State. (And Huxley still regarded 'the preservation of this Establishment' as unjustified.[3])

He was riding the Dissenting crest. The industrial barons were his family friends – steel tycoons who had come up the hard way, through the machine shops. These were the hard men who breathed open competition and enthused over Huxley's Great technocratic Britain. They had been marginals, like Huxley – men excluded from Oxbridge, the bench, the elite hospitals, indeed all aspects of the power of the State: but now they too were moving to the centre with their honorary LLDs and knighthoods for services to industry and Empire. It was telling that Hal and Nettie retreated to Sir Joseph Whitworth's 'lovely' Derbyshire pile after the 1870 BAAS presidential campaign. Here they spent five days relaxing, marvelling at the great iron machinery 'invented by himself'.[4] This marriage of Dissenting technology and marginal academia was the Victorian counter-culture come of age.

Whitworth was the embodiment of Northern industry – self-made son of a Congregationalist minister, a one-time journeyman-mechanic whose precision tools had made machine industry possible. The Crimean fiasco had him devising the devastating Whitworth .45 rifle for the War Office. A gruff committee-hating inventor still getting used to his baronetcy, he was happy to offer the Huxleys a wing of his Matlock mansion. His factory was turning out arms to extend Britannia's imperial reach. Special Whitworth steel was used to manufacture cannon and £100,000 of the profits went into science scholarships. Whitworth was a man for that dining coterie, the X-Club – John Tyndall (another friend) lectured on Whitworth's guns, and the Club's mathematician William Hirst was ultimately offered a directorship in the company. With Huxley articulating a radical Dissenting cause-and-effect view of the universe, they got on famously. The Huxleys spent two more 'truly enjoyable' days at Sir Joseph's Manchester town house.[5] Then it was off to Thomas Ashton's cotton mill before coming back to London. The journey was symbolic of Huxley's ideological trajectory.

Technology was making its extraordinary impact on the Victorian age. In 1871 the Huxleys had a nearby Underground, Marlborough Station, which meant that Sunday-evening guests arrived dappled in soot. In 1872 the mayors of London and Adelaide talked by telegraph, spanning the world in an electric click where Huxley's letters had once taken months. The machines lured a new generation. Young Jim – son of Huxley's 'broken down' and asylum-bound brother James – remained at the Royal School of Mines at Uncle Hal's expense. No high-flyer, he persevered at chemistry and metallurgy and would become an analytical chemist in a Sheffield steelworks. The industrial connections were riveted by marriage; the beaux were no longer doctors, even if 'Modern medicine', as Huxley said in industrial Manchester, was 'a kind of engineering'. Twenty-five-year-old Alice Cooke, daughter of Hal's tipsy sister Ellen, was walking out with Arthur Heath, who worked on the Great Northern Line.[6]

But Britain's industrial lead was vanishing. The prospect of losing their world supremacy shocked the mid-Victorians, and the flames of panic were fanned by Huxley's ginger group. He claimed that every 'third-rate, poverty-stricken German university' carried out more research than Oxford or Cambridge, overplaying this as the cause of her industrial might.[7] And yet there was no denying that Prussia's polytechnic schools were breeding a new dedicated industrialist, when Oxbridge disdained the factory manager (indeed, had barred him as a Dissenter to this time). Huxley's activists could now claim to speak in the national interest; the State needed them, needed their technical programmes and their expertise.

The theme was aired at Huxley's Working Men's College in Southwark. This self-betterment tech gave Huxley his 'plebeian' platform. He lured sympathetic speakers across the Thames: the *Fortnightly*'s editor John Morley, and the charismatic Yankee Unitarian Moncure Conway, that 'queer specimen of a latter day prophet', to discuss co-education among the sexes. The self-inflated poet Francis Palgrave came here to bemoan the national decline. With Germany moving ahead, Britain might be 'no longer the premier power', Principal Huxley piped up after Palgrave's warning, but we could 'become a greater nation' by developing every individual's faculties.[8]

Science would make the full man, hone his critical faculties, and it was in the national interest. This was Huxley's pitch in the 1870s. After a Transatlantic trip Whitworth too warned Manchester's foundrymen about America's capacity, pointing out the futility of matching her machines if 'you have not intelligent hands to work them'. The marginals – non-Oxbridge academics and chapel industrialists – were hammering on the government's door, demanding aid for training the 'intelligent hands'. The *Spectator* reminded Gladstone that the state had a duty to support science no less than to print money, and some saw the two as synonymous.

The clamour persisted during the Franco-Prussian war in 1870. Germany's was the 'most wonderful military engine ever seen on the face of the earth', Edwin Lankester told *Nature* readers. But then they were 'a scientific people', he added, rubbing it in. Every incident was played up to jolt a prickly government, including the capsizing of the revolutionary – and unstable – revolving-turret warship HMS *Captain* in 1870, which showed the need for physicists in the docks.[9] The tumult had its effect. Gladstone set up a Commission on Scientific Instruction, headed by the Duke of Devonshire, the President of the Iron and Steel Institute. Huxley, co-opted as a Commissioner, was tasting real power.

T. H. Huxley knew a family stability that the other Huxleys lacked. Home was a microcosm of advanced Victorian society, with an Anglican mother supporting an agnostic father. By 1870 the decade of baby-rearing was over. 'Babs' – the last baby, Ethel – had been baptized to Hal's usual growl, even though Nettie justified it as a vaccination against sin. A succession of ungodly Xs had compliantly stood as godparents: Busk for the lamented Noel, Hooker for Leonard, the Lubbocks for Nettie and Ethel, and Tyndall for Harry. This religious difference between husband and wife seemed surprisingly frictionless, as it did between Hal and the liberal Dean Stanley or Nettie's emancipist vicar Llewelyn Davies. For a supposedly anti-Christian bulldog, Hal had his Broad Church backers inside the family and out. Didn't he head a workers' college courtesy of the Christian Socialists? They supported his intellectual reformation and valued the bulldog's domesticated side. The publisher Alexander Macmillan saw 'so much real Christianity in Huxley that if it were parcelled out among all the men, women, and children in the British Islands, there would be enough to save the soul of every one'.[10]

Father was a mix of fun and formality. Incongruously, for a chap famous for his plebeian prose, he was called 'Pater' by the children (pronounced *Patter*). That was how he had referred to his own father, but it was a hard word which said something of his rising respectability. That brought its own worries: the higher he went, the greater his trepidation at the antics of the relations. Sister Ellen was unregenerate; a governess now, she was still begging and boozing. Her pay plus Hal's allowance 'ought to be sufficient for her wants', Nettie said, 'but somehow it never is'; and her own blowsy daughter Nelly bounced between gin and men in a 'deplorable, wasted life'. The lack of any welfare net had the overstretched *paterfamilias* helping where he could. When his old messmate Archie McClatchie died '& left a couple of boys without any adequate provision', Huxley pulled strings to get them into the Medical Benevolent College. The caring streak betrayed his own precarious past. At least brother George's widow, Polly, was off the family books now. In 1870 she married the ruddy-faced Patrick Duffy, a tax inspector. Nettie knew that pride and prejudice would bar 'any intimacy between Hal and him'.[11] There was a certain pique that an Irish Catholic had taken George's place. Polly too would slowly become estranged.

For the Agnostic Pope, intent on proving that Darwinians were not degenerates, drunken sisters and debauched nieces were to become a threat. An agnostic's respectability was always doubted, and it came as a surprise to bishops' wives that Huxley was 'an affectionate father'! Even the domestics held him in suspicion. The master, trying to prise the inebriate cook from the kitchen floor with 'Bridget . . . you ought to be ashamed of yourself', was put down with, 'I am not ashamed of myself, I am a good christian woman. I am not an infidel like you'.[12] That was the problem. For a man edging into society by preaching a new scientific morality, whose Sunday dining guests were the high and mighty, there could be no scandal.

Huxley's black eyes fixed on that unique colloquium, the Metaphysical Society, where the cardinals of knowledge decided the meaning of life. Unlike Darwin's his mind wasn't a whirl of evolutionary physics so much as existentialist metaphysics. On the second Tuesday each month he left his museum to go into conclave. The Metaphysical saw the great theologians and thinkers, politicians, poets and Positivists, men of science, letters and of the cloth, gather to ponder the great Victorian imponderables, the reign of law versus the grace of God, cosmic determinism versus free will. The society lacked only a Jew and a Muslim to make its denominational zoo complete, and like any zoo it was part forum for conservation in a changing world and part circus. As the two best debaters, Huxley and his opposite, the engaging Anglo-Catholic W. G. Ward, staked their positions, they developed a respect for one another that grew into personal warmth.[13] Of course the society never got past a hearty armistice.

Huxley thrived on the '"Oecumenical" freefight' on a Tuesday night. His 'new Nature', self-contained and evolving unaided, pulled the supernatural supports from a static Anglican (and Catholic) society. By 1870, as the Dissenters came in from the cold, Huxley's professionals were pushing a causal, determined science onto the cultural agenda. Here was the source of the Victorian 'crisis of faith': new social groups pitching for power in the name of the 'new Nature'. And the key issue – Free Will and future redemption versus cosmic uniformity – was the overriding concern at the Metaphysical. Agnosticism helped Huxley elude his detractors. It presented the man of science as non-aligned; it deflected any inquest from his own axiomatic beliefs (and Nature's undeviating causality was as unprovable as the Holy Ghost). And it allowed Huxley to take the offensive. He would sit scratching cartoons of his antagonists before cross-examining them in that 'rich and resonant voice'. Always he would steer the debate back onto the miraculous 'in the manner of a great criminal lawyer'. He traded on Hume's *reductio ad absurdums*; if the soul was immortal, it must be 'ingenerable', and thus have existed for an eternity independent of us. Or if it was somehow connected to our mental faculties, wouldn't animals have one? Hence Huxley's mocking Metaphysical paper, 'Has a Frog a Soul?'[14]

It was so congenial. It should also have been *in camera*, a private conclave of Church and Science. But word was out, and 'A lady told my wife all about these propositions of mine [against the soul's immortality]', he reported. Not that it mattered, for 'I cannot well be blacker than I am in the general mind'. Or greyer as society liberalized. A pale grey if Gladstone is to be believed. The Prime Minister apparently told Huxley's old Haslar Naval Hospital messmate and physician Dr Andrew Clark of the 'pleasure he had derived from your discourses'.[15] But the lion-hunting Clark would have said that. He was using Huxley to get into the Society himself.

That miraculous claims should be subjected to scientific scrutiny was a leitmotif of *Lay Sermons*. This potboiling book with a moral message 'will enrich you', Tyndall told Huxley (keeping his priorities straight). The riches were elusive, even with a reprint in four months, a cheap abridged edition in 1871, and a French translator lined up by Matthew Arnold.[16] But it was success enough for Huxley to start planning a series of volumes.

In America the response was as good, with the liberal *Nation* declaring Huxley a safe scientific guide. The *Nation* was moving for the South's post-war reconstruction, but in a bleak Montgomery, turned into a carpetbagging 'den of thieves', Huxley's sister Lizzie wondered whether the *Sermons* would not shatter the safeguards further. She wanted to know 'how far you carry your proposition of the regenerating effect of human discovery', and 'What you displace . . . by it'. It was a religious probing by the sister who had given him his religious training. 'I w^d have given any thing to be able to look up from the page, and ask you the questions', she said.[17]

America beckoned. He 'has had very pressing solicitations', Lizzie heard. Huxley was in the van of the Transatlantic science movement. He was on the committee of E. L. Youmans' International Science

Series – books which would give 'popular expression to the leading advances of thought'.[18] The American Youmans, despite bad sight, had gone into publishing, and he met many of his authors around Huxley's table. Huxley himself was slated to write the first, *Bodily Motion and Consciousness*. Not that it saw the light (nor did another, *The Races of Mankind*), but the series was Huxley to a tee. Its spirit was proselytizing, its territory was Darwinian, and its red covers promised a natural legitimation of social progress. Here were the pastors of science extracting moral and secular values from evolution and the 'Phenomena of Human nature'.[19] And with 40 million Americans it promised to be a lucrative business.

How much so became plain when Huxley hosted his New York publisher William Appleton at the Athenaeum in 1871. Appleton & Co. was a huge concern: its school department could sell a million copies of a single title. America shared Britain's love/hate relationship with Huxley and the firm was desperate for a publicity tour. American intellectuals were behind him. The Badlands explorer Ferdinand Vandiveer Hayden was typical in lapping up the latest Huxley article each time he returned to civilization. In 1870, back from Santa Fe and publishing his maps of Dakota and Nebraska, the chief of the US Geological Survey of the Territories saw Huxley's views being 'rapidly embraced among the Scientific and other Professional men of this Country'. Huxley was begged to make the crossing. Rumours were already sparking lunatic letters declaring that such 'ignorant jackanapes' as Huxley and Tyndall would be 'kicked out' if they dared to show their 'impudent faces on the American Continent', so Hal and 'brother John' were keen to get going. 'Perhaps in three or four years', Nettie told Lizzie, who had not seen her brother since 1846.[20]

The word 'evolution' became common currency in the 1870s. For a decade 'Darwinism' had been the term to cover a multitude of sins. But the 'Darwinians' had been an undifferentiated lot, who clustered for strength and tended to make little distinction between life's genetic development and Darwin's explanation of Natural Selection. Attracting radicals, atheists, socialists and free-traders, 'Darwinism became notorious as much for the friends it kept as for its political enemies'.[21] But at the end of the 1860s the groups were peeling off, emphasizing their internal differences. It was no coincidence that as the word 'evolution' came in and the dissidents fell out, Huxley devised his 'agnosticism' to legitimate only the secular and naturalistic end of the spectrum.

The lost souls were departing. The spiritualists and socialists regrouped behind that perpetual dissident Alfred Russel Wallace. (In 1869 Wallace suggested that the savage had an over-endowed brain for his simple life: so much grey matter was a spirit-bequeathed preadaptation for a civilized cooperative life. Wallace – the co-inventor of Natural Selection – had removed man from its arena.) The Spiritualists marched off to the Millennium.[22] The providential evolutionists went off in another direction, behind the Catholic St George Mivart, for whom life was a fulfilment of God's plan. After the shake-out, Darwinism remained an umbrella organization, and even Huxley diverged on key points. In the 1860s he had harped on the 'living fossils', creatures which had persisted unchanged through geological time. Where Darwin had nature select from tiny varia-tions, Huxley had been happy with larger jumps; where Darwin transported his species to islands by wind and raft, Huxley had invoked drowned continents. At times all they seemed to share was a faith in evolutionary naturalism.[23]

Given Huxley's own deviance, the problem is to understand how and why he designated other evolutionists as heretics. Take University College's pathology professor and rising star H. Charlton Bastian. He was just as materialistic, just as committed to nature's continuum. So much so that he insisted on the continuous chemical production of microbes at the fount of life, feeding Darwin's adaptive spread. In the 1860s Bastian too was part of that nebulous 'Darwinism', one of the new generation, younger than the young guard, and initially supported by Huxley.

'Transubstantiation will be nothing to this if it turns out to be true', Huxley laughed as Bastian went public on spontaneous genera-tion in 1870. Was the simplest life continually being generated from organic chemicals, all around us? Bastian's bottles of boiled hay bris-tled with microbes after a few days, and this evidence was good enough for part of London's medical community, traditionally an evolutionary hotbed. When the slanging started, the sharp Bastian traded on the clinician's superior experience. The doctors too could lay claim to experimental expertise, and they posed a professional threat to Huxley and Tyndall. Bastian ignored Huxley's advice 'not to publish till all results [were] retested'. This stung, and Huxley saw Bastian 'going out of his way to be . . . offensive'. In the territorial jockeying, Bastian was tarred as 'a clumsy experimenter & an uncrit-ical reasoner',[24] and Huxley pushed deep into a study of *Penicillium* and yeast to suggest that Bastian's spontaneously appearing bacteria were part of the mould's life-cycle. He wooed the electorate, travelling to Leeds and Bradford 'turning an honest penny out of Yeast',[25] and converting his talks into a *Contemporary* essay. Darwin's inner circle presented itself as more reliable than the established doctors.

The young guard was codifying Darwinism, hardening it into a Nicene creed. What had been nebulous became specific and doctrinal about 1870. Only by establishing a creed could the idea of a 'heretic' become real. A one-off matter-to-life event, deep in primeval times, was acceptable. Tyndall's purplest prose which made us children of the cosmos was acceptable. But a rival medical profession trading on the endogenous chemical production of fever-producing poisons and parasites was not (Huxley and Tyndall were singular in adopting the new germ theory of disease). Bastian was an Emperor Julian pointing back to the discredited transformism of the pagan years. Lamarck's crudities (as many saw them) had been kept alive through the dark ages at University College by Bastian's disreputable teacher, the atheist and reputed homosexual Robert Grant. Grant's 'advocacy was not calculated to advance the cause', said a prejudiced Huxley (intent on putting Darwinism on a more respectable footing). The Frenchman Lamarck had believed that life's evolutionary 'ascent' required a continual replenishment at the base. And the 78-year-old Francophile Grant was happy to see Bastian's atoms 'select their partners and waltz off in a quaternary danse of life' (note his French *danse*).[26] But old has-beens and young upstarts were no longer considered part of 'the cause'. 'Pope Huxley' was beginning to use his considerable powers of excommunication.

The General was angling for a new barracks. The Royal School of Mines in Piccadilly was cramped and he needed space, a certain sort of space. For a professional clawing power – no Darwin, with his country house for experiments, no clergyman in his pastoral realm – only the state could provide a rival laboratory space. The laboratory: it was a novel concept which signalled a new approach to education. Huxley's men denied Oxbridge claims that the Classics moulded a gentleman's character. Truth did not come from incestuously recycling Greek texts; it had to be found out, experimentally. The *arriviste* teachers contrasted this direct probing of 'reality' with Oxbridge pedagogy. It was their strategy for cultural domination; their truths would come from the 'new Nature'. The Department of Science and Art now had 30,000 students countrywide and the 1870 Education Act meant proliferating schoolmasters who needed training. More than anything Huxley needed a laboratory where they could be taught the practical Truths of the 'new Nature'. Their knowledge was to make all other "ologies ... so much book-wormery'.[27]

But a lab meant moving from Central London. Jermyn Street was a glorified geology museum. It had forced Huxley to knuckle down to taxonomic practice; and in arranging the fossils he had become a dedicated palaeontologist.[28] But it gave him no practical facilities. This was the more embarrassing because the vaunted superiority of science lay in its experimental verification.

By default he had come to see sprawling South Kensington as his only option. That strange *sui generis* suburb in the west, all empty plots, building tips and museums, was being turned into a Germanic 'culture centre' with the proceeds of Great Exhibition. The new Albert Hall stood at its north border, while the lot at the bottom was earmarked for the Natural History Museum. It met Huxley's territorial ambitions. With Richard Owen set to get his 'temple' here – that Romanesque Cathedral of Nature to snub the pagan Renaissance – Huxley could face the 'old fool', matching him building for building. It meant swopping Piccadilly for an unmade Exhibition Road (as it became).[29] But the drawbacks were outweighed by the prospect of labs and a proper red-brick science school. The move would symbolize the intellectual shift in the nineteenth century – the switch from museum display to that new knowledge-manufacturing site, the laboratory.[30]

He had close links with the empire-building Henry Cole, Secretary of the Department of Science and Art and South Kensington's effective creator (Cole even coined the name 'South Kensington'). And powerful allies inside the Whitehall machine had become family friends: the Liberal Minister and former Governor of the Bank of England, George Goschen, lobbied for him in Gladstone's Cabinet, while Lucy Goschen had the children to Admiralty parties. Hence one ironmaster's voice in the Commons exaggerating about 'Professor Huxley's anatomical preparations [having to be] made in a dark closet about eight feet square'.[31]

But Huxley had his own political machine. On the Devonshire Committee he was joined by X-Clubber and Liberal MP John Lubbock and his old examiner William Sharpey, with *Nature*'s editor Norman Lockyer as Secretary. Huxley led witnesses to condemn the cramped Jermyn Street, and he out-manoeuvred his old boss Murchison, the imperial swell with the Belgravia trappings. (Murchison had wanted to remain with the Geological Survey close to London's clubland.) Murchison died in 1871, and with this stiff-lipped military geologist went a world of upper-class values, and the

16. The young bearded lecturer at work, drawing a gorilla skull.

17. A 'grim and a grotesque procession', the Duke of Argyll called this skeletal troop, the clever frontispiece to Huxley's *Man's Place in Nature* in 1863.

18. The first known skull cap of Neanderthal Man. Huxley was given the cast by its discoverer Karl Fuhlrott.

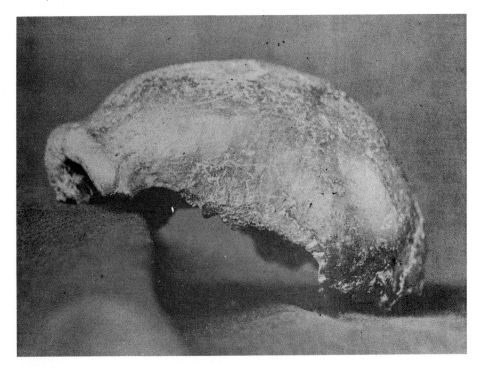

19. Not so grim: the discovery of another Neanderthal skull at Gibraltar in 1864 elicited this sketch of a hairy ape man. It was a joke: in reality Huxley was the first to show that Neanderthals were not 'ape men' at all, but large-brained humans adapted to a cold climate.

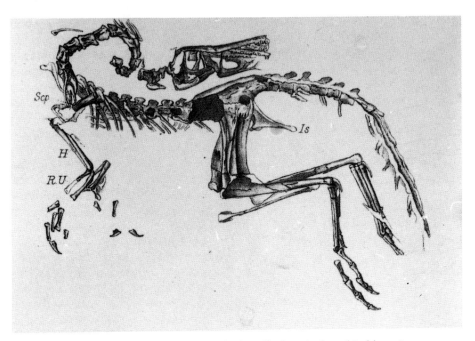

20. The tiny dinosaur *Compsognathus*, which walked on its long hind legs. It was crucial to Huxley's presentation of dinosaurs as the ancestors of birds.

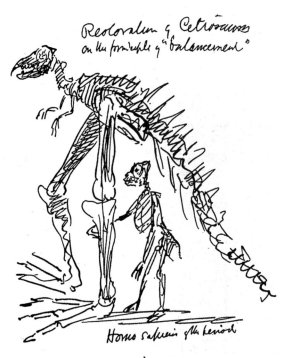

21. The concept of bipedal dinosaurs was novel in 1868. When John Phillips unearthed a five-foot *Cetiosaurus* thigh bone, Huxley dashed off this caricature. The arms were unknown; in the sketch Huxley shrank them by a corresponding amount as a tease. Note the ape-faced 'Homo sapiens of the period': Huxley had long believed that humans lived alongside dinosaurs.

22. Huxley on London's pace-setting School Board. He made science part of a modern curriculum, and had a touching faith that the Bible might be read in class for its poetry and selected ethics. 'He had a vision of heretical Huxleys instructing innumerable little Huxleys'.

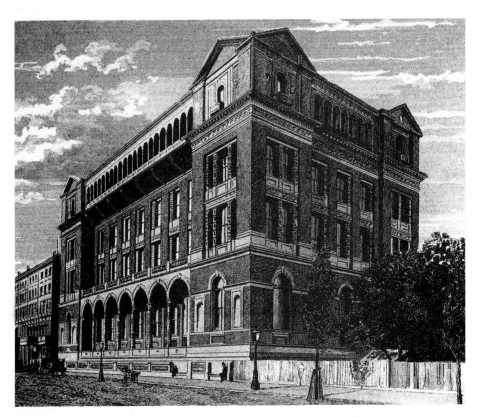

23. (*Above*) Shouting science's importance. The solid 'Science Schools Building' in South Kensington, finished in 1871. The discipline of 'Biology' was forged in Huxley's laboratory on the top floor.

24. (*Opposite, above*) The lab, with its regimented practical classes.

Huxley's reluctance to moot evolution in class belied his private pedigree-chasing in the 1870s. These family trees in his notebooks are typical.

25. (*Opposite, below, left*) A Haeckelian lineage for mammals.

26. (*Right*) The ancestral snail-like mollusc differentially curling its shell to produce a *Nautilus* or *Spirula* or straightening it to evolve a belemnite.

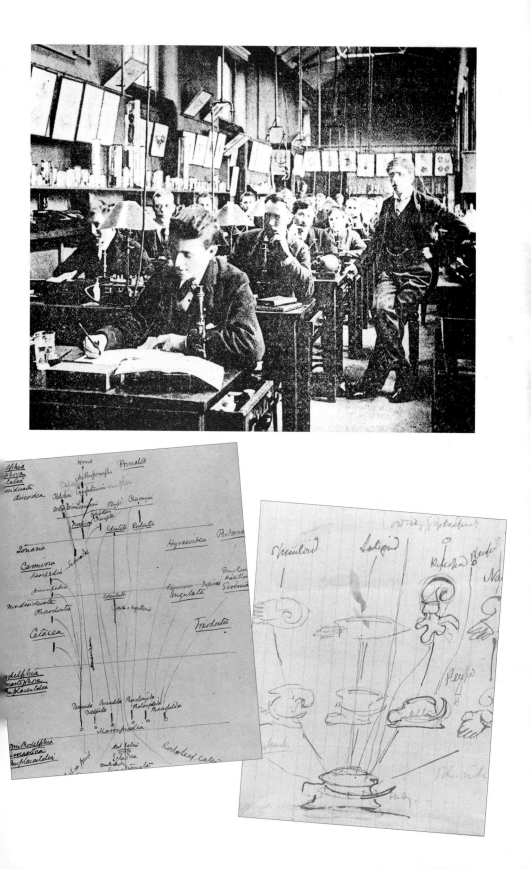

27. Huxley Eikonoklastes in New York, 1876. His irony and Ciceronian understatement confused Americans used to a Hell-fire style. But they gave him screaming headlines. Here he is battering at Moses with Milton's bust.

last major obstruction. The Committee recommended the amal-
gamation of the Royal School of Mines with the Royal College of
Chemistry and their removal to South Kensington. Still Huxley
pushed for more: he had always seen zoology and botany united at a
deep cellular level, and a botany department would make it 'a proper
Biological School'. 'It would be glorious', he told Hooker.[32]

His strategy paid off. The *Times* saw him inveigling the Committee,
and no protest of innocence could shake the feeling that his aim
was 'an imposing National College of Science'.[33] Even if the call for
laboratories came in a period of national frustration about American
advances and the German war-machine, the net result was more State
power to Huxley's group. Huxley, the mover and shaker who audited
the accounts and signed the cheques, who recast the prospectus and
liaised with commissioners, had always been powerful beyond his
teaching status. This proved it.

The government-built 'Science Schools' at South Kensington was
the first fruit of the politicking. Costing £66,000, with a 186-foot
frontage, the four-floor building shouted science's importance. It had
been intended as a Royal Navy school, but big labs could be made
out of the long rooms designed for naval models. With creamy terra-
cotta, ornate arcades and figures depicting the seven ages of man, it
was a match for Owen's projected museum over the road. Huxley
would be facing the 'old-fashioned' temple from his modern laboratory,[34] and two more different symbols could not be imagined.

In summer 1871 scaffolding still shrouded the edifice. The bewhiskered professor glowed in the building's red mottled tints. The
Times thought the façade 'a sight good for eyes tired of the endless
stucco'.[35] Inside he crossed the mosaic marble floor laid by convict
labour and swept up the huge central stairwell to his top floor. Peering over the balcony, he looked onto the glass dome of the 54-foot
lecture theatre below, whose 60-foot ceiling would give his mellifluous voice its accentuating echo. On the top floor was his joy: a
60-foot laboratory, based on the Berlin and Bonn models. This was
to be his biological seminary where he could turn the trainees 'into
scientific missionaries to convert the Christian Heathen'.[36]

If science was only '*trained and organised common sense*' (someone who saw himself as a self-educated 'plebeian' would say that) then
common sense would need training and organizing. Here he could
mobilize the teachers who would return to the factory towns. When
the first batch arrived for their practicals in June 1871, the interior
was still unfurnished.[37] As an interim measure, he had to requisition
the ground floor of the South Kensington Museum (the forerunner of

the Victoria and Albert). He jerry-built a lab here. Tables and apparatus were set up, preparations readied, 20 cheap, £6 microscopes laid on.[38] So much groundwork that Gladstone's Minister for Education was faced with a £750 bill. But he did sanction the employment of three demonstrators, each paid £100 for the six-week session.

The General's one-man army was a thing of the past. In came the succession of brilliant assistants. The adoring Michael Foster from University College, Professor William Rutherford, who had set up its own physiology labs at King's College London. And that bellicose giant, Ray Lankester. Like so many aspiring sons of Dissenting reformers, Ray had rung the social changes with a First from Oxford. The Congregationalist's son typified that second-generation social-climb to Oxbridge,[39] clambering into the Anglican seat of power where the boys dissipated their fathers' Nonconformist values. Not that Ray had anything but contempt for Oxford's 'disgusting toadying' elitism.[40]

Edwin and Phebe's son was naturally an adept microscopist, and the 23-year-old followed his hero Huxley with papers on monkey brains, fossil fishes and the invertebrate's cell layers. In 1870 the tyro had already published a crushing rebuke to the Darwinian apostate St George Mivart.[41] A freethinking evolutionist, and a fighting critic of Oxford's 'medieval folly',[42] the belligerent Ray was passed over at Oxford for a Readership in Anatomy (it did not help that his father had just blasted Oxford's Classicism in the *Quarterly Journal of Science*). So Ray – the boy who had played truant to hear Huxley lecture – toured the German pathology labs learning the latest staining techniques and returned fresh from Haeckel's Thuringian hills to his 'father-in-science' in June 1871.

He joined the team to drill the first 38 masters and solitary school-mistress. They were to be introduced to microscopes and taught the conventions in a crash course. Ironically, given the patronizing attitudes about the unsuitability of petticoats, the school-marm took the end-of-term prize. Lankester thought that the shock would spur the men on, so long as they did not set up a 'trades union' closed shop.[43] But there could be no lock-out.

The ramshackle beginnings reflected the scaffold-and-navvy state of South Kensington. Everywhere were shirt-sleeved Royal Engineers, drafted in by the War Office as free labour.[44] Swarms of squaddies completed the picture of regimented science on a war footing. South Kensington was militarized down to its very foundations (put in by the sappers).

Territorial rivalry with a wealthy Church accounted for Huxley's 'military metaphor' – that portrayal of rational science vanquishing the forces of obscurantism. It was a martial image he shared with street religions such as the Salvation Army. But *real* uniforms, those gave the image its authority and science its national purpose. Huxley likened himself to a shilling 'recruiting sergeant', enlisting men 'into the army of science'.[45] The blaze of red at South Ken gave this real meaning. And the Departmental barracks had more than shillings to give away: it had Whitworth's £100,000 in scholarships.

Military precision was admired by the Department's desk-bound head, Henry Cole. It was he who put the Crimean veterans into his top brass. First came Lieutenant John Donnelly, a Royal Engineer who had shown such initiative in clearing the site that Cole drafted him in as adjutant. The ebullient Donnelly would rise through the ranks without ever leaving South Kensington. With Huxley's backing he become the 'Secretary for Science', and he repaid his debt: 'why should you have [another] assistant?' he joked, mimicking the Treasury penny-pinchers. 'Is it not a complete waste of the money of the State? If you can black your own boots why should you not? No; there is no authority . . . Therefore if I were you I should engage Parker'.[46] And so Huxley took on W. K. Parker, professor-to-be at the College of Surgeons and an anatomical pedant with a wandering style (like a dog going home, sniffing everywhere, laughed Huxley). But he knew every millimetre of a bird's skull, and such confounding detail had won him a Royal Medal. Huxley's own team was becoming a crack unit.

The professionals played up their 'expertise' and linked it to national prestige, trying to make science indispensable. Their hijacking of the Devonshire bandwagon led to jibes about the 'Brompton pluralists' creating jobs for the boys. They wanted an expanded professional role: the replacement of Classics-trained advisers, a Ministry of Science, proper science schooling, even experts on public health authorities and as juries in cases involving insanity.[47]

Huxley's anthropological science too would follow Britannia's long reach. The Colonial Office in 1870–1 began its photographic round-up of the natives. Dispatches in diplomatic bags told of Huxley's needs, and governors photographed to his specifications, standing aborigines beside a rule. From Cape Town, Australia, Sierra Leone, the Falklands, West Indies, Ceylon, Formosa and Tierra del Fuego came sorry accounts of conquest, accentuated by photos of dejected faces. Here were Kandyan chiefs and Cape Town bushmen stripped naked in convict chains. Some enlightened governors would only photograph subjects unclothed with their permission; indeed, the missionaries having pointed out their shame, a few refused.[48]

Nothing like it had been tried. With the ladies gone from the societies, these brooding images could be used to render Huxley's talks on the geography of mankind more graphic. The London Stereoscopic and Photographic Company even sold its own 'extra-ordinary photographs', pandering to public voyeurism on Victoria's far-flung peoples.[49] Unclothed black men and women (white nudity was unthinkable) reinforced the image of their moral inferiority and child-like innocence. Ironically the new anthropology saw these peoples in a pre-Darwinian light as Stone Age survivors. They repres-ented the infancy of the human species. They were the emotional tykes of the Empire who needed stern guidance. Paternal respons-ibility was another attitude ushered into science by evangelicalism. But at the end of the day, Huxley's collation was part of a Colonial Office project to stamp the subject races as an aid to British rule.

Science pushed into the over-civilized areas at home as brusquely. As the Oxbridge colleges lost their religious bar, liberals such as Revd Benjamin Jowett tried to put science into the exams. Jowett had liberally kicked old Anglicanism in *Essays and Reviews* – and been liberally kicked back (he lost his fees for ten years as Greek Professor for heresy). The changing times told as he became the new Master of Balliol[50] and put Huxley up on his Oxford forays. Perhaps he put Huxley up for more. It was only the 'tremendous shindy' started by Revd Edward Pusey, the High Anglican who had charged Jowett with heresy, that stopped Oxford's revisionists nominating the agnostic for a Doctorate of Civil Laws in 1870. Darwin got it in order to keep a worse devil out, 'oh Coryphaeus diabolicus'.

At Cambridge too Huxley's word counted. He named the man for Trinity's new Praelectorship of physiology. Michael Foster, still grieving the death of his young wife and with 'two little bairns' to support, got the job. With the Tests Bill going through there was nothing to stop a Baptist-turned-agnostic. He joined that second-generation migration to the old seminaries, even though his father had set his heart on seeing him in a chair at University College.[51] With Foster went the London expertise to found a physiology lab in the virgin territory of the fens.

And at that birthplace of English academic physiology, University College, Huxley was just as active. When wealthy philanthropists wanted to do 'something more for science', he had them endow chairs here.[52] As an examiner, he boomed the need for physiological practice among its medical students, and he was in the thick of the politicking to establish a Faculty of Science.[53] Huxley put his money, or at least his son, where his mouth was. Len climbed out of the Gower Street tube daily and walked past UC's classical portico to his class at University College School. It seemed the natural choice, sharing the 'godless college's' Nonconformist origins and progressive regime. The boy did not have his father's lightning mind, but he was 'a miracle of steady perseverance' and topped his class.[54]

The old world scornfully eyed the new. In 1871 Professor Huxley presented the prizes at Charing Cross Hospital (in his own student days, that had been a clergyman's lot). His teacher, the tweedy Wharton Jones, that relic of Burke-and-Hare antiquity, still revelled in his protégé's success, even as he recoiled at a sullying ape ancestry.[55]

It was a typical reaction. The new science was a mix of lofty moral message and dirty substance. Huxley's postbag was full of letters from strangers who had 'great esteem towards you', but who drew the line at 'those "Lay Sermons &c on the Origin of Species"'. Kindly religious folk in awe of his 'great gifts' begged him not to get involved with Darwin's monstrous *Descent of Man*.[56] But radical social theory and evolution were all of a piece now, tied tightly in the *Fortnightly* and *Contemporary*, and there would be no spiking the Whitworth gun in liberalism's army.

Darwin's latest double-decker on mankind's ape ancestry and sexual selection was causing consternation. All pointed ears, hairy embryos and artful baboons, *The Descent of Man* combined anatomy and anecdote to establish that the morality of 'primeval men' grew from the social instinct of apes. A sad Emma Darwin saw her old husband 'again putting God further off'. For the sensitive even the title smacked of scientific man's descent into Hell. Hooker wished that Darwin had simply called it *The Origin of Man*. But the book was still titillating, and ladies had 'to order it on the sly!'[57]

The grand detour of Darwin's life was over; the affable naturalist had finally declared himself on the evolution of mind and morality. It had taken him 33 years to summon the courage for *The Descent of Man*, waiting until a cushioning Huxleyan community had made it quite safe. The poison had been drawn by *Man's Place* and Tylor's and Lubbock's ruminations. By now a flood of papers had inured the public: Wallace on the selection of savage morality and Galton on the selection of civilized character, Walter Bagehot on the evolution of prehistoric politics and W. R. Greg on the evolutionary fate of the low-birth-rate bourgeoisie.[58] These men, the last two an economist and mill owner, threaded class and politics into biological evolution and Darwin sealed the trend, weaving a white, wealthy, male outlook into the fabric of the *Descent*. Reviewers groaned with 'wrath, wonder, and admiration' at his lumpy tome, and predicted as usual that if morals were born of brute instinct 'a revolution . . . will shake society to its very foundations'.[59]

Talk of 'revolution' said more about the nation's nerves in 1871. The *Descent* had been published as those 'bloody Frenchmen' were being crushed at the climax of the Franco-Prussian war. Huxley had wanted the Germans to 'give that crowned swindler' Louis Napoleon and the whole syphilitic Second Empire 'such a blow' that they would 'never recover'. But by the time the *Descent* appeared even he wished the 'infernal war' at an end. Darwin's and Huxley's Russian translator Vladimir Kovalevskii, the nihilist who used science to undermine Tsarist Orthodoxy, had stayed at Downe and sat Huxley's lectures in the winter of 1869–70. Now he could be found carrying proofs of the *Descent* through the Prussian lines to the Dantonesque fortress of Paris. Russia, there too was a problem, a country reneging on the Crimean peace agreement. 'The Russian row is beginning', said Huxley, fearing a wider war. 'Bad days are I am afraid in store for all of us'.[60]

At such a time the *Descent* hit the bookstalls. Four months of siege had left the Parisians starving. The ravenous képi-hatted revolutionaries had even eaten the elephants in the zoo. With peace in February 1871 the Metaphysical antagonists Cardinal Manning and Huxley pulled together on their Paris Food Fund, adding to the 10,000 tons shipped across the Channel.[61] Unfortunately, as the reviewers got their teeth into the *Descent*, the Reds were distributing the parcels. Paris fell to the Communards in March 1871. Kovalevskii settled down to work in the Paris Muséum, laughing at British hysteria about the alleged 'brigands, assassins, [and] socialists' in control.[62] But the hysteria grew.

Huxley thought Darwin's timing 'too bad' because he was bogged down in more metaphysical warfare and 'You know I can't show my face anywhere in society without having read' the book. Not that he was left a free moment for promotion. But the press thought the timing atrocious because of the red skies: 'it is reckless', thundered the *Times*. Darwin expected 'execution' as a minimum, as he told Mivart just before the reactionary bloodbath in the French 'Sodom and Gomorrah'. For Mivart Good and Evil would lose their meaning and authority collapse if morals were made evolutionary products: 'God grant we in England may not be approaching a religious decay' of the sort 'which Frenchmen are now paying for in blood & tears!' he moaned to Darwin.[63]

European palaeontologists had already strung together bitty fossils to draw up genealogies for rhinos, pigs and elephants. With his publicist's flair, Huxley fixed on one creature, meaningful in an equestrian age. London was a din of iron-hoof clopping, a city congested at 8 am. by ten-horse buses and cabs. Ironically the trains had only increased the need for town horses and short-stop travel. On Fridays the swells arrived in hansoms at the Royal Institution to see Huxley. An equine pedigree was above all safe: a model of faithful subservience, the horse showed Nature in yoke. Huxley took 'one of the most beautiful animals in the world' and drew up the ultimate bloodstock. It was appealing, judging by the fact that Tyndall was 'torn to pieces by women in search of tickets'.

From a single-toed stallion, he worked back via the ass-like *Hipparion* with pronounced dew-claws to the three-toed *Anchitherium* of Miocene times. He cast further, past the tapir-ish *Palaeotherium* to an undiscovered five-toed agouti-shaped ancestor. His was a history of streamlined growth and toe-reduction, the making of society's 'exquisite running engine'.[64] He skirted the precise cause of this specialization towards one tip-toe, and it was left to Kovalevskii in the Commune, plunging into the 'adapt-or-die' Darwinian process, to explain it. He saw the Miocene forest ponies being forced onto the first grassy plains.[65] The old spread-toed tapir-like browsers gained long-striding legs on the hard meadows, and long grinders for grazing the tough grasses. No one had seen such a detailed calculus as he correlated toes and joints with survival potential. This was the palaeontology of the future.

The Descent of Man hardly diverted the public from the war. What did, the *Times* said, was the creation of a London School Board (not surprisingly with women voting for the first time in British history). With half the nation's children running loose, the Education Act enabled the setting up of education authorities (school boards) to sweep the street arabs into a countrywide system of schools. Radical London gave every ratepayer the vote in its school board election. The religious sects organized to return candidates. The women's bandwagon was unstoppable, given the chance to roll at last, and the first woman doctor, Elizabeth Garrett, ran in Marylebone. Huxley moved from the educational heights to the guttersnipes. He too contested Marylebone, running with a trade-unionist and carpenter William Cremer on a dream ticket, scientific training and artisan opportunity.

Huxley only had time for four rallies during the November 1870 hustings. London schooling was notorious, and on the platform he claimed that farmers would not rear pigs under such slum conditions. His star-studded (all-male) committee featured the X-Club's Tyndall, Lubbock and Busk, University College professors, J. S. Mill, Tom Hughes and endless foot-soldiers who traipsed from door to door. Two ragamuffins – 'a deputation from Huxley's Committee, or perhaps the Committee itself' – turned up at the house of the Endowed Schools Commissioner Arthur Hobhouse and asked him to be treasurer. He agreed, but first had to put £5 into the kitty.[66]

Unlike rivals, Huxley took no adverts in the papers, and he had few hours for canvassing. When he could manage it Nettie went 'with him in the ev^g to "stump"'. Here he fleshed out his educational scheme: science and modern studies for both boys and girls, 'drill' to get the street urchins healthy and housekeeping to teach the domestics their trade (applauded by a pernickety Nettie and the middle classes). 'I hope for Marylebone's sake he will be at the top of the poll – for his own at the bottom', said Foster, knowing what success would mean in lost time.[67] But everybody pulled, and Knowles, the new editor of the *Contemporary Review*, leaked extracts of Huxley's forthcoming essay on 'The School Boards' to the press.

The female vote, usually Huxley's, was siphoned off by Elizabeth Garrett's slick machine. He was up against his former pupil, and her supporters 'organised a complete system', Nettie reported, 'working down street after street & house after house'. Nettie admired her: she is a 'charming lady-like woman', 'one of those who does credit to us instead of damaging as many women do the cause they advocate'.[68] Garrett was triumphantly returned for Marylebone. And so was Huxley – in second place.

London's board saw labour, secularism and women well served, but even better served were the Anglicans, Methodists, Baptists, Congregationalists and Catholics, who ensured that factionalism prevailed. Many of the radical Dissenters, however, were secularists, some more so than Huxley. Nowhere could match 'Heterodox Hackney', and none admired Hal more than its Congregationalist delegate Revd James Picton. Hackney revelled in 'slummy' secularism. Its fanatics observed so close a 'connexion of cleanliness with godliness', a wag observed, 'that they abjured the former with the latter'. On Sundays the inns reverberated to speakers who would 'resolve Christ into a Solar Myth' or, in Picton's case, Christianity into Pantheism. Picton fancied that Huxley had underrated 'the revolution which modern discovery is working' on 'religious thought'.[69]

But if the *Lay Sermons* were casting their spell on society's under-belly, turning Congregationalists into Pantheists, Huxley was doing something else with the kids in the board's care. He wanted them taught the Bible. Hackney was bewildered.

Many Churchmen fought to keep the schools religious. The Board had the power to exclude theology altogether, but Huxley knew that making headway meant making compromises. He opted for selective Bible-reading, 'without any comment', to instil moral principles. He agreed with Birmingham's radical MP George Dixon 'the inex-pediency of attempting to exclude Bible reading' altogether. But it had to be selective: the Old Testament was as much vice as virtue. Who would want the lasciviousness of Lot's daughters or Joseph's seduction taught? 'As a French friend of mine observed, the stories of "Madam Potiphar et les demoiselles Lot" are not edifying for children'.[70]

On the one hand this was the Huxley who had sent a Bible to his godson Tom, Lizzie's boy. Having been a footloose 'young prig' him-self, he was not about to make others stand in moral isolation in a religious world. They 'should be brought up in the mythology of their own time', while being given the skills to question it. They should learn to recognize the 'moral beauty' in all religions. In the *Contem-porary* he warned the radical fire-bombers against 'burning your ship to get rid of the cockroaches!' Education was a more targeted toxin to eradicate the sectarian pests. Foster understood: strong medicine was needed to purge the extremists, and the *Contemporary* bait would prove 'Poisonous to snakes' of all shades.[71]

But it smelt of betrayal to out-and-outers, and the issue was to haunt him for life. Very few achieved Moncure Conway's degree of sympathy. For all of Huxley's vaunted familiarity with the 'dirt-eating' ways of the world, he remained curiously idealistic: 'he really believed that the Bible was to be read in the schools as he himself would use it', Conway noted, 'for its good English, its poetry, histor-ical value, selected ethics. He had a vision of heretical Huxleys instructing innumerable little Huxleys'.

The big Huxley held out 'to the disquiet of sundry of our liberal colleagues'. Still, the Sultan Schamyl in him rose at a sniff of doctrinal theology in school. He was the powerful pragmatist again. 'Fanatics on all sides abuse me', he said, 'so I think I must be right'.[72]

Because he occasionally sent small sums to the secularist George Holyoake and sought legal protection for freethinkers, agitators had Huxley pegged as an ally. But the agnostics were fighting their own professional corner. They had their agenda – creating a quasi-autonomous, state-paid scientific caste. No longer did they need this street-level secularist constituency. Holyoake, reporting Huxley's speeches in the American press and his *Reasoner*, celebrating 'your reign to the uttermost ends of the earth', never really understood. He asked Huxley to chair a meeting on the anniversary of the socialist Robert Owen's birth. But while Huxley praised Owen for having the 'courage . . . to work out his theory [of infant education] into a practical reality', his sympathy stopped there.[73] It led to a terrible disappointment when he compromised on the Bible.

Life was becoming topsy-turvy. Having snarled at patronage for so long, he found himself dispensing it in January 1871. George Eliot and Thomas Carlyle both approached him to get friends onto the School Board staff.[74] Huxley had a prodigious capacity for work, but he never seemed to know his limit. Between January and May 1871, as he reconstituted himself into the Board's administrative dynamo, he ran seven concurrent or consecutive courses. Workers' lectures, talks on biology at the London Institution; a Royal Institution course on Bishop Berkeley and the folly of contemplating the unknowable. Like an old-time Providentialist he would gallop up to a northern mining parish for a sermon weaving geological evolution and industry – telling of the aeons that the club mosses took to compact into the country's wealth, coal. Aeons, too, spellbound the children as he explained the origin of their world. In between came advanced physiology students and regular classes. The lectures continued literally *ad nauseam*. He was beginning to be sick. The public was fooled because the talks seemed to flow like 'conversation'. Giving them was 'perfectly easy to Huxley', everyone thought.[75] No one realized the strain.

Nor did home insulate him; the house was becoming a meeting place for the world's intellectuals. Do pop over, he wrote to James Knowles: 'Turguenief, the Russian [novelist], Tyndall, & I hope one or two other good folk are coming to dine with us'.[76] The 'good folk' were now the great. From the Underground the others trooped, Matthew Arnold and Herbert Spencer. And a sculptress: the dinners were rounded feasts, with painters and musicians for leavening. Huxley's wit was yearly in demand at the Royal Academy toasts, and the house welcomed the up-and-coming talent. Briton Riviere, whose syrupy scenes of sick children would come to typify Victorian sentimentalism, was cultivated by Nettie, who penned letters like hospital dispatches. The tall Jess (14) and frail 13-year-old Marian ('Mady') were arty. They would take the Underground to drawing classes at the new Slade School of Fine Art at University College. Mady was the skittish tease among the girls, waiting for Frank Darwin to visit to be on her 'dignity with him!' 'No more kissing, I can tell you', Huxley reported back to Darwin.[77]

The house was about to become their own home. After renting for 16 years, the Huxleys at 46 were finally to own a property. They could scarcely afford it (Hal was just breaking even) but another bank loan would see them through. Knowles now switched his publisher's for architect's hat. Having built Tennyson a house and made it fit for a Laureate, he planned to make Huxley's fit for a professional. In March 1871 Knowles obtained a 99-year lease on 4 Marlborough Place, minutes away in St John's Wood, and started an extension which would dwarf the original cottage.[78]

How to recoup was another matter. The Home Secretary had Huxley sitting (unpaid) on two Commissions. The BAAS President who had cursed epidemics as the 'bloodiest of all wars', and the father who had watched his own blond-tousled child die, had added the Contagious Diseases Committee to the Devonshire.[79] More aggravated (and unpaid) sittings overloaded him at the School Board. He ran its first Education Committee, which was to turn a few ragged schools into a London-wide system of education. After four gruelling months, on 13 June 1871, it published a 50-page plan for London's schooling, covering everything from optimum size to evening classes, and a broad curriculum spanning geography and history to six years of simple object-based science.[80]

The one-man think-tank dominated the meetings, building that ladder from the gutter to the university (his phrase which fired the nation). It was a massive job, and there weren't enough hours in the day. 'I fear for Huxley', Hooker told Darwin; 'his wife tells me' he 'is running a fearful rig of work . . . his love of exercising his marvellous intellectual power over men is leading him on – and on – and on – God knows to where'. Even Huxley saw the absurdity of being worked to death on 'two Royal Commissions & the School Board all sitting at once'.[81] Things had to calm down.

He was making Science rival Classics in the schools, usurping its prestige. Mass education also created a need for new textbooks. These had been the prerogative of country parsons and dame-school matrons, but Huxley's experts would edge them out. Only the 'interpreter of nature', he argued, could really popularize the 'scientific blue books' (academic monographs). And so grand schemes were hatched for a series of ninepenny 'science for beginners'. The best men were on board. The Owen's College chemist Henry Roscoe sent the proofs of his *Chemistry Primer* in August 1871 and chivvied Huxley for his scene-setting *Introductory Science Primer*.[82] But he was over-extended; the pages lay blank.

He was seizing up, like a millipede wondering which leg to move next. So many Commissions and controversies across such a broad front got in the way of construction. To Foster he was 'a brilliant David forbidden to build the Temple on account of the blood of the Philistines on his hands'.[83] At the British Association in Edinburgh it was the new President, Sir William Thomson, who had Huxley on his feet. Huxley loved giant intellects, and none was larger than Thomson's. They had been elected Fellows of the Royal Society together and enjoyed their affable sparring. Thomson had even invited Huxley on a Hebridean cruise, as if he had the time.[84]

But the Scottish physicists stood four-square against the London naturalizers. Not for them Tyndall's belief that mundane Earthly matter could generate 'all terrestrial Life'. Huxley had pinned his own Presidential faith on the chemical origin of primeval protoplasm. But for many the notion that 'dead matter' could crystallize into the 'germs of life' was preposterous. Thomson disliked Darwin's chancy natural selection, and he saw the Londoners' self-creating universe fasten man to Fate. It would deprive him of free will and redemption in a better world. But his own solution hardly helped. Thomson suggested that spore-bearing meteorites had seeded the cooled planet when it 'was ready to become a garden'.[85] The audience was shocked; a few laughed, thinking it was the start of 'some good joke'. And none roared more than Huxley: 'What do you think of Thomson's "creation by cockshy"', he asked Hooker. 'God almighty sitting like an idle boy at the sea side & slinging aerolites [at] . . . a planet!'[86] Shuffling the problem of origins off into the heavens showed the difficulty now for a Providentialist to get around Evolution.

Pater was forever jumping up. September found him still in Scotland, in St Andrews, supposedly relaxing. But he had little real rest. While the family swam and golfed, Hal went off to the Elgin fossil beds, the ancient tombs of his *Stagonolepis* 'crocodiles', there to sift 'tons of Elgin sandstone for bits of my dearly beloved reptiles with dear old Gordon of Birnie – the jolliest old brick of a Scotch minister'. A sackful of vertebrae meant more work. But the children were happy. Jess was enjoying herself 'much as I once used to', Nettie said revealingly, 'only unlike me . . . she has never known "hard times"'.[87] Even Hal was lured onto the 'Royal and Ancient' course by Thomson's colleague Professor Tait, only to be 'hopelessly bunkered three or four holes from home'.

Holidays were punishing rotas, and what snared Pater at St Andrews was scholasticism. Like any self-righteous sectarian, he was fully engaged in a religious age. He exploited society's prejudices against Papism, and made Science speak with a Protestant tongue. He had a 'sectarian keenness of scent for heresy',[88] and even on vacation sniffed his way into St George Mivart's *Genesis of Species*. This was liberal Catholicism come to meet Evolution, to make it progressive and directed. Only the production of preadapted organs could explain what Darwin's chancy mechanism couldn't – an incipient wing. Did natural selection have flight in sight, asked Mivart. If not, and if there was no functional value to half a wing, how could a whole one develop? For Huxley such problems were of no account in a book tainted by Catholicism. A hardening Vatican had given scholastic theology supreme authority over modern science, and the chaffing Mivart – the liberal caught between two infallible popes – had been forced to make the old Jesuits sanction evolution. Seeing the sixteenth-century Father Suarez pressed into service put the glow on Huxley's face. The cold warrior 'dived' into a dozen Latin folios in the university library, chasing Mivart's 'corky exposition of Catholic theology'. Huxley was making sure that 'Frater Suarez would have damned [Mivart] forty times over'.[89] He was keeping the Pope Catholic.

A prickly Darwin could only see the 'scorn & spite' in Mivart's review of *The Descent of Man*. He wanted revenge '& all the more, as I own I felt mortified'. Darwin was oversensitive. He felt betrayed by Huxley's pupil, and Huxley's policing was swift. Mivart was 'clever & not a bad fellow', but he was 'insolent to Darwin & I mean to pin him out'. A Manichaean Calvinist like Huxley needed a reactionary Catholicism. He needed a Jesuit militia to threaten Britain's modernity. It was Huxley's populist pitch: Science was protecting society against the menace of an infallible Papacy. A reconciliation between liberal Catholicism and providential Evolution threatened Huxley's naturalistic power base. Hence the relish at showing Suarez in all his orthodoxy, never the evolutionist: 'Only fancy my vindicating Catholic orthodoxy against one of the Papists themselves'. Darwin laughed until his 'stomach was contracted into a ball'.[90]

Knowles slotted 'Mr. Darwin's Critics' into November's *Contemporary*, when the season was back in swing. 'What a wonderful Essayist he is', said Hooker, passing the proofs to Darwin, this 'defender of the faithful'. Darwin, extending the imagery, thought 'it would be a sin & shame' not to reprint it in Huxley's next opus. Others were beginning to take all this religious imagery seriously. They were characterizing the 'faithful' as a Darwinian 'sect', which, like all beleaguered sects, had sought security in their Election. Or so one reviewer painted them. Those not born-again in Darwin were cast into a Dantean 'limbo of heretics'. Mivart was being excommunicated by bell, *Origin* and candle – publicly ostracized by Huxley, Hooker, Lankester and Flower to stiffen the resolve of the ranks.[91] Agnosticism had gone past Protestantism to become the hallmark of Huxley's profession – Nature pared to the bone, stripped of the last idolatrous trace in this 'New Reformation'. Huxley's supposedly non-aligned agnosticism kept showing its radical Dissenting roots. A secular, uniform Nature was now the unquestioned foundation of the Darwinian Temple.

This was one of five back-to-back reviews drafted on his holidays – so many social commentaries, sectarian interjections and demands for State aid that he returned from Scotland on 29 September 'as tired as two dogs'. Even so he dashed to Manchester within days to discuss exams as a Governor of Owen's College, then to lobby the government from that home of municipal socialism, Birmingham.[92] Talks were refined on the hoof, but the hooves were tiring as he drove himself on. The new opiate 'chloral' helped his sleep, but for the first time he had to cancel a public appearance for fear of dropping.

After lectures he would sit for hours on the School Board. The monumental task of establishing free primary schooling in London had become bogged down in religious bickering. Hardliners, throwing the fat into the fire, wanted the board to pay the fees of children at the existing Anglican and Catholic schools as well. Huxley dug in for a trench war, lampooning this 'outdoor relief' for the rich. The *Times* flapped at his anti-Catholic invective, but the Dissenters saw it as 'high time that *English Science* spoke out' against the 'impudence of the Ultramontanes'.[93] Huxley's speeches grew stirring and passionate until Gladstone took note. The cynical thought it a step to Parliament. But it was a school board, not a springboard, he told the *Daily News*, and 'not even the offer of a seat in the House of Commons' would lead him to forsake his 'proper occupations' again.[94] The grants were blocked to abbey and church schools. London was committed to a secular education.

It was a sign of the diminishing hold of the churches on education. But seven months of wrangling took its toll. Hobhouse wanted the board to switch 'its attention from Heaven to Earth'. So did Huxley. He was frustrated. 'I *cannot* and *will* not' sap 'my energies & waste my time in faction fights & administrative details', he swore.[95] He began clutching at fossil bones, desperate to pull himself out of the quagmire. He was losing precious time, and the wealthy Hobhouse, fearing he would resign, quietly offered him £100 a quarter from his own pocket to keep going. But Huxley turned the cash down to remain a free agent.

He only scrambled onto a higher plane to suffer more. From the chair of the School Board he switched to the chair of the Metaphysical Society, where the sects were locked in a more ethereal struggle. An agnostic on the throne caused consternation among the Catholics here too. 'Nothing could be better', Hooker crowed with Gillrayish crudity; it 'will send a bellyache all round the table. I think I now see the A. Bishops all bolting to the "Cabinets" with their aprons up & breeches down'.[96] F. D. Maurice turned up to read his misty paper encapsulating the quandary of the age, 'On the Words "Nature," "Natural," and "Supernatural"', and then left, never to reappear.

In an age of sects, sectarianism was at the root of Huxley's reviewing to an extent never really appreciated. A roll-call of his unpublished reviews revealed that the Catholic Mivart was not his only target; Huxley submitted papers on Anglican ritualism to the *Quarterly* and on the 'eloquence' of preachers (as he put it sarcastically) to the *Nonconformist Review*.[97] This was saturation publishing, and still the demands came in.[98]

It was too much. He staggered out of his London Institution lectures on mind and body in December, 'seedy to the last degree'. Mind might be a glorious epiphenomenon, like a steam whistle on a loco 'without influence upon its machinery', but Huxley's was whistling a warning. His hurtling express was careening off the rails. The machinery was 'grumbling like an ungreased block'. 'Don't know what is the matter with me except dyspepsia and a strong desire to do nothing', he told Hooker. 'D— everything an inch high and a year old – especially every Governmental thing'. That said it all: the School Board, Metaphysical strain, commissions, the chairs (Foster addressed him as 'The President of Most of the Societies'),[99] lectures on everything from consciousness to coral – the lot had drained him. By the end of 1871 he was crumpling. His diary, usually a splotchy mass of dates with the Victorian greats, from Gladstone to Elizabeth Garrett, fell blank. The listlessness of November gave way to depressions in December. He ran down to Brighton 'for a day or two to see if the sea breezes will set me up'. 'You will be right in a jiffy', Tyndall jollied him.[100] But he wasn't.

Incessant nausea left him looking haggard. On 3 January 1872 he admitted defeat. It seemed that 'weariness, incapacity & disgust' had got the better of him. The doctors said there was nothing organically wrong but they predicted a collapse if he carried on. Nettie was miserable about him, '& for once, he felt [that taking a rest] was a reasonable thing to do'. As usual, 'rest' meant work elsewhere. The Navy already had him studying a 'detestable grub', a maggot of the moth *Ephestia* which 'has been devouring Her Majesty's stores of biscuits at Gibraltar'.[101] So he contemplated a recuperative cruise via Gibraltar to the Mediterranean.

A day or two later his cavalier attitude shattered. 'Hal's health, his capital, suddenly failed'. The crash 'came all at once', Nettie said; 'he literally was unable to give his lectures, scarcely to write his letters'.[102] It left him momentarily incapacitated, unable even to stir from his seat. At short notice Nettie, ever the guardian, got him two months' leave from the School of Mines. Then she booked immediate passage on the steamer *Malta* to take him away from the winter fogs to Egypt.

He sent his resignation to the School Board on 6 January, only to have the Chairman Lord Lawrence try to refuse it. Even Huxley's opponents were mortified. He towered above them all in intellect, the Congregationalist minister Benjamin Waugh said, but never made them feel small. Waugh, the future founder of the Society for the Prevention of Cruelty to Children, had been antagonistic at the start; but he too had gravitated to this man whose 'motive in every argument, in all the fun and ridicule he indulged in', had been the welfare of the children.[103] Still, Huxley went.

The haste astonished everyone. 'Lowe will have to be quick if he wants the benefit of my discretion, piety & learning', Huxley said the next day on hearing that the Chancellor wanted a word, 'for I mean to be off by the P&O on Thursday'.[104]

So he left Nettie to deal with the children, Knowles to get on with the house, Foster to take over 'the SK lectures to womankind',[105] the Commissions to take care of themselves, Mivart to stew in his own juice, and stand-ins all over London to cover for him. He did the unimaginable, just stopped at the beginning of term and took an impromptu holiday.

21

From the City of the Dead
to the City of Science

P&O'S LINER WAS A far cry from the creaking, slack-canvas *Rattlesnake*. 'Fogs & calm' beset them but the sturdy steam pumps pushed them through. The Biscay swell was as horrid as ever, making the *Malta* 'very lively', and Huxley couldn't sleep. Past the Lisbon cliffs they ploughed, the last gale blowing them 200 miles in 16 hours into Gibraltar. He was on deck at 8 am. on a 'lovely morning', 16 January 1872, to see the Rock loom up.

Huxley began to revel in the leisure as he 'strolled into the market & devoured red oranges'. Then he presented his Admiralty letter and inspected the dockyard stores, only to find that 'nothing could be better in point of cleanliness & order'.[1] So he visited HMS *Hercules*, where the grumbling below deck about maggoty food was growing ominous. The flour was pure when it left Deptford, so he investigated the nearby sacks of cocoa and fruit, and finally traced the source of contamination: the moth eggs were being blown onto the flour from unpurified cocoa.

The former surgeon's relations with the top brass had equally changed. He was rowed over to the *Minotaur* to have breakfast with Rear-Admiral Hornby, commander of the Flying Squadron, whose warships could reach any trouble spot from Africa to India. Huxley enjoyed his new-found status, dining with colonial administrators and admirals. Hornby had him ferried to Tangier with the Bishop of Gibraltar. A week out and what a difference: he was 'wandering about Tangier', watching the Moors. His was a more admiring eye now, like Burton's, looking favourably on the Muslims in defiance of his own idolatrous culture. As he painted mosques his eye would catch 'a stately moor' wearing his *Haik* 'exactly in the manner of the

Roman toga ... hung in wonderfully graceful folds'. Britannia's reach was huge, and even in Morocco he had his contacts. 'Left Hooker's letter with Sir John D. Hay', he noted. Sir John was the consular minister and expert on the Barbary coast (although Hooker had been more interested in his daughter). The family had Huxley to dinner nightly and a son took him riding to Cape Spartel near the Cave of Hercules. But even here a depressed Huxley thought that 'the springs of [his] machine were finally smashed' and it reflected in his doom-laden sketches of medieval berber camps. The foul weather made him worse; 'rained Cats & dogs', he wrote, as his gloomy painting began to blotch.[2]

The Fates followed him on the *Nyanza* steaming for Malta. The Mediterranean was 'disagreeable, cold & wet'. His eight hours at Malta were 'rainy and cold', and he was blown on to Alexandria by gales. In Egypt on 1 February the downpours made a mockery of the travel brochures. Alex was a 'muddy hole', and so he took the 8 am. train the next morning up the Delta. From the windows the sleet made it seem more like a blustery Lincolnshire than a wondrous Nile, except for the palms reflecting in the pools.

At Cairo he checked into the palatial Shepheard's Hotel. Through its arabesque lobby passed all the Raj expats. With an English hotel, and almost English prices (14s a week), came more English rain. Walked in the bazaar '& went to bed early', he commented sourly. The disgruntled air gave way as he took a donkey and servant 'mosque hunting' the next morning. Always it was religion with him – before the pyramids, before the museum, before even the fossil-rich limestones. He went up to the Citadel, built by Saladin below the Mokattam hills, to take a kaleidoscopic view of the city's white domes. He saw Muhammad Ali's 'grand mosque', newly finished in an out-of-keeping Ottoman style. Through the crowded narrow streets of the Old City he ventured to the huge Sultan Hassan Mosque with its marble columns and fountain courtyard. Then to the beautiful eighth-century Tulun Mosque, where he sat in the enormous courtyard sketching the arches and wood friezes.[3] The noise, the smells, the competing chants from the minarets; the tasselled merchants, the crush of donkeys and traders: whatever the weather, it was the East.

Despite the British presence – the British hotels and British doctors (Dr James Grant, physician to the ruler, the Khedive, kept an open house for English savants) – the Nile was as deliciously mysterious as ever. Here the Orient merged into mystery, and only the matter-of-fact British thought to demystify the river by discovering its source. The impeccable Speke and outrageous Burton had done their job, describing Lakes Victoria and Albert as the White Nile's source, giving the great artery its imperial pedigree. As Huxley mooched around Cairo, a bumptious American reporter Henry Stanley was with Livingstone 2,500 miles to the south on the shore of Lake Tanganyika, having greeted him with the line that would become an imperial pun, 'Dr Livingstone, I presume?' And a weak, lion-savaged Livingstone was shortly to set off on his last journey to see if the Lualaba entered the Nile.

The Nile was a national obsession. The opening of the Suez Canal in 1869 made Egypt the strategic gateway to India. P&O was rebuilding its entire fleet for the Suez run and abandoning its Cape stations. So Egypt was both an easy and an exotic destination. It was also a *de facto* British outpost (becoming a partly official one three years later, when an opportunist Disraeli bought £4 million worth of shares in the French Suez Canal company from the bankrupt Khedive).

With cruise liners sporting lavish décor, and rail lines laid from Alexandria to Rodu, travel was more a 'question of time and money' than slog and slave, as the brochures put it.[4] Palace hotels were springing up to cater to Thomas Cook's trainloads. But most of all Egypt was a fashionable sanatorium for the intrepid who wanted to get away from the genteel spas. The pyramids promised a romantic resort for the wealthy who feared leisure. Here they could heal their congested lungs in the desert air, while losing no time to become more cultured.

Professor Huxley too was something of a national obsession. Doors opened even here. Sir William Gregory, erstwhile Chairman of the Commons Committee on the British Museum and the new Governor of Ceylon, escorted him round Bulaq Museum on the 5th, and the next day took him in his private train through the ancient capital of Memphis to see the world's oldest hewn-stone monument, the step pyramid at Sakkara. The museum housed Auguste Mariette's fabulous treasures, disinterred by his army of 3,000 diggers – Hyksos statues and scarabs, mummies and Meidum paintings. Of course, what stopped Huxley was a 'Sculpture in true bas relief from Memphis' showing 'man leading the apes!' 'Visit again & study carefully', he jotted in his diary.[5]

One afternoon he was in Cairo's City of the Dead, investigating the ornamented tombs of the Caliphs; another on Windmill Hill, littered with ancient potsherds. But much of his time was spent on the Mokattam hills to the east, looking at the limestone strata, drawing sections and ferreting in quarries of nummulite fossils.

Reports went back to Nettie, more about the terrain than the state of his brain. 'Cairo he says more than answers his expectations and at last he was in sun shine'. Unknown to Hal she had his doctor Bence Jones request a further month's leave, and 'I hope that he may see the wisdom of indulging himself'. She coped alone as the Marlborough Place tip was turned into an eight-bedroom home. She would visit it with Knowles and the builders to discuss baths and kitchen pipes. She met every crisis as the small house was expanded to include drawing room, dining room and bedrooms. Delays dogged them; London's planning authority, the Board of Works, halted the building because the extension went a foot over the approved plans. Then the labour costs overshot the estimate and Tyndall had to deposit £100 in Huxley's account.[6]

While Nettie was sitting on the Underground train, taking Jess and Marian to the Slade drawing classes, Hal was sketching in Cairo's Coptic churches. Here Christianity reached back to the third century. There were none of Llewelyn Davies' crucifixion scenes, only icons of a gentler beatific form. Then he popped back to the museum, to see 'the two statues recently discovered . . . at Meidum – 3rd Dynasty – 4800 B.C.' He had no schedules, no fixed itinerary, for once time was his own. When he should have been racing to give his Monday lectures he was taking a donkey across the desert to paint the remaining Wonder of the World, Cheops' pyramid.

It was too expensive to go up the Nile alone. But he fell in with fellow Athenaeum member Frederick Ouvry, the President of the Society of Antiquaries. (The Athenaeum was as much a social focus at Shepheard's as in Pall Mall.) He and a pleasant diplomat's son, Charles Ellis, had taken one of the shallow-draught houseboats, or *dahabiehs*, and invited Huxley along.[7] So on 15 February a fresh wind caught the big forward triangular sail and carried him at seven knots past the Meidum pyramid. Hal sat on deck, sketching, only diverted by a passing felucca boat, or a jackal scavenging on the bank. They saw their first pelicans. The days became hotter, the nights bright and moonlit. They stopped to buy oranges and bread in villages and to get a glimpse of rural life. And back on the boat they watched the dropping sun silhouette the palms with blood-red rays. At last Hal had his therapeutic heat.

They were 400 miles up the Nile by the 23rd. He arrived at Thebes in the evening and ambled about Karnak by moonlight. The great temple had been cleared of peasant huts by Mariette: here it stood, unbelievable, its hypostyle hall the largest in the world, 5,000 square feet, its 60-foot columns dwarfing the visitors with their flickering lights. The collapse of a mighty Pharaonic civilization seemed more real in the stillness, with only bats flapping through the ruins. In the fresh air of the morning Huxley rode with an old guide into the arid Valley of the Kings. First to the ramshackle temple of Kurna (Seti I), 'then to Kings tombs up an amazingly hot valley – visited Belzoni's, Bruces and No 9'. Belzoni's excavation (the tomb of Seti I) was on every tourist's itinerary; 'awe-inspiring', Flinders Petrie would call its paintings of the Book of the Dead. He rode over the hot sandy ridge, his donkey knowing each step, then across a 'plain to the Memnonium' (the Ramasseum, with its huge fallen statues of Rameses II). On he passed, to be surprised by the two stately 65-foot Colossi of Memnon, standing alone on the edge of the desert, all that remained of a vanished temple.

As they continued south he was beginning to sleep. He relished the '"always afternoon" sort of life'. The heat and laziness of *dahabieh* travel seem to massage away all cares. At El Kab they stopped to saunter round the old town with its 'thick crude mud walls' and see the graffiti-covered tombs cut into the cliffs. The heat was intense, and the surrounding hills were gradually lowering as the Nile became prettier. At Kom Ombo they visited the temple dedicated to the town's hawk and crocodile gods, and Huxley had a 'wonderful view of [the] desert from the top of the little hill on which the temple is placed'. Here he sat, pondering the fall of ancient worlds, 'very grateful to Old Nile for all that he has done to me – not least for a whole universe of new thoughts'.

Huxley's London lectures on race seemed a world away. On 1 March the Aswan bazaar showed them a real cultural crossroads. He stocked up with food, jostled by tall Abyssinians carrying bales, Nubians with lion skins and gun-toting Arabs. The next morning they visited the pretty temple of Isis at Philae, its columns still fresh with coloured depictions of Ptolemaic Egypt. Then the English Schamyl rode his camel to 'a point opposite Philae'. It seemed so remote, yet for all the spice and heat, they were never far from Britain. 'Sent letter IX [to Nettie] by Cooks steamer', he jotted.[8]

The return journey was even lazier, a dozen miles a day against hot headwinds. Each day brought more Ptolemaic temples, with their Greek and Roman influence, Edfu's, and then Esna's, with its relief of the Roman Emperor Decius. It was 'Exceedingly hot & close'; Huxley, his hair cropped short, brown skin and black beard, sat in the old *dahabieh*'s saloon scribbling notes: after a three-hour ride to Abydos to see the paintings on Seti's temple he jotted, 'Very hot, bad donkeys fatiguing'.[9] In truth, he was diverted but hardly better, whatever his protestations. On 16 March they reached Tel el Amarna. Huxley packed his paintings and books and left the old *dahabieh* at the railway terminus of Rodu.

The Nile brought time and tranquillity, but crumbling necropoli were no real cure for an obsessed mind. He left the cities of the dead as he stepped onto the Messina ferry on 19 March. Over the Mediterranean lay Sicily and then a more typical dash across Europe. He bounced from a hot past to an icy present. At Etna he found the 'old giant . . . half covered with snow'. But he had no heart to climb. On to Naples by train – he was there by the 27th, climbing the 160 steps to Anton Dohrn's mansion overlooking the beautiful bay. Fireworks heralded his arrival, with Vesuvius across the bay shooting molten rocks into the air. Dohrn was away, but Hal found his nimble 70-year-old father; and young Ray Lankester, his rooms looking like a marine laboratory, with the washbasins full of cuttle-fish larvae. More to the point he found the foundations of the Marine Station going in. Lankester and old Dohrn took Hal up to the north lip of the crater. The belching and 'blast furnace' explosions gave the Hell Gate a true Dantean image. At sunset the 'fiery stream found a lurid reflection in the slowly drifting steam cloud', while the exploding red-hot stones 'shone strangely beside the quiet stars in a moonless sky'.[10]

Through Rome and Turin he rushed, reaching Paris by 5 April. He got off the train in London the next day, a sunburnt face among the sombre throng. A waiting Nettie didn't recognize him,

> burnt to copper colour with beard moustache & short cropped hair! Jess & Mady were so disappointed at the change that they burst into tears when we got home! My great disapp[nt] was to find him still suffering from dyspepsia & . . . little the better for his trip.[11]

Hal diagnosed himself fitter than Nettie did: 'I am back; brown, bearded, & brutal in health', he informed Hooker. But it was touch and go, and even Hal had 'a sort of impression that I had better be prudent'. Prudent meant that he 'took to mineral waters & horse exercises & gave up all private dinner parties'. With his regimen he must have felt like sickly Darwin. He must have looked like the venerable old naturalist too, with 'such a beard & moustache that you w[d] hardly know him'.

But the hour's riding before work proved a bore, so he gave it up. And despite Foster's mineral-water cure Huxley still felt 'like a Holothuria' (a sea cucumber which squirted the contents of its stomach). In fact it was a time of relapses and depressions. He scared himself into taking life easy for a while. He published almost nothing for the year, and discarded and delegated where he could. Even looking back on the School Board wrangling sent a shiver, and 'I mean to keep clear of all that sort of semi-political work hereafter'.[12] But would the world let him?

He decelerated from the City of the Dead to the city of science, South Kensington. For a time life was unhurried, but the eternal afternoon did not last. How could it, with the Department of Science and Art conducting countrywide exams on a military scale? The number of students had increased fourfold in five years. 'Physical Geography' was the most popular subject, with Huxley's 'Animal Physiology' the fourth largest of the DSA's countrywide classes. Inspecting the 800 schools was itself a massive task, and 20 Royal Engineers were drafted in to police the students sitting Huxley's exams. From pacifying the Crimea to patrolling school halls, these uniformed invigilators completed the militarization of science. Huxley, a War Department examiner himself, thought the veterans perfect to mobilize the provincial irregulars.[13] A uniform gave science in the country its authority and national purpose. The *Pax Kensingtoniana* was ensured.

It was slow honing as he went back to the grindstone. 'I have just received a "missile" from My Lords', he told Foster in April 1872, 'to the effect that there will be about 5900 [exam] papers in Animal Physiology this year and that I shall therefore want 6 assistants'. So the General's own army expanded again, and down came Foster's Cambridge student, the 'young, energetic' Newell Martin. They were a socially cohesive group, and their lives intertwined at a family level. Foster even told Nettie of his engagement before his father, 'as the match is partly of your making'.[14]

They were a new breed of star demonstrators, Darwinians to the bone. Huxley's entrepreneurial flair for attracting Department grants paid their way. It was tough work for a man who had just broken down, but impossible to delegate. Behind the classes lay a vision. 'They are the commencement of a new system of teaching which if I mistake not will grow into a big thing', he told Tyndall, and for the present 'I am the necessary man to carry it out'.[15]

That loose cannon Ray Lankester joined him again. Edwin's son had a huge intellect and an irascibility to match. In the wake of the critical Commissions, Oxford's Exeter College had instituted a Natural Science Fellowship, and Huxley found himself examining his own demonstrator for it (Oxford was now routinely turning to Huxley for help). 'I should like to see him do well', Huxley admitted, 'but there is what we call "a screw loose" about him'. It showed. Ray got the post but turned round to roast the corruption 'and effete restrictions' of the place.[16] The Exeter post he dismissed as simply a sop to the science lobby in the wake of the Devonshire Commission.

With their different temperaments Huxley's men threw themselves differentially at Oxford and Cambridge. A reforming Cambridge had instituted the Natural Science Tripos in 1869. But while the affable Foster would attract a brilliant group here with his physiology practicals based on Huxley's pedagogical techniques, Lankester went off half-cocked. At Oxford he came up against the country gentlemen refining their morals and manners. Ray, another self-perceived 'poor' boy, damned this triumph of money and class over opportunity and merit, disdaining his cronies as 'flunkeys, snobs, spendthrifts and social bullies'.[17] Ray had found himself in a theological finishing school when he wanted a German science factory. He fell foul of Rolleston and was refused permission to teach in the museum. Latiny Oxford and obstinate Lankester saw science fail between them.

South Kensington's 'Science Schools' were to become the driving force of change. In June 1872 Huxley was ready to move. He finished his last Jermyn Street course, still a 'burnt sienna colour . . . and "bearded like the pard"'.[18] To the removals men he must have looked like a forensic boffin, as he spent his last days in Piccadilly picking at a macabre skeleton from King William's Sound, thought to be of one of Franklin's crew lost in the Arctic ice.

The hauliers carted truck-loads of apparatus through the unmacadamized Princes Gate in July. The experimentalists were moving in. Huxley would be joining with fellow X-man Edward Frankland with his relocated Royal College of Chemistry. 'The laboratory is a fine one', said Nettie, 'at the very top of a large building devoted to science. Below Hal's rooms are D^r. Frankland's for chemistry & beneath these D^r.Guthrie's for applied mechanics'.[19] Here Huxley would run his Summer crash course for the schoolmasters from the factory towns, required under the Education Act. His production-line turn-out would ultimately feed through, creating the need for science at the old Classics-based universities, underpinning his own profession and promoting scientific managers of industry. It was the vocational base of Huxley's dream of a liberal science college in South Kensington.

Older field naturalists spurned the laboratory for giving a distorted view of a dead, dismembered nature. And clerics celebrating the last Providential shreds of a happy contented Nature abominated it. But Huxley's new discipline of 'biology', created as a package that could be transmitted to the newly-built schools,[20] proclaimed the lab's privileged access to a deeper reality – a microscopic reality, comprehended by trained professionals. The laboratory, rather than the field, became the site for studying the new Nature. Indeed the 'field' was appropriated – Huxley not only brought Nature indoors, but put it under a cover slip, within the lens' 'field' of view. Here, deep down, one could see what the 'land is really like'.[21]

It was an irony that only in a congested city could real Nature be found. In the great age of burgeoning laboratories, designed to turn out hands-on schoolteachers wholesale, the microscope was portrayed as powerful and democratic, an open spyhole through to Nature's foundations. Really of course it offered no 'transparent' close-up. The tyros looking through an achromatic lens were baffled by the histological image. They had to learn the cognitive skills, learn to see and to stylize in diagrams, and it was a long regimented process. At South Kensington they first heard Huxley's morning lecture, where coloured blackboard drawings showed them what to expect (as, eventually, did giant papier-mâché models of sectioned snails and leeches, ears and brains). Then the students were expected to verify 'every material statement made in the lecture'. And yet, whatever was on the cover slide, the students tended to 'see' the picture drawn on the blackboard: they did 'not believe nature', Huxley admitted, they 'believed me'. The lab was as much a training ground for the demonstrators. Lankester, Foster, G. B. Howes and Thiselton-Dyer – the future professors – were 'generally up half the night rehearsing the demonstration for the following day', laying out Nature according to Huxley's Plan, rather than letting the students scramble it into chaos.[22]

The trainees' skills became instinctive through practice and exam reinforcement, when they too accepted the magnified image as obvious and 'natural'. Huxley was ruthless in his lighthearted way, and 'each visit inspired a certain amount of terror'. He would pause to look at a pupil's drawing, labelled 'sheep's liver' or whatever, and with that evil smile say, 'I am glad to know that is a liver; it reminds me as much of Cologne cathedral in a fog'.

He was teaching the teachers to see like him. They would sense Nature's iconoclastic strength. While older Classics dons objected to experimental studies because they encouraged students to question authority, Huxley actively turned the encounter with 'deep reality' into an attack on textbook tradition. He even relished it when advanced students questioned his own manuals: the wild-eyed Scot Patrick Geddes – the boy drawn from the Free Kirk to South Kensington by the *Lay Sermons* with their unimpeachable 'interpretation of existence' – teased apart a whelk's tongue and contradicted the master:

> 'Pon my word, you're right! You've got me! [Huxley told
> him] I was wrong! Capital! I must publish this for you!

His Nature became the new arbiter. Ultimately Huxley turned this virgin reality against a rival clerical authority – he used it against the priests in his attempt to claim territorial space, clearing out their supernature and usurping their authority to speak on the origin and meaning of life. Microscopic training became the academic's new credentials – his arcane entry card. A clergyman criticizing Darwin, and posting his articles to draw Huxley's fire, would receive the coded reply: 'Take a cockroach and dissect it!'[23] The cognoscenti saw 'truth' in those regions where only they were qualified to pursue it. It made microscopic training a perfect propaganda tool: Huxley was creating a legion of followers, looking at the world his way. The initiates were being taught the arcane skills of a new profession. The word 'biology' took root in the 1870s as the schoolmasters became the new authorities for Huxley's 'new Nature'. They had seen it for themselves.

Long-dead Edward Forbes had once thought that an 'educated youth ought, in a well-arranged museum, to be able to instruct himself'.[24] Twenty years on, Forbes' casual diorama experience was replaced by Huxley's experimental regime: a proper top-down training for students by State-paid professionals. The chaotic voluntarist aspect was waning. Nature ceased to be a spot of Sunday-afternoon recreation; an obligatory school science was being drilled into the nation.

That meant moving away from the crowded museum display. Laboratory logistics forced Huxley to minimize his exhibits. Where medical comparative anatomists like the old shabby-coated Lamarckian Robert Grant at University College had ploughed exhaustively through the animal kingdom – systematically following each organ system through the entire chain[25] – Huxley cut life up into a few exemplary 'types', and dealt with them as functioning wholes. And while at first he followed these old medical approaches by moving in a 'philosophical' way, from simple amoeba through to complex rats, that too would be reversed.

And still he overloaded his schoolmasters in the first years. In 1871 they had ten plant types, from yeast to conifers, and a dozen animals, from hydras to rabbits. There was a certain opportunism in his choice: his corpses had to be obtainable in quantity: amoebas, hydras and pond mussels were netted, frogs and rats caught in fields, and even the polyp *Cordylophora* was taken from Victoria docks.[26] But the skill required of novices to tackle minute yeast on their introduction to the microscope proved too much. So he reversed the order, starting them on the rat, and he cut the number of 'types' by a third. Expediency was at the birth of the modern biology practical.

No 'student of ordinary intelligence', one later said, 'could fail to see that the types were valuable, not for themselves, but simply as marking, so to speak, the chapters of a connected narrative'. But Huxley was teaching traditional morphology – the shape and structure of the basic 'types'; he kept one foot in the nineteenth-century morphological mainstream, which paid little heed to Darwin. And if there was any evolutionary 'narrative', it must have become hard to follow as he cut down the types and turned them around to start with the rat. In fact he first refused to 'mix up' evolution with his discrete types, fearing that it would 'throw Biology into confusion'.[27] He wanted his waters unmuddied and his types clear for the tyros. Ironically the need to simplify his school science left him looking less evolutionary than the old medical teachers.

He hurried daily out of South Kensington tube. Through the decorative arcade columns he marched up to his barren rooms, there to become engrossed in a cod dissection prior to his lectures. The fact that he started with no fittings at all forced him to requisition another £4,000 to furnish the natural history floor (which he wisely spent before the Treasury sanction was obtained).[28]

He tried to take life easily. He resolved 'to live scientifically & leave off politics which I suppose is, for me, the equivalent of "living cleanly & leaving off sack"'. His good intentions were for nought. Man was a born fighter, Carlyle said, but Huxley was a born general, ready to take on anybody's fight. For a year he had been trying to get Gladstone's bruising economizer Acton Smee Ayrton off Hooker's back. Ayrton was Hooker's Whitehall boss, and when he started pruning Kew Gardens, Huxley was on the garden gate. The 'idiotic mischief-making Ayrton' was sworn to cutting the public payroll. Kew to him was 'a semi-autonomous satrapy', rife with jobbers, and he sounded a threat to Hooker's independence. Huxley had rushed to 'make common cause and shew [Ayrton] that he has caught a Tartar in presuming to meddle with Science'.[29]

Thus began another debilitating fight to hold Science's territory. This time a hard one, for the case was about accountability. The professionals were using their claim to expertise to stand above the market-place. Now here was a new breed of populist cost-cutter who saw science as a tax drain. For years Huxley had been winning the Chancellor Robert Lowe over – wining him at the Royal, dining him at the X-Club, even escorting him on a pilgrimage to Downe. (He had met Lowe in Sydney with the future greats of Australian politics and knew him well.) Now he called in the chips, portraying Ayrton's action to Lowe as 'an affront to all the men of science'.[30] But others wondered if the scientific Establishment wasn't putting itself beyond parliamentary control. Like other professions science was setting its own standards and expecting a certain autonomy.

Huxley was dragged in by his camaraderie with Hooker. The lean Kew botanist had been his intellectual mainstay for 20 years. 'Like other good things you improve with age', Huxley told him: 'all but your handwriting which is horrid'. Kew Gardens had an international reputation: without it rubber would not have become established in the East Indies, nor cinchona (quinine) in Ceylon; and Hooker, famous for his work on Indian plants, shared in that reputation. Huxley hated to see him ground down by 'Ayrton the accursed (may jackasses sit upon his Grandmother's grave, as we say in the East)'.[31]

The Xs were turning science into a political force. It was not academic professionalism that bound them. After all, the group embraced philosophers and politicians and printers. But all saw science and industry as essential to the national health, and they supported an autonomous scientific civil service, based on specialist schooling and career opportunities. The group had the 'power of making ourselves unpleasant . . . and that is something the ministerial mind can appreciate'. They were 'wire-pullers', a critic said; and they proved it in every corridor. Tyndall waylaid Lord Derby at the Athenaeum and readied a petition against Ayrton for Parliament, which Huxley leaked to the press.[32] The story snowballed, and they made Hooker's hounding a national tragedy, even firing a debate in the Lords.

They had access to the Prime Minister through John Lubbock, himself in a rather invidious position as one of Gladstone's backbenchers. Not that it helped. Gladstone prevaricated, trying to avoid a Commons debate and a possible defeat. He preferred the preserves of Tradition to the pretensions of Science anyway. Huxley was infuriated by the PM's loquacious evasions: 'Some of these days he will turn himself inside out like a blessed Hydra, and I dare say he will talk just as well in that state . . . I never heard or read of any body with such a severely copious chronic glossorhea'.[33] It was the beginning of the Xs' growing disenchantment with Gladstone, and Gladstone's growing disenchantment with science. At best Hooker saw him as 'a craven bungler'; in time they would see him as something worse.

Old festering hatreds came to the fore when Ayrton had the haughty Richard Owen draw up a report on Kew to lay before Parliament: a report which reflected Owen's own imperial designs on Kew museum and accused Hooker of keeping an expensive herbarium for 'attaching barbarous binomials to dried foreign weeds'.[34] The Hookers of the world only knew about the law of science, Ayrton claimed in the House, while Ministers of the Crown were dwelling on the 'higher' science of law. He had a point but lost his seat at the General Election anyway. As *St James's Magazine* commented, a politician would henceforth 'as soon put his finger into a hornet's nest as treat a scientific man with contumely'. Corporate science emerged with its civil service ethos intact, in all its quasi-autonomous aspects.

Power continued accruing to the X-Clubbers. With four council seats in the Royal Society and the Secretary's chair, these senior statesmen oozed self-confidence. The next step, Huxley told Darwin in conspiratorial fashion, was to put Hooker in the President's chair. They managed it effortlessly and in 1873 Huxley was bidding Hooker, 'Oh King! come & reign over us'. With their man in front of the mace, the Xs could initiate their own Second Reform Bill. Hooker curtailed aristocratic privilege and – with the industrialists' money, £2,000 from Whitworth, £1,000 from the steel baron Sir William Armstrong – he set up a fund to subsidize poorer Fellows. As Huxley became the Biological Secretary in June 1872, the conservative Physical Secretary George Gabriel Stokes looked warily on the ginger group. He really 'dreads Huxley's being President', a fellow observed. Rather than cutting down work, Huxley cranked it up as he processed the Society's papers for publication. By now the Xs were divvying up posts almost by right. As Hirst informed Huxley of his election, Huxley was 'securing Hirst' – advising George Goschen (now Gladstone's First Sea Lord) over dinner to appoint Hirst Director of the Royal Naval College on its new Greenwich site.[35] And the Sea Lords were only too happy to install a physicist after the capsizing of HMS *Captain*. With George Busk settling in as President of the College of Surgeons (no worries here about having a gutsy wife), the Xs were becoming a sort of Institute of Scientific Directors.

Inside the *sanctum sanctorum*, they got things done. Huxley had the Royal Society's *Transactions* shipped off to Dohrn's marine station, that pan-European enterprise to unravel the embryology and evolution of life. And he liaised with Darwin to raise £500 from 'the land of fogs' to fund the Mediterranean enterprise. It was collected from 'each according to his ability': which meant that Darwin put in £75 while Huxley had 'no cash to spare'. But then Darwin was 'in all things, noble and generous', Huxley told Dohrn; 'one of those people who think it a privilege to let him help'.[36]

The new Secretary pushed open old creaky doors. No Royal Society paper had mentioned Darwinism (not even Huxley's). For ten years it had been shunned in the elite *Philosophical Transactions*, which remained factual, uncontroversial, anti-theoretical and aloof.[37] Evolution stayed on the literary fringes, in essays, press articles and reviews.

But the society's membership changes presaged new things. In came the academics and empire-builders, secular sons with their B.Sc.s, many echoing Tyndall's call for a new evolutionary imagination. Out went the marginalized clergymen (who dropped from 8 per cent to 5 per cent of the Fellowship in the 1870s).[38] Now the publication and grants committees gained a preponderance of Darwin sympathizers. But it still took a foreign revolutionary to break through the society's safe empirical confines. When the peripatetic Kovalevskii arrived in London to work on hippopotamus evolution, Huxley evidently persuaded him to submit his paper to the Royal. The revolutionary jumped at the idea, 'since "Phil. Trans." is a very stylish publication'.

Stylish or no, it still had a staid reputation. Huxley himself read the hippo paper at the society. But the Tory Anglican Stokes kicked up a kerfuffle at this first dazzling attempt at Darwinian palaeontology in England. He tried to cut out 'the objectionable passages', not wanting the society to sanction Kovalevskii's world of 'happy chances'. The Russian saw evolution in terms of chance modifications and changed terrains. But to Stokes this was 'flimsy to the last degree'. In his view, making speculative Darwinism as axiomatic as Newton's laws compromised the rock-like status of knowledge. How could a nihilist, known to Russia's secret police, be allowed to hail the 'complete revolution caused by Darwin's great work' in the *Phil. Trans.*? As befits Cambridge's Lucasian Professor of Mathematics, Stokes saw the 'continuous curve' joining the Creative

Acts as a piece of Divine Geometry. Life's course was planned. It was no 'Creation by Caprice'.[39] But Huxley pulled off the coup. He sent the paper out to sympathizers, who acted as referees, and they passed it. It was published intact to break the society's empirical impasse.

The high-pressure boiler whistled its warning again. Huxley teetered on the brink of a fragile recovery. He was unable to extricate himself from life, even its mundanities. Drink helped him to ease the pain, at least until Nettie hid the key to the cellar. The work piled up: during the June week that he posted the Ayrton petition, became the Royal Society Secretary, lobbied the Sea Lords for Hirst and started the teachers' practicals, he was trying to raise the cash for his house. He signed the contracts on 6 June 1872 and, with the extension costing over £4,000, he needed money. 'Brother John' came to his rescue: he placed £1,000 in Huxley's London & Westminster account. Unmarried and celebrated, Tyndall was 'perfectly secure' himself and could afford it.[40] It marked the start of a period of unprecedented help from Huxley's friends.

A year trying to move department, house and government alike left him complaining that his 'damnable bowels' were affecting his 'brains'. In August 1872 he migrated to a village outside Ilfracombe, on the rugged north Devon coast, to revise his *Lessons in Elementary Physiology*. He rented a house 'at the head of a ravine running down to the sea'; but there was no recuperation. The book simply kept the bustling world before him. Even reworking another textbook spoke of his dedication: while audiences were ready to fall at his feet at the sight of a blockbuster – a brilliant travelogue escorting them to an exotic Cretaceous age or Coal-swamp era – he was producing primers. And those in fast-moving fields. He knew that his *Physiology* might 'only stand for a year or two'.[41] He was sacrificing himself on the professional altar.

Sickness forced him back to London 'to recover from the effects of the country'! Crash diets followed; he left off 'meat, alcohol, & baccy' (to Nettie's pleasure) and improved for a while. 'I find that if I am to exist at all it must be on strictly ascetic principles', he told Tyndall, 'so there is hope of my dying in the odour of sanctity yet'.[42]

He was still discarding work where he could. In November he relinquished his Presidency of the Metaphysical Society 'with much joy'. He crawled to the end of the year trying to get the Marlborough Place house habitable, widening doors, worrying about the coal cellar, trying to fight his way into the wine cellar. They were kept out of the house until Christmas by the 'stupid delays of the workmen whom we had fairly to shove out'. It was hardly a pretty house, more a functional shrine to Victorian hard work and large litters, and big enough to accommodate visiting nieces or foreign dignitaries. The original white-painted cottage had become dwarfed by Huxley's uncompromising yellow-brick extension, the lot screened from the road by a row of ubiquitous Regent's Park lime trees.

It was Spring 1873 before the tiles were baked the right colour and they could move into the drawing room. On the walls went photos of friends and portraits presented by Royal Academy artists. Here the famous Sunday gatherings were to be held to the accompaniment of hymns from the Presbyterian church next door. Great men of science would sit with great poets. Robert Browning was a regular, as was the Shakespearean *grande dame* Helena Martin ('Helen Faucit'). Hal's study, the old dining room, was 'a mass of books – all round the walls, on the chairs and floor in heaps, everywhere'. Darwin sent Nettie a cheque to help with the furniture, but the rooms remained very simply furnished. The whole had a carefree cultured look, suggesting 'people of great refinement and with no pretensions'.[43]

Feeling 'such a dyspeptic hypochondriacal poor devil', the last thing Huxley wanted was a lawsuit. The builders had dug a well to improve the surface drainage and 'a knavish neighbour' claimed that it made his basement damp. The man was simply trying to swindle money out of Huxley, but it still went to court. 'Fancy finding myself a defendant in Chancery!' he wrote to Tyndall, on tour in America. The fees mounted as the case was put down to be heard before Vice-Chancellor Sir Richard Malins. James Knowles, his architect and *Contemporary* editor, heard about it all in each capacity. 'Macmillan wants another volume of essays of me', Huxley told him. 'I suppose you have no objection to my reprinting those I sent you for the Contemporary'?[44] Another compilation might at least help to defray the costs. He was set to call it prosaically *Critiques and Addresses*. It would still extol the moral and social force of science as he wove his way through the myriad tiny worlds of yeast, coal swamps or coral. But the new political tone was set by the opening pleas for State aid and State education.

On Thursday morning, 20 February 1873, Huxley won his case and was awarded £245 costs. It was a happier man who went off to the Royal Society that afternoon. 'You see that I have walloped my friend Mr Broad [the plaintiff]', he reported to Hooker. A huge weight was lifted; for an upright man, trying to disprove the myth that evolutionists inhabited a moral quagmire, the Court of Chancery was no place to be dragged over drains. But the euphoria ended when he found that 'the brute is impecunious & that I shall get nothing out of him. So I shall have had three months worry' and be left with court costs, though 'wholly & absolutely in the right'.[45]

Huxley was financially astute (even Matthew Arnold asked his advice about royalties on his poems). But money seemed to slip through his fingers. During the ordeal he tried to recoup with a new essay for the *Contemporary*. He jumped from hot water to the frozen deep. He did what he did best, act as science's salesman and glory in the first piece of 'Big Biology' sponsored by the State. The talk of technical decline and German competition had dented the national pride. Huxley now cheered as the government underwrote HMS *Challenger*'s voyage to sample the world's oceans. Science under the White Ensign could be rationalized as an assessment of global sea-bed resources, or sounding the depths for cable-laying. But in truth this was the first truly biological rather than Admiralty venture, and these were 'the best equipped voyagers who ever left the shores of England'. Later it would be heralded as the birth of modern oceanography.

The expedition under Captain George Nares would last four years and employ a host of civilian specialists. The 2,300-ton corvette set off with its cannon bays converted into labs. Criss-crossing the oceans, its dredge was hauled in from ever greater depths by the donkey engine. Up came bloated fishes from 1,000 fathoms, their eyes 'protruding like great globes from their heads'. The Victorians with their expanded evolutionary horizons were charting the last unknown. For Huxley it was a romantic trek: a quest in the unchanging depths for lost empires. Here might be living fossils, 'survivors of a world passed away', creatures from the dinosaurian Chalk Era. And why not? Wasn't the chalky *Globigerina* mud made up of microscopic shells like those in our Cretaceous rocks?[46] Might not other 'persistent types' lurk down there too? This hunt for past forms would become endlessly enmeshed in the science-fiction notion of prehistoric monsters dredged from the deep, but for a moment it seemed real.

The voyage cut to the heart of his own speculations. What of his primal-slime creature *Bathybius* (whose existence the Berlin protozoologist Christian Ehrenberg – revenging himself for Huxley's attacks? – had begun to doubt)?[47] Was the ocean floor carpeted by pulsating protoplasm as Huxley, Haeckel and almost everybody else now imagined? No secrets were to be left in the abyss.

The head of the *Challenger* staff was the rotund Charles Wyville Thomson (the new Professor of Natural History at Edinburgh). Interested in abyssal life, he had dredged with Carpenter as far as the Faroes and published *The Depths of the Sea*. He had sent Huxley armoured fossil fishes from Orkney's rocks and consulted him on the naturalists to take aboard. 'I rejoice that my friend Charlie has done so well', Huxley told Hooker, all thanks to 'the moral discipline he received from me'.[48] Now 'Charlie' was paid £1,000 a year on the *Challenger*, and he reported as faithfully to Huxley as to the Admiralty.

Others aboard the ship did too. The young German naturalist R. von Willemoës-Suhm sent reports from around the globe. He even had a talking parrot for Nettie, but neither of them reached port: Suhm died in the Pacific. With a chemist, artist, photographer and three naturalists aboard, every dredge sample was analysed and recorded. The records fell for life at the depths as tube worms came out of the peculiar red clay at 3,000 fathoms. The surprise was that there *was* a 'busy life which, contrary to all the beliefs of the naturalists of a past generation, blindly toils and moils in the darkness and cold'. These creatures of the abyss seemed to be continuous across all the oceans, but cut off from surface forms. It was as if, in Huxley and Thomson's view, the freezing uniform sea-bed had slowed evolution to leave a bizarre archaic population.

Huxley was the supreme publicist. But it was a case of two steps forward and one back. He sent the *Challenger* manuscript in April and received Knowles' contractor's bills by return. Knowles at least was relieved to find that Huxley's 'literary style is not badly affected by your blue devils – on the contrary one would swear from the print of your hoof that you were never stronger, more serviceable or more dangerous'. The *Review* reached the *Challenger* in Nova Scotia in May and was read by the naturalists 'with great satisfaction'.[49] Not so the ratings, evidently; they were unimpressed with the endless 'drudging' and five showed it by deserting.

But Huxley was unable to keep his head above water. Some £560 in contractor's bills were still outstanding and the money was due in late April 1873. Lady Lyell saw how 'harassed' he looked, and at her prompting the entire Darwinian–industrial complex paid its dues. She mooted starting a fund to Emma Darwin. Coincidentally Fanny Hooker too was proposing that the Xs cover Huxley's law expenses. The female household role was one of social support in the family, and the Darwinian brotherhood was a sort of extended intellectual family ('brother John', 'sister Nettie'). Clearly it was the women who were sensitive to Huxley's emotional state – and as the traditional givers of presents and philanthropy they were unabashed at the idea of a money gift. Yet the patriarch headed the family enterprise, whether intellectual or business, and the men now veiled the women off. The Huxleys visited the Downe hamlet on 8 March and probably gave the Darwins an account of the court case. Huxley clearly wasn't well. He was thin and haggard, and probably confessed (as he had to Foster) that he had 'to take the most absurd care of my eating & drinking – or I lapse from Grace'. He had a crushing feeling of 'everything having gone wrong in the world', Nettie confided to Lizzie, 'a profound melancholy' which made him wretched. Dr Clark had ordered him abroad for three months, and 'somehow it must be managed, tho' . . . money is not too plentiful'.[50]

Emma Darwin had Charles pass the plate around on 7 April. It piled high as it moved from X to X, and every deception was mooted for forcing the cash on Huxley. Darwin's brother Erasmus added £100, and so much enthusiasm had Darwin raising his own sub to £300. But he feared the female hand showing itself. Lady Lyell (the instigator) so disconcerted him by insisting on putting her own (rather than Sir Charles') money in that he resolved to 'keep her amount secret'.[51] This was to be a gift between 'brother' naturalists, and disguising Lady Lyell's role only emphasized the patriarchal prerogative. (And that was tragic because the day after Huxley received the money Lady Lyell died.)

Tyndall's 'magnificent success' with the ironmasters Sir William Armstrong and Sir Joseph Whitworth had the pot brimming with £1,700.[52] By the 11th Darwin was drafting a letter and quaking, but Tyndall thought that the 'brotherly spirit of the transaction' would win Huxley over.

On 23 April, £2,100 – two years' salary – was paid through Lubbock's bank into Huxley's account and Darwin posted 'the awful letter'. The 18 friends who subscribed refused to take 'no' for an answer; it was for his holiday and his health, and his acceptance would 'be a happiness to us to the last day of our lives'. The delicacy of it left them on tenterhooks. 'I tremble about his answer', Darwin told Tyndall, but 'it is a pleasure to think what a relief it will be to M^{rs}. H.'[53] 'I hope we may hear to-morrow', Darwin's daughter Etty wrote. 'It will be very awful'.

The sentiment overwhelmed Huxley that evening and turned his stern exterior to a shambles. After a sleepless night as he wondered 'what I have done to make my friends care so tenderly', he opened up groggily to Darwin in the morning:

I accept the splendid gift . . . for the first time in my life I
have been fairly beaten. I mean morally beaten. Through all
sorts of troubles & difficulties poverty illness, bedevilments
of all sorts have I steered these thirty years, and never lost
heart or failed to buffet the waves as stoutly as they
buffeted me . . . [But] I have for months been without
energy & without hope & haunted by the constant
presence of hypochondriacal apprehensions which my
reason told me were absurd but which I c^d not get rid of –
for I was breaking down; sliding into the meanest of
difficulties, the would be climber of heights, mired in a mere
bog . . . Well I have poured out all this Jeremiad that you
may understand what your . . . great gift will do for me . . .

Have I said a word of appreciation for your own letter?
I shall keep it for my children that their children may know
what manner of man their father's friend was & why he
loved him.[54]

It was 'so grand & sweet' that Darwin was quite affected.

There would have been more factory money. The Manchester mill
owner Thomas Ashton's 'only regret' was that he missed joining
'with your old friends in their bank operation'. But even £2,100
would see Huxley proud, relieve his house and court debts, and it
would prove to be the financial turning-point. 'I shall go & take a
long holiday in the summer now without feeling that I am particularly guilty of fraud, and when the blue devil dances about me . . .
I shall slap the cheque for £2100 at his head as Luther did the
inkstand'.[55]

Spencer, rejoicing 'that our plot has succeeded so well', wanted
Huxley to leave immediately. It was out of the question with 7,000
school papers to be marked. Anyway he was improving, and two new
books would show that life was returning to 'the old dog'. The
Physiology textbook had appeared in March, and he thanked his
benefactors with copies of *Critiques and Addresses* in late April.
That too was selling well, 'Bless the British Public', with booksellers
taking half the stock on publication day.[56]

His 48th birthday was heralded by apple blossoms in the back
garden. His new delight was to sit in the sun, smoking, a book open
– perhaps Fitzjames Stephen's conservative *Liberty, Equality and
Fraternity* with its 'world of muscular sense'. Or potter like Darwin;
sowing beans and pulling up bracken, the 'type' plants of his prac-

ticals. 'I am steadily mending', he told his 'doctor of doctors' Andrew Clark. Clark was glad of it. He was now standing on Huxley's shoulders to reach the highest intellectual echelons. Through Huxley he made contact with Tyndall, and ultimately with Darwin, whom he subjected to an 'abominable diet'. But Huxley was doing well under Clark's regime: riding 15 miles a day or walking around Regent's Park, and in bed by 10 to sleep 'like a top'. 'The animal part of me is really getting into first rate order', he reported. '"Ape & Tiger" (as Tennyson has it) very much alive', even if the critical faculty 'has shut up shop'.[57]

Money in the bank, success in the bookshops and one of Clark's diets saw him off on holiday in fine mood. He celebrated the 'wifes birthday' on 1 July and then set out with Hooker. He left a 'Black mug!' still full-bearded. But the 'beauty & geological interest' of the volcanic Auvergne capped his recovery, not to mention an ice-age human that the 'happy-go-lucky pair' stumbled on in Le Puy museum. No longer the 'broken-down old fellow', he was so buoyant that in Baden-Baden he felt 'ashamed of loafing about when I might very well be at work' (he had skipped the 1873 schoolmasters' course). The beard now symbolized that 'dreary illness' and it came off as he turned the corner.[58] It was his 'old original phiz' that greeted Nettie and Len when they joined him in Cologne with a celebratory box of Jamaica cigars.

Nettie was full of news: the King of Sweden had awarded the Order of the North Star to the evangelical triumvirate, Huxley, Hooker and Tyndall. Even as that sank in there was more, the death of an older evangelical. He heard of Bishop Wilberforce's sad passing, thrown from his horse. Wilberforce had been as busy a professional on the other side of the fence, organizing his clergy, visiting parishes and demanding information and statistics. The anti-racist son of a great abolitionist, Wilberforce had made humans one moral community, and had refused to place blacks nearer to apes or countenance an immoral anti-Christian evolution. Huxley, who had traded insults with him at the BAAS and organized exhibits with him at the Zoological Society, saw only his Tory reaction. 'Poor dear Sammy! His end has been all too tragic for his life', he said. 'For once, reality & his brains came into contact & the result was fatal'.[59]

His death as Huxley was honoured showed the tenor of the times. Honours as a sign of privilege and place Huxley abhorred. But the Swedish award for scientific merit was 'a good honest acknowledgment of one's work' – assuming that an English civil servant could actually accept it.[60]

So Huxley finished a frightful year. The 'wretched despondency' had passed; 'he is as bright & merry, as ever', Nettie rejoiced, and the 'Years only knit us together in closer & tenderer love'.

The government allowed Huxley his North Star insignia. He had survived his worst mental crisis and come out 'safe, sound & flourishing' and sporting a scientific knighthood. 'I really am wonderfully better, more myself than I have been for these two years'.[61]

22

Automatons

NOTHING SEEMED IMPOSSIBLE in the world's leading industrial nation. History was made as Crookes worked on cathode rays and Bell perfected the telephone. Britain even felt safe enough to begin test borings for a Channel Tunnel. Science and technology were making news.

By 1874 the restructuring of science was under way. It was becoming State-managed, with curriculums tightly prescribed and classrooms tightly policed. From the regimented lab to the patrolled exam hall, the regime was in place. The South Kensington professors were turning out their 'Whitworth Scholars' to run machine shops or teach in school.

It was no coincidence that this restructuring occurred as the traumas over evolution graduated into new concerns. Darwinism was becoming endurable, even natural for the industrial few. The histrionics caused by the *Origin* and *Essays* had passed. *The Descent of Man* went into a half-price second edition without a murmur, even though the mild Darwin – who could hate with the best of them – added Huxley's scalping 'supplement' on the outcome of the ape-brain debate to spite 'the fiend, Owen'. 'Denuded of its controversial spice', even a Brobdingnagian fossil world began to lose its fashionable interest in the 1870s.[1]

But the new concerns allowed Hal to keep his capacity crowds. An industrial-age evolution was supported on deep piles, rarely seen and never doubted. These axiomatic foundations – like the immense underground piles Londoners saw going under the new tall buildings – were massive load-bearers: an undeviating uniformity of nature, the exact interchange of all forms of energy, and human thought as a function of the brain chemistry. This axiomatic undergirding legitimized Huxley's power brokers. Tyndall went further. In his pantheon this Trinity was flanked by pagan lesser gods – Determinism and Necessity. Huxley at first banned these house deities, but they kept returning to haunt him. For a while he too saw a mechanical 'higher design' in a self-developing universe, where 'the existing world lay, potentially, in the cosmic vapour'. If 'we could project ourselves back' into the primal gas-cloud, he said, 'and then look forward we would be seen drinking our gin and water'.

From this scientific temple the 'priesthood of science', as Holyoake dubbed them, made their pitch for cultural leadership. The evangelical appeal of Tyndall's poetically self-flowering universe inured an intellectual and street culture against all supernatural interference. Matter itself had become one great miracle. There was a flamboyant assurance to it, a beguiling romance to Tyndall's story which made Everyone a child of the Sun.[2]

Many felt it, some vicarages began to waver. Letter after letter dropped through Huxley's mailbox from vicars with problems, vicars with doubts, vicars who held him responsible. Perhaps he felt it. They told of disillusion and anguish. Revd W. H. Dalton, a year after his Cambridge MA, wrote:

> I have no other excuse for thus trespassing on your time
> than the fact that thus early in life (27) religious convictions
> similar to yours & that of Professor Tyndall have prompted
> me to take what I consider a true step & resign what is in
> Ecclesiastical Language called 'holy orders' . . . & what I
> want is some work as secretary or manager of some sort
> . . . Can you offer me such a position? or tell me to whom
> to apply, & what you would advise under the
> circumstances?

Then came the vicar of St Pancras, Revd Anthony Thorold (shortly to become the Bishop of Rochester). He tackled Huxley as 'a kind-hearted and truly considerate man' because his curate had 'run so completely off the rails' after reading Huxley's *Lay Sermons* and Tyndall's books, with their pious aura of cosmic inevitability and new rationales for existence. The poor man was 'drifting fast towards utter "materialism"'. 'You are his Pope', Thorold pleaded, 'he thinks there is no one in the world like you'. It said much of an age in change that the tolerant Thorold asked the agnostic Pope to chat to his drifting curate.

That curate was a Yorkshire squire's son 'at once rather intelligent & totally unintellectual'.[3] Perhaps with the Church a dumping-ground for so many directionless sons of the gentry, this was to be expected. Even the law began to reflect it. Not only were the sons of the cotton kings now admitted to Oxford and Cambridge, but a Clerical Disabilities Act at last allowed vicars to resign their orders (they had not been able to before). Still, Huxley – that sweet voice of scientific reason – was as much symptom as cause.

The material cosmos with its mystical molecular potential came into vogue in the 1870s, as the territorial clashes over education and health between Huxley's professionals and a pastoral clergy peaked. Huxley and Tyndall's new religion lay in duty and agnostic morality – acquiescence before the fact – rather than superstitious reverence. These were the credentials for the thrusting professionals jealous of the State-endowed Church. Science had to be State-endowed too. The campaign swayed leading Tories. Lord Salisbury agreed before the Devonshire Commission that, like parish toil, 'research is unremunerative' but 'highly desirable for the community'.[4] Weren't men of science improving the moral, educational and medical state of the nation as they raised its international prestige?

Temporal benefits were the prize as a sectarian science contrasted itself with the wealthy Church. Never had the Church been richer. With universities, palaces, Lord Bishops and deep coffers, it was 'the most socially powerful group of intellectuals in the nation'. Never had it seemed richer: new seminaries were graduating more clergymen for dozens of new urban parishes. That expansion only increased the territorial tensions. The new science was deliberately made to tell against the clergy's supernatural sanction. The urban dissenters saw no descending spiral of power passing from God through this State priesthood into a capricious Nature. Nor did they doubt that the Church had lost its divine spark and become a place of idolatry. In contrast, Tyndall and Huxley drew their power from the universal soul – Nature would back their claim to 'domination over the whole realm of the intellect'.[5]

The propaganda peaked in an infamous challenge. A surgery professor at University College Hospital mooted a 'Prayer Gauge', to test the power of prayer on the sick in the wards. It was a disturbingly simple sign of the intensifying border dispute over public health. Despite the great sanitation movement, national days of prayer to check plagues were on the increase. Nettie's Marylebone vicar Llewelyn Davies was almost alone in dismissing these cosmos-diverting responses as a 'mechanical prophylactic'. For the rest, the Prince of Wales' recovery from typhoid after a day of prayers seemed proof enough. The *Guardian* even called for more of this 'moral regenerating power' in place of impious science. The last straw was the medical profession's virtual exclusion from the thanksgiving in St Paul's Cathedral, which turned into a celebration of the Divine power of Church and Throne. The doctors responded with the prayer test, to be conducted in the medical schools, hotbeds of materialism and cynicism by repute. (Huxley's Dr Clark had him ask Tyndall for a lecture on the pointlessness of prayer at his own London Hospital.)[6] No such test took place. But had it, Francis Galton was certain that it would have vindicated the insurance brokers, who offered no discounts to the 'praying classes'.

The brutal polemicist hardly seemed so brutal at home. Here Huxley appeared to visitors 'as tender as a woman'. The corpulent cosmic philosopher John Fiske made Marlborough Place his Mecca. He came over from Harvard, carting his *Cosmic Philosophy* manuscript, desperate to experience this 'clean-cut mind'. Having been warned by a cockney expat in New York about the ''orrid hold hinfidel 'Uxley', Fiske expected a baby-eating ogre. But he found 'a very gentle old chap, for such a savage controversialist'. By the New Year 1874 Fiske was coming each Sunday to the Huxleys' 'Tall Teas'. His infectious humour matched Huxley's flair for the absurd. Whatever Huxley's eager burning intensity, 'he was nothing if not playful', and no scientific salon was so thick with puns. Even the damp walls now had Huxley joking about the 'fresh water lake under the basement'. ('I did not covenant for this valuable water property when the house was built'.) Nor, these being Sundays, did the agnostic see anything incongruous in standing Fiske by the piano to sing psalms.

In the little library, Huxley sat by the fire smoking a narrow brier-wood pipe. He talked politics or theology with the same clinical precision as he discussed *Amphioxus* anatomy. He was 'alive in all directions', Fiske said – and peppy, judging by the pipe and 'noggin of Glenlivet'. Fiske's was a vibrant image of '*Patter*', learning Russian to read Kovalevskii, or burrowing into 'old Benedict' (Spinoza), his passion. (One corner was stuffed with crumbling old orthodox tomes, which he called the 'condemned cell'.) The heavens were over-hauled in that room. Huxley found rest in change and devoured books rapaciously. Straight from South Kensington he would settle in to Spinoza in Latin or 'Sybil's French Revolution . . . until the witch-ing hour'. Even novel-reading had the intensity of a dissection; still in love with strong women, he fell on George Sand's emotionally-soaked fiction as he would a new fish. ('She is bigger than George Eliot, more flexible, a more thorough artist'.) His encyclopedic recall and acerbic wit gave the common man an uncommon mind like 'Saladin's sword which cut through the cushion'. But Fiske's lasting impression, he told his wife on 15 January 1874, was of a 'lovely' man, even if the little 'Uxleys were used to seeing the chief cast as a 'cannibal'.[7]

The little Huxleys were not so little any more, even if *'Patter'* was still to be 'pulled about and tousled and kissed'. Len was already devouring Pater's and Tyndall's books. The girls were growing and life was sweet again. Jessie was turning 16. But it was Mady's contralto voice as she sang love songs that captivated Fiske. She was a delicate, sensitive girl. Privately her mental health left Hal and Nettie in 'constant terror', and each relapse caused Hal to 'collapse inwardly'. But to the world she was an artist with the mark of brilliance and she gave the exuberant Yankee a 'wonderful' painting of seven-year-old Ethel for his library. With their strong features the elder girls were already attracting admirers, chief among them the cheery illustrator Sam Waller and his architect brother Fred.[8] The Wallers, young Jim's distant cousins, were beginning to weave themselves into the family.

Spiritualism was all the rage in Britain. It had broken out of its confines among Pentecostalist plebeians and disillusioned socialists. Society swells now gave the manifestations a cachet. As religious authority outside the home declined, in darkened drawing rooms the spiritualist reaction to the materialism of the age intensified.[9] Wallace still awaited the spirit-delivered Millennium, but it was the conversion of William Crookes that really worried the professionals. Here was an elite chemist, Hofmann's one-time assistant, and the discoverer of the element thallium. Worse, he was a scrupulous experimenter.

Huxley was still fighting for the control of hearts and minds – still claiming cultural authority for his agnostic professionals. It required constant vigilance. Rival claimants to power ran from Scottish physicists with their unseen forces and romantic Owens with their Will-driven nature to these tricked-up table-turners. Agnosticism was a philosophic nicety and no threat to the wandering spirits manipulated by mediums. A more aggressive tack was needed to meet the new threat.

The mediums and their message had Huxley yawning. He could barely rouse himself to casual sarcasm; there was even a detectable ambivalence, for he had a 'sneaking admiration' for the real geniuses among the female fraudsters. Perhaps his problem was that so many mediums *were* women. When Ray Lankester did drag a psychic into court for a show trial on a charge of criminal fraud – duping the paying public – he made sure it was a man. (The original entrapment was set for the English medium Charles Williams, but the visiting American Henry Slade presented a bigger catch. He was sentenced to three months' hard labour, but got off on appeal.) Prosecuting a woman would have been inconceivable. But such a high-profile case belied the fact that spiritualism was a female preserve. In an age of sublimated sexual politics, when women's aspirations were high, when fathers and sons (judging by the Darwins and Huxleys, but it was probably true of much middle-class society) were agnostics while wives and daughters remained religious, mediumship became an autonomy-gaining, status-raising cottage industry which cashed in (literally) on the woman's traditional spiritual authority within the home.[10]

She was, in Tennyson's poetic stereotype,

> No angel, but a dearer being, all dipt
> In angel instincts, breathing Paradise,
> Interpreter between the Gods and men.[11]

The perfect medium.

Ghosts babbling like 'old women' did not appeal to Huxley. True, they argued eloquently against suicide. 'Better live a crossing-sweeper', he laughed, 'than die and be made to talk twaddle by a "medium" hired at a guinea' a time. He only attended the séance on 27 January 1874 after receiving the royal call. Darwin's son George was to hire Crookes' medium, Charles Williams – a psychic who had astonished Darwin's brother-in-law Hensleigh Wedgwood. They were to put Williams in a controlled situation at Wedgwood's house. As a rival experimentalist, Huxley had already learnt the black art: he could rap with his toes while his foot remained motionless. So he went incognito as 'Mr Henry'. He grasped Williams' hand in the dark and gauged the muscle strain as if he were testing a galvanized frog. Huxley's account of the trickery relieved Darwin. But Huxley's cover broke (he was spotted in the street), and all he got for his pains was Crookes' invitation to a six-week session with the psychic forces and a set of Wedgwood's best ghost photos.[12]

Public credulity showed how much further the New Reformation had to run. Always the educationalists wanted to sharpen Saladin's sword. Huxley was offered Playfair's Directorship of Science at the Department of Science and Art. But the Department had become byzantine in its complexity and impenetrable in its secrecy, and in 20 years Sir Henry Cole had turned from a 'bureaucratic reformer into a reformist bureaucrat'.[13] Besides, Huxley wanted to stay on the production side. So in civil service style Cole promoted a loyalist from within. Major Donnelly was upgraded with Huxley's blessing.

Huxley would have made a good organizer, but he was better spared for publicizing Nature's moral revelation. Not that anyone spared him. The Pope was expected to pontificate on every subject. The guardian of science had become Pythia's priest, with a status to match. From the sublime to the ridiculous, the requests rolled in. What did he think of free will and miracles, aquariums and *Amphioxus*? Would he go to the Lord Mayor's Dinner, or to the unveiling of Lord Derby's statue? What about an all-expenses-paid trip to India?[14] Would he review Mill's autobiography? Or write entries for the *Encyclopaedia Britannica*?

Huxley's illness had passed. Even so reports of his death were filtering across Europe, and he was being mourned by Kovalevskii in Russia. But his ghost was 'uncommonly lively',[15] and proved it by manifesting everywhere. He emerged at Aberdeen University to add a new post to his list. Here the Lord Rector was elected by the students and had real power in the Court. Huxley came in over a clansman, the Marquis of Huntley; and a Sassenach 'who stinketh in the nostrils of orthodoxy, beating a Scotch peer at his own gate . . . is a curious sign of the times'. Still, a dirty campaign had seen student intimidation and taunts, and the *Aberdeen Free Press* bewailed the 'deeper and darker blasphemies' which would creep north of the border with him. So much for abjuring the political arena. The students got what they wanted: a vigorous reformer rather than tartan title. And Huxley rang the changes – or tried to. 'I shall probably go down to posterity as the Rector who was always beaten', he prophesied to the students. Modernizing the medical curriculum was the least of it: 'I have been in Aberdeen fighting for the admission of Scotch dissenters to bursaries in my University & getting beaten', he told that English Dissenter Michael Foster, 'the parsons being too many for me. But we shall win yet'.[16]

A level playing field summed up his Rectorial Address. No religious or financial barriers; no Classics to the exclusion of Science and Art. The university had to be 'accessible to all comers'. Not that Aberdeen was a 'hot-bed of high-fed, hypercritical refinement', and he blessed its bursary system, which let poor boys trade their ploughshares for callipers. But the Rector was looking further afield. 'I have used the Aberdonians for the benefit of Oxford &

Cambridge', he told Foster, 'much as Tacitus drew the manners of the Germans for the benefit of the Romans'. The *Scotsman* called it wise and 'worth volumes of the emasculate stuff which the Lord Rector of Glasgow [Disraeli] recently' ventured. Still, said Huxley, 'I doubt if I shall be able to show my face in Oxford & Cambridge after it'.[17]

Huxley practised what he preached and returned to his workers' lectures. There was no wealth or rank test here; or rather there was, in reverse – only bona fide workers could get in. Occasionally students or reporters joined them, but, as Bernard Becker found on his survey of *Scientific London*, Huxley's theatre saw no '*Angot* caps and red opera cloaks'. It was crammed with real handicraftsmen. From the factory gates they trudged on Monday nights, not deterred by a 'Wild North-Easter', to hear his formidably titled 'On the Phenomena of Life as Motion and Consciousness'. Only in 1874 could such a penny-a-lecture series be a sell-out among such a class. Others tried to join them. His righteous science mated to social betterment had a stirring appeal. To young ordinands looking for a crusade it was irresistible. It wasn't only the freethinkers who infiltrated his lectures. One infatuated curate who spiced his sermons with science and knew the 'Physical Basis of Life' by heart begged a ticket, on the grounds that no man worked harder dashing around a parish of 17,000 souls.

The ease with which his lectures could be assimilated made them beguiling. Nettie said he had a sort of 'telepathic effect which enables you at once to perceive his meaning', or to think you do. There was no 'rustling, hushing, and settling down'. The artisans sat in deep silence as Huxley turned them into thinking automatons with an 'astounding bit of speculative philosophy'.[18]

But Huxley, becoming the solid middle-class professional, had a complex relationship with his factory hands. Some activists continued to cannibalize his science for their own co-operative ends. But he was a persuasive advocate; he made his labourers feel like a jury, and thus part of the process of scientific deliberation.[19] And many bearded workers tacitly accepted his lead and with it the hegemony of the Darwinian elite.

One can see why. By 1874 Huxley was becoming more the scientific determinist, making one's feeling of 'Free Will' simply an emotional warmth which accompanies some compunction. Yet only three years earlier, in 1871, his more cautious admission that the world was as likely to be the mental construct of a conscious mind as an objective material entity had brought jeers from the militant materialists on the street. They accused him of casting 'Idealistic dust in our eyes; seemingly to prevent the bigots calling him Materialist'.[20]

In 1874 Huxley's scientific dishes were spiced more to their taste. This March, he discussed Descartes' conception of brutes as self-adjusting machines. Epiphenomenal consciousness, reflex arcs, paraplegia: it seemed an unappetizing platter, but as always it came lightly served, and the factory hands had to like a lecturer who could moot the 'mechanical equivalent of consciousness'. Huxley was turning full-circle to his own back-street youth – to the radical Methodist Marshall Hall's reflex-arc concept at Sydenham College. After 30 years that Dissenting, alienating, Calvinistic concept had come to explain the very brain itself.[21] Huxley's automaton humans matched Tyndall's futuristic babies built from chemicals. And whatever Huxley's philosophic provisos, who among the godless unwashed would not have seen him throwing out free will and the threats and promises of an afterlife?[22]

America still beckoned. Tyndall had triumphantly toured from Boston to Baltimore. He had sold out $5 seats and the star treatment ended in him joining Emerson and Longfellow in their 'galaxy of genius'. The takings reflected it, and he had left $13,033 in trust, which would mature to endow Fellowships at Harvard, Columbia and Pennsylvania. Huxley organized the welcome-home party to hear about it. He was still a charity case himself: school fees, maids' salaries, meat bills and £150 cheques to drain the Marlborough Place 'lake' ate into his pay. Nettie could not even afford to go to the British Association with him. Huxley told Darwin that he had 'had an *awfully* tempting offer to go to Yankee-land', and 'two or three thousand pounds' was 'not to be sneezed at by a *père de famille*'. Rumour was rife in America: everyone thought that Harvard was about to make him a proposition. If they welcomed the 'raging infidel' Tyndall, Huxley's time had come.[23]

But where was the opportunity? He wanted Hooker to join him, but President and Secretary were held fast at the Royal Society. Every Thursday the senior statesmen did their duty. Hooker's lean figure could be seen swamped by the massive presidential chair, his worn face 'surmounted by a pair of those bushy eyebrows' which added gravity to his lean features. This was the imperial botanist who had just declined a knighthood as beneath the dignity of science. (Only Huxley approved, but, Hooker told Darwin, 'he *despises* Knighthood'.) Grave wasn't the word for the Secretary lounging in the armchair to his left, tweaking him that 'Sir Joseph looms in the future' so he had better practise kneeling in the bathroom mirror. The Royal was still a place of lords and commoners, but these two symbolized the careerists at the helm. And Huxley was for a continuing squeeze. As he said after one function: 'Noble Lords did not make good speeches. Plebeians, on the whole, distinguished themselves'.[24] He was in fine fettle again; and having done so much 'to gild the pill of science' he could afford to swank.

America was postponed for a year or so. Interminable lectures, 7,000 exam papers for school pupils and an oversubscribed course for their teachers required Olympian organization.[25] Huxley and Foster, the 'Best of Archangels', expanded their experimental work-force: the demonstrators now were of exceptional calibre – there was no team like it anywhere in the world. Rutherford had become the Professor of Physiology at Edinburgh; he brought his own pupil, the rising neurologist David Ferrier, already experimenting on the cerebral cortex for his book *The Functions of the Brain*. There was Martin, and the Gradgrinding Parker. More sons were co-opted. They were blooded young, and it was nothing for the 19-year-old Jeffrey Parker to be set marking the 'Elementary papers'. A corporate approach came with professionalization. Huxley began regimenting these research students, presenting each with an esoteric topic (the frog's larynx for young Parker) and coordinating the results.[26]

Huxley's heart was in London and his mind in the Black Country. An engineer he had wanted to be, and they were his men, with their frank, foundry-based, cause-and-effect universe. The family's indus-trial connections were being riveted tighter. In 1874 his niece Alice married the railway engineer Arthur Heath, who would go on to teach at Cooper's Hill (latterly the technological Brunel University). Steel towns welcomed Huxley: in 1874 he would speak as Governor of Owen's College in Manchester. Or he would take Nettie and the girls to his friend Sir William Armstrong, the munitions manu-facturer, at his Gothic manor house Cragside, amid the wild heather-covered hills of Northumberland (in what would be the first of almost yearly Summer visits). And while the children rode and boated, Hal wheeled money out of Armstrong's steelworks for Dohrn's marine station.[27]

But the telling connection was with Birmingham. Birmingham – with its vast social-engineering projects centred on Civic Hall. This 'experimental, adventurous' city – once the most sickly, polluted and ghetto-infested in England – was proclaiming the new civic gospel. Here the old Radicalism had flowered into a spending municipal socialism thanks to one man, the Unitarian Mayor Joseph Chamberlain. Chamberlain's caucus, fired by the Nonconformist hatred of Establishment inequalities, had squashed private interests to clear the slums and clean the sewage-choked river. It had municipalized the gas and water companies and ploughed the profits into new buildings. Chamberlain was a Cromwellian to his teeth, a Roundhead in his political imagination; Huxley's sort of leader. And Huxley lauded the proud Midlands town as a 'political laboratory'.[28] It was a crucible of civic achievement where 'local self government' was honing the new professional politician.

Here Huxley had delivered his famous 'Duties of the State' address, as President of the Birmingham and Midland Institute late in 1871. No talk was better tailored to time and place: as Chamberlain's city was being swept clean, Huxley appeared as the well-fledged State interventionist. He challenged Herbert Spencer's hands-off and do-nothing demand of government (Huxley published his paper under the title 'Administrative Nihilism'). The 'plebeian' praised the Education Act – something Chamberlain's Radical and Nonconformist National Education League had pressured for. He had no qualms about government running the Post Office or telegraph services, and he saw the State's vaccination, sanitation and road-building programmes (like Birmingham's) lessen the misery which had fuelled the revolutionary movements across Europe.[29]

A proud city gave Huxley his closest brush with municipal socialism. But it brought a mail full of love and hate. From friendly snipes by Spencer to abusive postcards from 'John Bull' ('*mere rot*'), the criticism rained down. Then again, he never went far enough for the socialists, and Wallace was for nationalizing land and mineral wealth immediately. But the South Kensington militia was behind Huxley. Get the Birmingham speech reprinted, Cole said, 'I am good to buy a hundred copies at a shilling a piece'.[30]

In 1874 Birmingham hosted Huxley again. The radical caucus was erecting a statue of Joseph Priestley, making a hero of the long-dead chemist, philosopher and materialist Unitarian preacher (he was their sort of man). So Huxley came to praise Joseph Priestley, and the city fathers 'hung breathless on his words'. And obviously, because 'Satan whispered that it would be a good opportunity for a little ventilation of wickedness'. Of course, Huxley recalled that the Church-and-King bigots – 'with that love for the practical application of science which is the source of the greatness of Birmingham' – had set 'fire to [Priestley's] house with sparks from his own electrical machine'. Priestley's hounding became another plea for 'rational freedom'. Even back in town, frail old Lyell, who had been 'taught to honour' Priestley as a child, chortled at the *Daily News* report of Huxley's 'splendid address'.[31]

Real notoriety awaited Huxley at Belfast in 1874, during the British Association week. It was hot, crowds of holidaymakers turned up in trams to see the savants; the rooms in Queen's College should have provided shade, but the temperature increased with the speeches. Tyndall's election as President had topped even Huxley's for intrigue. The Irishman was loved and loathed for his fiery materialism. And the fact that he *was* Irish caused ripples in sectarian Ulster. A 'blundering idiot' of a Belfast mayor started a '"Home Rule" agitation' to mark the event, leaving the unionist Tyndall positively livid.[32]

No pantheistic Orangeman could arouse more feeling. For every Arnold who embraced his religious 'reformation', there was a Ruskin who scorned it. (In fact there could only be one Ruskin who expected a second Joshua to make the sun stand still.) Ruskin hated the lot of them: he dug at Huxley, thought Darwin showed an unhealthy interest in monkey behinds, and now launched a 'slanderous attack' on Tyndall. Ignore 'that lunatic', was Huxley's order. 'Men don't make war on either women or Eunuchs'. But Belfast was 'flooded . . . with Ruskin's diatribe' to raise the temperature more.[33]

So it was already hot when Tyndall was elected. And with him at the dispatch box of the 'Parliament of Science' the deterministic philosophy of industrial Britain peaked. Nature was presented as a great ironclad bound fast to Fate.

Hal sat in the hot August fields poring over his own speech. He thought of the last time he was a Belfast Ass, as a callow 22-year-old, and wrote home sweetly to Nettie that 'you were largely in my thoughts' then too. Twenty years told in the crowds that packed the anatomy hall to see Huxley in action. The press thought him more interesting than his subjects: the smart prose, the 'well-simulated . . . modesty' of a 'dogmatist' who 'thinks . . . upon his feet'. The earnest looks and clenched lips gave him the manner 'of the Puritan', the effect ruined only by his irreverent jokes.[34] He knew how to hold the bus-loads. Talks here had to grip 'those who know nothing (ie 9/10th of the audience)', and he did that. Even if he tried to 'dance between the eggs', the crowds willed him to step on a few. He turned down his notes and gave a spellbinding 90-minute metaphysical oration which was totally out of keeping with the venue. He talked on animals – and humans – as conscious automatons, without any 'free-will' to break the body's physiological sequences. If swimming decerebrated frogs act as automatons, perhaps brain-damaged war veterans in their somnambulistic trances do too? He nudged his audience into believing that even they were thinking machines. Their thoughts were simply the mental reflections that accompanied an action, without influencing it or altering the body's physico-chemical action. There was a rock-bottom logic to it, and Darwin heard his 'Automaton' paper called the 'magnum opus' of the meeting.[35] But Tyndall's related talk had already eclipsed the proceedings.

'Johnny's' Presidential call had carried feelings to a fever pitch. It was an echo of Huxley's 'Science and "Church Policy"' editorial a decade earlier, the same territorial demand by a profession clearing space, just as pointed but more public. In Tyndall's words, 'We claim, and we shall wrest from theology, the entire domain of cosmological theory'. There spoke a former £1-a-week surveyor in a position to raise his lot. The pulpits claimed it was 'an abuse of his office'.[36] What they really feared was it becoming the badge of his office. Science in the industrial age was being demarcated. Professional boundaries were moving, and the self-taught surveyors were implementing a new Enclosure Act.

Tyndall had composed his Presidential Address during a 'barbarous' cold snap in the Bel Alp. Secreted away, he had been chilled to the bone and surrounded by snow. Huxley had received the drafts and counselled caution, but the Alpine air had given them a spartan feel. In the bleak snowscape one felt helpless against the elemental forces, and an overpowering fatalism carried the address: 'its very well done', Huxley admitted, but 'I wish he had taken another line'. 'Lord knows what will be the effect'. The two prophets of the new reformation went to Ireland together, 'as Luther did to Worms' – Tyndall said – to meet 'all the devils in Hell there'. The talk thickened the sulphurous atmosphere, and generated occasional bursts of applause like the crackle of thunder. Nettie, too poor to come, heard of the 'theological thunder', which rumbled around Hal's speech as well. Tyndall, the Protestant Orangeman, who had cut away at Catholicism's idolatries, had carried on hacking to the bedrock of Matter. Here he was, at one with the bloodstained martyrs who had sustained his youth. There was an awe in his address, and it horrified the Presbyterian *Witness*. This was a hymn to the glories of cosmic progress, and in a city of 'virile Calvinism' where Man was still Falling. The rival pulpits saw him hastening mankind's 'ruin'.[37] One unappreciative listener even demanded his prosecution for blasphemy.

Tyndall's was an evocative vision of almost hallucinogenic perfection – the sort everyone had expected of Huxley four years earlier.

It meshed mechanistic science with humanistic values, unifying them in the cosmic process, which evolved molecules and emotions alike. Cosmic evolution was treated as an organic unfolding, like a flower unfurling, self-contained and mysterious. Old Lyell, losing his sight, his speech slurred, called it a 'manly and fearless out-speaking', meaning over-the-top. And local Presbyterians feared from its cosmological completeness and religious tone that it would 'quench every thirst'.[38] To sophisticates it looked like the triumph of Calvin over Carlyle, or was it Carlyle over Calvin? To simpler souls it spelled the fantastic success of Democritean atheism over two millennia of Christianity. The majority thought it mad materialism, but no one could quite define his crime.

Tyndall had welded Carlyle's romanticism to Dissent's steam-enginery. Man and machine bowed to the same unyielding necessity. In the ultimate attenuation of Enlightenment radicalism, Tyndall gave molecules 'the promise and potency of every form and quality of Life', making 'all our poetry, all our science, all our art – Plato, Shakespeare, Newton, and Raphael – . . . potential in the fires of the sun'.[39] Amid the avalanches of the unforgiving Alps, the brooding Tyndall had had a stark vision, and no one was sure whether he should be damned as a materialist, a pantheist or a mystic.

Deterministic science and radical Dissenting politics were surging through Morley's *Fortnightly* and Knowles' *Contemporary* reviews. Evolution was 'made the illuminating explanation of all things on earth' and placed in happy proximity to radical programmes of 'social and political renovation'. With Morley soliciting papers and Knowles 'going about like a Raptorial Bird seizing on contributions', Huxley was as 'spoiled as a maiden with many wooers'. He was sworn to Morley's rag, 'which is my old love, and the *Contemporary* which is my new', and he promised 'to remain as constant as a persistent bigamist'.[40]

The monthlies were Hal's bread and butter and he liked the company. They thrashed over Tyndall's deterministic universe with its convertible forces, where the equivalence of motion and heat and electromagnetic force spoke of unbreakable causal sequences. Friends saw Huxley's 'Automaton' paper in November's *Fortnightly* moving the same way. Weren't his conscious robots shackled to fate? They operated without any interposition of the will. His old ally Carpenter – whose medical thesis 35 years earlier had been on reflex arcs – balked at the extremism. Having contributed so much himself he pulled back. Pithed frogs actually sit motionless unless stimulated, that was the crux. So what naturally stimulates an unpithed frog? For him 'a conscious determination of the Ego' initiates the body's repertoire of reflexes.[41] The Ego did not directly control every muscle; it triggered the pre-programmed behaviours. This too was heresy, of a Unitarian sort. The ghost was operating the machine. But Huxley had exorcized the ghost. He had ejected the spiritual entity with its transcendent allegiance, to leave a mental physiology in line with his anti-supernatural strategy.

With the school-marms outperforming the masters, it was not surprising that Huxley had a woman demonstrator in physiology by 1874. As Miss McConnish lent over the men to dissect a frog's urinogenitalia the writing was on the wall. Career women were overcoming the odds. And overthrowing the aristocratic ideal of the 'perfect woman': that helpless ornament, stuck in the 'doll stage of evolution', 'cribbed, cabined, and confined' at home to become the conventional mental invalid.[42]

But the cult of masculinity drove deep into Victorian science. The antithesis of coy home-maker and battling breadwinner was set hard in *The Descent of Man*. Intimidated by intellectual women (rather than fascinated, as Huxley), Darwin scorned them as bores. His 'Sexual Selection' had males peaking in perfection through their fight to possess submissive females. Men's intelligence increased further as they struggled to provide for their families, while the woman's stagnated. Darwin's was an image of ineradicable sexual difference. His science turned the stereotypes into seeming hard knowledge. That served to reinforce the Anthropological Institute's exclusion order against the 'ladies', barring their access to knowledge.[43] And so the thing turned in a vicious circle. The 'Woman Question' was pooh-poohed and equality declared unnatural, and a little learning was deemed not so much dangerous as pointless.

Huxley subscribed to much of this – it was the cultural standard, defied only by Mill's *Subjection of Women* and the emancipating socialists. But with something approaching scientific *noblesse oblige*, he pulled culture away from nature (a tactic he would perfect in the 1880s) and refused to make women's biological 'limitations' the basis of a discriminatory educational policy. The paternalist was *granting* opportunities, not accepting inalienable rights. Even acknowledging the prejudicial yardstick of gendered 'strength', he wondered why careers 'open to the weakest and most foolish of the male sex should be forcibly closed to women of vigour and capacity'.[44]

With girls ceasing to be educated at their mother's knee, careers and higher education would inevitably follow. In a decade most would be at the new High Schools (doing the Huxleys' German governess Miss Matthaei out of her supplementary income).[45] And the High Schools in turn would create that 'bicycles, bangs, and bloomers' New Woman.

Already some were earning, saving and delaying babies. Jobs, whether for weavers, teachers, clerks or domestics (Hal and Nettie made sure the nieces could stand on their own feet as governesses), meant money and security. And with these – or rather with the articulate Frances Cobbe, questioning the values of a culture which lumps women with criminals and idiots, and denies wives a legal existence – came the 1870 Married Women's Property Act, giving three million working wives a right to their possessions.[46] The 'Woman Question' was being resolved by the women themselves: they were taking charge of their own finances, their schooling, their access to the professions and their destiny.

Not all felt the need. Nettie's gentrified acquaintances (in this case Lady Portsmouth) thought that 'forcing . . . the brain' of 'young growing girls' will end up 'addling' it.[47] But that wouldn't have gone down well with Miss McConnish, or the graduates coming to study under Huxley, such as the American Sarah Stevenson, who went on to take the Chair of Physiology at the Women's Hospital Medical College in Chicago.

'Work and independence!' exclaimed Sophia Jex-Blake as she became a teacher. She was 'one of the band' with Elizabeth Garrett and Emily Davies, and had already written a book on her travels to America to study women's education. But her move into a male profession, medicine, was to point up Huxley's conflicting interests. Women were a minority who happened to be in a majority, and Jex-Blake knew that they wanted their own women doctors. She had enrolled at Edinburgh University (even though Garrett did not think her particularly suited), taking advantage of new regulations which allowed women separate medical instruction. There was high-level support, but also virulent opposition from the closed-shop consultants, who feared that the influx of women would take away their clientele. Jex-Blake did nothing to allay fears that the women had a political agenda: in her Huxleyan way, she shunned the side-door approach. She wanted women's rights to be recognized, and she attracted a dedicated group of women students around her. One came top in chemistry, but was refused the prize scholarship, while others were denied certificates of attendance.[48]

When the professors disbarred the women's anatomy teacher,

Jex-Blake appealed to Huxley. And why not? Weren't professionals dispassionate dealers in a neutral medical science? Didn't they transcend petty feelings of 'delicacy'? Shouldn't women sit alongside the men? The tangle of issues left the patriarch performing his old balancing act. He deplored the placing of any but 'natural' obstacles in the women's way. They should be able to take 'degrees upon the same terms as men'. But the issue of mixed classes was prickly. He said that he had kept women out of his winter biology course, 'with rare exceptions', but it is clear that he had increasing numbers paying 'homage at the Shrine of Huxley'.[49] So while he endorsed single-sex classes, he declined to slap down a rival professorate.

One can see why. Professional protocols and professional friendships were involved. Jex-Blake's supporters had been bringing Huxley her natural history exam papers since 1872, which suggested that everyone saw her as a test case. But these papers were set by his old friend Wyville Thomson, and Huxley confirmed that they had been marked correctly.[50] 'Charlie' Thomson's involvement added the final complication. The fact that Huxley himself would be asked in November 1874 to be an Edinburgh professor – to deputize for Thomson in Summer 1875 while he was on the *Challenger* – shows the delicacy of his situation. Lyon Playfair and Edinburgh's Principal Sir Alexander Grant (both of whom had sided against Jex-Blake) were wining and dining Huxley. He officially accepted because 'the University ... has been civil to me'. Privately nothing but mercenary considerations would force him to 'expatiate myself to the howling wilderness around Arthur's Seat'. But the sums to be pocketed were irresistible. Edinburgh was still the academic Eldorado, even if Hooker called it suicide. 'What does your wife say?'[51] But Nettie too appreciated the pay.

The women ended up suing Edinburgh University. What with firework attacks on her house, sexual harassment and a lawsuit, Jex-Blake failed her exams. She called it discrimination. So it was the professors, this time, who sent her papers to Huxley, and he endorsed their decision. But he told the *Times* that women *should* graduate; and Jex-Blake still sought his support. An apartheid scheme was her only recourse. She realized that women had to take charge of their own bodies. And so, with Elizabeth Garrett and Huxley on the coordinating committee in 1874, Jex-Blake became a pupil in her own London School of Medicine for Women.

This same year, 1874, the women sitting London University classes petitioned to be allowed to take the degree, and shortly the Senate changed its Charter. Just as it had opened its doors to Jews and

Dissenters when Huxley was a boy, now London would lead the way in granting degrees to women.[52]

Long-suffering Nettie bore the babies, ran the house, organized the maids and governesses, administered the liniment and the religion, and in her exclusive domain – from which her workaholic husband stood aloof in befuddled admiration – she led a life 'not only of super-human, but of super-feminine, activity'. But she could never escape the home: research kept Hal from going mad, and she envied him the digression. Still, she was his hidden aide. She drew the diagrams, checked the manuscripts and translated the German (the Goethe quote closing his 'Automatons' talk was hers).[53] They travelled to functions together, 'Regina mea et Ego', when money allowed. His emotional dependence was obvious: he admitted that 'Few people appreciate her at her real value, or dream what part she has played in my life'. And Nettie's submergence belied her active role. A German Moravian schooling had given her an interest in higher education and she put all her daughters through the Slade School, while Rachel sat the Senior Girls' Cambridge Exam (a school-leaver's proficiency test).[54] Notes from Spencer or Dohrn, Foster or Playfair, would come addressed to her, their messages to be passed on in supplicatory style. She was a conduit to Hal in more special ways: women's groups went through her, wanting, and getting, his support for the National Society for the Improvement of Women's Education or the Girls' Public Day School Company (both set up by the emancipist Maria Grey).[55]

The stereotype of the 'angel in the house' – the redoubtable wife giving moral succour while remaining the repository of 'parsonese superstition' – was honed from chauvinistic images. True, Nettie trotted the children to Lisson Grove Church on a Sunday – in fact, the conventional Misses took themselves off to church.[56] Hal was happy to wave them goodbye, and the religious issue was surprisingly frictionless – perhaps because, on the key issue of agnosticism, Nettie preferred to miss his point.[57] But her influence on his social views is difficult to gauge. What did she think of him dining with the unmarried George Eliot and G. H. Lewes at North Bank? Hal had no qualms, but he went alone, whether to protect her or because she was censorious is not clear. Certainly he shared the excitement in the Athenaeum smoking room at George Eliot's *Middlemarch*.[58] But there is a cryptic hint that Huxley might have thought it unseemly for Nettie to visit Eliot and Lewes.[59]

While Huxley was restricting participation in science, the women's home circle was expanding it. Lyell's secretary Arabella Buckley would drop in to have tea with Nettie. She was soon to join the best children's science writers. They were transformers rather than interpreters, not disseminators but cultural reshapers. They parablized and packaged stories 'fraught with cosmic significance' for the mother–child market.[60] These unsung women popularizers were as important in their way for reshaping the culture. Just as Huxley's labourers actively sculpted their evolutionary edifice, so middle-class women, the traditional moral teachers, used their skills to tailor Nature to the nursery. They made it pregnant with moral meaning and sympathy: an ugly Darwinism became divinely inspiring. Buckley's mass-market *Fairyland of Science* turned the invisible forces into wonder-working fairies. Here and in *Winners in Life's Race* (note the upbeat Darwinian connotation) she imbued Nature with love, mutual help and life-guiding precepts. Her story-book science carried a growing generation from the Darwinian arena towards the agnostic City of God – or the socialist *fin de siècle*. In early Victorian times science had been retailed in the pub, the church hall and the mechanics' institute, but the laboratory doors had shut out the public now.[61] The academics were drawing in the boundaries of expertise, turning the vicars, the socialists and the dame-school matrons into marginalized amateurs. But Arabella Buckley shows how Darwinism was still being actively recreated, and nowhere more importantly than in the kindergarten.

Evolution was a stimulus, and it presented great new challenges for eager young anatomists. More than anything it sparked the search for intermediate life forms, particularly those bridging the great chasms, creatures the old teachers said had never existed. Which group – worms or starfish or insects – had transmuted into fishes to start the vertebrate explosion? And how on earth had they made the change? This was the great prize. Everyone was on the scent, Dohrn in his marine station on the Med, Haeckel in Germany, Huxley in London. But it was Kovalevskii's brother Alexander in Russia who took the laurel.[62] Huxley had sniffed close to the clues: off New Guinea the sailor had noted that the peculiar, sessile, sack-like tunicate or sea squirt had a free-swimming larva with a tadpole-like tail. And he had long held that the adult sea squirt's branchial region was equivalent to the fish's gill slits. And so it turned out. But Kovalevskii's coup was a decidedly Darwinian triumph: the young Kovalevskii was educated into German *Darwinismus* and had worked with Dohrn, who had committed his station to the study of marine embryos and evolutionary ancestries.

More and more of Huxley's research became part of the trend towards exploring links. In 1874 he and Lankester were sectioning that primitive sand-burrowing *Amphioxus*, another creature that had fascinated the sailor in his dredging days. It was fish-like but had no proper skull or brain or renal organs. Huxley's dissection showed that it did have an enlarged cranial development and antecedents of kidney tubes: in other words, rudiments of skull and brain, 'shut up like an opera-hat'. It was the sort of anatomical finding to 'take your breath away'.

His class heard it first. The tunicate larva's stiffened tail, with its dorsal nerve cord and muscles and fish-like development, had a 'fundamental resemblance ... [to] the Vertebrata'.[63] Sea squirts passed via an *Amphioxus*-like form to the jawless lampreys and hagfishes and ultimately all higher life. This was very satisfactory for Huxley. Behind it stood his original suggestion that the two body layers (ectoderm and endoderm) of the medusae and sea nettles were analogous to the cell layers in the vertebrate embryo, a point that Haeckel and Lankester were now busily working up.[64]

Darwinism was having the same impact on Huxley's fossil work. Despite the fact that for 15 years he had been harping on the prodigious time that crocodiles had persisted unchanged, continual study of that 16-foot Elgin *Stagonolepis* had him rethinking crocodiles. Now he saw them putting on a spurt in Mesozoic times. He traced their progressive acquisition of a secondary palate (the bony roof of the mouth that separates off the nasal passage). Quite whether it went with a modified lifestyle, or had something to do with the reptile being able to drown its newly-evolved mammalian prey without shipping water, Huxley wasn't sure. (Owen was far more adept at this sort of thinking.)[65]

In a sense, it was outside his jurisdiction. The *Origin of Species* had caught the medically-trained comparative anatomists on the hop. Its unusual ecological and population approach was quite alien to these dead-room men, interested in whole-body design. There was no study of the *Origin* in Huxley's class – that was something the students read at home, as they would a novel. The book simply stood outside the disciplinary norm. Ironically there was no space for it in a biology laboratory, no way that conventional anatomists could get to grips with its competition and geographical isolation. That would require a wholesale reorientation, and it would take Huxley years to integrate elements of an evolutionary view into his academic discipline.[66]

It certainly made little impact on his unsung work at the chalk-face. He delivered some 120 stock lectures a year to students and masters. This is what the public didn't see: the weekly haul through the animal and plant kingdoms, starting with mould and ending with monkey brains. Then came the practicals, themselves a dash to prepare slides of bacteria, sections of ferns, demonstrations of bat anatomy (or, opportunely in 1874, dissections of a porpoise).[67] This was the business of biology, not Darwin's book.

True, Huxley emphasized the meeting point between plants and animals. Algae, unicellular animals and moulds preponderated in these lectures, partly because of Huxley's interest in the similarities of animal and plant cells. That was part of the synthetic tendency of the age, and went with Darwin's own interest in the almost animal-like activity of insectivorous sundews and flytraps. After this fundamental divergence, the plants had gone on to become 'the ideal *prolétaire* of the living world, the worker who produces; the animal, the ideal aristocrat, who mostly occupies himself in consuming'.[68] And Huxley saw his job as enumerating the types for the tyros.

In 1874 he was still telling them that 'all hypotheses [like Darwin's, were to be] . . . carefully kept in the back-ground, because theories on these matters are "excellent servants, but very bad masters"'.[69] This Jekyll and Hyde attitude to evolution – championing it outside, disdaining it in – confused many people. Darwinism was an ideological cannon to be fired in the street (at least until after his American trip, when one palaeontological big gun was hauled inside the walls). But for the moment Darwin's bulldog was content to confuse. There he was, shunning the 'bad master' in class, while defending Darwin in print.

So the students saw one Huxley, the 'neutral', tolerant professional, as Mivart's son Frederick testified. (He came home after his first day at South Kensington in October 1874 full of Huxley's kindness and carrying a note: 'Dear Mivart, – Wolves do not prey upon wolves, and I can accept no payment from you for your son's work with me'.)[70] But the public saw another: the ferocious carnivore in the evolutionary circus who, within eight weeks, would be savaging the boy's inept father.

Causes célèbres had a habit of seeking Huxley out. This one started with George Darwin. He was stomachy like his father, and like his father mending under 'D^r. Andrew' (Huxley's doctor Clark). At a loose end while recuperating, he had written an article on cousin Galton's eugenics, to the disapproval of his prim sister Etty. His first *Contemporary* piece advocated divorce in cases of wife battering, sexual abuse or mental breakdown (to stop bad traits being passed on). St George Mivart, working in Germany from muddled notes, saw family values under attack and the sanctity of marriage succumbing to Darwinian bestiality. In a defamatory aside he even accused George of *encouraging* vice. What 'hideous sexual criminality of Pagan days' could not be defended 'by the school to which this writer belongs'? A stunned Charles Darwin made the *Quarterly* run George's rebuttal, but Mivart's 'apology' only rubbed salt in the wound. Darwin, unequal to the social fray, sought Huxley's advice on this 'Papist' matter. Remain aloof, counselled Huxley, 'like one of the blessed gods of Elysium, and let the inferior deities' stand in.[71] But a Victorian raw nerve was tingling. Talk of 'unrestrained licentiousness' transfixed a generation that dare not speak of sex.

Huxley emerged from his classes, read the reviews and found an old bogey: the Darwinians cast as evil corrupters. 'If anybody tries that on with my boy L. the wolf will show all the fangs he has left', he commiserated with Darwin. As it was, the wolf would savage any predator approaching the pack's cubs. So it was Huxley who promised not to 'leave a square inch of unwaled skin upon his idolatrous carcass'. To have 'slandered Darwin once' was disgraceful; to have repeated it 'in a more aggravated form' was unforgivable.[72]

Huxley had his pretext. 'Unless I err', he responded in print, Mivart includes 'me among the members of that school' which is to return us to the 'gross profligacy of Imperial Rome'. Forensic dissection was Huxley's forte, not that much was needed for this blundering breach of etiquette. A red-faced Mivart watched the issue turn to his perversion of the truth. And that pointed to something more vile than Nero's profligacy, namely 'the secret poisonings of the Papal Borgias'. 'Tremendous', cried Darwin, wallowing in the reproof, 'it is tremendous'. And George was proud to have Huxley take 'up the cudgels for me'. The clique acquired its identity and cohesion from this sort of posturing. The Mivarts and Bastians focused the party's gaze, and it watched spellbound as Huxley's lacerating tongue took off Mivart's hide. Glad to 'see that you haven't forgotten how to be 'orrid', crowed Fiske.[73]

Father Roberts, the priest who had coaxed Mivart from Darwin's explanation of ethics, was auditing Huxley's lectures at that moment. Roberts' ascetic life in a slum school appealed to Huxley. (As did his 'brain sharpener' cleverness, not to mention his unhappiness over Papal infallibility.)[74] And so through his favourite priest Huxley rid himself of a turbulent pupil: he severed all relations with Mivart. Darwin followed suit. Mivart's bitter regrets were to no avail. As

Father Roberts eventually left the Church of Rome, so Mivart was excommunicated from the Church of Science.

The Church Scientific was about to get its bible. The four years of experience with schoolmasters went into Huxley and Martin's book of '*practical dodges*' (Foster's apt description), the seminal 'how-to' lab manual, *A Course of Practical Instruction in Elementary Biology*. It was distilled by Huxley and his demonstrators from the Kensington course. They all had a hand in it, and Martin got his name on the title-page in 1875 through Foster's angelic intercession.[75] They knew it would increase his prospects of a job.

As dynasties changed the book became the standard. At University College the 80-year-old radical Robert Grant had died at his post. Innovative in his day, the only Lamarckian academic in England, he had become a deaf, dejected atheistic anachronism, his frayed French coat as funny as his archaic Restoration lectures.[76] One bull-headed professor replaced another, but the students noted the difference. The huge, domineering Ray Lankester swept in with Huxley's help. He was 'like those winged beasts from Nineveh', someone said. 'What you feel is just immense force'. The blustery, womanizing Lankester had hated Oxford, where 'life amidst old bachelor clergymen and a few cynical young classics is not normal'. He had been desperate for UCL. Once in, he refurbished the museum, introduced the latest embryological and morphological approaches and initiated practical work 'from 12 to $4\frac{1}{2}$ twice a week', using Huxley's *Elementary Biology*.[77] He turned the department's fortunes around and put University College back at the forefront of evolutionary research in Britain.

With the rise of the new went the demise of the old. There was 'a regular clearing out of the old philosophers', as Hooker put it. Saturday 23 January 1875 was the day Charles Kingsley had awaited with 'reverent curiosity' all of his life. So passed the friend who had restored Hal after Noel's death. Not that their differences were ever resolved: 'You were one of the people he loved & honoured', Fanny Kingsley wrote to Hal, '& does still'. It made the point. Others were ready to smile down on Hal. Lyell's decrepitude had Huxley craving a 'speedy end whenever my time comes'. Huxley's soft spot showed as he loyally repeated his latest lecture on the *Challenger* at his old mentor's bedside. In a month he was bearing Lyell's body to the nave of Westminster Abbey. When Nettie saw the snowdrop-sprinkled coffin she felt an 'inexpressible pain' at Sir Charles' burial so far from his wife. But Lyell had to be enshrined here. His *Principles of*

Geology, with its grindingly-slow evolution of the earth's surface, might have troubled an older generation, but the Darwinians were securing its immortality. Huxley bore the old-world gent who had influenced and sustained him, equivocated and hesitated, and finally died believing that science must not 'disturb any man's faith, if it be a delusion which increases his happiness'.[78]

That was the concern of the age: the search for moral meaning. Were there transcendent truths freeing mankind from this cruelly-fatalistic cosmos? Huxley gave the unpalatable answer, pleasantly dressed up. An impenetrable net lay at the sensory extremity: there was no knowing beyond, and little point in hoping. Agnosticism provoked Christian fears that individual life would become purpose-less. Was mankind at the end of an exotic evolutionary journey, or questing towards some future exotic end? With no object of veneration, no spark of divinity, and Huxley making a desert of the Unknowable, many despaired of a secular humanism.[79] The Positivists tried to put back the spark, Spencer tried to upgrade the Unknowable, but Huxley braved the task of giving a new meaning to morality itself, seeing virtue and worth in acquiescence to evidence. He too was trying to put the meaning back into life – it was the light shining from his *Lay Sermons* and *Critiques and Addresses*.

Lists of prospective books tumbled out of him, none to material-ize: on 'Consciousness' for the International Scientific Series, on 'Ethnology', on the 'Classification of Birds', and (one Darwin wanted) a revamping of his workers' 'Lectures on the Origin of Species'. Too many; he hardly knew which way to turn. They were screaming for his *Introductory Science Primer*. The others in the series were appearing (Balfour Stewart's *Physics* had sold 7,000 copies in six months). Henry Roscoe urged him to finish because 'the Christian Knowledge Society & other Sinners' were pirating the idea, printing 'whitened sepulchre' imitations that were 'hideously bad'. The pro-fessional fortifications were still precarious in the 1870s and encroaching commercial and religious interests remained a hazard. Even shilling crammers for Huxley's exams were selling in 'enor-mous numbers & we ought to try to put them out'.[80]

Too many books and too much bureaucracy. Like Dick Swiveller in the chips, he would pay off an old debt only to run up two others. The Devonshire Commission was over: it had detailed the needs of a new scientific culture – university research, Oxbridge laboratories, a Natural History Museum, schoolteaching and the creation of jobs – and Huxley wrapped up its final report in 1875 with a call for public money to match.[81] 'Thank Heaven the Science Committee is over &

done with', he told the zoo's Philip Sclater. 'But it is one down & another to come on'. He was already sitting on the Royal Society's 'Polar-Committee' and poaching Sclater's zoologists for Captain Nares' voyage to the North Pole. February found Nares at Marlborough Place, planning. Bureaucracy was at least broadening Huxley's ecological outlook; he was taxing the ornithologists on Arctic birds to be observed, and Darwin on glacial phenomena to be noted.[82] But his real 'weary work' in 1875 was on a different committee, countering public hostility on the most divisive aspect of the new science.

Women were not only penetrating science, but intent on altering its practice. Frances Cobbe's anti-cruelty alliance was targeting live animal experiments and tearing at the nation's heartstrings. Her campaign was made for the moment: a new laboratory culture encouraged vivisections, and they were more tolerable to younger physiologists with the use of anaesthesia after 1870. Then there was a growing stratum of non-medical biologists, who experimented, not to alleviate human suffering, but to further knowledge. Cobbe 'would have gladly died' to save the suffering cats, and such martyrdom moved families. Sickly Etty Darwin signed Cobbe's petition; in Victorian semis where ailing was normal, hypochondriacal housewives were empathizing with the torture victims. Cobbe's Victoria Street Society for the Protection of Animals from Vivisection raised deep questions about the emerging profession: how accountable was it? And to whom? Should there be lay scrutiny, parliamentary control or self-regulation?

Cobbe would extend RSPCA surveillance from the cat-skinning hovel to South Kensington. Huxley had his own horror of experiments on *conscious* animals and forbade them. He always pithed or anaesthetized his frogs before showing teachers the blood flow or muscle action. But this wasn't a line Cobbe cared to draw; and even Huxley defended those who went further if they were intent on 'alleviating human suffering'.

Cobbe began drafting a banning Bill. But laws were for publicans and prostitutes, not the professional elite of the nation! The Darwinians called for pre-emptive action, 'or else these beggars will steal a march on us'. For Darwin the vivisectionist's gains were tangible, in medical care, humanitarian sympathy and pure science. But pamphleteers denied that animal sacrifice led to medical advance. And they denounced a 'Demoniacal Physiology' for its dehumanizing effect on students. Huxley wasn't squeamish, but 'the doctrine that men may suffer & knowledge stand still rather than dogs & rabbits should be made uncomfortable, makes me sick'.[83] As a non-medical teacher, he saw experiential learning – his fundamental track to true knowledge – threatened by Cobbe's 'fanatical following'.

Her broad alliance feared science's claim to cultural leadership. Many of her petition-signers were alienated, shut out as the lab doors closed, and horrified by the nihilistic implications of chance evolution and its moral vacuum. It showed in the vilification of the '*parvenu* profession'. The campaign was hurting. Huxley's State aid now brought State restrictions with it: an order rather pointedly banning vivisections in his lab. With Hutton's *Spectator* standing for Cobbe and Christianity, Huxley warned Foster not to do anything in the schoolmasters' course 'that could be laid hold of by Hutton & the "foolish fat scullion"'.[84]

Questions of pain and responsibility racked the nation. The Queen had a sermon preached on 'Vivisection, in which H.M. is *very* strongly interested'. And she had it sent to Huxley, who gave it the shortest shrift in the politest way. The women, so long lauded by the patrician Darwins and Huxleys for their moral superiority and concern with suffering, were turning this very aspect of femininity against an exclusive male profession.[85]

The socialists too became odd bedfellows, siding with the Crown and Church philanthropists against Darwin's Malthusian Nature progressing through cruelty and culling. Ironically the Darwinians, who embraced the kinship of all life, were justifying its mutilation, while Christians, given dominion over the animals, felt Methodism's sympathy for suffering creation. But Huxley the cat-lover left his sentiment at the lab door. He joined the squeamish dog-loving Darwin to propose a self-regulating system for licensing experimenters. They would make it part of the professionals' accrediting procedures.

Huxley went to Downe on 17 April 1875. Here he joined one of Foster's physiologists on his first visit, George John Romanes. This stuffshirt was a young Darwin, wealthy, a failed Cambridge ordinand subverted by Nature's creation. The evangelical had transferred the devotional power of his student essay *Christian Prayer and General Laws* to Darwin's altar (the book had taken the Burney Prize at Cambridge, its topic a response to the 'Prayer Gauge Debate'). Here was another whose home was a workshop where he could pick jellyfish apart. Darwin had asked them not to mention animal experiments in the 'presence of my ladies'.[86] But they mooted potential sponsors (Lubbock suggested Playfair), and Darwin sent their draft report to the Foreign Secretary, Lord Derby. Huxley knew that the fox-hunting MPs would rally to save their own skins.

The result was another Royal Commission, instigated by Disraeli at the Queen's suggestion, which seemed a further slight on the profession. But this one they turned to advantage. Huxley was adept at leading witnesses, and for once he was happy to be co-opted by the Home Secretary.[87]

Huxley was 'enlightening the Caledonians' by the time it convened. On 4 May 1875 he turned 50, one day into his Edinburgh lectures, standing in for that 'zoological Ulysses' Wyville Thomson. No longer the brooding romantic, Huxley was jolly and jowly, and as cleverly teasing as ever. He was away on his birthday for the first time, but what a present! The fame which had brought the autograph hunters – everybody from Millais to the charwomen – brought the students: 600 on his opening day. The Northern Athens was regaining its reputation, with a new zoology lab and new chairs of geology and engineering. He was among a staunch set of research-orientated professors. With no admissions tests the medical school alone attracted 900 students. It made Huxley's work pleasant, but 'still pleasanter was the pay'.

His star billing led the throng to expect a blast on Darwinism (his old friend Dyster's nephew among them). And for once he obliged, at least on his opening day. Dressed unfamiliarly in a gown, he gave them the icing from the cake first. He stroked Scottish vanities by holding up a single fossil as his emblem, the great Triassic 'crocodile' from the Elgin rocks. Then he conducted them through untold prehistoric aeons, as the crocodiles became more and more like those of the present day. He used it to explain the origin of birds, and to ask the fundamental question: how did this life transform? The audience was in his palm. Imagine, he said, a marsh – and there, suddenly, a crocodile springing

> into existence without anything to precede it – (laughter) – which was hard to believe, at least to an unimaginative person like himself. (Renewed laughter and applause.)
> Or . . . they might take what seemed to him the simple and natural explanation . . . that some primitive stock [like] . . . the crocodile of the trias, had in that long course of ages undergone those modifications which had converted it into the crocodile of the present day. (Great applause.)

The cheers showed the passing years. By 1875 the mood had changed. The students wanted to hear of life's variability and 'The production of Races in Nature & by Artificial condition'.[88]

Of course they had to eat the cake afterwards, 53 doses of 'dry facts'. But the parsons who mustered strong on the first day 'came to curse and didn't remain to pay'. Those who stayed were worked hard; 'panting' students found the daily pace 'awful' and crept out exhausted. But 353 stuck as the professor 'positively polished off the Animal Kingdom'. And had his talks been 'ten times as difficult', said one, they would still have been 'something glorious'.

Paying £4 each for the anaerobic exercise, they contributed substantially to a poor man's coffers. Huxley cleared about £1,000, a huge sum for a Summer course. He joked that it was 'one of the few examples known of a Southern coming north & pillaging the Scots'.[89]

Helping Thomson out, Huxley hardly expected the *Challenger* to torpedo him amidships. The corvette had left Cape York in sweltering north Queensland, a 'horrid place so close and muggy' that drained Thomson, as it had once Huxley. By June 1875 it had made Japan, and from Yeddo (Tokyo) Thomson sent the depressing news. The note was marked 'private'. 'None of us have ever been able to see a trace of *Bathybius*'. They had scrutinized every sea floor for three years, but without sight of Huxley's living gelatin, and they had lost faith that 'such a thing exists'.[90] So what was this enucleate jelly, christened by Huxley and considered by Haeckel to hold the key to the origin of life? The crew was perplexed until it was realized that *Bathybius haeckelii* only appeared when the ooze was bottled in alcohol. A precipitate!

Thomson's private note was to forewarn Huxley, to enable him to beat his breast before the news broke. And this he did, telling *Nature*'s Norman Lockyer that 'My poor dear *Bathybius* appears likely to turn out a "*Blunderibus*"'. *Nature* was more and more the professionals' mouthpiece, its success due to the judicious Lockyer (renowned himself now for studies of the sun's spectrum and discovery of helium). It was the place for a recantation. To stop enemies saying that '*Bathybius*' had been deliberately precipitated from his evil imagination 'I shall eat my leek handsomely'. And quickly. He published Thomson's letter and took responsibility for 'introducing this singular substance into the list of living things'.[91] And so perished a perfect fiction, a primal blob spontaneously generated by Huxley's sparks in the Victorian soup: a phantasm too easily seen during the 'protoplasmic' fever, when Haeckelian protozoology and Darwinian evolution conspired to make it real.

The 'Frau-widow' Nettie saw Hal twice during the Edinburgh Summer, as the penitent dashed back to Town for committee meetings. But Marlborough Place was like a university dorm – girls coming and going to University College soirées, and the Fosters living in, while Michael conducted the masters' course.[92]

He conducted it cagily while Cobbe's feathers were ruffled. Other feathers were looking equally dishevelled. Lord Arthur Russell, three-year-old Bertie's uncle, defended vivisection at the Metaphysical Society. As a good Deist and Darwinian, he believed that sacrificing 'the life of animals, for food or for knowledge ... is the birthright of man in his struggle for existence'. Huxley had a preview of Lord Arthur's paper, and wrote to Knowles that it was

> refreshing to read his fair & manly statement after being
> wearied by the venomous sentimentality & inhuman
> tenderness of the members of the Society for the infliction
> of cruelty on Man, who are ready to let disease torture
> hecatombs of men as long as poodles are happy.
> Let Art & Science, Men & Women die
> But let no tear suffuse a lap dog's eye!

Wickedly, Knowles read out Huxley's letter after Lord Arthur's paper. Hutton flew into a 'white rage' and thought it 'ought to be "burnt by the common hangman"'. Of course it was aimed at him. Hutton, ordinarily a generous critic, was on his own diametric journey from Unitarianism to Anglo-Catholicism. It showed in the *Spectator*'s growing readership of 'gentle souls ... declining gracefully', the doily set who 'looked askance at a Huxley travelling roughshod over their dearest orthodoxies' and awaited each Saturday when Hutton would put the world to rights. But vivisection was no party issue; in this rarefied atmosphere, Huxley had a degree of support that surprised even Knowles. Old enemies showed a friendly face. The Catholic Mivart rose to say 'how much & how far he agreed' with the letter's tone. And in the rumpus a sympathetic Gladstone in the Chair asked for it to be read again. Lord Arthur, said Knowles, 'is so much in love with it that he begged me hard to give it to him' as a 'certificate of character'.

> I have no doubt Hutton would like to see other productions
> of mine dealt with by some common or uncommon
> Hangman [Huxley replied]. Yet I know he has a kindness
> for me and when he looks down upon me from Abraham's
> bosom, he will beg the Cardinal [Manning, Catholic
> Archbishop of Westminster] hard to be allowed to fetch
> me a bottle of Apollinaris water out of the celestial cellar –
> if only to cool my tongue. But the Cardinal will see me —
> [damned] first.[93]

461

Huxley's friends would make matters worse. He was actually shot in the back by one witness before the Vivisection Committee. The bacteriologist Emanuel Klein was a Vienna MD who realized Hutton's nightmare. He should have been a safe expert, the co-author of the leading experimental physiology textbook. Klein had taken the name Edward on settling in London, but his pidgin English pointed up his Slav origins, and he showed a Viennese contempt for State interference. Huxley was absent when Klein provoked the committee and 'professed the most entire indifference to animal suffering'. He 'only gave anaesthetics to keep animals quiet!' Huxley snorted. 'I did not believe the man lived who was such an unmitigated cynical brute . . . I would willingly agree to any law which would send him to the treadmill'.

Commissioner Hutton stood shaken but vindicated. The ultimate horror – and the thing that should have made Klein a safe witness – was his job at London University. He was deputy director of its new philanthropically-endowed Brown Animal Sanatory Institute. He had the capital's horses and dogs in his care! His work on the sheep-pox virus here had been appreciated by Huxley. Now the man had 'done more mischief than all the fanatics put together'. Darwin was 'astonished & disgusted' and only 'glad he is a foreigner'. But it hit home: young Francis Darwin was actually working on his MD degree under Klein at the veterinary institute, and Darwin too had 'liked the man'.[94]

There was the solution. Nothing short of a voice from the Mount could sooth the Commission. Darwin was no authority on physiology, but he was an expert on life and death, and his word was sacrosanct. Encouraged by Huxley, he emerged from his country exile to testify. On 3 November 1875 Lord Cardwell greeted him like a duke and Huxley saw the craggy patrician to their largest seat. And from it the squeamish evolutionist talked nervously on the beneficent necessity of sacrifice. It worked.

23

The American Dream

'MY HEART DANCED WITHIN me', wrote Fiske at the news. Huxley was 'A1 copper bottomed' and set to sail for America in 1876. Nautical language was in the air again. In three decades he had swapped his surgeon's lowly rank for celebrity status. But he never forgot that day when, as a Naval hopeful, he had waved goodbye to his favourite sister, Lizzie. 'It is . . . thirty years since I left you at Antwerp, a boy beginning life', he wrote. 'Now I am a grey man looking towards the end of it . . . What ghosts we shall seem when we face one another!'

The 'whole nation is electrified', said an American banker. Fiske offered the Huxleys a drive through the 'glorious hill-country' of Massachusetts, where Fall brought 'the nearest approach I know to heaven'. The Huxleys, always interested to know what Heaven was like, accepted. Appleton began planning a press reception, and lectures. President Gilman of the new Johns Hopkins University, discussing Martin as the possible professor of biology, realized a coup and snatched Huxley to inaugurate a guest lecture series. As Huxley's plans firmed up, the 'flying visit' for a family reunion became a royal walkabout. Dickens and the literary greats had all toured, often with typical British hauteur. Even Prince Edward had crossed the Canadian border in 1860, but for some with long memories Huxley's was the eclipsing visit: 'We will make infinitely more of him than we did of the Prince of Wales, & his retinue of Lords & Dukes'.[1]

Preparations took place amid the usual turmoil. The 'hurry and worry of life' might increase 'with the square of your distance from youth', but even this formula looked simplistic by 1876, as new whirlwinds rose out of the steady turbulence.

The year had started off reasonably enough with a miracle and two fishes. Christmas found the family 'up to our necks in snow & over them in fog'. Huxley was locked in his study, revelling in Arnold's Spinozaist attack on the Philistines in *God and the Bible*, and contemplating the Catholic Wilfred Ward's challenge at the Metaphysical Society.[2] The rotund Ward, like a gentleman farmer pooh-poohing Biblical fads, had goaded doubters to forsake theory and grapple with a real miraculous fact. The austere agnostic was preparing to do just that. He drew gasps by taking up *the* miracle, the Resurrection.

But his widowed sister Ellen interrupted. She staggered in on Christmas Day and keeled over drunk. With her came the familiar stench of family decay. Boarding in West Brompton, the old crone had spent Hal's rent money on gin and run up a huge slate as 'Professor Huxley's sister'. Landlords, butchers, drapers and shopkeepers all collected from Huxley. 'Humiliating', Nettie called it, but even she was unprepared for the worst. Ellen's 35-year-old daughter Nelly had just had an illegitimate son by a Captain Seaton. Now Nelly and Ellen split the gin and pawned their clothes for more. In debt, in bare rooms, in an alcoholic stupor, they were tempting Nelly's teenage daughter Mabel into 'wickedness'. It was less a case of dead-drunk-for-tuppence than paralytic on Hal's £60. The iniquity was Ellen's taking a further 10s weekly from Huxley to 'educate' Mabel, and frittering it in a gin palace while Mabel minded the bastard.[3] Demoralized, he banned Ellen from the house. Here was the Professor, defining the new moral norm for a polite society, proving that agnosticism and depravity were not correlates, waiting for the sweaty hand to pull him back into the morass. Waiting for the scandal.

It was sickening. Nettie took to her bed ill and headachy for the rest of Christmas, only rising for New Year's dinner with Tyndall and Spencer. But there were stronger devils than Ellen to drive Hal. Knowles was impatiently awaiting to see Huxley's paper on Christ's alleged Resurrection, which threatened to do to Ward's Catholics what Klein had done to the Vivisection Commission. 'I have not written a line', Huxley apologized.

> Don't scream. I am subject to Demoniacal possession and
> the devil which came into me about ten days ago was a Fish
> – the most suggestive interesting brute that ever existed
> since the time of the old serpents. Like the latter my Fish is
> full of revolutionary ideas. I have been working twelve
> hours a day to get them into shape for a paper.[4]

Nature still took precedence. What diverted Huxley was a newly-discovered fish with lungs from Queensland. *Ceratodus*, with its ability to gulp air and walk on sturdy fins between drying pools, blotted out all other considerations. He had two corpses, 30 inches long, one from the Zoological Society and another especially procured by Sir George Macleay (the Speaker in the New South Wales House when Huxley was in Sydney, and W. S. Macleay's brother). Huxley noted *Ceratodus*' similarity to the two other surviving species of lungfish, while its skull-bones were like an amphibian's. Here was the interest. This was a very primitive lung-breather – so primitive that Haeckel's colleague Gegenbaur in Jena considered its lobe-fin as something like the first paired fin to evolve in the fishes. Behind all the excitement there was a sense that *Ceratodus* gave anatomists another lead on amphibian origins – pointing to the source of all higher vertebrates and mankind.

Huxley specialized in the shiny-scaled, fringe-finned (and, he guessed, lung-breathing) fishes from the Devonian period, that great age of fishes. But where before he had simply brought the relevant species together as 'Crossopterygeans', which he likened to the living lungfishes, now there was an evolutionary imperative to his studies.[5] He created the conditions for the later belief that the world's three remaining lungfish were relics of this Devonian group – living cousins of the stagnant-water air-gulpers which had evolved into the amphibians. As always, there was a chauvinistic excitement about it, a tingle, because this was the human line, *our* line.

It took precedence over the Resurrection. Through Christmas, through the Ellen fiasco, Huxley had his nose deep in the dismembered *Ceratoduses*, adding the stench of preserving spirits to the smell of family decay. 'I have been working tremendously hard', he told Sclater at the zoo, '& have been getting some good results'. On New Year's Eve he had mudfishes and primitive sharks sent from the zoo to South Kensington and the next morning was drawing the result. Len would collect shark foetuses from the British Museum to save time. As always Huxley could see past his scalpel and projected 'a series of papers', and as usual this was the first and last in the series. Even then he had to limit himself 'to the Brain & Skeleton' in order to have his paper ready for the Zoological Society on 4 January 1876.[6]

A week after one delicate dissection he was engaged in another. His forensic report on the alleged Resurrection was causing the squeamish to groan at the Metaphysical. Huxley, the genial chairman in 1876, kept his meetings at 'a high level of discursive analysis and witty repartee'. But if his geniality put everyone at ease, his topics made hairs stand on end. By now the Metaphysical had become a factional ecclesiastical court, adjudicating agnosticism and belief, spiritual interference and natural uniformity, experience and intuition. The very agenda was an epistemological sign of a industrializing culture thrown into professional turmoil.

Miracles were essential to Huxley's method. He always kept the onus on his rival's beliefs, never his own. And his rivals found his playful, mock-consensual rhetoric so easy and so hard to deal with. With Kant he pronounced nothing impossible and, as that Reverend heretic Moncure Conway laughed, he 'told the theologians that science had plenty of miracles, and would willingly add theirs, if proved'. But could they be? Could one seismic rupture at the fount of Christianity be verified? On 11 January 1876, vacating the Chair for Gladstone, he took to the floor to dissect the testimony of the Resurrection. He brought the most notorious test case in the Metaphysical's history. Old Father Newman – whose evangelical impulse had come from Huxley's Ealing school – was shocked that Manning had actually sat through it, wondering if it wasn't 'a ruse of the Cardinal to bring the Professor into the clutches of the Inquisition'.[7] Not that Manning had actually sat unaffected. It was 'pathetic' to see his 'ill-disguised amazement' as he 'listened to the ruthless and cold-blooded denials of what to him were self-evident and eternal truths'. For the first time a debate ran into the next meeting, and there was a detectable stiffening of attitudes. Huxley had gone too far.

Huxley returned to his High Chair to watch Gladstone, who was waging his own pamphlet war on Manning over Papal Infallibility. The raptorial anatomist peered down on the Grand Old Man's head. With a mortician's eye he sized up its 'curious breadth of parietals, & flatness', and imagined with undue phrenologicalness that its feline shape explained his 'eccentricities'.[8] These were intensifying yearly. Even now Gladstone was seeking some obscure link between Genesis and Homer's *Iliad*. He never understood the new science, nor the growing disenchantment with mankind's religious 'treasure'. Having dispensed with the Pope, Gladstone now invited the devil to one of his Thursday breakfasts. Huxley had to accept.

Huxley's Resurrection paper was too hot to handle. Even Morley declined such a 'deadly routing of the most sacred article in theology'. It was for scholars in conclave, not 'the profane crowd'. Morley had already burnt his fingers with the incorrigible William Kingdon

Clifford. This consumptive, Proudhon-reading, atheistic 30-year-old (for whom Nettie had a particular soft spot), was dabbling in the uncertainties of non-Euclidean geometry at University College and lambasting the certainties of Christian cosmogony in the *Fortnightly*. But the catcalls would be as nothing to the outrage if an idol like Huxley were to unstitch society's 'whole system of belief'. It would land 'the rotten egg and dead cat' on his doorstep.[9] It would enrage the Christian, said Morley, more aptly than he knew, as much as by calling his sister a slut. Huxley looked at Ellen and took the point.

Jessie was tall, striking, and 18 years old in February. Her dance was the 'brightest & pleasantest' anyone could remember. The dining room was turned out, and shimmering candlelight played on exotic blooms, sent specially from Kew. The party went on till 3.30, and even Nettie could not resist a waltz, although it was 'shocking' to be 'dancing at 50.' They looked at Jess in her mousseline-de-soie dress and realized that she had grown up. Not that it prepared them for the announcement of her engagement to Fred Waller. But Hal, forgetting his 'hatred of possible sons-in-law', was overjoyed (even if he did set his 'face against her marrying before she is Twenty'). Fred had a 'sterling character', Nettie said, and 'Hal & I both love him very much'.[10]

Nothing should have surprised them any more, but one thing did. At 55 Tyndall showed all the signs of confirmed bachelorhood: absent-mindedness, unnatural work-hours, a death-wish attitude to safety – in his speeches no less than his Alpine skirmishes. Huxley had received nothing but bottles of bacteria from him for months, so everything seemed normal. Tyndall was obsessively experimenting to prove that germs fill the air and were the cause of disease, and sending on the flasks. Huxley, his interest rekindled, at one point observed that *Penicillium* mould stopped bacterial growth. This would be the real medical moment for Fleming with his twentieth-century understanding of antibiosis and 'penicillin'-extraction techniques. But Huxley and Tyndall had their distinct nineteenth-century preoccupations. Huxley was concentrating on *Penicillium*'s life stages, and Tyndall was still consumed with the need to debunk the spontaneous generation of life. Obsession was driving the bachelor to live as an 'ascetic, to clear away this "Bastian fog"'.[11]

But an admirer sat weekly in Tyndall's audience, the imperturbable Louisa Hamilton. Through concerts and climbs the plain 30-year-old daughter of Lord Claud Hamilton pulled the abstemious Professor out of himself. Her parents bravely wafted aside their differences in age and class. The X thought she was dicing with death herself in trying to turn Tyndall into something approaching married normality. Nettie pondered the age gap, and 'considering what a radical & independent nature our brother John is, it is amusing that his wife is cousin to half the dukes in England'. Tyndall treated the wedding as rather a nuisance which got in among the germ experiments. 'After discussing the registrar, Moncure Conway & Gretna Green', he explained to Huxley, 'we turned ... to Stanley'. The Dean's wife was dying, but it was her wish that he not 'lose sight of the men of science', and so he created an à la carte service almost tolerable to a freethinker.

The bells of Westminster Abbey pealed for the infidel who would seize the cosmos from theology. Clutching him was old Carlyle in a shabby black felt hat, nothing but a clean face and collar to suggest any preparation. There was no sign of Spencer. He had refused to soil his boots on hallowed ground. And the Dean's spirit was elsewhere (the wedding flowers would be on his wife's coffin the next day). It was a mercy to all that the service was shorn. Even so, Tyndall's ringing 'I will' contrasted with his sheepish 'Father, Son, and Holy Ghost'.[12] And so it was a card for 'D^r. & M^{rs}. Tyndall' to join Browning, Morley and Lord and Lady Arthur Russell at the next Marlborough Place dinner.

Nor was that the last surprise. America liked Huxley as the industrialists did. And as the factory bosses became powerful they showed their gratitude. 'God bless my soul', exclaimed Hal as £1,000 tumbled out of a letter on 21 March. It was a bequest from the Bolton cotton king Thomas Thomasson. He had been the retiring money-man behind the free-trade agitation. His coffers had kept Cobden afloat and the Anti-Corn Law League solvent, and in death the Quaker was keeping faith with the cause. Flush Dissenters put their trust in individual conscience rather than State-privileged Church, and their faith in a wheeze-and-snort world run by impartial law rather than miraculous whim. They understood *Lay Sermons* (it was Thomasson's favourite book). Around the Lord's table they praised Huxley's school drive and sought legitimacy in his democracy of knowledge. The cash, Thomasson's son said, was in 'appreciation of your services'. It 'was on account of Hal's religious opinions . . . & high moral nature', Nettie heard, 'that M^r. Thomasson admired & esteemed him'.[13] The Dissenters were paying their dues.

With the cash in hand Hal and Nettie immediately bought tickets for America. It was time to do something for themselves. Huxley tied up loose ends. He gave addresses, accepted prizes,[14] dotted the i's and crossed the t's of his 600-page *Anatomy of Invertebrated Animals*, only 20 years late (his publisher John Churchill had died waiting). And as for 'that pietistic old malefactor, Shaftesbury', with his slur in the Lords that Huxley encouraged children to vivisect animals, Huxley made his 'Evangelical soul' shake with a thunderous rebuke in the *Times*. That was the last gasp of the vivisection debate before a compromise Cruelty to Animals Act was passed. In future only the licensed would be able to experiment, while their Lordships remained free to inflict more pain in a day's shooting than the physiologists did in a year's research. The Duke of Somerset had the temerity to say it, and Huxley thought him 'the only man who talked sense'.[15] That done, Huxley had only to deliver his Edinburgh course.

With Hal away, Nettie bore the brunt. She was of that powerful breed which carried Victorian families. She spent weeks organizing the troop, the Transatlantic trip and two months' wardrobe. What with the logistics and worrying about woollen shifts in the Southern sun, while seeing to adolescent daughters during the London Season, she 'had a very hard time' of it. In a year of betrothals the last word came just before she left: from the widower Hooker, about *his* engagement to Lady Jardine, an ornithologist's widow and bred-in-the-bone naturalist. The X-Club patriarchs undertook marriage with professional detachment: Tyndall wanted a domestic lab assistant, Hooker a replacement mother and scientific secretary, and the ladies obligingly jettisoned their titles to join the intellectual aristocracy. With that news, plain Mrs Huxley trundled off in a 'huge omnibus, with luggage piled to the top, & a cab besides', marshalling a governess, three servants and five children (the elder girls having gone ahead) to meet Hal at Armstrong's Northumberland estate.

Sir William and Lady Armstrong had no children, and his enormous engineering works on the Tyne, ever experimenting with breech-loaders and iron-clad cruisers, had left the industrial baronetcy in luxury. They could afford to lavish care on the hard-pressed Huxleys. With the children settled, Hal and Nettie set off for the New World. Nettie – her 'seven darlings' lined up at Rothbury station to be kissed in turn – hated leaving them, and the emotional Mady as always 'sobbed bitterly'.[16] They were leaving the children for the first time. But in a year of marriages they were due their own second honeymoon.

On 27 July 1876 they were at Queenstown, in Co. Cork, settling into their berths on the *Germanic*. It 'must be a delightful trip nowadays, such splendid ships', an expectant Lizzie wrote, recalling her own seven-week ordeal on a tramp sailing ship. Indeed £63 tickets bought them a bit of gracious living. The liner ploughed through the Atlantic waves at an unprecedented 13 knots. Nettie was seasick but the old sailor relished the salt air. The huge funnels belched smoke from the furnaces, the foghorns blasting every few minutes through the first night. The next morning Hal and Nettie woke to the sight of icebergs, a reminder of the Atlantic's hazards.[17] But the weather calmed and warmed and after a week of deck reading they sighted Manhattan.

America lay waiting, wondering. English intellectuals had a reputation for airs and graces, but would the new moralist be grave and the philosopher high-falutin? American culture had itself become scientific and exciting. No longer was English fiction the staple. The post-Civil War years had a new way of rationalizing the hope and progress of reconstruction. 'Now it is English science. Herbert Spencer, John Stuart Mill, Huxley, Darwin, Tyndall, have usurped the places of Tennyson and Browning, and Matthew Arnold and Dickens'. Appleton's red-cloth books had carried the Word, and the archangel Edward Youmans had heralded the Coming. As a result Huxley's democratic depiction of knowledge and his musings on the pain of existence were acclaimed by Californian miners and Kentuckian bankers; his worldly piety fired Boston intellectuals and New York businessmen; his profane Calvinism explaining man's hard relation to Nature could discipline a new industrial workforce. The Gilded Age welcomed this 'monumental embodiment of rational energy'. They had read him to find American values, and they had done so through Spencerian spectacles. The New World was riding the evolutionary torrent 'onward and upward to ever higher and better manifestations'.[18] They had taken what they wanted; they had taken it aplenty and now they prepared a handsome reception.

He reciprocated in his rational admiration. Catching his first sight of the Manhattan skyline on 5 August he asked about the two conspicuous towers. Told they were the *Tribune* and Western Union Telegraph buildings, 'Ah,' he replied, 'that is American. In the Old World the first things you see as you approach a great city are steeples; here you see ... centres of intelligence'. He had endeared himself before he put a foot ashore. And more than he knew: the new *Tribune* tower had been inaugurated amid speeches by Darwinians exalting the new scientific progress. No wonder the hacks had forgotten the Prince of Wales and were awaiting Huxley's royal progress.

The couple were whisked from the sultry quayside to the Appletons' 'beautiful place on the Hudson'. In an exceptionally hot Centennial Summer their country estate was cooler, and it gave the Huxleys a glimpse of the 'wild scenery'. After a night's sleep they braved the 'broiling' city. It was sticky and bustling, 97° on the sidewalk, a crush of carriages and people, with looming telegraph poles sending the eye up the tall, flagstrewn buildings. He fought his way to Appleton's office on Broadway. Like a good publisher Appleton had lined up the press, and the newsmen were as surprised by the philosopher as he was moved by the razzmatazz. The *World* found him of the 'commercial' class, and not 'highfalutin' at all. He was proud of that. 'We may be rich yet', he laughed to Nettie. Reports said he was 'good-humoured, and exceedingly unpretentious', and it showed in the squibs about Professor Protoplasm and skits about the discoverer of the 'life principle' ('Anything to do with insurance?').[19] In New York science came with a pinch of salt, but wisecrackers still made a meal of it.

Now there was 'nothing but solid railwayable ground' separating him from Lizzie. Seeing her was a 30-year dream, but his schedule was packing out impossibly. He was reduced to a lightning visit; and even then, 'to economise time', he asked her to meet him in Nashville. The fact that he could only spare her four days in six weeks showed how much more the tour had become. Proselytizing now ruled his 3,000-mile itinerary. And Hal's diary totting showed the money to be pocketed. Offers still came in: would he lecture in St Louis for $1,000? Nettie, watching the purse, knew from Appleton that they could have gone 'home with £10,000 in the Spring'.[20]

Huxley hurried along with the New Yorkers, listening to the paperboys shout of the latest banking scandals. Urban America was vibrant, its technology entrepreneurial. Here venture capital was set to illuminate the modern world. Edison was already in his private laboratory over in New Jersey, perfecting the phonograph and light bulb, and ensuring the boom for consumer gadgetry. Trains were furbished for businessmen in a hurry. Huxley saw the future as he tried the new-fangled 'drawing room car' on his way to New Haven.

Yale gave him the best week of his trip. The Peabody's fossils alone were 'worth all the journey across'. Othniel C. Marsh, the 'magician' in charge, had the robust looks of a Western explorer, and he could produce any number of exquisite fossils from his frontier forays. But it was one in particular that Huxley had come to see.

Marsh was the solid product of Peabody money. He had been installed at Yale as America's first professor of palaeontology by his tycoon uncle George Peabody, and the millionaire's money had paid for five expeditions to the parched Badlands. The steadfast fellow was surprisingly 'full of stories about his Western adventures', Huxley regaled Nettie. Marsh was a new breed of palaeontological robber baron, whose plunder Huxley had come to see. He held Huxley captive with talk of his trek with Pawnee scouts, Buffalo Bill and cavalry troop into the Rockies in 1870, and again to the Smokey river in western Kansas in 1871. He had scoured Dakota like a frontiersman, slaughtering buffalo indiscriminately in Oglala Sioux territory. But his meeting with Red Cloud in 1874 and discovery of the scale of the swindling and treachery by traders and agents had turned him into a passionate campaigner for the Indian nations. They had shown him the 'thunder beasts' (huge fossil titanothere skulls washed out of Badland rocks) – creatures of legend which roamed the plains during storms – and he had been adopted into the Oglala tribe as 'the man who chops out bones'. Marsh's hectoring of President Grant over their plight was to little avail (although he did get the Secretary of the Interior fired). Even as he was telling Huxley, the news was of Custer's massacre two weeks earlier. The Sioux' fury had been unleashed after the invasion of gold miners into their sacred Black Hills.

Huxley experienced a little of the Peabody hospitality. Marsh installed him in Uncle George's apartment, lavish enough for Connecticut's Governor to pay court. Most evenings Huxley dined in Marsh's mansion and sashayed along the elm-lined avenues afterwards. But from 9 to 6 it was business.

While roaming the Smokey in 1871 Marsh had found the fossil that had brought Huxley so far. It was an extraordinary Cretaceous bird, still with teeth, but only a stumpy tail. The six-foot *Hesperornis* had vestigial wings but powerful legs, and the fact that Marsh called it a 'carnivorous swimming ostrich' piqued Huxley's interest.[21] It fitted his evolutionary genealogy – from strutting bipedal dinosaurs to struthious flightless birds. Marsh, custodian of the key evolutionary link, prided himself on agreeing.

Links were in their mind as they travelled 60 miles to Springfield on 14 August. Huxley had used the Connecticut fossil footprints for years as proof of the ostrich-like gait of many dinosaurs. Now he walked with them; along the sandstone bank of the Connecticut river, beside the primeval three-toed tracks. Here Triassic dinosaurs had once trotted.[22] It was grist to the mill and he would grind it well for American consumption.

The West was putting American palaeontology on the map. Huxley was set to extol evolution in his US lectures. He had started writing one, on elephants, almost nostalgically: he reminisced about sleepy Ealing and the Summer fairs of his boyhood, full of 'red-faced & top-booted farmers' and lads charging past 'canvas booths stocked with gilt gingerbread'. He recalled a Wild Beast show, with its awesome hoardings of pythons devouring oxen. He looked on himself as an inquisitive stripling, armed with 'nuts & buns', beckoned into a dark foreboding tent by the unearthly 'roars & grunts' to see his first towering elephant. That was the way to start a lecture.

Marsh interrupted the day-dream. He cantered out his fossil horses. Box after box of bones, real fossil gold from the Nebraska hills. Huxley's elephants vanished like his reverie. Marsh seemed to have everything, from yesterday's pony-like *Pliohippus* with a single toe, down to the sheep-sized *Miohippus* with three toes, and ultimately the four-toed, fox-sized *Orohippus*. The collection was 'the most wonderful thing I ever saw'. It overhauled the horse's supposed European ancestry; indeed 'The more I think of it the more clear it is that your great work is the settlement of the pedigree of the horse'. Marsh's horses came from progressively older rocks. *Orohippus*, the oldest, went back to Eocene times. But Marsh thought that an even older five-toed ancestor might have lived in the shadow of the dinosaurs. To cap his conversion Huxley dashed off a cartoon of this conjectural pygmy '*Eohippus*', and added a conjectural rider, a pygmy '*Eohomo*'.[23]

He pored over the fossils. He would call for a *Protohippus* hoof or a *Miohippus* molar. Line up Marsh's 30 species and it made Kovalevskii's point: tiny browsers had changed with the Miocene grassy plains into swift grazers, their molars enlarging and faces lengthening to deal with the tough meadow grass. 'I believe you are a magician', Huxley told his host, 'whatever I want, you just conjure it up'. Marsh's was a pedigree in the truest sense, an American bloodline for a noble thoroughbred. He had jettisoned the confusing variants to leave a neat image. From a tiny forest dweller to today's high-stepping sprinter: the horses had stretched their legs, fused the lower limb bones, evolved the single tip-toe and grown tall on the high plains. In the Centennial year American palaeontology was proving its independence. With Marsh proclaiming Wyoming and Nebraska the 'true home of the Horse', Huxley could puff America and Darwin in the same breath.[24] He had the perfect lectures for a continent that was being conquered in the saddle.

His rounds continued with the sea-urchin expert and mining entrepreneur Alexander Agassiz, a troubled man torn between Darwin's evolution and his father's memory. The late, dynamic Louis Agassiz, founder and general factotum of Harvard's Museum of Comparative Zoology, had given the world Ice Ages, but it wasn't the cold his son feared. Old Louis had died within a week of Alex's wife, and in an act of self-immolation Alexander had thrown himself into managing the museum. He was 'a driven man', he told Huxley, 'trying to keep all [of his father's] irons hot'.

Then came a *de rigueur* meeting with the botanist Asa Gray at Harvard. Gray had done sterling service selling an insipid theological version of Darwinism to waverers. He had even visited Downe, still looking to pump a little Design into Darwin, only to find the *Origin* commandeered and smothered by infidel connotations by the 'Huxley set'. Still, the fogeyish Darwin was attached to the fogeyish Gray, and that was enough for the visiting diplomat. There was more wholesome enjoyment among Fiske's 'sweet-scented pine-woods' of northern Massachusetts on 21 August, and ne'er a word on infidelism: Fiske knew that there was more real religion in Huxley's 'honest scepticism' than in any 'timorous assent to a half-understood creed'. The jovial cosmic philosopher, the most corpulent in America, laid on a gourmet feast to repay all those convivial high teas, before giving Huxley a taste of 'primitive New England life'.[25]

And so to Buffalo, where the British Ass saw how the American Asses advanced their science. His renown preceded him. So did Marsh, who was to be his rugged chaperon for much of the trip. The ambitious Marsh could see off the unwelcome attention of rivals (the race for dinosaurs was deteriorating into a range war against his erratic foe E. D. Cope). Marsh needed Huxley's imprimatur as Huxley needed Marsh's bones. Having given Huxley his theme, Marsh was on hand for the plaudits. Huxley's remarks at the American Association for the Advancement of Science came off-the-cuff. He moved from New York's preternatural press corps to America's revelation in the wilderness. The high plains had turned evolution from informed speculation into 'matter of fact'. To reassure their guest at Buffalo, Louis Agassiz's old students admitted that they were all now for Darwin. The euphoria lingered in Buffalo after the delegates had packed and gone, at least until the revivalists Moody and Sankey arrived to sanitize the city with battle-hymn and harmonium.

Like all second honeymooners Hal and Nettie stayed at nearby Niagara. They lay low for a week, Hal writing his lectures, trying not to create the sort of stir associated with the dare-devil tightrope walkers at the Falls. The couple braced themselves in the 'roaring of the winds & waters & tempestuous spray'. Ahead lay a gruelling

30-hour train journey via Cincinnati to Nashville, and the moment
of reunion.

The damage of time showed in both brother and sister. Lizzie's
'thin grave face' told of a struggle in the carpetbagging South:
'there's nothing young about me', she had warned Tom, 'but love and
sympathy'. She was 62, with bad eyes; Scott's death in 1872 had
ended a tragic era and left her dependent on the children. Yet time
had not erased her 'old motherly feelings towards you'. There was
apprehension on both sides. Never mind that 'he is grey, and 50',
Nettie wrote ahead from Niagara, 'your hearts will bridge across the
years'.[26]

They did. At dusk on Monday 4 September the New Orleans
Lightning Express pulled into Nashville. England still provided cultural leadership, even in the South, and the visit of a British Great
was an occasion for a turn-out. Among the waiting crowd at the
Church Street depot, Lizzie was instantly recognizable by her jet-
black eyes. It was a poignant moment. Lizzie clasped her brother and
in the lantern light saw 'the most lovable . . . face in the world'.

He had last seen her on that fateful day 30 years before, as they
fled across the Channel carrying two-year-old Flory and newborn Edith. Now the girls were Southern Belles. Tears probably
clouded the family's journey to Edith's South Vine Street house. But
it had the warmth of home, with English books, the 'racket' of three
small children, and now laughter and singing (although Lizzie's voice
– so evocative for Tom – had gone). Edith's husband, the urbane
and humorous Albert Roberts, ran the city's cosmopolitan *Daily
American*. As 'John Happy' Captain Roberts had been the rebs'
rousing pamphleteer. The veteran of Shiloh was now the great conservative campaigner for a new industrial South.[27] His training and
investment schemes, and schooling and health-care campaigns, put
him squarely behind Hal, whose speeches he had reprinted. For a
moment Hal could have been in any developing city. But this was
Nashville, the 'buckle on the Bible belt', heartland of the 'Lost
Cause': his nieces had grown into Presbyterian churchwomen, and
Roberts' vision had a dark underbelly. The jobs and education were
for whites – and when his ethnically-cleansed Tennessee was mooted
the air must have chilled.

All was newspaper talk. Flory's own husband Robert Roberts was
the *American*'s business manager – the sisters had married brothers
and ran their lives according to deadlines. Lizzie's son Tom, working
on the Mobile and Montgomery Railroad, was there to meet his
uncle and namesake. But it was Lizzie whom Huxley had come so far

to see. These two, always so close, were the polished mahogany flotsam washed up from the wreck of a family. There was no one else now. 'George, poor fellow, is dead. William I have not seen for twenty years. Jim is as near mad as a sane man can be' and Ellen was lost in 'drink quarrels debt & vice'. Lizzie told of her own heavy-hearted years and the hopes for her sons. And she still worried over the golden boy, knowing that 'all the world watches what you do'.[28]

Despite having only four days with Lizzie, Tom's time wasn't his own. Trying to keep his visit low key had proved futile, for the Governor requested his pleasure the next morning. Governor Porter, up for re-election on a better-schooling ticket, saw no votes lost in hobnobbing with Huxley. And so the visiting dignitary was honoured by a state tour, covering everything from the Federal Courts to Fisk, the South's new black university (built with money raised by the Jubilee Singers, who had entertained Britain with their Negro Spirituals in 1874). On Wednesday the widowed Mrs Scott saw nothing for it but to join the entourage. They all walked a bit taller after coming face to face with a bust of Tom at the new Vanderbilt University. And this, Lizzie must have noted, in a Methodist school under Bishop McTyeire's Board! They visited the European-style science departments. Then hearty theology professors showed Huxley where they beat the rhythm of old-time religion, and 'where we should be glad to have the opportunity of beating a little into you'. 'Ah, sir', said their guest, 'if I were here I should give you novel theology'. He slapped backs at Fogg High School for its physics and chemistry classes, claiming that Tennesseans could show the backwoods British a thing or two. He was so courteous. Lizzie was lost in admiration, desperately pleased that her baby brother was not the 'pugilistic Boanerges he had been painted'. If only 'old Vanderbilt would leave Hal a couple of his superfluous millions'.

Tom was unable to shake his civic tail. It had taken him 30 years to reach Lizzie's doorstep, only to be whisked away. A deputation dragged the 'Great Scientist' off for another appearance. The good folks, equally sceptical of his son-of-thunder notoriety, wanted his 'view from his own lips'. Whether Huxley acquitted himself in the 700-seater Masonic Hall is debatable. Still, the South's lushest theatre outside of New Orleans resonated to his 'Sermon in Stone'. Bewhiskered preachers and professors in kid gloves sat amid scarlet drapery; judges strained to hear from their gold boxes; Southern beauties fanned themselves; and an Ealing Englishman showed them the real rock of ages: a little Lyell, a little Darwin and a lacing of local geology. Look at the aeons that Niagara has been cutting its gorge, and the ages since mastodons roamed the region – look beneath Nashville to the Pharaonic dynasties of life. In half an hour he had covered the history of the world. Then suddenly realizing his place, he apologized for appearing 'a sort of fanatic in these matters'.[29] Tennessee forgot itself too and cheered at evolution, led on by the *American* – but then Edith's husband was editor.

Too soon, the next morning, he was gone. His motherly sister had lived to see him praised by the God-fearing South as the 'great apostle of modern science' and the 'whole-souled' missionary of education. She hoped they would meet again, but both seem to have doubted it. The parting opened Lizzie's old wounds as she returned to Alabama and reflected on 'the sins that drew down on me the discipline of being banished from the land I love'. She could never quite close 'that page of my inner life'. Tom too was lost as the 'wild wooded scenery' of Kentucky flashed past his carriage window.

He awoke to the vastness of the continent. Having spent long hours behind great locomotives, with their kerosene headlamps and balloon smokestacks bellowing out black clouds, it was fitting that he should be met by President Garrett of the Baltimore & Ohio Railway on 9 September. Marsh joined Hal and Nettie in Garrett's 'Montebello' mansion in Baltimore. Adjoining their grounds was the Hopkins estate, another product of railroad money. The Baltimore & Ohio had been the first passenger line in America, and opening up the Midwest farm belt had made Johns Hopkins a fortune. Some $3.5 million of it were now building the new university. The money had come across as railway shares. In America real steam was being turned into real intellect.

The Huxleys were in a Quaker community of liberal emancipists. Their hostess, Mrs Garrett, let them know 'that all women sh^d get better educated'.[30] The university was itself an experiment. It was no architecturally-resplendent mausoleum, but a vital think-tank. Boom money was bouncing Baltimore into the vanguard of American higher education. Johns Hopkins' President Gilman projected an advanced graduate school to staunch the flow of students to Europe, a Ph.D. factory to meet the nation's needs. Behind his thinking lay the strange concept of organized research, and he cited Huxley's biological workshop as a prime example. Hopkins professors were to be paid to research and, with the largest bequest in US history, paid well. The Trustees saw friend Huxley as their man.

He was to open the guest lecture series on 12 September, on the eve of the first enrolment. With his awe of science, Gilman would make Hopkins a 'shrine for her worship'. And who better to stamp his assent than the agnostic Pope? Gilman had seen Huxley perform in London, where Huxley's deliverance from grace was only matched by 'the grace of his delivery'. Gilman also knew of the standard sectarian problems with universities. So Johns Hopkins would have no 'sectional bias'. Gilman the lapsed Congregationalist had learned from his ally President White, frustrated with the sectarian sniping at Cornell. White's myth-making *Warfare of Science* in 1876 reflected his anger at all this religious bickering. It was a book, and a programme, Huxley could endorse.

But friend Huxley was flagging; more than that, for the first time he was flummoxed. Gilman escorted him onto the Hopkins stage at 11 o'clock, trailing the Governor, Mayor, state and federal officials, a Japanese Minister and university presidents, who tailed away to sit in the orchestra pit. Gilman, already praised and abused for his celebrity choice, promptly exacerbated matters by opening the proceedings without the rudiments of a religious blessing. Go-ahead Quakers had seen no need of a prayer, and even critics perceived the giant incompatibility. 'It was bad enough to invite Huxley', one snorted. 'It were better to have asked God to be present. It would have been absurd to ask them both'.[31] Instead Gilman quoted the Quaker poet on America's Saxon debts, and Huxley stepped forth. His benedictions were famous for soothing the wrinkled brow. Then he looked at his notes.

He had made a stupid mistake. To get an accurate transcription into the papers, he had summoned up heroic strengths and dictated it to an Associated Press stenographer the day before. But the fair copy arrived too late, on flimsy paper; standing before the 2,000 he couldn't read a word of it. And he couldn't improvise with his speech being *reported* across the land. Stymied, he tried to recall his dictated words, so as not to deviate from the printed version. Even the unostentatious Quaker ladies thought the result was too, well, unostentatious. It 'had no glow', said a puzzled Gilman.

Glow or no, it was quintessential Huxley: the poor man praising a brains before bricks policy (Hopkins' money was going into research, not a fabulous façade); the intellectual commending America's steel barons for founding secular academies. If it wasn't the 'vigorous & exhaustive' triumph that the loyal Nettie claimed, it was redeemed by his 'noble & touching conclusion'. In the last minutes the golden touch returned, the prophetic glint. The voyager had seen eight states, and with 30 more (Colorado was the new 38th state) he sensed an awakening giant. But size and territory do not a nation make: 'The great issue, about which hangs a true sublimity, and the terror of overhanging fate, is what are you going to do with all these things?' He had a touching faith that America was a Greater Britain bent on 'a novel experiment in politics'. So what of the 200 millions he predicted by the bicentenary of 1976? Would they hold together under 'a republic, and the despotic reality of universal suffrage'? As the cities burgeon 'and the pressure of want is felt, the gaunt spectre of pauperism will stalk among you, and communism and socialism will claim to be heard'. A deathly hush crept over the audience at the prospect of a Communist America. No, of course; with 'fortresses . . . of the nation' like the Hopkins providing inspiration 'America has a great future before her'. And may the university's Renaissance freedom draw students 'from all parts of the earth, as of old they sought Bologna, or Paris, or Oxford'.[32] With that he sat down. Nettie gave him kiss and was quietly proud.

As so often at home, his old demonstrator H. N. Martin was in the audience. Or rather Professor Martin. The young, dedicated Martin had come over to head up the Hopkins Biology Department and adapt the Kensington laboratory technique 'in usum studiosum Yankietatis'.[33] Huxley was leaving him in charge, a sturdier reminder of the way things were done in London.

The next day they took Gilman's private railway carriage for four hours of sightseeing in Washington. After the 'magnificent' domed Capitol building there was the Smithsonian Institution, and they still fitted in the 'very theatre where poor Lincoln was shot'. The exhaustion was showing by the 14th as they took in more anatomical theatres in Philadelphia. Here were American fossil mastodons and sloths, and the doyen himself, Joseph Leidy, to show Hal around the museum of the Academy of Natural Sciences. Old Leidy was a dry anatomist, but he had seen the light: for him, the *Origin of Species* was 'a meteor [that] flashed upon the skies'. Huxley was in seventh heaven himself: here the prize exhibit was a 25-foot dinosaur skeleton, the *Hadrosaurus*, which had been cast standing on its hind legs by Huxley's book engraver and friend Benjamin Waterhouse Hawkins, the first such mount in the world. It had proved so great a crowd-puller that another had been made for the Centennial Exposition in Fairmount Park. Hal and Nettie were escorted there too, to see the new-age wonders, including Bell's patented talking telephone. The Californian exhibitors, tickled that Huxley should stop to talk to them, told of 'how the miners read his books & by their fires talked over his deepest problems'.[34] Perhaps they really did.

The 15th saw them in New York's Westminster Hotel. Nettie was now 'tired & stupefied' by the constant 'sightseeing & travelling'.

But the stream of visitors only increased, and the requests. The Professor was taxed on the sublime and the ridiculous: would he comment on the evolution of the heavens? And on chimney ventilation? Would he discuss Biblical exegesis and fossil fish? A bevy of 'Fannies' and 'Lucys' besieged him for autographs, and august bodies besieged him for lectures. Finally Nettie mounted guard in the sitting room, barring all entry, and for five hours on Sunday the 17th Hal shut himself away in the dressing room to finish his lectures.[35]

He needed to. Horace Greeley's progressive *Tribune* was zealously trailing Hal's appearance. The newspapers had reported each speech and raised expectations of his three New York lectures. The *Herald* proclaimed him one of the world's great exponents of science. Even as the letters pages countered with thoughts on Genesis, the *Times* prided itself that Huxley would find no English-style prejudice in this secular, ticker-tape city. To prove it a preacher at the Church of the Strangers refused to call him an atheist. These 'scientists' 'are nothing of the kind', he conceded. 'They have a religion of their own'.[36] They did, and the crowd was baying for it. The evangelism of science was beginning to produce its own Great Awakening. Appleton felt the rush for the $5 tickets at his Broadway office, and astutely brought out Asa Gray's theistic *Darwiniana* to cash in on Huxley-mania.

Chickering Hall, on 5th Avenue and 18th, was packed to capacity the next night. The entrance was thronged with top hats and feather bonnets. Here were 'New-York's best', the 'familiar faces' of the Social Register set. It was a 'highly respectable crush'. Tactically adept (some said inept), Huxley had only to walk out holding Milton's *Paradise Lost* (with its epic depiction of Creation) to make the next day's headlines: 'The Gauntlet Thrown Down by Modern Science' screamed the *Herald*. It made good copy. The *Herald* assumed that Milton was a 'courteous' cover, to save Huxley mentioning Moses, and even then warned him that Milton-lovers would not stand by and 'see him cuffed over the ears to make a scientific lecturer's holiday'.[37] If he meant the Good Book, why didn't he say the Good Book? The story grew in the telling, until the *Daily Graphic* capped it with a full-cover cartoon of 'Huxley Eikonoklastes' battering a statue of Moses with Milton's bust.

Huxley talked quietly, gravely, and listeners found it difficult to get his measure. These weren't his working clods, whose colloquialisms he could capture, or his West End toffs ready for buttering. He lacked the American stump-style perfected by hellfire preachers. He seemed reserved, English, 'unimpassioned and deliberate'. His incisive hits came understated, his humour had an unaccustomed irony. There was drama in there, in his seemingly common-sense demands for an orderly universe undisturbed by 'external agencies'.[38] And in his theatrical juxtaposition – setting this off against *Paradise Lost*'s earth-shaking Sixth Day of Creation: 'out of the ground up rose' each beast, 'The tawny lion, pawing to get free . . . ' He gave science its moral solemnity, where the press was expecting histrionics. It was clever, but confusing. Wasn't he an 'intellectual athlete who is shaking the old beliefs'? How to report his subtleties, where a sardonic glance doubled for a wild flourish? He seemed measured, but surely he wasn't. The *Times* came closest to unravelling his rhetoric, his 'Ciceronian way of saying that he will not denounce such and such an hypothesis', while damning it by his very denial.[39] At breakfast New Yorkers read of the brouhaha about Darwin's vicar and Milton's idolatry. It ensured a packed second night.

On Wednesday the 20th came the 'favourable' evidence for evolution. Not for Darwin's mechanism, but for the belief that life was a connected whole. For once Huxley did not overplay his 'persistent types'. The fact that American scorpions had not altered since coal-swamp times simply showed that change was not inevitable. But change there had been elsewhere, spectacular change – tails shortened, teeth lost, scales turned into feathers. This was his sensational bird ancestry. Behind him were pictures of the chicken-sized dinosaur *Compsognathus* and the Connecticut footprints, and America's fossil toothed birds. Marsh had blown them up, and Marsh and America collected the kudos as Huxley showed how Nebraska's toothed divers could have evolved from free-armed dinosaurs. And what of that unique feature, feathers? Whether the delicate dinosaur *Compsognathus* 'had them we don't know', he admitted, but merely to moot the possibility of a feathered dinosaur made an avian descent seem so plausible.

He talked cagily of the famous *Archaeopteryx* with its bony tail and three wing-fingers. Later in print he still expressed doubts that *Archaeopteryx* was on the direct route to birds. It was a cousin, the royal line having already run from the 'bird-leg' dinosaurs to ostrich-like birds.[40] It was one more piece of circumstantial evidence that this real bloodline had existed.

Only a direct sequence of fossils could provide the 'Demonstrative Evidence of Evolution', and that he saved for Friday's finale. The socialites escaped from New York's 'threatening skies' to the prairies of Nebraska. Past them cantered the horses from Marsh's palaeontological stable – first high-stepping modern thoroughbreds, then tapir-toed proto-ponies, and bringing up the rear the miniature

Orohippus. What would be found next? An older Eocene forerunner with a fifth toe? The prediction gave the *Herald* its headline: 'Horses with Fingers and Toes Discovered in America. The Last Toe Wanting'. Even that caught the serious side. Huxley was applauding the United States for providing the real palaeontological proof of evolution, important during the centenary as the nation counted its achievements. Marsh, emboldened by Huxley's talk of 'Demonstrative Evidence', would henceforth tell Americans that 'to doubt evolution . . . is to doubt science'.[41]

At the finish Huxley apologized for his gravity. These were not issues, he said, digging at his critics, to be 'dealt with by rhetorical flourishes'. The shoe was now on the other foot: the man of science had emerged as the true Puritan in a nation proud of its heritage. The alienated, Dissent-backed activist clawing power in his own fragmenting Anglican culture had emerged in Manhattan as the true voice of Nature. Here the press had a word to match the incarnation: in America he was first called a 'scientist'.[42]

It was 'splendid', said Nettie, 'he was in great form'. Notes of congratulation poured in, talking of the 'profound impression' he had made. Everyone migrated back to the hotel '& drank our health in champagne'. There was the indefatigable Youmans, conniving with Marsh to get Huxley's lectures into book form with the Yale illustrations. The Appletons, too, were relishing a rise in sales as the pulpiteers declared 'war against Hal'. But the patriotic Nettie was sanguine, 'they cannot crush facts'.[43]

A 10¢ commemorative issue of the *Tribune* containing all of Huxley's speeches was on the streets at 8.30 the next morning, Saturday 23 September. The couple were already on board the liner *Celtic*, saying goodbye to Youmans and Appleton, and Professors Marsh and Martin. Thirty minutes later the great ship slipped its moorings.

Their spirits were dampened by a cold, cheerless, 12-day voyage home. For three of them Hal lay in bed 'wrapped in linseed & mustard poultices'. Exhausted, and always 'rebellious ab' overcoats', he had walked the stormy decks and caught a chill. But the mulligrubs passed on sighting land. And the ledger looked good: £915 8s 6d for Hal's cut of the profits, minus £300 expenses, 'Say £600 profit on the whole Transaction'. And by the time he got home he pronounced the 'Wife younger by ten years'.

'Never did I so love, or so appreciate the quiet loveliness of England' said Nettie of the green fields.[44] The Pope too, glad to see his 'dear native mud again', figuratively kissed the ground.

24

A Touch of the Whip

IN MARCH 1877 the eagle-eyed raptor nodded off on his Secretary's perch and slept through Frank Darwin's paper on teasel plants. The Royal Society was rather astonished. It wasn't the Huxley of old. 'I am not quite happy about Hal', Nettie told Lizzie as the inner man sagged, 'but don't say so beyond yʳ home'.[1] Others saw his candle burning down fast.

Huxley was a glutton for punishing work, with endless opportunity to indulge himself. Thursday, his last free night, was finally sacrificed when Stanley started his meet-the-eminent evenings for young clerks and shop assistants at Westminster Deanery. Nettie was furious. Even the Professor was finding 'that as I get older doing more than two or three things at once becomes somewhat troublesome' – or so he told the Quekett Microscopical Club (of which of course he took the Presidency). And the 'Government never gives Hal any peace'. It co-opted him now onto his eighth Royal Commission, to look into the Scottish universities. Thus began more trips to Edinburgh and 'much work & no pay'. Even then the Treasury had the gall to query his expenses. But he had to get aboard to push through his reforms, and take 'up the case of you troublesome women', as he told the wife, 'who want admission into the University (very rightly too I think)'.[2]

Nettie sat at home awaiting the daily numbered letter. A genteel circle came to her aid: Lord Arthur Russell would arrange a ducal box at Covent Garden, or she would accompany the older girls to the Season's soirées. By day the younger, boisterous Nettie and brother Len would 'chase & battle' about the house. 'The rushing, the screams . . . ' and their mother laughing too much to be able to stop them. And the youngest of all, Harry, 12 in 1877, was 'wonderfully affectionate'. His father thought that 'women will play the devil with him, & he with them'.[3]

Overextension was a lifelong problem. In Huxley's study papers lay part-finished, like 'full many a flower, born to blush unseen'. Among them was his *Lessons in Elementary Psychology*, umpteen years old, and each year reduced the chance of him catching up. Work was 'a debt which whatever payments you may make grows continually vaster'. He began to lay a dead hand on precious specimens, like a secret collector with a priceless painting. With that modern *Argo*, the *Challenger*, back in port, and Thomson dubbed Sir Wyville by the Queen, Huxley had his pick of the prizes. The hold was loaded: 6,257 casks and jars full of the world's sea-bed treasures, enough to keep Europe's biologists busy for a generation and fill 50 volumes of reports. From the 4,000 new species Huxley picked a tentacled cephalopod, a cuttlefish relative with a flesh-covered coiled shell, *Spirula*. In 69,000 nautical miles they had found only one, and Huxley had another from the Governor of the Windward Islands. These smelly, preserved specimens lay dissected on his desk through 1879, a 53-page manuscript almost complete, plates engraved. But somehow the last heroic effort seemed to elude him.[4] Always there was some new challenge, some hidden hand beckoning him away.

Nor was it surprising, given the work he *did* wrap up in '77. Book after book came out, generating review after review. In May his 'wonderfully clear and rich' *American Addresses* brought 'the doctrine of evolution to the house'. Marsh's diagrams were fuller; and it was the first British book to make the fossil case for evolution. Marsh's archaic toothed birds reinforced Huxley's dramatic avian ancestry (which, joked J. A. Froude, resolved the chicken-and-egg question). A month later Huxley was putting the preface to his technical *Anatomy of Invertebrated Animals*: two decades on the desk, that one! Then there was that 'priceless gem', as sister Lizzie called it; the best of the crop, in Nettie's words: the *Physiography*, the book that spoke to the little ones, a mere seven years late. To stretched parents that spotter's guide to the land, the rocks, the weather and the world was 'worth silver and gold'. And that was what Huxley received for it, with tills ringing up 3,386 sales in six weeks. It was a bedtime book that turned from tiny everyday observations to gigantic prehistoric explanations. Radical in its conception, the *Physiography* set the trend for post-Darwinian geography. It took children from their parish to the outer reaches of the solar system. Huxley stood the old geography on its head: making local events the launch point was revolutionary, even if his strategy was to subordinate a distant

Jewish geography on the school syllabus. In line with this, the book looked to the causal connection of things rather than their Divine harmony. Morley's stepson couldn't be prised from it: Oh no, he would say, offered a novel in exchange, 'I'm at an awfully interesting part, and I can't leave off'. Morley saw it as 'a real service to the human race'. By Christmas there was a second printing and *American Addresses* had sold out. So, said Hal, 'I hope to tap Macmillan pretty freely'.[5]

Nettie gave thanks, and she chose a new shrine. Lisson Grove was too long a walk and she switched to St Mark's Church in the next road. The big spire promised wealthy pews for the socially mobile St John's Wood set. It was an upmarket move. The Revd Robinson Duckworth was the Queen's Chaplain, and fresh from his trip to India with the Prince of Wales. (They had long known Canon Duckworth; he was Ethel's godfather.) Not that Nettie's observance here was so fulfilling, or so central any more. Hal saluted the Sunday troop off. He had been open about his doubts, but he thought 'self-righteousness . . . worse than any wrong religious beliefs', and he knew that 'Their mother has a sneaking love for the old story'. St Mark's never fostered it. The church was uninspiring, so was Duckworth. And on sunny days Nettie could admit that

> I get more good out of Nature than, by going to church &
> hearing things put in such a way that they are simply
> irritating – or hearing things that to my mind are untrue
> & heathenish.[6]

Hal found his own Kingdom of Heaven in the New World. The prophecy was fulfilled. Seven weeks after waving goodbye in New York, Youmans announced Marsh's discovery of his five-toed 'dawn horse' *Eohippus*. In fact, Marsh had it all the time:

> I had him 'corralled' in the basement of our Museum when
> you were there, but he was so covered with Eocene mud that
> I did not know him from *Orohippus*. I promise you his
> grandfather in time for your next Horse Lecture if you will
> give me proper notice.[7]

If Huxley had any faith, it was in 'the inexhaustibility of the contents of those boxes', he told Marsh. So it was back to the circuit, with more talks on American horses and American birds with teeth. The Badlands horses changed Huxley's understanding of evolutionary timing yet again. Watching their growth from dog-sized ancestors to today's thoroughbreds, he began to contemplate a parallel series of human fossils. No talk now of Silurian men, or lost pre-Cambrian ancestors. After the Pliocene, Miocene and Eocene horses he could suggest that 'when we obtain the remains of Pliocene, Miocene, and Eocene *Anthropidae*, they will present us with the like series of gradations'.[8] He joined Wallace and Darwin to await the discovery of ape-men.

'So far as animals are concerned I am quite satisfied that Evolution is a historical fact', he now said, adding cryptically, 'What causes brought it about is another matter'.[9] There was the rub. While Hooker – or rather Sir Joseph, for he had caved in and accepted the Star of India, recommended by Lord Salisbury for his monumental work on the Himalayan flora – got to grips with Natural Selection in his Presidential Address to the Royal Society, his Secretary was distancing the fact of evolution from putative 'physiological' causes. It showed in the first-ever article on 'Evolution', which Huxley wrote for the *Encyclopaedia Britannica*. Darwin was nonplussed to find himself the culmination of Cartesian philosophy and biological discovery. His contingent and chancy Natural Selection was mentioned once, only to be neutered by talk of some innate tendency for organisms to vary.[10] Huxley had managed to portray 'Evolution', not only without 'Natural Selection', but without any 'Natural History' either.

But for better or worse Pope Huxley was Darwin's representative on Earth. When an admiring solicitor Anthony Rich offered to leave Darwin his fortune, it was Huxley who went to Worthing to check on the donor's respectability. Back went a report to the Darwins on the odd gent's bachelor house with its fine-lawned two acres:

> Well he is an alert, bright-eyed little man with a long beard
> & croaky voice – very frank & straightforward and with a
> sort of abrupt courtesy & kindness, that's rather taking . . .
> He seems to have had a loose ended sort of life – spending
> many years in Italy & studying art – and is about as
> pronounced a heretic, theologically morally & politically as
> I have yet met with – which you will allow is saying a good
> deal for him. But the man is a gentleman in the best sense
> of the word [this was Darwin's main worry, having spent a
> life trying to avoid being tarred with the disreputables].[11]

Huxley's report on the 'man who had strayed so eccentrically into the path of wisdom' gave the Darwins 'a real good laugh'. Huxley, seeing the rich get richer, 'had half a mind to try & cut you out', a joke with an edge that would come back to haunt him.[12]

When Darwin and Huxley were put up in opposition for the Académie Française in 1877 – with Huxley offered the better odds 'as being more orthodox!' (as George Darwin laughed, another joke with an edge) – Huxley quietly withdrew.[13] The world had a habit of genuflecting and withdrawing before Darwin. Even Gladstone, spending the weekend at John Lubbock's High Elms estate with those other Liberal deities Playfair and Morley, and descending on Darwin's hamlet on Saturday 10 March 1877, was chaperoned by Huxley to ensure proper etiquette in a superior deity's presence.[14]

New forums were opening up. Knowles' monthly, the *Nineteenth Century*, which he established in March 1877 after falling out with his old publisher, was an instant success. Tennyson plotted its course in his opening poem, where Huxley was one of those 'wilder comrades, sworn to seek'

> If any golden harbour be for men
> In seas of Death and sunless gulfs of Doubt,[15]

while its opening symposium on 'The Influence upon Morality of a Decline in Religious Belief' caught the anxieties of the 1870s. And of course it had Huxley throwing his agnostic spanner into the works, suggesting as ever that 'Religion is the affair of the affections, theology of the intellect' – meaning it was the latter that was declining as real religion reflected the awe of modern science.[16]

So Huxley the persistent bigamist switched one of his partners and spread his favours liberally. From now on Morley's *Fortnightly* and the *Nineteenth Century* were to 'occupy the best place (for every body but parsons & country squires) in England'. Morley and Knowles were still rending contributors in twain like 'ravening lions'. If Knowles had the bigger mane, Morley had the radical cunning. 'Why should Knowles – with all his flocks and hens, some of them uncommonly bovine and ovine – grudge me my one ewe lamb?' Morley asked Huxley: 'Were you ever mistaken for so gentle a beast before?'[17] So Huxley sent Morley his contribution to the tercentenary of William Harvey's birth. Harvey's discovery of the circulation of the blood became another platform for Huxley's justification of vivisection and the right method of doing science, vindicating not only Harvey, but implicitly Darwin as well.[18]

More justification for 'torturing' angered the *Spectator*. But Huxley declared with a twinkle that 'Controversy is as abhorrent to me as gin to a reclaimed drunkard'.

The abstemious pugilist prepared more screeds for Morley. Nettie was a scientific widow: Hal's dinners, meetings and lectures kept him out till all hours. The ewe wrote on the hoof. His 'Technical Education' was finished on the morning of 1 December 1877 and read at teatime at the Working Men's Club. That paper too fitted Morley's radical design. It made the mechanic one with the anatomist, who dissected with the finesse of a monocled watch-maker. Vocational training was as necessary for the lab as the work-bench, and in both the 'empyreal' mists of speculation were wafted up the ventilation shaft. 'Mother Nature is serenely obdurate to honeyed words', he said; she respects only the craftsman's 'tangible facts'. He made it his licence to speak to the workers.[19]

The wealthy City livery companies had prompted his talk. The Clothworkers Guild was now investing in the Yorkshire College of Science (to become the University of Leeds). The Grocers Company was awarding science scholarships. But they sought their own vocational college, and they had Huxley do a feasibility study. He knew the needs of heavy industry. Yearly the family stayed with the steel magnate Sir William Armstrong. And if Huxley was partly responsible for the theoretical – rather than hands-on – bent of technical education, the big guns were behind him on that too. Armstrong, shown Huxley's report, was even more adamant on the need for pure science, and more 'competent teachers' to teach it.

This *theoretical* bent was part of the professional scientists' strategy. They were equating science's moral training with the Classics' character-forming ability. It was their pitch for power. Pure science was escaping its sordid image, hitching itself to traditional values. And so a theory-based education for mechanics and man-agers became the norm. Huxley's men were elevating the mind, rather than teaching 'fingers to earn money'.[20]

If Huxley's industrial ties haven't been noted before it is because his family hasn't been set in the foreground. Armstrong's ballistics expert Captain Noble – the man to put modern breech-loading can-non onto Her Majesty's warships – had Huxley's eldest son Len to stay with his boys. And when the family were with Armstrong Mady and Jess would go to Newcastle balls in mob caps with Noble's daughter Lily. The Huxleys kept close to Pater's Coventry roots, even to his old factory mentor George May (the ribbon-master with whom he had pondered the divine government). Len, at University College School with May's boy, was sweet on 16-year-old Margery May. He would bicycle 120 miles in a day, and on iron wheels! setting off from London before sunrise, passing through Coventry, to stay with her.[21] Professional welding and family rivets locked these industrial connections tight. Huxley was a unique institution: a sort of cultural Telford bridge between the old steel Dissent and new professionals.

University College seemed the natural home for Huxley's son. Mady was there, studying art at the Slade School. She had grown more talented, judging by the prizes, and more stunning, judging by the stupefied men. The governess was appalled to see one in the street 'literally stopped with his mouth partially open' as she passed. The skittish beauty dangled suitors. It was unseemly for a Victorian Miss to have had three proposals of marriage by 19, and Nettie foresaw 'trouble . . . with her & her admirers'. Mady's work caused the same flutter. In 1877 she took the composition prize for her *Death of Socrates*, and another for etching the following year. At the 'Tall Teas' there was admiration for her sketch of her father, ironically because it gave him the 'look of the B^p. of Oxford'.[22] (There was a resemblance: Huxley had actually been mistaken for Wilberforce's son shortly after the 1860 fracas.)

Len was 'a good steady worker'. But he was aimless, and his mother wished 'he had a decided turn for some one thing'. Professor Huxley was the exponent of exams as the gates to professional excellence, and London University had the stiffest in Britain. Len passed the 15 hours of tests in 1877, despite an attack of mumps that left him feeling 'as if the back of his head were coming off'.[23] But he would not join the professionals' sons in godless Gower Street. The boy had been rather shepherded; he clearly had no scientific bent, and he was using the exam to gain a diploma of school achievement – common practice in London. His parents were left wondering what to do with him.

The solution came from Huxley's broadest of Broad Church admirers, Revd Benjamin Jowett. Such was the liberal ascent that the Greek professor who had been accused of heresy for analysing the Bible historically was the Master of Balliol now. He was still trying to inject science into the Oxford degree (and still being opposed by his own science dons, 'on the ground that it will lower the character of [science] studies'). What better than to have the son of Britain's most famous scientist under him? Jowett advised two terms at St Andrews in Scotland, which was cheap and small 'so that the pupils get more careful grinding'. It was a preparing school where Len could work for a Scholarship to Balliol. Jowett accordingly arranged tutors in Classics and mathematics. And so, instead of walking across Regent's Park, Len travelled to the North. But he remained his father's son and complained that the Rector's opening address 'contained a lie on Evolution'.[24]

If there was a feeling that this was second best, there was also an awareness that the old dames of Isis and Cam were changing their clothes. Huxley the Devonshire Commissioner had helped to pay the costumier. Science, seen on all sides as an authority-questioning upstart, was rudely pushing beneath the spires. The £120,000 belatedly pumped by Oxford's fat colleges into laboratories would surely have an effect – notwithstanding the physics professor's feeling that it was 'not etiquette' to enter a dirty lab. No one had yet said 'to punish a scientific man ... appoint him to an Oxford professorship'.[25] Perhaps science could prosper here, as at Cambridge.

Darwin's Alma Mater signalled the changes by awarding him an honorary doctorate in November 1877. Cambridge was committing herself to the future. The traffic between Kensington and Cam said as much. Foster's eager students came down yearly to help run Huxley's courses, and Cambridge got that 'sharp fellow' Patrick Geddes in return. (The wild-eyed son of the Kirk had left his Positivist Church in Chapel Street, but Cambridge seemed dismal without Huxley's moral light and he moved on, ultimately to transfer Huxley's physiographical analysis to urban development and develop an unlikely career in town planning.)[26]

Foster's team was happy to see Darwin invested. At exam times they were taxing students on the struggle for existence (which was more than Huxley was doing), and Darwin's crown legitimated their claim on the new biological laboratory being built on Downing Street.[27] There was home-grown talent too, it wasn't all coming up from London. One student stood out, Frank Balfour. Such was the brilliance of Balfour's Trinity College Fellowship exam that Foster told Huxley (an examiner) not to bother coming up for the *viva*. Balfour was a man after Huxley's heart. And Nettie's: she saw in his 'dash and verve' Hal in his *Rattlesnake* days, and Foster noticed it too. The brilliant Balfour had an 'old head on his young shoulders'.[28] He had been to the Naples station to study marine larvae, and he was now lecturing on animal relationships as revealed by their embryological development.

They all watched Darwin's crowning in a packed Senate House. Rowdy undergrads perched irreverently on statues and raised a monkey-puppet to roars. An embarrassed Darwin was lauded in Latin for works that the wrinkled dons had once damned as 'grievously mischievous'. If the Public Orator could not quite relate Moral Man to 'the unlovely tribe of apes', the anatomy professor George Humphry could. He claimed that 'the University has by todays proceedings committed itself to the doctrine of evolution'. It was a 'great step for Cambridge', said Huxley, 'though it may not seem much in itself!'[29]

But Huxley could not resist the snipe that would never have occurred to the affable squire. He 'chaffed the dons so sweetly':

> Mr Darwins work had fully earned [the] distinction you
> have today conferred upon him four & twenty years ago . . .
> [With 'wise foresight', instead] of offering her honours
> when they ran a chance of being crushed beneath the
> accumulated marks of approbation of the whole civilized
> world[,] the University has waited until the trophy was
> finished & has crowned the edifice with the delicate wreath
> of academic appreciation.

It was a mere 'touch of the whip', which 'was so tied round with ribbons that it took them some time to find out where the flick had hit'. But the sight of pink hides had Frank Darwin 'boiling over with enthusiasm' and his father bubbling about his 'generous friend'.[30]

Yet Huxley's own haggling over evolution continued to confound. He had broken his *Spirula* work to make the gesture at Cambridge. But what was he doing with the tentacled molluscs? He had moved on to the related belemnites, those rod-like cuttle-bones from the blue-lias cliffs. The shirt-sleeved prof, relishing a Bohemian seaside existence, had taken the family to the Esplanade at Whitby for their holidays, close to the cliffs, where presumably he had picked up the Jurassic fossils. Before he knew it he was sucked into an encompassing history of all the nautiluses and ammonites. Sea-slug shipments arrived from Naples, and he set in for the duration, devising a novel combination microscope, a simple lens for gross dissections with a compound lens that could be swung on top for detailed work. The result, in class, was the sober Dr Jekyll, still damning the 'growing tendency to mix up [evolutionary] speculations with morphological generalizations'. But madly, brilliantly and privately he fleshed out evolutionary trees.[31] He depicted ancestral snail-like molluscs differentially curling their shells like *Nautilus* or *Spirula* or uncurling them like certain ammonites or even straightening them like cuttlefish and belemnites. And this wild Mr Hyde then escaped the theatre and burst onto the London Institution stage to talk on the 'Probable Causes of Evolution'. Dr Jekyll seemed the strange *alter ego* of the flamboyant Mr Hyde of these populist moments.[32]

The *doppelgänger* confused Darwin, as it did later historians, who saw only Huxley's monographs (no evolution) and popular essays (championing evolution). Yet buried away was the link: his private research notes were littered with phylogenetic tree trunks: every mammal group was followed to the flowering branches of its existence, so were reptiles and amphibians, and the sudden efflorescence as birds evolved out of reptiles – these evolutionary diagrams came to dominate his notes. They were the heuristic link. The evolutionary trees underwrote, perhaps even drove, much of his work from the later 1870s, but they left barely a trace in his class lectures or his stripped-down descriptive papers. So much of each pedigree was informed guesswork, as it had to be. Such genealogies were ephemeral, liable to change – simply lightning sketches to investigate possibilities. Made public, they would imperil the public image of the solid bedrock of biological knowledge. So they remained hidden.

Nothing could be allowed to jeopardize the new professionals' claims. Dr Jekyll's solid image of science matched his new face of bronze. Thomas Woolner had fixed on Hal's stern lines for immortalization. Who better to sculpt him than one of the original Pre-Raphaelite Brethren? Long before, Hal had seen Nettie's mournful look in their ethereal paintings, now his own bust would go on show at the Royal Academy. With art fastened to anatomy, and the artists fastened to Mady's skirt-tails, Marlborough Place was every bit the fashionable salon. The Victorian Masters of the languid graced Nettie's table – Lawrence Alma-Tadema, with his eye for a classically-draped figure, and her favourite neighbour Briton Riviere, whose scenes of ill children moved an infirm nation. William Roden slipped from Gladstone's lopsided head to Huxley's setjawed features (slyly hoping to sell a few reproduction paintings on the side). In an age when Science – not Art – was daring, Huxley was the darling of Academy dinners. Here he exhibited the Great and Good to his New World friends. 'When I was in America, you showed me every extinct animal', he told that 'large hearted' blood brother of the Sioux, Prof. Marsh. 'Now, if there is a single living lion in all Great Britain that you wish to see, I will show him to you in five minutes'.[33]

Sundays' 'Tall Teas' could still be a refuge for an alienated world. Leslie Stephen, lonely now after the death of his wife Harriet (Thackeray's daughter), became a regular.[34] And in the late seventies as the elite correspondents sat in – George Smalley (*New York Tribune*), Archibald Forbes (*Daily News*), that old Africa hand Henry Morton Stanley, and J. R. Young (*New York Herald*) – the cigar talk became more expansive.

With a maimed British lion savaging the Zulus, and the British in Kabul under siege, it dissolved into imperial deliberation. 'Catch me discussing the Afghan question with you you little pepper pot', Pater would declaim to Jess, before holding forth on the Khyber Pass tribes as 'a pack of disorderly treacherous blood-thirsty thieves'. The Tories had discovered jingoism, and so, it seemed, had Huxley. But Nettie could only 'wish that we had never had a Clive in our History'. The exotic Disraeli was making the Empire central to Toryism, but he was hard pressed to keep that minor jewel, the mountain stronghold of Kabul, in the crown. And by flattering the Queen as Empress of India he even turned discussions to the monarchy itself. Huxley buttressed the palace so backhandedly in his flippant sexist way that guests wondered if he wasn't a republican at heart. 'So long as the throne is held by the present Royal family, in which the intellect is entirely confined to the females', he said, 'the monarchy is quite safe'.[35]

Ten thousand feathered Zulus slaughtered in defence of their 'hearths and homes' brought Gladstone alive. The groans of the dying evoked during his Midlothian campaign helped to sweep him back into power. Huxley too found Sir Bartle Frere's invasion of Zululand unacceptably genocidal and pulled out of an association backing him. But he shared the nation's conceit about its civilizing influence, even if moral duty meant a heavy hand. The '"family" declare I am becoming a Jingo!' he exclaimed, surprised that the minors could show the Huxley bent for independence. With the *Daily News* war correspondent Archibald Forbes besotted by Mady and enticing the girls to his campaign briefings, the cadets put up spirited resistance to the General. At times Midlothian sentiments positively swept the ranks to insubordination. 'Pater is becoming quite a conservative', said Mady. 'Fancy, Prof Huxley a "true blue"!'[36]

That was qualification enough to put him on the Eton governing board. Actually what put him there was the Public Schools Act. It allocated one seat to a Royal Society nominee in an attempt to force changes on Eton. But Huxley might well have stumbled into a Zulu kraal, considering the resistance he met. With Rorke's Drift fortitude he overcame the odds to get a science block built, imagining that this would breed sweet reason into the twentieth century's generals. They were out there, on the playing fields.

'I think I commenced to become respectable when I was elected a Governor of Eton College', he later confirmed. He had followed a line of Deans and Divines, who found the devil rather a charming chap, and he too could not help thinking them 'nice fellows'. The girls feared the worst. The outsider was now in the heart of the Establishment. But it was not easy to convince uncomprehending Churchmen, who saw the Classics as the mark of culture, that

Science added anything to the national character. Some schools prevaricated, notably Westminster, which insisted that the Royal Society nominee be an Anglican.[37] But Huxley shrugged them off. Politics was now against the older monopolies, and with him.

Whatever his unbecoming hue, Hal still took royal hob-nobbing a mite less seriously than Nettie. Her family letters were beginning to ooze stately acquaintance. He endured invitations to dine with the Crown Prince and Princess, or attend M'Lady's reception, or call on the 'Rootle-Tootles', who, he was astonished to learn, 'have a bigger drawing-room than ours' ('perhaps', he asked Jess, 'you will tell them to have it made smaller before I visit them'). One confidence trickster even used him to prey on passing countesses.[38] The 'Comte de Veysey' got close by offering to translate one of his books into Russian, but niggling doubts sent Huxley to Chief Superintendent Williamson at Scotland Yard where he saw the arrest warrants.

The con men at least had begun to appreciate his new standing.

25

A Person of Respectability

HUXLEY'S SCIENTIFIC BROTHERHOOD gathered on a warm sunny Saturday 4 May 1878 – Hal's 53rd birthday – for Jess's wedding to her young architect Fred Waller. Only an unwell Tyndall was missing, but Louisa carried his blessing, which was 'as good as the parson's'. Hooker sent 'heaps of lovely flowers from Kew' and the bride wore the Darwins' gift, a ruby and diamond star. 'It is the first break in our family', Huxley told Haeckel, and he felt it. He 'was grey in colour from the suppressed emotion' as he walked Jess towards Canon Duckworth. Naturally this 'ecclesiastical part' was 'quite out of the question' for the blimpish Spencer, but he deigned to attend the 'social part' afterwards in his 'passive' way.[1] He milled with the barons of science and industry. And at least one Right Honourable artist, John Collier, 'Jack' to everybody, son of a former Attorney-General and a constant presence in the lives of the arty girls.

'Married & done for' pronounced a footloose Mady, dangling her bevy of men. But the footsteps of fortune are slippery. Days later the marriage was overshadowed as the children came down with diphtheria, Mady dangerously so. Her throat was an agony. She was gasping and feverish. Her blood poisoned, she 'lost her sight her speech, & lastly the use of her legs'. Clark and the family doctor stood by helpless. By 17 May Nettie was fraught and 'worn out with nursing'. By the 20th she herself had not had an hour's undisturbed sleep for a week. Hal's face showed the desperation as he watched Mady 'for several days hovering between life & death'. 'I never saw a man more crushed', said his lab technician Jeffrey Parker.[2]

The day Mady began fighting for her life Huxley tore himself from her bedside to deliver the first of his Davis Lectures at the Zoological Society. He started to talk on the common crayfish as a key to the relationship of the crustaceans, but he was close to breaking down, and his mellifluous voice choked. The gallery listeners, not realizing, pressed him to 'speak a little *louder*'. But by the time he came to give a workers' lecture on 20 May (everything was now crustaceans) the worst was over. Four hours later he returned home to 'find a wonderful & blessed change'.[3] Mady would still have three weeks of excruciating pain, but she had turned the corner. As Huxley went back to crayfish he was also chairing a public meeting to discover the cause of the diphtheria ravaging St John's Wood (he tracked its source in the contaminated milk coming from a Kilburn farm).

Crayfish were the 'hidden hand' which drew him from *Spirula*. He veered off, lured by a new promise and would never finish the tentacled molluscs.[4] Crayfish acquired their own momentum and for an instant invertebrates again took over his life. His absorption was evident. Devotees approached seeking enlightenment on some backboned animal only to be outrageously deflated: 'Codfish?' he mumbled at Parker, 'that's a vertebrate, isn't it?'

By the time he had finished his five-week working men's course on crayfish he had two weeks of his concurrent Davis Lectures to run. Mady was still paralysed but recovering as he topped his work off. He had started from the commonplace, the dinner-table familiar, the edible crayfish bought from a French vendor. These had two rudimentary filaments, one-tenth of an inch long, next to the gills. He moved to the exotic, looking at primitive Australian crayfish to see perfectly developed gills in these slots. Then he cast his net wider, to lobsters and marine crays. At the zoo he used these varying gill plumes to investigate the 'Morphological relation of all the forms', and to draw a full 'Phylogeny' – as he had done with the coiling shells of *Spirula*'s relatives. It was a logical pedigree or Haeckelian family tree. 'I need hardly say that the bearing of all this upon the theory of evolution from a common type was very important'.[5] He might say it, but when he came to summarize his conclusions on gills and classification on 4 June 1878 in a paper to be published in the Zoological Society's *Proceedings* he remained his usual factual self. By and large, evolution was reserved for a public canvas.

The Crayfish might not sound like a stimulating book. But it was destined for the International Scientific Series. The ISS now stretched from physics to psychology and beyond. It outdid the evangelical presses in pumping out rationalist books for Everyman. A huge force for deterministic and social evolution, it mixed modernity and notoriety to sell titles through umpteen editions. Science was becoming 'mightier and forever mightier' and flaunting its celebrities. Here was

Spencer's influential *Study of Sociology*, Bagehot's *Physics and Politics*, Bain's *Mind and Body*, Tyndall's *Forms of Water*. And the most successful, by a Methodist, University College-trained, Yankee emigrant, John Draper – a bullish mood-catcher, a warmongering account of 'contending powers' to rival his own *History of the American Civil War*. A book to cap the professionalizing, dissenting militancy against Rome. This was Draper's *History of the Conflict Between Religion and Science*.

These were Huxley's people with their own provocative encyclicals. He started *The Crayfish* after the Summer holidays in 1878, giving his own text an alluring evolutionary gloss. He intended it as the beginning of his own series.[6] He would take readers from the 'insignificant' and common-or-garden into the profound depths. The crab-stall was the portal into an exotic invertebrate kingdom. Next would come the fireside *Dog*,[7] an open sesame into the world of vertebrates, and *Man* would complete the trio. It was another forlorn hope, for he only ever prepared the *Crayfish* hors-d'œuvre. Although the starved customers found that so tasty that they came back for seven editions.

If the evolutionary agnostics were rewriting the times, they were rewriting history to match. Huxley's long dalliance with the sceptical philosopher David Hume would become a stronger engagement with Morley's bribe: £150 if he would add *Hume* to his new *English Men of Letters* series. Morley, who had made the *Fortnightly* the most discussed and doctrinaire organ of literary radicalism, was adding saltpetre to sulphur. Hume was an 'easy, sensible, compatible . . . sort of man', and with Huxley a model of rational lucidity, he had the mix. Huxley's homily-clad style would put the final torch to Hume's powder-dry rationalism for the 'ordinary person'. Would Huxley plebeianize Hume's logical remonstrance against miracles? and ready the manuscript for the 1878 Christmas rush? 'It would be a seasonable book for that holy time'.[8]

Huxley's eyes were bigger than his mouth. Nothing could be done on the *Crayfish* until *Hume* had been finished. So a few weeks later he packed his family and himself off to North Wales at Penmaenmawr, Gladstone's favourite village, squeezed between mountain and sea. The holiday was a furious excuse to fill 200 sheets in a bid to subdue Hume into Victorian respectability.

There was to be no holiday for Len. He was dispatched to Herr Professor Haeckel to 'to pick up your noble vernacular'. In Jena the 'German Darwin' was firing students with his declamatory style; not that everyone wanted a 'Darwin' in Deutschland, and one critic considered his *Evolution of Man* a 'fleck of shame on the escutcheon of Germany'. It was Haeckel's new *Freedom in Science and Teaching* that absorbed Pater back home. *Darwinismus* in the classroom had acquired political overtones in Germany, and in his preface to the English translation Huxley, for the first time, defended the principle of teaching evolution in school. (Although in practice he knew that children needed nature lessons before answering more ineffable questions, making his *Physiography* – now in its third printing – the essential grounding.) In a famous speech, reported in the *Times*, the steadfast Rudolf Virchow, Professor of Pathology at Berlin, wanted *Darwinismus* proscribed, ostensibly because of its degree of uncertainty. And yet, countered Huxley in his introduction, dropping his School Board moderation, how much greater the uncertainties about 'the linguistic accomplishments of Balaam's ass' that Christianity subjects schoolchildren to![9]

Huxley's *Hume* was to cut the ground from these 'preposterous fables'. His Hume was a mental anatomist, whose epistemological dissections would legitimize 'the laboratory [as] . . . the fore-court of the temple of philosophy'. It did not take Nettie to see that the book had 'as much of Huxley's as of Hume's' philosophy. On holiday mornings he made Hume's scepticism 'police . . . the whole world of thought'.[10] Then a pause for inspiration on a brisk walk into the mountains. Under this regime a modern Hume emerged whose behaviourist arguments for animal thought were given physiological grounding; a Hume who sounded like Huxley demanding evidence for miracles; and a Huxley who saw like Hume that good religion should be devoid of bad theology.

For a week Huxley drew breath. He crossed the Irish Sea, to be heralded by a Public Orator in formidable Latin as an Honorary Doctorate was bestowed by Dublin University. Then it was on to the British Association stage in the university, to talk a little evolution in Ireland as President of the Anthropology Section. His eyes still burned, even if the silvery sideburns aged him: 'See there is Huxley', said a gent behind Nettie; 'there is such a fascination in his face I cannot keep my eyes off him'. But oh! replied a lady. 'He looks faded'.

With that, the family's deflation of his proud headship began. The girls ribbed him as 'fascinating but faded'. The cockerel's coxcomb drooped. (In an easy house, he 'loved to imagine that he was entirely ruled by his family', observed a student, horrified into disbelief, 'and spoke of himself as chicken pecked as well as hen-pecked'.) Back in Wales he continued to boil 'at high pressure'. By day he made *Hume* a paragon of Victorian sense, but at night the safety valves blew in his sleep as the pressure left him 'grinding his teeth, or scratching his head!'[11]

Middle-aged, post-Mill, post-*Descent of Man*, Huxley was an uncomfortable utilitarian. He had no 'great respect for . . . mere knowing as such', he said. Knowledge had to pay, less in 'pudding or praise', in its fight against germs or farm pests, as in laying a foundation for life. David Hume had made social and personal benefit the utilitarian explanation of morality. *Hume* inched Huxley closer to Darwin, who had made the utilitarian moral instincts evolutionary products.[12] But primarily *Hume* celebrated the Victorian sense of the material world. It put out of mind what was 'out of reach'. Morley had his tract for the times. The contemporary frock-coat made 'the old sage' into 'a new figure'. That was 'capital'.[13]

As the troop decamped for home the potboiler lacked only one detail, the Life. And Huxley, sympathizing with the struggling man, while the fêted 'David . . . begins rather to bore me', added that peremptorily. Morley was staggered at the turnaround. 'I'm a pretty rapid worker myself', but he confessed 'to some amazement' at this.

Advance copies were in hand by Christmas Day. Old Darwin uttered dire prognostications: philosophy left him cold and, apart from the 'interspersed flashes of wit', he saw nothing to suggest a sale. How wrong. Morley capitalized on the Christmas sale with a 5,000 print-run, and Huxley declared the book 'a measure of what the public will stand in frank speaking'. For the Twelve Days of Christmas *Hume* went 'with a fine rush'.[14] By 26 January 1879 4,400 copies had crossed the counter and it was still selling 50 a day, with a reprint in hand. (Ten thousand sold over the next 18 months, making the sceptical philosopher more famous than in his own lifetime.)

The book sold on Huxley's name, but the figures also suggest that it caught the mood of moralizing materialism of the mid-Victorian public. Critics praised its jargon-free tone, if not its dogmatism. 'Twenty years ago I should have been posted for it', said Huxley, yearning for the old martyrdom. 'Now, respectability itself pats me on the back'. 'There must be something wrong somewhere'. Copies went out to the literary elite, the Arnolds and Stephens, who found it a bit short on actual biography. More were dispatched as printed replies to troublesome pamphleteers. George Stokes, sending his *Conditional Immortality* (which admitted that there was no *natural* evidence for the soul), got *Hume* by return. But the book itself leached through these literary strata to petit-bourgeois levels. Blue-collar staff debated its sceptical sanctity, and the poor chemist's assistant 'w^d cheerfully pay three times the price of "Hume" for a book even half as good'.[15] This wide constituency confirmed that Huxley's impact extended much deeper than ever Arnold's or Stephen's.

Morley's success even had Huxley mooting a profile-raising 'English Men of Science' series in imitation. He fancied himself editing 'à la Knowles', and collecting a 5 per cent royalty à la Morley.[16] Such a series would have reinforced his ascendant cultural tradition. But Huxley's potential contributors despaired at seeing him knock off *Hume* in a month, and they quickly killed the project.

No matter, *Hume* itself did the promotional job. Hume's powder-puff wig and knee-breeches had been whipped off and the philosopher who died in the year of the American Revolution had become the voice of Victorian scientific agnosticism. It was another pitch for Huxley's specialists, who were to patrol the outer limits of legitimate knowledge. Huxley still distinguished his pure agnosticism from rival products. He scorned the religious observance of Positivism, with its vacuous Host, abhorred Bradlaugh's atheists hammering on the Establishment door and eyed socialism warily. When the social missionary and father of secularism George Holyoake went blind, Huxley was invited to join a fund-raising committee. The distant cordiality between Huxley and Holyoake could be touching; Holyoake would giftwrap his *History of Co-operation*, and Huxley wished him 'with all my heart a speedy return to the visible world, which is on the whole a pleasant spectacle'. But while Huxley contributed for the man 'who has so long & so faithfully served the cause of Free thought', he knew that a committee seat would send the wrong signal.[17]

The signals were important. In Germany Virchow, taunted by the Social Democrats, was making *Darwinismus* look like a terrorists' manual. Evolutionary godlessness had led to the Commune, and it pointed to the apocalypse now that 'Socialism has established a sympathy with it'. At home an unctuous Tory *Quarterly* rebroadcast the message to scientists 'playing with edged tools'. Huxley froze at this scare-mongering. It was scurrilous 'to frighten sober people by the suggestion that evolutionary speculations generate revolutionary schemes in Socialist brains'. Having sanitized evolution for the scullery and study, he wasn't about to be made 'answerable for the horrors of the Paris Commune'.[18]

Nettie rather sweetly wanted him to encapsulate his own philosophy in a book. Arabella Buckley did too, an exploration of his agnostic world. 'No one w^d make a greater mark', Nettie said patriotically, but 'he laughs & asks how he is to get time'. Still, he was 'sowing good seeds', which was 'greater work' than 'writing a system of philosophy'. She saw the seeds germinating in a rounded scientific humanism; and even Hal accepted that 'freethought' would ultimately 'organise itself into a coherent system embracing human life & the world as one harmonious whole'.[19]

But how? Huxley's base was never the secular networks or radical chapels. His was a cerebral freethought suited to the agnostic literati – to an elite sub-class, not to the streets. There were attempts to cast the net wider. Moncure Conway founded an Association of Liberal Thinkers in June 1878, grandly calling it 'the first effort ever made to unite persons interested in the religious sentiment and the moral welfare of mankind on a plan absolutely free from considerations of dogma, race, names, or shibboleths'.[20] In an emancipating, imperial Britain, the socialists and humanitarians led the way towards racial and sexual tolerance, and a steering committee of deists and Jews, Unitarians and secularists, a Hindu, a Parsee and four ladies invited Huxley to be president. But he shared the doubts of Morley, Stephen and Tyndall (a Vice-President). When the council met in Nettie's dining room on 25 January 1879 it was clear they had no common vision, and the mere attempt at a mission statement saw the association fly apart. Huxley's 100-day 'Ministry' collapsed and he resigned. This, the shortest Presidency of his life, illustrated the difficulty of organizing a 'coherent' humanism across classes, races and religions.

It was an Honorary Doctorate from Cambridge a few months later that really rang the social changes. Huxley's men were in place, part of the new hegemony. The modernizing university had been willing to use him, now it was willing to honour him. Huxley, splendid in red gown, hereafter looked 'to be treated as a PERSON OF RESPECTABILITY. I have tried to avoid that misfortune, but it's of no use'.[21] And having honoured him, they made use of him, wanting his views on the abolition of compulsory Greek for entrants to Honours courses.

Pater's choice of Oxford for Len said even more about the tide of change. The status-conscious mandarins of science were renouncing their outsider origins and recolonizing the old seminaries. The Lankesters, Fosters and Carpenters, those sons of Dissent, were seeking legitimation at Oxford and Cambridge. Where once the 'monks of Oxford' were 'sunk in prejudice and port', now Jowett's tipple was Biblical criticism and science. And his 'experiment' with Len worked. Not even the Paternal embodiment of Science, or the more declamatory reasoning of Herr Haeckel, could steer Len from his course. With further Classics-cramming under Jowett's appointed tutor Len gained an Exhibition – a fee-paying scholarship – which would 'lighten Pater's cares'. What was an odd turnabout for the world turned out to be a coup for Jowett, who was 'very much pleased to have a son of Professor Huxley's at Balliol'.[22]

Huxley and Society met in a liberal confluence, and marriage mixed the rivers into a mighty torrent. The artist Jack Collier came with the radical flow. Forty years earlier, in the great parliamentary debates on Church monopolies and Dissent's disabilities, his grandfather had voted to exclude bishops from the Lords. Jack happily suffered in the family tradition. Jack's proposal to the daughter of the MP Joseph Hardcastle had her outraged father scalding this 'half playwright half art set' Bohemian 'who has the contemptible conceit to profess himself an unbeliever'.[23] No gruff Hardcastle protestations from Hal, of course. He found Jack a 'right good fellow'. Collier had long been a brotherly presence around the Slade girls, and there was no greater 'friend of the house'.

No one would forget his kindness in taking Clifford to Madeira on the mathematician's last journey. The consumptive Clifford, at 33 the most cynically brilliant and playful Spinozaist, had set off with Jack, chloroform bottle in hand to ease the pain: 'you always were goodness itself', Clifford had told 'moo'. (Nettie was *Moo* to her brood and becoming a universal mother to the materialist brotherhood.) From Clifford's 'lung mischief' Huxley feared the worst. 'It is a thousand pities, for . . . time would have ripened him into something very considerable'.[24] The group paid Clifford's fare to the dry air of the Mediterranean, where Jack had watched over the dying man.

Secretly Moo was pleased to see the teasing Miss Mady tied down – never mind being bound in such splendour. Jack's father was building a luxury house in Chelsea where they would join the family, with their own maid and footman and fine studio.[25] The Colliers were even further past the wig-maker stage on their own evolutionary journey towards the woolsack. Wasn't Jack's father Sir Robert a former Attorney-General and now a judge of the Court of Appeal? The small, fair, bespectacled, stuttering artist was made for the tall, striking Mady. The Victorian marriage of art and radicalism took place on 30 June 1879.

Hal felt the loss of Mady and Jess, and the next day asked for the flowers to be taken away. A holiday in Devon only confirmed that they were getting old. Nettie was laid up with swollen ankles, and that kept Hal in the house. So he taught himself Greek. 'It is quite wonderful the freshness & directness with which Hal goes into a new thing!' she said, still astonished after all the years.[26] He wanted to find out at first hand why Aristotle apparently saw only three chambers in the human heart. Of course what started in Teignmouth as background to his paper on William Harvey and the blood circulation took on a life of its own and pushed him into Aristotelian studies.

He ploughed on to finish his long-overdue *Introductory Science Primer*. Finally the children's series would have its opener, written expressly to retain control of the dissemination of elite knowledge and preempt the motherly vulgarizations and Christian manipulations.[27] Technology was visible, telephones were a novelty, Siemens' electrical trams were experimental, electric companies were the rage. Even the stodgy *Quarterly Review* saw the need for primers now that science has 'ceased to exist only for the few'. But exponents should fire the 'popular imagination', not abuse it by debasing 'the highest problems of life'. The shire Tories were still twitchy about science as subversion, still apprehensive as Huxley and Tyndall spoke in the industrial Midlands. They feared the baseness of Tyndall's man 'bound fast in fate'. They hated the new scientist whose own 'soul is not above the level of a laboratory'.[28] Huxley was in the black belt again in 1879, visiting the steel town of Sheffield as Vice-President of the BAAS. Nettie stayed with young Jim the industrial chemist and his wife Gaite. The shock of finding Jim already balding only reinforced her autumnal view of life. Amid the threatening smokestacks of chemical factories, she blamed his unhealthy workplace.

The Tory critics of the new science need hardly have worried. If Darwinism had moved from the radical fringe towards the central stage by 1880, it was because of its anodyne social presentation. In popular books and lectures evolution was talked up positively, as a history of meritorious promotion: 'we who are now "foremost in the files of time" had come to the front through almost endless stages of promotion from lower to higher forms of life', as Tyndall phrased it.[29] Benignity had replaced Darwin's bloody struggle; optimism and merited progress suited a striving middle-class audience. The sanitization came with a soothing social message.

The image was even more enthusiastically played up in America's Gilded Age, where evolution promised an onward-and-upward sweep. And reinforcement came with the fossils streaming into Yale and Philadelphia from the West. In 1877 a buckskinned Marsh had opened up the Morrison formation in Colorado with its mountainous dinosaurs: first *Titanosaurus*, with foot-long vertebrae, eight-foot thigh-bones – the largest land animal ever known at 60 feet.[30] Then came the first *Stegosaurus* with plates down its back. The rush was on for the fantastic wealth of the Rocky Mountain states. These extraordinary Jurassic finds turned the rivalry between Marsh's and Cope's quarry gangs into bone warfare. Pot-shots, bribes and desertions on the sites were only matched by dirty tricks in the press as the priority-grabbing Cope and Marsh traded insults. Then came the Como Bluff site in Wyoming and *Brontosaurus*; indeed, in a few years, a hundred sites were being strip mined for their prestigious fossils.

The Como Bluff bonanza threw up tiny intruders in 1878 – the first American Jurassic mammals.[31] As the news came in, Huxley was lecturing on that most primitive mammal, the egg-producing platypus, and thinking on its origin. What had that waddling, duck-billed enigma, marooned in Australia, actually evolved from? Like a biological Occam he flashed his pen across the page on 29 January 1879, sketching the logical family tree. He visualized twin branches, one passing from the amphibians through reptiles to birds (his 'Sauropsida'). The other from amphibians via 'some unknown "promammalian" group' (Haeckel's term) to the platypus.[32] It was eminently logical – all sauropsid skulls had a single condyle (or ball articulating with the first vertebra), all the mammals had a double condyle. And the aortic arches leading from the heart are so different in birds and mammals that the split must have occurred in extremely ancient stock. The solution was neat and tidy – and totally avoided fossils.

And this from a biologist who had insisted that evolutionists had to back their claims with 'title-deeds', fossils. In truth Huxley was trying to scotch Richard Owen's rival image: the festering hatreds after the ape-brain debate had never healed, and Huxley held Owen high in his demonic pantheon. Owen at the British Museum had endless mammal-like reptiles from the Cape – by 1876 a whole *Illustrated Catalogue* full of *Lycosauruses* ('wolf-reptiles') and *Tigrisuchuses* ('tiger-crocodiles'). Some were formidable predators: *Cynodraco* was a reptilian 'big cat', the size of a lion, with a sabre-tooth's canines and a flexible paw for lacerating flesh. He spotlighted them in a new order – the Theriodontia ('beast tooth') – and took a bow at the Geological Society for showing the 'great gains' Triassic reptiles had made towards the mammalian constitution. And he kept the supply of fossil skulls coming from South Africa by having the Treasury fund ox-cart expeditions onto the parched Karroo plateau.[33] Imperial science was marching with the Redcoat's rifle to bring home bones to order.

Huxley had the logic, but Owen had the fossils. Actually Owen's image was much fuzzier. He believed that the erect-standing dinosaurs approached the mammalian grade too, and used his mammal-like reptiles as more proof. As always Huxley's coterie kept their intellectual distance from Owen; indeed, they kept their physical distance: in 1879 Hooker was only elected to 'The Club' (London's ultimate club, founded by Dr Johnson, so exclusive it could shut its door on a Lord Chancellor) after Tyndall gave the all-clear that 'Owen rarely appears'. Huxley waited to join until Owen was all but gone.[34]

Logic is dicey where the exigencies of life are concerned. Owen, told of the impossibility of reptilian forebears, merely had to walk to his drawer of *Cynodracos*.[35] Huxley's was Tweedledee logic, as it turned out: 'If it was so, it might be . . . but as it isn't, it aint'. The fossil past was a Wonderland where one independent reptile group could grow skulls and hearts like mammals. In 1878 Cope described even older (Permian) mammal-like reptiles from Texas, typified by that great sail-backed predator *Dimetrodon*. Clearly the mammal-ancestors were a well-marked fossil lineage. As an idealistic Harry Seeley said (and it took an archetypal realist to say it), reptiles were a *grade*, and while some filled the 'morphological interval between Amphibians and Mammals', others appeared between amphibians and birds.[36]

Huxley had trouble with Platonic grades of existence. Cope appreciated his rival logic, but he took Huxley's clever Penelope's web and rewove it. He envisaged two streams: one from archaic armoured amphibians through mammal-like reptiles to the platypus, and the other via small dinosaurs to the birds. As the evidence tumbled about him Huxley began to waver.[37] Evidently two great empires of unrelated fossil reptiles *had* once thrived, the dinosaur bird-ancestors, and Cope's *Dimetrodons* on their way to the furry mammals.

As the past expanded the present world contracted. Space and distance were collapsing. Only in 1878 had University College students packed a room to see a telephone working. Two years later there was an exchange operating in London. How much more could the planet shrink? Once the forlorn sailor had waited eight months for his fiancée's replies from Australia, now the 'phone promised 'to bring the whole world within speaking distance'. The 60-year-old physicist George Stokes, Huxley's fellow Secretary at the Royal Society, was already practising on his newfangled typewriter. But Huxley retained his drunken-crayfish approach to creative calligraphy. At 55 he was burning out faster than most. He had worn out more professors' caps and Commissioners' chairs and pumped out more memoirs and essays than any five rivals. He reckoned he had but 'ten years of activity left'.[38]

With the *Science Primer* published and his school regime sinking in, he began to brush off posterity. Over 19,000 *Primers* sold at the turn of 1880, and a generation of schoolchildren were setting in.[39] He told a trade-unionist that 'if I am to be remembered at all, I would rather it should be as a "man who did his best to help the people"'. He had helped. His carrot and stick goading on technical education had shifted the sluggish beast. He was already liaising with the government and City Guilds on blueprints for a Central Institution for Technical Education (the 'City and Guilds'). It wasn't going to be an apprentice-shop – he was adamant that industrial skills should be taught close to the engineering plants. His idea was a red-brick tech to turn out teachers in applied physics and mechanics. Locating this college up the road in salubrious South Kensington might breed sneers about 'Art and Science among the roses', and have the *Electrician* pondering the heroic efforts of handicraftsmen to reach it, but it would keep the professionals in control of the educational infrastructure. Huxley still had his territorial ambitions. In the event his 'pet institution', the City and Guilds Institution, built by Alfred Waterhouse close to his Natural History Museum, ended up turning out industrial managers. Even then, Huxley said, it might nurture 'another Faraday or Whitworth or Armstrong'.[40]

Always he left others to finish the building. So much was rubble, and around it the 'ghosts of unfinished work flitter threateningly': tentacled molluscs, lungfishes, educational books, 'English Men of Science', more promises unfulfilled. The spirit was so willing and the flesh growing so weak. His sharp features in portraits were starting to acquire that resigned sadness. An equally sad Foster listened to his papers on mammal ancestry. They were so 'full of suggestive thought' and yet the master seemed 'to suggest that others, and not he himself, were to carry out the ideas'. The intimations of mortality were creeping in.

> It is a curious thing [Huxley told Morley] that I find my dislike to the thought of extinction increasing as I get older and nearer the goal.
> It flashes across me at all sorts of times with a sort of horror that in 1900 I shall probably know no more of what is going on than I did in 1800. I had sooner be in hell . . . at any rate in one of the upper circles, where the climate and company are not too trying.[41]

26

The Scientific Woolsack

HELL HAD TO WAIT while there was a flicker of 'life in the old dog'.[1] He was a Janus-faced sentinel now, guarding the professional portal. In the 1880s he watched his legions march out to meet sacrilegious agnostics on one side and pious Prime Ministers on the other. He looked to the future as the ethical implications of Evolution and Socialism became pressing concerns, and then back again to the beginning of the Darwinian era.

Huxley himself had become part of history, and the passing years showed. Jessie's baby Oriana, born on 11 February 1880, made them grandparents at last. Hal felt a grandfatherly creakiness. He was 'very tired & worn out', and with Nettie suffering from bronchitis, the couple took off for the Surrey countryside early in April 1880. Here he devised a surprise blessing for Darwin. Excruciating toothache ruined his break and a local dentist had to extract two teeth. Inflamed gums or not, he dressed in evening costume to come up to the Royal Institution on the 9th. The perk of power was munificence, and he showered it in his Darwinian benediction. Huxley called his talk 'The Coming of Age of the "Origin of Species"'.

Darwin was at first perplexed, '& then . . . the meaning of your words flashed on me!' It had been 21 years since Murray had chanced his arm on that royal green 15s *Origin*. Huxley was giving Darwin the key to Science's door. It was a political gesture, suggesting Darwinian maturity; a celebration of the 'prodigious change in opinion' which had left many 'worshipping that which they burned, and burning that which they worshipped'. The 'Coming of Age' masqueraded as history. It had the *Origin* sweeping away antique notions in 1859, of 'Great and sudden physical revolutions' causing global extinctions, and equally sudden and supernatural reCreations. But had it? Rewriting history was one of the spoils of victory, and Huxley's reinvention of geology showed how false his memory played him. When the *Origin* appeared in 1859 no Londoner was still clinging to a 'catastrophic' past. Foreign extremists such as Louis Agassiz, who had indeed sent ice-sheets sweeping across the planet 'like a sharp sword' to sever past and present life – using his Ice Age to entomb the planet and kill off all prehistoric life prior to God's next Act of Creation – had long been declared 'glacier-mad', a lunatic doting on 'moonshine'.[2] The mighty Owen was already talking of life's spreading tree, growing slowly and continuously, like a stately old oak.

Huxley was relocating the extremists on centre stage to give the old squire a dramatic cast. This wasn't history; it was propaganda which turned the past to advantage. But it started the trend for reducing the pre-Darwinian era to 'fragmentary' debris in order to highlight the 'simple, unified and comprehensive cosmos' of the 1880s.[3] From the moment Huxley opened his talk, picturing himself as the 'under-nurse' at the *Origin*'s birth, viewing the 'pretty turmoil about its cradle', his whimsy released the tension. Ape-ancestry embarrassed, titillated and shocked the tight-laced matrons, but Huxley's pantomime performance caught them offguard. In the stalls they laughed at the baby's 'naughtiness', the *Standard* said. He had them in the palm of his hand. It was a confidence-building trick, a way of smuggling in the new evolutionary certainties. He was meeting an emotional need as the old standbys vanished: making Darwin a new Rock. And yet in private he was more circumspect. Guests at his High Teas still heard that the *Origin* had been 'difficult to understand. When it first came out, H. said "This will take me about seven years' fighting", & so it did'.[4] Huxley was coming up from behind, reinventing himself as Evolution's midwife.

With no room for equivocation he made no mention of Natural Selection in 'Coming of Age'. The neurotic Darwin still feared Huxley was 'giving it up'. But he was simply making evolution indispensable, telling old war stories lest a new generation forget, knowing – as he put it in one of those enduring aphorisms – that the 'customary fate of new truths' is 'to begin as heresies and to end as superstitions'. Some already saw a new superstition in the making. For years Froude had been wondering if Huxley could 'elevate Evolution into a theory which will satisfy the eagerness of the imagination' while making it an ethical foundation for life. If so, 'then science has the world in its hands. If not, I cannot shake off the fear that we may have another era of . . . superstition before us'.[5]

And so the *Origin* had come of age. Evolution, the word and the deed, was accepted. As partial proof of it, the Metaphysical Society wound itself up. Huxley said that its top-heavy protagonists had embraced one another to death and 'died of too much love'.[6] But 'voluntary euthanasia' was the only course with the revolution complete. The issues they had thrashed out had become clear-cut and the protagonists stalemated. The painful birth pangs of the first industrial revolution were over; Dissent was emancipated; the 'Scientist' was established. The social changes that carried Darwinism were complete.

The issue now was less the fact of evolution than Darwin's originality. That was the point scored by Samuel Butler. His *Evolution Old and New* made Darwin steal the credit from his evolutionary forebears by an 'intellectual sleight of hand' and then insult them with his mindless universe. Butler liked a row. A gifted writer who craved Rome's 'conservative stronghold' (and only wished the Pope would give up miracles), a Pantheistic Lamarckian who enjoyed Mivart's put-down of the *Origin* as 'puerile', he had Huxley's sort of incendiarism. 'Has Mivart bitten him and given him Darwinophobia?' asked Huxley. 'Its a horrid disease and I would kill any son of a [*drawing of bitch*] I found running loose with it without mercy'. Not that Huxley would let Darwin do the culling. He was too protective of his untarnished image. 'If I say a savage thing, it is only "pretty Fanny's way"', Huxley once told him, 'if you do, it is not likely to be forgotten'. But they thought Butler was craving notoriety and refused to rise. It angered Butler even more to be ignored like his pre-Darwinian evolutionists. And for Huxley 'the best thing that could happen is that he should get madder'.[7] Butler never knew that Huxley was behind the boycott, but he did know that the bishops posed no threat: 'Men like Huxley and Tyndall are my natural enemies'.

With evolution commonplace, it was also time for Huxley to remake his own discipline – palaeontology. He remade it as the inductive foundation of evolution. The *Times* editor, Thomas Chenery (another dinner guest), recruiting the best pens to broaden the paper's political base, had him show what he meant – show how our spyholes on to the past had enlarged, to reveal the cavalcade of life in its true evolutionary light. Huxley peered through, to see the tapirs, rhinos and horses converge in the past, the lungfish and coelacanths close ranks, the birds merge with the gracile dinosaurs – like the branches of a tree traced to the stem. It was so obvious that 'if the doctrine of Evolution had not existed' the modern 'palaeontologist would have had to invent it'.

This planetary lifeline provided a secure anchorage for an uncertain age. Huxley's Church Scientific, with its canonizations and demonizations, invited a sublimated form of worship. He talked in parables. At the Working Men's College, he retailed Voltaire's legend of the Babylonian Zadig, who predicted the sex, size and stance of missing royal pets from their tracks (which left the 'magi with the desire to burn' him, seeing their ruin in his 'carnal common sense'). In the same way Huxley's own caste of Zadigs had told of five-toed horses browsing the Eocene foliage before a single bone had been seen. Science's 'retrospective prophecies' showed that its mundane powers could appear magical.[8] Huxley gave no sense of the long training required before a tyro could actually understand fossil bones in an evolutionary way. His rhetoric played up the self-evident, the transcendence of common sense. Evolution was the Victorian revelation, its prophets the new magi.

'Huxley is the king of men!' Darwin told Marsh, *Eohippus*' stable keeper. Huxley relished his role as Darwin's Protector, and the students recognized it, even if none had ever seen Darwin. Each day the Professor briskly entered his class (about 90-strong now), with an oppressive expression, starting the lecture before he reached his chair. Then one day all changed. He ambled in with a bearded stranger, Huxley leading, chatting, pointing out the new apparatus. 'Darwin was instantly recognized by the class . . . and sent a thrill of curiosity down the room, for no one present had ever seen him before'. Darwin's blue eyes were beaming, emitting a saintly 'benevolence', recalled a student, and Huxley's 'piercing black eyes . . . were full of admiration, and at the same time protection of his older friend'.[9]

It wasn't only the *Origin* Huxley was celebrating, but his own silver wedding. He liked anniversaries, he told Darwin, 'being always minded to drink my cup of life to the bottom'. He didn't need excuses. A steady stream of politicians, littérateurs, artists and scientists graced his 'Tall Teas'. There might be the Tyndalls to talk Physics, Alma-Tademas to talk Art; the US Ambassador James Lowell to hammer out a Transatlantic copyright agreement, and Henry James, agreeing to make it known to American authors.[10] The intimate circles of 30 years had become a galactic spiral, and among the risen stars Huxley interspersed the small asteroids – perhaps his 'clever' American lab worker Emily Munn, or the 'pleasant . . . & well informed' Henry Fairfield Osborn, who would take the 'Huxley method' back to Princeton to create the future nucleus of a distant galaxy.[11]

By contrast, the relatives were walking embarrassments and segregated to their own parties. Those that could walk, that is. The 'enormously stout & very emotional' Polly, brother George's widow, was flying high, disgusting Hal and engrossing the children with her pie-eyed antics (woozy on her three daily bottles of the morphine-based sedative 'chlorodyne' – an addict, clearly[12]). Ellen had crashed: the latest policeman to evict her after she had 'neglected & beaten' her grandchild '& pawned every thing' found her 'tipsey in bed'.[13] The boy eventually died and she begged more money to bury him. Not even Nettie's secret cheques could now save the 69-year-old from starving in a coffee-house.

The children remained Huxley's strength. Rachel at 17 was about to join her sisters at the Slade when Mady made the break. Her lot was 'easy & pleasant' in Chelsea, working on a painting already acclaimed by Alma-Tadema. The highly-strung Mady was Huxley's real heir. 'She was not only beautiful, with a strong likeness to her father', said the *Illustrated London News*, 'but she had genius'. And devilment. This picture, 'The Sins of the Father', was hung at the Academy as she turned 21 and sold before it went on public show.[14] To her father's horror, for it showed Nettie and 14-year-old Ethel gambling with cards. And 'the father' a good evangelical who held betting in abhorrence! Later, Mady's nude lying lasciviously on a beach had one outraged lady at the Grosvenor Gallery exhorting the subject, 'Get up you slut, and dress yourself'.[15] Artistic licence and Huxley latitude had combined to breed a sensation-loving New Woman, the sort who raised eyebrows by riding atop the open buses.

The loss of four more teeth under laughing gas left Darwin's bull-dog a toothless old hound. A new set of false teeth saw Hal off on holiday to south Devon in August. The more the old man craved escape from the 'workaday harness', the more he succumbed to the 'exquisite views of hill & dale & sea under the louchest of cloud flecked blue skies'. He would walk for miles with Nettie and then lie on top of the red cliffs in the evening sun. It seemed symbolic of their autumn years. But he could never escape the work, and interminable dissections of Cape lobsters were interrupted by endless Home Office or India Office calls to discuss compulsory vaccination or ways of improving Indian agriculture.[16]

As Huxley slowed, the age seemed to rush past. His had once been a hectic life driven by steam. Others saw the new technology as symptomatic of an age out of control, overridden by great imper-sonal forces. Every August saw the awful crashes, after the summer heat buckled rails; and they were topped in 1879 by the terrible Tay

Bridge disaster, when a train careered off the track during a storm, killing everyone in a 'mighty crush of iron & humanity'.[17] Instead of the carnage being Providential, deaths were becoming statistical, insurance problems, part of the randomness of a Darwinian order.

The big institutions were already installing Siemens dynamos. Spottiswoode had two to light the Royal Society, but then Siemens was a Fellow. The rich were fitting them at home, despite the danger here too. Mrs Spottiswoode fell and dislocated her shoulder while showing off her electric lights to Huxley.[18] Technology was impinging on life. It was exciting, frightening, new. Huxley wasn't asserting science's cultural hegemony against Theology and the Humanities alone. His harping on the integrity of pure science in education was as much a reaction to the overpowering threat of technology, precisely because it was so successful. Of the two, only science could enable us to evaluate life and its problems, to usher in the moral reformation, to criticize beliefs – in short to challenge Classics as the stamp of the cultured man.

'Science and Culture' was his theme at the opening of Josiah Mason's Science College in Birmingham on 1 October 1880. Birmingham, that national showpiece of social engineering: 'parked, paved, assized, marketed, gas-and-watered and *improved*'. Chamberlain's city cried out for Huxley's scientific legitimation. And how alike were Chamberlain and Huxley, as became apparent when the politician turned up at Marlborough Place for tea – frank, with that ironic look and cynical turn of Scriptural phraseology, mated to a Church-disestablishing sense and attention to public duty.[19] Chamberlain had demanded a liberating education to unite the classes, and Josiah Mason was realizing it, putting up £180,000 for the new science college.

Mason had come up the hard way. Starting on Kidderminster's streets selling cakes, he had ended with a factory producing four million steel-nibbed pens a week. His wealth was financing a Dissenting 'guerilla force' in applied science, according to Huxley. The Birmingham faithful gave Huxley a podium to justify Science's enlightening role against the Oxbridge Classicists, those 'Levites in charge of the ark of culture'. His success in breaking the Classical mould – in pitting hands-on experience against Latin learning – was finally being reflected in curriculums from Clifton to Eton. Indeed, Matthew Arnold, so supportive for so long, was beginning to sense an all-devouring monster and to reassert literature's humanizing aspect. But the industrial Midlands was standing up for itself. Granting that 'culture' gave us the means to criticize life and society,

Huxley wondered whether Greek and Judaic literature did the job. Wasn't an expansive science, with its anti-authoritarian spirit, its child's innocence before the 'fact' and its ethical obligations towards free expression, the supreme critic? And didn't it provide a devastating critique of this ancient literature itself? That was intellectual manna to Mason's Trust, which had excluded 'mere literary education' from its college.

Huxley was in his constituency, among Unitarian factory bosses and social engineers. He spoke to them all. The manufacturer was told that the learned 'seek for truth not among words but among things'; rational Dissent was reassured that science shuns the dogmatic Word and makes a democratic appeal to Nature. Huxley was in his muddy boots, moving the centre of the world, making the dead Oxbridge outer planets revolve round the solar furnace of the Black Country. And where better to harmonize class relations, to teach 'the capitalist and the operative' that the 'common principles of social action' were an 'expression of natural laws'?[20] Never would he give Nature such a social spine again. Even now, the socialist clouds were gathering.

The first spots of rain could be felt. Within weeks he was helping Darwin arrange a pension for Alfred Wallace. They all worried about the implacable old chap's spiritualism, which had to be concealed.[21] While his socialism was unmentionable even among themselves. Wallace, the rank outsider, the President of the Land Nationalization Society, was already touting the American Henry George's *Progress and Poverty* as the most 'original book of the last twenty years', with its cure for chronic poverty in the common ownership of land. Not for him Darwin's Malthusian defence of property as the honing stone of social fitness.[22] It would be a few years before scientific socialism flowered in Britain, but Wallace was already looking forward to the operatives harvesting the full crop.

Huxley was thinking more of the fish harvest as he did his own bit for the sluggish economy. He was at home during Christmas 1880, supposedly working on shrews, but contemplating the expense as the water pipes froze. With the door blocked by a snowdrift, he took to his desk, trying to earn more, writing on education for the *Times*,[23] putting his essays into a new volume, *Science and Culture*. Hack work was still a necessity with his lecturer's pay seeping through the vast pyramid of dependent relatives.

Two days before Christmas the Government stepped in. Gladstone's radical Home Secretary, Sir William Harcourt, was for positive discrimination, securing jobs for the scientists. He offered Huxley the Inspectorship of Fisheries, and then fought the Treasury for £700 a year and lightened his duties to make the offer attractive. After all the unpaid seats on Royal Commissions Huxley was at last offered a decent supplementary income. *Punch* saw the radicals finding jobs for the boys in its skit on the oilskinned 'Professor Huxley, LL.D., F.R.S., £.s.d.' The *Athenaeum*'s, too, was a 'carping' announcement. But, he explained to Darwin,

> whereas for the last twenty years I have been obliged to make as much again as my official income in order to live decently & do justice to my children – the new appointment . . . will about do that business & relieve me from the necessity of bread-making.[24]

'So three cheers for Harcourt'. Nettie rejoiced at the end of the scrounging 'to make up enough', little realizing how much work the new job would entail. Thus Huxley settled part-time in another set of rooms with a prestigious Whitehall frontage. Afternoons would be spent at the Home Office, listening to fisheries deputations and Billingsgate fishmongers, followed by weeks on the rivers and coasts, investigating pollution and dwindling stocks. The job might have been created under the Salmon Fisheries Act of 1861 but he told his son that 'you are not to expect salmon to be much cheaper just yet'.[25] And in late 1880 Huxley's remit was much wider.

The post was given him by a Government hopelessly bogged down on the Irish question. As Irish peasants starved and 10,000 tenant farmers were evicted during a year of plummeting agricultural prices, Fenian terrorism increased. Gladstone had failed to pass a Coercion Bill compelling landlords to compensate evicted tenants, and was even now alienating back-bench Liberals (no less than Huxley[26]) by drafting a new Land Bill. Britain needed to increase yields during the Depression, including fish, and part of Huxley's job was to study fish diseases and increase North Sea catches. He had no time for those who feared the depletion of stocks from over-fishing (although he did extend in-shore restrictions, because too many lobsters and crabs were clearly being taken).

No sooner was the Inspector's job secure than there was more money in the offing. The old solicitor Anthony Rich was so taken with Darwin's emissary that he added a codicil to his will bequeathing Huxley his house on the Worthing coast, as a base 'for your Fishery work'. The canny Darwin, a wealthy absentee landlord, reckoned that Huxley could realize £3,000 on the lot. But it was the generosity which struck Huxley. 'If all the sea & fresh water fishes together had tumbled on to my head I could not have been more astonished'. Nettie was over the moon, even if Hal saw this particularly 'tough old gentleman . . . outliving his legatee'.[27]

It seemed likely given Huxley's tearing lifestyle. Added to his other work, he was dissecting herrings and pilchards, taking shipments of diseased salmon (and taking abuse from fishermen for being too 'scientific' and un-practical), studying the Black Country's river pollution or standing at exhibitions 'until my back is broken'.[28] Everything had to be fitted around fish. Robert Browning persuaded him to let the realist painter Alphonse Legros paint his portrait, but time permitted only a single sitting. Squeezing more hours for the inevitable Boehm bust was as hard. Edgar Boehm's self-confident statues dominated imperial London, and everyone tried to slow Huxley to a speed the sculptor could capture. It took a year and still did not do him justice. But then it had to be fitted around research, Home Office bureaucracy, and dashes to seaside inns to listen to rancorous old fisherfolk.[29] Every family jaunt – to Worthing to the delight of the lonely old bachelor Mr Rich, or a day return from Waterloo with Herbert Spencer – had to be wrung out of a tight schedule.

Huxley never knew his limits. The archetypal scientific civil servant found that Commissions were endemic in his constitution. The word from Lord Spencer that they wanted him on yet another – to examine the medical qualifications offered by Britain's 19 licensing bodies and establish a uniform licensing control by the State – gave him more work and no pay and chopped up his holiday on Lake Windermere still further.[30] As the State encroached more on every aspect of life, the scientist was penetrating deeper into the byzantine bureaucracy of the State.

By the time he got back to Windermere after delivering the last day's lecture to the Seventh International Medical Congress, Nettie threw up her hands: 'Poor darling! he looked so worn & tired'. Holidays were now patchy affairs, but Nettie knew that even a few days in the 'peaceful beauty & sweet air will do him good'. It also gave him time to catch up with Len. Despite Jowett's goading essay topics on the origin of morality in the individual and the race – giving the Professor's son his evolutionary rope[31] – there was no hanging a young Huxley. Len had gone over totally to the Classics. Each term Jowett had pronounced him better, and at Windermere came the news that he had got his First at Oxford. He had gone over to the enemy in another way. From Windermere he was cycling to nearby Rydal, where he was sweet on Matthew Arnold's niece Julia.

By contrast, the old seminaries were trying to tilt towards science. They were struggling to come to grips with an alien culture. Cambridge succeeded, and Huxley designed Trinity College's Fellowship exam, building an unprecedented three days of practicals into it to ensure 'that the College shall have either a good man or none'. With science came a new rigour. Struggling was the operative word for Oxford. But he had allies in place. The Broadest of Churchmen Revd George Bradley – like Stanley, a good intellectual friend (Huxley had put him up for the Athenaeum) – also took his advice on Science Fellowships. With these clergymen the broad and agnostic churches developed an ecumenical spirit. It showed in the Huxleys' 'great grief' at Stanley's funeral in 1881. 'No one can replace him', said Nettie, 'not one'.[32] But one man could. Another of his ilk would keep Westminster Abbey's door open to the agnostic scientists: George Bradley.

The *Essays and Reviews* set – that gifted group of rationalist clergy – were now powerful and making overtures. When the Linacre Professor George Rolleston died word was flashed to the Huxleys. Mrs Rolleston was 'out of her mind' from the trauma, making the funeral 'one of the most tragic scenes' Huxley had ever witnessed. 'We have been so mixed up in this woe', explained Nettie (Rolleston's daughter Rosie had recently been staying at Marlborough Place). Jowett doubted that the plummy Rolleston had ever really had 'the spirit of a Scientific man' – but he knew who was its living incarnation. The day after the death the Oxford liberals offered Huxley the chair. Having lured Len to Oxford, Jowett thought his father's acceptance would be the 'very best thing that could happen to the University'. There would be no sniff of '"odium theologicum": Nous avons change tout cela'. But they appreciated the impudence of asking a London intellectual to deign to grace Oxford – let alone be assessed for an anatomy chair by the Archbishop of Canterbury![33] Huxley was a Londoner through and through: the modern Babylon had the vibrancy, the science, arts, the clubs; it was the revolving hub of the Empire. The dank seminarian surroundings would never have suited. Of course he politely declined.

The maudlin Nettie was lapping on the edges of agnosticism herself now, only ebbing away at the thought of extinction. 'The old question', she mused on Rolleston's death, 'Wherefore this world, its creatures?' Do we all just 'shrivel up'? Does destiny lie 'in some sun', '& what is the good of it all . . . if we with all our aspirations are to perish for evermore, only living on through the race . . . And yet in spite of all these feelings, I have faith that all is wisely planned, however inexorable its details'. And the Victorian grand matriarch threw up her hands in Christian exclamation, '& any way I have my work to do, part of which is submission, the hardest part of all'.[34] In duty she could agree with her husband.

With the offers coming in, South Kensington opportunely increased the incentive for their own man. The next month, August 1881, 'after 9 years of shilly shally on the part of Gov.' the 'Science Schools' was renamed 'The Normal School of Science' (Huxley's idea, after the French *École Normale*). It became independent of the Geological Survey, all fees went to the government and the professors were put on fixed salaries. Huxley officially became the 'Professor of Biology' and Dean of the School. It was a dignified title which simply meant more work, but he milked it for all of its ecclesiastic worth. Don't you know, he told Donnelly, 'that a letter to a Dean ought to be addressed "The Very Revd."'? The school was shaping up. It wasn't training 'scientists', but creating the middle-class infrastructure upon which corporate science could develop. The *Prospectus* saw its clientele as the future science teachers and industrial managers.[35] Hal's son Harry with his mechanical bent would join them for a few terms, before switching to surgery as a career.

The bribes increased. Would Huxley like the cushy Mastership of University College, Oxford (£1,200 tax free, a house and 'no fixed duties'), made vacant when Bradley left for Westminster Abbey? That said it all. The Masters, usually clergymen, corruptly sinecured as many saw it, had done little to manage their colleges. Gripped by reaction, seized by an anti-science movement as Depression and radicalism racked the country, the University had dropped 'behind the general current of thought', and reformers implored Huxley to drag it towards the twentieth century. But his name wasn't for sale. Nor could he swap the 'inestimable freedom' of London for a cloistered existence. 'I do not think I am cut out to be a Don nor your mother for a Donness', he explained to Len. Still, his astonishment was unfeigned, 'and I begin to think I may yet be a Bishop'. Astronomic sums, pulled out of hats, failed to shift him. Agassiz at Harvard supposed it was no use offering 'say $10,000 a year for the benefit of your presence'.[36]

'I find I am regarded by the outside world as a sort of King-Maker', he said. Certainly the eternal acolyte Michael Foster – in 1883 elected as Cambridge's first Professor of Physiology – was ready to 'follow your bidding'. As Huxley tried to clear some of the decks by resigning from his Working Men's College and his office at the Royal Society, Foster was ready to keep the Secretary's cushion warm.[37] But still Huxley had more livings than was good for a man. As he let the chair go in 1881, the Fisheries Inspector had to set off for a cold Christmas in the Welsh valleys. It was like the old days, marching along riverbanks, except for 16-year-old Harry in tow. The man famous for his elegant essays was a very muscular littérateur: with an epidemic of salmon disease, father and son walked 'ten miles between 3 pm & 5.30' each day, examining infected fish. He discovered the fungal cause of the sores, and the growing culture in his lab led to his prediction that he would soon be able 'to furnish Salmon Disease wholesale, retail, or for exportation'.[38]

The kingmaker considered others too hot-headed for a crown. Or, in Lankester's case, with screws so loose that they left the upper regions unstable. Having impetuously thrown over University College London for the lucrative Edinburgh Chair at Christmas 1881, despite Huxley's caution, the fickle Lankester about-faced before his induction, declared the University not to his taste, and returned south. Lord Rosebery at the Home Office had been wary of arming this loose cannon, and probably only appointed Lankester on Huxley's word that he was 'far & away the best man'. The fiasco left Huxley with egg on his face and Hooker reassessing their credibility as government advisers. The kingmaker penned an apologetic letter to the *Scotsman* and exonerated Rosebery. The throne had been made a laughing-stock, and the mad Regent's attempt to 'cut his own throat' did nothing for the scientists' carefully cultivated image.[39]

The new Dean was slitting more exotic throats. He had to run a school now, as well as his classes, and cram his research and his rivers in between. In February 1882 he was dismembering assorted sauropsids from tortoises to ostrich chicks, searching for the common features of bird and reptile lungs.[40] A new intake of scientific sappers was anatomizing this huge vertebrate group, while the General dissected a kiwi's lungs to refute Owen's claim that New Zealand's furry-feathered bird could be a link to the mammals.

He was ageing badly. 'I see it', said Nettie, '& it goes to my heart'. The work was overpowering him. The passing time was registered by a second grandchild. Jess named him Noel 'after our lost darling' (even now Nettie could barely 'bring my lips to utter the name'). And even more by an old messmate's painting of the donkey frigate *Rattlesnake*, recalling that 'peculiar kind of life' on the high seas. The days of self-taught warship scientists were long gone. Huxley had only to look around at his students dissecting in rows. A pump-and-grind drilling of graduates was breeding a new civil service. The memories made him feel 'confoundedly old – 150 at least, and I talk seriously of putting up the shutters, as it becomes a double bundled Grandfather to do'.[41]

As 72-year-old Darwin, the great evolutionary theorist, confounded the world with his *Formation of Vegetable Mould, Through the Action of Worms*, the redoubtable Emma came up for Noel's christening. She joined John Tyndall to renounce the devil. Jessie, like her mother, swore by this inoculation against sin, and Emma endorsed such preventive spiritual medicine. A heart attack at Christmas had left Darwin invalided into her care. Her home remained a sanatorium, where she ministered to her old husband, wretched with angina pains and fainting fits. His life was emptying of experiments, and he 'looked forward to Down graveyard as the sweetest place on earth'. Huxley sent his latest collection, *Science and Culture*, with its plea for technical education and celebration of the *Origin*'s Twenty-First. But it was the *tour de force* on 'Automatism' that bucked the old man up. He saw his disciple going on 'ad infinitum to the joy & instruction of the world'.[42] But his own day was done.

A seizure on the Sandwalk in March 1882 had Darwin lurching into the house to collapse in Emma's arms. Morphia eased the pain, but the attacks left him decrepit and frightened. Huxley tried to be cheery as he advised on the cleverest young doctors. As always your words are the 'real cordial to me', Darwin wrote on 27 March. 'I wish to God there were more automata in the world like you'.[43] Those were the last words to his disciple of 30 years.

The letter dropped through Huxley's door on Thursday afternoon, 20 April 1882. Frank Darwin concealed his grief in the clinical details:

> He died yesterday afternoon about 4 o'clock; he was not unconscious except for the last $\frac{1}{4}$ hr. He had an attack in the middle of Tuesday night in which he had some pain which was continuous but not severe. He fainted and soon regained consciousness and remained in a condition of terrible faintness and suffered very much from overpowering nausea interrupted by retchings. He more than once said 'if I could but die'.

Trauma had left Emma 'very calm'. Frank, trying to give Huxley that desperate reassurance he needed, added, 'how often I have heard him express his affectionate regard for you. We all feel your friendship was an unvarying cause of real happiness to my father'.[44]

Darwin was dead. It had been almost 40 years since he had confessed his 'murder' – his belief in evolution – to that other sea-dog Joseph Hooker. The years had firmed their friendship into something immutable, and the shock left Hooker 'utterly unhinged'. He was incapable even of penning a few words for *Nature*. As Hooker collapsed at the thought, Huxley buried his grief in action. The consummate politician, he went into conclave with Darwin's cousin Francis Galton, agreeing on the cultural import of a public burial for this 'royal character', as Galton had it – for the man who had delivered up a new Nature for the new priesthood. He had died, fêted abroad but unrecognized at home; even now his body lay in a rough oak coffin ready for interment in Downe churchyard. As Huxley said, '50 or 100 years hence it would seem absolutely incredible to people that the state had in no way recognised his transcendent services to Science'. On Friday night Huxley sought to remedy this. At the Athenaeum he and Spottiswoode talked to Canon Farrar of Westminster Abbey (Huxley's old supporter on scientific schooling) about the ultimate recognition. Meanwhile Lubbock, another of Downe's great folks and now MP for London University, whipped up Liberal support in the Commons. The night-time plotters brought off a coup to deposit the agnostic in the Abbey. The alliance of Broad Church and liberal science sealed 'the Westminster Abbey business', Huxley informed Hooker.[45] Dean Bradley, who had tapped Huxley's brains and tipped him as his Oxford successor, gave his blessing.

Grand pall-bearers were summoned: the Dukes of Argyll and Devonshire (head of Huxley's influential Commission) and Lord Derby. 'I have written to Lowell [Huxley's friend, the American Ambassador] & Sir JH telegraphs consent', George Darwin told Huxley. He added embarrassingly: 'It has suddenly flashed across me that Wallace is a man whom it w^d be gracious to ask to be a pall-bearer. What do you think. The only objection that I know of is that H. Spencer might think it more his place'.[46] Huxley knew that it would be hard to lure Spencer into the Abbey, let alone to the altar. And so Wallace, that perennial afterthought in the Darwin story, prepared to bear the body. The bells pealed in Darwin's praise, and the *Times* declared the Wilberforce clash in 1860 so much ancient history. While sermons up and down the country talked of Natural Selection fulfilling Divine Destiny, Huxley dashed off a chivalrous leader for *Nature*, mourning the saintly naturalist who had captured the heart of Christendom

And so the rough box gave way to a magnificent coffin. On Wednesday 26 April the X-Club, Huxley, Hooker, Spottiswoode and

Lubbock, bore it in solemn procession, arms locked with the Church (Farrar) and their Lords. Past a black-draped Nettie and her boys – Leonard was Darwin's godson – and on in sombre procession to the north-east corner of the nave, beneath Sir Isaac Newton's monument. The aristocracies of birth, spirit and intellect were proclaiming their faith in evolution as a preserver of the social order and a provider of future glory. Perhaps, the *Times* surmised, the 'Abbey needed it more than it needed the Abbey'. In the canonization they had snatched the body from the heretics: the Moncure Conways, the old Chartist leaders, all there, in the back rows, radicals who might have appropriated it for more subversive ends.

Canon Farrar invited Huxley to his 7 pm. service that Sunday to hear the final benediction. The ascent of the liberal clergy gave science its spiritual recognition. As the religious press praised Darwin's exemplary character, they linked conventional mores and social stability to his Malthusian gospel. That gospel of struggle and reward had become the sacred book of the liberal meritocracy. Darwin's thought reappeared 'under a hundred disguises in works on law and history, in political speeches and religious discourses', said Morley. 'If we try to think ourselves away from it we must think ourselves entirely away from our age'.[47] Darwin's clever, competitive, uncharitable Whig-workhouse motor for moving life forward summed up the century.

In the will there was £1,000 for Huxley, and the day after hearing of this tax-free legacy he started repaying. Iron Dukes had their imperial monuments as the conquerors of nations; why not one to the fallen hero for his 'conquests over the realm of Nature'? Huxley primed the pump with 10 guineas and even Spencer managed £2. The fund overflowed as word spread world-wide: 2,300 subscriptions came from Sweden alone and the Finns raised £94. Within a year they had £3,300,[48] enough for a marble statue by Boehm, who made the old recluse a commanding public figure, something he never was in life.

With deification, the very scraps that Darwin hoarded became prized. In life he had been George Romanes' father confessor, absolving the desperate sceptic, whose godless cosmos had lost 'its soul of loveliness'. Romanes craved the evangelical comfort of evolutionary certainty. It showed in his anguished *Candid Examination of Theism*, a book that became the talking point at Huxley's 'Tall Teas'. It showed in the way he brought morality firmly under the yoke of selection. He probed the minds of savages and the insane to prove that 'man and brute have much more in common . . . morally, than is dreamt of'. Darwin's death shattered the adulatory Romanes. His was 'the sorrow of a heart broken as it never has been before'. Not even his own father's passing had left 'a desolation so terrible'. In his blinded state he planned his own memorial. Darwin had passed on the 'Instinct' chapter from his manuscript *Natural Selection*. Romanes now planned to publish it. Huxley, invited to a reading at the Linnean Society, thought this a 'crude & unfinished piece' which would do Darwin an injustice.[49] 'Colossal', Romanes had called Darwin's intellect; every snippet carried the mark of genius. But the years had given Huxley a fuller understanding. A 'clear rapid intelligence', yes – but 'tenacious industry' backed by a 'passionate honesty' had been Darwin's strength. The probing Socrates, disdaining the clouds, had humbly ploughed the earth to find 'a great truth trodden underfoot'. Darwin's published works were his epitaph.

Darwin's death set a sombre tone for events at home. Mady had been the highly-strung daughter, the one 'painfully attached' to Nettie, clinging and crying if she were sent to Downe or the Armstrongs. The insecure daughter with the knife-edged emotions: she shared her father's brilliance and she suffered his psychology. In the Spring she collapsed: 'first she lost her sight, & for three months, c^d not . . . read or write & even had her food cut up for her'. Then came stomach problems, and the 'racking headaches'.[50] No one at first appreciated the danger for the girl with the Pre-Raphaelite looks.

Huxley ploughed on with the Darwin Memorial as she regained her sight. Poignantly, her old Pre-Raphaelite mentor John Everett Millais had him preside over the Artists Benevolent Institution dinner. Here struggling Science sympathized with struggling Art, and Huxley's growing anti-Darwinian belief that 'blood is thicker than water, but sympathy is thicker than blood' netted £1,600 for the orphans.[51] But from now on Mady's tightrope walk would transfix him as he widened the divide between a harsh Darwinian Nature and benign human ethics.

It was a sad Huxley who gave his Summer course in 1882. Among the 31 teachers dissecting rabbit capillaries was the chameleon-like Annie Besant, a 35-year-old who had left her parson husband to become an atheist missionary. Science had always seemed liberating to staff writers on the *National Reformer* like Besant. Huxley found her a 'well-conducted lady-like person', and 'very hard-working'.[52] But Tory MPs took exception to her penny blasts on republicanism, atheism, female emancipation and worse, and prevented her from receiving her teacher's pay, even though qualified from the Science and Art Department. It was a sign of the sharpening antagonisms of the 1880s.

The day Huxley's lab course finished Frank Balfour was killed in an Alpine fall. It seemed a bleak end to a bleak Summer. Seven weeks earlier Balfour had been given a special Chair of Animal Morphology at Cambridge and with his death Pope Huxley saw the demise of his Cardinal successor. And so his short life passed from rumour to legend in a brilliant flash. Nettie had asked Balfour as he set off to be especially careful. 'To me he was very dear', she said, 'as well as to Hal'.[53] Huxley, bogged down in interminable Fisheries work, could not get the image of Balfour's frozen body out of his mind.

The bleakness was affecting. He moved towards his own bitter Winter probing diseased oysters. For a time it was fish with everything, lectures on eels for the workers, herring for his students, oysters for the Royal Society. He managed to write on the smelt's oviducts, but growing paperwork ruled out any more scientific memoirs for four years. The fisheries were taking over his life. Free days would see him dissecting his way from primitive sturgeons to modern salmons; Christmas caught him in a sou'wester gazing from a desolate Cromer hotel onto the 'wintry sea'.[54] And then his briny face would reappear in class for lectures on fish anatomy.

Work was his anaesthetic, but he kept awakening to think of Mady. She had regained some strength and had become pregnant, giving hope that motherhood would soothe her spirit. But losing the baby only heightened her hysteria. Nettie, whose nightly thoughts were of her own Noel, watched in 'sickening anxiety' as Mady's 'nerves began to give way'. She would get 'despairing' notes from Jack and rush to Chelsea to find her 'grown darling sobbing bitterly, very frightened at the constant palpitations she suffers from'.[55] Nights camped by her bedside were wearing Nettie down.

Huxley's world had forged closer to Mady's. On Royal Academy nights the eminent would pinch his sleeve to enquire of her. Jack, in between arranging country convalescences and live-in nurses, was painting the definitive portrait of the battered patriarch, skull in hand, shadows disguising his worried eyes. As Hal's old sparkle vanished, one ontologically-confused artist 'remarked that it was a better likeness of me than I was'.[56] So close was the scientist now to the Academy professors that he even sat for group portraits.

Jack's painting was hanging behind him as he talked at the Academy banquet on 5 May 1883. It was part of his continuing engagement with Matthew Arnold over the nation's education. That engagement had a literal aspect now: Len had continued to manoeuvre adroitly around his intimidating father. His betrothal to Julia, the daughter of fellow Balliol man Thomas Arnold – Matthew's brother – rather shocked them. He was too young, too aimless, and they made him promise a long engagement. But it was his filial way of making Matthew Arnold's point. Jowett had encouraged him to become a master at a public school, so Len took a post unannounced at Charterhouse.[57] He too was escaping a domineering Science. The oddity of Professor Huxley's eldest son becoming a Classics master to the upper classes was striking, but Pater never gave any signs of disappointment.

Arnold at a former banquet had looked sceptically on Science, as it barged forward to rival Art and Literature 'in the pursuit of the eternal and unseizable shadow, beauty'. But Huxley continued to soothe the spirit. Science was no 'monster rising' to devour 'the Andromeda of Art'. Or, if a monster, it was 'a very *débonaire* and gentle monster'. Nor was he among the 'scientific Goths and Vandals' who would desecrate other forms of culture. The real vandals were those Classical seminaries at Oxford and Cambridge, which still shunned modern English studies. That gents could be turned out 'epopt and perfect', and ignorant of the past three centuries of literature or history, was 'a fraud practised upon letters'.[58]

Huxley would have science deep inside One Culture, not suzerain of a breakaway province. Evolution was secure by the 1880s, so there was no fearing a *rapprochement*. Indeed it was becoming necessary as Huxley pulled ethics out of Nature and offered it to the humanities. But with Arnold reasserting Art's role in a technocratic age, and the fight for educational resources during the Depression fuelling the Classical reaction of 'Young Oxford',[59] the cultural split only increased.

Spottiswoode died of typhoid in June 1883, the first member of the X to break ranks. Headstrong old men now, his X-colleagues rampaged like 'rogue elephants' around the body. Spottiswoode was one of 'us', and he died as President of the Royal Society. Busk was for social recognition in an Abbey burial, but Hooker hated 'touting for the Abbey graves' and was for saving 'poor Spottiswoode's bones', while the old bull Spencer simply gave an anti-clerical bellow. They reflected the nation's confusion. What was the Abbey, a State Pantheon or a Christian Shrine, the social Establishment or the Church Established? The two were no longer one, and the divorce was disorientating. In the end Spottiswoode, the Queen's Printer and stolid mathematician, was rather bizarrely buried there, but it threatened to 'smash the x completely'.

There would be no communal elephants' graveyard for the remaining rogues as they ambled off to their retirement homes. At 66 Hooker was waiting to 'throw off the trammels of official life' and retire from Kew. Darwin's £1,000 enabled him to plan a bigger house in six acres of Scots-pine country at Sunningdale in Berkshire, and to pay Huxley's son-in-law Fred Waller to build it. The Tyndalls' house too was 'going on prosperously' at Hindhead, atop the plummeting Devil's Punchbowl of the North Downs, and they too dreamt of 'escaping from London'.[60]

Spottiswoode's accolade said so much about these erstwhile dinner-conspirators. More *anciens honorables* than *enfants terribles* now. It was hard to believe that they were ever agitprop activists, looking at Princess Louise's screen embellished with their photo-silhouettes (courtesy of Mrs Spottiswoode). It was even harder to imagine it on looking at Mrs Huxley, making satin heliotrope dresses for her Court presentation. And at the Palace she found the new royals more *au fait* than the old Queen, with the Princess of Wales immersed in *Science and Culture*.[61] Few appreciated how much scientific agnosticism was being cut into the Establishment cloth. The *Times*, unable to credit it, misheard Bradley's funeral eulogy to say that Spottiswoode 'regarded Science as the "handmaid of religion"', where the Dean had really said that Spottiswoode 'never followed science in the spirit of that "often misused phrase"'![62]

And for a Dean to say it showed the temper of the times. But agnosticism was being sanctioned in the highest courts.

The Huxleys were still straddling worlds in 1883. Just how short the distance from the Royal court to the law court was shown by the letters in the post: would the agnostic champion raise his voice against 'cruel and barbarous sentence' – a year in Holloway jail – imposed on G. W. Foote for the blasphemous cartoons in his penny *Freethinker*? (He did, quietly, petition the Home Secretary with Leslie Stephen, Spencer and Llewelyn Davies on its severity, but he deplored Foote's own 'coarsely & brutally insulting' behaviour and gave the begging writers short shrift.)[63]

This was the Foote who lambasted the 'ghoul-like . . . twaddle of the clergy over Darwin's tomb', who made evolution the shell in the atheist's breech-loader – and who quoted the writings of Huxley and other 'high-class heretics' in his defence. But exactly why Huxley snubbed Foote's henchmen was revealed in the landmark ruling following the case. The Old Etonian Chief Justice Coleridge for the first time agreed that Christianity was *not* 'part of the law of the land'. Simply disavowing it was no longer an offence. How could it be with Jews and Unitarians having civil equality? He talked instead of the *manner* rather than the substance constituting a blasphemous libel. And since scurrility had always been abhorrent to Huxley, he could agree with the judiciary on Foote's offensiveness. While the bench would reciprocate by de-privileging Christianity. The Judge actually contrasted 'the great writers alive' who show

> a grave, an earnest, a reverent, I am almost tempted to say, a
> religious tone in the very attacks on Christianity itself, that
> shows that what is aimed at is not insult to the opinions of
> the majority of Christians, but a real, quiet, honest pursuit
> of truth. If the truth at which these writers have arrived is
> not the truth we have been taught . . . they are not to be
> exposed to a criminal indictment.[64]

Huxley's professional strategy was being sanctioned by the law. His tomes were legitimized, while the political atheism of the penny trash was outlawed. Foote seethed that 'respectable Agnosticism' got away scot free because it 'is more cultured'. Lord Coleridge was living up to his reputation. He had piloted the Bill abolishing the Anglican monopoly at Oxbridge and had succeeded Collier's father as Gladstone's Attorney-General. He was an FRS, inducted into the Royal Society by Huxley himself; more, he was a friend who relished Huxley's complimentary books.[65] Through this suave old boy, high society was throwing a protective cloak around its agnostic elite. It was redrawing the red line, redefining the class divide. It was permitting its aristocrats of intellect to question Christianity, while threatening rougher working-class attacks. The pact was sealed.

'The law's a hass', as Mrs Bumble said, but it was now Huxley's 'hass'. Never mind that his moral vision was leaving a trail of unemployable ex-clergymen – men who had seen it destroy their cosmic theodicy.[66] That might have lengthened the welfare queues, but it never threatened the social fabric. Quite the reverse, he was aligning agnosticism with conventional family pieties. Sixteen months before securing Darwin's place in the Abbey he had refused to press for George Eliot's plot in Poets' Corner. On that occasion he told Spencer that the Abbey was 'a Christian Church & not a Pantheon' and that her life was 'in notorious antagonism [to] Christian practice in regard to marriage'. Propriety before greatness. Sanctification would invite public muck-raking about her cohabitation with Lewes.

Such was old Dean Stanley's liberality that he would have taken her on Huxley's say-so. But Huxley refused to ask Stanley to read words she considered lies, and for which he would 'be violently assailed'. If 'peace & honour' were to 'attend George Eliot to her grave', hers should be the unconsecrated infidel plot in Highgate.[67] And that is where he stood over her coffin, one snowy December's day, this woman whose perceptions had long pierced his own armour. After 30 years he was still trying to unhitch freethought from free love, still trying to decontaminate agnosticism.

The realignment was accelerated by the militant upsurge on the streets. Huxley found himself outflanked by a wave of young agnostics led by the rationalist publisher Charles A. Watts. Watts & Co. had moved away from the *Freethinker*'s Bible-bashing to trade on agnosticism's respectability. It promised intellectual upward mobility; it was proven to penetrate the Establishment, and it was ripe for exploitation. Piracy was still part of street publishing: Watts canvassed Huxley's views and coolly printed his reply without leave in the first *Agnostic Annual* in November 1883. Huxley, outraged at the way 'that free thinkers "make free"', found himself 'paraded . . . as a "contributor" among as queer a crew as Jack Falstaffs'. But his imprimatur looked genuine: Watts had the man who had coined the word to dignify our ignorance about matters on 'which Metaphysicians & Theologians both orthodox & heterodox dogmatise'. The letter appeared on the *Annual*'s title-page. As Huxley had said, 'I have a sort of patent right in Agnosticism – it is my "trade mark" ',[68] and with his seeming endorsement the logo was passing to Watts' populist press.

Falstaff's crew had a flair for retailing science. They turned 'agnostic' into a buzz-word. Huxley lost control as the monthly *Agnostic* in 1885 preceded a spate of books capitalizing on the need for agnostic texts, all following *The Creed of a Modern Agnostic* by a black-smith's son with a London B.Sc., Richard Bithell. The *Secular Review* became the *Agnostic Journal* and 'Saladin' (Watts' satirical side-kick W. S. Ross) produced his apologetic *Why I am an Agnostic*. This was entrepreneurial agnosticism, given mass appeal by its rich blend with Spencer's synthetic evolution, itself the determinant of life, religion and ethics. Huxley's ascetic method lumbered under continuing accretions. The movement turned religious, with exhortations to worship the wondrous 'Unknowable'. Disciples even began plans for an Agnostic Temple in Brixton, where incantations on Nirvana as the evolutionary goal might be chanted. Watts '*must* be a lineal descendant of Watts' Hymns', Huxley steamed, 'nobody could be such a knave without pietistic blood in him'. For Huxley agnosticism wasn't a creed. It was 'the essence of Science', the sensual veil, the correlate of a knowledge-seeking method – making it a tenuous host for an Agnostic Temple. But he recognized the public thirst and knew that 'If there were a General Council of the Church Agnostic, very likely I should be condemned as a heretic'.[69] The revolution was consuming its leaders.

Watts' search for respectability had been a reaction to the atheist Charles Bradlaugh – the reviled street hero, the *National Reformer*'s founder, the former Dragoon Guard whose tactics were splitting the movement. Malevolent papers portrayed Bradlaugh as an 'Alpine bandit'; in fact he was a self-immolating, sad-eyed martyr to the cause, the evangelist of confrontation who invited howls of 'Kill the Infidel'.[70] He was still grabbing headlines, still in and out of court (a former solicitor's clerk, he knew all the tricks). As Northampton's new MP, he would be the first open atheist in Parliament. But not yet; the Sergeant-at-Arms was still barring his way, and inviting Tory MPs to throw him into the street.

Bradlaugh's was political atheism, a frontal assault on the privileges of Church and Throne. Huxley wearily restated his opposition to 'Bradlaugh & Co – For whom & all their ways & works I have a peculiar abhorrence'. Telling Watts that agnosticism undermines 'not only the greater part of popular theology but also the greater part of popular antitheology', he was fingering Bradlaugh. But philosophy meant nothing in the slums, and it was here that Bradlaugh had his impact. The atheists had about-faced on one pivotal issue: after a century of abusing the 'revolting' Malthus, they now accepted that population outran food supply. It explained Mrs Besant's horrifying statistic that a third of the children were dying in Britain's worst ghettos. The population had risen 3.4 million in a decade. London was growing at 1,000 a week and the East End was at crisis point. Exposés like *The Bitter Cry of Outcast London* in 1883 were shocking, but not as much as Bradlaugh's solution. If his 'Neo-Malthusians' now accepted Darwin's analysis of struggle and destruction, they deplored his assumption of its continuing necessity. If mouths outstripped food supply, decrease the mouths. 'Neo-Malthusian' became a euphemism for birth control – 'Bradlaugh & Co' were advocates of contraception to break the poverty trap. Besant's 6d worth of sexual advice and adverts for intimate appliances, *The Law of Population*, made the *Origin of Species* an argument for birth control.[71] For a few pence the atheists would supply 'one pound weight of Malthusian Leaflets', in an effort to end the perpetual-pregnancy condition of womenkind and raise the quality of life.

Darwin, the cocooned, wealthy patriarch, had feared that birth control would 'spread to unmarried women & would destroy chastity'. So did a genteel nation, which considered six months in jail quite fair for Bradlaugh and Besant. They received it for reprinting an old birth-control pamphlet *Fruits of Philosophy*, described on the Old Bailey charge sheet as 'indecent, lewd, filthy, bawdy and obscene', and Besant lost custody of her daughter. But the convicts never lost faith in rational science as a route to liberation. Besant had passed the first part of her London B.Sc. exams, taking honours in botany. Now, refused entry into the Botanic Gardens in Regent's Park for her practicals because of the 'opinions attributed to me', she begged Hooker let her come to Kew.[72] The fallout from the case was still being felt in May 1883 when even University College forgot its godlessness and banned Besant and Bradlaugh's daughter from its botany classes 'without reason'. Huxley signed a protest petition and summoned an extraordinary council meeting, on the pretext that this was an infringement of religious liberties. But privately he admitted that

> freedom of thought should be carefully distinguished from
> laxity in morals. Freethinking does not mean Free love . . .
> [and if the banned *Fruits*, which he had never read,
> undermined] the safeguards of sexual intercourse among
> unmarried people . . . we are out of the region of
> speculation and into that of practice – and I have no
> objection to her exclusion.[73]

Huxley was tying Darwinian agnosticism to middle-class values. It was a genteel stand, something he could luxuriate in, not a problem of agonizing death in the ghetto. He had to manoeuvre adroitly to champion 'philosophical freedom, without giving other people a hold for saying that I have identified with Bradlaugh'.[74] The Darwinians ensured the undefiled purity of Malthusian views, dreading Bradlaugh's sexual contagion which would rot the respectable evolutionary edifice.

Upholding the social conventions gave Huxley an air of moderation. He perfected the rhetoric of neutrality and balance. He said he had witnessed 'every form of human society from the uncivilised savage of Australia and the civilised savage of the slums' and still saw nothing to commend the 'somewhat over-civilised members of our upper ten thousand'. But in truth his professionals were becoming central to the Establishment's reforms, based on education and competition. He was functioning among the 10,000, but only the context shows how well. Wasn't his talk to the Eton boys on Nile geology early in 1883 innocence itself? Not if one looks at the radicals' condemnation of General Wolseley's recent defeat of the Egyptian nationalists. They slated this 'war of aggression' in Britain's Suez interests. By contrast Huxley was celebrating victory with a briefing to the future generals in the Eton Volunteer Corps, passing, in his slick 'physiographic' way, from the strategic history of the Nile to the geological explanation of its topography. Every General his own scientist, it was a simple message if Britain was to win 'the terrible [and ultra-Darwinian] game of war'.[75]

By tightening his grip on the Establishment he changed part of its nature. That was true of his own Presidential period. The Royal Society mace was beginning to look like the X's mascot. Huxley had heard the whispers, that 'Some time or other you ought yourself to be President'.[76] On Spottiswoode's death Huxley slid easily onto the throne as caretaker President. And so, at 58, he sat on the woolsack of the Scientific 'Lords', guardian of the *sacred penetralia*, staring at the mace in front of his massive Presidential chair. Oddly it was an anticlimactic moment, one Nettie almost feared.

And 'like Johnny Gilpin', Tom Huxley had 'little thought when he set out (some forty years ago) of running such a rig'. The rig had been run hard along a stony track. The last of his old Christian Socialist comrades, Frederick Dyster, guessed 'that a certain Lady is prouder of "Hal" . . . (if that be possible) than she was when I found her up to the elbows in a Devil fish' (on their honeymoon). Proud or no, Nettie was still 'dead against it'. Her worries over the extra work and financial strain gave Huxley 'a cold fit', even if the world's support was '"grateful & comforting" like Epp's Cocao'.

Science paralleled Parliament, whose Members were expected to finance themselves. This had always tipped the scales in favour of the grandees, who considered trusteeship of the nation's moral and material treasures part of their public calling. Noble Presidents could spend time and money, entertain lavishly and liaise with ministers. But just as more commoners took government posts, so the Royal Society was finishing with 'Lord Presidents'. The workers in the intellectual factory wanted 'to keep out [the rich] traders on the one hand and mere noblemen on the other'. Science needed no social sanction, nor should it dignify wealthy dilettantes. Huxley's term would be proof 'that a poor man – who does not mean either to entertain . . . one whit more than before – can hold the post'. The nobility of poverty was a nice principle, but it left a drooping Nettie wishing 'we were rich' with a budget for outside caterers.[77]

The press announcement on 6 July 1883 brought a note from Jim, not so mad that he couldn't congratulate Tom on the woolsack. 'The family is ennobled', he mumbled, as if in sad compensation for the drugs and drink: the unworldly son's science had provided a moral purity, just as in olden days the seminary boy had been the family beacon. 'You have now the highest scientific distinctions and will sit where Newton sat'. Huxley's control of the Upper House of Science was supported by 'all the younger & working' Fellows. The rumour that G. G. Stokes–called 'Gabriel' behind his back for his angelic Christian conservatism–might run in the November elections, backed 'by the "goodies" to keep such a d—d infidel ...out'[78], had the backbenchers raising such a 'howl' that Hal's interim period was made permanent. Nettie wailed the more.

Not without cause. The Chair automatically entailed new duties, including Trusteeship of the British Museum. But it also gave Huxley the ear of Prime Ministers and Privy Councillors. And he used it to see scientists honoured, not for great science – that came from 'the verdict of their peers' – but for public sacrifice. He plumed the hats of those who gave 'their knowledge energy time & money to the service of the country'. Roscoe became 'Sr'enery' for a life's work in Manchester, and, with Owen retired, Huxley slipped the courtly Flower into the Director's office at the Natural History Museum and recommended a title to match.[79] He had the gall of a cultural politician. With Owen out and Flower in, Huxley sensed the ultimate conquest. He was in charge of the Darwin Fund, with a Committee that included the Xs, 61 FRSs, five MPs, the legally-compliant Lord Coleridge and the theologically-acquiescent Dean Bradley. Thumbing his nose at Owen's statue of Adam, guarding the portal to this gothic Cathedral of Science, he suggested Darwin's shiny white statue take central place in the nave. And that piece of Darwinolatry concluded Evolution's institutional conquest of London.

The knights of science were taking their place alongside the great statesmen and military figures. But the man who had sacrificed most health and time to make the New Nature serviceable to the new State was Huxley, and the press continually announced his own honours. 'I think we will be "Markishes"', he laughed at the latest rumour, 'the lower grades are getting common'.[80] The jest oozed an uneasy contempt.

Nor would he succumb to Palace pressure to put Court favourites into the Royal Society. Rather, he tried to open the gates wider to careerists. His was an easy, open regime. The cold meeting room put on a friendlier face. Above his Chair in Burlington House Newton still gazed sternly, and the weary-looking Robert Boyle glared down in full-bottomed wig. But no bigwig solemnity for the new President. The young bloods were encouraged to turn the committee chamber into a smoking room and open the library in the evenings (this reflected a changing social composition, with fewer FRSs joining the London clubs). Foster brought in cosy chairs for 'Free & Easy' nights 'where they may do what they d— please'.[81] Stiff upper lips quivered. Huxley even tried the ultimate reform – to abolish fees altogether to level the field for the poorer Fellows. Armstrong offered £7,000 to start a fund, but matching it proved too hard and the scheme collapsed.

With his poor-toiler ethos Huxley invited Chamberlain to the anniversary dinner on 30 November. The railer against the idle rich who, 'like the lillies of the field . . . toil not', was putting his principles to work nationally as President of the Board of Trade. There was no more charismatic leader of the radicals. Chamberlain's National Liberal Federation lured many away from Gladstone. Morley was with them. He had left the *Fortnightly* and been elected by Armstrong's factory workers as Newcastle's MP. He was one of the affirmative-action intellectuals who called for religious liberty, free schools and land for the poor. Chamberlain's contempt for the G.O.M.'s tepid reforms rivalled Huxley's for his torpid piety. Huxley, 'who vies with the Tories in hating Gladstone', was ready to put 'Science . . . in league with the Radicals'.[82]

Chamberlain had once produced cheers for declaring a republic inevitable. With Morley sharing this republican strain, Liberal Federation thought infected the X. President Huxley sat in judgment on the immortal status of minor associations. The Meteorological Society wanted the *Royal* prefix, but Huxley's caucus thought that they should be 'content to worship in a Republican form'. This 'multiplication of "Royal" Societies is an evil', Hooker said; 'give us decent weather' and he would 'consider their claims not only to Royalty, but to Divine honours'.[83]

Quality of life was at the core of the new civic pride, and Huxley's school campaigns and fisheries work, combined with his suite of unremembered chairs, from economic entomology – looking at food pests – to the London Sanitary Protection Association – looking into drains – made the rational scientist the civic darling. For his own technocratic principles he was made a Freeman of the City of London in 1883, sponsored by the Salters Company. And while he took the freedom of the City, future cities were exercising a certain freedom in taking his name. Pioneers had carried it West; maps of the newest state, Dakota, showed a frontier town called 'Huxley'. Be thankful, joked Fiske, that it 'escaped the everlasting Yankee final syllable' and wasn't called 'Huxleyville'.[84]

The Summer produced posts like administrative plums, too juicy to turn down. Satiated, and still offered a seat on London University's Senate, he pushed it away because he would rarely be able to attend. But the Chancellor, that tactful old Whig Lord Granville, called his bluff:

> Clay the great whist player once made a mistake and said to his partner 'My brain is softening' the latter answered 'never mind, I will give you 10,000£ down for it, just as it is'.[85]

And on that principle they co-opted him. The University was leading the rolling revolution in higher education. This was Huxley's moment. The Senate had just started Graduate Teaching Diplomas, and a new D.Sc. by research thesis, and passed out its first woman in medicine. 'Haul down your flag', *Punch* told the men, as women took 10 per cent of the B.Sc. degrees – a fact which would liberalize the curriculums of the girls' schools. Huxley joined the other liberal patriarchs trying to cope.

By the time he faced the first woman D.Sc. in 1884 his stomach ached from all the plums. The Fisheries were drudgeries: paperwork, conferences, speeches and exhibitions left him 'dog-tired'. The man organizing D.Sc.s in his off-moments had drifted from his own research. Was this how he would end a 'misspent life'? How could it be 'frittered away in all this drivel'? As his automaton body ground to a halt from 'the awful friction' the epiphenomenal nightmare began.[86] He had become a 'yes' man; even as he sank in the Summer 1884 his gluttony led to more punishment.

Lankester's bulldozing agitation for a Marine Laboratory, similar to the Naples one, was paying off. He was summarily conscripting lords of the manor, scientists, the Fishmongers Company and anybody with money into a Marine Biological Association. Obviously he installed his father-in-science as President.[87] A sinking Huxley joked that he would do as little as possible to deserve the honour, but he stayed at the helm trying frantically to collect £10,000 to build a Marine Station at Plymouth.

'Huxley looks fagged', Hirst noted in his diary. Not even the Fenian bomb attacks in Pall Mall and Scotland Yard could shake

Huxley in his Home Office rooms. Exhaustion had got the better of him. 'I don't like to see him working like this', Nettie sighed as she watched him trudge between Commissions, Senates, Whitehall, the Royal Society, the Normal School and the Fisheries, while juggling 'tens & tens of letters' daily with their demands or their damnations; 'oh how I wish he c^d give up this rush'. Everything was suffering: the students only saw him in the lab once a week and he was beginning to lose contact. A cab would dash him from Whitehall to Kensington at night, where he would try to snatch half an hour for dissecting before staggering home at midnight. But depression left his scalpel hand leaden.

Trapped by a 'thousand and one entanglements', all he could think of was Mady. The birth of baby Joyce had left her in a 'deplorable state', nervous, her sight failing again as 'the old hysteria' returned: 'her mind is affected', admitted Nettie. She was 'a prey to gloom & horrors', and it left her father an emotional cripple. London became 'a perfect loathing' to him. He yearned for flight, escape, the old cathartic smell of wood-smoke. Nettie arranged continual trips to the Downs, or to country farms. Hal even hankered to buy one. 'How I long to live in the country', she said after each pick-me-up, '& so does Hal'. September was spent on Surrey's sandy heaths discussing his quitting work on his 60th birthday.

He had his last four teeth extracted, and the bulldog who had cut them on clerical opposition was reduced to mushy puddings. The mirror each morning revealed a sunken-jawed depressive. The Fisheries was a quagmire of 'Jackass' poachers and squabbling squires. He tried to rationalize the feeling of wastage and void, to subdue them by that famous scientific mind, but the thought of Mady's frailty brought nihilistic waves. Swamped, he saw the coming term's work as 'the death of me'. On 19 September he left for the Devon fisheries, to see if he could cast the blue devils into 'a herd of Cornish swine'. But he returned in 'terrible anxiety' about the girl. 'It is a pain eating into our hearts', Nettie admitted.[88] A few days later, on 1 October, he tried to start his lectures.

1885–1895

The Old Lion

27

Polishing off the G.O.M.

HUXLEY'S BREAKDOWNS were peculiar. A mental lethargy left him unable to face the world. He had no 'positive complaint', just a 'deadness that hangs about me'. His haggard looks had Matthew Arnold in tears after a chance meeting. The 'great anguish about Mady' had immobilized Hal again. And yet, ordered off to sunny climes, and told by his adoring superiors to '*at once* act upon Sir A Clarke's [sic] advice', he had the will to work his way to Venice. He should have been fighting through the snarled-up traffic to his office. Instead mid-October found him sitting in a gondola.[1]

Nettie remained, left with her own burden of organizing Rachel's wedding. She never forgot 'the agony of that time, Hal away, in torture of mind & weak in body', as she too 'lost hope'. A bleak telegram told them of Mady's total mental collapse, turning Hal into a silent 'wounded beast'. He slunk back for the wedding on 6 November. Rachel was marrying a blue-eyed civil engineer Alfred Eckersley, on a contract to build a railroad across southern Spain. But the wedding was a tortured dream: a flounce of feather-hatted bridesmaids, the shower of rice vexing the bride, Nettie in her Court dress trying to seat 90 to breakfast. By 3 o'clock it was all over and Rachel on her way to Spain. The worry returned as Nettie looked at Hal. 'Between him & Mady, my soul has been torn'. Like a typical depressive, Huxley was unable to cope with it in his daughter. The *Times* reported his flight, leaving the Fisheries men flummoxed. But Gladstone's Ministers agreed on the need for a 'Coercion Bill first in his case'.[2] Not that it proved hard to evict him from Britain.

The couple returned to Italy as Britain froze. They left Foster editing a new edition of the *Lessons in Elementary Physiology* and looking after affairs. He dropped in to Marlborough Place to find

Miss Nettie the 'mistress of the House doing accounts on the drawing room table'. And he took Sir Andrew's note to the Home Office and with Donnelly got Huxley's 'banishment ... prolonged till April'.³ And so two months' leave turned into six, giving the Lotus-Eaters time to roam.

Roam they did. From Locarno they took a steamer up Lake Maggiore to a chilly Pallanza. On they pressed, to the picturesque Verona, with its tombs of La Scala and monument to Dante.⁴ And on, to find Milan freezing, Bologna too cold, Ravenna too snowy. They rarely stopped a day or two until Clark's pills and the autobiography of 'that delightful sinner', the courtly Renaissance artist Benvenuto Cellini, carried them to Naples.

A thousand miles away South Kensington woke up to its loss. Huxley had left announcing his intended resignation. But 'what the devil shall we do for a Biology Professor'? Donnelly asked. Huxley left a well-oiled machine at the Royal Society. His ally Sir John Evans, a pulp-mill manager and expert on coins and *Archaeopteryx*, 'seemed to enjoy sitting in the big chair'. He told Huxley 'on no account to hurry back'.⁵

They escaped Naples' filthy backstreets by sightseeing in Dohrn's steam launch. Huxley's ups and downs were hitched to the telegrams about Mady, and when they reached that city frozen in pumice, Pompeii, Nettie was 'terribly anxious' about him. Even Huxley thought 'he was sinking'. The dead sentinels of Pompeii seemed to shriek of mortality, and Nettie looked on a world without health as 'tasteless ashes'. Hal joked about the expense of bringing him home in a box. But it wasn't needed, a local quinine pick-me-up 'worked wonders':⁶ whether it cured any organic disorder or not, the stimulant brought him back to life.

Their drug-raised spirits entered Rome, and Hal's gravitated to the 'gruesome' catacombs, where, he said, his Puritan soul might be protected from the 'pagan' Papacy. In reality he relished the Papal appeal to his prejudices on the streets above. These returned to their healthy level as strychnine supplements toned up his system. Nettie marvelled at the faun of the Vatican, while he mocked the festival of St Peter's Chair with its 'devout adorations addressed to that venerable article of furniture'.⁷ And no morally-indignant Protestant could pass the Vatican without reassuring himself that the wispy-haired Galileo had suffered that the Inquisitors' Earth might stand still.

While Huxley pored over skulls in Roman museums, England was stunned into 'mourning, humiliation and rage' at the news of the Gordon massacre at Khartoum. 'I wonder if he has entered upon the "larger sphere of action" which he told me was reserved for him in case of such a trifling accident as death', Huxley mused. Huxley had known Major-General Gordon as Donnelly's friend. He was another Royal Engineer, and 'a great soul . . . sacrificed' by Gladstone's dithering. The mystic with the cold blue eyes 'filled with the beauty of holiness' became an imperial martyr, praised for his fights against the slave trade and searches of the Holy Land. Idiosyncrasy only coloured the legend. He once sent Huxley a photo of the 'Forbidden Fruit' from Mauritius, which he had settled as the site of Eden. It was typical that, of the two men, Gordon and Darwin, who struck Huxley as having 'something bigger than ordinary humanity . . . a sublime unselfishness' and sense of purpose, one was a Christian General in the field.[8] Donnelly, the Crimea veteran who would soon retire himself with the rank of Major-General, saw another comparison: he had his boy christened 'Gordon Huxley'.

The Huxleys left Rome after the Carnival with a trunkload of Italian books on neolithic artifacts. Through the hills of Tuscany they returned, and a few days in Florence saw them 'with minds enlarged and backs broken' as they took in the art treasures. Hal was degenerating again. The train journeys, flat out at 'fully twenty-five miles an hour' – and 'very few donkeys could have gone faster' – were excruciating. When they landed in Folkestone on 8 April after a four-day trip, he was barely able to dress himself. Clark, reading of a new drug, put him on coca extract – 'the plant of which the S Amer Indians chew the leaves'. Cocaine fortified him for his last set of lectures.[9]

They had returned a week before Len's wedding. There was a discernible sense of disappointment about the boy. He had a 'lack of ambition', noted their Fabian friend Beatrice Webb. But marriage to a dynamic Julia Arnold, who was well educated, 'clever & possesses a strong character' would provide a compensating spur.[10] Huxley could not wish a better match than Matthew Arnold's niece.

Then Professor Huxley dragged himself into his final biology course. It would be the last time for those unique lectures which had become the template worldwide.[11] He was drugged and fighting despondency. It showed in H. G. Wells' portrayal of a 'yellow-faced' teacher fastidiously dusting the chalk from his hands. Even so Wells was in awe of the old man, clubbing with his friends to buy each *Nineteenth Century* with a Huxley broadside; and he became 'excessively agitated with pride' the first time he spotted Huxley's 'drab spatterdashes' next to his own table. Huxley's strict morphological course taught him 'coherence and consistency', while the Dean's liberating articles revealed the prehistoric panorama of an ocean bed or flayed a decaying culture from behind the cloak of biblical criticism. But most of all Wells was moved by Huxley's new ethos, which saw research – unlike Oxbridge textual criticism – as an open-ended voyage of discovery, full of unpredictable possibilities. For the 'fragile, unkempt' trainee teacher, these few weeks under Huxley in Spring 1885 were themselves liberating; it became, 'beyond all question, the most educational year of my life'.[12] And to remember it, he had himself photographed laconically apeing Huxley's lecturing style, arm around a gorilla.

Pater was more touchingly captured by daughter Nettie, another aspiring artist at the Slade. She sketched pigs in the zoo and her father snoring in a chair. Her fast friends breathed the new decadence, that self-obsessed hedonism soon to break. The girl was 'mad with restless vanity', public singing and partying; a 'handful' for her father, and outside the family ménage now, another reason Beatrice Webb noted for Huxley's 'wearing anxiety'. The art-set returned with her one night. In came Oscar Wilde, that blasé presage of the naughty nineties, although not, presumably, in his plum velveteen suit. Into the house of propriety, with his risqué quips; a house reacting to the drink and drugs outside; an upright house, as it had to be, headed by a Darwinian agnostic who spoke for the new morality. And Wilde, at 30, a homosexual who projected all the 'petulances and flippancies of the decadence, the febrile self-assertion, the voluptuousness, the perversity' of the new Hedonism. In slouched the epitome of reaction to two decades of Puritan naturalness, who would make his exotic Art a celebration of Nature's death. An incongruous meeting, surely, verging on the absurd, something confirmed by Huxley's order: 'That man never enters my house again'.[13]

At 30 a brash Tom Huxley had talked of the rarity of any 'enduring work after the age of threescore'. It were better that scientists be throttled at 60. 'So the "day of Strangulation" has arrived', wrote the irreverent Foster on 4 May 1885. He implored 'your Sixty-ship' to keep the Presidency of the Royal Society but give up the Fisheries and the 'Black Board at S.K.' But the General lived up to his word. On 11 May he penned the awful letters. He resigned as professor at the Normal School of Science, and as Inspector of Fisheries, and warned the Royal Society that he would resign there too.

> I would rather step down from the chair than dribble out of
> it. Even the devil is in the habit of departing with a
> 'melodious twang,' and I like the precedent.[14]

Oxford's announcement that it was conferring on him a Doctorate of Civil Laws was 'a sort of apotheosis coincident with my official death'. 'In fact I am dead already', he added, 'only the Treasury Charon has not yet settled the conditions upon which I am to be ferried over to the other side'. Whitehall was working on his pension, responding to the roar from all sides for the man who had forced science and modernism on a backward British culture. Donnelly reminded them that Huxley had steered ten Commissions, made economies in the Fisheries Department, driven the School Board, taught publicly for 30 years, and put science at the heart of the imperial nation. The Treasury was chivvied, and the outgoing Gladstone – shamed by Khartoum, failing to get local Home Rule in Ireland and defeated on his budget – bowed to the clamour with £1,200-a-year. Not to be outdone, the Tories came in and Sir Stafford Northcote – now Lord Iddesleigh – dropped a note from 10 Downing Street asking if Huxley would accept a further £300 Civil List Pension for 'distinguished services'. The Civil List had always been for indigent gents who were eminent, worthy and acceptable, and an *enragé* who could savage Gladstone was quite acceptable. Of course it cut deeper. The cosmic evolutionary world that Huxley had 'opened up' was beginning to seem universal, non-partisan, as attractive to blue-chip Tories as blue-collar radicals.[15]

He had made his sectarian world-view seem neutral and unproblematic. What had been damnable for 30 years appeared natural now. His philosophy looked positively inoffensive. After all, science could say nothing about ultimate Matter or ultimate Spirit; the argument for a deterministic universe stood exactly where it had in Thomas Aquinas' day, morality lay in acquiescence to evidence, and the agnostic's lips were sealed where that writ ran out. Phrased like that, 'Radicals and Conservatives alike agreed in praising it'.[16] It was agnosticism for the floating voter.

Their Excellencies were waylaid in official corridors. The British had been shamed by bestowing no honour on Darwin during his life, Donnelly told Lord Spencer. Now Huxley 'holds a position scarcely inferior to Darwin'. They knew Huxley's abhorrence of bits of ribbon and 'CB ships & KCB ships', but he had once joked that

> the only kind of honour I should care about as a man of science – for there is not the *slightest fear* of its ever being offered me – . . . is a Privy Councillorship. There is a possible appropriateness in that, a kind of fiction that one was called to the Councils of the State on behalf of Science.

Donnelly reported this verbatim to the government.[17] Shouldn't Science, the new Baron of culture, be summoned to the inner sanctum to advise the Crown? Ought it not sit where the old Norman squires sat, at the highest council table? Linking a Privy Council seat to Huxley's services to science – something inconceivable a generation earlier – might make it the ancient order he *could* accept. And what less for the man who had scientifically stiffened the nation's spine?

The General left a modern command structure in South Kensington, with proliferating ranks of assistant professors and demonstrators.[18] The modern university was taking shape: a labyrinth of labs and theatres, and modern offices where 'Providence & the Telephone was agin' you. He said goodbye to South Kensington as the axis of the Victorian scientific empire: where his 'pet institution', the City and Guilds Institution, was about to open, and a £390,000 budget was already earmarked for a twentieth-century Science Museum. Not quite goodbye. As Honorary Dean he still kept a room in the Normal School 'with all appliances about him'.[19] But his day was over.

The last act was to defile Owen's Temple of Nature. Through the Natural History Museum's gothic arch he trooped on 9 June 1885, four days after his last lecture. Owen had gone, but even he might have admired Huxley's retinue of three earls, even more lords, the Archbishop of Canterbury and Prince of Wales. They heard Huxley eulogize Darwin for irrevocably changing the way men thought.[20] He handed over Boehm's statue of the minor squire who had presented the new professionals with their new sanction. And thus, in the nave, the marble Charles Darwin sat, the host in Owen's Cathedral.

Then the Huxleys beat a retreat to the south coast – to Bournemouth, 'the "English Naples"'. There the husk of a man could be seen sitting by the sea. Not even cocaine could keep him upright now. He passed his days dissecting 'Tusk Shells', tapering white-shelled molluscs, while wishing he were a sea cucumber 'and could get on without my viscera'. They tried to put the thought of Mady's dreadful decline 'away from us as much as we can & live on from day to day', but it was stirring the pit of his stomach. Even here, on the far side of the Styx, or as near as a geriatric could get, he still guarded the evolutionary portals. He muted Mivart's proofs where they criticized Darwin. But, looking back now, he admitted that in protecting Darwin he had perhaps struck 'much harder at his adversaries' than he should have done.[21]

Huxley had been ferried away to the wails of the Royal Society radicals. He resigned the woolsack on 30 November with one last act, getting Ray Lankester the Royal Medal. Lankester's touching response was faintly echoed by so many: 'Since the day when I brought to you 25 years ago the jaw of Stereognathus [one of the first Jurassic mammals] you have been the chief actor in every event which has seemed to me of importance in the chronicle of my life'. In his valedictory address Huxley looked back twice as far, to his own youth when 'there was no such thing as a physical, chemical, biological, or geological laboratory' in Britain[22] – when aspiring chemists looked to Giessen, and Tyndall's physicists travelled to Marburg. Now a laboratory made the school and pure research was a driven activity. The university was becoming 'a factory of new knowledge' in the urbanized, labour-intensive 1880s. Knowledge had become a commodity, to be brokered by the State. Lankester talked of '*creating new knowledge*' as if it were production-line goods. Yet the research factory was an industrial metaphor utterly alien to an old Oxbridge generation, which had prided itself on creating the perfect drawing-room ornament.[23] Dissent's industrial ideology cast the very soul of corporate man.

The relief as he shed jobs was immense. With Mady stabilizing again he began 'to feel thoughts rushing through his mind as they used to'. The grandparents wintered in Bournemouth, where they were joined by Jess and Fred and their three children, including little Noel or 'Buzzer', a 'regular pickle', and already at kindergarten. 'It is 25 years yesterday 15th Sep.', Nettie wrote, looking at the little chap with twinkling eyes, 'since our sweet Noel was taken away from us – & still the memory of that day is keen & bitter'. The thought turned her mind to Mady with a shudder. Jack's mother brought down Mady's baby Joyce, blue-eyed and with that 'determined Huxleyan mouth'. Bournemouth and babies were an escape, and Hal would have been happy 'to remain buried here' far from all responsibility.[24]

The best of the Xs had dispersed, ending an era. The old men were breaking the 'thraldom of official life', and Hooker's advice was to '*soak* in that freedom, get it well into your capillaries and lymphatics'. Hooker had left Kew one of the capital's great attractions, with over a million visitors each year. A restless Tyndall, taking drugs to help him sleep, escaped to the devil's punchbowl wilderness at Hindhead. 'Wicked people have spread the report that "a colony of heathens" is being established' here, he laughed, inviting Huxley down. 'Your presence . . . would complete the evidence'. He bade farewell to the Royal Institution, and at a glittering farewell looked back at his own climb 'from the modest Irish roof under which I was born' to the top of the world. Friends dropped away, although the 'sad & cruel' manner of Carpenter's passing stunned them all. (The lively 72-year-old kicked over the burning gallipot under his vapour bath and died enveloped in flames.)[25] But he had lived to see his deterministic Unitarian universe become the scientific norm and his modern London University curriculum set the Empire's standard.

Huxley was anticipating a tranquil pasturage. It should have been a quiet time to contemplate fossil insects for their own sake. But once more it was controversy that drove him to it. Gladstone, 76, out of office himself, sat dejected in the shadow of Khartoum. Isolated, the Grand Old Man toyed with Home Rule for the spiritual advance of Ireland, while relieving his frustration by torturing God's Word. England's first statesman made the Genesis verses on the creation of fishes, fowl, cattle and creeping things so many 'astonishing anti-cipations' of Victorian palaeontology. Here was proof that the Good Book was 'God-given'. Gladstone was putting down the theologian Albert Réville's *Prolégomènes de l'Histoire des Religions*, which made Genesis 'a venerable fragment' to be surrendered to Science. Many saw him putting down modernity itself. 'Even I saw his gross errors', said Nettie, but Hal! 'It roused Hal to fury'. He went 'blaspheming about the house with the first healthy expression of wrath known for a couple of years'. Gladstone's

> ignorance of the present attitude of Natural Science in this matter is as the Yankees say phenomenal [Huxley told Oxford's expert on Oriental mythology Max Müller, who had brought Réville out in English] – and his grand argument about the 'fourfold order' is utter bosh. I really cannot use respectful language about this intrusion of an utter ignoramus into scientific questions.[26]

And that was the gist. A Statesman had presumed to talk for Science with 'magisterial gravity'. Added to this mortal sin the venial contraventions of a Home Ruler, anathematized by the Unionist intelligentsia, a man who had turned the 'stupendous' ignorance of the upper classes into a force to break up the United Kingdom, and Huxley sensed the political payoff in pinning out this 'copious shuffler'.

Max Müller knew that the religious portions of Gladstone's 'brain are petrified; hard as rock', rendering any factual 'Dynamite . . . useless'. But he encouraged Huxley's Fenian exercise. Huxley was adept at scientific terrorism. In December's *Nineteenth Century* he pointed out that the 'fowl' – the Jurassic first bird, *Archaeopteryx* – appeared after every manner of 'creeping thing', from Silurian 'scorpions' to Triassic mammals, and not before.[27] He lampooned Gladstone's morality of elastic interpretation – and the audacity of Classicists who reduce the complex, tree-like branching of hundreds of thousands of evolving, retrogressing, adapting fossil dynasties to a banal axiom. The professional hauteur was obvious in his discussion of the latest Silurian scorpions; and in the gusto with which he announced that the origin of birds from terrestrial reptiles was in every tyro's text-book. It was a show of moral authority. The solid geological column was the new totem. It gave no leeway for shaky exegetics, even from shaky PMs.

The battle 'stirred his bile as to set his liver right'. Gladstone provided the cure that quinine and cocaine couldn't. The New Luther lived for the moment of nailing his proclamation. As energetically as Gladstone threw himself into textual contortions, Huxley threw himself into fossil scorpions. The toothless bulldog could still leave a mark. He too sublimated his existential worries into an exuberant theological warfare. Knowles was exultant over Huxley's 'Interpreters of Genesis and the Interpreters of Nature'. 'It is as if all the fire which has been kept in so long & smothered in uncongenial work, had at length burst out again'.[28]

The fee of £25 seemed cheap for an article which pushed Britain's thinking monthly into a second edition and spawned a debate in the *Times* on the meaning of 'creeping things'. Spencer never understood Huxley's 'appetite for . . . fairy stories [Christian myths]', but he too 'chuckled' over Huxley's ridiculing of Gladstone's literalism. A surprising assortment of people did: the old Kirk preacher who would substitute Huxley's religion of love for Gladstone's ritual incantation, the Broad Churchman who relished his higher criticism, the Catholic Mivart who was blinded by his brilliance[29] – where was the enemy for a cold warrior in 1886?

'Alas for Gladstone!' Armstrong wrote. 'You have extinguished him in first rate style'. Privately, Gladstone admitted his haste and turned for help. Where else could one extinguished Grand Old Man go but to another? The retired Sir Richard Owen – Vice-President of Richmond Liberal Association – was newly knighted by Gladstone. He was a sad octogenarian in a skullcap whose only child would shortly commit suicide. Surely help was on hand from Sir Richard, whose new armorial crest proclaimed '*Scientia et Pietate*'? It would have been invaluable support, too. Owen was still Britain's premier palaeontologist. Into the 1880s, while Huxley vainly hunted for his hypothetical 'protomammals', Owen was etching out a new fossil 'Cat Reptile', *Aelurosaurus felinus* from the Cape, which fitted the bill. He had the ancestor of the mammals. But only a greater deference distinguished Owen's response to Gladstone from Huxley's. Triassic mammals *had* emerged before the Jurassic *Archaeopteryx*, reversing the sacred order. And what of the oldest unicellular fossils, which appeared 'ere the distinction of animal and vegetal'? For Owen the flow of life pointed to a continuous Presence rather than an Old Jehovah. The Bible was a moral guide for the masses, 'intelligible to the age it addressed'.[30] But palaeontology's precise findings should not be muddled with it. Gladstone never received a politer hands-off notice.

But Gladstone was on his own moral crusade. He inserted a rather squirming paragraph and posted off his unrepentant 'Proem to Genesis' after receiving Owen's last letter. An astute Knowles slipped Huxley an early copy to ensure the monthly parry. Another furious turnaround: on 31 December Huxley had the 'Proem', and a week later his rejoinder was typeset. Part smart parody of a demagogue, part forensic dissection of a wheedler, it oozed mock bewilderment that the Grand Old Man should pin the truth of revelation on a palaeontological howler. 'M^r. Gladstone & Genesis', Knowles called the piece, which even he considered ' "pulverizing" & final'. But too earnest. This was, after all, Gladstone. Would Huxley 'be a little less fierce' in his 'vivisection'? Huxley 'tamed his wild cat', but he still played the infuriating heckler with his trick questions: if Gladstone now saw Genesis as a sermon, not a lecture, does he mean that the latter, 'so far as it deals with matters of fact, may be taken seriously . . . while a sermon may not'?[31] He was impugning the integrity of the nation's leader-in-waiting.

The General Election in January 1886 ended the fray. The vote was a plebiscite on Gladstone's Irish Home Rule and, if it hadn't been for the science-grant-slashing Randolph Churchill, Huxley would have voted Tory for the first time in his life. As it was he abstained. Gladstone re-entered No 10, leaving the wild cat with his bloodlust up. Knowles' suggestion of a more general article resulted in such a manuscript on 'The Evolution of Theology' – the longest Huxley had ever written for him: '40 pages long! double my maximum' – that it had to be split across the March and April issues of the *Nineteenth Century*. It was a palaeontological peep into someone else's *sacred penetralia*. In white coat, Huxley hammered at the rich 'fossiliferous strata' of the eleventh- to twelfth-century BC Books of Judges and Samuel. He reconstructed the ancient genus of Elohim ghosts of the polytheistic Israelites of the land of Goshen – making them a sort of child-sacrificing Tongan race of antiquity. (A fundamentally pre-Darwinian concept, based on the premiss that all peoples passed through the same 'grades of social organization'.)[32] He left unsaid that one superior species of deified ancestral ghost, Jahvah, evolved under cultural pressure into the Israelites' supreme deity and Christianity's sole god.

He planned to say it. He would begin chiselling away at Christendom's ancient strata in a 34-chapter book, 'The Natural History of Christianity'. It would show the religion becoming associated with society's ethical code – show this Elohim ghost-deity, 'thoroughly human' in its feelings, policing moral behaviour with promises of rewards and threats of unearthly torment. He drew on the Book of the Dead (the indefatigable Amelia Edwards was already signing him up to her Egypt Exploration Fund) and his voluminous readings in the Valley of the Kings, to suggest that the moral code itself, if not a number of Commandments, came to Moses from his 19th Dynasty Pharaonic foster-parents. Here was the first reformation, when Moses refined the Book of the Dead into the Book of the Covenant, and the Egyptian ethics into the Jewish social code – just as Calvin 'built up a puritanic social organisation' from the remains 'of the ethics and theology of the Roman Church'. Such parables made Huxley's sermons comprehensible and uplifting. It was Whig history writ large: the Victorian age was the culmination of a succession of reformations. History was read backwards: the eighth-century BC prophets Isaiah and Jeremiah had tried 'to free the moral ideal from the stifling' old idolatry. They

> pour scorn upon the whole sacrificial system . . . To them
> there is no atonement save the offering of a contrite spirit
> . . . They ignore the priest; & have no manner of respect for
> decorative theology – neither for incense, nor for music . . .
> Their sole guide is the inner light of reason & conscience
> . . . The prophets of Israel are the earliest & the extremist
> of Protestants.[33]

Refleshing the sacred fossils – making Isaiah as Victorian a cultural construct as Owen's rhino-like dinosaurs – the modern patriarch was preparing the way to detach the ethics and destabilize the theology for the final revolt: the 'New Reformation'. With this the Positivist strategy of the age peaked. The 'Evolution of Theology' was 'thin & pretentious' in Gladstone's view. But Huxley's homespun higher criticism, Knowles enthused, had the 'invincible strength of common sense'.[34]

It was a chilling Winter. Around him frustration was turning to rage as 1886 scooped a deep trough in the Great Depression. In a freezing

February, the coldest for 30 years, Carpenter's widow Louisa was helping to feed 8,500 ragamuffins in a Leeds soup kitchen. The mood turned ugly as begging gave way to rioting, and the wrench opened up the Darwinian divide. After the evictions in Ireland the socialist Wallace had founded his Land Nationalisation Society. Huxley shuddered. He saw 'the "earth hunger" of the many' as a 'plea for the spoliation of the landowning few'. He feared the false millennium, 'when the "Have-nots," whether they lack land, or house, or money, or capacity, or morals, will have parted among themselves all the belongings of the "Haves" – save the last two'. Socialism's head was above the parapet now. The Fabians were appealing to the genteel classes, while Wallace's *Bad Times* attacked speculators and million-aires. Huxley was suddenly in unfriendly terrain. And he felt the power of the Marxist-led Social Democratic Federation.

On an icy 8 February 1886, 'Black Monday', the emeritus professor tore himself from the revises of 'The Evolution of Theology'. He was busing through the West End as it fell to the mob. Already stiffening against demagogues and ultra-democracy, he was caught as the starving East End rampaged West. A bad tip-off had sent the police to protect Buckingham Palace, but the crowd ransacked Piccadilly instead. The Social Democratic Federation lost control. Omnibuses were overturned, people robbed, the gentlemen's clubs attacked in London's worst riot for 50 years. He 'escaped unhurt from the wanton outrage' on his bus. But he sensed an ominous force as thousands smashed and looted.[35] He retreated from the war zone to salubrious Bournemouth.

Socialism was drawing sustenance from secularism. The usual sus-pects went over. Aveling – already translating Marx's *Kapital* – was in the crowd. Annie Besant was singing duets with George Bernard Shaw at Fabian meetings. 'Why I am a Socialist' was her latest pam-phlet – and the answer was '*because I am a believer in Evolution*'. But her sort of 'Evolution' pushed on from Darwin's bestial world of 'individualistic anarchy' to produce a more efficient State organism. Huxley was mulling over his contribution on 'The Progress of Science 1837–1887', just commissioned for the jubilee volume, *The Reign of Queen Victoria*. How had the agitators missed the point? Hadn't the 'new Nature begotten by science' given Victorian England its social and technological 'revolution'? And 'worked miracles', breaking the bounds of time and space – a revolution that could put men 12,000 miles apart in instant touch, and through steam-print 'destroy the effect of inequalities in wealth among learning men'? Education would liberate people to rise, according to their ability, and no artificial redistribution was needed. This age which could detect a new planet, or the chemistry of stars, or equate magnetism and motion, or look to its evolutionary history – it still hadn't learnt that the common 'gifts of science are aids in the process of levelling up',

> of removing the ignorant and baneful prejudices of nation against nation, class against class; of assuring that social order which is the foundation of progress . . . and against which one is glad to think that those who, in our time, are employing themselves in fanning the embers of ancient wrong, in setting class against class . . . are undertaking a futile struggle.[36]

But the Great Depression had dampened the public's faith. Few saw material progress promise a political New Jerusalem any more. Or science offer a chimerical stabilizing equation. And without jobs, what hope that technology could satisfy the workers' material demands?

Meanwhile a broad alliance was forming against Gladstone's Home Rule Bill. For X-Clubbers the final reformation sat ill with idolatrous Papists in an Irish Parliament. One fanatical Unionist told the *Times* that, 'sooner than hand over the Loyalists of Ireland to the tender mercies of the priests and Nationalists I would shoulder my rifle among the Orangemen'.[37] That was Tyndall, and like Huxley he was arming.

Huxley thought the destruction of the Union a 'cowardly wickedness'. Breakaway Liberal Unionists regrouped around Joseph Chamberlain, who wanted social reform in an Ireland that remained part of the State. They contacted Huxley. Would he help in 'fighting the enemies of the Union'? His word meant so much in America, where sympathizers were funding the Irish Nationalists. Could he 'get behind their supplies & cut them off'? Huxley loathed that 'profligate old demagogue' Gladstone, and if democracy meant an Irish Parliament then it showed that 'government by average opinion is merely a circuitous method of going to the devil'. They elicited such a bilious lament that his letter was passed around the Liberal Unionist MPs.[38] No sooner had Gladstone introduced his Home Rule Bill on 8 April 1886 than they placed it in the *Standard* (itself founded 50 years earlier to thwart Catholic Emancipation). From there it was waved alongside the Union Jack in every paper through to the *Monthly Record of the Protestant Evangelical Mission*.

In an extremist age it seemed 'the quintessence of the political wisdom of today', an antidote to 'outrage & Dynamite'. But it showed the same hysterics that he deplored in the *enragés*. For two months the country went mad. Pro-Union speeches in the House even had 'the unimpassioned Lubbock waving his hat above his head'. To a nation reclining with pride as its searchlight swept the world, Gladstone was a fanatic breaking up the Empire: 'Have you read Gladstone's *Genesis*?' ran the joke; 'No, I'm waiting for his *Exodus*!'[39] They didn't have to wait long.

Huxley's view of Irish aspirations was coloured by the pervasive anti-Catholic prejudice. The butt of his perennial Paddy quips, the navvies had come to sum up a menial, superstitious culture. The 'careless, squalid, unaspiring Irishman' was the '*less* favoured race' of Darwin's *Descent of Man*. And although Huxley avoided talking of an Irish 'race' or 'Celtic blood'[40] (that was the Nationalists' warrant for a separate state), the stereotype still allowed him to damn the Parnellites as a pack of 'ingrained liars'. But not their Protestant, Cambridge-educated leader. Charles Stewart Parnell was cold and mesmerizing. Democracy and riots had left a reactionary nation looking again for heroes. Huxley was no different. He sympathized with strong intellects, and despite the anger caused by the Fenian murders (he knew Lord Frederick Cavendish, who had been stabbed to death in Dublin in 1882), he recognized Parnell's 'great qualities'. It was a back-hander, but he conceded that at last 'the Irish malcontents have a leader who is . . . honest'.[41]

The X had regrouped behind Chamberlain. Tyndall wanted them to draw up 'a scientific declaration' for the Union. His signatories would be the 'unbiased sons of science', true men who championed 'true liberty of thought'. Dispassionate science was to denounce Gladstone's 'tyranny'.[42] No such damning sectarian document ever went off. It was scuppered by a more realistic Huxley, who knew the groundswell of Separatist feeling among the younger FRSs.

The X was 'going to smithereens', said Huxley amid the Fenian blasts. There never had been any new members admitted, and attendances by the old rogues were spasmodic now, although none could 'bear to think of its extinction'. The odd Thursday saw a 'doleful' meeting of Dad's Scientists. Half stayed out at pasture. The 66-year-old Tyndall looked 'very worn' amid the Hindhead gorse. And Hooker in Sunningdale was trying to finish his *Flora of British India* and get a life devoted to imperial botany rewarded by a decent pension. (Considering the £40,000 and untold lives he saved the Bengal Government yearly by transplanting quinine-producing cinchona from South America to India, along with the rubber, it should have been easy, but it was not.) While a blimpish Spencer was going about Brighton in a bath chair, threatening to write his autobiography. At one point he tried to inveigle Huxley onto a yacht for a therapeutic two-month sail. 'Just fancy' being cooped up 'with H.S. in a yacht', exclaimed Hooker: 'I should go before the mast, & stay there'. Once the X could have staffed a scientific university, now their aches and pains could complete a clinician's manual. They were decrepit and, for each of them, Death had a stalking-horse. Tyndall's bosom friend Hirst was emaciated, 14 pounds down in seven months. Busk would be dead by the summer, 'Poor dear old Busk', that shoulder Hal had once leant on.[43] They prepared another notice for the *Times*.

Over summer 1886 the X took the airs in their codgerly ways. Switzerland was now the playground of Thomas Cook's tourists. Columns of them could be seen snaking over the glaciers. Even the old mountain goat Tyndall, who had built a chalet on the breathtaking Lusgen Alp, now felt grateful to Cook's agents for helping him along. The Huxleys made their own snake on 2 August. They came up 18 miles and 2,000 feet in a caravan – 'four mules & five bipeds' – from Evolena to Arolla, off the Rhône valley. Here, 'at the tail of a glacier in the midst of a splendid amphitheatre of 11–12000 feet snow heights' they settled. It 'suits us to a T', he told Tyndall. If religion could not supply a religious experience, the Alps could. This was the sublime 'dream region', Leslie Stephen's 'sacred place' which evoked pure unrefined emotion. Here faithless Victorians could worship the indomitable force of Nature.

Amid the splendour the old man sat among the purple flowers sketching. He took 'a sudden mania' for the trumpet-shaped gentians, Alpine herbs whose tubular flowers show different adaptations to insect pollinators. 'I have become great on the varieties of Gentiana purpurea', he told Tyndall. 'Satan doth not find my hands idle'. Life near the snowline left him in fine fettle; the world seemed brighter, the reports of Mady were better; and he had to look in the mirror at 'the increasing snow cap on the summit of my Tête noire (as it once was), to convince myself I am not twenty years younger'.

We 'shall catch you with the spade before long', said Foster on his return. True, Huxley was soon planting specimens from Kew. Nettie was happy to see him 'madly working at botany' if it kept him 'free from his "blues"'. The pottering turned serious of course. 'I am amazed at your taking to Botany in your old age', Hooker wrote, as Huxley plundered his library and recaptured the botanical infatuation of his long-haired days. Being 'unanointed and unannealed' in the ways of plant systematics, he swept past the experts to assemble the flowers into morphological groups. The Linnean gents were nonplussed to see him draw a tree-like chart showing the gentians' increasing differentiation. It was all à la Haeckel, down to the extrapolation of a hypothetical 'ancestral' herb.[44]

Gentians gave way to reflections. Frank Darwin's *Life and Letters of Charles Darwin* would start the public glorification of the 1860 Oxford confrontation. Huxley's chapter on the 'Reception of the Origin of Species' made it a moral 'victory' to be proud of, so important in an age of imperial defeat, with Gordon fresh in the memory. The General was elegant and heroic as he backslapped old friends and crushed old enemies and moved salt cellars around the table. But a mite too indignant; even Frank thought him a bit 'hard upon the "Quarterly Article"'. But Wilberforce's 25-year-old review was still 'absolutely scandalous' to Huxley's mind. With Huxley's 'Reception' Whig history was issuing a caution: it would apprise the 'villifiers of the present day . . . that they may yet hang in chains'.[45]

The Alps put a spring in his step. His tripping-up of Cardinal Newman's advocate W. S. Lilly in November's *Nineteenth Century* reminded Spencer 'of the way a good-tempered Newfoundland knocks over & tumbles about an impertinent puppy'. Lilly joined a long line of Catholics to portray Huxley as immoral. 'With whatever rhetorical ornaments he may gild it', Huxley's agnosticism was plain materialism, and to see what that meant Lilly looked to Revolutionary France: a country whose godless excesses ran to placing 'natural children' on 'a footing of almost complete equality with children born in wedlock'. It was the old bogey, materialism sapping the strength of establishment ritual, and it had some foundation. Huxley responded with his own *Apologia*, 'Science and Morals'. It was the last act of that divine comedy which began with the Wilberforce drama, when a powerful theology with its eyes to heaven met a carnal science sifting through the 'mole's earthheap'. The sublime and ridiculous, angels and apes, were Huxley's trademark, and his undercutting sense of moral authority gripped a nation. The boy from the back-street school made a comic absurdity of scholastic authority. Huxley's morality plays portrayed the winning ways of innocence. The young waif Science eyed her old sisters, Theology and Philosophy.

> Cinderella . . . lights the fire, sweeps the house, and
> provides the dinner; and is rewarded by being told that she
> is a base creature, devoted to low and material interests.
> But in her garret she has fairy visions out of the ken of the

pair of shrews who are quarrelling downstairs. She sees the
order which pervades the seeming disorder of the world; the
great drama of evolution, with its full share of pity and
terror, but also with abundant goodness and beauty . . . ;
and she learns . . . that the foundation of morality is to have
done, once and for all, with lying; to give up pretending to
believe that for which there is no evidence.[46]

Cinders, ground down in menial reality, slaving for others, had her
visions of beauty and truth, and Society's Prince Charming would
make her the Princess.

'I have painted that Lilly:' he crowed to Tyndall, ' – with nitrate of
silver'. Of all people, it was Mivart who admired Huxley's caustic
ink. Never had he read a Huxley critique 'with more relish'. But
Catholicism's liberal son was under siege himself. He was feeling the
chills in an increasingly inquisitorial climate. This 'Pontificate of
Pius IX' was 'calamitous', he told Newman.[47] Mivart would be
excommunicated by Rome for liberalizing Hell as he had been by the
Darwinians for liberating the soul. Huxley's 'constant reader' would
die in no man's land, in defiance of any authority. He was more an
heir than either of them would admit.

'I know only too well *I* have made mistakes', Mivart confessed, '&
life is short'. Others were feeling it. On 25 November an envelope
popped though the door bearing a strange hand. Inside, it began 'My
Brother'. It was from Tom's long-lost brother William. Ostensibly it
was a request to have a friend's Geological Society certificate signed;
in fact William at 67 knew that his 'sands of life are running low' and
he was making overtures after 40 years.[48] And so the two brothers
spoke again for the first time since 1845.

The calls on Huxley's time had scarcely diminished. On 12 January
1887, the Prince of Wales had him speak at the Mansion House in
the City on a new pet project for South Kensington. The Prince's new
complex would celebrate the Jubilee, and herald science, industry
and empire in an 'Imperial Institute'. It was a Scientific Age, Huxley
agreed, and such an Institute would 'mark the Victorian epoch in history' as the Parthenon had marked the ancient world. Huxley's was
'the most interesting speech', according the *Pall Mall Gazette*. But
then his Darwinian diatribe blew away all the dreary talks. He
depicted the industrial competition with Germany and America as
international 'warfare', with starvation befalling the losers. The
'Imperial Institute' was to help Britain win the industrial 'war'. It
was a line which appalled socialist economists.[49]

There was the 'war' again. Huxley's Nonconformist generation had written competition large on the world. It had made technical education the *sine qua non* of imperial success. The boy had not been born with a silver spoon in his mouth, but the Salters Company in the City presented him with a pair to mark the Jubilee.[50] Even if the socialists shunned his science as a deceptive panacea (a fact that would push Huxley more and more into politics itself), the Liberals echoed his industrial 'war' cry. Lord Hartington, Gladstone's Minister of War before his defection to the Unionists, talked of 'famine, indigence, and starvation' as the price of economic defeat. And the Chancellor, Goschen, waded in to deplore the prevailing Oxbridge manorial mentality which regarded business as a necessary evil. *Nature* applauded Huxley's application of 'Darwin's great theory to commercial competition'. While the *Times* advocated 'spending freely [on science] to protect ourselves from [economic] aggression'. They understood Huxley's image of the Imperial Institute as 'the drill-grounds of the army of industry'.[51]

The General had turned Dissent's competitive ethic into the military image of the day. Darwin had blooded it with his 'concealed war of nature'. The age had seen South Kensington being built by Crimea vets and patrolled by Royal Engineers. It had tingled at Huxley's Total War with Theology, itself awash with Church Armies and Salvation Armies marching as to war.[52] The uncontrolled – or rather conscripted – metaphors had taken on a life of their own in this propaganda-saturated environment.

Huxley's only scruple was about the Prince's proposed site for the Imperial Institute – in South Kensington. Huxley backed big business, which wanted it in 'the heart of our . . . mercantile organism – the City of London'. The City had expanded enormously, sucking in provincial banks and foreign financiers to become the centre of the world's money markets, and here the trade guilds were solidly based. Over in leafy South Kensington the City & Guilds 'Tech – 'so portly outside and . . . so . . . starved within' – was struggling. The *Times* thundered its backing for Huxley, but he was in bad 'odour at Court'. Pledges of £10,000 'at a packed meeting of stockjobbers' saw the Imperial Institute founded on Exhibition Road despite him. (This 'industrial University'[53] – the Imperial Institute – would ultimately amalgamate with Huxley's Normal School and the City and Guilds Institute as Imperial College.)

Huxley seemed a solid presence at the Mansion House. But he was collapsing inwards: those around him were becoming 'all shadows',

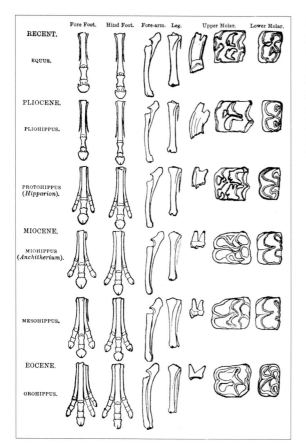

	Fore Foot.	Hind Foot.	Fore-arm.	Leg.	Upper Molar.	Lower Molar.
RECENT.						
EQUUS.						
PLIOCENE.						
PLIOHIPPUS.						
PROTOHIPPUS (*Hipparion*).						
MIOCENE.						
MIOHIPPUS (*Anchitherium*).						
MESOHIPPUS.						
EOCENE.						
OROHIPPUS.						

28. Huxley found his palaeontological proof of evolution at Yale. O. C. Marsh drew up this table of his fossil horses to accompany Huxley's lectures. The oldest horse is at the bottom with four toes and low-crowned teeth, the latest, tip-toeing plains-runner at the top.

29. Projecting backwards to an even older five-toed ancestor, Huxley dashed off this sketch of the anticipated '*Eohippus*', with a suitable rider, '*Eohomo*'. Ironically, the dog-sized *Eohippus* was already in Yale's basement, waiting to be unpacked. Marsh's horses forced Huxley to reconsider the timing of human evolution.

Eohippus + Eohomo

30. T. H. Huxley in Birmingham. He was the darling of the city's slum-clearing Unitarian fathers. Like the mayor Joseph Chamberlain, Huxley was a Cromwellian to his teeth.

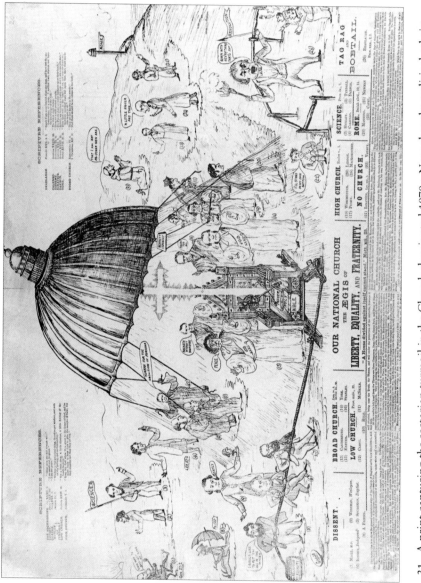

31. A print capturing the sectarian turmoil in the Church-dominated 1870s. Note that the political atheists stand fenced in at the bottom right. By contrast, Huxley, the monkey Darwin, and flag-waving Tyndall appear top left on the side of Dissent, here seen pulling the chocks away from the State-supported Church.

PROFESSOR HUXLEY, LL.D., F.R.S., L.S.D.,

32. The Scientist as Public Servant. With a radical Home Secretary discriminating to get scientists jobs, Huxley added the Inspectorship of Fisheries in 1881 to his teaching load and Royal Commissions. *Punch* cynically appended '£.s.d' to his name, but the extra work drained his energy and drove him towards another breakdown.

33. Huxley's true heir was his talented, unstable daughter Marian ('Mady'). She was an inspired artist – a girl, admitted her paternalist father, with a 'career' before her. She married the artist John Collier, shown here painting her – but the painting itself is by Mady. She would die mad in 1887.

34. H. G. Wells was among Huxley's last students. He is apeing Huxley, who mesmerized his class by lecturing with his arms around the gorilla.

35. The Right Honourable T. H. Huxley, spokesman for Science at the Councils of the State. Having ridiculed Gladstone's Scripturalism and impugned the Home Ruler's judgment, Huxley was made a Privy Councillor by Lord Salisbury's Tories in 1893.

36. Behind the stern portraits of the savage controversialist lay the droll, good-natured chap of this rare photograph.

ghosts receding into the twilight. He was dropping 'back into the unreal world he lives in'. 'The old lion is broken down', Beatrice Webb noted after a meeting in May, 'he has only the remains of greatness'. Alternately animated and depressed, he opened a little in her presence. He seemed to scream failure, as he did during his depressions; 'melancholy has haunted his whole life', she said, and with skewed insight blamed his 'indifferently dutiful' and 'dull' children for lacking any understanding of their father. Twenty-three-year-old Nettie had 'taken without a care to public singing'. (She had impulsively – and expensively – apprenticed herself to the London Symphony Concert's founder George Henschel, and accompanied him to Boston in Spring 1887. Henschel had been the first conductor of the Boston Symphony Orchestra, and the Agassizes, who funded it, helped her settle, only to find Oscar Wilde's *amie* making herself the belle of Boston's balls.) Another, 'his brilliant and gifted child has sunk into hysterical imbecility'. There was the real reason. Huxley was crushed by worry. He 'dreams strange things', noted Webb, 'carries on lengthy conversations between unknown persons living within his brain. There is a strain of madness in him'.[54] There was at this moment.

The dreamer could still pick at a fossil reptile skull.[55] But mostly he lost himself in metascientific thought on fate and determinism. Still, anyone who tried to beard the broken old lion in his philosophical den 'got his reward'. The Duke of Argyll declared that a Darwinian 'Reign of Terror' was stifling creative science. The Duke had borne Darwin's body into the Abbey, but he stood on the Ministerial fringe of science. In fact His Grace was the noblest of Owen's supporters, and he disparaged the *Origin* as 'a guess which includes a few *bits* of the truth'. The Duke was 'a clever man', growled Huxley, 'who thinks he is much cleverer than he is'.[56] The ageing lion was 'out of patience with his meddling' and 'not exactly sorry for the provocation he offered'. It was an excuse to unsheathe his feline claws.

Birth was no longer an open sesame into science, and the Duke's Totalitarian accusation came as the professionals shut the laboratory door. Against these experts Argyll offered a nobler vision which reinforced an older order. Evolutionary change reflected a Decree from On High, rather than any self-development. His Grace's 'natural law' was the Will of God, whose Writ still ran from the great dome of St Paul's to Inverary Castle. As Canon Liddon affirmed, God's was the highest Law, the illimitable Royal Edict. It could suspend 'lower' ones, and in the case of Lot's wife turn living tissue into chemical residue. It could guide evolution, or stop it at Armageddon.

This conservative mannikin view of God and his creation had been laughed out of court by radical Dissenters in the 1830s. Nor had they viewed Owen's Law-as-Divine-Fiat more sympathetically. Argyll was restaging the Romantic fight with radical Dissent's cold, determined universe. And just as the Unitarians had considered old S. T. Coleridge 'half-crazed' for his aristocratic Willed Nature, so Huxley was predisposed to think His Grace no saner. Providential Evolution seemed, after 40 years, 'rather flabby'.[57]

It was so much 'Pseudo-Scientific Realism'. Argyll's own pot-boiling *Reign of Law*, written while the Duke was juggling Reform Bills 20 years earlier, described the descent of power from God down through Nature. His Grace was making 'Natural Laws' the instruments of Divine legislation and evolution the 'fulfilment of Creative Purpose'.

Huxley had not bothered with the book before. And he only waded in now on being fingered as a new Danton. His response was radical Dissent's: to laugh at a marionette Nature, capriciously manipulated from above. The idea of laws tugging and pulling one another seemed the 'acme of absurdity'. The Royal Laws were like so many 'Eastern despots' who 'descend in wrath among the middle-class and plebeian laws, which have hitherto done the drudgery of the world's work'. Laws *cause* nothing, neither the fall of apples nor the descent of men. They are 'a mere record of experience', a sign of the constant conjunction of events, a symbol of universal order.[58] The professional was snatching the passionless cosmos away from the reconciler who has not 'undergone the discipline' necessary to understand it.

There was a certain cachet in being 'abused by a Duke'. As usual Huxley felt 'wonderfully better' for it. So good, he told old comrade Holyoake, that 'I may yet serve the good cause by something better than chastening impatient Dukes'. Radical evolutionism was corroding the aristocratic foundations of science, just as the democratic acids were etching away at old political privileges.

In this area too Huxley was clapped by the old comrades. He chaired a public meeting to collect £20,000 for a free Public Library in his borough of St Marylebone. It was vintage Huxley as he persuaded the council to put a halfpenny on the rates to run it. It was the old Nonconformist ethic: free education, helping the best to bob up to the surface. There was to be a leavening of talent in the Duke's top-heavy society. Huxley did not

believe that if 100 men were picked out of the highest
aristocracy in the land and 100 out of the lowest class, there
would be any difference of capacity among them. (Cheers.)
Men of mark and capacity were rare animals. Perhaps one
in ten thousand . . . and if all the cost of the Education Act
and all the money spent on free libraries enabled them to
catch two of such men a year . . . the thing would be dirt
cheap. (Cheers and laughter.)[59]

'She was a brilliant creature', he said of 28-year-old Mady. The world
saw her as his gifted heir. What more could a patrician father admit?
She was a woman with 'a career before her'. Once, with the Chelsea
art-set, life had 'smiled on her from all sides'. But the sun faded with
the suffering, and in 1887 she plunged 'down hill'. Nettie was terribly
shocked that for a time 'she did not know me'. Hal privately feared
'the worst of all ends – dementia'. Mady knew that 'she was going
mad and I knew it too by her look of melancholia'.[60]

In desperation they contacted the great neurologist and specialist
in 'hysteria', Jean-Martin Charcot. It was Charcot who had dignified
it as a serious mental illness, characterized by the blindness and loss
of voice that Mady suffered. Freud, studying hysteria under Charcot,
stood in awe. He watched Charcot hypnotize his female 'hysterics' to
reveal the powerful mental processes hidden from consciousness.
Despite the hundreds flocking to him, Charcot came to England
to examine Professor Huxley's daughter. He invited Mady to Paris,
where he planned to use hypnotic suggestion to remove the emotional 'conflicts' causing her brain disorder.

Mady hardly knew her three-year-old Joyce, the tot who had
'wound herself about' Nettie's heart. The grandchildren gave the
family ballast. (Julia and Leonard, in their rose-clad cottage close to
his Charterhouse school, had Julian in 1887.) They needed the ballast
with so many buffeting relations. Polly, deranged by her second husband's death, became wild on morphia and brandy and punched
Hal, screaming, 'No wonder you drove Mady mad!' It hurt. Such was
the end of George's wife, the scamp who had fussed over him after
the *Rattlesnake* voyage. He continued to pay a doctor £20 a year to
look after her, but 'I don't think Hal will ever go near her again'.[61]
Hal's cash was still a featherbed, and illness was still their lot. His
own fight against pleurisy this summer portended difficulties, and
Nettie was growing apprehensive about her own bladder operation.

Some invitations couldn't be shirked. Industrial Manchester too
was raising taxes to fund local technical education, and Huxley had

agreed to inaugurate the scheme. On 13 November Sir Henry Roscoe was preparing his room. Jack had taken Mady and two nurses to Charcot's Salpêtrière Hospital, a huge 40-building medical complex devoted to women's diseases. 'It was a forlorn hope', sighed her father. The telegram arrived a week later, on the morning of 20 November. Run down, she had died from pneumonia before Charcot had even managed to see her.

'Oh Lizzie', cried Nettie, 'I know that it is for the best – her sufferings are ended – but I want her so'. Her father, bitterly stoical, knew that she was 'spared that most miserable of endings', madness. But he was ashen-faced, and lost. Mady had passed 'beyond his veil', Knowles said, feelingly. Nettie gave an inner scream; she desperately wanted to believe in 'another happier world that shall make up for all the cruelties of this'.[62]

The black-edged envelope brought a touching response from 'brother' John. Being childless, he had always suffered 'with your sufferings', and 'I have been drawn towards you, in feeling and affection, more than you are aware of'. So it would be 'to the end'.[63] With Mady were buried rare gifts, and many of Huxley's hopes. The blow symbolized the loss of all the optimism born in that year of her birth, the Victorian *annus mirabilis* 1859. But there would be reminders. In one of the kindest acts, the owner returned Mady's painting 'The Sins of the Father'. It would now be hung over the big fireplace in the drawing room.

Everything was cancelled, Nettie put back her operation to get over the funeral. Nobody expected Huxley in Manchester on the 29th. Yet he felt honour bound, having fired them up – and he was incapable 'of chalking up "no popery" and running away'. Nettie, finding no distraction, watched him scribbling grief-stained lecture notes and could only 'envy him his work'. But the bitterness exploded in his spattered image of nature's butchery. Mady's death blackened his soul; and the more he was politicized by the Depression, the more he damned Nature's violence. Was it Huxley or Darwin who depicted the deceptive calm masking the massacre of the innocents?

> You see a meadow rich in flower & foliage and your
> memory rests upon it as an image of peaceful beauty. It is a
> delusion . . . Not a bird that twitters but is either slayer or
> [slain and] . . . not a moment passes in that a holocaust, in
> every hedge & every copse battle murder & sudden death
> are the order of the day.[64]

It was Huxley in a riot-torn 1887, but it could have been Darwin in a Dickensian 1837. The two men were mirror-image dancing, one in his storm-tossed morning before the sunny Victorian Noon and the other with the coming dark night. Malthusianism was back in contention in the socialist 1880s. But Huxley saw continual over-population as a spanner in the co-operative works, forcing unending competition which defied any egalitarian socialist solution. Blood-thirsty Darwinian struggle was inevitable in Nature: Huxley was swearing to the 'primacy of Satan in this world' where once he had faced a calm angel.[65] But the bloodier he made Nature, the more it forced him to fortify a pure human ethics. His Darwinian world was peeling apart. Nature was losing its moral spine.

It was torn out in the scrum of overpopulation, competition and culling. Where Huxley had been loath to mention natural selection in an evolutionary context, politics and personal tragedy had him thrusting it into a social context. With increasing Atlantic and European rivalry it was a case of retooling and retraining or die, he said. This was the 'fatal necessity' of business existence. His theme returned with a vengeance: industrial competition was war by another name. Darwin, cocooned with his £¼ million, had welcomed the human struggle, but for Huxley to embrace a 'humanity doomed forever to be at war' was an act of cynical desperation. And utopian promises of

> The improvement of morals, the advances of science, the
> universality of that Liberty Equality & Fraternity to which
> many look as to a new Heaven & new Earth will do
> nothing for us here.[66]

He had hoped to make Nettie's 'later days peaceful & happy – but such plans are folly'. Cynicism carried him to Manchester. The fury of it – 'I travelled 400 miles and made a speech of fifty minutes in a hot, crowded room, all in about twelve hours' – tinged his words.[67] The Town Hall meeting, hosted by the Mayor and trades leaders, was exposed to an apocalyptic justification for technical education.

Grief gave his tendency to distance human ethics from Nature's carnage a dramatic wrench. The toned-down essay, published in February's *Nineteenth Century*, and retitled 'The Struggle for Existence in Human Society',[68] still evoked the strife-torn side of Nature. His world of brooding malevolence damned 'the optimistic dogma, that this is the best of all possible worlds'. By cursing Nature for the Darwinian carnage and Mady's death, Huxley was *having* to detach his own ethics, wherein rested the beauty of a flower or the goodness of a young girl.

This was deep in the Great Depression. The streets swarmed with the starving. Growing numbers of socialists were besieging science and society demanding co-operation and redistribution. Huxley was using a competitive biology to police and pacify the crowds – the rioters who had attacked his omnibus. But he could only defend the capitalist war in nature and industry by dubbing it, as Kingsley had once done, a 'gladiator's show'. He bowed to its brutal Darwinian necessity as he detached his ethical sorrow for its dead victims. Kingsley's moral duty was to a Beneficent Deity promising rewards. But Huxley recognized the indiscriminate meddlings of a different divinity: the Babylonian goddess of war and lustful mother of renewed life, Ishtar. To her were the first-born sacrificed. To her we owe the deafening shrieks as she ravaged the land. Their million wails crescendoed above every field. Darwin had taken bleak consolation in the struggle honing a better-specialized descendant. But to the cynic 'it is not clear what compensation the *Eohippus* gets for his sorrows in the fact that, some millions of years afterwards, one of his descendants wins the Derby'. Darwin had looked to the species, Huxley looked to the individual. And what does it profit a species anyway? With the globe ultimately heading for an ice death, life will devolve and degenerate in a final 'universal winter' and end in the meanest of Hooker's Antarctic diatoms. A death shroud descended over Huxley's philosophy.

'Huxley looked upon creation and saw that it was bad'. There was no compensation, even in a favoured imperial nation. Ishtar added a new mouth every hundred seconds and demanded her sacrifice accordingly. And increasing the output to keep up meant an 'internecine struggle' with other nations for markets. Moral man abhorred it, but Ishtar dictated it. No 'fiddle-faddling with the distribution of wealth' would help. Population drove the war on. The speed of technological change, which was already breaking the traditional apprenticeship system, demanded greater technical mobilization. The government was right to allow the manufacturing districts to raise new rates to pay for new training. Manchester's, he said, was a sort of 'war tax . . . for purposes of defence'.

He was rationalizing pain in an industrial nation and policing the masses with Malthusian biology. It was too much. Reviews of 'The Struggle for Existence in Human Society' were crushing from Right to Left, from the Christian anti-protectionists to the socialist co-operators. 'Since Elisha prescribed for the leprosy of Naaman never was a simpler remedy offered for a terrible disorder', moaned the *Standard*. It was a calumny that 'evolution has nothing better to offer'.[69]

But his own mind would revolt against it too. Overpopulation might have demanded a continuing evolutionary struggle, leading to the survival of the Darwinian Elect. But he was beginning to eschew this Biological Calvinism, and to think that all men might be saved. As he mellowed he would have ethical man reject Ishtar's savagery. Moral *Homo sapiens* was trying 'to escape from his place in the animal kingdom', as Huxley was trying to escape the pain. Nature's Darwinian outrage had hurt him, and he was beginning to look inward.

But for now there was grief. A day or so later Nettie had her tumour removed. As she went 'icy cold' under the ether her last word was 'Mady'.[70]

28

Christic Was No Christian

HEART TROUBLE CONDEMNED old Huxley 'to the life of a prize pig': 'corporeal stuffing with meat and drink' and 'as few manifestations of intelligence as possible'. In 1888 he was at last forced to take it easy. That January came another warning, a second dose of pleurisy, which left him gasping and as 'melancholy as a pelican in the wilderness'. 'Bellows very creaky', he reported to Hooker.[1] His doctor, George Hames, ordered him out of London's smog to Bournemouth, and thus began the great cosmopolite's final exile.

They were all fleeing in their own ways. Jack left for Egypt, supported by Fred Waller and Harry, where he was to sublimate his grief in temple sketches for his painting of 'The Death of Cleopatra'. Nettie pored over Mady's childhood letters, retreating into the past, where she was 'quite happy'. Torn from the Good and Great, a croaky Hal vowed to attend no more banquets. He resigned his last posts – the governorships of those diametric bulwarks of his educational empire, Eton and University College. In maudlin mood he would 'jog along the declining path of life'. He hardly needed Nettie's confirmation that 'Old age is not exhilarating'.[2]

He remained the figurehead President of the Marine Biological Association long enough to see a fine Marine Laboratory built on Citadel Hill overlooking Plymouth Sound.[3] That too took him back to old Plymouth and his *Rattlesnake* adventure. London officialdom was now like the outback's snagging vines; having cut them with a machete chop, he was free to roam as a cultural ambassador for science.

When he could roam, that is. He was confined to his seaside digs through the Spring, coughing, the 'dreadful oppression' of his lungs lifting only slowly. The 'hermit life' depressed him, away from the

562

clubs and gaiety of home. He survived the days of tight-chested pain by writing a long Royal Society obituary of the man who had scientized the liberal struggle, Charles Darwin. A little every day got him through. He read the '"Origin" for the sixth or seventh time', grumbling at Darwin's higgledy-piggledy ways to the truth 'as dark as those of the Heathen Chinee'. He dug into the book daily, laying out the bare bones of the argument. The Royal Society had never honoured Darwin for his *Origin of Species*, and so Huxley was deliberately giving the dead hero the society's imprimatur.[4] He was officially gazetting the book after the society's years of cavilling.

Darwin was cast in the heroic mould. It was a life for the times. Darwin's had been a paradigm struggle to overcome a stunting Classical education. The youngster had forced his way through the extra-academical byways at school and Edinburgh, via that peculiar apprenticeship on HMS *Beagle*, to a career in science. As Huxley was writing, word from one of Darwin's midshipmen, Huxley's friend from his outback days, Philip King, reached him from Australia. For '4 years we occupied opposite corners of the Beagles poop', King recalled. 'He at his microscope and books and I making charts'. But that was an ancient world. Philip's brother Robert, who had gazed at tropical horizons from the *Rattlesnake*'s stern, was 'now a full blown archdeacon with breeches and gaiters'. Huxley found it hard to look back on the scuttle-bucket without the sensation of 'studying a fly in amber'. Outside the resin preserve the ageing Professor saw his own extinction. He wanted Hooker's reassurance that the obituary was sound. 'I am getting nervous over possible senility', he explained on 4 May 1888, '63 today & nothing of your Evergreen ways about me'.[5]

Huxley's 'Struggle for Existence' had met a resounding response from Right and Left. It had been one thing for Darwin to advocate the human struggle in the stable, affluent, Victorian Noon, that Age of Equipoise, but quite another for Huxley as the Depression crushed spirits in the mid-1880s. Right-wing individualists and left-wing anarchists railed hard. He knew Spencer would be 'in a white rage' at any talk of State-sponsored technical training, 'but he knows I think he has been doing mischief this long time' with own hands-off call to government.[6] Spencer was exiled to Brighton for his health (travelling back and forth to his guest house in a 'hammock slung diagonally in an invalid carriage'). He hated the corporatist, State-spending solution of Huxley the Chamberlainite. But there were more interesting exiles to the salubrious suburbs.

Britain now hosted one of the most famous revolutionary refugees, Peter Kropotkin. The amiable red-bearded Kropotkin – looking, said George Bernard Shaw, like a 'shepherd from the Delectable Mountains' – was responding to the deepening crisis with his *Conquest of Bread*. This was the first full-blown exposition of anarchist communism, in which fair distribution by local communes was to replace wages and property. Russia's revolutionary Prince and Ealing's rational Pope came from different worlds.

The Prince, once the personal page of Tsar Alexander II, had seen the world in exile. He had started in the gulag-wastes of Siberia, where he had become revolutionized by the rotting human flesh of the labour camps (and where his 50,000-miles study of tundra life from the Steppes to the Far East had made his reputation). He had travelled an equal intellectual distance towards a mutual-aid anarchism with a biological base. He was the propagandist, not of treason and terror, but of humanity's fraternal growth. Nurtured in a Darwinian age, familiar with Huxley's works (the *Science Primers* were even now being sought for Russian schools),[7] Kropotkin saw revolution as accelerated evolution, speeding us towards a benign Kingdom of Man. He projected benevolence onto Nature, as Darwin had projected bloodletting.

From Clairvaux prison in France (convicted of being a member of the International) he had written for Knowles' *Nineteenth Century*. Pardoned after an international outcry he moved to England in 1886. No sooner settled than Huxley's 'Struggle for Existence' had him planning a reply and putting the biological base to his anarchism. Kropotkin's 'Mutual Aid among Animals' in the *Nineteenth*, Knowles told Huxley, was 'one of the most refreshing & reviving aspects of Nature that ever I came across'. It was the first of a series of articles which would become the classic *Mutual Aid*.

Huxley portrayed primal man's savagery as a 'gladiator's show', a 'continual free fight'.[8] Darwin had seen morality develop from the social instincts, but for Huxley the instincts were antisocial, an amoral vestige to be repressed, the primeval lusts. Moral man was trying to escape them, trying to escape to his new kingdom.

For a Russian anarchist it was so different. His 'primitive' living tribes had always been bonded by customs into co-operative groups. So it was for many other species. The underpopulated tundra had shown the cossack a different nature, where mutual support among ants or yaks helped them in a hostile terrain. Sociability was the driving force, something played down by the English Malthusians. It destroyed Huxley's divide between savage and civilized man. Social cohesion was rooted in our biological past and the sanction of our future ethics. Instinct and morality were one, on a continuum, not on a war footing.[9] Man wasn't trying to *escape* his place in nature. He was trying to re-establish the primal balance destroyed by the capitalists who had caused mass starvation in Huxley's industrial 'war'. Overpopulation and starvation weren't the necessary correlates of progress, but a hideous corruption of an unjust technological society.

Huxley's writings started Kropotkin's search for a new moral philosophy based on a co-operative Nature. The two men showed how malleable Nature was, as easily appropriated by capitalist as anarchist. The age of extremes was nearing now; indeed, having over-elaborated the struggle in the days after Mady's death, Huxley with his meliorative tendencies and Chamberlainite sympathies was never that unsympathetic: Kropotkin was wrong, but his work was 'very interesting and important'.[10]

Switzerland was a familiar destination in Summer 1888. Huxley's life was now a perennial holiday in search of mountain sun. Away with Jack and Ethel, he had the physiological job of exercising one ventricle in the high dry air. He got his legs back, eventually 'going up 1500 or 2000 ft & walking 12–14 miles a day!' He swept back home to pick up the 'two or three cwt. of letters', only to be engulfed in the London fog. The black sooty vapour might have been the sublime canopy of the World City, but it belched from Hell's grate to kill the old. Everything beyond the front door disappeared and the suffocating stuff 'got down into the house & choked us'. It fouled Huxley's lungs and Hames ordered him out again. So they tried coastal Eastbourne for the Winter. 'I shall not have been home a month all the year', he told Hooker, but it was paying off. He went down 'weak, silent & depressed but gradually he became merry'. Striding out from his clifftop guest house over the Downs or up to Beachy Head saw him returning to normal.[11] The Mady crisis was finally over.

The Royal Society's troop of emancipated Huxleyites (or 'scientists' as they called themselves, although Huxley avoided the word) paid its parting respects in November 1888. The Copley Medal was its prestigious crown, the laurel of high rank. It was a sign that 'the scientific *orbis terranum*' now encircled the Huxleyan Sun. The medal would fill the gap on the mantelpiece where the nugget-like Royal Medal had stood before George's death. This one the old man would not have to hock. Hooker had taken the Copley in '87, and Huxley relished their 'niches in the Pantheon' together.[12] Sir Joseph was himself an aged idol turned to bronze and oil. He too could be seen on the Royal Academy walls, wedged between the nudes, incongruously wrapped in Lyell's old fur coat (a legacy) in Herkomer's portrait. The old sea dogs, whose 40-year masonic bond came from being salted on creaking ships, were the last of their Senior Service generation.

Deafness was forcing Huxley to fight shy of society, and he ceased public speaking. 'It irritates me not to hear – it irritates me still more to be spoken to as if I were deaf – & the absurdity of being irritated on the last ground irritates me still more'. But, for all the indignities, the spirit was kicking, and 'age hath not cooled the Douglas blood'. He proved it on front pages and letters pages, remaining a pillar of disbelief in the absurd. The cynic was incapable of letting the ludicrous pass. There were epistles to split sides: 1889 opened with him showing *Pall Mall Gazette* readers how to employ the tendons of the big toe like 'delicate Ariels' to produce spirit raps. There were rants in the *Times* on the 'cock and bull' about steam trawlers depleting fish stocks. And he snapped his fingers at the evangelical myth-makers. He squashed the rumours of Darwin's death-bed conversion, only to face American reports that he himself 'had been at Lourdes', seen the light, and was about to enter the 'Catholic Church!'[13]

The barbarians were on his borders, pressing at his own Hadrian's Wall. The agnostic populists shunned his scientific sackcloth-and-ashes approach. They arraigned Huxley for sticking to 'phenomenal evidence'. On Huxley's cleared ground they were busy erecting an Agnostic Temple to Spencer's 'Great Unknown' – the Thing on the far side of the sensory veil. The 'Jewish tribal God' might be dead, but in this temple 'our best feelings, such as love, hope, conscience, and reverence' might 'find reflections of themselves in the Unseen World'.[14] This urge for a 'super-phenomenal' Something to satisfy the emotions led to new catechisms from the new Saladins, even a graft of Zoroastrianism from the agnostic chairman of the London and Brighton Railway Samuel Laing. It was a mockery, a new idolatry, as the rationalist priests made 'metaphysical teraphim out of the Absolute, the Unknowable, the Unconscious'.

This perversion of agnosticism heated him to 'boiling pitch', and 'I really can't keep the lid down any longer'. The Puritan lashed the market traders from the Temple, furious at the pagan idols. He met them with a rambling exegesis of 'Agnosticism' in 1889, surprisingly his first. He romanticized his own search for a new authority, and told how, coming out of the trap of youth like the fox shorn of its tail, he had invented the term *agnostic* 'to show that I, too, had a tail'.

(He had coined the word privately, at the Metaphysical Society in 1869, but until this moment not even his X-Club friend Hirst had realized that it was Huxley's neologism.) Boiling away happily, Huxley almost vaporized the concept. Agnosticism was 'not a creed', he said, 'but a method'.[15] It was a Socratic questioning, the 'axiom' of science, a holding fast only to what is good, the 'foundation of the Reformation', a demand that every man 'give a reason for the faith that is in him'. And in keeping this faith 'a man . . . shall not be ashamed to look the universe in the face'.

His blunderbuss shot peppered the fat Church Congress on one side and faddist Church Agnostic on the other. The Positivists were hit by the ricochet. (As Huxley dug at them: 'Charles the Second told his brother, "They will not kill me, James, to make you king"'. Nor was science 'destroying the historical foundations of the noblest ideal of humanity [Christianity]', to put Positivism's 'incongruous mixture of bad science with eviscerated papistry' in its place.) The 'Agnosticism' article was pure Huxley, so full of 'tender devotedness', said Knowles, that he would 'win souls' 'even from Baptists'.[16] It was 'about the very finest article you ever wrote'.

The ascetic sceptic was thoroughly ashamed of the pleasure he took. The more so because Dr Wace at the 1888 Church Congress had had the temerity to call him an 'infidel', a sorry 'unbeliever' in Biblical authority. That gave Huxley the excuse to shift the article onto Biblical ground to attack that rival authority. Through the years of Mady's madness he had buried himself in ancient demonology, studying that 'preposterous and immoral' story of the devils cast by Jesus into the Gadarene Swine. In 'Agnosticism' he made Jesus just another orthodox Jewish teacher, a product of his culture with a contemporary faith in unclean spirits. Indeed, for holding that Gentile converts had to obey the Jewish Law, Christ was portrayed as another 'infidel' himself in Wace's book. As possessed pigs became the nation's dinner talk, Huxley separated Jesus' Nazarene beliefs from the later Christianity fashioned by Paul.[17] Here was the leitmotif of his 'Natural History of Christianity', if he could write it.

In the 1880s no elite scientist accepted a literal Day of Creation or a Deluge that left a geological trace.[18] (Sounded out by No 10, Huxley called the President of Canada's McGill University, William Dawson, the colonies' last 'Mosaic Geologist'. Thereupon Gladstone promptly knighted Dawson, but not before echoing his claim that palaeontology proved the Divine inspiration of the Pentateuch.) If the Bishop of Oxford had tried to revive exorcism in the 1850s,[19] Jowett's *Essays and Reviews* had buried it. By the 1880s Huxley was simply exploiting miracles and demons to market his rival agnostic product. His technique was to make contemporary religious testimony tell against venerable traditions – testimony retrieved by the historical and scientific expert.

These clever digressions into first-century events were a sign of science's new cultural authority. Scientific naturalism had been part of urban industrialism's assault on the old landed interest, but now the new professionals claimed to speak on the country's behalf. By contrast, the Church of England was portrayed as a party organ, 'not the Church of a nation but of a class'. This class aspect was complicated as the situation blackened in the 1880s. In the Depression, bread rioters and socialist agitators menaced the Establishment from below. The theological spine noticeably stiffened, and there were concerted efforts to discredit Huxley's rival naturalistic morality. Lilly saw the moral bud blighted in the theological darkness, and the 'Baal of Dead Mechanism' degrade children and ruin women. For Mallock 'the miserable [moral] rags ... [with] which [Huxley] attempts to cover the life which he professes to have stripped naked of superstition are part and parcel of that very superstition'. Morality and social safety were impossible without a supernatural sanction. From the Godhead a descensive spiral of power passed through his Church – indeed the 'whole structure of society is pervaded by the will and power of God'.[20] His presence is revealed in a sequence of miracles from the Creation to the Resurrection.

Huxley was kicking away the supernatural props of a rival profession. It was a social response, a ratification of a new cultural order. The Church had used its supernatural sanction against socialism; now Huxley would be forced to find new arguments. Having tarred the theological despots who ruled through the 'terror of possible damnation', he would have to make Nature rule against the revolutionaries too.

Agnosticism's weak freedoms had been hard won: freedom to follow the evidence, a freedom sanctioned by the Protestant appeal to private conscience.[21] Vigilance was wanted to protect them. Jowett, 'a coward of a man of peace', marvelled at Huxley's martial attitude. 'What a tremendous controversialist he is!' 'Such smashing blows!'[22] He took it as a sign of renewed health, and he was right. Huxley considered it almost indecent to have gone through so much and still be 'above ground'.

He was 'wonderfully well'. Just as Kingsley had revived him after Noel's death, so 'Agnosticism' was balm for his weak joints. According to Nettie, the paper 'seemed to run from the end of his pen &

gave him inexpressible pleasure'.[23] In late January 1889, Hal sat by the wintry sea, wallowing in an infernal Dantean world. He was dutifully discrediting medieval witnesses to the miraculous when the family news completed the spring in his step. Having doubted Church authority, Pater now found himself in and out of Church. Ethel, their youngest, not yet 23, had been Jack's companion in the dark days after Mady's death. She had shared his love of painting and taken over Mady's toddler Joyce. They became engaged.

It was a 'noble thing' to take charge of Joyce, said Ethel's god-mother, Lady Armstrong. (Sir William had capped the industrialists' rise with a peerage.) Ethel was 'undoubtedly the proper person'. Proper or not, it was still illegal. Jack was her brother-in-law. Marrying him was against the law. The Deceased Wife's Sister Bill sought to change all that, but it was still before the Lords and being resisted ferociously. The law was 'an ageing iniquity', said Hooker, but it was the law.[24] The bishops would uphold it on a reading of Leviticus, although their real concern was for that Victorian custom of chaste girls keeping house for their married sisters. Their Lordships were removing temptation.

Huxley found the 'Bishops and their aristocratic *clientèle*' patronizing. Might not the sister be the best stepmother, making the arrangement 'eminently beneficial'? Friends rallied round. Hooker took Collier's devotion to the family as 'a strengthening of an old undying love'. Jack had 'been tried by fire, & come out pure gold', said Nettie, happy to see him accompany Ethel 'in life's journey'. And unlike Mady, Ethel was 'absolutely fearless'. She was prepared for the snubs of parsons' wives.[25] There was no better match.

Pater had hardly got back to impugning the saints when the impulsive Nettie became engaged to a mining engineer. The rugged Harold Roller had done well in America, and he was on a private income. He was introduced at dinner on 23 January. During the dreaded 'mauvais quatre [sic] d'heure' in Professor Huxley's study, Roller found the paterfamilias 'completely patched up – seams caulked and made seaworthy'. The terror of Mady's madness was receding, even if they thought of her 'every moment of the day'.[26]

But the old ship was still docked in the Thames fog. Now, with the last girls engaged, and Harry preparing to go into practice with Dr Hames, they could search for a seaside mooring.

The sea had its attractions. Huxley still dreamed about those New Guinea palms. Amid the din of a glittering reception, he would see himself 'waking up on the flat plank . . . in the bright dawn of a tropical morning . . . when every noise was hushed except the lap lap of the waves'. But no Mauritian paradise for them – it would have to be the Channel coast at Eastbourne. Beachy Head would provide a continuity with those gale-tossed days on Caldy cliffs. And if the rolling Downs did not quite evoke the Alps, they served to blow away the same London ills. The mountaineer was a little stooped now, and comical as he trailed a pack of sheepdogs over the hills, attracted by his undressed wool coat. With his aching ears protected by huge cap flaps, he looked a bit 'doggy' himself.[27]

The chicks had fledged. Some were flying. Rachel was accompanying Alfred to Mexico on rail construction business. Len was about to start a school in New York. Jess, sharing her mother's Moravian interest in education, was writing an article for the *Nineteenth Century* on the moral training of children. With the last engagements announced, Huxley bought a plot high above Eastbourne near Beachy Head, and Fred Waller drew up the plans for a house. Huxley would call it 'Hodeslea' (the archaic name for 'Huxley', he supposed). Although one of the first men to know his ancestry back to Devonian days, he did not know where he came from. The man from nowhere was inventing a somewhere. He was pushing down ersatz roots. Hodeslea – 'temp. Henry IV' – was a last-minute legitimation, even though he could trace no farther back than his innkeeping grandfather. Nettie was no different. She knew now that she was illegitimate and was scouring the imperial fringes for her forebears. With Lizzie's son sailing to the Caribbean, she asked him to make enquiries about her mother, 'a Miss Thomas', born in Antigua, and her grandmother, three times married in the colony.[28]

People wanted to know about Huxley. But he had to be 'bothered . . . out of my life' before he would supply the most perfunctory autobiography to accompany a published portrait. And then the few pages were curiously truncated – as lamentably short-breathed as Spencer's was laughably long-winded. What passed as an autobiography was a pastiche of anecdotes and smokescreens through which he remained invisible. Nothing was given away. He felt like Dr Johnson, ready 'to take Boswell's life' on hearing of any biography. The autobiography fizzled out even before Darwin's début. The pages were published without his knowledge in an obscure 'who's who' and reprinted in the Normal School's own magazine, greedy for crumbs from the Dean's table.[29] But the students were none the wiser.

'Agnosticism' had pushed the *Nineteenth Century* through four editions. Everyone had been reading it: at Windsor Castle M'Ladies had been astonished, and Knowles goaded Huxley to lash the bishops and get Wace into the 'witness-box' again to convict himself on 'all that herd of swine' stuff. And so 'Agnosticism: A Rejoinder' was set going in February. Knowles rubbed his hands. Others saw what was happening. Hooker wasn't alone in his dismal view of 'Editors, who feed like maggots on controversial articles'. The confrontations were stage-managed. Knowles even hung pictures of his participants on the wall, and now added a new sketch of Huxley bought at Christie's. Given a lull in the fighting, he would drop in Mrs Humphry Ward's article on the 'New Reformation', using Len's sister-in-law (herself under a cloud at the Church Congress for her loss-of-faith novel *Robert Elsmere*) to start a second front. The frisson increased his circulation. And Huxley loved every moment. 'You can't think how I enjoy writing now'. One last 'little shove to the "New Reformation"' and 'I shall think the fag-end of my life well spent'.[30]

It was a case of consecutive articles and marriages. In the buoyant mood he sailed through Nettie's wedding on Shrove Tuesday, 5 March. It was the last time they would see Marlborough Place decked out in palms and flowers. Nettie, tall and gangly, wafted down the aisle waving her bouquet, looking, a friend said, 'like some handsome giraffe'. The wedding gifts were laid out in the front room, and with the rising crime rate in the Depression they were watched over by a detective.[31] With 200 guests, it doubled as a farewell party for their London friends. The next day Huxley 'bolted' back to Eastbourne to finish his 'Rejoinder'.

Knowles had it four days later, and his £44 cheque paid the wedding bills. To his joy he found it more 'A Rejoinder' and less 'Agnosticism'. Huxley was now camped so securely in the first century – making Christ's Nazarene sect so many more 'infidels' – that it was doubtful if he would ever escape back to the real world of Devonian swamps. Christ no Christian! 'The Church founded by Jesus . . . became extinct in the country of its birth'! No wonder the April *Nineteenth Century* shot through two editions in days. Biblical criticism became Huxley's *cheval de bataille*, revealing him for the old stump orator he was. The Pauline religion which 'coalesced with the State in the 4th century . . . is Alexandrian Judaism and Neoplatonic mystigogy', mixed with 'much of the old idolatry', and its success owed little to 'the truth or falsity of the story of Jesus'. By now Huxley, the pure popularizer, was muscling in on the assyriologists' work – using it to pound the historical authority of a rival profession. He was exploiting esoteric German sources to score points against Wace and Gladstone. His was still a Manichaean world of 'us' and 'them', and on the question of who was 'to have the confidence of the general public',[32] the *arriviste* agnostic made sure it was 'us'.

Knowles dubbed it Huxley's 'Gospel of Common Sense'. But it wasn't a gospel. There were no rival articles of faith; nothing on that holy trinity of scientific naturalism: physical causation, the uniform order of nature, and an objective world. And wisely so, given his pitch to the public. For Huxley had the same faith that 'order is lord of all' that Wace had in Our Lord as the cause of order. It was simply an axiom underpinning his deconsecrated cosmos. It 'cannot be proved', as he knew, even if deductions from it 'are always verified by experience', and so his onus remained on discrediting witnesses who claimed to find any miraculous deviation. But Knowles was right in using Huxley's favourite term, 'Common Sense'. This was how he struck the gadget-marvelling Victorian public. He made them feel that 'the whole edifice of practical life is built upon our faith' in an unbroken chain of causation.[33]

There were fewer clergy to face now. With no chance of passing the Deceased Wife's Sister Bill – and the English 'fanatics' getting even 'the Swiss Gov. to forbid such marriages' – Jack and Ethel sailed to Norway on 29 March to marry. A frail Nettie was unhappy at not making the North Sea crossing, but Hal, who sailed with them to Christiania, thought it 'quite unfitting for her to go'. He got back to watch Joe Chamberlain fight the 'bigotry & opposition' against this 'much needed social reform'.[34] Huxley put pressure on the Liberal Unionist Lord Hartington to get Lord Salisbury to allow a free vote, but the Bill was defeated on 9 May.

With his fourth article in five months the critical response began to pall. 'Agnosticism and Christianity' appeared in June's *Nineteenth Century*. Leslie Stephen had alerted him to one of Newman's old Tracts, and the Cardinal's denial that 'evidence [was] the test of [religious] truth' served to hang every ecclesiastical iniquity. But the relentless impeachment of faith was wearing thin. Hooker really thought 'you have exhausted the subject, & completely vindicated our position'. Tyndall saw him 'hacking a dead horse'. The high-flyers of the fifties had become the old fogies of the eighties. Gone were the glory days of Darwin and Lyell, Colenso and *Essays*, when the miraculous base of the powerful State Church was eroded by radical Nonconformists, when the boom economy allowed new professionals the luxury of looking for a New Reformation. The interminable Depression had coincided with a specialist age, as young Gradgrind scientists put their heads down and looked to their pay packets. 'They shut their eyes to the obstacles which clericalism raises', Huxley moaned.[35] They were not following him.

Huxley's age was passing: the Dissenters' meritocracy was yesterday's victory. In the gloomy Depression many who had sought scientific redemption turned to the new politics, to socialism, suffrage, the New Woman. Those 'dirty Radicals', Hooker seethed to Tyndall. 'It makes one weary of life to see the spread of democracy and socialism'. The world was sweeping past the old cronies. Socialism was questioning the Malthusian core of Darwin's eternally struggling Nature. Technology at its finest hour, as the great boring machines worked under the sea (the Channel Tunnel was already a mile long), was failing to feed the masses.

The literati were getting blasé about Huxley's onslaughts. The new *Review of Reviews* abstracted his explanation of Biblical miracles in one word: 'lies'.[36] He was stymied by his own success. He had made doubting a middle-class virtue. Even as he denounced sweeping devils into the Gadarene swine as a violation of Victorian property rights, he was being cited as a 'well-behaved blasphemer' by MPs trying to extend legal protection to non-Christian faiths after Lord Coleridge's judgment.[37]

A divisive politics was even shaking Huxley's social group. The X-Club was 'almost in xtremis'. Two or three would struggle in to St George's Hotel, down the road from the Royal Institution; sometimes Hooker would 'sit-alone at table'. Hirst, 'shrunk to a skeleton', hardly presented a corporeal presence.[38] But the old rogues would still clash tusks over politics. By November the ivory giants, Spencer and Huxley, were locked in their death-throes. The sexagenarians were fractious, sensitive to the slightest lapse of protocol (Huxley even stopped reading Spencer's proof 'Autobiography' in October after it arrived second-hand from a daughter of one of Spencer's friends!). High dudgeon became high drama in November as Huxley waded into a *Times* dispute over land socialism with a series of letters which cuffed Spencer's *a priorism* in politics and science. They made Spencer 'treat cholera by deductions from physiological principles'. A smarting Spencer took it as a public slap, thinking that Huxley was 'making me look like a fool to a hundred thousand readers'.[39] An extremist age had simply exposed the political gulf. The two old friends had diverged. From a common reaction to a strangling Church monopoly, Spencer had gone on to make his Nonconformist fair-competition ethic a total government hands-off call: no State favouritism, no State spending, no endowments, whether of Church or Science. But Huxley the government scientist, the State Commissioner, clawing professional power, wanted a State-paid education, a 'ha'pny' on the rates for libraries, spending on science, on schools, on the modern State Secretariat.

It 'abruptly ended' a 35-year friendship. Spencer's letter of resignation from the X sent the others into a spin. Intellectually ponderous, he was unequal to his nimble antagonist, and Hooker thought it incumbent on Huxley to say something 'soothing'. Spencer was a sensitive anachronism in a growing social democracy. Do not further 'aid in his downfall', they pleaded. Be 'merciful as you are strong'.[40]

But Huxley wondered how he had put up for so long with that boorish 'long winded . . . pedant', who had 'about as much tact as a hippopotamus'.[41] He, of course, was tact itself.

Knowles wormed his way in, sniffing controversial carrion. Already in November he had convinced Huxley to follow up his *Times* letters on the 'New Radicalism', upping the ante to £3 a page. It led to a set of essays that had Huxley applying the brake to socialism's demands. Henry George's land-nationalizing *Progress and Poverty* 'has had an *immense* effect', agreed Knowles, and Huxley could see no 'more damneder nonsense'.

George's *Progress* was an attack on property, competition and Malthus: the whole Darwinian establishment. It was being touted by none other than Alfred Russel Wallace, the co-inventor of natural selection, now a pensioner living in Dorset. Wallace was an outsider to the end. A renegade on Human Darwinism, he remained true to socialism and spiritualism, which he used to redress the political balance. To him they were all of a piece: the spirit powers made economic competition redundant by guiding society. He even saw the economically free woman as the way ahead, the sexual selector, the chooser, not the feeble chosen of Darwin's *Descent of Man*. Wallace had always been interested in the political goal of human existence. Ever the propagandist, he had posted Huxley books (the latest was Arthur Bell's *Why Does Man Exist?*). Though never daunted by Darwin, he had 'never got over a feeling of awe for Huxley'. Now the outsider was in Huxley's sights – or rather his egalitarian ideal.

This was the world to play for. Huxley's manuscript, said Knowles, receiving it on 13 December, 'makes a final end . . . of the tom-foolery'. But the title, 'Rousseau & rousseauism'! Knowles saw his profits dribbling away, and since 'I especially want working men to read the paper' he turned it into a blatant 'On the Natural Inequality of Men'.[42] There was no disguising their intent.

Never once was *Progress and Poverty* mentioned, but he made it fall with 'Rousseau's blether'. Huxley set into noble savagery, ancient communes, free-born men and dreams of primeval equality. Rousseau *was* George, a 'stalking horse' for the revolutionized masses maddened by hunger, the dreamer who 'clothed passion in the garb of philosophy' and would end injustice by the 'perpetration of further injustice'. Huxley's 'savage' was a slave to inheritance and circumstance, a gritty survivor in a primevally privatized world, never the egalitarian of Wallace's 'land socialists' or Kropotkin's 'primitive communism'. Society had to be ruled by 'sound judgment', not the 'despotism of a majority'. The 'cook and the loblolly boys' could no more countermand the Captain's orders on a man-o'-war than the ship of state – and so saying Huxley echoed the top brass which had damned his own shipmates' demands 45 years earlier. He was accused by the Left of latter-day hero-worshipping,[43] but Huxley really had in mind a latter-day Benthamism: rule by a technical elite.

The phrase 'Social Darwinism' was just coming into use – first in France, whence it spread to England (the French translated 'The Natural Inequality of Men' specifically to meet their own labour unrest).[44] Until this time 'Darwinism' had subsumed the social dimension; the Darwinians had never doubted that animals and society were to be explained in the same biological terms. Huxley was ripe for translation as the expanding Continental industries tried to pacify their own labour forces; his papers had honed the political edge of Darwinism – and 'Social Darwinism' carried a new anti-socialist intent.

For him overpopulation was the serpent in the Socialist Eden. For a Darwinian, the unprecedentedly high growth rates of the 1870s[45] confirmed the Malthusian prediction. Peace and plenty in a socialist arcadia would only increase the number of births and start the struggle for resources all over again. Huxley had no faith that even a 'despotic government' could control population by a eugenics programme. (Nor would it be desirable: coming from a family having its share of failures, he knew how minuscule a change could turn the 'unfit' into successes.)[46] Birth control with its threat to chastity was no option. Yet it was becoming one for the younger generation, even for his own civic-reforming pupils. Patrick Geddes, a maverick professor who looked like a Greek Orthodox bishop, had become Besant's friend and Kropotkin's host, and he was considering it in *The Evolution of Sex*.[47] Ultimately Huxley, like Darwin before him, was asserting mid-Victorian, male-governing, family values.

Knowles was engineering events furiously. He was running Kropotkin's papers on co-operation in animal communities, and urging them on Huxley as the most uplifting articles on Nature that he had ever read. Then he had Spencer fire salvoes from the other side. Spencer's own elephant's memory went back two decades to Huxley's attack in 'Administrative Nihilism'. Relations were at a low ebb now; 'for a man who goes whining about that I have killed him', noted Huxley, Spencer could still summon up an 'allowance of spite'.[48] Too many years of benign indifference towards Spencer's epistemological shortcomings turned to contempt for his *a priori* ethics and politics.

Others saw the futility of the two men bickering when the nation 'seems ready to thrust itself into the arms of the Socialist'. Huxley's politics were unmasked now. Some asked his views on socialism, or the Southampton dock strike. Others didn't any more. For them his materialistic science remained a potent force, spreading 'the common particles of Light', but it was becoming 'a gigantic Mrs. Pardiggle . . . assuming the airs of a social censor'. Malthus and Darwin had canonized the struggle for resources, restraining the altruists who would wade into the 'social swamp' to save the drowning. But this uncharitable Malthusianism was under attack; Darwin was under attack. Huxley, having struggled himself to accept Darwin's desperate Malthusianism, ironically found himself under attack. His own Darwinian diktat had the Left grieving 'that the religion of Science, hailed by all of us as the birth of a new day, is fossilising already into a religion of despair'. What 'sadder sight' than

> Professor Huxley fighting for the *status quo* in Politics . . .
> the man who argues in favour of Force as a proof of
> ownership, and of a statute of limitations in matters of
> secular wrongdoing, will one day have to cast in his lot
> with Ecclesiasticism and the Bishops . . . for Church and
> State stand or fall together.[49]

The glint of truth shone from those menacing words. The professionals were defending their hard-won stake in society. Had the rioters peered through the smashed windows of the Pall Mall clubs, they would have seen the liberal scientists hobnobbing with the liberal clergy.

Deep in the 'Class *v.* Mass' debate, Huxley was revealing the politics that lay behind his supposedly 'neutral' science. Knowles cleverly corralled him with the 'Classes'. The editor ignored the response of the Social Democratic Federation's Henry Hyndman, a former City gent converted by Marx's *Kapital*, and a 'poor fool' in his view; he ran instead a poorer fool's reply – a pastry-cook's. Huxley had dared to damn land nationalization in the people's interest, dared to speak 'for them, of them, and at them'. Huxley and 'his bosom friend the Duke of Argyll' were simply 'too high up in the social scale' to see why 'millions of thoughtful working men' saw hope in Henry George's doctrine of the 'natural rights of man'. From the jam-puff shop he was just another of the 'dukes, earls, professors, ministers, lawyers, soldiers' who 'produce next to nothing' and yet 'are all well housed, clothed, and fed'.

Huxley was horrified. Knowles had printed the pastry-maker's 'passionate prejudices' to expose the 'mind of his masses'. But impassioned prejudice could look like a passionate plea. 'It is very easy for well-fed dukes and professors to philosophise', seethed the cook. Just give them

> 20s. per week of sixty or seventy hours' hard labour, and
> give them a wife and four or five children to provide for out
> of this magnificent income. Just give them five years of this
> life – as a very interesting experiment, you know

and when they are screaming for justice quote them Huxley's high-sounding words. The scientist had 'got out of his groove in taking up politics'. Pleas from the gut always touched Huxley. Now an extremist age had marked him as the oppressor whose highfalutin tongue justified 'bâtons, bayonets, bullets, and battering rams to keep the power to rob'.[50] Knowles had turned the tables, throwing a bolshy cook into the plush-leather heart of the Establishment to draw *Huxley* out.

Wasn't he the popular champion, wafting away priestly hobgoblins, levelling the vaunted aristocracy, twitting the bishops, welcoming a secular State? The workers did not realize that he was clearing a professional space, making a middle-class revolution. False expectations led to fierce denunciations: from the anarchists' *Commonweal*, which saw equality and suffrage, 'the Professor's bugbears', as the driving 'forces in the evolution of modern society', to 'the servant gal's' *Daily Telegraph*, where Henry George's friends berated him as the 'specialist transformed into the dilettante'.[51] Sitting at Beachy Head, the old chap in the shaggy wool coat watched society drift past with equanimity.

Another blast, 'Natural Rights and Political Rights', would blow the misty vapours from 'men's eyes – even the "Socialists"', said Knowles. Huxley was left defending the 'might and right' of an amoral Darwinian nature to undermine the dream. But the more he stressed inequality and struggle, the more he had to salvage human ethics. It was the relentless pressure of socialism with its assumption about *natural* rights that made him drive the wedge deeper between

Darwin's 'ceaseless and pitiless' civil war, as the *natural* state of things, and the civilized curbing of these 'anti-social and anarchic tendencies'. By 1890 a bloody Darwinism and buffeting socialism had pushed him into the ethical realm. No longer could a cut-throat Nature provide the rules of ethical conduct. He was still intent on stabilizing society, but Nature would henceforth play a vastly different role in his lay sermons. The question became how far *moral* rights should infringe on a natural 'unmitigated selfishness'.[52]

Huxley could not even sail off to Madeira in early April without revises of 'Government: Anarchy or Regimentation' chasing him to Plymouth. The trip was to give 25-year-old Harry a holiday in the sun before he started in medical practice. It was a far cry from 1846 when bishops blessed creaking wooden ships and Anglicans ruled the waves. In Plymouth the latest shrine to science was suitably hewn from Devonian coral limestone. He paid a visit to the new Marine Station on Citadel Hill, with its labs and aquariums, his last as President of the Marine Biological Association.[53]

Luxury liners were also a far cry from donkey frigates. But Hal could show his son up on the four-day run: 'head wind all the way', he reported home, 'and enough rolling to make Harry take to his berth'. No swabbing decks, no sick-room muster, but deckchairs and sea air, and the luxury of poring over botany books and putting the finishing licks to his paper. On deck he tore at both Spencer's deregulation – no taxes, no State aid, no State education – and socialism's 'despotism of the "general will"'.[54] So what was *his* solution to social regeneration, critics asked. It was the sum of all he had stood for: an open, competitive meritocracy, overseen by a strong progressive government counselled by experts. His technocracy was Chamberlain's, the stuff of public libraries, compulsory education, Council water and lighting. Perhaps it was the way of the future, between the extremes.

The beginning and end of life were spent sailing from political turmoil. Now a queasy son joined him at the rails as the ship steamed into Funchal on 3 May. 'The last time I saw the place was in December 1846. All my life lies between the two visits. I was then $21\frac{1}{4}$ & I shall be 65 tomorrow'. The sleepy town was a bit bigger now, with a few English villas dotting the hills. Otherwise half a century hardly told. Wheeled carriages were still unknown, and the daily pace was dictated by the plodding oxen. It was a last nostalgic look back. The memory gave him a sprightly air. The 65-year-old proved it on his cob mare, as he took Harry for a five-hour

ride up to the Great Curral . . . – about 10 miles . . . &
3500ᶠ. up. We started at 11. the weather looking very
doubtful and heavy clouds overhanging the mountain top.
We passed the little Curral up to which I, and a party of
mad middies rode 44 years ago – (I wonder we did not all
break our necks) and then rode on & on, through fine
forests.

The staid Harry already had the makings of a 'worthy but dull'
doctor. By comparison Huxley felt 'the youngest man of the family'.
'When you & I were five and twenty, my pet, there was a sort of go in
both of us', he wrote to Nettie, 'which I do not observe in any of our
children'. Harry was no mad middy, but he had the Huxley independence. The casual mention of his engagement to a nurse before he
left elicited his father's wry promise 'to be the young lady's slave . . .
By the way, you might mention her name; it is a miserable detail, I
know, but would be interesting'. This last fling took them both over
breakneck passes. Harry, seeing his father's burnt sienna face and
flashing eye, must have sensed his exotic past. Atop the volcanic
crater with its deep ravines a puff of 'wind cleared the clouds away
and the whole basin . . . – the bottom 1500 fᵗ. below us & the top of
its great wall 2000 fᵗ. above us – was revealed. It was a wonderful
sight'.[55] A religious scene of subtropical splendour: Huxley had the
21-year-old's fire in his belly again.

The zest showed in his 'itch to be fighting'. That was 'always a safe
& good sign', agreed Knowles. The cold warrior returned to trot out
more £70 articles. The editor kept putting up 'targets', showing how
routine the pot-shots were becoming, making him a mill for cranking
out controversy. How about that shocker in the *Essays and Reviews*
mould, *Lux Mundi*? Here was a collection by Church progressives
who treated miraculous Floods and Daily Creations as allegorical.
Revd Aubrey Moore, the Oxford Reformation historian and fearless
Darwinian, was among them. He could happily follow Huxley in
tracing our image of Creation to Milton's poetry. Moore's God
worked within Darwin's nature. But for Huxley, at the end of his life,
the real issue was the critical approach to sacred texts. That is what
made the 'antagonism between Science & Theology' so complete.[56]
The *Lux Mundi* progressives had 'distilled away every inconvenient
matter', wafted aside the salty 'transubstantiation' of Lot's Wife, dismissed Jonah's 'submarine navigation', made the Deluge a bogey
used by Jesus as a moral tale, and yet they 'continue to pay divine
honours to the residue'.[57]

Huxley stiffened with every year of controversy. Even his last-ditch Unitarian belief – that Jesus' personality had been cause of Christianity's departure from Judaism – melted away. Christ's Nazarenes were just another unoriginal Jewish sect.[58] Huxley's hardening showed as he started funding secular societies. He put money into the ailing *Agnostic Journal* to keep it afloat. (Given his stand-offish nature, the editors were 'surprised to notice how accurate was his knowledge of the work we belligerent Agnostics were carrying on'.) And he was projecting a 'strict secularity in State education' – no more Bibles.[59] He was harder, cynical still, and older by far. That is how Jack Collier painted him in 1890, as a subject fitting his own anti-clerical themes, to be followed appropriately by his painting of 'The Inquisition: Waiting for the Accused'.

He was an old Ironsides – the solid Puritan with a 'military bearing', wanting only the clunking metal. There was no need to run his pike through *Lux Mundi*; Canon Liddon in his fine 'silvery voice' did the job at St Paul's, insisting that Jesus wasn't 'accommodating' himself to a rude age. The 'trustworthiness of the Old Testament is', insisted Liddon, 'inseparable from the trustworthiness of our Lord Jesus Christ'. Huxley liked self-immolating deductions. It was his warrant to turn Noah's Flood into a 'Bowdlerised version' of an older Babylonian fable and hang Christian theology. It was slick and sensible and it caused as much fright as popping a balloon: and yet '30 years ago no decent magazine would have dared to publish such articles'. By now a scientific world-view had become the *de rigueur* perception for all things. He was a victim of his own success. One acolyte saw him as the 'High Priest of the New Religion' whose sermons grew slicker and more predictable by the day.[60] 'The Lights of the Church and the Lights of Science' passed without a stir in July's *Nineteenth Century*.

The decadent nineties hardly noticed. The new Hedonism was already flushing out his old Puritanism. Society was lost in *fin de siècle* abandonment. People wanted fun. Freak and perversity were the order of the day. Oscar Wilde was outraging London. Beardsley returned the exotic to Art. The Gadarene devil reappeared in *The Picture of Dorian Gray*; and, said Dorian in his topper, 'Life is a great disappointment'.[61] Nothing shocked the Upper Classes.

But old men are serious and this one wandered off to Stonehenge. He stood alone, between the megaliths on a wind-swept Salisbury Plain, far from any gaiety. Perhaps he was thinking of his deep ancestry, of a distant migration of peoples from the East. He was striking out in a last ethnological paper. With the young Oxbridge anthropologists disappointingly looking on anthropology as a background to the Classics, Huxley held to a multi-factored evolutionary method. He drew wide – prehistoric climates and archaeology, ethnology and philology, Ice Age glacial boundaries and Mediterranean changes – to pinpoint the cradle of the Aryans just west of the Urals.[62] Like a giant Gulliver, he watched swarms of men, the ants of neolithic history, migrating, diverging in peripheral pockets, evolving proto-languages, discovering copper. The detail blurred into his profoundly secular image of the immense human journey since the emergence of Europe's beetle-browed Neanderthals (then definitely known, from two skeletons found in Belgium in 1886, to be palaeolithic hunters of extinct mammoths).

He had an evolutionary belief that other modes of thought – like older forms of life – had existed in the past and persist as living fossils into the present. His positivist justification for wiping out these religious relics – born of Dissent's mid-century campaign against entrenched Anglican power – made prehistory more an ammunition dump to be mined than the basis for a proper sociology of religion.[63]

Knowles called him 'one of my chiefest pillars', and considering that his *Nineteenth Century* stable ran from Oscar Wilde to Bram Stoker, and Gladstone to Kropotkin, that was saying something. Seven articles in 1890 gave Huxley £500 to plough into his East-bourne garden. He poured it into levelling land, building conservatories and paths, and planting shrubs from Kew. The house was planned with the large rooms at the back looking onto the South Downs, and with an attic playroom for Joyce. Nettie scooted around in a bath chair choosing tiles and placing electric 'burners', tickled by the novelty of the new touch-of-a-switch lighting. But the delays in finishing: 'fitters, paperers, and polishers are like bugs or cock-roaches, you may easily get 'em in, but getting 'em out is the deuce'. The couple had to live out of suitcases in the Grand Hotel until November. Hal swore that this was his last move, 'except to a still smaller residence of a subterranean character!'[64]

London was no place any more. The city had lost its sobriety and charm and honesty; it was a city in search of the bizarre and exotic, its dandy shallowness a reaction to two decades of staid Puritanism. It were better to be in Eastbourne. Leaving Marlborough Place distanced them further from the Mady tragedy. It would still break Nettie's heart: 'every room is brim full of memories', of daughters and sons traipsing off to school, Hal coming home full of news, Mr Darwin popping around on Sunday morning. That world was gone. And its finality was confirmed at Christmas when sister Ellen and George's widow Polly died within days of one another. Naturally, the 'details were ghastly', the one scrounging money to die drunk, the other 'morbidly hysterical' and reeking of drugs.[65] But that cut the millstones from Hal's neck, the financial weight and worry dropped and he sprang back.

Death brought a clarity to times past. The Puritan's cosmos was blackening as sun after sun went cold. The endless losses, 'One feels them awfully on wakening every morning', said Hooker. And as Hal stood over the grave of Ellen Busk, his Egyptian priestess, the loss was 'grievously painful'.[66]

Gladstone's accusatory finger in *The Impregnable Rock of Holy Scripture* had Huxley making a rival gesture. He relished the G.O.M.'s 'rough coming on'. He was morose without a crusade, and delivered thanks to Providence for sending Gladstone to keep ''ome 'appy for me'. Again he would rubbish Gladstone's first-century beliefs – delivering theological right hooks and political lefts. Gladstone was being 'spread eagled' as much for his Irish politics; he sensed it, he saw his character being 'besmirched'. Tyndall's cheers accompanied the pounding of the Home Ruler. '*Hit this man*', he shouted from the ringside, seeing each punch lead to his political weakening.[67] And so it was Gadarene pigs again, or rather a Galilean foreigner's legality in sending them over a cliff (which was justified by Gladstone). Huxley made it a comment on the Home Ruler's cavalier attitude to the law of the land.

Huxley was a heathen foreigner himself in Eastbourne and the nosey locals kept an eye on him. The Professor had arrived fighting the greatest statesman of the century. This was the gossipy sticks, not the anonymous metropolis, and the *Sussex Daily News*, having witnessed the unholy onslaughts on Noah and Jonah, was reassured to see Huxley's daughters in church. Still the yokels thought these Grand Old Men could be better occupied than fighting over swine.

But Huxley could not 'give up tormenting ces drôles'.[68]

29

Combating the Cosmos

OF COURSE THE HATE MAIL started arriving. He was 'the Infidel and enemy of mankind' whose depraved writings 'are of the devil'.[1] And the Salvation Army was marching out to meet him.

The Army was led by another General. 'General' Booth's Army had a massive military field structure by 1890, with 9,400 officers commanding 1,375 corps and three-quarters of a million recruits. Having spent his later life studying the origins of sects, Huxley found one springing up under his nose: 'a new Ranter-Socialist sect', whose spine-tingling trombone parades and hymn-singing corybantism was so much 'sanctified buffoonery'. The two autocratic Generals, sharing so much and so little, prepared to do battle for the imperial spoils of the hinterland, the souls of the dispossessed. Their armies stood poised, their rival flags of Spiritual Democracy and Technocratic Professionalism fluttering, the one with its street carnivals, the other with its Darwinian promises. It was horribly uneven, for 'not even a Salvation Army of Huxleys' could stop the simpletons singing along with Booth.[2]

General Booth was four years younger. When Tom was in his back-street anatomy school run by that democratic New Connexion Methodist Marshall Hall, the working-class Booth was living up to Hall's democratic 'Methodist Jacobinism'; he too had joined the New Connexion; he too was a Chartist supporter. Like Tom, the evangelist was a prey to despondency and sought regeneration in a crusade. His Methodists denied the Anglicans' providentially happy world teeming with 'delighted existence'; for them, 'the whole creation travaileth and groaneth'. In his war cry, *Darkest England*, Booth could speak with Darwinian vigour of the weakest going 'to the wall'. But he was another whose radical religious duty was to aid this suffering creation. *In Darkest England and the Way Out* was an affir-mation that all life could be redeemed. Booth's image of a tormented Creation was little different from Huxley's. But he demanded some-thing more than Darwin's struggle and Huxley's Calvinist resignation. The fittest were not the Elect. For Booth, 'Everybody might be saved'.[3]

Booth had begun his East End social work in the 1860s as Huxley (20 years out of Rotherhithe himself) was preaching scientific salva-tion. And as Huxley had shouldered his rifle in the Volunteers, so this mobilization became Booth's inspiration, and he renamed his mission the 'Salvation Army'. This other shilling sergeant recruited to the razzmatazz of military bands. With mass unemployment and the socialists marching, Booth's Jacobinism emerged as 'social salvationism'. Day centres and hospices were set up. Hand-outs to striking dockers' families gained socialist sympathy. Shelters for battered women brought suffragette approval. (*Darkest England* even envisaged vigilantes to hunt rapists and force them to pay main-tenance.)[4] The East End's no-go ghettos were 'as unexplored as Timbuctoo'. But the Army's revivalism was a sort of 'moral coca', giving it the strength to march into *Darkest England* as Stanley had penetrated 'Darkest Africa'. Had this been an educational or sanita-tional reclamation Huxley would have cheered – but he saw it as a soul-saving militia parading with socialist regimentation, and he was horrified.

In Darkest England was published on 20 October 1890. Booth's name was on the title-page, but many doubted his primary author-ship. Beside him stood the former *Pall Mall Gazette* editor with the literary know-how, W. T. Stead – the founder of the *Review of Reviews* (which had infuriated Huxley by abstracting his articles on miracles under the rubric 'lies'). Stead the spiritualist stood on the other side of 'a gulf'. The 'filthy ex-convict' was loathed by Knowles for dealing in 'stolen goods', pirated abstracts in his *Review*. *Darkest England*, Knowles tipped off Huxley, 'was written & boomed by that most accursed of all Iscariots'. His 'hoof-prints are on every page'. Certainly two days after publication Stead had sent Huxley a copy, explaining that he 'had some hand in licking it into shape'.[5] What-ever the truth, Knowles cranked up the antagonism, adding a literary dimension to the political and religious friction.

Booth's campaign plan was to feed and reclaim the under-class in 'City Colonies', send them to the depopulated countryside for moral and agricultural training, and finally – under the influence of Stead's social imperialism – ship them out to the real colonies (and hadn't Huxley on the *Rattlesnake* seen the potential for new Indian empires started by the hungry millions from home?)[6] The scheme, said a rival missionary, was 'sensational through its very *audacity*'. Talk of shuffling off the rioting hordes made the book a huge seller. Its publication coincided with two months of the worst weather anyone could remember. Huxley's pipes froze, and the cold, angry jobless frightened his middle-class constituency. *Darkest England*'s promise of deliverance ensured that the funds flowed in; £750,000 found their way into the General's military chest. Riots and strikes threatened the well-to-do, who turned against the means-testing miserliness of the existing Charity Organisation Society, with its targeting of the deserving poor.[7] More and more went over to the Army.

A philanthropic Mrs Crawshaw was set to buy her place in heaven by popping £1,000 into Booth's account. But she asked Huxley to vet the scheme first, and thereby triggered the chain of events. The lack of safeguards for Booth's projected Poor Man's Bank were not what really frightened Huxley when he started digging. It was the scale of its 'socialist' organization. Beneath this cymbal-bashing 'corybantic Christianity' was a regimentation of enthusiasts 'pledged to blind and unhesitating obedience'. He cynically imagined a runaway machine, powered by 'unchastened religious fanaticism', drawing on slush funds and using 'Sicilian Mafia' tactics. The nightmare scenario culminated in evangelical socialist cadres 'with barracks in every town' threatening the liberal State itself. He told Jack Collier that

> The ultimate object of their plots is the establishment of a sort of Methodist Jacobin club with vigilance committees, under the name of 'Salvation Army corps' scattered all over the country. Decent men would not be able to call their souls their own if the plot succeeded – and Stead would have his Laboratories for Experimental investigation of the possibilities of Rapes all over the country.[8]

Why this extreme reaction? Was it because the tables had been turned: the ascetic scientist had been outmanoeuvred by a worldly salvationist? Whistle-blowing pamphlets encouraged the paranoia. Even some rival missionaries denounced Booth's 'dangerous autocracy'. Army watching became a national pastime, but then the uniforms were so visible on the streets. Continual scuffles in Huxley's own seaside town of Eastbourne between Salvationists and goading youths made the daily papers and led to calls for bans on Army marches (the *Eastbourne Gazette* spotted Huxley on the edge of a crowd watching one brawl). Even the socialists eyed the Salvationists warily. Booth, rather than saving the deserving paupers in the pool, like the charities committed to the free market, or fishing out the activists, as the socialists were doing, would share his resources with the 'dregs' at the very bottom.[9] It smacked of primitive Christian communism.

Years of political bickering had affected Huxley. He had seen the newly created London County Council fall to 'Radicals and Socialists', heard the curdling yells against the 'robber knights of capital' and 'brigand aristocracy of the Stock Exchange'. Socialism was evocative, and it was moving the masses. His fears heightened with trade-unionist hopes that Booth's 'autocratic Socialism' would eventually lose its '"fantastic" religious skin' to leave a standing Red Army. Already the socialists were emulating Booth by setting up their rival 'Labour Army' and heralding a quasi-religious new dawn to rival Christianity's. But Huxley's was a bizarre nightmare: it had Booth centralizing power, controlling the press and floating his own bank to process the millions and finance his militias. Letters from disaffected Army lieutenants told of vigilantes. The highest-ranking defector, a Major, Booth's private secretary, exposed the cashiering practices of the Chiefs of Staff. But only Huxley saw the Red menace. To the end he was telling Hooker that 'the Papistical & Socialistic schemers who were rubbing their hands in the hope of profiting by his mad project & the "Army" organization, are sold'.[10]

He sent a stream of letters to the *Times* on the Army in December. It was no good telling him to 'neglect it & so give it the best chance of an earlier death', as Knowles tried. Knowles refused to dignify that 'blackguard Stead's last swindle' by printing a rebuttal. So Huxley took up the street technique; he turned the letters into a shilling pamphlet. These could be shifted in huge numbers at these evangelical moments. Macmillan had 2,000 out by January 1891, with a second edition in February. And in reply came the 'heaps of abusive letters'. 'I have not been so well abused for an age', Huxley claimed, revelling in it. 'It's quite like old times'.[11]

The Darwinian 'workhouse' solution was to help the deserving fight their own way out. Do not herd the moral sheep into Booth's 'narrow theological' pen, pleaded Huxley: 'self-respect and thrift are the rungs of the ladder by which men may most surely climb out of the slough of despond'.[12] Liberalism had been hardened on the Darwinian proving ground.

But through the crises a more sympathetic explanation of the hovel-dwellers was growing. The poor were not moral cretins, not atavists by 'nature'; in the socialists' view they were stunted by their 'nurture'. They were deprived rather than depraved. The State had to better their squalid conditions, lest the whole race 'degenerate'. Others thought that the race would degenerate if the slum-dwellers *were* cosseted in an egalitarian society. There was the apocalyptic backdrop to the *fin de siècle*. Huxley had emphasized the 'persistence' of life – how a living Mesozoic world might survive in the unchanging oceanic depths. But as the decadent art of Beardsley and Oscar Wilde shocked and Lankester saw stagnation as the fate awaiting a society that failed the industrial race, another pupil raised on Huxley's proving ground projected a different collapse. The leisured classes would degenerate into effete Eloi, taking to 'art and eroticism . . . languor and decay', to be bred in herds and devoured by the troglodyte masses.[13] H. G. Wells – having absorbed Huxley's message of a hostile universe honing mankind – had begun his book in Huxley's nemesis year, 1887. It would become *The Time Machine*. Science fiction was coloured by Huxley's pessimism.

By now Nettie was begging him 'to give up controversy'. But to no avail, and March 1891 found him settling 'accounts with that little cad of a duke & the G.O.M.' In the *Nineteenth Century* he was still running rings around Gladstone as he had once Owen, with that facetious glee in the face of grave absurdity. Policing the intellect, he called it. He was now carving ideological weapons from the esoteric work of the assyriologists. He used the Babylonian myths of a flood and half-mile-long ark to discredit the Biblical plagiarism. Gladstone 'you will find like a dead dog with a stone tied to his neck in March number of XIX', he alerted Hooker. And then he declared himself 'as sick of controversy as a confectioners boy of tarts'. Lord Armstrong did not believe it for a minute. He knew that this intellectual Gordon would ' "die happy" on the field of literary battles'.[14]

The 74-year-old secularist George Holyoake watched Huxley's five-year 'duel with Gladstone, Wace and the Duke of Argyll', staggered at the impunity of it – the way Huxley made Christianity just another regional religion, with a largely borrowed mythological base. What was atheist fanaticism in the 1840s had become mainstream pulp by the 1890s. Holyoake had been jailed 50 years earlier (to deny God then was treasonous in an Anglican State). Now working-class political weaponry had become middle-class professional ideology, and he gave up editing the *Reasoner* 'because his views were abundantly advocated in the most respectable Quarterlies'. There was no incarceration for Huxley. Science, the professions and suffrage had etched away so many Anglican-State standards that pious blasphemers were now patted. Hence his gall in telling Holyoake that this fighting was 'hard upon a poor man who has retired to "make his sowl" as the Irish say, in the sea side hermitage'.[15]

His 'sowl' had all the security of home life. Nothing was allowed to disturb it. Privacy meant keeping out the searching spotlights. And with his refusal to expose himself in an autobiography or be featured in the *World*'s 'Celebrities at Home' spot, it was maintained.[16]

Large Victorian families were always edged by grief. The Huxleys were reminded of Mady every day. The fair-haired Joyce was her spitting image. The seven-year-old spent six months of each year at Eastbourne, trailing around as grandmoo's 'constant companion'. Not that a bundle of fun couldn't try the pensioners, especially given her 'rich inheritance of the family volition'.[17] Joyce had her own sage observations on being brought up by ageing grandparents. She declared her intention to remain a child, noticing 'that grown-up people have a great deal of trouble'.

Once a visitor chanced on Huxley and Joyce, lying on the floor, moving planetary pellets of paper around a large screwed-up ball of a Sun. On clear nights he would take the little girl out with a telescope to show her the other worlds.[18] The old hulk had 'come about' in an emotional calm after her mother's death. Retirement brought a certain equanimity, and with it his awe at this great universe returned.

> If there is anything I thank the Gods for (I am not sure there is, for as the old woman said when reminded of the goodness of Providence: 'Ah but he takes it out of me in the corns') it is a wide diversity of tastes [he told the 75-year-old public health campaigner Sir John Simon]. Barred from scientific work, I should be miserable, if there were not heaps of other topics that interest me, from Gadarene pigs & Gladstonian psychology, upwards. No one who has lived in the world as long as you & I have, can entertain the pious delusion that it is engineered upon principles of benevolence – and I suppose I may assume you to have reached my conviction that of all the fiends dangled before us as by hope, the 'peaceful old age' delusion is one of the most fraudulent. But for all that, the cosmos remains always beautiful and profoundly interesting in every corner – and if I had as many lives as a cat I would leave no corner unexplored.[19]

With equanimity came reflection. He was hanging photos and paintings above his chimney breast: *Rattlesnake* on top, Darwin on the bottom, von Baer (the founder of developmental biology) and Faraday (without whom Nettie would not have the 'unspeakable convenience' of electric lights) to the left, Hooker and Sir John Richardson, the 'founder of my fortunes', to the right. And in the middle? – the man who had taken Hal to Hell and back, Dante.[20]

The Huxleys visited Downe for the first time in years, but it was 'rather sad' – even if Parslow the butler, looking in on old Emma, reminded them of the glory days. 'What times those days were!' Huxley reminisced.[21] He conjured up Homeric images, as if 'warfare has been my business', something forced on him by the times. In a sense it had been: hadn't the great generals been thrown up by Dissent's industrious ranks to lead its New Model Army? He was the Puritan strategist to substitute its cause-and-effect universe for the supernaturally sanctioned Anglican status quo. He was the man who had symbolized the hopes of the Unitarian and secularist manufacturers, the man whose coming had been dreaded by the old Iron Duke of Wellington. But in the naughty nineties no one cared – except, it seems, the new cook. She walked out on learning of the godless household she was expected to cater to.

At least the life in debt ended. The two mortgages were paid off with the sale of Marlborough Place and Rich's bequest. The eccentric died in April 1891, leaving them his bachelor house along the coast, much as a devoted parishioner would leave the Church his worldly goods. Hooker ribbed Huxley about his 'estate', bemused by his evangelical power to fill the platter. 'My "estate" is somewhat of a white elephant', Huxley replied, 'unluckily, in building the house dear old Rich thought of his own convenience & not mine'. But there was an attraction, not three acres and a cow, as the Irish tenants demanded, but two acres and a coach house. Shrubberies and forest bordered beautiful lawns, which looked across to a church. 'What could pious reclusives desire more?' he asked the publisher Macmillan, who was searching for a seaside house. It fetched a handsome £2,800 and Huxley ploughed some of the money into a piece of land, 'a Naboth's vineyard' adjacent to Hodeslea, so he could 'turn horticulturist. I find nailing up creepers a delightful occupation'.[22] But he still thought of little Joyce and the stars – he drew up a new will, leaving her £500 in trust.[23]

The garden became the old man's love, and summers were for showing visitors around. Down came the men of their age. It 'would amuse you to see him going about with the hose and watering pot', Hooker told Tyndall, 'petting weak plants . . . and coaxing shrubs'. Hours were lost in the sunshine, potting the saxifrages from Kew.

The sanctuary was a far cry from the bitter streets, and the 'insane' acts of the 'new unionism', whose bus strikes for a 12-hour day could cripple a city.[24] Labour was making its own history now and passing him by. To talk of it there was John Morley, radical Liberal MP, down in the recess. And a decrepit Benjamin Jowett visited, the old *Essays* author, pleading that Huxley's last task was to locate the foundations of a humanistic morality outside of the old theological traditions. Perhaps that was what Huxley thought of as he contemplated extinction. Not that it held any terrors; humour as always deflected thoughts on that final 'small & commodious residence 7 feet by 2'.[25]

'Dad', he was signing himself now to the children, in that modern middle-class way. They were scattering. Harry the doctor got £500 for six winter weeks in Egypt with a wealthy patient, 'which is not bad for a beginner'.[26] Egypt was even more fashionable now. Young Nettie's husband Harold was out too, photographing the pharaonic frescoes for a British Museum book.

Dad was seeing too many of London's own fashionable Sphinx tombs through yellowy eyes. Hirst, his mind wandering in February 1892, had had his last smoke with the X. His life of unfulfilled promise had been 'more or less of a tragedy' after the early loss of his wife. The mathematician had typified the X as untrammelled by theology. Huxley was fittingly in a *Times* dispute on Genesis when news of Hirst's death from prostate cancer came. Tyndall was affected most. He too was ill, 'another fallen leaf'; another preparing to send his enriched atoms back to the sun: 'it will be neck and neck ... which of us will reach the winning post ... of the gate of Heaven', he wrote gamely to Hooker.[27] 'If I get in first . . . I shall take care to prepare comfortable berths for you and Huxley'.

But Huxley's mortal fears had moved closer to home. 'With the best will a man is but a helpless creature', he admitted as Nettie started suffering from stabbing pains (diagnosed as a 'loose kidney'). Blinding giddiness knocked her down and she had to have morphine injections. The stern patriarch was unnerved. 'I keep my head level about most things', he told Ethel, 'but I am afraid not when your mother is ill'.[28]

Spring 1892 was divided between the fruit trees in his kitchen garden and devotions in his private chapel, his stained-glass study. Here he collected his polemics against Gladstone, Wace and Argyll into what the *Times* described as a 'fugitive' volume of daring opinions, *Essays upon some Controverted Questions*. Conscious of the last grains slipping through the timer he took great pains over the

Prologue. It was eloquent on the continuing exorcism of the ghosts of medieval Christianity by a 'scientific Naturalism', and on the Victorian Reformation which illegitimated this old 'Supernature'. Ultimately it made 'intelligent work . . . the only acceptable worship'.[29] His own veneration told in the Prologue's final mythopoeic history of mankind's rise from savagery. The last revises were posted on 4 May 1892, his 67th birthday.

George Romanes was a tragic soul, terrified at his own atheism. He gazed forlornly on a godless universe which had 'lost its soul of loveliness'.[30] Yet Sunday had remained a Church day and in the decade after Darwin's death the despair had slowly subsided. His return to an appreciation of Christian moral beauty made his rehabilitation at Oxford possible. Even now he was joining Christ Church High Table and moving into Cardinal Wolsey's old oak-beamed house opposite the College.

Darwin's tortured protégé had been *plus loyal que le roi*. If Romanes had quibbled with August Weismann's theory of the continuity of germ-plasm (which denied that bodily changes during an individual's life can influence the offspring: variations result only from the 'spontaneous variation' in the chromosomes of the cell nucleus), he still saw himself holding Darwin's brief. Huxley had no truck with Lamarck's (and Darwin's) inheritance of acquired characters, unlike Spencer, who was 'bound to it *a priori* – his psychology goes to pieces without it'. Romanes sent Huxley his historical *Darwin and After Darwin* to prove 'that I have no way departed from my allegiance to Darwinism'. And he made Huxley an offer he could not refuse. Wealth had allowed Romanes to endow an Oxford lectureship, like the yearly 'Rede Lecture' at Cambridge.

> M[r]. Gladstone has agreed to give the lecture for this year
> next term; and if you could possibly bring yourself to
> address once more a cultivated audience, there would not
> only be something appropriate in your following the
> champion of Adam and of swine, but you might really do
> much good in this seminary of ecclesiasticism. Actual
> theology is excluded by the Statute; but much may be
> consigned under 'Science' and 'Philosophy'.[31]

Dangling Gladstone hooked Huxley. He was lured out by his political contempt for the G.O.M. – despite deafness, despite a fading voice, and his blanket ban on lecturing for five years, on doctor's orders. ('Hames will countersign that statement if necessary'.) Huxley drolly told Frank Darwin that a 'Puck like spirit of mischief' forced him on, but he added seriously that 'he did want to say this thing about Ethics'.[32] And this was the other draw: he and Spencer were now 'speculatively poles asunder' and it would be a chance to voice his opposition to the 'ethical & political' nonsense stemming from Spencer's ultra-*laissez-faire* world-view.[33] So Huxley accepted his first lecture since Manchester and Mady's death.

Romanes was haunted by the moral meaning of evolution. He took a quintessential Darwinian approach, dispatching intimate question-naires to see if there were racial differences to suffering, death and release, and immersing himself in books on the *Ethical Purport of Darwinism*. All the time he was moving from Darwin's racial cost–benefit explanation of morality to a more feeling religious under-standing. So he was euphoric that Huxley's 'Romanes Lecture' would be a *fin de siècle* statement on 'Evolution and Ethics'. Given a looming election and Gladstone's age, he even begged Huxley to ready himself as the Grand Old Man's stand-in. For Huxley, dou-bling for Gladstone was a piquant thought. And were it to happen, Romanes 'would not be altogether sorry'.[34]

Salisbury's Tories had survived on a wafer-thin majority, helped by Parnell's divorce scandal. The Huxley–Tyndall–Hooker triumvirate gloated as 'the Gladstone-Parnell bubble burst' and the Irish alliance exploded from the 'pressure of the mephitic gases' built up by its 'internal putrefaction'.[35] Parnell had died exhausted after marrying his mistress, leaving Gladstone to fight the Tories.

Another trough in the terrible Depression brought a new extrem-ism. In the 1892 election Gladstone was deserted by the 'Classes' and appealed to the 'Masses' – those who had told Huxley that they would soon be running the country,[36] and proved it by electing a Scottish miner, Keir Hardie, as the first Independent Labour MP. Gladstone half believed his own pandering promises of reform, disestablishment and suffrage. 'If the devil that is in him could be transferred', Huxley told Tyndall, 'there would be enough to send 2,000,000 pigs headlong, instead of a poor 2000!'[37] He hoped for a tiny Liberal majority, to keep the G.O.M.'s hands tied by the Unionists.

On 18 June 1892 Romanes thanked Huxley 'for the large and latest instalment of your wisdom'. *Controverted Questions* was out. It was a huge book, 625 pages of gilded controversy, a piece of evangelic rationalism that had one worshipper demanding a society be formed to propagate Huxley's wisdom.[38] Ironically, after a life in science, his biggest book was of Biblical criticism. But it left an overall impression of ridiculing, not clerical naivety so much as Gladstone's obscurantism.

Two days later Lord Salisbury's Tory government sounded him out about a Privy Councillorship. Donnelly had tipped Salisbury off, even telling him that he was sure Huxley would accept, 'so', he said, 'do not through any blooming *agnostic* ideas make me look a fool'.[39] Donnelly wanted 'such a note of acceptance' as he could send on. 'You have been and done me', Huxley replied, which was hardly the word to pass on, never mind his banter on this reward for the 'wicked'.

He was to be the first Crown adviser on science. Nominally, at least, this was an office, a seat in that great baronial chamber, not a title (something he had always refused); and although that might salve the conscience of a Puritan 'dead against' decorations, it was still very nominal. Knowing Huxley's predilection, the physicist William Thomson, now Lord Kelvin and 'the biggest of all the big swells', assured him that it was something he could accept. And for all the Rt Hon.'s merriment at the etiquette – searching for a 'table of precedence' to see who passed through the door first – Nettie revelled in it: sister Lizzie heard that it ranks 'above Baronetcies & titular Lordships'.[40] 'You never thought Lizzie when you threw yʳ slipper after the boy . . .'

Parliament dissolved on 29 June amid election fever. Gladstone called again for Home Rule, and the Queen called the prospect of an 82-year-old governing 'with the miserable democrats . . . a bad joke'. The Liberals won, with more than the sliver Huxley had hoped for. Salisbury stood down on 11 August and five days later he told Huxley that his PC would be 'public evidence that the Government which is now resigning are not insensible to the great renown which you have conferred on English science, or to the services which you have rendered to your country more'.[41] Huxley had made science patriotic in the industrial 'war' with Germany, raising it with the Union Jack. So in a feverish election period, with the Grand Old Man committed to hauling down the flag, the Tories' last act was to put Huxley on the Honours List.

He and 'Mrs. Right Honourable' were away touring Wales, and 'every now and then had to laugh' at this reward for 'plain-spoken wickedness'. He declared the 'Archbishopric of Canterbury' his only ambition left, and so saying ran off into scorching parody. Of course Salisbury had no need to press for that particular spiritual peerage, knowing that

as Evolutionism is rapidly gaining ground among the
people who have votes [working classes] . . . his eminent
successor [the 'demagogue' Gladstone] . . . would become
a hot evolutionist . . . And when [Gladstone] goes out, my
bishopric will be among the Dissolution Honours. If H.M.
objects she will be threatened with the immediate abolition
of the H. of Lords, and the institution of a social
democratic federation of counties.[42]

A Wonderland world of Archbishop Huxley in a socialist arcadia
highlighted the underlying fears as the country continued its Leftward drift.

It was an edifying spectacle on 25 August 1892: Huxley, rigged up
in his Court dress 'ablaze with gold', gilt sword, the lot 'costing a
sum with which I could buy, oh! so many books'. The royal train, the
grand procession of officers at Osborne House (Her Majesty's
Palazzo Mansion): it was so quaint. 'We knelt as if we were going to
say our prayers', he recounted, as though reporting the latest dance
steps; swore an oath, 'advanced to the Queen, knelt and kissed her
hand, retired backwards, and got sworn over again (Lord knows
what I promised and vowed this time also)'. With natural irreverence
he glanced up at Queen Victoria – only, to his 'great discomforture',[43]
to find her studying this interloper from another culture.

Here was final proof that he was no social pariah: science was
being fêted. Not that smashing Gladstone's *Impregnable Rock* had
harmed him; nor had his disbarring of socialism gone unnoticed. Of
course Huxley saw nothing 'queerer' than 'that a Tory & Church
Government should have delighted to honour the worst famed
heretic in the three Kingdoms' – and truly it must have made some
back-benchers crawl.[44] But at the end of the day, although the PC was
given for Huxley's scientific status, party tensions and fear of socialism made it easier for the Conservatives. They were themselves
pledged to private property and the Union.

It is just thirty years now since I published 'Man's Place in
Nature' which some of my anxious friends declared would
ruin me altogether. And considering my long series of
aggravated offenses since that time I should have expected
the offer of a bishopric as soon as that of a Privy
Councillorship.[45]

But their Lordships leaving the Dispatch Box were happy to honour
the Devil, so long as he tormented 'pious William' and played havoc

with the socialists. The 'anomaly' simply ignores the increasingly conservative function of Huxley's agnostic science. This particular Liberal Unionist had been making a wasteland of the Grand Old Man's scripturalism for seven years – impugning the Home Ruler's judgment in the best part of 600 reprinted pages. And who mistook Huxley's company at Court?[46] The other PCs were political functionaries, a Liberal Unionist MP and the next Tory Home Secretary. That made 'three hot Unionists' and the gift more than politically suspect. Gladstone, hearing of Salisbury's gesture, was livid.

It was The Right Honourable T. H. Huxley who attended Tennyson's funeral two months later. Tennyson had found Huxley 'chivalrous, wide, and earnest', and the Volunteer had raised his rifle in one hand and *Idylls* in the other. In June he had sent the poet his *Controverted Questions*. Now he joined the Royal Society elite over his bier. 'Tennyson had a right to that as the first poet since Lucretius who has understood the drift of science'.[47]

Huxley did not double for Gladstone at Oxford. Ten days later the Prime Minister delivered the first 'Romanes Lecture'. Under penalty to avoid religion, he dressed up his 'impassioned plea for conservative ways of thinking about Religion and Morals' as a pandering history of university education. It drew chauvinistic cheers. Lankester called it 'George's Show' for its stagey enthusiasm, and 'as a show it was well worth seeing', added Romanes. But away from the scene Huxley wondered how the great orator could say so much 'without ever rising above the level of antiquarian gossip'. The worst of it was Gladstone's leading the church parade and reading the lessons! That had Huxley pleading that 'I couldn't – really'. The horrified clergy excused him, being happily 'disposed to regard such an exhibition as the profanation of Scripture'.[48]

With the last rays of Autumn sunshine came a restless desire to re-enter the fray. He started lobbying for the reform of that colossus which bestrode the Empire, London University. He wanted a tighter co-ordination between the scattered teaching colleges and examining Senate House, to be achieved by increasing the professors' power on the executive. He busied himself so much, leading deputations and presenting evidence to the Gresham Commission on London University (indeed suggesting the Commissioners), that he seemed his old self. He told the professors 'that this old hulk is ready to be towed out into line of battle, if they think fit', which was more public-spirited than prudent. They thought him 'seaworthy enough to fly the admiral's flag' and made him President of a group intent on marshalling the 'chaotic' London colleges into a coherent whole.

From the prow the deaf Admiral led the motley flotilla towards his modern university ideal. *His* university was not to train clerics, lawyers or doctors, but 'pioneers in the exploration and settlement of new regions' of knowledge.[49]

The smart PC suit could not mask the Rt Hon.'s irreverence. 'Don't ask anybody above the younger son of a peer', he told Romanes, referring to the lecture, 'because I shall not be able to go into dinner before him'.[50]

With socialism strengthening, the first Independent Labour member in Parliament, and Kropotkin stealing the nation's heart, the great argument was the sort of ethics and evolution a democratic nation should adopt. Huxley would talk at Oxford, not on the evolution of ethics, but the ethics of evolution. He would look at whether Darwin's Nature gave any sanction to human values. It is 'very courageous of you to lecture on Morals & Evolution', said Benjamin Jowett. 'No one has yet expressed adequately the antithesis of the moral & the physical'.[51] For Jowett a weak-to-the-wall Darwinism was countered by society's wall to protect the weak.

After the blistering attacks on Gladstone's demonology Oxford was petrified at what Huxley might say. Having encouraged him, Romanes got cold feet and reminded him of the prohibition on religion and politics. If people applied what he said to religion, replied Huxley, 'that is not my affair. To be honest, however, unless I thought they would, I should never have taken all the pains'. That unleashed two more letters begging him to be circumspect. Only the arrival of Huxley's manuscript allayed the fears. It was so discursive that not even Mrs Romanes' 'fine nose for heresy' could sniff any.[52] Oxford's sensibilities were respected.

On his 68th birthday, 4 May, Nettie was in bed, the stabbing pains eased by morphine. Huxley was readying the typescript, which was to be printed and 1,000 copies put on sale prior to the lecture. Three days before the event he posted one to Tyndall. 'There are not many apples (& those mostly of the crab sort) left upon the old tree but I send you the product of the last shaking'.[53]

It was his first time on any stage for six years, and on *that* stage since 1860. The 'flu had left him a red-nosed 'disreputable Captain Costigan-looking' character, and reduced his weak voice to a whisper. Romanes had the Public Orator stand by, just in case.[54]

At 2.15 on Thursday 18 May 1893 the last students piled in to the Sheldonian Theatre. They were after 'splendid rhetoric' more than angst and insight, and more had turned out for the sacerdotal Prime

Minister than science's 'High Priest'. Huxley, silver hair flowing over his 'gorgeous D.C.L. robes', proceeded in a quiet voice. Romanes called it 'genial and "mellow"'. The students called it 'almost inaudible' and cries of 'speak up' accompanied a shuffling as they migrated forward.⁵⁵ But those in front of the stage appreciated how skilfully the injunction to avoid politics had been skirted.

The cunning disguise of 'Evolution and Ethics' was completed by its sparkling language: it was 'one of the most brilliant gems in the prose literature of the nineteenth century'. But still 'a regular egg-dance' for all that, as Huxley admitted. He was staking his Liberal political ethics midway between the Spencerian and socialist extremes without being able to mention either. The dance said less about the dons' sensibilities than Huxley's. At bottom of it he was responding to the politics of the age – to the socialism that had almost crushed him in his bus, to communist cooks who damned his uncaring Darwinism, to Labour's attacks on his Malthusian views. He was meeting the calls to pronounce on 'Socialism and Darwinism'.⁵⁶

The theme had been set in the dark days of Mady's death. But a deeper theme was older. Fifty years on, he was still rationalizing a planet which had seen so much pleasure and pain without merit or desert. Suffering evolved with consciousness; it appeared, not because of a Fall, but with the rise of brain complexity. Sacrifice and death were the 'necessary concomitant' of evolutionary progress, part of an amoral Darwinian process. But for Huxley the price of progress had become too high.

He portrayed ethical man revolting 'against the moral indifference of nature'.⁵⁷ Care had replaced the crushing competition, altruism the competitive aggression. The flight was not to the swift, nor the battle to the strong; among humans a mitigating ethics dictated that the weak be rescued from the wall. 'Evolution and Ethics' was the missing chapter of *Man's Place in Nature*, filled in after 30 years' digestion of Darwinism.

The justice Huxley and Carlyle had seen in the soul of the universe was gone. The truth of Darwinism and fear of Socialism had forced Huxley to demur. Natural Selection, that 'calm strong angel' who had once played chess for love, had crashed in tatters, feathers scattering. And beneath them he found 'Satan, the Prince of this world'. Nature's vicious disregard in killing his daughter among the unsung myriads in the Depression was the tragedy that gave his lecture its poignancy. Still, the bitterness of 1887 was softening. That 'bloody rum world' was receding, and he was levelling out in 1893. He now bolstered a competitive Darwinism, to make it immune to mutualist attacks, while denying that it could provide any natural basis for our ethics of love. 'Evolution and Ethics' split the world; it separated a wild zoological nature from our ethical existence. 'Social progress means a checking of the cosmic process'. It selects not the 'fittest' but 'ethically the best'.[58] Man came of age when he ceased emulating Nature and started 'combating it'.

It wasn't what was being said, but *who* was saying it: the 'prophet of evolution', as *Blackwood's Magazine* called him. Spencer bristled at this further onslaught on his naturalistic ethics – his belief that the struggle for survival could be the only true foundation for ethics. He called Huxley's distinction between cosmic strife and a combating morality his own 'Pauline dogma of nature and grace'.[59]

At the end of his days Huxley could find no 'sanction for morality in the ways of the cosmos'. He had come full circle to Southwood Smith's *Divine Government*, which had taught the boy that tackling social evil was a divine responsibility. Huxley's whole life had revolved around pain and duty. He had taken the hard road back to his Unitarian and Latitudinarian allies, to Kingsley's refusal to sacrifice humanity in Nature's arena. 'Just so!' cried Mivart, with a hint of glee. Wasn't Huxley admitting an Absolute ethics outside Nature? Wasn't it *really* grace from God? Of course Huxley saw human ethics still as 'part and parcel of the general process of evolution', evolved by natural selection to defy natural selection. Man's 'nature within nature' was a strange microcosm spinning counter-clockwise. But by refusing to see human ethics as Absolute or God-given, he nonplussed many critics, who saw him plunging into paradox.[60]

Huxley the political animal was facing up to Darwin's dog-eat-dog Nature. Instinctive man was at war with ethical man in the same corporeal frame. It was no good cutting the umbilical cord to the cosmos like the Buddhists (suddenly fashionable in a humanistic age), or trying for salvation by total renunciation. Man had the mark of Cain; beneath the civil surface lay the bestiality of his savage forebears. The ferocious instincts of his 'hot youth' were struggling against his social upbringing. Huxley had internalized the 'war', satisfying his battling mentality to the end. The pugilist was leading a new fight against the savage within. Owen had once talked of original sin as the malingering ape in our constitution.[61] But the bestiality had not quite washed off with our social baptism. The old General on Oxford's stage had an air of 'militant heroism' as he faced an unequal battle against overpowering cosmic forces.

Nature's injustice 'has burned itself deeply into the writer's soul', said one critic. Some took his talk of suffering as a 'scathing attack' on 'all possible Theodices'. Others saw it as an 'indictment' of the Darwinian terrors.[62] They were too close to see him bolstering the Darwinian cosmos, whose ruthlessness could now be accepted because he had detached human ethics.

He *needed* a competitive Nature. He needed to undercut the socialist legions. 'Evolution and Ethics' was the General's final effort to save the political day. The essay was conceived in terms of competition and struggle, as were all his anti-socialist essays. He ignored 'adaptation': only in a published note did he admit that human social cohesion was of use, 'just as the gregarious habit of innumerable plants and animals . . . has been of immense advantage to them'. Ethics had evolved, Leslie Stephen said, expanding on Huxley's note, on 'purely prudential grounds', as a sort of parental altruism writ large. Our welfare, our sanitary reforms, our smallpox vaccines, all increased the health of the species. Morality benefited us. But Stephen, just as aware of the political undercurrent, was quite happy to 'stimulate "collectivism" at the expense of a crude individualism'.[63] Huxley was on harder ground. Though a little mutualism might bolster his professional State bureaucracy against Spencer, he knew from experience that too much might justify Wallace's and Kropotkin's collectivist ideals – the very targets he was trying to destroy by strengthening Darwinian nature.

He was boxed in, surrounded by invisible political walls. Praised for his stand against the 'fanaticism of individualism',[64] congratulated for his buttress against socialism in this 'muddled and aspiring epoch', he showed how difficult it was to steer a straight course. Struggling in white water, avoiding the eddies of Spencer's ultra-selfish ethics, and the whirlpool of Wallace's and Kropotkin's harmonious socialist Nature, Huxley was forcing his ethical Ark against the Darwinian current which had brought him so far.

30

Fighting unto Death

THE OLD INTELLECTUALS were in their red-brick homes. Out in the sticks, away from London. Out of time now. Doomed like Beardsley and Wilde, in a moribund decade, watching decadent London living frantically as if on borrowed time. The naughty nineties, reacting so raucously against their staid Puritanism, seemed like a distant country. Huxley escaped the shallowness in Eastbourne. Here the anatomist watched his body crumble. His yearly fights against 'flu had become a wretched struggle. The old man, huddled over the winter fire devouring Aristotle, was buying time.[1]

No manor retreats for the X-Club stragglers, no grand piles. Huxley's house on the corner of Staveley Road was overlooked on two sides. The tormented, sleepless Tyndall in the Devil's Punch Bowl of Hindhead was an equal prey to peeping fans and screened off the bottom of his garden. They seemed such ordinary men gone such ordinary ways.

And yet Huxley the ageing matinée idol still made guest appearances. At Gonville and Caius College in Cambridge he played the part and 'Loaded himself with champagne' before another Harvey dinner on 21 June 1893.[2] He looked 'tired out'. But with his tubes lubricated he could still evoke the old scientific patriotism in his homage to the discoverer of the blood's circulation.

Death's hand touched them all. Almost monthly it left friends to be mourned and memories to be enshrined. Huxley helped Lord Coleridge arrange a 'Jowett Memorial Fund'. He was astonished that his old society doctor Sir Andrew Clark, grown 'pompous' since his Haslar days, had left £250,000 from the practice among the swells. Annihilation had once filled Huxley with 'horror unspeakable': 'whether or not Nature abhors a vacuum', Romanes remembered him saying, 'I know that the soul of man does'.[3] But age had bred a certain equanimity. And anyway in 1893 it seemed to the old war-horse that 'F.M. General Death had forgotten me'.

Immortality – if Weismann was right – was a little of one's chromosomes corrupting slowly through the generations.[4] Or perhaps it was a larger uncorrupted corpus of published work. Macmillan had remained with Huxley, liberal to the century's end. Now the publisher would see a lifetime's proselytizing capped by the obligatory *Collected Essays*. Huxley joined Arnold, Kingsley and Morley, with nine volumes – a million words – the first off the press in September 1893, 40 years of bread-and-butter journalism amassed into canonical form. They ranged from Darwin's defence to the agnostic's apology, the sea of doubt to the sin of faith, from the vivid opening of the dinosaurian past to the veiling off of an immortal future. No set so amply testified to the Victorian naturalistic world and its meaning. For his prose alone he was lauded as 'perhaps the greatest virtuoso of plain English who has ever lived'.[5] The style was the man – the *bon viveur*, the twinkling, the suave hectoring, the apology that of course he was really peace-loving. Such prose only made the message more beguiling; here was the emergent scientist ratifying a new social order. Critics read the 5s volumes as war memoirs by a valiant 'old contemptible' (with all the propagandist connotations of that Great War image). And by the *fin de siècle* it was obvious that the moralizing Huxley had inherited the natural theologian's mantle: the publicist was appearing in new red covers to reassure another disorientated generation.

If sin did not bring its own desert, the avenging Huxley was on hand to help. It was Sir Richard Owen's misfortune to die first. They had preyed on the same fossil animals, but run with diametric packs across a changing social landscape. The sad old man was 88, demented at the end, destroyed by his only son's suicide. That was December 1892. It should have ended the hatreds. Indeed Huxley accepted an invitation to the Black Knight's funeral. But biting winds brought the reflection that Owen would end up killing him too, and so he telegraphed his apologies.[6]

Diplomacy did dictate his presence at a memorial – and a few words. But though he came to praise Owen, not to bury him, there was grim hypocrisy in his seconding the proposal for a statue in the Natural History Museum. Even his admission that the man 'did a lot of first rate work and now that he can do no more mischief he has a right to his wages',[7] made it sound like the wages of sin. The blackened bronze statue close to Darwin's shining white marble only served to rub in Owen's tarnished reputation. In truth, the great cathedral of a museum was his monument.

Owen's grandchildren buried the old man better than they knew. 'Three, or thirty, guesses & you shall not guess', Huxley wrote to Hooker. 'Rev Richard Owen has written to me to ask me to write a concluding chapter for the biography of his grand father – containing a "critical estimate" of him & his work!!!!!' There was no crueller irony. The simple curate knew little of Owen, nothing of biography, and he was 'incompetent to deal with his Grandsire's character under any aspect'. Owen's successor at the museum, Sir William Henry Flower, had refused any help. And so the Revd Richard had turned to Huxley to make the biography 'as impartial & authentic as possible'! The hapless curate should never have asked, and Huxley should never have accepted. He did turn down a personal estimate as 'I was never in your grandfather's house nor he in mine', but after twinges of doubt he agreed to assess Owen's science – and he expected 'poor old Richard's ghost' to haunt him for his pains.[8]

Luck had distributed the last spoils of victory. Huxley stopped planting his rockery to inter Owen properly. Few scientists could see past Owen's quirks to his wondrous world of dinosaurs (his word) and mammal ancestors (his work): the Grand Old Man of palaeontology had opened up the lost tropical planet during the Age of Reptiles. But Nettie revealed the home spirit. 'It is quite comic', she said of the offer: this the 'man who did his best, to prevent Hal from coming to the front, in every mean, & untruthful way'. The phobia turned on the biography itself. Flower was suspicious. Hooker had heard that it 'is likely to bubble over with unveracity – being grounded on R.O.'s estimate of his modest self & his intercourse with mankind, as contained in an autobiography which he has left'.[9] It conditioned Huxley's mood, as he imagined Owen's 'ghost in Hades' preparing a posthumous strike. In reality there was no autobiography; no stabbing from beyond the grave. The grandson simply turned the old man into a laughable 'social fop'.[10] But fear of the dead scorpion's sting affected Huxley's writing.

He wrote watching his back. In 1894 new radical evangelicals, admitting that 'Evolution is . . . a Vision – which is revolutionizing the world of Nature', were cashing in. In the age of the New Woman, the hot author Henry Drummond – Moody and Sankey's scientist – saw the *Ascent of Man* culminate in motherly love, and through the altruism of the 'Holy Family' the perfection of morality. 'Nature is the Garment of God', Drummond claimed, as Owen might have, its process His 'Eternal Will'. To naturalize the spirit – to make 'Christianity . . . as old as Nature' – was to contest secular authority once more. From another side came Benjamin Kidd's denunciation of dry agnosticism in *Social Evolution* (1894). Where the novelist Grant Allen had called religion a 'grotesque fungoid growth' disguising a primeval 'Ancestor Worship', Kidd would treat it seriously as the ethical regulator of social evolution. Such books might have been an 'anaesthetic which a clement Providence has administered to orthodoxy during the excision of its diseased organs',[11] but they were the backdrop to Owen's autopsy. The split-loyalty spiritualizers were vipers at the biologist's bosom.

Huxley finished his Darwinian business by burying Owen's Nature of Divine Archetypes. He strained to be fair and let the strain show. Even knowing that 'all the things we fought about, belong to antiquity', he continued to reslay the slain. To old hands like Flower it was the only way: 'You have been very judicious in devoting 31 out of your 57 pages to Owen's predecessors, and thus avoiding all details regarding your hero'.[12] But young adjutants who had seen victory a thousand times over wondered at the sods being thrown onto Owen's white face.

> Pp. 1–40 – very good and very interesting.
> 41–8 you praise Richard *seven pages*
> 48–66 *18 pages*(!), you damn him

Better not to 'dwell on his philosophy', thought Foster, who knew that Huxley should have concentrated on the crowning fossil edifice.[13] But 'the apostle Paul of the new teaching' was performing the last rite of purification. The remnants of a rival Coleridgean world were destroyed – a might-have-been Nature, obeying the divine Edict, legitimating the National Church. Huxley was finishing what the industrial Unitarians had begun with their resistance 60 years earlier to a reactionary old S. T. Coleridge, who had damned the Dissenting technocracy and 'Ouran Outang theology'.[14] The 'new Nature' – that lawful, causal, agnostic bundle – had triumphed. It was called Science.

And so Huxley left the late twentieth century with the daunting task of hacking through the partisan myths to rehabilitate that giant of modern palaeontology, Richard Owen.[15]

Wednesday morning's paper, 6 December 1893, said that Tyndall had taken an overdose of drugs and there would be an inquest. 'I suppose it was Chloral at the last – & all along', Hooker sighed. It was. Louisa telegraphed the Huxleys on Thursday night and the next morning they were at Hindhead. 'Poor woman, it was a terrible meeting', said Nettie, 'She clung to us'. 'The circumstances of his death were so ghastly'.[16] Louisa had mixed up John's medicine bottles on Monday morning and given him a massive dose of the opiate sleeping draught chloral by mistake. Stomach pumps, emetics and coffee failed to keep him conscious. He had died that night.

On Saturday Huxley walked behind the hearse to Haslemere churchyard. Louisa poured out her heart about 'John's love for you & me beyond any others', Hooker told Huxley, but the tragedy left her in a 'dangerous' traumatic state. Huxley went to see a half-finished Tyndall bust for Louisa, but it only helped 'to tear her to pieces', and it was heart-rending for him. He placed a remembrance in the *Nineteenth Century* – a final board report on the 40-year-old 'firm'. Castor and Pollux had had their adventures, and come a long way since losing their Toronto chairs – through the *Reader* and X-Club to the joint LL.D.s and North Stars. One 'abusive sermon on the subject of the "late Professor Huxley"' showed that even in death they could not part. The firm had been the defining voice of the new scientific naturalism, that religion of cosmic evolution. 'People don't get their heart-strings tugged at my time of life without knowing about it',[17] Huxley said as he sipped his own tonic and spent Christmas week in bed, 'running up a little account over poor old Tyndall'.

Age brought a numbing resignation, and the Spring saw him out hoeing his sylvan patch on Staveley Road. After three years of clearing and planting, the old gardener had the rustic metaphor to introduce his 'Evolution and Ethics' in the ninth volume of essays, due out on 28 August 1894. His Kew outpost of foreign delicate shrubs was maintained against an encroaching Nature, just as care for the weak made human ethics an exotic nook in a brutal cosmos. Even this ethical corner was held like a valiant imperial conquest. Huxley's life had been a homage to heroism, and at the end he stood for man's epic fight against the universe. Nettie thought it 'a gem of [an] argument'.[18]

He was received as a hero himself now. A cameo appearance was called for at the BAAS in August 1894, which after 34 years was returning to Oxford. The students were steeped in the mythology of 1860. Revd George Brodrick, the Warden of Merton, had the Huxleys' room ready and headed a new phalanx of liberal dons ready to be 'signally honoured' by a visit. Even if Brodrick was no

more 'sound on the doctrine of Evolution' than his liberal predecessors in 1860, he appreciated 'how many doors it has appeared
to unlock'.[19] Hesitancy had been Oxford's lot. It still was.

Huxley should have been the silent star bathing in the adulation.
But the gods had a way of intervening, and at the last moment he was
asked to second the vote of thanks for Lord Salisbury's Presidential
speech. 'Hal's wrath was great', said Nettie, as he read the draft with
its backhanded compliment to evolution and slight on natural selection. On the platform, Salisbury talked of that 'comforting word,
evolution', although he took more comfort from the latest disputes
over heredity which made the thing look tottery. Huxley sank into
his chair. At the end the ovation for him began. He stood, 'looking
kinglike in his red gown', said a proud Nettie: 'the applause was
deafening – again & again it rose & fell'. He was on the stump again,
managing the crowd. And on this occasion the *Times* reported every
word of clever repartee in the face of aristocratic ignorance. He spoke
amid laughter as one who 'had made a pretty free use of the comfortable word "evolution"'. Then he politely rapped Salisbury's
knuckles for confusing Darwin's and Weismann's theories with the
historical fact of evolution, and went on to welcome 'so distinguished
a convert' to his comfortable world. He sat down drowned by cheers.
For a last time he was the 'hero of the day in the Sheldonian Theatre'.[20]

The 'old Adam' reconstructed himself in these mythic moments.
He retailed the day's events to Louisa Tyndall (and Hooker, and
Lockyer, and Lewis Campbell), overplaying them awfully:

> Lord Salisbury was clever as usual; but knowing nothing
> about the topic, in reality, he makes an awful hash of this
> attempt to deal with Darwins views. If the address had only
> been a paper in section D [the working Zoology Section],
> I think the massacre would have been worse than that of
> 'Sammy' 34 years ago – always excepting that Ld Salisbury
> was courteous & indeed generous to Darwin personally.

But for all of Salisbury's caveats Huxley took satisfaction in His
Lordship's acceptance of evolution, telling Hooker, 'It was very
queer to sit there and hear the doctrines you & I were damned for
advocating 34 years ago at Oxford, enunciated as matters of course –
disputed by no reasonable man! – in the Sheldonian theatre by the
Chancellor'.[21]

It was clearly 'rather a risky thing to entrust the Presidentship to a
layman'.[22] *Lay* said it all: after 34 years the professionals no longer
needed these stately sanctions.

The next afternoon at Christ's garden party – as if to remind them of the passing time – they were handed tea by the son of Hal's *Rattlesnake* superior, John Thomson. A baby then, he was in his 50s now and had Nettie reminiscing about all the shore leave his father had given Hal to 'come & see me'.[23] Those courting days seemed far off to the bundled old lady, now with 14 grandchildren (Aldous had been born to Len and Julia two weeks earlier).

Every event was to be Huxley's last, but the indomitable old chap had become a stately institution. Up to town he would trot, there to be cared for by the Donnellys 'as if I were a piece of old china'. His 'swellness' would don his gilt sword to dine with the Prime Minister, Lord Rosebery. The puffing reached gigantic proportions after the Liberal PM begged 'the smallest of your works with my name written in it', to be 'cherished by your . . . lifelong admirer'.[24] (After 30 years Huxley thought an original *Man's Place in Nature* suitable for a Prime Minister.) He made an appearance at the Savoy to mark the 25th anniversary of *Nature*. In a quarter of a century he had seen his broad-forum weekly become the organ of the specialist. But no more romantic aphorisms of Goethe's and accusations of madness; he marked the completion of 50 volumes with a rallying retrospective of evolution. It was his 'anti Salisbury manifesto', to counter Oxford's faint praise – a rummage through his old scientific drawers to peruse the fossil title deeds once more.[25]

Up he went again to collect his long-service award. He had hoped that the Royal Society's new Darwin Medal would be used to fire the young bloods, not bedeck the 'useless old extinct volcanoes'. But the prize went to him anyway for his comparative anatomy and 'intimate association with Mr Darwin' – 'it was inevitable', said Foster by way of comprehensive explanation.[26] It showed that he was not quite shelved. 'Old age brings mere calm isolation to us all', he mused in the New Year 1895. 'When I am well, I am capable of forgetting my antiquity and then the many reminders that I am regarded by my younger contemporaries as a relic of the past (more or less venerable) have a very droll effect'.[27] And in that vein he gamely led a London University deputation to Lord Rosebery at No 10 through the January snow, which of course gave him a chill and put him in bed. It was the chance to plan a tenth volume of essays.

Meanwhile students at the College of Surgeons were arguing over an extraordinary monograph just received from Java. A short, bow-legged, heavy-browed ape-human had been announced by Eugène Dubois. Haeckel had guessed that a hypothetical *'Pithecanthropus'* would be found in the East, and Dubois, inspired to search, accord-

ingly named his find *Pithecanthropus erectus*. He placed it close to
the ape-human fork. But the skullcap, said Arthur Keith – a latter-
day impecunious Huxley hoping to make a penny popularizing this
'real "missing link"' – showed it to be a true early human, with a
900cc brain, midway between a chimpanzee's and a modern
human's. On 13 February young Keith read a paper at Bart's on it.
The next day Huxley wrote to Hooker that 'The Dutchman seems to
have turned up something like the "missing link" in Java . . . I expect
he was a Socratic party with his hair rather low down on his forehead'.[28] By 1895 it was so matter-of-fact. Huxley had lived long
enough to see the first ape-man – indeed hear about a Far Eastern
cradle for humankind, where these bent, small-brained ape-people
had retreated in the face of the northern ice sheets. Suddenly the
Owen fracas seemed positively prehistoric.

Oscar Wilde's decadence was a release from two decades of Puritanism. But there was a final and more pointed challenge to Huxley's
moral agnosticism. In February 1895, as the students contemplated
Java Man's villainous low brow, the high-brow Arthur Balfour on the
Tory Front Bench delivered the strongest rebuttal yet. An aristocrat,
'bolder but less brilliant' than his uncle Lord Salisbury (or so said
Gladstone), Balfour was destined to succeed him as Tory Prime
Minister. The agnostics related his metaphysical *excursus* to the
milk-and-water Oxford praise. 'He & Salisbury run on the same
lines'. 'Is this the basis of Conservative statesmanship?' asked Foster.
'Thank Ether I am a radical'.[29]

In ten years the Tories, unsettled by Fenian terrorism, socialism,
secularism and other manifestations of the 'class war' (Salisbury's
term), had become the Law and Order party of the Union. 'Bloody
Balfour's' bolstering of United Kingdom should have endeared him
to the X-Club. They shared interests – indeed as extreme Unionists
the Xs even deplored his sop to the Nationalists in the shape of a
proposed Irish Catholic University. And the collectivist threat to
property struck Tory Anglicans and Liberal Scientists alike. But
Huxley's men were themselves targeted by Balfour's Conservatives.
Scientific 'Naturalism' was thought to feed Socialism. It reduced
morale and an effective theological policing, destroying the safeguards of the established order. Balfour had already dubbed it a
'contemptible fetish' at that famous 1888 Church Congress.[30] By
removing God's Personal sanction and the threat of His punishment,
Naturalism opened the gates to the gothic hordes.

Balfour's *Foundations of Belief* was a Shadow Cabinet censure motion on all the secular '-isms'. The book berated Huxley's regrounding of morality and association of agnosticism with 'real' science. An election was looming; *Foundations* spoke for moral fibre, Anglican authority and a higher sphere of class union. It attempted to unstitch the scientific warp from the naturalistic weave (by questioning Huxley's own faith in an undeviating causality and uniform nature), and then reweave science into a supernatural pattern.

Politicians held sway with the 'wandering British public', said Knowles. 'Since you have forsaken the Constable's Beat the loose characters of thought have plucked up too much courage'. Gagged at Oxford before Balfour's uncle, Huxley did not need luring. Feeling chipper, already thinking about a summer holiday in Wiesbaden, he was eager to respond to the *Foundations*. The *Times* on 8 February had incensed him with its talk of the 'little Bethels of . . . Agnosticism' quaking in Balfour's wake.[31] Balfour liked his rapier with its button off; for all his breeding, he held Dr Johnson's belief that to respect an enemy is to give him the edge. He deplored the agnostics' 'parasitic' moral life on the Christian rump; and like all Tories he thought that without Christian blood the parasite would perish.[32] *Christ* was Morality. Huxley took his own button off. The professional 'Constable' was not prepared to see Tory recidivists go about questioning the new State of science.

Fashionably elegant, one of the wealthiest men in England (he had inherited £4 million on coming of age), Balfour had patronized Drummond's evangelical lectures. He had been active in cultivated Cambridge, itself resisting the vulgar professionals. The counter-'Revolution of the Dons' saw them infiltrating the Cavendish Laboratory and endorsing a Physics based on that universal supramundane stuff, the 'ether' (which could knit the seen and unseen kingdoms into the 'living garment of God'). The physicists in the Society for Psychical Research used Cambridge's scientific apparatus to probe the unseen, invoking a sort of 'transcendent naturalism' to trump the Londoners' materialism. By 1895 Balfour was 'President of the Spook Society' and Knowles expected Huxley's blow against 'Spook-speculation, in all its forms'.[33] He would not be disappointed.

With Naturalism hurting Tory Anglican interests, Balfour gave it a tinny materialistic ring. Old Huxley put on his spectacles and repolished his trumpet. Agnosticism had been his strength in an alien world – his moral shield against the medieval powers – and it had inspired his Cossacks. This time 'Mr. Balfour has acted like the French in 1870', he observed, and 'gone to war without any ordinance maps'. Clamping his teeth on, Huxley found 'the cleverest exhibition of philosophical ineptitude'. But his teeth were false now, the book was gristly, and chewing would be a long process. So he split his review into two. He posted the first part on 18 February. 'I think the cavalry charge in this months XIX will amuse you', he told Ethel in March.[34]

The indignant General laid about the *fin de siècle* with a vengeance. In the 1890s everything seemed up for grabs. A restlessness gripped the nation. Hedonism and theosophy railed against the Puritan years. Socialism had weakened the political structures as well as science's voice. Nietzsche was making 'truth' another moral prejudice, and Ibsen saw the need for 'vital lies' to enrich life. Everywhere was change and disillusionment, while the people looked 'in vain to science and authority for any hint as to duty'. Victorian Science and Victorian Statesmen, Huxley and Balfour, were like dinosaurs, struggling in their dying world. Huxley was 'fighting for his life'.[35] As evening crowns the day so 'Mr. Balfour's Attack on Agnosticism' would be his last testament.

Foster wanted 'a parody on B's book bolstering up some d—d idiocy'. Huxley gave him a Swiftian satire on the whole d—d society. He made profligate Imperial Rome stand for Balfour's Britain, in which the 'refined depravity among the upper classes' was matched by the hypocritical priests' winking as they performed sacred rites, no longer believing their own fables. With the moral rot had come the barbarian superstitions, Oriental religions and 'criminal impostures, analogous to so much of modern spirit-rapping' (the 'Spooks'). In his bankrupt Rome, the 'half-cretinised products of over-civilisation' had become sensually indulgent, 'flabby' and 'weak minded', led by clever *littérateurs* who substituted smart prose for substance (Wilde was about to be sentenced to hard labour in Pentonville for homosexuality).[36] Never had he crafted such blistering Swiftian prose. The tables were turned on an effete Establishment (Balfour himself had been accused of effeminacy). It dwarfed the critique of the Eloi's decadent eroticism in *The Time Machine*, which his old boy H. G. Wells would post him in three months.[37]

Balfour's society smelt of decay. By substituting illicit faith for pious ignorance it had kicked away its foundations in 'solid and stern' reality and abdicated its moral responsibility. Even now the 'shepherds of the people' would jeopardize the 'future of our civilisation' by reinstating the old pagan gods.[38]

'Delightful', said Donnelly of the therapeutic rant. But even if Hooker assured Huxley that 'You have probed his weak places with effect', it was a wonderfully quixotic tilt. Not that this was true disembowelling, he told Ethel: the proper 'bayonets will be brought into play next month'.[39] Then he would slice through Balfour's misreading of 'Agnosticism' line by line.

But the Winter 'flu swept through Eastbourne. Nettie caught it in late February and took to her bed. Hal struggled on, 'so anxious to finish the 2nd part of his article on Balfours book, that he fought against the pains in his limbs'.[40] He posted off Part II early in March only to collapse into bed. There he stayed, with no heart for the proofs.

The weathercocks pointed due east. The 'flu turned into bronchitis and 14-hour bouts of coughing damaged his weak heart. Night and day the nurses tended him. Always there was Brace, the sweet maid, smiling through her hospital chores. The 'anxiety & misery' reached a peak for Nettie as Hal's lungs became infected. It left him sitting up all night, deranged by fevers and head pains. Harry's wife Sophie – a former nurse – came to help. Three times – 'three terrible scares' – he seemed on a knife's edge and the girls telegraphed Harry.[41]

All the while Sophie and Ethel intercepted the mail, only to discover how much of it was malignant. The fanatics had heard that Huxley was dying and on his way to Hell.

The shock of white hair tossed and turned on the pillow. For 29 days in bed, hallucinating, sweating, the back of his head pounding, he fought the lung infection. Wasted and weak, he nevertheless survived, a 'mere carcass, which has to be tended by other people'. The children had taken shifts, with Harry and Ethel coming down as Sophie and Rachel left. By his 70th birthday on 4 May 1895 he could just about walk from the terrace to the lawn in the sunshine to see his saxifrages. Foster and the faithful had watched 'from afar all these dreadful weeks'.[42] They feared the General had reached his Khartoum.

Half a century earlier, Huxley used to wake in his *Rattlesnake* alcove on stormy nights and, hearing the duty officers coping, fall asleep again. In the same way he trusted the doctors. But he watched his decline and wondered why the kidney complications had not put him in a coma. The country watched too. After an alarming report in the *Times* he wrote to Hooker on 26 June that he didn't 'feel at all like "sending in my checks"'.[43]

The two old salts were the last of the '"thick and thin" companions'. The surgeon's mates would reminisce about wooden ships and weevily biscuits, and Huxley's terrace at Hodeslea became his 'Quarterdeck', where he paced in the sea breeze. There was no pacing now. Each day in June he had been borne down to a garden tent, where he basked in the sun. It had been a lovely hot Summer and he thought he was mending, despite the 'beastly nausea' on any exertion. The nurses knew he was dying. Hooker guessed it too from Nettie's scribbled words on his 26 June envelope.

Huxley was 'still clinging to hope', but his was a 'sad hand'. The last news was of Rachel's husband dying of yellow fever in San Salvador, like so many sons of the Empire – leaving her and the three children with little provision. Grief would be Hal's to the end. For two days the agnostic 'stood alone with his dead before the abyss of the Eternal'.[44]

For those 48 hours nausea would strike him for long periods. In between he was indomitable. He read, seemingly equanimical about stepping into Nature's vacuum. Nettie fussed about him; she had waited almost as long as Rachel to marry her Jacob and the tenderness showed them as 'lovers to the end'. On the summery Saturday morning, 29 June 1895, he had a heart attack. Painkillers eased his last seven hours.[45] The doctors declared him dead at 3.30 in the afternoon.

Rachel had lost her Jacob. 'May we love to grow old together and dying may we meet again in Heaven', the star-crossed lover had written almost 50 years earlier. 'I am alone!' the old lady scribbled against these words. She was lost in his love letters, as if Sydney was more tangible than Heaven. Then in Hal's secret belongings she came across a 48-year-old bloom.[46] It was the red camellia that the black-eyed surgeon had begged after their parsonage dance.

How to honour 'the Apostle Paul of the new teaching'? Some proposed a State funeral in Westminster Abbey, where he might join Darwin. But Huxley had anticipated and scotched that idea. It might have been fitting for the Pope of Science, but it was absurd in its way. Wilder calls were heard for a Pantheon for these new men,[47] but that was very unBritish, and there was a stubborn Britishness to Huxley.

Nor would Highgate's infidel plot do. Clifford, George Eliot and G. H. Lewes had already colonized the north-east corner, ultimately to be joined by Spencer, Holyoake and Watt's agnostics. But Huxley had been the intelligentsia's 'finest free lance',[48] and a lifetime's lonely furrow in gentlemanly engagement would have made him uncomfortable there too.

His own 35-year wish would be respected – to lie alongside his little son Noel. And so on Thursday morning, 4 July, the wreath-covered oak coffin travelled by train to London Bridge, thence by hearse past quiet fields to Finchley.

There was 'no pageantry', no eulogy, the *Times* noted, and 'little that was even official'.[49] A simple blessing was given by that stalwart friend Revd Llewelyn Davies, who had come down from his parish in Westmorland. Heterodox himself, Davies was that last remnant of Christian Socialist stock with no scruples about evolution or emancipation, and no notion that his prayers could alter the physical universe.[50]

The *Telegraph* noted that the grave had been 'deeply excavated'.[51] Of course, the golden-haired three-year-old had been interred 12 feet down that his father and mother might rest just above him. It had always been intended as a family plot. At 3 o'clock Huxley was laid close by his brother George, next to his son Noel.

No invitations had been sent out. It was to have been a quiet funeral for the family. But the veiled Nettie, standing beneath the oak that had been a sapling at Noel's death, turned round to see the last and greatest constellation of Victorian scientists ever to gather on one spot. Two hundred had made their individual ways there. In front stood Sir Joseph Hooker, Lord Kelvin, Sir Joseph Lister, Michael Foster and Ray Lankester. With them were sombre heads of untold Physics, Chemistry and Biology Labs, the 'Professors', the South Kensington militia led by Major-General Sir John Donnelly, Sir William Henry Flower and the museum directors, Presidents and Councils of every learned society, the great hospital surgeons: all friends who were positively embarrassed by their admiration. Then the faceless men from the institutes, trainloads from the Midlands and North. It became a 'military' burial in Science, missing only a fusillade from the Royal Engineers. There was no government or Church presence, and none was wanted, the obituarists agreed. During an election, mud-slinging politicians would have sullied the agnostic shroud. Instead artists mixed with writers, Alma-Tadema with Henry James; 'the commanding figure of Lecky' was spotted,[52] sad-faced at the Christian recital, the fine-browed Leslie Stephen, and Darwin's sons. And, to comfort Nettie, Lucy Clifford and Louisa Tyndall.

Unknown mourners mingled, covens from the *Agnostic Journal* and *Liberty Review* and Rationalist Press, there to record events in reverent detail. For them it was 'painful' to hear the '*sure and certain*' when Huxley was so unsure and so uncertain – a 'cruel mockery' one called it. With fine-honed sarcasm Moncure Conway, reading the lesson from Huxley's works at his South Place Chapel, found that the doctrine ' "he that believeth not shall be damned" – is reserved for common people; it does not apply to Fellows of the Royal Society'.[53]

Had they returned a few days later, they would have found the wreaths removed to Huxley's old hospital, Charing Cross.[54] And carved on the tombstone were lines from Nettie's poem on 'Browning's Funeral'. The original had begun appropriately

> And if there be no meeting past the grave,
> If all is darkness, silence, yet 'tis rest.

But there followed the three lines on the headstone:

> Be not afraid, ye waiting hearts that weep;
> For still He giveth His beloved sleep,
> And if an endless sleep He wills, so best.

Nettie, still with that 'sneaking love for the old story', had covered her options.[55]

The sects were already tugging at Huxley's corpse, with the *Freethinker* laughing at the *Catholic Review*'s comment, 'He is no longer an Agnostic; he knows now that the Christian revelation is true'. But a grief-stricken Nettie jealously guarded Hal's intellectual remains. Through his Eastbourne retirement she had begged him to give up controversy.[56] Now she would see it stopped at the grave. That Swiftian satire would have no conclusion.

The old story jostled uncomfortably with the new in her mind. No cajoling could persuade her to release the unrevised Balfour finale. There would be no last charge, no bayoneting from beyond the grave. Knowles' plea that Hal had been 'fighting even *with* Death to accomplish it' had no effect.[57] Huxley had gone down like his hero Gordon, sword in hand, and death brought all controversies to rest.

Afterword

Huxley in Perspective

'READ NO HISTORY', advised Disraeli, only 'biography, for that is life without theory'. Good enough, perhaps, for the posing *littérateur*; but it would be a rash biographer today who ignored the new contextual and sociological approaches to science in 'Darwin's Century'. Isn't the modern function of biography to carve a path through brambly contexts? To become a part of history? Without comprehending Huxley, the *Times* said, no one could estimate the century's intellectual and social transformation. And isn't that our ultimate aim, to understand the making of our world?

Not only did the cultural landscape transform between 1840 and 1890, along with the city skyline – indeed the emergence of South Kensington testified to the rise of the professional and decline of the gentleman – but 'the very foundations of human thought' were 'rebuilt'. One Victorian concept above all would shake the complacency of ages. Evolution, Benjamin Kidd said, 'has affected the entire intellectual life of our Western civilization'.[1] At its visceral edge was T. H. Huxley – evolutionary propagandist and proselytizer of a new scientific authority – and it is impossible to separate his story from that of the 'Wonderful Century'.

Huxley is part of the new contextual history of science. This itself is a reaction to the old history of ideas, which *dis*placed the person, made him or her a disembodied ghost, a flash of transcendent genius. Only by embedding Huxley can we appreciate his role in the vast transformation that staggered our great-grandfathers. It is an irony that many historians who gravitated to the sociology of knowledge in the 1980s, trying to understand why different sorts of knowledge were produced by different social groups, have come out seeing their subjects as individuals. For me this is particularly true. Perhaps it is because, as a beleaguered minority, we have been forced to follow our subjects so closely – the onus lay on us to prove that science really was socially contingent.[2] It meant ever more microscopic examination of unique contexts, leading 'to the point at which each individual has "his" science – almost a pulverizing pluralization of the concept'.[3] This put the burden back on biography to explain scientific originality in terms of individual social trajectories. The upshot is a revitalized interest in scientific biography in the 1990s.[4]

At the same time a recognition that there is no such thing as value-free history has made biographies more personal. Given my apprenticeship – charting the radicals' fight against Anglican monopoly in *Politics of Evolution*, the street use of science in 'Artisan Resistance and Evolution', and the way Victorians reconstructed their dinosaurs using social cement in *Archetypes and Ancestors* – *Huxley* had to be an ideological portrait. While 'confrontationist' histories ('Science vs. Religion') are deeply unfashionable, it unashamedly digs into the roots of Huxley's gladiatorial antagonism. It is a book about Class and Power.

Frank Turner rightly berates an older genre, based on the Victorian *Lives and Letters*, which themselves assumed an ahistorical and hagiographical air.[5] Today's goal is to relate Huxley to the alienated Dissenters, to the rising industrialists and to the retrenching gentry who sought safety in Church. We have to understand his origins and audience. We must travel incognito on mud-spattered streets, pick up our *National Reformer* and don our wideawake hats to appreciate his workers' lectures, or buy a *Macmillan's Magazine* and mingle with the feather and sable fashionables at the Royal Institution. More than anything we have to understand how the man of science rode the political and religious crest to power.

'Servants talk about People: Gentlefolk discuss Things' ran the Victorian proverb. And since my grandparents and their parents were cooks and grooms in the great manors, my history is a maelstrom of motivated people and social action.

HUXLEY'S SOCIAL HISTORY

[The *Origin of Species* and *Man's Place in Nature*], which were anathema to the generation passing away, have become the standards of scientific thought to-day, blessed by bishops and quoted by rural deans. The times are changed more than we can appreciate.

Pall Mall Gazette, 1 July 1895

The 1850s were the time to be young, wrote G. M. Young in *Portrait of an Age* – to be one of Thackeray's flashing blades. Tom Huxley had the keenest edge of them all, honed to a glint in the hungry forties. The 1860s and 1870s were the 'glorious hour of crowded life' – the years of the liberal intelligentsia, the *Origin of Species* and *Essays and Reviews* and the fall of Anglican monopoly. Then came the storm clouds of the recessionary 1880s with their socialist riots. This is our time – a huge span. Just as the Chartists of the forties seemed remote from the equipoised Darwinians of the sixties, so Britain in the 1890s with its secularism, socialism and rediscovery of sexuality seemed another world again. Each age shocked, and was shocked in turn. 'To dip into the current literature of the "sixties"', said the *Pall Mall Gazette* on Huxley's death, 'is like plugging into a burning fiery furnace'.[6] I have tried to show the famous rapier being tempered in this oven: to grasp T. H. Huxley's role in half a century which saw the emancipation of Dissent and rise of the professions.

He lived long enough to see the scandalous sexual experimentation. The naughty nineties arrived after decades of belief that morality was fixed. Women in knickerbockers on bikes, women climbing the winding stairs of open-top buses, men complaining that 'their privileges are going'. The hedonism of Wilde's London was a furious reaction to the old guard's Puritanism. The long years of salvation by reason had led the unsatisfied spirit to try salvation by sin. Or salvation by social action, or spiritualism – Huxley bowed out amid the decadence, the new mystifications, Annie Besant's final migration to theosophy, and science going private as political activism assumed its public function. He left amid the *fin de siècle* restlessness, 'pregnant of great changes'.[7]

There was a flawed perfection to his messy life: the conquering heights, the prehistoric visions, the quixotic tilts and medieval excursions, the visionary who 'dreams strange things', the inward collapses and outward bravura. His life was lived like a hurtling express, and it periodically careened off the tracks. The speed and sublimation, Beatrice Webb thought, were something to do with 'his early life' being 'supremely sad'. Speed from a full head of steam was his diversion. But the energy he expended on School Boards, Commissions and intellectual theatricality left everyone excusing the defects; anyway, said Moncure Conway echoing Shakespeare, 'Best men are moulded of their faults'. For Webb they were what made Huxley fascinating. Even Catholic contessas were drawn to this religious smiter of Papal perversions, to this Reformer from the North with no god and no heaven; and still there was 'something so attractive in Prof Huxley'.[8]

To many the assertive 'masculine' prose suggested that there were no hidden depths. Steely imagery for the Victorians meant intellectual power and virility (an equation itself that was no longer adding up by the 1890s).[9] 'Pope Huxley' exuded certainty and reassurance. He provided the totemic strength to face up to our animal past and face down an Immortal future. It was a magnificently efficient façade, put up to comply with Victorian codes of behaviour. Men did not gush out their feelings in public; and when one did, like Froude, Carlyle cursed him for 'vomiting up his interior crudities'. But an acute Beatrice Webb saw the frail veneer over the seething depths, while Len's sister-in-law Mrs Humphry Ward extracted Huxley's revealing self-perception:

> Beneath the cooled logical upper strata of my microcosm, there is a fused mass of prophetism and mysticism, and Lord knows what might happen to me, in case a moral earthquake cracked the superincumbent deposits, and permitted an eruption of the demonic element below.[10]

The currents visible in the 1850s were still swirling after a generation.

Always the self-perceived 'plebeian',[11] Huxley was a prey to the pressures of Victorian uprightness. Using Darwinism to claw more power only exacerbated his predicament. With evolutionists widely held to be wicked, his life had to be an exemplary open book. Hence the appearance of a model family, above reproach. Indeed it was a stable, close-knit, free household glossed by Pater's 'warm, indulgent, loving nature',[12] even if, as Webb said, none of the children understood his intellectual struggle.

It explains why the sober Huxley, keeper of the agnostic moral flame, was wary of the family skeletons rattling in the closet. The poor boy was conscious of his origins. George's banking scandal and Ellen's drunken debauchery threatened him like a dropped accent. Ellen's and Polly's deaths removed the peril of exposure, but only their gin-sodden corpses explained his accepting an Honorary Membership of the suitably distant 'American Society for the Study and Cure of Inebriety' in 1893, with a coy admission that he knew something 'of its very worst consequences'. Still, 'No scandal ever had the name' of Huxley 'for its butt', concluded one admirer.[13] And from our century there never did appear 'such worthy representatives of frock-coated respectability as those terrible scientists'. But the struggle for respectability had taken its toll.

He had to erect formidable defences. A lacerating tongue was for conquering and repelling; a scalpelled pen saw him cutting up men more than monkeys. Many approached but few touched him. There was a frightening presence. Young Oliver Lodge felt it. He once plucked up courage at a soirée to ask Mrs Huxley about the dying Clifford. Through the noise she thought he was asking about the children, and the 'General' 'stiffened in a manner appropriate'. Poor Lodge, 'too shy to explain, slunk away' and it took him 20 years to overcome the 'twinge' and write to explain.[14]

Only to strong women did Huxley open up – the dark priestesses like gutsy Ellen Busk, to be adored and feared. George Eliot in the 1850s saw him blindly driven, aloof, while Beatrice Webb in the 1880s penetrated the smouldering vulnerability. She saw the insecurities beneath the life of conquest. His were philosophic dashes between disabling fits. Just as he had no time to earn money, he had no money to buy him time: he could never luxuriate like Darwin in sustained research. It was all *ad hoc*, squeezed in. His science suffered. 'He is greater as a man than as a scientific thinker', Webb said, and more interesting. He had 'None of the enthusiasm for "what is", or the silent persistency in grasping truth'. His was 'the eager rush of the conquering mind, loving the fact of conquest more than the land conquered'. And behind him was a trail littered with half-finished work which generations would try to mop up.[15] Publishers understood and cajoled him: Macmillan once sent him a bound, embossed *Lessons in Elementary Physiology* – completely blank-leaved, with a reminder to write the book. But the dashes enabled Huxley to scout beyond society into strange regions, back to ape-men, forward to the ice death of planet, out to the lonely cosmos, inward to the 'abyss of the Eternal'.[16]

The voyager acquired a cynicism as he was blown about 'among the grains of human dust on our speck of a planet'. The anguished soul had discovered the gloomy wastes of an uncaring cosmos and was venting his evangelical anger. This was Victorian man on the edge, lashing out, as George Eliot noted. Such 'melancholy has haunted his whole life', Webb added. Hence the paradox: he was 'never at peace unless he was fighting', never alive unless he was slaying. The poor boy broke lances in religious aggression. And the alienated outsiders who had risen with him indulged his mock modesty. 'What an unfortunate man you are!' said Lecky as Huxley stood before the Salvation Army. And 'With your deep "sense of the blessedness of peace"'. Ultimately his 'controversial manner' became as 'polished as his literary style',[17] but that does not disguise his religious need to engage.

Science did bring the 'solace of fame', but it barely satisfied. Huxley, the most ascetic of sceptics, the most relativistic of agnostics, laughing at materialism, knowing nothing of necessity, the man who stood alone with no Humanist Church or Agnostic Temple, found less and less to cling to. He had left the 'Unknowable' a desert, the Laws of Nature merely the relations of events passing our vision. Yet through all, the 'Cynic and sceptic' clung to love as the one 'mysterious reality'.[18] It was this that pulled him back from the brink. And it was this that saved mankind in 'Evolution and Ethics'.

But personality is not the most interesting level of explanation. 'Men of genius', said the *Times*, contemplating Huxley's shooting star, 'come no one knows whence or when'.[19] But we can appreciate the social forces they ride to power. To start, we might ask why the *enfant terrible* felt himself part of excluded England, alienated and angry. And why he felt the need to forge *Science* as his rapier.

THE ROUNDHEAD WHO LOST HIS FAITH

The question . . . is how British intellectual life marked by a
predominance of Anglican institutions, ideas, and ideology in 1830
moved by 1870 to a culture in which Nonconformity . . . played an
important part and one in which scientific naturalism had replaced
natural theology.

Frank Turner[20]

Twenty years ago Arnold Thackray brilliantly analysed Manchester's Unitarians. He made their Dissenting drive the motor force of the 'transformation of natural knowledge'.[21] In the industrial heartland, the Chapel elite had developed a wheeze-and-snort Nature wilfully at odds with the supernatural props of Anglican power. The Black Country democrats legally bound Nature, made it subject to law and order. The most radical of them denied that it was subject to Divine aristocratic whim. Thus they refused any miraculous support for the bishops' status quo. With the institutions of power – the universities, the bench and the hospitals – in Anglican hands, these *arriviste* industrialists forged a rival outsider-knowledge. To these excluded, marginal men the democratic republic of science was appealing.

Now consider Huxley. True, his father – that shadowy presence – taught in an Anglican public school (taught the future Cardinal Newman no less). But if Ealing School had been part of the nation's evangelical backbone, it was in decline in Tom's day and 'as bad as any of them'.[22] Nor should this blind us to the teenager's sensitivity

to religious injustice. It was shown in the ease with which he learnt
the morality of resistance from the handicapped Dissenters. Those
are the unexplored years of Huxley biographies: the lost background,
the missing key, the trajectory away from Anglicanism. The years in
cotton-spinning Coventry reading Southwood Smith's fatalistic,
reforming Unitarian bible, *The Divine Government*, and in Marshall
Hall's cut-price medical school, cast a new light on the development
of Huxley's science and agnosticism. No one had even correctly
identified Huxley's first anatomy school before, the short-lived
'Sydenham College' in London. And yet it was the institution that
pioneered the study of reflex arcs and automaton biology and led the
dirty war against Anglican privilege.

Huxley's radical teachers were waging a campaign of disobedience
against the Anglican-run, power-grabbing College of Physicians.
Huxley in the forties was among radical Methodists and rational
Dissenters – activists whose culture of resistance and scientific
Calvinism had matured around the Lord's table. Houston Peterson
once said that Huxley's mind was fixed about 1840. Peterson knew
nothing of Huxley's radical schooling, but I think he was right.[23]
Young Huxley became heir to the Dissenting resistance of cotton
kings and medical activists. Without this insight his lifelong struggle
simply makes no sense.

The ultra-radicals accepted a sovereign, self-regulating Nature.
Not for them a supernatural command structure descending from
the Godhead through the State priesthood (as L. S. Jacyna has shown
in a series of stunning papers). The radical Dissenters were disabling
this divine sanction of Anglican repression. They were taking their
orders direct from God's Works, His natural order. The new causal,
natural science became the 'social legitimation of marginal men',
their 'mode of cultural self-expression', the means to paint Tory
Anglicans themselves as idolatrous '*pagani*'.[24] Huxley and Spencer
would make it the cosmic norm; and with Darwin's competitive
Origin of Species sanctioning the Nonconformist meritocratic ideal,
a new intellectual aristocracy would be born around Science.

In the 1840s evolution had been a nail-studded club hidden in
the street atheist's coal-hole; by 1870 it was being polished as a
Whitworth gun in the imperial armoury. By any account this was
a telling crossover. Thirty years of Dissenting liberation and professional changes had eased the way for Darwin's *Origin of Species*.
Jim Secord calls Darwin's the 'palace coup'.[25] It took the winter
palace after the battle had been won by the urban Dissenters and
professionals.

Twentieth-century scientists have taken Huxley's non-partisan self-image on trust. He became iconic as *the* ideologically untainted Scientist. But historians have become cautious. Bernie Lightman has pointed out the theological structures behind Huxley's thought. Lightman's *Origins of Agnosticism* makes Huxley a transitional figure whose agnosticism had *religious* qualities. And this was how Huxley was seen in his own day – as 'a lineal descendant of the Protestant Reformation', steeped in Biblical lore. 'He may have inverted orthodox theology, he may have blessed what it bans', said the *Times*, but he shared its 'temper'.[26] He commanded 'the sect of the Darwinian evolutionists', whose converts would revere evolution's 'grandeur and power'. In short, he made an undercast feel first class through his holier-than-thou attitude. Scientists, he said, had a higher 'standard of veracity'. That in itself, critics argued, bred a 'spirit of latent intolerance':

> his nature is essentially Puritanic, if not Calvinistic. He has the moral earnestness, the volitional energy, the absolute confidence in his own convictions, the desire and determination to impress them upon all mankind, which are the essential marks of Puritan character. His whole temper and spirit is essentially dogmatic of the Presbyterian or Independent type, and he might fairly be described as a Roundhead who had lost his faith.[27]

So we have Huxley decrying the 'sin of faith', descending on the apostate Mivart. We have the righteousness, the prophetic 'tide of matter' drowning unregenerate 'souls'. He was a good hater, with a 'scientific hell, to which the finally impenitent, those who persist in rejecting the new physical gospel, might be condemned'.[28] We have to beware of this Dissenting imagery becoming one-sided. What he actually retained was the 'temper' and the deconsecrated theological shell, a sort of evacuated Calvinistic antigen in the shape of a deterministic Nature.[29] But mate this Dissenting husk to Turner's Carlylean living host, fire it with the residual romanticism described by James Paradis in his superb *T. H. Huxley: Man's Place in Nature*, and you have the roots of young Huxley's scientific secularism.

It went to cement his Cromwellian image – and Chamberlain's Unitarian Birmingham loved him for it. But it was a religious reputation he had to shake if Science was to seem untarnished. Not that that was hard. Ultimately, with the success of Dissent, his Nonconformist virtues – earnestness, duty, moralism – became the middle-class norm in the Victorian Noon. They no longer stood out.

In some ways Agnosticism *was* the apotheosis of Dissent. It was the last act of the Protestant Reformation. To that other Ealing graduate John Henry Newman it was as *'clear as day'* in 1840 'that Protestantism leads to infidelity'. By then Huxley – that most 'radical among Protestant Whigs', as Chalmers Mitchell called him – was treading the path.[30] He was cutting and trimming to the knowable border. He carried freedom of conscience to the limit. This was his 'New Reformation' – the freeing of Nonconformity from its final idolatrous anchor.

From dog-collar to white-collar: subtly his 'sect' absorbed the old priesthood's functions. Morality became acquiescence to scientific evidence. The social order was sustained by the Laws of Biology. The unemancipated women and workers were held to their stations. Order remained as the classes toppled one another (or ultimately merged into a higher hegemony). Industrial-age Science, hitching itself to the State, was called upon to curb insurrection and maintain national security. It explains why the pious old 'Pope' – who castigated the clergy for climbing over their side of the fence – felt free to roam into politics, theology, morality and education himself. And why it was impossible to open a journal 'without feeling his hand in all the moving subjects of the day'.[31]

The Nonconformist motor had carried Huxley to power. And Nonconformist money kept him there – bequests from Quaker manufacturers, Cobden's free-traders and Congregationalist steel barons, all of whom understood his *Lay Sermons*. The seditious Unitarian science of 1800 had become the deconsecrated universal by 1900. Southwood Smith's deterministic *Divine Government* became Huxley's *Natural Government*. (Not for nothing was Huxley's Jubilee address on the 'Progress of Science in the last Half Century' cemented into the foundation of the All Souls Universalist Church in Grand Rapids, Michigan, by a 'thorough evolutionist' pastor who preached humanitarian sermons.[32]) By 1887 the Nonconformists had their open society, their access to power. Indeed, they had their new universities in the industrial towns, Birmingham, Liverpool, Manchester, Leeds, Nottingham, Sheffield, all giving science prominence and Huxley his due.[33]

So Huxley's 'New Reformation' was synonymous with the liberation of the industrial and professional classes. It made evolutionary naturalism the serviceable way of thought in a free-trading nation. As he modernized history – making ape ancestors for mankind as unproblematic as dinosaur ancestors for birds – he camouflaged the tainting metaphysics while putting the 'new Nature' into the professionals' hands. He left an image of neutral science soaring like Pegasus to unknown regions.

All of this suggests that Evolution had an overriding social import-ance. While he had difficulty reconciling himself to Darwin's bloody Natural Selection in biology, the competitive struggle could legit-imate a meritocratic order or combat socialism. To this extent 'Darwin's Bulldog' was a misnomer (as Michael Bartholomew said long ago). In the final analysis Huxley comes across as a complex figure coping with the shift from a Romantic 1840s to a Socialist 1880s. He repackaged Darwinism for his dissolvent armoury. Both to fire off its shells at a rival Anglican edifice, and to sustain a form of Calvinist fatalism: justifying resignation on earth rather than redemption in heaven. His prose was called 'masculine English' because it squared up to the 'abysmal griefs hidden under the current of daily life'.[34] His 'masculine vigour' was a hard-edged uncom-promising style, a clenched-jaw attitude to the horror of pain and death in nature and the sentimental supernatural fictions which sur-round it. His evolutionary Nature was harsher than Calvin's, and his hard-nosed science hinted at a similar religious forbearance.

A SALVATION ARMY OF HUXLEYS

We begin to sense how science in Huxley's hands had a religious potency. The fact that it acquired a non-aligned image made it even better to ratify the new social order and sanction the seizing of Church assets. The State Church, portrayed as a rival 'branch of the Civil Service',[35] lost its monopoly on Oxbridge, the bench and the hospitals.

Huxley's men were being puffed as a 'priesthood of science' as early as 1868 by the secularist George Holyoake. Not only were they usurping Dissent's dispute with the Anglicans, they were turning it into a territorial claim over health, education and morality (making the common culture of scientific, social and sectarian thought at once larger than R. M. Young envisaged in *Darwin's Metaphor*). This explains why Huxley so easily turned theological questions into scientific ones, why he plumbed 'the whence and whither of mankind, the limitations of knowledge, the sanctions of conduct', while challenging the Church's 'monopoly of serious and constant reflection upon the terrible problems of existence'.[36] Even the title of his book *Lay Sermons* said so much: a century later it sounds plummy, strange, even dusty for a *scientist's* work, but its double meaning was provocative in 1870: suggesting secular sermons to rival those from the pulpit, or professional addresses to the laity adoring at the scientific altar. Like the old Paleyites who had made known God's way through Nature, Huxley was making Nature's known through Science. The 'garment of God' had become the scientific priest's robe. And like the old priesthood he saw nothing insignificant in nature. Every coral polyp in a reef or *Globigerina* in the Chalk was pregnant with moral meaning.

The outsiders hitched their demands for State employment to an image of science as a national asset.[37] The result was a swelling 'Salvation Army of Huxleys': a middle-class profession. It was self-sustaining through its teacher-training programme, and self-validating through its university restructuring. It left a growing corps of biology professors who swore (as an eavesdropping Chalmers Mitchell heard at a Royal Society soirée) that 'it was Huxley who made all of us possible'.[38]

Scientific research became free-ranging, open-ended, itself a novel concept. Huxley's professionals in their 'knowledge factories' would become 'pioneers in the exploration and settlement of new regions'. It was exciting, modern. H. G. Wells tingled at the thought that he might 'do Research. Research!' A buzz surrounded the word. Wells was in awe of Huxley, and the frisson shows at his prospect of voyaging into the unknown, at 'any moment' to 'make a Discovery!!!' Such open-ended research broke the seminary tradition of incestuously-recycled Classicism. Vulgar nature had been by-passed by the Classics-dominated Anglican Universities, with their dedication to rank and wealth. But Huxley exploited this shunned and sordid Nature to legitimate his scientific 'priesthood', using it to build a rival base in secular London and the industrial Midlands. From here he turned the instruments of government against the Anglican universities. The Classics *had* been the mark of a Gentleman, but the 'Gentleman' as an occupational category was dead. And as Ruth Barton says, Huxley portrayed Science as more rigorous, more critical, and equally character-forming.[39]

This was already evident when 'Theology' was 'massacred', as the legend had it, at the 1860 Oxford British Association meeting. In fact, Archdeacon Farrar remembered it as a question of manners. Wilberforce's 'flippant' question on grandma Huxley's descent from apes showed that 'the Bp. had forgotten to behave like a gentleman'. Huxley for once refused to cap the tackiness, leaving a question hanging about the bishop's taste. An Oxford audience of 'gentlefolk, not prepared to endorse anything vulgar', contrasted the worldly bishop, his 'splendid nature debauched by society', with this plain-dressed Puritanical unknown. The manners themselves reflected a wide sectarian divide. The jest was innocuous to Wilberforce because his distinguished grandmother was related to bankers and archbishops. The venerable old lady being akin to apes was ludicrous. But Huxley knew nothing of his grandmother, and it stung to be the brunt of High Church hauteur. Puritans made virtue the true nobility; and Huxley's gravity showed the man of science, Cockshut said in *The Unbelievers*, to be 'the more faithful heir of the heroes of the Reformation and Civil War'.[40]

The Puritans slid their men into the Oxbridge seminaries. Here the professionals created a unique space for themselves. Laboratories were built to enclose Nature. The 'field' reappeared under the lens, as Graeme Gooday puts it. Here the 'new Nature' could be jealously guarded. But the laboratory's deadroom air gave it a very different feel from Paley's happy parsonage. That is because Huxley's 'Biology' – that unique South Kensington development – was carved out of medical comparative anatomy.[41] It remained a dead, dissected nature, relocated from the anatomy schools, and simplified by means of 'type' specimens so that it could be transmitted to the schoolmasters. The geography of science had changed dramatically by the mid-1870s. The industrial fringes had coalesced into centres of laboratory excellence within the old universities.

Huxley called the 'Victorian epoch' the 'age of science'. It was only a beginning, he argued. Since 'Nature is limitless', the free-roaming enquirer would never come up against a boundary.[42] Securely institutionalized in the universities, funded by the State, the emergent scientific enterprise had become a self-sustaining exploration.

Inside its great institutions, the 'scientific priesthood', quasi-autonomous like so much of the civil service, would continue the old patrician ethos. There was a grand imperial, paternal arrogance in Victorian Britain. It was not only the age of science, but the Age of the Father.[43] The *men* of science were chary of letting even their talented daughters near the altar or workers do more than swing thuribles. Against this backdrop one has to judge Huxley's attitude to women.

Evelleen Richards talks of the 'scientific onslaught' on women's emancipation. The onslaught was sanctioned by a nascent, worried profession backed by Darwin's *Descent of Man*, and it was the Darwinians who 'articulated the dominant constructions of femininity . . . and naturalized the barriers against feminine intellectual and social equality'. Women bought the Darwinian commodity, figuratively and literally. Despite the stereotype of stay-at-home, religiously demure wives, many paid for the *The Descent of Man*, even if they had 'to order it on the sly!' And amid the 'pretty hubbub' at Huxley's Royal Institution talks Tyndall was 'torn to pieces by women in search of tickets. Anything that touches progenitorship interests them'. But for all that was religiously liberating or titillating (it is difficult to capture the frisson about 'evolution' except by this word), would-be emancipists were being bound by its prejudicial laws. They had a doubly hard time of it. Darwin had branded them as biologically inferior because of their exclusion from the competitive arena, yet in medicine they were seen as undesirable economic competitors, rivalling men for the few paying jobs. The men simply did not want them as contenders.

But women were prising open the doors – Huxley even thought his talented Mady had a brilliant 'career' in prospect. In the 1860s he had put biological limitations on women's capacity; but as a liberal paternalist he was willing to grant them the privilege of sitting in class.[44] And *yet*, allowed to compete, the women came off well, confounding his stereotype: the sole woman in his first practical class at South Kensington took the prize. And Huxley soon had Miss McConnish demonstrating. By H. G. Wells' day Huxley's audience was a normal cross-section, including women, vegetarians and socialists. Interestingly, when Huxley died the papers juxtaposed the successive Darwinian and suffragettist revolutions: 'we have now got over' the shock of the *Origin of Species* and *Man's Place*, said a syndicated obituary, 'just as we . . . may, perchance, get used to the "new woman" '.[45] It was as if Huxley was responsible for the first and consumed by the second.

The Nemesis of growing knowledge was its fractionalization. Huxley's age had created the specialists. In the 1860s came a few Generals. By the 1890s whole squads of sappers were spending their lives watching amoebas or weighing gases, their research papers being valued 'in proportion as the corner of the world with which they deal is dark and minute'. Knowledge, said the *Times*, had 'already become too vast to be manageable'. Huxley had been the last to manage it, indeed the last to view Art, Literature and Science as a whole. In Royal Academy talks he visualized each of them stopping the flux of life to fix its order and beauty momentarily. David Roos has him keeping faith with the broad-based monthly magazines and demanding a larger purview for culture. Out there, in public, as Edward Clodd observed, Huxley was 'free from that curse of specialism which kills all sense of proportion'.[46] But that was ironic, because it was Huxley's training that created the boffins.

Of course he outlived his time, and it showed in his superannuated Church-bashing in these monthlies. He 'continued his method of controversy after its justification had ceased', unable to shake off his old political mentality. Even as the Right Honourable T. H. Huxley grew staid he clung to an old radical sectarianism. A second generation never followed him. His students were the specialists now: winning their own Royal Medals or studying heredity in Weismann's Germany. They kept their religious sense of belonging to him. As was true 'of Pius IX when he wrote to the Emperor of Germany, saying "everyone who was baptised belonged to the Pope"', wrote one admirer, 'so every student of science belongs to you'. But few became miracle-denouncing publicists, and he lamented the fact. They were professionally secure, with his scientific naturalism written into their accredition procedures.

The years of science's heady excitement were over. After he died, there was only the 'deadly dulness of the mere workshop'.[47] On the eve of the twentieth century science was specialized and esoteric; it shut itself away in the laboratory and lost its public appeal. Its radicalism passed to politics, its moral drive to humanism; and the poison bombs raining death in the Great War finally killed its nineteenth-century promise.

AGNOSTICISM

. . . the word had to him a deep and solemn meaning.

Michael Foster[48]

Something more surrounded the man of science's credentials – an agnostic moral aura. 'Pope Huxley' had fused the little sciences into a universal corpus – the One Catholic Apostolic Church of True Knowledge. Science, with a capital 'S' now, a monolithic entity matched by a name for its acolyte, the 'Scientist'. Its method of enquiry set limits to the knowable, and acquiescence to those limits earned initiates moral dispensation. Indeed the acceptance of physical evidence became a religious imperative itself. It was what gave Huxley, in Bishop Magee's words, his 'bumptious air of omniscience'. Huxley had at last found his 'saving belief'.[49]

Agnosticism was a product of circumstance. It was already evident in the young surgeon's letters of 1847. Here it appears as much a response to the seditious street atheists, bent on destroying the social fabric, as to Carlyle's ideal of a theology-less religion. Frank Turner sees the 'cultural apostasy' of the Arnolds and Stephens as 'different from the direct social and political protests' of the 1840s. So it was for them, but Huxley's outsider education put him closer to the protesters. If Matthew Arnold's 'cultural apostates' were fifth columnists destroying the Church from within, Huxley was digging up the foundations from without. He *would* later seek a gentlemanly engagement, but the boy among cotton spinners and medical destructives was steeped in the dissident sub-culture. It had turned him into an 'agnostic' in all but name before he set foot on the *Rattlesnake*. From the chaos of the 1840s came a Calvinistic upstart quoting Luther, a sceptic who sought the burden of evidence, a nonconformist who refused to equate the 'Truth' with Anglican authority.[50] Agnosticism was fashioned from a Dissenting lawful secularism to give the State Church its moral come-uppance.

Twenty years later, in 1869, the word was added to the deed. 'Agnosticism' became his 'apologetic tool', Lightman says. He consecrated doubt and wielded it with political bravado. In those 20 years the tainting sectarian connotations had started to wear off. The word would appear *de novo*, signifying the scientist with clean hands. It would make the agnostic a moral cut above all the sectarian 'ists' – Atheist or Anglican, Positivist or Spiritualist. 'What does nature want with me?' the young romantic had asked in 1851.[51] By 1869 he knew; he had become Nature's prophet, Her voice in the wilderness of men.

Agnosticism became a secure port, Tennyson's 'golden harbour'. Scientific method defined the limits to the sensory orb, beyond which it was immoral to stray. Acquiescence to the unpalatable sublunary truths about apes or ancestors became a baptism by fire for tyros, and for them 'veracity [lay at] the heart of morality' and at the centre of a new religion. While Mallock and Hutton slashed at secularism for making life meaningless,[52] Huxley put the meaning back with his essays, equating worth and purpose with duty and honesty.

Science's *method*, not its glitzy applications. offered redemption. It became a harder and harder line to hold. Faced with the technological marvels of the 1880s and 1890s – motorbikes, the first petrol-driven cars, moving pictures and electric underground trains – he had to ensure the purity of Science. Where once he had attacked 'aristocratic flunkeyism' in the Royal Society, now he lashed the techno-flunkeys from the temple – the 'Engineers, Chemical traders

& "Experts" (who have sold their souls for a good price) and who find it helps them to appear to the public as if they were men of science'. He feared the veneration switching to Science's products – 'its froth and scum', its engines and telegraphs, as he angrily put it answering Disraeli. Science's ascetic method was the real 'foundation of its human worth'. Science had been sanctified for its agnostic moral purity. It had acquired something of the holy. 'Science takes the place of dogmatic religion', noted the *Tablet* in 1871, 'Mr. Huxley is the favourite and popular apostle of this new creed'.[53] And the 'holy' had to be preserved to bind the profession in an age of religious revivals.

Method and agnostic moralism were his professionals' *raison d'être*. Science was no longer a revelation of God's handiwork, but a search for the Eternal in a fact. It was an image powerful enough to make agnosticism the intellectual's credentials by the 1880s. Huxley took it 'out of the wilderness of Sinai', said a follower.[54] He made a Promised Land of Science.

KENSINGTON BARRACKS:
THE SOCIAL ROOTS OF THE MILITARY METAPHOR

> The ascendancy of an unambiguously militaristic ethos [in the Department of Science and Art] . . . raises a number of troubling questions . . .
>
> > Rafael Cardoso Denis on the role of the
> > Royal Engineers at South Kensington[55]

There is no doubt that Frank Turner is right: the 'war' between science and religion was a professional territorial dispute. By the 1870s this 'military' image was being hyped by Huxley's group and universalized by Draper's blockbuster *History of the Conflict Between Religion and Science* into the battle of all time. Jim Moore decisively deconstructed the 'war' scenario in his 'non-violent' *Post-Darwinian Controversies* (1979). It was a book born of the anti-Vietnam War years, as he says himself. And he has gone on to give a more gutsy political *re*construction. Through the 1980s, while I was looking at the medical radicals for *Politics of Evolution* – the antagonistic under-class – Moore was re-evaluating the intellectuals' crisis of faith. He saw it as a result of the elite's attempt to rationalize the industrial dislocations while retaining their grip on power. The Victorians created and resolved their crisis by naturalizing religious beliefs, putting God's power into Nature and making Scientists the new priests. Moore too saw it as a case of new physical gospels for a new social order.[56] We arrived at the same spot, which is why we could sit down to collaborate on *Darwin*.

But what stimulated this 'War' propaganda? Why did students dub Huxley the 'General'? Why did he see himself as a shilling sergeant, enlisting men 'into the army of science'? We need to get back beyond the 1870s. Too much talk of the 'military metaphor' has been about a bloodless paper war. Not only must we penetrate the radical Dissenting campaign headquarters, but we need to look at real warfare. For the slippage between a metaphoric and literal militarism was surprising; indeed there was a common basis. While Huxley called evolution his Whitworth gun, he aligned himself with the gunsmiths. South Kensington had its military underbelly.

We must go back further still, to Huxley the young war reporter on the *Westminster Review*. Already we see the metaphor acquiring its military edge as he identified with Sultan Schamyl's guerrilla resistance to the Cossacks. This was more than reportage in 1854, in the patriotic prelude to the Crimean War. Huxley *lived* the Islamic *jihad*, contrasting Islam's 'youthful vigour' with the 'degraded idolatry' of the Russian Orthodox Church. He sided with the ascetic Sufi, who damned Orthodoxy's 'besotted priests' with their 'gew-gaw saints'. His report was a displaced attack on a corrupt theology at home. He had Schamyl standing 'beside our own Cromwell' as a liberator. Huxley was already deep in his own holy war. The 'prophet-warrior' taught that to resist oppression was a religious duty, and Huxley sought to bind his 'scientific Young England' as the Sultan was uniting his Muslim nation, by meeting an orthodox 'threat'.[57]

Huxley the teacher was surrounded by Crimea veterans. Troops fresh from the front were seconded as free labour to the Kensington site. The Royal Engineers turned the 'sword into the reap-hook' and gave the Department of Science and Art its military mind. The DSA had Major-General Donnelly as chief of staff, and six similar ranking officers among its inspectors by the 1880s. With War Office personnel, and soldiers patrolling the exam halls, the regimental colours waved over South Kensington. Huxley was a War Department examiner himself. He lectured at the Royal Engineer Institute in Chatham (making the Forces the naturalist's eyes abroad) and was 'all for an R.E.' to drill the students.[58] The uniform suited his purpose. In an age when the Salvation Army cadres were setting up their own recruiting tents, Science acquired real military authority and an air of national purpose.

The Whitworth gun was a product of Dissenting industry, and its designer backed the Kensington corps. Sir Joseph Whitworth put £100,000 into the DSA's science scholarships and joined the steel magnate Sir William Armstrong to fill Huxley's purse. This was armaments money. While the gun-toting Volunteer put Darwin's Whitworth into the liberal armoury, his sponsors were producing weapons to police an empire. Whitworth and Armstrong supported Huxley's technical education, and in return got science teachers for their factory towns. The Huxleys would enjoy a wing in Whitworth's Matlock mansion. Working trips to Newcastle, to pore over Permian reptiles, gave way to annual holidays at Armstrong's Gothic manor. The *paterfamilias* toured the plants, looking at the experimental breech-loaders and iron-clad cruisers. The families became close – Lady Armstrong was Ethel's godmother – while the misses donned mob caps to go dancing with Captain Noble's daughter.

The metaphor of the *Origin* as a 'Whitworth gun in the armoury of liberalism' – the Darwinian muzzle-loader to keep Britain Great – had complex social roots in an age of gun-toting Volunteers. Huxley was updating Dissent's intellectual weaponry. He was allying the *Origin* to patriotism and secular competitive progress – shouldering his .45 to shoot over the ranks of obstructive Anglicans. Society's 'crisis of faith' was a collision of creeds accompanying the professionalizing of society. Huxley's evolutionary oiling of the industrial rents both speeded the cultural transition and made the crisis so much worse for many. It goes to reinforce the image of Science's 'war' with the Church as an extension of industrial Dissent's struggle, born of an era, in Gilley and Loades' words, when the Churches themselves 'were at war'. It was 'part of a wider battle'.[59]

Dissent's demand for fair competition – meritocracy rather than Anglican monopoly – was fulfilled by the *Origin of Species* (1859). But then that too was a belated piece of Reform Age business, crafted in 1837–9 when the Dissenting struggle was at its height (and supported by Darwin's Whigs). Darwin's book was itself built on 'death, famine, rapine, and the concealed war of nature' (as he said in that turbulent year 1842). It gave a scientific sanction to competition; the best survived to carry the species forward, both among animals and humans. Darwin had been bathed in economic individualism; the *Origin* recast Nature in its light, and in 1872 he was expressing dismay that the unions opposed piece-work and competition, and that so many saw the 'Cooperative Societies . . . as the main hope for the future'. Given all this it was easy for Huxley to re-politicize the *Origin*'s competitive aspect a decade later to use against the socialists who had attacked his bus. New contexts required new conceptualizations of Darwin's opus, and the 'new debates', as Asa Briggs has called them, were 'about the nature not of the Universe but of society'. Huxley turned full circle and used Darwin's 'neutral' science to justify a property-owning capitalist economy. It was at this point, around 1890, as the Malthusian aspects of the *Origin of Species* were being used to quell the socialist masses, that the term 'Social Darwinism' was first coined.[60] The very words had anti-socialist connotations.

The international situation was by then becoming tense. The 'war' – initially between a competitive, evolutionary Science and a monopolistic Anglicanism – was extended yet again. Huxley now *nationalized* the Darwinian struggle. There were dangerous currents beneath the gay nineties. Paul Crook has dipped his toes into these darker waters in *Darwinism, War and History*: the arms race was on, military budgets were staggering and peace seemed increasingly dependent on 'sheer force'. This was the age of Krupp's Ruhr works; Germany had the best-equipped army in the world, and its militarists would come to see war as a civilized nation's 'highest expression of strength'. Europe's industrial growth supported the scramble for Africa (in the last 15 years of the century Germany and France added 4.5 million square miles of colonial territory). The flood of imports marked 'Made in Germany' left Britons with a foreboding. In 1887 Huxley called this competition among the great powers industrial 'warfare'. A 'war' footing demanded better technical education and the stabilizing of class relations within a capitalist economy. British universities would have to become 'the drill-grounds of the army of industry'.[61] A former Minister of War echoed Huxley's warning that 'famine, indigence, and starvation' would accompany economic defeat.

Crook's analysis of the 'peace' books of the period – which declared war to be economically unviable and genocidal – showed the fears as Anglo-German relations deteriorated after 1893. This was the backdrop to the final act in Huxley's 'war' drama. Or rather the final proof that there were practical ramifications of his Darwinian 'war' metaphor. For in 1894 he refused to sign a moratorium on the European arms race. Though an 'International Arbitration' agreement had the backing of trade unions and Churches, he declined to sign because industrial competition was natural and Darwinian – 'merely the superficial expression of social forces the operation of which can not be sensibly affected by agreements between governments'.[62]

His belief that governments could not moderate these large-scale Darwinian struggles forces us to re-evaluate his ethical position at the end. Clearly the post-Mady Huxley was restricting mankind's anti-Darwinian ethics (care rather than competition) to a very tight *personal* sphere. Not even governments could take a moral stand (that smacked of socialism). Michael Helfand called 'Evolution and Ethics' an essay on the 'limits of political activism', and he is right.[63] And there was a sad irony to it all. The romantic who was originally so suspicious of Darwin's bloody Malthusianism was trapped by it at the end. Hatred of socialism had him bowing to an inevitable Darwinian arms race 20 years before the Great War.

Huxley slid easily from one 'war' footing to another. Perhaps it is too glib to make the 'war' between Science and Theology a transformed case of the radical Dissenting campaign of the hungry thirties, with its demand for fair competition to free up a static Anglican society. Perhaps it is too ambitious to see the same political Dissent create the structure for Huxley's Darwinian and International 'war' images, to make them all of a piece. Yet surely some such larger picture will ultimately prove more satisfying than simply accepting Science's 'War' with Theology as an inevitable development of the rational mind.

SCIENCE ON THE STUMP

In England when people say 'science' they commonly mean an article by Professor Huxley in the *Nineteenth Century*.[64]

Canvassing votes for the profession – by selling the *Origin of Species* or condemning a benighted theology – meant reaching out. Almost all of Huxley's famous articles were campaign speeches, positively plebeian and crafted for accessibility. They were beguiling, having that 'telepathic effect which enables you at once to perceive his meaning'[65] – an apparent opaqueness suggesting that he was a neutral conduit for the social precepts of the 'new Nature'.

Historians have long accepted Huxley's claim that the 'work of the popular expositor' was simply the conversion 'of the hieratic language of the experts into the demotic vulgar tongue'.[66] Nothing more. It was to retail the latest discoveries, package them in paper of 'colourless brilliancy' which declared a transparent intent. Such diffusion required a sponge-like absorption by the audience. That is what he meant by oiling the bolus of evolution to stuff into the 'ecclesiastical swallow'.

But surely there was much more than a simple *diffusion*.[67] Neither

Huxley nor his audience was disinterested. He was refracting the light of science through an ideological lens. The Huxleys and Tyndalls were reaching out with evangelical fervour, outdoing the pamphleteering Methodist fanatics. This is how people knew them, on the stump: 'Science' was the latest harangue in the *Nineteenth Century*. Ray Lankester went so far as to call his hero only 'accidentally a zoologist'. Huxley's real work was as a publicist – a one-man lobbying machine.[68]

It helped that Huxley and Tyndall were among the few scientists who could actually turn a phrase. In an age when the ubiquitous W. T. Stead, editor of *Cassell's Magazine*, *Pall Mall Gazette* and *Review of Reviews*, refused to commission scientists because they talked gobbledegook, Huxley's scintillating prose was converting mundane matters into thrilling parable. He did not need an interpreter. A *Daily News* wag said that Huxley 'would have known how to make Herbert Spencer readable'.[69] It reinforced the belief that Science was coming undiluted from the fountainhead. The message was made more pleasurable by Huxley's Ciceronian irony and cautious claims dressed in outrageous garb. Not to mention his wit, the distanced intellectual word-play that punctuated his essays. Even ticklish events, like Hooker's son Brian falling into a salt vat, would have Huxley waxing:

> Abram, Abraham became
> By will divine:
> Let pickled Brian's name
> Be changed to Brine![70]

This fast wit weaving around Old Testament allusions greased a social edge; it made the prose frictionless. 'I always admire & envy you', Leslie Stephen wrote; 'no English writer, alive or dead, could ever put his points better'. His seemingly see-through style was designed to keep the spotlight on the dramatization of Nature in his 'proletarian theatre', where, as Paradis says, it was reworked in the way of an old morality play. He saw himself merely encapsulating 'great emotions & great thoughts in such form that they touch the heart'.[71]

For him popular lectures were never hors-d'œuvres but meals in their own right. Even the act of reaching out was seen to be virtuous: the *Illustrated London News* praised him for not joining those who 'keep their name as scientific hierophants unsullied'. The fine-honed prose made his worldwide reputation. But if he was the man 'who brought down science from the skies',[72] he distributed his manna in revealing ways. From the young Volunteer's patriotic panegyric on Science as his profession formed,

> Cherish her, venerate her, [or] . . . the day will come when
> our children will see the glory of England vanishing like
> Arthur in the mist[73]

to the pensioner's use of Social Darwinism to debunk

> that Liberty Equality & Fraternity to which many look as
> to a new Heaven & new Earth[74]

the last thing he was selling was disinterested science. His science was instrumental, it had a political payoff that changed with the context. He was cajoling, social grooming, promising greatness, pacifying or damning. The world's greatest scientific synthesizer was easing the social dislocations of industrial society. His common-sense cleverness was committed to the creation of a new moral society, a New Reformation.

HUXLEY AND HIS WORKERS

'Did they get "the message"?'

Roger Cooter and Stephen Pumfrey challenging the traditional 'diffusionist' model of popular science.[75] How did Huxley's workers take his parables?

If one element missing from studies of science and religion is radical Dissent, another is the political atheism of the workers. The factory hands are still ignored by historians of science. The absence is more glaring for the fact that they were Huxley's sounding board.

The curiosity is not that Victorians lectured the workers, but that the bearded men turned up in droves. It suggests that they weren't passive recipients, but that they *wanted* something. And their penny prints showed what it was. In a growing democracy they saw them-selves preparing for power. The labour elite knew that 'political free-dom and general ignorance are incompatible' and that to redirect industrial society they needed to be masters of politics and science.[76] Flaming democrats growled that science was 'a matter of traffic and trade among the *savants* . . . who are interested in keeping up the usual common-place go in society'.[77] So the workers appropriated it, turning it into the scientific patois of the street prints. Early socialists harnessed social Lamarckism to justify co-operation and female emancipation. They made it an anti-Creationist force to overthrow 'Priestcraft' and 'Old Corruption'. Into the 1860s they exploited any materialistic science with socially-regenerative properties. Huxley's talk of the rising underworld of life suited perfectly.

Even in the 1840s the convicted agitator Richard Carlile was looking to 'bring the Spiritual World and all Religion within the boundaries of science'.[78] No wonder that his heirs saw Huxley 'confirming our own view of the universe'.[79] Both Huxley, gaining a constituency, and his workers, gaining a serviceable science, benefited by the transaction.[80]

Because (as Cooter and Pumfrey say) so little is known of what *audiences* got out of science lectures, I have broached Huxley's workers and their indigenous literature throughout. We can triangulate to determine their beliefs, knowing that Huxley's tickets were touted at secular societies, his books were shifted in the Socialist Halls of Science, his 'brigandlike' auditors were largely freethinkers, and his lectures were reported in the *Reasoner* and *National Reformer*.[81] In the 1860s he made evolution appeal to this radical interest. He enlisted its support in his territorial dispute with the clergy and put its strength behind his nascent profession. Opposed by the powerful Church and Anglican universities, he had to be able to speak in the name of the nation and its people. He talked the radicals' language, duplicated their cynicism (to the extent that he was accused of nihilism) and depicted a history of revolutionary scientific bursts. In turn they reshaped his progressive evolution on their co-operative march to the Millennium. It dignified humble origins and allowed them to project 'forward, with inexorable confidence to the achievements of the future'.[82] 'Darwinism' was continually reconfigured as it passed across these political boundaries. A self-propelling evolution was stirred into the old seditious literature of innately-powered atoms. The result was a science to liberate the sovereign 'social atoms' from spiritual tyranny and sanctify democratic equality.

It gave Huxley a ready-made street audience, unlike, say, Matthew Arnold or Leslie Stephen. His Darwinians captured this constituency so successfully through the 1870s that the workers' old pirated literature was pushed to the back shelves. Mechanics' Institutes traded up to Darwin's *Descent of Man*, Huxley's *Man's Place in Nature* and *Lay Sermons*, as well as Wallace, Haeckel and the International Scientific Series. John Laurent shows that Huxley's *Physiography* was possibly the most borrowed book in the northern institutes. Later Huxley even projected workers' lectures on the New Testament, portraying the Bible as the Magna Carta 'of the poor and the oppressed', to stir them to insurrection 'against the worst forms of clerical and political despotism'.[83]

One understands how he became a working-class hero, why cabbies refused his fare and delegations petitioned him as they once would have nobility – supplication that showed the tremendous power acquired by the scientist. In Manchester the old Chartist George Howell, soon to be a Trade Union MP, would be stopped by cheers mid-lecture when he mentioned Huxley's name. (More touching still, Howell's son died tragically asking his father to thank Huxley for the pleasure his talks had given him.) In the 1860s an uplifting evolution filled an almost religious need among the oppressed. Science became a devotion, and one chemist's dispenser, in awe of Huxley's books, willed his body to Huxley for dissection.[84]

There was no doubting Huxley's sincerity. His belief that Science would uplift the masses was genuine. He put it with his usual apocalyptic flair: if the conquest of Nature could not better mankind's condition, he intended to hail 'some kindly comet which would sweep the whole affair away as a desirable consummation'. 'When the poor have cried, Caesar hath wept', said an admirer.[85] The legend grew with his largesse. Like his kindness in 1894 to the pound-a-week coffee unloader in Southampton docks, George Sparks. The casual docker had sent him such promising observations of the fission of pond organisms (made with a sixpenny 'toy-glass') that Huxley pulled strings to locate the man (who had given no address). The two regional networks – Donnelly's School Inspectors and the Solent clergy – were co-opted, and the local St Luke's vicar reported back on finding Sparks, clearly captivated himself. Here was a self-educated haulier, with a knowledge of advanced biology that was 'something astounding'. He was, 'as one might expect, a socialist in politics', the vicar said, 'and in religion as one would also expect, a free-thinker ... But what does that matter! He is a truly sincere seeker after demonstrable Truth'. Having tracked down his docker, Huxley sent books and an achromatic compound microscope through the priest, marking them 'from a friend'. 'Ah', said the docker, 'I know who that must be; it can be no other than the greatest of living scientists'. Then came Huxley's own telescope to enable him to see the sun spots – and 'I', said Sparks, moved by it all, 'who carries nothing but negative recommendations, such as poverty and obscurity'.[86] The rapport was unfeigned, whatever the ideological cross-currents.

And yet those cross-currents were already evident during the dock strikes, as Huxley's *ad hoc* coalition with the workers peeled apart.

From the late 1880s he met the reinvigorated socialism by emphasizing the Malthusian competitive aspects of Darwinism. The old man was seeming to harden – but in truth it was working-class society changing, drifting to the Left and forcing a reaction. Letters began to complain that he was looking, not from 'the point of view of the "masses" [but] rather of the "classes"'.[87] He ended the scientific *alter ego* of Joseph Chamberlain, a 'benevolent Conservative', said the *Spectator*'s R. H. Hutton with satisfaction. But it was with a very small 'c', and of the most idiosyncratic sort. Like Chamberlain Huxley had been pushed into conservative Unionism by Home Rule, and to a defence of property by socialism. The old bull elephants of the X-Club found themselves in unfamiliar terrain, surrounded by Hooker's 'dirty Radicals'. The lab doors shut and the profession became unresponsive to the needs of women and workers. New flanking dissidents accused his Royal Society of elitism, of becoming a professors' forum. Huxley's response made him sound like his old Hero-worshipping self: he defended the high institutions inside science; while outside he wanted the municipal 'laboratories' of politics (as he called the town halls) to breed decisive leaders for the Commons, men 'who have clear heads, a strong sense of right, and the courage to stand alone with their backs to the wall'.[88] By the new democratic standards, his out-of-step Puritans had become old reactionary patriarchs. Science had lost its street credibility.

Huxley made 'Social Darwinism' the stern taskmaster to reconcile the workbench to capitalism. He still promised melioration through technical education, but even that was challenged. Can 'pauperism . . . be cured by technical education'? the socialist Walter Crane asked him. By 1890 the intellectual and political freedoms had eroded faith in a Divinely or even Darwinianly-instituted social order. Kropotkin, Henry George and the Fabians jostled on the institutes' shelves with tracts on 'Evolution and Socialism'.[89] The masses were on the move, pointing the way to a Labour twentieth century.

The class divide was glaringly obvious even in 1883, when the crude G. W. Foote was jailed for blasphemy while Lord Justice Coleridge declared Huxley's reverent agnosticism no offence. The cultured and now powerful professionals had switched their coalition partners, and high society threw its protective cloak around them. Science no longer needed its old bedraggled backers. The red line was redrawn as the aristocrats of intellect were permitted to question Christianity, while street scurrility commanded a year in prison.

The agnostics had became part of the new class hegemony. The second-generation Dissenters were entrenched at Oxbridge; the industrialists were living a baronial life on big profits (which, as Martin Wiener says in *English Culture and the Decline of the Industrial Spirit*, was the start of the rot – that developing 'culture of containment' which saw the bourgeoisie absorbed and gentrified and industrialism arrested by the patrician order).[90] The politicized workers had become a liability to Science. As natural history overtly resumed its old policing function, Darwin's influence declined on the street. There was even a residual bitterness at the greats around Huxley's grave. One radical stated starkly that, had Huxley

> put forward his Agnosticism . . . in some mere penny
> journal, had he, instead of occupying a Government
> Professorship, and writing in the leading (*i.e.* high-priced)
> reviews, addressed the democracy, not only would there
> have been no such funeral demonstration, but, on the
> contrary, he would have stood a remarkably good chance of
> interviewing some Justice North or other at the Old Bailey,
> and of enjoying subsequently a twelvemonth's hospitality
> at the expense of his country at Holloway or Pentonville.[91]

Huxley died in honour, not in Holloway jail, because he had so successfully consolidated science as a civil service profession. He had made it part of the State apparatus, and Roy MacLeod has shown the extent of its tentacles in Whitehall. In 1890 Huxley's 'Normal School' (the French name never took) had become the impressively titled Royal College of Science, its walls adorned with portraits of Huxley and Tyndall and the old professorate. Rising status was revealed in the Honours Lists. The men heading up the big institutions were dubbed, from that 'over-rated old Saint Flower', through Sr'enery at Manchester, and Sir Archibald Geikie at the Geological Survey, to Sir John Donnelly at South Ken.[92] Their prestige showed at that other social node of Victorian Science, the Athenaeum Club. By the nineties his scientists were no longer an indistinguishable part of the general culture, as they had been 60 years earlier. Now they acted as a bloc to elect representatives on the Club's committees.

As the specialists looked inwards, Huxley's romantic mantle was assumed by the novelists. It became the new science fiction. H. G. Wells' *Time Machine* explored the theme of human degeneration in a society stripped of competition. The dark side of the deranged automaton was exploited in Stevenson's *Dr Jekyll and Mr Hyde*. While the lost worlds motif was plumbed by Conan Doyle, whose

Sherlock Holmes became the apotheosis of Zadig's clinical detective, the scientist-sleuth as a 'fictional superman'.[93]

As the superman in Huxley becomes fictional, we begin to see the flawed greatness of this Schamyl binding his nation through science. He was an intellectual bruiser who 'warmed both hands at the fire of life'. That, ultimately, is what makes Thomas Henry Huxley so interesting. He was in the thick of the nineteenth century. He was crucial to that social transformation towards the modern world. Without comprehending his Darwinian campaigns or agnostic polemics, the *Times* wrote, it would be impossible 'to estimate the forces which have been at work to mould the intellectual, moral, and social life of the century'. He shaped our vision, closing one window onto future immortality as he opened another on our prehistoric past. There was no looking beyond for him. And yet, *Punch* said in the best epitaph, when he magically carried readers to exotic dinosaurian worlds, or conjured up pithecoid people,

> The great Agnostic, clear, brave, true,
> Taught more things may be, than he deemed he knew.[94]

Abbreviations

CORRESPONDENTS

AD	Anton Dohrn
BJ	Benjamin Jowett
CD	Charles Darwin
CK	Charles Kingsley
CL	Charles Lyell
CWT	Charles Wyville Thomson
ERL	Edwin Ray Lankester
ES	Eliza Salt, later Scott (sister)
FD	Frederick Dyster
GJR	George John Romanes
GR	George Rolleston
HAH	Henrietta Anne Huxley, née Heathorn
HS	Herbert Spencer
JD	John Donnelly
JH	Joseph Dalton Hooker
JK	James Knowles
JM	John Morley
JT	John Tyndall
MF	Michael Foster
NL	Norman Lockyer
RIM	Roderick Impey Murchison
WBC	William Benjamin Carpenter
WHF	William Henry Flower

Abbreviations

MANUSCRIPT SOURCES

AD	Huxley family letters being transcribed by Angela Darwin
APS	American Philosophical Society
BL	British Library
BM(NH)	British Museum (Natural History)
CCH	Charing Cross Hospital Medical School, Minutes of School Committee of Management
CUL	Cambridge University Library
GSM	British Geological Survey, records of the Government School of Mines
HH	T.H.Huxley - Henrietta Heathorn Correspondence, Imperial College, Huxley Archives (catalogued in Pingree, *T.H.Huxley: Correspondence with Henrietta Heathorn*)
HM	T.H.Huxley Manuscripts, Imperial College, Huxley Archives (catalogued in Pingree, *T.H.Huxley: List of his Scientific Notebooks*) HM series:volume:folio
HP	T.H.Huxley Papers, Imperial College, Huxley Archives (catalogued in Dawson, *Huxley Papers*)
LS	Linnean Society of London
OUM	Oxford University Museum
RCS	The Royal College of Surgeons of England
UCL	University College London
ZSL	Zoological Society of London

PRINTED SOURCES

CCD	F. Burkhardt and S. Smith, eds, *The Correspondence of Charles Darwin* 9 vols (Cambridge University Press, 1985–1994).
CE	T.H.Huxley, *Collected Essays* 9 vols (Macmillan, 1893).
Diary	J.Huxley, ed., *T. H. Huxley's Diary of the Voyage of H. M. S. Rattlesnake* (Chatto & Windus, 1935).
LCK	F.Kingsley, ed., *Charles Kingsley: His Letters and Memories of his Life* 2 vols (Kegan Paul, 1881).
LGR	E. Romanes, ed., *The Life and Letters of George John Romanes* (Longmans, Green, 1896).
LHS	D.Duncan, ed., *The Life and Letters of Herbert Spencer* (Methuen, 1908).
LJH	L.Huxley, ed., *Life and Letters of Joseph Dalton Hooker* 2 vols (Murray, 1918).
LJT	A.S.Eve and C.H.Creasey, eds, *Life and Work of John Tyndall* (Macmillan, 1945).
LLD	F.Darwin, ed., *Life and Letters of Charles Darwin* 3 vols (Murray, 1887).

Abbreviations

LLL   K.Lyell, ed., *Life, Letters and Journals of Sir Charles Lyell* 2 vols (Murray, 1881).

LRO   R.S.Owen, ed., *The Life of Richard Owen* 2 vols (Murray, 1894).

LTH   L.Huxley, ed., *Life and Letters of Thomas Henry Huxley* 2 vols (Macmillan, 1900).

MLD   F.Darwin and A.C.Seward, eds, *More Letters of Charles Darwin* 2 vols (Murray, 1903).

Narrative   J.MacGillivray, *Narrative of the Voyage of H. M. S. Rattlesnake, Commanded by the late Captain Owen Stanley, R.N., F.R.S., &c. during the years 1846–1850 including discoveries and surveys in New Guinea, the Louisiade Archipelago, Etc* 2 vols (T. & W. Boone, 1852).

SM   M.Foster and E.R.Lankester, eds, *The Scientific Memoirs of Thomas Henry Huxley* 5 vols (Macmillan, 1898–1902).

Notes

Part One:
The Devil's Disciple

THE APOSTLE PAUL OF THE NEW TEACHING

1. H.F.Jones, *Butler*, 1:385; CCD, 8:316.
2. Owen, 'Affinities', 4–8.
3. TH to JH, 19 Dec. 1860, HP 2.79; Hutton, 'Pope Huxley', 135–6; Haight, *Eliot Letters*, 8:89–90.
4. Fiske, *Personal Letters*, 121–2.
5. Understanding scientific ideas in their original production site is now a prime concern of historians: Ophir and Shapin, 'Place of Knowledge'; Desmond, 'Author's Response'.
6. Webb, *My Apprenticeship*, 25.
7. CE, 2:52.
8. As David Knight spotted: 'Huxley', 34.
9. Roos, 'Neglected', has made a start. By contrast the mature Huxley has proved perennially interesting, for his theological 'warfare' (Gilley and Loades, 'Huxley'; Barton, 'Evolution'), his humanistic milieu (Paradis, *Huxley*), his educational endeavours (Bibby, *Huxley*), his rhetoric (Jensen, *Huxley*) and his science (di Gregorio, *Huxley*).
10. Bourdieu, *Outline*, 177ff; Turner, *Contesting*, 39–40.
11. Roderick and Stephens, *Scientific*, 29–31.
12. MacLeod, *Public Science*; E.Richards, 'Huxley', on the anti-feminist ethos among the Darwinians.
13. Lightman, *Origins*, 117–21, 146.
14. Van Riper, *Men among the Mammoths*.
15. Harris, *Private Lives*, 19.
16. Pedersen, 'Rathbone'.
17. Desmond, 'Darwin, Huxley'.
18. Clodd, 'Huxley'; *Times*, 1 July 1895.

1 PHILOSOPHY CAN BAKE NO BREAD

1. Huxley, 'Thoughts & Doings', HM 3:123, f.10. This notebook has been transcribed with an excellent commentary by Roos, 'Neglected', 416. *LTH*, 1:15–16; sensitive: TH to HAH, [?27 Mar. 1850], HH 79–80.
2. CE, 1:2–5; 'tone': TH to HAH, 7 Sept. 1851, HH 163; 'passion', 'active':

648

4–7 May 1851, HH 147; *LTH*, 1:1–4; 'Cockney': ES to HAH, 16 Mar. 1883, AD; Bibby, *Huxley*, 1–4; Ker and Gornall, *Letters*, 5:267; Murphy, 'Ethical Revolt', 802.

3. TH to HAH, 18 Aug. 1851, HH 162; 'sage': 31 July 1851, HH 160; 'can't': 14 Mar. 1851, HH 140; 'one': 23 Nov. 1848, HH 40; 24 Dec. 1850, HH 134; 16 Oct. 1851, HH 169; Paradis, *Huxley*, 19.

4. TH to ES, 27 Mar. 1858, HP 31.27; 'of the': TH to ES, 8 June 1876, HP 31.44; Bibby, *Huxley*, 4–5; *LTH*, 1:35; Davidoff and Hall, *Family Fortunes*, 281; Angela Darwin, pers. comm.

5. *CE*, 1:5–6; on Poideoin: TH to George Huxley, 24 Apr. 1848, HP 31.47; curriculum: Ker and Gornall, *Letters*, 1:4, 6–9, 31; *LTH*, 1:5, 8–10; 2:145.

6. Ker and Gornall, *Letters*, 5:267.

7. Prest, *Industrial Revolution*, 73 passim; Davis, *Every Man*, 3–4; *Diary*, 333; Gaskell, *Mary Barton*, 5; Eliot, *Middlemarch*, 122; 'large': ES to HAH, 16 Mar. 1883, AD.

8. TH to HAH, 23 Nov. 1848, HH 40–1; *LTH*, 1:6, 35; 2:145; opium: Gaskell, *Mary Barton*, 22, 53; Paradis, *Huxley*, 19–20.

9. K. Jaggard to TH, 11 May 1852, HP 19.13: *LTH*, 1:8–9; Bibby, *Huxley*, 6–7; Huxley, 'Tyndall', 3; 'pursuits': TH to HAH, 23 Nov. 1848, HH 40; Turner, 'Victorian Scientific Naturalism', 330, 340–1; Carlyle, *Heroes*; Prest, *Industrial Revolution*, 1, 71.

10. Huxley, 'Thoughts & Doings', HM 3:123, ff.6–7; *LTH*, 1:6; Gallenga, 'Age', 4; Thackray, 'Natural Knowledge', 678–87; *LTH*, 1:35; Haight, *Eliot*, 19–24, 36–9; 'was': TH to HAH, 23 Nov. 1848, HH 40.

11. Huxley, 'Thoughts & Doings', HM 3:123, f.2; Prest, *Industrial Revolution*, 20, 48–9; Rolt, *Victorian Engineering*, 68; *LTH*, 1:7; *CE*, 1:6–7.

12. Huxley, 'Thoughts & Doings', HM 3:123, f.2; *LTH*, 1:36; Tugwood, *Coventry Hospital*, 1–12; Prest, *Industrial Revolution*, 28–9.

13. Robertson, 'Elliotson', 205, 257; Elliotson, *Lectures*; sacking: *Lancet*, 1 (1838–9), 561–2, 590–7; on Cooke: Allen, 'Huxley's Brother-in-Law'; *London Medical Directory*. 1845, 36; *LTH*, 1:15.

14. K. Jaggard to TH, 11 May 1852, HP 19.13: *LTH*, 1:8; *CE*, 1:7–8; Richardson, *Death*, 30ff; cf. Audubon's reaction, *Audubon*, 1:146; farms and other times: Gaskell, *Mary Barton*, 3; F. Smith, 'Darwin's Ill Health', 455.

15. Huxley, 'Thoughts & Doings', HM 3:123, f.4–5; T. S. Smith, *Divine*, viii; 'commit': Epps, *Church*, 3; Halevy, *Triumph*, 150; Cowherd, *Politics*, 155.

16. 'Seat of the Soul', *Medico-Chirurgical Review*, 12 (1830), 461; Desmond, *Politics*, chap. 4; Huxley, 'Thoughts & Doings', HM 3:123, ff.7–8, 10.

17. *CE*, 9:217; Poynter, 'Smith', 389; Briggs, *Victorian Cities*, 311–15; Engels, *Condition*, 73–4; Norton, *Victorian London*, 17–18, 35–6; Raumer, *England*, 2:111.

18. I assume it was Cooke's doing. Both Cooke and Chandler had worked with John Elliotson, Cooke as co-editor of Elliotson's *Lectures* in 1839, and Chandler, House Surgeon at University College Hospital in 1834–5, as a mesmerist: Chandler, 'Cases of Mesmerism', 189; *London Medical Directory*. *1845*, 31.

19. Chandler, 'Rheumatism', 81–3. He used mesmerism to cure epilepsy, tics, fits and insanity: *Zoist*, 1 (1843), 174; 2 (1844), 373; 3 (1845), 189, 486.

20. Mayhew, *London Labour*, 104; Winter, 'Island', 19–24; Parssinen, 'Professional Deviants', 113–14.

21. TH to Rachel Huxley, 23 Apr. 1841, AD.
22. Mayhew, *London Labour*, 48, 51, 174; *LTH*, 1:15–16; Tristan, *London Journal*, 7.
23. Chesney, *Victorian Underworld*, 105, 378; 'in that': Huxley, 'Thoughts & Doings', HM 3:123, f.9; Roos, 'Neglected', 416; *LTH*, 1:15; Carlyle, *Essays*, 6:110.
24. T. S. Smith, *Divine*, 104; 'I see': Huxley, 'Thoughts & Doings', HM 3:123, f.10; 'deep': TH to HAH, 28 Aug. 1852, HH 222; 'I confess': TH to CK, 23 Sept. 1860, HP 19.176; *LTH*, 1:220; Chesney, *Victorian Underworld*, 105, 378. By 15 Huxley had only a residue of Calvinistic 'moderate' evangelicalism left in him (in Hilton's sense, *Age*, 8–11) but growing rationalist and romantic streaks.
25. Huxley, 'Thoughts & Doings', HM 3:123, ff.9–13, 30; Weiner, *War*, 171; Vincent, *Bread*, 114ff; Desmond, *Politics*, 120; Sheets-Pyenson, 'Popular Scientific Periodicals', 550; 'I got': TH to Rachel Huxley, 23 Apr. 1841: AD.
26. *Diary*, 94, 97; *LTH*, 1:17, 19, 36; James Huxley to John Salt, Aug. 1842, HP 31.55–7.
27. Cooke was here by 15 December 1840, when two fellow teachers at Sydenham College, Sigmond and Heming, put him up for the Linnean Society: Certificate of Fellowship, LS. Sydenham College was in Grafton Street, off Gower Street. Cope, 'Private Medical Schools', 106. Cooke taught anatomy and physiology here in 1840–1: 'Sydenham College', *Lancet*, 1 (1840–1), 14. 'loudly': Thackeray, *Pendennis*, 330.
28. 'Sydenham College', *Lancet*, 1 (1841–2), 15, 61. It enrolled about 175 pupils: *Lancet*, 2 (1838–9), 176; 'dingy', *Lancet*, 1 (1842–3), 29.
29. 'Metaphysics', *Punch*, 2 (1842), 149; Dickens, *Pickwick*, 493.
30. McMenemey, 'Education', 145; Desmond, *Politics*, chap. 4.
31. 'Poverty and Religious Bigotry of the College of Physicians', *Lancet*, 1 (1840–1), 556–8; 'Sydenham College – Experiments on the Nervous System in the Turtle', *Lancet*, 1 (1837–8), 166–7; Manual, 'Hall', 139–51; Desmond, *Politics*, 124–34; Hall, *Memoirs*, 4, 60, 87–8, chaps 4–5, 145, 150, 157–9.
32. TH to HAH, [?27 Mar. 1850], HH 79–80; 'isolated': 16 Oct. 1851, HH 169; *Lancet*, 1 (1842–3), 29, 100–2; *Medico-Chirurgical Review*, 17 (1832), 574.
33. Huxley, 'Thoughts & Doings', HM 3:123, ff.14–16.

2 SON OF THE SCALPEL

1. TH to HAH, [?27 Mar. 1850], HH 79–80.
2. *Diary*, 94; *LTH*, 1:17; prize-giving was usually in April, e.g. 'Sydenham College', *Lancet*, 2 (1838–9), 176.
3. 'Sydenham College', *Lancet*, 1 (1841–2), 15; *LTH*, 1:17, 19 n. Cooke joined the Council of the Botanical Society in 1844. He taught materia medica at University College Hospital and elsewhere: *London Medical Directory*. *1845*, 36; Allen, 'Huxley's Brother-in-Law', 191–3; David Allen pers. comm. Cooke–Hoblyn partnership: Rachel Huxley to TH, 15 Mar. 1847, 13 Sept. 1848, AD.
4. *Diary*, 95; Harte and North, *World of UCL*, 37; Goodway, *London Chartism*, 49–51. Omnibuses: Mayhew, *London Labour*, 347.
5. *Diary*, 95; Jackson, *Scharf's London*, 96–101. On the Apothecaries:

Holloway, 'Medical Education', 307–17; Waddington, *Medical Profession*, chap. 3. Carlyle: Huxley, 'Thoughts & Doings', HM 3:123, ff.17–18.

6. Huxley, 'Thoughts & Doings', HM 3:123, f.22; *LTH*, 1:19n; *Diary*, 95.

7. *Diary*, 95–6; *LTH*, 1:34.

8. Huxley's Sydenham College teacher, George Sigmond, had been physician at Charing Cross Hospital (before being sacked for financial irregularities): Sigmond was Cooke's friend and proposer for the Linnean Society, 15 Dec. 1840, LS Archives; Minney, *Two Pillars*, 66–7. Golding, *Origin*, 64–5 on the scholarships. *Lancet*, 1 (1842–3), 24, on the fees.

9. Charing Cross Hospital Regulations for Applications for Free Scholarship, 1842, HP 31.97; Golding, *Origin*, 64. 'The Pharmaceutical Society', *London Medical Gazette*, 28 (1840–1), 726–30, on the druggists; Desmond, *Politics*, 154, 196, on the move to drive out the working classes.

10. Jenkins, *General Strike*, 95–104, 165–71, 270–2; *Illustrated London News*, 20 Aug. 1842; Goodway, *London Chartism*, 51, 106–11.

11. James Huxley to John Salt, 11, 22 Aug. 1842, HP 31.55, 57; *Times*, 17, 18 Aug. 1842; Holyoake, *History*; Moore, *Religion*, 340–50; Desmond, 'Artisan Resistance', 85ff.

12. CCH, Vol. 1, f.330; *LTH*, 1:19–20; *Diary*, 97; TH to W. Burnett, 31 Jan. 1846, HP 11.194.

13. On the hospital: Golding, *Origin*, 41; Minney, *Two Pillars*, 46–77.

14. Minney, *Two Pillars*, 51–3, 56–7; Hart, *Roots*, 18; Golding, *Origin*, 60; Hunter, *Historical Account*, 194.

15. Minney, *Two Pillars*, 24–6; Jackson, *Scharf's London*, 74–5; Hilton, *Age*, 206–7, 270; Stigginses: *Diary*, 224; Dickens, *Pickwick*, 449, 452, 729.

16. Hart, *Roots*, 14; Jackson, *Scharf's London*, 28–9, 58; Minney, *Two Pillars*, 23–4.

17. *Lancet*, 1 (1842–3), 28. Debts to Cooke and George: HP 31.5–6.

18. Casualties: Golding, *Origin*, 75, 175; *Lancet*, 2 (1846), 138. Dickens, *Sketches by Boz*, 286–7; Minney, *Two Pillars*, 61; Jackson, *Scharf's London*, 72; 'miserable': 'Advice to Students', *Lancet*, 1 (1837–8), 20.

19. Minney, *Two Pillars*, 30, 53, 91; Hart, *Roots*, 9, 17–22, 25–6.

20. Richardson, *Death*, 265. The Strand's workhouses supplied more corpses for dissection than almost any other London parish: Durey, 'Bodysnatchers', 218.

21. This was a common reaction: Audubon, *Audubon*, 1:146. In 1843 the School's President W. D. Chowne warned of the unpleasantness of dissection: *Lancet*, 1 (1843–4), 17.

22. 'Advice to Students', *Lancet*, 1 (1837–8), 18–22; also 2 (1844), 20.

23. *Diary*, 97.

24. Huxley, 'Thoughts & Doings', f.51, HM 3:123; Jessie Rachel Salt, Death Certificate, 17 Nov. 1842: General Register Office, London.

25. Huxley in 'Thomas Wharton Jones', *British Medical Journal*, 2 (1891), 1176; Godlee, 'Wharton Jones', 97–105; Lonsdale, *Life*, 97. Lecture times: *Lancet*, 1 (1842–3), 24. Mob poetry: 'Dr. Knox', *Medical Times*, 10 (1844), 245–6.

26. Huxley in 'Thomas Wharton Jones', *British Medical Journal*, 2 (1891), 1176; *CE*, 1:9; Godlee, 'Wharton Jones', 99. On Wharton Jones' appointment in May 1841: CCH, Vol. 1, f.306. Huxley's student notebook, c. 1845, HM 3:124 (misdated '1847' in Pingree, *Huxley. Scientific Notebooks*, 62),

shows him studying shark's teeth (ff.22–3, using Richard Owen's *Odontography* as a guide), feather ontogeny (ff.24–7, after Theodor Schwann and Frédéric Cuvier), and the perch (ff.46–79, following Georges Cuvier and Achille Valenciennes).

27. Jones, 'Development', 261; Huxley's student notebook, c. 1845, HM 3:124, ff.11–15 for Henle, Rudolph Wagner, etc. on blood corpuscles; ff.34–6 for Theodor Bischoff on the ovum; f.83 for Albert Kölliker on nucleoli. These German anatomists based their work on Schwann's cell theory and accepted a mechanistic explanation of cell growth. On the increasingly mechanistic outlook in Germany during the 1840s see Lenoir, *Strategy*, chaps 3 and 4; and Jacyna, 'Romantic Programme', for the cell theory's reception in Britain.

28. McMenemey, 'Education', 138–9, 145; Chesney, *Victorian Underworld*, 7, 398; Minney, *Two Pillars*, 59, 89–90; *LTH*, 1:21.

29. TH to HAH, 2 Dec. 1850, HH 132; *Lancet*, 2 (1844), 19; 'Charing-Cross Hospital School', *Lancet*, 1 (1842–3), 24 on his classes.

30. TH to HAH, 8 Feb. 1848, HH 7; *CE*, 1:8–9.

31. Fownes' former teacher, Justus von Liebig, was now breaking protein into amino acids. Huxley was reading Liebig's journal, *Annalen der Chemie und Pharmacie*, while breaking up albumen himself: Huxley's student notebook, c. 1845, HM 3:124, ff.3–9. President: *Lancet*, 1 (1843–4), 18. Fownes was at the school from 1840–3: CCH, Vol. 1, ff.284, 347. On his 9 am. lectures: *Lancet*, 1 (1842–3), 24.

32. Huxley's student notebook, c. 1845, HM 3:124, f.1. Huxley quoted more from Henle's *Allgemeine Anatomie* (*General Anatomy*) (1841); but the tenor of Henle's piece, as Nordenskiöld, *History*, 398, shows, was mildly antivitalist. Rowe, 'Life', 423–4, 432; Godlee, 'Wharton Jones', 102; Lonsdale, *Life*, 402; Knox, 'Contributions', 501, 529. For the radical satires on 'design': Desmond, *Politics*, 56, 73, 110–17, 181–2. Fownes took the first Acton Prize in 1844; Wharton Jones the second in 1851.

33. Huxley, 'Thoughts & Doings', HM 3:123, f.18.

34. *LTH*, 1:23; CCH, Vol. 1, ff. 331–2, 336–7, 341; Hunter, *Historical Account*, 195. The exams were held on Monday 17 Apr. 1843.

35. Knight, *London*, 3:200–3; Carus, *King*, 60; Desmond, *Politics*, 251–3; Richard Owen's testimony: *Report from the Select Committee on British Museum* (Parliamentary Papers, 14 July 1836), 10: 44–6; *LTH*, 1:15–16; Richardson, *Death*, 57–8 on O'Brien.

36. *CE*, 1:7; Jones, 'Muscle', 77 (this was his introductory lecture on 3 Oct. 1843); Huxley's student notebook, c.1845, HM 3:124, ff.37–43.

37. Huxley, 'Thoughts & Doings', HM 3:123, f.4; 'Law': Carpenter, *Animal Physiology*, 2:viii; Grainger, *Observations*, 47–8; Fletcher, *Rudiments*, 1:78; *CE*, 1:7. Recent research has shown how powerful philosophical anatomy was in London around 1840: Jacyna, 'Principles'; Desmond, *Politics*.

38. Monk, *Journals*, 113, 138; *LRO*, 1:197; 'brains': W. Broderip to W. Buckland, 27 Dec. 1844, BL Add. MS 40,556, f.314. The young Owen is discussed in Sloan, *Owen*, 3–72; Rupke, *Owen*, chaps 1, 4; Desmond, *Politics*, chaps 6–8. Hugh Torrens, 'When did the Dinosaur', suggests that Owen did not introduce his 'dinosaurs' until 1842.

39. Fayrer, *Recollections*, 22; Jackson, *Scharf's London*, 86–8; Dickens, *Sketches*, 60–2.

40. 'The Medical Student', *Punch*, 2 (1842), 71; Minney, *Two Pillars*, 27. J. Browne, 'Squibs', 166 for a wonderful study of this 'counter-culture of caricature'.

41. *LTH*, 1:15–16; Minney, *Two Pillars*, 26–7; Mayhew, *London Labour*, 284; Chesney, *Victorian Underworld*, 3–5; Richardson, *Death*, 278; G. M. Young, *Portrait*, 17, 20–1.

42. *Lancet*, 1 (1830–1), 4; *Medical Gazette*, 29 (1841–2), 117–20; Desmond, *Politics*, chaps 3–6, 9.

43. CCH, Vol. 1, f.333, 334; Hart, *Roots*, 12.

44. Elliotson, 'More', 490; Chandler, 'Extraordinary Effects', 3; Winter, 'Ethereal Epidemic', 1, 6–11. Chandler was now experimenting with phreno-mesmerism. With his patients in a trance, he would touch the 'bumps' on the skull to have them sing, fume, dance or whatever (touching the Veneration bump produced clasped hands): Chandler, 'Cures', 376; Cooter, *Cultural Meaning*, 150. Operating theatre: Harte, *University*, 38.

45. CCH, Vol. 1, ff. 341, 350; *LTH*, 1:36.

46. Fayrer, *Recollections*, 10; Tristan, *London Journal*, 7; Dickens, *Bleak House*, 49.

47. Altick, *Shows*, 377–80; Jackson, *Scharf's London*, 95.

48. TH to HAH, n.d. [?27 Mar. 1850], HH 79–80; Jackson, *Scharf's London*, 86; Fayrer, *Recollections*, 21–2. Fayrer's prizes: CCH, Vol. 1, f.357; *Lancet*, 1 (1845), 545.

49. TH to HAH, 16 Nov. 1850, 2 Jan. 1851, HH 129, 134; Bibby, *Huxley*, 4.

50. TH to HAH, 14, 23 Mar. 1851, HH 140, 141.

51. Rachel Huxley to TH, 23 Aug. 1849, AD.

52. Huxley's student notebook, c. 1845, HM 3:124, following George Newport on the myriapods and scorpions (ff.89, 135), Meckel on snails (f.106), W. B. Carpenter on shell structure (f.111), Edward Forbes on echinoderms (f.129). His readings on 'Alternation of Generations' (to be taken up so controversially later), especially Steenstrup's book, are on 118ff (cf. Winsor, *Starfish*, 61).

53. He was attacking Martin Barry, himself a leading importer of German embryology: Huxley in 'Thomas Wharton Jones', *British Medical Journal*, 2 (1891), 1176; Jones, 'Development', 258–9; Godlee, 'Wharton Jones', 98, 105; 'Mr. T. W. Jones's Manual', *Medical Gazette*, 39 (1847), 1046.

54. Huxley, 'Hitherto Undescribed Structure', 1341. The original MS, with his draft letter to the *Gazette*, is in HM 3:122 ff.1–6. For the research behind it see his student notebook, c. 1845, HM 3:124, ff.16–17. 'Thomas Wharton Jones', *British Medical Journal*, 2 (1891), 1176; *CE*, 1:9.

55. Sharpey's testimonial, HP 19.85; TH to W. Burnett, 31 Jan. 1846, HP 11.194; *LTH*, 1:23; *CE*, 1:9; Harte, *University*, 92, 101.

56. Candidates had to be 21: *Regulations of the Council Respecting the Professional Education of Candidates for the Diploma of Members* (15 Aug. 1843), i, RCS Library; *LTH*, 1:20; *CE*, 1:9; TH to W. Burnett, 31 Jan. 1846, HP 11.194. On his bills: HP 35.1.

57. James Huxley to TH, 30 July 1848, AD.

3   THE SURGEON'S MATE

1. CE, 1:9–10; Desmond and Moore, *Darwin*, 313, 326; Fayrer, *Recollections*, 23.

2. 'Assistant-Surgeons in the Navy', *Lancet*, 1 (1847), 685; also 1 (1840–1), 869; 1 (1841–2), 630; 2 (1840–1), 639, 933. 'Surgeon's Mate' was by the 1840s a colloquialism for assistant surgeon, who was in effect the junior surgeon aboard. Compare Huxley's 7s 6d a day (£138 per annum: HP 31) with a seaman's 26s a month: Rasor, *Reform*, 104.

3. TH to W. Burnett, 31 Jan. 1846, HP 11.194 (misdated in Dawson, *Huxley Papers*); Fayrer, *Recollections*, 24–5; CE, 1:10.

4. W. Sharpey's testimonial, 7 Feb. 1846; Wharton Jones's, 9 Feb. 1846, both HP 19.85. TH to W. Burnett, 31 Jan. 1846, HP 11.194. On the Navy's requirements: 'Naval Medical Service, Regulations', *Lancet*, 2 (1846), 342. Candidates also had to be between 20 and 24 and unmarried.

5. CE, 1:10.

6. *Lancet*, 2 (1846), 342.

7. TH to ES, 20 Feb. 1846, AD; also ES to TH, 20 Oct. 1846, AD, on the family fights; Clark, *Huxleys*, 14–15.

8. TH to W. Burnett, 25 Feb. 1846, HP 11.193a; Court of Examiners Ledger, 6 Mar. 1846, f. 51, RCS Library; Ian Lyle, RCS Library, pers. comm.

9. TH to ES, 20 Feb. 1846, AD; Clark, *Huxleys*, 15; CE, 1:10; date of enrolment and pay: HP 31.5; landladies' bills: HP 31.9–12; debts and drafts, HP 31.6; Cooke's £16 debt was repaid during the voyage: HP 21.181.

10. Gillot's bill, 7 Apr. 1846, HP 31.13; *Diary*, 351. He mentions borrowing from an agent to buy the outfit in TH to HAH, 21 July 1851, HH 159; *LTH*, 1:118n. The agent was Goode & Lawrence: HP 21.181.

11. Rasor, *Reform*, 10–12; *Lancet*, 2 (1840–1), 482.

12. CE, 1:11–12. One of his messmates was his later physician Andrew Clark, at Haslar from 1846–1853. On Haslar Hospital: Coad, *Royal Dockyards*, 295–7.

13. TH to ES, 22 Apr. 1846, HP 31.15; CE, 1:11; *LTH*, 1:25. On the West African postings: 'Naval Assistant Surgeons', *Lancet*, 2 (1840–1), 639.

14. TH to ES, 22 Apr. 1846, HP 31.15; TH to ES (addressed to Miss Knight), 12 Mar., 3 May 1846, AD; ES to TH, postmarked 12 Apr. 1846, AD.

15. 'Naval Assistant-Surgeons', *Lancet*, 2 (1840–1), 875–8, 935.

16. *LTH*, 1:25; CE, 1:12; Lubbock, *Stanley*, 163, 170–1.

17. *LTH*, 1:25; Lubbock, *Stanley*, 2, 19–24, 28, 33, 39, 72–5, 90, 119, 144, 148–9, 152, 155, 169, 278; CE, 1:12.

18. Lubbock, *Stanley*, 163, 170–2; *LTH*, 1:25.

19. *LTH*, 1:25, 27. On Owen: *Diary*, 16; Rupke, 'Owen's Hunterian Lectures'; Desmond, *Politics*, chap. 8. Wilson and Geikie, *Memoir*, 61, 250–1, 274, 359; On Forbes: Mills, 'View'; Rehbock, 'Early Dredgers', and *Philosophical Naturalists*, chaps 4–5; Browne, *Secular Ark*, chap. 6.

20. 'Naval Assistant Surgeons', *Lancet*, 1 (1840–1), 869; 2 (1840–1), 283, 444–5, 525–7, 767, 875–8; 1 (1841–2), 628–30; 2 (1844), 302; 2 (1846), 280, 306; 1 (1847), 288, 293, 345, 680, 685. Some middies were the sons of sea captains, being shown the ropes, such as Philip King on Darwin's *Beagle*; others were

placed in the gunroom by the Captain's friends, such as Philip Sharpe in Huxley's mess.

21. HM Notebook R1, ff.3–5, 24–5 July, 27 Sept. 1846, on bee, slug and snail nerves; £13 15s microscope, HP 31.6; 1 July pay, £37 7s 7d, HP 31.5.
22. Huxley, 'Science at Sea', 100; *LTH*, 1:27; on his book buying, HP 31.6, which also lists his mess bills, which averaged about £5 a month.
23. Lubbock, *Stanley*, 169; Huxley, 'Science at Sea', 100, 108.
24. Kirby, 'Introductory Address', 2, 5; Desmond, 'Making', 168, 174–5, on imperial London zoology. *Narrative*, 1:2–9; Huxley, 'Science at Sea', 102–3.
25. Matthews, *Emigration Fields*, vi–9; *Narrative*, 1:3–6.
26. Wilson and Geikie, *Memoir*, 190–202, 399; Rehbock, 'Early Dredgers', 323–40; *Amphioxus*: *SM*, 1:4–5; *LTH*, 1:28.
27. Lubbock, *Stanley*, 179, 182; *LTH*, 1:26; on his 2 Oct. commission, HP 31.8; 'Am': TH to George Huxley, n.d. 'The Hulks', AD; Lloyd, *British Seaman*, 209; Hughes, *Fatal Shore*, 138.
28. *LTH*, 1:26, 491; see the illustration in *Diary*, 177.
29. *LTH*, 1:27; 'Naval Medical Intelligence', *Lancet*, 2 (1846), 306; Lubbock, *Stanley*, 180–81; on Sharpe: TH to HAH, 2 Dec. 1850, HH 132.
30. Lubbock, *Stanley*, 170, 179–80; *Narrative*, 1:16 reports that the *Rattlesnake* carried 15 government chronometers and 2 private ones, although Lubbock gives the total number as 28.
31. TH to Rachel Huxley, 24 Mar. 1847, AD; Allen, 'Huxley's Brother-in-Law', 192. Gray was apparently piqued because many of MacGillivray's specimens from the *Fly* expedition failed to reach home: Ralph, 'MacGillivray', 185–9; *LTH*, 1:26, 33; Lubbock, *Stanley*, 171, 180; Whittell, *Literature*, 110–11, 465; *Narrative*, 1:179.
32. *LTH*, 1:32; *Diary*, 305, 326, 364; Whittell, *Literature*, 110–11.
33. ES to TH, 20 Oct. 1846, AD; 'gut': James Huxley to TH, 20 Nov. 1846, AD; E. Forbes to TH, 11 Nov. 1846, HP 16.151; Lubbock, *Stanley*, 182–6; Fayrer, *Recollections*, 24–5.
34. Lubbock, *Stanley*, 174–6, 181–3. On the Kings: Nicholas and Nicholas, *Darwin*, 130–8.

4   MEN-OF-WAR

1. 'Degradation of Naval Surgeons', *Lancet*, 1 (1847), 680. Jim sent out reports of the *Lancet*'s fight for the assistant surgeon's 'right of space cabins & the wardroom': James Huxley to TH, 30 July 1848, 22 Apr. 1849, AD.
2. *Lancet*, 2 (1840–1), 876; Ralph, 'MacGillivray', 188–9.
3. *LTH*, 1:28; Lubbock, *Stanley*, 183–5; Coad, *Royal Dockyards*, 15 pl.7, 136–8.
4. *Diary*, 15–17; *SM*, 1:198.
5. Huxley, 'Science at Sea', 100; *Diary*, 362–3; *Narrative*, 1:10.
6. *Diary*, 18; Seaman, *Victorian England*, 233.
7. *Diary*, 19; *Narrative*, 1:13.
8. *Diary*, 17–18.
9. Darwin, *Journal*, 4; Barrett, *Collected Papers*, 1:199–203; *Diary*, 18, 22.
10. 'The Naval Medical Service', *Lancet*, 2 (1844), 302; *Diary*, 22–3, 141; arrow-worms: HM R1 Notebook, f.11; *LTH*, 1:32. One notebook from his Charing Cross days that he had aboard is in HM 3:124, see ff. 155–72.
11. *Narrative*, 1:14–15; *Diary*, 19, 23.

12. *Diary*, 24, 27, 363; Rasor, *Reform*, 16–22; *Narrative*, 1:16; Lubbock, *Stanley*, 187; *LTH*, 1:31–2.

13. HM R1 Notebook, ff.11–14; *Diary*, 26.

14. *Diary*, 27, 29–30; *Narrative*, 1:17–21; *LTH*, 1:31.

15. *LTH*, 1:32; *Diary*, 30; *Narrative*, 1:23; Lorimer, *Colour*, 101–3 on the comparison of blacks and the English agricultural poor.

16. TH to Rachel Huxley, 24 Mar. 1847, AD; ES to TH, 6 Dec. 1846, AD; Allen, 'Huxley's Brother-in-Law', 192. *Amphioxus:* HM R1 Notebook, f.16; *Diary*, 28–31; *Narrative*, 1:22–5, 329.

17. *Diary*, 28–31; *Narrative*, 1:24–7; Gould, 'Ingenious Paradox'.

18. TH to Rachel Huxley, 15 May 1847, AD; 'Salpae': HM R1 Notebook, f.17; *Diary*, 31–3.

19. *Diary*, 34–5; *Narrative*, 1:29–30; HM R1 Notebook, ff.35–45.

20. *Diary*, 32–6. MS, 'On the Anatomy and Physiology of *Physalia*', HP 34.1; abstract, *SM*, 1:361–2; HM R1 Notebook, ff.21–5, 31–2; Winsor, *Starfish*, 61–2.

21. *Diary*, 36; Gage and Stearn, *Bicentenary History*, 36, 43, 47. On the aristocrat's role in science: Desmond, 'Making of Zoology', 224–43; *Politics*, 135–7, 145–51, 223–34; MacLeod, 'Whigs'. Morrell and Thackray, *Gentlemen*, 25–9, on Bishop Stanley and liberal Anglican science.

22. *Diary*, 37–8, 40; *Narrative*, 1:30–33; Darwin, *Journal*, 570.

23. *Diary*, 39–40; *Narrative*, 1:34, 36, 38; *LTH*, 1:34.

24. *Diary*, 40–3, 45–9; *LTH*, 1:34–5; Darwin, *Journal*, 573; *Narrative*, 1:35–6; Saint-Pierre, *Paul*, 65.

25. HP 30.14; *Diary*, 37; HM R1 Notebook, ff.46–72; *SM*, 1:363–4.

26. *Narrative*, 1:41; *Diary*, 44–5, 49; Lubbock, *Stanley*, 188–9; Keynes, *Darwin's 'Beagle' Diary*, 406–7.

5 AN ARK OF PROMISE

1. *Diary*, 81; Winter, 'Ethereal Epidemic', 18–23; Lubbock, *Stanley*, 191; *CCD*, 1:490; Keynes, *Darwin's 'Beagle' Diary*, 406–10.

2. *Diary*, 81; H. A. Huxley, 'Pictures', 770.

3. Marshall, *Darwin*, 10–15; Nicholas and Nicholas, *Darwin*, 23–4; Lubbock, *Stanley*, 86–7; Darwin, *Journal*, 515–16; Keynes, *Darwin's 'Beagle' Diary*, 395–6; *CCD*, 1:482–5, 492; Desmond and Moore, *Darwin*, 175–6; *Diary*, 81.

4. *Diary*, 81–2; *LTH*, 1:37.

5. Lubbock, *Stanley*, 197–200; *Narrative*, 1:98n, 117; *Diary*, 98.

6. *LTH*, 1:33; HM R1 Notebook, ff.73–6.

7. TH to E. Forbes, [Sept. 1847], HP 16.154; Winsor, *Starfish*, 66, 76, 88.

8. HAH's Reminiscences, HP 62.1; *Diary*, 81, 338.

9. HAH's Reminiscences, HP 62.1; H. A. Huxley, 'Pictures', 781; Hughes, *Fatal Shore*, 344.

10. *Diary*, 81–2; P. P. King to TH, 30 Apr. 1850, HP 19.154. Nicholas and Nicholas, *Darwin*, 130–3. On King, Darwin and zoology: Desmond and Moore, *Darwin*, 109, 178–9; Darwin's notes on preserving specimens, DAR 29.3:78ff, CUL; *Report of the Council and Auditors of the Accounts of the Zoological Society of London* (London, Taylor, 1832), 9–10; Desmond, 'Making', 169n. Darwin also visited Captain King in Australia: *CCD*, 1:481, 483.

11. HAH's Reminiscences, HP 62.1; *Diary*, 82–3.

12. HAH's Reminiscences, HP 62.1; *LTH*, 1:37; Clark, *Huxleys*, 21; TH to HAH, 31 July 1851, HH 160 on her German school.

13. TH to Rachel Huxley, 1 Feb. 1849, HP 31.60; *LTH*, 1:38; Lubbock, *Stanley*, 198.

14. Bayley, *Blue Haven*, 20–3; Henrietta's Kent ancestry, HP 62.18; Clark, *Huxleys*, 21; her mother's ancestry, HAH to ES, 15 Jan. 1891, AD.

15. H. A. Huxley, 'Pictures', 772–4, 779–81.

16. *SM*, 1:6–8; HM R1 Notebook, f.77 (dated 'September' 1847); 'You': TH to HAH, 6 Oct. 1847, HH 1; *Diary*, 84–8; *LTH*, 1:37.

17. *Diary*, 80, 88.

18. TH to HAH, 16 Oct. 1847, HH 2; *Diary*, 88–9, 294, 303; *Narrative*, 1:43–4; Lubbock, *Stanley*, 197, 200, 214. Comb jelly *Cydippe* (=*Pleurobranchia*): HM R1 Notebook, ff.79–81.

19. In her first letter to him (14 Oct. 1847, HH 5) she pleaded: 'There is but one thing in our short acquaintance that I look upon with pain. It is our conversation last Sunday Afternoon. I cannot review it without sadness. I have thought over all you said and though in your presence unable to reply I may say almost without the power of reflection I have since weighed all your arguments yet cannot think you right. Do not I beseech you let years role by and still find you unfixed. Give much of your thought to this important subject, and oh whatever your ultimate convictions God grant they may be right, not alone in your eyes but in His.'

20. TH to HAH, 16–17 Oct. 1847, HH 2–3; Bainton, *Here I Stand*, 144; *CE*, 5:235–6; Carlyle, *Heroes*, 10. 'Law and Order' were the words of the Unitarian W. B. Carpenter, *Animal Physiology*, 2:viii, later to become Huxley's ally in London. On Carpenter's deterministic physiology and theology, Desmond, *Politics*, 211–22. Paradis, *Huxley*, 92–3; Lightman, *Origins*, 96–7.

    Since so little is known of Huxley's early scepticism, and since it reflects so strongly on his later scientific and agnostic stand, I quote this passage to Henrietta in full:

    I have thought much of our afternoon conversation, and I am ill at ease as to the impression I may have left on your mind regarding my sentiments. If there be one fact in a man's character rather than another, which may be taken as a key to the whole, it is the tendency of his religious speculations. Not by any means, is the absolute nature of his opinions in themselves a matter of so much consequence, as the temper and tone of mind which he brings to the inquiry. Opinion is the result of evidence. From a given amount and strength of evidence, as cause, a certain belief must, in all minds, always follow as effect. The intellect here acts passively, and is as irresponsible for its conclusion as a jury, who convict a man on the strength of certain evidence are irresponsible for their conclusion should that evidence turn out to have been unworthy of trust. For the verdict they are not responsible, for the manner in which they found it they are deeply & heavily so. It is the same with individuals. The opinion a man has, once more, neither is nor can be a matter of moral responsibility. The extent to which he deserves approbation or reprobation depends on the mode in which he has founded his opinion – and of this the Almighty search of hearts can alone be the efficient judge.

May his fellowmen then form no judgment upon the point? Surely they must and will do so, and so long as they confine themselves to their proper sphere of judgment nothing can be more fit than that they should do so. But let them not judge him by his agreement or disagreement with their own ideas however venerable and raised the latter may appear to them – let them rather inquire whether he be truthful and earnest – or vain and talkative – whether he be one of those who would spend years of silent investigation in the faint hope of at length finding truth, or one of those who conscious of capability would rather gratify a selfish ambition by adopting and defending the first fashionable error suited to his purpose.

Whether again he be one who says I doubt, in all sadness of heart, and from solemn fear to tread where the fools of the day boldly rush in – or whether he be one of those miserable men, whose scepticism is the result of covetousness & who pitifully exhibit their vain ingenuity for the mere purpose of puzzling and disturbing the faith of others.

On grounds of this kind only can a judgment be justly formed. On these my own dear one must you form your judgment of me.

As for my opinions themselves, I can only say in Martin Luther's ever famous words, "Hier Steh Ich – Gott helfe mir – Ich kann nicht anders". Perhaps after all they are not so different from yours as you may imagine . . .

Had I space I would write you much more on this matter which so deeply interests us both . . .

21. *Narrative*, 1:48–9, 168; TH to HAH, 18 Oct. 1847, HH 3.
22. *Diary*, 89–91; *Narrative*, 1:45; Nicholas and Nicholas, *Darwin*, 56; Hughes, *Fatal Shore*, 441. 22.
23. TH to HAH, 14, 17, 27 Nov. 1847, HH 4; HAH to TH, 14, 17, 23 Oct. 1847, HH 5.
24. *Narrative*, 1:50–3, 56–7; Lubbock, *Stanley*, 201; Hughes, *Fatal Shore*, 551–2.
25. HM R1 Notebook, ff.82 and 85 (Sertularidae); f.84 Brachiopod *Lingula*.
26. HM R1 Notebook, ff.86–97; *Narrative*, 1:54–8.
27. *Diary*, 91–2. Megapodes and sunbirds at Port Molle: *Narrative*, 1:59–63. Whittell, *Literature*, 111; J. Gould, 'On New Species', 201.
28. Carlyle, *Heroes*, 93, 209–10; Huxley, 'Tyndall', 3; Turner, 'Victorian Scientific Naturalism', 329–34; *LTH*, 1:237; *Diary*, 92–4; *Narrative*, 1:63–6; HM R1 Notebook, f.97.
29. Eliza Knight to TH, 27 Jan., 3 Apr., 11 May 1847, AD; 'with': ES to Rachel Huxley, 20 Dec. 1846, AD; 'God': Rachel Huxley to TH, 26 Oct. 1847, AD: 'from': George Huxley to TH, 27 June 1847, AD; *Diary*, 92–4. The 'Scotts' had sailed two months after Tom, on 27 January 1847, the only private passengers on the US merchantman *Thomas Wright*, landing in New Orleans on 21 March.
30. HAH to TH, 23 Dec. 1847, HH 6; *Diary*, 98–9.
31. *Diary*, 32. The *Physalia* paper was read at the Linnean Society on 21 November and 5 December 1848, but attributed to 'Willm. Huxley': LS Minute Book; HP 34.1; abstract: *SM*, 1:361–2.
32. TH to HAH, 6, 10 Feb. 1847, HH 7–8; *Diary*, 99–100; *Narrative*, 1:66–7. HM R1 Notebook, ff.108–17 for the Strait's jellyfish.

33. HM R1 Notebook, ff.123–8. *Narrative*, 1:67–8, 71; *Diary*, 100–1.
34. *Diary*, 100–6; *Narrative*, 1:68–70; Whittell, *Literature*, 111–12.
35. *SM*, 1:9–11, 23; draft MS, 'On the Anatomy and the Affinities of the Family of the Medusae', HP 34.127; *LTH*, 1:36, 39–40; *Diary*, 66–9; Winsor, *Starfish*, 61, 75ff; di Gregorio, *Huxley*, 5ff.
36. MacLeod, 'Whigs', 56–7, 70–80; Crosland, 'Explicit Qualifications', 179–83, Desmond, *Politics*, 222–34, 393–4.
37. *Diary*, 103–9; *Narrative*, 1:73–4; Lubbock, *Stanley*, 205–6; on his obstinacy: TH to HAH, 8 Feb. 1848, HH 8.

6 THE EIGHTH CIRCLE OF HELL

1. Rachel Huxley to TH, 26 Oct. 1847, AD. On Sharpe: *Diary*, 315; HAH to TH, n.d., HH 97; priests: 25 Feb. 1848, HH 13.
2. HAH to TH, 6 Feb. 1848, HH 10; H. A. Huxley, 'Pictures', 771; George Street: 12 Apr. 1848, HH 15.
3. TH to George Huxley, 21, 24 Apr. 1848, HP 31.47; *CE*, 1:6; *Diary*, 275–6; W. Poideoin to TH, n.d. postmark 4? Apr. 1848, AD; gun: HAH to TH, 17 July 1848, HH 29. Hughes, *Fatal Shore*, 163, 299–300, 307, 347, and 340, 487, 635–6 on Wainewright.
4. *LTH*, 1:37–8; TH to George Huxley, 21 Apr. 1848, HP 31.47; 'You': James Huxley to TH, 22 Apr. 1849, AD; Ralph, 'MacGillivray', 188, 190. George financing Cooke: George Huxley to TH, 27 June 1847, AD. On Britain's growing civic ceremony: Best, *Mid-Victorian Britain*, 82.
5. HAH's Reminiscences, HP 62.1.
6. TH to George Huxley, 27 Apr. 1849, HP 31.52; *LTH*, 1:38.
7. Quotes from Desmond, 'Making', 161–4, which also deals with the ideological impact of Macleay's system; Macleay, *Horae Entomologicae*, 1:332–3; Winsor, *Starfish*, 82–97; Stanbury and Holland, *Mr Macleay's Cabinet*, 19–34.
8. *LTH*, 1:38; 'strong': TH to HAH, 1 July 1849, HH 70.
9. *SM*, 1:24; the MS (HP 34.127) was endorsed 'Finished & sent to R. S^y. in April 1848' (f.157 on jellies and vertebrate germs); *LTH*, 1:40; *Diary*, 69; Macleay was not so happy about Huxley's developmental approach: Winsor, *Starfish*, 92.
10. Rachel Huxley to TH, 26 Oct. 1847, and Rachel Huxley in George's letter to TH, 27 June 1847, AD.
11. TH to George Huxley, 21 Apr. 1848, HP 31.47; TH to J. Richardson, n.d., HP 25.68.
12. Lubbock, *Stanley*, 205–6.
13. TH to George Huxley, 21 Apr. 1848, HP 31.47; *CE*, 1:13.
14. HAH to TH, 14 Oct. 1847, HH 5.
15. *Narrative*, 2:119, 133; *Diary*, 125; Lubbock, *Stanley*, 209–14; Bassett, *Behind*, 24–5.
16. HM R1 Notebook, f.133–7; *LTH*, 1:38; *Diary*, 125–6; *Narrative*, 1:77.
17. *Diary*, 128–9, 363–4; Lewes, *Ranthorpe*, 68, 110–11, 351; *Narrative*, 1:78–80; Italian: TH to HAH, 22 May 1848, HH 20.
18. *Diary*, 126–7; MacGillivray, *Narrative*, 1:125, 145–6; *LTH*, 1:44.
19. *Narrative*, 1:83, 2:119–25; *Diary*, 127–8; Lubbock, *Stanley*, 217.

20. *Diary*, 129–36; *Narrative*, 1:82–3, 2:123–33; 'the Service': TH to HAH, 28 May 1848, HH 23.
21. Huxley, 'Science at Sea', 112; *Narrative*, 1:84, 106.
22. Huxley, 'Science at Sea', 108.
23. J. Gould, 'On New Species', 111, 201, and Whittell, *Literature*, 112; *Narrative*, 1:85–6, 90; *Diary*, 128.
24. *Diary*, 135–8; *Narrative*, 1:90–91, 93–6, 2:377–8. MacGillivray's efforts were rewarded, Forbes later named his new snail *Helix Macgillivrayi*. J. Gould, 'On New Species', 109–10, for the flying fox.
25. Huxley, 'Science at Sea', 104–5.
26. Huxley, 'Science at Sea', 99; Rasor, *Reform*, 82–3 on the rum; *Diary*, 138–42; *Narrative*, 1:93, 97–9, 112, 123; TH to HAH, 26 June 1848, HH 24.
27. TH to HAH, 2 July–27 Oct. 1848, HH 35–7; *Narrative*, 1:100–4; *Diary*, 141; HM R1 Notebook, ff.153–61; HM B 43.2, 46.1.2, 56–7.
28. Huxley, 'Science at Sea', 112; *LTH*, 1:44; *Diary*, 141–2; *Narrative*, 1:106–8; cowrie *Cypraea*, HM R3 Notebook, f.112.
29. *Narrative*, 1:110–16, 120; *Diary*, 143–5; Dante, *Inferno*, 233, 235, 240, 269–70, 347, 353, 383.
30. *Narrative*, 1:121–32; J. Gould, 'On New Species', 110–11; Lubbock, *Stanley*, 208; Huxley, 'Science at Sea', 109.
31. J. Gould, 'On New Species', 109–12 (1849), 200–1 (1850); ZSL Minutes of Scientific Meetings, 13 November 1849, f.15; 23 July 1850, f.59. Beauty was crucial to Gould, whose sales reflected the exotic splendour of his birds. The names he chose, like *Ptiloris Victoriae*, Queen Victoria's rifle bird, also implied conquest; and associating 'this lovely denizen of the Australian forests', shimmering in iridescent green, 'with our most gracious Queen', added to the bird's imperial appeal (p. 111).
32. Rachel Huxley to TH, 22 Feb. 1848, AD; HAH to TH, 21 June 1848, HH 26; Bassett, *Behind*, 30.
33. Rachel Huxley to TH, 31 May 1848, AD; James Huxley to TH, 27 Mar. 1848, AD.
34. Rachel Huxley to TH, 31 May 1848, AD; 'who': TH to George Huxley, 27 Apr. 1849, HP 31.52.
35. *Diary*, 136n, 146–9; TH to Rachel Huxley, 2 Feb. 1849, HP 31.60; *LTH*, 1:43–4; Lubbock, *Stanley*, 90–6, 108–11; *Narrative*, 1:135–9; Bassett, *Behind*, chap. 5.
36. *Narrative*, 1:153–9; Morris, *Heaven's Command*, 302; HM R3 Notebook, ff.33–51; *Diary*, 148; *SM*, 1:33.
37. TH to HAH, 24 Dec. 1848, HH 39; *Diary*, 150–2, 364–5; *Narrative*, 1:157–60.
38. *Diary*, 146, 152–3; HM R3 Notebook, ff.67–99.
39. TH to George Huxley, Apr. 1849, HP 31.50; Lubbock, *Stanley*, 243–4.
40. TH to Rachel Huxley, 2 Feb. 1849, HP 31.60; H. A. Huxley, 'Pictures', 771.
41. George Huxley to TH, 27 June 1847, AD; Rachel Huxley to TH, 13, 22 Sept. 1848, also 15 Mar., 12 May 1847, AD; TH to George Huxley, 27 Apr. 1849, HP 31.52.
42. TH to Rachel Huxley, 1 Feb. 1849, HP 31.60; *LTH*, 1:39; 'there': TH to George Huxley, 27 Apr. 1849, HP 31.52.
43. TH to George Huxley, 27 Apr. 1849, HP 31.52; Ralph, 'MacGillivray', 190.
44. TH to Rachel Huxley, 1 Feb. 1849, HP 31.60; *LTH*, 1:39, 45; *Diary*, 298.

45. TH to George Huxley, 27 Apr. 1849, HP 31.52; Rachel Huxley to TH, 7 Dec. 1848, AD.
46. *Diary*, 293, 328.
47. Lubbock, *Stanley*, 240–1; *LTH*, 1:44; *Narrative*, 1:82–3, 162–6, 2:133–276; *Diary*, 111–12, 244; Bassett, *Behind*, chaps 7–9.

7 SEPULCHRAL PAINTED SAVAGES

1. *Diary*, 172–3; *Narrative*, 1:166, 181; Lubbock, *Stanley*, 244; 'then': TH to HAH, 10 May 1849, HH 57; 'fierceness': HAH to TH, 21 Jan. 1849, HH 46.
2. *SM*, 1:33; HM R5 Notebook, f.16 *Tubularia* (f.99 ship's bottom); f.27 *Echinus* larvae; f.29 Diphydae; f.31 comb jelly. *Diary*, 174, 296.
3. *Diary*, 175–9; *Narrative*, 1:4, 183; Lubbock, *Stanley*, 177, 246–50; 'sweated': TH to George Huxley, April 1849, HP 31.50; HM R5 Notebook, f.33 *Pteropoda*; f.35 spiny crustaceans.
4. *Diary*, 182–5, 191–200; *Narrative*, 1:168–73, 186–91, 201, 277; Lubbock, *Stanley*, 245.
5. Lubbock, *Stanley*, 246; *Narrative*, 1:200, 208; *Diary*, 191–2; Huxley, 'Science at Sea', 117; Desmond and Moore, *Darwin*, 174.
6. *Narrative*, 1:189, 196–8, 208–12, 243–4, 246; *Diary*, 184–6, 188, 190.
7. TH to HAH, 1 July 1849, HH 70; *Diary*, 186–98, 209, 297–8; TH to HAH, 26 Apr. 1849, HH 51; *Narrative*, 1:4; Lubbock, *Stanley*, 256–7.
8. Huxley, 'Science at Sea', 112; *Diary*, 190, 197–207; *Narrative*, 1:215, 223, 228–37, 280–1.
9. HM R5 Notebook, f.50; also f.56, 65 crustaceans; f.62 worms; f.72ff, jellies and sea nettles; Notebook HP 51.1; *Diary*, 156, 209.
10. *Diary*, 209–10.
11. Huxley, 'Science at Sea', 115; *Narrative*, 1:238, 248.
12. *Narrative*, 1:254–84; *Diary*, 212–30; 'I never': Huxley, 'Science at Sea', 115–16 quoting Stanley's journal.
13. *Diary*, 215, 218–20, 223–9; *Narrative*, 1:233, 255–6, 260–4, 271–4; Lubbock, *Stanley*, 252.
14. *Diary*, 223–5, 231–2; *Narrative*, 1:283.
15. TH to HAH, 1 Sept. 1849, HH 71; 'sitting': TH to Rachel Huxley, 17 Sept. 1849, AD; HM R5 Notebook, ff.20ff; Notebook HP 51.12–22.
16. *Diary*, 211, 232–3; Lubbock, *Stanley*, 253; *Narrative*, 1:285. On the euphemisms 'unclean' and 'indecent', and the dying use of the 'cat': Rasor, *Reform*, 49–51, 98.
17. *Narrative*, 1:241, 285–90; *Diary*, 154n, 235–8; Lubbock, *Stanley*, 255; naming: Kirby, 'Introductory Address', 5.
18. TH to Goode & Lawrence, Navy Agents, 11 Oct. 1849, HP 181. *Diary*, 239–40, 366–7; *Narrative*, 1:293–301; HAH to TH, 31 Aug. 1849, HH 68; *LTH*, 1:64.
19. James Huxley to TH, 22 Apr. 1849, AD; TH to HAH, 6 Oct. 1849, HH 71. The Linnean paper was only published in abstract. Forbes read Huxley's notes on *Trigonia* at the Zoological Society: *SM*, 1:6–8, 363–4.
20. *SM*, 1:33–5; Winsor, *Starfish*, 77–8, 87ff; Huxley, *Oceanic*, 1.
21. *Diary*, 241–8; *Narrative*, 1:301–7, 2:277; Lubbock, *Stanley*, 258–61; Bassett, *Behind*, chap. 11.

22. *Narrative*, 1:317–26; J. Gould, 'On New Australian Birds', 276–9; Whittell, *Literature*, 116.
23. 'Sketch of a Classification of the Ascidians', HP 34.168; *SM*, 1:69–74; Redscar: HM R5 Notebook, f.100; HP 74; *SM*, 1:38–9.
24. *SM*, 1:38–53; Winsor, *Starfish*, 64; *Diary*, 56–60. What he did not set out to publish were his diagrams, drawn at the Cape, slotting the 'Nematophora' – indeed all animal life – onto Macleay's circles (HP 50.3).
25. *Diary*, 165–6, 248–62; *Narrative*, 1:307–8, 318–20, 2:8–15, 35–49; Lubbock, *Stanley*, 261–3; TH to HAH, 20 Oct. 1849, HH 73.
26. *Diary*, 262–5; *Narrative*, 2:29, 35, 49–66; Lubbock, *Stanley*, 265.

8   HOMESICK HEROES

1. TH to HAH, 4 Feb. 1850, HH 74; *Diary*, 265, 367–8; *Narrative*, 2:67; Lubbock, *Stanley*, 265–8.
2. *Diary*, 301, 368; Lubbock, *Stanley*, 261, 266–7; *Narrative*, 2: 67–9; 'Lioness': TH to HAH, 20 Oct. 1849, HH 73.
3. *Diary*, 288, 294, 302.
4. TH to HAH, n.d. (endorsed Feb. 1850), HH 75; *Diary*, 276, 281–2. On Darwin's trip: Keynes, *Darwin's 'Beagle' Diary*, 396–400; Nicholas and Nicholas, *Darwin*, 3, 13, 23–5, 68–9. Hughes, *Fatal Shore*, 262–3.
5. George Huxley to TH, 3 Nov. 1849, AD; Halevy, *Victorian Years*, 197; Rachel Huxley to TH, 30 Jan. 1848, AD; 'my': James Huxley to TH, 30 Jan. 1848, AD; 'Dʳ': A. McClatchie to TH, 24 Sept. 1849, HP 22.119. Cooke resigned from the Linnean Society because of 'circumstances which I cannot control' (presumably financial): J. C. Cooke to LS, 31 Jan. 1848, LS Archives.
6. *Diary*, 290, 299, 302.
7. Huxley, 'Science at Sea', 103; Lubbock, *Stanley*, 266–9.
8. *LTH*, 1:46; *Diary*, 303; Lubbock, *Stanley*, 270–1.
9. *Diary*, 303–5, 312; HAH to TH, n.d. [20 Mar. 1850], HH 78; *Narrative*, 2:86; Lubbock, *Stanley*, 270n.
10. *Diary*, 305–10; HAH to TH, n.d., HH 91.
11. *Diary*, 265–7, 308–13.
12. HAH to TH, Tuesday noon, Tuesday evening [30 Apr. 1850], HH 94, 95; TH to HAH, Tuesday morning [30 April 1850], HH 92.
13. Huxley's MS Diary, HH 128, f.1; *Diary*, 313, 317–18.
14. TH to HAH, [2 May 1850], HH 99; Huxley's MS Diary, HH 128, ff.1–6; *Diary*, 318–20; Whittell, *Literature*, 116; *Narrative*, 2:86.
15. Huxley's MS Diary, HH 128, ff.2–4; *Diary*, 317–19.
16. Huxley's MS Diary, HH 128, f.4; *Diary*, 319.
17. Huxley's MS Diary, HH 128, ff.4–8; *Diary*, 312, 319–22, 323.
18. Lubbock, *Stanley*, 272. On alcoholism in the Service: Rasor, *Reform*, 81.
19. TH to HAH, 14 May 1850, HH 101; Huxley's MS Diary, HH 128, ff.8–10; *Diary*, 322–3, 336; diagrams: HP 50.20–2.
20. TH to HAH, 18, 21 May 1850, HH 103–5; *LTH*, 1:52–3; *Diary*, 313, 323–5; *Narrative*, 2:87–94; Morris, *Heaven's Command*, 302–3; rats: Huxley, *West. Rev.*, 63 (1855), 252–3. Cf. Darwin's view, Desmond and Moore, *Darwin*, 174–6.

21. HP 51.63–70; *SM*, 1:53–9; *Narrative*, 2:95–6; Huxley's MS Diary, HH 128, ff.15–16, 19; *Diary*, 326–9.
22. Huxley's MS Diary, HH 128, ff.20, 24–6; *Diary*, 329, 332–3; *LTH*, 1:54.
23. TH to HAH, 12 July 1850, HH 111–12; *LTH*, 1:53–4; *Narrative*, 2:99–107; Desmond and Moore, *Darwin*, 336–7; *CCD*, 2:109–11; 3:109–26.
24. Huxley's MS Diary, HH 128, ff.28–30; *Diary*, 334–5; TH to HAH, 8 Aug. 1850, HH 115; siphonophores: HP 63.1–14; *Narrative*, 2:112–13.
25. James Huxley to TH, 22 Apr. 1849, AD; Huxley, 'Science at Sea', 98–9, 104, 106; *CE*, 1:12–13; 'Service': TH to HAH, 27 Mar. 1850, HH 79–80; *Diary*, 24, 338, 350.
26. TH to HAH, 27 Mar. 1850, HH 79–80; 'sick': 8 Feb. 1848, HH 7–8.
27. Huxley, 'Science at Sea', 117–19. The Quaker physician Thomas Hodgkin and William Wilberforce's heir in the anti-slavery movement, Thomas Fowell Buxton, had formed the 'Aborigines Protection Society' in 1837, and published the *Colonial Intelligencer and Aborigines Friend*. Hodgkin was guardian of an aboriginal boy brought to England by Eyre: Rose, *Curator*, 31–8, 104–17; Stocking, 'What's', 369–72.
28. *Narrative*, 1:343–402, 2:387–95.
29. TH to HAH, 28 Aug. 1852, HH 222; *LTH*, 1:57.
30. James Huxley to TH, 22 Apr. 1849, AD; Rachel Huxley to TH, 23 Aug. 1849, AD; George Huxley to TH, 3 Nov. 1849, AD.
31. Huxley's MS Diary, HH 128, ff.26, 55; *Diary*, 333, 350; *LTH*, 1:45, 54.

9 THE SCIENTIFIC SADDUCEE

1. TH to HAH, 16 Nov. 1850, HH 129; *LTH*, 1:60; Desmond and Moore, *Darwin*, 189.
2. *Lancet*, 2 (1840–1), 552–3; *LTH*, 1:57–8.
3. TH to HAH, 16 Nov., 24 Dec. 1850, HH 129, 134; *LTH*, 1:60, 63.
4. TH to ES, 21 Nov. 1850, AD; *LTH*, 1:61.
5. TH to HAH, 1 Mar. 1851, HH 139; Tristan, *London Journal*, 1–2; Norton, *Victorian London*, 31, 55, 73; Best, *Mid-Victorian Britain*, 51, 76; Huxley 'had a grand view of some of the celebrities' (including Disraeli) in the Commons: TH to HAH, 1 Feb. 1851, HH 136.
6. *LTH*, 1:56; 'approved': TH to HAH, 16 Nov. 1850, HH 129; Huxley, *Oceanic*, ix–x; Desmond and Moore, *Darwin*, 226–7; *CCD*, 2:26, 34, 37–9.
7. TH to HAH, 21 July 1851, HH 160; *LTH*, 1:118n; Desmond and Moore, *Darwin*, 226, 292, 396; Owen's paper: E. Sabine to TH, 30 Oct. 1853, HP 26.6; Desmond, *Archetypes*, 28. £120 pay per annum: HH 145.
8. TH to HAH, 31 Mar. 1851, HH 143; *LTH*, 1:95, 116; Forbes, *Literary Papers*, 119; Mills, 'View', 372–85; Wilson and Geikie, *Memoir*, 480. On C. *Huxleyi*: Forbes, 'On the Mollusca', 385.
9. TH to HAH, 16 Nov. 1850, HH 130; *CE*, 1:14; *Diary*, 354; 'Willm Huxley': LS Minutes, 21 Nov. 1848; HP 34.1.
10. TH to HAH, 16 Nov. 1850, HH 130; 15 June 1851, HH 153 on Murchison; *LTH*, 1:62–3; Secord, 'King'; 'Sang froid', 'Pompeii': Secord, *Controversy*, 43ff, 118–23; Stafford, *Scientist*, 7; Secord, 'Geological Survey', 233; 'dingy': Geikie, *Memoir*, 30.
11. TH to HAH, 16 Nov. 1850, HH 130; MacLeod, 'Royal Society', 325ff; Geikie, *Life*, 1:118–19; Geikie, *Memoir*, 197; Lyell, *Manual*, vi–viii; Bowler,

Fossils, 75; R. Porter, 'Gentlemen', 824. Lyell's fears: Desmond, *Politics*, 327–31; Desmond, 'Artisan Resistance', 108–9; Bartholomew, 'Lyell', 263–9; Bartholomew, 'Non-Progress'; Bartholomew, 'Huxley's Defence', 527–8; Lyell, *Principles*, 2:20–1. Lyell's palaeontology: Rudwick, *Meaning*, 181ff; Gould, *Time's Arrow*, 137ff. As President of the Geological Society, Lyell was preparing his final address on the subject of fossil stasis (Lyell, 'Anniversary Address').

12. *LTH*, 1:60–1; TH to HAH, 16 Nov. 1850, HH 129.

13. TH to HAH, 16 Nov. 1850, HH 129; n.d. [pre-30 Jan. 1851], HH 137; HP 31.115 for his zoo season ticket. Thylacines and hippopotamus: *Reports of the Council and Auditors of the Zoological Society of London, Read at the Annual General Meeting, April 29th 1851* (London, Taylor, 1851), 14–15.

14. *LTH*, 1:61–3; G. M. Young, *Portrait*, 7; TH to HAH, 28 Nov. 1850, HH 131; 16 Nov. 1850, HH 130.

15. Rupke, *Owen*, 21; Desmond, *Archetypes*, 40; W. S. Macleay to R. Owen, 28 Apr. 1850, BM(NH) OC 18.331; G. M. Young, *Portrait*, 76–7.

16. *LTH*, 1:59–62; TH to Admiralty, 20 Nov. 1850, HP 30.1. On Bell: MacLeod, 'Whigs', 77; Desmond, *Politics*, 393–4.

17. J. Parker to R. Owen, 29 Nov. 1850, BM(NH) OC 21.135; *Diary*, 353; *LTH*, 1:60; Huxley's official notification came on 3 Dec. 1850, HP 32.1.

18. TH to HAH, 2 Dec. 1850, HH 132; *Lancet*, 1 (1840–1), 869; 2 (1840–1), 876, 878.

19. *Diary*, 353; TH to HAH, 24 Dec. 1850, HH 133–4; 2 Dec. 1850, HH 132. Geikie, *Memoir*, 145; Huxley, 'Tyndall', 6. G. M. Young, *Portrait*, 13 on sermonizing. TH to J. Goodsir, 20 Jan. '1850' [1851], HP 17.72.

20. TH to HAH, 16 Dec. 1850, HH 133; 'Sisyphus': 28 June 1851, HH 155; *LTH*, 1:63.

21. *LTH*, 1:64; TH to HAH, 1 Feb. 1851, HH 135; 16 Dec. 1850, HH 133. This fight or succumb theme occurs in Thackeray's *Pendennis*, 306.

22. HAH to TH, 17–27 July 1850, HH 113–14; 5 Sept., HH 116; TH to HAH, 2 Jan. 1851, HH 134. Keynes, *Darwin's 'Beagle' Diary*, 403–8; Darwin, *Journal*, 527–8; Nicholas and Nicholas, *Darwin*, 63–4.

23. TH to HAH, 30 Apr. 1852, HH 200–1; Jane Eyre: n.d., HH 137 (also HH 184); 'cares': 1 Feb. 1851, HH 135.

24. *Diary*, 355–6; TH to HAH, 24 Dec. 1850, HH 134; 1 Feb. 1851, HH 135; Mrs Charles Stanley to TH, 12 Feb. 1851, HP 26.253.

25. TH to HAH, 1 Feb. 1851, HH 136; 7 Sept. 1851, HH 163–4. Tillotson and Hawes, *Thackeray*, 14, 46–7, 90, 107–8; Sutherland, *Thackeray*, 46; Hardy, *Exposure*, 12. *Pendennis* was dedicated to Chandler's friend John Elliotson.

26. Bibby, *Huxley*, 184; *LTH*, 2:423; Goodrich, 'Lankester', x; English, *Victorian Values*, chaps 1–5; 'my sort': TH to HAH, 7 Sept. 1851, HH 163; 'blades': Thackeray, *Pendennis*, 225.

27. TH to HAH, 7, 23 Sept. 1851, HH 163–5; 'fair': 15 Mar. 1854, HH 266; Jensen, *Huxley*, 39. Busk translated Steenstrup's *Alternation of Generations* in 1845. Busk, 'Account', 388, on *P. Huxleyi*. Thackeray, *Pendennis*, 106–7.

28. TH to HAH, 23 Sept. 1851, HH 165; Thackeray, *Pendennis*, 646–9; Murphy, 'Ethical Revolt', 800–11; on Holyoake, Desmond, 'Artisan Resistance', 107–8. For newer socially based approaches to the Victorian crisis of faith, see Moore's 'Crisis', 59–68; 'Freethought', 279–89; and 'Theodicy'.

29. TH to HAH, n.d. HH 138; *LTH*, 1:66–7; MacLeod, 'Whigs', 72–4; Crosland, 'Explicit', 181–2.

30. TH to HAH, 14, 23 Mar. 1851, HH 140–1; *LTH*, 1:66; Geison, *Foster*, chap. 2, on the parlous state of experimental physiology in the 1850s and the lack of paid openings.

31. TH to HAH, 31 Mar. 1851, HH 142; *SM*, 1:38; Geikie, *Memoir*, 145; 'farmer': TH to HAH, 15 June 1851, HH 153.

32. TH to HAH, 14 Apr. 1851, HH 144; 1 Mar. 1851, HH 139; *LTH*, 1:65; 'splashed': Dickens, *Bleak House*, 49.

33. *Diary*, 356–7 (Thomson's reply, HP 27.328); TH to HAH, 15 Apr., 6 June 1851, HH 144, 152; *LTH*, 1:67, 96. Museum: Geikie, *Memoir*, 184–5; Wilson and Geikie, *Memoir*, 447–9, 452, 469–70, 485–7; Flett, *First Hundred Years*, 65; Secord, 'Geological Survey', 227, 257–8; R. Porter, 'Gentlemen', 833. Huxley was elected FRS with the physicists G. G. Stokes and William Thomson, chemist A. W. Hofmann, and Admiral FitzRoy: Hall, 'Royal Society', 155.

34. TH to HAH, 22 Apr., 4 May 1851, HH 145–7.

35. TH to HAH, 4 May 1851, HH 146; 'sick', 28 June 1851, HH 155; 'bullfinch', 31 Mar. 1851, HH 142; *LTH*, 1:67–9.

36. TH to ES, 20 May 1851, AD; 'I said': TH to HAH, 4 May 1851, HH 146; 'utter': 28 June 1851, HH 155; *LTH*, 1:67–9, 95.

37. TH to HAH, 4 May 1851, HH 146; *LTH*, 1:67–9; Grant's pay: Desmond, *Politics*, 392 n.59 (358, on Owen's total income of £700); Desmond, 'Grant's Later Views', 396; Council Minutes, vol. C, f.135 (1839): King's College London Archives; Dickens, *Sketches*, 313; Beddoe, *Memories*, 32–3; Harrison, *Early Victorian Britain*, 131–2; Best, *Mid-Victorian Britain*, 107–9; G. K. Clark, *Making*, 119; *LLL*, 1:161.

38. TH to HAH, 23 Sept. 1851, HH 165–6; *Diary*, 356, 358. The family even took his imbecile father to see it (HP 31.62). Harrison, *Early Victorian Britain*, 173; Briggs, *Victorian Things*, 34; D. Thomson, *England*, 99.

39. TH to HAH, 15, 28 June 1851, HH 153–5; *SM*, 1:104–20; *CCD*, 5:49.

40. TH to HAH, 8 June 1851, HH 152; *Diary*, 358; *LTH*, 1:72. Huxley's request for funding, 26 May: HP 30.2. MacLeod, 'Royal Society', 328–9.

41. *Diary*, 357, 359; Ralph, 'MacGillivray', 191.

42. J. Richardson to TH, 24 June 1851, HP 25.70; TH to HAH, 8 June 1851, HH 152; 28 June 1851, HH 155; Thackeray, *Pendennis*, 648; *Diary*, 358; *LTH*, 1:87n.

43. Barton, 'Tyndall', 124–8; *LJT*, 1–2, 6–7, 17, 21–34; Huxley, 'Tyndall'; Turner, 'Victorian Conflict', 363; 'I know': TH to HAH, 12 July 1851, HH 156–7; *LTH*, 1:88–90; *SM*, 1:98.

44. TH to HAH, 12 July 1851, HH 156–7; 31 Mar. 1851, HH 143; *LTH*, 1:88–90. *LJH*, 1:62, 66–71, 122–3, 167, 219, 223, 312; Hooker, *Himalayan Journals*, 2:206. Dayman had been a mate on Hooker's *Erebus* voyage. The *Erebus* and its sister ship the *Terror* were subsequently lost during Franklin's expedition in search of the North-West Passage. At Greenwich Dayman was to show Huxley over 'the Search Ship that went out after poor Sir John Franklin and his comrades': TH to HAH, 16 Oct. 1851, HH 169.

45. TH to HAH, 12 July 1851, HH 156–7; 'An account of researches into the Anatomy of the Hydrostatic Acephalae', HP 37 ff.13, 35; *SM*, 1:98–101;

Winsor, *Starfish*, 77–9, 93–7; *LTH*, 1:89; *LJH*, 1:347–50, also 39–40, 161, 170.

46. TH to HAH, 16 July 1851, HH 158; *LTH*, 1:90–1; E. Sabine to TH, 14 July 1851, HP 26.1.

47. TH to HAH, 12 Oct. 1851, HH 168; 31 July 1851, HH 160; 'happier', '350£': 21 July 1851, HH 159. Sharpey (HP 26.64) warned him that 'local interest' would win out. *LJT*, 35. Morris, *Heaven's Command*, 202. Writing to the Bursar of Toronto University (18 Aug. 1851, HP 28.27) Huxley scratched out 'R.N.' and put 'F.R.S.' after his name. That tailpiece, as he had promised, was talking for him. It was a symbolic switch, and diplomatic, since an officer could not apply for a job! (HP 26.254). Bell (18 Aug. 1851, HP 10.274) even had the printer rush his new Royal Society paper so that he could send out the sheets.

48. TH to HAH, 23 Sept. 1851, HH 165–6. He continued: 'They say "how shocking, how miserable to do without this or that belief!" Surely this is little better than cowardice … The intellectual perception of truth and acting up to it, is so far as I know the only meaning of the phrase "one sees with God". So long as we attain that end does it matter much whether our small selves are happy or miserable?' 'Missionariness': G. M. Young, *Portrait*, 2–3; Jensen, *Huxley*, 39–41; 'In fact': TH to HAH, 1 Feb. 1852, HH 185; *Diary*, 359; *Hydra* and *Spongilla*, HP 63.16–28.

49. TH to HAH, 12 Oct. 1851, HH 168; 16 Oct. 1851, HH 169; *LTH*, 1:78. The testimonials are printed in HP 31.68.

50. TH to HAH, 12, 16 Oct. 1851, HH 168–9. TH to the Bursar, Toronto University, 17 Oct. 1851, HP 28.31. C. Stanley to TH, n.d., HP 26.250; TH to Mrs Charles Stanley, 15 Oct. 1851, HP 26.254; Lord Stanley to the Earl of Elgin, n.d., HP 26.256; TH to Elgin, 6 Nov. 1851, HP 30.47. *Diary*, 361.

51. W. Fanning to TH, 23 Oct. [1851], HP 16.5; 'Old': TH to HAH, 16 Oct. 1851, HH 170; Marshall, *Darwin*, 117–20.

52. HAH to TH, 22, 31 May, 2, 9 June 1851, HH 148–51; 'pick': TH to HAH, 7 Sept. 1851, HH 164; Schiller: TH to HAH, 26 Oct. 1851, HH 171. Hughes, *Fatal Shore*, 561–2.

53. TH to HAH, 12 Oct., 7 Nov. 1851, HH 167, 172.

54. *SM*, 1:140–4; 'Arrangement of the Radiata', HP 37.43; G. Allman to TH, 28 Sept. 1851, HP 10.46; Winsor, *Starfish*, 102–17.

55. TH to HAH, 7 Nov. 1851, HH 172–3; *LTH*, 1:69–70; TH to W. S. Macleay, 9 Nov. 1851, HP 30.3; *LTH*, 1:91; MacLeod, 'Of Medals', 83.

56. TH to W. S. MacLeay, 9 Nov. 1851, HP 30.3; *LTH*, 1:91.

10 THE SEASON OF DESPAIR

1. TH to HAH, 29 Nov., 25, 31 Dec. 1851, HH 175–7. 'Brother': P. McGill to TH, 10 Dec. 1851, HP 22.129; TH to W. S. Macleay, 9 Nov. 1851, HP 30.3; *LTH*, 1:91, 100.

2. TH to HAH, 7 Nov., 11 Dec. 1851, HH 173, 176; Thackeray, *Pendennis*, 45.

3. *CCD*, 1:481–92, 2:345, 5:74; Keynes, *Darwin's 'Beagle' Diary*, 395–403; Desmond and Moore, *Darwin*, 124, 176–8; Nicholas and Nicholas, *Darwin*, 20–1, 45–54; Burstyn, 'If Darwin', 62–9; 'key': Gallenga, 'Age', 3. On

Tyndall: JT to TH, 2 Dec. 1851, HP 1.1; TH to JT, 4 Dec. 1851, HP 9.1; *LTH*, 1:79.

4. TH to HAH, 1, 6 Jan. 1852, HH 178, 181; 'purpose': TH to ES, 9 May 1852, HP 31.20; *LTH*, 1:80–2, 100; *Diary*, 360. For details of the *Narrative* copy inscribed 'H. A. Heathorn from T. H. Huxley 1852 & bound for her 1894' I am indebted to Mr William Collier.

5. TH to HAH, 1, 10 Feb. 1852, HH 185–6; 'that': 6 Jan. 1852, HH 181.

6. TH to HH, 15 Mar. 1852, HH 191; *SM*, 1:153, 173, 176–7; TH to W. Macleay, 9 Nov. 1851, HP 30.3; *LTH*, 1:91; Paradis, *Huxley*, 4ff. The Unitarian Joseph Maclise made the archetype a 'mathematical axiom': Desmond, *Politics*, 368; and the positivist G. H. Lewes ('Goethe', 498–9; Desmond, *Archetypes*, 49) derided its Platonic reality. For a rival idealized conception see Broderip and Owen, 'Generalizations'.

7. TH to HAH, 1, 27 Feb. 1852, HH 185, 189; n.d., HH 138; Berman, *Social Change*, chap. 4; G. Staunton to TH, 5 Feb. 1852, HP 26.274.

8. TH to HAH, 27 Feb. 1852, HH 189; TH to W. S. Macleay, 9 Nov. 1851, HP 30.3; *LTH*, 1:93–4; Owen, 'Metamorphosis', 12–16; Flower, 'Owen', xiii.

9. *SM*, 1:190–2; Huxley, *West. Rev.*, 63 (1855), 242–3; Ospovat, 'Darwin'.

10. TH to HAH, 15 Mar. 1852, HH 191. This letter was bowdlerized in *LTH*, 1:97–8; Desmond, 'Darwin, Huxley', 595. The Ehrenberg paragraphs were shorn, leaving the impression of gratuitous aggression on Owen's part (so successfully that Bibby, *Huxley*, 25, believed that an 'increasingly jealous Owen' *had* 'tried to prevent publication'!). The missing paragraphs are proof that Owen's heels were being nipped by the bulldog pup, as revisionist historians had suspected: Ruse, *Darwinian Revolution*, 142–4; Desmond, *Archetypes*, 21, 28–9. On Ehrenberg: Winsor, *Starfish*, chap. 2.

    Huxley (taking his cue from Siebold) attacked Ehrenberg in *SM*, 1:89; 'man's': *West. Rev.* 63 (1855), 558–60; and 'Lectures', *Medical Times and Gazette*, 12 (1856), 507, where he broke up Ehrenberg's Polygastria, removing the algae and combining the amoeba-like forms with the Foraminifera, sponges and Gregarinidae in the new sub-kingdom 'Protozoa'.

    On the Anglican and Coleridgean view of nature, law and society: Jacyna, 'Immanence', 325–6; Desmond, *Politics*, 114–15, 254–74, 358–72. Ibid, 331–2, and *LRO*, 1:167, 321 on the Honourable Artillery Company.

11. R. Owen to TH, 15 Mar. 1853, HP 26.6. Forbes and Bell refereed the paper.

12. TH to HAH, 15 Mar. 1852, HH 192; 'nursery': 16 Apr. 1852, HH 195–6; TH to ES, 17 Apr. 1852, HP 31.17; *SM*, 1:197; Wallace, *My Life*, 1:323.

13. TH to the Duke of Northumberland, 28 Mar. 1852, HP 30.10; TH to G. Airy, [Mar. 1852], HP 30.9; Admiralty to TH, 24 Apr. 1842, HP 30.12; *LTH*, 1:72, 100.

14. TH to HAH, 5, 16 Apr. 1852, HH 195–6, 218; *LTH*, 1:81.

15. TH to ES, 17 Apr. 1852, HP 31.17; 'hideous', 'She': TH to HAH, 16 Apr. 1852, HH 195–6; J. Barlow to TH, 24 Apr. 1852, HP 10.229; B. Vincent to TH, 24 Apr. 1852, HP 28.73.

16. 'Animal Individuality' draft, HP 38.10–13, 15; *SM*, 1:146; Jensen, *Huxley*, 56; 'heart', 'whole', 'break': TH to ES, 3 May 1852, HP 31.17; *LTH*, 1:98–100; 'ever': TH to HAH, 30 Apr.1852, HH 200; Flower, 'Reminiscences', 285.

17. TH to HAH, 30 Apr., 23 May 1852, HH 200, 206; 'triumphantly': G. Allman to TH, 30 May 1852, HP 10.63.

18. Carpenter, *Remarks*, 2–3; Carpenter, 'Dubois', 203; Desmond, *Politics*, 210–22; WBC to TH, HP 12.61–6; referee: TH to T. Williams, 7 July 1852, HP 29.45; TH to T. Bell, n.d., HP 30.9; 'my': TH to HAH, 13 June 1852, HH 209.

19. TH to HAH, 23 May, 13, 24 June, 5, 11 July, 5 Aug. 1852, HH 206, 209–10, 215–18; *LTH*, 1:81; also on the grant: HP 30.12–16.

20. His archetype was based on the sedentary adults. He was now dismissing his tadpole-like larval 'Appendicularia as an aberrant form': 'Sketch of a Classification of the Ascidians', HP 34.168; HP 35; *SM*, 1:194; 'fresh': TH to HAH, 28 Aug. 1852, HH 221. He earned his keep by reporting the 1852 BAAS meeting for the *Literary Gazette*.

21. HAH to TH, 11 May 1852, HH 203; 'deep', Owen: TH to HAH, 28 Aug., 16 Sept. 1852, HH 222–3; T. Chandler to TH, 12 Sept. 1852, HP 12.166.

22. *LTH*, 1:83; C. Aldis to TH, 8 Sept. 1852, HP 10.33; J. Bishop to TH, 6 Sept. 1852, HP 11.3; Cope, 'Private Medical Schools', 105–6; Clarke, *Autobiographical Recollections*, 128–32; 'boiling': TH to HAH, 30 Oct. 1852, HH 229. On Dermott's school, which changed its name to the 'Hunterian' after he died: Desmond, *Politics*, 166ff.

23. TH to HAH, 30 Oct. 1852, HH 229–30. HP 10.212, 16.168, 23.245, 24.107, 27.281; *LTH*, 1:79, 107.

24. *LTH*, 1:101, 105; C. R. Weld to TH, 7 Nov. 1852, HP 28.230; 'scientific knighthood': Desmond, *Politics*, 232; MacLeod, 'Of Medals', 83, 92. Floods and Forbes's Ark: R. Austen to E. Forbes, 29 Nov. 1852, HP 10.179.

25. R. Austen to E. Forbes, 22 Nov. 1852, HP 10.177; *LTH*, 1:102–3; Briggs, *Victorian People*, 9–10, 62.

26. Draft of Huxley's reply, HP 31.139; E. Forbes to TH, 16 Nov. 1852, HP 16.170; *LTH*, 1:103, 105.

27. E. Forbes to TH, 2 Dec. 1852, HP 16.174; 'I was': TH to E. Forbes, 27 Nov. 1852, HP 16.172; TH to R. Owen, 17 Nov. 1852, HP 23.247; 'How': L. Horner to E. Forbes, 17 Nov. 1852, HP 18.224, referring to Owen's miserable *Literary Gazette* obituary of Gideon Mantell. Owen's callousness cost him the chair of the Geological Society: W. Hopkins to E. Forbes: 4 Dec. 1852, HP 18.224; Desmond, *Archetypes*, 26–7, 208 n13; Benton, 'Progressionism'.

28. G. Busk to TH, 16, 22 Nov. 1852, HP 11.210–12; TH to HAH, 20 Dec. 1852, HH 238; A. Kölliker to TH, 31 Dec. 1852, HP 19.276, reply, 278. Huxley tried to interest Longman in a translation of Karl Theodor Siebold's book – presumably his and Friedrich Stannius's *Lehrbuch der Vergleichenden Anatomie* – on which see Huxley, *West. Rev.*, 61 (1854), 583; W. Longman to TH, 8 Mar. 1852, HP 22.9.

29. TH to HAH, 10 Feb. 1852, HH 186; Angela Darwin, pers. comm.; *LTH*, 1:106.

30. HS to TH, 25 Sept. 1852, HP 7.94; *LHS*, 64–5; Spencer, *Autobiography*, 1:368, 402, 2:24; Desmond, *Archetypes*, 97–9; Kennedy, *Spencer*, chap. 6.

31. *LHS*, 65, also 35, 41, 45, 49, 56, 61; Irvine, *Apes*, 10; Spencer, *Autobiography*, 1:201, 218–21, 227–8, 237, 246; Spencer, 'Theory'. On phrenology's use to the outsiders: Shapin, 'Phrenological Knowledge'.

32. Peel, *Spencer*, 97, 132; Wiltshire, *Social*, 66; R. M. Young, 'Development';

Desmond, *Archetypes* 96–8; Desmond and Moore, *Darwin*, 393; C. U. M. Smith, 'Evolution', 59–60; R. J. Richards, *Darwin*, 246ff.

33. Haight, *Eliot and Chapman*, 3–4, 14–23 and *passim*; Poynter, 'Chapman', 4–5, 18–19; Spencer, *Autobiography*, 1:347, 386–8, 394–5, 2:33; *LHS*, 40, 60, 65; Desmond and Moore, *Darwin*, 379.

34. TH to HAH, 9 Jan. 1854, HH 261; J. Chapman to TH, 12 Aug., 23, 26 Oct. 1853, HP 12.168–70; TH to Chapman, n.d., HP 12.169; Van Arsdel, 'Westminster Review', 547; Poynter, 'Chapman', 6–8; Spencer, *Autobiography*, 1:226, 372; Moore, *Religion*, 432; Huxley, 'Science at Sea', 99, 107, 112, 119.

35. J. Chapman to R. Owen, 13 Jan. 1848, BM(NH) OC 7.26; *LRO*, 1:390; 'I say': Huxley (quoting Lewes) in *West. Rev.*, 61 (1854), 257; Haight, *Eliot and Chapman*, 68; Haight, *Eliot Letters*, 2:89, 8:89; Desmond, *Archetypes*, 29–32; Spencer, *Autobiography*, 1:347–8, 377–8; Poynter, 'Chapman', 5; Ashton, *Lewes*, 4, 72; Bell, 'Lewes', 277.

36. Ashton, *German Idea*, 94–101, 126; Gregory, *Scientific Materialism*, 2, 29ff; Lenoir, *Strategy*, 197ff; Broderip and Owen, 'Generalizations', 80–1; 'greatest': Lewes, 'Goethe', 481, 498–9; Bell, 'Lewes', 288–94; Wilson, *Lyell's Journals*, 54–60; 'We find': Burrow, *Evolution*, 106; 'speculation': Huxley, *West. Rev.*, 61 (1854), 255–6; zoo: HS to TH, n.d., HP 7.96; *LHS*, 63; Ashton, *Lewes*, 96; Spencer, *Autobiography*, 1:348, 377, 403; 'paradox': Haight, *Eliot Letters*, 8:89–90.

37. *CCD*, 5:130–1, 133–5; Desmond, *Archetypes*, 49–50.

38. TH to HAH, 20 Dec. 1852, HH 236; the King's chair: HP 11.215, HP 24.5, HP 16.178, HP 12.67–71, HP 23.126, HP 21.175, *LTH*, 1:79, 84, 107.

39. JT to TH, 22 Feb., 5 Mar., 11 Nov. 1853, HP 1.4, 6, 8; 'looking';: TH to JT, 25 Feb. 1853, HP 9.5; *LJT*, 38–41, 45–9; *LTH*, 1:79–80, 114–15.

40. Irvine, *Apes*, 32; MacLeod, 'Visiting', 2–3, 8–9; *LTH*, 1:84.

41. TH to JT, 25 Feb. 1853, HP 9.5; 'difference': Huxley, *West. Rev.*, 62 (1854), 255; Cardwell, *Organization*, 80–1, 87–9; Bibby, *Huxley*, 124; Secord, 'Geological Survey', 255.

42. TH to ES, 22 Apr. 1853, HP 31.21; *LTH*, 1:106–7; Hardy, *Exposure*, 69–70; Thackeray, *Pendennis*, 335; 'jackal', 'red': Huxley, *West. Rev.*, 61 (1854), 260–1; *LTH*, 1:85, 104.

43. Haight, *Eliot Letters*, 8:51; Paxton, *Eliot*, 19; Spencer, 'Progress', 448–9; Spencer, *Autobiography*, 1:377, 384; *LHS*, 61; C. U. M Smith, 'Evolution', 58; Desmond, *Archetypes*, 97; Ospovat, 'Influence'; Ospovat, *Development*, chap. 6; di Gregorio, *Huxley*, 28; Gould, *Ontogeny*, 109–14; E. Richards, 'Question', 134ff; R. Richards, *Meaning*, chap. 5.

44. Broderip and Owen, 'Generalisations', 50, 56; Owen, 'Lyell', 449; Ospovat, 'Influence', 10, 17–24; Ospovat, *Development*, 117–40; Desmond, *Archetypes*, 44.

45. Huxley, *West. Rev.*, 61 (1854), 581, 585, 593; 'aberrant': 62 (1854), 247; Geikie, *Life*, 1:119.

46. HAH to TH, 10 Sept. 1853, HH 250; 'honour': TH to ES, 22 Apr. 1853, HP 31.21; *LTH*, 1:73–4, 106–7.

47. Ashton, *Lewes*, 143–7; 'purely': Haight, *Eliot Letters*, 2:132–3; 'Witch': Huxley, *West. Rev.* 61 (1854), 255–6, 266, 268; Barrow, *Independent Spirits*, chaps 1–2.

48. Huxley, 'Vestiges', 425–33, 438–9; Secord, 'Behind the Veil'; Bartholomew, 'Huxley's Defence', 526–8. Huxley listed *Vestiges'* howlers in HP 41.57–63.
49. *LTH*, 1:85–6; TH to HAH, 1 Jan. 1854, HH 259.

11   *THE JIHAD BEGINS*

1. TH to HAH, 3 Sept. 1854, HH 286; 'Cape Horn': *LTH*, 1:117.
2. Sheets-Pyenson, 'Horse Race', 464; 'baked': Geikie, *Memoir*, 165; 'monster', '£100': TH to HAH, 9 Jan. 1854, HH 260–1; 30 Apr. 1854, HH 275; *LTH*, 1:86; Godlee, 'Wharton Jones', 102.
3. TH to HAH, 9 Jan. 1854, HH 260–1; Huxley, *West. Rev.*, 61 (1854), 264.
4. Huxley, *West. Rev.*, 63 (1855), 562; TH to HAH, 9 Jan. 1854, HH 260.
5. TH to HAH, 16 Feb. 1854, HH 262–3; Seaman, *Victorian England*, 101, 127–9.
6. TH to HAH, 8 Apr. 1854, HH 271; 15 Mar. 1854, HH 267; J. Chapman to TH, 5 Mar. 1854, HP 12.171; Huxley, 'Schamyl', 491–2, 496, 500–17; Moore, *Post-Darwinian Controversies*, 19–100, on the 'warfare' with theology; Briggs, *Victorian People*, 62–4; 'Young England': TH to JH, 5 Sept. 1858, HP 2.35; *LTH*, 1:160 – this was a play on Disraeli's exercise in popular Toryism, the 'Young England' movement, designed to bolster the Church and Crown, for which Huxley would substitute Science and State.
7. TH to HAH, 15 Mar., 8 Apr., 12 Oct. 1854, HH 267, 270, 288.
8. *LTH*, 1:117; Admiralty: HP 30.18–27; TH to HAH, 8 Apr. 1854, HH 270.
9. TH to HAH, 8 Apr. 1854, HH 271; brachiopods: *SM*, 2:325; HM Box B:8.2–17; A. Hancock to TH, 23 Apr., 11 May 1854, HP 17.271–3.
10. TH to HAH, 15 Mar., 30 Apr., 4 May 1854, HH 266, 275–6; HAH to TH, 30 Dec. 1853, HH 258; Harrison, *Early Victorian Britain*, 139–40, 170; Davidoff and Hall, *Family Fortunes*, 222 passim.
11. TH to HAH, 30 Apr., 4 May 1854, HH 275–6; *SM*, 1:281; *LTH*, 1:138–9.
12. TH to HAH, 3 June 1854, HH 277; *LTH*, 1:108; E. Forbes to TH, 2 July 1854, HP 16.181.
13. TH to HAH, 3 June 1854, HH 277–8; Bibby, *Huxley*, 124; Hays, 'Science', 148, 151, 160; *Historical Account of the London Institution*; 'Lecturing': JT to TH, 31 May 1854, HP 1.11.
14. *CE*, 3:60, 62; Paradis, *Huxley*, 24–5; TH to FD, 10 Oct. 1854, HP 15.38; *LTH*, 1:113.
15. TH to HAH, 30 July 1854, HH 280; *LTH*, 1:109; E. Cardwell to TH, 20 July 1854, HM 3:121:38; TH to RIM, 17 May 1862, HP 30.63; GSM 1/ 7.141–2. John Morris was the University College professor, a good field palaeontologist well known for his *Catalogue of British Fossils*. On his decision: JH to TH, 1 Aug. 1854, HP 3.3; E. Forbes to TH, 31 July 1854, 16.183. Secord, *Controversy*, 271–2; Secord, 'Salter', 63, 65–6, 72; Secord, 'Geological Survey', 233, 243–50; 'simply': J. B. Jukes to TH, 1 June 1862, HP 19.110.

    Huxley's autobiography has been misunderstood. He recalled that Sir Henry

    offered me the post vacated of Paleontologist and Lecturer on Natural History. I refused the former point blank, and accepted the latter only provisionally, telling Sir Henry that I did not care for fossils, and that I should give up Natural History as soon as I could get a physiological post. (*CE*, 1:15)

This has been taken to mean that he wanted nothing to do with palaeontology. But he did want the palaeontological *lectureship*, and only turned down the museum job.

As for giving it up for a physiology post, the letters show only enthusiasm for his new job. He quickly saw the post as permanent, so much so that when Forbes tried to lure him to Edinburgh two months later 'to take part of the duties of the Professor of Physiology there who is in bad health, with the ultimate aim of succeeding to the chair', he turned it down, telling Nettie that he was fixed in 'London [and] I hope to remain there for my life long in *our* house': TH to HAH, 12 Oct. 1854, HH 287.

16. Cardwell, *Organisation*, 81–5; G. K. Clark, *Making*, 43–4; Briggs, *Victorian People*, 71–2, 85–7; G. M. Young, *Portrait*, 81; Turner, 'Victorian Conflict', 363ff; Stafford, *Scientist*, 18; 'imbecility': Huxley, *West. Rev.*, 63 (1855), 563.

17. TH to HAH, 30 July, 3 Sept., 1854, HH 280, 285; St Thomas': R. G. Whitfield to TH, 22 Aug. 1854, HM 3:121:114; Marlborough House: H. Cole to TH, 21 Sept. 1854, HP 12.265; *LTH*, 1:117–18. Earnings generally: Best, *Mid-Victorian Britain*, 110; Harrison, *Early Victorian Britain*, 131, 136.

18. TH to FD, 10 Oct. 1854, 5 Jan. 1855, HP 15.38, 46; TH to HAH, 30 July, 3 Sept. 1854, HH 280, 285; *LTH*, 1:109, 113. A. Hancock to TH, 8 Sept. 1854, HP 17.275, on his nudibranchs; HP 35 for the ascidians; Huxley, 'Report on Tenby Bay', n.d., HP 43.149. Secord, 'Geological Survey', 237–8; English, *Victorian Values*, 67–70. Tenby was no fortuitous choice. It had been De la Beche's headquarters when surveying Wales, and his director, Andrew Ramsay, had started as an assistant there: Geikie, *Memoir*, 28, 31–3.

19. TH to FD, 10 Oct. 1854, n.d., 5 Jan., 6 May 1855, HP 15.38, 42, 46, 62; *SM*, 1:337; *LTH*, 1:113, 121–2. HAH's Reminiscences: HP 78.81–3; Raven, *Christian Socialism*, 126, 159, 376.

20. Huxley, *West. Rev.*, 62, (1854), 574; 'Lower': 64 (1855), 568; Secord, *Controversy*. Other worlds: 61 (1854), 593–4; 62 (1854), 242–6; Brooke, 'Natural Theology and Plurality'.

21. Huxley, *West. Rev.*, 62, (1854), 575–6; Bartholomew, 'Huxley's Defence'; Desmond, *Archetypes*, chap. 3.

22. Huxley, *West. Rev.*, 62 (1854), 249, 253, reviewing J. C. Nott and G. R. Gliddon's *Types of Mankind*; Lorimer, *Colour*, 51, 72, 82–6, 123.

23. TH to JT, 17, 22 Oct. 1854, HP 9.12, 15: *LTH*, 1:85n, 120–1; Van Arsdel, 'Westminster Review', 458–9; Haight, *Eliot and Chapman*, 75–9.

24. TH to JH, 6 Nov. 1854, HP 2.7; JH to TH, 7 Nov. 1854, HP 3.13; *LTH*, 1:110–11; *LJH*, 1:416; *LJT*, 45–9.

25. TH to JH, 19 Nov. 1854, HP 2.1; subscription: HP 40.265; TH to FD, n.d., 24 Nov. 1854, HP 15.40–2; 'His': TH to JH, 24 Nov. 1854, HP 2.4; *LTH*, 1:116–17; E. Forbes to TH, 2 July, 8 Nov. 1854, HP 16.181, 192.

26. TH to FD, 5 Jan., 13 Feb., 1855, HP 15.46, 50; *LTH*, 1:117, 119, 122; TH to JH, 24 Nov. 1854, HP 2.4; Sheets-Pyenson, 'Horse Race', 465, 468.

27. TH to FD, 13 Feb. 1855, HP 15.50; *LTH*, 1:119, also 109, 123–4; Geikie, *Memoir*, 224. TH's Report to the Director of the Geological Survey, 3 Nov. 1854, HP 44.1. Geological justification: TH to RIM, [April–June 1855], HP 23.143; GSM 1/7.159–63. Edinburgh fell to his friend George Allman (G. Allman to TH, 20 May 1855, HP 10.71). And Huxley was right in his fears, Allman all but gave up original work: 19 Dec. 1855, HP 10.76.

28. TH to FD, 1 Apr. 1855, HP 15.56; *LTH*, 1:124. He tried unsuccessfully to marshal local helpers: A. Hancock to TH, 7 Apr. 1855, HP 17.280.

29. TH to HAH, 22 Nov. 1851, HH 174; HAH to TH, 3, 5, 18 Nov. 1854, HH 289–90; HAH's Reminiscences, HP 31.84; Mayhew, *London Labour*, 347.

30. Huxley, 'Lectures', *Medical Times and Gazette*, 12 (1856), 431–2, 483–4, 563; Winsor, *Starfish*, 117–19; di Gregorio, *Huxley*, 14. George Allman coined the terms 'ectoderm' and 'endoderm' for Huxley's two layers in 1853.

31. TH to JT, 13 Feb. 1855, HP 9.20; Tyndall replied 'I breakfasted with Owen a few days ago and ventured at the time upon one or two of your "heretical" remarks' (14 Feb. 1855, HP 1.233). *London Institution. 1855. Syllabus of a Course of Six Lectures on The General Laws of Life ... by Thomas H. Huxley*: HM 3:122.7 (8 Feb.–29 Mar. 1855). Hays, 'London', 100; Hays, 'Science', 151, 160.

32. TH to FD, 27 Feb. 1855, HP 15.54; Wilson and Geikie, *Memoir*, 497, 517; Geikie, *Memoir*, 196; Secord, 'Geological Survey', 230–1, 258.

33. LCK, 1:184, 201, 313–17; Backstrom, *Christian Socialism*, 37; Raven, *Christian Socialism*, 343–60; 'Nature's': Huxley, *West. Rev.*, 64 (1855), 240–55 (reviewing *Glaucus*); Allen, *Naturalist*, 125–37. On Dyster's role in connecting Huxley with the Christian Socialist leaders F. D. Maurice, Charles Kingsley and J. M. Ludlow see, TH to FD, 30 Nov. 1854, 6 May, 28 June 1855, 29 Feb. 1860, HP 15.42, 62, 66, 110. F. D. Maurice to TH, 19 Dec. 1854, HP 22.200; Hilton, *Age*, 271. Huxley himself gave lectures in Red Lion Square.

34. TH to FD, 6 May 1855, HP 15.62; *LTH*, 1:138; 'idolatrous': Huxley, *West. Rev.*, 63 (1855), 562; spirit-rappers: 64 (1855), 254–5; CE, 3:61.

35. 'Origin of Man', *The London Investigator* 1 (1854–5), 8ff; Desmond, 'Artisan Resistance'; Johnson, 'Really Useful Knowledge'; sacking: Cooper, *Immortality*, 76; Briggs, *Victorian People*, 36, 90; Seaman, *Victorian England*, 17; G. K. Clark, *Making*, 149–50.

36. Huxley, *West. Rev.*, 63 (1855), 250, reviewing Robert Latham's *Native Races of the Russian Empire*; 63 (1855), 563 on Sebastopol; E. Richards, 'Moral Anatomy', 391–6; 'confidence', 'working': TH to FD, 10 Oct. 1854, 27 Feb. 1855, HP 15.38, 15.54; *LTH*, 1:113; CE, 3:59.

37. He was too astute not to see that 'our knowledge is the knowledge of our time – that absolute truth is unattainable – that all our theories, however well founded, and however grand, are but myths, which enable us to grasp for awhile that fragment of the incomprehensible universe which has presented itself, – to float thereby on the surface of the great abyss until some larger fragment come within our reach and the old is deserted for the new': Huxley, *West. Rev.*, 63 (1855), 559; 'special': Backstrom, *Christian Socialism*, 29.

38. TH to FD, 27 Feb. 1855, HP 15.54; *LTH*, 1:87–8, 138; Shapin and Barnes,

'Science', 37, 39, 48, 52–4. Huxley's lectures, says Paradis, *Huxley*, 42, were old morality plays with new props.

39. TH to FD, 6 May 1855, HP 15.62; *LTH*, 1:126.

40. TH to JH, n.d., 7 June 1855, HP 2.10–12; *LTH*, 1:127–8; Angela Darwin, pers. comm.

41. JH to TH, n.d. [Oct. 1854], HP 3.5; n.d. [Oct. 1855], HP 3.18; Gage and Stearn, *Bicentenary History*, 49, 53; *LJH*, 1:352, 355; F. Hooker to TH, 11 May 1855, HP 3.30; '1000': JH to TH, n.d., HP 3.15; 11 May 1855, HP 3.30; TH to JH, n.d., HP 2.10.

42. TH to JH, 6 July 1855, HP 2.14; *LTH*, 1:126, 128; 'intense': WBC to TH, 6 July 1855, HP 12.76; 'Oh': TH to FD, 28 June 1855, HP 15.66; 'May': JT to TH, 4 July 1855, HP 1.19; Fullerian chair, 3 July 1855, HP 32.2.

43. TH to FD, 9 Apr., 6 May 1855, HP 15.60–2; *LTH*, 1:125; Wilson and Geikie, *Memoir*, 444–6; Secord, 'Geological Survey', 237–8.

44. *CCD*, 5:213–14; 'blindness': Owen, *Lectures*, 493; di Gregorio, *Huxley*, 37–9. Owen had complained (W. Sharpey to R. Owen, 12 [?Feb.] 1855, BM(NH) OC 23.376) of Huxley's error concerning the brachiopod (lamp-shell) heart, which underrated his own work, forcing Huxley into a retraction (*SM*, 1:335); 'There': TH to HAH, 8 Feb. 1848, HH 7.

45. WBC to TH, 16 July 1855, HP 12.78; Ospovat, 'Influence'.

46. HAH's Reminiscences, HP 31.79–80; *LTH*, 1:128–9; Pevsner, *Buildings*, 326; Angela Darwin, pers. comm.

47. HAH's Reminiscences, HP 78.81–4; tapeworm *Tetrarhynchus*: HM 3:125:2; also *Chondracanthus* (fishlouse), HM Box C 39 and HM 3:125:7; *CCD*, 5:442; 'Darby', TH to JH, 16 Aug. 1855, HP 2.16; *LTH*, 1:130.

48. TH to JH, 16 Aug., 14 Dec. 1855, HP 2.16, 198; *LTH*, 1:129–30; Notes on dredging specimens, 6 Aug.–6 Nov. [1855], HM 3:125:1–12.

49. 'Determined the develop^t. of the true ovaria in the peduncle & made out that the "true ovaria" of Darwin are not ovaria at all': Notes on dredging specimens, HM 3:125:1 (12–13 Aug. [1855]); Huxley, 'Lectures', *Medical Times and Gazette*, 17 (1857), 238–9; Richmond, 'Darwin's Study', 389, 398; Desmond and Moore, *Darwin*, 368–9, 408–9; *CCD*, 5:200, 262, 281. Huxley dropped Darwin a note about his findings: *CCD*, 5:441–2. Darwin's views were shortly undercut still more: *CCD*, 6:301–2 n10; Huxley, *Manual*, 257.

50. *CCD*, 5:351; *LJH*, 1:375; *SM*, 1:300. On Owen's and Darwin's science: Bowler, *Fossils*, chap. 5; Desmond, *Archetypes*, 69; Desmond, *Politics*, 360–72; Ospovat, *Development*, 137–9; R. Richards, *Meaning*, chap. 5.

12   THE NATURE OF THE BEAST

1. HAH's Reminiscences, HP 31.84–5, 95–6; HP 62.1–5; 'what', TH to ES, 27 Mar. 1858, HP 31.24; 'In this': TH to HAH, 26 Oct. 1851, HH 171; *SM*, 1:307–12. FGS, 9 Apr. 1856: admission form, Geological Society of London.

2. TH to HAH, 14 Apr., 22 Nov. 1851, 27 Feb. 1852, HH 144, 174, 189; 'Bloaters': JH to TH, 14 Dec. [1855], HP 2.198; *Diary*, 314–15; MacGillivray: TH to JH, 17 Nov. [1855], [19 Nov. 1855], HP 2.196, 110; J. Gray to TH, 17 Mar. 1856, HP 17.109; *LTH*, 1:232; Ralph, 'MacGillivray', 192, who states that Hooker's father put up the money.

3. Huxley, 'Owen & Rymer Jones', 26–7; WBC to J. Chapman, 1 Sept. 1855, HP 12.80. Huxley also slated Owen's protégé Thomas Rymer Jones, 20 years professor of comparative anatomy at King's College, London, for his failure to keep pace with research: Huxley, *West. Rev.*, 65 (1856), 261–5.

4. WBC to TH, 22 Oct. 1858, HP 12.94; Desmond, *Archetypes*, 38–40. *LTH*, 1:93; *LJH*, 1:520; 'unscientific': Huxley, 'Lectures', *Medical Times and Gazette*, 12 (1856), 432; Turner, 'Victorian Conflict'; Wiener, *English Culture*, 15–16 on the destructive cleavage of the middle class caused by professionalization.

5. TH to RIM, 15 Oct. 1855, HM 3:125:8; [c.April–June 1855], HP 23.143; *LTH*, 1:132–3; Geikie, *Life*, 1:190; Secord, 'Salter', 66; *CE*, 8:274.

6. Huxley, *West. Rev.*, 63 (1855), 243–5; 64 (1855), 571; CL to TH, 29 Aug. 1855, HP 6.9; *LLL*, 2:183, 185–6; R. Richards, *Meaning*, 116, 148.

7. Darwin, *Origin*, 329–33, 435–50; Darwin's notes on Huxley's review of Carpenter's *Principles of Comparative Physiology*, DAR Box B.C. 40f, CUL; Ospovat, 'Darwin'.

8. *CCD*, 3:2, 211, 5:201, 345, 372; *LJH*, 1:474.

9. Napier, *Selections*, 491; Barrett et al., *Darwin's Notebooks*, C76; *CCD*, 3:43–4.

10. Holt, *Unitarian Contribution*, 132; Darwin, *Origin*, 56, 380; Schweber, 'Darwin', 212; Browne, *Secular Ark*, 210–16; Kohn, 'On the Origin', 250. Barnacles: Darwin, *Monograph*, 2:155; *CCD*, 4:344; Ospovat, *Development*, 85.

11. *CCD*, 3:211, 336–7, 5:403, 498–9, 6:66, 361; Browne, *Secular Ark*, 65–8, 77–80; T. V. Wollaston, *Variation*, 186, 189.

12. *CCD*, 2:324, 352; 6:66–7, 74.

13. JH to TH, [4 Apr. 1856], HP 3.23; n.d., HP 3.21; TH to JH, [31 Mar. 1856], HP 2.21; HP 31.142; WBC to TH, 9 July 1856, HM 3:121.93; *LJH*, 1:368–9; *LJT*, 60–3; *LTH*, 1:111; Harte, *University*, 102.

14. Atkins, *Down*, 97 passim; Desmond and Moore, *Darwin*, chap. 20, also 296, 397; *CCD*, 2:324–5, 6:113–14; Harte, *University*, 82–3.

15. *CCD*, 3:345, 6:74, 87, 197; J. Lubbock to TH, Dec. 1856, HP 22.53–7.

16. Owen, 'Lyell', 449–50; Owen, *Fossil Mammalia*, 55; Ospovat, *Development*, 134–9; Rachootin, 'Owen'; Stauffer, *Natural Selection*, 384; Desmond and Moore, *Darwin*, 145, 235; Desmond, *Archetypes*, 44; Bowler, *Fossils*, 102ff; *LLD*, 2:26–7.

17. This was an idiosyncratic mix of Macleay's circles and von Baer's archetypes: Huxley, *West. Rev.*, 63 (1855), 242–3; Darwin's notes on this interview: DAR Box B.C. 40e, CUL; Ospovat, 'Darwin'.

18. *LLD*, 2:196 for Huxley's wrongly dated recollection of this meeting.

19. *CCD*, 5:83, 338–9, 363–7, 370, 374–5, 477, 483, 500, 6:122; *LJH*, 1:494; *LLD*, 2:26–7; Barrett, *Collected Papers*, 1:255–8, 261–3, 264–73; Browne, *Secular Ark*, 196ff; Desmond and Moore, *Darwin*, 418, 423–4, 444.

20. *CCD*, 5:352, 386, 492, 508, 6:58, 152, 236; Darwin, *Expression*, 259; *LLL*, 2:213; Wilson, *Lyell's Journals*, 54; Secord, 'Darwin and the Breeders'; R. Richards, *Meaning*, 151–2; Ospovat, *Development*, 156–7.

21. Wollaston, *Variation*, 35, 186–9; *CCD*, 6:134, 147; Desmond and Moore, *Darwin*, 434–6.

22. Huxley, *West. Rev.*, 67 (1857), 281–2; *LJH*, 1:367; *CCD* 6:100.

23. Bunbury, *Life*, 2:90, 99–100; *CCD*, 6:89, 91 note 7; *LLL*, 2:212.

24. Huxley, 'Lectures', *Medical Times and Gazette*, 12 (1856), 482–3; Wilson, *Lyell's Journals*, 54–60.

25. CCD, 6:103, 106–7, 109–12; 'old': TH to JH, 30 Jan. 1858, HP 2.29; *LTH*, 1:157; JH to TH, [Oct. 1855], HP 3.18; *LJH*, 1:375; Huxley, 'Lectures', *Medical Times and Gazette*, 12 (1856), 430, 432, 484, 507. CE, 2:12. The savaging of Owen was deliberate policy: TH to JH, n.d., HP 2.77.

    Huxley was also demolishing Louis Agassiz's evidence for progression. Agassiz saw fish maturing equally in geological and individual time. His argument involved changes in fish tails. He believed that in the embryo, as well as in ancient fish, the tip of the backbone turned up ('heterocercal'), whereas living adult fish have 'homocercal' tails, where the vertebrae fuse and rays come off as a uniform fan. But Huxley dissected perch and mackerel embryos and found them to be homocercal from the first: *West. Rev.*, 63 (1855), 244–6; *SM*, 2:271.

26. TH to JH, 3 Apr. 1857, HP 2.23; *LTH*, 1:149; JH to TH, n.d., HP 3.66; *LJH*, 1:427; CCD, 6:112, 147, 175–6; Huxley, 'Method of Palaeontology', 43–5; CL to TH, 13 July 1856, HP 6.11; Falconer, 'Huxley's Attempted Refutation', 476–90; Morris, *Heaven's Command*, 267–71.

27. CCD, 6:109, 161, 173, 178, 304; Stauffer, *Natural Selection*, 45–6, 73, 89.

28. TH to FD, 10 Oct. 1856, HP 15.74; 'knocked': TH to JH, 3 Sept. 1856, HP 2.19; *LTH*, 1:145–6; *LJT*, 50, 64–5, 342–4, 353; 'biggest': HAH's Reminiscences, HP 31.87–91; Ramsay Diary, 15 Mar. 1856, Ramsay Papers 1/24, Imperial College, London.

29. *LTH*, 1:143; HP 31.99; TH to FD, 10, 28 Oct. 1856, HP 15.74, 78.

30. CCD, 6:260; 'congenital': Owen, 'Affinities', 4–8; 'There': TH to FD, 3 Nov. 1856, HP 15.78.

31. HAH's Reminiscences, HP 31.91; *LTH*, 1:151.

13 EMPIRES OF THE DEEP PAST

1. TH to FD, [Jan. 1857], HP 15.80; Owen, 'Conclusion', 115; *LRO*, 2:60; Rupke, *Owen*, 93–5. Owen's title in the *Medical Directory*: TH to J. Churchill, 22 Jan. 1857, HP 12.194; reply, HP 12.195.

2. 'The Physiology of Sensation and Motion', Royal Institution, Jan.–Apr. 1857, HP 38.53, ff.146–7; 'fellows', 'I will': TH to FD, [Jan. 1857], HP 15.80; *LTH*, 1:138; HS to TH, 14 Jan. 1857, HP 7.102; Spencer, *Autobiography*, 2:11.

3. TH to FD, [Jan. 1857], HP 15.80; *LTH*, 1:137, 143.

4. Owen, 'On the Orders', 154–6; Owen, 'Conclusion', 115; Desmond, *Politics*, 254ff; 'Synopsis of a Course of Lectures on Fossil Birds and Reptiles', Museum of Economic Geology, Lectures 3 and 4, 25–6 Mar. 1858, in 'Richard Owen: Manuscripts, Notes, and Synopses of Lectures', Vol. 3 (1849–64), BM(NH); Meyer, 'Reptiles', 52, 55; Meyer, 'Reptilien'; Desmond, *Archetypes*, 65–71; Bowler, *Fossils*, 101–6.

5. Owen, 'Reptilian Fossils', 59–60. *Galesaurus* arrived in 1858; Owen read his paper on 20 April 1859, while Huxley was the G.S. Secretary. Bain, 'Discovery'; 'richer': A. G. Bain to R. Owen, 25 Sept. 1848, BM(NH) OC, 2.32; Owen, *Descriptive*, iii; Desmond, *Archetypes*, 195–6; Gruber and Thackray, *Owen*, 44–7. In 1858 Huxley was working on the Karroo two-

tusker *Dicynodon*: *SM*, 2:130; HM 2:96, and f.26 for his own later drawing of *Galesaurus*.

6. *SM*, 1:320; Buckle, *History*, 3:486; 'Buckle': TH to JT, [Mar. 1857], HP 9.22; Spencer, 'Progress', 450; *LHS*, 83; Spencer, *Autobiography*, 1:505; T. M. Porter, *Rise*, 60–5; Ruse, *Darwinian Revolution*, 145–6.

7. Portlock, 'Address' (1857), cvii, cxliv–v; (1858), lxxxii, clvii–iii; Murchison, 'Portlock', cxviii. Portlock recommended Huxley for the FGS: Huxley's admission form, 5 March 1856: Geological Society of London.

8. Colp, *To be an Invalid*, 59; *CCD*, 6:335, 366, 452; Stauffer, *Natural Selection*, 92–4, 134–8, 214, 223–4, 380; Kohn, 'Darwin's Ambiguity', 229–32; Ospovat, *Development*, chap. 9; F. Darwin, *Foundations*, 52.

9. *CCD*, 6:420, 424–8; Stauffer, *Natural Selection*, 275–9, 303–4; Ospovat, *Development*, chap. 7.

10. *CCD*, 6:456, 461–3; Darwin, *Origin*, 420; Winsor, 'Impact', 63–72; Di Gregorio, 'Order', 227–33.

11. Stauffer, *Natural Selection*, 379; *CCD*, 6:454; Huxley, 'Lectures', *Medical Times and Gazette*, 15 (1857), 238; *SM*, 1:311.

12. Cardwell, *Organisation*, 92–5; Harte, *University*, 107–12; A. W. Hofmann to TH, 20 June 1857, HP 18.208; CL to TH, 9 July 1857, HP 6.16; Linnean: A. Henfrey to TH, 13 Mar. 1857, HP 18.109; *LJH*, 1:410; Gage and Stearn, *Bicentenary History*, 53–5.

13. TH to JH, 3 Apr. 1857, HP 2.23; 'God': JH to TH, 2 Apr. 1857, HP 3.33; *CCD*, 6:451; *LTH*, 1:149. Diploma, 1 Oct. 1857: HP 32.4–7. He had already been elected to the Microscopical Society of Giessen on 7 Jan. 1857: HP 32.3.

14. Huxley's Deep Sea Soundings Notebook: HM 2:116; Pingree, *Huxley: Scientific Notebooks*, 48–9; Huxley, 'Chalk', 501; *CE*, 8:11–17; Rehbock, 'Huxley', 511–12; Rice, 'Huxley', 169–71. Darwin thought it 'the *gravest of errors*' that mid-oceanic mud could preserve remains as fossils: *CCD*, 6:506. Huxley disagreed: *Manual*, 79–82. Briggs, *Victorian Things*, 377; Young, *Portrait*, 16; Briggs, *Victorian People*, 23; Rolt, *Victorian Engineering*, 215–17; Paradis, *Huxley*, 75.

15. HAH to JT, 30 Aug. 1857, AD; 'on a': TH to JH, 16 Aug. 1857, HP 2.25; 'weary': TH to FD, 16 Sept. 1857, HP 15.86; 'rascally': JT to TH, [Jan. 1858], HP 1.221; Huxley's notebook: HM 3:126; *SM*, 1:482–501; TH to ES, 27 March 1858, HP 31.24; JT to TH, 19 July 1857, HP 1:21; TH to JT, 3 Sept. 1857, HP 8.29; *LTH*, 1:145–6, 159.

16. *CCD*, 6:419, 484, 7:58–9; Owen, 'Characters', 19–20; Wilson, *Lyell's Journals*, 86, 153. *SM*, 2:30, 51–6; 'Polemically': TH to FD, 10 Dec. 1857, HP 15.94.

17. Owen, 'Osteology', 343, 354–5, 370–2; Desmond, 'Owen's Reaction', 40–2.

18. Wilson, *Lyell's Journals*, 86, 157, 183; Lartet, 'Note'; Owen's marked copy of Lyell's *Supplement*, 14–15, BM(NH) Palaeontology Library; Owen, *On the Classification*, 86–7.

19. Owen, 'Osteological Contributions', 414–17; T. Savage to R. Owen, 24 Apr. 1847, BM(NH) OC, 23.103; Lamarck, *Philosophie Zoologique*, 1:349–57.

20. Desmond, 'Artisan Resistance'; Watts, 'Theological Theories'; Chilton, 'Geological Revelations'; 'Origin of Man', *London Investigator*, 1 (1854–5), 8ff. Wombwell's gorilla: T. J. Moore, 'Gorilla', 474; *LLL*, 2:358; S. S. Flower, *List*, 1:2; Barnaby, *Log Book*, 36–7; Barber, *Heyday*, 276, 310 n18.

21. W. Whewell to R. Owen, 3 Apr. 1859, BM(NH) OC 26.285.

22. Owen's Notebook 1 (Oct.–Dec. 1830), BM(NH), 27 Oct. 1830; Lankester, 'Flower', 254; *CCD*, 6:419; 'like': TH to JH, 5 Sept. 1858, HP 2.35; Gross, 'Hippocampus', 408, 413 suggests that Owen latched onto the ventricles because of their classical importance as body-soul interfaces.

23. Huxley, 'The Principles of Biology', Royal Institution, 19 Jan.–23 Mar. 1858, Lecture 10, 16 Mar. 1858, HP 36.97–100; Vevers, *London's Zoo*, 66.

24. *CCD*, 6:515; *LTH*, 1:143; Stauffer, *Natural Selection*, 10.

25. TH to FD, 27 Feb. 1858, HP 15.98; 'Hoorar': JH to TH, [26 Jan. 1858], HP 3.28; 'I had': RIM to TH, 26 Jan. 1858, HP 23.151; *LTH*, 1:150; *LJT*, 76; JT to TH, [Feb/Mar. 1858], HP 1.158; TH to JT, [March 1857], HP 9.22.

26. JT to TH, n.d., HP 1.158; 'corps': TH to JT, 20 Apr. 1858, HP 9.24; Bevington, *Saturday Review*, 277–80; Briggs, *Age*, 451; G. K. Clark, *Making*, 48; TH to JD, 20 Apr. 1858, HP 2.33; *LTH*, 1:139; *LJH*, 1:412.

27. TH to ES, 27 Mar. 1858, HP 31.24; HAH to ES, ibid.; *LTH*, 1:157, 159–60; 'travel', France: TH to FD, 18 Aug. 1858, HP 15.102; 'editor': TH to JH, 5 Sept. 1858, HP 2.35; 'Pon': JT to TH, 17 Feb. 1858, HP 1.22; fisheries: HP 43.76; also HP 20.23, 30.29.

28. Jensen, *Huxley*, 43; dinner guests in the 1860s: Watterson, *Marse*, 1:103.

29. TH to JH, 18 June [1858], HP 2.153; Spencer, 'Owen', 400, 415–16; *LTH*, 1:161; *LHS*, 87; Spencer, *Autobiography*, 2:24–5; Desmond, *Archetypes*, 95–9; Kennedy, *Spencer*, 72; *SM*, 1:571; Hall, 'Royal Society', 155–6; Stanley, 'Huxley', 121.

30. *CCD*, 6:290, 387–8, 457, 514–15, 7:107; R. Smith, 'Wallace', 178ff; Kottler, 'Darwin', 374; Durant, 'Scientific Naturalism', 35ff; Brooks, *Just Before the Origin*, chaps 1, 4; Wallace, *My Life*, chap. 6 et seq.

31. *CCD*, 7:116–25, 142, 507–11, 514, 520; Wallace, *Contributions*, 29, 42; Gage and Stearn, *Bicentenary History*, 57.

32. TH to JH, 5 Sept. 1858, HP 2.35; *LTH*, 1:159–60; *CCD*, 7:127, 137–8, 140, 161, 165, 222, 230, 270.

33. Owen, 'Presidential', li; Desmond, *Archetypes*, 61–4; Brooke, 'Natural Theology of the Geologists', 41, 56 n14. *LHS*, 81–97, 550–1; HS to TH, 31 Dec. 1858, HP 7.104; Spencer, *Autobiography*, 1:498–9, 503, 2:3, 8–16.

34. Dean, 'Through Science', 115, 121–4; Shatto, 'Byron', 151; Rudwick, *Scenes*, 80ff; Lightman, *Origins*, 6ff, on Mansel.

35. Huxley, *West. Rev.*, 64 (1855), 571–2; Hitchcock, 'Attempt', 250–1; Dean, 'Hitchcock's Tracks'; *London Quarterly Review*, 3 (1854), 238; Desmond, 'Designing'.

36. *LHS*, 91; *SM*, 2:112–13; notes on *Stagonolepis* and clippings on the GS meeting, HM 2:92; Geikie, *Life*, 2:120, 244, 311; Lyell, *Manual*, Postscript, x; CL to TH, 30 Nov. 1858, HP 6.18, for fears about dating; 'fairest': 'Death of the Rev. Dr Gordon', *Moray & Nairn Express*, 16 Dec. 1893; Desmond, *Archetypes*, 100, 171; Benton, 'Progressionism', 124–32; 'tooth': Collie, *Huxley*, 18–19, 30, 99–105.

37. HAH to ES, [Jan.–Feb. 1859], HP 31.29.

14 THE EVE OF A NEW REFORMATION

1. *LTH*, 1:161; 'bright': TH to ES, 28 Mar. 1859, HP 31.32; HAH to ES, [Jan.–Feb. 1859], HP 31.29.

2. TH to JH, 5 Sept., 2 Dec., n.d., 1858, HP 2.35, 39, 61; *LTH*, 1:133–4, 160; WBC to TH, 22 Oct. 1858, HP 12.94; also HP 3.36, 41, 43, 49, 10.302, 15.193, 17.143, 30.52; 'temple': Rupke, 'Road', 81–2; Rupke, *Owen*, 34–46, 97ff; memorial: HP 49.1–19.

3. CCD, 7:531; TH to JH, 29 Jan. 1859, HP 2.53; JH to TH, 22 Dec. 1858, 25 Jan. 1859, HP 3.45, 59; *LTH*, 1:165; 'Biologist': Huxley, 'Lectures', *Medical Times and Gazette*, 12 (1856), 429.

4. Huxley, 'Science and Religion', 35–6.

5. TH to FD, 30 Jan. 1859, HP 15.106.

6. TH to JH, [Apr. 1859], HP 2.43; 'By': JH to TH, [Apr. 1859], HP 3:47; *LJH*, 1:495–6; *LTH*, 1:165; *CCD*, 7:246–7, 252–4, 263–4, 270, 284–5; Colp, *To Be an Invalid*, 64ff.

7. CCD, 7:255–62, 272, 279, 299, 301–3, 308, 451.

8. CL to TH, 1 Oct. 1859, HP 6.27; TH to CL, 10 Oct. 1859, HP 30.33 (original APS); *LLL*, 2:325. Owen accepted the dating: 'On the Orders', 163; 'down': Collie, *Huxley*, 107–8. Huxley recognized *Hyperodapedon*'s similarity to the Triassic rhynchosaurs, the living Tuatara's ancestors, and this pushed him into a study of *Rhynchosaurus* itself in 1860 (Huxley's Diary, 22 Oct. 1860: HP 70.3; TH to CK, 4 Oct. 1860, HP 19.198). Other saurian studies: HM 2:89, 2:90–1; 2:94, 2:96; *SM*, 2:118–57; *LTH*, 1:154. Persistence: *SM*, 2:90; Huxley, 'Time', 144–6; Wilson, *Lyell's Journals*, 240; Desmond, *Archetypes*, 93–4, 102, 104, 171.

9. TH to CL, 26 June 1859, APS; *LTH*, 1:173; CL to TH, 17 June 1859, HP 6.20. Lyell was responding to Huxley's caricature of atoms flashing into elephants first mooted in his 'Lectures', *Medical Times and Gazette*, 12 (1856), 482–3; cf. *CCD*, 7:305–7; 'reptilian': R. Chambers to R. Owen, 6 Mar. 1849, BM(NH) OC 7.19; Darwin, *Origin*, 483; *CE*, 2:35–41, 53–4; Ospovat, 'Perfect Adaptation', 49.

10. *LTH*, 1:162, 164; *CCD*, 6:101; TH to E. Lankester, 1 Aug. 1859, Richard Milner Collection; TH to JH, 22 Apr. 1859, HP 2.49.

11. WBC to TH, 26 Sept. 1855, HP 12.82; 'Paradise': RIM to TH, 11 Oct. 1855, HP 23.147; *LTH*, 1:155.

12. JH to TH, [19 Nov. 1859], HP 3.63; *LJH*, 1:428; *CCD*, 7:328, 332, 336, 350–1, 362; Desmond and Moore, *Darwin*, 476ff.

13. CCD, 7:305, 340, 354; Wilson, *Lyell's Journals*, 227, 330–2, 335–6; 'race', CL to TH, 17 June 1859, HP 6.20; Bartholomew, 'Lyell'.

14. CCD, 7:368, 371, 375, 377, 392.

15. CE, 2:21, 24, 78–9, 448, 475; *CCD*, 7:383, 437; Irvine, *Apes*, 89; *LTH*, 1:170–1, 2:190–1; Bartholomew, 'Huxley's Defence', 529. Huxley's annotated copy of the *Origin of Species* with Darwin's covering letter is in the possession of the Huxley family.

16. Hull, *Darwin*, 114; *CCD*, 7:382–3, 387; *Athenaeum*, 19 Nov. 1859, 659–60.

17. CCD, 7:260, 390–1, 398–400, 404–5, 428, 434, 447; Carlyle, *Heroes*, 96.

18. CCD, 7:412–15; Hull, *Darwin*, 81–4, 93–4; Ellegard, *Darwin*, 37–8, 55, 367; D. Masson to TH, 10 Nov. 1859, HP 22.192; Huxley, 'Time', 145–6.

19. Haight, *Eliot and Chapman*, 102–4, 228–33, 237; TH to JH, [2 Jan. 1860], HP 2.59.

20. CE, 2:22–3, 51–3; Barton, 'Evolution'; Himmelfarb, *Darwin*, 216; Seaman, *Victorian England*, 144–5.

21. *CCD*, 7:356, 391, 398, 432, 434; *CE*, 2:34–49, 74–7; Bartholomew, 'Huxley's Defence', 529.

22. *CCD*, 7:379–80; 'startled': CK to TH, 7 Dec. 1859, HP 19.160; *LCK*, 2:66–7.

23. *CCD*, 7:324, 373, 413, 422–3.

24. Huxley, 'Darwin', cutting HP 41.1; cf. *CE*, 2:1–21; *CCD*, 7:457–8; 'I wrote': TH to JH, 31 Dec. 1859, HP 2.57; *LTH*, 1:176–7. The *Times* reviewer was Samuel Lucas: S. Lucas to TH, 9 Jan. 1860, HP 22.105.

25. *CCD*, 7:451, 458–9.

26. W. Elwin to J. Murray, 3 Dec. 1859, John Murray Archives; 'heard': TH to JH, [2 Jan. 1860], HP 2.59; TH on Elwin, HP 2.39, 2.43; Paston, *At John Murray's*, 174; *CCD*, 7:288–90, 359 n6.

15 BUTTERED ANGELS & BELLOWING APES

1. *CCD*, 7:396, 8:35, 81, 87, 97, 113, 119; Hull, *Darwin*, 138; 'stupid': TH to FD, 29 Feb. 1860, HP 15.110; *LJH*, 1:513; Mayhew, *London Labour*, 106–7.

2. RIM to TH, 14 Apr. 1860, HP 23.154; Geikie, *Life*, 2:321–2; *Athenaeum*, 19 Nov. 1859, 659–60; Secord, 'Geological Survey', 224, 260.

3. *CCD*, 8:97–8, 112–13, 176, 189 n7.

4. Mrs Dyster to HAH, 9 Apr. 1860, HP 15.108; *CCD*, 8:4–5, 25, 43. Huxley's 1860 diary lists 'Darwin' on 25 Jan., but arrows it to Thursday 26th (HP 70.3). E. Lankester, 'Lecture'.

5. TH to FD, 29 Feb. 1860, HP 15.110; Cunningham, *Volunteer*, 11, 113, 153.

6. *CCD*, 8:35, 52. Huxley's 1860 Diary on tickets: HP 70.3.

7. 'On Species and Races' MS, HP 41 ff.29, 30, 43–6, 49; cf. *SM*, 2:389, 391. The manuscript version (HP 41.9–56), which I have used, differs from the later printed abstract.

8. 'On Species' MS, ff.51–6; cf. *SM*, 2:392–4, quoting Tennyson, *Idylls*, 286; *CCD*, 8:80, 117 n11; 'I had', TH to FD, 29 Feb. 1860, HP 15.110; 'Professor Huxley at the Royal Institution', *Reasoner*, 25 (1860), 125; 'High': GR to TH, 13 Apr. 1860, HP 25.142.

9. *CCD*, 8:80, 84; TH to FD, 29 Feb. 1860, HP 15.110.

10. *CE*, 3:62; 2:59; *CCD*, 8:238; Dean, 'Through Science', 121. Huxley's failure to assimilate Darwin's 'selectionist' – or more accurately utilitarian – programme, while exploiting the *Origin* for ideological ends, has led Bowler (*Darwin*, 142–8) to call him a 'pseudo-Darwinian'.

11. *CCD*, 8:81, 109, 115, 124, 216, 320, 345, 405; Hull, *Darwin*, 201–2; D. Livingstone to R. Owen, 29 Dec. 1860, BM(NH), OC 17.415; Argyll to R. Owen, 2 Dec. 1859 and 27 Feb. 1863, OC 1.230.

12. TH to CL, 17 Mar. 1860, HP 30.34 (original APS); CL to TH, 16 Mar., 21 May 1860, HP 6.32–4; E. Richards, 'Huxley', 253–7; Harte, *University*, 122; Bibby, *Huxley*, 217; *LTH*, 1:211–12, 289, 310. Lyell shared Huxley's political view of Victorian women as conservative church-goers, and he feared that giving them the vote would 'delay educational reforms': *LLL*, 2:446.

13. *CCD*, 8:130, 150–4, 157, 160, 162, 190, 224, 247, 405, 490, 525; *CE*, 2:28, 61; Hooker, 'Reminiscences', 187; 'I have': GR to TH, 13 Apr. 1860, HP 25.142; Owen, 'Darwin', 500–1; Owen, *On the Anatomy*, 3:796 n6; Hull, *Darwin*, 177, 181–2; 'Palaeontology', *Athenaeum*, 7 Apr. 1860, 478–9.

14. G. Grote to TH, 23 Nov. 1860, HP 17.150; *SM*, 2:174; Schama, *Citizens*, 778; Huxley, *Lay Sermons*, 104–5, 117–18 (14 May 1860, not '1861']; *CCD*, 5:83, 8:474.

15. GR to TH, n.d., 13, 23 Apr., 13, 20 May 1860, HP 25.142–53; Pembroke dinner: TH to HAH, 27, 28 June 1860, AD; Rolleston on brains in HM 1.14.283–93; Rolleston, *Scientific Papers*, 1:ixff, 56, 61; *CE*, 2:61; Cunningham, *Volunteer*, 1.

16. Trains: Diary HP 70.3; A. Thomson to TH, 24 May 1860, HM 2:118:99; *SM*, 2:323–4, 400, 481; *LTH*, 1:179, 187; TH quotes: TH to HAH, 28, 29 June 1860, AD; 'So you': HAH to TH, 29 June 1860, AD; Jensen, *Huxley*, 79; *CCD*, 8:244–5; 265, 268, 270, 282; *Athenaeum*, 7 July 1860, 26; Ellegard, *Darwin*, 66. I assume Owen was responding to Huxley's comparison of apes and humans at the Royal Institution in 1858, but cf. Rupke, *Owen*, 272.

17. *Daily Telegraph*, 10 Apr. 1863, 4; 'finished': Gardiner, *Harcourt*, 1:247; 'to look', 'Vice': TH to HAH, 29 June 1860, AD; Gilley, 'Huxley–Wilberforce', 326–36; *LLL*, 2:335; Morrell and Thackray, *Gentlemen*, 395–6; *CCD*, 8:270; *LTH*, 1:181, 187; Wilberforce, *Pride*, 15–20; Desmond and Moore, *Darwin*, 348; Ellis, *Seven*. Huxley had openly castigated *Vestiges* only months before in 'Time and Life', 147.

18. TH to FD, 9 Sept. 1860, HP 15.115. Huxley was criticizing loose reports like the *Guardian*'s, which talked of the sad day 'when Professors lose their tempers and solemnly avow they would rather be descended from apes than Bishops': Ellegard, *Darwin*, 68. A. Wollaston, *Newton*, 119 for an eye-witness account that related the famous ape jibe to the Huxley–Owen clash on the preceding Thursday. Jensen, *Huxley*, 70–3, 76; Sedgwick, 'Natural History', 3; *LTH*, 1:183–4, 188; Lucas, 'Wilberforce,' 317, 327; Altholz, 'Huxley–Wilberforce', 315; Phelps and Cohen, 'Wilberforce–Huxley', 58–9; Sidgwick, 'Grandmother's Tale', 433; *LLL*, 2:335; *Athenaeum*, 14 July 1860, 65.

19. Wrangham, 'Wilberforce', 192; *CCD*, 8:270–1; 'position', TH to FD, 9 Sept. 1860, HP 15.115; Jensen, *Huxley*, 71–7; Gilley, 'Huxley–Wilberforce', 336–7; Lucas, 'Wilberforce', 323; Altholz, 'Huxley–Wilberforce', 315; Gould, 'Knight'; 'splendid': Gardiner, *Harcourt*, 1:247. Janet Browne reconstructs the Wilberforce-smashing legend in 'Darwin–Hooker Correspondence'.

20. TH to FD, 9 Sept. 1860, HP 15.115; 'slap': GR to TH, n.d., HP 25.150; *CCD*, 8:277, 280–1, 285, 306, 319; *LLL*, 2:335; *Athenaeum*, 7 July 1860, 19; Lucas, 'Wilberforce', 316; Himmelfarb, *Darwin*, 240; *LTH*, 1:188; Sidgwick, 'Grandmother's Tale', 434.

21. TH to JH, 27 Apr. 1861, HP 2.98; *LTH*, 1:191; GR to TH, n.d., 13 Apr. 1860, HP 25.142, 148, 150.

22. JH to TH, 4 Jan. 1860, HP 3.81; *LJH*, 1:414; *SM*, 2:471–2.

23. A. Thomson to TH, 24 May 1860, HM 2:118:104; di Gregorio, *Huxley*, 135–6; W. Sharpey to TH, 8 Nov. 1860, HM 2:118:116; Rolleston: HM 1.14.288–93; *CCD*, 8:171, 189; Gross, 'Hippocampus', 408.

24. G. Rorison to R. Owen, 25 Apr. 1860, BM(NH), OC 22.379; Rorison, 'Creative Week', 322; for more on this see Desmond, *Archetypes*, 79–80. Ellegard, *Darwin*, 294–5, 304.

25. Darwin's annotations on Wilberforce, 'Darwin's Origin', 239, 255, 259, Darwin Reprint Collection, R. 34, CUL; 'Article': JH to J. Murray, n.d., John Murray Archives; Paston, *At John Murray's*, 176.

26. *LJH*, 1:516; *CCD*, 8:294, 316, 516; Fawcett, 'Popular Exposition', 83. On the rector Henry Tristram's reconversion: Cohen, 'Three Notes', 598; A. Wollaston, *Newton*, 120–2.

27. JH to TH, [18 July 1860], HP 3.119; 'you': TH to JH, 17 July, 2 Aug., 1860, HP 2.67, 70; TH to P. L. Sclater, 16 Oct. 1860, APS; *CCD*, 8:294–6, 527; *LTH*, 1:209–10; *LLL*, 2:366; *LJH*, 1:413. At first Huxley really did want articles pro and con. He told the Oxford geologist John Phillips (20 Nov. 1860, OUM Loe/16) that if 'you or any one else with your knowledge & spirit, will favour us with the most anti Darwinian of articles, it shall receive the place of honour'.

28. *SM*, 2:446–7; *HM* 2:86–8 (Crossopterygians would come to be seen as the ancestors of the amphibians); 'more': TH to JH, 2 Aug. 1860, HP 2.70; *LTH*, 1:210, 215; *CCD*, 8:295; di Gregorio, *Huxley*, 73–4.

29. TH to FD, 9 Sept. 1860, HP 15.115; 'Honeymoon': TH to JH, [8 Aug. 1860], HP 2.74; 'deep', '99': TH to CK, 23 Sept. 1860, HP 19.176–7; *CE*, 2:59. Lightman, 'Pope Huxley', 150–2; Lightman, *Origins*, 7–10, 71ff.; *LLL*, 2:322–3; *LTH*, 1:212–13, 220; HS to TH, 11 Sept. 1860, HP 7.108; Harrison, 'Radicals,' 206; Turner, 'Victorian Scientific Naturalism', 334–9; Brown, *Metaphysical Society*, 139; Pevsner, *Buildings*, 328–9; Angela Darwin pers. comm.

30. TH to FD, 16 Sept. 1860, HP 15.119; *LTH*, 1:152, 213.

31. TH to CK, 23 Sept. 1860, HP 19.169–76; *LTH*, 1:151–2, 213, 217–22; 'up': HAH's Reminiscences, HP 31.92; 'stunned': JT to TH, 17 Sept. 1860, HP 1.32; *LJH*, 1:528; 'four': TH to FD, 16 Sept. 1860, HP 15.119; Huxley's Diary, HP 30.3 for 11 o'clock procession; grave: Angela Darwin pers comm.

32. CK to TH, 21 Sept. 1860, HP 19.162; 'Spinozaist': CK to TH, 16, 31 Oct. 1860, HP 19.193, 195.

33. TH to CK, 23 Sept., 4 Oct. 1860, HP 19.169, 191, 198; *LTH*, 1:217; Gilley and Loades, 'Huxley', 304.

34. *CCD*, 8:438, 475, 522–3, 527; 'coming': TH to E. P. Wright, 20 Nov. 1860, HP 29.102.

35. TH to CK, 4 Oct. 1860, HP 19.191, 198; *LCK*, 2:112–15; *LLL*, 2:336; 'useless': TH to CK, 23 Sept. 1860, HP 19.169; *LTH*, 1:217; 'Theology': CK to TH, 26 Sept. 1860, HP 19.180.

36. *LTH*, 1:214, 216, 222–3, 225; *LJH*, 1:536; *CCD*, 8:483; birth, travel: Huxley's Diary, HP 70.3; TH to JH, 19 Dec. 1860, HP 2.79; 'because': HAH's Reminiscences, HP 31.92. G. S. Jones, *Outcast London*, 45. It had been an emotionally turbulent year. Brother Jim had married Mary Anne Coleman after his first wife died.

37. JH to TH, n.d. HP 3.83; 'public': CL to TH, 5 Jan. 1860 [1861], HP 6.36; TH to S. Wilberforce, 3 Jan. 1861, HM 3:121.118; reply 30 Jan. [1861], HP 29.25; Blinderman, 'Oxford Debate', 126. 'What': CD to TH, 3 Jan. 1861, HP 5.155; 'mends': TH to JH, 3 Jan. 1861, HP 2.83; *LTH*, 1:224.

38. JH to TH, 4 Jan. 1861, HP 3.81; 'You': TH to JH, 3 Jan. 1861, HP 2.83; *LTH*, 1:223, 2:59.

39. TH to JH, 12 Feb. 1861. HP 2.91; also 6 Jan. 1861, HP 2.85; *LTH*, 1:224.

40. TH to HAH, 19 Mar. 1861, AD; 'suffering': E. Darwin to CD, [June 1861], DAR 210.10, CUL; 'dear': HAH to TH, 22 Mar. 1861, AD; 'House': CD to TH, 22 Feb. 1861, HP 5.157; Colp, *To Be an Invalid*, 69; *LLD*, 1:136; *MLD*, 1:460; Litchfield, *Darwin*, 2:176–7.

16 RESLAYING THE SLAIN

1. *CE*, 7:81; Cooper, *Immortality*, 15; Chilton, 'Geological Revelations'; Desmond, 'Artisan Resistance', 96, 100; Watts, 'Theological Theories'; *Reasoner*, 26 (1861), 62; R. D. N. , 'Place of Man'; 'Cook', 'My': TH to HAH, 'Friday' [15], 22 Mar. 1861, AD; *LTH*, 1:190; 'Rifle': Huxley's Diary, 13 Mar. 1861, HP 70.4.

2. *CE*, 7:79–81, 146, 153–5; Eng, 'Huxley's Understanding', 300; Desmond, *Archetypes*, 170; 'progress': Watts, 'Theological Theories', 134; 'absolute': TH to CK, 23 Sept. 1860, HP 19.169; 'cynics': TH to JH, 6 Jan. 1861, HP 2.85; *LTH*, 1:219, 224; Chilton, 'Theory'; Becker, *Scientific London*, 186; T. J. Parker, 'Huxley', 164. Secord, 'Geological Survey', 260–1; Geikie, *Memoir*, 276–7. Only workers could attend; they had to give their occupation on buying a ticket: J. P. A., 'Huxley', 2. According to this workers' source, the 'majority' at Huxley's lecture were freethinkers.

3. TH to HAH, [15], 19, 22 Mar., 1861; HAH to TH, 14, 20, 22 Mar, 1861, AD.

4. HAH to TH, 17 Apr. 1861, AD; CD to TH, 1 Apr. [1861], HP 5.162; *MLD*, 1:185. On du Chaillu and Owen: *LRO*, 2:115; J. Murray to R. Owen, BM(NH), OC 20.130–3. Owen, 'Gorilla', 395–6; Huxley, 'Man', 433. By now the argument had degenerated to Huxley's use of the word 'rudiment' to describe the ape's hippocampus. To Owen the idealist *philosophical anatomist* that was sloppy – a 'rudimentary organ' was a collapsed representation of the whole normal organ, like the human appendix; whereas Huxley the *transmutationist* meant the homological antecedent of the human hippocampus. Ideological differences cut to the very core of their neuro-anatomical language.

5. JH to TH, [18–27 Apr. 1861], HP 3.86; *MLD*, 1:185.

6. TH to JH, 18 Apr. 1861, HP 2.95; 'ill': HAH's Reminiscences, HP 31.92–5.

7. Egerton, 'Monkeyana'; TH to JH, 18 Apr. 1861, HP 2.95; Huxley, 'Man', 498; *LTH*, 1:191.

8. TH to JH, n.d., HP 2.100; *LTH*, 1:192; CD to TH, 22 May 1861, HP 5.164. Within weeks Huxley was to visit Egerton's country seat in Chester to examine his Devonian fish (Huxley's Diary, HP 70.4: 31 July 1861).

9. *CE*, 7:71–2; Du Chaillu meetings 4, 8, 18 Apr., 4 July 1861: Huxley's Diary, HP 70.4; *Punch*, 14 Dec. 1861; Ellegard, *Darwin*, 43, 295; 'The Gorilla and the Mbouve', *National Reformer*, 1 June 1861, 4; 'relieve': TH to JH, 18 Apr. 1861, HP 2.95; HAH's Reminiscences, HP 31.92–5; *LTH*, 1:225. Du Chaillu (to R. Owen, 19 Aug. 1864, BM(NH), OC 10.173) caught a live gorilla.

10. Owen, 'Gorilla', 395; Huxley, 'Man', 498; Desmond, *Archetypes*, 75; Blake, 'Huxley', 563–4; Rolleston, *Scientific Papers*, 1:21, 52; GR to [*illegible*], 1 Oct. 1861, Wellcome Institute, London, AL 325619; Carlyle: Huxley's Diary, HP 70.4.

11. HAH to TH, 17 Apr. 1861, AD; Huxley, *Evidence*, 118; TH to HAH, 16 Apr. 1861, AD; *LTH* 1:191–2; *MLD*, 1:185.

12. TH to HAH, 16 Apr. 1861, AD; A. Stanley to TH, [15 Apr. 1861], HP 26.217; Moore, *Religion*, 26, 40; JH to TH, 11 Apr. 1861, HP 3.89; TH to JH, 18 Apr. 1861, HP 2.95. Powell, in *Essays*, 139; Corsi, *Science*, 283–4; Gilley and Loades, 'Huxley', 289; *LLL*, 2:351.

13. J. Lubbock to TH, 28 Feb. 1861, HP 22.61; A. Stanley to TH, 25 Mar. 1861, HP 26.218; Moore, *Religion*, 425, 435–7; *LJH*, 1:514, 2:54–6; *MLD*, 2:266–7; 'Memorial', HP 22.63; Ellis, *Seven*, 62.

14. TH to JH, 27 Apr., n.d., HP 2.98–100; 'cut': JH to TH, n.d. [after 18 Apr. 1861], HP 3.86; *LTH*, 1:191, 225.

15. TH to E. P. Wright, 11 May 1861, HP 29.107; *LTH*, 1:210, 231, 235; 'only': TH to FD, n.d. [early 1862], HP 15.113; brewery: Angela Darwin pers. comm.

16. Bynum, 'Lyell's *Antiquity*', 161, 171; Grayson, *Establishment*, 120ff; Boylan, 'Controversy', 174. TH to CL, 26 June 1861, HP 30.35; *LLL*, 2:341, 344; *LTH*, 1:174; Desmond, *Archetypes*, 83–6.

17. TH to CL, 25 Jan. 1862, HP 30.38; *LTH*, 1:197; K. Fuhlrott to CL, 13 Nov. 1861, 2 Jan. 1862, HM 3:121:68; *CE*, 7:169, 182, 184; CL to TH, 4 July 1862, HP 6.63. *LHS*, 102; Grayson, *Establishment*, 212; Rudwick, *Scenes*, 168.

18. CL to TH, 10 Jan. 1862, HP 6.53; *SM*, 2:558; *CE*, 8:158; 'If': TH to CL, 25 Jan. 1862, APS, also HP 30.38; Jenny Lind: Huxley's Diary 70.4; *LTH*, 1:197, 231; 'First': HM 2:58:76; 'mere': TH to FD, n.d., HP 15.113.

19. TH to FD, [early 1862], HP 15.113; *LTH*, 1:192–5; *Witness*, 11, 14 Jan. 1862; 'I told': TH to JH, 16 Jan. 1862, HP 2.112; 'sinners': JH to TH, 20 Jan. 1862, HP 3.98; *LJH*, 2:25; Himmelfarb, *Darwin*, 216; R. W. Clark, *Huxleys*, 66.

20. E. W. Cooke to TH, 8 Feb. 1862, HP 12.314; *SM*, 2:509–11; 'Neanderthal': TH to CL, 25 Jan. 1862, APS, also HP 30.38; CL to TH, 26 Nov. 1861, 10 Jan. 1862, HP 6.40, 53; *LTH*, 1:197; *CE*, 7:164, 168, 178–81, 192, 204.

21. TH to JH, n.d. [May 1861], HP 2.102; Secord, 'Salter', 67–8; TH to RIM, 17 May 1862, HP 39.60–3; TH to G. G. Leveson-Gower, [13 June 1861], HP 30.56; Bibby, *Huxley*, 114; Bibby, 'Huxley and University Development', 111.

22. ZSL Minutes of Scientific Meetings, 6 (1857–68), ff.237, 239–41 (cf Owen's more negative *public* pronouncement: 'Characters of the Aye-Aye'); Huxley's spider monkey paper was read on 28 May 1861, not 11 June as stated in *SM*, 2:493: ff. 213–16. Gross, 'Hippocampus', 409–10 on its importance in distinguishing the calcarine sulcus. Wallace: ZSL Minutes of Council, f.462. Huxley and Wilberforce were elected VPs on 15 May 1861: f.381. They worked together on at least five occasions during their 1861–2 term.

23. Bunbury, *Memorials*, Middle Life, Vol.3, pp. 204, 335–7; *LLL*, 2:356; *LTH*, 1:204; *CE*, 8:288ff; 'reconstruct': TH to W. J. M. Rankine, 18 Jan. 1862, HP 9.291; L. Horner to TH, 12 June 1861, 27 Feb., 21 Mar., 1862, HP 18.231–4. Despite Huxley's harping on 'persistence', when an out-of-sequence specimen did turn up, such as O. C. Marsh's supposed Carboniferous 'ichthyosaur' (a reptile associated with much later deposits), Huxley routinely suspected that it was a misidentified labyrinthodont: TH to CL, 5 May 1862, APS, also HP 30.40; O. C. Marsh to CL, 16 May 1862, HP 22.170.

24. CD to TH, 10 May 1862, HP 5.171; *LTH*, 1:205; *MLD*, 2:234; Desmond, *Archetypes*, 85–8; Lyons, 'Huxley', 556; *SM*, 2:530; *LLL*, 2:356. He went to Edinburgh looking for the fossil fish *Rhizodus* (on which he was working: Diary, HP 70.5; TH to W. J. M. Rankine, 18 Jan.–9 Dec. 1862, HP 9.291–

304) and ended up naming two new amphibians *Loxomma* and *Pholidogaster*.

25. Huxley's Diary, HP 70.5; *CE*, 7:147; TH to CL, 5 May 1862, HP 30.40; *LTH*, 1:199; *MLD*, 1:237.

26. *CE*, 7:204, 208; 'was': CK to TH, 28 Feb. 1862, HP 19.203; 18 July 1862, HP 19.205; Bowler, *Theories*, 65–6.

27. TH to E. P. Wright, [Feb. 1862], HP 29.111; Huxley's Diary, HP 70.5.

28. W. H. Flower, 'Introductory Lecture', 196, 199; Cornish, *Flower*, 43–6, 92–3; W. H. Flower, *Essays*, 43–7, 51, 133–4; 'Was': GR to TH, 1 Jan. 1865, HP 25.167.

29. Rolleston, *Scientific Papers*, 56, 61; Cornish, *Flower*, 100; *LTH*, 1:249; Desmond, *Archetypes*, 52–5.

30. W. H. Flower to TH, 11 July 1862, HP 16.117; *LTH*, 1:235–6; HM 2:58:15, 62; 2:97; *SM*, 2:546.

31. TH to CL, 17 Aug. 1862, HP 30.41; L. Playfair to TH, 29 Mar. 1861, HP 24.132; minutes: HP 43.3–49; *LTH*, 1:198, 201, 234; Huxley's Diary, HP 70.5.

32. TH to FD, 11 Oct. 1862, HP 15.123; Blake, 'Huxley', 563; Huxley, *Evidence*, 113–18.

33. CL to TH, 11 Oct. 1862, HP 6.76; CK to TH, 4 Aug. 1862, HP 19.207; *LTH*, 1:198; Ellegard, *Darwin*, 71–3. Flower went on to describe dissections of 16 ape and monkey brains at the Royal Society, using Huxley's terminology (e.g. of the calcarine sulcus): Gross, 'Hippocampus', 410; TH to W. Flower, 29 Aug. 1862, APS. A. Wollaston, *Newton*, 122–3, on Owen's indifference to the refutations. For a good account of the cerebral debate sympathetic to Owen, see Rupke, *Owen*, chaps 6–7.

34. Rupke, *Owen*, 295.

35. TH to FD, 11 Oct. 1862, HP 15.123; CL to TH, 9 Aug., [Oct.], 1862, HP 6.66, 70; TH to CL, 17 Aug. 1862, APS, also HP 30.41; *LTH*, 1:200; *LJH*, 2:32. Huxley also showed the proofs to Sir William Lawrence, who admitted their truth but advised him against publication to protect his reputation. Lawrence should have known: 40 years earlier, during the reactionary Regency, he had been accused of blasphemy and humiliated for his materialist *Lectures on Man*, but times were very different now: Agnosco, 'Huxley'; Desmond, *Politics*, 117–20.

36. TH to W. Sharpey, 13, 16 Nov. 1862, Sharpey Corres. MS. Add 227, Nos. 122, 124, University College London; E. Sabine to W. Sharpey, ibid., No. 121, UCL; Sharpey, 'Address'.

37. Bunbury, *Memorials*, Middle Life, Vol. 3, 276–7; 'And yet': HAH's Reminiscences, HP 62.1; Ellegard, *Darwin*, 51; Dyster, 'Evidence', 234.

38. TH to JH, n.d., HP 2.125; *LTH*, 1:206–7, 245; English, 'Hardwicke', 29–31, 35; Sheets-Pyenson, 'Popular Science', 567–9; piracy: Desmond, *Politics*, 163, 231, 412; 'confirming': J. P. A., 'Huxley', 2; Laurent, 'Science', 596. Huxley, *On Our Knowledge*, 51; Huxley's Diary, HP 70.5; Syllabus: HM 2.58.9; 'spirited': *British Controversialist*, 9 (1863), 300.

39. CL to TH, 23 Jan. 1863, HP 6.78; *LTH*, 1:207–8; CD to TH, 7 Dec. 1862, HP 5.179; *LLD*, 3:3; *MLD*, 1:215, 229; Huxley, *On Our Knowledge*, 126–30, cf. *CE*, 2:439–44; 'far', 'Professor Huxley's Lectures to Working Men', *Reader*, 1 (1863), 99–101; *Am. J. Sci.*, 36 (1863), 312 for a September 1863 listing of Appleton's edition.

17 MAN'S PLACE

1. CD to TH, 18, 26 Feb. 1863, HP 5.173, 191; *LTH*, 1:204; *MLD*, 1:238; *LJH*, 2:34; Himmelfarb, *Darwin*, 209; di Gregorio, *Huxley*, 153–4; Straus, 'Huxley's *Evidence*'; 'Evidence as to Man's Place in Nature', *Athenaeum*, 28 Feb. 1863, 287. Haight, *Eliot Letters*, 4:11. Industrial readers: Lyell's evidence before the Public Schools' Commission, in Tyndall *et al.*, *Culture*, 461; depression: CL to TH, 9 Sept., 11 Oct. 1862, HP 6.72, 76.

2. Watts, 'Man's Origin'; 'Man's Place in Nature', *National Reformer*, 14 Mar. 1863; 'best': TH to FD, 12 Mar. 1863, HP 15.125; Dyster, 'Evidence'; Torr, *Marx*, 141; Draper, *Marx*, 116.

3. R. Godwin-Austen to TH, 30 Mar. 1863, HP 10.183; 'astonished': TH to FD, 12 Mar. 1863, HP 15.125. *Athenaeum*, 28 Feb. 1863, 287–8; *LTH*, 1:201–3; Ellegard, *Darwin*, 165; GR to TH, 20 Mar. 1863, HP 25.163; 'find': H. Acland to TH, 22 Nov. 1863, HP 10.8; Moore, *Post-Darwinian Controversies*, 94.

4. R. King to TH, 8 July 1863, HP 19.155; casts: GR to TH, 20 Mar. 1863, HP 25.163, 159; G. Grote to TH, 16 June 1862, HP 17.152; Reeve: TH to FD, 22 Mar. 1864, HP 15.127; royals: J. Clark to TH, 25 Mar. 1863, HP 12.209.

5. CL to TH, 9 Aug. 1862, HP 6.66; Bartholomew, 'Lyell', 296.

6. 'Evidence as to Man's Place in Nature', *Athenaeum*, 28 Feb. 1863, 287–8.

7. Morris, *Heaven's Command*, 323–8.

8. T. Oldham to TH, 8 Apr. 1863, HP 23.236. Colenso presumably sat Huxley's first Hunterian lectures, on classification (17 Feb.–28 Mar. 1863: HM 2.58.11–37; Huxley, *Lectures*, 85, 100–1); Winsor, 'Impact', 72. By now Huxley had given the sea squirts primary status, and split his 'Annulosa' into echinoderms and arthropods. Coleman, 'Morphology', 155–60 on the break-up of typal divisions in this period.

9. J. W. Colenso to TH, 28 Mar. 1865, HP 12.274; GR to TH, 20 Mar. 1863, HP 25.163. Visits: Huxley's Diary, HP 70.6 (15 Feb., 18 June 1863). *Telegraph*, 10 Apr. 1863, 4. Huxley brought Colenso to the Athenaeum Club and forced a furious Lord Overstone to resign from the Visitors Committee: TH to S. J. Loyd, 12 Oct. 1864, HP 22.47–51; CD to TH, 22 May [1864], HP 5.174; *LLL*, 2:360.

10. 'Report of a Sad Case', HP 79.(6); 'Professors Huxley and Owen in the Police Court', *National Reformer*, 9 May 1863, 5. Kingsley's *Water Babies*, 172–3, parodied the 'hippopotamus major' debate for children.

11. R. Wagner to TH, 4 Jan. 1863, HP 28.88; R. Wagner to R. Owen, 30 Nov. 1860, BM(NH) OC 26.12; Wagner, 'Upon the Structure'; Gregory, *Scientific Materialism*, 32, 44; Dana, 'Evidence', 452; *MLD*, 1:236.

12. W. C. Thomson to TH, 26 Nov. 1863, HP 27.332; Melbourne *Argus* clipping, 'The Gorilla on its last legs', HP 40.249, also 40.251; C. S. Wood to TH, 24 Feb. 1864, HP 29.86; Butcher, 'Gorilla Warfare', 157, 159, 164. Mozley, 'Evolution', 422, 427 on old Macleay's view: he would only back Huxley's classification in so far as man was considered '*materially*'.

13. C. Vogt to TH, 23 Mar. 1863, HP 28.77; Vogt, *Lectures*, 378; 'contemptuous', *Reader*, 1 (1863), 99; Kelly, *Descent*, chap. 2.

14. L. Büchner to TH, 6 July 1863, HP 11.179; Montgomery, 'Germany', 82ff;

Gregory, *Scientific Materialism*, chaps 3, 5. The translation appeared as *Zeugnisse für die Stellung des Menchen in der Natur* (Braunschweig, Vieweg & Sohn, 1863).

15. Todes, 'Kovalevskii', 104–5; Todes, *Darwin*; Vucinich, 'Russia', 228, 235–6, 245–6; Vucinich, *Darwin*; Rogers, 'Reception', 496, 501–2; Bibby, *Huxley*, 101.

16. JT to HAH, n.d., 'Monday night', AD; Barton, 'Tyndall', 129–32; *LTH*, 1:231.

17. TH to CK, 30 Apr., 22 May 1863, HP 19.212, 229; *LTH*, 1:239, 242–3.

18. *CCD*, 6:184; Wilson, *Lyell's Journals*, 57–8, 94–8; Blake, 'Man', 153; E. Richards, 'Moral Anatomy', 376, 388–402, 410–19; E. Richards, 'Huxley', 264–6; Lorimer, 'Theoretical Racism', 412; Lorimer, *Colour*, 138, 143; Stocking, 'What's', 376–9; Rainger, 'Race', 60–4; Huxley, 'Negro's Place', 335; Mill, 'Mill on the Negro'; Paradis, *Huxley*, 64. According to 'Professor Huxley and the Anthropologists', *National Reformer*, 12 Mar. 1864, Huxley was offered the Presidency of the Anthropological Society in 1863 and declined it.

19. Blake, 'Huxley', 566–9; di Gregorio, *Huxley*, 154–5; d'Holbach's *System of Nature* had just been reissued: *National Reformer*, 2 Jan. 1864, 6. TH to C. C. Blake, 2 May 1863, HP 11.17; *LTH*, 1:274; GR to TH, n.d., HP 25.159.

20. E. Richards, 'Moral Anatomy', 421; E. Richards, 'Huxley', 262, 266ff; Stocking, 'What's', 375–9; Stocking, *Victorian Anthropology*, 248–56.

21. *LTH*, 1:210, 238, 245–6, 256n; HM 2:58:38; HM 2:58:10, 38–53; nights: HM 2:58:96; TH to E. P. Wright, 31 Dec. 1863, HP 29.122; 'appeal': TH to JH, 21 July 1863, HP 2.120; Huxley and Hawkins, *Elementary Atlas*.

22. TH to JH, 18 Aug. 1863, HP 2.123; 'been': TH to ES, 27 Mar. 1858, HP 31.24; Huxley's Diary HP 70.6 (earnings, 70.5); Clark, *Huxleys*, 73–4; Angela Darwin, pers. comm.; TH to the father of a boy engaged to Katy Huxley, 3 July 1874, HP 9.253; *LTH*, 1:248, 250. George died on 1 Aug. 1863.

23. *LTH*, 1:236, 244; Cornish, *Flower*, 75–6; Flower, 'Reminiscences', 284; HM 2:58:58, 63; 2:119; 1:14:166.

24. HAH to ES, 7 Mar. 1875, AD; 'Had': HAH to ES, 14 Aug. 1881, AD; 'eaten': TH to FD, 22 Mar. 1864, HP 15.127; *LLL*, 2:366; *LTH*, 1:202, 251; 'I wish', CD to TH, 5 Nov. [1864], HP 5.207; *LLD*, 3:3.

25. E. L. Youmans to TH, 9 Apr. 1864, HP 29.256; *LTH*, 1:247.

26. Lorimer, *Colour*, 168, also 12, 14, 55, 73, 76, 81, 107, 118, 124, 165, 171; *LHS*, 106–7; *LLL*, 2:360; *LLD*, 3:11.

27. *LTH*, 1:251; Angela Darwin, pers. comm.; McPherson, *Battle Cry*, chap. 22.

28. Taylor, *Huxley*, 8–13 (HM 1:16:88); Huxley, 'Professor Huxley's Lectures', 267–8; Huxley, 'Negro's Place'; TH to FD, 22 Mar. 1864, HP 15.127; GR to TH, 1 Jan. 1865, HP 25.167: Lorimer, *Colour*, 48, 140, 149; Craft: 'Science and Slavery', *National Reformer*, 9 Apr. 1864 (also 12 Mar. 1864 and 19 Sept. 1863).

The Colonel who commanded the 1st South Carolina Volunteers, the first regiment of freed slaves, wrote to confirm Huxley's observations that black ankles were normal. Not only could his troops stand to attention, but they fought like the best and earned their citizenship: T. W. Higginson to TH, 23 June 1867, HP 18.167; McPherson, *Battle Cry*, 564–5.

29. King, 'Reputed', 92, 96; Ellegard, *Darwin*, 165; *LLL*, 2:382–3; Stafford, *Scientist*, 148; 'midway': HM 1:14:170.

30. HP 31.158; Busk, 'Ancient Human'; *SM*, 2:589; Argyll, *Primeval Man*, 73; Gillespie, 'Duke', 44ff.

31. Best, *Mid-Victorian Britain*, 27; fisheries: V. H. Hobart to TH, 19 Sept. 1864, HP 18.184; TH to P. Wright, 3 Aug. 1864, HP 29.124; R. J. Coward to TH, 6 Apr. 1864, HP 12.324; HP 43.69ff.

32. After the ape-brain debate with Owen, Huxley had founded a 'Thorough Club' in 1862, for 'the propagation of common honesty', which pushed profundity towards the glib. It was a broad evolutionary coalition, and included Kingsley on one side and those cosmic theorists Spencer, Lewes and Chambers on the other. The club quickly withered. Haight, *Eliot Letters*, 4:66; *LTH*, 1:199; Huxley's Diary, 7 Oct. 1862, HP 70.5; HP 31.120–1.

33. Public Schools' Commission extracts in Tyndall *et al.*, *Culture*, 461; *LLL*, 2:359; Sir John Wrottesley consulted Huxley (23 May 1865, HP 29.250) as the Public Schools Bill passed through the Lords; 'Note of conversation with [Henry] Cole & [John] Donnelly', 30 Nov. 1864, HP 42.194; TH to JH, 6 Oct. 1864, HP 2.127; *LTH* 1:237, 254; 'concerns': JH to TH, 7 Feb. 1864, HP 3.105; 'have': TH to JH, 4 Dec. 1862, HP 2.114.

34. Brock and MacLeod, 'Scientists' Declaration', 41, 48, 50; Ellis, *Seven*, 109–11, chap. 4; Jensen, *Huxley*, 143; Huxley, 'Tyndall', 6.

35. Barton, 'Influential Set', 54, 58, 61–4; MacLeod, 'X Club'; *LJH*, 1:542; Jensen, *Huxley*, 143, 150; Spencer, *Autobiography*, 2:115–16; Huxley, 'Tyndall', 10; TH to GR, n.d., HP 25.180.

36. *LLL*, 2:369, 385; Geikie, *Memoir*, 284; *LJT*, 119, 125; Cornish, *Flower*, 79–87; Flower, 'Reminiscences', 281; A. P. Stanley to TH, 29 Nov. 1869, HP 26.226.

37. CD to TH, 5 Nov. 1864, HP 5.207; *LLD*, 3:5, 29; *LTH*, 1:254–5; *MLD*, 1:252–6, 258; MacLeod, 'Of Medals', 83; Bartholomew, 'Award'; Desmond and Moore, *Darwin*, 526; *LJH*, 2:75–6; *LLL*, 2:384; TH to JH, 3 Dec. 1864, HP 2.129; Barton, 'Influential', 61; *LJT*, 92.

38. TH to FD, 26 Jan. 1865, HP 15.129; Pearson, *Life*, 2:67–8; Roos, 'Aims', 162–5; Meadows, *Science*, 17–22; *LHS*, 117; Spencer, *Autobiography*, 2:118–20; 'heart', 'pig': T. Hughes to TH, 22 Nov. 1864, HP 18.326.

39. TH to FD, 26 Jan. 1865, HP 15.129; 'matured': *Times*, 25 May 1864, 8–9; Ellegard, *Darwin*, 168; *LLL*, 2:386; Chadwick, *Secularization*, 111; J. Moore, *Post-Darwinian Controversies*, 25; Ridley, *Palmerston*, 770; 'disgrace': TH to FD, 27 Feb. 1858, HP 15.98; Bradford, *Disraeli*, 254–5.

40. Huxley, 'Science and "Church Policy"'; Barton, 'Evolution', 263–4; Barton, 'X Club', 225; Moore, 'Deconstructing Darwinism', 376–7; Lightman, 'Pope Huxley', 158–9; *LHS*, 118; 'encyclical': TH to FD, 26 Jan. 1865, HP 15.129; cf. Roos, 'Aims', 164. Huxley's diatribe was more characteristic of overt secularist papers. Compare it to the hit at Wiseman in 'Science, and the Church of Rome', *National Reformer*, 25 June 1865.

41. GR to TH, 4 Jan. 1865, HP 25.171, 178; *LTH*, 1:265; *LJT*, 115.

42. TH to GR, n.d., HP 25.180.

43. CD to TH, 4 Jan [1865], HP 5.211.

44. TH to FD, 26 Jan. 1865, HP 15.129; 'hot': TH to HAH, 16 Apr. 1861, AD; HAH to TH, 17 Apr. 1861, AD; *LTH*, 1:265.

45. W. B. Clarke to TH, 6 May 1864, HM 1:16:181; C. Aplan to TH, 16 Dec. 1864 HM 1:16:143; E. Brown to TH, 10 Apr. 1865, HM 1:16:188–94; W. Turner to TH, 16 Nov. 1865, HM 1:16:32. Anthropometric studies: HM 2:105:50.

46. J. P. A., 'Huxley', 2; Bibby, *Huxley*, 100; Clark, *Huxleys*, 44; course: *LTH*, 1:264–5; J. Williams to TH, 5 Dec. 1864, HM 3:121:120; HM 2:102:1–13.

47. GR to TH, 1 Jan. 1865, HP 25.167.

48. Lewis, 'Japanese Connexion'; Lewis, 'Black'; Desmond, *Politics*, 36n; Lorimer, *Colour*, 56–7, 60, 68, 101, 113–14; *National Reformer*, 12 Mar. 1864; collection: Huxley, 'Government'.

49. TH to HAH, 17 Apr. 1861, AD.

50. *CE*, 3:66–7, 73; Harte, *University*, 114–15; E. Richards, 'Huxley', 260ff; Desmond, *Archetypes*, 159; Paradis, *Huxley*, 64–5.

18 BIRDS, DINOSAURS & BOOMING GUNS

1. MF to TH, 20 Aug. 1866, HP 4.157; Geison, *Foster*, chap. 3; Huxley, 'How to Become'; Mivart, 'Reminiscences', 990–1; Parker, 'Huxley', 161–5; Osborn, 'Memorial', 46; Fiske, 'Reminiscences'; A. Wollaston, *Newton*, 46; Block, 'Huxley's Rhetoric', 373; Gardner, 'Huxley Essay', 177.

2. St G. Mivart to CD, 22 Apr. 1870, 10 Jan. 1872, DAR 171, CUL; Mivart, 'Reminiscences', 985–8, 993; Gruber, *Conscience*, chaps 1–3; *CE*, 3:120; Howes, 'Mivart', 100.

3. E. H. Giglioli to TH, 4 Apr. 1865, HP 17.44; Corsi, 'Recent', 714; 'opposed': J. Young to TH, 14 July 1867, HP 29.271; 'tooth': TH to E. P. Wright, 30 Oct., 2 Nov. 1863, HP 29.116–18.

4. Bynum, 'Lyell's *Antiquity*', 178, 182; *LLD*, 3:39; *LJH*, 2:53; 'like': TH to JH, 12 June 1865, HP 2.131; *LJT*, 115; Harte, *University*, 114–15, 128.

5. *LLD*, 3:40; *LJH*, 2:47–8, 71; Hutchinson, *Life*, 1:74.

6. Tylor, *Primitive Culture*, 1:6; Burrow, *Evolution*, 229–30, 254–6; Lorimer, *Colour*, 140–60; Stocking, *Race*, 97–8; *LLD*, 3:40; 'really': JH to TH, 14 July 1865, HP 3.107; 'just': TH to JH, 15 July 1865, HP 2.134.

7. MF to TH, 1 July 1865, HP 4.151; 'out': TH to E. P. Wright, 4 Jan. 1866, HP 29.175.

8. TH to E. P. Wright, 4 Jan. 1866, HP 29.175; TH to CD, 4 Oct. [1865], HP 5.223; 'bound': MF to TH, 23 Oct. 1865, HP 4.153; TH to J. N. Lockyer, 22 Aug. 1865, HP 21.242; Roos, 'Aims', n16; Meadows, *Science*, 21–2; Pearson, *Life*, 2:69.

9. J. Lubbock to TH, 2 Aug. 1866, HP 22.65; 'Turkey': GR to TH, 1 Jan. 1865, HP 25.167; JH to TH, n.d., HP 3.85; 'scandal': TH to JH, 24 Jan. 1868, HP 2.140; '700': J. Crawfurd to TH, 6 Oct. 1866, HP 12.335; E. Richards, 'Moral Anatomy', 422–30; E. Richards, 'Huxley', 264–7; Stocking, 'What's', 380–5; Green, 'Huxley', 692; *CE*, 7:209; Lorimer, 'Theoretical', 412; di Gregorio, *Huxley*, 160ff. TH's 1865 ethnology notes, HM 1:16:119–41; HM 2:103.

   For Wallace's attempt to produce a mediating science see: Wallace, *Contributions*, 303–31; Durant, 'Scientific Naturalism', 40–5; R. Smith, 'Wallace', 179–80; Kottler, 'Darwin', 388; Schwartz, 'Darwin', 283–4.

10. A. R. Wallace to TH, 26 Feb. 1864, HP 28.91; *LTH*, 1:324; E. Richards, 'Huxley', 262–4.

11. *English Leader*, 13 Jan. 1866; *CE*, 1:37–40; TH to FD, 4 Jan. 1866, HP 15.131; flyer: HP 31.189; Draper, *Chronicle*, 120; Turner, *Between Science*, 18.

12. TH to JT, [Nov. 1867], HP 9.35; G. H. Lewes to TH, n.d., HP 21.220; Haight, *Eliot Letters*, 4:192, 214, 8:360; Jenny Marx, 29 Jan. 1866, in Lefebvre, *Marx–Engels* (Simon Schaffer's translation). Paradis, *Huxley*, 76–8 on the religious awe of infinite space and life's eternal flux which gave this lecture its impact.

13. Owen, 'The Reign of Law', Autograph Manuscripts of Sir R. Owen, BM(NH), Owen Coll. 59.1–2, 17; Huxley, 'To the Editor'; *English Leader*, 3, 24 Feb. 1866; *LTH*, 119.

14. CL to TH, 28 Nov. 1865, HP 6.192; E. P. Wright to TH, 1865–6, HP 29.128–237; HM 2:33:1–14, 2:89; W. Brownrigg to TH, 29 Nov. 1865, HP 11.125; *SM*, 3:180; *LTH*, 1:263.

15. Bibby, *Huxley*, 196; *LTH*, 1:275; Irvine, *Apes*, 242; W. C. H. Peters to TH, 3 July 1865, HP 24.109; *LJT*, 120–1.

16. *LTH*, 1:276; 1866 Hunterian Lectures HM 2:58:109; fellows: *English Leader*, 5 May 1866; 'What': G. M. Humphrey to TH, 22 Mar. 1866, HP 18.332; *SM*, 3:60–77; A. Wollaston, *Newton*, 133–5; O'Connor, *Founders*, chap. 11; *CE*, 3:79.

17. F. Burr to RIM, 19 Sept. 1866, HM 3:121:29; *SM*, 3:326–7; *LTH*, 1:276, 312; on *Toxodon*: CD to TH, 4 July [1866], HP 5.231. E. Lynn to TH, 11 Nov. 1868, HP 21.223; RI course on ethnology 3 May–9 June 1866, HM 1:16:171, 2:58:116, 2:60:1–93, 2:102:14; HP 33.74.

18. TH to ES, 18 Mar. 1866, HP 31.34; *LTH*, 1:273; Angela Darwin, pers. comm.

19. TH to ES, 18 Mar., 1 Dec. 1866, HP 31.34–6; *Times* notice, HP 9.243; Watterson, *Marse*, 1:97–9; Angela Darwin, pers. comm.; *LTH*, 1:273.

20. F. Burr to RIM, 19 Sept. 1866, HM 3:121:29; 'you': H. M. Hozier to TH, 20 June 1866, HP 18.314; V. Carus to TH, 15 Nov. 1866, HP 12.140.

21. The spread of liberalism gave the British a new European identity. The free-trader Richard Cobden even set up an International Education Society, planning parallel schools in Bonn, Paris and a London one in Isleworth. Modern languages and a liberal education were to ready the sons of professionals and businessmen for a new European role. Huxley and Tyndall became Governors of the London school in 1865 and planned its science teaching: HP 1.55, 1.57, 22.223–5, 34.35, 43.25, draft programme, 42.37, 42.46, 42.50, 42.51; *LTH*, 1:269–70, 308; Bibby, *Huxley*, 168–72.

22. *LTH*, 1:266–7; Weindling, 'Haeckel', 314, 317; E. Haeckel to TH, 17 May 1865, HP 17.170.

23. Gasman, *Scientific Origins*, 17–18; Weindling, 'Darwinism', 689, 694; Weindling, 'Haeckel', 311, 318–20; Bölsche, *Haeckel*, 133ff, 150; Kelly, *Descent*, 22; Coleman, 'Morphology', 150; Haeckel, *Generelle Morphologie*, 2:451; Haeckel, *History*, 1:1–2, 295; S. Gould, *Ontogeny*, 78, 170; E. Haeckel to TH, 4 May 1866, HP 17.174.

24. Marsh, 'Huxley', 182.

25. Grove, *Correlation*, 346; Ellegard, *Darwin*, 78–9; *LJH*, 2:102.

26. F. W. Farrar to TH, 24 Sept., 1 Oct. [1866], HP 16.21–3; HP 42.1–28; W. Smith to TH, 4 Dec. 1866, HP 26.129; *MLD*, 2:43; *LTH*, 1:277.

27. J. Hunt to TH, 6, 12 Oct. 1866, HP 18.334, 340; TH to J. Hunt, 9 Oct.

1866, HP 18.335; Stocking, 'What's', 382; E. Richards, 'Moral Anatomy', 426; J. Lubbock to TH, 2 Aug. 1866, HP 22.65; A. R. Wallace to TH, n.d., HP 28.93.

28. TH to CK, 8 Nov. 1866, HP 19.243; *LTH*, 1:279–82; HP 8.47; Jamaica Committee to JT, 12 Oct. 1866, HP 8.315; HP 8.331; Morris, *Heaven's Command*, 303–17; di Gregorio, *Huxley*, 172–3; Paradis, *Huxley*, 63–4; Lorimer, *Colour*, chap. 9; Bolt, *Victorian Attitudes*, chap. 3; Semmel, *Eyre*, chaps 4–5.

29. JH to JT, 13 Nov. 1866, HP 8.318 (also 'sight'); CK to TH, 6 Nov. 1866, HP 19.241; *LCK*, 1:3; '*naturally*': F. W. Farrar to JT, n.d., HP 8.342; HP 8.334; 'Professor Tyndall's Reply to the Jamaica Committee', HP 8.316; JT to HAH, n.d., AD; Spencer, *Autobiography*, 2:139; *LTH*, 1:279; *LJT*, 122–3; Huxley, 'Tyndall', 4.

30. Lorimer, *Colour*, 150–9, 195; Hunt's attack: W. B. Hodgson to TH, 3 Nov. 1866, HP 18.201; F. W. Chesson to TH, 20 Oct. 1866, HP 12.184. January 1867 Mechanics' Institute talks: *LTH*, 1:287; HM 1:16:142; 2:59:10; W. B. Carpenter to TH, 20 June 1866, HP 12.100; 'personally': TH to JH, 24 Jan. 1868, HP 2.140. M. Moore to TH, 9 Aug. 1867, HP 23.3, possibly having read of Huxley's May–June 1867 Fullerian course on Ethnology: HM 2:59:32; HP 33.73; di Gregorio, *Huxley*, 170ff. Stocking, *Victorian Anthropology*, 62 on 'Anglo-Saxon' self-imagery.

31. TH to ES, 1 Dec. 1866, HP 31.36; Briggs, *Age*, 492–7; 'denouncing' quoted in Collie, *Huxley*, 89 n59.

32. CD to TH, 12 Jan., 21 Feb. 1867, HP 5.235, 260; *MLD*, 1:281; HAH to ES, 20 Sept. 1869, HP 31.40; Becker, *Scientific London*, 248; Bibby, *Huxley*, 114–15.

33. Bölsche, *Haeckel*, 242; *MLD*, 2:350; Huxley, 'Natural History', 13–14; *LTH*, 1:289; E. Haeckel to TH, 12 May, 28 June 1867, HP 17.177–82; Haeckel, 'Huxley', 464–6.

34. Huxley, 'Natural History', 41; *LTH*, 1:288–90; 'German': CD to TH, 10 June 1868, HP 5.239, also 5.196; *MLD*, 1:274; Coleman, 'Morphology', 164, 171–3; di Gregorio, 'Dinosaur', 398, 415–16.

35. Benson, 'Naples', 332–3; *LTH*, 1:290–1; Groeben, *Darwin*, 10, 22; TH to A. Dohrn, 9, 22 Sept. 1867, HP 13.156–9.

36. *MLD*, 1:277–8; *LTH*, 1:288, 305; *LLD*, 3:69; Haeckel, *Generelle Morphologie*, 1:90, 173–4n; E. Haeckel to TH, 11 Aug., 21 Sept. 1868, 28 Feb. 1869, HP 17.187, 198. Nyhart, 'Disciplinary Breakdown', 374.

37. Huxley, 'Natural History', 40–2; Desmond, *Archetypes*, 89; *LLD*, 3:105.

38. *SM*, 3:238, 305; Workingmen's Lectures on 'Birds and Reptiles', 29 Oct.–3 Dec. 1866, HM 2:59:8.

39. *SM*, 3:241; cf. Seeley, 'Epitome', 326; Padian, 'Pterosaurs'; Hull, *Science*, 114, 348. (Huxley was in touch with Seeley, who sent him his book *Ornithosauria*: e.g. TH to H. Seeley, 20 July 1866, 27 Apr. 1870, APS.) Huxley's 1867 RCS syllabus HM 2:59:16. He had first mooted the 'Sauropsida' at the College of Surgeons in 1863–4: HM 2:58:94; Huxley, *Lectures*, 69; and his pupils were already using the word in 1864: W. Parker, 'Remarks', 57. For Owen's reasoning on the relationship of reptiles to *mammals*, based on his dinosaur and mammal-like reptile studies: Desmond, *Archetypes*, 119, 197–9, 246 n53–4.

40. *SM*, 3:238; interleaved copies: HM 2:36, HM 2:40; *LTH*, 1:285, 290. On

the response to his re-classification of birds, drawing in the clawed-wing hoatzins and mound-incubating megapodes, see HP 15.225, 22.237–9, 23.212–14, 24.35–7; A. Wollaston, *Newton*, 215.

41. HM 2:40:33, 43, 47; also volumes 41–3. The immediate cause of these avian classificatory trees, the first dated 22 Jan. 1868, was the need to respond to Newton's criticisms in the *Ibis*. (Newton, a Darwinian, liked to stir up controversy to keep his paper lively: A. Wollaston, *Newton*, 66.)

42. SM, 3:296, 365; Huxley, 'Reply', 361; interleaved 'Reply', HM 2:40:48; Allen, *Naturalist*, 190; O'Connor, *Founders*, 165; di Gregorio, *Huxley*, 79ff.

43. TH to RIM, 2 Oct. 1866, HM 2:33:15; *LTH*, 1:275; SM, 3:90, 198; G. Gordon to TH, 2 Nov. 1867, HM 2:59:45; 'incubus': TH to P. Sclater, 10 June 1867, ZSL.

44. Desmond, 'Owen's Response'; Desmond, *Archetypes*, 115–20; Padian, 'Pterosaurs'.

45. HM 2:93:70; SM, 3:465.

46. CCD, 7:409, 532. Only five years earlier, before Huxley had assumed his partisan role, he praised Phillips precisely for his avoidance 'of party prejudice': *West. Rev.*, 64 (1855), 565.

47. TH to MF, 26 Nov. 1867, HP 4.5; 'like': TH to A. Dohrn, 15 Jan. 1868, HP 13.160; *LTH*, 1:304.

48. TH to J. Phillips, 31 Dec. 1867, OUM 29.

49. Joan Evans, *Time*, 115–16; John Evans, 'Portions', 418–19; Mackie, 'Aeronauts'; Woodward, 'Feathered Fossil'; Owen, 'Archaeopteryx'; CL to TH, [Oct. 1862], HP 6.70; Rupke, *Owen*, 71–5.

50. SM, 3:345; Huxley, *American Addresses*, 241; notes on *Archaeopteryx*, 25 Dec. 1867, HM 2:40:7; Desmond, *Archetypes*, 124–30.

51. TH to J. Phillips, 28 Apr. 1870, OUM 29.1; Phillips, 'Cetiosaurus'; Phillips, *Geology*, 254–94; SM, 3:241, 311; Huxley, *American Addresses*, 65.

52. Huxley, 'On the Animals'; SM, 3:303, 366; HM 2:59:48; Di Gregorio, 'Dinosaur', 407–8. Huxley did not announce it that night, but he had another ancestor. Christmas 1867 in the British Museum had been celebrated with a turkey-sized dinosaur. Owen's so-called baby *Iguanodon* from the Isle of Wight was, Huxley realized, an adult of an unknown species, which he called *Hypsilophodon*. With an even more avian hip, it brought dinosaurs 'a further step towards the bird': SM, 3:482; Desmond, *Archetypes*, 144; HM 2:93:31; TH to J. Phillips, 31 Dec. 1867, OUM 29; SM, 3:458; TH to CL, 23 July 1868, APS, also HP 30.45.

53. J. Phillips to TH, 14 Oct., 19 Nov. 1869, HP 24.119, 121; SM, 3:466–70, 476–80. Huxley went on to amend dinosaur classification, rubber-stamping his ornithic product by uniting *Compsognathus* with the big dinosaurs in a new group, the 'Ornithoscelida' ('bird-leg'): SM, 3:487. Cf. Owen, *Monograph on the Fossil Reptilia*, 87–93. E. D. Cope to TH, 28 Nov. 1866, HM 2:33:21–2; Cope, 'Remains'; Osborn, *Cope*, 157; Leidy, 'Hadrosaurus'.

54. *LTH*, 1:303; Uschmann and Jahn, 'Briefwechsel zwischen', 15; E. Haeckel to TH, 27 Jan. 1868, HP 17.183. Haeckel (*History*, 2:226–7) interposed the beaked anomodonts (e.g. *Dicynodon*) between dinosaurs and birds. But Owen ('Description', 423) saw the anomodonts leading to mammals, showing that his and Huxley's divergence over the kinship of birds, reptiles and mammals was never as clear-cut as it later seemed.

19 EYEING THE PRIZE

1. Bibby, 'South London', 211; Hutton, 'Pope Huxley', 135–6; Lightman, 'Pope Huxley', 161.

2. Davies, *Heterodox London*, 1:111–12; G. S. Jones, *Outcast London*, 40, 85; Gilley and Loades, 'Huxley', 305; Gardner, 'Huxley Essay', 179–80; Stanley, 'Huxley's Treatment', 122; Paradis, *Huxley*, 58–9 offers the best analysis of the chess analogy. *CE*, 3:78–9, 82–3; Bibby, 'South London', 212; *'your'*: W. F. Rae to TH, 6 Jan. 1868, HP 25.11. On Christian Socialism: TH to CK, 23 Sept. 1860, HP 19.169; *LTH*, 1:222.

3. JT to TH, 8 Jan. 1868, HP 1.45; Barnes and Shapin, *Natural Order*, 93; R. Young, *Darwin's Metaphor*, 190ff; *CE*, 3:88–9.

4. J. H. Titcomb to TH, 22 Nov. 1867, HP 28.25; Green, 'Huxley'; *CE*, 3:119–20; *LTH*, 1:302; Gilley and Loades, 'Huxley', 295–6.

5. *LTH*, 2:297; M. Kalisch to TH, 8 May 1868, HP 19.122; JT to TH, 22 Apr. 1869, HP 1.59.

6. Ellegard, *Darwin*, 82; *LJH*, 2:114–21; Holyoake, 'Priesthood', 1–3; J. V. Carus to TH, 30 July 1868, HP 12.142; *LLD*, 3:48–9; 'duty': JT to JH, n.d., HP 8.344; *LTH*, 1:301–2; 'out': TH to A. Dohrn, 7 July 1868, HP 13.166.

7. TH to W. C. Williamson, 16 Oct. 1869, APS; Rehbock, 'Huxley', 508–18; Rupke, *'Bathybius'*, 54–6; Rice, 'Huxley', 171–3; Gould, *'Bathybius'*, 198; *LTH*, 1:295–6; *SM*, 3:330; 3:454, and Fox, 'Skull', on his bird-like dinosaur *Hypsilophodon*.

8. Tyndall, *Fragments*, 92–3, 130, 163–4, 198, 441; Huxley, 'Tyndall', 4; Turner, *Between Science*, 25–7; *LJT*, 131, 148, 150; Mivart, *Essays*, 2:228. Ellegard, *Darwin*, 83; *LTH*, 1:297; Holyoake, 'Priesthood', 4–5.

9. Holyoake, 'Priesthood', 5–6; *CE*, 8:1–4, 7, 27, 35; *LTH*, 1:297. The prehistory of this talk can be seen in Huxley, 'Chalk', and in his London Institution lecture on cosmogony, 14 Oct. 1867, HM 2:59:40.

10. Baynes, 'Darwin', 505–6; Cockshut, *Unbelievers*, 91; Lightman, *Origins*, chap. 5; G. M. Young, *Portrait*, 96; Barton, 'Tyndall'; *CE*, 5:319–20.

11. E. M. Schmitz to HAH, 15 Nov. 1868, HP 26.43 (the eye witness); *CE*, 1:131–60; Geison, 'Protoplasmic Theory', 273–84; 'pouring': J. Young, 'Huxley', 242; Gardner, 'Huxley Essay', 182ff; Calderwood, 'Huxley's Sermons', 197; Weindling, *Darwinism*, 45–6; Gilley and Loades, 'Huxley', 298, 302; Morley, *Recollections*, 1:88, 90; Brown, *Metaphysical Society*, 51; J. Morley to TH, 31 May, 12 Nov. 1869, HP 23.14–15; J. Cranbrook to TH, 2, 23 Oct. 1868, HP 12.328–32; *LTH*, 1:299.

12. CD to TH, 19 Mar. [1869], HP 5.266; *LLD*, 3:113; HAH to ES, 7 Nov. 1869, HP 31.40; J. Morley to TH, 31 May 1869, HP 23.14; 'lunar': E. Frankland to TH, 16 Feb. 1869, HP 16.251; Geison, 'Protoplasmic Theory', 279, 284; J. Young, 'Huxley', 244; 'Protoplasm at the Antipodes', *Nature*, 1 (1869), 13.

13. St G. Mivart to CD, 25 Apr. 1870, DAR 171, CUL. Huxley, *Prove di Fatto Intorno al posto che L'Uomo Tiene Nella Natura* trans. Pietro Marchi (Milan, Treves, 1869). It also went into French as *La Place de l'homme dans la Nature* (Paris, Baillière, 1870).

14. HAH to ES, 7 Nov. 1869, HP 31.40; *LTH*, 1:307–10; syllabus, HM 2:63; MS, HM 2:64–5; Huxley, *Physiography*, vii; *CE*, 3:87, 111, 116, 129.

15. HAH to ES, 20 Sept.–7 Nov. 1869, HP 31.40; *LTH*, 1:305–6; 'definitely': TH to FD, [28 Sept. 1869], HP 15.133; 'I often': CD to TH, 10 June 1868, HP 5.239; TH on Jim's health problem: HP 9.253.

16. HP 31.101; CL to TH, 13 Feb. 1868, HP 6.126; RIM to TH, 18 Feb. 1869, HP 23.184.

17. Tait, 'Geological Time', 407, 422, 438; *MLD*, 1:314; Jenkin, 'Origin', 301; W. Thomson, *Lectures*, 2:64; *CE*, 8:306, 327–9; C. Smith and Wise, *Energy*, chaps 15–17; Burchfield, *Kelvin*, chaps 2–4; Jensen, *Huxley*, 171.

18. On 29 Apr., 5 May 1869: Huxley's Diary, HP 70.9; R. H. Meade to TH, 30 June 1869, HP 22.206; TH to G. G. Leveson-Gower (Granville), 12 Aug. 1869, HP 30.75; *SM*: 3,427; *LTH*, 1:306, 2:451; Stocking, *Victorian Anthropology*, 108. Later letters, e.g., HM 1:16:110, 168; HP 25.43, 28.192–4, 30.65.

19. P. M. Duncan to TH, 8 Sept. 1868, HP 15.26–8; also HP 10.267–9; 12.211–13; 15.26–35; 18.355–7; 21.29–38; 23.112; 27.261; 30.160; 33.1–31. Stocking, 'What's', 382–3; Rainger, 'Race', 68; purging: TH to D. W. Nash, 17 Nov. 1868, HP 23.196, also 23.98; E. Lynn to TH, 11 Nov. 1868, HP 21.223; E. Richards, 'Huxley', 269–75.

20. *LTH*, 1:292, 312; TH to MF, n.d., HP 4.3, 15.

21. Nobody had tried allegiances more than J. S. Mill with his call for black suffrage and Eyre's prosecution. But sympathies ran deep in this aristocracy of intellect. When Mill lost his Parliamentary seat, even though Tyndall reckoned he 'deserves what he has got', he added 'but if I had a pocket borough at my disposal he is the first man that I should choose to represent it': JT to TH, 19 Nov. [1868], HP 1.228.

22. JT to TH, 13 Mar. [1868], HP 8.345.

23. HAH to ES, 7 Nov. 1869, HP 31.40; Heyck, *Intellectual Transformation*, 178, 215–17; Roos, 'Aims', 165–71; *MLD*, 1:317; Huxley, 'Nature', 9; Meadows, *Science*, 25–31.

24. *LCK*, 2:214; Dockrill, 'Huxley', 470–3; Eisen, 'Huxley', 338–42; Lightman, *Origins*, 23ff; Paradis, *Huxley*, 80–5; 'hard': E. S. Beesly to TH, 8 Feb. 1869, HP 10.270; *CE*, 1:156; J. Morley to TH, 12, 13 Jan. 1869, HP 23.11–12; 'superstitious': Wollaston, *Newton*, 244; Huxley, 'Chalk', 500; Haight, *Eliot Letters*, 4:214–15; J. R. Moore, 'Theodicy', 173; Turner, *Between Science*, 22; nihilist: J. Young, 'Huxley', 257. Huxley echoed Carlyle, who was 'neither Pantheist nor Pottheist, nor any *Theist* or *ist* whatsoever, having the most decided contempt for all manner of System-builders and Sectfounders': Turner, 'Victorian Scientific Naturalism', 336–8.

25. J. Lubbock to TH, 16 Apr. 1869, HP 22.68; Huxley's Diary, HP 70.9; Brown, *Metaphysical Society*, 15, 21–7; J. P. A., 'Huxley', 2.

26. Hutton, 'Pope Huxley', 135; Lightman, 'Pope Huxley', 155, 157; *CE*: 1:195, 5:238–9; J. R. Moore, 'Deconstructing Darwinism', 388–9, 394; Dockrill, 'Huxley', 464–9; J. R. Moore, 'Theodicy', 177–9; Cockshut, *Unbelievers*, 92; 'Professor Huxley's Doctrine', *English Leader*, 3 Mar. 1866, 101–2; Kottler, 'Wallace'.

27. JT to TH, [Sept. 1869], HP 1.60; TH to JT, 30 Sept. 1869, HP 8.75; *LTH*, 1:313; *Times*, 25 Aug. 1869, 6; 'repudiated': JH to TH, [Aug. 1869], HP 3.126; 'President Huxley', *Spectator*, 42 (1869), 1108–10; S. Northcote to TH, 19 Apr. 1869, HP 23.226.

28. 'President Huxley', *Spectator*, 42 (1869), 1108–10; Ellegard, *Darwin*, 65, 85;

'big wig': TH to HAH, 12 July 1851, HH 156; *LTH*, 1:89; 'like': TH to FD, [28 Sept. 1869], HP 15.133.

29. Ralph, 'MacGillivray', 185, 193; Collie, *Huxley*, 89 n59; 'President Huxley', *Spectator*, 42 (1869), 1108.

30. HAH to ES, 20 Sept.–7 Nov. 1869, HP 31.40; *LTH*, 1:231.

31. Hutton, 'Pope Huxley', 135; 'jacket': TH to HAH, 16 Feb. 1854, HH 262; Morris, *Heaven's Command*, 265–6; G. Young, *Portrait*, 72.

32. J. R. Moore, 'Theodicy', 173–4; G. Young, *Portrait*, 95; 'President Huxley', *Spectator*, 42 (1869), 1108; Morley, *Recollections*, 1:88–9; Cockshut, *Unbelievers*, 87.

33. HAH to ES, 19 Mar. 1873, AD; Heyck, *Intellectual Transformation*, 13, 138–9; J. R. Moore, 'Crisis', 68; J. R. Moore, 'Freethought', 308; '220': HAH to ES, 20 Sept.-7 Nov. 1869, HP 31.40.

34. *CE*, 1:270–1; Bibby, *Huxley*, 30–1; *LTH*, 1:16, 334–5.

Part Two:
Evolution's High Priest

20 THE GUN IN THE LIBERAL ARMOURY

1. 'Men of the Day, No. 19', *Vanity Fair*, 28 Jan. 1871; *Illustrated London News*, 17 Sept. 1870; 'noble': TH to MF, 2 Oct. 1875, HP 4.109; 'great': HAH to ES, 8 Feb. 1871, AD.

2. Dennis and Skilton, *Reform*, 104.

3. TH to unknown corres., 8 Jan. 1871, APS; G. M. Young, *Portrait*, 83.

4. HAH to ES, 8 Feb. 1871, AD.

5. HAH to ES, 8 Feb. 1871, AD; T. A. Hirst, Journal 15, 13 Mar., 14 June 1884: Royal Institution; *LJT*, 200; wing: J. Whitworth to TH, 3 May 1873, HP 29.20.

6. HAH to ES, 8 Feb. 1871, 22 Sept. 1872, AD; Rolt, *Victorian Engineering*,

216; Underground: TH to JK, 9 Jan. 1871, APS; 'Modern': Huxley, 'Professor Huxley at Manchester'.

7. *CE*, 3:104; Brock, 'Patronage', 174; Cardwell, *Organisation*, 111–26; Dennis and Skilton, *Reform*, 188; Turner, 'Public Science', 592; Alter, *Reluctant Patron*, chap. 2.

8. Bibby, 'South London', 213; F. Palgrave to TH, 6 Jan. 1867 [1868], HP 24.16; on Palgrave: TH to JH, 15 July 1865, HP 2.134; 'queer': TH to G. J. Holyoake, 2 Aug. 1873, Holyoake Collection 2178, Co-Operative Union, Manchester.

9. MacLeod, 'Support', 202–7; MacLeod, 'Ayrton', 46–7; Cardwell, *Organisation* 125; 'you', 'most': E. Lankester, 'Representation', 509.

10. Fiske, 'Reminiscences'; HAH's Godparents Notebook, AD; Bibby, *Huxley*, 151.

11. HAH to ES, 8 Feb. 1871, 22 Sept. 1872, 16 Apr. 1874, AD; 'ought': 20 Sept. 1869, HP 31.40; A. Huxley, 'Grandfather', 147; Fiske, 'Reminiscences'. Huxley's solicitor E. F. Burton (17 Aug. 1870, HP 11.199) made it plain that Duffy's 'Cash and Catholicism' were the jarring points. McClatchie is presumably the 'shipmate' whose wife was 'a very old & dear friend of my wifes', referred to in TH to WHF, 17 Oct. 1871, APS.

12. Osborn, 'Enduring Recollections' 727; HAH's Reminiscences, HP 62.1.

13. Brown, *Metaphysical*, 10, 23, 29, 32, 41, 111–12; *LTH*, 1:313–21.

14. Brown, *Metaphysical*, 50–56, 65, 94, 103, 139–40, 318–20; *CE* 6:201; 'Oecumenical': TH to JK, 27 Apr. 1870, APS; J. R. Moore, 'Deconstructing Darwinism', 365. Tener and Woodfield, *Victorian Spectator*, 180 reprint Hutton's 'Pope Huxley' article. Lightman, *Origins*, on Huxley's resistance to analysing his own axioms.

15. A. Clark to TH, [pre-1874], HP 12.198. Gladstone was present at Huxley's 17 Nov. 1869 talk: Brown, *Metaphysical*, 146, 319; 'A': TH to JK, 15 Nov. 1869, APS.

16. M. Arnold to TH, [1870], HP 10.151. *Lay Sermons* was published in July 1870; by 15 November there were 'not more than 150 copies left'. In 1871 came the abridged *Essays Selected from Lay Sermons, Addresses and Reviews*: HP 52.1–4; 'will': JT to TH, 16 June 1870, HP 1.67.

17. ES to HAH, 4 Mar. 1869, AD; *LTH*, 1:323.

18. Youmans' prospectus, HP 21.262; E. L. Youmans to TH, [Aug. 1871], HP 29.261–2. Henry S. King was to publish the books in England first, then send the plates to Appleton, see HP 19.145ff; TH to JT, 31 Oct. 1874, HP 8.167; 'has': HAH to ES, 8 Feb. 1871, AD; TH to E. Delafield, 24 Aug. 1870, APS.

19. Circular 'To British Scientific Authors', 28 Dec. 1871, HP 30.92; MacLeod, 'Evolutionism', 65, 67–72; Youmans: Fiske, *Century*, 71; TH to NL, 21 Nov. 1868. HP 21.248.

20. HAH to ES, 8 Feb. 1871, AD; 'ignorant': JT to TH, 24 Sept. 1873, HP 1.113; encl. 1870 letter 1.115; 'rapidly': F. V. Hayden to TH, 20 Dec. 1869, HP 18.89; Goetzmann, *Exploration*, 406–7, 490–502; Appleton: E. L. Youmans to TH, 7 Apr. 1868, 28 Apr. 1871, HP 29.259, 10.105–7.

21. J. R. Moore, 'Deconstructing', 365.

22. J. R. Moore, 'Wallace's Malthusian Moment' on the original Darwin–Wallace common culture; Wallace, 'Principles', 392; R. Smith, 'Wallace'; and Kottler, 'Wallace' on its break-up.

23. Bartholomew, 'Huxley's Defence'; Desmond, *Archetypes*, chap. 3; di

Gregorio, *Huxley*, 60–8; Lyons, 'Origins', on Huxley's saltationism as an attempt to square evolution with an older morphology based on discrete types.

24. TH to JH, 10 Aug. 1870, HP 2.163. The institutional aspects are nicely brought out in James Strick's Princeton Ph.D. thesis on the spontaneous generation debates in 1860–80. *CE*, 8:136; *LTH*, 1:333; 'going': TH to NL, 8 Oct. 1870, HP 21.252; 'not': TH's annotation on H. C. Bastian to TH, 2, 12 May 1870, HP 10.238–40; Bastian, 'Reply'.

25. TH to MF, 2 Jan. 1871, HP 22.27; HM 2:3; *CE*, 8:110; bacteria as mould: TH to JH, 20 July 1870, HP 2.157; *SM*, 3:606; HM 1:1:1–66, 2:1:1ff.

26. R. E. Grant to H. Bastian, 26 June 1872, Wellcome Institute Library, London. Grant, *Tabular View*, 3, 5–6, 9, had a continually originating microbial life giving rise to independent 'trees of life', a strikingly pre-Darwinian concept, as explained in Hodge, 'Universal'. Farley, *Spontaneous*, 124, on Bastian's Lamarckism. Bastian won Grant's gold medal in 1859; Grant's previous winner, the revolutionary's son Alexander Herzen, offered to translate Bastian into French: A. Herzen to H. Bastian, 15 Dec. 1877, Wellcome Institute. *LTH*, 1:168.

27. E. R. Lankester, 'Instruction', 362; Gooday, 'Nature'; Barton, 'Scientific Opposition'; Chadarevian, 'Laboratory'; Meadows, *Science*, 84–5.

28. Forgan and Gooday, 'Constructing South Kensington'.

29. Forgan and Gooday, 'Constructing South Kensington'; Girouard, *Waterhouse*, 26–33; *Survey of London*, 74; Rupke, *Owen*, 36ff. Huxley's Devonshire Commission examined the plans for the Natural History Museum, which led to a scrap when Owen the 'old fool' appeared: TH to JH, 18 Mar. 1871, HP 2.172.

30. On the cognitive and architectural changes accompanying the switch from museum to lab, which was not so much a replacement as an expansion: Pickstone, 'Ways of Knowing', 442–52; Forgan and Gooday, 'Fungoid Assemblage', 158–60; Nyhart, 'Natural History'. In some senses Huxley's lab for beginners was a simplified museum laid open, with the corpses made accessible to trainees. It was not designed for control over, or alteration of, Nature (as in the later, research-driven, vivisection programmes), even if it did foster new manipulative skills. This blurs the socio-cognitive categories in 1870: Pickstone, 'Museological Science', 113, 131–2.

31. The voice was that of the Middlesbrough ironmaster, and shortly Huxley's fellow Devonshire Commissioner, Bernhard Samuelson MP: *Hansard*, 198 (19 July 1869), 160; L. Goschen to HAH, 1 Aug. [1871], 24 June [1871–4], HP 17.94–7; G. Goschen to TH, n.d. [*c.*1870?], HP 17.89; *Survey of London*, 234.

32. TH to JH, 7 Jan. 1872, HP 2.189; Forgan and Gooday, 'Constructing South Kensington'; Meadows, *Science*, 85–7; TH to NL, 20 Apr. 1871, HP 21.270; Bibby, *Huxley*, 116.

33. Huxley, 'Royal School of Mines', *Times*, 11 Apr. 1871; TH to NL, 20 Apr. 1871, HP 21.270; Gooday, 'Nature', 334; Bibby, *Huxley*, 113.

34. Forgan, 'Architecture', 154.

35. *Survey of London*, 234–7; 'The Creation of Albertopolis', *Jarvis Journal*, 54 (1978), 4–6; 'New Science Schools for the Department of Science and Art, South Kensington', *Builder*, (2 Sept. 1871), 687; Forgan and Gooday, 'Fungoid Assemblage', 162–4. Huxley's friend, the chemist A. W. von Hofmann, had visited the German laboratories and reported back to Cole.

36. TH to AD, 7 July 1871, HP 13.202; *LTH*, 1:361.

37. TH to MF, 5 Jan. 1871, HP 4.29; 'The Creation of Albertopolis', *Jarvis Journal*, 54 (1978), 4–6; Gooday, 'Nature', 334–5; *CE*, 3:45.

38. TH to MF, 5 Jan. 1871, HP 4.29, initially projected 15 microscopes; Gooday, 'Nature', 336; E. R. Lankester, 'Instruction', 362; Geison, *Foster*, 132; *LTH*, 1:378. These were possibly Hartnack microscopes (mentioned in JD to TH, 27 Jan. 1894, HP 14.171) – cheap students' models of typical Continental design, made by Edmund Hartnack in Paris until 1870 and then in Potsdam (Eric Hollowday, pers. comm.).

39. Haters of Oxbridge-exclusivity such as the radical Methodist Marshall Hall and Unitarian W. B. Carpenter also saw their sons at Cambridge (Philip Carpenter won a scholarship to Trinity College in 1871). Lankester studied zoology under Huxley's plummy protégé George Rolleston in the new University Museum, but why he chose Oxford rather than University College or Jermyn Street is puzzling. Wiener, *English Culture*, 13–14 on this dilution of Nonconformity. Howarth, 'Science Education', 334–5.

40. Lester and Bowler, *Lankester*, 19.

41. E. R. Lankester, 'Use', 34–5; Desmond, *Archetypes*, 138. He purged the idealist word 'homology', which took its meaning from Owen's Platonic archetype, replacing it with 'homogeny', meaning structural affinity through descent.

42. ERL to TH, 18 Dec. [1872], HP 21.39; Lester and Bowler, *Lankester*, 23, 27, 39.

43. E. R. Lankester, 'Instruction', 362–4; Gooday, 'Nature', 336.

44. Denis, 'Brompton Barracks'; Cardwell, *Organisation*, 116.

45. Huxley, 'President's Address', *Journal of the Quekett Microscopical Club*, 6 (1879), 251; Denis, 'Brompton Barracks', 11–12. J. R. Moore, *Post-Darwinian Controversies* on the 'military metaphor'.

46. JD to TH, 22 Sept. 1871, HP 14.4; *Survey of London*, 86ff; Denis, 'Brompton Barracks', 11–14. *LTH*, 1:415; T. J. Parker, *Parker*, 31–2; Desmond, *Archetypes*, 51, 216–17.

47. Huxley, 'Contemporary Literature', *West. Rev.*, 65 (1856), 269. Huxley had the UCL physiology professor Burdon Sanderson and hygiene professor at the Army Medical School Edmund Parkes appointed to Liverpool's health authority: E. A. Parkes to TH, 3 Dec. 1870, HP 24.62. MacLeod, 'Support', 212, 224.

48. Fuegians, Maltese and British Columbian 'Indians' refused to be photographed nude: HM 1:15:158–9; HM 1:16:1, 180. The Central Board for Aborigines in Melbourne would only photograph willing subjects naked: HM 1:15:117. Chains: HM 1:15:2–8, 155. See HM 1:15:4, 113–52; also HM 1:16:23, 60, 85–6, 118, 186, 196; photographs in HM Boxes G and H. Di Gregorio, *Huxley*, 175.

49. HM 1:16:172. Ethnological Society talk, 7 June 1870, HM 2:103:170; *SM*, 3:564; Huxley's race typology: Lorimer, 'Theoretical Racism', 408–13; di Gregorio, *Huxley*, 162ff; his sexism: E. Richards, 'Huxley'; paternalism: Lorimer, *Colour*, 148–9. On the geopolitical aspects of ethnography and biogeography: Browne, 'Biogeography', 314; Desmond, *Archetypes*, 102–3; and the origin of questionnaire-type collations in government surveying voyages: Beer, 'Travelling', 327; Bravo, 'Ethnological', 344.

50. BJ to TH, 14 Jan. 1870, HP 7.3; Howarth, 'Science Education', 335; *LTH*, 1:330.

51. M. Foster Sr to TH, 3 May 1870, HP 4.176; 'two': MF to HAH, 10 Feb.

1870, HP 16.205; Huxley's influence: W. G. Clark to TH, 2 Apr. [1870], HP 4.172; Geison, *Foster*, 76–7, 100.

52. G. Young to TH, 17 Jan. 1879, HP 29.266; T. J. P. Jodrell to TH, [1872?], HP 19.70–2; Huxley's 1872 Diary, HP 70.12 (26 Nov. 1872). On Jodrell's chairs: Bibby, *Huxley*, 216–17; Harte, *World*, 86.

53. A. W. Williamson to TH, 8 July [1870], HP 29.58; *CE*, 3:308ff; Bibby, 'Huxley and Medical Education', 193.

54. HAH to AD, 20 May 1872, postscript to HP 13.214; HAH to ES, 8 Feb. 1871, 22 Sept. 1872, AD.

55. Godlee, 'Jones', 102.

56. M. Fox to TH, 16 Mar. 1871, HP 16.245. Morley, *Recollections*, 1:88–90; Jacyna, 'Science'. Huxley's radical social and scientific blend was reflected in his alignments. When a new club, designed 'to bring into contact the Radical members of the House of Commons, the representatives of the Liberal press, and the leaders of liberal thought in the universities & elsewhere' (circular HP 16.52) was mooted, with Mill, Cairnes, Morley, Stephen and Dilke signed up, Huxley was invited to join: H. Fawcett to TH, 14 Jan. 1870, HP 16.51.

57. *LJH*, 2:125; Burkhardt and Smith, *Calendar*, 7323; Darwin, *Descent*, 62, 95–6; Desmond and Moore, *Darwin*, chap. 38.

58. Greene, 'Darwin', 7–16; Gruber and Barrett, *Darwin*, 24; Durant, 'Ascent', 285; G. Jones, 'Social Darwinism Revisited', 771.

59. This was W. B. Dawkins ('Darwin', 195–6), the Huxley-nominated geology curator at Owen's College, Manchester. E. Richards, 'Darwin' and 'Redrawing the Boundaries'; Erskine, '*Origin*'; and Jann, 'Darwin', for the most recent feminist studies on Darwin's selection scenario which upheld the Victorian commonplace of female inferiority.

60. TH to AD, 18 July, 17 Nov. 1870, 7 Jan. 1871, HP 13.177, 183, 189; *LTH*, 1:334, 336–7, 361; 'bloody': TH to JH, 20 July 1870, HP 2.157 – and on 10 Aug. 1870, HP 2.163, he was wishing 'they would hang the Emperor at the nearest Camp'; JD to TH, 19 July 1870, HP 14.1. Kovalevskii: CD to TH, 1 Oct. [1869], HP 5.275.

61. Bibby, *Huxley*, 144; Owen, 'Fate'.

62. Todes, 'Kovalevskii', 119; Horne, *Fall*, 45–6, 229–31, 246ff, 341.

63. St G. Mivart to CD, 24 Jan. 1871, DAR 171, CUL; Horne, *Fall*, 520, 556; *Times*, 8 Apr. 1871, 5; *LTH*, 1:359.

64. 'The Pedigree of the Horse', (Royal Institution Lecture, 8 Apr. 1870), HP 44.7–42, ff.14 ('one'), 18, 30; *CE*, 8:358–61. Huxley was following the French – Albert Gaudry, Paul Gervais and Edouard Lartet – and Richard Owen (*Anatomy*, 3:825): on which see Ospovat, *Development*, 137–40, and Desmond, *Archetypes*, 165–9. HM 2:100 notebook; 'torn': JT to TH, 6 Apr. 1870, HP 1.65; *LTH*, 1:329; Ritvo, *Animal Estate*, 18–20; Read, *England*, 61–3.

65. Kovalevskii, 'Osteology', 21; Todes , 'Kovalevskii', 130–3.

66. Bibby, *Huxley*, 146–7. Committee and speeches: 'Election of London School Board. Addresses to the Ratepayers of the Marylebone Division from T. H. Huxley and W. R. Cremer', HM 3:122:11.

67. MF to HAH, 28 Nov. [1870], HP 16.211; curriculum: 'Election of London School Board . . .', HM 3:122:11, also *CE*, 3:389ff; *LTH*, 1:338; 'with': HAH to ES, 8 Feb. 1871, AD.

68. HAH to ES, 8 Feb. 1871, AD; Bibby, 'Huxley and Medical Education', 194; Blake, *Charge*, 62.

69. J. A. Picton to TH, 24 Mar. 1873, HP 24.126; Davies, *Heterodox London*, 1:351–5.

70. TH to G. Dixon, 20 Feb. 1871, APS; referring to Genesis 19:32, 37:12; 'without': Huxley, 'Election of London School Board . . .', HM 3:122.11. The Bible-reading compromise that won was brought in by W. H. Smith, son of the newsagent, which allowed for principles of religion and morality suitable to the children to be drawn from the readings: Coleman and Mansell, 'Science'; Bibby, *Huxley*, 150, 153; *LTH*, 1:346; CE, 3:396ff.

71. MF to HAH, 26 Feb. 1871, HP 16.213; CE, 3:395; 'should': Mivart, 'Reminiscences', 993; Tom: TH to ES, 26 Nov. 1854, AD.

72. TH to AD, 7 Jan. 1871, HP 13.189; *LTH*, 1:361; 'to': TH to G. Dixon, 20 Feb. 1871, APS; 'really': Conway, 'Huxley', 73–4.

73. TH to G. J. Holyoake, 21 Apr. 1871, Holyoake Collection 2001, Co-Operative Union, Manchester; 2 Aug. 1873, Holyoake Collection 2178, on protecting freethinkers, funding; 'your': G. J. Holyoake to TH, 21 June 1871, HP 18.211. The divide between the scientific agnostics and Holyoake's secularists was shown in Holyoake's ill-treatment by the BAAS in 1870, even though Holyoake was there to report Huxley's Presidential Address.

74. TH to F. Sandford, 5 Dec. 1870, HP 26.21; T. Carlyle to TH, 5 Jan. 1871, HP 12.33. George Eliot recommended John Nassau Senior (whose wife was a close friend) for Chief Secretary of the School Board: G. E. Lewes to TH, 2 Jan. 1871, HP 21.221; Haight, *Eliot Letters*, 9:5–6.

75. JD to MF, 20 Feb. 1872, HP 14.8; HP 70.14 ff.1–28; HM 2:65; *LTH*, 1:309–10; Huxley, *Physiography*, vii; CE 6:282, 8:137; HP 39.58; A. Buckley to TH, 22 May 1871, HP 11.182; HP 52.4–5; J. C. Brough to TH, 10 Aug. 1870, HP 11.97.

76. TH to JK, 9 Jan. 1871, APS; I. Turguenieff to TH, 10 Jan. 1871, HP 28.43; HAH to ES, 8 Feb. 1871, AD.

77. *LTH*, 1:360–1; Slade: HAH to ES, 22 Sept. 1872, AD; HAH to AD, 19 Jan. 1872, HP 13.205. Huxley was introducing Riviere with his sketch pad at the Zoo: B. Riviere to TH, 9 May 1871, 30 Apr. 1873, HP 25.92–3; RA: HP 49.36; HM 3:122:13; Roos, 'Arnold', 316.

78. TH to E. F. Burton, 20 Mar. 1871, HP 11.198; TH to JK, 8 July 1871, APS; *LTH*, 1:383; HAH to ES, 22 Sept. 1872, AD.

79. H. A. Bruce/TH, 14 Nov. 1870, HP 11.132.

80. Huxley *et al.*, *School Board*, 2–6; Bibby, *Huxley*, 155–60; Coleman and Mansell, 'Science', 150.

81. TH to AD, 7 July 1871, HP 13.202, *LTH*, 1:362; *LJH*, 2:125; Burkhardt and Smith, *Calendar*, 7627; CE, 3:424.

82. H. E. Roscoe to TH, 10 Aug., 19 Oct. 1871, HP 25.267, 273; *LTH*, 1:360; 'interpreter': undated fragment, HP 49.55. Children's popularizations: Lightman, 'Voices'; Tener and Woodfield, *Victorian Spectator*, 169.

83. MF to HAH, 10 Feb. 1870, HP 16.205.

84. W. Thomson to TH, 9 Apr. 1871, HP 27.265. They also dined 'without ceremony' at the Taits, and Nettie too liked 'Mⁿ Tait very much for so short an acquaintance': HAH to AD, 6, 8 Sept. 1871, HP 13.209.

85. Smith and Wise, *Energy*, 633–45; CE, 8:256–7; SM, 3:607.

86. TH to JH, 11, 28 Aug. 1871, HP 2.177–9; *LJH*, 2:126–7, 165–6; Burkhardt and Smith, *Calendar*, 7905; Ellegard, *Darwin*, 89.

87. HAH to AD, 6, 8 Sept. 1871, HP 13.209; 'tons': TH to JH, 11 Sept. 1871, HP 2.181; *LTH*, 1:363; Collie, *Huxley*, 135–6.

88. Baynes, 'Darwin', 502–6.

89. TH to JH, 11 Sept. 1871, HP 2.181; *LTH*, 1:364; *LLD*, 3:147; Mivart, *Genesis*, 19, 67–73, 239, 302; Gruber, *Conscience*, 52ff; Vorzimmer, *Darwin*, 230ff; Hull, *Darwin*, 351; J. R. Moore, *Post-Darwinian Controversies*, 62–4; *CE*, 2:125ff; Huxley, *Critiques*, ix–xi.

90. CD to TH, 21, 30 Sept. 1871, HP 5:279, 283; *LLD*, 3:148–9; *LTH*, 1:365; 'clever': TH to JH, 11 Sept. 1871, HP 2.181.

91. E. R. Lankester, 'Use of the Term', 342; Flower, 'Introductory', 199; Desmond, *Archetypes*, 138–9; *LJH*, 2:128–30; 'limbo': *Times*, 1 July 1895; 'sect': Baynes, 'Darwin', 506; 'sin': CD to TH, 5 Oct. [1871], HP 5.287; JK to TH, 22 Sept. 1871, HP 20.1.

92. This was 'Administrative Nihilism', delivered in Chamberlain's Birmingham on 9 Oct. 1871, to be discussed below. Manchester: Huxley's Diary, HP 70.11 (6 Oct. 1871); H. E. Roscoe to TH, 15 Oct. 1871, HP 25.269; governor, chloral: HAH to ES, 8 Feb. 1871, AD; 'as': TH to JH, 11 Aug. 1871, HP 2.177.

93. M. Foster Sr to TH, 30 Oct. 1871, HP 4.180; *LTH*, 1:349–55; Bibby, *Huxley*, 153–5; C. J. Herries to TH, 28 Oct. 1871, HP 18.137.

94. TH to J. Carr, 18 Nov. 1871, HP 9.249; published in the *Daily News* and reproduced in the *Reasoner*, (Dec. 1871), 183, which identifies the recipient.

95. TH to JH, 7 Jan. 1872, HP 2.189; A. Hobhouse to TH, 25, 29 July, 15, 24 Nov. 1871, HP 18.188–92, 196; bones: TH to J. Phillips, 10 Nov. 1871, OUM 1871/66.

96. JH to TH, 25 Oct. 1871, HP 3.153; Brown, *Metaphysical*, 118, 139, 323; JK to TH, [Nov. 1871], HP 20.2.

97. TH to MF, 27 Oct. 1871, HP 4.31; Bibby, *Huxley*, 54.

98. Knowles had him write up 'Yeast' for the next *Contemporary* number: JK to TH, [Nov. 1871], HP 20.2; *CE*, 8:110.

99. MF to HAH, 28 Jan. 1870, HP 16.202; 'Don't': TH to JH, 31 Dec. 1871, HP 2.187; Huxley's 1871 Diary, HP 70.11; 'seedy': TH to MF, 18 Dec. 1871, HP 4.34. Mind: *CE* 1:240; London Institution lectures on 'Bodily Motion and Consciousness', 30 Oct.–4 Dec. 1871: HM 2:67; HP 70.14, ff.1–23.

100. JT to TH, 24 Dec. [1871], HP 1.79; TH to JH, 22 Dec. 1871, HP 2.185; TH to JT, 22 Dec. 1871, HP 9.48.

101. TH to AD, 3 Jan 1872, HP 13.213; *LTH*, 1:367–8; Burkhardt and Smith, *Calendar*, 8136, 8139; F. Brady to TH, 23 Nov. 1871, HP 11.65; H. T. Stainton to TH, 3, 22 Dec. 1871, HP 26.211–12; Huxley's notes HP 26.214–16; '&': HAH to AD, 19 Jan. 1872, HP 13.205.

102. HAH to ES, 22 Sept. 1872, 16 Apr. 1874, AD.

103. *LTH*, 1:351; J. H. Lawrence to TH, 9 Jan. 1871, HP 21.178; replying to 6 Jan. 1872, HP 21.176; HAH to AD, 19 Jan. 1872, HP 13.205.

104. TH to JH, 7 Jan. 1872, HP 2.189.

105. TH to MF, 8 Jan. 1872, HP 4.35; MF to HAH, 12 Jan. 1872, HP 16.219.

21   FROM THE CITY OF THE DEAD
TO THE CITY OF SCIENCE

1. Notes on Egypt, 11 Jan.–16 Mar. 1872, HP 70.13, ff.1–6; HAH to AD, 19, 24 Jan. 1872, HP 13.205; *LTH*, 1:367.

2. Notes on Egypt, HP 70.13, ff.6–8. JH to HAH, 3 Feb. 1872, HP 3.154; TH to JH, 9 Apr. 1872, HP 2.192; *LTH*, 1:368; 'springs': TH to FD, 9 June 1875, HP 1.135. Sir John would dine with the Huxleys in London: TH to JT, 28 May 1872, HP 9.54; J. D. Hay to HAH, [May 1872], HP 18.87.

3. Notes on Egypt, HP 70.13, ff.9–11; 'disagreeable', 'muddy': HAH to AD, 13 Feb. 1872, HP 13.207.

4. Pang, 'Social Event', 264; Blake, *Disraeli*, 581–7; Morris, *Heaven's Command*, 290–5, 417–19.

5. Notes on Egypt, HP 70.13, ff.12–22; Drower, *Petrie*, 35–6. Sir William Gregory would later ask Huxley's advice on a Director for his proposed natural history museum in Colombo: TH to AD, 20 May, 5 June 1872, HP 13.214–18; *LTH*, 1:374.

6. JT to [HAH], endorsed 23 Feb. 1872, HP 1.82; JK to HAH, 26 Jan., 16, 20 Feb. 1872, HP 20.6–10; JK to TH, 23 Feb. 1872, HP 20.12; 'Cairo': HAH to AD, 13 Feb., 20 May 1872, HP 13.207, 214; JT to TH, 14 Feb. 1872, HP 1.80; HAH to ES, 22 Sept. 1872, AD; 'Friend', 'Huxley's Homes'.

7. TH to JT, 31 Mar. 1872, HP 9.50; *LTH*, 1:371; TH to HAH, 11 Feb. 1872, AD; Notes on Egypt, HP 70.13, ff.30–42; C. Ellis to TH, n.d., HP 18.180.

8. Notes on Egypt, HP 70.13, ff.44–56; *LTH*, 1:370; Drower, *Petrie*, 36, 56, 112–14, 221; Kamil, *Luxor*, 112; 'always': TH to JT, 31 Mar. 1872, HP 9.50; TH to MF, 5 Apr. 1872, HP 4.36.

9. Notes on Egypt, HP 70.13, ff.56–9, 63–4; TH to JT, 31 Mar. 1872, HP 9.50; *LTH*, 1:371.

10. TH to JT, 31 Mar. 1872, HP 9.50; *LTH*, 1:371–3; Huxley's Diary, HP 70.12; TH to AD, 20 May 1872, HP 13.214; AD to HAH, 7 Mar. 1872, HP 13.210; Lester and Bowler, *Lankester*, 42–7.

11. HAH to ES, 22 Sept. 1872, AD; Huxley's Diary, HP 70.12; TH to MF, 5 Apr. 1872, HP 4.36.

12. TH to JT, 31 Mar. 1872, HP 9.50; *LTH*, 1:371; 'like': TH/HAH to MF, 21 Apr. 1872, HP 4.39; 'took': HAH to AD, 20 May 1872, HP 13.214; 'I am': TH to JH, 9 Apr. 1872, HP 2.192.

   Delegating proved a disaster. His *Introductory Science Primer* for children was not finished. Roscoe's chemistry volume and Stewart's physics were ready, and Geikie was writing on geology. They needed Huxley's to launch the series. He tried farming it out to James Ward, but Ward's work was useless, so Huxley had to take it up again later: H. E. Roscoe to HAH, 20 Feb. 1872, HP 25.275; J. C. Ward to TH, 1 Apr. 1873–14 Mar. 1874, HP 28.157–65; A. Macmillan to TH, 31 May, 3 June 1872, HP 22.144–6; *LTH*, 1:381.

13. Denis, 'Brompton Barracks', 12–15, 19, 22; Stoddart, 'That Victorian Science', 23. *Physiography*'s popularity in the Mechanics' Institutes also testified to Huxley's pedagogical success: Laurent, 'Science', 592; Becker, *Scientific London*, 156; Meadows, *Science*, 84.

14. MF to HAH, [Jan. 1872], HP 16.217; HAH to MF, 21 Apr. 1872, HP 4.39;

'missile': TH to MF, 15, 21 Apr. 1872, HP 4.38–9; 'young': TH to D. C. Gilman, 20 Feb. 1876, Milton S. Eisenhower Library, Johns Hopkins University.

15. TH to JT, 4 June 1872, HP 9.56; *LTH*, 1:379; JT to TH, 3 June [1872], HP 1.105.

16. ERL to TH, 18 Dec. [1872], HP 21.39. Lankester was cranky, but others too told of how alien the science Fellow felt at Exeter College, which belied the talk of Oxford's scientific promise: Howarth, 'Science Education', 334–5, 348, 353. 'I should': TH to AD, 5, 22 June 1872, HP 13.218, 222.

17. Lester and Bowler, *Lankester*, 47–57; Gooday, 'Nature', 334.

18. TH to MF, 5 Apr. 1872, HP 4.36; skeleton: G. H. Richards to TH, 22, 24 June 1872, HP 25.66–7; also HP 19.3–5, 25.5, 33.70–2.

19. TH to ES, 22 Sept. 1872, AD; Bibby, *Huxley*, 117; Gooday, 'Nature', 334; Forgan and Gooday, 'Constructing South Kensington'.

20. Caron, 'Biology', 240–53, relates the emergence of 'biology' to Huxley's 'vocal and aggressive group' at South Kensington. But he fails to note that it was forged as part of Huxley's strategy for the remoulding of State education. Huxley was designing a transmittable basic biology for the new school curriculum. That explains Caron's otherwise anomalous observation that this 'biology' was 'introductive and elementary' and spawned no research tradition. It *had* to be simple, synthetic and assimilable. It was to train teachers and had no other heuristic function. (In the same way, Gooday, 'Precision', 48–50, shows how the new school physics teachers were part of the driving force for the creation of the physics labs.)

Huxley's comprehensive 'biology' united a study of plants and animals on the basis of their common protoplasmic structure and function. It was formed not from natural history but from physiology, structural botany, and pre-eminently comparative anatomy, which gave the new 'biology' its distinctive morphological aspect. 'Biology' retained medical comparative anatomy's lineaments as analytic and descriptive (Desmond, *Politics*), even as it moved sites from the anatomy theatre and Professor-only museum to trainee-accessible laboratory. Indeed this comparative-analytic approach dominated medicine itself until the mid nineteenth century: Pickstone, 'Ways of Knowing', 437, 442–9.

But then the 'lab' culture itself developed largely from medicine. The General Medical Council had first recommended compulsory physiology practicals for student MDs in 1869. (Butler, 'Centers', 475; Geison, *Foster*, 148–56) The College of Surgeons followed suit in 1870 and UCL in 1871 (after receiving Huxley's report: 'Human Physiology', [1870] HP 42.34).

21. Gooday, 'Nature', 313. Of course there was a long haul between 'real' nature and the enclosure of the 'field' under the microscope. In between lay the more visible enclosures in zoos and museum gardens and galleries (Outram, 'New Spaces', 251–3) as well in as the medical theatres noted above.

22. Thiselton-Dyer, 'Plant', 711; Bower, 'Teaching', 712; 'not': Huxley, 'Distribution of Awards'; Forgan and Gooday, 'Constructing South Kensington'; Gooday, 'Nature', 327, 332; *CE*, 3:284–5. The come-apart papier-mâché models were from L. Auzoux's workshop in Paris. Later glass animals were added as teaching aids, supplied by Leopold Blaschka's Dresden works (pers. comm. Anne Barrett). The British and Continental dealers who supplied specimens are listed in HM 2:71:2.

23. Fiske, 'Reminiscences'; Mairet, *Pioneer*, 1, 15; Geddes, 'Huxley', 742; 'glad': Osborn, 'Memorial Tribute', 46; Gooday, 'Nature', 330–40; Howarth, 'Science Education' 349.

24. Forgan, 'Architecture', 149, 153.

25. Grant, 'Lectures'.

26. E. R. Lankester, 'Instruction', 362–3; Huxley and Martin, *Course*, v–vi; *LTH*, 1:378; Lester and Bowler, *Lankester*, 41. That Huxley had access to quantities of seaside and field animals is obvious from his 1873 Diary (HP 70.15A): 'Ask Lloyd about getting Hydra/ Hydratula/ Actinia/ Ascidian/ Green Lizards / . . . / Whelks /Cephalopods /Echinoderms /Dogfish'.
    Physiological experiments followed the anatomical dissections: the masters experimented on the frogs' heartbeats and so forth.

27. Huxley, *Manual of the Anatomy of Invertebrated Animals*, 4; Lyons, 'Origins', 466–7. Ironically, it was the young T. J. Parker ('Huxley', 163) who 'saw' these evolutionary connections and Parker who insisted on reversing the order: *LTH*, 2:405, 411.

28. *Survey of London*, 234–5; Whitrow, *Centenary*, 14; cod: HM 2:31.

29. TH to JH, 11, 28 Aug. 1871, HP 2.177–9; JH to TH, 2, 19, 31 Aug. 1871, HP 3.142–6; *LJH*, 2:59, 161, 165; MacLeod, 'Ayrton Incident', 51–7; 'live': TH to MF, 5 Apr. 1872, HP 4.36.

30. TH to R. Lowe, 4 May 1872, HP 22.22. He had dined with Lowe in Nelson's Bay, Sydney, along with Nicholson (the future Speaker), Donaldson (the future Premier of New South Wales) and W. S. Macleay (or perhaps his brother George Macleay, the then Speaker). 'I have met with many of the best men of my time since – but I have never listened to better talk than at that table': TH to A. P. Martin, 14 Nov. 1893, HP 22.176. A. P. Martin to TH, 13 Nov. 1893, HP 22.174 on Lowe's visit to Darwin, whom he came to 'hero-worship'. MacLeod, 'Ayrton', 59–69; MacLeod, 'Science and the Treasury', 138; Wiener, *English Culture*, 15; TH to AD, 5 Aug. 1872, HP 13.226.

31. TH to AD, 23 Aug. 1872, HP 13.232; 'Like': TH to JH, 31 Dec. 1871, HP 2.187; *LTH*, 1:376.

32. He targeted the *Telegraph*, *Daily News* and *Spectator*, and Hutton 'had very great pleasure in firing off a double shot at that wretch Ayrton, one in this paper & one in the Economist': TH to R. H. Hutton, 9 July 1872, APS; reply 12 July 1872, HP 18.364. JT to TH, 19, 20 June [1872], HP 9.56, 1.109–11; TH to JT, 20 June 1872, APS; JH to JT, 9 May 1872, HP 1.246; MacLeod, 'Ayrton', 58, 61; *LTH*, 2:112.

33. TH to JH, 11 Sept. 1871, HP 2.181; MacLeod, 'Ayrton', 70, 72 n9; 'craven': JH to HAH, 19 Apr. 1872, HP 3.156. On Lubbock's role: HP 22.72–9; 1.110, 248; *LJH*, 2:171.

34. MacLeod, 'Ayrton', 61–5; *LJH*, 2:176; Huxley, 'Kew', which shows how much Owen's intervention polarized the community. Owen's act finally appalled Tyndall. He had remained friendly with Owen through the ape-brain fiasco, and had even urged him to heal the breach with Huxley (R. Owen to JT, 14 June 1871, BM(NH) Owen Corres., vol. 21, f.28; Desmond, *Archetypes*, 143; Rupke, *Owen*, 295). 'I never broke with that man, as you know', he told Huxley. 'But this last trick makes me feel that those who broke with him knew him better than I did. It will greatly augment his isolation': JT to TH, 5 Sept. 1872, HP 1.87; reply HP 9.58.

35. G. J. Goschen to TH, 19 June [1872], HP 17.85; TH to G. J. Goschen, 30 Nov. 1872, HP 17.87; Huxley's Diary, HP 70.12 (28 Nov. 1872); TH to JT, 1 Jan. 1872 [1873], HP 9.63; *LTH*, 1:389; T. A. Hirst to TH, 9 Dec. 1872, HP 18.174; 'Oh': TH to JH, [June 1873], HP 2.208; Burkhardt and Smith, *Calendar*, 8761; 'dreads': Barton, 'Influential', 66–9, 73–5; *LJH*, 2:135. Barton sees Hooker's Presidency as the reforming high spot of the Xs' term of office.

    Ironically, the Naval College had originally been destined for the 'Science Schools' building that Huxley was now in. On Huxley as RS Secretary: T. A. Hirst to TH, 20 June 1872, HP 18.173; *LTH*, 2:451; Hall, 'Royal Society', 157. He succeeded William Sharpey.

36. TH to AD, 24 Feb. 1873, HP 13.236; 'no': 15 Nov. 1873, HP 13.249; 'each': 24 June 1874, HP 13.268; *LTH*, 1:400, 417; Desmond and Moore, *Darwin*, 601.

37. Burkhardt, 'England', 33–8.

38. Turner, 'Victorian Conflict', 367; MacLeod, 'Royal Society', 341.

39. G. G. Stokes to TH, 16 Jan. 1873, HP 27.87. Huxley read the paper on 6 February 1873. The referees, W. H. Flower and W. B. Dawkins, were both comfortable with evolution (RR 7.250–1, RS). Kovalevskii, 'Osteology', 20; Todes, 'Kovalevskii', 128.

40. JT to TH, 3, 19, 20 June [1872], HP 1.105, 110–11; TH to JT, 20 June 1872, APS. The £1,000 was repaid on 11 Jan. 1875, HP 9.90. £4,000: Huxley's 1872 Diary, HP 70.12; JK to TH, 23 Feb. 1872, HP 20.12; wine cellar: Angela Darwin, pers. comm.

41. TH to MF, [Sept. 1872], HP 4.57; 'head': TH to AD, 5 Aug. 1872, HP 13.226; *LTH*, 1:375; 'damnable': TH to JT, 9 Sept. 1872, HP 9.58.

42. TH to JT, 1 Jan. 1872 [1873], HP 9.63; 'meat': TH to MF, [Sept. 1872], HP 4.57; TH to JK, 18 Sept. 1872, APS; 'recover': TH to JT, 9 Sept. 1872, HP 9.58; *LTH*, 1:382, 388. The beneficial effect of Huxley's 'cocoa and Revalenta' diet could support Fabienne Smith's belief ('Darwin's Ill Health') that Huxley, like so many Victorians, suffered from an allergenic disorder, which was aggravated by stress.

43. Friend, 'Huxley's Homes'; CD to HAH, 16 Oct. [1872], HP 5.291; 'stupid': TH to JT, 1 Jan. 1872 [1873], HP 9.63; 'joy': TH to JK, 18 Sept., 2 Nov. 1872, 25 Apr. 1873, APS; TH to AD, 24 Feb. 1873, HP 13.236; TH to MF, 28 Apr. 1873, HP 4.53; *LTH*, 1:383, 388, 399, 403. R. Browning to HAH, 1875–8, HP 11.118–21; H. F. Martin to HAH, 17 Feb. [1875], HP 22.181.

44. TH to JK, 2 Nov. 1872, APS; 'such': 18 Sept. 1872, APS; TH to AD, 24 Feb. 1873, HP 13.236; 'Fancy': TH to JT, 1 Jan. 1872 [1873], HP 9.63; *LTH*, 1:384, 388, 399; HAH to ES, 29 Mar. 1873, AD for the details of the case.

45. TH to JH, n.d., HP 2.208; TH to AD, 24 Feb. 1873, HP 13.236; E. F. Burton (Huxley's Solicitor) to TH, 19 Feb. 1873, HP 12.318; M. H. Cookson (Counsel) to E. F. Burton, 19 Feb. 1873, HP 12.318; E. F. Burton to HAH, 'Monday night', HP 11.201; *LTH*, 1:384, 399.

46. *CE*, 8:37–8, 41, 48, 52–60; 'best': Huxley, 'First Volume'; Deacon, *Scientists*, chap. 15; Linklater, *Voyage*, 15–16; 'Rice, 'Oceanographic', 213; Rehbock, *At Sea*; MacLeod, 'Ayrton', 46–7; Morrell, 'Patronage', 356–7, 383–4. Poems: M. Arnold to TH, 22 Nov. [1873], HP 10.157.

47. C. G. Ehrenberg to TH, 13 Jan. 1873, HP 15.172; TH to MF, 2 Mar. 1873, HP 4.44, 47; Rehbock, 'Huxley', 519–29. Others who had Huxley's Atlantic

mud samples were not too sure of *Bathybius* either: Huxley, 'Deep-Sea Soundings'.

48. TH to JH, 25 July 1871, HP 2.174; C. W. Thomson to TH, 23 Sept. n.y., n.d., 13 Oct. 1871, 10 Oct. 1872, HP 27.283–7, 291; Morrell, 'Patronage', 383. Huxley's word had put Thomson in the chair: H. A. Bruce to TH, 26 Oct. 1870, HP 11.131.

49. C. W. Thomson to TH, 19 May [1873], HP 27.303; see 13 Feb. [1873] on, HP 27.293ff; 'literary': JK to TH, 28 Apr. 1873, HP 20.23; R. von Willemoes-Suhm to TH, 11 Feb. 1873, 5 June 1874, 2 Sept. 1874, HP 29.31–7; Huxley, 'Dinner'; Huxley, 'First Volume'; Deacon, *Scientists*, 338; Linklater, *Voyage*, 35. On the *Challenger*'s results, particularly as they affected Huxley (proving, for example, that *Globigerina* was planktonic and not benthic), see *CE*, 8:89–109.

50. HAH to ES, 29 Mar. 1873, AD; 'take': TH to MF, 2 Mar. 1873, HP 4.44; *LJH*, 2:184; Davidoff and Hall, *Family Fortunes*, 279–81, 313; bills: JK to TH, 2, 23, 28 Apr., 19 June 1873, HP 20.20–6.

51. CD to JT, 8, 11 Apr. 1873, Down House MS 8:13–14; G. H. Darwin to JT, [7 Apr. 1873], Down House MS 8:12; *LLL*, 2:451; *LJH*, 2:184; Litchfield, *Emma Darwin*, 2:212; Burkhardt and Smith, *Calendar*, 8843.

52. CD to JT, 11 Apr. 1873, Down House MS 8:14; Burkhardt and Smith, *Calendar*, 8852, 8855, 8860, 8870.

53. CD to JT, 18 Apr. [1873], Down House MS 8:15; 'be': CD to TH, 23 Apr. [1873], HP 5.295; *LTH*, 1:367; Litchfield, *Emma Darwin*, 2:212.

54. TH to CD, copy dated 'April 25ᵗʰ. 1873', HP 9.198.

55. TH to CD, copy dated 'April 25ᵗʰ. 1873', HP 9.198; 'so': CD to TH, 25 Apr. [1873], 5.297; T. Ashton to TH, 30 Apr. 1873, HP 10.171.

56. TH to MF, 25, 28 Apr. 1873, HP 4.51–3; CD to TH, 28 Apr. 1873, HP 5.299; 'old': TH to JT, 1 Apr. 1873, HP 8.138; *LHS*, 167.

57. TH to A. Clark, 8 May 1873, APS (also 'world'); 'doctor': TH to JT, 2 July 1873, HP 8.150. A. Clark to TH, 25 Sept. 1873, HP 12.199; plants: Huxley and Martin, *Course*; Desmond and Moore, *Darwin*, 601, 608; Colp, *To Be an Invalid*, 88–9; *LTH*, 1:384.

58. TH to JH, 24 Aug. 1873, HP 2.202; 'beauty', 'ashamed': TH to JT, 30 July 1873, HP 9.72; *LTH*, 1:390–5; 'wifes': TH to MF, 27 June 1873, HP 4.60.

59. TH to JT, 30 July 1873, HP 9.72; Blinderman, 'Oxford Debate', 127.

60. Hooker was for sending the ribbon back, even if it meant being in 'the black-books of all the crowned Heads': JH to TH/HAH, 4, 6, 8 Aug. 1873, HP 3.194–202; *LJH*, 2:186–7; 'good': TH to JH, 8 Aug. 1873, HP 2.200.

61. TH to JK, 18 Oct. 1873, APS; TH to JH, 25 Sept. 1873, HP 2.206; TH to Count Steenbock, [Sept. 1873], HP 30.141; 32.13–14; 'wretched': HAH to ES, 16 Apr. 1874, AD.

22 AUTOMATONS

1. Becker, *Scientific London*, 48–9; 'fiend': CD to TH, 5 Dec. [1873], 20 Mar. [1874], HP 5.293, 305; *LTH*, 1:418–19. Cosans, 'Anatomy', for a recent highly-charged defence of Owen's neuroanatomy and 'holistic biology'.

2. Barton, 'Tyndall'; Turner, *Contesting*, 21; Turner, 'Victorian Scientific Naturalism', 349; Lightman, *Origins*, chap. 6; Holyoake, 'Priesthood'. Design: *CE*, 2:86, 109; Paradis, *Huxley*, 99. Huxley talked on evolution

and design in Glasgow on 15 Feb. 1876 (Diary 70.18; *LTH*, 1:456–7; J. S. Blackie to TH, 22 Feb. [1876], HM 3:121:11) and in his Working Men's College (Bibby, 'South London', 216); 'we': Thiselton-Dyer, 'Plant Biology', 711.

3. A. Thorold to TH, 27 Dec. 1871, HP 27.342; 'I have': W. H. Dalton to TH, 19 Nov. [1874], HP 13.3, endorsed 'An⁴. Dec 9ᵗʰ 1874'.

4. MacLeod, 'Science and the Treasury', 135; Turner, 'Public Science', 592; Turner, 'Victorian Conflict', 375.

5. Huxley, 'Science and "Church Policy"'; Barton, 'Evolution', 263–4; Jacyna, 'Immanence'; Turner, 'Victorian Scientific Naturalism', 334–42; Turner, 'Victorian Conflict', 371; Turner, *Contesting*, 157–8.

6. TH to JT, 2 July 1873, HP 8.150; Galton, 'Statistical Inquiries', 134; Turner, *Contesting*, 153–4, 162–70 for a full analysis.

7. Fiske, *Personal Letters*, 121–2, 146–8; Fiske, 'Reminiscences'; J. Fiske to TH, 22 Dec. 1873, 9 Feb. 1874, HP 16.80–3; 'condemned': Clodd, 'Huxley'; 'fresh': TH to JK, 5 Dec. 1873, APS. Tyndall wanted Huxley to write on Spinoza's 'notorious' contemporary influence: JT to TH, 29 Aug. [1875], HP 1.139, also HP 9.91; *LTH*, 1:447, 458. Jacyna, 'Physiology', 119, on the Victorian monists' love of Spinoza.

8. HAH to ES 22 Sept. 1872, AD; 7 Mar. 1875, AD. The publisher Alexander Macmillan met Sam through Nettie and used his book illustrations: A. Macmillan to HAH, 25 July, 26 Sept. 1873, HP 22.147–9. J. Fiske to TH, 31 Jan. 1875, HP 16.86; TH to AD, 24 Feb. 1873, HP 13.236; *LTH*, 1:399; JH to TH, 4 Aug. 1873, HP 3.195; *LTH*, 1:396; Len: TH to JK, 16 Mar. 1874, APS; Fiske, 'Reminiscences'.

9. There is a growing literature on the ideologies of spiritualism: Barrow, in *Independent Spirits*, investigates this plebeian and socialist road to power, and A. Owen, in *A Darkened Room*, explains the sexual politics of female mediumship.

10. A. Owen, *Darkened Room*, chap. 1; Slade: Milner, 'Darwin for the Prosecution'; sneaking admiration: Huxley, 'Spiritualism Unmasked'.

11. Tennyson, *The Princess*, quoted in Erskine, 'Origin', 102.

12. G. Darwin to TH, [22, 28, 30 Jan. 1874], HP 13.87–91; Huxley, 'Report on Séance Janʸ. 27 1874', HP 49.121; CD to TH, 29 Jan. [1874], HP 5.377. Huxley's rapping: Conway, 'Huxley', 74. 'Better': *LTH*, 1:419–20; *LLD*, 3:187. W. Crookes to W. Huggins, 9 Feb. 1874, HP 12.352; W. Huggins to TH, 11 Feb. 1874, HP 18.318; H. Wedgwood to TH, [Mar. 1874], HP 28.209, 215; TH to H. Wedgwood, 14 Mar. 1874, HP 28.213; spirit photographs: HP 28.221.

   Another worry was Carpenter, who seemed 'on the brink of spiritualism or something equally absurd': JT to TH, 27 Oct. 1876, HP 1.148; reply HP 9.101.

13. Denis, 'Brompton Barracks', 14, 17–18. Sir James Kay-Shuttleworth, founder of Battersea teacher-training college, was overjoyed at the prospect of Huxley at the Department: JH to TH, [5, 14 Oct. 1873], HP 3.212–16.

14. Huxley's Aberdeen predecessor, the Under-Secretary of State for India, Grant Duff, was making his first visit to the subcontinent and Liverpool's MP offered to pay Huxley's expenses if he went along: M. Grant Duff to L. Huxley, 4 Nov. 1898, HP 30.178; other requests: HP 19.132–4, 23.17, 28.56, 187; JT to HAH, 25 Apr. 1874, HP 1.118; TH to JT, 22 July 1874, HP 9.84; *LTH*, 1:355, 410.

15. TH to AD, 5 March 1874, HP 13.260; JM to TH, 23 Dec. 1874, HP 23.21; Burkhardt and Smith, *Calendar*, 9469.

16. TH to MF, 22 Apr. 1873, HP 4.50; TH to JK, 25 Apr. 1873, APS; 'deeper': Bibby, *Huxley*, 201–11; 'stinketh': TH to JT, 1 Jan. 1872 [1873], HP 9.63; *LTH*, 1:389; 'shall': *CE*, 3:191. A. Harvey to TH, 25 Apr. 1873, HP 18.68. Huxley wanted botany and zoology removed from Aberdeen's medical examinations and put in a new Faculty of Science, to free up time for 'finger-end' clinical studies (*CE*, 3:217, 222–3; 'On the Medical Curriculum', *Nature*, 9 [1873], 21–2), and he suggested that German or French be substituted for ancient Greek.

17. TH to MF, 23 Feb. 1874, HP 4.73; Bibby, *Huxley*, 205; *CE*, 3:191, 202.

18. Becker, *Scientific London*, 185–7. Frederick Harrison, Lyell, John Chapman and Spencer had at times sat in on the workers' lectures (Peterson, *Huxley*, 139), and the student Thiselton-Dyer ('Plant Biology', 709); curate: R. England to TH, 7 Mar. 1874, HP 15.194; 'telepathic': HAH to ES, 31 Dec. 1865, AD.

19. Knight, 'Getting Science', 136. We have to recognize the needs of Huxley's workers in order to understand his gentle hegemonic hijacking. True, many *Reasoner* readers relished Darwinism's dissident image, seeing the *Origin* bypass the Creative props of a static Anglican society. But others saw lecturer and lectured as a sort of coalition and continued on their co-operative evolutionary track. While Huxley was trying to mobilize this constituency, radicals were incorporating the congenial parts of his science, sustaining them within socialist programmes in the Halls of Science. It was a case of working-class 'appropriation, and transformation', rather than passive diffusion: Cooter and Pumfrey, 'Separate Spheres', 242–9.

20. L. L. D., 'Huxley', cf. *CE*, 6:279, 1:241.

21. Carpenter, 'Doctrine', 400–2, reminded Huxley of his debt to Hall; *CE*, 1:191, 199ff, esp. 244; Jacyna, 'Physiology', 111–16; R. Smith, 'Human Significance'; Tyndall, *Fragments*, 92–3, 441.

22. By 1874 he had become more deterministic, making the feeling of free will an emotional warmth which accompanies some compunction (*CE*, 1:241). In 1871, his more cautious admission that the mentally-constructed world of a conscious mind was as likely as the material world of our subjective being brought jeers from the militant materialists. By making it impossible to disprove free will, he was casting 'Idealistic dust in our eyes; seemingly to prevent the bigots calling him Materialist': L. L. D., 'Huxley', cf. *CE*, 6:279.

23. TH to JT, 25 Sept. 1873, HP 9.77; *LTH*, 1:401, 418; Sopka, 'Tyndall'; Harvard: TH to C. E. Appleton, 8 July 1874, APS; *LJT*, 167–73; party: TH to MacGregor, 14 Mar. 1873, APS; £150: JK to TH, 5, 8 June 1874, HP 20.38–9. HAH to ES, 16 Apr. 1874, AD.

24. TH to JH, 4 Dec. 1874, HP 2.216; 'Sir': 31 Mar. 1874, HP 2.210; *LJH*, 2:148–9; Becker, *Scientific London*, 23–5.

25. Over 70 masters had applied for the June 1874 course; 40 were accepted, double the usual number: TH to MF, 18 May 1874, HP 4.84.

26. T. J. Parker to TH, 7 May 1875, HP 24.23; 'Elementary', 'Best': TH to MF, 5 May, 4 July 1874, HP 4.81, 86; T. J. Parker, 'Huxley', 165; O'Connor, *Founders*, 188–202.

27. W. G. Armstrong to TH, 3 July 1874, HP 10.116. Huxley tapped both Armstrong and Whitworth for the Dohrn appeal: TH to MF, 26 Apr. 1874,

HP 4.180. Heath: HAH to ES, 16 Apr. 1874, 7 Mar. 1875, AD. Huxley, 'Professor Huxley at Manchester'.

28.   TH to unknown corres., 30 June 1894, APS; Briggs, *Victorian Cities*, chap. 5; G. M. Young, *Portrait*, 109.

29.   *CE*, 1:256–9, 282. While there has been considerable exegesis of this essay, e.g. Helfand, 'Huxley's "Evolution"', Paradis, *Huxley*, 173–7, no one to my knowledge has emphasized its telling Birmingham location.

For a subtle analysis of Spencer's Lamarckism and Huxley's non-Lamarckian naturalism, and the way this led to human nature being fixed for Huxley, with social progress being brought about by the 'transformation of the environment', i.e. a Chamberlainite technocracy, see Paradis, '*Evolution*', 31–5.

30.   H. Cole to TH, 3 Nov. 1871, HM 3:121:43; A. R. Wallace to TH, 27 Sept. 1873, HP 28.96; 'John Bull' to TH, 16 Oct. 1871, HP 9.278; TH to AD, 3 Jan. 1872, HP 13.213; Huxley, *Critiques*, vi–ix; *LTH*, 1:368; *LHS*, 150; Spencer, *Autobiography*, 2:232.

31.   K. M. Lyell to HAH, 5 Aug. 1874, HP 22.111; 'Satan': TH to JT, 22 July 1874, HP 9.84; *LTH*, 1:410; *CE*, 3:2, 30; 'hung': HAH to ES, 7 Mar. 1875, AD.

32.   TH to JT, 25 Sept. 1873, HP 9.77; *LTH*, 1:401; replying to HP 1.113; JH to JT, 16 Oct. [1873], HP 8:356; *Belfast News-Letter*, 21 Aug. 1874, 5; Burkhardt and Smith, *Calendar*, 9063.

33.   JT to TH, 14 May 1874, HP 1.119; 'lunatic': TH to JT, 13 Nov. 1873, HP 9.79; 'slanderous': JT to JH, 25 Oct. 1873, HP 8.357; Burkhardt and Smith, *Calendar*, 12220, 12230; M. Arnold to TH, 13 Oct. 1873, HP 10.155; Brown, *Metaphysical Society*, 65–6. Alexander Agassiz told Tyndall (10 June 1874, HP 6.143) to 'Cowhide Ruskin' the 'scientific Charlatan'.

34.   *Belfast News-Letter*, 21 Aug. 1874, 5; *LTH*, 1:414.

35.   *LJH*, 2:158; *LTH*, 1:413; *CE*, 1:241; 'dance': TH to MF, 12 Aug. 1874, HP 4.90; Barton, 'Tyndall', 115–16; 'those': TH to W. H. Williamson, 24 Aug. 1873, APS.

36.   Barton, 'Tyndall', 113; Tyndall, *Fragments II*, 199; *LTH*, 1:413. Calderwood, 'Present Relations', 225, had long seen such imperial pretensions and the 'strong hand of conquest' in Huxley's work.

37.   Livingstone, 'Darwinism', 411–12, 418; *LJT*, 187; Barton, 'Tyndall', 116; Gillespie, 'Duke', on disputes about mankind's rise from savagery; HAH to ES, 7 Mar. 1875, AD; 'as Luther', quoted by Lightman, 'Pope', 156; 'its': TH to MF, 12 Aug. 1874, HP 4.90; drafts: JT to TH, 1, 15 July 1874, HP 1.128–9.

38.   Livingstone, 'Darwinism', 419; *LLL*, 2:455; Barton, 'Tyndall', 121. Tyndall's cosmos had its teleological aspect, as Huxley ('Natural History of Creation', 40–3) knew.

39.   Tyndall, *Fragments*, 163–4; Barton, 'Tyndall', 117; *LJT*, 183. With Tyndall bathing Lucretius' atheistic *De rerum natura* in the new atomic light, Classicists made the Roman poet denounce a stale modern naturalism. One anonymous potboiler (written by Balfour Stewart and P. G. Tait), *The Unseen Universe*, expanded Tyndall's cosmos into a greater Whole. Here energy flowed back and forth between Providential and natural realms to square conservation principles with immortal promises: Turner, 'Lucretius', 330–8; Heimann, '*Unseen Universe*'.

40. *LTH*, 1:424; JM to TH, 12 Nov. 1874, HP 23.20; 'going': TH to P. L. Sclater, 24 Apr. 1875, APS; Brown, *Metaphysical Society*, 224–30; Morley, *Recollections*, 1:88–90.

41. Carpenter, 'Human Automatism', 397, 413–15, and esp. 943; Desmond, *Politics*, 214–15; V. M. D. Hall, 'Contribution'; Wace, 'Scientific Lectures', 42. Jacyna, 'Physiology', 111–12, 124–6, for a superb study on the new 'physiological psychology' of Spencer, Huxley, Bain, Ferrier, Clifford *et al.*, with its epiphenomenal mind and anti-Church political connections.

42. Perkins, *Origins*, 158–9; 'doll': TH to CL, 17 Mar. 1860, HP 30.34, *LTH*, 1:212; McConnish: Becker, *Scientific London*, 182. Huxley would be a Trustee for the George Henry Lewes Studentship for physiology at Cambridge in 1879, which was open to women and men: Haight, *Eliot Letters*, 7:117, 177.

43. E. Richards, 'Huxley', 276; E. Richards, 'Darwin', 60ff for a convincing study of the 'congruence of *The Descent* with dominant Victorian social and political assumptions' (79); Erskine, 'Origin', 97–103; Jann, 'Darwin'; Darwin, *Descent*, 563–6.

44. Huxley, 'Miss Jex-Blake'; *LTH*, 1:417; Bibby, *Huxley*, 35–6.

45. HAH to ES, 10 Feb. 1883, AD; Erskine, 'Origin', 105.

46. Dennis and Skilton, *Reform*, 148.

47. E. A. J. Wallop to HAH, 21 Oct. 1874, HP 28.107; Stevenson: HAH to ES, 16 Apr. 1874, AD. For the Huxleys at the Earl of Portsmouth's mansion: *Brighton Herald* press cutting, July 1895, HP 81.94.

48. Blake, *Charge*, 90–2, 96, 104, 114, 123.

49. One was Mary Whitfield: M. Whitfield to TH, 9 Aug. 1894, HP 29.14; *LTH*, 1:386–7; E. Richards, 'Huxley', 278; Blake, *Charge*, 117–18.

50. 'X.Y.Z.' to *Times*, 2 June 1874.

51. JH to TH, 25 Nov. 1874, HP 3.222; 'University': TH to MF, 1 Dec. 1874, HP 4.100; L. Playfair to HAH, 30 Nov. 1874, HP 24.140.

52. Harte, *University*, 126–8; Blake, *Charge*, 135, 167; *LTH*, 1:417.

53. HAH to ES, 7 Mar. 1875, AD; 'not': TH to AD, 24 Feb. 1873, HP 13.236; *LTH*, 1:400. Nettie's submergence matched Emma's in Charles Darwin (E. Richards, 'Darwin', 80), even though she too disagreed with her husband on religious matters. Despite writing to Lizzie, 'You touched me deeply when you said that you believed dear Hal's "principles aims & hopes and mine were the same" – I can truly say that indeed they are' (HAH to ES, 8 Feb. 1871, AD), there was never quite the congruence that she implied on the deepest issue, agnosticism.

54. HAH to ES, 13 Sept. 1879, AD. Rachel failed. The Cambridge local exams admitted women from 1865: Brock, 'School Science Examinations', 171–2. Martin Cooke is currently looking at Henrietta's Moravian education. 'Regina': TH to MF, 5 May 1874, HP 4.81; 'Few': TH to MF, 5 Apr. 1872, HP 4.36.

55. M. G. Grey to HAH/TH, 12 June, 13 July 1871, HP 17.144–8; Bibby, *Huxley*, 36.

56. HAH to TH, 7–8 July 1873, AD.

57. In HAH to TH, 7 July 1873, AD, Nettie saw Hal founding 'a new school of thought where the materialists & spiritualists shall be united in brotherhood – or if not this, your creed shall give peace to those whose souls are unsatisfied with the doctrines alike of materialist or spiritualist', which missed his

point entirely. Indeed his reply (TH to HAH, 8 Aug. 1873, AD; *LTH*, 1:397) made plain that he was not reconciling 'the antagonisms of the old schools', 'nor is any reconcilement possible between free thought and traditional authority. One or other will have to succumb', and he had no more doubt that 'freethought will win in the long run than I have that I sit here writing to you'. She evidently preferred not to see his work this way.

58. Haight, *Eliot Letters*, 5:365. But then there was the odd echo of his own reverie in 'Physical Basis of Life' in *Middlemarch*: Adam, 'Huxley'.

59. I have only been able to trace one undated HAH reminiscence on the point, written late in life (HP 62.21):

> Geo. H Lewes. Pater w^d tease me by repeating his compliments which I loathed. – Pater goes thrice to the Lewes but not allowing me to call.

The first statement suggests Nettie's dislike of the coarse G. H. Lewes, the second that Huxley would not allow her to visit George Eliot.

60. Lightman, 'Voices'; Gates, 'Revisioning', 762ff; Cooter and Pumfrey, 'Separate Spheres'. Buckley's visits: HAH to TH, 7 July 1873, AD.

61. A. Secord, 'Science in the Pub', for a sophisticated look at the manual workers' co-operative botany in Victorian Lancashire, with its Sunday pub meetings, Methodist organization and craft pride, and the way this had once allowed the weavers to share the cultural property of the educated classes.

62. *CE*, 2:236; Weindling, *Darwinism*, 47–8; cf. Dohrn's rival work on an annelid ancestry for vertebrates: Groeben, *Darwin*, 34–5; TH to AD, 30 Apr. 1870, HP 13.174; *LTH*, 1:332; Maienschein, 'It's a Long Way'.

63. Abstract of Huxley's Lectures on Biology, South Kensington, Oct. 1874, by W. W. Cobb, HP 68.41–2; *SM*, 4:51, 128; ERL to TH, 11 June [1875], HP 21.45; 'shut', 'take': *LTH*, 1:398, 416–17, 425; HM 1:5:83, 2:16.

   Huxley was also attempting to homologize the lamprey's and tadpole's skulls, to show that the jawless fish shared the normal vertebrate plan (contra Gegenbaur and Haeckel): *SM*, 4:128–44; HM 2:17–18.

64. E. R. Lankester, 'On the Primitive', 'Notes on the Embryology'; Lester and Bowler, *Lankester*, 82–3. Haeckel, 'Scientific Worthies', was quick to point out that Huxley's suggestion that the two layers of the coelenterates were analogous to the germinal layers of the vertebrate embryo was at the root of his 'Gastraea' theory in 1874, which hypothesized a two-layered remote ancestor for all metazoa (Gould, *Ontogeny*, 170).

65. *SM*, 4:66ff, esp. 82–3, 175, 227–32. For a study of the meaning of Huxley's crocodile work and its contrast to Owen's, see Desmond, *Archetypes*, 170–4; also Collie, *Huxley*, 60ff; and di Gregorio, *Huxley*, 95–7.

66. Ruse, 'Booknotes', 250.

67. HM 2:69:24ff.

68. *CE*, 8:176. Huxley's was also partly influenced by Haeckel's monographs on the 'monera'; hence his own work on the ciliates in late 1874. He was cadging *Paramecium* from Foster (who had a Muscovy duck pond), and devising new techniques to preserve the related unicellular *Nyctotherus* and *Balantidium*: TH to MF, 20 Oct. 1874, HP 4.94; HM 2:6:2, 5, 7ff.

69. Cobb's notes, HP 69.8. By 1879 – after America and Marsh's horses – he was prepared to use the 'good servants and bad masters' metaphor in a way more positive to evolution: Huxley, 'Prefatory Note', xi.

70. Mivart, 'Reminiscences', 996; St G. Mivart to TH, 6 Oct. 1874, HP 22.261; Gruber, *Conscience*, 237 n32.

71. *LTH*, 1:425; 'Papist': TH to JH, 27 Dec. 1874, HP 2.220; Gruber, *Conscience*, 99–101; G. Darwin to TH, 28 Dec. 1874, HP 13.94.

72. TH to C. E. Appleton, 28 Jan. 1875, APS; 'leave': TH to JH, 27 Dec. 1874, HP 2.220; Gruber, *Conscience*, 102–4; *LTH*, 1:425; also HP 2.218, 3.225. Huxley only caught up with the offending review on 17 December 1874: TH to JH, 19 Dec. 1874, HP 2.214.

73. J. Fiske to TH, 31 Jan. 1875, HP 16.86; CD to TH, 24 Dec. [1874], HP 5.311; G. Darwin to TH, 28 Dec. 1874, HP 13.94; Huxley, 'Anthropogenie', 16–17; Gruber, *Conscience*, 102, 109.

74. Mivart, 'Reminiscences', 994, 997; St G. Mivart to TH, 20, 24 Dec. 1874, HP 22.263, 267; reply HP 22.265; Burkhardt and Smith, *Calendar*, 9768, 9770, 9777, 9780, 9800; CD to TH, 6 Jan. 1875, HP 5.313; TH to JH, 27 Dec. 1874, HP 2.220; JH to TH, 28 Dec. 1874, HP 3.229; Gruber, *Conscience*, 102–10.

75. MF to TH, 19, 27, 31 Jan. [1875], HP 4.192–4, 200; TH to MF, 1 Feb. 1875, HP 4.102; Geison, *Foster*, 142–3. Foster thought Martin's name on the cover would increase his job prospects; that it did was evident from Huxley's sending Johns Hopkins a copy in 1876, as a reference for Martin. He became the biology professor there: Benson, 'American', 166–7.

    'Lord how I wish that I had gone through such a course', said Darwin as he read it (CD to TH, 12 Nov. [1875], HP 5.324). In fact Darwin was being polite – his morphologically-undisciplined mind would have hated it, and his stomach would have reacted to the gore, as it did during his student days in Edinburgh.

76. Poore, 'Grant'; Schafer, 'Sharpey'.

77. ERL to TH, 11 June [1875], HP 21.45; Lankester was appointed on 20 Feb. 1875; 'life': ERL to TH, [*c.* 1873], HP 21.48; 'like': Lester and Bowler, *Lankester*, 61–7.

78. *LLL*, 2:452, 460; bedside: Judd, *Coming*, 80; *LTH*, 1:361, 448; *LJH*, 2:199; *LCK*, 2:343; 'You': F. Kingsley to TH, 16 Nov. 1876, HP 19.261; 'pain': HAH to ES, 7 Mar. 1875, AD.

79. Tener and Woodfield, *Victorian Spectator*, 28; desert: *CE*, 6:319.

80. H. E. Roscoe to TH, 24 Jan. 1875, HP 25.277; E. Becker to TH, Feb. 1875, HP 10.261–2 on the *Primers'* German translation; MacLeod, 'Evolutionism', 74. Book list: HP 52.9, cf. 30.92.

81. Meadows, *Science*, 88–92; TH to NL, 31 Jan., 3 Feb. 1875, HP 21.266–7.

82. 'Thank': TH to P. L. Sclater, 22 Jan., 14 Aug. 1875, ZSL; 29 Apr., 11 May 1875, APS; TH to JH, 3 Nov. 1875, APS; *LTH*, 1:447, 450; Burkhardt and Smith, *Calendar*, 9827, 9831, 9843. The Polar Committee also fought for Treasury funding to make Carpenter's son Philip the naturalist on the 1875 *Valorous* expedition to the Arctic: WBC to TH, 20 Jan. 1876, HP 12.105; A. Gunther to TH, 1 Dec. 1875, BM(NH) L MSS Gunther Coll. 27, box 1, folder 9. Huxley had already backed a private attempt to get a screw steamer through the Spitzbergen ice to the unconquered Pole: *Proposed Arctic Expedition, via Spitzbergen* (Jan. 1873): flyer in BM(NH), Z. Keeper's Archives 1.1.

    And he encouraged military efforts to record information. At the Royal Engineer Institute, Chatham, he talked on 'The geographical distribution of animals; and on collecting and observing . . . ', 3 Apr 1878, HM 1:4:131.

83. TH to FD, 9 June 1875, HP 1.135; antivivisection flyers: HP 49.143; 'or else': MF to TH, 27 Jan. [1875], HP 4.194; Ritvo, *Animal Estate*, 160–4; 'alleviating': TH to JD, 12 Feb. 1874, HP 30.85; *LTH*, 1:431; Harrison, 'Animals', 791; O'Connor, *Founders*, 132; French, *Antivivisection*, 100.

84. TH to MF, 16 Apr. 1875, HP 4.106. The Council on Education minute on vivisection was recorded on 10 Feb. 1874 and evidently changed to cover only conscious animals after Huxley protested: TH to Lord Aberdare (H. A. Bruce), 14 Feb. 1874, HP 30.87; TH to JD, 12 Feb. 1874, HP 30.85; *LTH*, 1:430–3; French, *Antivivisection*, 95; 'parvenu': Ritvo, *Animal Estate*, 157–65; E. Richards, 'Redrawing the Boundary' on the class edge to Cobbe's feminist attack.

    Ironically, having clawed State funding, the Xs were soon to start worrying that it might bring with it State interference: Barton, 'Influential', 76–7.

85. To explain the sympathy of women with the antivivisectionist movement one must look to Evelleen Richards' work on the Victorian categorizing of women, as a lower form, like 'dogs' possessing 'dangerous sexualities that necessitated control'. Women accepted that inferior position, while sharing a sympathy with other denigrated races brutalized by men: E. Richards, 'Redrawing the Boundary'. Coral Lansbury, 'Gynaecology', goes further to suggest slippage between the anti-pornography and antivivisectionist protest, in both cases the victims being tied down and violated.

86. Burkhardt and Smith, *Calendar*, 9849, 9916, 9923, 9933–5, 9938, 9948; *LLD*, 3:204; French, *Antivivisection*, 62–79; *LGR*, 7–8, 15–22; R. Richards, *Darwin*, 334ff; sermon: Countess Camperdown to TH, 7 July [1875], HP 15.23–5. Playfair's reworded Bill in the Commons proved unsatisfactory: a clause allowing vivisection only for the purpose of scientific discovery would have outlawed Huxley's schoolmasters' demonstrations: *LTH*, 1:436–9; CD to TH, 21 May 1875, HP 5.316.

87. R. A. Cross to TH, June 1875, HP 12.353–6; *LTH*, 1:438–9; HP 10.204–6; E. Cardwell to TH, 1, 6 July 1875, HP 12.29–32; French, *Antivivisection*, 91ff, and 93 on the fox-hunting MPs on the Commission.

88. Huxley, Edinburgh lectures, 3 May–23 July 1875, HM 2:70:4; 'University of Edinburgh – Opening of the Natural History Class by Professor Huxley', newspaper cutting, HM 2:70:4a. Cf. his letter to Spencer, in which he jokingly claimed that he had warned the students 'to keep free of the infidel speculations which are current under the name of evolution': Caron, 'Biology', 250. TH to FD, 9 June 1875, HP 1.135; 'still': TH to JH, 10 Oct. 1875, HP 2.222. Rice, 'Oceanographic', 216. Morrell, 'Patronage' 360–78; autograph hunters: J. E. Millais, HP 22.232–3; also HP 15.224, 22.12.

89. TH to JT, 13 Aug. 1875, HP 9.91; *LTH*, 1:443–6.

90. CWT to TH, 9 June 1875, HP 27.312; 'horrid': 5 Sept. 1874, HP 27.310; Rehbock, 'Huxley', 527–9; Linklater, *Voyage*, 121ff.

91. Rehbock, 'Huxley', 528–9; Rupke, '*Bathybius*', 60; Rice, 'Huxley', 173; Huxley, 'Notes from the "Challenger"'; *LTH*, 1:480; 'My': TH to NL, 13 Aug. 1875, HP 21.268; Meadows, *Science*, 31–6.

92. TH to MF, 29 Nov., 1 Dec. 1874, HP 4.96, 100; ERL to TH, 11 June [1875], HP 21.45; HAH to ES, 3 Apr. 1876, AD.

93. TH to JK, 14 June 1875, APS; 'white': JK to TH, 9 June 1875, HP 20.42; 'refreshing': TH to JK, 5 June 1875, APS; Catlett, 'Huxley', 184–6; 'gentle': Tener and Woodfield, *Victorian Spectator*, 9.

94. CD to TH, 1 Nov. [1875], HP 5.322; *LTH*, 1:440; sheep-pox: TH to JT, 9 Nov. [1874], HP 9.88; O'Connor, *Founders*, 133, 137, 155–7, 254; Harte, *University*, 125–6; Litchfield, *Emma Darwin*, 2:221; French, *Antivivisection*, 103–6. Klein, Burdon-Sanderson, Brunton and Foster, *Handbook for the Physiological Laboratory* (1873) was the standard text on the experimental method.

23 THE AMERICAN DREAM

1. F. Harrison to TH, 30 Aug. 1876, HP 18.48 (also 'whole'); Martin, 'flying': TH to D. C. Gilman, 20 Feb., 23 Apr. 1876, Milton S. Eisenhower Library, Johns Hopkins University; D. C. Gilman to TH, 14 Mar. 1876, HP 17.51; 'heart', 'glorious': J. Fiske to TH, 1 Mar. 1876, HP 16.89; 'thirty': TH to ES, 8 June 1876, HP 31.44; Jensen, 'Huxley's Address', 259; *LTH*, 1:446, 459–60.

2. TH to JK, 4 Dec. 1875, APS, reply, 7 Dec., HP 20.44; M. Arnold to TH, 8 Dec. 1875, HP 10.159; *LTH*, 1:319, 448, 457; 'up': TH to MF, 4 Dec. 1875, HP 4.111.

3. HAH to ES, 3 Apr. 1876, 2 Sept. 1878, AD; creditors: J. W. Johnson to TH, 15 Nov. 1875, HP 19.79; W. C. Norton to TH, 16 Nov. 1875, HP 23.230.

4. TH to JK, 4, 31 Dec. 1875, APS.

5. *SM*, 4:36, 84–124, esp. 101, 121; Woodward, 'Contributions', 729; di Gregorio, *Huxley*, 72–4. Yet he suggests elsewhere that, despite the remarkable similarity to the Devonian fringe-finned fish *Dipterus* (now known to be a lungfish), *Ceratodus* was possibly not related to it 'in the way of ancestry': *SM*, 4:166.

   Nyhart, *Biology*, 251–62 on Gegenbaur's 'archipterygium' theory: his attempt to show how *Ceratodus*' 'archetypal fin' had developed; Huxley was not too happy about Gegenbaur's conclusion: *SM*, 4:118. Di Gregorio, 'Wolf', on Gegenbaur as a go-between bridging the archetypal idealists such as Owen and the Darwinians with their evolutionary theory.

6. TH to P. L. Sclater, 21, 31 Dec. 1875, APS; Len: TH to A. Gunther, 3 Jan. 1876, Z Keeper's Archives 1.9, Letters 1876 no 279; *LTH*, 1:398; Drawings of *Polypterus*, 1 Jan. 1875, HM Box D:54; Notes on *Ceratodus Forsteri*, HM 2:22:1.

7. Brown, *Metaphysical*, 31, 89, 140, 329; *LTH*, 1:319, 457; JK to L. Huxley, 23 Feb. 1899 HP 20.200; Conway, 'Huxley', 74; Peterson, *Huxley*, 170.

8. Anne Evans' Diary, HP 31.105; Magnus, *Gladstone*, 229, 233–7; W. E. Gladstone to TH, 24 Feb. 1876, HP 17.67; Huxley's Diary, 2 March 1876, HP 70.18.

9. JM to TH, 9 Jan. 1876, HP 23.24; *LTH*, 1:458. Huxley (Diary, HP 70.18) met Morley on 18 January 1876 and presumably discussed the paper. W. K. Clifford to HAH, 7, 19 Apr. 1876, HP 12.240–2; J. L. Richards, 'Reception', 152–6.

10. HAH to ES, 3 Apr. 1876, 14 Nov. 1877, AD; 'face': TH to AD, 13 Jan. 1877, HP 13.272; JH to HAH, 1 July 1876, HP 3.245; Countess of Portsmouth to HAH, 2 Aug. 1876, HP 28.109; TH to JT, 13 Aug. 1875, HP 9.91; *LTH*, 1:447. Huxley was soon introducing Waller to the people of note: TH to H. Cole, 6 July 1877, APS.

11. JT to TH, 15 Oct. [1875], HP 1.92, also 1.91–7; 9.38, 94–6; *LTH*, 1:449;

Friday, 'Microscopic Incident', 65–9; TH's notes, HM 1:1:67, 2:2; *CE*, 3:280.

12. *LJT*, xxi, 202–6; *LHS*, 182; 'After': JT to TH, 4 Feb. 1876, HP 1.141–3, also 1.145, 151; JH to JT, 10 Mar. 1876, HP 8.368; 'considering', 'D': HAH to ES, 3 Apr. 1876, AD.

13. HAH to ES, 3 Apr. 1876, AD; J. P. Thomasson to TH, 20 Mar. 1876, HP 27.243, see also 244–7; W. Brimelow to TH, 30 Mar. 1876, HP 11.76; Morley, *Cobden*, 687.

14. Huxley was awarded the Geological Society's Wollaston Medal in 1876: H. Woodward to TH, 2 Feb. 1876, HP 29.92.

15. TH to MF, 25 May 1876, HP 4.120 (also 'pietistic'); *Times*, 23 May 1876; Huxley's letter, *Times*, 26 May; Shaftesbury's reply, *Times*, 27 May, in HP 49.140–2; TH to Shaftesbury, 29 May 1876, HP 12.320; *LTH*, 1:427–30; *CE*, 3:310. Sir William Smith urged Huxley (21 Feb.–19 Mar. 1876, HP 26.131–49) to write on vivisection in the *Quarterly* to sway Parliament.

16. HAH to ES, 3 Apr., 9 Aug. 1876, AD; Huxley's Diary HP 70.18; *LTH*, 1:460. Hooker: *LJH*, 2:202; JH to JT, 26 June 1876, HP 8.369; JH to HAH, 1, 4 July 1876, HP 3.245–6.

17. HAH to ES, 9 Aug. 1876, AD; cartoon of ship, 2 Aug. 1876, Huxley's Diary HP 70.19; 'must': ES to TH, 26 June 1876, AD. They sailed with friends, George Smalley of the *New York Tribune* and Newell Martin, on his way to Johns Hopkins: Maienschein, *Transforming*, 25; *LTH*, 1:461.

18. King, 'Catastrophism', 469–70; Pfeifer, 'United States', 199–200; Irvine, *Apes*, 289; MacLeod, 'Evolutionism', 66; Hofstadter, *Social Darwinism*, 6–10, 41; F. Harrison to TH, 30 Aug. 1876, HP 18.48; *LTH*, 1:460.

19. Randel, 'Huxley', 75–81; *LTH*, 1:461, 463; 'beautiful': HAH to ES, 9 Aug. 1876, AD; Hofstadter, *Social Darwinism*, 24.

20. W. H. Appleton to HAH, 22 Aug. 1876, HP. 10.108; 'to': TH to ES, 8 June 1876, HP 31.44.

21. Marsh, *Introduction*; Marsh, *Odontornithes*; and Marsh, 'Discovery', 56–7 – a paper earmarked in Huxley's Diary HP 70.15A: 'Marsh – Bird from Upper Cretaceous shale of Kansas . . . Annals Jny 1873'. *LTH*, 1:462–3; Randel, 'Huxley', 78–80. Background: Schuchert and LeVene, *Marsh*; Ostrom and McIntosh, *Marsh's Dinosaurs*; Goetzmann, *Exploration*, 421–9.
    After Huxley left America Marsh continued to work on the toothed, flight-less *Hesperornis* and to reaffirm that its primitive characters were those of ratites, in effect confirming Huxley's dinosaur–*Hesperornis*–ostrich link: O. C. Marsh to TH, 12 Jan. 1877, Yale University Library.

22. Dinosaurs alone were responsible for the prints, Marsh now believed: *Introduction*, 11; Dean, 'Hitchcock's Tracks'; Desmond, *Archetypes*, 129; Randel, 'Huxley', 80; *LTH*, 1:462.

23. Schuchert and LeVene, *Marsh*, 236–7; 'more': TH to O. C. Marsh, 17 Aug. 1876, Yale University Library; *LTH*, 1:463; 'red-faced': HP 89.39.

24. Marsh, *Introduction*, 27; Marsh, 'Huxley'; Marsh, 'Notice', 255; *LTH*, 1:463; Rainger, 'Paleontology', 282–4.

25. J. Fiske to TH, 1 Mar. 1876, HP 16.89; Fiske, *Darwinism*, 54. Fiske named his own son Herbert Huxley: Randel, 'Huxley', 75, 82; 'driven': A. Agassiz to TH, 14 July 1874, HP 6.144; Winsor, *Reading*, chaps 5–6; Desmond and Moore, *Darwin*, 562–3; Dupree, *Gray*, 337–41.

26. HAH to ES, 2 Sept. 1876, AD; 'thin': ES to TH, 26 June 1876, AD; Randel,

'Huxley', 82–4. Winsor, *Reading*, 42. The Director of Buffalo Museum wrote of how the 'pulpiteers' struck up after Huxley left. Their arguments 'smell badly' and it takes 'all Moody & Sankey and Mrs. Van Cott can do to make them neutral in their odor'. A. R. Grote to TH, 13 Mar. 1878, HP 17.149. On Moody and evolution: J. R. Moore, *Post-Darwinian Controversies*, 55; J. R. Moore, *Darwin Legend*, 83ff.

27. Summerville, 'Roberts', 18–22, 30–6, 180–2; J. M. Smith, 'Huxley', 191–8; 'most': ES to HAH, 30 Oct. 1876, AD. The 'buckle on the Bible belt' is Jim Moore's expression.

28. ES to TH, 6 July 1874, 26 June 1876, AD; 'George': TH to ES, 8 June 1876, HP 31.44; 'drink': HAH to ES, 3 Apr. 1876, AD; J. M. Smith, 'Huxley', 193.

29. Randel, 'Huxley', 85–6; J. M. Smith, 'Huxley', 200–1, 322–7, 330–40; 'pugilistic': ES to HAH, 30 Oct. 1876, AD. Fisk: Lorimer, *Colour*, 63.

30. HAH to ES, 17 Sept. 1876, AD; 'page': ES to HAH, 30 Oct. 1876, AD; J. M. Smith, 'Huxley', 334, 336; Flexner, *Gilman*, 35.

31. Randel, 'Huxley', 88–9; Jensen, 'Huxley's Address', 257–64; Flexner, *Gilman*, 23–5, 35, 48, 50, 55–9, 63–4; White, *History*, 22ff; and see J. R. Moore, *Post-Darwinian Controversies* on White's military metaphor.

32. CE, 3:236, 256, 260–1; 'vigorous': HAH to ES, 17 Sept. 1876, AD; Jensen, *Huxley*, 98; Jensen, 'Huxley's Address', 265; Huxley, 'How to Become', 2.

33. TH to H. N. Martin, 2 Apr. [1879], Milton S. Eisenhower Library, Johns Hopkins University; Jensen, 'Huxley's Address', 258–60; Randel, 'Huxley', 90; Caron, 'Biology', 243–5. On Martin at Hopkins, and his lab-based physiological approach: Pauly, 'Appearance', 378–9; Benson, 'American', 166–7; Benson, 'Museum Research', 66ff. As in London, so Martin here too started practical lab classes for teachers with a microscope as the exam prize: Maienschein, *Transforming*, 27–8.

34. HAH to ES, 17 Sept. 1876, AD. The Smithsonian zoologist Spencer Fullerton Baird (the man who commissioned the Centennial *Hadrosaurus*) escorted Hal and Nettie around the exhibits. Rainger, 'Rise', 9–12. Huxley presumably never met the Philadelphian E. D. Cope. Even Agassiz had warned him off the erratic Cope, who had gained 'the contempt of all the scientific men of the country': A. Agassiz to TH, 14 July 1874, HP 6.144.

35. HAH to ES, 17 Sept. 1876, AD. Requests: HP 11.106, 13.135, 15.7, 15.36, 15.223, 21.173, 23.207, 24.108, 24.192, 25.1, 26.159, 27.121, 29.100.

36. Randel, 'Huxley', 91–3. Greeley himself had been ever ready to 'lend an attentive and unprejudiced ear to the bold speculations of our Darwins and Huxleys, wherein they almost seem to lay a confident finger on the very heart of the great mysteries of life', quoted in *New-York Daily Tribune*, 18 Sept. 1876.

37. Randel, 'Huxley', 92–4; *New-York Daily Tribune*, 19 Sept. 1876; *Daily Graphic*, 27 Sept. 1876, HP 79.16.

38. Huxley, 'Evidences'. This press transcript differs from Huxley's MS (HM 2:82:38ff), showing that he extemporized on the night. He modified the text further for *American Addresses*. He changed the expression to 'extranatural', and strengthened it by talking of supposed events 'many thousand years ago ... utterly foreign to and inconsistent with the existing laws of Nature': CE, 4:48–9. This pointed reference to the miraculous base of Christianity was not made on the night.

39. Jensen, *Huxley*, 101–4; Randel, 'Huxley', 93–5; *New York Daily Tribune*, 19 Sept. 1876; Huxley, 'Evidences'; CE, 4:53–4.

40. Desmond, *Archetypes*, 128–30. The suggestion that *Archaeopteryx* was an 'intercalary' (not a 'linear') type was not made on the night but appeared in print in *American Addresses*. Cf. *CE*, 4:102ff with Huxley, 'Evidences'. *Compsognathus* diagram: TH to O. C. Marsh, 17 Aug. 1876, Yale University Library.

41. Marsh, *Introduction*; *CE*, 4:132; *New-York Daily Tribune*, 23 Sept. 1876; Randel, 'Huxley', 96; Pfeifer, 'United States', 197. Desmond, *Archetypes*, 167, and Bowler, *Fossils*, 132, for the scientific context of Huxley's discourse.

42. Huxley, 'Evidences'; *CE*, 4:137. The *Times* (23 Aug. 1878, p.10) called the word 'scientist' 'a horrible, but handy Americanism'. In fact the word had been coined by William Whewell in Britain in 1834, but it only caught on in the US in the 1870s.

43. HAH to ES, 23 Sept. 1876, 4 Jan. 1877, AD; E. L. Youmans to TH, 17 Nov. 1876, HM 3:121:122; 'profound': P. Jackson to TH, 22 Sept. 1876, HP 19.11.

44. HAH to ES, 8 Oct. 1876, AD; 'dear': Clark, *Huxleys*, 93; 'Wife': TH to MF, 12 Oct. 1876, HP 4.133; '£600': Huxley's Diary, 70.19; Randel, 'Huxley', 96; Jensen, *Huxley*, 109.

24 A TOUCH OF THE WHIP

1. HAH to ES, 4 Jan. 1877, AD; Burkhardt and Smith, *Calendar*, 10873.

2. *LTH*, 1:477–8; Bibby, *Huxley*, 211–14; expenses: HP 30.105–12; 'Government': HAH to ES, 3 Apr. 1876, AD; 'that': Huxley, [Speech], *Journal of the Quekett Microscopical Club*, 5 (1878), 48; Deanery: A. Stanley to TH, 18 Oct. 1876, HP 26.237; HAH to ES, 4 Jan. 1877, AD.

3. TH to MF, 29 June 1876, HP 4.129; 'rushing': HAH to ES, 4 Jan. 1877, AD; A. Russell to HAH, 4 Jan. 1877, HP 25.309.

4. Plates of *Spirula*: CWT to TH, 1877/8, HP 9.314–18, 27.322, 326; Huxley, 'Dinner'; drawings, HP 78; MS: HP 40.1–53; J. P. Hennessy to TH, 30 Jan. 1877, HP 18.112; 6257: Huxley, 'First Volume'; 'debt': Anne Evans' Diary, HP 31.105; Manual: HAH to ES, 4 Jan. 1877, AD; *LTH*, 1:399, 491. Seventeen years later (by which time the old Huxley seems to have forgotten that he had written this much manuscript) the plates were turned over to P. Pelseneer, who started afresh: J. Murray/TH, 29, 30 Sept. 1894, HP 23.190; *LTH*, 2:361–2.

5. TH to JT, 7 Dec. 1877, HP 8.203; JM to TH, 14 Dec. 1877, HP 23.36; *LTH*, 1:476–7; HAH to ES, 14 Nov. 1877, AD; ES to HAH, 11 Feb. 1879, AD; J. A. Froude to TH, 3 June 1877, HP 16.284; Stoddart, 'That Victorian Science', 18–22; Jensen, *Huxley*, 108. Marsh completed the horse teeth-and-toes diagram in *American Addresses* by putting the pattern on the grinders: TH to O. C. Marsh, 27 Dec. 1876, Yale University Library.

6. HAH to ES, 13 Sept. 1879, AD; walk: 7 Mar. 1875; godfather: HAH's Godparent's Notebook, AD. The switch occurred late in 1876: Duckworth christened Alice Heath's baby (with Nettie godmother) on 26 December 1876: HAH to ES, 4 Jan. 1877, AD; 'self', 'Their': Anne Evans' Diary, HP 31.105. Pevsner, *Buildings*, 330.

7. O. C. Marsh to TH, 12 Jan. 1877, Yale University Library; E. L. Youmans to TH, 17 Nov. 1876, HM 3:121:122. Marsh had also worked out ancestries for tapirs and rhinoceroses, and Huxley incorporated them into his lectures: 'The Succession in Time of the Form of Ungulata' (HM 1:10:37–45).

8. Huxley, 'Prefatory Note', xiv. (In 1892 he was still assuming that our primate ancestors would be found in the strata that yielded the horses: *Controverted Questions* 45.) Cartoon, HP 79.18; Marsh, *Introduction*; 'inexhaustibility': TH to O. C. Marsh, 27 Dec. 1876, Yale University Library; *LTH*, 1:469.

9. TH to A. W. Williamson, 27 June 1877, APS.

10. *CE*, 2:187; *LTH*, 449–54; HM 2:32; CD to TH, 11 June [1878], HP 5.331; Hooker's address: TH to JH, 8 Dec. 1877, HP 2.227; Star: *LJH*, 2:147, 150. The way evolution triumphed without natural selection is chronicled in Bowler, *Non-Darwinian Revolution*.

11. TH to CD, 28 Dec. 1878, CUL DAR 210.12:8 (my thanks to Perry O'Donovan for sending me a transcription). Darwin's maintenance of respectability is at the crux of Desmond and Moore, *Darwin*.

12. TH to CD, 6 Mar. 1881, HP 9.209; gave: CD to TH, 29 Dec. 1878, HP 5.329.

13. Burkhardt and Smith, *Calendar*, 10933; TH to H. Milne Edwards, 1 June 1877, HP 30.102, 22.248–52; F. Lacaze-Duthiers to TH, 21 June 1877, HP 22.250.

14. Colp, 'Notes on Gladstone', 181–2; Irvine, *Apes*, 211; Huxley's Diary, 10 Mar. 1877, HP 70.20.

15. Tennyson, 'Prefatory Poem'; Brown, *Metaphysical*, 180ff; JK to TH, 26 Apr. 1876, HP 20.46.

16. Huxley, 'Modern "Symposium"'; HAH to ES, 15 July 1877, AD. Huxley also became a fixture on the 'Recent Science' column: TH to JT, 2 Dec. 1880, HP 9.130, also 1.173.

17. JM to TH, 16 Jan. 1878, HP 23.39; 'ravening': 27 Nov. 1877, HP 23.33; Bibby, *Huxley*, 104; *LTH*, 1:483; 'occupy': TH to AD, 12 June 1880, HP 13.289.

18. *LTH*, 1:485–8; *SM*, 4:319–44; Huxley, 'Scientific Worthies'. Darwin had been hurt by the slurs about his 'anti-Baconian' method. J. S. Mill had early defended him (*CCD*, 9:204) and now Huxley used 'Harvey' to show that '*the worm has turned*', implying that Darwin's was *the* scientific method. J. Spedding to TH, 28 Jan. 1878, HP 26.179, 181.

19. *CE*, 3:407–8; HAH to ES, 14–27 Dec. 1877, AD; *LTH*, 1:488.

20. Barton, 'Scientific Opposition', 16; W. G. Armstrong to TH, 26 Nov. 1877, HP 10.118; *CE*, 3:425; *LTH*, 1:474, 484; Grocers: TH to JT, 19 May 1883, 22 May 1884, HP 9.136, 146; Cardwell, *Organisation*, 139.

21. HAH to ES, 3 Apr. 1876, 4 Jan., 15 July 1877, 2 July 1878, 13 Sept. 1879, AD; *LTH*, 2:35; Clark, *Huxleys*, 99.

22. Anne Evans' Diary, HP 31.105; HAH to ES, 3 Apr. 1876, 14 Nov. 1877, AD; also 15 July 1877, 2 July, 2 Sept. 1878, AD.

23. HAH to ES, 4 Jan., 15 July 1877, AD. AnneMarie Robinson, University of London Archives, provided confirmation of Leonard Huxley's matriculation. On the practice of using the university's 'highly valued' matriculation exam to gain a proficiency certificate, see Brock, 'School Science Examinations', 173.

24. HAH to ES, 26 Nov. 1878, AD; Jowett's role: HAH to ES, 15 July, 14 Nov. 1877, AD; 'on': BJ to TH/HAH, 23 Apr., 6 May 1877, HP 7.9–11; 'so': 19 July 1877, HP 7.13; tutors: 7, 23 May [1878], HP 7.15–17; Howarth, 'Science Education', 364–5.

25. Howarth, 'Science Education', 335, 347, 353; *CE*, 3:214.

26. Mairet, *Pioneer*, 19ff; 'sharp': TH to MF, 12 Oct. 1876, HP 4.133; H. N. Martin, Sydney Vines, Emily Munn came down from Cambridge.
27. O'Connor, *Founders*, 162–3; exams: Ruse, *Darwinian Revolution*, 262.
28. TH to AD, 5–6 Mar. 1874, HP 13.260–2; 'dash': *LTH*, 2:37; HAH to ES, 3 Sept. 1882, AD; *viva*: MF to TH, 1 Oct. [1874], HP 4.188; Bowler, 'Development', 290.
29. TH to AD, 21 Nov. 1877, HP 13.280; Desmond and Moore, *Darwin*, 629–30; 'University': HP 41.151; *LTH*, 1:479–81; *CCD*, 7:396.
30. CD to TH, 19 Nov. [1877], HP 5.328; 'M': HP 41.151; *LTH*, 1:479–80, 483.
31. 'The Extinct Animals termed Belemnites and their Ancient & Modern Allies', London Institution, 17 Dec. 1877, HM 2:82:16–37, ff.20–8. See also HM 1:3:179, 189; *CE*, 4:14–16; HP 40.64–9; Naples: HP 13.272, 280; 'growing': Huxley, *Anatomy of Invertebrated Animals*, 4 (only days after the publication of this book he delivered his 'Extinct Animals' talk). Huxley, 'New Arrangement of Lenses'; *SM*, 4:316–18; G. B. Howes to L. Huxley, 9 Jan. 1900, HP 18.264; Hollowday, 'Huxley', 451–2.
32. Interestingly Robert Louis Stevenson's *Strange Case of Dr Jekyll and Mr Hyde* (1886) could have been based on the case studies popularized by Huxley in his famous 1874 essay on 'Automatism' (*CE*, 1:235). Stevenson was an Edinburgh University engineer by training and a close friend of Huxley's 'Tall Teas' regular Henry James.
33. Marsh, 'Huxley', HP 82; *LTH*, 1:494; W. T. Roden to TH, 16 Jan. 1879, HP 25.129, also 131–3; S. Evans to TH, 31 Dec. 1881–4 Jan. 1882, HP 15.220–2; Anne Evans' Diary, HP 31.105; T. Woolner to HAH, 5 Dec. 1877, HP 29.95, also 96; 'large': HAH to ES, 14 Nov. 1877, AD. An analogy of phylogenetic trees with the ephemeral 'fabled "bean-stalk"' was drawn by Mivart, '*Lepilemur*', 506.
34. L. Stephen to HAH, 28 Nov., 18 Dec. 1877, HP 27.44–6; correspondents, HAH to ES, 4 Jan. 1877, AD; Stanley: Anne Evans' Diary, HP 31.105.
35. Anne Evans' Diary, HP 31.105; *LTH*, 1:488–9; HAH to ES, 4 Jan. 1880, AD.
36. Marian Huxley to ES, 26 Nov. 1878, AD; A. Forbes to TH, n.d. [1878], HP 16.143; *LTH*, 1:489; Frere: JM to TH, 16 Mar. 1879, HP 23.57. Morris, *Heaven's Command*, 384; Magnus, *Gladstone*, 261–4.
    Huxley met war veterans at Forbes' house and had explorers to his own, including the small, taciturn Henry Morton Stanley – who left with egg on his face, having brought two chimpanzee skulls in bandboxes, only to have them pronounced human, 'with some amusement': Anne Evans' Diary, HP 31.105; H. M. Stanley to TH, [Mar. 1878], HP 26.270. The Queen asked Huxley about Stanley's skulls: F. I. Edwards to TH, 18 Feb. 1880, HP 15.162.
37. H. W. Smith/TH, 27, 28 Jan. 1881, HP 26.123; maths at Eton: Revd R. Okes to TH, 18 June 1881, HP 23.232; 'I': E. Clayton, 29 Sept. 1890, HP 12.220; Bibby, *Huxley*, 172–5.
38. TH to JH, 9 Nov. 1878, HP 2.229; 'Victor, Comte de Veysey' to TH, 19 Sept., 26 Oct. 1878, HP 28.69–70; also HP 2.236, 11.111, 24.278. The *Globe*, 14 Mar. 1879, reported Veysey in a Rome jail. Crown Prince: Viscountess Goschen to HAH, 28 May 1878, HP 17.99. *LTH*, 1:445, 458.

25 A PERSON OF RESPECTABILITY

1. HS to HAH, n.d., HP 7.143; 'grey': HAH to ES, 2 July 1878, 8 July 1879, AD; *LTH*, 1:492; 'as': JT to TH, 3 May 1878, HP 1.152.

2. Parker, 'Huxley', 166; *LTH*, 1:492–4; 'worn': TH to AD, 16 Feb. 1879, HP 13.284; TH to JT, TH to JT, 16–20 May 1878, HP 9.112–16; 'Married', 'lost', 'for': Marian Huxley/HAH to ES, 2 July, 2 Sept. 1878, AD. Parker was about to go out to New Zealand as the first Professor of Zoology at Otago University: CWT to TH, 14 Jan. 1880, 27.324; HM 3:121:99

3. TH to JT, 20 May 1878, HP 9.114–16; CD to TH, 11 Aug. [1878], HP 5.326; Huxley, Davis Lectures, ZSL, 17 May–21 June 1878, HM 1:4:2–13; 'speak': 'FZS' to Council, 23 May 1878, ZSL; farm: HAH to ES, 2 July 1878, AD; *LTH*, 1:492–4.

4. He did pick up *Spirula* in Summer 1880, but the momentum was lost (HM 2:15). *LTH*, 1:399–401.

5. Huxley, 'President's Address' (1879), 255; 'Morphological': Huxley, Davis Lectures, ZSL, HM 1:4:5, 'Phylogeny', f.8: this genealogy is reproduced in di Gregorio, *Huxley*, 110, who gives a detailed discussion; cf. *SM*, 4:300–14.

6. Plan for an educational series, 9 Oct. 1878, HP 52.11; Huxley's 1878 Diary, HP 70.21; 'mightier': MacLeod, 'Evolutionism', 72; Hofstadter, *Social Darwinism*, 33ff; Draper, *History*, iv, viii. For contextual studies of Draper's 'conflict' thesis, see Brooke, *Science*, 34ff; Barton, 'Creation'; and esp. J. R. Moore, *Post-Darwinian Controversies*, 20ff.

In Huxley's popular ISS book, *The Crayfish*, 320–46, the evolution of the crays takes on a diffusionist, geographical orientation, in line with his growing 'physiographic' approach. The increasing biogeographic interest also reveals Wallace's influence. Indeed, Jane Camerini ('Evolution', 700 n1) suggests that it was Huxley who coined the term 'Wallace's Line' (dividing the Australian and Asian faunal zones), in his work on the classification of gallinaceous birds in 1868. And significantly, shortly after this, Huxley began to use global maps of human stocks to accompany his Ethnological Society lectures.

7. He did start a sort of Darwinian programme in late 1879 as a prelude to writing this book. He collated information on domestic breeds from Hungary to India, and had expats searching for Bengal foxes, Burmese jackals and African foxes for his ultimate canine pedigree (HM 1:12:105–216; 1:13:1–14; *SM*, 4:404). He talked on 'Dogs and their History' at the London and Royal Institutions (HP 39.198; HM 1:12:216ff, 2:56), or 'Dogs and their Forefathers', as he called it in his more homely 'anthropological' style in his working-class lectures in February 1880. But the book itself remained unwritten.

8. JM to TH, 28 Mar., 29 Sept. 1878, HP 23.41, 47; *LTH*, 1:424–5, 495–7.

9. Huxley, 'Prefatory Note', xvi–ix; 'fleck': McCabe's introduction to Haeckel, *Evolution*, ix; *LTH*, 1:492; Tyndall, *Fragments II*, 397; Wace, 'Scientific Lectures', 52–61. Haeckel was to complain of Virchow's blocking his access to funds: TH to CD, 28 June 1881, HP 9.211, 5.364. Huxley, *Physiography*, v; this book was reprinted yearly until 1885. By 30 July 1878 (HP 12.326) his Macmillan statement was looking eminently 'respectable'.

10. CE, 6:51, 61–3, 69–70, chaps 5, 7–8, esp. 152, 166.

11. HAH to ES, 2 Sept. 1878, AD (also 'See', on which cf. HP 62.1); 2 July, 26 Nov. 1878, AD; *SM*, 4:265; 'and': Osborn, 'Enduring Recollections', 728; Webb, *Diary*, 203.

12. Yet *Hume* never quite made contact with Darwin. At one of Huxley's 'Tall Teas' Romanes questioned 'the omission of the inheritance-theory of innate ideas [from *Hume*]', having heard Huxley criticize 'the lack of that idea in J. S. Mill's "Utilitarianism"': Anne Evans' Diary, HP 31.105. 'Pudding': *CE*, 3:272, 280; Paradis, '*Evolution*', 22–34 on Huxley's later revolt against utilitarianism in the moral realm.

13. JM to TH, 26 Oct., 6 Nov. 1878, HP 23.49–50; *CE*, 6:211, 226.

14. JM to TH, 26 Jan. 1879, HP 23.54; 'I'm': 26 Oct. 1878, HP 23.49; 10,000: 25 Sept. 1880, HP 23.64; 'measure': Anne Evans' Diary, HP 31.105; *LTH*, 1:496–7; *CE*, 6:43.

15. H. F. Peck to TH, n.d., HP 24.93; JM to TH, 14, 26 Jan. 1879, HP 23.53–4; CD to TH, 18 Jan. 1879, HP 5.333; *MLD*, 1:381; *LTH*, 1:501; dogmatism: Veitch, 'Huxley's Hume'; 'Twenty': TH to H. N. Martin, 2 Apr. [1879], Milton S. Eisenhower Library, Johns Hopkins University. List of recipients: HP 31.109. M. Arnold to TH, 17 Oct. 1880, HP 10.163. G. G. Stokes to TH, 10, 13 Jan. 1882, HP 30.190–1. Revd Henry Wace even quoted *Hume* in his Bampton lectures: Wace to TH, 23 June 1881, HP 28.84.

16. TH/JT, HP 9.118–26; 1.160–3; *LTH*, 1:498–500; projected series: HP 52.12. Huxley himself was set to turn in a volume on William Harvey: HP 39.154ff. H. E. Roscoe to TH, 24 Dec. 1878, HP 25.281. Collini, *Public Moralists*, 316.

17. TH to J. S. Stone, 31 Jan. 1875, HP 27.103, replying to HP 27.102; 'with': TH to G. J. Holyoake, 2 Nov. 1875, Holyoake Collection 2338, Co-Operative Union, Manchester, replying to HP 18.213.

18. Haeckel, *Freedom*, xxvii; Huxley, 'Prefatory Note', xviii–xx; R. Richards, *Darwin*, 526–8; Kelly, *Descent*, 123–41; 'Socialism': Wace, 'Scientific Lectures', 59.

19. TH to HAH, 8 Aug. 1873, AD; *LTH*, 1:397; 'sowing': HAH to TH, 7 July 1873, AD; 'No': HAH to ES, 26 Nov. 1878, AD.

20. M. Conway to TH, 13 Nov 1878, HP 12.298, also 12.300–12; Conway, 'Huxley', 73; broadsheet HP 30.10. The Old Testament scholar Marcus Kalisch (to TH, 17 Jan. 1879, HP 19.124) wanted 'the principles of the "Lay Sermons" . . . acted upon', but Huxley had his own agenda for that. Doubts: L. Stephen to TH, 19 Nov.–17 Jan. 1878, HP 27.50–3; JM to TH, 26 Jan. 1878, HP 23.54; JT/Louisa Tyndall to TH, 25 Jan., 7 Feb. 1879, HP 1.167, 179; TH to M. Conway, 24 Feb. 1879, HP 12.311; *LTH*, 2:3–4.

21. *LTH*, 2:4; J. Power to TH, 12 May 1879, 24.193–4, also 30.113; Bibby, *Huxley*, 187.

22. BJ to HAH, 21 Dec. 1879, HP 7.26; tutor A. M. Bell: 22 Apr., 5 Aug. 1879, HP 7.22–4; BJ to A. M. Bell, 13 Aug. [1879], HP 7.21. At St Andrews Leonard gained the Guthrie Scholarship: L. Campbell to TH, 5, 11 Apr. 1879, HP 12.12; *LTH*, 2:8; F. Pollock to TH, 22 Apr. [1879], HP 24.158. Exhibition: GR to TH, 27 Nov. 1879, HP 25.195; HAH to ES, 4 Jan. 1880, AD; 'monks': *CE*, 3:214. Hooker's son Reggie would also go to Cambridge: JH to TH, 19 June 1889, HP 3.344.

23. J. Hardcastle to E. Hardcastle, 12 Sept. 1874; bishops: R. Collier to J. Collier, 1 May 1836, both in the possession of William Collier; Collier, *Religion*, 56; 'friend': HAH to ES, 8 July, 1879, AD; *LTH*, 1:454.

24. *LTH*, 1:495–6, 501–2; 'moo': W. K. Clifford to HAH, 25 June 1878, HP 12.244; 'you', 7 Apr. 1876, HP 12.240; JM to TH, 3 Apr. 1878, HP 23.44; TH to JT, 2 Apr., 6 May 1878, HP 9.108, 110.

25. HAH to ES, 8 July, 28 Sept. 1879, 4 Jan. 1880, AD.

26. HAH to ES, 13 Sept. 1879, AD; *SM*, 4:380; HM 2:106.

27. H. E. Roscoe to TH, 24 Jan. 1875, HP 25.277; JD to TH, 16 Sept. 1879, HP 14.18; *LTH*, 2:2; Lightman, 'Voices'; Cooter and Pumfrey, 'Separate Spheres', for an exceptional study of science popularization.

28. Wace, 'Scientific Lectures', 36, 45–6; tram: WBC to TH, 29 Nov. 1883, HP 12.113; HAH to ES, 2, 13, 28 Sept., 26 Nov. 1879, AD.

29. Tyndall quoted in Wace, 'Scientific Lectures', 51.

30. Marsh, 'Notice of a New and Gigantic Dinosaur'; Marsh, 'A New Order'; Schuchert and LeVene, *Marsh*, 189ff; Ostrom and McIntosh, *Marsh's Dinosaurs*, 2–47; Colbert, *Men*, 82ff; King, 'Catastrophism', 469.

31. Marsh, 'Fossil Mammal' 459. In England in 1879 the Platonist and Archetypalist Harry Seeley ('Note on a Femur'), happy with a 'grade' concept of organization, (Desmond, *Archetypes*, chap. 6; Padian, 'Pterosaurs') relocated these early mammals into a low, sub-marsupial, 'generalized order'. Marsh ('Notice of Jurassic Mammals') followed suit, calling them 'Pantotheria'.

32. Forking phylogenetic tree, 29 Jan. 1879: HM 1:10:5. It shows the 'Monocondylia' passing from the Amphibia to the Sauropsida (reptiles and birds), and the 'Dicondylia' leading via 'Promammalia unknown' to the monotremes. (The monotremes, incidentally, give rise independently to the edentates and marsupials – and, through the latter, the rest of the mammals.) He read a paper at the Royal Society on 3 February giving this conclusion: Huxley, 'Characters of the Pelvis', 404. Haeckel, *History*, 2:233 on 'Promammalia'.

    Winsor, 'Impact', 78–82 has looked at Huxley's attempt at an evolutionary classification of the mammals (Huxley, 'Application', 658–9). Her analysis suggests that he was addressing the issues of species' multiple origins and convergence (then being discussed by P. M. Duncan, St G. Mivart, H. Seeley and E. D. Cope: Duncan, 'Anniversary Address', 85–7; Mivart, '*Lepilemur*', 506–10; Desmond, *Archetypes*, 183–4; Bowler, 'Cope'). But Huxley's notes with their branching trees show, I think, that he was engaged in a 'conventional' Haeckelian phylogenetic programme. He simply allowed that each group, like his paradigm, the horse, had a long 'peculiar line of ancestry', and that the common ancestors lay deep in the past – and that classification must reflect this.

33. T. Bain to R. Owen, 15 Dec. 1878, BM(NH), Owen Corres. vol. 2, f.61; Owen, *Descriptive*, iii–iv, 76; Owen, 'Evidence of a Carnivorous Reptile'; Desmond, *Archetypes*, 197–9. John Evans, the President, was praising Owen's work at the Geological Society (*Quart. J. Geol. Soc.*, 32 [1876], 112) the day Huxley was awarded its Wollaston Medal.

34. Hooker's election: JT to JH, 17 Feb. 1879, HP 8.388; Huxley's: JH to TH, 26 Feb. 1884, HP 3.279; reply, 27 Feb. 1884, HP 2.446 on potential blackballing; P. G. Hewett to TH, 2 Apr. 1884, HP 18.166. Rupke, *Owen*, 56–8 for interesting insights on Owen's four decades in The Club.

35. Even if Huxley noted some 'Simosaurian and Nothosaurian analogies' (*SM* 3:117) of Owen's paradigm specimen, the weasel-reptile *Galesaurus*, presumably in an attempt to undermine their mammal-likeness.

36. Seeley, 'Ornithosaurian', 238; Cope, 'Descriptions', 529; Cope, 'Second Contribution', 38–40. Desmond, *Archetypes*, chap. 6; and Padian, 'Pterosaurs', for the way social and biological philosophy prestructures perceptions of fossils.
37. Cope, 'Relations', 480. Although in Huxley's lectures on 'Sauropsida', Feb. 1882 (HM 2:75:10) he includes

    Theriodontia?? Copes Pelycosauria [*Dimetrodon*] comp[are]
    Protorosauria
    Anomodontia [i.e. Rhynchosaurus]?

    with the dinosaurs (his old view, lumping *all* reptiles as Sauropsida), his '??' show his growing uncertainty, and indeed in pencil next to them is written 'doubtful'. He was moving to a recognition that some reptiles might not be sauropsids, but be on a line to mammals.
        Later in the 1880s teeth were detected beneath the bony plate of the duck-billed platypus and its egg-laying was confirmed. This evidence for its reptilian ancestry swayed Mivart ('Possibly Dual Origin') among Huxley's disciples.
38. *LTH*, 1:476; G. G. Stokes to TH, 14 Jan. 1878, HP 30.180; 'to': Wace, 'Scientific Lectures', 35; University College: W. D. Halliburton to TH, 8 May 1878, HP 17.236.
39. A. Macmillan to TH, 23 Apr. 1880, HP 22.154.
40. Forgan and Gooday, 'Constructing South Kensington', 'Fungoid Assemblage', 166–9; Barton, 'Scientific Opposition'; *Survey of London*, 237–42; 'pet': JD to TH, 13 Feb. 1885, HP 14.48; on trade schools next to factories: HP 42.52–7; 'Art': Denis, 'Brompton Barracks', 17; 'if': *LTH*, 1:476, reply from the labour leader George Howell, 26 Jan. 1880, HP 18.241.
41. *LTH*, 1:398, 455, 2:62

26 THE SCIENTIFIC WOOLSACK

1. TH to FD, 30 Dec. 1881, HP 15.138.
2. Desmond, *Archetypes*, 58–9; *CE*, 2:230–1; '&': CD to TH, 11 [Apr.] 1880, HP 5.340; *LLD*, 3:240; *LTH*, 2:416; 'very': HAH to ES, 4 Apr. 1880, AD. Murchison was the elite geologist who came closest to retaining a catastrophic impression of the past.
3. E. g. Grant Allen cited in MacLeod, 'Evolutionism', 76.
4. Anne Evans' Diary, HP 31.105; 'Professor Huxley on the Origin of Species', *Standard*, 10 Apr. 1880; HM 1:12:198; *CE*, 2:227.
5. J. A. Froude to TH, 3 June 1877, HP 16.284; *CE*, 2:229; CD to TH, 11 May [1880], HP 5.342; *LTH*, 2:12–13.
6. Brown, *Metaphysical*, 34, 104.
7. TH to CD, 8 Jan. 1881, HP 9:203; *LTH*, 2:14; Burkhardt and Smith, *Calendar*, 12815; Darwin, *Autobiography*, 211; Butler, *Evolution*, 346; H. F. Jones, *Butler*, 1:272, 277, 291, 299ff, 318–28, 340–4, 349, 372, 385.
8. *CE*, 2:241, 4:6, 18, 44; HP 44.118, 59.40; Paradis, *Huxley*, 34. T. Chenery to TH, 28 Apr.–31 Aug. 1880, HP 12.179–82; A. Macmillan to TH, 23 Apr. 1880, HP 22.154; Escott, *Masters*, 183; CD to TH, [24 Dec. 1880], HP 5.363; Becker, *Scientific London*, 48–9.
9. Osborn, 'Memorial Tribute', 47; Marsh, 'Huxley'.

10. J. R. Lowell to TH, 27 Aug. 1880, HP 22.29, reply 22.30; H. James to TH, 17, 28 Nov. [1880], HP 19.23; Huxley, 'Olive Branch', 620–4; *LTH*, 2:15.

11. Osborn, 'Enduring Recollections', 728; Rainger, 'Vertebrate Paleontology' on the American institutional infrastructure created by Osborn and his 'Huxley method', which made palaeontology more zoology than geology. Munn: TH to AD, 18 Jan. 1882, HP 13.291; 'clever', 'pleasant': HAH to ES, 4 Jan. 1880, 8 Feb. 1882, AD.

12. Chlorodyne – containing morphia, chloroform and hemp – was in vogue among women, who became habituated and constantly increased their dosage. Addicts 'behave like morphinists', and in extreme cases 'women sell . . . property and steal in order to obtain the drug': Lewin, *Phantastica*, 75; White, *Materia Medica*, 618–19; sources provided by Ralph Colp.

13. Ellen begged money to bury her grandson: HAH to ES, 15 Jan., 3 Sept. 1882, 6 Dec. 1885, 1 July 1887, AD.

14. Friend, 'Huxley's Homes'; 'easy': HAH to ES, 4 Jan., 4 Apr. 1880, AD. William Collier kindly identified the subject of 'The Sins' for me.

15. T. A. Hirst, Journal XV (1884), 2151, Royal Institution.

16. And also of the peculiar *Peripatus* sent by Lloyd Morgan, who had worked in Huxley's lab: L. Morgan to TH, 2 Aug. 1880, HP 23.5; R. Trimen to TH, 19 Aug.–30 Dec. 1880, HP 28.39–42, 6 Jan. 1881, HM:4:59ff: 'workaday': HAH to ES, 13 Aug. 1880, AD; Home Office: R. Strachey, 14, 19 Aug. 1880, HP 27.106–9.

17. HAH to ES, 13 Aug. 1880, AD; J. R. Moore, 'Theodicy', 160.

18. W. Spottiswoode to HAH, 13 Aug. 1881, HP 26.203; Hall, 'Royal Society', 137; Jones, *Butler*, 294; Barton, 'Scientific Opposition'.

19. Morley, *Recollections*, 1:150–3; Spencer, *Autobiography*, 2:206; tea: J. Chamberlain to HAH, 23 Feb. 1881, HP 12.159; 'parked': Briggs, *Victorian Cities*, 231.

20. *CE*, 3:135–7, 140–50, 153, 158, 290; Paradis, *Huxley*, 166–8, 177, 188; Roos, 'Arnold', 317; Sanderson, 'English Civic Universities', 92–5.

21. JH to TH, 26 Nov. 1880, HP 3.259; JH to CD/CD to TH, 26 Nov. 1880, HP 5.349; *LTH*, 2:14–15. Huxley was still exposing Carpenter's demonstrations by card-sharps of the supposed transference of thought, never mind Wallace's full-blown spiritualism: WBC to TH, 16 June 1881, HP 12.108.

22. Wallace, *My Life*, 2: chap. 34; Durant, 'Scientific Naturalism'.

23. A. F. Walter to TH, 6 Jan. 1881, HP 28.155; HAH to ES, 18 Jan. 1881, AD; HM 2:46–52.

24. TH to CD, 24 Jan. 1881, HP 9.205; W. Harcourt/TH, 23 Dec. 1880 on, HP 18.5–18; 'carping': ERL to TH, 23 Jan. [1881], HP 21.77; warrant, 29 Jan. 1881: HP 32.(27). MacLeod, 'Government', on the State's use of expertise to investigate pollution and fish stocks.

25. *LTH*, 2:21–2; S. Walpole to TH, 17 Feb 1881, HP 28.122 (Spencer Walpole was his fellow Inspector); 'to make': HAH to ES, 18 Jan. 1881, AD; 'So': TH to CD, 24 Jan. 1881, HP 9.205.

26. Clipping from *Pall Mall Gazette* [1880], quoting Huxley in regard to the Evicted Tenants Bill, HP 49.62; Magnus, *Gladstone*, 295–8. The day after Gladstone introduced his new Land Bill, Disraeli (Lord Beaconsfield as he had become) was in communication with the Huxleys and discussing the question: J. Hawthorne to HAH, 8 Apr. 1881, HP 18.84.

27. TH to CD, 6 Mar. 1881, HP 9.209; CD to TH, 5 Mar. 1881, HP 5.359; Burkhardt and Smith, *Calendar*, 13046, 13071–2, 13080.

28. *LTH*, 2:27–9; *SM*, 4:473–92; HM 2:27–9; TH to H. G. Hensmen, 5 July 1881, APS; MacLeod, 'Government', 140.

29. HAH to ES, 14 Aug. 1881, AD. Trips: Burkhardt and Smith, *Calendar*, 13202; CD to TH, 9 Sept. 1881, HP 5.368; HS to HAH, 6 July 1881, HP 7.149. R. Browning to TH, 8, 10 Feb. 1880, HP 11.122–4. Bust: L. Russell to TH, 20 May 1881, HP 25.321 (it was Lady Laura Russell who also had Huxley ask Darwin to sit); TH to J. E. Boehm, 31 May 1881, HP 11.23; J. E. Boehm to HAH, 12 May 1882, HP 11.25; G. Howell to TH, 3 May 1882, HP 18.247.

30. HAH to ES, 14 Aug. 1881, AD; *LTH*, 2:36, 40–1; J. P. Spencer to TH, 30 Mar. 1881, HP 26.190. While not exactly endorsing a free-market approach to medicine, Huxley thought that attaching Medical Council examiners to each licensing board would be a less disruptive way to obtain the minimum qualifications than to start afresh with State 'Divisional Boards': *CE*, 3:323; cf. Cowen, 'Liberty', 34–5.

31. BJ to L. Huxley, n.d., HP 7.47; BJ to HAH, 8 May 1881, HP 7.29; HAH to ES, 14 Aug. 1881, AD. Congress: *SM*, 4:493–507; HP 59.41; *LTH*, 2:33–4.

32. HAH to ES, 14 Aug. 1881, AD; G. G. Bradley to TH, 24 Mar. 1881, HM 3:121:19; J. R. Moore, 'Darwin Lies', 99; 'that': TH to J. H. Thompson, 19 Dec. 1880, HP 30.119.

33. G. C. Broderick to TH, 21 June 1881, HP 11.85; 'spirit', 'very': BJ to HAH, 17 June, 4 July 1881, HP 7.35–7; H. J. S. Smith to TH, 10 June, 12 July 1881, HP 26.118–19; *LTH*, 2:30; 'We': HAH to ES, 14 Aug. 1881, AD.

34. HAH to ES, 14 Aug. 1881, AD.

35. *Prospectus of the Normal School*, 5; E. Frankland to TH, 11 Oct. 1882, HP 16.252. Dean: J. P. Spencer to TH, 18 Aug. 1881, HP 26.192; *LTH*, 2:36; salaries: TH to C. J. Faulkner, 9 Oct. 1881, HP 16.34 (£1,500 a year: £800 at the Normal School and £700 as Inspector: *LTH*, 2:20); 'after': HAH to ES, 14 Aug. 1881, AD.

36. A. Agassiz to TH, 8 Nov. 1882, HP 6.146, reply in Clark, *Huxleys*, 93; Winsor, *Reading*, 133; Oxford: C. J. Faulkner/TH, 9–18 Oct. 1881, HP 16.34–50; Howarth, 'Science Education', 351; *LTH*, 2:32.

37. MF to TH, 3 Jan. 1881, HP 4.216; TH to W. Spottiswoode, 15 Feb., 7 Oct. 1881, HP 26.203–6; TH to J. Paget, 27 Apr. 1881, Sir James Paget Papers, APS; 'I find': TH to FD, 30 Dec. 1881, HP 15.138; Bibby, 'South London', 216.

38. *LTH*, 2:24; 'ten': TH to FD, 30 Dec. 1881, HP 15.138. Disease: HP 15.3–5, 23.188; HM 1:1:88, 1:7:230, 2:57; *SM*, 4:520–8, 540–62; Huxley, *Twenty First Annual Report*, 11.

39. Lester and Bowler, *Lankester*, 98–101; 'far': GJR to TH, 25 Dec. 1881, HP 25.210; ERL to TH, 17 Apr. [1882], HP 30.122; W. Thiselton-Dyer to TH, 18 Apr. 1882, HP 27.193. TH to *Scotsman*, 22 Apr. 1882, HP 21.81; in the *Scotsman* he praised Rosebery, who remained cordial (Lord Rosebery to TH, 26 Apr. 1882, HP 24.209).

40. HM 1:9:99; HM 2:36:14; HM 2:37; HM 2:39:12, 16, 22–45; *SM*, 4:529; HM 2:75.

41. TH to FD, 30 Dec. 1881, HP 15.138; 'peculiar': G. H. Inskip to TH, 13 June 1881, HP 19.9; 'I': HAH to ES, 8 Feb., 3 Sept. 1882, AD.

42. CD to TH, 12 Jan. 1882, HP 5.370; *LLD*, 3:251; *LTH*, 2:38; Desmond and Moore, *Darwin*, 652; HAH to ES, 8 Feb. 1882, AD.

43. CD to TH, 27 Mar. 1882, HP 5.371; *LLD*, 3:358; Desmond and Moore, *Darwin*, 659.

44. F. Darwin to TH, [20 Apr. 1882], HP 13.10.

45. TH to JH, 21 Apr. 1882, HP 2.240; JH to TH, 21 Apr. 1882, HP 3.261, also 263; *LJH*, 2:259; '50': JD to J. P. Spencer, 26 Aug. 1882, HP 30.131; J. R. Moore, 'Darwin Lies', 98ff.

46. G. Darwin to TH, [22 Apr. 1882], HP 13.96; TH to JH, 23 Apr. 1882, HP 2.238; *CE*, 2:244–7; GJR to TH, 25 Apr. 1882, HP 25.216–18; J. R. Moore, 'Darwin Lies', 102.

47. J. R. Moore, 'Darwin Lies', 98–110; Desmond and Moore, *Darwin*, 677; F. W. Farrar to TH, [Apr. 1882], HP 16.26; Chartist: G. Howell to TH, 28 Apr. 1882, HP 18.246.

48. TH to NL, 11, 16 July 1883, HP 21.283–5; J. Evans to TH, 12 July 1883, HP 15.208; Stearn, *Museum*, 73; J. R. Moore, 'Darwin Lies', 107; Moore, pers. comm.; W. E. Darwin to TH, 28 Apr., 6 July 1882, 2 May [1883], HP 13.106–9; *CE*, 2:247.

    Closer to home, son-in-law Jack Collier was ploughing £500 into having his 1881 portrait of Darwin etched, and Huxley used Marsh to open up the American market for these prints of the fallen hero: TH to O. C. Marsh, 17 June 1882, Yale University Library.

49. GJR to TH, 25 Apr. 1882, 10 Nov., 6 Dec. 1883, HP 25.218–22 (also 'sorrow'); *LTH*, 2:39; *CE*, 2:245–7; R. Richards, *Darwin*, 339–52; *LGR*, 71–88, 135–6; Schwartz, 'Romanes's Defense', 307; Teas: Anne Evans' Diary, HP 31.105; 'man': *Times*, 22 Aug. 1878, 8.

50. HAH to ES, 3 Sept. 1882, 29 Jan. 1883, 21 June 1885; and Mady's psychology: 27 June 1865, AD. Ralph Colp (pers. comm.) suggests that this violent attack of 'hysteria' in a young and peculiarly sensitive girl, stressed perhaps by leaving home and her new marriage, reflected the onset of acute schizophrenia, which would become chronic with her approaching insanity and death.

51. Address, 13 May 1882, HP 49.31; J. E. Millais to TH, 20 Jan., 14 May 1882, HP 22.233–6.

52. He told Edward Aveling, then writing on Darwin in the *Reformer* and soon to be Besant's lover: Tribe, *Bradlaugh*, 220, 227; Desmond and Moore, *Darwin*, 643–5; TH, Physiology course, 28 June–18 [20th practicals] July 1882, HM 2:76–7; *LTH*, 2:56.

53. HAH to ES, 3 Sept. 1882, AD; TH to AD, 24 Sept. [1882], HP 13.293; *LTH*, 2:37–8; TH to JH, 28 July 1882, HP 2.246.

54. TH to HAH, 12 Jan. 1883, AD; *LTH*, 2:48; HM 1:7.26–7; HM 2:21, 23–4, 26; *SM*, 4:563–609; E. Johnson to TH, 28 Oct. 1882, HM 1:3:161–3.

55. HAH to ES, 18 July 1883, 21 June 1885, AD.

56. *LTH*, 2:63; HAH to ES, 10 Feb. 1883, AD; group: W. P. Frith to TH, Feb. 1882, HP 16.282–3.

57. BJ to L. Huxley, [21 Nov. 1881], HP 7.40; BJ to HAH, n.d., HP 7.49; Clark, *Huxleys*, 99; Webb, *Diary*, 203; HAH to ES, 3 Sept., 8 Feb. 1882, 7 Feb. 1884, AD. Matthew Arnold was a regular diner at the Huxleys': e.g. 4 July 1884, with Hirst, Noble and Alma-Tadema: T. A. Hirst, Journal XV (1884), 2150, Royal Institution.

58. Huxley, 'English Literature'; Huxley, 'Prize Distribution'; *CE*, 3:163; Roos, 'Arnold', 319–22; Bibby, 'Huxley and University', 102. This was a response to Oxford's manoeuvre of putting a *philologist* into the new Chair of English Language and Literature (which had been endowed in response to Royal Commission suggestions).

59. Howarth, 'Science Education', 351.

60. JT to TH, 24 Mar. 1884, HP 1.171; JH to JT, 20 May 1882, HP 8.401; *LJH*, 2:246; HAH to ES, 10 Feb. 1883, AD; 'rogue': TH to JH, 30 June 1883, HP 2.250; also HP 11.70, 21.282, 26.209, 27.95; 'poor: JH to TH, 29 June 1883, HP 3.268; *LJH*, 2:256.

61. M. Holzmann to TH, 9 Mar 1882, HP 18.223; Court: F. Lowell to HAH, 25 Feb. [1883], HP 22.27; Lord Kenmore to J. R. Lowell, 5 May 1883, HP 11.117; J. R. Lowell to HAH, 7 May 1883, HP 22.34; HAH to ES, 25 Jan. 1885, AD; screen: W. Spottiswoode to TH, 6 July 1882, HP 26.207.

62. G. G. Bradley to TH, 9 July 1883, HP 11.59, also 61.

63. C. J. Steinberg to TH, 8 Feb. 1883, HP 27.38; reply, 12 Mar. 1883, HP 27.40; *LTH*, 2:406; J. Sully to L. Huxley, [1900], HP 27.131; H. T. Mosley to TH, 4 Apr. 1884, HP 23.100; reply, 8 Apr. 1884, HP 23.101; Lightman, 'Ideology', 301.

64. J. R. Moore, *Religion*, 339–40, 353–60, esp. 357; 'ghoul-like': J. R. Moore, 'Freethought', 313; Tribe, *Bradlaugh*, 224–6; Foote, *Defence*, 9, 25: I should like to thank Jim Moore for showing me a copy of this book.

65. J. D. Coleridge to TH, 19 Dec. 1869, HP 12.276; Lord Coleridge had been sponsored for the FRS in 1877 by Huxley, Hooker, Galton and Spottiswoode among others: Certificate at Election, X.292, Royal Society Archives. Foote, *Defence*, 9. Jowett would invite the Huxleys to Oxford to dine with Coleridge and his daughter: BJ to HAH, 16 Apr. [1880], HP 7.28.

66. E. Scammell to TH, 25 Nov., 31 Dec. 1881, HP 26.39–41; 'The': TH to JH, 10 Nov. 1887, HP 2.295.

67. TH to HS, 27 Dec. 1880, HP 7.247; *LTH*, 2:18, 31, replying to HS to TH, 24 Dec. 1880, HP 7.246; Haight, *Eliot*, 548–50.

68. TH to C. A. Watts, 10 Sept. 1883, HP 28.196 (draft, the final version was longer and printed in *Agnostic Annual*, 1 (1884), 5–6); 'paraded', TH to JT, 25 Nov. 1883, HP 9.144; 'that': TH to G. J. Holyoake, 9 May 1884, Holyoake Collection 2935, Co-Operative Union, Manchester. Lightman, 'Ideology', 286; J. R. Moore, 'Freethought', 308. Huxley's protest about the use of his letter gave Annie Besant on the *National Reformer* an excuse to return Watts' advert for the new edition of the *Agnostic Annual*, marking it 'declined on account of the fraud on Prof. Huxley': A. Besant to TH, 22 Dec. 1883, HP 10.307; reply, 24 Dec., HP 10.308. As Bernie Lightman points out to me, ten years later Watts was still using Huxley's name as bait to catch writers of Karl Pearson's calibre: K. Pearson to TH, 15, 20 July 1894, HP 24.89–90.

69. TH to C. A. Watts, 10 Sept. 1883, HP 28.196; '*must*': TH to JT, 25 Nov. 1883, HP 9.144. Temple: *Agnostic Annual*, (1885), 54, back cover – Bernie Lightman kindly provided this reference, and his 'Ideology', 288–301 and *Origins*, 116ff are my main sources. On the need for agnostic 'books of reference': R. T. Wright to TH, 22 July 1882, HP 29.240. So little faith did Huxley have in Watts that he later refused to back him as Finsbury's Secular Education Candidate to the School Board: R. Bithell to TH, 30 Sept. 1894, HP 11.5; reply, 22 Sept., HP 11.6.

70. Bonner, *Bradlaugh*, 1:26, 41, 75, 98, 192; Tribe, *Bradlaugh*, 210–11.
71. Besant, *Law*, 6, 10, 14, 17; *CE*, 9:210; *LGR*, 145; Jones, *Outcast London*, chap. 11; Desmond, 'Artisan Resistance', 79; 'Bradlaugh': TH to G. J. Holyoake, 2 Aug. 1873, Holyoake Collection 2178, Co-Operative Union, Manchester; 'not only': TH to C. A. Watts, 10 Sept. 1883, HP 28.196; *LTH*, 1:56. E. Richards, 'Gendering', is a rich study of Besant, Aveling, birth control and the socialists' use of Darwin.
72. A. Besant to JH, 23 Oct. [1882], Director's Corres., 79 (386), Archives of the Royal Botanic Gardens, Kew; Tribe, *Bradlaugh*, 178–83; Royle, *Radicals*, 12–19; J. R. Moore, 'Freethought', 305–7; Desmond and Moore, *Darwin*, 627–8.
73. Tribe, *Bradlaugh*, 220, 226–7; *LTH*, 2:56; 'without': memorial signed by Huxley (a UCL Councillor) and other members of University College: College Correspondence AM/C/125, 160, UCL: E. W. Aveling to the Council, 23 June 1883, University College London. There was a plethora of complaints about the exclusion, and Huxley had to keep on the right side of the Council, and at the same time try to elicit acceptable reasons for the banning order.
74. *LTH*, 2:56–7.
75. Huxley, 'Unwritten History'; cf. Besant, 'Egypt', in *Selection*; Tribe, *Bradlaugh*, 221; 'every': Huxley, 'Prize Distribution'. Huxley ('President's Address' (1883), 66), also took advantage of the Egyptian occupation by having the War Office begin a series of geological borings in the Delta.
    Huxley's clever rhetorical stance and changing alliances help to explain why he was invited to deliver the annual Rede Lecture at Cambridge in 1883. It was 'the cordial manner' in which he spoke of the university during a talk at the Cambridge Philosophical Society in 1881 (where he had been invited by Frank Balfour [F. M. Balfour to TH, 4 Nov. 1881, HM 3:121:6]) that had the Vice-Chancellor issuing the invitation (Revd J. Porter to TH, 7 Dec. 1881, HP 24.171).
76. H. J. S. Smith to TH, 5 May 1878, HP 26.112. Huxley was eased into the Presidency by Hooker, Foster and John Evans: JH to TH, 1, 6 July 1883, HP 3.270, 274; Becker, *Scientific London*, 22–5.
77. HAH to ES, 19 Apr. 1884, AD; 'that', 'keep', 'dead': TH to JH, 30 June, 6 July 1883, HP 2.250, 256; 'cold': TH to WHF, 8 July 1883, APS; *LTH*, 2:52–3; 'like': TH to FD, 10 July 1883, HP 15.141; 'certain': FD to TH, 6 July 1883, HP 15.140; 'Lord': H. E. Roscoe to TH, 13 Nov. 1887, 25.287. Barton, 'Influential', 70.
78. TH to JH, 23 Oct. 1883, HP 2.262, also 3.277; 'all': MF to TH, 22 Sept. 1883, HP 4.218, also 220–5; 'family': J. E. Huxley to TH, 7 July 1883, HP 31.59. Barton, 'Influential', 71.
79. TH to A. J. Mundella, [1884], HP 23.130; TH to Marquis of Salisbury, 29 Nov. 1885, HP 12.146; WHF to TH, 28 Nov. 1883, 16.125, and TH to WHF, 3 Dec. 1883, APS (marked 'Privatissime') for the manoeuvring to get Flower into Owen's old job; *LTH*, 2:66; J. R. Moore, 'Darwin Lies', 107; Stearn, *Natural History Museum*, chap. 7.
80. *LTH*, 2:69; TH to JH, 6 Dec. 1883, HP 2.266.
81. MF to TH, 7 Feb., 8, 20 Mar. 1885, HP 4.246, 250–2. W. G. Armstrong to TH, 25 Oct., 9 Nov., 1 Dec. 1885, HP 10.128–32, HM 3:121:1; Huxley, 'President's Address' (1885), 283. TH to 'Her Royal Highness', 6 Feb. 1884,

HP 9.259. Becker, *Scientific London*, 22. As Barton, 'Influential', 79, says, Huxley's absence made his term an anticlimax, and it was Foster who took the smoking-room and library initiative.

82. *LTH*, 2:60–1; *LJT*, 232; 'vies': E. Hamilton to HAH, 5 Feb. 1881, HP 17.246; TH to JT, 9 Nov. 1883, HP 9.138; 8.234–7. Morley, *Recollections*, 1:184–5, 201; Magnus, *Gladstone*, 277, 339. The changes were reflected in the birth of the Liberal Club in 1883, whose building, thanks to Nettie's whispers in influential ears, and Huxley's and Hooker's testimonials, was designed by son-in-law Fred Waller: HAH to ES, 10 Feb. 1883, AD.

83. TH to JH, 22 Aug. 1883, HP 2.260; JH to TH, 23 Aug. 1883, HP 3.276; *LJH*, 2:264; 'content': R. Strachey to TH, 23 Aug. [1883], HP 27.109; Magnus, *Gladstone*, 207.

84. J. Fiske to TH, 17 Sept. 1883, HP 16.101; *LTH*, 2:50; *LJH*, 2:265; sanitation: A. Wills to TH, 4, 6, 10 Mar. 1881, 26 Mar. 1882, HP 29.66–72; pests: H. M. Jenkins, 28 Apr. 1883, HP 19.50–2.

85. G. G. Leveson-Gower, Earl Granville, to TH, [25–8], 28 July 1883, HP 21.212–13; *LTH*, 2:59; Harte, *University*, 127–37.

86. MF to TH, 18 Sept. 1884, HP 4.227; *LTH*, 2:49; TH to F. Knollys, 7 May 1883, HP 19.268, also 270–2, 30.134.

87. ERL to TH, 12 Oct. [1883], 19 June 1884, HP 21.83–7; TH to President of the Zoological Society, 30 July 1884, ZSL; Lester and Bowler, *Lankester*, chap. 9.

88. HAH to ES, 9 Apr., 19 Aug. 1883, 19 Apr., 24 May, 9, 14 Sept. 1884, 3, 25 Jan. 1885, AD; *LTH*, 2:20, 42, 71–6. 'Huxley': T. A. Hirst Journal, XV (1884), 2145, 2147, Royal Institution; lab: Osborn, 'Enduring Recollections', 726. Buying a farm: Angela Darwin, pers. comm. Home Office letters continued to report the squabblings while he was away: HP 16.293–303, 22.106.

27 POLISHING OFF THE G.O.M.

1. A. J. Mundella to JD, 10 Oct. 1884, HP 23.132. The radical Mundella, who had pushed through the 1881 Compulsory Education Act, 'could not more *earnestly* express my wishes for Huxleys health . . . if I filled a sheet of foolscap'. *LTH*, 2:81; 'great': HAH to ES, 3 Jan. 1885, AD; Arnold: Peterson, *Huxley*, 219; Notebook of journey: HM 3:128.

2. J. W. Ramsay to TH, 16 Oct. 1884, HP 25.25; S. Walpole to HAH, 15, 20 Oct. 1884, HP 28.125–8; *LTH*, 2:81–2; 'Between': HAH to ES, 11 Sept. 1885, AD; wedding: 25 Jan. 1885, AD; Ralph Colp, pers. comm.

3. MF to TH/HAH, Nov. 1884–Jan. 1885, HP 16.228, 4.238–43; JD to TH, 27 Dec. 1884, 13 Jan. 1885, HP 14.42,46; *LTH*, 2:82, 110. Clark's word in official ears helped, and the doctor cannily applied for a Fellowship of the Royal Society at the same moment, which put the returning President in a quandary: TH to JH, 25 Apr. 1885, HP 2.274.

4. TH to Ethel Huxley, 18 Nov. 1884, APS; *LTH*, 2:83–5; HAH to ES, 3 Jan. 1884, AD.

5. J. Evans to TH, 30 Oct. 1884, HP 15.210; 'seemed': MF to HAH, 21 Nov. [1884], HP 16.228; 'what': JD to TH, 18 Sept. 1884, HP 14.34, 'I won't have Lankester', Donnelly continued.

6. HAH to ES, 25 Jan. 1885, AD; TH to Ethel Huxley, 22 Dec. 1884, APS;

LTH, 2:85–90. A tonic, quinine was also used for bad digestion ('dyspepsia'), coughs and debilitation: Estes, *Dictionary*, 48; Ralph Colp, personal communication.

7. *LTH*, 2:86–92, 113; HAH to ES, 25 Jan. 1885, AD. Galileo: TH to St G. Mivart, [12 Nov. 1885], HP 22.272; reply 13 Nov. 1885, HP 22.274.

8. *LTH*, 1:94–5, 139; 'great': JD to TH, 13 Feb. 1885, HP 14.48; C. Gordon to TH, 17 Jan. 1882, HP 17.81; 'mourning': MF to TH/HAH, 7 Feb. 1885, HP 4.246. The relief expenses: J. W. Ramsay to TH, 27 Dec. 1884, HP 25.27. Morris, *Heaven's Command*, 496–7.

9. He sensed how cocaine worked: he talked in the wake of Mady's death of the 'moral coca' which sanitary reformers needed to stomach the stinking ghettoes: *CE*, 9:217; 'plant': HAH to ES, 21 June 1885, AD; 'fully': TH to Ethel Huxley, 30 Mar. 1885, APS; *LTH*, 2:100–1; HM 2:101; HP 31.113.

10. HAH to ES, 8 Feb. 1882, 28 Mar. 1886, AD; BJ to L. Huxley, 17 Mar. 1885, HP 7.56; Webb, *Diary*, 203.

11. HM 2:79:51, 2:80. This was the course H. G. Wells sat.

12. Wells, *Experiment*, 1:201, 207; 'yellow', 'excessively', research: Wells, 'Huxley', 210. Wells studied Biology Part 1 at the Normal School in December 1884 (while Huxley was away) and Part 2 beginning February 1885; and Advanced Zoology in June 1885. So he was describing Huxley during his last term of teaching (pers. comm. Anne Barrett).

13. Clark, *Huxleys*, 111; Jackson, *Eighteen Nineties*, 62, 69–72, 106–7; 'mad': Webb, *Diary*, 203. Sketching: TH to P. L. Sclater, 28 Mar. 1884, ZSL; Nettie's sketches of Huxley are in the possession of Hilary Buzzard.

14. *LTH*, 2:106, 109; TH to C. S. Parkinson-Fortescue, 11 May 1885, HP 30.137; TH to W. Harcourt, 11 May 1885, HP 30.136; 'So': MF to TH, 4 May 1885, HP 4.254; 'enduring': Huxley, 'Contemporary Literature', *Westminster Review*, 64 (1855), 241.

15. S. H. Northcote/TH, 20, 24 Nov. 1885, 23.227–8; HAH to ES, 6 Dec. 1885, AD; A. J. Mundella/TH, 19, 20 June 1885, HP 23.134–5; JD to C. S. Parkinson-Fortescue, 18 May 1885, HP 24.64; HP 30.138–40; 'sort': TH to B. Price, 20 May 1885, HP 24.206; *LTH*, 2:107–10; MacLeod, 'Science and the Civil List', 51.

16. F. Harris to TH, 7 Dec. 1886, HP 18.38; *CE*, 9:117. As Darwin in the *Origin* had traded off familiarity (e.g. pigeon selection) rather than novelty to get his message across (Ritvo, 'Classification', 60), so Huxley hoodwinked conservatives that there was nothing new, philosophically, under the Empire's never-setting Sun.

17. JD to J. P. Spencer, [sent 15 May 1885], HP 30.131. Hooker had always wanted Huxley 'made a P. C., on public grounds': JH to TH, 27 Dec. 1883, HP 3.278. Soon the Prime Minister would be sounding Huxley out on instituting a new honour as a 'formal recognition of distinguished service in Science Letters & Art': Lord Salisbury to TH, May–June 1887, HP 12.148–53; *LTH*, 2:164.

18. Huxley's assistant T. G. B. Howes became his successor, amid opposition, and the botanist D. H. Scott, who was promoted by Thiselton-Dyer, became one of the two assistant professors: W. Thiselton-Dyer/TH, 15 Aug., 4 Sept. 1885, HP 27.201–5; D. H. Scott to TH, 8 Aug 1885, HP 26.49.

19. HAH to ES, 11 Sept. 1885, AD; budget: JD to TH, 13 Feb. 1885, HP 14.48; 'Providence': 16 Feb. 1888, HP 14.91.

20. *CE*, 2:248–52; J. R. Moore, 'Darwin Lies', 107; Minutes of 'Special General Meeting, 9th June, 1885', BM(NH).
21. TH to St G. Mivart, [12 Nov. 1885], HP 22.272, also 22.271, 274–8; *LTH*, 2:113, 123; Notes on Dentalium, 31 Aug. 1885, HM 1:3:171; 'away': HAH to ES, 21 June 1885, AD.
22. *Times*, 1 Dec. 1885; Huxley, 'President's Address (1885), 294; L. Playfair to TH, 7 Dec. 1885, HP 24.142; 'Since': ERL to TH, 8 Nov. 1885, HP 21.88; Royal Society: W. G. Armstrong to TH, 28 May, 9 Nov. 1885, HP 10.126, HM 3:121:1; MF to HAH, 21 Sept. [1885], HP 4.263.
23. E. R. Lankester, *Advancement*, 89; *LTH*, 2:309–10; Desmond, *Politics*, 254–75.
24. *LTH*, 2:106; HAH to ES, 11–16 Sept., 6 Dec. 1885, AD.
25. HAH to ES, 6 Dec. 1885, AD; J. E. Carpenter to TH, 15 Nov. 1885, HP 12.35; JT to TH, 24 Mar. 1884, 5 May, 22 Aug. [1886], HP 1.180–2; 8:241; TH to JH, 24 Oct. 1885, HP 2.276; *LJT*, 253. Kew: JH to TH, 9 May 1884, HP 8.405; 'thraldom': JH to JT, 26 Mar. 1887, HP 8.408.
26. TH to F. Max Müller, 1 Nov. 1885, HP 23.118; *LTH*, 2:115; 'Even': HAH to ES, 6 Dec. 1885, AD; *CE*, 4:141; J. R. Moore, *Post-Darwinian Controversies*, 65; Magnus, *Gladstone*, 333–40. Gladstone was taking Sir William Dawson's line.
27. *CE*, 4:145–7, 151, 156–7, 171; 'brain': F. Max Müller to TH, 6 Nov. 1885, HP 23.120; HAH to ES, 6 Dec. 1885, AD; *LTH*, 2:115, 122.
28. JK to TH, 12 Nov. 1885, HP 20.50; HP 44.162; *CE*, 4:148–9; *LTH*, 2:114.
29. St G. Mivart to TH, 31 Mar. 1886, HP 22.280; Revd C. F. Gunton, 5 May 1886, HP 17.162; Revd R. M. Spence to TH, 9 Jan. 1886, HP 26.185; HS to TH, 19 Jan. 1881, 7 Dec. 1885, HP 7.146, 168; *LTH*, 2:115; JK to TH, 16 Dec. 1885, HP 20.51.
30. R. Owen to W. E. Gladstone, 5 Jan. 1884, 7, 14 Dec. 1885, BL Add. MS 44,485, f.32, 44,493, ff.188, 223; Foot and Matthew, *Gladstone*, 11:445; Desmond, *Archetypes*, 196–203, 218; Rupke, *Owen*, 340–1; Gruber, 'Owen and his Correspondents', 45–6; Owen, 'Description of . . . an Anomodont', 423; Owen, 'Order Theriodontia'; Association: R. Owen to J. K. Langdon Edis, 1882–5, BM(NH) Owen Corres.; 'Alas': W. Armstrong to TH, 3 Dec. 1885, HP 10.132.
31. *CE*, 4:180; *LTH*, 2:116, 122; 'pulverizing', 'be': JK to TH, 31 Dec. 1885, 6, 14 Jan. 1886, HP 50.52, 55, 58; Magnus, *Gladstone*, 340; Peterson, *Huxley*, 229 on Gladstone's additional paragraph after hearing from Owen.
32. Which reflected as much in global human architecture. Huxley, back from Italy, explained to children how today's Papuan pile-dwellers were at the same 'grade' as the hut-builders of Stone Age Italy who would one day build the Parthenon: Huxley, 'From the Hut', 282. *CE*, 4:290, 301, 308, 350–2; '40': JK to TH, 1, 6 Jan., 10 Feb. 1886, HP 20.53–5, 61; Magnus, *Gladstone*, 341–3.

    Churchill: TH to A. Grey; Huxley, 'Home-Rule Bill'; *LTH*, 2:125; 'Lord Randolph Churchill on Science and Art Instruction', *Times*, 27 Oct. 1887.
33. ['The Natural History of Christianity'], HP 48, f.5, 30. This was intended to be bound as a book with the 'Evolution of Theology' (f.15). The evidence suggests that he may only have started, or continued, this book after 1889 (e.g. *LTH*, 2:229). *CE*, 4:349, 354, 358, 361–2.

    A. Edwards to TH, 28 July, 11 Sept. 1886, HP 15.154–6. In 1887 Huxley was drafting Royal Society reports on future borings in the Delta to date the Nile deposits, and suggesting that its Delta Committee work with the Egypt Exploration Fund (HM 2:85:2–6).

34. JK to TH, 10 Feb. 1886, HP 20.61. Foot and Matthew, *Gladstone*, 11:505.

35. L. Carpenter to HAH, [Feb.1886], HP 12.48; 8 Mar. [1886], HP 12.50 on Leeds; G. S. Jones, *Outcast London*, 227, 291, 344–5; Wallace, *My Life*, 2:104, 240; 'earth': TH, 'Olive Branch', 620–1.

36. *CE*, 1:43, 51, 108; commissioned: J. Caird to TH, 12 Dec. 1885, HP 12.2; *LTH*, 2:146–7; Besant, 'Why I am a Socialist', 2–3, in *Selection*; Tribe, *Bradlaugh*, 229–52.

37. Tyndall, 'Political Situation'.

38. A. Grey to TH, 19, 23 Mar. 1886, HP 17.128, 123; 'cowardly', 'government': TH to A. Grey, 21 Mar. 1886, HP 17.132; Huxley, 'Home-Rule Bill'; *LTH*, 2:124; 'profligate': TH to JT, 7 May 1886, HP 9.150; 'Professor Huxley on Government', *Monthly Record of the Protestant Evangelical Mission*, Aug. 1887, p.122, HP 49.65; Escott, *Masters*, 193, 202–3.

39. Magnus, *Gladstone*, 345–9; 'unimpassioned': A. Grey to TH, [1886], HP 17.142. The Liberal Unionists begged him to join their committee: A. Grey to TH, 24 Apr. 1886, HP 17.140; 'quintessence': G. Smith to TH, 12 Apr. 1886, HP 26.109; 'outrage': E. A. J. Wallop to TH, 16 Apr. 1886, HP 28.113; *LTH*, 2:168.

40. Huxley, 'British Race-Types'; Rich, 'Social Darwinism', for the wider basis of the shifting attitudes towards the Celtic and Saxon 'races'. Huxley had long dismissed the idea of pure 'Celtic blood' or distinct Celt and Saxon 'races' (breaking Europeans down instead into broader morphological groups – the northern fair Xanthochroi and southern darker Melanochroi). But he had always done this against the explicit backdrop of the Irish question: e.g. in 1870 when he transferred his 'Sunday Evenings for the People' to Moncure Conway's South Place Chapel and talked on 'The Forefathers ... of the English People' (9 Jan. 1870: HM 2:61:16; *CE*, 7:260; Huxley, 'Forefathers'; Keith, 'Huxley', 722). And by 1886 Huxley was arguing that something other than 'race' explained the negative Irish traits.

   By removing 'race', he undercut Nationalist demands for a homeland while leaving English prejudices intact. That spare-time anthropologist John Lubbock knew that, as a Liberal Unionist MP, his science would be discredited if he talked in the House on race, so he asked Huxley to point out the 'large admixture of Celtic, Scandinavian & Germanic' blood throughout England and Ireland, which he (Lubbock) could then quote in Parliament in order to assert one 'nationality': J. Lubbock to TH, 24 Jan. 1887, HP 22.96. Darwin, *Descent*, 138; Desmond and Moore, *Darwin*, 557; di Gregorio, *Huxley*, 178.

41. TH to A. Grey, 21 Mar. 1886, HP 17.132; Huxley, 'Home-Rule Bill'; *LTH*, 2:45, 124; 'ingrained': TH to JH, 2 Dec. 1890, 2.373.

42. JT/TH, 27 Dec. 1887, 1, 4, 8 Jan. 1888, HP 1.199, 102, 9.166–8; E. Frankland to TH, 5 Nov. 1887, HP 16.272.

   Contrast the support for this political 'scientific declaration' with the furore when Stokes, Huxley's Presidential successor at the Royal Society, ran for Parliament. Up went cries that science was 'above' politics and that Stokes was compromising his office. Huxley's Liberal academics advised the President to resign, rather than have 'all the dirt of politics imported into

Science'. (TH to NL, 6, 10 Nov. 1887, HP 21.291; TH to JH, 6 Nov. 1887, HP 2.293, reply 3.305, also 9.224–6, 25.287, 1.198.) Although Huxley's group was opposed by Evans' businessmen, Lubbock's MPs and Conservative FRSs: HP 3.316, 4.294–307, 21.297, 22.98–100, 27.209. The problem was partly Stokes' *Tory* candidature. After reading Stokes' election address, Huxley deemed that the President – who had already 'abused us' by accepting the Chair of the Victoria Institute, founded in defence of Revealed Truth – was pulling the Society behind 'everything Churchy & reactionary', and he even vented his feelings in an anonymous leader in *Nature*, 'drawn mild but with a head to it!' (TH to NL, 10, 13 Nov. 1887, HP 21.293–5; reply 21.296; Huxley, 'M. P. '; TH to JH, 6, 14 Nov. 1889, HP 2.293, 297, reply 3.308; TH to G. G. Stokes, 1 Dec. 1887, HP 30.192; *LTH*, 2:173–5; Meadows, *Science*, 226).

43. TH to JH, 11 Sept. 1886, HP 2.280, reply 3.288; T. A. Hirst to TH, 9 May 1886, HP 18.177; yacht: JH to TH, 27 Mar., 6, 7 July 1886, HP 3.281, 284–7; TH to JH, 26 Mar. 1886, HP 2.272; HS to TH, 19, 23, 24 Mar., 19 May, 11 Oct. 1886, HP 7.172–83; *LTH*, 2:119, 127; 'bear': JH to TH, 30 Apr. 1886, HP 3.283; 'doleful': TH to JH, 3 May 1886, HP 2.278; *LJH*, 2:1–7

44. G. B. Howes on Huxley's unconventionality, HP 40.282; *SM*, 4:612; 'amazed': JH to TH, 12 Sept. 1886, HP 3.288; 'catch': MF to TH, [12 Sept. 1886], HP 4.275; 'madly': HAH to ES, 8 Oct. 1886, AD; HM 2:107–11; *LJT*, 391; *LTH*, 2:137–8; 'suits', 'I have': TH to JT, 19 Aug. 1886, HP 9.152; Cook: JT to TH, 22 Aug. [1886], HP 1.182. Huxley's Diary, 1887, HP 70.30 – this also contains a heart-rending account of the English climber whose life Huxley tried to save. On the agnostics and the Alps: Lightman, *Origins*, 150.

45. TH to JH, 20 Oct. 1886, HP 2.287; *LTH*, 2:144; Browne, 'Charles Darwin', 361–2 on the making of the Oxford legend. Hooker concurred with Huxley: 'The Quarterly does not get one iota more than it deserves, or than the public should see it gets': JH to TH, 21 Oct. 1886, HP 3.292; *LJH*, 2:301. Wilberforce's 1860 query – 'How would the Professor like to reckon apes among the progenitors of his father or mother?' – was routinely recounted during the Huxleys' 'Tall Teas': Anne Evans' Diary, HP 31.105. Huxley's 1887 'Reception' caused a sharp exchange in the *Times* with Wilberforce's son: R. G. Wilberforce, 'Professor Huxley'; Huxley, 'Bishop Wilberforce'.

46. *CE*, 9:146; Lilly, 'Materialism', 576, 586; Paradis, *Huxley*, 43–5; 'of': HS to TH, 11 Dec. 1886, HP 7.189.

47. Gruber, *Conscience*, 153–70; St G. Mivart to TH, 31 Dec. 1886, HP 22.284; 'I': TH to JT, 24 Nov. 1886, HP 9.154. Mivart was *still* being blackballed at the Athenaeum for his sins: JH to TH, 28 Nov. 1888, HP 3.335. Mivart's undoing in the eyes of the Church came with his 'Happiness in Hell' in 1892. No sooner was it out in the *Nineteenth Century* than Knowles was trying to goad Huxley into responding to it: JK to TH, 6 Dec 1892, HP 20.166.

48. W. Huxley to TH, 24 Nov. 1886, HP 31.64, reply 65.

49. Huxley, 'Queen's Jubilee'; L. Playfair to TH, 1 Jan. 1886 [1887], HP 24.144, also 146. The notion of institutional struggle was taken up by another moderate State interventionist, D. G. Ritchie, in *Darwinism and Politics* (1891): Paradis, *'Evolution'*, 40; G. Jones, *Social Darwinism*, 57–62.

50. E. L. Scott to TH, 15 July 1887, HP 26.51.

51. Huxley, 'Organization'; editorial, *Times*, 18 Mar. 1887; 'Lord Hartington on our Industrial Position', *Times*, 18 Mar. 1887; 'Messrs. Goschen and Huxley on English Culture', *Nature*, 37 (1888), 337–8.

52. J. R. Moore, *Post-Darwinian Controversies*, 51–3ff, is still brilliant on this imagery; Denis, 'Brompton Barracks'; Crook, *Darwinism*, 12ff for a counter-balance to the 'war' image; Beer, *Darwin's Plots*, 9; Stauffer, *Natural Selection*, 92–4, 134–8, 214, 223–4, 380.

53. Huxley, 'Imperial Institute', *Times*, 20 Jan., 19 Feb. 1887; *LTH*, 2:151; *Times*, 17 Feb. 1887, HP 42.159; also HP 14.76, 12.189, 23.191, 18.139; Huxley, 'Queen's Jubilee'; 'odour': HAH to ES, 1 July 1887, AD; Harris, *Private Lives*, 19.

54. Webb, *Diary*, 202–3; Nettie: HAH to ES, 6, 28 Apr. 1887, AD; A. Agassiz to TH, 31 Jan., 8 Mar. 1887, HP 6.159, 163; J. R. Lowell to HAH, 23 May 1887, HP 22.45; E. C. C. Agassiz to HAH, 19 Apr. [1887], HP 10.25.

55. Or rather belligerently reattribute a skull – which 83-year-old Owen had just diagnosed as the remains of an extinct Australian monitor lizard – as a turtle's skull. Owen responded, showing that rivalries still existed: HM 2:99 notebook on *Ceratochelys*; SM, 4:232.

56. TH to G. J. Holyoake, 24 Apr. 1887, Holyoake Collection 3080, Co-Operative Union, Manchester; CE, 5:122, 4:284; 'guess': G. J. D. Campbell (Argyll) to R. Owen, 27 Feb. 1863, BM(NH) Owen Corres. vol. 1, f.230; 'got': JK to TH, 18 Mar. 1887, HP 20.70; G. J. D. Campbell to TH, 4 Mar., 3 Apr. 1886, HM 3:121:32, HP 12.4, for their disagreement on Argyll's 'Predestined Potentiality' of evolving life – whatever its potentiality, Huxley did not think it was 'predestined'.

57. J. Skelton to TH, 7 Mar. 1887, HP 26.93; CE, 5:69–75; Jacyna, 'Immanence'; Desmond, *Politics*, 114–16, 216, 257, 263.

58. CE, 5:75–80, 104–16; Argyll, *Reign*, 294. Owen praised the *Reign* as a 'wholesome antidote': R. Owen, 'The Reign of Law' (1867), 'Autograph Manuscripts of Sir R. Owen', BM(NH) OC 59. R. Smith, 'Background', 97–105, on the distinction between Huxley's use of Hume's 'constant conjunction' theory of causation, and the Romantic belief in law as an efficient cause equivalent to a Divine force.

59. Huxley, 'Free Libraries'; HP 42.168–75. Huxley's Working Men's College had amalgamated with the South London Free Library on his retirement in 1880: W. Rossiter to TH, 7 Dec. 1880, HP 25.300; Bibby, 'South London', 216–17. 'I may': TH to G. J. Holyoake, 24 Apr. 1887, Holyoake Collection 3080, Co-Operative Union, Manchester, reply to HP 18.216; 'abused': J. Skelton to TH, 7 Mar. 1887, HP 26.93.

60. Clark, *Huxleys*, 109; 'smiled', 'worst': TH to FD, 25 Nov. 1887, 15.143; 'She', 'down': TH to JH, 21 Nov. 1887, HP 2.299; HAH to ES, 11 May 1886, AD.

61. HAH to ES, 11 May 1886, 6 Apr., 1, 24 July 1887, 4 Mar. 1888, AD; E. A. J. Wallop to HAH, 29 Oct. 1887, HP 28.118; JD to TH, 22 June 1887, HP 14.79. Charcot: TH to JT, 26 Nov. 1887, HP 9.164; Sulloway, *Freud*, 15–35.

62. HAH to ES. 15 Dec. 1887, AD (also 'Oh'); TH to JH, 21 Nov. 1887, HP 2.299; 'beyond': JK to TH, 23 Nov. 1887, HP 20.77; TH to JT, 26 Nov. 1887, HP 9.164. Manchester: A. H. D. Ackland to TH, 24 Oct. 1887, HP 10.6; H. E. Roscoe to TH, 13 Nov. 1887, HP 25.287.

63. JT to TH, 23 Nov. 1887, HP 1.196; picture: 'Friend', 'Huxley's Homes'.

64. Huxley, draft of Manchester Address 1887, HP 42.58–67, f.61; 'envy': HAH to ES, 15 Dec. 1887, AD; TH to NL, 27 Nov. 1887, HP 21.297, reply 299; JD to TH, 21, 23 Nov. 1887, HP 14.83–5; TH to JH, 21 Nov. 1887, HP 2.299;

  LTH, 2:180. Paradis, *Huxley*, 142–8 considers Huxley's 'Evolution and Ethics' the culmination of alienation, but surely it lies here, in 1887, rather than in a mellower 1893.

65. Huxley, 'Apologetic', 569.

66. Huxley, early draft of Manchester Address 1887, HP 42.58–67, f.67. Helfand, 'Huxley's "Evolution"', 167–8; R. Richards, *Darwin*, 331–2.

67. TH to JH, 4 Dec. 1887, HP 2.301; *LTH*, 2:181; *Manchester Guardian*, 30 Nov. 1887; 'later': TH to FD, 25 Nov. 1887, 15.143.

68. Huxley's working title had been 'Programme of Industrial Development'. It pushed February's *Nineteenth Century* into an immediate second edition and was 'greatly talked about': JK to TH, 12 Dec. 1887, 4 Feb. 1888, HP 20.83, 90.

69. McCready, 'Worship'; *CE*, 9:196, 199–200, 210–11, 229, 232; 'Huxley': Gilley and Loades, 'Huxley', 303, 307.

70. HAH to ES, 15 Dec. 1887, AD; *CE*, 9:202–5; Helfand, 'Huxley's "Evolution"', 169–70.

28 *CHRIST WAS NO CHRISTIAN*

1. *LTH*, 2:186, 198–9; TH to JH, 29 Jan., 12 Apr. 1888, HP 2.309, 318.

2. HAH to ES, 4 Mar., 29 July 1888, 2 Jan. 1889, AD; J. Paget to TH, 28 Apr. 1888, HP 24.12; TH to J. J. Horny, 5 Nov. 1888, HP 18.226. In an age of civic pride and acquisition, 'The Death of Cleopatra' was bought by the Municipal Art Gallery in Oldham: William Collier, pers. comm.

3. ERL to TH, 1885–8, HP 21.90–121, 30.146, Lester and Bowler, *Lankester*, 110–13. But he was still dogged by controversy in the MBA. With the government mooting a Fisheries Department, Lankester – more a corporatist than Huxley – canvassed so raucously for a staff of scientists that Huxley had to slap him down in the *Times* (Huxley, 'Proposed Fishery Board'; *LTH*, 2:128). Huxley's 'Don't Meddle' policy was due in part to his *laissez-faire* heritage; but it was also the pragmatic response of an inspector who knew that trawlermen paid no heed to scientists. He thought that biologists should be sought for advice, not to run the Fisheries Department. See TH/ A. J. Mundella, 15, 16, 18 Mar. 1886, HP 30.142, 23.137–9; H. T. Wood to TH, 23 Mar. 1886, HP 29.87; MF to TH, 3 Apr. [1886], HP 4.271.

  The President permanently teetered in his inclination to resign over Lankester's bull-headedness. But he was convinced to stay on to keep Lankester in check until the Plymouth lab was functioning. (J. Evans to TH, 19 June 1887, HP 15.218; TH to H. N. Moseley, 20 June 1887, HP 23.98–9; MF to TH, 9 Apr. [1888], HP 4.325.)

4. MF to TH, 14 Apr. 1888, HP 4.328; 'hermit': HAH to ES, 4 Mar. 1888, AD; 'Origin': TH to JH, 23 Mar. 1888, HP 2.316; *LTH*, 2:190–3.

5. TH to JH, 4 May 1888, HP 2.322; *CE*, 2:258–61, 270; F. Darwin to TH, 10 Apr. 1888, HP 13.72 supplied the details; '4': P. G. King to TH, 8 Feb. 1888, HP 19.152; *LTH*, 2:183. Leslie Stephen shortly asked Huxley to write Darwin's entry in the *Dictionary of National Biography*, but Huxley had clearly had enough: L. Stephen to TH, [1889], HP 27.61.

6. *LTH*, 2:184–8; HS/TH, 6, 9, 10 Feb. 1888, HP 7.209–12; 'hammock': HS to TH, 16 Nov. 1887, HP 7.204.

7. L. Boguslavsky to TH, 12 Sept. 1888, HP 11.27. Woodcock, *Anarchism*, 172–6, 190–5, 206; Todes, 'Darwin's Malthusian Metaphor', 545–8 on

mutualist biology as both the Russian socialist 'national style' and a response to life on the tundra wastes.

8. *CE*, 9:200, 204; 'one': JK to TH, 27 Oct. 1890, HP 20.139.

9. Paradis, *Huxley*, 149–50; Kropotkin, 'Mutual Aid'.

10. *LTH*, 2:199; JK to TH, 2 June 1888, HP 20.93. Crook, *Darwinism*, 106–9 discusses 'peace' biology's debt to Kropotkin in his opposition to Huxley's industrial 'war'.

11. HAH to ES, 29 July 1888, 2 Jan. 1889, AD; TH to JH, 23 Oct. 1888, HP 2.326; *LTH*, 2:206–7, 210. Huxley was using Oertel's graduated exercise technique to strengthen his heart: *British Medical J.*, 6 July 1895.

12. TH to JH, 15 Nov. 1888, 6, 9 May, 19 June 1889, HP 2.332, 342–4; *LTH*, 2:211; MacLeod, 'Of Medals', 83–99; HM 3:121:92.

13. L. Playfair to TH, 3 Jan. 1889, HP 24.147; J. R. Moore, *Darwin Legend*, 82–3, 143; Huxley, 'Sea Fisheries'; H. Ffennell to TH, 9 Jan. 1889, HP 16.68; Huxley, 'Spiritualism Unmasked'; HP 49.128–33; 'age': TH to AD, 1 Dec. 1886, HP 13.299; 'It': TH to JH, 28 Oct. 1888, HP 2.328; *LTH*, 2:148, 208.

14. [Ross], 'Huxley', HP 47.62–3; W. S. Ross to TH, 25 Apr. 1889, HP 25.297; Lightman, 'Ideology', 291, 296, 301; Lightman, *Origins*, 143–4; *CE*, 1:421, 5:245–6. Only when Huxley published 'Agnosticism' in 1889 did Watts' group really begin to appreciate his distance from Spencer and his 'Unknowable Noumenon': F. J. Gould/TH, 23 Dec. 1889, 2 Jan. 1890, HP 17.106–8.

15. Eisen, 'Huxley', 352; Ashforth, *Huxley*, 117–22; *CE*, 5:239, 245; *LTH*, 2:221. Dockrill, 'Huxley', 461, is right: this was only a different emphasis from his 1869 understanding, when his focus was on the outer veil this method revealed. He had not switched definitions. Indeed, the letters show Huxley still defining 'agnostic' as a 'confession of ignorance': TH to J. A. Skilton, 10 Dec. 1889, HP 30.152.

16. JK to TH, 14 Jan. 1889, HP 20.99; Lightman, *Origins*, 141; *CE*, 5:255; Eisen, 'Huxley', 351. Sir Spencer Walpole wondered why Achilles was bothering with the 'small fry of the Trojan Army' (Positivism) when he should be sticking to his battle with Hector (Christianity): S. Walpole to HAH, 10 Feb. 1889, HP 28.143. But Huxley was in continual engagement with the Positivist Frederic Harrison, who defined agnosticism as a 'paralysis of religious faith' (Harrison, 'Future', 144). But Huxley was showing by contrast that it was an active, elevating moral position.

17. *CE*, 5:218, 230–1; *LTH*, 2:70–1; TH to MF, 9 Aug. 1884; Barton, 'Evolution'.

18. One second-eleven exception was Huxley's Methodist friend William Kitchen Parker, a rustic pietist and anatomical pedant whose every second was coloured by an 'abiding sense of the Divine Presence'. He alone could believe that Elisha's axe-head swam and that no law of hydrostatics could explain it. There being no rationale, he compartmentalized his beliefs and accepted Huxley's positivist biology. More, he idolized Huxley, naming one son after him, and putting another, Jeffrey, under him. And all along the 'cunningly contrived deceptions of the four gospels', which according to Huxley 'it is immoral to believe . . . have been the strength of my life': T. J. Parker, *Parker*, 125; T. J. Parker, 'Huxley', 125; Desmond, *Archetypes*, 51–2.

19. G. A. Kendall to TH, 6 Apr. 1889, HP 19.127; Gladstone's enquiry after Dawson: E. W. Hamilton/TH, 15 July 1884, HP 17.248–9; Livingstone, *Darwin's Forgotten Defenders*, 80–5.

20. Jacyna, 'Science', 13, 21; Jacyna, 'Immanence'; Peterson, *Huxley*, 236, 251. Turner, *Contesting*, and MacLeod, *Public Science*, are collected essays exploring these larger themes.

21. Huxley's 'private conscience' Protestantism never went so far as to support anarchism or ultra-democracy. He was scathing on 'the coach-dog theory of premiership', where the Prime Minister seems 'to look sharp for the way the social coach is driving, and then run in front and bark loud' (*CE*, 5:252).

22. BJ to HAH, 26 Feb. 1889, HP 7.66; *CE*, 5:242; *LTH*, 2:289.

23. HAH to ES, 22 Jan. 1889, AD; JK to TH, 13 Feb. 1889, HP 20.102; *CE*, 5:160.

24. JH to TH, 25 Jan. 1889, HP 3.339; M. Armstrong to HAH, 15 Jan. 1889, HP 10.114; W. G. Armstrong, 23 June 1887, HP 10.133.

25. TH to JH, 14 Jan. 1889, HP 2.336; JH to TH, 25 Jan. 1889, HP 3.339; *LTH*, 2:217; 'Bishops': TH to P. Allen, 28 Mar. 1889, HP 30.163; HAH to ES, 25 Jan. 1885, 22 Jan., 19 Mar. 1889, AD.

26. HAH to ES, 21 June 1885, 2, 22 Jan., 3 Nov. 1889, AD; TH to G. H. Hames, 20 Aug. 1889, HP 17.242; Huxley's 1889 Diary, HP 70.33; *LTH*, 2:221, 229.

27. *LTH*, 2:216–17; Lightman, *Origins*, 149–52; 'waking': Huxley, 'Prize Distribution'; HP 42.153; *CE*, 3:164–5.

28. HAH to ES, 15 Feb. 1883, 22 Jan., 19 Mar., 3 Nov. 1889, 10 Nov. 1890, 15 Jan. 1891, AD; TH to JH, 25 June 1889, HP 2.346; HP 62.6 Eastbourne house advert; *LTH*, 2:277.

29. *LTH*, 2:230, 265; TH to HAH, 2 Mar. 1889, AD; H. von Herkomer to TH, 23 May 1890, HP 18.135; *CE*, 1:1–17; Roos, 'Neglected', 405–6. The autobiography was 'rather too short', said Hooker in a masterly understatement (JH to TH, 28 Sept. 1893, HP 3.328). It was read aloud in one biology society, like some venerable text, to cries of 'Huxley has not done himself justice' (S. F. Clarke to TH, 17 Sept. 1894, HP 12.214).

    Another autobiography was commissioned by the 'British Biographical Company': E. W. Scott Martin to TH, 1 Aug. 1894, HP 22.179; reply 11 Nov. 1894, APS.

30. *LTH*, 2:221–4; 'witness-box', Christie's: JK to TH, 1, 9, 17 Mar., 18 Nov. 1889, HP 20.103–6, 114; *CE*, 5:262; 'Editors': JH to JT, 11 Dec. 1889, HP 8.421. *Robert Elsmere*'s hero was like one of Huxley's apostate Anglican vicars imploring his help (in the novel he ended up a Unitarian doing social work). The novel explored the value of testimony to the miraculous, Huxley's monthly theme in the *Nineteenth Century*: Peterson, *Huxley*, 243–4.

31. HAH to ES, 19 Mar. 1889, AD; M. Armstrong to HAH, 15 Jan. 1889, HP 10.114; *LTH*, 2:224; Huxley's 1889 Diary, HP 70.33.

32. *CE*, 5:270, 285, 289–97; *LTH*, 2:223, 228–30; JK to TH, 9 Mar., 11, 22 Apr. 1889, HP 20.104, 108, 110.

33. *CE*, 1:176, 5:73, 6:153, 9:121; Lightman, *Origins*, chap. 6; Gospel: JK to TH, 17 Mar. 1889, HP 20.106.

34. J. Chamberlain to TH, 14 Apr. 1889, HP 12.162; JD to TH, 21 Apr. 1889, HP 14.101, also 103; *LTH*, 2:219; R. A. T. G. Cavendish (Hartington) to TH, 7 May 1889, HP 12.145; *LTH*, 2:219; 'fanatics': HAH to ES, 19 Mar. 1889, AD; 'unfitting': TH to JH, 22 Mar. 1889, HP 2.338; Huxley's 1889 Diary, HP 70.33. William Collier, pers. comm., assumes that it was a civil ceremony.

35. *LTH*, 2:223–7, 234; Eisen, 'Huxley', 351; 'hacking': Lightman, *Origins*, 141; 'you': JH to TH, 19 June 1889, HP 3.344; L. Stephen to TH, 8 Apr., 5 May 1889, HP 27.57–9; TH to JH, 30 May 1889, HP 2.344; *CE*, 5:334.

36. TH to W. T. Stead, 8 July 1890, HP 27.5–9. Tunnel: Bradlaugh, *Channel*; JK to TH, 6 June 1890, HP 20.134; 'dirty': JH to JT, 14 Nov. 1891, HP 8.429.

37. *Hansard*, 335 (13 April 1889), 459; *LTH*, 2:225. By contrast, the socialist atheists wanted all blasphemy laws swept away: Royle, *Radicals*, 274. Huxley tried to indict Gladstone for justifying the loss of a pig herd (a violation of property) to score a point: it was Gladstone the Home Ruler who would dispossess the great estate owners in Ireland (*CE*, 5:369).

38. JH to TH, 4, 25 Mar., 11 Apr. 1888, HP 3.320–1, 260; *LJH*, 2:304–5.

39. HS to JH, 5 Dec. 1889, HP 7.243. Huxley, 'Mr. Spencer', 'Political Ethics', 'Ownership'; TH to HS, 19 Oct. 1889, HP 7.230 (not sent); *LTH*, 2:242–3. On Spencer's early belief in land socialism, which came back to haunt him: *CE*, 1:297.

40. JH to TH, 6 Dec. 1889, HP 3.352; JH to JT, 6, 11 Dec. 1889, 1 Jan. 1890, HP 8.420–2; HS to JH, 5 Dec. 1889, HP 7.243; TH to HS, 9 Dec. 1889, HP 7.244; 'abruptly': TH to F. H. Collins, 3 Dec. 1889, HP 12.286.

41. TH to JH, 1 June, 26, 29 Sept. 1890, HP 2.361, 365–7.

42. Huxley too had planned to republish his political essays as *Letters to Working Men*. It was Nettie's idea again: a socially-quieting 'Primer of Politics' for the masses. (And the come-hither '*Letters*', said Knowles, was 'a bit of inspiration in itself'.) JK to TH, 18 Nov., 13, 16 Dec. 1889, HP 20.114–19; *LTH*, 2:223–5, 245; TH to JH, 17 Jan. 1890, HP 2.346.

    A. R. Wallace to TH, 22 Nov. 1891, HP 28.100; Wallace, *My Life*, 2:14, 38–9; Wallace, 'Human', 336–7; Helfand, 'Huxley's "Evolution"', 163–6; E. Richards, 'Gendering', on Wallace the feminist.

43. Flürscheim, 'Huxley's Attacks'; *CE*, 291–3, 308–9, 313; *LTH*, 2:245.

44. M. Halboister to TH, 18 Feb. 1894, HP 17.229–231; also A. Tille to TH, 20 Jan.–14 Dec. 1894, HP 28.6–9. J. R. Moore, 'Socializing Darwinism', 61–6.

45. Huxley was not to know that middle-class family sizes would decrease continually from that time on: Ashworth, *Economic History*, 41; *CE*, 9:20–2.

46. *CE*, 9:39 is a very subtle piece of autobiography.

47. Helfand, 'Huxley's "Evolution"', 170. Geddes' book, co-authored with his pupil J. Arthur Thomson – himself critical of the Romanes lecture (J. A. Thomson, 'Huxley') – is all but ignored in Mairet, *Pioneer*, 45–50, 61–9, 100. E. Richards, 'Gendering'.

48. TH to JH, 13 Jan. 1890, HP 2.354; Spencer, 'Absolute Political Ethics'; JK to TH, 27 Oct. 1890, HP 20.139.

49. Buchanan, 'Are Men Born Free'; E. Jeffrey to TH, 29 Sept. 1890, HP 19.42; 'seems': A. Herbert to TH, 17 Feb. 1890, HP 18.126; *CE*, 9:216.

50. Christie, 'Working Man's Reply'; 'passionate': JK to TH, 20 Mar. 1890, HP 20.129; 'poor': 20 Jan. 1890, HP 20.123; *LTH*, 2:219; G. A. Gaskell to TH, 23 Jan. 1891, HP 17.20.

51. Buchanan, 'Are Men Born Free'; 'servant': JK to TH, 3 Feb. 1890, HP 20.125; Huxley, 'Are Men Born Free'. Lafargue, 'Primitive Communism'; the SDF *Commonweal* was captured by the anarchists in 1889: Cole and Postgate, *Common People*, 422.

52. *CE*, 1:336–58, 428, 9:154: 'men's': JK to TH, 20 Jan. 1890, HP 20.123.

53. On his resignation, HP 21.135–50; 10.265–6; HM 3:121:16; Lester and Bowler, *Lankester*, 110–12. HAH to ES, 19 Mar. 1890, AD; *LTH*, 2:251–7; JK to TH, 26 Mar., 3 Apr. 1890, HP 20.131–2.

54. *CE*, 1:393–5, 402, 424–5; Paradis, *Huxley*, 182; botany reading: W. T. Thiselton-Dyer to TH, 12 Jan. 1890, HP 27.222; 'head': TH to HAH, 3 May 1890, AD.

55. TH to HAH, 3 May 1890, AD; TH to Ethel Collier, 6 May 1890, APS; TH to JH, 18 May 1890, HP 2.359; HAH to ES, 19 Mar. 1890, AD; *LTH*, 2:252, 255–7; 'worthy': Webb, *Diary*, 203.

56. TH to A. L. Moore, 15 Mar. 1888, APS on Moore's *Guardian* review of Darwin's *Life and Letters*; A. L. Moore, 'Evolution', 154; A. L. Moore, *Science*, 184ff; J. R. Moore, *Post-Darwinian*, 259–69; 'itch': JK to TH, 19 May 1890, HP 20.133.

57. *CE*, 1:210, 232–3, 237. He had set out to write exclusively on *Lux Mundi* (his MS, 'Educated Circles; and their Modes of Reasoning', is in HP 46.125) but presumably reset his sights after reading Liddon's sermon in 1890.

58. As he told Carpenter's son Estlin (*LTH*, 2:266), a Unitarian minister whose *First Three Gospels* he rated 'the best popular statement I know of the result of criticism': TH to JH, 29 Nov. 1890, HP 2.371. Romanes too saw Christ's personality securing the acceptance of his ethical teachings (*LGR*, 227).

59. *LTH*, 1:321–2, 343; P. Bayne to TH, 1892–4, HP 10.248–55; C. A. Watts to TH, 23 May 1892, HP 28.199. Funding: Agnosco, 'Huxley'; TH to Leicester Secular Society, 12, 17 Feb. 1891, Holyoake Collection 3307, Co-Operative Union, Manchester, also HP 9.262–3; G. J. Holyoake to TH, 26 Mar. 1891, HP 18.218. William Collier, pers. comm., on Jack Collier's paintings.

60. E. Clayton interview, 29 Sept. 1890, HP 12.220 (also 'military', '30'); *CE*, 4:207–29; *LGR*, 160; JK to TH, 8 July 1890, HP 20.135. 'The Lights of the Church' probably caused more stir in the Hispanic American magazine *El Pensamiento Contemporánea*: A. Llano to TH, 10 Dec. 1891, HP 21.229.

61. Jackson, *Eighteen Nineties*, 17–26.

62. Reviving Latham's 'Sarmation hypothesis', which he had first met as a young *Westminster* reviewer: this disputed a dispersal point in the 'Hindoo-Koosh'; *CE*, 7:305–6; HP 33.156ff; *LTH*, 2:259–60; di Gregorio, *Huxley*, 181. Classics: Burrow, *Evolution*, 238.

63. TH to JH, 29 Sept. 1890, HP 2.367; *LTH*, 2:269; *CE*, 7:321–2; Bowler, *Theories*, 34, 81; Burrow, *Evolution*, 263.

64. TH to JH, 26 Sept. 1890, HP 2.365; *LTH*, 2:221, 263, 267, 274, 277; HAH to ES, 19 Mar., 10 Nov. 1890, AD; garden: HP 31.123; 'one': JK to TH, 8 July 1890, HP 20.135.

65. HAH to ES, 22 Jan. 1889, 20 July 1890, 15 Nov. 1891, AD; Jackson, *Eighteen Nineties*, 106–10.

66. TH to JH, 2 Nov. 1890, HP 2.369; reply 3 Nov. 1890, HP 3.365; *LJH*, 2:346.

67. JT to TH, 20 Dec. 1890, HP 1.205; *CE*, 5:374, 393, 415; ''ome': TH to JH, 29 Sept. 1890, HP 2.367; *LTH*, 2:269; 'spread eagling': TH to J. Collier, 16 Dec. 1890, in the possession of Hilary Buzzard.

68. TH to JH, 29 Sept. 1890, HP 2.367; *LTH*, 2:269. Church: *Sussex Daily News*, 15 Oct. 1890: cutting courtesy of Angela Darwin. The Wallers, Jess and Fred, were Christians, and Fred was finishing the house.

29 COMBATING THE COSMOS

1. H. G. Sharp to TH, 23 Jan. 1891, HP 26.61.
2. JK to TH, 9 Dec. 1890, HP 20.144; Huxley, *Social Diseases*, 54–5, 63, 73.
3. Hodges, *Booth*, 12–13, 27; Huxley, *Social Diseases*, 44. On Hall and the New Connexion: C. Hall, *Hall*, 1–4; Hepton, *Methodism*, 67–9, 104; Desmond, *Politics*, 156, 184.
4. Greenwood, *Booth*, 44–5; Huxley, *Social Diseases*, 66; J. R. Moore, *Religion*, 305; Briggs, *Victorian Cities*, 314.
5. W. T. Stead to TH, 22 Oct. 1890, HP 27.11; evidently Booth 'drafted' the book and Stead 'settled' it: Greenwood, *Booth*, 98; 'gulf': 29 Oct. 1890, HP 27.12; 'filthy': JK to TH, 8 Jan., 9, 12 Dec. 1890, HP 20.121, 144–6.
6. The Colonial Office was shortly to tax Huxley on this part of Booth's scheme: C. E. H. Hobhouse/TH, 28, 30 Oct. 1892, HP 18.198–200.
7. Huxley was familiar with the work of C. S. Loch and the Charity Organisation Society: *Social Diseases*, 55, 61, 106; TH to J. Collier, 16 Dec. 1890, in the possession of Hilary Buzzard; 'sensational': 'Watchman', *Darkest England*, 5; worst weather: TH to JH, 2 Dec. 1890, HP 2.373; T. A. Hirst to TH, 20 Jan. 1891, HP 18.183.
8. TH to J. Collier, 16 Dec. 1890, in the possession of Hilary Buzzard; Huxley, *Social Diseases*, 10–11, 53–8. Mrs Crawshaw was possibly Catherine Crawshaw, wife of the Liberal Unionist Thomas Crawshaw: TH to JH, 2 Dec. 1890, HP 2.373; *LTH*, 2:271–3; JK to TH, 12 Dec. 1890, HP 20.146.
9. Greenwood, *Booth*, 29, 82; Hodges, *Booth*, 38ff; Eastbourne: R. P. Martin to TH, 12 Mar. 1892, HP 22.183; *Eastbourne Gazette*, 3 July 1895. Tyndall's alignment: TH to JT, 18 Dec. 1890, HP 9.176; 'dangerous': 'Watchman', *Darkest England*, 14.
10. TH to JH, 4 Jan. 1891, HP 2.375; Huxley, *Social Diseases*, 7, 72–9; Hodges, *Booth*, 52; Kidd, *Social Evolution*, 9; 'Labour Army': Yeo, 'New Life', 27. Talk by the dock-strike leader John Burns, on the London County Council's far Left, of 'corybantic' conservatives hampering the LCC (Briggs, *Victorian Cities*, 334–9), suggests that the socialists were still reading Huxley.
11. TH to JH, 30 Jan., 17 Feb. 1891, HP 2.377–9; *LTH*, 2:274; T. A. Hirst to TH, 20 Jan. 1891, HP 18.183; 'heaps': HAH to ES, 15 Jan. 1891, AD; 'neglect': JK to TH, 9 Dec. 1890, HP 20.144. Greenwood's pamphlet on *General Booth and . . . the Criticisms of Professor Huxley* had advance orders for 10,000.
12. Huxley, *Social Diseases*, 65.
13. Bowler, 'Holding', 332, 336–8; E. R. Lankester, *Degeneration*; E. R. Lankester, *Advancement*, 349–50; Desmond, *Archetypes*, 108; Jones, *Outcast London*, 313.
14. W. G. Armstrong to TH, 8 Jan. 1891, HP 10.138; 'accounts', 'you': TH to JH, 30 Jan., 17 Feb. 1891, HP 2.377–9; *LTH*, 2:274–6; *CE*, 5:414; 'to give': HAH to ES, 5 Apr. 1891, AD.
15. TH to G. J. Holyoake, 1 Apr. 1891, Holyoake Collection 3293, Co-Operative Union, Manchester; 'because': TH to H. Thompson, 27 Aug. 1892, APS. Huxley was discussing Holyoake and the rationalism of the times with the surgeon Henry Thompson, who had started the infamous 'Prayer Gauge Debate' in 1872: Turner, *Contesting*, 151.

16. J. F. Boyes/TH, 12, 13 Nov. 1892, HP 11.57–8.

17. TH to J. Collier, 16 Dec. 1890, in the possession of Hilary Buzzard; 'constant': TH to E. Collier, 4 May 1891, APS; 'that': TH to JH, 27 Mar 1892, HP 2.411; *LTH*, 2:333; TH to JT, 14 Feb 1892, HP 8.275.

18. TH to E. Collier, 14 Aug. 1891, APS; *LTH*, 2:435; Joyce Kilburn, letter in *Sunday Times*, 19 Apr. 1870; *LTH*, 2:293.

19. TH to J. Simon, 11 Mar. 1891, HP 26.82.

20. TH to JH, 17 May 1891, HP 2.383; HAH to ES, 10 Nov. 1890, AD.

21. TH to JH, 3 July 1891, 11 Jan. 1892, HP 2.385, 395; *LTH*, 2:213, 232, 287, 291.

22. TH to JH, 17 May, 3 July 1891, HP 2.383–5; 'What': TH to [F. or G. A.] Macmillan, 26 Apr. 1891, APS; *LTH*, 2:286–7; mortgages: HAH to ES, 12 July 1891, AD.

23. 'Professor Huxley's Will', *Globe*, 5 Aug. 1895. Will dated 29 Oct. 1891. He died leaving £8,907, wealth by his standards.

24. Huxley, [Bus Strike], *Trade Unionist*, 20 June 1891; 'Professor Huxley on the Bus Strike', *Pall Mall Gazette*, 27 June 1891; HP 49.117; Pelling, *History*, 97–102; 'would': JH to JT, 20 June 1892, HP 8.439; JH to TH, 27 June, 15 Aug. 1892, HP 3.392–4; JH to TH, 29 June 1892, HP 2.417.

25. TH to JH, 10 July 1891, HP 2.389; BJ to HAH/TH, 4 Aug. 1891, 3, 9 Feb., 8 July 1892, HP 7.77, 81–3, 88; JM to TH, 13, 15 June 1891, 5 Mar. 1892, HP 23.83–5.

26. TH to JH, 27 Nov. 1891, HP 2.391; HAH to ES, 5 Jan. 1892, AD; TH to E. Collier, 17 May 1892, APS.

27. JT to JH, 21 June 1892, HP 8.440; 'more': JT to TH, 18, 19 Feb. 1892, HP 1.211; reply, HP 9.182; also HP 8.434–6, 3.381–4. Genesis: *LTH*, 2:296–7; HM 3:121:72, 88–90, 97–8.

28. TH to E. Collier, 28 May 1892, APS; 'With': 18 Mar. 1892, APS; HAH to ES, 24 Apr., 22 Aug. 1892; TH to JH, 26 May 1892, HP 2.415.

29. Huxley, *Controverted*, 7, 35; TH to E. Collier, 5 May 1892, APS; Prologue: TH to N. P. Clayton, 4 Jan. 1893, HP 12.231; *LTH*, 2:298; *Times*, 1 July 1895. Lightman, 'Fighting', Paradis, *Huxley*, 178, and Turner, *Between*, 11, on the introduction of the word 'Naturalism'. While many intellectuals saw *Controverted Questions* as a superannuated book by an old general wallowing in past campaigns, it did have influence in unsuspected areas. It taught the new men like Ben Tillett, the 1889 dock-strike leader, 'to puzzle my ill-trained brain': Laurent, 'Science', 607.

30. *LGR*, 87–8, 153–6, 256–7; Desmond and Moore, *Darwin*, 632–4.

31. GJR to TH, 31 May 1892, HP 25.232; *LGR*, 240, 274–6; *LTH*, 2:267; Spencer's Lamarckism: Freeman, 'Evolutionary Theories', 216–17; TH to JH, 30 Dec. 1893, HP 2.440, where Huxley calls Spencer (who was disagreeing with Weismann) a 'poor fool of [a] man . . . He does not know what he is talking about'. Schwartz, 'Romanes's Defense', 314–15, on Romanes' denial, too, that non-adaptive traits were a refutation of natural selection.

   The freethought journalist W. Platt Ball wrote what Huxley considered an excellent book against the inheritance of acquired characteristics (*Are the Effects of Use and Disuse Inherited*), while defending Huxley in the *National Reformer*: Ball, 'Hebrew Prophecy'; W. P. Ball to TH, 24 Oct. 1890, HP 10.217; F. Darwin to TH, 15 Nov. 1890, HP 13.76. On Romanes and acquired characteristics: Ridley, 'Coadaptation', 59–63; R. Richards, *Darwin*, 350–2.

32. Marginalia in F. Darwin's copy of *The Romanes Lecture*, DAR pamphlet G2136, CUL (Perry O'Donovan's transcription). Mario di Gregorio kindly alerted me to this note. Hames: TH to J. Collier, 16 Dec. 1890, in the possession of Hilary Buzzard; *LTH*, 2:350.

33. Huxley, 'M'. Balfour's Attack on Agnosticism II', MS HP 47.73–4; Peterson, *Huxley*, 315–16; Huxley, 'Apologetic', 568; Gilbert, 'Altruism'; Paradis, '*Evolution*', 31–4. Three weeks after accepting Romanes' offer, Huxley received Spencer's *Principles of Ethics* and a note from Spencer trying to heal the breach. But it was too late 'for I really do not care one straw about his friendship or his enmity now': TH to JH, 29 June 1892, HP 2.417; HS to TH, 2 July 1892, HP 7.231. The rupture became final as Huxley composed 'Evolution and Ethics': TH to HS, 20 Oct. 1893, HP 7.242; TH/JH, 20, 25, 27, 29 Oct. 1893, HP 2.433, 3.410, 2.435, 3.412.

34. GJR to TH, 5, 10 June 1892, HP 25.234–6; Schurmann's *Ethical Purport*: 4 Jan. 1888, HP 25.224; *LGR*, 144, 188; *LTH*, 2:350; R. Richards, *Darwin*, 332.

35. TH to JT, 18 Dec. 1890, HP 9.176.

36. Christie, 'Working Man's Reply'; G. A. Gaskell to TH, 23 Jan. 1891, HP 17.20.

37. TH to JT, 10 July 1892, HP 9.186. On the rise of Keir Hardie: S. Walpole to TH, 23 Aug. 1892, HP 28.146.

38. F. C. Holland to TH, 27 Sept. 1892, HP 18.210; 'for': GJR to TH, 18 June 1892, HP 25.238.

39. JD to TH, 20 June 1892, HP 14.136–8; *LTH*, 2:323–4.

40. HAH to ES, 22 Aug. 1892, AD; *LTH*, 2:322–3; W. Thomson to TH, 21 Aug. 1892, HP 27.275; 'biggest': *LGR*, 91; H. Roscoe to TH, 25 Aug. 1892, HP 25.294; 'table': TH to E. Collier, 22 Aug. 1892, APS.

41. Lord Salisbury to TH, 16 Aug. 1892, HP 12.153–5; 'with': Magnus, *Gladstone*, 397.

42. *LTH*, 2:323–5; TH to JH, 20 Aug. 1892, HP 2.419.

43. *Westminster Budget*, 8 August 1895: *LTH*, 2:324–8; *LGR*, 287; HP 32.95–6.

44. TH to E. Collier, 22 Aug. 1892, APS; *LTH*, 2:345; Jacyna, 'Science', 20ff. The science should not be underplayed; Salisbury, on Huxley's long-standing recommendation, now gave Flower, up to this point a CB, his KCB – although even this was for heading the Natural History Museum, rather than for actual scientific work.

45. TH to H. Thompson, 27 Aug. 1892, APS.

46. Donnelly did not: 'I wish you were not mixed up with a lot of your politicians', he said after seeing the Honours List in the *Times*: JD to TH, 19 Aug. 1892, HP 14.140; *LTH*, 2:329; Magnus, *Gladstone*, 407; 'pious': TH to JT, 7 May 1886, HP 9.150. There were five PCs, and the *Times* (19 August 1892) allowed that 'The Privy Councillors are interesting, if only because they include the name of Professor Huxley. We are far from the Platonic ideal State in which philosophers shall be Kings; but it is something to find the foremost man of science . . . becoming a Councillor of the Queen'.

47. TH to JT, 15 Oct. 1892, HP 9.188; *LTH*, 2:337–8; A. Tennyson to TH, 21 June 1892, HP 27.166.

48. GJR to TH, 25, 31 Oct. 1892, HP 25.242–4; *LTH*, 2:350; *LGR*, 286; Magnus, *Gladstone*, 404; 'impassioned': *Oxford Magazine*, 11 (24 May 1893), 380.

49. On this Association for Promoting a Teaching University in London,

Huxley, 'Professorial University'; HP 42.93–144. Commissioners: JD to TH, 29 Mar. 1892, HP 14.118, reply *LTH*, 2:311, 333; Harte, *University*, 150–6; Bibby, *Huxley*, 221–30 ('seaworthy', 225) for a full discussion.

50. *LGR*, 287; *LTH*, 2:352.

51. BJ to TH, 18 Apr. 1893, HP 7.91.

52. GJR to TH, 21, 25, 27 Apr. 1893, HP 25.250–4; *LTH*, 2:353–4.

53. TH to JT, 15 May 1893, HP 9.190; *LTH*, 2:356; GJR to TH, 19 Apr. 1893, HP 25.248; TH to E. Collier, 4 May 1893, APS; 2,673 copies of the 'Evolution and Ethics' pamphlet sold in a month: F. Macmillan to TH, 16 June 1893, HP 22.156.

54. GJR to TH, 27 Apr. 1893, HP 25.254. TH to J. Collier, 9 May 1893, APS; TH to JT, 15 May 1893, HP 9.190; *LTH*, 2:355–6.

55. 'The Romanes Lecture', *Oxford Magazine*, 11 (24 May 1893), 376, 380–1; *LGR*, 303; 'voice was weak from Influenza – couldn't be heard', was Frank Darwin's comment: marginalia in Darwin's copy of 'Evolution and Ethics', DAR pamphlet G2136, CUL (Perry O'Donovan's transcription).

56. H. de Varigny to TH, 8 Nov. 1892, HP 28.67; 'one': 'The Romanes Lecture', *Oxford Magazine*, 11 (24 May 1893), 376, 380–1; HP 45.28; 'regular': TH to J. Collier, 9 May 1893, APS; *LTH*, 2:355; Helfand, 'Huxley's "Evolution"', 159–60. Paradis, *'Evolution'*, 6–7, 33, dissents from much of Helfand's thesis. For him the thrust of 'Evolution and Ethics' is against 'the romantic a priori arguments of the social idealists', whether of Right or Left (in line with his political writings of the 1880s). In the end Paradis (p.55) sees (as I do) Huxley fighting for the political 'middle ground'. He was neutralizing nature's restraints to allow the technocratic transformation of society.

57. *CE*, 9:58–9; Huxley, *Controverted Questions*, 44.

58. *CE*, 9:81–3; Paradis, *Huxley*, 148; Gilley and Loades, 'Huxley', 305; Turner, 'Victorian Scientific Naturalism', 342; 'bloody': TH to JH, 6 Nov. 1887, HP 2:293. Evelleen Richards sees a methodological similarity between Huxley's ability to *allow* a benign human ethics, despite the lack of any Darwinian sanction, and his liberal paternalist tactic in the 1860s of *granting* the emancipation of women and workers, even though 'biology' vouched for male supremacy in a competitive Darwinian universe (E. Richards, 'Gendering'). For 30 years he had stood apart from the socialists on this score. *He* was granting a favour, against his better Darwinian Nature; *they* were demanding a right sanctioned by a different egalitarian science.

59. Seth, 'Man's Place', 823–5.

60. He was a believer in 'an *a priori* Moral law discerned by Reason', said the *Oxford Magazine*, rather than in the sensationalism of his *Hume* period (*Oxford Magazine*, 11 (24 May 1893), 381). Seth, 'Man's Place', 825; *CE*, 9:53, 114, 205; Mivart, 'Evolution', 203–6.

61. R. Owen to G. Rorison, [April 1860], BM(NH) Owen Corres., vol. 22, f.379; *CE*, 9:52; his peer-group fascination for Buddhism: JH to TH, 18 May 1893, HP 3.404; 'militant': Seth, 'Man's Place', 825. Huxley's approach to 'instinct' had changed dramatically since writing *Hume*.

62. Seth, 'Man's Place', 823; 'The Romanes Lecture', *Oxford Magazine*, 11 (24 May 1893), 380–1.

63. Stephen, 'Ethics', 163–7, 170; *CE*, 9:114–15.

64. W. P. Ward to TH, 19 May 1893, HP 28.173; *CE*, 9:82; A. M. Curtis to TH, 19 Aug. 1893, HP 12.371.

30   FIGHTING UNTO DEATH

1. HP 45.42–231, and HP 53–55 for his 'physiographical' or spatial, map-based, approach to the ancient philosophies.

2. Marginalia in F. Darwin's *Evolution and Ethics*, pamphlet 2136, Darwin Coll. CUL. Huxley's speech at Gonville and Caius College, 21 June 1893, HP 39.183; MF to HAH, [22 June 1893], HP 16.235. Screened: Press cutting, HP 82.32.

3. GJR to TH, 9 Oct. 1893, HP 25.265; 'pompous': JK to TH, 14 Nov. 1893, HP 20.169; *LTH*, 2:367–8; Fund: C. S. C. Bowen to TH, [Nov. 1893], HP 11.45–7.

4. Huxley had intended 'gathering up the threads of the Weismann question' and tying them together in an essay (GJR to TH, 26 Sept. 1893, HP 25.263; *LTH*, 2:368). His notes on Weismann's 'Continuity of Germ plasm' show that he was contrasting it with Owen's *Parthenogenesis*: HP 41.118.

5. H. L. Mencken, quoted in Fawcett, 'Huxley', 208; *LTH*, 2:371; Roos, 'Aims', on Huxley's steadfast public platform; R. M. Young, *Darwin's Metaphor*, 126 on the common context of early Victorian natural theology and late Victorian naturalism.

6. TH to E. Collier, 25 Dec. 1892, APS; *LTH*, 2:340.

7. TH to JH, 22 Jan. 1893, HP 2.421; MF to TH, 15 Jan. [1893], HP 4.367; J. Paget to TH, 19 Jan. 1893, HP 24.14; *LTH*, 2:340–1; Rupke, *Owen*, 3.

8. TH to JH, 1 Oct. 1893, HP 2.429; 'as': R. S. Owen to TH, 25 Sept. 1893, HP 23.251; 'I': TH to R. S. Owen to TH, 26 Sept. 1893, HP 23.253; WHF to TH, 9 Feb. 1895, HP 16.136; *LTH*, 2:364; 'incompetent': JH to TH, 8 Oct. 1893, HP 3.408.

9. JH to TH, 8 Oct. 1893, 4 Feb. 1894, HP 3.408, 444; WHF to TH, 1 May 1894, HP 16.134; 'man': HAH to ES, 29 Dec. 1893, AD; *LTH*, 2:373

10. Gruber, 'Owen Correspondence', 3–7: the *Life* was 'an unconscious parody' of filially-devoted biographies. Its bowdlerized letters were used to curry science's good favour while grandfather was jockeyed into the highest echelons – 'a successful imposture, quite worthy of the subject', said Flower: WHF to TH, 7 Feb. 1895, HP 16.135.

11. J. R. Moore, 'Evangelicals', 390, 393, 408, 412; Kidd, *Social Evolution*, 17, 21, 23, chap. 5; Drummond, *Lowell*, 9, 34, 73, 342ff, 406, 414, 426, 441.

12. WHF to TH, 1 May 1894, HP 16.134; 'all': TH to JH, 4 Feb. 1894, HP 2.444; *LTH*, 2:373.

13. MF to TH, 30 June 1894, HP 4.379; Huxley's notes on Owen's work, HP 39.186.

14. Coleridge, *Constitution*, 1972, 51–2; Desmond, *Politics*, 237; 'Apostle': Clodd, 'Huxley'.

15. The more sympathetic re-evaluation was begun in the 1970s by Dov Ospovat, 'Influence', Ospovat, *Development*. It is now a rolling movement: Desmond, *Archetypes*; Rehbock, *Philosophical*; Sloan, 'Darwin'; E. Richards, 'Question'; Desmond, *Politics*; Sloan, *Owen*; Gruber and Thackray, *Commemoration*; Rupke, *Owen*; Padian, 'Hunterian Lecture'; Desmond, 'Foreword'.

16. HAH to ES, 29 Dec. 1893, AD; TH to JH, 8 Dec. 1893, HP 2.437; 'I': JH to TH, 5 Dec. 1893, HP 3.413; JD to TH, 6 Dec. 1893, HP 14.159.

17. TH to [L. Tyndall], 9 Jan. 1894, HP 9.184; 'tear', 'abusive': TH to E. Collier, 24 Dec. 1893, APS; 'dangerous': TH to JH, 8, 15 Dec. 1893, HP 2.437–8; 'John's': JH to TH, 10 Dec. 1893, HP 3.414; *LTH*, 2:369; Huxley, 'Tyndall'; JK to TH, 15, 19, 21 Dec. 1893, HP 20.171–4; bed: HAH to ES, 29 Dec. 1893, AD.

18. HAH to ES, 6 Feb. 1895, ES; *CE*, 9:17; G. A. Macmillan to TH, 16 Aug. 1894, HP 22.156.

19. G. C. Brodrick to TH, 5 Dec. 1893, 3 Sept. 1894 HP 11.88–91.

20. G. C. Brodrick to TH, 3 Sept. 1894, HP 11.91; 'wrath', 'looking': HAH to ES, 18 Aug. 1894, AD; Osborn, 'Memorial Tribute'; J. R. Moore, 'Deconstructing', 354.

21. TH to JH, 12 Aug. 1894, HP 2.452; *LTH*, 2:378–9; Lord: TH to [L. Tyndall?], 20 Aug. 1894, HP 9.269.

22. E. Frankland to TH, 2 Sept 1894, HP 16.276.

23. HAH to ES, 18 Aug. 1894, AD.

24. A. P. Primrose/TH, 1, 2, 9 June 1894, HP 24.212–14; *LTH*, 2:362, 373.

25. Historians have disagreed about Huxley's 'Past and Present' retrospective. The letters show that he was limiting the damage done by Salisbury: 'Oh that my hands had not been tied & I could have shown up the rottenness of the thing': TH to MF, 28 Oct. 1894, HP 4.144 (also 'anti'); TH to NL, 28 Oct. 1894, HP 21.318; Turner, 'Conflict', 369, cf. Roos, 'Aims', 176, n48; Meadows, *Science*, 217.

26. MF to TH, 2 Nov. 1894, HP 4.384, also 383; Lord Rayleigh to TH, 1 Nov. 1894, HP 27.122; *LTH*, 2:386–7.

27. TH to N. P. Clayton, 2 Jan. 1895, HP 12.234; deputation: A. P. Primrose to TH, 6 Dec. 1894, HP 25.215; A. W. Rucker to TH, 10 Jan. 1895, HP 25.307; HAH to ES, 17 Dec. 1894, 6 Feb. 1895, AD.

28. TH to JH, 14 Feb. 1895, HP 2.460; *LTH*, 2:394; Keith, *Autobiography*, 172–4; Dubois, 'Place'; Bowler, *Theories*, 34–5; McCabe, *Prehistoric Man*, 17–20.

29. MF to TH, 7 Mar. 1895, HP 4.248; Magnus, *Gladstone*, 402.

30. R. F. Carpenter to TH, 10 Feb. 1889, HP 12.55; Catholic University: JH to TH, 26 Sept. 1889, HP 3.346, reply 29 Sept. 1889, HP 2.350; *LTH*, 2:241–2; Magnus, *Gladstone*, 368; Jacyna, 'Science', 20–3, 27.

31. Lightman, 'Fighting'; 'wandering': JK to TH, 13 Feb. 1895, HP 20.177. Donnelly said the reviews made *Foundations* sound like one 'long wail as to how dreadful the truth about things was and therefore it could not be true': JD to TH, 5 Mar. 1895, HP 14.188. Holiday: TH to E. Collier, 5 Feb. 1895, APS.

32. Peterson, *Huxley*, 302; Morley, *Recollections*, 1:226–7.

33. JK to TH, 9 Feb. 1895, HP 20.176; 'living': Wynne, 'Physics', 179–80; Drummond: J. R. Moore, 'Evangelicals', 389.

34. TH to E. Collier, 6 Mar 1895, APS (also 'cleverest'); JK to TH, 22, 24 Feb. 1895, HP 20.178–9; *LTH*, 2:396–8.

35. Lightman, 'Fighting'; 'look': Kidd, *Social Evolution*, 5; Turner, *Between*, 228; Jackson, *Eighteen Nineties*, 126; Peterson, *Huxley*, 195.

36. Huxley, 'Mr. Balfour's Attack', 527–9 – the 'Second Revise' is in HP 47.65; 'parody': MF to TH, 7 Mar. 1895, HP 4.248.

37. H. G. Wells to TH, May 1895, HP 28.233; effeminate: Magnus, *Gladstone*, 368.

38. Huxley, 'Mr. Balfour's Attack', 530–2.
39. TH to E. Collier, 6 Mar. 1895, APS; 'You': JH to TH, 27 Mar. 1895, HP 3.425; 'delightful': JD to TH, 28 May 1895, HP 14.194. Lightman, 'Fighting', by contrast suggests that Balfour had probed the weak spots of Naturalism – its unquestioned axioms. Peterson, *Huxley*, 315–27 finally published the galley proofs of part II; the original MS is Huxley, 'M^r. Balfour's Attack on Agnosticism II', HP 47.72.
40. HAH to ES, 30 Mar. 1895, AD; TH to E. Collier, 6 Mar. 1895, APS; cf. *LTH*, 2:400; JK to TH, 9 Mar. 1895, HP 20.182.
41. HAH to ES, 30 Mar. 1895, AD; poison pen letters (thought to have been from the Salvationists), Martin Cooke, pers. comm., and Clark, *Huxleys*, 119; Brace: TH to E. Collier, 5 Feb. 1895; E. M. Thompson to TH, 12 Mar. 1895, HP 27.248; *LTH*, 2:400.
42. MF to HAH, 26 May 1895, HP 4.390; *LTH*, 2:401–2; HAH to ES, 30 Mar. 1895, AD.
43. *LTH*, 2:402; *British Medical Journal*, 6 July 1895.
44. Clodd, 'Huxley' (the expression comes from Huxley, 'Apologetic'); *LTH*, 2:402, 442; *LJH*, 2:328, 357–9; 'beastly': TH to JH, 10 June 1895, HP 2.462. Ships: JH to TH, 7 June 1895, HP 3.427.
45. 'Death of Professor Huxley', *Observer*, 30 June 1895; 'lovers': *Daily Chronicle*, 1 July 1895. The immediate cause of death was a pulmonary embolism – a blood clot in the pulmonary artery causing a heart attack: *British Medical Journal*, 6 July 1895.
46. HAH reminiscences, HP. 62.1; HAH to TH, 23 Dec. 1847, HH 6.
47. *Folkstone Express*, 6 July 1895; Abbey: Marsh, 'Huxley'; *Daily Telegraph*, 5 July 1895; 'Apostle': Clodd, 'Huxley'.
48. Conway, 'Huxley', 75.
49. *Times*, 5 July 1895; *Eastbourne Chronicle*, 6 July 1895.
50. Revd L. Davies to TH, 2 June [1889], HP 13.123.
51. *Daily Telegraph*, 5 July 1895.
52. *Agnostic J.*, 1 Aug 1895; e.g. on politicians *Eastbourne Guardian*, 10 July 1895; list of mourners: *Times*, 5 July 1895; *Nature*, 11 July 1895.
53. Conway, 'Huxley', 73; *Agnostic J.*, 13 July, 20 July, 1 Aug. 1895; *Literary Guide*, 1 Aug. 1895.
54. *Daily Telegraph*, 5 July 1895.
55. That Nettie was still a church-goer and Hal observed the 'Christian' pieties helped to explain why their Eastbourne vicar Revd Bickersteth Ottley gave Huxley a fine memorial sermon at St Mary's Church, an 'unholy panegyric' according to one horrified member of the congregation: 'The Vicar of the Late Professor Huxley', *Eastbourne Guardian*, 10 July 1895; 'A Protest by Mr. G. F. Chambers', *Eastbourne Gazette*, 9 July 1895.
56. HAH to ES, 5 Apr. 1891, AD; 'He': HP 81.26.
57. JK to HAH, 16, 20 Aug., 11 Oct. 1895, HP 20.184 Ostensibly Nettie objected that the proof was unrevised. But I think it cut deeper. Len and Fred Pollock were certainly for publication: F. Pollock to HAH, 30 Sept. 1895, HP 24.160; Lightman, 'Fighting'.

AFTERWORD: HUXLEY IN PERSPECTIVE

1. Kidd, *Social Evolution*, v, vi.
2. Shapin, 'History'.
3. This was Grene's ('Recent Biographies', 664) comment on *Politics of Evolution*. Like other historians, I have come to see that the actors we once lumped together – the 'Darwinians' of the 1860s or the morphologists of the 1830s – consisted of heterogeneous, politically-allied individuals whose constructions of Nature were as unique as their embedding contexts.
4. It is shown in the current symposia, e.g. Shortland and Yeo, *Telling Lives in Science* (1996) and La Vergata, *Le Biografie Scientifiche* (1995).
5. Turner, *Contesting*, 40.
6. *Pall Mall Gazette*, 1 July 1895; G. M. Young, *Portrait*, 67, 145.
7. Kidd, *Social Evolution*, 3; Jackson, *Eighteen Nineties*, 30, 126; 'their': HAH to ES, 1 July 1887, AD. The old Puritans, disliking the nineties, looked back to a time of higher morality. 'I remember one exhibition in which there were portraits of FD Maurice, Carlyle, JH Newman & of J. S. Mill & each one was sadder than [the] other', said T. H. Farrer (to TH, 6 Jan. 1894, HP 16.33), '& yet' those were the men who had moved 'mankind towards better things'.
8. E. R. Pisani to HAH, 9 Mar. 1894, HP 24.129; Conway, 'Huxley', 75; Webb, *Diary*, 202.
9. Green, 'Strange [In]difference', 531.
10. Ward, *A Writer's Recollections*, quoted in Peterson, *Prophet*, 13, 268.
11. *CE*, 3:189.
12. Webb, *Diary*, 203.
13. Agnosco, 'Huxley'; Peterson, *Huxley*, 83; 'American': G. F. Ormsby/TH, [Dec. 1893], 3 Jan. 1894, HP 23.238–9.
14. O. Lodge to TH, 17 July 1893, HP 22.1.
15. Webb, *Diary*, 202; Jensen, *Huxley*, chap. 1. As late as 1899 Sclater at the Zoological Society gave young Arthur Keith (*Autobiography*, 193) four large lithograph plates of ape anatomy which Huxley had prepared in 1864 for an unwritten paper, asking him to supply the 'missing text'. It took Keith 50 years.
16. Clodd, 'Huxley'. The blank *Lessons* is now owned by Sir Andrew Huxley.
17. *Pall Mall Gazette*, 1 July 1895; 'What': W. Lecky to TH, 20 Jan. 1891, HP 21.191; 'never': Clodd, 'Huxley'; Webb, *Diary*, 202; 'among': Huxley, 'Mr. Balfour's Attack on Agnosticism II', HP 47.83.
18. TH to HAH, 28 June 1851, HH 155; desert: *CE*, 6:319; 'solace': *CE*, 5:60.
19. *Times*, 5 July 1895.
20. Turner, *Contesting*, 44.
21. A. Thackray, 'Natural Knowledge', 764.
22. TH to E. W. S. Martin, 11 Nov. 1894, APS. Huxley's mother too was High Anglican. Despite the sinking fortunes of the family, it evidently had once had gentlemanly origins, judging by the fact that Huxley's brother George was using the family crest of the Cheshire Huxleys in the 1840s: information from Angela Darwin.
23. Peterson, *Huxley*, 20; Desmond, *Politics*, chaps 3–4, on the radical medical milieu.
24. *CE*, 5:143; 'social': A. Thackray, 'Natural Knowledge', 678; Jacyna, 'Immanence', 321–8.

25. Secord, 'Behind', 166.
26. *Times*, 1 July 1895; Jensen, *Huxley*, calls Huxley a 'secular theologian', and, although one understands what he means, the term strikes me as wrong; 'lineal': Mitchell, 'Huxley', 148–9. Lightman, *Origins*, 3–5, 6–9, 30, made Huxley a transitional figure in religion as my *Archetypes and Ancestors* made him a transitional figure in palaeontology. But where Lightman emphasizes Huxley's use in 1859 of Mansel's 'orthodox' logic to chop away at Anglicanism, I see this as a late *ad hoc* sarcastic rationalization, with the real origins of his agnosticism back in the Dissenting 1840s.
27. Baynes, 'Darwin', 502–6; 'standard': *CE*, 5:140–1.
28. Baynes, 'Darwin', 506; *Times*, 1 July 1895.
29. Ruth Barton, 'Evolution', calls Huxley's a 'sterilized' Calvinism, with 'little to commend it to Calvinist theologians'; di Gregorio, *Huxley*, 192–3 for a good discussion.
30. Mitchell, 'Huxley', 148–9; '*clear*': Briggs, *Age*, 484.
31. *Pall Mall Gazette*, 1 July 1895.
32. C. Fluhrer to TH, 2 June 1892, HP 16.140.
33. Sanderson, 'English Civic Universities', 91.
34. *LTH*, 2:392; 'English': Tener and Woodfield, *Victorian Spectator*, 141; 'vigour': *Oxford Magazine*, 11 (24 May 1893), 381. Bartholomew, 'Huxley's Defence'; Barton, 'Evolution'.
35. *CE*, 5:92.
36. *CE*, 5:140; 'whence': E. R. Lankester, 'Huxley'; R. M. Young, *Darwin's Metaphor*, 23; Heyck, *Transformation*, 102. Turner talks of Huxley's men removing theology's 'social vision from the cocoon of eternity' and dragging it 'into the saeculum of history': *Contesting*, 118.
37. MacLeod, *Public Science*; Turner, *Contesting*.
38. Mitchell, 'Huxley', 147.
39. Barton, 'Scientific Opposition', 16; Wells, 'Huxley', 209; 'pioneers': Huxley, 'Professorial University'.
40. 'The worldly, flippant Anglican is being rebuked by one of the ranting Colonels of Cromwell's army': Cockshut, *Unbelievers*, 91, 93. Wilberforce's grandmother: J. Stephen, 'Wilberforce', 469–70; 'splendid': Gardiner, *Harcourt*, 1:247; 'the Bp.': A. S. Farrar to L. Huxley, 12 July 1899, HP 16.13.
41. *Standard*, 1 July 1895; Caron, 'Biology'; Gooday, 'Nature'; Forgan and Gooday, 'Constructing South Kensington'.

    While some of the best literature contrasts the science in the gentry's country house with that in the academic's laboratory (Chadarevian, 'Laboratory Science'; Secord, 'Extraordinary Experiment'), the more representative path for the social transference of science occurred lower down the social scale, between London's medical schools with their radical comparative anatomy courses (Desmond, *Politics*; Pickstone, 'Museological Science') and the laboratories of Huxley's South Kensington, Rolleston's Oxford and Foster's Cambridge.
42. Huxley, undated fragment, HP 49.55; 'age': Huxley, 'Royal Academy'.
43. Pedersen, 'Rathbone', 98–9.
44. E. Richards, 'Gendering', E. Richards, 'Huxley'; E. Richards, 'Redrawing'; E. Richards, 'Darwin'; Erskine, '*Origin*'; Blake, *Charge*; *LJH*, 2:125; 'torn': JT to TH, 6 Apr. 1870, HP 1.65; *LTH*, 1:329.
45. E. g. *Cambridge Express*, 6 July 1895; Wells, 'Huxley', 209.

46. Clodd, 'Huxley'; Roos, 'Aims', 176; 'corner': *Times*, 5 July 1895.

47. *Hospital*, 13 July 1895; 'Pius': R. T. Wright to TH, 22 July 1882, HP 29.240. News from his last group of students: H. M. Ward to TH, 20 Nov. 1893, HP 28.157; C. H. Hurst to TH, 7 Sept. 1894, HP 30.201; W. J. Sollas to TH, 14 July 1894, HP 26.167; 'continued': Mitchell, 'Huxley', 149.

48. Foster, 'Few More Words', 320.

49. Dale, *Pursuit*, 5; Peterson, *Huxley*, 253.

50. TH to HAH. 16–17 Oct. 1847, HH 2–3; Turner, *Contesting*, 44–5.

51. TH to HAH, 16 Oct. 1851, HH 169; Lightman, *Origins*, 28–9; Dockrill, 'Huxley', 470; J. R. Moore, 'Deconstructing'.

52. Tener and Woodfield, *Victorian Spectator*, 28; 'veracity': CE, 3:205.

53. Ellegard, *Darwin*, 61; 'froth': Huxley, 'Science and "Church Policy"'; 'Engineers': TH to JH, 26 Mar. 1889, 2.340; *LTH*, 2:231; Barton, 'Scientific Opposition'; E. R. Lankester, 'Huxley'.

54. Agnosco, 'Huxley'.

55. Denis, 'Brompton Barracks', 11.

56. J. R. Moore, 'Theodicy'; Moore, 'Crisis', 59–68; Moore, 'Freethought', 279–89; Moore, *Post-Darwinian Controversies*; Desmond, 'Author's Response'; Brooke, *Science*, 34; Turner, *Contesting*, 171; Barton, 'Evolution'. The war metaphor, as Barton so rightly says, was itself Huxley's major weapon.

57. Huxley, 'Schamyl', 491–517; TH to HAH, 8 Apr. 1854, HH 271; 'scientific': TH to JH, 5 Sept. 1858, HP 2.35; *LTH*, 1:160.

58. *LTH*, 2:46–7; Chatham: HM 1:4:131; Denis, 'Brompton Barracks', 12–22. The Forces' support of science is an unplumbed area (Brock, 'Patronage', 199; although Hearl, 'Military Examinations', has investigated one aspect). By contrast, much work has been done on the Navy's surveying voyages (Deacon, *Scientists*; Browne, 'Biogeography', 307–10; Desmond, 'Making', 229–30).

59. Gilley and Loades, 'Huxley', 287–9. Huxley's looking over the Permian *Protorosaurus* in Newcastle: A. Hancock to TH, 15, 20 Dec. 1869, HP 17.324–7; TH to CL, 4 Jan. 1870, HP 30.45.

60. J. R. Moore, 'Socializing Darwinism'; Briggs, *Age*, 488. The *Origin* as unfinished 1830s business: Desmond, *Politics*, 398–414; Desmond and Moore, *Darwin*, chaps 15–18; 'death': F. Darwin, *Foundations*, 52; 'Cooperative': Weikart, 'Recently Discovered'. Greene, 'Darwin', for an overview.

61. Huxley, 'Organization'; 'Lord Hartington on our Industrial Position', *Times*, 18 Mar. 1887; Ashworth, *Economic History*, 37; Roberts, *Europe*, 78, 101; Crook, *Darwinism*, chap. 3, esp. 65, 82–3.

62. TH to W. T. Stead, 21 June 1894, HP 27.32 draft; cf. *LTH*, 2:374–5; Crook, *Darwinism*, 103, and 99 on Stead's peace brokerage; Roberts, *Europe*, 113, 117–18.

63. Helfand, 'Huxley's "Evolution"', 160; but cf. Paradis, '*Evolution*', 6–7. Helfand was first to challenge the received wisdom that Huxley's lecture was 'a humanistic statement against the use of [Darwin's] authority' in science. He reinterpreted it contextually, as part of a six-year critique of Spencer and socialism by a reinvigorated Darwinian. Helfand made Wallace stand in for socialism, but I have tried to show that Huxley's exposure to socialism was in fact much more extensive in 1886–93.

64. Lang, 'Science'.

65. HAH to ES, 31 Dec. 1865, AD.
66. Undated fragment, HP 49.55; *LTH*, 2:16n, 56.
67. Hilgartner, 'Dominant View', 519; Cooter and Pumfrey, 'Separate Spheres', 248; Lightman, 'Voices'.
68. E. R. Lankester, 'Huxley'; Knight, 'Getting Science'; Turner, *Contesting*, 171ff.
69. *Daily News*, 1 July 1895; Stead: Lightman, 'Voices'.
70. TH to JH, 4 Dec. 1894, HP 2.454; *LTH*, 2:391.
71. Undated fragment, HP 49.55; see also the undated cutting, Huxley, 'Good Writing: A Gift or an Art', HP 49.58; L. Stephen to TH, 14 Oct. 1894, HP 27.66. Paradis, *Huxley*, 37, 42, on the 'dramatization'.
72. *Daily News*, 1 July 1895; *Illustrated London News*, 20 July 1895.
73. Huxley, 'On Species and Races' MS, HP 41, ff.51–6.
74. Huxley, early draft of Manchester Address 1887, HP 42.58–67, f.67.
75. Cooter and Pumfrey, 'Separate Spheres', 243.
76. Detrosier, *Lecture*, 5–8; Desmond, 'Artisan Resistance', 82–3, 89–92. While I have dealt with science at an ideological level, as seems appropriate with London's radical workers (Huxley's audience was composed of radical free-thinkers: J. P. A., 'Huxley', 2), Anne Secord ('Science in the Pub') has exquisitely investigated the relations of the non-radical artisan botanists in the Midlands.
77. Chilton, 'Geological Revelations'.
78. R. Carlile to F. Place, 5 Aug. 1841, BL Add. MS 35144, f.340.
79. J. P. A., 'Huxley', 2.
80. As such, Huxley had something of an older patron–client relationship as well as a newer canvasser–electorate alliance with his workers: Pickstone, 'Museological Science', 114 for discussions of lay patronage.
81. Davies, *Heterodox London*, 1:112; J. P. A., 'Huxley', 2; Cooter and Pumfrey, 'Separate Spheres', 249–50; Hilgartner, 'Dominant', 531.
82. Watts, 'Theological Theories', 134; nihilism: Kidd, *Social Evolution* 3.
83. Huxley, *Controverted Questions*, 52; HP 56.10; Laurent, 'Science', 595–7.
84. W. C. Meakin to TH, 25 Feb. 1894, HP 22.207; Richardson, *Death*, on the poor and dissection; G. Howell to TH, 1 Sept. 1880, 10 July 1883, HP 18.244, 248; *LTH*, 1:476; cabbies: Mivart, 'Reminiscences', 996; petitioned: HP 32.11–12.
85. Agnosco, 'Huxley'; 'hail': Kidd, *Social Evolution*, 3.
86. G. Sparks to F. G. M. Powell/TH, Feb.–Apr. 1894, HP 26.174–7 (also 'toy', telescope); Revd F. G. M. Powell to *Spectator*, clipping in HP 81.91; reproduced in *Eastern Morning News*, 16 July 1895; MF to TH, 1 Jan. [1894], HP 4.377; 'something', 'as': F. G. M. Powell to JD/TH, Jan. 1894–Jan. 1895, HP 24.179–190; *LTH*, 2:365–7, 382; Holloway, 'Huxley', 437–8. Huxley tried to get Sparks a job in Foster's lab: L. Shore to TH, 3 Apr. 1894, HP 26.75.

    Donnelly, put on the search for Sparks (JD to TH, 5, 27 Jan. 1894, HP 14.165, 171, 175), offered to lend Huxley one of the Royal College's old Hartnack microscopes – a cheap student's instrument (Eric Holloway, pers. comm.) – for the docker.
87. G. A. Gaskell to TH, 23 Jan. 1891, HP 17.20.
88. TH to unknown corres., 30 June 1894, APS; Hutton, 'Great Agnostic'. On his anonymous response to the Royal Society critics: Huxley, 'Criticism'.
89. Laurent, 'Science', 601–7; 'pauperism': Crane, 'Marriage'.

90. Wiener, *English Culture*, 10–14; cf. Edgerton, *Science*, 8, 19.
91. *Daylight*, 13 July 1895.
92. JD to HAH, 29 May 1893, HP 14.146; A. Geikie to TH, 31 May 1891, HP 17.39; 'over-rated': W. T. Thiselton-Dyer to TH, 24 Dec. 1894, HP 27.232; portraits: TH to JT, 8 Mar. 1891, HP 9.173. Athenaeum: H. E. Roscoe to TH, 22 Jan. 1891, HP 25.291.
93. Rose, 'Huxley', 23; Bowler, 'Holding'.
94. *Punch*, 13 July 1895; 'to': *Times*, 1 July 1895; 'warmed': *Saturday Review*, 6 July 1895.

Bibliography

Anonymous press articles are cited fully in the notes. Place of publication is London unless otherwise stated.

AMNH	*Annals and Magazine of Natural History*
ANH	*Archives of Natural History*
AS	*Annals of Science*
BFMCR	*British and Foreign Medico-Chirurgical Review*
BJHS	*British Journal for the History of Science*
CR	*Contemporary Review*
CUP	Cambridge University Press
ER	*Edinburgh Review*
FR	*Fortnightly Review*
HS	*History of Science*
JHB	*Journal of the History of Biology*
NC	*Nineteenth Century*
NR	*National Reformer*
NRRS	*Notes and Records of the Royal Society*
OUP	Oxford University Press
QJGS	*Quarterly Journal of the Geological Society*
QR	*Quarterly Review*
Report BAAS	*Report of the British Association for the Advancement of Science*
UCP	University of Chicago Press
UP	University Press
VS	*Victorian Studies*
WR	*Westminster Review*

Adam, I., 'A Huxley Echo in "Middlemarch"', *Notes and Queries*, 209 (1964), 227.

Agnosco, 'Professor Huxley', *Agnostic J.*, 37 (1895), 1–2.

Allen, D.E., *The Naturalist in Britain: A Social History* (Penguin, 1978).

——, 'Huxley's Botanist Brother-in-Law', *ANH*, 11 (1983), 191–3.

Alter, P., *The Reluctant Patron: Science and the State in Britain 1850–1920* (Oxford, Berg, 1987).

Bibliography

Altholz, J.L., 'The Huxley-Wilberforce Debate Revisited', *J. Hist. Med. & Allied Sciences*, 35 (1980), 313–16.

Altick, R.D., *The Shows of London* (Cambridge, Mass., Harvard UP, 1978).

Amigoni, D., and J.Wallace, eds, *Charles Darwin's The Origin of Species. New Interdisciplinary Essays* (Manchester UP, 1995).

Appel, T.A., *The Cuvier-Geoffroy Debate* (New York, OUP, 1987).

Argyll, Duke of, *The Reign of Law* (Strahan, 1867).

——, *Primeval Man* (Strahan, 1869).

Ashforth, A., *Thomas Henry Huxley* (New York, Twayne, 1969).

Ashton, R., *The German Idea: Four English Writers and the Reception of German Thought 1800–1860* (CUP, 1980).

——, *G.H.Lewes, A Life* (Oxford, Clarendon, 1991).

Ashworth, W., *An Economic History of England 1870–1939* (Methuen, 1960).

Atkins, H., *Down, the Home of the Darwins* (Royal College of Physicians, 1976).

Audubon, M.R., ed., *Audubon and his Journals* 2 vols (Nimmo, 1898).

Backstrom P.N., *Christian Socialism and Co-operation in Victorian England* (Croom Helm, 1974).

Bain, A.G., 'On the Discovery of the Fossil Remains of Bidental and other Reptiles in South Africa', *Trans. Geol. Soc.*, 7 (1854), 53–9.

Bainton, R.H., *Here I Stand: A Life of Martin Luther* (New York, Mentor, 1950).

Ball, W.P., 'Hebrew Prophecy', *NR*, 15, 29 Mar. 1891.

Barber, L., *The Heyday of Natural History* (New York, Doubleday, 1980).

Barnaby, D., ed., *The Log Book of Wombwell's Royal No. 1 Menagerie, 1848–1871* (Sale, Cheshire, ZSGM Publications, 1989).

Barnes, B., and S.Shapin, eds, *Natural Order: Historical Studies of Scientific Culture* (Sage, 1979).

Barr, A., ed., *Thomas Henry Huxley's Place in Science and Letters: Centenary Essays* (Athens, Univ. Georgia Press, 1997).

Barrett, P.H., ed., *The Collected Papers of Charles Darwin* (UCP, 1977).

——, P.J.Gautrey, S.Herbert, D.Kohn and S.Smith, eds, *Charles Darwin's Notebooks, 1836–1844* (British Museum [Natural History]/CUP, 1987).

Barrow, L., *Independent Spirits: Spiritualism and English Plebeians 1850–1910* (Routledge & Kegan Paul, 1986).

Bartholomew, M., 'Lyell and Evolution', *BJHS*, 6 (1973), 261–303.

——, 'Huxley's Defence of Darwin', *AS*, 32 (1975), 525–35.

——, 'The Award of the Copley Medal to Charles Darwin', *NRRS*, 30 (1976), 209–18.

——, 'The Non-Progress of Non-Progression: Two Responses to Lyell's Doctrine', *BJHS*, 9 (1976), 166–74.

Barton, R., 'Scientific Opposition to Technical Education', in M.D.Stephens and G.W.Roderick, eds, *Scientific and Technical Education in Early Industrial Britain* (Dept Adult Education, Univ. Nottingham, 1981), 13–27.

——, 'Evolution: The Whitworth Gun in Huxley's War for the Liberation of Science from Theology', in Oldroyd and Langham, *Wider Domain*, 261–86.

——, 'The Creation of the Conflict Between Science and Theology', in C.Bloore and P.Donovan, eds, *Science and Theology in Action* (Palmerston North, New Zealand, Dunmore, 1987), 55–71.

——, 'John Tyndall, Pantheist', *Osiris*, 3 (1987), 111–34.

Bibliography

——, '"An Influential Set of Chaps": The X-Club and Royal Society Politics 1864–85', *BJHS*, 23 (1990), 53–81.

Bassett, M., *Behind the Picture: H.M.S. Rattlesnake's Australia-New Guinea Cruise 1846–1850* (Melbourne, OUP, 1966).

Bastian, H.C., 'Reply to Professor Huxley's Inaugural Address at Liverpool on the Question of the Origin of Life', *Nature*, 2 (1870), 410–13, 431–4.

Bayley, W.A., *Blue Haven: History of Kiama Municipality New South Wales* (Kiama, Kiama Municipal Council, 1976).

[Baynes, T.S.], 'Darwin on Expression', *ER*, 137 (1873), 492–508.

Becker, B.H., *Scientific London* (King, 1874).

Beddoe, J., *Memories of Eighty Years* (Bristol, Arrowsmith, 1910).

Beer, G., *Darwin's Plots: Evolutionary Narrative in Darwin, George Eliot and Nineteenth-Century Fiction* (Ark, 1983).

——, 'Travelling the Other Way', in Jardine, Secord and Spary, *Cultures*, 322–37.

Bell, S., 'George Henry Lewes: A Man of His Time', *JHB*, 14 (1981), 277–98.

Benson, K. R., 'American Morphology in the Late Nineteenth Century: The Biology Department at Johns Hopkins University', *JHB*, 18 (1985), 163–205.

——, 'The Naples Stazione Zoologica and Its Impact on the Emergence of American Marine Biology', *JHB*, 21 (1988), 331–41.

——, 'From Museum Research to Laboratory Research', in Rainger, Benson and Maienschein, *American Development of Biology*, 49–83.

Benton, M.J., 'Progressionism in the 1850s: Lyell, Owen, Mantell and the Elgin Fossil Reptile *Leptopleuron* (*Telerpeton*)', *ANH*, 11 (1982), 123–36.

Berman, M., *Social Change and Scientific Organization: The Royal Institution, 1799–1844* (Heinemann, 1978).

Besant, A., *The Law of Population* [1877] (Freethought Publishing Co., 1887).

——, *A Selection of the Social and Political Pamphlets* (New York, Kelly, 1970).

Best, G., *Mid-Victorian Britain 1851–70* (Fontana, 1979).

Bevington, M.M., *The Saturday Review 1855–1868* (New York, Columbia UP, 1941).

Bibby, C., 'The South London Working Men's College', *Adult Education*, 28 (1955), 211–21.

——, 'T.H.Huxley and Medical Education', *Charing Cross Hospital Gazette*, 54 (1956), 191–5.

——, 'Thomas Henry Huxley and University Development', *VS*, 2 (1958), 97–116.

——, *T.H.Huxley: Scientist, Humanist and Educator* (New York, Horizon, 1960).

Blake, C., *The Charge of the Parasols: Women's Entry to the Medical Profession* (The Women's Press, 1990).

[Blake, C.C.], 'Man and Beast', *Anthropological Review*, 1 (1863), 153–62.

[—], 'Professor Huxley on Man's Place in Nature', *ER*, 117 (1863), 541–69.

Blake, R., *Disraeli* (Univ. Paperbacks, 1969).

Blinderman, C.S., 'The Oxford Debate and After', *Notes and Queries*, 202 (1957), 126–8.

Block, E., 'T.H.Huxley's Rhetoric and the Popularization of Victorian Scientific Ideas: 1854–1874', *VS*, 29 (1986), 363–86.

Bölsche, W., *Haeckel: His Life and Work*, trans. J.McCabe (Unwin, 1906).

Bolt, C., *Victorian Attitudes to Race* (Routledge & Kegan Paul, 1971).

Bonner, H.B., *Charles Bradlaugh* 2 vols (Fisher, Unwin, 1898).

Bourdieu, P., *Outline of a Theory of Practice*, trans. R.Nice (CUP, 1977).

Bower, F.O., 'Teaching of Biological Science', *Nature*, 115 (1925), 712–14.

Bowler, P.J., *Fossils and Progress* (New York, Science History Publications, 1976).

——, 'Edward Drinker Cope and the Changing Structure of Evolutionary Theory', *Isis*, 68 (1977), 249–65.

——, *Theories of Human Evolution* (Oxford, Blackwell, 1986).

——, *The Non-Darwinian Revolution* (Baltimore, Johns Hopkins UP, 1988).

——, 'Development and Adaptation: Evolutionary Concepts in British Morphology, 1870–1914', *BJHS*, 22 (1989), 283–97.

——, 'Holding your Head up High: Degeneration and Orthogenesis in the Theories of Human Evolution', in Moore, *History*, 329–53.

——, *Charles Darwin. The Man and His Influence* (Oxford, Blackwell, 1990).

Boylan, P.J., 'The Controversy of the Moulin-Quignon Jaw: The Role of Hugh Falconer', in Jordanova and Porter, *Images*, 171–99.

Bradford, S., *Disraeli* (New York, Stein & Day, 1982).

Bradlaugh, C., *The Channel Tunnel: Ought the Democracy to Oppose or Support It?* (Bonner, 1887).

Bravo, M.T., 'Ethnological Encounters', in Jardine, Secord and Spary, *Cultures*, 338–57.

Briggs, A., *The Age of Improvement 1783–1867* (Longman, 1979).

——, *Victorian People* (Penguin, 1990).

——, *Victorian Cities* (Penguin, 1990).

——, *Victorian Things* (Penguin, 1990).

Brock, W.H., 'The Patronage of Science', in Turner, *Patronage*, 173–206.

——, 'School Science Examinations', in MacLeod, *Days of Judgement*, 169–88.

——, and R.M.MacLeod, 'The Scientists' Declaration: Reflexions on Science and Belief in the Wake of *Essays and Reviews*, 1864–5', *BJHS*, 9 (1976), 39–66.

——, N.D.McMillan and R.C.Mollan, eds, *John Tyndall: Essays on a Natural Philosopher* (Royal Dublin Society, Historical Studies 3, 1981).

[Broderip, W., and R. Owen], 'Generalizations of Comparative Anatomy', *QR*, 93 (1853), 46–83.

Brooke, J.H., 'Natural Theology and the Plurality of Worlds: Observations on the Brewster-Whewell Debate', *AS*, 34 (1977), 221–86.

——, 'The Natural Theology of the Geologists', in Jordanova and Porter, *Images*, 39–64.

——, *Science and Religion* (CUP, 1991).

Brooks, J.L., *Just Before the Origin: Alfred Russel Wallace's Theory of Evolution* (New York, Columbia UP, 1984).

Brown, A. W., *The Metaphysical Society* (New York, Columbia UP, 1947).

Browne, J., 'The Charles Darwin - Joseph Hooker Correspondence', *J. Soc. Bibphy Nat. Hist.*, 8 (1978), 351–66.

——, *The Secular Ark: Studies in the History of Biogeography* (New Haven, Yale UP, 1983).

——, 'Squibs and Snobs: Science in Humorous British Undergraduate Magazines around 1830', *HS*, 30 (1992), 165–97.

——, 'Biogeography and Empire', in Jardine, Secord and Spary, *Cultures*, 305–21.

Bibliography

Buchanan, R., 'Are Men Born Free and Equal?', *Daily Telegraph*, 16, 27 Jan., 3 Feb. 1890.

Buckle, H.T., *History of Civilization in England* 3 vols (Richards, 1903–4).

Bunbury, C.J.F., ed., *Memorials of Sir Charles J. F. Bunbury* 9 vols (Privately Printed, 1891).

——, ed., *Life, Letters and Journals of Sir Charles J.F.Bunbury* 3 vols (Privately Printed, 1894).

Burchfield, J.D., *Lord Kelvin and the Age of the Earth* (UCP, 1990).

Burkhardt, F., 'England and Scotland: The Learned Societies', in Glick, *Comparative Reception*, 32–74.

——, and S. Smith, eds, *The Correspondence of Charles Darwin* 9 vols (CUP, 1985–94).

——, *A Calendar of the Correspondence of Charles Darwin, 1821–1882, With Supplement* (CUP, 1994).

Burrow, J.W., *Evolution and Society* (CUP, 1966).

Burstyn, H.L., 'If Darwin wasn't the *Beagle*'s Naturalist, Why was he on Board', *BJHS*, 8 (1975), 62–9.

Busk, G., 'An Account of the Polyzoa, and Sertularian Zoophytes, Collected in the Voyage of the Rattlesnake', in MacGillivray, *Narrative*, 1:343–402.

——, 'On a very ancient Human Cranium from Gibraltar', *Report BAAS, Bath, 1864*, (1865), Notices 91–2.

Butcher, B.W., 'Gorilla Warfare in Melbourne: Halford, Huxley and "Man's Place in Nature"', in R.W.Home, ed., *Australian Science in the Making* (CUP, 1988), 153–69.

Butler, S., *Evolution Old and New* (Hardwicke & Bogue, 1879).

Butler, S.V.F., 'Centers and Peripheries: The Development of British Physiology, 1870–1914', *JHB*, 21 (1988), 473–500.

Bynum, W.F., 'Charles Lyell's *Antiquity of Man* and its Critics', *JHB*, 17 (1984), 153–87.

Calderwood, H., 'Professor Huxley's Lay Sermons', *CR*, 15 (1870), 195–206.

——, 'The Present Relations of Physical Science to Mental Philosophy', *CR*, 16 (1870–1), 225–38.

Camerini, J.R., 'Evolution, Biogeography, and Maps: An Early History of Wallace's Line', *Isis*, 84 (1993), 700–27.

Cardwell, D.S.L., *The Organisation of Science in England* (Heinemann, 1972).

Carlyle, T., *Critical and Miscellaneous Essays* 7 vols (Chapman & Hall, 1894).

——, *On Heroes, Hero-Worship, and the Heroic in History* (New York, Chelsea House, 1983).

Caron, J.A., '"Biology" in the Life Sciences', *HS*, 26 (1988), 223–68.

Carpenter, W.B., *Remarks on Some Passages in the Review of 'Principles of General and Comparative Physiology'* (Bristol, Philip & Evans, 1840).

——, 'Dubois and Jones on Medical Study', *British and Foreign Medical Review*, 10 (1840), 175–203.

——, *Animal Physiology* 2 vols (Orr, 1843).

——, 'On the Doctrine of Human Automatism', *CR*, 25 (1875), 397–416, 940–62.

Carus, C.G., *The King of Saxony's Journey through England and Scotland in the Year 1844* (Chapman & Hall, 1846).

Catlett, S., 'Huxley, Hutton and the "White Rage": A Debate on Vivisection at the Metaphysical Society', *ANH*, 11 (1983), 181–9.

Chadarevian, S. de, 'Laboratory Science versus Country-House Experiments. The Controversy between Julius Sachs and Charles Darwin', *BJHS*, 29 (1996), 17–41.

Chadwick, O., *The Secularization of the European Mind in the Nineteenth Century* (CUP, 1975).

Chandler, T., 'Rheumatism, with Periodical Fits of Delirium, Treated by Animal Magnetism', *Lancet* 2 (1837–8), 81–3.

——, 'Cures of Various Diseases with Mesmerism', *Zoist*, 2 (1844), 373–6.

——, 'Cases of Mesmerism', *Zoist*, 3 (1845), 189–95.

——, 'Extraordinary Effects of Mesmerism on a Gentleman, PERFECTLY BLIND for Eleven Years', *Zoist*, 5 (1847), 1–11.

Chesney, K., *The Victorian Underworld* (Penguin, 1972).

Chilton, W., 'Theory of Regular Gradation', *Oracle of Reason*, 27 Nov. 1841.

——, 'Geological Revelations', *Oracle of Reason*, 29 July 1843.

Christie, J.D., 'A Working Man's Reply to Professor Huxley', *NC*, 27 (1890), 476–83.

Clark, G.K., *The Making of Victorian England* (Methuen, 1962).

Clark, R.W., *The Huxleys* (Heinemann, 1968).

Clarke, J.F., *Autobiographical Recollections of the Medical Profession* (Churchill, 1874).

[E.Clodd], 'The Right Hon. Thomas Henry Huxley', *Daily Chronicle*, 1 July 1895.

Coad, J.G., *The Royal Dockyards 1690–1850* (Aldershot, Scolar Press, 1989).

Cockshut, A.O.J., *The Unbelievers: English Agnostic Thought 1840–1890* (Collins, 1964).

Cohen, I.B., 'Three Notes on the Reception of Darwin's Ideas on Natural Selection', in Kohn, *Darwinian Heritage*, 589–607.

Colbert, E.H., *Men and Dinosaurs* (Penguin, 1971).

Cole, G.D.H., and R.Postgate, *The Common People 1746–1946* (Methuen, 1966).

Coleman, D., and T.Mansell, 'Science, Religion and the London School Board', *History of Education*, 24 (1995), 141–58.

Coleman, W., 'Morphology between Type Concept and Descent Theory', *J.Hist. Med. & Allied Sciences*, 31 (1976), 149–75.

Coleridge, S.T., *On the Constitution of the Church and State* (Dent, 1972).

Collie, M., *Huxley at Work: With the Scientific Correspondence of T.H.Huxley and the Rev. Dr George Gordon of Birnie, near Elgin* (Macmillan, 1991).

Collier, J., *The Religion of an Artist* (Watts, 1926).

Collini, S., *Public Moralists: Political Thought and Intellectual Life in Britain 1850–1930* (Oxford, Clarendon, 1993).

Colp, R., *To Be an Invalid: The Illness of Charles Darwin* (UCP, 1977).

——, 'Notes on William Gladstone, Karl Marx, Charles Darwin, Kliment Timiriazev, and the "Eastern Question" of 1876–78', *J. Hist. Med.*, 38 (1983), 178–85.

Conway, M., 'Huxley', *South Place Magazine*, 1 (9) (1895), 73–5.

Cooper, R., *The Immortality of the Soul* (Watson, 1853).

Cooter, R., *The Cultural Meaning of Popular Science: Phrenology and the Organization of Consent in Nineteenth-Century Britain* (CUP, 1984).

——, and S.Pumfrey, 'Separate Spheres and Public Places: Reflections on the History of Science Popularization and Science in Public Culture', *HS*, 32 (1994), 237–67.

Cope, E.D., 'Remains of a Gigantic Extinct Dinosaur', *Proc. Acad. Nat. Sci.*, Philadelphia (1866), 275–9.

——, 'Descriptions of Extinct Batrachia and Reptilia from the Permian Formation of Texas', *Proc. Am. Phil. Soc.*, 17 (1878), 505–30.

——, 'Second Contribution to the History of the Vertebrata of the Permian Formation of Texas', *Proc. Am. Phil. Soc.*, 19 (1882), 38–58.

——, 'The Relations Between the Theromorphous Reptiles and the Monotreme Mammalia', *Proc. Am. Assoc. Adv. Sci.*, 33 (1884), 471–82.

Cope, Z., 'The Private Medical Schools of London (1746–1914)', in Poynter, *Evolution of Medical Education*, 89–109.

Cornish, C.J., *Sir William Flower* (Macmillan, 1904).

Corsi, P., 'Recent Studies on Italian Reactions to Darwin', in Kohn, *Darwinian Heritage*, 711–29.

——, *Science and Religion: Baden Powell and the Anglican Debate, 1800–1860* (CUP, 1988).

Cosans, C., 'Anatomy, Metaphysics, and Values: The Ape Brain Debate Reconsidered', *Biology and Philosophy*, 9 (1994), 129–65.

Cowen, D.L., 'Liberty, Laissez-Faire and Licensure in Nineteenth Century Britain', *Bull. Hist. Med.*, 43 (1969), 30–40.

Cowherd, R.G., *Politics of English Dissent* (New York UP, 1956).

Crane, W. 'The Marriage of Science and Industry', *Pall Mall Gazette*, 20 Jan. 1887.

Crook, P., *Darwinism, War and History* (CUP, 1994).

Crosland, M., 'Explicit Qualifications as a Criterion for Membership of the Royal Society', *NRRS*, 37 (1983), 167–87.

Cunningham, H., *The Volunteer Force* (Hamden, Conn., Archon Books, 1975).

Dale, P.A., *In Pursuit of a Scientific Culture: Science, Art and Society in the Victorian Age* (Madison, Univ. Wisconsin Press, 1989).

Dana, J.D., 'Evidence as to Man's Place in Nature', *Am. J. Sci.*, 35 (1863), 451–4.

Dante, *The Divine Comedy. Volume 1, Inferno*, trans. M.Musa (Penguin, 1984).

Darwin, C., *Journal of Researches* (Colburn, 1839).

——, *Monograph on the Sub-Class Cirripedia* 2 vols (Ray Society, 1851–4).

——, *On the Origin of Species by Means of Natural Selection* (Murray, 1859).

——, *The Expression of the Emotions in Man and Animals* (Murray, 1872).

——, *The Descent of Man, Selection in Relation to Sex* (Murray, 1877).

——, *The Autobiography of Charles Darwin 1809–1882*, ed. N.Barlow (New York, Norton, 1958).

Darwin, F., ed., *The Foundations of the Origin of Species. Two Essays Written in 1842 and 1844* (CUP, 1909).

——, ed., *The Life and Letters of Charles Darwin* 2 vols (Murray, 1887).

——, and A.C.Seward, eds, *More Letters of Charles Darwin* 2 vols (Murray, 1903).

Davidoff, L., and C. Hall, *Family Fortunes: Men and Women of the English Middle Class, 1780–1850* (UCP, 1987).

Davies, C.M., *Heterodox London* 2 vols (Tinsley, 1874).

Bibliography

Davis, M., *Every Man his own Landlord: A History of Coventry Building Society* (Warwick, Coventry Building Society, 1985).

[Dawkins, W.B.], 'Darwin on the Descent of Man', *ER*, 134 (1871), 195–235.

Dawson, W.R., *The Huxley Papers* (Imperial College, 1946).

Deacon, M., *Scientists and the Sea 1650–1900* (Academic Press, 1971).

Dean, D.R., 'Hitchcock's Dinosaur Tracks', *Am. Quart.*, 21 (1969), 639–44.

——, '"Through Science to Despair": Geology and the Victorians', *Ann. N.Y. Acad. Sci.*, 360 (1981), 111–36.

Denis, R.D., 'The Brompton Barracks: War, Peace, and the Rise of Victorian Art and Education', *Journal of Design History*, 8 (1995), 11–25.

Dennis, B., and D.Skilton, eds, *Reform and Intellectual Debate in Victorian England* (Croom Helm, 1987).

Desmond, A., 'Designing the Dinosaur', *Isis*, 70 (1979), 224–34.

——, *Archetypes and Ancestors: Palaeontology in Victorian London 1850–1875* (Blond & Briggs, 1982; UCP, 1984).

——, 'Robert E. Grant's Later Views on Organic Development', *ANH*, 11 (1984), 395–413.

——, 'Richard Owen's Reaction to Transmutation in the 1830's', *BJHS*, 18 (1985), 25–50.

——, 'The Making of Institutional Zoology in London 1822–1836', *HS*, 23 (1985), 153–85, 224–50.

——, 'Artisan Resistance and Evolution in Britain, 1819–1848', *Osiris*, 3 (1987), 77–110.

——, *The Politics of Evolution: Morphology, Medicine, and Reform in Radical London* (UCP, 1989)

——, 'Darwin, Huxley, and the Natural Sciences', *Isis*, 84 (1993), 594–5.

——, 'Foreword' to Ospovat, *Development of Darwin's Theory* (CUP pbk, 1995).

——, 'Author's Response' in 'Huxley, A.D.', *Metascience*, 7 (1995), 27–55.

——, and J.Moore, *Darwin* (Michael Joseph, 1991).

Detrosier, R., *Lecture on the Utility of Political Unions . . . and on the Political Influence of Scientific Knowledge* (Brooks, 1832).

Dickens, C., *The Posthumous Papers of the Pickwick Club* [1836–7] (Penguin, 1972).

——, *Sketches by Boz* [1839] (Mandarin, 1991).

——, *Bleak House* [1853] (Penguin, 1971).

Di Gregorio, M., 'Order or Process of Nature: Huxley's and Darwin's Different Approaches to Natural Sciences', *Hist. Phil. Life Sci.*, 3 (1981), 217–41.

——, 'The Dinosaur Connection: A Reinterpretation of T.H.Huxley's Evolutionary View', *JHB*, 15 (1982), 397–418.

——, *T.H.Huxley's Place in Natural Science* (New Haven, Yale UP, 1984).

——, 'A Wolf in Sheep's Clothing: Carl Gegenbaur, Ernst Haeckel, the Vertebral Theory of the Skull, and the Survival of Richard Owen', *JHB*, 28 (1995), 247–80.

Dockrill, D.W., 'T.H.Huxley and the Meaning of "Agnosticism"', *Theology*, 74 (1971), 461–77.

Draper, H., *The Marx-Engels Chronicle, Volume 1* (New York, Schocken, 1985).

Draper, J.W., *History of the Conflict Between Religion and Science* (New York, Appleton, 1874).

Drower, M.S., *Flinders Petrie: A Life in Archaeology* (Gollancz, 1985).

Drummond, H., *The Lowell Lectures on the Ascent of Man* (Hodder & Stoughton, 1894).

Dubois, M.E.F.T., 'The Place of "*Pithecanthropus*" in the Genealogical Tree', *Nature*, 53 (1896), 245–7.

Duncan, D., ed., *The Life and Letters of Herbert Spencer* (Methuen, 1908).

Duncan, P.M., 'Anniversary Address', *QJGS*, 33 (1877), 41–88.

Dupree, A.H., *Asa Gray, 1810–1888* (New York, Athenaeum, 1968).

Durant, J., 'Scientific Naturalism and Social Reform in the Thought of Alfred Russel Wallace', *BJHS*, 12 (1979), 31–58.

——, 'The Ascent of Nature in Darwin's *Descent of Man*', in Kohn, *Darwinian Heritage*, 283–306.

Durey, M.J., 'Bodysnatchers and Benthamites', *London J.*, 2 (1976), 200–25.

Dyster, F.D., 'Evidence as to Man's Place in Nature', *Reader*, 1 (1863), 234–5.

Edgerton, D., *Science, Technology and the British Industrial 'Decline' 1870–1970* (CUP, 1996).

[Egerton, P.], 'Monkeyana', *Punch*, 18 May 1861, 206.

Eisen, S., 'Huxley and the Positivists', *VS*, 7 (1964), 337–58.

Eliot, G. *Middlemarch* [1871–2] (Penguin, 1985).

Ellegard, A., *Darwin and the General Reader* (UCP, 1990).

Elliotson, J., *Lectures on the Theory and Practice of Medicine*, ed. J.C.Cooke and T.G.Thompson (Moore, 1839).

——, 'More painless Amputations and other Surgical Operations in the Mesmeric State', *Zoist*, 3 (1845), 490.

Ellis, I., *Seven Against Christ: A Study of 'Essays and Reviews'* (Leiden, Brill, 1980).

Eng, E., 'Thomas Henry Huxley's Understanding of Evolution', *HS*, 16 (1978), 291–303.

Engels, F., *The Condition of the Working Class in England* [1845] (Penguin, 1987).

English, M.P., 'Robert Hardwicke (1822–1875), publisher of biological and medical books', *ANH*, 13 (1986), 25–37.

——, *Victorian Values: The Life and Times of Dr Edwin Lankester M.D., F.R.S.* (Bristol, Biopress, 1990).

Epps, J., *The Church of England's Apostasy* (Dinnis, 1834).

Erskine, F., 'The *Origin of Species* and the Science of Female Inferiority', in Amigoni and Wallace, *Darwin's Origin*, 95–121.

Essays and Reviews, 4th ed. (Longmans, 1861).

Escott, T.H.S., *Masters of English Journalism* (Westport, Conn., Greenwood, 1970).

Estes, J.W., *Dictionary of Protopharmacology. Therapeutic Practices, 1700–1850* (New York, Science History Publications, 1990).

Evans, Joan, *Time and Chance: The Story of Arthur Evans and his Forebears* (Longmans, 1943).

Evans, John, 'On Portions of a Cranium and of a Jaw, in the Slab Containing the Fossil Remains of the Archaeopteryx', *Nat. Hist. Rev.*, 5 (1865), 415–21.

Eve, A.S., and C.H.Creasey, eds, *Life and Work of John Tyndall* (Macmillan, 1945).

Falconer, H., 'On Prof. Huxley's attempted Refutation of Cuvier's Laws of Correlation, in the Reconstruction of Extinct Vertebrate Forms', *AMNH*, 17 (1856), 476–93.

Farley, J., *The Spontaneous Generation Controversy from Descartes to Oparin* (Baltimore, Johns Hopkins UP, 1977).

Fawcett, H., 'A Popular Exposition of Mr. Darwin on the Origin of Species', *Macmillan's Magazine*, 3 (1860), 81–92.

Fawcett, J.W., 'Thomas Henry Huxley', *Unity*, 95 (1925), 207–10.

Fayrer, J., *Recollections of My Life* (Edinburgh, Blackwood, 1900).

Fiske, J., 'Reminiscences of Huxley', *Ann. Rep. Smithsonian Inst.*, (1901), 713–28.

——, *Darwinism and Other Essays* (Boston, Mass., Houghton, Mifflin, 1902).

——, *A Century of Science and Other Essays* (Boston, Mass., Houghton, Mifflin, 1902).

——, *The Personal Letters of John Fiske* (Cedar Rapids, Iowa, Torch Press, 1939).

Fletcher, J., *Rudiments of Physiology* 3 Parts (Edinburgh, Carfrae, 1835–7).

Flett, J.S., *The First Hundred Years of the Geological Survey of Great Britain* (H.M.Stationery Office, 1937).

Flexner, A., *Daniel Coit Gilman* (New York, Harcourt, Brace, 1946).

Flower, W.H., 'Introductory Lecture', *Medical Times and Gazette*, 1 (1870), 195–200.

——, 'Reminiscences of Professor Huxley', *North American Review*, 161 (1895), 279–86.

——, 'Richard Owen', *Proc. Roy. Soc.*, 55 (1894), i–xiv.

——, *Essays on Museums* (Macmillan, 1898).

Flower, S.S., *List of the Vertebrated Animals Exhibited in the Gardens of the Zoological Society of London, 1828–1927* (Zoological Society, 1929).

Flürscheim, M., 'Professor Huxley's Attacks', *NC*, 27 (1890), 639–50.

Foot, M.R.D., and H.C.G.Matthew, eds, *The Gladstone Diaries* 15 vols (Oxford, Clarendon, 1968–1994).

Foote, G.W., *Defence of Free Speech: Being a Three Hours' Address to the Jury in the Court of Queen's Bench before Lord Coleridge on April 24, 1883* (Progressive Publishing Co., 1889).

Forbes, E., 'On the Mollusca', in MacGillivray, *Narrative*, 2:360–86.

——, *Literary Papers by the Late Professor Edward Forbes* (Reeve, 1855).

Forgan, S., 'The Architecture of Display: Museums, Universities and Objects in Nineteenth-Century Britain', *HS*, 32 (1994), 139–62.

——, and G.Gooday, '"A Fungoid Assemblage of Buildings": Diversity and Adversity in the Development of College Architecture and Scientific Education in Nineteenth-Century South Kensington', *History of Universities*, 13 (1994), 153–92.

——, 'Constructing South Kensington: The Buildings and Politics of T.H.Huxley's Working Environment', *BJHS*, 29 (1996), 435–68.

Foster, M., 'A Few More Words on Thomas Henry Huxley', *Nature*, 1 Aug. 1895, 318–20.

Fox, W., 'On the Skull and Bones of an Iguanodon', *Report BAAS, Norwich, 1868*, (1869), Sections 64–5.

Freeman, D., 'The Evolutionary Theories of Charles Darwin and Herbert Spencer', *Current Anthropology*, 15 (1974), 211–37.

French, R.D., *Antivivisection and Medical Science in Victorian Society* (Princeton UP, 1975).

Friday, J., 'A Microscopic Incident in a Monumental Struggle: Huxley and Antibiosis in 1875', *BJHS*, 7 (1974), 61–71.

Bibliography

'Friend, A', 'Professor Huxley's Homes', *Illustrated London News*, 6 July 1895.

Gage, A.T., and W.T. Stearn, *A Bicentenary History of the Linnean Society of London* (Academic Press, 1988)

[Gallenga, A.], 'The Age We Live In', *Fraser's Magazine*, 24 (1841), 1–15.

Galton, F., 'Statistical Enquiries into the Efficacy of Prayer', *FR*, 18 (1872), 125–35.

Gardiner, A.G., *The Life of Sir William Harcourt* 2 vols (Constable, 1923).

Gardner, J.H., 'A Huxley Essay as "Poem"', *VS*, 14 (1970), 177–91.

Gates, B.T., 'Revisioning Darwin, With Sympathy', *Hist. Eur. Ideas*, 19 (1994), 761–8.

Gaskell, E., *Mary Barton* (Dent, 1967).

Gasman, D., *The Scientific Origins of National Socialism: Social Darwinism in Ernst Haeckel and the German Monist League* (Macdonald, 1971).

Geddes, P., 'Huxley as Teacher', *Nature*, 115 (1925), 740–3.

Geikie, A., *Life of Sir Roderick I. Murchison* 2 vols (Murray, 1875).

——, *Memoir of Sir Andrew Crombie Ramsay* (Macmillan, 1895).

Geison, G.L., 'The Protoplasmic Theory of Life and the Vitalist-Mechanist Debate', *Isis*, 60 (1969), 273–93.

——, *Michael Foster and the Cambridge School of Physiology* (Princeton UP, 1978).

Gilbert, S.F., 'Altruism and Other Unnatural Acts: T.H.Huxley on Nature, Man, and Society', *Perspectives in Biology and Medicine*, 22 (1979), 346–58.

Gillespie, N.C., 'The Duke of Argyll, Evolutionary Anthropology, and the Art of Scientific Controversy', *Isis*, 68 (1977), 40–54.

Gilley, S., 'The Huxley-Wilberforce Debate: A Reconsideration', in K.Robbins, ed., *Religion and Humanism* (Oxford, Blackwell, 1981), 325–40.

——, and A.Loades, 'Thomas Henry Huxley: The War between Science and Religion', *Journal of Religion*, 61 (1981), 285–308.

Girouard, M., *Alfred Waterhouse and the Natural History Museum* (British Museum [Natural History], 1981).

Glick, T.F., ed., *The Comparative Reception of Darwinism* (UCP, 1988).

Godlee, R.J., 'Thomas Wharton Jones', *Brit. J. Ophthalmol.*, 93 (1921) 97–117, 145–56.

Goetzmann, W.H., *Exploration and Empire: The Explorer and the Scientist in the Winning of the American West* (New York, Norton, 1978).

Golding, B., *The Origin, Plan, and Operations of the Charing Cross Hospital, London* (Allen, 1867).

Gooday, G., 'Precision Measurement and the Genesis of Physics Teaching Laboratories in Victorian Britain', *BJHS*, 23 (1990), 25–51.

——, '"Nature" in the Laboratory: Domestication and Discipline with the Microscope in Victorian Life Science', *BJHS*, 24 (1991), 307–41.

Gooding, D., T.Pinch and S.Schaffer, eds, *The Uses of Experiment* (CUP, 1989).

Goodrich, E.S., 'Edwin Ray Lankester', *Proc. Roy. Soc.*, 106B (1930), x-xv.

Goodway, D., *London Chartism 1838–1848* (CUP, 1982).

Gould, J., 'On New Species of Mammalia and Birds from Australia', *Proc. Zool. Soc.*, 17 (1849), 109–112.

——, 'On New Species of Birds from Australia', *Proc. Zool. Soc.*, 18 (1850), 200–201.

——, 'On New Australian Birds in the Collection of the Zoological Society of London', *Proc. Zool. Soc.*, 18 (1850), 276–9.

Gould, S.J., *Ontogeny and Phylogeny* (Cambridge, Mass., Harvard UP, 1977).
——, '*Bathybius* and *Eozoon*', in *The Panda's Thumb* (Penguin, 1983), 196–202.
——, 'Knight Takes Bishop?', *Natural History*, 95 (5) (1986), 18–33.
——, *Time's Arrow, Time's Cycle: Myth and Metaphor in the Discovery of Geological Time* (Penguin, 1990).
——, 'A Most Ingenious Paradox', in *The Flamingo's Smile* (Penguin, 1991), 78–95.
Grainger, R.D., *Observations on the Cultivation of Organic Science* (Highley, 1848).
Grant, R.E., 'Lectures on Comparative Anatomy and Animal Physiology', *Lancet*, 1–2 (1833–4), 60 lectures.
——, *Tabular View of the Primary Divisions of the Animal Kingdom* (Walton & Maberly, 1861).
Grayson, D.K., *The Establishment of Human Antiquity* (Academic Press, 1983).
[Green, J.R.], 'Professor Huxley on Science and the Clergy', *Saturday Review*, 24 (1867), 691–2.
Green, L., '"Strange [In]difference to Sex": Thomas Hardy, the Victorian Man of Letters, and The Temptations of Androgyny', *VS*, 38 (1995), 523–49.
Greene, J.C., 'Darwin as a Social Evolutionist', *JHB*, 10 (1977), 1–27.
Greenwood, H, *General Booth and His Critics: Being an Analysis of the Scheme and an Enquiry into the Value of the Criticisms of Professor Huxley, Mr. C.S.Loch, "The Times" Newspaper, and Other Critics* (Howe, n.d.).
Gregory, F., *Scientific Materialism in Nineteenth Century Germany* (Dordrecht, Reidel, 1977).
Grene, M., 'Recent Biographies of Darwin: The Complexity of Context', *Perspectives on Science*, 1 (1993), 659–75.
Groeben, C., ed., *Charles Darwin - Anton Dohrn Correspondence* (Naples, Macchiaroli, 1982).
Gross, C.G., 'Hippocampus Minor and Man's Place in Nature', *Hippocampus*, 3 (1993), 403–16.
Grove, W.R., *The Correlation of Physical Forces* (Longmans, 1867).
Gruber, H.E., and P.H.Barrett, *Darwin on Man* (New York, Dutton, 1974).
Gruber, J.W., *A Conscience in Conflict. The Life of St. George Jackson Mivart* (New York, Columbia UP, 1960).
——, 'The Richard Owen Correspondence', in Gruber and Thackray, *Owen Commemoration*, 1–24.
——, 'Richard Owen and his Correspondents', in Gruber and Thackray, *Owen Commemoration*, 25–93.
——, and J.C.Thackray, *Richard Owen Commemoration* (Natural History Museum, 1992).
Haeckel, E., *Generelle Morphologie der Organismen* 2 vols (Berlin, Reimer, 1866).
——, 'Scientific Worthies II. - Thomas Henry Huxley', *Nature*, 9 (1874), 257–8.
——, *The History of Creation* 2 vols (New York, Appleton, 1876).
——, *Freedom in Science and Teaching* (Kegan Paul, 1879).
——, 'Thomas Huxley and Karl Vogt', *FR*, 58 (1895), 464–9.
——, *The Evolution of Man* (Watts, 1907).
Haight, G.S., *George Eliot and John Chapman* (New Haven, Yale UP, 1940).
——, *The George Eliot Letters* 9 vols (New Haven, Yale UP, 1954–56, 1978).
——, *George Eliot* (Penguin, 1985).

Halevy, E., *The Triumph of Reform, 1830–1841* (Benn, 1950).

——, *Victorian Years, 1841–1895* (Benn, 1951).

Hall, C., *Memoirs of Marshall Hall* (Bentley, 1861).

Hall, M.B., 'The Royal Society in Thomas Henry Huxley's Time', *NRRS*, 38 (1983–4), 153–8.

Hall, V.M.D., 'The Contribution of the Physiologist, William Benjamin Carpenter (1813–1885), to the Development of the Principle of the Correlation of Forces and the Conservation of Energy', *Med. Hist*, 23 (1979) 129–55.

Hardy, B., *The Exposure of Luxury: Radical Themes in Thackeray* (Peter Owen, 1972).

Harris, J., *Private Lives, Public Spirit: Britain 1870–1914* (Penguin, 1994).

Harrison, B., 'Animals and the State in Nineteenth-Century England', *Eng. Hist. Rev.*, 88 (1973), 786–820.

Harrison, F., 'The Future of Agnosticism', *FR*, 45 (1889), 144–56.

Harrison, J.F.C., *Early Victorian Britain 1832–1851* (Fontana, 1979).

——, 'Early Victorian Radicals and the Medical Fringe', in W.F.Bynum and R.Porter, eds, *Medical Fringe and Medical Orthodoxy 1750–1850* (Croom Helm, 1987), 198–215.

Hart, F., *The Roots of Service. History of Charing Cross Hospital 1818–1974* (Charing Cross Hospital Trustees, 1985).

Harte, N., *The University of London 1836–1986* (Athlone Press, 1986).

——, and J. North, *The World of UCL 1828–1990* (University College London, 1991).

Hays, J.N., 'Science in the City: The London Institution, 1818–40', *BJHS*, 7 (1974), 146–62.

——, 'The London Lecturing Empire, 1800–50', in Inkster and Morrell, *Metropolis and Province*, 91–119.

Hearl, T., 'Military Examination and the Teaching of Science, 1857–1870', in Macleod, *Days of Judgement*, 109–49.

Heimann, P.M., 'The *Unseen Universe*', *BJHS*, 6 (1972), 73–9.

Helfand, M.S., 'T.H.Huxley's "Evolution and Ethics"', *VS*, 20 (1977), 159–77.

Hepton, D., *Methodism and Politics in British Society, 1750–1850* (Hutchinson, 1984).

Heyck, T.W., *The Transformation of Intellectual Life in Victorian England* (Croom Helm, 1982).

Hilgartner, S., 'The Dominant View of Popularization', *Soc. Stud. Sci.*, 20 (1990), 519–39.

Hilton, B., *The Age of Atonement: The Influence of Evangelicalism on Social and Economic Thought 1785–1865* (Oxford, Clarendon, 1988).

Himmelfarb, G., *Darwin and the Darwinian Revolution* (Chatto & Windus, 1959).

Historical Account of the London Institution (1835).

Hitchcock, E., 'An Attempt to Discriminate and Describe the Animals that made the Fossil Footprints of the United States, and Especially in New England', *Mem. Am. Acad. Arts Sci.*, 3 (1848), 129–256.

Hodge, M.J.S., 'The Universal Gestation of Nature: Chambers' *Vestiges* and *Explanations*', *JHB*, 5 (1972), 127–51.

Hodges, S.H., *General Booth: 'The Family', and the Salvation Army* (Manchester, For the Author, 1890).

Bibliography

Hofstadter, R., *Social Darwinism in American Thought* (Boston, Mass., Beacon Press, 1955).

Holloway, S.W.F., 'Medical Education in England, 1830–1858', *History*, 49 (1964), 299–324.

Hollowday, E.D., 'Thomas Henry Huxley and the Microscope', *Quekett Journal of Microscopy*, 37 (1995), 437–54.

Holt, R.V., *The Unitarian Contribution to Social Progress in England* (Allen & Unwin, 1938).

Holyoake, G.J., *The History of the Last Trial by Jury for Atheism in England* (Watson, 1850).

——, 'The Priesthood of Science', *Reasoner Review*, 1 Nov. 1868, 1–8.

Hooker, J.D., *Himalayan Journals* 2 vols (Murray, 1855).

——, 'Reminiscences of Darwin', *Nature*, 60 (1899), 187–8.

Horne, A., *The Fall of Paris: The Siege and Commune 1870–71* (Pan, 1968).

Howarth, J., 'Science Education in Late-Victorian Oxford: A Curious Case of Failure?', *English Historical Review*, 102 (1987), 334–71.

Howes, G.B., 'St. George Mivart', *Proc. Roy. Soc.*, 75 (1905), 95–100.

Hughes, R., *The Fatal Shore: A History of the Transportation of Convicts to Australia 1787–1868* (Pan, 1988).

Hull, D.L., *Darwin and his Critics* (UCP, 1983).

——, *Science as a Process* (UCP, 1988).

Hunter, W., *Historical Account of Charing Cross Hospital and Medical School* (Murray, 1914).

Hutchinson, H.G., *Life of Sir John Lubbock*, 2 vols (Macmillan, 1914).

[Hutton, R.H.], 'Pope Huxley', *Spectator*, 29 Jan. 1870, 135–6.

[—], 'The Great Agnostic', *Spectator*, 6 July 1895.

Huxley, Andrew, 'Grandfather and Grandson', *NRRS*, 38 (1983–4), 147–51.

Huxley, Henrietta A., 'Pictures of Australian Life, 1843–1844', *Cornhill Magazine*, 31 (1911), 770–81.

Huxley, Julian, ed., *T. H. Huxley's Diary of the Voyage of H. M. S. Rattlesnake* (Chatto & Windus, 1935).

Huxley, Leonard, ed., *Life and Letters of Thomas Henry Huxley* 2 vols (Macmillan, 1900).

——, ed., *Life and Letters of Sir Joseph Dalton Hooker* 2 vols (Murray, 1918).

Huxley, Thomas Henry, 'On a Hitherto Undescribed Structure in the Human Hair Sheath', *Medical Gazette*, 36 (1845), 1340–1.

[—], 'Science at Sea', *WR*, 61 (1854), 98–119.

[—], 'Contemporary Literature: Science', *WR*, 61 (1854), 254–70, 580–95; 62 (1854), 242–56, 572–80; 63 (1855), 239–53, 558–63; 64 (1855), 240–55, 565–74; 65 (1856), 261–71; 67 (1857), 279–88.

[—], 'The Vestiges of Creation', *BFMCR*, 26 (1854), 425–39.

[—], 'Schamyl, the Prophet-Warrior of the Caucasus', *WR*, 61 (1854), 480–519.

[—], 'Owen and Rymer Jones on Comparative Anatomy', *BFMCR*, 35 (1856), 1–27.

——, 'On the Method of Palaeontology', *AMNH*, 18 (1856), 43–54.

——, 'Lectures on General Natural History', *Medical Times and Gazette*, 12 (1856), 429 - 15 (1857), 471 passim.

[—], 'Chalk, Ancient and Modern', *Saturday Review*, 6 (1858), 500–502.

——, 'Science and Religion', *The Builder*, 15 Jan. 1859.

——, 'The Government School of Mines', *The Builder*, 22 Jan. 1859.

——, *The Oceanic Hydrozoa* (Ray Society, 1859).

——, 'Time and Life: Mr. Darwin's "Origin of Species"', *Macmillan's Magazine*, 1 (1859), 142–8.

[—], 'Darwin on the Origin of Species', *Times*, 26 Dec. 1859.

——, 'Man and the Apes', *Athenaeum*, 30 Mar., 13 Apr. 1861, 433, 498.

——, *On Our Knowledge of the Causes of the Phenomena of Organic Nature* (Hardwicke, 1862).

——, *Evidence as to Man's Place in Nature* (Williams & Norgate, 1863).

——, *Lectures on the Elements of Comparative Anatomy* (Churchill, 1864).

——, 'Professor Huxley's Lectures on "The Structure and Classification of the Mammalia" at the Royal College of Surgeons', *Reader*, 3 (1864), 266–8.

——, 'The Negro's Place in Nature', *Reader*, 3 (1864), 334–5.

[—], 'Science and "Church Policy"', *Reader*, 4 (1864), 821.

——, 'To the Editor of the "Spectator"', *English Leader*, 24 Feb. 1866.

——, 'Reply to Objections on my Classification of Birds', *Ibis*, 4 (1868), 357–61.

——, 'Nature: Aphorisms by Goethe', *Nature*, 1 (1869), 9–11.

——, 'The Natural History of Creation', *Academy*, 1 (1869), 13–14, 40–3.

——, *Lay Sermons, Addresses, and Reviews* [1870] (New York, Appleton, 1882).

——, 'The Forefathers of the English People', *Nature*, 1 (1870), 514–15.

——, 'The Deep-Sea Soundings and Geology', *Nature*, 1 (1870), 657–8.

——, 'To the Ratepayers of the Marylebone Division', (1870), flysheet.

——, 'The Royal School of Mines', *Times*, 11 Apr. 1871.

——, 'Kew Gardens', *Times*, 31 July 1872.

——, *Critiques and Addresses* (Macmillan, 1873).

——, 'Professor Huxley at Manchester', *Nature*, 10 (1874), 455–7.

——, 'Miss Jex-Blake and Her Examiners', *Times*, 8 July 1874.

——, 'Anthropogenie', *Academy*, 7 (1875), 16–18.

——, 'Notes from the "Challenger"', *Nature*, 12 (1875), 315–16.

——, 'The Article "Birds" in "Encyclopaedia Britannica"', *Nature*, 13 (1876), 247.

——, 'Professor Huxley on Lord Shaftesbury', *Times*, 26 May 1876.

——, 'Dinner to the Challenger Staff', *Nature*, 14 (1876), 238–9.

——, 'Evidences of Evolution', *New-York Daily Tribune*, 19, 21, 23 Sept. 1876.

——, *American Addresses* (Macmillan, 1877).

——, *Physiography: An Introduction to the Study of Nature* [1877] (Macmillan, 1887).

——, 'A Modern "Symposium"', *NC*, 1 (1877), 536–9.

——, *A Manual of the Anatomy of Invertebrated Animals* (New York, Appleton, 1878).

——, [Speech], *J. Quekett Microscopical Club*, 5 (1878), 47–9.

——, [On a New Arrangement of Lenses for Dissecting], *J. Quekett Microscopical Club*, 5 (1878), 144–5.

——, 'Scientific Worthies XII. - William Harvey', *Nature*, 17 (1878), 417–20.

——, 'Prefatory Note' in Haeckel, *Freedom in Science*, v-xx.

——, 'On the Characters of the Pelvis in the Mammalia, and the Conclusions Respecting the Origin of Mammals which may be based on them', *Proc. Roy. Soc.*, 28 (1879), 395–405.

——, 'President's Address', *J. Quekett Microscopical Club*, 6 (1879), 250–5.

——, 'On the Application of the Laws of Evolution to the Arrangement of the Vertebrata, and more particularly of the Mammalia', *Proc. Zool. Soc.*, 43 (1880), 649–62.

——, *The Crayfish: An Introduction to the Study of Zoology* (Kegan Paul, 1880).

——, 'The First Volume of the Publications of the "Challenger"', *Nature*, 23 (1880), 1–3.

——, *Twenty First Annual Report of the Inspector of Fisheries (England and Wales)* (1881).

——, 'Distribution of Awards, Normal School of Science and Royal School of Mines', *Nature*, 26 (1882), 233–5.

——, 'Prize Distribution at the Liverpool Institute', *Liverpool Mercury*, 17 Feb. 1883.

——, 'Unwritten History', *Macmillan's Magazine*, 48 (26 Apr. 1883), 26–41.

——, 'President's Address', *Proc. Roy. Soc.*, 36 (1883), 60–73.

——, ['Agnosticism', pirated letter], *Agnostic Annual*, (1884), 5–6.

——, 'President's Address', *Proc. Roy. Soc.*, 39 (1885), 278–99.

——, 'Professor Huxley and the Proposed Fishery Board', *Times*, 30 Mar. 1886.

——, 'The Home-Rule Bill', *Standard*, 13 Apr. 1886.

——, 'English Literature and the Universities', *Pall Mall Gazette*, 22 Oct. 1886.

——, 'The Queen's Jubilee', *Pall Mall Gazette*, 13 Jan. 1887.

——, 'The Imperial Institute', *Times*, 20 Jan., 19, 22 Feb. 1887.

——, 'The Organization of Industrial Education', *Times*, 21 Mar. 1887.

——, 'Royal Academy Address', *Times*, 2 May 1887.

——, 'On Free Libraries', *Daily Chronicle*, 8 June 1887.

——, 'From the Hut to the Pantheon', *Youth's Companion*, 23 June 1887, 281–2.

——, 'An Olive Branch from America', NC, 22 (1887), 620–4.

——, 'British Race-Types of To-Day', *Times*, 12 Oct. 1887.

——, 'On the Reception of the Origin of Species', in F.Darwin, *Life*, 2:179–204.

——, 'Bishop Wilberforce and Professor Huxley', *Times*, 1 Dec. 1887.

[—], 'M.P., P.R.S.', *Nature*, 37 (1887), 49–50.

——, 'How to Become an Orator', *Pall Mall Gazette*, 24 Oct. 1888, 1–2.

——, 'Spiritualism Unmasked', *Pall Mall Gazette*, 1 Jan. 1889, 1–2.

——, 'Sea Fisheries', *Times*, 4, 8 Jan. 1889.

——, 'Mr. Spencer on the Land Question', *Times*, 12 Nov. 1889.

——, 'Political Ethics', *Times*, 18 Nov. 1889.

——, 'The Ownership of the Land', *Times*, 21 Nov. 1889.

——, 'Are Men Born Free and Equal?', *Daily Telegraph*, 27, 29, 30 Jan. 1890.

——, *Social Diseases and Worse Remedies* (Macmillan, 1891).

——, [Letter on the Bus Strike], *Trade Unionist*, 20 June 1891.

——, *Essays upon some Controverted Questions* (Macmillan, 1892).

——, 'The Royal School of Mines', *Times*, 16 Jan. 1892.

——, 'An Apologetic Irenicon', FR, 52 (1892), 557–71.

——, 'Professorial University for London', *Times*, 7 July, 6 Dec. 1892.

[—], 'Criticism of the Royal Society', *Nature*, 47 (1892), 145–6.

——, *Collected Essays* 9 vols (Macmillan, 1893–4).

——, 'Professor Tyndall', NC, 35 (1894), 1–11.

——, 'Past and Present', *Nature*, 51 (1894), 1–3.

Bibliography

——, 'Mr. Balfour's Attack on Agnosticism', *NC*, 37 (1895), 527-40.

——, *The Scientific Memoirs of Thomas Henry Huxley*, ed. M.Foster and E.R.Lankester, 5 vols (Macmillan, 1898-1903).

——, and B.W.Hawkins, *An Elementary Atlas of Comparative Osteology* (Williams & Norgate, 1864).

——, *et al.*, *School Board for London. First Report. The Scheme of Education Committee. 13 June 1871* (Yates & Alexander, 1871).

——, and H.N.Martin, *A Course of Elementary Instruction in Practical Biology*, rev. G.B.Howes and D.H.Scott (Macmillan, 1888).

Inkster, I., and J. Morrell, eds, *Metropolis and Province: Science in British Culture, 1780–1850* (Hutchinson, 1983).

Irvine, W., *Apes, Angels, and Victorians* (Cleveland, Meridian, 1959).

Jackson, H., *The Eighteen Nineties* (Pelican, 1950).

Jackson, P., *George Scharf's London* (Murray, 1987).

Jacyna, L.S., 'Science and Social Order in the Thought of A.J.Balfour', *Isis*, 71 (1980), 11–34.

——, 'The Physiology of Mind, The Unity of Nature, and the Moral Order in Victorian Thought', *BJHS*, 14 (1981), 109–32.

——, 'Immanence or Transcendence: Theories of Life and Organization in Britain, 1790–1835', *Isis*, 74 (1983), 311–29.

——, 'The Romantic Programme and the Reception of Cell Theory in Britain', *JHB*, 17 (1984), 13–48.

——, 'Principles of General Physiology: The Comparative Dimension to British Neuroscience in the 1830s and 1840s', *Stud. Hist. Biol.*, 7 (1984), 47–92.

Jann, R., 'Darwin and the Anthropologists', *VS*, 37 (1994), 287–306.

Jardine, N., J.A.Secord and E.C.Spary, eds, *Cultures of Natural History* (CUP, 1996).

[Jenkin, F.], 'The Origin of Species', *North British Review*, 46 (1867), 277–318.

Jenkins, M., *The General Strike of 1842* (Lawrence & Wishart, 1980).

Jensen, J.V., *Thomas Henry Huxley: Communicating for Science* (Associated Univ. Presses, 1991)

——, 'Thomas Henry Huxley's Address at the Opening of the Johns Hopkins University in September 1876', *NRRS*, 47 (1993), 257–69.

Johnson, R., '"Really Useful Knowledge": Radical Education and Working-Class Culture, 1790–1848', in J.Clarke, C.Critcher, and R.Johnson, eds, *Working-Class Culture* (Hutchinson, 1979), 75–102.

Jones, G., *Social Darwinism and English Thought* (Brighton, Harvester, 1980).

——, 'Social Darwinism Revisited', *Hist. Eur. Ideas*, 19 (1994), 769–75.

Jones, G.S., *Outcast London* (Penguin, 1984).

Jones, H.F., *Samuel Butler* 2 vols (Macmillan, 1920).

Jones, T.W., 'Abstract of a Report on the Development of the Ovum of Man and the Mammifera', *Lancet*, 1 (1843–4), 258–62, 293–5.

——, 'Muscle a Neuro-Magnetic Apparatus', *Medical Gazette*, 33 (1843–4), 77–8.

Jordanova, L.J., and R.S.Porter, eds, *Images of the Earth* (Chalfont St. Giles, British Society for the History of Science, 1979).

J.P.A., 'Professor Huxley on Darwin's "Origin of Species"', *NR*, 31 Jan. 1863, 2–3.

Judd, J.W., *The Coming of Evolution* (CUP, 1911).

Kamil, J., *Luxor: A Guide to Ancient Thebes* (Longman, 1973).

Keith, A., 'Huxley as Anthropologist', *Nature*, 115 (1925), 719–23.

——, *An Autobiography* (Watts, 1950).

Kelly, A., *The Descent of Darwin: The Popularization of Darwinism in Germany, 1860–1914* (Chapel Hill, Univ. North Carolina Press, 1981).

Kennedy, J.G., *Herbert Spencer* (Boston, Twayne, 1978).

Ker, I., and T.Gornall, eds, *The Letters and Diaries of John Henry Newman* (Oxford, Clarendon) Vol. 1 (1978); T.Gornall, ed., Vol. 5 (1981).

Keynes, R.D., ed., *Charles Darwin's 'Beagle' Diary* (CUP, 1988).

Kidd, B., *Social Evolution* (Macmillan, 1895).

King, C., 'Catastrophism and Evolution', *Amer. Nat.*, 11 (1877), 449–70.

King, W., 'The Reputed Fossil Man of the Neanderthal', *Quart. J. Sci.*, 1 (1864), 88–97.

Kingsley, C., *The Water Babies* [1863] (Macmillan, 1883).

Kingsley, F., ed., *Charles Kingsley* 2 vols (Kegan Paul, 1881).

Kirby, W., 'Introductory Address', *Zool. J.*, 2 (1825), 1–8.

Knight, C., ed., *London* 6 vols (Knight, 1841–4).

Knight, D., 'T.H.Huxley: The Devil's Disciple?', *Dialogue*, 5 (1995), 31–4.

——, 'Getting Science Across', *BJHS*, 29 (1996), 129–38.

Knox, R., 'Contributions to Anatomy and Physiology', *Medical Gazette*, 32 (1843), 463–7, 499–502, 529–32, 554–6, 586–9, 637–40, 860–2.

Kohn, D., 'On the Origin of the Principle of Diversity', *Science*, 213 (1981), 1105–8.

——, ed., *The Darwinian Heritage* (Princeton UP, 1985).

——, 'Darwin's Ambiguity: The Secularization of Biological Meaning', *BJHS*, 22 (1989), 215–39.

Kottler, M.J., 'Alfred Russel Wallace, the Origin of Man, and Spiritualism', *Isis*, 65 (1974), 145–92.

——, 'Charles Darwin and Alfred Russel Wallace', in Kohn, *Darwinian Heritage*, 367–432.

Kovalevskii, V., 'On the Osteology of the Hyopotamidae', *Phil. Trans. Roy. Soc.*, 163 (1873), 19–94.

Kropotkin, P., 'Mutual Aid among Animals', *NC*, 28 (1890), 337–54.

Lafargue, P., 'Primitive Communism', *Commonweal*, 6 (12 Apr. 1890), 114–15.

Lamarck, J.-B.-P.-A., *Philosophie Zoologique* 2 vols (Paris, Dentu, 1809).

Lang, A., 'Science and Demonology', *Illustrated London News*, 30 Jan. 1894, 822.

Lankester, E., 'Dr. Edwin Lankester's Lecture on the Origin of Species', *NR*, 20 Apr. 1861, 8.

——, 'The Representation of Science at the School Board', *Nature*, 2 (1870), 509–10.

Lankester, E.R., 'On the Use of the Term Homology in Modern Zoology', *AMNH*, 6 (1870), 34–43, 342.

——, 'Instruction to Science Teachers at South Kensington', *Nature*, 4 (1871), 361–4.

——, 'On the Primitive Cell-Layers of the Embryo as the Basis of Genealogical Classification of Animals', *AMNH*, 11 (1873), 321–38.

——, 'Notes on the Embryology and Classification of the Animal Kingdom', *Quart. J. Micros. Soc.*, 17 (1877), 399–454.

——, *Degeneration: A Chapter in Darwinism* (Macmillan, 1880).

——, 'William Henry Flower', *Nature*, 60 (1899), 252–5.

——, *The Advancement of Science* (Macmillan, 1890).

——, 'The Right Hon. T.H.Huxley', *Athenaeum*, 6 July 1895.

Lansbury, C., 'Gynaecology, Pornography, and the Antivivisectionist Movement', *VS*, 28 (1985), 413–37.

Lartet, E., 'Note sur un Grand Singe Fossile', *Comptes Rendus de l'Academie des Sciences*, 43 (1856), 219–23.

Laurent, J., 'Science, Society and Politics in Late Nineteenth-Century England: A Further Look at Mechanics' Institutes', *Soc. Stud. Sci.*, 14 (1984), 585–619.

La Vergata, A., *Le Biografie Scientifiche, Intersezioni*, 15 (1995), 1–184.

Lefebvre, J.P., ed., *Marx-Engels: Lettres sur les Sciences de la Nature* (Paris, Editions Sociales, 1973).

Leidy, J., 'Hadrosaurus and its Discovery', *Proc. Acad. Nat. Sci.*, Philadelphia (1858), 213–18.

Lenoir, T., *The Strategy of Life: Teleology and Mechanics in Nineteenth-Century German Biology* (UCP, 1989).

Lester, J., ed. P.J.Bowler, *E. Ray Lankester and the Making of Modern British Biology* (Faringdon, British Society for the History of Science, 1995).

[Lewes, G.H.], *Ranthorpe*, [1847] ed. B.Smalley (Athens, Ohio UP, 1974).

[—], 'Goethe as a Man of Science', *WR*, 58 (1852), 479–506.

Lewin, L., *Phantastica: Narcotic and Stimulating Drugs* (Kegan Paul, 1931).

Lewis, A., 'Black Letter Day', *UCL Bulletin*, 7 (15) (1989), 18–19.

——, 'The Japanese Connexion', *UCL News* 1 (8) (1990), 4–6.

Lightman, B., 'Pope Huxley and the Church Agnostic', *Historical Papers* (1983), 150–63.

——, *The Origins of Agnosticism* (Baltimore, Johns Hopkins UP, 1987).

——, 'Ideology, Evolution and Late-Victorian Agnostic Popularizers', in Moore, *History*, 285–309.

——, '"Fighting even with Death": Balfour, Scientific Naturalism, and Thomas Henry Huxley's Final Battle', in Barr, *Huxley's Place*, 323–50.

——, '"The Voices of Nature": Popularizing Victorian Science', in Lightman, *Victorian Science*, 187–211.

——, ed., *Victorian Science in Context* (UCP, 1997).

Lilly, W.S., 'Materialism and Morality', *FR*, 40 (1886), 575–94.

Linklater, E., *The Voyage of the Challenger* (Murray, 1972).

Litchfield, H., ed., *Emma Darwin* 2 vols (Murray, 1915).

Livingstone, D.N., *Darwin's Forgotten Defenders: The Encounter Between Evangelical Theology and Evolutionary Thought* (Edinburgh, Scottish Academic Press, 1987).

——, 'Darwinism and Calvinism: The Belfast-Princeton Connection', *Isis*, 83 (1992), 408–28.

L.L.D., 'Professor Huxley as Schoolmaster', *NR*, 31 Dec. 1871, 422–3.

Lloyd, C., *The British Seaman 1200–1800 A Social Survey* (Paladin, 1970).

London Medical Directory (Mitchell, 1845).

Lonsdale, H., *A Sketch of the Life and Writings of Robert Knox* (Macmillan, 1870).

Lorimer, D.A., *Colour, Class and the Victorians* (Leicester UP, 1978).

——, 'Theoretical Racism in Late Victorian Anthropology, 1870–1900', *VS*, 31 (1988), 405–30.

Lubbock, A., *Owen Stanley R.N Captain of the 'Rattlesnake'* (Melbourne, Heinemann, 1968).

Bibliography

Lucas, J.R., 'Wilberforce and Huxley', *Hist. J.*, 22 (1979), 313–30.

Lyell, C., *Principles of Geology* 3 vols (Murray, 1830–33).

——, 'Anniversary Address', *QJGS*, 7 (1851), xxxii-lxxvi.

——, *A Manual of Elementary Geology*, 4th ed. (Murray, 1852).

——, *Supplement to the Fifth Edition of a Manual of Elementary Geology* (Murray, 1859).

Lyell, [K.M.], *Life, Letters and Journals of Sir Charles Lyell, Bart* 2 vols (Murray, 1881).

Lyons, S.L., 'Thomas Huxley: Fossils, Persistence, and the Argument from Design', *JHB*, 26 (1993), 545–69.

——, 'The Origins of T.H.Huxley's Saltationism: History in Darwin's Shadow', *JHB*, 28 (1995), 463–94.

McCabe, J., *Prehistoric Man* (Milner, 1912).

McCready, T.L., 'The Worship of Istar', *Standard*, 17 Mar. 1888.

MacGillivray, J., *Narrative of the Voyage of H. M. S. Rattlesnake* 2 vols (Boone, 1852).

Mackie, S.J., 'The Aeronauts of the Solenhofen Age', *Geologist*, 6 (1863), 1–8.

Macleay, W.S., *Horae Entomologicae* 2 vols (Bagster, 1819).

MacLeod, R.M., 'Government and Resource Conservation: The Salmon Acts Administration, 1860–1886', *J. Brit. Stud.*, 7 (1968), 114–50.

——, 'The X Club', *NRRS*, 24 (1970), 305–22.

——, 'Science and the Civil List, 1824–1914', *Technology and Society*, 6 (1970), 47–55.

——, 'The Support of Victorian Science', *Minerva*, 4 (1971), 197–230.

——, 'The Royal Society and the Government Grant', *Hist. J.*, 14 (1971), 323–58.

——, 'Of Medals and Men: A Reward System in Victorian Science 1826–1914', *NRRS*, 26 (1971), 81–108.

——, 'The Ayrton Incident', in A.Thackray and E.Mendelsohn, eds, *Science and Values* (New York, Humanities Press, 1974), 45–78.

——, 'Science and the Treasury', in Turner, *Patronage*, 115–72.

——, 'Evolutionism, Internationalism and Commercial Enterprise in Science: The International Scientific Series 1871–1910', in A.J.Meadows, ed., *Development of Science Publishing in Europe* (Amsterdam, Elsevier, 1980), 63–93.

——, ed., *Days of Judgement: Science, Examinations and the Organization of Knowledge* (Driffield, Studies in Education, 1982),

——, 'On Visiting the "Moving Metropolis": Reflections on the Architecture of Imperial Science', *Historical Records of Australian Science*, 5 (1982), 1–15.

——, 'Whigs and Savants: Reflections on the Reform Movement in the Royal Society, 1830–48,' in Inkster and Morrell, *Metropolis*, 55–90.

——, *Public Science and Public Policy in Victorian England* (Variorum, 1996).

McMenemey, W.H., 'Education and the Medical Reform Movement', in Poynter, *Evolution of Medical Education*, 135–54.

McPherson, J.M., *Battle Cry of Freedom. The Civil War Era* (Penguin, 1990).

Magnus, P., *Gladstone* (Murray, 1963).

Maienschein, J., *Transforming Traditions in American Biology, 1880–1915* (Baltimore, Johns Hopkins UP, 1991).

——, '"It's a Long Way from *Amphioxus*": Anton Dohrn and Late Nineteenth Century Debates about Vertebrate Origins', *Hist. Phil. Life Sci.*, 16 (1994), 465–78.

Mairet, P., *Pioneer of Sociology: The Life and Letters of Patrick Geddes* (Lund Humphries, 1957).

Manual, D.E., 'Marshall Hall, F.R.S. (1790–1857)', *NRRS*, 35 (1980), 136–66.

Marsh, O.C., 'Discovery of a Remarkable Fossil Bird', *Am. J. Sci.*, 3 (1872), 56–7.

——, 'Notice of New Equine Mammals from the Tertiary Formation', *Am. J. Sci.*, 7 (1874), 247–58.

——, 'Notice of a New and Gigantic Dinosaur', *Am. J. Sci.*, 14 (1877), 87–8.

——, 'A New Order of Extinct Reptilia (Stegosauria) from the Jurassic of the Rocky Mountains', *Am. J. Sci.*, 14 (1877), 513–14.

——, 'Fossil Mammal from the Jurassic of the Rocky Mountains', *Am. J. Sci.*, 15 (1878), 459.

——, 'Notice of Jurassic Mammals Representing Two New Orders', *Am. J. Sci.*, 20 (1880), 235–9.

——, *Introduction and Succession of Fossil Life in America: An Address Delivered Before the American Association for the Advancement of Science, at Nashville, Tenn., Aug. 30, 1877*, offprint, pp.1–50.

——, *Odontornithes: A Monograph on the Extinct Toothed Birds of North America* (Washington, Government Printing Office, 1880).

——, 'Thomas Henry Huxley', *Am. J. Sci.*, 50 (1895), 177–83.

Marshall, A.J., *Darwin and Huxley in Australia* (Sydney, Hodder & Stoughton, 1970).

Matthews, P., *Emigration Fields* (Edinburgh, Black, Longman, 1839).

Mayhew, H., *London Labour and the London Poor* (Penguin, 1985).

Meadows, A.J., *Science and Controversy: A Biography of Sir Norman Lockyer* (Macmillan, 1972).

Meyer, H. von, 'The Reptiles of the Coal Formation', *QJGS*, 4, pt. 2 (1848), 51–6.

——, 'Reptilien aus der Steinkohlen-Formation in Deutchland', *Palaeontographica*, 6 (1856–8), 59–220.

Mill, J.S., 'On the Negro Suffrage', *NR*, 12 Nov. 1865, 723.

Mills, E.L., 'A View of Edward Forbes, Naturalist', *ANH*, 11 (1984), 365–93.

Milner, R., 'Darwin for the Prosecution, Wallace for the Defence', *North Country Naturalist*, 2 (1990), 19–50.

Minney, R.J., *The Two Pillars of Charing Cross* (Cassell, 1967).

Mitchell, P. C., 'Huxley', *New Review*, 13 (1895), 147–55.

Mivart, St G., *On the Genesis of Species* (Macmillan, 1871).

——, 'On *Lepilemur* and *Cheirogaleus*, and the Zoological Rank of the *Lemuroidea*', *Proc. Zool. Soc.*, (1873), 484–510.

——, 'On the Possibly Dual Origin of the Mammalia', *Proc. Roy. Soc.*, 34 (1888), 372–9.

——, *Essays and Criticisms* 2 vols (Osgood, 1892).

——, 'Evolution in Professor Huxley', *NC*, 34 (1893), 198–211.

——, 'Some Reminiscences of Thomas Henry Huxley', *NC*, 42 (1897), 985–98.

Monk, W., ed., *The Journals of Caroline Fox, 1835–71* (Elek, 1972).

Montgomery, W.M., 'Germany', in Glick, *Comparative Reception*, 81–116.

Moore, A.L., 'Evolution and Christianity', in *Oxford House Papers* (Rivingtons, 1889), 148–182.

——, *Science and the Faith* (Kegan Paul, 1889).

Moore, J.R., *The Post-Darwinian Controversies* (CUP, 1979).

——, 'Charles Darwin Lies in Westminster Abbey', *Biol. J. Linn. Soc.*, 17 (1982), 97–113.

——, 'Evangelicals and Evolution: Henry Drummond, Herbert Spencer, and the Naturalisation of the Spiritual World', *Scot. J. Theol.*, 38 (1985), 383–417.

——, 'Socializing Darwinism', in L.Levidow, ed., *Science as Politics* (Free Association Books, 1986), 38–80.

——, 'Crisis without Revolution: The Ideological Watershed in Victorian England', *Revue de Synthèse*, 4 (1986), 53–78.

——, 'Freethought, Secularism, Agnosticism: The Case of Charles Darwin', in G.Parsons, ed., *Religion in Victorian Britain. Volume 1* (Manchester UP, 1988), 274–319.

——, ed., *Religion in Victorian Britain. Volume 3: Sources* (Manchester UP, 1988).

——, ed., *History, Humanity and Evolution* (CUP, 1989).

——, 'Theodicy and Society', in R.Helmstadter and B.Lightman, eds, *Victorian Faith in Crisis* (Macmillan, 1990), 153–86.

——, 'Deconstructing Darwinism', *JHB*, 24 (1991), 353–408.

——, *The Darwin Legend* (Grand Rapids, Baker Books, 1994).

——, 'Metabiographical Reflections on Charles Darwin', in Shortland and Yeo, *Telling Lives*, 267–81.

——, 'Wallace's Malthusian Moment', in Lightman, *Victorian Science*, 290–311.

Moore, T.J., 'The Gorilla', *AMNH*, 10 (1862), 373–4.

Morley, J., *The Life of Richard Cobden* (Fisher Unwin, 1903).

——, *Recollections* 2 vols (Macmillan, 1917).

Morrell, J.B., 'The Patronage of Mid-Victorian Science in the University of Edinburgh', *Science Studies*, 3 (1973), 353–88.

——, and A.Thackray, *Gentlemen of Science* (Oxford, Clarendon, 1981).

Morris, J., *Heaven's Command: An Imperial Progress* (Penguin, 1979).

Mozley, A., 'Evolution and the Climate of Opinion in Australia, 1840–76', *VS*, 10 (1976), 411–30.

Murchison, R.I., 'Major-General Portlock', *J. Roy. Geogr. Soc.*, 34 (1864), cxv–cxviii.

Murphy, H.R., 'The Ethical Revolt against Christian Orthodoxy in Early Victorian England', *Am. Hist. Rev.*, 60 (1955), 800–17.

Napier, M., *Selections from the Correspondence of the Late Macvey Napier*, (Macmillan, 1879).

Nicholas, F.W. and J.M., *Charles Darwin in Australia* (CUP, 1989).

Nordenskiöld, E., *The History of Biology* (New York, Tudor Publishing, 1942).

Norton, G., *Victorian London* (Macdonald, 1969).

Nyhart, L., 'The Disciplinary Breakdown of German Morphology, 1870–1900', *Isis*, 78 (1987), 365–89.

——, *Biology Takes Form: Animal Morphology and the German Universities, 1800–1900* (UCP, 1995).

——, 'Natural History and the "New" Biology', in Jardine, Secord and Spary, *Cultures*, 426–43.

O'Connor, W.J., *Founders of British Physiology* (Manchester UP, 1988).

Oldroyd, D., and I.Langham, eds, *The Wider Domain of Evolutionary Thought* (Dordrecht, Reidel, 1983).

Ophir, A., and S.Shapin, 'The Place of Knowledge', *Science in Context*, 4 (1991), 3–21.

Osborn, H.F., 'Memorial Tribute to Prof. Thomas H. Huxley', *Trans. N.Y. Acad. Sci.*, 15 (1895), 40–50.

——, 'Enduring Recollections', *Nature*, 115 (1925), 726–8.

——, *Cope: Master Naturalist* (Princeton UP, 1931).

Ospovat, D., 'The Influence of Karl Ernst von Baer's Embryology, 1828–1859', *JHB*, 9 (1976), 1–28.

——, 'Perfect Adaptation and Teleological Explanation', *Stud. Hist. Biol.*, 2 (1978), 33–56.

——, 'Darwin on Huxley and Divergence: Some Darwin Notes on his Meeting with Huxley, Hooker, and Wollaston in April, 1856 (typescript).

——, *The Development of Darwin's Theory* (CUP, 1981).

Ostrom, J.H., and J.S.McIntosh, *Marsh's Dinosaurs* (New Haven, Yale UP, 1966).

Outram, D., 'New Spaces in Natural History', in Jardine, Secord and Spary, *Cultures*, 249–65.

Owen, A., *The Darkened Room: Women, Power and Spiritualism in Late Victorian England* (Virago, 1989).

Owen, R., 'On the Osteology of the Chimpanzee and Orang Utan', *Trans. Zool. Soc.*, 1 (1835), 343–79.

——, *Fossil Mammalia.* Pt. 1, *The Zoology of the Beagle Voyage of H.M.S. Beagle*, ed. C.Darwin (Smith, Elder, 1840).

——, 'Osteological Contributions to the Natural History of the Chimpanzee', *Trans. Zool. Soc.*, 3 (1849), 381–422.

[—], 'Lyell - on Life and Successive Development', *QR*, 89 (1851), 412–51.

——, 'On Metamorphosis and Metagenesis', *Proc. Roy. Inst.*, 1 (1854), 9–16.

——, *Lectures on the Comparative Anatomy and Physiology of the Invertebrate Animals* (Longman, 1855).

——, 'On the Affinities of the *Stereognathus ooliticus*', *QJGS*, 13 (1857), 1–11.

——, 'On the Characters, Principles of Division, and Primary Groups of the Class Mammalia', *J. Proc. Linn. Soc.* (Zool.), 2 (1858), 1–37.

——, 'Presidential Address', *Report BAAS, Leeds, 1858*, (1859), xlix-cx.

——, 'Conclusion of the Twelfth Lecture of a Course "On Fossil Mammals"', *Proc. Roy. Inst.*, 3 (1858–62), 109–16.

——, *On the Classification and Distribution of the Mammalia* (Parker, 1859).

——, 'On the Orders of Fossil and Recent Reptilia, *Report BAAS, Aberdeen, 1859*, (1860), 153–66.

——, 'On Some Reptilian Remains from South Africa', *QJGS*, 16 (1860), 49–63.

[—], 'Darwin on the Origin of Species', *ER*, 111 (1860), 487–532.

——, 'The Gorilla and the Negro', *Athenaeum*, 23 Mar. 1861, 395–6.

——, 'On the Characters of the Aye-Aye, as a Test of the Lamarckian and Darwinian Hypothesis of the Transmutation and Origin of Species', *Report BAAS, Cambridge, 1862* (1863), 114–6.

——, 'On the Archaeopteryx of Von Meyer', *Phil. Trans. Roy. Soc.*, 153 (1863), 33–47.

——, *Monograph on the Aye-Aye* (Taylor & Francis, 1863).

——, 'Instances of the Power of God as Manifested in His Animal Creation', in *Lectures Delivered before the YMCA* (Simpkin & Marshall, 1864).

——, *On the Anatomy of Vertebrates* 3 vols (Longman, 1866–8).

——, 'The Fate of the "Jardin d'Acclimatation" during the late Siege of Paris', *Fraser's Magazine* (1872), 17–22.

——, *Monograph on the Fossil Reptilia of the Mesozoic Formations* (Palaeontographical Society, 1874–1889).

——, *Descriptive and Illustrative Catalogue of the Fossil Reptilia of South Africa* (Taylor & Francis, 1876).

——, 'Evidence of a Carnivorous Reptile (Cynodraco Major, Ow.) about the Size of a Lion, with remarks thereon', *QJGS*, 32 (1876), 95–101.

——, 'Description of Parts of the Skeleton of an Anomodont Reptile (Platypodosaurus Robustus, Ow.) from the Trias of Graaf Reinet, S. Africa', *QJGS*, 37 (1880), 414–25.

——, 'On the Order Theriodontia, with the Description of a new Genus and Species (Aelurosaurus Felinus, Ow.)', *QJGS*, 37 (1881), 261–5.

Owen, R.S., ed., *The Life of Richard Owen* 2 vols (Murray, 1894).

Padian, K., 'Pterosaurs and Typology: Archetypal Physiology in the Owen-Seeley Dispute of 1870', in W.A.S.Sarjeant, ed., *Vertebrate Fossils and the Evolution of Scientific Concepts* (Reading, Harwood, 1995).

——, 'A Missing Hunterian Lecture on Vertebrae by Richard Owen, 1837', *JHB*, 28 (1995), 333–68.

Pang, A.S.-K., 'The Social Event of the Season: Solar Eclipse Expeditions and Victorian Culture', *Isis*, 84 (1993), 252–77.

Paradis, J.G., *T.H.Huxley: Man's Place in Nature* (Lincoln, Univ. Nebraska Press, 1978).

——, 'Evolution and Ethics in Its Victorian Context', in J.G.Paradis and G.C.Williams, eds, *Evolution and Ethics* (Princeton UP, 1989), 3–55.

——, and T.Postlewait, eds, *Victorian Science and Victorian Values, Ann. N.Y. Acad. Sci*, 360 (1981).

Parker, T.J., *William Kitchen Parker* (Macmillan, 1893).

——, 'Professor Huxley', *Natural Science*, 8 (1896), 161–7.

Parker, W.K., 'Remarks on the Skeleton of the Archaeopteryx; and on the Relations of the Bird to the Reptile', *Geol. Mag.*, 1 (1864), 55–7.

Parssinen, T.M., 'Professional Deviants and the History of Medicine: Medical Mesmerists in Victorian Britain', in R.Wallis, ed., *On the Margins of Science* (Keele, Univ. Kent, 1979), 103–20.

Paston, G., *At John Murray's: Records of a Literary Circle 1843–1892* (Murray, 1932).

Pauly, P.J., 'The Appearance of Academic Biology in Late Nineteenth-Century America', *JHB*, 17 (1984), 369–97.

Paxton, N.L., *George Eliot and Herbert Spencer: Feminism, Evolutionism, and the Reconstruction of Gender* (Princeton UP, 1991).

Pearson, K., ed., *The Life, Letters and Labours of Francis Galton* 3 vols (CUP, 1914–30).

Pedersen, S., 'Rathbone and Daughter: Feminism and the Father at the Fin-de-siècle', *Journal of Victorian Culture*, 1 (1996), 98–117.

Peel, J.D.Y., *Herbert Spencer* (Heinemann, 1971).

Pelling, H., *A History of British Trade Unionism* (Penguin, 1971).

Perkins, H., *The Origins of Modern English Society 1780–1880* (Routledge, 1972).

Peterson, H., *Huxley: Prophet of Science* (Longman, 1932).

Pevsner, N., *The Buildings of England: London, except the Cities of London and Westminster* (Penguin, 1952).

Pfeifer, E.J., 'United States', in Glick, *Comparative Reception*, 168–206.

Phelps, L.A., and E.Cohen, 'The Wilberforce-Huxley Debate', *Western Speech*, 37 (1973), 56–64.

Phillips, J., 'Cetiosaurus', *Athenaeum*, 2 Apr. 1870, 454.

——, *Geology of Oxford and the Valley of the Thames* (Oxford, Clarendon, 1871).

Pickstone, J., 'Ways of Knowing: Towards a Historical Sociology of Science, Technology and Medicine', *BJHS*, 26 (1993), 433–58.

——, 'Museological Science? The Place of the Analytical/Comparative in Nineteenth-Century Science, Technology and Medicine', *HS*, 32 (1994), 111–38.

Pingree, J., *Thomas Henry Huxley. A List of his Scientific Notebooks, Drawings and Other Papers* (Imperial College, 1968)

——, *Thomas Henry Huxley. List of his Correspondence with Miss Henrietta Anne Heathorn, later Mrs. Huxley, 1847–1854* (Imperial College, 1969)

Poore, G.V., 'Robert Edmond Grant', *University College Gazette*, 2 (34) (1901), 190–1.

Porter, R., 'Gentlemen and Geology', *Hist. J.*, 21 (1978), 809–36.

Porter, T.M., *The Rise of Statistical Thinking 1820–1900* (Princeton UP, 1986).

Portlock, J.E., 'Anniversary Address', *QJGS*, 13 (1857), xxvi-cxlv.

——, 'Anniversary Address', *QJGS*, 14 (1858), xxiv-clxii.

Poynter, F.N.L., 'John Chapman (1821–1894)', *J. Hist. Med.*, 5 (1950), 271–90.

——, 'Thomas Southwood Smith', *Proc. Roy. Soc. Med.*, 55 (1962), 381–90.

——, ed., *The Evolution of Medical Education in Britain* (Pitman, 1966).

Prest, J., *The Industrial Revolution in Coventry* (OUP, 1960).

Prospectus of the Normal School of Science, and of the Royal School of Mines (Science and Art Department, 1881).

Rachootin, S.P. 'Owen and Darwin Reading a Fossil: *Macrauchenia* in a Boney Light', in Kohn, *Darwinian Heritage*, 155–83.

Rainger, R., 'Race, Politics, and Science: The Anthropological Society of London in the 1860s', *VS*, 22 (1978), 51–70.

——, 'Paleontology and Philosophy: A Critique', *JHB*, 18 (1985), 267–87.

——, 'Vertebrate Paleontology as Biology: Henry Fairfield Osborn and the American Museum of Natural History', in Rainger, Benson and Maienschein, *American Development of Biology*, 219–56.

——, 'The Rise and Decline of a Science: Vertebrate Paleontology at Philadelphia's Academy of Natural Sciences, 1820–1900', *Proc. Am. Phil. Soc.*, 136 (1992), 1–32.

——, K.Benson, and J.Maienschein, eds, *The American Development of Biology* (Philadelphia, Univ. Pennsylvania Press, 1988).

Ralph, R., 'John MacGillivray - His Life and Work', *ANH*, 20 (1993), 185–95.

Randel, W.P., 'Huxley in America', *Proc. Am. Phil. Soc.*, 114 (1970), 73–99.

Rasor, E.L., *Reform in the Royal Navy: A Social History of the Lower Deck 1850 to 1880* (Hamden, Conn., Archon Books, 1976).

Raumer, F. von, *England in 1835*, 3 vols (Murray, 1836).

Raven, C.E., *Christian Socialism 1848–1854* (Cass, 1920).

R.D.N., 'The Place of Man in the Animal Kingdom', *NR*, 29 June 1861, 6–7.

Read, D., *England 1868–1914* (Longman, 1979).

Rehbock, P.F., 'Huxley, Haeckel, and the Oceanographers: The Case of *Bathybius haeckelii*', *Isis*, 66 (1975), 504–33.

——, 'The Early Dredgers: "Naturalizing" in British Seas, 1830–1850', *JHB*, 12 (1979), 293–368.

——, *The Philosophical Naturalists* (Madison, Univ. Wisconsin Press, 1983).

——, ed., *At Sea with the Scientifics: The* Challenger *Letters of Joseph Matkin* (Honolulu, Univ. Hawaii Press, 1992).

Rice, A.L., 'Thomas Henry Huxley and the Strange Case of *Bathybius haeckelii*; A Possible Alternative Explanation', *ANH*, 11 (1983), 169–80.

——, 'Oceanographic Fame - and Fortune; The Salaries of the Sailors and Scientists on HMS *Challenger*', *ANH*, 16 (1989), 213–20.

Rich, P.B., 'Social Darwinism, Anthropology and English Perspectives of the Irish, 1867–1900', *Hist. Eur. Ideas*, 19 (1994), 777–85.

Richards, E., 'Darwin and the Descent of Woman', in Oldroyd and Langham, *Wider Domain*, 57–111.

——, 'A Question of Property Rights: Richard Owen's Evolutionism Reassessed', *BJHS*, 20 (1987), 129–71.

——, 'The "Moral Anatomy" of Robert Knox', *JHB*, 22 (1989), 373–436.

——, 'Huxley and Woman's Place in Science', in Moore, *History*, 253–84.

——, 'Gendering the Romanes Lecture: The Sexual Politics of T.H.Huxley's "Evolution and Ethics"', paper delivered at Huxley Conference, Imperial College, London (April 1995).

——, 'Redrawing the Boundaries: Darwinian Science and Victorian Women Intellectuals', in Lightman, *Victorian Science*, 119–142.

Richards, J.L., 'The Reception of a Mathematical Theory: Non-Euclidean Geometry in England, 1868–1883', in Barnes and Shapin, *Natural Order*, 143–66.

Richards, R.J., *Darwin and the Emergence of Evolutionary Theories of Mind and Behavior* (UCP, 1987).

——, *The Meaning of Evolution* (UCP, 1992).

Richardson, R., *Death, Dissection and the Destitute* (Penguin, 1989).

[Richmond, M.], 'Darwin's Study of Cirripedia', in Burkhardt and Smith, *Correspondence*, 4:388–409.

Ridley, J., *Lord Palmerston* (Panther, 1972).

Ridley, M., 'Coadaptation and the Inadequacy of Natural Selection', *BJHS*, 15 (1982), 45–68.

Ritvo, H., *The Animal Estate: The English and Other Creatures in the Victorian Age* (Cambridge, Mass., Harvard UP, 1987).

——, 'Classification and Continuity in *The Origin of Species*', in Amigoni and Wallace, *Darwin's Origin*, 47–67.

Roberts, J.M., *Europe 1880–1945* (Longman, 1970).

Robertson, J., 'Dr. Elliotson on Life and Mind', *Medical Gazette*, 17 (1835–6), 203–10, 251–7.

Roderick, G.W., and M.Stephens, *Scientific and Technical Education in 19th Century England* (New York, Barnes & Noble, 1973).

Rogers, J.A., 'The Reception of Darwin's *Origin of Species* by Russian Scientists', *Isis*, 64 (1973), 484–503.

Rolleston, G., *Scientific Papers and Addresses* 2 vols (Oxford, Clarendon, 1884).

Rolt, L.T.C., *Victorian Engineering* (Penguin, 1988).

[Romanes, E., ed.], *The Life and Letters of George John Romanes* (Longman, 1896).

Roos, D.A., 'Matthew Arnold and Thomas Henry Huxley: Two Speeches at the Royal Academy, 1881 and 1883', *Modern Philology*, 74 (1977), 316–24.

——, 'Neglected Bibliographical Aspects of the Works of Thomas Henry Huxley', *J. Soc. Biblphy Nat. Hist.*, 8 (1978), 401–20.

——, 'The "Aims and Intentions" of *Nature*', in Paradis and Postlewait, *Victorian Science*, 159–80.

Rorison, G., 'The Creative Week', in *Replies to 'Essays and Reviews'* 2nd ed. (Oxford, Henry & Parker, 1862), 277–345.

Rose, M., *Curator of the Dead: Thomas Hodgkin (1798–1866)* (Peter Owen, 1981).

Rose, P., 'Huxley, Holmes, and the Scientist as Aesthete', *Victorian Newsletter* 38 (1970), 22–4.

[Ross, W.S.], 'Professor Huxley and Agnosticism', *Agnostic J.*, 27 Apr. 1889, 261.

Rowe, J.S., 'The Life and Work of George Fownes', *AS*, 6 (1949), 422–35.

Royle, E., *Radicals, Secularists and Republicans* (Manchester UP, 1980).

Rudwick, M.J.S., *The Meaning of Fossils* (Macdonald, 1972).

——, *Scenes From Deep Time* (UCP, 1992).

Rupke, N.A., '*Bathybius Haeckelii* and the Psychology of Scientific Discovery', *Stud. Hist. Phil. Sci.*, 7 (1976), 53–62.

——, 'Richard Owen's Hunterian Lectures on Comparative Anatomy and Physiology, 1837–55', *Medical History*, 29 (1985), 237–58.

——, 'The Road to Albertopolis: Richard Owen (1804–92) and the Founding of the British Museum of Natural History', in N.A.Rupke, ed., *Science, Politics and the Public Good* (Macmillan, 1988), 63–89.

——, *Richard Owen: Victorian Naturalist* (New Haven, Yale UP, 1994).

Ruse, M., *The Darwinian Revolution* (UCP, 1979).

——, 'Booknotes', *Biology and Philosophy*, 8 (1993), 249–54.

Saint-Pierre, J.-H.B. de, *Paul and Virginia*, trans. J.Donovan (Penguin, 1989).

Sanderson, M., 'The English Civic Universities and the "Industrial Spirit", 1870–1914', *Historical Research*, 61 (1988), 90–104.

Schafer, E.A., 'William Sharpey', *University College Gazette*, 2 (36) (1901), 215.

Schama, S., *Citizens* (Penguin, 1989).

Schuchert, C., and C.M.LeVene, *O.C.Marsh* (New Haven, Yale UP, 1940).

Schwartz, J.S., 'Darwin, Wallace, and the *Descent of Man*', *JHB*, 17 (1984), 271–89.

——, 'George John Romanes's Defense of Darwinism', *JHB*, 28 (1995), 281–316.

Schweber, S.S., 'Darwin and the Political Economists', *JHB*, 10 (1977), 229–316.

Seaman, L.C.B., *Victorian England* (Methuen, 1973).

Secord, A., 'Science in the Pub: Artisan Botanists in Early Nineteenth-Century Lancashire', *HS*, 22 (1994), 269–315.

Secord, J.A., 'King of Siluria: Roderick Murchison and the Imperial Theme in Nineteenth-Century British Geology', *VS*, 25 (1982), 413–42.

——, 'John W. Salter', in A.Wheeler and J.H.Price, eds, *From Linnaeus to Darwin* (Society for the History of Natural History, 1985), 61–75.

——, 'Darwin and the Breeders', in Kohn, *Darwinian Heritage*, 519–42.

——, 'The Geological Survey of Great Britain as a Research School, 1839–1855', *HS*, 24 (1986), 223–75.

——, *Controversy in Victorian Geology: The Cambrian-Silurian Dispute* (Princeton UP, 1986).

——, 'Behind the Veil: Robert Chambers and *Vestiges*', in Moore, *History*, 165–94.

——, 'Extraordinary Experiment: Electricity and the Creation of Life in Victorian England', in Gooding, Pinch and Schaffer, *Uses of Experiment*, 337–83.

[Sedgwick, A.], 'Natural History of Creation', *ER*, 82 (1845), 1–85.

Seeley, H.G., 'An Epitome of the Evidence that Pterodactyles are not Reptiles, but a New Subclass of Vertebrated Animal Allied to Birds', *AMNH*, 17 (1866), 321–31.

——, 'Note on a Femur and a Humerus of a Small Mammal from the Stonesfield Slate', *QJGS*, 35 (1879), 456–63.

——, 'The Ornithosaurian Pelvis', *AMNH*, 7 (1891), 237–55.

Semmel, B., *The Governor Eyre Controversy* (McGibbon & Kee, 1962).

Seth, A., 'Man's Place in the Cosmos', *Blackwood's Magazine*, 154 (1893), 823–34.

Shapin, S., 'Phrenological Knowledge and the Social Structure of Early Nineteenth-Century Edinburgh', *AS*, 32 (1975), 219–43.

——, 'History of Science and its Sociological Reconstructions', *HS*, 20 (1982), 157–211.

——, *A Social History of Truth* (UCP, 1994).

——, and B.Barnes, 'Science, Nature and Control: Interpreting Mechanics' Institutes', *Soc. Stud. Sci.*, 7 (1977), 31–74.

Sharpey, W., 'The Address in Physiology', *Brit. Med. J.*, 2 (1862), 162–71.

Shatto, S., 'Byron, Dickens, Tennyson, and the Monstrous Efts', *Yearbook of English Studies*, 6 (1976), 144–55.

Sheets-Pyenson, S., 'Popular Scientific Periodicals in Paris and London', *AS*, 42 (1985), 549–72.

——, 'Horse Race: John William Dawson, Charles Lyell, and the Competition over the Edinburgh Natural History Chair in 1854–55', *AS*, 49 (1992), 461–77.

Shortland, M., and R.Yeo, eds, *Telling Lives in Science: Essays on Scientific Biography* (CUP, 1996).

[Sidgwick, I.], 'A Grandmother's Tale', *Macmillan's Magazine*, 78 (1898), 425–35.

Sloan, P.R., 'Darwin, Vital Matter, and the Transformation of Species', *JHB*, 19 (1986), 367–95.

——, ed., *Richard Owen. The Hunterian Lectures in Comparative Anatomy. May and June 1837* (UCP, 1992).

Smith, C., and M.N.Wise, *Energy and Empire: A Biographical Study of Lord Kelvin* (CUP, 1989).

Smith, C.U.M., 'Evolution and the Problem of Mind: Part 1. Herbert Spencer', *JHB*, 15 (1982), 55–88.

Smith, F., 'Charles Darwin's Ill Health', *JHB*, 23 (1990), 443–59.

Smith, J.M., 'Thomas Henry Huxley in Nashville', *Tennessee Historical Quarterly*, 33 (1974), 191–203, 322–41.

Bibliography

Smith, R., 'The Background of Physiological Psychology in Natural Philosophy', *BJHS*, 6 (1973), 75–123.

——, 'Alfred Russel Wallace: Philosophy of Nature and Man', *BJHS*, 6 (1972), 177–99.

——, 'The Human Significance of Biology: Carpenter, Darwin, and *vera causa*', in U.C.Knoepflmacher and G.B.Tennyson, eds, *Nature and the Victorian Imagination* (Berkeley, Univ. California Press, 1977), 216–30.

Smith, T.S., *The Divine Government*, 5th ed. (Trübner, 1866).

Sopka, K.R., 'John Tyndall: International Populariser of Science', in Brock, McMillan and Mollan, *John Tyndall*, 193–203.

Spencer, H., 'A Theory Concerning the Organ of Wonder', *Zoist*, 2 (1844), 316–25.

——, 'Progress: Its Law and Cause', *WR*, 67 (1857), 445–85.

——, 'Owen on the Homologies of the Vertebrate Skeleton', *BFMCR*, 44 (1858), 400–416.

——, 'Absolute Political Ethics', *NC*, 27 (1890), 119–30.

——, *An Autobiography* 2 vols (Williams & Norgate, 1904).

Stafford, R.A., *Scientist of Empire: Sir Roderick Murchison, Scientific Exploration and Victorian Imperialism* (CUP, 1989).

Stanbury, P., and J. Holland, *Mr Macleay's Celebrated Cabinet* (Sydney, Macleay Museum, 1988).

Stanley, O., 'T.H.Huxley's Treatment of "Nature"', *J. Hist. Ideas*, 18 (1957), 120–7.

Stauffer, R.C., ed., *Charles Darwin's Natural Selection* (CUP, 1975).

Stearn, W.T., *The Natural History Museum at South Kensington* (Heinemann, 1981).

Stephen, J., 'William Wilberforce', in *Essays in Ecclesiastical Biography* 5th ed. (Longman, 1867), 469–522.

Stephen, L., 'Ethics and the Struggle for Existence', *CR*, 44 (1893), 157–70.

Stocking, G.W., 'What's in a Name? The Origins of the Royal Anthropological Institute (1837–71)', *Man*, 6 (1971), 369–90.

——, *Race, Culture, and Evolution* (UCP, 1982).

——, *Victorian Anthropology* (New York, Free Press, 1987).

Stoddart, D.R., '"That Victorian Science": Huxley's *Physiography* and Its Impact on Geography', *Trans. Inst. Br. Geog.*, 66 (1975), 17–40.

Straus, W.L., 'Huxley's *Evidence as to Man's Place in Nature* - A Century Later', in L.G.Stevenson and R.P.Multhauf, eds, *Medicine Science and Culture* (Baltimore, Johns Hopkins UP, 1968), 160–7.

Sulloway, F.J., *Freud: Biologist of the Mind* (Fontana, 1980).

Summerville, J., 'Albert Roberts, Journalist of the New South', *Tennessee Historical Quarterly*, 42 (1985), 18–38, 179–202.

Survey of London, The, Vol. 38: The Museums Area of South Kensington, ed. F.H.W.Sheppard (1975).

Sutherland, J.A., *Thackeray at Work* (Athlone Press, 1974).

[Tait, P.G.], 'Geological Time', *North British Review*, 11 (1869), 406–39.

Taylor, P.A., *Professor Huxley on the Negro Question* (Ladies' London Emancipation Society, Tract 10, 1864).

Tener, R.H., and M.Woodfield, eds, *A Victorian Spectator: Uncollected Writings of R.H.Hutton* (Bristol, Bristol Press, 1991).

Tennyson, A., 'Prefatory Poem', *NC*, 1 (1877), 1.

——, *Idylls of the King* (Penguin, 1983).

Thackeray, W.M., *The History of Pendennis* [1850] (Penguin, 1972).

Thackray, A., 'Natural Knowledge in Cultural Context: The Manchester Model', *Am. Hist. Rev.*, 79 (1974), 672–709.

Thiselton-Dyer, W.T., 'Plant Biology in the 'Seventies', *Nature*, 115 (1925), 709–12.

Thomson, D., *England in the Nineteenth Century* (Penguin, 1950).

Thomson, J.A., 'Huxley as Evolutionist', *Nature*, 115 (1925), 717–18.

Thomson, W., *Popular Lectures and Addresses* 3 vols (Macmillan, 1889–1894).

Tillotson, G., and D.Hawes, eds, *Thackeray: The Critical Heritage* (Routledge, 1968).

Todes, D.P., 'V.O.Kovalevskii: The Genesis, Content, and Reception of his Paleontological Work', *Stud. Hist. Biol.*, 2 (1978), 99–165.

——, 'Darwin's Malthusian Metaphor and Russian Evolutionary Thought, 1859–1917', *Isis*, 78 (1987), 537–51.

——, *Darwin Without Malthus* (OUP, 1989).

Torr, D., ed., *Karl Marx and Frederick Engels. Selected Correspondence 1846–1895* (Lawrence & Wishart, 1936).

Torrens, H., 'When did the Dinosaur get its Name?', *New Scientist*, 4 Apr. 1992.

Tribe, D., *President Charles Bradlaugh, M.P.* (Elek, 1971).

Tristan, F., *Flora Tristan's London Journal* (Prior, 1980).

Tugwood, D.T., *The Coventry and Warwickshire Hospital 1838–1948* (Lewes, Sussex, Book Guild, 1987).

Turner, F.M., 'Lucretius Among the Victorians', *VS*, 16 (1973), 329–48.

——, *Between Science and Religion: The Reaction to Scientific Naturalism in Late Victorian England* (New Haven, Yale UP, 1974).

——, 'Victorian Scientific Naturalism and Thomas Carlyle', *VS*, 18 (1975), 325–43.

——, 'The Victorian Conflict between Science and Religion: A Professional Dimension', *Isis*, 69 (1978), 356–76.

——, 'Public Science in Britain, 1880–1919', *Isis*, 71 (1980), 589–608.

——, *Contesting Cultural Authority: Essays in Victorian Intellectual Life* (CUP) 1993)

Turner, G.L.'E., ed., *The Patronage of Science in the Nineteenth Century* (Leiden, Noordhoff, 1976).

Tylor, E.B., *Primitive Culture*, 5th ed., 2 vols (Murray, 1913).

Tyndall, J., *Fragments of Science*, 2nd ed. (Longman, 1871).

——, *Fragments of Science, II*, 6th ed. (Longman, 1879).

——, 'On the Political Situation', *Times*, 3 June 1886.

——, A.Henfrey, T.H.Huxley *et al.*, *The Culture Demanded by Modern Life* (New York, Appleton, 1867).

Uschmann, G., and Jahn, I., eds, 'Der Briefwechsel zwischen Thomas Henry Huxley und Ernst Haeckel', *Wissenschaftliche Zeitschrift der Friedrich-Schiller-Universität Jena*, Mathematisch-Naturwissenschaftliche Reihe, Heft 1/2, 9 (1959–60), 7–33.

—Van Arsdel, R., 'The Westminster Review, 1824–1900', in W.E.Houghton, ed., *The Wellesley Index to Victorian Periodicals 1824–1900 Volume 3* (Toronto, Univ. Toronto Press, 1979), 529–58.

Van Riper, A.B., *Men among the Mammoths: Victorian Science and the Discovery of Prehistory* (UCP, 1993).

Veitch, J., 'Prof. Huxley's Hume', *Nature*, 19 (1879), 453–6.

Vevers, G., *London's Zoo* (Bodley Head, 1976).

Vincent, D., *Bread, Knowledge and Freedom: A Study of Nineteenth-Century Working Class Autobiography* (Europa, 1981).

Vogt, C., *Lectures on Man*, trans. J.Hunt (Longman, 1864).

Vorzimmer, P.J., *Charles Darwin: The Years of Controversy* (Univ. London Press, 1972).

Vucinich, A., 'Russia', in Glick, *Comparative Reception*, 227–55.

——, *Darwin in Russian Thought* (Berkeley, Univ. California Press, 1988).

[Wace, H.], 'Scientific Lectures - Their Use and Abuse', QR, 145 (1878), 35–61.

Waddington, I., *The Medical Profession in the Industrial Revolution* (Dublin, Gill & Macmillan, 1984).

Wagner, W., 'Upon the Structure of the Brain in Man and Monkeys, and its bearing upon Classification, with Special Reference to the Views of Owen, Huxley and Gratiolet', *Am. J. Sci.*, 34 (1862), 188–99.

[Wallace, A.R.], 'Principles of Geology', QR, 126 (1869), 359–94.

——, *Contributions to the Theory of Natural Selection* (Macmillan, 1875).

——, 'Human Selection', FR, 48 (1890), 325–37.

——, *My Life: A Record of Events and Opinions* 2 vols (Chapman & Hall, 1905).

'Watchman', *In Darkest England. A Reply to 'General' Booth's Sensational Scheme for 'Social Salvation'* (Kensit, 1890).

Watterson, H., *Marse Henry* 2 vols (New York, Doran, 1919).

Watts, J. 'Theological Theories of the Origin of Man', *Reasoner*, 26 (1861), 102–4, 119–21, 132–4.

[——], 'Man's Origin and Nature', NR, 28 Mar., 4 Apr. 1863.

Webb, B., *My Apprenticeship* 2nd ed. (Longmans, Green, 1945).

——, *The Diary of Beatrice Webb. Vol. 1: 1873–1892*, ed. N. and J. MacKenzie (Virago, 1982).

Weikart, R., 'A Recently Discovered Darwin Letter on Social Darwinism', *Isis*, 86 (1995), 609–11.

Weindling, P.J., 'Darwinism in Germany', in Kohn, *Darwinian Heritage*, 685–98.

——, 'Ernst Haeckel, Darwinismus, and the Secularization of Nature', in Moore, *History*, 311–27.

——, *Darwinism and Social Darwinism in Imperial Germany: The Contribution of the Cell Biologist Oscar Hertwig (1849–1922)* (Stuttgart, Gustav Fischer, 1991).

Weiner, J.H., *War of the Unstamped: The Movement to Repeal the British Newspaper Tax, 1830–1836* (Ithaca, Cornell UP, 1969).

Wells, H.G., 'Huxley', *Science Schools Journal* (April 1901), 209–11.

——, *Experiment in Autobiography* 2 vols (Gollancz, 1934).

White, A.D., *A History of the Warfare of Science with Theology in Christendom* (New York, Free Press, 1965).

White, H.H., *Materia Medica Pharmacy, Pharmacology and Therapeutics*, ed. R.W.Wilcox, 3rd American ed. (Philadelphia, Blakiston, 1897).

Whitrow, G.J., *Centenary of the Huxley Building* (Imperial College, 1972).

Whittell, H.M., *The Literature of Australian Birds* (Perth, W.A., Paterson Brokensha Pty, 1954).

Wiener, M.J., *English Culture and the Decline of the Industrial Spirit 1850–1980* (Penguin, 1992).

Wilberforce, R.G., 'Professor Huxley and the Life and Letters of C.Darwin', *Times*, 29 Dec. 1887.

Wilberforce, S., *Pride a Hindrance to True Knowledge* (Rivington, 1847).

[—], 'Darwin's Origin of Species', *QR*, 102 (1860), 225–64.

Wilson, G., and A. Geikie, ed., *Memoir of Edward Forbes* (Macmillan, 1861).

Wilson, L.G., ed., *Sir Charles Lyell's Scientific Journals on the Species Question* (New Haven, Yale UP, 1970).

Wiltshire, D., *The Social and Political Thought of Herbert Spencer* (OUP, 1978).

Winsor, M.P., *Starfish, Jellyfish, and the Order of Life* (New Haven, Yale UP, 1976).

——, 'The Impact of Darwinism upon the Linnean Enterprise, with Special Reference to the Work of T.H.Huxley', in J.Weinstock, ed., *Contemporary Perspectives on Linnaeus* (Lanham, Md, Univ. Press of America, 1985), 55–84.

——, *Reading the Shape of Nature: Comparative Zoology at the Agassiz Museum* (UCP, 1991).

Winter, A., 'Ethereal Epidemic: Mesmerism and the Introduction of Inhalation Anaesthesia to Early Victorian London', *Soc. Hist. Med.*, (1991), 1–27.

——, '"The Island of Mesmeria": The Politics of Mesmerism in Early Victorian Britain' (St. John's College, Cambridge, Ph.D Thesis, 1992).

Wollaston, A.F.R., *Life of Alfred Newton* (Murray, 1921).

Wollaston, T.V., *On the Variation of Species* (Van Voorst, 1856).

Woodcock, G., *Anarchism* (Penguin, 1963).

Woodward, A.S., 'Contributions to Vertebrate Palaeontology', *Nature*, 115 (1925), 728–30.

Woodward, H., 'On a Feathered Fossil from the Lithographic Limestone of Solenhofen', *Intellectual Observer*, 2 (1862), 313–9.

Wrangham, R.W., 'Bishop Wilberforce: Natural Selection and the Descent of Man', *Nature*, 287 (1980), 192.

Wynne, B., 'Physics and Psychics: Science, Symbolic Action, and Social Control in Late Victorian England', in Barnes and Shapin, *Natural Order*, 167–86.

Yeo, S., 'A New Life: The Religion of Socialism in Britain, 1883–1896', *History Workshop*, 4 (1977), 5–56.

Young, G.M., *Portrait of an Age* 2nd ed. (OUP, 1989).

Young, J., 'Professor Huxley and "The Physical Basis of Life"', *CR*, 11 (1869), 240–63.

Young, R.M., 'The Development of Herbert Spencer's Concept of Evolution', *Congrès International d'Histoire des Sciences*, 11 (1965), 273–8.

——, *Darwin's Metaphor: Nature's Place in Victorian Culture* (CUP, 1985).

Index

Abbey Place 298, 348, 354, 357, 369, 377
Aberdeen Free Press 439
Aberdeen University 47, 124, 182, 439
Aborigines 11, 68, 76, 78, 92, 101, 104, 108-10, 124-6, 301, 333, 342, *see* Savages
Aborigines Friend 144
Aborigines Protection Society 144
Abraham 637
Abydos, Egypt 415
Abyssal life 427-8, 460, 484
Académie Française 487
Academy 372
Academy of Natural Sciences 479
Acorn barnacles 214
Acton Prize, Royal Institution 27
Adam 591; from womb of ape 283; statue 531
Adaptation 221, 230, 235, 245, 258, 262, 392, 401, 407, 551, 599; imperfect 235; cumulative 244
Adelaide Gallery 32
Admiralty 37, 39, 43-5, 48-9, 54-5, 64, 73, 79-80, 133, 142, 149, 151, 394, 411, 427, 428
Adventure, HMS 48
Aelurosaurus felinus 545
Afghanistan 493
Africa 272, 315, 584; first dinosaur 357; du Chaillu in 296; scramble for 635
Agassiz, A. 473-4, 517, 555
Agassiz, L. 188, 324, 474, 508
Age of earth 370
Age of Fishes 465
Age of Reptiles 602

Agnostic Annual 527
Agnostic Journal 527, 580, 612
Agnostic Temple 527, 566, 622
Agnostic, The 527
Agnosticism, agnostics, 374-6, 378, 398, 434, 451, 464, 478, 487, 497, 520, 571, 592, 593, 603, 607, 611, 612, 613, 622, 643; Balfour on 608-9; Buckley on 500-1; Darwinism and 391; definition 456, 500-1, 527-8, 541, 566-7, 568, 624-5, 630-2; and Dissent/Protestantism 385, 407-8, 568, 623-5, 630-2; and family 388, 436, 438; Foster 398; Hume and 498, 500; and the law 526, 641; and life's meaning 456, 631; Lilly on 552; and liberal Churchmen 516, 520; for literary elite 437, 501, 642; at Metaphysical Society 374, 409, 466, 566-7; and miracles 567-8, 570-1; morality and 435, 456, 464, 540-1, 608, 620, 630-2; and naturalistic science 389-90, 391, 408, 456, 500-1, 527-8, 566-7, 572, 603, 607-9; Nettie on 450, 516-7; neutral image 374, 389-90, 408, 541, 595, 624, 631; new hegemony 525-6, 642; onus on evidence 456, 498-500, 541, 553, 566, 568, 572, 625, 630, 631; origin of Huxley's 623-5, 630-2; populists 507, 527-8, 566-7, 580, 611; and Positivism 500, 567; and professionalism 374, 403, 408, 437, 630-2; and respectability 389, 464, 525-9, 540; and spiritualism 437; the word 567

Airdrie Iron and Steel works 300
Airy, G. 167
Alabama 325, 477
Albany Island 101, 110, 125
Albert Hall 394
Albert, Prince 11, 164-5, 167, 251
Alexandria 412
Alfred, Nettie's cousin 181
Algae 177, 453
Alice, Princess 314
All Saints Church, Finchley Road 213
All Souls Universalist Church, Grand Rapids 625
Allen, G. 603
Alma-Tadema, L. 492, 510, 511, 612
Alps 228-9, 237, 290, 305, 467, 523, 551, 570
Alternation of Generations 34, 126, 160, 165, 173, 175, 180
Alton Locke (Kingsley) 208
Altruism 576, 597, 599, 602
America 48-9, 80, 140, 146, 247, 313, 317, 322-4, 334, 359, 372, 387, 390-1, 426, 441-2, 448, 463, 468-82, 492, 503, 549, 550, 553, 569; Huxley in 469-82
American Addresses (Huxley) 484
American Association for the Advancement of Science 474
American Society for the Study and Cure of Inebriety 620
Ammonites 491
Amoeba 83, 177, 421, 629
Amphibian fossils 232-3, 255, 300, 303, 306, 321, 346, 355, 465, 492, 504-5

Index

Amphioxus 45, 59, 436, 439, 452
Anaesthetic 66, 237, 457
Anarchism 184, 186, 563–4, 575, 577
Anatomy of Invertebrated Animals (Huxley) 469, 484
Anatomy schools 9–10, 15–16, 19, 20–34, 43, 75, 181, 628
Ancestor worship 603
Ancestors, Darwin on 188; based on embryos 349; of white man, 335; of humans, *see* Human origins; Mammal-like reptiles; Birds; Amphibian fossils
Anchitherium 401
Ancient environments 207
Ancon sheep 256, 262
Andean uplift 173
Anemones 59, 61, 69, 123
Angelo, Father 104
Anglicans, Church of England 4, 6, 10–13, 16, 20–1, 42, 69, 75, 83, 139, 152, 154, 160, 177, 186, 197, 202, 204, 209–10, 213, 220–1, 224, 230, 252–3, 256, 269, 277–8, 283, 285, 287, 296–7, 305–6, 309, 316, 328, 330–1, 346, 365, 373; agnostic scientists v. 389–90, 397, 424, 435, 468, 482, 494, 568–9, 572, 573, 576, 581, 587, 589, 607–8, 618–9, 623, 626–8, 631, 634–9, *see* Wilberforce, S; Gladstone, W.E., Balfour, A., Miracles; apostates 434–5, 631; Bradlaugh and 528; radical Dissent v./attacks on 10–12, 16, 21, 75, 86, 89, 160, 177, 184, 186, 197, 210, 220, 230, 232, 240, 252–3, 256, 259, 269, 292, 313, 316, 335, 339, 343, 346, 364, 370, 373–4, 376, 378–9, 385–6, 389–90, 435–6, 443, 468, 482, 512, 572, 573, 581, 583, 589, 618, 622–3, 626, 631, 634–6; displaced from town halls 6, 11, 220; Ealing School 4, 622–3; liberal/Broad Church 42, 69, 203, 208–9, 218, 263, 276–8, 280, 285, 297–8, 305–6, 309, 313, 315–6, 329, 343, 350, 361–3, 388, 398, 489, 516, 520, 521, 530, 545, 572, 579, 612, 619; Huxley's daughters 582; law of the land 526, 587, 641; London School Board 402–3, 408; Nettie's 72, 75, 77, 81, 86–7, 132, 285–6, 131, 388, 450, 485; party organ 568; privileges 10–12, 16, 75, 160,
177, 184, 252–3, 256, 285, 330, 346, 373, 385–6, 396, 494, 502, 526, 573, 578, 581, 618, 619, 622–3, 626–7, 634–6; ritualism 409; Romanes 591; wealth 435
Anglo-Catholics 86, 185, 275, 373–4, 389, 461
Animal Morphology, Cambridge Chair 523
Animal Physiology, DSA exam 417
Annales des Sciences Naturelles 19
Annals and Magazine of Natural History 152, 359
Annuloida 170
Annulosa 208
Antarctic 36, 42, 141, 167–8, 560
Anthracosaurus 300, 303
Anthropidae 486
Anthropological Institute 447
Anthropological Review 320
Anthropological Society 320, 326, 343–4, 351, 371
Anthropology, 397–8, 580–1
Anti-Catholicism 86, 131, 388–9, 407, 408, 409, 445, 461, 466, 497, 538, 549, 550, 552–3, 557, 586, 607
Anti-Corn Law League 468
Anti-protectionists 560
Anti-Vietnam War movement 632
Anti-vivisection 459–69
Antigua 72, 570
Antiquity of Man (Lyell) 292, 299, 312, 315, 329, 341
Antislavery Reporter 352
Ants 564
Apes 90, 153, 225, 238–41, 266–7, 271, 274, 276, 278–83, 288, 290, 292–7, 299–301, 304–5, 307, 312–18, 320, 325–6, 330, 333, 341, 353, 354; ape·brain debate, 238–41, 276, 282–3, 290, 295–7, 307, 316–17, 433, 453, 504; *Dryopithecus*, 239; gorilla 240–1, 295–6; Huxley on, 240–1, 271, 274, 276, 278–83, 288, 290, 292–7, 299, 301, 304–5, 307. 312–18, 320, 325–6, 333, 354; Kingsley on 288, 304; Lamarck on human ancestry 90, 239; Lyell on human ancestry 225, 239, 314–15; origin of mankind 90, 153, 225, 238–40, 266–7, 271, 274, 276, 278–83, 288, 290, 292–4, 297, 301, 304, 307, 313, 315, 317–18, 320, 333, 341, 382, 399, 431, 486, 490, 508, 552, 598, 606–7, 621, 625, 627–8, 631, 643; Owen
on 238–41, 271, 274, 276, 278, 283, 290, 295–7, 316–17; radical workers on human ancestry 90, 239–40, 292–3
Aphids 126, 179, 238
Apostles' Creed 281
Apothecaries Hall 19, 162
Apothecaries medal 21, 37
Appendicularia 125
Appleton, W. 311, 315, 323, 391, 463, 470, 471, 480, 482
Apprenticeship system changing 560
Apriorism, Spencer's 573, 576, 591
Aquinas, T. 541
Archaeology 333, 581
Archaeopteryx 358, 359, 364, 481, 538, 544, 546
Archbishop of Canterbury 370, 516, 542
Archegosaurus 232
Archencephala 238
Archetype, ascidian 181; Darwin on, 188, 254, 258; Huxley on 72, 174, 176, 181, 187, 190–1, 200, 223, 218, 226–7, 235, 244, 254, 258, 273, 315, 603; idealism derided 184, 187–8, 218, 226, 244, 275, 306; mollusc 174, 176; Owen on 29–30, 45, 177, 184, 187, 191, 218, 226, 243–4, 256, 273, 275, 281, 308, ·315; Sharpey on 308; siphonophore 69; Von Baer on 191; *see* Owen, R.
'Archetype', Nettie's name for Owen 277
Arctic 40, 41, 457
Argus, Melbourne 317
Argyll, Duke of 231, 272, 326, 520, 555–6, 577, 587, 590
Aristotle 503, 600
Ark 587
Armadillo, fossil 28, 305, 306, 321
Arms race 635, 636
Armstrong, Lady 569, 634
Armstrong, Sir W. 423, 429, 442, 469, 488, 506, 522, 532, 545, 569, 587, 634
Arnhem Land 103
Arnold, J. 516, 524, 539, 557, 606
Arnold, M. 378, 390, 404, 427, 444, 464, 470, 499–500, 512, 516, 524–5, 537, 539, 601, 631, 639
Arnold, T. Dr, 16
Arnold, T. 524
Arolla 551
Arran 257
Arrow-worms 56–7, 145, 166
Arthur, King 270, 324, 638
Artificial selection 245, 262, 264, 268–9, 310

Artists 426, 428, 437, 492, 495, 502, 510, 522, 523, 538, 540, 612

Artists Benevolent Institution 522

Aryans 581

Ascent of Man, Lowell Lectures on the (Drummond) 602

Ashton, T. 386, 430

Asia 197

Asiatic Society of Bengal 347

Asp 47, 76, 77, 79, 96, 125

Assistant Surgeons 36, 40, 43, 46, 53

Association of Liberal Thinkers 501

Assyriologists 571, 587

Astor, Mabel, daughter of Nelly Astor, née Cooke 469

Astronomer Royal 167, 178

Astronomy 588

Aswan, Egypt 415

Atheism 16, 20–1, 75, 153, 185–7, 205, 209, 220–1, 232, 240, 258, 269, 285, 292, 306, 309, 320, 324, 332–3, 346, 372–3, 391, 393, 446, 455, 467, 480, 500, 522, 528–9, 535–6, 587, 591, 623, 631, 638, 642; Bendyshe 343; Bradlaugh 500, 529; Cooper 240; equated with immorality 309, 332; Foote, G.W. 525–6, 641; in Germany 187; middle-class 185; Huxley accused of 320, 346; Martineau 185, 187, 205; French Revolution 269; red republican banner 373; slated by Tories 324; Watson 221; Watts 240; *see* Working classes; Holyoake, G.J.

Athenaeum 123, 159, 168, 259–60, 266, 272, 274, 295, 315, 317, 514

Athenaeum Club 226, 241, 298, 391, 414, 422, 450, 516, 520, 642

Atkinson, H. 185

Atlanta 348

Atlantic cable 237, 351, 370

Atlantic Monthly 324

Atlantic mud 237, 365, 366

Atlas of Comparative Osteology (Huxley and Hawkins) 321

Atoms, atomism 318, 366, 393, 446, 639

Attorney-General 495, 502, 526

Audience, Huxley's 208–11, 252, 292–3, 344–5, 362–3, 367, 425, 440, 444–5, 459, 479, 503, 591, 627–9, 636–8; historical sensitivity to 618, 636–9

Australia 11, 41, 44–5, 48, 65–137, 144, 145, 150, 173, 180, 185, 217, 255, 397, 504, 505, 529, 563

Australian Agricultural Company 71

Australian bustard 78

Autobiography (Spencer) 573

Autograph hunters 459, 480

Automatism 440, 444, 446, 519, 623, 642

Auvergne 431

Aveling, E. 548

Aye-aye 302

Ayrton, A.S. 421–3, 425

Azores 223

Baboons 241

Babylon 510, 560, 580, 587

Bacteria 392, 453, 467

Bad Times (Wallace) 548

Baden-Baden 431

Baer, K.E. von 190–1, 199, 208, 232, 260

Bagehot, W. 242, 374, 399, 497

Baily, W. 219

Bain, A. 340, 497

Baker Street Bazaar 264

Bakunin, M. 318

Balfour, A. 607–10, 613

Balfour, F. 490, 523

Balliol College, Oxford 398, 489, 502, 524

Baltimore & Ohio Railway 477

Baltimore 441, 477

Bank of England 131, 394

Banking collapse (1847) 131; scandal 198, 620

Baptists 215, 252, 340, 351, 363, 398, 402, 567

Barbados 72

Barming Churchyard, Kent 178

Barnacles 42, 54, 71, 98, 173, 188, 195–6, 214–5, 220, 225, 235, 263, 355

Barnard Islands 97

Barrier Reef 44, 47, 54, 68–9, 74, 79, 91–2, 96–9, 100–1, 123, 129, 165

Bartholomew, M. 626

Barton, R. 627

Basle 228

Bass Strait 81–2

Bastian, H.C. 392–3, 454, 467

Bathurst 158, 161, 170, 173

Bathybius 365, 427, 460

Bats 453

Battered women 584

Bavaria 232

Bay of Islands, New Zealand 139

Beachy Head 565, 570, 577

Beagle, HMS 41, 48, 56, 67, 71, 105, 114, 142, 151, 156, 173, 188, 563

Beam-trawling 327

Bear, fossil 227

Beardsley, A. 580, 587, 600

Beaufort, Sir F. 91, 133, 149, 151

Beauty, explanation of 200, 236

Beche, Sir H. de la 153, 162, 189, 201, 203, 207–8, 212

Becker, B. 440

Bedford Square, women's college 272

Bee 43, 273

Beesly, E. 372

Beetles 221

Bel Alp 445

Belemnites 491

Belfast 444

Belgium 301, 581

Bell, A. 574

Bell, A.G. 433, 479

Bell, T. 156

Belzoni, G. 415

Bendyshe, T. 343

Bengal 357, 550

Benthamism 14, 575

Berbers 412

Beresina, metaphor for selection 310

Berger, C. 328

Berkeley, Bishop 404

Berlin 329, 364, 498

Bermuda 32

Besant, A. 522, 528–9, 548, 575, 619; 'Why I am a Socialist' 548

Bethnal Green 333

Bible 13, 210, 247, 252, 275, 298, 302, 351, 364, 403, 480, 489, 527, 546, 567, 573, 580, 587

Biblical criticism 185–6, 298, 501, 540, 547, 568, 571, 593

Bicycles 488, 619

Billingsgate 514

Biogeography 452, 457, 617–8

Biologists, biology 252, 395, 404, 419–21, 427, 449, 452–3, 455, 457, 463, 477, 486, 517, 538–9, 543, 560–1, 564, 575, 589, 612, 623, 625–8, 640; new discipline 419; non-medical 457; practicals 393, 418–20, 455; transmissible to schoolmasters 628; the word 420

Birds, anatomy 397; Arctic 457; classification 355–6, 456; dinosaur ancestry 357, 365, 377, 459, 472, 481, 484, 492, 504–5, 509, 545, 625; fossil 472, 481, 485, 538, 544, 546; Owen on relation to mammals 518; related to reptiles 518, 355–61

Birds of Paradise 302

Birds of Australia (Gould) 145

Birmingham 352, 403, 408, 442, 443, 512, 624, 625

Birnie 247, 406

Birth control 528, 575

Birth rates 575
Bishops, on Deceased Wife's Sister Bill 569; of Gibraltar 411; in Huxley's audience, 268–9; of London 309; of Natal 315–6, 318–9, 321, 327; mitre, 340; Magee 630; McTyeire 476; of Norwich, 41, 47–9, 53, 62, 69, 83–4, 90–1, 116, 119, 130, 132, 141, 152; of Oxford, *see* Wilberforce, S.; of Rochester 434; sneer at Huxley 271; Wilkin, 266
Bismarck, O. von 350
Bithell, R. 527
Bitter Cry of Outcast London 528
Black Sea 196
Blacks, anatomy normal 325; compared to working classes 59, 353; slavery, 58–9, 205, 324–6, 333, 348; Huxley sees slaves 58–9; Huxley on 205, 324–6, 333–5, 397–8; Jamaica uprising 351; racists on 320, 324–6; as separate species 320, 325; take prize at UCL 334
Blackwood, Captain F. 41–2
Blackwood's Magazine 598
Blake, C.C. 320, 325–6, 337
Blasphemy 20–1, 525, 526, 641
Blastoderm 328
Blood circulation 503
Bloomsbury 334
Board of Excise 26
Board of Trade 207, 532
Boehm, E. 515, 521, 542
Boers 61, 233
Bologna 479, 538
Bombay 74
Book of the Dead 415, 547
Book of the Covenant 547
Book trade, transatlantic 312
Books of Judges and Samuel 546
Booth, General 583–6
Borneo 118, 326
Boston 441, 470, 555
Boston Symphony Orchestra 555
Boswell, J. 570
Botafogo Bay 59
Botanic Gardens, Regent's Park 529
Botanical Gardens, Sydney 125, 132; Calcutta 227
Botanique, La 19
Botany, Huxley's work on 18–19, 395, 421, 430, 453, 529, 550–2, 578, 589, 604
Botany Bay 46
Bougainvillia 104
Bournemouth 542, 543, 548, 562
Bowen 79
Bower birds 125, 145

Boyle, R. 532
Brace, maid 610
Brachiopod 198, 204, 213, *see* Lamp-shell, *Lingula*
Bradford 393
Bradlaugh, C. 500, 528–9
Bradlaugh, H. 529
Bradley, Revd G. 516–7, 520, 525, 531
Brain, *Amphioxus* 452; apes and men 238–41, 276, 282–3, 290, 295–7, 307, 315–17, 433, 504; *Archaeopteryx*, 358; *Ceratodus* 465; chemistry 433; damaged 445; Ferrier on 442; Lankester on 396; mental materialism, 9, 16, 319, 366–7; model 419; monkey 396, 453; Neanderthal, 304, 326; *Pithecanthropus* 607; reflex arc 441, 446–7; rising complexity 597; Wallace on size 392
Bramble (tender) 68, 74, 77, 80, 106, 109, 111, 121–3, 127, 136
Bramble Key, Torres Strait 123, 127
Brayley, E. 208
Brazil 58–9
Breech-loading guns 469, 488, 634
Breslau 236
Brewster, Lady 280
Brierly Island 116
Brierly, O. 74, 113, 115–16
Briggs, A. 635
Bright, J. 352–3, 370, 375
Brighton 151, 409, 551, 563
Brisbane 76–7, 80, 111
Bristle worm 214
British Association for the Advancement of Science 157, 169, 206, 314; Southampton (1846) 45, 166; Oxford (1847) 277; Ipswich (1851) 166; Belfast (1852) 181; Leeds (1858) 246; Oxford (1860) 275–8, 431, 489, 512, 552, 604, 627–8; Cambridge (1862) 305, 307; Newcastle (1863) 320, 325; Bath (1864) 328; Nottingham (1866) 350–1; Norwich (1868) 365; Exeter (1869) 375–6; Liverpool (1870) 375, 385, 386, 405; Edinburgh (1871) 406; Belfast (1874) 441, 444–6; Dublin (1878) 498; Sheffield (1879) 503; Oxford (1894) 604, 608
British Medical Association 16
British Museum 19, 38, 42, 45, 47, 62, 125, 156, 178, 202, 215, 218, 221, 251, 274, 295, 358, 364, 412, 465, 504, 531, 590

Britomart, HMS 41, 69
Brixham cave 299
Broad, Mr (plaintiff) 426
Broad Street pump, source of cholera 203
Broadway 471
Brodrick, Revd G. 604
Brontosaurus 504
Brooke, Rajah 118
Brown Animal Sanatory Institution 462
Browning, R. 426, 468, 470, 515
Brumer Island, New Guinea 118
Brunel, I.K. 351
Brush turkeys 78
Büchner, L. 318
Buckingham Palace 318, 548
Buckland, W. 357, 360
Buckle, H. 233–4, 242, 318
Buckley, A. 450, 500
Buddhists 366, 598
Budgerigars 131, 141
Buffalo 474
Buffalo Bill 472
Buffon, Comte de 56
Builder 252, 254
Bulaq Museum, Cairo 412–14
Bullfinch 163
Bulwer-Lytton, E. 214
Bunbury, Lady 307
Bunbury, Sir C. 225, 232, 303, 307, 309, 313–4
Bunsen, R.W. 166
Burke and Hare scandal 25, 27, 210, 399
Burlington House 236, 243, 532
Burma, Burmese 41, 371
Burnett, Sir W. 36, 39, 83, 140, 151
Burney Prize, Cambridge 458
Burton, D. 22
Burton, R. 343, 411, 413
Bus strikes 590
Bushmen 397
Busk, E. 160, 168, 189, 214, 243, 328, 341–2, 582, 621
Busk, G. 159–60, 168–70, 173, 183, 189, 197, 203, 211, 213–4, 236, 238, 241, 243, 245, 261, 284, 290, 298–9, 317, 321, 326–30, 341, 388, 402, 423, 524, 551
Butler, S. 509

Caffre War 61, 62
Cairns 97, 99
Cairo 412
Calculating machine, Babbage's 189
Calcutta 227, 347, 366
Caldy cliffs 229, 232, 570
California 123, 172, 470, 479
Calvados Group, Louisiade 122
Calvin, J., Calvinist 407,

445–6, 470, 547, 561, 584, 623, 624, 626, 631
Cambrian-Silurian debate 204
Cambridge local exams 450
Cambridge, Mass. 324
Cambridge University 14, 151, 167, 221, 225, 240, 253, 260, 267, 288, 304–5, 307, 329, 346, 356, 385, 387, 398, 417, 418, 424, 434, 435, 440, 458, 490–1, 501, 516, 517, 523, 524, 550, 591, 600, 608
Campbell, L. 605
Canada 168, 463, 567, *see* Toronto
Cancer 590
Candid Examination of Theism (Romanes) 521
Cannibal Club 343
Cannibalism 112, 114
Cape Brett, New Zealand 139
Cape Colony 45, 60–2
Cape Flattery 100
Cape Horn 140–1, 195
Cape Howe 85
Cape of Good Hope 60, 158, 255, 357, 365, 397, 504, 511, 545
Cape Rodney, New Guinea 122
Cape Spartel, Morocco 412
Cape Town 60–2, 315, 397
Cape Tribulation 99
Cape Upstart 79
Cape Verde islands 57
Cape York 91–2, 94, 101–2, 109, 122–6, 152, 460
Capitol building, Washington 479
Captain Cook's Whitsunday Passage 78
Captain, HMS 388, 423
Captains, naval 40
Carboniferous fossils 232, 260, 267, 300, 313, 346
Cardigan, Lord 202
Cardwell, Lord 462
Carlile, R. 639
Carlyle, T. 7, 13, 19, 28–9, 75, 79, 135, 166, 186–7, 200, 258, 260, 275, 285, 297, 346, 351, 404, 421, 446, 468, 597, 620, 624, 631
Carnival, Rome 539
Carpenter, L. 548
Carpenter, P. 501
Carpenter, W.B. 180, 186, 212–3, 218–9, 221, 230, 236, 243, 252, 257, 260–1, 267–8, 272, 284, 298, 328, 428, 446, 544, 548
Carron, W. 92, 94, 108, 109, 118
Carus, V. 318, 349, 365
Casale 341
Cassell's Magazine 637
Cassowary 119–20
Catacombs, Rome 538

Catamarans, New Guinea 118
Catastrophism 153, 507
Cathode rays 433
Catholic Review 613
Catholic University, Ireland 607
Catholics 4, 55, 85–6, 104, 130, 185, 260, 301, 340–1, 373–5, 389, 392, 402, 407–9, 445, 454, 461, 464, 509, 545, 547, 549, 552–3, 566, 607, 613, 619, 630
Caucasus 196
Cause and effect, invariant causation 386, 389, 390, 442, 485, 556, 572, 589, 603, 608, 622–3
Cave bears, fossil 299
Cave of Hercules, Morocco 412
Cave tigers, fossil 309
Cavendish Laboratory, Cambridge 608
Cavendish, Lord Frederick 550
Cavin Cross Island 101
Cell layers 208, 396, 452
Cell theory 26, 183; protoplasm 367
Cells, unity of animal and plant 395, 453
Celtic, steamer 482
Celts 550
Census 209, 235
Centennial Exposition, Philadelphia 479
Central Institution for Technical Education 506, 542, 554
Cephalopods 174, 176, 484, 491
Cephea 78
Ceratodus 465
Cerebellum 240
Cerebral hemispheres 240–1, 276, 283, 295, 297, 314, 317
Cetiosaurus 358
Ceylon 397, 413, 422
Chaillu, P. du 295–6
Chalk 237, 365–6, 309, 380–1, 427, 245
Challenger, HMS 427–8, 449, 455, 460, 484
Chamberlain, J. 443, 512, 532, 549–50, 563, 565, 572, 578, 624, 641
Chambers, R. 193, 251, 256, 277
Chambers' Journal 251
Chance, and Evolution 228, 234, 245, 263, 370, 406, 407, 424, 458, 486
Chancellor of the Exchequer 151, 251
Chancellors 151, 410, 422, 554
Chancery, Court of 426
Chandler, T. 11–12, 32, 66, 181
Channel Tunnel 433, 573

Chapman, J. 185, 190, 193, 196–7, 205, 216, 261
Charcot, J.-M. 557–8
Charing Cross Hospital 20–35, 38, 114, 347, 399, 613
Charity, and Darwinism 521, 576, 585–6
Charity Organisation Society 585
Charles II 567
Charter, Chartism 13, 15, 18–20, 29, 31, 86, 102, 143, 177, 184, 220, 353, 521, 583, 619, 640
Charterhouse 524, 557
Chartism (Carlyle) 13
Chatham 149–50, 154, 633
Chattanooga 325
Chelotropis Huxleyi 152
Chelsea 502, 523, 557
Chemistry as Exemplifying the Wisdom . . . of God (Fownes) 27
Chemistry Primer (Roscoe) 406
Chemists, evangelical 328
Chenery, T. 509
Chickering Hall, New York 480
Children, education, 369, 391, 393–4, 396, 397, 401–5, 408, 417–21, 430, 442, 448, 450, 451, 455, 456, 468, 475, 485–6, 493–4, 498, 503, 506, 520, 532, 533, 570, 573, 622, 628
Children, savages as 144, 342, 353
Children's books 451, 484, 503, 506, 564
Chile 138
Chimpanzee 28–9, 239–41, 276, 288, 295, 299, 304, 306, 352, 607
China 69, 117; Opium Wars 44
Chloral 408, 603
Chlorodyne 511
Cholera 203
Chopin 222
Christ Church, Oxford 164, 275–6, 298, 591, 606
Christ Church, Lisson Grove 285, 450, 103
Christ, Jesus 266, 332, 567, 571, 579–80, 608
Christian Prayer and General Laws (Romanes) 458
Christian Socialism 203, 208–9, 218, 263, 285, 313, 343, 350, 361–3, 388, 530, 612
Christiania 572
Christianity, law of land 526, 587, 641
Christie's 571
Chromosomes 591, 601
Chronometers 47
Church Army 554

Church Congress (1888) 567, 571, 607
Church Convocation (1864) 328
Church of England, *see* Anglicans
Church of Scotland 206
Church of the Strangers, New York 480
Church rates 10
Churchill, J. 202, 321, 323, 469
Churchill, R. 546
Cinchona 422, 550
Cincinnati 475
Circular system, classification 89, 124, 167, 176
Circulation of the blood 487, 600
City and Guilds Institution 506, 542, 554
City Colonies, Booth's 584
City of London, Guilds 488, 506, 532, 553-4
Civic pride 442-3, 532, 575
Civil List 183, 252, 541
Civil Service 202; science part of 422, 423, 431, 439, 515, 518, 626, 628, 642
Civil War, American 234, 312-13, 320, 324, 334, 343, 353, 371
Civil War, English 628
Civilization in Europe (Guizot) 14
Clairvoyants 192
Clapham School 354
Claremont Islands 101
Clark, A. 390, 429, 431, 436, 453, 495, 537-9, 600
Class, explanations 618
Class v. Mass 576, 592, 607, 641
Classes, evolution of animal 256, 357
Classics, anthropology part of 581; character forming 393, 488, 493-4, 512-13, 524, 627; Darwin on 275; at Oxbridge 393, 396, 418, 419, 455, 489, 501, 512-13, 515, 524, 545, 563, 627; v. experimental science 393, 396, 397, 405, 418, 419-20, 488, 512-13, 524, 545, 627
Classification, circular system 89-90, 124, 167, 176; genealogical 235, 262, 354-5, 356; Huxley on, 138, 167, 208, 226, 235, 262, 315, 323, 354-6
Clayton, E. 48
Clerical Disabilities Act 435
Clerks 293, 310, 483
Clifford, L. 612
Clifford, W.K. 467, 502, 611, 621
Clifton 512
Climates, prehistoric 581

Clive, R. 493
Clodd, E. 630
Clothworkers Guild 488
Club-mosses 247, 255, 404
Club, The 505
Clunn's Hotel 152, 154
Co-education 387
Coal 404; mining 201, 232, 300
Coal Hole, London 22
Coast Survey, Huxley's plans 207
Cobbe, F.P. 448, 457-8, 461
Cobden, R. 241, 253, 334, 362, 468, 625
Coca 539, 542, 545, 584
Cochlospermum 100
Cockatoo Island, near Sydney 74
Cockroaches 79, 97, 106, 260
Cockshut, A.O.J. 628
Cod 421, 496
Coelacanths 284, 509
Coelenterata 69, 83, 123, 167, *see* Jellyfish, Sea nettles
Coercion Bill 514, 537
Colchester 371
Cole, H. 394, 397, 439, 443
Colenso, J.W. 315-6, 318-19, 321, 327, 572
Coleridge, J.D. 526, 531, 573, 600, 641
Coleridge, S.T. 179, 556, 603
Collected Essays (Huxley) 601, 604, 606
Collier, John, 'Jack' (son-in-law) 495, 502, 523, 526-7, 543, 558, 562, 565, 569, 572, 580, 585
Collier, Joyce (granddaughter) 534, 543, 557, 569, 581, 588, 589
Collier, Sir. R. 495, 502, 526
Collins, W. 313
Cologne 431
Colonial Office 169, 371, 377, 397-8
Colonialism, and anthropology 397-8; and Booth 584-5
Colorado 478, 503
Colossi of Memnon 415
Columbia University 441
Comb jellies 74, 112
Commandments 547
Commentary on Leviticus (Kalisch) 364
Commissions, sale of 202
Committee on the British Museum 413
Commonweal 577
Commune, Paris 363, 400, 500
Communists 209, 344, 479, 564, 575
Como Bluff 504
Comparative anatomy 28, 42, 190, 202, 218, 221, 231, 323, 628
Competition, demand for in society 184, 202, 211, 220-1,

245, 260-1, 268, 271, 334; in Darwin's Nature 223, 234-5, 258-60, 263, 271, 318, 452, 521, 559-60, 574, 597-9, 623, 626, 629, 634-6, 641-2; and Dissent 16, 31, 160, 184, 252, 260, 386, 554, 556, 573, 578, 596, 634-6; Establishment ideal 530, 578, 597-9, 626, 629, 634-6; foreign industrial 386, 387, 553-4, 559-60, 635-6; v. socialism 559-60, 574, 597-9, 626, 634-5, 641-2
Compsognathus 359, 481
Comte, A. 187, 193, 372-3, 375
Comte de Veysey 494
Conditional Immortality (Stokes) 499
Confederacy 320, 324-6, 334, 344
Confidence trickster 494
Confucians 64
Congregationalists 386, 396, 402, 410, 478, 625
Congress of Naturalists, German 349
Congreve, R. 373
Connecticut 247, 472, 481; Governor of 472
Conolly, J. 31
Conquest of Bread (Kropotkin) 564
Consciousness, physical basis 367
Conservation of Energy 433, 446, 549
Conservatives, Tories 11, 16, 29, 77, 151, 177, 212, 221, 240, 266-7, 271, 278-9, 283, 292, 317, 324, 328, 330, 333, 364, 366, 375, 378, 423-4, 430, 431, 435, 475, 493, 500, 503, 509, 522, 528, 531, 532, 541, 546, 556, 592-5, 607-8, 623, 641
Contemporary Review 393, 399, 402-3, 407, 426-7, 446, 453
Contextual approaches to history 617
Continents, sunken 223, 392
Continuity of germ-plasm 591
Continuous creation 232, 234, 246-7, 263, 274, 281, 304
Contraception 528
Convicts 46, 63, 66-7, 77, 87, 125
Conway, M. 387, 403, 466, 468, 501, 521, 612, 619
Cook, Captain 55, 100
Cook, T. 413, 415, 551
Cook's River, Sydney 70
Cooke, Alice (niece), 322, 387, 442

Cooke, Ellen (sister) 6, 9, 48, 106, 213, 242–3, 322, 376, 378, 387, 388, 464, 465, 467, 476, 511, 582, 620
Cooke, J.C. (brother-in-law) 9, 11, 15, 18–21, 23, 35, 47–8, 54, 60, 88, 106–7, 131, 150, 181, 213, 242–3, 248, 322, 376
Cooke, Nelly (niece) 388, 464
Cooks 389, 589
Cooper, R. 240
Cooper's Hill 442
Cooperative Societies 7, 634, *see* socialism
Cooter, R. 638, 639
Cope, E.D. 359, 474, 504–5, 533, 537
Copernicus, N. 304
Copley Medal 329, 565
Copper mines 172
Coptic churches, Cairo 414
Copyright law 510
Coral 54, 77, 79, 92, 96–8, 113, 133, 142, 173, 627
Coral Haven, Louisiade 113, 116–7
Cordylophora 421
Cork 469
Cornell University 478
Coronation Stone 329
Corrallines 145
Cortes, H. 118
Cosmic Philosophy (Fiske) 436
Cossacks 196, 633
Course of Practical Instruction in Elementary Biology (Huxley and Martin) 455
Court, law 426–7, 430, 438, 525–8
Court of Appeal 502
Court of Chancery 427
Court, Royal 314, 525, 531, 537, 554, 594–5
Covent Garden 30, 344, 483
Coventry 6, 8–10, 60, 94, 141, 488, 623
Cowrie 100
Crabs 114, 145, 156, 219, 371, 514
Craft, W. 325
Crammers, for Huxley's courses 456
Crane, W. 641
Crawford, Mrs 138
Crawshaw, Mrs 585
Crayfish (Huxley) 497
Crayfish 495–7, 505
Creation, Baden Powell on 298; Carpenter on 261; Days of 154–5, 204, 283, 364; Flower on 306; Hooker on 219; student Huxley on 8, 10; Huxley's view in 1856 225–6; Huxley's caricature 256, 274, 459, 480–1, 507, 556, 567–8, 639; Huxley polarises options, Evolution or Creation, 253,

366; miraculous acts 424–5, 508, 544, 555–6, 567–8, 579; Owen's continuous creation 232, 234, 246–7, 263, 274, 281, 304; as support for status quo 220, 240, 269
'*Creation*' (Haydn) 345
'Creative Week' (Rorison) 283
Creed of a Modern Agnostic (Bithell) 527
Creeping things 544, 545
Cremer, W. 401
Cretaceous fossils 366, 427, 472
Crimean War 196, 202, 210, 223, 268, 305, 386, 397, 400, 417, 539, 554, 633
Crinoids 205
Critiques and Addresses (Huxley) 426, 430, 456
Crocodile 99, 103, 248, 275, 300, 303, 355, 358, 406, 452, 459
Cromer 523
Cromwell, O. 197, 624, 633
Crook, P. 635
Crookes, W. 433, 437, 438
Croonian Lecture 243–4
Crossopterygians 284, 355, 465
Crown Prince 494
Cruelty to Animals Act (1876) 457, 469
Crustacean 29, 56, 61, 79, 97, 112, 117, 142, 145, 208, 214, 496
Crystal Palace 164, 247, 357
Cultural evolution 244
Curral Mountain, Madeira 55, 228, 579
Curtis Island 79
Cuscus 121, 125, 127
Custer, G.A. 472
Cuttlefish 484, 491
Cuvier, G. 227
Cyclone 111
Cyclops, HMS 237
Cynocephalus 241
Cynodraco 504, 505

Daguerreotype 47
Dahabieh 414, 415
Daily American 475, 477
Daily Graphic, New York 480
Daily News 159, 408, 444, 492, 493, 637
Daily Telegraph 577, 612
Dakota 391, 472, 533
Dalton, Revd. W.H. 434
Dana, J.D. 317
Dante 57, 99–101, 106, 112, 164, 257, 357, 538, 569, 589
Danton, G.J. 146, 251, 556
Dark Ages 293, 318
Darling Downs 77
Darnley Island, Torres Strait 127, 144
Darwin and After Darwin (Romanes) 591
Darwin, Annie 291
Darwin, Charles Robert

Private life: wealth 4, 151, 173, 222, 284, 323; son dies 245; illness 254–5, 257–8, 277, 291; visits spa 235, 238, 254, 257, 258, 261, 277; absenteeism 257; on classical education 275; ethical departure from Christianity 291; Justice of the Peace 258; convalescent atmosphere of house 291
Career: Cambridge 167, 221; Zoological Society 71; *Beagle* voyage 41, 56, 62, 64, 67, 76–7, 105, 114, 119, 131, 142, 151, 156, 173; *Zoology* of voyage 151, 156; elected to Imperial Academy in Breslau 236; Copley medal 329–30; in German encyclopaedia 349
Early contacts with Huxley: Huxley sends papers 165, 188; gives Huxley reference 169; meets Huxley 188; Huxley reviews barnacle monographs 195–6; resites their cement glands 213–4; on Huxley's archetype 188; on Huxley vs Owen 213, 215, 230, 238; on Huxley's non-progressionism 215, 219, 222–4, 303–4; on Huxley vs Falconer 227; on Huxley's switch to transmutation 225, 254, 257–8; taxes Huxley on jellyfish 228; sends pages of *Natural Selection*, 234–5, 260; queries Huxley on embryology 235; disagree over genealogy 235, 262, 303, 356, 359; reads Huxley's *Builder* article 254
Family friendship: on Huxley's marriage 214; the Huxleys at Downe 219–24, 273–4; does not put Huxley up for Athenaeum 226; on Huxley's brusqueness 226–7; Leonard Huxley's godfather 290–1; Nettie at Downe 291, 294–5; on Marian Huxley 294; on Harry Huxley 369; Nettie reads him Tennyson 294; tours School of Mines with Huxley 267, 354; at Abbey Place 369
Other scientific contacts: on Owen's archetype 188, 223; Owen's congenial palaeontology 215, 233–4; Owen on human brain 238–40; Forbes' death 206; Rolleston's FRS 306; on Haeckel 349, 354–5; on Phillips 357
Origin of Species: conditions ripe for *Origin* 188, 220; plans to publish 225, 227–8;

writes *Natural Selection* 241; on Lyell's creative cause in evolution 258; hears from Wallace 244–5; writes *Origin* 246; Huxley reads proofs 257; Huxley on 'flaws' 254–5, 262, 268–9; uses Huxley's Creationist caricature 256, 274; publication of *Origin* 257–8; German translation 274; Russian translation 318; Huxley on *Origin* 258–9; *Athenaeum* on 259–60, 266–7; Carpenter on 260; Huxley's 1860 lecture on 259–60, 266–72; Darwin attends 268, 270–1; Huxley's *Macmillan's Magazine* review 260–1, 263; School of Mines lecturers on 261, 267; Huxley's *Westminster* review 261–2, 273; Kingsley on 263; Owen on 263, 265, 272, 273–4; Huxley reviews in *Times* 263–5, 266; *Quarterly Review* on 265, 283; Wollaston on 266; Murchison on 267; Ramsay on 267; E.Lankester on 267; Dyster on 267; attacks on 266, 272; Wilberforce on 278, 283, 298; *Natural History Review* on 284; Sharpey on 308; Tyndall on 319; Princess Royal of Prussia on 329; the Pope on 331; Thomson on 370
Science: early science 173, 195–6; barnacles 173, 188, 214–5, 220, 235–6, 263; fancy pigeons 223–4, 226, 260, 264, 267–8; caricatured in squib 317; on Huxley's zöoids 165; variations 220, 224; theory of evolution 188, 219–20, 224, 234–5, 245–6, 258–9; support at BAAS 350, 365–6; Huxley's metaphor for selection 363; origin of man 119, 241, 267, 269; avoids in *Origin* 253–4; age of earth 370–1
On Nature: bloody ethic 197, 228, 234–5, 245; utilitarianism 200, 220, 223, 234–6, 245–6, 258–9, 263, 271; competitive individualism 223, 235; dignity of man 282
Post-Origin period: pushes Huxley on 260, 295; on Huxley's 'Zoological Relations of Man' 289–90; on ape-brain debate 295, 297; on Owen's 'basting' at BAAS 1860 281; on Wilberforce 281, 283; Huxley's talks on human origins 301; on *Athenaeum* 272; bishops sneering at Huxley 271; on atheism 185, 258; reads Lecky 342; collapse of

Reader 343; signs *Essays* petition 298; loathes Owen 290, 295, 297; on Huxley's 1862 Geological address 303–4; on *On Our Knowledge* 310–11; sends Farrar Huxley's pamphlets 350; Emma reads pamphlets 323; on Lyell's *Antiquity of Man* 312; on *Man's Place* 312–13; on Huxley's 'encyclical' 332; on Huxley's opening of *Nature* 372; on Huxley's 1869 Geological address 371; on Huxley's essays 368; and racists 320; on abolition 324; Jamaica Committee 352
Post-1870: 389, 393, 400, 407–8, 416, 420–1, 423–4, 430–1, 441, 444–5, 453–4, 456–8, 470, 473–4, 476, 481, 486–7, 491, 499, 503, 507, 510–11, 514, 525, 528–9, 541–2, 570, 572, 574–5, 579, 581, 588, 591, 596, 601, 606, 611, 634, 642; Abbey burial 520–1, 525–6, 555, 611; elected to Académie 487; adaptive spread 392; DCL 398; bequest to Hooker 525; bequest to Huxley 521; on birth control 528–9; and Butler 509; death 519–22; deathbed legend 566; *Descent of Man* 399–401, 433, 550, 574, 628–9, 639; ecological approach 452; evolution of morality 400–1, 499, 564, 592; finances Dohrn's Marine Station 424; finances Huxley 426, 428–30; on female inferiority 447, 629; *Formation of Vegetable Mould* 519; gift to Jess 495; Gladstone visits 487; on *Hume* 499; on Huxley 510; Huxley's obituary 563; Huxley on 522, 529; inheritance of acquired characters 591; insectivorous plants 453; 'Instinct' chapter 521–2; on Klein 462; LL.D. 490–1; Lowe visits 422; Malthusian 458, 513, 576, 636; Memorial 521–2, 531, 542, 602; and Mivart 407–8, 454, 509, 542; on 'Mr Darwin's Critics' 407–8; Natural Selection 391, 392, 406, 407, 447, 453, 520–1, 548, 554, 605, 626; *Origin* 453, 507–9, 510, 563, 623; on Owen 433; Rich legacy 486, 514–5; séance 486; sexual selection 447; at South Kensington 510; species dispersal 392; translation 400; on unions 634; on vivisection 457–8, 462; Wallace pension 513; war of nature 554,

558–60, 563–4, 573, 576, 578, 584, 598, 635–6; wealth 393, 559, 621
Darwin, Charles Waring 245
Darwin, Emma 222, 242, 291, 294, 323, 342, 399, 428–9, 519, 589
Darwin, Erasmus A. 187, 429
Darwin, Francis 223, 405, 462, 483, 491, 519, 552, 592
Darwin, George 223, 438, 453, 487, 520
Darwin, Henrietta 291, 294, 429, 453, 457
Darwin, Horace 323, 354
Darwin Medal 606
Darwin's Metaphor (Young) 626
Darwiniana (Gray) 480
Darwinians, begin differentiating 391, as a sect 407–8, 435, 541, 624–5, 626, 628, 630–1; palaeontology 424
Darwinism, the term 391, 575
Darwinism, War and History (Crook) 635
Darwinismus 498, 500
Davies, E. 448
Davies, Mrs L. 372
Davies, Revd L. 285, 330, 372, 388, 414, 435, 525, 612
Dawson, W. 567
Dayman, J. 42, 64, 74, 82, 100, 116, 158, 174, 237, 365
'Death of Socrates', painting 489
'Death of Cleopatra', painting 562
Deceased Wife's Sister Bill 569, 572
Deep sea soundings 57, 60, 64, 237
Degeneration 587, 642
Deists 461, 501
Democracy 13, 20–1, 102, 186, 209, 220, 242, 267, 320, 324, 334, 353, 363, 479, 548–50, 556, 573–7, 587, 592–4, 596, 638–9, 641; of intellect, 63, 242, 252
Democritus 446
Demography 221
Demonstrators, Huxley's 396–7, 417, 419, 442, 447, 490, 510, 629
Denis, R.C. 632
Department of Science and Art 189, 199, 202, 217, 274, 327, 393–4, 397, 417, 430, 438–9, 442, 523, 632–4
Department of Woods 167
Depletion of fish stocks 566
Depression, economic 3, 15, 19, 21, 24, 25, 31, 45, 514, 517, 524, 534, 547, 549, 558, 560, 563, 568, 571, 572–3, 585, 592, 597, 619
Depths of the Sea (Thomson) 428

Derby, Lord 422, 458, 520
Dermott, G. 181
Descartes, R. 441, 486
Descent of Man (Darwin) 399–401, 407, 433, 447, 499, 550, 574, 628–9, 639
Descriptive and Illustrated Catalogue of the Fossil Reptilia of South Africa (Owen) 504
Design, providential 27, 227–8, 230, 235, 392, 407, 424, 434, 437, 474, 555–6, 622, 627–8
Detective 571
Determinism 318, 366, 389, 434, 440–1, 444–7, 496, 503, 541, 544, 555–6, 624, 625–6
Development 184, 186, 191, 193, 224, 226, 232–5, 246, 265, 266, *see* Evolution
'Development Hypothesis', Spencer 184
Devil 573, 580, 592
Devil fish 530
Devon 229, 502, 511, 534
Devonian fossils 247–8, 255, 267, 284, 303, 346, 465, 578
Devonport 54, 149
Devonshire, Duke of 388, 520
Diatoms 560
Dickens, C. 11, 23, 159, 164, 237, 252, 340, 463, 470
Dicynodonts 255, 357
Diffusion, critique of 636, 638
Dijon 306
Dimetrodon 505
Dinosaurs 247–8, 257, 356–9, 363–5, 427, 473, 601, 618, 643; American 472, 474, 479, 481, 503–4; ancestors of birds, 356–7, 365, 377, 472, 481, 505, 509, 625; bipedal 247, 257, 358, 472, 479, 481; *Brontosaurus* 504; *Cetiosaurus* 358; *Compsognathus* 359, 481; *Euskelesaurus* 357; feathered 481; *Hadrosaurus* 479; *Iguanodon* 358; *Laelaps* 359; *Megalosaurus* 357; *Stegosaurus* 503; *Titanosaurus* 503; Owen on 29, 153, 218, 247, 306, 357, 504–5, 547, 602
Diphyes 65, 69, 123, 152
Disestablishment 10, 186, 385, 512, 592
Dispenser, wills body 640
Dispersal of species 392
Disraeli, B. 330–1, 339, 370, 375, 413, 440, 459, 493, 617, 632
Dissent, Dissenters 7–8, 14, 16, 31, 42, 69, 75, 159–60, 181, 184, 252, 256, 260–1, 267, 275, 285, 361, 364; and agnosticism 408, 624–5, 631;

attack Anglican monopolies 10–12, 16, 21, 75, 86, 89, 160, 177, 184, 186, 197, 210, 220, 230, 232, 240, 252–3, 256, 259, 269, 292, 313, 316, 335, 339, 343, 346, 364, 370, 373–4, 376, 378–9, 385–7, 389–90, 435–6, 443, 468, 482, 502, 512, 556, 572, 573, 581, 583, 589, 603, 618, 622–3, 626, 631, 634–6, 638; back Huxley 429, 468, 489, 512–13, 625; and Catholicism 408, 497; competitive ethos 16, 31, 160, 184, 252, 260, 386, 554, 556, 573, 578, 596, 634–6; missing from history of science 638; Scottish 439; secular, causal science 8, 16, 75, 184, 256, 386, 402, 435, 441, 446, 468, 556, 589, 603, 622–4, 631, 633–4; social rise 385–7, 389, 402, 509, 619, 622–5, 642; sons at Oxbridge 396, 398, 501, 642; University College and 399, 450; and 'war' metaphor 634, 636
Dissolvent literature 160, 315
Divine Government (Smith) 10, 200, 598, 623, 625
Division of labour 191, 220
Divorce 453
Dixon, G. 403
Dock strikes 640
Dockers 584, 640
Doctor of Science degree 533
Dogs, Huxley's work on 497
Dohrn, A. 355, 416, 424, 442, 450, 451, 538
Donnelly, G.H. 539
Donnelly, J. 397, 439, 517, 538–9, 541–2, 593, 606, 609, 612, 633, 640, 642
Down House, Downe 173, 215, 219, 221–2, 226, 254, 266, 273, 291–2, 294, 400, 422, 429, 458, 474, 520, 522, 589
Doyle, C. 642
Draper, J, 497, 632
Dreadnought, HMS 159
Dredging 42, 45, 59, 61, 78, 97, 152, 168, 203, 205–7, 212, 214, 219, 237, 257, 355, 427
Drift-netters 306
Drowned forest 214
Drummond, H. 602, 608
Drunkenness 9, 16, 24, 26, 30, 48, 68, 87, 106, 121, 130, 145, 150, 166, 210, 242, 376, 388, 464, 476, 531, 540, 557, 582, 620
Dryopithecus 239
Dublin 284, 305, 348, 374, 498, 550

Dublin Review 374
Dublin University 498
Dubois, E. 606
Duchateau Island, New Guinea 128
Duckworth, Revd R. 485, 495
Duffy, P. 389, 262
Dugongs 76
Duncan, P.M. 371
Dunk Island 93, 97
Dyaks 326
Dyster, F. 203, 208, 210, 212, 214, 218, 232, 238, 253, 267–8, 286, 292, 301, 313–4, 345, 459, 530
Dyster, Mrs 267

Ealing 473
Ealing School 4, 6, 466, 622, 625
Early History of Mankind (Tylor) 342
Earthquake 57
East End, London 3, 11, 155, 181, 184, 353, 528, 548, 584
East India Company 233
East Indies 103
Eastbourne 565, 570–1, 581–2, 585, 588, 600, 610, 613
Eastbourne Gazette 585
Echinoderms 96
Eckersley, A. 537, 570, 611
École Normale 517
Economic entomology 532
Economist 183, 374
Ectoderm 208, 452
Eden, Gordon on 539
Edfu, Egypt 415
Edinburgh 25, 193, 195, 206–7, 277, 300–1, 303, 305, 346, 367, 428, 442, 448, 459, 483, 518, 563
Edinburgh Review, 273, 298, 320
Edison, T. 471
Education Act (1870) 393, 401, 418, 443, 557
Education, American higher 477–8; v. Arnold on 523–4; *see* Children; London School Board; co-education 387; compulsory free 393ff, 401–5, 443, 556, 578; higher 523, 562; lab and 393–4, 396–7, 405, 418, *see* Schoolmasters; Nettie's interest 570; professionals and 435, 626; resources 524; secular 408–9, 580; technical 488, 506, 512–13, 519, 554, 557, 559, 634–5, 641; textbooks 405–6; white only, in Tennessee 475; and women 447–50, 477, 483, 533
Education Committee, London School Board 405
Edwards, A. 547
Eels 523

Egerton, Sir P. 296
Egg nucleus, source of first embryonic cells 277
Egypt 410, 412–16, 530, 547, 562, 590
Egypt Exploration Fund 547
Ehrenberg, C. 177, 226, 427
Eiger 229
El Kab, Egypt 415
Electric companies 503; lights 471, 512, 581, 589; trains 631
Electrician 506
Electro-biologists 192
Electro-magnets 372
Electrophysiology 28
Elementary Physiology (Huxley) 350
Elements of Physiology (Müller) 14
Elephant, 473; fossil 309, 366; genealogy 401
Elephantiasis 114
Elgin 247, 255–6, 275, 365, 406, 452, 459
Elgin, Earl of 169
Eliot, G. 8, 93, 185–6, 189, 191, 193–4, 342, 345, 373, 404, 436, 450, 526, 611, 621
Elisha 560
Elizabeth Bay House, Sydney 89
Elizabeth, Salt's maid 38
Elliotson, J. 9, 12, 32, 66
Ellis, C. 414
Elohim ghosts 546
Elwin, W. 265
Embryology, embryos 25–6, 39, 83, 90, 125, 184, 190–1, 199, 219, 224, 232, 235, 244, 271, 304, 349, 355, 399, 424, 451–2, 455, 490
Embryonic cells, first to appear 277
Emerson, R.W. 441
Emigration 45, 49, 164, 170, 180, 184
Empire 377, Huxley's photographic record of races 371
Encyclopaedia Britannica 439, 486
Endoderm 208, 452
Endowed Schools Commission 402
Endymion (Keats) 180
Engels, F. 313
Engis skull 301
English Churchman 365
English Culture and the Decline of the Industrial Spirit (Wiener) 642
English Men of Letters 497
English Men of Science 506
Environments, ancient 153
Eocene fossils 222, 473, 482, 485–6, 510
Eohippus 473, 485, 510, 560
Ephestia 410, 411

Erebus, HMS 36, 42, 167–8, 174
Esna, Egypt 415
Essays (Macaulay) 138
Essays and Reviews 278, 280, 283, 297–8, 315, 318, 328, 330, 398, 433, 516, 568, 572, 579, 590, 619
Essays upon some Controverted Questions (Huxley) 590, 592, 595
Ether, supramundane matter 607, 608
Ether, anaesthetic 66, 179
Ethical Purport of Darwinism (Schurmann) 592
Ethics, Bible and 403; Christianity and 253, 547, 598, 603; evolution and 454, 507, 508, 522, 524, 559–61, 577–8, 592, 596–9, 604, 622, 635–6; Kingsley on 263; science and 513; Spencer and 527, 573–4, 576, 592, 597–9; socialism and 507, 564–5, 597–9
Ethnological Society 321, 333, 343–4, 347, 353, 358, 371, 376
Ethnology 144, 391, 397–9, 415, 546, 550, 580–1, 592
Etna 416
Eton College 328, 493, 512, 526, 530, 562
Euclid 14
Eugenics 453, 575
Euskelesaurus 357
Evangelicalism, 4, 13, 55, 167, 144, 201, 209, 300, 302, 304, 314, 324, 328, 332, 376, 398, 466, 480, 511, 602–3, 621–2, 637
Evans, J. 358, 538
Evans, M., *see* Eliot, G.
Evidence as to Man's Place in Nature (Huxley) 304, 306–7, 311, 312–18, 320, 324, 329, 333, 340–3, 368, 399, 594, 597, 606, 618, 629, 639
Evolena 551
Evolution; Before the *Origin*: Lamarck's 89, 393, 509; working classes on 21, 209–10, 292–3; democratic metaphor 210; *London Investigator* promotes 21; *Oracle of Reason* 21; Chapman on 186, 256, 261, 267; Lewes 187, 191; Spencer 184, 186, 191, 244, 246; *Vestiges* 193, 215, 244; Huxley on transmutation 187, 193, 224–6, 235–6; Lyell on 187, 225, 239
Origin of Species: see Darwin, C.R., Wallace, A.R.; Huxley comes to grips with 245–65, 268–70ff, *see* Hux-

ley, T.H.; Hooker on 261; Carpenter on 261; support for Darwin 261, 267; Kingsley 263, 288, 304; Owen on 263, 272ff; Wollaston on 266; Murchison on 267; Ramsay on 267; Salter on 267; Dyster on 267; Flower on 305; BAAS 1860 276ff; Oxford dons on 313; Germany 317–8, 349–50, 354–5; Russia 318; Italy 341, 355; Tyndall on 319; racists on 320; Huxley keeps out of class 340; of language 350; *Archaeopteryx* verifies 358; of dinosaurs into birds 358–60, 459, 472, 481, 484, 492, 504–5, 509, 518, 545, 525; of one class into another 256, 358; ideology of industrial order 364; evolutionary naturalism 366; Huxley opposes to Creationism 253, 256, 274, 366; *Fortnightly's* creed 367; origin of mankind 90, 153, 225, 238–40, 266–7, 271, 274, 276, 278–83, 288, 290, 292–4, 297, 301, 304, 307, 313, 315, 317–18, 320, 333, 341, 382, 399, 431, 486, 490, 508, 552, 598, 606–7, 621, 625, 627–8, 631, 643
After 1870: in America 470ff; anthropology and 581; and *Bathybius* 460; Cambridge commits itself to 490; chance 406–7, 424, 458, 486; of crayfish 496; crocodile 452, 459; Darwin's statue caps 531; as drama 553, 637; and embryology 424; entry in *Encyclopaedia Britannica* 486; ethics and 507, 508, 524, 592, 496–8, 603, 604, 622, 636; evangelical 602–3; a fact 486; fossil case for 470ff, 484, 509; on fringe of academia 424, 453; geological 404, 455; horse 401, 473, 481, 485, 509–10; hippopotamus 424; Huxley's reticence about selection 420–1, 452–3, 486, 491, 496, 508, 626; immoral 427, 454, 552, 620; and industry 404, 428, 433–4, 445, 509, 559–61, 565, 575, 587, 625–6, 634–5; and International Scientific Series 496; Jowett on 515; and liberal clerics 515, 604–5, 612, 625; as life's genetic development 391, 486; Kidd on 617; Kovalevskii on 401, 424; of mammals 452, 492, 504–6, 518, 545–6, 602; and mean-

792

ing of life 456; and medical community 392; of mind/morality 399, 400, 499, 521, 581, 592; and mores 528–9; naturalism 385, 389, 391–2, 406–7, 434, 466, 555–6, 568, 572, 591, 597–8, 601, 603–4, 607–8, 622–3, 625, 629–30, 632, 635; neutral seeming 541; for nursery 451; origin of life 392–3, 406; and old universities 489, 605; in *Philosophical Transactions* 424; presentation of 503, 508, 510, 636, 639; providential 392, 396, 406, 407, 424–5, 555–6, 602–3; and radical politics 385, 391, 399, 408, 446, 455, 503, 532, 541, 556, 577, 623, 639; religion of 406–7, 604, 640; religious certainty 521, 527–8; respectability of 426–7, 431; Salisbury on 605–6; on seabed 427–8; in school 498; search for intermediate life-forms 451–2, 465; social evolution 399, 496, 596–8, 603; and social order 513, 521, 549, 559–60, 597, 625–6; social values and 391, 399–400, 603, 626; and socialism 500, 548–9, 559–61, 564, 577, 641; of theology 546–7; timing 485–6; titillating 629; Tyndall on 424, 446, 503; and type system 421; at University College 393, 455; of vertebrates 451–2; and Watts' agnostics 527–8; Whitworth gun 399, 623, 633–4; women and 401, 447–8, 450–1, 528–9, 568, 625, 628–9; the word 391, 509; working classes and 451, 525, 556, 592, 623, 639
Evolution of Man (Haeckel) 498
Evolution of Sex (Geddes and Thomson) 575
Evolution Old and New (Butler) 509
Examinations, and professionalism 202, 327; Cambridge University 490, 516; Cambridge local 450; Department of Science and Art, 417–19, 433, 442, 456, 633; Edinburgh University 449; London University 221–2, 489, 529, 595; Oxford University 398, 417–18; War Department 221, 417, 633
Excommunication, Mivart's 553
Exeter 375
Exeter College, Oxford 417

Exeter Hall, London 22, 120
Exodus 253
Exorcism 567
Expertize, scientific 387, 392, 397, 405, 422, 451, 568, 578
Extra-terrestrial life 204
Eyre Arms (pub) 207
Eyre Defence Fund 352
Eyre, E.J. 104, 139, 351–2

Fabians 539, 548, 641
Facing Island 78
Fairyland of Science (Buckley) 451
Falconer, H. 227, 232, 258, 260, 276–7, 281, 299
Falkland Islands 141, 397
Family Islands 93
Fanning, Alice 108
Fanning, Oriana, 'Ory' (Nettie's half-sister) 70, 73, 108, 155, 181, 242, 251
Fanning, William (Nettie's brother-in-law) 70–3, 107, 116, 130, 155, 157, 165, 168–9, 172–4, 180, 200, 213, 251
Fanning, Willie (Fanning's son) 155
Faraday, M. 171, 175–6, 179, 189, 371, 506, 589
Farnborough, Battle of 280
Farrar, Revd F. 350, 362–4, 520–1, 627
Faucit, H. 426
Faust 318
Fayrer, J. 32–3, 36, 38–9, 48, 347
Felixstowe 168
Fellowships, Cambridge 490, 516; Columbia 441; Harvard 441; Oxford 417–18, 516; Pennsylvania 441
Female Factory, Parramatta 131
Fenians 514, 533, 544, 550, 607
Fergusson, J. 366
Ferns 453
Ferrier, D. 442
Filippi, F. de 341
Finchley, Finchley Road 199, 207, 213, 346, 287, 612
Finland 521
Finsteraarhorn 229
First International 344
First Principles (Spencer) 285
First Sea Lord 156, 178, 423
Fisguard, HMS 156, 162
Fish, anatomy 496, 523, 530; abyssal 427; *Ceratodus*/lungfish 233, 247, 258, 303, 355, 464–5, 506, 509; diseases 514, 518; fossil 193, 284, 303, 321, 355, 396, 428, 465, 480; origin of 451–2; salmon 514–15; stocks 566

Fisheries Department/work 514, 523, 533–4, 537, 540–1, 566
Fishmongers Company 533
Fisk University 476
Fiske, J. 436–7, 454, 463, 474, 533
Fitzroy Island 97
FitzRoy, R. 41, 105, 151
Flatworm 170, 214
Fleming, A. 467
Flint axes 299
Flood 567, 579–80, 587
Flora Antarctica (Hooker) 167
Flora of British India (Hooker) 550
Flora of Tasmania (Hooker) 257–8
Florence 539
Flower, W.H. 305–7, 315, 323, 329, 347, 371, 408, 531, 602–3, 612, 642
Flukes 34, 173, 175
Fly, HMS 41–2, 45, 47, 68, 79
Flycatchers 97
Flying fox 98, 100, 102
Flying Squadron 411
Flytraps 453
Fogg High School, Nashville 476
Folkestone 295–6, 539
Foote, G.W. 525–6, 641
Footprints, fossil 247, 358, 472, 481
Forbes, A. 492, 493
Forbes, E. 42, 45, 48, 59, 69, 73, 81, 123, 140, 152, 154, 156–7, 161–2, 166, 168, 170, 179, 182–3, 195–7, 199, 201, 205–6, 212, 223, 248, 420
Forbes Medal 206
Foreign Office 169
Formation of Vegetable Mould (Darwin) 519
Formosa 397
Forms of Water (Tyndall) 497
Fortnightly Review 329, 345, 367–8, 387, 399, 446, 467, 487, 497, 532
Fossilization, process 214
Fossils, *see* entries for Palaeontology in Huxley, T.H., Owen, R., and specific fossil animals
Foster, M. 340, 343–4, 358, 371, 396, 398, 402–3, 406, 409–10, 416–19, 429, 439–40, 442, 450, 455, 458, 490, 501, 506, 517, 518, 532, 537, 540, 547, 551, 603, 606–7, 609–10, 612, 630
Foster, M. Snr 398
Foundation membranes, Coelenterate 90, 123, 208
Foundations of Belief (Balfour) 607–8
Fownes, G. 27

France, French 5, 14, 28, 41, 44, 58, 63, 73, 87, 89, 102, 104, 122, 130–1, 169, 187, 196, 204, 214, 220, 239, 243, 251, 253, 272, 292–3, 296, 299, 320, 324, 363, 368, 374, 381, 400, 564, 575, 608, 635; 1789 Revolution 436, 552; Commune 400, 500
Franco-Prussian War 379, 387, 400, 608
Frankland, E. 327, 418
Frankland Island 97
Franklin, Sir J. 36, 39, 174, 418
Fraser's Magazine 289
Free love 184–5, 209, 324, 527, 529
Free Public Library movement 556
Free trade 261, 253, 349, 468, 625
Free-will 28, 389, 406, 439–41, 444
Freedom in Science and Teaching (Haeckel) 498
Freethinker 525, 613
Freethinkers 160, 184–5, 188, 209, 363, 396, 403, 440, 468, 500–1, 525, 527, 529, 613, 639–40, *see* Atheism
French Revolutions (1789) 89, 220, 269, 272, 292–3, 320, 375, 552; (1848) 102, 131, 317, 364; (1871) 400
Frere, Sir B. 493
Freud, S. 557
Frogfish 114
Frogs 421
Froude, J.A. 185–6, 484, 508, 620
Fuegian 'savages' 41, 347
Fuhlrott, K. 299–300
Fullerian Chair, Royal Institution 195, 199, 212, 227, 347, 371
Funchal, Madeira 56, 578
Function, explanation of structure 200, 223, 227, 230, 236, 246
Functions of the Brain (Ferrier) 442

Gadarene Swine 567, 571, 573, 580, 582, 588, 591
Galenstock 329
Galesaurus 233
Galileo 269, 538
Galton, F. 330, 350, 399, 436, 453, 520
Galway 341
Gambling 511
Gardeners' Chronicle 261, 266, 295
Garibaldi, G. 330
Garrett, E. 334, 342, 401–2, 409, 448–9
Garrett, J.W. 477

Geddes, P. 420, 490, 575
Gegenbaur, C. 359, 465
Geikie, A. 642
General Elections (1874) 423; (1886) 546; (1892) 592, 593; (1895) 608, 612
General Practitioners 12, 16, 19, 31
General Strike (1842) 20
Generelle Morphologie (Haeckel) 349, 354, 355–6
Genesis 75, 204, 253–4, 262, 272, 278, 314–15, 331, 351, 466, 480, 544–6, 550, 590
Genesis of Species (Mivart) 407
Geneva 317
Gentiana purpurea 551
Gentians 551
Gentleman, occupational category 617, 627
Geoffroy, E. 190
Geographical isolation 452
Geographical Society 158
Geography 484
Geological Magazine 359
Geological Society 152–3, 217, 229–30, 233–4, 248, 255, 272, 303, 370, 376, 504, 553
Geological Survey 42, 152–3, 162, 201, 203, 207, 212, 214, 217, 394, 517, 642
George, H. 513, 574, 577, 641
Germ theory of disease 393, 467
Germans, Germany 5, 7–8, 14, 26–8, 40, 57, 70, 72, 159, 166, 183, 187, 190–1, 236, 244, 274, 306, 317–18, 322, 327–8, 346, 348–50, 354, 372, 387, 394–6, 400, 418, 427–8, 440, 448, 450–1, 453, 497–8, 500, 553, 571, 593, 630, 635
Germanic, steamer 469
Germs 499
Giant armadillo 28
Giant sloth 152
Giant's skeleton 323
Giants Causeway 181
Gibbon 315
Gibraltar 326, 410, 411; bishop of 411
Giessen 27, 543
Giglioli, E. 341
Gilley, S. 634
Gilman, D.C. 463
Girls' Public Day School Company 450
Glaciers 173, 228, 237, 457, 551
Gladstone, North Australia 77
Gladstone, W.E. 77, 240, 312, 333, 353, 385, 387, 388, 390, 394, 396, 408, 409, 421–3, 461, 466, 487, 492, 493, 497, 513, 514, 526, 532, 537, 539, 541, 544–7, 549, 550, 554, 567, 571,

581, 582, 587, 590–6, 607; 'Proem to Genesis' 546
Glasgow 257, 276, 341
Glaucus (Kingsley) 208
Globigerina 237, 366, 377, 427, 627
Gloucester 15, 20, 21
Glyptodon (giant armadillo) 28, 306
God and the Bible (Arnold) 464
Godparents, for Huxley children 290–1, 388, 485, 519, 521, 569, 634
Goethe, J.W. von 14, 121, 349, 372, 450, 606
Gold rush 170, 172, 180
Gonville and Caius College, Cambridge 600
Gooday, G. 628
Goodsir, H.D. 36, 53
Goold Island 93
Goose barnacles 214
Goose Island 84
Gordon, General C.G. 538, 552, 587, 613
Gordon, Revd G. 247, 255, 356, 406
Gordon, W. 351
Gorilla 239–41, 274, 276, 278, 292, 295–6, 299, 304, 312, 314, 326, 341, 540
Goschen, G. 394, 423, 554
Goschen, L. 394
Goshen 546
Gosport 38
Göttingen 69, 317
Gould, J. 47, 166
Government, and social Darwinism 635
Government House, Hobart 66; Sydney 67–8, 132
Government School of Mines, 162, 189, 199, 201–2, 206–7, 228, 231, 267, 287, 296, 300, 302, 317, 340, 347; then Royal School of Mines 354, 369, 386–7, 393–5, 410; *see* Museum of Economic Geology; Geological Survey; Science Schools
Governor-General of Canada 169
Governor of New South Wales 80, 81, 169
Grade, fossil 505
Graduate Teaching Diploma 533
Grand Hotel, Eastbourne 581
Grant, A. 449
Grant, J. 412
Grant, President U.S. 472
Grant, R.E. 164, 354, 393, 420, 455
Grant, U. 325
Granville, Lord 371, 533
Grasshoppers, fossil 346
Gray, A. 474, 480
Gray, J.E. 42, 47, 60

Great auk 339
Great Australian Bight 104, 351
Great Bight of New Guinea 122
Great Eastern 351
Great Exhibition 151, 162, 164, 189, 247, 394
Great Northern Railway 222
Great Northern Line 387
Great War 601, 630, 636
Greek, compulsory 501; Huxley learns 502
Greeley, H. 480
Greenwich 156, 159–60, 174, 183, 423
Greg, W.R. 399
Gregory, W. 413
Gresham Commission on London University 595
Grey, M. 450
Griffiths, Mr 134
Griffiths, Mrs 130
Grindelwald 228
Grocers' Company 488
Grosvenor Gallery 511
Grote, G. 275, 292, 314, 336
Ground sloth fossil, *Megatherium* 28, 305
Grove, W. 350
Grut, Mrs 254
Guardian 365, 435
Guiana 352
Guizot, F. 14
Gulf of Carpentaria 103
Guthrie, F. 418

Hackney 402
Hadrosaurus 479
Haeckel, E. 349, 354–6, 359–60, 362–3, 365, 372, 374, 396, 427, 451, 452, 460, 465, 495, 496, 497–8, 501, 504, 552, 606, 639
Hagfishes 452
Haiti 351
Halcyon kingfisher 100
Halford, G. 317
Hall, M. 16, 441, 583, 623
Halls of Science 239, 244, 310, 639
Hames, G. 562, 565, 569, 591
Hamilton, L. 467
Hamilton, Lord C. 467
Hamilton, Sir W. 75
Harcourt, Sir W. 513–14
Hardcastle, H. 502
Hardie, K. 592
Hardwicke, R. 310
Harrison, F. 373
Harrow School 350–1, 378
Hartington, Lord 554, 572
Harvard University 436, 441, 474, 517
Harvey, W. 487, 503, 600
Haslar Naval Hospital 38–40, 43, 134, 390, 600
Hawkins, B.W. 479
Hay, J.D. 412

Hayden, F.V. 391
Heart, chambers 503
Heath, A. 387, 442
Heathorn, Henrietta Anne (wife), *see* Huxley, H.A.
Heathorn, Henry (Nettie's father) 131, 158, 198, 298, 322
Heathorn, Isabel, 'Isy' (Nettie's half-sister) 107, 133, 276–7
Heathorn, Oriana, *see* Fanning, Oriana
Heathorn, Sarah (Nettie's mother) 133, 298
Hebrew 364
Hedonism 540, 580, 600, 607, 609, 619
Heidelberg 159
Heki, Maori chief 139
Helfand, M. 636
Helium 460
Hell 100–1, 209, 239, 266, 271, 288, 328, 357, 553
Henle, J. 28
Henschel, G. 555
Henslow, F. 167
Henslow, J.S. 151, 278
Hercules, HMS 411
Heredity 605, 630
Herkomer, H. von 566
Herring 203, 515, 523
Herzen, A. 318
Hesperornis 472
Hexadactyly 256
High Church 21, 69, 269, 285
High Elms, Lubbock's mansion 222, 487
High Schools 448, 533
Higher animals, concept of 191, 204
Highgate 611; cemetery 371, 527
Himalayas 167, 227, 486
Hindhead 525, 543, 550, 600, 604
Hindus 64, 334, 366, 501
Hipparion 401
Hippocampus 240, 293, 295–7, 302, 307, 316
Hippopotamus 155, 424
Hirst, T.A. 237, 243, 298, 327, 328, 386, 423, 425, 533, 551, 567, 573, 590
Histoire des Girondins (Lamartine) 141
History, lawbound, 233
History, no value-free 618
History of Civilization (Buckle) 233
History of Co-operation (Holyoake) 500
History of Great Britain (Hume), 13, 14
History of Greece (Grote) 275
History of Rationalism (Lecky) 342
History of the American Civil War (Draper) 497
History of the Conflict Between

Religion and Science (Draper) 497, 632
History of the Warfare of Science with Theology in Christendom (White) 478
Hitchcock, E. 358
Hobart 48, 64–6, 67, 338
Hobhouse, A. 402, 408
Hoblyn, R. 18, 106
Hodeslea 570, 589, 610
Hoffmann, A.W. 437
Holbach, Baron d' 320
Holloway jail 525, 642
Holmwood 71, 76, 130
Holyoake, G.J. 20–1, 160, 186, 380, 403–4, 434, 500, 556, 587–8, 611, 626
Home Office 183, 511, 514–15, 518, 534, 538
Home Rule, Irish 444, 514, 541, 544, 546, 549, 582, 592–3, 595, 641
Home Rule Bill (1886) 549
Home Secretary 405, 459, 525, 595
Homer 466
Homo neanderthalensis 326
Homologies 254, 321, *see* Archetype, Unity of Plan
Honey-eaters 125, 145
Honey-suckers 102
Honourable Artillery Company 177
Honours Lists 593, 642
Hooker, B. 637
Hooker, F. 428
Hooker, J.D. 36, 173, 205–6, 211–14, 217–26, 230, 236, 238, 241, 243–6, 251–2, 254, 257–9, 261–2, 265, 269, 271–2, 277–80, 282–4, 287, 289–90, 295–6, 298, 301, 307, 312, 317, 321, 327, 329, 341–2, 350, 352, 365, 375, 395, 406, 409, 416, 426, 428, 441, 449, 455, 518, 560, 562, 563, 565, 586, 587, 589, 590, 602, 605, 607, 610, 637; anticlericalism 218, 283–4, 365; assistant surgeon, 36, 53; Athenaeum 241–2; Ayrton incident 421–3; at BAAS (1860) 277–80; BAAS (1866) 350; BAAS (1868) 365; on A.Balfour 609; Besant 529; British Museum 251–2; Copley Medal 565–6; Darwin's death 520–1; deaths of friends 582; Deceased Wife's Sister Bill 569; on *Descent of Man* 399; 'dirty Radicals' 573, 641; at Downe 219–25; on editors 571; on *Essays* petition 298; on evolution/*Origin* 226, 245–6, 254, 258–9, 261, 272, 283; on Eyre 352; Gladstone 423; godfather

388; J.D. Hay 412; meets Huxley 167; holiday with Huxley 431; at Huxley's wedding, 213; on Huxley's 'Zoological Relations' 282; on Huxley's 1860 lecture on the *Origin* 269; on *Man's Place* 307, 312; Leonard's godfather 290–1; Huxley's BAAS Presidency 375; Huxley's botany 551–2, 589; Huxley's essays 407; Huxley on miracles 572; Huxley's Rich legacy 589; Huxley's health 405; Huxley dying 611; Jess' wedding 495; at Kew 212, 327, 342, 421–2, 543; knighthood 441–2, 486; on Lady Lyell 341–2; Metaphysical Society bishops 409; Mivart 408; on *Natural History Review* 290; North Star 431; on Owen 230, 244; Owen's supposed autobiography 602; pension 550; picture on Huxley's wall 589; portrait 566; at Royal Society 205–6, 211–12; President 423, 441–2, 486; reforming societies 212, 221, 236, 238; remarries 469; retirement 525, 543; on Rolleston 295; royal prefix for societies 532; on Spencer 551, 574; Stanley 298; Star of India 576; The Club 505; Tyndall's death 603–4; Unionism 592; on Westminster Abbey 524; Wilberforce, 283; X-Club 327, 329, 573

Hooker, Sir W. 342

Hope Islands 99

Horace 57

Hornbill 119

Hornby, Rear-Admiral 411

Horse lineage, evolution 191, 222, 268, 271, 401, 473, 481, 485, 509–10

Horton, J. 325

House of Commons 23, 151, 296, 370, 394, 422, 520, 528, 530, 550, 593, 641

House of Lords 23, 151, 175, 314, 422, 469, 502, 569

Household Words 252

Housekeepers, sisters as 569

Howell, G. 640

Howes, T.G.B. 419

Howick Islands 100

Hudson, River 471

Hughes, T. 313, 330, 352, 362, 402

Hulks, Portsmouth 46

Human evolution 90, 153, 191–2, 225, 238–41, 252–3, 266–7, 269, 271–2, 274, 276, 278–83, 288, 290, 292–7, 299, 301, 304, 307,

313–18, 320, 333, 341, 382, 399, 431, 486, 490, 497, 508, 552, 598, 606–7, 621, 625, 627–8, 631, 643

Human fossils 239, 257, 298–301, 304–5, 313–5, 326, 333, 581, 606–7

Human, ice-age 431

Hume (Huxley) 497

Hume, D. 13, 14, 390, 497–500

Hummingbird 236

Humphry, G. 490

Hungerford Market, London 23

Hunt, J. 320, 325–6, 343, 353, 371

Hunterian Chair, Royal College of Surgeons 29, 156, 164, 196, 306, 323, 325, 341, 362

Hunterian Museum, Glasgow 341

Huntley, Marquis of 439

Hutton, J. 7, 14

Hutton, R.H. 374, 458, 461–2, 631–41

Huxley, Aldous (grandson) 606

Huxley, Eliza 'Lizzie' (sister), *see* Salt, Lizzie

Huxley, Ellen (sister), *see* Cooke, Ellen

Huxley, Ethel (daughter) 348, 377, 388, 437, 485, 511, 565, 569, 572, 590, 609, 610, 634

Huxley, Gaite (nephew Jim's wife) 503

Huxley, George (father), 4–7, 10, 20–1, 48, 106, 131, 145–6, 150, 163, 178–9, 622

Huxley, George Knight (brother) 5, 23, 33, 35, 46–7, 80, 88, 90, 106–7, 131–2, 140, 145, 150, 155, 168, 170–2, 179, 182, 197–8, 200, 207, 211, 248, 296, 321–2, 388, 476, 511, 557, 565, 612, 620

Huxley, Henry, 'Harry' (son) 332, 348, 355, 369, 388, 483, 517–18, 562, 569, 578, 579, 590, 610

Huxley, James (brother), 5, 9, 12, 15, 20–1, 28, 31–3, 35, 37, 48, 88, 102, 123, 131, 143, 146, 150, 178, 322, 348, 354, 369, 386, 476, 511

Huxley, Jessie Oriana (daughter) 242–3, 285–6, 294, 348, 369, 404, 406, 414, 416, 437, 467, 488, 493–5, 502, 518, 543, 570

Huxley, Jim (nephew) 354, 369, 386, 437, 503

Huxley, Julian (grandson) 557

Huxley, Katy (niece), 88, 322, 348

Huxley, Leonard (son) 289–90, 332, 369, 388, 399, 431,

437, 454, 465, 483, 488–9, 497, 501, 515–17, 521, 524, 539, 557, 570, 571, 606, 620

Huxley, Marian, 'Mady' (daughter) 285, 294, 369, 404–5, 414, 416, 437, 469, 488–9, 492–3, 495–6, 502, 511, 522–3, 534, 537–8, 542–3, 551, 555, 557–9, 561–2, 565, 567, 569, 581, 588, 592, 597, 629, 636

Huxley, Mary, 'Polly' (sister in-law, George's wife) 33, 150, 155, 162, 168, 170, 179, 207, 211, 296, 322, 388, 389, 511, 557, 582, 620

Huxley, Mary (sister-in-law, Jim's wife), 33

Huxley, née Heathorn, Henrietta Anne (wife)

Ancestry/Life in Australia: 70, 72–3, 87, 115–6, 130, 138, 170; illegitimate 570; early life 406; Aunt Kate 157; father's arrest 158; Moravian schooling 450

With Huxley in Sydney: 70–4, 81, 83, 86–91, 99, 102, 106–8, 111–12, 123, 129–37, 606

Separation (1850–55) 138, 141, 143–6, 150–2, 154–5, 157–9, 161–3, 165–70, 173–4, 176, 178–81, 185, 188, 192, 194–6, 198–203, 207–8

Marriage/Family life 211–14, 216–17; friction with Ellen Busk 243; envy of Darwins' wealth 323; mother moves in to Abbey Place 298; illnesses 502, 507, 557–61, 590, 596, 610; on money 388, 441, 445, 449, 468–9, 471, 514, 515, 530–1; on Noel 230, 286–7, 289–91, 294–5, 298, 518, 523, 543; in Folkestone 295; Jessie 242; Leonard 289–90, 369; Mady 294; Mady's admirers 489; Mady's health 437, 492–3, 534, 537, 543, 557–62; Henry 332; Ethel 348; growing children 369, 377; daughters' education 404, 414, 448, 450, 489; Waverley Place 298, 300; domestics 217, 314, 322, 332, 334, 402; educating nieces as governesses 448; illnesses 211, 214, 348, 377, 557, 561, 590; nurses Hal 333; family's scarlet fever 286, 357–8; seaside 364–5; Alps 228–9; on the climbs 237–8; 'moo' 502; Rachel's wedding 537; Collier 569; Ethel's wedding 572; in US 469ff; Vatican 518; Ellen's drunkenness 464, 511; family role 450,

469, 495; furnishes house
426, 581; electric lights 589;
the Privy Councillorship 593;
Thomasson's gift 468; Waller 467; waltzing 467; young
Jim 503; Huxley's drinking
425; Huxley's health 410,
416, 429, 432, 483, 515,
518, 534, 537–8; on old age
562; Huxley's death 610–12;
'Browning's Funeral' poem
on tomb 613
Friends: Alice Radford 77,
150, 170; the Griffiths, 130,
134; Foster 358; F.Balfour
490, 523; A.Buckley 451,
500–1; on Clifford 467; does
not visit George Eliot 450;
E.Garrett 402; on B.Riviere
404, 492; Rolleston's death
516; Dean Stanley 483, 516;
stately acquaintances 448, 494
Religion: 72, 75, 77, 81,
86–7, 132, 285–6; Church
going 285; and Llewelyn
Davies 285–6; anti-
Catholicism 86, 131; Duffy's
Catholicism 389; on baptism
388; church-goer 388, 435,
450, 485; on agnosticism 450,
485, 501, 506, 516–7, 568
Science: draws diagrams for
Hal's lectures 216, 260, 268,
272; translates German for
him 450; suggests *Lay Sermons* book 368; at Downe
221, 291, 294; scientific
widow 460, 483, 487–8; 'Evolution and Ethics' 604;
reads Tennyson at Downe
294; on Darwinism 267;
Tyndall on *Origin* 318–9; on
1860 BAAS meeting 276–7;
on ape-brain debate 295–7;
on Owen 277, 602; on Gladstone 544; on Salisbury 605;
on Tyndall and Eyre 352;
Tyndall 468, 604; on *Hume*
498; on *Physiography* 484;
on the stump 402; Huxley's
botany 551; Huxley's lecturing style 440, 478, 482; the
laboratory 418; Huxley's
Presidency of Royal Society
530–1; Liverpool 1870 385;
Lyell's funeral 455; Huxley
in Oxford 1894 605; begs
Huxley to cease controversy
587; refuses to publish rejoinder to A.Balfour 613
Huxley, Nettie (daughter) 322,
388, 483, 538, 540, 555,
571, 590
Huxley, Noel (son) 230–1, 251,
285–6, 295, 322, 379, 388,
455, 518, 523, 543, 568, 611
Huxley, Rachel (daughter) 304,

358, 450, 511, 537, 570,
610, 611
Huxley, Rachel (mother) 4–5,
10, 12, 14, 33, 39, 48, 54,
59–60, 63, 80, 86, 88, 90,
102, 103, 106–7, 126,
131–2, 146, 150, 163, 178–9
Huxley, Sophie (daughter-in-
law) 610
Huxley, Thomas (grandfather)
6, 570
Huxley, Thomas Henry
Personal:
Family origins 4, 570; in Ealing 3ff, 622–3; Coventry 6ff;
appearance 4, 18; bullied 6;
poverty 5, 17; affected by
death 25, 99, 117, 138, 143,
153; by cadaver 9; reminisces
about boyhood 473; schooling 4–6, 15, 16–19; learns the
morality of civil disobedience
10; self-educated 13
  Psychology: 4, 5, 7, 16, 25,
157, 163, 186, 192, 217,
226, 251, 253, 376; aesthetic
sense 90; alienation 78, 159,
182, 200, 247; ambition 19,
61, 84, 174, 361; artistic 4,
115; black moods, break-
downs and self-doubt 62, 65,
97, 99, 116, 155, 163, 172,
174, 178, 188, 192, 195,
409–10, 429, 534–9, 555,
619, 621; George Eliot on
186, 450, 621; loneliness
158; cynicism 7, 62, 68, 72,
117, 140, 157–9, 164–6,
171, 211, 228, 248, 293,
324, 369, 559, 560, 566,
580, 585, 621–2, 639; guilt-
ridden 13, 84; temper 4, 47,
67, 105, 140, 177–8, 195,
213, 230, 279, 290; tyrannizing 134; wit and sarcasm
115, 158, 186, 193, 204,
235, 339, 354, 404, 436–7,
444, 637; playful 436; irony
481, 637; worries about
pride 19, 25, 28, 84, 107,
140, 163; martial self-image
397; always fighting 621;
military bearing 580; Lecky
on 621; religious need to engage 621; roots of his lifelong
struggle 623; evangelical anger 621; Puritan righteousness 566, 580, 619, 624,
627–8; air of omniscience
630; and Victorian codes of
behaviour 620; need for uprightness 620; Beatrice Webb
on 540, 555, 619–21; on love
622; electric presence 621;
Lodge on 621; strain of madness 555; self-perceptions
620; 'mass of prophetism and
mysticism' 620

Medical education:
Apprenticed to Chandler 11;
to Cooke 9; Rotherhithe 11;
East London's hovels 3, 11;
Sydenham College 15–19,
441, 583, 623; Hoblyn's Prize
19; Apothecaries' medal 19,
25; Charing Cross Hospital
20–34; Wharton Jones 25;
Bachelor of Medicine exam
34; gold medals 34, 37; publishes on hair follicle 34; 'Huxley's Layer' 35; debts, 21,
35, 36, 38, 43, 53, 88, 123
Naval Travels:
Assistant Surgeon RN 36; at
Haslar Naval Hospital
38–45; Haslar museum 39;
HMS *Rattlesnake* 44ff; voyage 53–150; Madeira 55; Rio
de Janeiro 58; Cape colony
60; Mauritius 62; Tasmania
65; New South Wales 67ff;
New Guinea 112ff; New
Zealand 139; Falklands 141;
nostalgia for *Rattlesnake*
518, 563, 578–9, 584–5,
606, 610; daydreams of New
Guinea 569–70
Additional Assistant Surgeon
156; scratched from Navy
List 1854 198
London life:
Referee 180; proofs Carpenter's
Principles 180; translations 159,
183, 190–1; illustrates *Narrative*
158; contemplates emigrating
172–4, 202, 211; gold mining
speculations 172. Anonymous
Westminster reviewer 185, 190,
192–3, 195–6, 204–5, 208, 224;
subsequently writes for *Saturday
Review*; *Natural History Review*, *Reader*, *Nature*; *Contemporary Review*; *Nineteenth Century*; *Fortnightly Review*;
courted by editors 446, 487, 581
- *see* separate entries
  Long-distance walker 229,
232, 370; love of mountains
55; Alps 228ff - *see* Alps;
climbs Snowdon 290
Marriage and Family:
Meets Henrietta Heathorn
70; engaged 72–3, 88, 107;
delayed marriage 132–3; reunited with Nettie 211; marriage 207, 212–13, 376;
dredging honeymoon 212,
214, 530
  Birth of children: Noel
(1856) 230; Jessie (1858) 242;
Marian (1859) 285; Leonard
(1860) 289; Rachel (1862)
304; Nettie (1863) 322; Henry
(1865) 332; Ethel (1866) 348
  Family man 216; Huxley
as godfather 108, 154;

'young Jim' with the family 369; Katy (niece) joins them 322; Hal the 'lodger' 300, 333; Mrs Tait on Huxley as a husband 309; homes: lodgings 163, 172; 41 North Bank 155; 14 Waverley Place 207; Abbey Place 298, 377; uses Bence Jones' Folkestone house 295; their cook illiterate 334; overworked 200, 205; travels 4,000 miles in 1862 305; family's scarlet fever 286, 357; Noel's death 286; brother George's death 321; sells Royal Medal 322; with children 369, 377; holiday in Swanage 355; in Littlehampton 364; lack of leisure 323; Huxley ageing 243, 369, 370, 377

Home life 251, 388, 436, 450, 460, 464, 483–4, 537–8; Fiske on 436; out till all hours 488, 534; on baptism 388; sends Bible to godson Tom 403; called Pater 388; on Ellen's drunkenness 48, 242, 388, 464, 511, 582, 620; Mabel's 'wickedness' 464; need for propriety 464, 620; family warmth 620; relations in engineering 387, 442, 488–9; Polly's remarriage 388–9; plays golf 406–7; working holidays 406–7, 497

Move to 4 Marlborough Place 405, 414, 425–6, also 436, 441, 457, 460, 468, 492, 512, 516, 537, 571, 581, 589; wall photos 426; Tall Teas 404–5, 426, 436, 489, 492, 510, 512; Lizzie on *Lay Sermons* 390; Len at University College School 399, 488–9; children 388, 404–6, 436–7, 450, 467, 483–4, 488–9, 495, 511, 540, 569–70, 590; governesses 448; domestics 389, 441, 450, 502, 589, 610; novel reading 436–7; learns Russian 436; learns Greek 502; Wallers 437; George Eliot's co-habitation 450; Lyell's funeral 455–6; Jess' engagement 467, wedding 495; Tyndall's marriage 467–8

Contemplates trip to America 390–1, 441, 453, 463; *Nation* on 390; hosts Appleton 391; Hayden on 391; Nettie prepares 469; in America 1876 468–82; New York 470–1, 479–82; New-haven/Yale 471–3; New England/Harvard 474; Buffalo 474; Niagara 474; Nashville

475–7; meets Lizzie 463, 475; Baltimore/Johns Hopkins 463, 477–9; 'Sermon in Stone' 476; Washington 479; Philadelphia 479; *American Addresses* 484; Dakota town named 'Huxley' 533

Asleep at Royal Society 483; Len and Oxford 489, 501–2; Mady's diphtheria 495–6; chairs public health meeting 496; London Sanitary Protection Association 532; Marsh in London 492; newspaper correspondents 492–3; dines with Crown Prince 494; confidence trickster 494; to Penmaenmawr 497–8; faded but fascinating 498; ruled by his family 498; on Collier 502; Mady's marriage 502; Devon holidays 502, 511; The Club 505; worn out 507, 518; grandfather 507, 518, 543, 557, 606; silver wedding 510; on anniversaries 510; Lowell and copyright 510; Polly's drug addiction 511; daughters at Slade 404–5, 414, 450, 489, 502, 511, 540; Huxley at the Royal Academy 404, 426, 492, 511, 523, 629; presides over Artists Benevolent Institution dinner 522; Mady's art 511; day-trips with Spencer 515; Lake Windemere 515; Rolleston tragedy 516; takes Harry to Wales 518; work as President of Royal Society 530–1; at the Royal Court 525, 532; loss of Mady's baby 523; Joyce born 534; teaches Joyce astronomy 588; George Eliot's burial 526–7; breakdown and retirement 534, 538, 540; recuperates in Italy 537–9; Rachel's wedding 537, 570; Len's wedding 539; Oscar Wilde in house 540; winters in Bournemouth 542–3, 548, 562; Busk's death 551; Switzerland 551, 565; botany keeps away his blues 551; hears from brother William 553; Prince of Wales has him speak 553; Salters Company presents silver spoons 554; Nettie's singing 555; Polly punches him 557; Mady's madness and death 437, 522–3, 542, 555, 557–8; Huxley throws himself into 'Struggle' speech 558–61; leaves Marlborough Place 571

Boehm bust 515; Collier portraits 523, 580; Legros portrait 515; Roden portrait 492; Woolner bust 492

Move to Eastbourne 565, 569–70, 581–2, 600; Waller builds 'Hodeslea' 570; hangs photos 588–9; watches Salvationist scuffles 585; Ethel's marriage in Norway 569, 572; Deceased Wife's Sister question 569, 572; Nettie's marriage 569, 571; Harry in practice 569, 579; Jess writing for *Nineteenth Century* 570; writes autobiography 570, 588; Madeira with Harry 578–9; Harry engaged 579; visits Stonehenge 580; Ellen and Polly die 582; accepts membership of American Society for the Study and Cure of Inebriety 620; Ellen Busk dies 582

Hate mail 583, 610; Nettie wants him to give up controversy 587; the wonder of the universe 588; visits Downe 589; reminisces about Darwinian warfare 589; buys land 589; turns gardener 589, 590, 604; visitors 589–90; signs himself 'Dad' 590; Hirst's death 590; on Nettie's illness 590; his Privy Councillorship 593–5; Queen eyes him 594; Tennyson's funeral 595; loads himself with champagne at Cambridge 600; Jowett's death 600; Clark's death 600; thoughts on death 600–1; *Collected Essays* 601, 606; Tyndall's death 603–4; Owen's death and *Life*, 601–3; a piece of old china himself 606; dines with Prime Minister Rosebery 606; at Savoy on *Nature* anniversary 606; calm isolation 606; parody of *fin de siècle* society 609

Finances: debts 152, 168, 172, 174, 202, 217, 270, 298, 322; pay 151, 157, 162, 183, 185, 190, 195, 198–203, 206, 207, 212, 376; earnings in 1862 322; family banker 322, 387, 388, 464, 513, 557; Ellen's £60 allowances 322, 388, 464; Mabel's 10s a week 464; sends Lizzie cheques 190, 322; Hobhouse offers £100 a quarter 409; contractors' bills 425, 428; Tyndall loans £1,000 414, 425; Darwin's housemoving cheque 426; lawsuit 427–8; Arnold asks about royalties 427; collection for Huxley raises £2,100 428–30, 625; expenses 441; Nettie too poor to go to BAAS 441; appreciates extra pay 449, 514; £1,000 for summer Edinburgh course 460; Thomasson's £1,000 bequest 468, 625; £600 profit in America 482; Rich bequest 486, 514–15, 589; £700 a year Fisheries pay 514; £1,000 in Darwin's will 521; burden of Presidency of Royal Society 530–1; pension £1,200 541; £300 Civil List 541; pay for review articles 545, 571, 574, 579, 581; pays doctor £20 a year to treat Polly 557; inherits Rich's house 589; debt ended 589; mortgages paid off 589 *Illnesses*: 10, 203; dyspeptic 203, 205, 425, 542; headaches 217, 232; mumps 142; nervous palpitation 73; rheumatism 71, 333; overworking 404–6, 409, 417, 423, 425, 483–4, 511, 513–14, 518, 523, 530, 533–4; Dr Clark trading off Huxley 390, 431, 436; takes chloral 408; breakdowns 409–10, 429, 534, 537, 554–5, 619; recuperates in Egypt in 1872 410–16; at Vesuvius 416; regime 416–17, 421, 425, 431; drink 425; recuperates in Ilfracombe 425; diets 425, 429; recovers in Germany 431–2; reports of his death 439; burning out 505; sleep pattern 499; loss of teeth 507, 511, 534; 'fagged' 533–4; breakdown and retirement 534, 537; recuperates in Italy 537–9; tries quinine and strychnine 538; coca 539, 542; Webb on his breakdown 555; pleurisy 557, 562; heart condition 562, 565; deafness 566, 591; 'Agnosticism' perks him up 568–9; lung infection 610; bronchitis 610; heart attack, death 611; funeral 611–12, 642

Science as a career:
Problem of career 107, 123; science as vocation 181; applies to Toronto 168; Aberdeen 182; King's College 188; difficulty of obtaining a grant 151, 154, 156, 165, 167, 178, 180, 182, 183, 196, 198; justfying career in 'The Educational Value of the Natural History Sciences' (1854) 200
Professional strategy:
Against privilege - Dissenting ethos of his science: wants talent rewarded 12, 16, 31, 54, 62, 73, 83–4, 93, 108, 154–6,

158, 163, 169, 172, 177, 180, 188, 202, 226, 242, 261–2, 361, 385–6, 389, 408, 441, 446, 468, 482, 513, 543, 554, 556, 581, 589, 603, 618–19, 622–6, 631, 632–6; ousts those with dual calling 283; confrontational strategy 298, 308; professionalization 202, 327, 389–90, 392–3, 397, 404, 408, 418–20, 422, 425, 435, 437, 440, 442, 445, 449, 453, 456, 457, 458, 488, 489, 506, 526, 530, 545, 556, 568, 571, 573, 576–7, 587, 599, 617, 619, 622–32, 634, 636, 638–9, 641–2; imputes moral order to Nature 174, 200, 210, 288, 293, 345, 363; definition of science 395; fulfils religious need 407–8, 434, 468, 526–7, 624, 626, 629–32, 640

On a causal uniform nature 385, 386, 389, 392, 433–4, 442, 466, 468, 555–6, 568, 572, 589, 603–4, 607–8, 622–3, 625, 630–1; and agnosticism 385, 389, 391, 403–4, 408, 437, 456, 487, 525, 528, 541, 566–8, 603, 608, 622–5, 630–2; profile raising International Scientific Series 391, 496–7; 'Progress of Science' 548, 625; moots 'English Men of Science' 500; cultivates non-partisan image 453, 503, 529, 541, 576, 624–6, 631, 635–6; method of science 487; agnosticism synonymous with 567, 631–2; accountability 421–5, 457; and national interest 387, 397, 417, 422, 427, 435, 494–5, 625, 627, 633–4, 638–9, 643; and philanthropists 399; militarism and 396–7, 417, 443, 554, 632–6; Whitworth gun metaphor 261, 399, 623, 632–6; research ethos 387, 435, 442, 456, 477, 533, 540, 543, 627; specialization 572, 606, 629–30, 642; the word 'Scientist' 482, 509, 565, 630

On science at Cambridge 387, 398, 417–18, 439–40, 490–1, 501, 516, 523, 608; at Oxford 387, 396, 398, 417–18, 439–40, 489–90, 501–2, 516–17, 541, 579, 605–7; wants modern languages at Oxbridge 524

Territorial dispute with Church 397, 420, 435, 445, 456, 488, 568, 571, 572, 622–6, 632–4, 639; 'Science

and "Church Policy"' (1864) 331–2, 445; as character forming as Classics 387, 397, 405, 418, 439, 488, 493–4, 512–13, 524, 627; engages Arnold over Science v. Humanities 512, 523–4; 'Science and Culture' 512; Ruskin a eunuch 444; *Lay Sermons* 344, 368, 377, 390, 399, 403, 420, 434, 468, 625, 626; *Critiques and Addresses* 426, 430, 456
Scientific Society:
Professorships and posts: *see* Government School of Mines; Fullerian Professor, Royal Institution 212, 227, 347, 371, 401, 404, 507, 618, 629; Hunterian Professor, Royal College of Surgeons 305, 371; holds three professorships 347; Edinburgh University chair 448–9, 459–60, 469; Rector at Aberdeen 439; Governor of Owen's College, Manchester 408, 442; examiner in Physiology and Comparative Anatomy, London University 221, 222; examiner for University College 398; for Owen's College 408; examines 'Animal Physiology' for DSA 417, 442; examiner for War Department 221, 417, 633; for Exeter College, Oxford 417–18, 516; for Trinity College, Cambridge 490, 516; Edinburgh University 449; South Kensington 456. Councillor University College London 529, 562; London University Senate 533, 595–6, 606; Trustee of British Museum 531; offered Linacre Chair, Oxford 516; offered Mastership of University College, Oxford 517; offered $10,000 by Harvard 517

Learned Societies: Royal Society: Fellow 162, 406; Royal Medal 171, 182; Council 189, 215, 329; Biological Secretary 423–5, 441, 483, 505, 518; Polar committee 456–7; President 423, 530–2, 540, 542–3; his regime 532; resigns chair 542–3. Geological Society: Fellow 234; Council 233; Secretary 248, 255, 303; President 370. Linnean Society: 236, 245. Zoological Society: Vice-President 302. Ethnological Society: Council 321; President 371

Elected to Athenaeum 241
BAAS, Chairman of the

Zoology Section, 1862 307; President Liverpool 1870 375, 378, 385–6, 405–6; VP Sheffield 1879 503; *see* separate entries for yearly BAAS meetings

President of Marine Biological Association 533, 562, 578; Davis Lecturer at Zoological Society 495–6; chairs economic entomology 532; President of Quekett Microscopical Club 483

Elected to Imperial Academy in Breslau 236; Göttingen Royal Society 317; German academies 346; Société d'Anthropologie 346; St Petersburg's Imperial Academy 346; Microscopical Society of Giessen

Royal Commissions: Trawling and Fisheries (1862–5) 243, 305–6, 321, 323, 327; Contagious Diseases Acts (1870–1) 405; on Scientific Instruction (Devonshire) (1870–5) 388, 394, 397, 405, 418, 435, 456, 490; on Vivisection (1876) 458–62; Universities of Scotland (1876–8) 483; Medical Acts (1881–2) 515

Inspector of Fisheries 513–14, 518, 523, 533–4, 537, 540–1; at Home Office 511, 514, 534; Colonial Office 397–8; India Office 511

Teaching:
Joins School of Mines 199; palaeontology lectureship 201; *see* Government School of Mines; Naturalist with Geological Survey 207; *see* Department of Science and Art; Marlborough House; moves to South Kensington 394–5; laboratory ethos here 393–5, 418–21, 498, 543, 628; called the 'General' 339, 633; 'Science Schools' routine 419, 442, 510, 518–19; Royal Engineers patrol 396–7, 417, 554, 633; summer course in SK Museum (1871) 395–6; 1872 417–21; classroom persona 510; demonstrators 396–7, 417, 419, 442, 447, 490, 510, 629; trains schoolmasters 189–90, 272–3, 274, 327, 350, 368–9, 393–6, 418–21, 431, 447, 452–3, 455, 458, 628, 634; teaching microscopic techniques 396, 420; devises a combination microscope 491; *Course of Elementary Instruction in Practical Biology* (1875) 455; runs seven

courses in 1871 404; delivers 120 lectures a year 452–3; offered Directorship of Science at DSA 439; Professor of Biology at Normal School 517; Dean 517–18, 540, 551, 570; Honorary Dean 542; 1882 course 522–3; 1885 course 539–40; resigns from Normal School 538, 540; it becomes Royal College of Science 642

Students: Mivart's son 453; Foster's students help 490; Geddes 420; Jeffrey Parker 442; H.F.Osborn 510; H.G.Wells 539–40, 587, 609, 627, 642; last students 630

BAAS Committee on education (1866) 350; London School Board 401–6, 408–9, 410, 417; 'The School Boards' 402; Eton governing board 493–4, 530, 562; Westminster School 494; children's lectures 273, 369, 404; 'Physiography' (1869) 369; *Physiography* (1877) 484–5, 490, 498, 530, 639; textbooks 405–6, 425, 456; *Introductory Science Primer* (1880) 406, 456, 503, 506, 564; preface to Haeckel's *Freedom in Science and Teaching* 498; on evolution in school 498

Science
Comparative Anatomy: Archetypal body plans 69, 72, 174, 176, 181, 187, 190–1, 200, 223, 218, 226–7, 235, 244, 254, 258, 273, 315, 603; derides zoological idealism 184, 187–8, 218, 226, 244, 275, 306; vertebral theory of skull, 243–4; 'Croonian Lecture' (1858) 243; *Atlas of Comparative Osteology* (1864) 321; publishes Royal College of Surgeons lectures 321; *Lectures on the Elements of Comparative Anatomy* (1864) 323

On embryology 83, 90, 235, 244, 260, 265, 271; archetypal-circular geometry of nature 176, 223; derides functional explanation of structure 200, 227; classification 208: five subkingdoms 208; seven primary groups 315

Making of 'biology' 395, 419–21, 628; botany and zoology integrated 453; type system 420–1, 430–1, 453, 628; in morphological mainstream 421

On physiology 217, 221, 232, 300, 350, 398–9, 404, 417–19, 425, 430, 447, 484; 'First Principles of Physiology' (1861) 300; *Lessons in Elementary Physiology* (1866) 340, 425, 430, 484, 537, 621; on Cobbe and vivisection 457–62, 469, 487; Klein 462; Aristotle and the heart 503, 600; Harvey 487, 503, 600

Protoplasm 365, 367–8, 372, 380, 406, 427, 460, 471; 'On the Physical Basis of Life' (1869) 367, 440; *Bathybius* 365, 427, 460

Botany: 18–19, 395, 421, 430, 453, 551–2, 578, 589, 604; yeast 392–3, 421, 426; mould 392–3, 453, 467; *Penicillium* 392, 467; takes up gentians 551–2

Invertebrate anatomy:
Foundation membranes in coelenterates 83, 90, 208, 248, 254; new class 'Nematophora' 69, 83, 123, 167; human embryo homology of coelenterate membranes 90, 254, 452

Archetypal ascidian 181; mollusc 174, 176; siphonophore 69; papers 107, 123, 134, 145, 152; Men-of-war 61, 81, 152, 168; *Diphyes* 69, 69, 123, 152; jellyfish 82, 88, 152; *Trigonia* 73, 123; sea squirts 141, 161; oysters 523; molluscs 174, 176, 177, 188; Tusk Shells (*Dentalium*) 542; belemnites 491; *Spirula* 484, 491, 496; cyclopaedia article 190; *Oceanic Hydrozoa* (1859) 178, 243, 248, 257, 259; *Globigerina* and Chalk, 237, 365–6, 377, 427, 627; 'On a Piece of Chalk' (1868) 365; dissecting technique 323; *Anatomy of Invertebrated Animals* (1877) 469; crayfish 495–7, 511; *Crayfish* (1880) 497

For individual invertebrates, *see* separate entries
Palaeontology:
Moves into palaeontology 204, 218; on Cambrian-Silurian debate 204; view of geology 303; draws up 'Report on the Recent Changes in Level in the Bristol Channel' 229; disdains fossil curation 201; fossil record has no Christian meaning 205; debates Owen on palaeontology 229; on School of Mines fossil catalogues 219; courses on fossils 232; fossil

diles 248, 275; changing views of fossil succession 264; fossil fish 284, 303, 321, 355; Crossopterygians 284, 355, 465; *Pteraspis* 284; fossil amphibians 255, 300, 303, 321, 346, 355; *Stagonolepis* 248, 406, 452, 459; *Hyperodapedon* 255; turtle *Ceratochelys* 555; dinosaurs and the origin of birds 356–60, 377, 459, 472–3, 481, 484, 492, 504–5, 509, 518, 545, 625; mammal-like reptiles 504–5; *Glyptodon* 306; fossil horses 268, 401, 473, 481–2, 485–6, 509–10; Neanderthal man 299, 301, 304, 326–7; - *see* Evolution; entries for individual species

Anti-progressionist 176, 191, 204, 208, 215, 219, 222, 248, 255, 258, 303, 305; addresses to Geological Society on palaeontology and persistent types 303, 370; persistence of crocodiles 248; 'Persistent Types' 255, 259, 303, 358, 392, 427, 452, 481, 485–6, 587; attacks Carpenter's progressionism 219; origins 174; Palaeozoic man 192, 204, 248, 257; persistence of humans 257, 305; mankind an aberrant modification 191; adopts a more progressionist vision of life 226, 255–6, 258–9, 293–4, 356, 401, 473, 481–2, 485–6

Evolution

Meets Darwin 188; praise for him 195; goes to Downe in 1856 221; reviews Darwin's barnacle monographs 195, 235; reviews *Vestiges* 193, 213, 277; early views on transmutation 187, 193, 223, 225; 1856 lectures broach evolution 225; reviews Hooker and Wollaston 224; anti-utilitarian 200, 201, 216, 235–6, 246, 258, 271; on Darwin's fancy pigeons 226, 245, 255, 260, 264, 267–8, 310; disagrees with Darwin on embryology 224; classification 235; sunken continents 392; innate tendency to vary 486; saltation 256, 262, 392; reads pages of *Natural Selection* 234, 235; gets overview of natural selection 245; halfway house to Darwin's theory 255; reads *Origin* 257–60; difficulties with Natural Selection 188, 254, 258, 262, 269, 270–1, 303,

486, 508, 626; *Origin* explains persistent types 261; endorses Darwin's naturalism 262; ideological use of *Origin* 246, 259, 261, 271; reviews *Origin* 260–1, 263, 265–6, 273, 276; at Downe in 1860 273; Royal Institution lecture on *Origin* 259, 266–8; plebeianizes the *Origin* 310 - *see* On Our Knowledge; evolution's 'ladder' 293, 342; ecdyses metaphor for human progress 293; connects artificial and natural selection 310; makes 'angel' of natural selection 363; on Darwin's Copley Medal 329; defends Darwin against Sir W. Thomson 370; Darwin at School of Mines 354; on genealogy and Haeckel's *Generelle Morphologie* 349, 354–6, 360, 372; on 'phylum' 356; keeps evolution out of classroom 340, 420–1, 452–3, 491, 496, 508; social instincts and morality 564, 598; amoral Darwinian cosmos 597; growing ecological outlook 457; ice death of planet 560

On Grant 393, 420, 455; anti-Lamarckism 393, 420, 591; spontaneous generation/origin of life 392–3, 406; Bastian 392–3; Sir W. Thomson 406; Huxley's pre-Darwinian imagery 398, 508, 546–7; rewrites pre-Darwinian geology 507–8; on providential evolution 407, 556

Darwinians as a 'sect' 408, 624; on *Descent of Man* 400, 433; takes Lowe to Downe 422; Gladstone to Downe 487; 'Coming of Age of the "Origin of Species"' 507–8; protective of Darwin 509–10, 542; behind Butler's ostracism 509; introduces Darwin in class 510; on Darwin's LL.D. 491; Darwin's intellect 522, 539; Darwin's method 487; Darwin's death, burial 519–21, 531; obituary 563; 'Instinct' chapter 522; Darwin statue 542; chapter for Darwin's *Life* 'Reception of the Origin of Species' 552

Codifying evolution 393; lectures on in Edinburgh 459; at Royal Institution 401, 507, 629; London Institution 491; in America 476–7, 480–2; Cambridge accepts 491

'Evolution' in *Encyclopae-*

dia Britannica 486; privately draws evolutionary trees 491–2, 496–7, 504; gets Kovalevskii's paper into *Philosophical Transactions* 424–5; Malthusian struggle in man 529, 559–61, 563–5, 573–7, 584, 597–9, 626, 635–6, *see* Social Darwinism

Evolution a fact 474, 486; palaeontology and evolution 357–60, 377, 401, 424, 452, 459, 472ff, 484, 491, 504–5, 509–10; Zadig and retrospective prophecy 510; 'living fossils' 392, 427

Phylogenies: origin of life 392–3, 406; phylogeny of crustaceans 496–7; molluscs 491; *Amphioxus* 452; sea squirts and the origin of vertebrates 451–2; lungfish and origin of amphibians 465, 509; crocodile evolution 406, 452, 459; dinosaur origin of birds 356–60, 377, 459, 472–3, 481, 484, 492, 504–5, 509, 518, 545, 625; bird family trees 356; bird-reptile group 'Sauropsida' 355–6, 504, 518; *Archaeopteryx* 358; rebuilds dinosaurs as bipeds 358; mammal ancestry 452, 492, 504–6, 545–6; horse evolution 268, 401, 473, 481–2, 485–6, 509–10; Darwinian programme on dogs 497; timing of 486; evolution of gentians 551; *see* Humans and apes below

On Weismann 601; responds to Salisbury on evolution 605–6; retrospective of evolution in *Nature* 606

Evolution and ethics 507, 508, 522, 524, 559–61, 565, 576–8, 592, 596–9, 604, 622, 635–6; Romanes 591–2, 595, 596–9; 'Evolution and Ethics' 592, 597–9, 604, 622, 636

Humans and apes:

Ideological reason for tackling human evolution 253; similar human and animal mental faculties 241; religious implications 252; mankind's ape ancestry 267, 269, 271, 290–305, 399, 413, 431, 486, 508, 598, 606–7, 625, 627–8, 631; 'The Distinctive Characters of Man' (1858) 240; Royal Institution lecture (1858) on gorilla and human brains 276; 'On the Zoological Relations of Man' (1861) 281; ape-brain debate with Owen 238–40,

276, 282–3, 290, 295–7, 307–8, 316–7, 433, 504; dissects spider monkey 302; Neanderthal man 299, 301, 304, 326–7; cast of brain 326; on Engis skull 301; 'On the Fossil Remains of Man' 301; on *Pithecanthropus* 606–7; *Evidence as to Man's Place in Nature* (1863) 304ff
Human Races:
On human races 205, 333, 347–8, 397–8, 498, 580–1; Anthropological/Ethnological Society hatreds 320–1, 333, 343–4, 351, 353; scorns philanthropy 324; on race 210, 325, 334, 521, 550; pioneers skull bisecting techniques 301, 333; obtains Patagonian skulls 347; Fuegian skulls 347; on 'persistent' races 344; calls them 'stocks' 344; supports American Union 324; against slavery 205, 325; in *Antislavery Reporter* 352; attacked by racists 320; on Jamaica Committee 351–2; 'Emancipation—Black and White' (1865) 334; 'The Races of Mankind' (1865) 333; on Aryans 580–1; Nile geology and military strategy 530; joins Egypt Exploration Fund 547; later views on primitive society 529, 564–5, 574–5, 591, 598; studies Arctic skeleton 418; Ice-Age skeleton 431
On human automatism 440–1, 444–7, 450, 519, 623; mind an epiphenomenon 409, 433, 441, 445; mechanical equivalent of consciousness 441; 'The Physiology of Sensation' (1857) 232; 'On the Phenomena of Life as Motion and Consciousness' 400; 'On the Hypothesis that Animals are Automata' 446, 450, 519; scientific determinism 389–90, 433–4, 440–1, 444–7, 496, 541, 544, 555–6, 624–5; on Spinoza 436, 464
Religion and Theology:
3, 8, 63, 73, 75–6, 79, 81, 86, 104, 197, 252–3, 285, 331–2, 345, 372–3; evangelical 13, 285, 181; Calvinism 75, 200; Puritan 8, 14, 280, 285, 340, 345, 366; a Sadducee 166, 204; New Reformation 4, 253, 260, 270, 293, 367, 408, 547, 571, 572, 625, 638; military metaphor/martial imagery 104, 269, 331, 397, 554, 632–6;

against orthodoxy 169, 276 - see Disraeli, B., Wilberforce, S.; attacks 'Parsonism' 253, 269, 271; lectures clergy at Sion House 364; aims remarks at bishops in audience 268; on Bible's moral truths 252; on Genesis 253, 262; on biblical chronology 364; on immortality 288; on moral government of the world 288; on prayer 289; on Unknowable 285, 319, 332, 345, 374; on true religion 331; religion distinct from theology 7, 79, 186, 252–3, 285, 487, 498, 547, 631; a new rationale for belief 345; avoids religion in class 340; apostate vicars 434–5, 526; Lord Coleridge, Anglicanism no longer law of land 526, 573, 641–2; religious press sneer 308, 314; his 'Priesthood of Science' 365, 434, 626–8; dubbed 'Pope Huxley' 375; unpublished sectarian reviews 409; on disestablishment 385–6; clings to radical sectarianism in old age 630; his 'Christianity' 388; Lizzie on *Lay Sermons* 390; relativistic 622; Tennyson on 487; Association of Liberal Thinkers 501; liberal Anglican alliances: *see* Arnold, M.; Bradley, G.; Brodrick, G.; Christian Socialists; Colenso, J.W.; *Essays and Reviews*; Farrar, F.; Jowett, B.; Kingsley, C.; Moore, A.; Stanley, A.
On Creation 225, 256, 424–5, 480–1, 507–8, 567–8, 579; caricature of Creationists 256, 274; polarizing options Evolution or Creation 253, 256, 274, 366
Genesis and Miracles: v. Gladstone on Genesis 466, 544–6, 550, 567, 571–2, 582, 587, 590, 594–5; 'Interpreters of Genesis...' 545; 'Mr Gladstone and Genesis' 546; Biblical criticism 480, 540, 546–7, 567, 571, 573, 580, 587, 593; 'Evolution of Theology' 164–6, 567; 'Natural History of Christianity' 547, 567; Flood 567, 579–80, 587; Babylonian fables 580; 'Lights of the Church...' 580; Dawson's Scripturalism 567; Gadarene Swine 567–8, 570–1, 573, 580, 582, 588; and property rights 573, 582; miracles 390, 466, 498, 567–9, 572,

579, 630; Jesus and Nazarenes 567, 571, 580; Resurrection 464, 568; Morley refuses Resurrection paper 466; supernaturalism and policing 568; young scientists not copying his public anti-Scripturalism 572; *Review of Reviews* on 573; *Essays upon Some Controverted Questions* 590–1, 592–3, 595
On Argyll 555–6, 587, 590; Liddon 555–6, 580; law as Divine Will 555–6; 'Pseudo-Scientific Realism' 556; higher design 434
Unitarians: Priestley 443–4; Southwood Smith 10, 11, 14, 200, 598, 623, 625; Universalist Church 625; heterodox Hackney 402; *see* Unitarians
Bible-reading in schools 403, 498, 580; among workers 639–40
At Metaphysical Society 373, 389–90, 400, 509, 567; Huxley's Presidency 409, 425, 465; 'Has a Frog a Soul?' 390; on the Resurrection 464, 465–7
Anti-Catholicism: visits Catholic seminary 341; Cardinal Wiseman 331; Pope Pius IX 331; Mivart 340–1, 368, 392, 396, 400, 407–9, 453–4, 461, 509, 542, 545, 553, 598, 624; 'Mr. Darwin's Critics' 407; Duffy's Catholicism 389; at Vatican 538; Newman on 466, 552–3, 572; Lilly 552, 568; 'Science and Morals' 552; Mallock 568; scholasticism 407; books in his condemned cell 436; also 445, 464, 538, 549–50, 607, 619–20
Salvation Army 583–6; Stead 584; Mrs Crawshaw 585
Spiritualism 192, 209, 437–8, 608–9; perfects spirit raps 566; at Wedgwood séance 438
Atheists: 285, 320, 346; Bradlaugh 500, 528–9; Foote 525–6, 641; on freethought 501; and free love 527, 529, 552; secular State education 580; funds secular societies 580; religious ideas as living fossils 581; hardens against Christianity 580
Russian Orthodox Church 633; Islam 29ff, 633; Buddhism 598
Agnosticism
Early scepticism 8, 75–6, 79, 86–7, 132, 154, 159–60,

165–6, 168–9, 185–6, 204, 210, 228, 252–3, 285–7, 293, 307–8, 319, 331–2, 345–6, 367, 373–5; 'sin of faith' 184, 288, 340, 345, 346, 385, 624; agnosticism 374, 378, 389, 391, 456, 527–8, 566–72, 623–5, 630–2; agnosticism and Dissent 385–6, 407–8, 468, 556, 568, 622–6, 630–2; and scientific method 567, 631–2; and naturalism 391, 408, 466, 572, 591, 607–8; and materialism 552; and evidence 456, 498, 499, 541, 553, 566, 568, 572, 625, 630–1; contrasted to secularism 403–4; and Positivism 456, 500, 567; new morality of 435, 456, 487, 540–1, 553, 568, 590, 608, 625, 631; Buckley wants book on 500–1; demands family propriety 388–9, 526–7, 620; and Hume 497–500; *Hume* 499; neutral image 389–90, 408, 541, 595, 624, 631; and Church Congress 1888 567, 607; Wace 567, 570, 590; Watts' agnostics 527–8, 566–7, 580; agnostics use workers' weapons 587; funds *Agnostic Journal* 580; 'Agnosticism' 184–6, 570, 610; 'Agnosticism: A Rejoinder' 571; 'Agnosticism and Christianity' 572; and A. Balfour 607–10; 'Mr. Balfour's Attack on Agnosticism' 609
Talks/Essays:
Popularizer 175–6, 179–80, 199, 208–10, 231, 252, 292–4, 309, 333–4, 344–5, 362, 391, 401, 405–6, 428, 491, 503, 571, 636–8; Lankester on 637; *Daily News* on 637; L. Stephen on 637
Prose: tailored to audience 208–11, 252, 292–3, 344–5, 362–3, 367, 425, 440, 444–5, 459, 479, 503, 591, 618, 627–9, 636–8; 'plebeian' 388; proletarian theatre 637; 'masculine' 620, 626; agnosticism and pain 626; essays best sellers 367; as an essayist 377; disguising message 601; use of parable 510, 552–3, 560, 637–8; drama 637; lecturing style 339, 366; like revivalist meetings 345; greatest virtuoso 601; brilliance 597; Swiftian 609; rapier-like 491, 605, 608, 619, 621; and Victorian codes of behaviour 620; lec-

turing style 444, 480; simulated modesty 444; 'telepathic' 440, 636; Hooker on 407–8; air of omniscience 630
Working class talks:
208–9, 231, 252, 292, 309, 333, 362, 376, 404, 440–1, 456, 488, 496, 523, 618, 638–40; on mankind's animal ancestry (1859) 252; on men and apes 292, 300, 313; on evolution 309; on birds and reptiles 355; on ethnology at the Mechanics' Institute 353; 'Sunday Evenings for the People' (1866) 344; at Norwich 1868 366; on automatism 440–1; crustaceans 496; eels 523; projects lectures on Bible 639; on working class political power 362; piracy of his 1862 lectures 310; Marx on his lectures 313; Dissenting image of science 252; workers reactions to 333, 440–1, 638–40; dialectical relationship with workers 211; chess match metaphor 362; description of audience 373, 440, 639; swings masses behind Darwinian professionals 362, 440, 576, 638–40; Sparks 640; on *Hume* 499–500; Howell 640; dispenser wills body to Huxley 640, *see* Working Classes
Working classes missing from history of science 638; School Board and 401–2; Huxley Principal of South London Working Men's College 361–2, 387, 388, 510; resigns 517; Working Men's Club 488; at Westminster Deanery 483; Mechanics Institutes 639, 641
Coalition with workers collapses 440–1, 561, 576–8, 638, 641–2; held to their station 625, 628, 641–2; *see* Social Darwinism
Social Darwinism:
Phrase coined c.1890 575, 635; repoliticizes Darwin's Malthusian struggle 534, 558–61, 563, 574–8, 599, 626, 634–6, 641; 'Struggle for Existence in Human Society' 559–60, 563–4; policing function 560, 575–6, 607, 625, 635–6, 638, 641; overpopulation 559, 561, 565, 575; on birth control 528–9, 575; Ishtar 560; Darwinian image of war 530, 554, 558; and charity 586; industrial

competition as Darwinian warfare 553–4, 559–61, 593, 635; H.G.Wells on 587; Christians on 560–1; cynicism attacked 560–1; v. Kropotkin's mutualism 564–5, 575; socialists attack 554, 560, 573, 575–7, 597, 641; nationalizes 'war' metaphor 635–6; no faith in eugenics 575; governments cannot control social Darwinian forces 575, 635–6; refuses to sign moratorium on arms race 635
Falls out with Spencer on State intervention 563, 573–4, 575–6, 578, 591–2, 598; stops proofing Spencer's *Autobiography* 573; on Spencer's *a priorism* 573, 576, 591
National Politics:
See Competition; Meritocracy; Democracy; Liberalism. A Liberal Unionist 544, 549–50, 572, 595, 607, 641; a Chamberlainite 442–4, 512–13, 532, 549–50, 563, 565, 572, 578, 624, 641; Chamberlain on Deceased Wife's Sister Bill 572; on state intervention 443, *see* Falls out with Spencer above; compulsory vaccination 511; free Public Libraries 556–7; rates for libraries and education 556–8, 560, 563, 573; on municipal politics 408, 442–4, 641; town halls as 'laboratories' of politics 641; strong leaders needed 575, 578, 641; Benthamism 575; on monarchy 493; 'Royal' prefix for societies 532
Home Rule and the Irish 389, 444, 514, 544–6, 549–50, 582, 592, 593, 595, 607, 641; would vote Tory 546; Parnell 550, 592
And Gladstone 388, 390, 394, 396, 408, 409, 421–3, 461, 466, 487, 513–14, 532, 539, 541, 544–6, 549–50, 567, 571, 582, 587, 590–6; Disraeli 331, 339, 413, 440, 459, 493, 617, 632; Goschen 394, 423, 554; Lowe 410, 422; Ayrton 421–5; Harcourt 513–14; Granville 271, 533; Iddesleigh (Northcote) 375–6, 541; Hartington 554, 572; Salisbury 435, 572, 592–5, 605–7; Rosebery 518, 606; A.Balfour 607–10
War, imperialism: 398, 492–3, 553, 584–5; patriotism 252, 361; joins Volun-

teers 268, 284; on Tennyson 268, 294, 341; on Schamyl's war against Russians 196, 633; Franco-Prussian war 379, 387, 400; Zulu war 492–3; Afghan war 493; jingoism 493; Suez 530; Gordon's massacre 538–9; offered trip to India 439; German industrial threat 387–8, 395, 427, 553, 593, 635–6

On socialism 75, 184–6, 209–10, 293, 310, 317–8, 361, 374, 404, 440, 443, 447, 451, 458, 479, 500, 501, 507, 513, 548–9, 553–4, 559–61, 568, 573–8, 583–6, 594–7, 599, 607, 626, 629, 634–6, 638–41; Commune 500; Robert Owen 404; Holyoake 403–4, 434, 500, 556, 587–8, 626; in 'Black Monday' riot 548, 597; Land Nationalization 513, 548, 573–6; 'earth hunger' 548; Wallace 443, 450, 486, 513, 548, 574–5, 599; Henry George 513, 574–5, 577; 'Rousseau and Rousseauism' 574; 'On the Natural Inequality of Men' 574–5; French translation to meet labour unrest 575; Crane on 641; Kropotkin on 564–5, 575, 599; pastry cook 576–7; *Commonweal* 577; Huxley attacked 576–7; 'Natural Rights and Political Rights' 577; 'Government: Anarchy or Regimentation' 578; and Salvation Army 583–6; London County Council 586; new unionism 590; bus strikes 590
Technical Education and Industrialism
Befriends industrialists 385–7, 429, 442, 468, 469, 488–9, 569, 633–4; Armstrong 429, 442, 469, 488, 506, 522, 532, 545, 569, 587, 634; Ashton 386, 430; Whitworth 386–7, 429, 506, 633–4; May 8, 10, 319, 488; Noble 488, 634; in Birmingham 408, 442–3, 512–13, 624; Bradford 393; Leeds 393; Manchester 386–7, 408, 430, 442, 557–60, 592, 640; Sheffield 387, 503; on German industrial research 387; President of the Birmingham and Midland Institute 443; 'Duties of the State', retitled 'Administrative Nihilism' 443–4, 576; 'Technical Education' 488; report for livery compa-

nies 488; industrial 'war' and technical education 553–4, 559–60, 632–6; theoretical bent of technical education 488; Crane on 641; City and Guilds Institution 506, 542, 554; at Mason's College 512–13; on Imperial Institute 553–4; Manchester raising taxes for technical education 557–8, 560; technical change breaking apprenticeship system 560
Woman Question: see Women
Honours/Awards:
Despises State honours 441, 541, 593; rumour of honours 531; arranges knighthoods for scientists 531, 642; Swedish Order of the North Star 431–2; Académie Française 487; honorary doctorate from Edinburgh 346; Hon. LL.D. Cambridge 501, Dublin 498; DCL Oxford 398, 541; Freemen of the City of London 532; Royal Society's Royal Medal 565, Copley 565, Darwin Medal 606; Privy Councillor 541–2, 593–5
Huxley, William (brother) 5, 33, 476, 553
Huxley, town 533
Huxley Island, Louisiade 122
Hyde Park 151, 276, 316
Hydra 69, 83, 126, 168, 175
Hydroids 145
Hyndman, H. 576
Hyperodapedon 255
Hypnotism 557
Hysteria 522, 523, 534, 557

Ibsen, H. 609
Ice Ages 474, 508, 581, 607
Ichthyosaurs 309
Iddesleigh, Lord 541
Idealism 152, 174, 187–8, 213, 232, 244, 305–6, 505
Idylls of the King (Tennyson) 268, 595
Iguanodon 358
Ilfracombe 425
Iliad (Homer) 466
Ilkley 257–8, 263
Illiteracy, his cook's 334
Illustrated London News 385, 511, 637
Illustrious, HMS 196
Immortality 9, 75, 239, 266, 288, 341, 379, 390, 499, 601, 620, 643
Imperial Academy, St Petersburg 346
Imperial Academy of Naturalists, Breslau 236
Imperial College, London 554

Imperial Institute 553, 554
Imperial Rome 454, 609
Imperialism 41, 44–5, 72, 122, 125, 167–8, 315, 326, 386, 394, 397–8, 413, 441, 492–3, 501, 504, 515, 521, 539, 541, 550, 552–4, 560, 570, 584, 623, 628; and human progress 197; geological 153; zoological 45, 227, 302, 347, 377
Impregnable Rock of Holy Scripture (Gladstone) 582, 594
In Darkest England and the Way Out (Booth) 583–5
Income tax, British 202; American 323
Independent Labour Party 592, 596
Independents 8, 624
India 44, 59, 62–5, 151, 185, 233, 347, 485, 493, 550, 584; 'Mutiny' 233
India Office 511
Indians, South American 539
Individuality, animal 60, 65, 126, 145, 160, 165, 175, 179, 208
Industry, industrialists 31, 45, 120, 160, 164, 177, 187, 191, 201, 220, 239, 261, 300, 312, 327, 333, 364, 428, 438, 475, 495, 509, 522; competition 387, 422, 553–4, 559–61, 565, 587, 593, 635; support Huxley 428–9, 468, 625, 634; finance science 386, 397, 423, 442, 512, 532, 633–4; Huxley's friends 386–7, 442, 468–9, 488–9, 503, 569, 587, 634; Huxley trains 404, 418, 470, 503, 506, 512–13, 517, 543, 553–4, 557, 575, 627, 628, 632, 634, 638; Oxbridge disdains 387, 543; science and 385, 433, 444–5, 488, 512–13, 543, 548, 554–5, 575, 603, 622–2, 633–5; social rise 386, 469, 618, 622–5, 642
Inequality, human 574–7
Inferno (Dante) 100, 101, 104
Ingham 91
Inheritance of acquired characteristics 244, 591
Inner passage, Coral Sea 44, 74, 81, 92, 96
Innisfail 97
Inns of Court 202
Inquisition 538
'Inquisition: Waiting for the Accused', painting 580
Insectivorous plants 453
Insects 89, 451; fossil 544
Inspectors, DSA 417, 633, 640

Inspectorship of Fisheries 514, 518, 540
Instinct 71, 234, 239; morality evolves from 399–400, 499, 522, 564–5, 598
Intellectuals, emerging 378
Interlaken 228
International Scientific Series 391, 456, 496, 639
International, The 564
Introductory Essay on the Flora of New Zealand (Hooker) 225
Introductory Science Primer (Huxley) 406, 456, 503, 506
Ipswich 166, 167
Ireland, Irish 45, 49, 55, 68, 142, 161, 166, 206, 229, 296, 305, 346, 351, 389, 444, 445, 498, 514, 541, 543–4, 546, 548, 549–50, 582, 588, 589, 592, 607
Irish fossils 346
Iron and Steel Institute 388
Isaiah 547
Ishtar 560
Islam 196, 411, 633
Isle of Wight 246, 305
Israelites, polytheistic 546
Italy, Italian 57, 92, 100, 162, 261, 313, 330–1, 341, 349, 355, 368, 537

Jackey Jackey (aborigine) 92, 109, 110
Jacyna, L.S. 623
Jahvah 547
Jail, for blasphemy 20–1, 525–6, 587, 641, 642
Jam makers 362
Jamaica 32, 351
Jamberoo, New South Wales 72
James, H. 327, 510, 612
Jameson, R. 195, 199
Jane Eyre (Brontë) 158
Japan 460
Japanese students 334
Jardine, Lady 469
Java Man 607
Jellyfish 34, 45, 54, 56, 59–61, 63, 69, 74, 78, 81–3, 88, 90, 92–3, 99, 104, 112, 117, 123, 145, 170, 208, 228, 248, 254, 257, 354, 458
Jena 349–50, 359, 465, 497
Jenkin, F. 370
Jeremiah 547
Jerusalem 165
Jesuits 341
Jeune, F. 276–7, 280
Jewish Law 567
Jews 165, 253, 330, 364, 369, 449, 501, 526, 571, 580
Jex-Blake, S. 448–9
Jingoism 493
Joannet Island, Louisiade 116
John Bull 45
John Bull (pseudonym) 443

Johns Hopkins University 463, 95–7
Johnson, Dr 23, 46, 505, 570, 608
Jonah 579, 582
Jones, B. 414
Jones, T.W. 25–8, 33–5, 37–9, 179, 195, 399
Joshua 444
Journal (Linnean Society) 212, 246
Journal of Anatomy and Physiology 346
Journal of Researches (Darwin) 62, 67
Jowett, Revd B. 398, 489, 501–2, 515–16, 524, 567, 590, 596, 600
Jubilee 548, 553, 625
Jubilee Singers 476
Judiciary, Dissenting inroads 253
Jurassic fossils 153, 229, 257, 306, 358–9, 491, 504, 543–4, 546
Juries, experts on 397

Kabul 492
Kalisch, M. 364
Kangaroo 98
Kansas 472
Kant, I., 466
Kapital (Marx) 548, 576
Karnak 414
Karroo 233, 504
Kean, E. 30
Keats, J. 91, 180
Keith, A. 607
Kelvin, Lord 593, 612; *see* Thomson, Sir W.
Kennedy, E. 92, 94–6, 99, 101–3, 108–10, 112, 124–5, 144
Kentucky 470, 477
Keppel Island 79
Kew Gardens 36, 167, 212, 327, 342, 421–3, 495, 525, 529, 543, 551, 581, 589, 604
Khartoum 538, 541, 544
Khedive, Egyptian 412
Khyber Pass tribes 493
Kidd, B. 603, 617
Kidi Kidi river, New Zealand 139
Kindergarten, in Huxley's college 362
King crabs 219
King, P.G. 71, 563
King, P.P. 48, 70, 89
King, Revd R. 48, 64, 70, 130, 133, 314, 563
King William's Sound 418
King's College London 152, 164, 188, 209, 396
King's Cross station 151
Kingfishers 100, 102, 125
Kingsley, F. 455
Kingsley, Revd C. 208–10,

218, 263, 285, 288–9, 304, 307, 313, 319, 320, 351–2, 364, 373, 455, 560, 568, 598, 601
Kiwis 359, 518
Klein, E. 462, 464
Knight, Eliza (cousin) 12, 40, 146
Knighthoods for scientists 431–2, 441, 484, 486, 531, 545, 567, 642
Knowledge, a commodity 394, 543; democratizing 310, 363, *see* Science
Knowles, J. 373, 402, 404–5, 407, 410, 414, 426, 428, 446, 461, 464, 487, 500, 545–7, 558, 564, 567, 570–2, 574–7, 581, 584, 586, 608, 613; 'Influence upon Morality of a Decline in Religious Belief' 487
Knox, R. 25, 27, 37, 38, 210
Kölliker, A. 183
Kom Ombo, Egypt 415
Königgrätz, Battle of 349–50
Königsberg 244
Kovalevskii, A. 436, 451
Kovalevskii, V. 318, 400–1, 424, 439, 451, 473
Kropotkin, P. 564–5, 575, 581, 596, 599, 641; 'Mutual Aid among Animals' 564
Krupp 635
Kurna, Egypt 415

La Scala 538
Laboratories 393–6, 398, 416, 418–20, 433, 451–2, 455–9, 469, 471, 479, 488, 490, 498, 503, 510, 518, 523, 533–4, 542, 543, 555, 562, 578, 608, 612, 628–30, 641
Labour Army 586
Labyrinthodont 300, 303, 321, 355
Ladies College, Bedford Square 272
Ladies' London Emancipation Society 326
Laelaps 359
Laing, S. 566
Lake Maggiore 538
Lake Tanganyika 413
Lake Victoria 413
Lake Windermere 515
Lamarck, J.-B., Lamarckians 29, 89–90, 209, 232, 239, 252–3, 292, 393, 420, 455, 509, 591, 638
Lamlash Bay, Arran 257
Lamp-shell (brachiopods) 59, 213, 267
Lampreys 452
Lancet 24, 26, 31, 43, 53, 317
Land nationalization 443, 513, 548, 573–6

Land Nationalisation Society 513, 548
Language, evolution 350; relationship of words 199
Lankester, Edwin 159–60, 165, 168, 170, 202, 212, 267, 387, 396, 417
Lankester, E. Ray 159, 396, 408, 416–19, 438, 452, 455, 501, 518, 533, 543, 587, 595, 612, 637
Lankester, P. 160, 212, 396
Large genera 234
Larks 283
Larvae 112, 126, 170, 175, 196, 257, 355, 416, 451–2, 490
Latin 198, 201, 270, 350, 512
Laughing gas 511
Launceston, Tasmania 82
Laurent, J. 639
Law of correlation 227
Law of Population (Besant) 528
Lawrence, Lord 410
Laws of Nature, *see* Natural Law
Lay Sermons (Huxley) 368, 377, 390, 399, 403, 420, 434, 456, 468, 625, 626, 639
Le Puy museum 431
Leader 160, 184, 186, 191, 209, 345
Leather traders 362
Lebanon 287
Lecky, W. 342, 612, 621
Lectures on Man (Vogt) 317
Lectures on the Elements of Comparative Anatomy (Huxley) 323
Lectures on the . . . Invertebrate Animals (Owen) 213, 218
Lectures on the . . . Vertebrate Animals (Owen) 42
Lee, General 334
Leeds 393, 548, 625; University 488
Legal protection to non-Christian faiths 573
Légion d'Honneur, Owen's 239
Legros, A. 515
Leidy, J. 479
Leipzig 349, 365
Lemur 276, 340
Lepas 214
Lepidosiren 258
Lessons in Elementary Physiology (Huxley) 340, 425, 430, 484, 537, 621
Letters on the Laws of Man's Nature (Martineau and Atkinson) 185
Leuckart, R. 69, 167
Leviticus 569
Lewes, G.H. 93, 160, 186–7, 189, 191, 193, 209, 329, 345, 372, 450, 526, 611

Liberal Unionists 549, 554, 572, 592, 595, 607, 641
Liberalism, Liberals 41, 143, 156, 190, 260–1, 268, 276–8, 280, 283, 297–8, 306, 313, 328–31, 334, 340, 343, 349–50, 352, 372–3, 394, 487, 514, 520, 545, 554, 590, 592, 593, 597, 606, 607; attacks on it, 320, 328, 330–1; and Darwinism 261, 268, 349; and women's rights 334; liberal Anglicans, 41–2, 276–8, 280, 297–8, 306, 328–30, *see* Christian Socialists, *Essays and Reviews*, Stanley, A.
Liberty, Equality and Fraternity (Stephen) 430
Liberty Review 612
Libraries 573, 578; free 556
Licensing bodies, medical 515
Licensing, for vivisection 458
Liddell, H. 276
Liddon, Revd H.P. 580
Life and Letters of Charles Darwin (F.Darwin) 552
Life of Jesus (Strauss) 185
Life of Richard Owen (Owen) 601–3
Light Brigade 202
Light, electric 471, 512, 581, 589
Lightman, B. 624
Lignite 326
Lilly, W.S. 552–3, 568
Limits of Religious Thought (Mansel) 247, 285
Linacre Chair, Oxford 275, 516
Lincoln, A, 324, 479
Lincoln's Inn Fields 30, 323, 339, *see* Royal College of Surgeons
Lincolnshire, Darwin's farm 222
Lind, J. 300
Lindley, J. 18, 30
Lingula 78, 255
Linnean Society, 62, 69, 81, 123, 152, 212, 236, 238, 245–6, 522, 552
Lion 227
Lisson Grove 285
Lister, Sir J. 612
Literary Gazette 168, 206
Literary Papers (Forbes) 248
Literature, humanizing 512
Littlehampton 364
Liverpool 168, 240, 375, 378, 385, 625
Liverpool Mercury 378
Lives and Letters, Victorian 618
Living fossil 78, 255, 259, 392, 427, 581
Livingstone, D. 231, 272, 292, 413

Lizard Island 100
Lizard, supposed Devonian fossil 247
Llamas 223
Loades, A. 634
Lobe-fin fish 465, *see* Crossopterygian
Lobster 274, 496, 511, 514
Locarno 538
Lockyer, N. 330, 343, 372, 394, 460, 605
Lodge, O. 621
London and Brighton Railway 566
London-Birmingham railway 8
London County Council 586
London Hospital 436
London Institution 199, 202, 208, 369, 404, 409, 491
London Investigator 210
London, Rotherhithe 3, 11–15; West End 11, 151; Euston Place 15, 20; Chelsea 18; Charing Cross 22–6; Strand 22–3; Trafalgar Square 23, 151; Drury Lane 23, 30–1; Hyde Park 151; Regent's Park 155ff, 207ff; Piccadilly 162ff; Finsbury 199; Blackfriars Road, Southwark 361–3; Thames Embankment 377; South Kensington 377, 394ff; size 11, 151, 327; commuters, traffic jams 151, 233, 327; sprawling suburbs 327
London Sanitary Protection Association 532
London School Board 401, 404–5, 408, 410, 417, 498, 541, 619
London School of Medicine for Women 449
London Stereoscopic and Photographic Company 398
London Symphony Orchestra 555
London University 18, 34, 206, 221–2, 236, 267, 334, 449, 462, 489, 520, 533, 544, 595, 606
Longfellow, H.W. 441
Lord Derby 439
Lord Mayor of London 439
Lord Privy Seal 326
Lord's Day Observance Society 346
Lost worlds 642
Lot 555, 579
Louis Napoleon 102, 130, 261, 268–9, 400
Louisiade archipelago 44, 112, 129, 185
Lourdes 566
Lovely wrens 125
Low Island 99
Lowe, R. 410, 422
Lowell, J. 510, 520

Lubbock, J. 222, 279, 284, 298–9, 313, 321, 327–9, 329, 341–4, 361, 363, 373, 375, 378, 381, 388, 394, 399, 402, 422, 429, 458, 487, 520, 521, 550
Lubbock, Sir J. (Snr) 222
Lucasian Professor of Mathematics, Cambridge 424
Lucretius 230, 595
Lungfish 233, 247, 258, 303, 355, 465, 506, 509
Lungs, Devonian fish with 284, see Crossopterygian
Lungs, sauropsid 518
Lusgen Alp 551
Luther, M. 1, 76, 88, 166, 195, 430, 445, 631
Lux Mundi 579–80
Lycosaurus 504
Lyell, Lady M. 341, 428
Lyell, Sir C. 153–4, 175, 187, 206, 215, 219, 225, 236, 238–9, 245, 247–8, 255–8, 267, 271–3, 282, 284, 290, 292, 294, 298–301, 303, 307–8, 311–16, 318, 320, 323–4, 326, 328–9, 341, 352, 358, 370, 429, 444, 446, 455, 476, 566; on evolution 187, 256–7, 267; on progressionism 152–3, 219, 247–8, 255–6; on human origins 187, 238–9, 256–8, 272, 282, 299, 307, 312, 315, 320, 326
Lynn, E. 347, 371

Macaulay, T.B. 138
MacGillivray, J. 47, 53, 59–60, 63, 76, 78, 82, 88, 96–8, 100–2, 104–5, 107, 113, 115, 119–20, 124–5, 127, 129, 136, 138, 143, 145, 152, 158, 166, 173–4, 181, 185, 196, 217, 376
MacGillivray, W. 181
Macleay, G. 465
Macleay, W.S. 89–90, 92, 176, 465
MacLeod, R. 642
Macmillan, A. 321, 372, 388, 426, 485, 586, 589, 601, 621
Macmillan's Magazine 260, 263, 363, 618
Macquarie River 158
Macrauchenia 223
MacWilliam, Dr 134
Mad-doctors 31, 88
Mad-house, Haslar's 39
Madeira 48–9, 55, 58, 221, 228, 502, 578
Magee, Bishop 630
Magic lantern 119
Maidstone 72, 150
Malay Archipelago 244, 302
Malins, Sir R. 426
Mallock, W.H. 568, 631

Malta 410
Malta, steamer 410, 411
Malthus, T., Malthusian 88, 199, 220, 458, 513, 521, 528–9, 558, 560, 563, 573–6, 597, 635, 641
Mammal-like reptiles 233, 504, 545, 602
Mammals, fossil, 218; Triassic 192, 544, 546; Jurassic 29, 153, 229, 306, 504, 543; origin of 233, 377, 504–6, 545–6, 602; Owen v. Huxley on *Stereognathus*, 229; Owen on relations to bird 518; phylogeny 492; platypus 504–6; prey for Mesozoic crocodiles 452
Mammoths 301, 581
Manchester 160, 386, 387, 408, 430, 442, 531, 557–60, 622, 625, 640, 642
Manhattan 470, 482
Manning, Cardinal H. 400, 461, 466, 374
Mansel, H. 247, 285
Mansion House, City of London 553–4
Manual of Human Histology (Kölliker) 183
Maoris 41, 139
Marburg 166, 327, 543
Mariette, A. 413, 414
Marine Biological Association 533, 562
Marine officers, privileges 43
Marine Station, Naples 416, 424, 451, 490, 533
Marine Station, Plymouth 533, 578
Marki 94, 124–5, 127, 142
Marlborough House 199–200, 202, 217, 274
Marriage, attacks on 186
Married Women's Property Act (1870) 448
Marsh, O.C. 471–4, 477, 481–2, 485, 492, 503–4, 510
Marsupials 29, 121, 218
Martin, H.N. 417, 442, 455, 463, 479, 482
Martin, Helena 426
Martin, J. 247
Martineau, H. 185, 187, 205, 374
Martineau, J. 374
Marx, J. 344
Marx, K. 313, 344, 548, 576
Marxists 548
Mary Barton (Gaskell) 141
Mason, J., 512
Mason's Science College, Birmingham 512
Masonic Hall, Nashville 476
Massachusetts 256, 463, 474
Mastodons 477, 479
Materialism, 8–9, 16, 28, 187, 213, 232, 285, 297, 318–20,

330, 366–8, 372–4, 392, 434, 436–7, 440–1, 443–6, 499, 502, 541, 552, 576, 608, 622, 624, 639
Matterhorn 228, 229, 305
Matthaei, Miss (governess) 448
Maurice, F.D. 208–9, 218, 350, 361, 364, 409; 'On the Words "Nature," "Natural," and "Supernatural"' 409
Mauritius 45, 62, 64, 539, 570
May, G. 8, 10, 319, 488
May, M. 488
Mayflies, fossil 346
McClatchie, A. 77, 82, 132, 150, 170, 388
McConnish, Miss 447–8, 629
McGill University 567
McTyeire, Bishop 476
Meander, HMS 133–4
Mechanics Institutes 202, 293, 353, 639, 641
Medical Benevolent College 388
Medical Directory 231
Medical Gazette 34–5, 37
Medical reform 12, 15–16, 31, 36, 43, 53, 159, 515
Medical schools 9, 15–16, 19, 20–34, 43, 75, 181, 392–3, 420–1, 446, 448–9, 452, 457, 459, 467, 515, 558, 623
Medical students 15–16, 19
Medical Times 225
Mediterranean 410, 502, 581
Mediums, see Spiritualism
Medusae 69, 81, 83–4, 90, 92, 98, 104, 126, 152, 165, 175, 254, 340, 452, see Jellyfish
Megaliths 580
Megalosaurus 357
Megapodes 78, 88, 98, 114, 364
Meidum pyramid 413–14
Melbourne 82, 317, 341, 368
Melbourne, Lord 11, 42
Memnonium (Ramasseum) 415
Memphis, Egypt 413
Men of Eminence (Reeve) 314
Meritocracy 146, 161, 273, 418, 431, 503, 521, 573, 578, 623, 626, 634
Merton College, Oxford 604
Mesmerism 12, 15, 19, 32, 39, 66, 192
Metaphysical Society 373, 389, 390, 400, 409, 425, 461, 464–6, 509, 567
Meteorological Society 532
Methodists 139, 363, 366, 402, 441, 458, 476, 497, 583, 585, 623, 637
Methodist Jacobinism 583
Meuse valley 301
Mexico 118, 570
Microscope, microscopic work

26, 43, 46, 56–7, 61–2, 69, 112, 159, 163, 170, 396, 419, 421, 491, 563, 640
Microscopical Society 170
Middle class 11, 13, 31, 72, 164, 208, 314, 327, 355, 361, 364
Middle Island 117
Middlemarch (Eliot) 450
Midlothian campaign, Gladstone's 493
Midshipmen 32, 43, 46, 53, 55, 57–8, 68–9, 71, 78, 86, 101, 106, 121, 138, 143, 155, 173
Midwifery 32
Milan 368, 538
Militarism, military metaphor 197, 331, 397, 554, 632–5
Militarization, of South Kensington 396–7, 417, 554, 632–5
Mill, J.S. 186, 242–3, 320, 340, 352–3, 402, 439, 499
Millais, J.E. 158, 459, 522
Millennial, millennium 8, 209, 210, 223, 236, 293, 333–4, 374
Millipedes 208
Milton 480, 579
Mind, an epiphenomenon 409, 433, 441, 445
Mind and Body (Bain) 497
Miners 300, 592
Minister for Education 396
Minister of War 554, 635
Ministry of Science demanded 397
Minnamurra river, New South Wales 79
Minotaur, HMS 411
Miocene fossils 227, 239, 305, 401, 473, 486
Miohippus 473
Miracles 8, 10, 29, 75, 180, 204, 220, 233, 252–3, 261, 267, 278, 297, 297, 305–6, 328–9, 342, 385, 390, 399, 434, 439, 464, 466, 468, 497–8, 509, 548, 568–9, 572–3, 579, 584, 622, 630
Missing link, concept of 326, 607
Missionaries 11, 22, 104, 120, 125, 139–40, 144, 255, 320, 398, 585
Mitchell, P.C. 625, 627
Mitral valve 340
Mivart, F. 453
Mivart, St G. 340–1, 366, 368, 392, 396, 400, 407–10, 461, 509, 542, 545, 598, 624
Moa 29, 218, 306, 358
Mobile and Montgomery Railroad 475
Mohammed 260
Mokattam Hills, Cairo 412–13
Molecular forces, basis of life 367

Molluscs 29, 54, 59, 61, 71, 90, 96, 125, 145, 152, 174–7, 188, 191, 199, 208, 214, 223, 254, 256, 491, 496, 506, 542
Monkey, fossil 227; spider monkey 302; *see* Apes
Monstrosities 256
Mont Blanc 237
Montgomery 325, 348, 390
Montgomery Mail 348
Monthly Record of the Protestant Evangelical Mission 549
Montmartre, Eocene fossils 227
Moody and Sankey 474, 602
Moore, F. (maid) 314
Moore, J. 632
Moore, M. (slave) 352
Moore, Revd A. 579
Moors 411
Morality, cultural product 16–17, 245; problem with ape ancestry 239, 266ff; Huxley on, compares humans and apes 240–1, *see* Apes, Darwin, C.R., Evolution; new agnostic meaning 389, 390, 391, 426, 435, 456, 464, 470, 481, 512, 540–1, 547, 553, 568, 590, 592, 596, 597–9, 607–8, 625, 630–2; evolution of 399–400, 515, 521–2, 560–1, 564, 577–8, 597–600; and religion 403, 435–6, 456, 487, 546–7, 568, 579–80, 590, 595, 607–8; utilitarian explanation 499, 592, 599; Kingsley on 288; Mivart on 341; women as teachers of 451, 458
Morant Bay 351
Moratorium on the arms race 635
Moravians 450, 570
Moreton Bay 76, 80, 111, 124
Morley, J. 367–8, 372, 380–2, 387, 446, 466–8, 487–8, 497, 499–501, 521, 532, 590, 601
Morning Advertiser 314
Morning Chronicle 22
Morphia, morphine 511, 519, 557, 590, 596
Morrison Formation 503
Morton Island 76
Mosaic Geologists 567
Moscow 310
Moses 204, 232, 321, 352, 354, 480, 547
Mosman Bay, Sydney 106
Moss animals (Bryozoa) 145
Motorbikes 631
Mould 392, 453, 467
Mount D'Urville, New Guinea 127

Mount Ernest Island, Torres Strait 126
Mount Valentine, Tasmania 82
Mount Wellington, Hobart 66
Moving pictures 631
Mudie, C.E. 316
Mudskippers 114
Muhammad Ali's mosque, Cairo 412
Mulgrave Island 125
Müller, J. 14, 170
Müller, M. 544
Municipal socialism 408, 443
Munn, E. 510
Murchison Sir R. 152–4, 159, 165, 192, 204, 212, 219, 241, 248, 267, 370, 394
Murray, J. 254, 265, 283, 507
Museum, contrasted to laboratory 394, 420
Muséum d'Histoire Naturelle, Paris 89, 400
Museum of Economic Geology 162, 195, 201, 354, *see* Government School of Mines
Museum of Comparative Zoology, Harvard 474
Muslims 64, 197, 411, 633
Mussels 176, 421
Mutton bird 84
Mutual Aid (Kropotkin) 564

Naaman 560
Naples 58, 355, 363, 416, 451, 490–1, 533, 538, 542
Napoleon I 39, 310
Napoleonic Wars 89
Nares, Capt G. 427, 457
Narrative of the Voyage of H.M.S. Rattlesnake (MacGillivray) 158, 166, 173, 185
Nashville 471, 475
Nassau, HMS 347
Nation 390
National Gallery 23
National Liberal Federation 532
National Reformer 292, 313, 336–9, 362, 522, 528, 618, 639
National Society for the Improvement of Women's Education 450
Native Baptist 351
Natural children 552
Natural History Review 284, 289–90, 295, 299, 312, 321, 342
Natural History Museum, London, *see* British Museum; 394–5, 456, 506, 531, 542, 601–2
Natural Law, as Divine Fiat 177, 191, 200, 232, 246, 256, 304, 437, 555–6; immanent in Nature, 200; and social inequality 334; and social action 513, 625, 629;

ultimate authority 275, 352; precept for behaviour 210; Martineau on 187; as rules of a game 319–20, 362–3; Darwinism as 424; v. miraculous grace 389, 468; and prayer 458; Law causes nothing 556, 622
Natural rights 577
Natural Science Tripos, Cambridge 418
Natural Selection 224, 232, 234–6, 238, 241, 245–6, 258–60, 269–71, 283, 303, 310, 363, 370, 391, 392, 399, 406–7, 447, 486, 508, 520–2, 559, 574, 597–8, 605, 626
Natural Selection (Darwin) 234, 522
Natural theology 154, 230–1, 247, 298, 365, 392, 407, 424, 434, 437, 474, 555–6, 622, 627–8
Naturalism, cf supernaturalism 591, 604, 607, 622
Naturalist, career description 252
Nature 372, 387, 394, 460, 520, 554, 606
Nature, romantic 79, 83, 174, 216, 236, 244, 362; as poem 83, 216, 236; expression of Divine Intelligence 174, 230, 232, 253, 392, 406, 407, 409, 419, 451, 542, 555–6, 583, 598, 602–3, 627; justice of 293; Huxley first imputes moral order to 174, 200, 210, 288, 345, 363; game-playing analogy 319–20; chessboard analogy 362–3; Darwin on 224, 228, 234, 271, 363; uncaring 56, 200, 228, 234, 247, 271; law and order 75; non-miraculous 75; democratic 252; no absolute monarchy 234; geometry of, *see* Circular system; Huxley the Darwinian on 385, 389–94, 408, 419–20, 435, 439, 444, 458–9, 465, 470, 482, 488, 513, 520–2, 524, 531, 545, 548, 551, 556, 558–61, 564–5, 568, 573, 578, 596–9, 602–4, 622, 624–8, 631, 632, 634–7, 640; Nettie on 485; socialists on 564–5, 568, 573, 575
Nautilus 491
Nazarenes 567, 571, 580
Neanderthal Man 299–301, 304–5, 313–5, 326, 333, 581
Nebraska 391, 473, 481
Necessity 319, 434, 446, 622
'Negro's Place in Nature' (Hunt) 325
Nelson, Lord 38–9, 151

Nematocysts 123
Nematophora 83, 123, 167
Nemesis of Faith (Froude) 185
Neo-Malthusians 528
Neolithic 539, 581
Neoplatonism 571
Nepotism 62, 168, 172, 202
Neuwied 72
New England 474
New Guinea 40–42, 44, 45, 74, 111–13, 117, 118, 120–2, 125–7, 130, 135, 144, 179, 451, 569
New Jersey 359, 471
New Orleans 80, 475–6
New Poor Law 22
New Reformation 4, 253, 260, 270, 293, 367, 408, 438, 445, 547, 571, 572, 625, 638
New South Wales 67, 82, 87; Parliament of 465
New Testament 639
New Woman 511, 573, 602, 629
New York 32, 192, 311, 368, 391, 436, 470–1, 474, 479–81, 485, 492, 570
New-York Daily Tribune 470, 480, 482, 492
New York Herald 480, 482, 492
New York Times 480–1
New York World, 471
New Zealand 41, 104, 139–40, 114, 167, 218, 225, 255, 306, 351, 518
Newcastle 333, 488, 532, 634
Newcastle, New South Wales 70
Newfoundland 351
Newhaven 471
Newman, F. 185–6, 352
Newman, J.H. 4, 6, 21, 466, 552–3, 572, 622, 625
Newport, G. 171
Newspaper tax 14
Newton, A. 339, 356
Newton, I. 315, 521, 531, 532
Newts 303
Niagara 474–6
Niblet, C. 96, 108–10, 125
Nietzsche, F.W. 609
Nihilists 318, 400, 424, 639
Nile 37, 364, 412–16, 530
Nineteenth Century 487, 539, 544, 546, 552, 559, 564, 570–2, 580–1, 587, 604, 609, 636–7
Noah 580, 582
Noble, Capt A. 488, 634
Noble, L. 488
Non-Euclidean geometry 467
Non-progressionism 153, 176, 191, 204, 208, 215, 219, 222, 248, 255, 258, 303, 305; *see* Lyell, C., Huxley, T.H.
Nonconformist Review 409

Nonconformity, *see* Dissent
Norfolk Island 125
Normal School of Science 517, 534, 540, 542, 554, 570, 642
North Australia 77
North Bank 132, 155, 162, 213, 322, 345
North Cape, New Zealand 139
North, Justice 642
North Pole 457
North Sea 327; fish stocks 514
North-West Passage 36, 41, 174
Northampton 528
Northcote, Sir S. 375–6, 541
Norway 572
Norwich 90, 119, 365–6
Norwich, Bishop of 41, 47–9, 53, 62, 69, 83–4, 90–1, 116, 119, 130, 132, 141, 152
Not Like Man (Halford) 317
Nottingham 625
Nova Scotia 219, 428
Novelists, Huxley and 93, 185–6, 189, 193–4, 345, 373, 404, 427, 436, 450, 470, 571, 587, 642–3
Nucleus 26, 208, 277, 591
Nummulite fossils 364, 413
Nyanza, steamer 412

O'Brien (giant) 28
Oceanea 81
Oceanic Hydrozoa (Huxley) 243, 248, 257, 259
Oceanic islands, colonization of 223
Oceanography 427, *see Challenger*
Oglala Sioux 472, 492
Oken, L. 190
Old Bailey 529, 642
Old Red Sandstone 274
Old Testament 312, 330, 366, 580, 637
On Our Knowledge of the Causes of the Phenomena of Organic Nature (Huxley) 310–11, 456
Opium, opiates 7, 9, 32, 44, 48, 150, 213, 222, 242, 377, 408, 604
Oracle of Reason 21
Orange River, Cape 357
Orangemen 549
Orangs 205, 239, 256, 264; extinct, 326, *see* Apes
Order of the North Star 431, 604
Organic chemistry 27
'Origin of Man' (*London Investigator*) 210
Origin of Species (Darwin) 233, 246, 253–4, 256–74, 278, 283–4, 292–3, 298, 302, 305, 310, 312, 318, 329, 349, 355, 358, 368, 433, 452, 474, 479, 507–10, 519,

528, 555, 563, 618–19, 623, 629, 634, 636
Original Sin 598
Origins of Agnosticism (Lightman) 624
Orkney Islands 327
Orohippus 473, 482, 485
Orthodox, Christians in Turkey 196; Russia 318, 633
Osborn H.F. 510
Osborne House 594
Ostrich 315, 355, 358, 360, 472, 481, 518
Ottoman Empire 196
Ouvry, F. 414
Overpopulation, human 245, 559–61, 565, 575
Overproduction of life 228, 234, 245, 271
Owen, Revd R.S. 602
Owen, Richard
  Relations with Huxley: meets Huxley 42, 54, 71, 156, 163–4, 181; gives him references 140, 163, 169, 182–3; Huxley refutes 61, 174–7, 180; called a Conservative by Huxley 177; derided by Huxley 193, 208, 213, 226, 279, 339; rift 193–4, 208, 213; its cause 218, 238, 308; disagreement over lamp-shell, 213; on Owen's *Lectures on the ... Invertebrate Animals* 218; on Huxley's lectures 226; on Huxley's adaptation views 229–30; on parthenogenesis 226, 238; on vertebral skull, 243–4; on method of palaeontology 229; on British Museum plans 251–2; on Owen's classification 226; archetype 273, 603; on his Platonic idealism 174, 218; on skull 244; on *Archaeopteryx* 358; Huxley slates Owen in *Vestiges* review 213; in his lectures 226; fury at Owen's lecturing at the School of Mines 231; clash on *Origin of Species* 263, 265, 271–4; Owen's creationist language 304; on Huxley's 1860 Royal Institution lecture 268, 271–2; on candidates for Oxford's Linacre Chair 275–6; at BAAS 1860 276–7, 278; Owen on Huxley's actions 307; Huxley's 'defect of mind' 230; his 'extremist views' 346; encouraged by *Athenaeum* 274; Huxley on Owen's Royal Society Council seat, 308
  Psychology 29, 163–4, 175–7, 183
  Human/Ape Distinctions: on apes 29, 238–40, 271, 276, 283, 295–7, 306–8, 316–7; Archencephala 238; aye-aye 302; brain ventricles, 240; hates human transmutation 239, 247, 271–2, 274, 276, 297; man's cerebral uniqueness 238–40, 276, 283, 290, 295–7, 307–8, 316–7, 433, 504, 587, 607
  Classification of Life: 208, 238, 240, 315
  Development of Life: archetypes 29–30, 45, 174, 184, 187–8, 200, 216, 218, 244, 256, 273, 306, 315, 603; change of species 186, 256, 302–3, 306; continuous creation 232, 234, 246–7, 263, 274, 281, 304; hates transmutation 191, 193, 232, 239, 246–7; original sin and ape within 598; idealism 29–30, 174, 184, 187–8, 200, 216, 218, 226, 230, 244, 283, 305; Natural Law as a Divine Fiat 174, 177, 191, 200, 230, 232, 246, 256, 304, 556, 602; on the *Origin* 263, 265, 266, 272–4
  Parthenogenesis: 156, 175, 180, 226, 238
  Palaeontology: fossils 29, 193, 218, 229–33, 234, 274, 303, 377; 'annectant' amphibian *Archegosaurus* 232–3, 303, 306, 355; *Archaeopteryx* 358; dinosaurs 29, 153, 218, 247, 306, 356, 357, 359, 547, 602; ecological explanations of crocodile progression 452; horse lineage 191; mammallike reptiles 233, 377, 504–5, 545–6, 602; Mesozoic mammals, 229–30, 306; reptilemammal relationships, 356–7, 359, 504–5, 545–6; mammalbird relationships 518; progressive specialization of life 191, 193, 204, 215, 244, 263, 281, 508, 546; developmental views 234, 302
  Social Position: 29, 151, 156, 159, 163–4, 218, 231, 239–40, 263, 265; and Argyll 555; at BAAS 45, 238, 246–7; and British Museum 215, 218, 251–2, 274; Natural History Museum 394–5, 531, 542; College of Surgeons 29, 156, 305–6, 323; Crown pension 164; Geological Society 229–30, 233; and Gladstone 545–6; knighted 545; on Kew 423; Royal Institution 175; at Royal Society 243, 308; at School of Mines 231–2, 240;
at Zoological Society 302; honours 171, 239; pay 164, 207, 215; protégés, Halford 317; Rymer Jones, 218; insensitivity to audience 333; at The Club 505; and Wilberforce 281, 283, 290; death 601–3; supposed autobiography 602; *Life* 602; Huxley on Owen's work 602
  Books: *On Parthenogenesis,* 175; *Lectures on the ... Vertebrate Animals* 42; *Lectures on the ... Invertebrate Animals* 213, 218
Owen, Robert 404
Owen Stanley's Range, New Guinea 122
Owen's College, Manchester 406, 408, 442
Oxford, Bishop of 431, 489, 520, 552, 567, 605, 627–8
Oxford Movement, *see* Anglo-Catholics
Oxford Street 22
Oxford University 14, 18, 42, 86, 164, 239, 253, 267, 271, 275–81, 290, 298, 313, 316, 330, 346, 352, 357, 372–3, 378, 385, 387, 396, 398, 417–18, 435, 439–40, 455, 479, 489–90, 501–2, 515–16, 517, 520, 524, 541, 544, 552, 579, 591, 595–8, 604–8, 627
Oxford University Museum 277–8, 357, 418
Oysters 523

P&O Steam Navigation Company 410–11, 413
Paddington 155, 314, 340
Pain, and suffering 10, 14, 200, 458, 583–4, 597–8, 626
Paired fins, origin 465
Palaeolithic 581
Palaeontology (Owen) 274
Palaeontology, *see* entries in Huxley, T.H., Owen, R., Lyell C.
Palaeotherium 222, 268, 271, 274, 401
Palate bones, basis of bird classification 356
Paley, Revd W., Paleyites 363, 627–8
Palgrave, F. 387
Pall Mall Gazette 352, 361, 553, 566, 584, 618–19, 637
Pall Mall 533, 576
Pallanza 538
Palm Islands 99
Palmerston, Lord 326, 341
Pantheism 166, 184, 189, 229, 318, 372–3, 381, 402, 446, 509
Pantheon, Paris 269
Papal infallibility 331, 454, 466
Papal States 331, 355

Index

Papier-mâché models 419
Papuans 45, 101, 111, 113, 118–9, 121–2, 142, 144–5, 161
Paradis, J. 624, 637
Paradise Lost (Milton) 480
Paradiso (Dante) 99, 100
Parasites 54, 98, 117, 178
Paris 89, 102, 269, 274, 342, 344, 346, 362, 378, 400, 416, 479, 500, 557; siege of 400
Paris Food Fund 400
Parker, T.J. 442, 495–6
Parker, W.K. 397, 442
Parnell, C.S. 550, 592
Parrots 78, 125, 136, 138
Parsee 501
Parslow, Darwin's butler 589
Parthenogenesis (Owen) 175
Parthenogenesis 126, 156, 176, 179, 226, 238
Parthenon 553
Partridge 356
Pastry cook, replies to Huxley 576–7
Patagonia 41, 141, 304, 347
Patriot 309
Patriotism 197, 202, 261, 268, 270–1, 349, 361, 493, 593, 633–4, 638
Patronage 11, 29, 36, 83–5, 93, 108, 151, 154–6, 202, 218, 239, 302, 317, 329, 361; paternalism, patriarchy 398, 429, 447, 449, 529, 533, 575, 628–9
Paul and Virginia (Saint-Pierre) 63
Paul, St 567, 571, 598
Pauper press, 14, 209, 239, 253, 292, 310, 317, 368, 375, 377 *see* Working classes
Pawnees 472
Peabody, G. 472
Peabody Museum, Yale 471, 485
Peel, Sir R. 11, 29, 197, 240, 370, 372
Pelvic girdle, dinosaur's 357
Pembroke College, Oxford 203, 275–6, 292
Pendennis (Thackeray) 159–60
Penguins, fossil 255
Penicillin 467
Penicillium 392, 467
Peninsular War 39
Penmaenmawr 437
Pennsylvania, University of 441
Penny Cyclopaedia 14
Penny Magazine 14
Pentateuch (Colenso) 315, 316
Pentecostalism 192, 437
Pentonville prison 609, 642
Percy Islands 78
Perfect adaptations, Darwin denies 228
Perfection of man 184, 193, 210, 233, 245, *see* Socialism

Periwinkles 174
Perkin's machine gun 32
Permian fossils 505, 634
Persian Gulf 365
Persistent types, Huxley's 255, 257, 259, 260–1, 344, 358, 427, 481, 587; humanity as, 257, 344; *see* Non-progressionism
Perth 81, 105
Perthes, B. de 299
Peterson, H. 623
Petrie, F. 415
Petrol-driven engines 631
Phalangers 102, 121
Pharaohs 547
Phases of Faith (Newman) 185
Philadelphia 479, 503
Philae, Egypt 415
Phillips, J. 357–9
Philology 581
Philosophical anatomy 29, 38, 54, 175, *see* Archetype
Philosophical Club 211, 225, 298
Philosophical Institution, Edinburgh 300
Philosophical Transactions of the Royal Society 123, 152, 424
Phoenician (ship) 142
Phonograph 471
Phosphoridae 69
Photographs, anthropological 371, 398
Phrenology 184
Phylogenetic trees 401, 465, 491–2, 496, 504, 508–9, 552
Phylum 350, 356, 360
Physalia, see Portuguese man-of-war
Physic Garden, Chelsea 18, 30
Physical geography 369
Physician General of the Navy 36
Physics and Politics (Bagehot) 497
Physics Primer (Stewart) 456
Physiographic approach 490, 530
Physiography (Huxley) 369, 484, 498, 639
Physiology 14, 25–28, 32–3, 42, 138, 180, 200, 217, 221, 232, 300, 321, 340, 346, 350, 396, 398, 404, 417, 418, 425, 430, 442, 447, 448, 457, 462, 484, 517, 537, 621
Piccadilly 144, 162, 175, 201, 203, 267, 293, 309–10, 314, 329, 334, 548
Pickwick Papers (Dickens) 22
Picton, Revd J. 402
Picture of Dorian Gray (Wilde) 580
Pietermaritzburg 316
Pig 264; ancestors 229, 401

Pig Island, Louisiade 115
Pigeon clubs 264, 267
Pigeons, fancy 222–4, 226, 245, 255, 260, 264–5, 267–9, 271, 274, 278, 310, 317, 355–6
Pigeons, Torres Strait 101
Pilchards 515
Piracy, by press 310, 527
Pithecanthropus 606
Pitt Street, Sydney 87
Plankton 174, 188, 237, 305
Platonism 152, 174, 187–8, 213, 232, 244, 305–6, 505
Platypus 29, 173, 240, 306, 504–5
Playfair, L. 189–90, 232, 236, 306, 438, 449–50, 458, 487
Pliocene 305, 486
Pliohippus 473
Plumularia 78, 83, 159; *P. Huxleyi* 159
Plymouth 53, 65, 142, 533, 562, 578
Plymouth Brethren 328
Poet's Corner 526
Poideoin, W. 6, 87
Polar-Committee, Royal Society 457
Politics, and natural selection 558–60, 564–5, 574–8, 591–9, 623ff
Polygenism 317, 320
Polygraphic Hall 26
Polyps 60, 69, 78, 83, 90, 96, 98, 112, 145, 421, 627
Polytheism 346
Pompeii 153, 538
Poor Man's Bank 585
Poor, nature v. nurture explanation 586
Pope 407, 466, 509, 553, 630; Pius IX 130, 331, 368, 440, 553
Pope, A. 314
Popular Science Review 310, 359
Popularization 175–6, 179–80, 199, 208–10, 231, 252, 292–4, 309, 333–4, 344–5, 362, 391, 401, 405–6, 428, 440, 444, 451, 491, 503, 571, 607, 636–8
Population rise 528, 575
Pornography 343
Porpoise 76, 453
Port Bowen 92
Port Curtis 77
Port Dalrymple, Tasmania 82
Port Essington 103, 136
Port Jackson Harbour, Sydney 67, 74, 131, 137, 170
Port Louis, Mauritius 62
Port Phillip 81
Port Stanley, Falklands 141
Port Stephens, New South Wales 71
Porter, Governor of Tennessee 476

811

Portlock, J. 234
Portrait of an Age (Young) 619
Portsmouth 38, 39, 41, 44, 48, 196
Portsmouth, Lady 448
Portuguese man-of-war, *Physalia* 58, 60–2, 65, 83, 90, 105, 152, 159, 167–8, 179, 202, 208
Positivism 187, 193, 372–3, 375, 456, 490, 500, 567, 631
Post-Darwinian Controversies (Moore) 632
Post Office 443
Posts, ten a day 151
Powell, B. 298, 305
Prayer 289, 329, 435, 612
Prayer Gauge 435, 458
Pre-adaptation 407
Pre-Cambrian 486
Pre-Darwinian ladder 398, 508, 546–7
Pre-Darwinian era, historical distortion of 508
Pre-Raphaelites 158, 492
Prehistoric Times (Lubbock) 342
Presbyterian Church, Melbourne 317
Presbyterians 204, 367, 426, 445–6, 475, 624
Preston 20, 122
Prevenient Grace 165
Priesthood of Science 187, 335, 365–7, 434, 626
Priestley, J. 443
Primers, science 406, 425, 456, 503, 506, 564
Prince of Wales Island, Torres Strait 124
Prince of Wales 435, 463, 470, 485, 542, 553–4
Princess Louise 525
Princess of Wales 525
Princess Royal of Prussia 329
Princeton University 510
Principles of Comparative Physiology (Carpenter) 180
Principles of Geology (Lyell) 153, 455
Principles of Psychology (Spencer) 232, 246
Privilege, Anglican 10–12, 16, 75, 160, 177, 184, 252–3, 256, 285, 330, 346, 373, 385–6, 396, 494, 502, 526, 573, 578, 581, 618, 619, 622–3, 626–7, 634–6
Privy Council 531, 541–2, 593
Proceedings of the Zoological Society 152, 496
Professionalization of science, Professionals 202, 218, 221, 236, 253, 279, 376, 421, 425, 453, 466, 492, 507, 530, 542, 599, 605, 608, 617, 619, 623, 625–6; and

agnosticism 374, 404, 408, 437, 526, 632; anti-Catholicism 497; autonomy 404, 422, 457–8, 628; clawing power 393, 397, 404, 418, 422, 435, 437, 451, 456, 573, 576, 627–8, 632, 636; and deterministic science 389, 408, 437, 556; and education 418–20, 442, 488, 506, 627–8; and exams 43, 327; expertise 397, 420, 422, 489; and industry 418, 422, 440, 488, 506; law and 526; and medicine 392–3; *Nature* and 460; new hegemony 526, 530, 576, 641–2; Oxbridge disdains 490, 608; rise of 530, 617, 619, 623; and State 393, 397, 404, 420, 422, 506, 526, 530, 568, 599, 642; strategy 256, 279, 283–4, 291, 298; territorial rivalry with Church 397, 420, 435, 445, 456, 488, 568, 571, 572, 625–6, 632–4, 639; women and 273, 448–9, 451, 457–8, 555, 628, 641; and workers 576–7, 587, 638
Professions 9, 20, 43, 53, 67, 146, 160, 173–4, 202, 236, 253; science not yet one 34, 67, 146, 189, 192, 218, 221, 236, 246, 253, 268, 361
'Professor Long' (Darwin) 214
Progress and Poverty (George) 513, 574
Progress, social 144, 184, 210, 233–4, 244, 271, 282, 293–4, 314, 325, 331, 334, 349, 391, 513, 549, 565, 574, 597, 634; social v. cosmic 598
Progression, life's 153–4, 176, 191–3, 204, 208, 215, 219, 223, 226, 230, 232–4, 244, 248, 256, 258, 260–1, 271, 303, 349–50, 356; Darwin on, 215, 223–4, 234–6, 258–60, 282, 303–4; through cruelty 458, 503, 597; Lyell against 153–4, 255–6; Huxley against 176, 191, 193–4, 204–5, 208, 213, 215, 219, 223, 248, 260–1, 303; Huxley's change 226, 255–6, 258–9, 293–4, 356, 401, 473, 481–2, 485–6; Owen on, 191, 193–4, 204, 230, 232–4; Spencer on 184, 190–1, 244, 248; *Vestiges* on 193, 215, 232, *see* Specialization
Prolégomès de l'Histoire des Réligions (Réville) 544
Promammalia 504, 545
Property, abolition 513, 564,

574, 607; defence of 513, 573, 594, 607, 635, 641; women own 448
Proserpine 78
Prospective Review 205
Protein 27, 365, 367–8
Protohippus 473
Protoplasm 365, 367–8, 372, 380, 406, 427, 460, 471
Protoplasmic unity, plant and animal 395, 453
Protozoa 83, 177, 208
Protula Dysteri 203
Proudhon, P.-J. 467
Prudery, society's 273, 344
Prussia 348, 387, 400
Pteraspis 284
Pterodactyl 232, 356
Pterygotus 274
Public health authorities 397
Public schools 275, 350
Public Schools Act (1868) 493
Publishing, cost of 152; Hardwicke 310
Pumfrey, S. 638–9
Punch 15, 17, 30, 123, 196, 295–6, 330, 514, 533, 643
Puritanism, Huxley's 444, 482, 540, 566, 580–1, 589, 593, 600, 607, 609, 619, 624, 628, 641
Purple-throated orioles 102
Pusey, Revd E. 398
Pyramids 364, 412, 414
Pyrosoma 141, 157

Quakers 314, 333, 342, 359, 468, 477–8, 625
Quarterly Journal of Science 396
Quarterly Review 187, 251, 265, 283, 454, 500, 503, 552
Queen Street Hall, Edinburgh 300
Queen's Chaplain 485
Queen's College, Belfast 181, 444
Queen's Printer 328, 524
Queensland 460, 465
Queenstown 469
Quekett Microscopical Club 483
Quinarian classification 89–90, 124, 167, 176
Quinine 422, 538, 545, 550

Rabbit 522
Race, racism 199, 205, 210, 320, 344, 353, 391, 397–9, 415, 475, 501, 546, 550, 592
Radford, A. 77, 150, 170
Radiata 83, 170
Radical and Nonconformist National Education League 443
Radicals 9–10, 13–14, 16–17, 27, 29, 62, 75, 160–1, 184–7, 189–90, 200, 208, 221, 233, 253, 261, 269, 272, 292–3,

310, 314, 333, 340, 349, 352-3, 364, 378, 385-6, 391, 399, 401-2, 403, 408, 441-3, 446, 455, 468, 488, 497, 501-3, 513-14, 517, 521, 530, 532, 541, 556, 572-4, 583, 586, 590, 607, 618, 622-3, 625, 630, 632-3, 636, 638-9, 641-2
Railways 8, 151, 184, 222, 233, 237, 305, 537; Australian 81; Indian 347; Italian, 368; shares 131, 222; underground, 314
Rain, Steam, and Speed (Turner) 237
Rameses II 415
Ramsay, A. 217, 228, 232, 267, 298, 329
Ramsay, L. 228
Ranthorpe (Lewes) 93, 160, 186
Rapes 584-5
Rates, 573; for education 557, 560; libraries 556
Rathke, M. 244
Rationalist Press 612
Ratitae 358, 360
Rat, laboratory 421
Rattlesnake, HMS 41-8, 53-146 passim, 150, 158-9, 166, 171, 174, 182, 203, 208, 314, 321, 350, 411, 490, 518, 557, 562-3, 584, 588, 606, 610, 631
Ravenna 538
Ravensworth, Lord 333
Ray Society 202, 257, 259
Reader 313, 316, 326, 330-1, 334, 343, 372, 604
Reading 276, 277, 281
Reasoner 240, 269, 292, 365-6, 404, 587, 639
Red Cloud 472
Red Lion Square (Working Men's College) 208
Red Lion Club 157, 159, 161, 168, 208, 218
Rede Lecture, Cambridge 591
Redscar Point, New Guinea 122, 124-5, 127
Reeve, L. 314
Reflex arc 15-16, 441, 446, 623
Reform Bills 556; (1832) 12; (1867) 354, 363; Gladstone's 385, 524
Reform League 353
Reformation 76, 166, 367, 547, 579, 625, 628
Regency 90, 163, 314, 376
Regent's Park 11, 47, 155, 163, 211
Reign of Law (Argyll) 556
Reign of Queen Victoria, jubilee volume 548
Religion, distinct from theology

7, 79, 186, 252-3, 285, 487, 498, 547, 631
Religion of Humanity, Comte's 187, 372
Renaissance 293
Replies to 'Essays and Reviews' (Wilberforce) 283
Reptiles 126, 127, 156, 235, 274, 275-6; fossil 29, 193, 218-9, 233, 247-8, 255-6, 306, 356, 366, 406, 452, 504-5, 555, 634; Age of 602; classification 223, 355-60; relationship to birds 355-60, 365, 492, 504, 518, 545, *see* Dinosaurs, Sauropsida; ancestors of mammals 233, 377, 504-5, 545-6, 602; phylogeny 492; a grade 505
Republicanism 522, 532
Research, Huxley on 387, 442, 459, 477-8, 540, 543, 596, 627; Devonshire Commission on 435, 456; Gilman on 477; Lankester on 543; D.Sc. by 533; Wells on 540, 627
Resurrection 464-5, 568
Retrospective prophecies 510
Revelation 247, 285
Review of Reviews 573, 584, 637
Réville, A. 544
Revolution, and evolution 350, 498, 500
Rheas 359
Rhinoceroses 268, 401, 509
Rhizostoma Mosaica 82
Rhône valley 229, 551
Rich, A. 486, 514-15, 589
Richards, E. 628
Richardson, Sir J. 39-40, 42, 90, 149, 156, 166, 589
Richmond Liberal Association 545
Richmond, Virginia 326
Riffelberg 229
Rifle bird 97
Rifle clubs 261, 268
Rights of Man, attacked by racists 320; defended by socialists 577
Rio de Janeiro 56, 58-9
River pollution 515
River Tamar, Tasmania 82
Riviere, B. 404, 492
Robert Elsmere (Ward) 571
Roberts, A. 348, 475
Roberts, Father 454-5
Roberts, R. 475
Robots 366
Rochester, Bishop of 434
Rockingham Bay 91
Rocky Mountains 472, 504
Roden, W. 492
Rodu, Egypt 413, 416
Roller, H. 569, 590
Rolleston, G. 274-6, 280-1, 283-4, 295, 297-8, 306,

313, 317, 326, 329, 332, 344, 418, 516
Rolleston, R. 516
Roman sarcophagus 329
Romanes, G.J. 458, 521-2, 591-2, 595-7, 600
Romanes Lecture 591, 595-7
Romanticism 7, 56, 166, 174, 187, 200, 244, 271, 362, 446, 556, 624, 626
Rome 21, 86, 130, 331, 340-1, 368, 373, 416, 454, 497, 509, 538-9, 553, 609, *see* Catholicism
Roos, D. 629
Roscoe, H. 406, 456, 531, 558, 642
Rosebery, Lord 518, 606
Ross, J. 42
Ross, W.S. 527
Rosse, Lord 161, 165, 180, 182
Rossel Island (New Guinea) 112
Rotherhithe 11, 13, 584
Rotifers 170-1, 236
Rousseau, J.J. 163, 574
Royal Academy 87, 404, 426, 492, 511, 523, 566, 629
Royal and Ancient golf course 406
Royal Artillery 221
Royal College of Chemistry 395, 418
Royal College of Physicians 12, 16, 623
Royal College of Science 642
Royal College of Surgeons 12, 28-31, 35, 37-8, 156, 239, 301, 305-6, 315, 321, 325-6, 339, 347, 355, 363, 397, 423, 606
Royal Commissions on Trawling and Fisheries (1862-5) 243, 305-6, 321, 323, 327
Royal Commission upon ... the Contagious Diseases Acts (1870-1) 405
Royal Commission on Scientific Instruction, 'Devonshire Commission' (1870-75) 388, 394, 397, 405, 417-18, 435, 456, 490, 520
Royal Commission on the Practice of Subjecting Live Animals to Experiments (1875-6) 458-62, 464
Royal Commission to inquire into the Universities of Scotland (1876-8) 483
Royal Commission on the Medical Acts (1881-2) 515
Royal Engineer Institute, Chatham 633
Royal Engineers 396-7, 417, 539, 612, 632-3
Royal Institution 27, 175, 179-80, 189, 195, 199, 212, 216, 221, 231-2, 240-2,

255, 259, 267–71, 276, 291, 295, 301, 327, 347–8, 356, 359–60, 371–2, 401, 404, 507, 543, 573, 618, 629
Royal Medal 397, 543, 565, 630
Royal Naval College 395, 423
Royal Navy 36, 38–9, 395, 410, 488, *see Rattlesnake*, HMS
Royal School of Mines, *see* Government School of Mines
Royal Society of London 83–4, 90, 107, 123, 126, 141, 152, 154, 156–8, 161–2, 165, 167–9, 171, 173, 175, 180, 182, 188–9, 198, 205–6, 211–12, 215, 243, 306, 308, 329, 350, 426, 523, 595, 613, 627; Huxley's papers, 83–4, 90, 107, 123, 126, 141, 152, 156, 161; Huxley's grant, 154, 156, 165, 167, 180, 198; Huxley's FRS 162, 406; Huxley's Royal Medal 171, 182; Copley Medal 565–6; Darwin Medal 606; on Council 189; Huxley as Secretary 423–5, 441, 505, 518; President 530–2, 534, 538, 540, 542–3; Huxley's Croonian Lecture 243; Philosophical Club 211–12; aristocratic flunkeyism 631–2; decline of clergymen 424; Lord Coleridge at 526; Darwinism at 424, 563; Darwin obituary 563; elitism 641; Hooker's Presidency 423, 486; Huxley asleep 483; lighting 512; nominates Eton governor 493–4; Polar-Committee 456; Spottiswoode 524
Royal Society for the Prevention of Cruelty to Animals 457
Rubber 422, 550
Rugby School 16
Ruhr 635
Ruskin, J. 153, 247, 362, 444
Russell, B. 461
Russell, Lord A. 461, 468, 483
Russell, New Zealand 139
Russia 153, 196, 318, 400, 404, 424, 436, 439, 451, 494, 564, 633
Russian Orthodox Church 400, 633
Rutherford, W. 396, 442
Rydal 516

Sabbatarian Bill 209
Sabine, E. 167, 174–5, 308, 329
Sacred kingfishers 114
Saint-Pierre, J.-H. B de 63
Saints, miracles of 569
Sakkara pyramid 413

Saladin 412
Saladin, pseudonym of Ross, W.S. 527
Salamander 232, 300
Salamis (fisheries vessel) 327
Salisbury, Lord 435, 486, 572, 592–3, 595, 605–7
Salisbury Plain 580
Salmon 514–15, 518, 523
Salmon Fisheries Act, 1861 514
Salpae 60, 125, 126, *see* Sea squirts
Salt, Edith, later Scott (niece) 38, 348, 475, 477
Salt, Eliza, 'Lizzie', later Scott (sister) 5–6, 9, 15, 18–19, 21, 25, 32–3, 37–41, 47–8, 68–9, 80, 88, 90, 123, 146, 149, 154, 183, 190, 242, 322–5, 348, 353, 376–7, 390, 391, 403, 429, 463, 470–1, 475–7, 483–4, 558, 570, 593
Salt, Flory, later Scott (niece) 32, 38, 123, 154, 475
Salt, J.G., later Scott (brother-in-law) 9, 11, 15, 19–21, 33, 37, 40, 73, 146, 198, 323, 325, 348, 376, 475
Salt, Jessie (niece) 15, 25, 242
Salt, Tom, later Scott (nephew) 325, 403, 475
Saltation 256, 262, 392
Salter, J. 201, 212, 219, 267, 302
Salters Company 532, 554
Saltpêtrière Hospital 558
Salvation Army 397, 554, 583–5, 621, 626–7, 633
San Salvador 611
Sand, G. 436
Sanskrit 312
Santa Fe 391
Saturday Review 242, 324, 330, 333, 344, 364, 372
Saul 339
Sauropsida 355, 504, 518
Savages, Huxley's view 11, 41, 45, 61, 65, 76, 91, 93–4, 99, 104, 113–16, 118–21, 124–5, 127–8, 135, 144, 150, 161, 315, 347, 371, 392, 399, 521, 529, 564, 574–5, 591, 598; considered as 'children' 144, 342, 353; equated with white working classes, 59, 353; kill Kennedy, 109–11; as stone-age relics 342; as white ancestors, 258, *see* Aborigines, Papuans
Savoy 606
Saxifrages 589, 610
Scarlet fever 245, 286, 357, 379
Schaafhausen, H. 299
Schamyl, Sultan 196–8, 200, 276, 633, 643
Schiller, J.C.F. 83, 116, 170
Scholasticism 407
School boards 401

School Inspectors, DSA's 417, 633, 258
Schoolmasters, training in science 189–90, 272–4, 327, 350, 368–9, 393, 395, 418–21, 431, 455, 457–8, 460, 628
Schools, reforming curricula 189–90, 272–4, 327, 350, 368–9
Science, books aimed at industrial areas 312; in the metropolis 189; under-capitalized 365; poor pay 117, 145, 164; need for upgrading 180; difficulties of career 161ff; professionalizing 146, 202, 205, 218, 221, 236, 253, 256, 279, 283–4, 291, 298, 376; and exams 43, 327; amateurs ousted 193; territorial 'war' with Church part of strategy 197, 253, 269, 279, 331, 397, 435–6, 445, 466, 487, 494, 512–13, 544, 567–8, 579, 608, 623, 626, 628, 632–6, 639, 641; and Catholicism 341, 407, 496; new 'Priesthood' 187, 335, 365–7, 434, 439, 606, 626; rapprochement with progressive Christianity 364; artisan image of 198; democratic Dissenting image 8, 252; as method 374, 487, 631–2; as reason 192, 209; as Truth 160, 187, 308; as tested knowledge 210; experimental 393–6, 417–19, 421; as salvation 165; as patriotism 270, 275; as struggle and 'combat' 150, 272; as common sense 395; and moral authority 160, 187; need for in schools 189–90, 272–5, 327, 350, 368–9, 372; women must be taught 273; and social ends 373; popular magazines 310; accountability 422–3; and agnosticism 374, 385, 389–91, 403–4, 408, 435, 437, 487, 500–1, 525, 528–9, 541, 566–7, 595, 603, 607–8, 622–5, 630–2; autonomy 423; Big Science 427; and Chamberlain's radicals 443, 512, 532, 550; as character forming as Classics 387, 397, 405, 418, 439, 488, 493–4, 512–13, 524, 627; Cobbe on 457–8; at Eton 493, 512; evangelical paternalism 398; Gladstone on 466, 544; honours for 441–2, 531, 541–2, 593–4; Lyell on 456; male preserve 273, 447, 450, 628–9; morality and 399;

and national prestige 427, 435, 568, 593, 627, 638; naturalistic 385, 389–90, 444–6, 503, 552–3, 576, 603, 608, 623, 639; neutral image 389–90, 449, 503, 529, 541, 576, 624–6, 631, 635–6; and nobility 530–1, 555–6, 631; ratifier of social order 601, 622–7, 638; religious aura 344, 408, 446, 526–7, 624, 626, 630, 632–3, 639–40; regimentation 396–7, 416, 420, 433, 632–6; in school 397, 402, 405, 420–1, 433, 498; and social progress 391, 440, 548–9; and social stability 548–9, 625, 638; specialization 284, 629–30, 642; Stanley on 468; State support demanded 387–8, 397, 426, 433, 435, 514, 573, 625, 642; Tennyson on 595; textbooks 405–6, 456, 503, 506, 564; training teachers 393–6, 418–21, 447, 453, 458, 460, 488, 512, 517, 522, 540, 628, 634; Watts' popularizers 527–8; women popularizers 450–1; authority waning in 1890s 609, 619, 630, 641

Science and Culture (Huxley) 513, 519, 525

Science fiction 587, 642

Science Gossip 310

Science Museum, South Kensington 542

Science scholarships 386, 397, 488, 634

Science Schools 395, 418, 421, 517, 264

Scientific London (Becker) 440

Scientist, the word 252, 480, 482, 565, 630; concept 376

Sclater, P.L. 457, 465

Scorpions, fossil 481, 544, 545

Scotland 305–6, 327, 370

Scotland Yard 494, 533

Scotsman 440, 518

Scott family, *see* Salt

Scott, Sir G. 371

Screw-propellers 39, 44

Sea butterflies 112, 174

Sea cows 76

Sea cucumbers 96, 165

Sea fans 96

Sea ferns 145, 159

Sea firs 78, 145

Sea lilies 257

Sea Lords 44–5, 55, 74, 88, 140, 146, 149, 151, 156, 167, 185, 192, 196

Sea nettles 58, 60–1, 92, 112, 117, 123, 145, 243, 452

Sea slugs 42, 54, 69, 96, 99, 121, 176, 180, 203, 491

Sea squirts 56, 60, 141, 145,

157, 181, 183, 188, 202–3, 214, 277, 451

Sea urchins 99, 112, 236, 473

Seabed 427–8, 460, 484

Séances 192, 374

Seaton, Capt. 464

Sebastopol 210

Secondary palate, crocodile 452

Secord, J. 623

Secretary for Science 190, 397

Secretary of the Interior, US 472

Sect, Darwinians as 407–8, 435, 541, 624–6, 628, 630–1

Sectarianism 10, 69, 104, 187, 206, 373–5, 401–3, 409, 444, 478, 550, 583, 613, 628, 630–1

Secular Review 527

Secularism 16, 85–6, 160, 184–7, 192–3, 200, 205, 226, 232, 244, 349, 365–6, 372–3, 385, 391, 402–4, 408, 424, 456, 478, 480, 500–1, 527, 548, 577, 580–1, 587, 589, 603, 607–8, 619, 624, 626–7, 631, 634, 639

Sedgwick, Revd A. 204, 220, 260, 279, 329

Seeds, Darwin's experiments 223

Seeley, H. 356, 505

Self-Help (Smiles) 233

Senior Girls' Cambridge Exam 450

Sermons, influence of 157

Servants 87, 130, 322, 389, 441, 450, 502, 589, 610

Seventh International Medical Congress 515

Sewage systems 23, 314

Sexual mores 344, 454, 527, 529, 540

Sexual selection 399, 447, 574

Sexuality, rediscovery of 619

Shabby-genteel men 164

Shaftesbury, Lord 469

Shakespeare Head (pub) 30

Shakespeare, W. 214, 619

Sharks 303, 465

Sharpe, P. 46, 53, 58, 69, 74, 86, 106, 157, 217

Sharpey, W. 34, 37, 308, 340, 394

Shaw, G.B. 548, 564

Sheep-pox virus 462

Sheerness 149

Sheffield 387, 503, 625

Shelburne Bay 109

Sheldonian Theatre, Oxford 330, 596, 605

Shepheard's Hotel, Cairo 412, 414

Sherlock Holmes 643

Shetland Islands 327

Shiloh 475

Shrews 513

Siberia 564

Sicily 416

Siemens dynamos 512

Siemens, Sir W. 503

Sierra Leone 397

Sikkim 167

Silk weavers 6

Silurian strata, fossils 152–4, 204–5, 245, 248, 255, 257, 267, 312, 486, 544

Simon, Sir J. 588

Simon's Bay 60

Simpson, H.G. 113, 115, 137

Singapore 44, 103

'Sins of the Father', painting 511, 558

Sion House 364

Siphonophores 60–1, 98, *see* Sea nettles

Sivatherium 227

Siwalik foothills 227

Skull, vertebral theory of 243

Slade, H. 438

Slade School of Fine Art 405, 414, 450, 489, 502, 511, 540

Slaves, slavery 58–9, 205, 313, 320, 321, 324, 324–6, 333–4, 344, 348, 352–3, 539

Sloths, fossil 479

Slug 43

Slums 3, 12–13, 16, 23, 30–1, 45, 75, 220, 353, 374, 378, 528–9, 584

Smalley, G. 492

Smelt 523

Smiles, S. 233

Smith, T.S. 10, 11, 14, 200, 598, 623, 625

Smithsonian Institution 479

Smokey River 472

Snails 98, 100, 174, 419, 489

Snowdon 290

Social Darwinism, phrase 575, 635, 638, 641, *see* sub-entry under Huxley, T.H.

Social Democratic Federation 548, 576

Social Democrats, German 500

Social Evolution (Kidd) 603

Social Lamarckism 638

Social Statics (Spencer) 185

Socialists 75, 153, 184, 186, 209–10, 219, 244–5, 293, 310, 317–8, 320, 324, 344, 354, 361, 374, 388, 391–2, 400, 404, 408, 437, 443, 447, 451, 458, 479, 500–1, 507, 513, 530, 548, 553–4, 559–60, 564, 568, 573–8, 583–7, 594–9, 607, 609, 612, 619, 626, 629, 634–6, 638–41

Société d'Anthropologie 346

Societies, reform of 62, 156, 212, 236

Society for the Prevention of Cruelty to Children 410
Society for the Promotion of Christian Knowledge 456
Society for Psychical Research 608
Society of Arts 202
Society of Antiquaries 414
Society, statistical regularity 233
Sociological approaches to science 617
Solar spectrum 460
Solnhofen 359
Somerset, Duke of 469
Somerset House 34, 37, 161, 182
Soul 8–9, 239, 271, 314, 324, 362, 390, 499, 553
South Africa, Huxley in 60–2
South America, Huxley in 58–9, 140
South Kensington 377, 394–7, 417–21, 433, 436, 443, 453, 455, 457, 465, 479, 490, 506, 517, 534, 538, 542, 553–4, 612, 617, 628–9, 632–4
South Kensington Museum 395–6
South London Working Men's College 361–2, 387, 388, 510, 517
South Place Chapel 612, see Conway, M.
Southampton 45, 640
Southampton dock strike 576, 640
Spain 118, 537
Sparks, G. 640
Specialization, of fossil life 188, 190–1, 213, 215, 219, 224, 235, 401; during embryonic growth 188, 190–1, 224, see Progress, Non-Progressionism
Specialization, in science 629–30, 642
Spectator 186, 346, 361, 374–377, 382, 387, 458, 461, 487, 641
Speech, human 241, 315
Speke, J.H. 413
Spencer, H. 160, 183–7, 191, 217, 232–4, 236, 243–4, 246, 248, 268, 285–7, 299, 312, 323, 327–8, 330, 340, 352, 404, 430, 443, 450, 456, 464, 468, 470, 495, 497, 515, 520–1, 524–7, 545, 551–2, 563, 566, 570, 573–6, 578, 591–2, 597–9, 611, 623, 637
Spencer, Lord 515, 541
Spencer, S. 470
Spermatic force 238
Spider monkeys 302
Spiders 208
Spinoza 288, 436, 464, 502, 275

Spiral-shells 152
Spirit rappers 192
Spiritualism 192, 209, 374, 392, 437–8, 513, 566, 574, 584, 608–9, 619
Spirula 484, 491, 496
Spitalfields 224
Spontaneous generation 365, 392, 406, 467
Sporocysts 175
Spottiswoode, Mrs 512, 525
Spottiswoode, W. 328, 512, 520, 524–5, 530
Springfield 472
Squatters 68, 76–7, 144, 351
Squids 174, 176
St Andrews University 406, 489
St Bartholomew's Hospital 275, 607
St George's Hotel 327, 573
St Helena 365
St James's Magazine 423
St John's Wood 155, 207, 298, 405, 485, 496
St Louis 471
St Luke's Church, Southampton 640
St Mark's Church, St John's Wood 485
St Martin's Hall 200, 344
St Mary's Hospital 340
St Marylebone 556; cemetery 287
St Paul's Cathedral 182, 274, 436, 555, 580
St Peter's Chair, festival 538
St Petersburg 190
St Thomas' Hospital 202
Stagonolepis 248, 406, 452
Standard 324, 508, 549, 561
Stanley, Captain Owen, 40–2, 44–9, 53, 55, 57, 61–2, 64, 66, 68–9, 74, 76, 78, 81, 84, 90–2, 96, 101, 103, 105, 110, 112–16, 118, 120–2, 124–5, 127–30, 133–4, 298
Stanley, Catherine 48
Stanley, Charles 48, 64, 66, 122, 124
Stanley, Edward John, 2nd Lord Stanley 169
Stanley, H.M. 413, 492, 584
Stanley, Lord (Edward, 14th Earl of Derby) 375
Stanley, Lord, see Norwich, Bishop of
Stanley, Mary 48
Stanley, Mrs Charles (Eliza) 48, 64, 66, 124, 133, 136–7, 141, 154, 158, 160, 169, 199
Stanley, Revd Arthur 42, 124, 298, 329, 370, 374, 388, 468, 483, 516, 527
Star of India 486
Starfish 29, 42, 45, 59, 83, 89, 97, 165, 170–1, 175, 180, 191, 208, 257, 451
Stars, chemistry of 549

State, interventionism 162, 201–2, 443, 515, 548, 563, 573, 578, 587, 599; scientific claim on 387, 393, 395, 404, 408, 420, 426–7, 433, 435, 443, 458, 515, 531, 541, 543, 573, 578, 625, 628–9, 642
Statistical laws 233
Statistics, death 512
Staunton, Sir G. 175
Stead, W.T. 584–6, 637
Steam, engines 18, 32, 73, 79, 151, 155, 237, 245, 331; factories 8; powered gun 32; ships 32, 39, 44–5, 74, 76, 81, 82, 91, 101, 196, 255, 257, 326; presses 14, 34, 310
Stegosaurus 503
Stephanomia 92
Stephen, F. 430
Stephen, H. 492
Stephen, L. 353, 376, 492, 499, 501, 525, 551, 572, 599, 612, 631, 637–9
Stephenson, R. 8, 233
Steppes 564
Stereognathus 229, 543
Stettin 349
Stevenson, R.L. 642
Stevenson, S. 448
Stewart, B. 456
Stoker, B. 581
Stokes, Captain P. 105
Stokes, G.G. 423–4, 499, 505, 531
Stone-age, savages represent 342
Stonehenge 580
Stork 355
Storm Bay, Tasmania 65
Straits of Magellan 347
Strand 22–3, 31–2, 34, 37, 93, 114, 152, 185, 188
Stratford 213
Strikes 576, 585, 590, 640
Stroud, New South Wales 71
Struggle for resources 228, 234–5, 245–6, 263, 271, 310, 349–50, 461, 490, 503, 521, 528, 559–61, 563–4, 573–5, 584, 598–9, 626, 635–6
Strychnine 538
Students, Huxley's 393–4, 404, 419–21, 439–40, 442, 447–8, 452–3, 459–60, 490, 498, 510, 518, 523, 534, 570, 629–30, 633
Study of Sociology (Spencer) 497
Sturgeons 523
Suarez, Father 407
Subjection of Women (Mill) 447
Submarine telegraph cables 237
Suckling, W. 121, 158, 166
Suez Canal 413, 530

Suffragettes 584, 629
Sufis 197, 633
Sugar Loaf Mountain, Rio 59
Sulivan, B.J. 142
Sultan Hassan Mosque, Cairo 412
Sunbirds 145
Sunday Evening lectures, Edinburgh 367
'Sunday Evenings for the People' 344–6
Sunday Island 101
Sunday League 344
Sunday trading 209
Sundews 453
Sunningdale 525, 550
Supernaturalism 220, 226, 376, 389, 409, 434–5, 447, 466, 507, 568, 589, 591, 608, 622–3, 626, *see* Miracles
Survivals, pre-Darwinian concept 398
Sussex Daily News 582
Swan River Settlement 81, 105
Swanage 355
Sweden 521; King of 431
Switzerland 306, 365, 551, 565, 572
Sydenham College 15–16, 18–21, 441, 623
Sydney 44, 65, 67–75, 79–81, 84–92, 99, 102, 105–11, 117, 125, 128, 129–37, 142, 144, 146, 158, 167–73, 211, 217, 251, 298, 326, 376, 422, 611
Sydney Morning Herald 69
Sydney University 67, 169, 172
Syllabus of Errors 331
'Synthetic Philosophy' (Spencer) 285
System of Nature (d'Holbach) 320
System of Philosophy (Spencer) 312

T. H. Huxley: Man's Place in Nature (Paradis) 624
Tablet 632
Tahlee, King's house in Australia 71
Tait, Mrs 309
Tait, P.G. 371, 407
Tall Teas 426, 436, 489, 492, 508, 510, 521
Tam O'Shanter 91
Tangier 411
Tapeworm 178, 214
Tapirs 223, 268, 271, 509
Tasmania 64–6, 77, 81, 82, 124, 257, 258
Tasmanian tigers 155
Tay Bridge disaster 512
Teasel 483
Technical education 488, 506, 519, 554, 557, 559, 634–5, 641
Tecnic Institute, Casale 341

Teignmouth 503
Tel el Amarna, Egypt 416
Telegraph 178, 206, 210, 237, 351, 373, 386, 443, 470–1, 577, 612, 632
Telegraph 278, 316
Telephone 433, 503, 505, 542; exchange 505
Telescope 588, 640
Tenby 203, 212–13, 217, 286, 313
Tennessee 80, 149, 154, 183, 325, 475–6
Tennyson, A. 235, 247, 261, 268, 292, 294, 341, 373, 374, 405, 431, 438, 470, 487, 595, 631
Teoma 124–6, 130, 144, *see* Thompson, B.
Terrorism 514, 533, 550, 607
Texas 352, 505
Textbooks 405, 420, 425, 456, 462, 545
Thackeray, W.M. 159–60, 166, 492, 619
Thackray, A. 622
Thallium 437
Thames 12, 23, 149, 156, 183, 195, 302, 341, 361, 369, 377
Thames Embankment 377
Thebes 414
'Theological Theories of the Origin of Man' (Watts) 292
Theory of the Earth (Hutton) 7
Theosophy 609, 619
Theriodontia 504
Thirty-Nine Articles 165
Thiselton-Dyer, W. 419
Thomas, Sarah Henrietta (Henrietta's mother) 570
Thomasson, T. 468
Thomson, A. 276
Thomson, C.W. 428, 449, 459–60, 484
Thomson, J. 42, 47, 93, 96, 114–15, 120, 122, 129–30, 134, 140, 156, 606
Thomson, Sir W. 370–1, 406, 593
Thorold, Revd A. 434
Thuringia 349, 396
Ticket-of-leave convicts 66, 87–8, 96, 130
Tierra del Fuego 105, 397
Tigrisuchus 504
Time Machine (Wells) 587, 609, 642
Times 19–20, 100, 123, 251, 261, 263–4, 266, 307, 348, 375–6, 395, 400, 401, 408, 449, 469, 480, 498, 509, 513, 520, 521, 525, 537, 545, 549, 551, 554, 566, 573, 574, 586, 590, 605, 608, 610, 612, 617, 622, 624, 629, 643
Timor 105

Titanosaurus 503
Titanotheres 472
Tithes 10
Tokyo 460
Tom Brown's Schooldays (Hughes) 313
Tongan race 546
Toronto University 168–9, 172–3, 175, 188, 189, 604
Torquay 208
Torres Strait 44, 101, 103, 124, 125
Tortoises 518
Tow netting 56, 60, 64, 78, 97, 179
Town halls, democratization 160, 253; Dissenters invade 220, 253; as 'laboratories' of politics 641
Town planning 490
Toxodon 347
Toy Pigeons 268
Tracts for the Times 572
Trade Unionism 46, 203, 335, 353, 401, 444, 506, 586, 590, 635, 640; Darwin on 634; Trades Union Congress 363
Trafalgar, Battle of 37, 39
Trafalgar Square 23, 151
Trams, electric 503
Transmutation 153, 173, 193, 219, 225–6, 232, 234, 247, 256, *see* Evolution
Transportation 46, 87
Treasury 166, 180, 397, 421, 483, 504, 514, 541
Trepang 54
Trevelyan, Sir C. 180
Triassic fossils 192, 255, 358, 459, 472, 504, 544, 546
Trigonia 73, 152
Trilobites 153, 192, 205, 219
Trinidad 334
Trinity Bay 99
Trinity College, Cambridge 398, 490, 516
Trollope, A. 242
Truth, from research not authority 393, 420, 513, 572, 631
Tsar 143, 196, 318, 400; Alexander II 564
Tube-worm 203, 428
Tubularia 112
Tulun Mosque, Cairo 412
Turguenieff, I. 404
Turin 341, 416
Turks, Turkish 93, 196, 210
Turner, F. 618, 622, 624, 631, 632
Turner, J.M.W. 237
Turtles 99–101, 127, 555
Tuscany 539
Tusk Shells 542
Twofold Bay, New South Wales 74
Tylor, E.B. 342, 350, 399

Tyndall, J. 166, 173, 184, 188–9, 190, 200, 205, 211–13, 217, 221, 225, 228–9, 232, 234, 236–7, 241–3, 261, 272, 287, 290, 298, 318–9, 327, 329–30, 345–6, 352, 361, 364–6, 370, 372, 375, 386, 388, 390–3, 401, 402, 404, 406, 409, 414, 417, 422, 424–6, 429, 431, 434–7, 441, 444–6, 464, 467–70, 495, 501, 503, 505, 509, 510, 519, 525, 543, 549–51, 553, 572, 573, 589, 582, 590, 592, 596, 600, 603–4, 629, 637, 642; 603–4; *Forms of Water* 497

Tyndall, L. 467, 495, 604–5, 612

Tyneside 321, 323, 333, 469

Type specimens 420–1, 430–1, 453, 628

Typewriter 505

Typhoid 435, 524

Ulster Loyalists 549, *see* Unionists

Unbelievers, The (Cockshut) 628

Uncle Tom's Cabin (Stowe) 205

Underground railway 314, 386, 404, 631

Unicellular animals 453, 546

Uniformity of nature 389, 408, 433, 466, 556, 572, 608

Unionists 444, 544, 549–50, 554, 572, 592, 595, 607

Unitarians 8, 10, 14, 27, 29, 180, 187–8, 205, 213, 220, 244, 252–3, 261, 272–3, 283, 306–7, 328, 373–4, 387, 443, 447, 461, 501, 513, 526, 544, 556, 580, 589, 598, 603, 240–3

Unity of life 367

Unity of Plan 29, 69, 199, 208, 227, 274, *see* Archetype, Philosophical Anatomy

Universalist Church 625

Universities Tests Acts (1871) 385, 398, 526

University College Hospital 15, 435

University College London 9, 12, 14, 15, 18–19, 21, 34, 146, 164, 180, 201, 327, 334, 340, 354, 372, 392–3, 396, 398–9, 402, 405, 420, 455, 461, 467, 489, 497, 505, 518, 529, 562

University College School 399, 488

University College, Oxford 517

Unknowable, Huxley on 319, 374, 456, 527, 566, 622; Rolleston on 332; Spencer on 285

US Ambassador 510, 520

US Geological Survey of the Territories 391

Utilitarianism 79, 175, 200–2, 223, 246, 271, 499

Vaccination 443, 511, 599

Valley of the Kings 415, 547

Valparaiso 105

Vanderbilt, C. 476

Vanderbilt University 476

Vanity Fair 385

Variation, Darwin on 220, 224, 234, 271; Wollaston on 221, 225; Hooker on 225; functional 262; Huxley on innate tendency to vary 486; *see* Chance

Variation of Species (Wollaston) 221

Vatican 407, 538

Vegetarians 629

Velella 60, 105, 142, 167, 179

Venice 537

Verona 538

Versailles 90

Vertebral theory of skull 244

Vertebrate embryo, cell layers 452

Vertebrates, origin of 451

Vestiges of the Natural History of Creation (Chambers) 193–4, 213, 215, 244, 277, 279, 292

Vesuvius 416

Vicars, apostate 434–5

Vice-Chancellors, Oxford University 277; London University, 222

Victoria (ship) 38

Victoria and Albert Museum 396

Victoria docks 421

Victoria, Port Essington 103

Victoria, Queen 11, 38, 54, 103, 153, 156, 177, 233, 276, 329, 356, 370–1, 458, 484–5, 493, 525, 548, 593–4

Victoria, State of 82

Victoria Station 291

Victoria Street Society 457

Victory, HMS 38

Vigilantes, Salvation Army 585–6

Virchow, R. 498, 500

Vital Forces 208

Vitality 367

Vivisection 457–9, 461–2, 464, 469, 487, 546

Vogt, C. 317–8, 354, 365

Volcanoes 173

Voltaire 163, 331, 510

Volunteer Review 280

Volunteers 261, 268, 284, 584, 595, 634, 638

Von Baer, K.E. 589

Wace, Revd H. 567, 570–2, 587, 590

Wagner, R. 317

Waimate, New Zealand 139

Wainewright, T.G. 87

Wakley, T. 31

Wales 203, 214, 229, 497–8, 518, 593

Wall, T. 92, 110, 125

Wallace, A.R. 178, 244–6, 254, 302, 326, 344, 350, 352, 374, 392, 399, 437, 443, 450, 486, 513, 520, 548, 574–5, 599, 639

Waller, Fred 437, 467, 495, 525, 543, 562, 570

Waller, Noel (grandson) 518, 543

Waller, Oriana (granddaughter) 507

Waller, Sam 437

War, Darwinian metaphor 235, 530, 554, 565, 578, 598, 623, 632–6; industrial competition as 553–4, 559–60, 632–6

War Office 221, 330, 386, 396, 417, 633

War with the United States (1812) 234

Ward, Mrs H. 571, 620; 'New Reformation' 571

Ward, W.G. 374, 389, 464

Warwick 213

Washington 190, 479

Waterfleas 222

Waterhouse, A. 506

Waterloo (ship) 207

Waterloo, Battle of 163, 182, 516

Waterloo Station 151, 266

Watson, Captain 347

Watson, H.C. 221

Watts, C.A. 527–8, 611

Watts, J. 240

Waugh, Revd B. 410

Waverley Place 207, 212, 216, 218, 243, 298

Weavers 6–7, 9, 30, 76, 224, 288, 294, 353

Webb, B. 539–40, 555, 619–21

Wedgwood, H. 438

Wedgwood, J. 222

Weismann, A. 591, 601, 605, 630

Wellington, Duke of 182, 220, 589

Wells, H.G. 539–40, 587, 609, 627, 629, 642

Wengern Pass 228

West India Docks 352

West Indies 22, 36, 72, 397

West Mariposa, gold mine 172

Western Union Telegraph 470

Westminster Abbey 233, 329, 371, 455, 468, 483, 516–17, 520, 524, 526, 555, 611

Westminster Publishing Company 261

Westminster Review 185, 190,

192–3, 195–7, 202, 204–5, 219–20, 224–5, 234, 261–2, 265, 273, 276, 330, 633
Westminster School 494
Weymouth Bay 109
Whales 347
Whelks 174, 176, 203, 420
Whigs 11, 29, 41, 42, 62, 67, 69, 77, 89, 138, 173, 175, 220, 253, 330, 341, 378, 634
Whitby 491
White, A.D. 478
White, G. 222
Whitechapel 353
Whitehall 23, 151, 180, 377, 514, 534, 541, 642
Whitworth gun 261, 268–9, 283, 331, 339, 386, 623, 633
Whitworth Scholarships 433
Whitworth, Sir J. 386, 506, 634
Why Does Man Exist? (Bell) 574
Why I am an Agnostic (Ross) 527
Wiener, M. 642
Wiesbaden 608
Wilberforce, Bishop S. 271, 273, 276–81, 283, 290, 293–4, 298, 302, 307, 313, 315–6, 328, 330, 352, 431, 489, 520, 552, 567, 605, 627–8
Wilberforce, W. 431
Wilcox, J. 47, 125
Wild Beast show 473
Wilde, O. 540, 555, 580–1, 587, 600, 607, 609, 619
Wilhelm Meister (Goethe) 121
Wilkin, Bishop 266
Willemoes-Suhm, R. von 428
William the Conqueror 314
William's Town 82
Williams & Norgate 304, 312, 321, 342
Williams, C. 438
Williamson, Chief Superintendent 494
Willis' Rooms 374
Windsor Castle 570
Windward Islands 484
Winners in Life's Race (Buckley) 451
Wiseman, Cardinal 301, 331
Witness 300–1, 305, 445
Wollaston, T.V. 220–1, 224–5, 266
Wolseley, General 530
Wolsey, Cardinal 591
Wombwell's menagerie 240
Women, younger Huxley on 119–20, 137, 144, 168, 207, 212, 272–3; Lyell on, 272–3; barred from learned societies 272–3, 343–4, 371, 398, 447, 447, 450, 625, 628–9, 641; conservative, 341; 'natural'

limitations/ 'inferiority' stereotype 334, 371, 447–8, 628–9; his liberal paternalism 429, 447, 625, 628–9, 641; family role 450; mediums 437–8; hospices 584; prudery, 272–3, 344; and chlorodyne 511; war not made on 444; in Huxley's college 362; in Huxley's classes, 273, 362, 396, 410, 447–9, 510, 629; Miss McConnish 447, 629; Sarah Stevenson 448; Emily Munn 510; buy tickets for his courses 401, 629; on evolution 401, 629; on *Descent of Man* 399, 629; making their own way, 342; Married Women's Property Act 448; careerists 438, 447–48, 557, 629; education of 272–3, 334, 342, 362, 447–50, 477–50, 477, 483, 533; Senior Girls' Cambridge Exam 450; in medicine 448–50, 483, 533, 629; at London University 449–50, 533; in Scottish Universities 448–9, 483; Jex-Blake 448–50; single sex classes 449–50; London School of Medicine for Women 449; Maria Grey 450; on London School Board 401–2; Elizabeth Garrett 401–2, 449; in Association of Liberal Thinkers 501; take collection for him 428; money gifts 429; New Woman 448, 511, 573, 602, 619, 629; Cobbe 448, 457–8, 460; anti-vivisection 447–8, 457–8; opens up to strong women 436, 447, 620–1; on Huxley's emotional state 428–9, 540, 555, 619–20; Ellen Busk 621; Beatrice Webb 540, 555, 619–21; mediums 437–8; novelists 436; George Eliot 404, 436, 450, 526–7, 621; Arabella Buckley 450–1, 500; children's writers 405, 450–1, 503; Annie Besant 522–3, 528–9; neo-Malthusians and birth control 528–9, 575; women's rights/emancipation 273, 285, 324, 334, 447–50, 477, 522, 619, 628, 639; Drummond on 602; Wallace on 574
Women's Hospital Medical College, Chicago 448
Woodstock Mill, Jamberoo 72
Woolloomooloo, Sydney 67, 130, 136–7
Woolner, T. 492
Woolpark Inn, Parramatta 131
Woolwich arsenal 47

Words, phylogeny of 199
Wordsworth, W. 244
Workhouses 20, 22, 24, 37, 88, 217, 220, 271
Working classes 3–4, 7, 13, 20, 24, 49, 54, 59, 75, 141, 153, 203, 208–11, 215, 224, 231–2, 239–40, 252, 263, 269, 292–5, 300–1, 309–10, 313, 333–5, 344, 353, 355, 361–3, 366, 376; atheists/freethinkers 75, 153, 209, 232, 240, 269, 292, 333, 363, 402–3, 440–1, 500–1, 515–19, 522, 525–9, 540–1, 576, 587, 623, 631, 638–9, 641–3; agnosticism 527–8, 567, 580; compared to blacks 59, 334, 353; cynicism 292; education 203, 210, 363; served by London School Board 402; on evolution 153, 209–10, 231, 239–40, 263, 292–3, 310; on human evolution 239–40, 292; accept Huxley's lead 440, 576, 639–40; on *Hume* 499–500; description of Huxley's audience 440, 639; Huxley on 401, 488, 557, 618, 625, 627–30; disillusioned with Huxley 440–1, 561, 576–8, 638, 641–2; pastry cook 576–7, 597; Huxley sees poverty 3–4, 7, 13, 24, 49, 141, 361; neo-Malthusians 528–30; anti-Malthusian socialists 75, 153, 209, 239, 293, 440, 500, 513, 548–9, 554, 559–60, 568, 573–8, 576–7, 587, 594–7, 599, 619, 634–5, 638–40; Sparks 640; Social Darwinism and 560, 568, 574–8, 594, 599, 625–6, 634–6, 638, 641–2; dispenser wills body to Huxley 640; missing from history of science 638
Working Men's College, Blackfriar's Road 361–3, 387, 388, 510, 517
Working Men's College, Red Lion Square 208, 488
Working Men's Club 488
Workingmen's lectures, Huxley's 208–11, 215, 252, 292–5, 300–1, 309–10, 313, 333, 355, 361–3, 366, 404, 440, 456, 488, 496, 510, 523, 618, 625, 638–42
World, The (New York) 368
World, The 588
Worms 54, 89–90, 96, 116–7, 170, 173, 199, 200, 203–4, 208, 212, 214, 257, 451

Worshipful Company of Apothecaries 19
Worthing 514
Worthington, J.W. 28
Würzburg 190
Wyoming 473, 504

X-Club 327–30, 332, 342, 354, 364, 368, 371–2, 377, 386, 388, 394, 402, 418, 422–4, 428–9, 468–9, 520, 524–5, 530–2, 543, 549–51, 567, 573–4, 590, 600, 604, 607, 641

Yaks 564
Yale University 317, 471, 482, 485, 503

Yeast 379, 392–3, 421, 426
Yedo 460
Yellow-breasted sunbird 78
Yellow fever 611
York 326
Yorkshire College of Science 488
Youmans, E.L. 323–4, 337, 390, 391, 470, 482, 485
Young, G.M. 619
Young, J.R. 492
Young Men's Christian Association 374
Young Oxford movement 524
Young, R.M. 626
Yule, C.B. 74, 121–2, 134, 136–7, 139, 143, 149, 158

Yule Island, New Guinea 122

Zadig 510, 643
Zambezi 231
Zebra 178
Zoöids 126, 165, 238
Zoological Gardens, London 155, 186–7, 239–40, 302, 540
Zoological Society, London 47, 62, 71, 82, 102, 107, 130, 152, 178, 240, 302, 356, 431, 465, 495
Zoology, adjunct of medicine 189
Zoology of the Beagle Voyage (Darwin) 151
Zoroastrianism 566
Zulus 315, 492, 493